The Encyclopedia
of
American
Intelligence
and Espionage

The Encyclopedia of American Intelligence and Espionage

From the Revolutionary War to the Present

G. J. A. O'Toole

Facts On File®
New York · Oxford

The Encyclopedia of American Intelligence and Espionage
From the Revolutionary War to the Present

Library of Congress Cataloging-in-Publication Data

O'Toole, G. J. A. (George J. A.), 1936–
    The encyclopedia of American intelligence and espionage: from the
Revolutionary War to the present / G.J.A. O'Toole.
      p. cm.
    Bibliography: p.
    Includes index.
    ISBN 0-8160-1011-0
    1. Espionage, American—History—Dictionaries. 2. Espionage—
United States—History—Dictionaries. I. Title.
UB271.U5085 1988   87-30361
327.1′2′0973—dc19   CIP

Printed in the United States of America

10 9 8 7 6 5 4 3 2 1

For Lucy,
of cherished memory

CONTENTS

INTRODUCTION

That which has been called the world's second oldest profession has lately become one of its newest fields of scholarly study. More than forty American colleges and universities now offer courses in espionology,* ranging from "Espionage in the Ancient World," taught at Georgetown University through "Espionage and History" at the University of New Hampshire, to Yale University's "Intelligence and Covert Operations." The Defense Intelligence College, an accredited educational institution operated by and for the U.S. government, grants the degree of Master of Science of Strategic Intelligence to those government employees and military personnel who complete its twelve-month program.

Several private organizations are dedicated to the advance of espionology. The National Intelligence Study Center, the Consortium for the Study of Intelligence, and the Hale Foundation (named after Nathan Hale, the patriot spy of the American Revolution) encourage and sponsor the study of intelligence and the teaching of espionology in colleges and universities, and work to improve public understanding of the role of intelligence in national security.

The literature of espionage, long the exclusive province of novelists, journalists, and memoirists, has taken on a serious academic tone in recent years. Today, for example, few books about the Central Intelligence Agency will be taken seriously unless they come complete with source notes, index, and bibliography. A periodical literature of espionology has begun to appear, and the interested reader can find such articles as "Empathy as an Intelligence Tool" in the *International Journal of Intelligence and Counterintelligence*, "Sun Tzu's 'Revolutionary' Principles" in *Military Intelligence*, "The Roman Secret Service" in *Intelligence Quarterly*, and news and reviews of the latest crop of books on the subject in the *Foreign Intelligence Literary Scene*. There is also the *American Intelligence Journal*, a publication of the National Military Intelligence Association; and *Periscope*, the journal of the Association of Former Intelligence Officers. And, for those who hold the appropriate clearance, there is *Studies in Intelligence*, a scholarly journal produced by the CIA's Center for the Study of Intelligence and distributed within the U.S. intelligence community.

As yet, however, there are few reference works in espionology. Several excellent bibliographies have appeared in the last few years, most notably George Constantinides's *Intelligence and Espionage: An Analytical Bibliography* and the *Bibliography of Intelligence Literature*, prepared by Walter Pforzheimer for the Defense Intelligence College. But the handful of lexicons, biographical dictionaries, and encyclopedias available all tend more to the popular than the scholarly in tone and substance, and in attempting to encompass intelligence worldwide are far too diffuse to be very helpful to the serious scholar.

It was in hope of filling at least a small part of this vacuum that I undertook the project several years ago, which bears its first modest fruit in this volume, an attempt to digest what has been published about American intelligence and espionage from the American Revolution onward, to organize it in a useful way, and to present it between the covers of a single book.

Sources

I must make it clear that my own brief service with the Central Intelligence Agency long ago is absolutely incidental to the contents of this book. Even were my memory of matters that I learned about while with the CIA two decades ago sufficiently reliable to serve as a source for a current work—and it is not—hardly any of those matters bears on the topics covered in this encyclopedia. All of the information presented in this work is derived from openly available sources; the sources I used in compiling each entry may be found listed at the end of that entry, and a full bibliography of the works I consulted is included at the end of the book. (However, many of the Civil War entries incorporate information furnished in personal letters by historian and espionologist Edwin C. Fishel, based on his extensive archival research into Civil War intelligence and espionage; of course, even this information was obtained by Fishel from readily available archives.)

To satisfy the formal requirements of the secrecy agreement that binds every former employee of the Central Intelligence Agency, I have submitted the

---

*Espionology: the study of intelligence and espionage. See the entry under this term.

manuscript of this book to the CIA's Publications Review Board. However, I must point out that the board's function unfortunately does not include advising the author of any errors of fact he may have committed. Therefore the CIA's nihil obstat permitting the publication of this work means only that it contains no classified information; it should not be construed as a confirmation or endorsement of anything to be found in the book. Let no user of this encyclopedia be misled, then; the work carries no greater authority than that of the published and open archival sources upon which it has been based, and it is subject to the same pitfalls of error and omission as any other scholarly work.

Such pitfalls are formidable in the study of intelligence and espionage. Of course, all historical research is subject to errors and omissions in the surviving record, to the self-serving mendacity of some memoirists and other participants in events, and to simple human frailty; but the espionologist is confounded further by the very nature of the thing he tries to study. Truth itself is the prize in the intelligence game; secret services strive to acquire it or deny it to their adversaries just as opposing armies contend for territory in war. Silence and deception are the most basic weapons in the intelligence armamentarium. To the intelligence officer the needs of future historians, if he thinks of them at all, are completely eclipsed by the demands of current operations and the subsequent security of the results. Much of the true record disappears up the chimney forever, therefore, while an astonishing amount of mythology, fanciful invention, and deliberate lying is published with the silent acquiescence or active encouragement of those few who know better.

Beyond the secrecy and deception that are the by-products of intelligence activity, there is still another source of error in the literature: the politically controversial nature of post-Second World War intelligence operations and the consequent temptation—too rarely resisted by authors of works on cold war espionage—to slant their work to the left or right by omitting or distorting some of the facts.

Espionology, then, is a very elusive thing.

Acknowledgments

In the face of such hazards I have proceeded with caution. The Constantinides and Pforzheimer bibliographies have provided invaluable guides through some passageways in the labyrinth of the intelligence literature. Authors who have closely studied parts of the story of American intelligence have created a small body of well-researched and carefully drafted literature of which I have made liberal use. I am grateful to many of the authors of these works for generously clarifying for me a variety of matters both great and small. In this regard I wish especially to thank Dr. Ray S. Cline, Mr. George Constantinides, Col. William R. Corson, Mr. David Atlee Phillips, Mr. Edward F. Sayle, Prof. Meriwether Stuart, Maj. Gen. Edmund R. Thompson, and Mr. Thomas F. Troy for their kind responses to my inquiries.

I am very specially indebted to Edwin C. Fishel for permitting me to draw upon his encyclopedic knowledge of, and voluminous files of, Civil War intelligence and espionage, and other matters, and for his review of many of the Civil War entries.

Of course, I am solely responsible for all errors and other deficiencies that may be found in the text.

Organization of the Encyclopedia

It may be helpful to the user of this encyclopedia to understand its general organization (beyond the simple alphabetical order in which the entries appear). There is a central core of articles on:

1 American intelligence organizations (e.g., the CIA, Army Intelligence, Naval Intelligence, the OSS, etc.)
2 The role of intelligence in the principal wars of American history
3 Subjects of predominant importance in American intelligence history (e.g., Overhead Reconnaissance, Cryptology, Covert Action, Air Proprietaries, etc.)
4 Events or incidents in American intelligence history (e.g., the Northwest Conspiracy, the Pearl Harbor Attack, the Bay of Pigs Invasion, the Cuban Missile Crisis, etc.)
5 Biographies of major figures of American intelligence (e.g., William J. Donovan, Allen Dulles, Ralph van Deman, etc.)

Beyond this central core there is a large collection of entries that further explicates incidents, persons, organizations, and terminology mentioned in the major articles. These are, in effect, footnotes to the major articles.

Finally, there is an assortment of peripheral entries on persons and other topics relevant to American intelligence but more or less incidental to the central core of the encyclopedia. More often than not I elected to include them simply because the information was readily available. Many of these are biographic entries for prominent persons who have had some affiliation with American intelligence, but who are notable for some other pursuit, e.g., Ralph Bunche, Julia Child, Arthur Goldberg, Sterling Hayden, and Herbert Marcuse, all of whom served in the OSS; William F. Buckley, Jr., and the Reverend William Sloan Coffin, two CIA veterans; and publisher Frederick A. Praeger, who served in Army Intelligence.

Biographic Entries

Early in the project I had hoped to include in this peripheral collection brief entries for all of the "semifamous," i.e., sometime intelligence people whose relatively modest claims to celebrity in other pursuits earned them inclusion in *Who's Who in America* or some similar biographical dictionary. I abandoned this plan when I saw that such persons are truly legion, but I left in the manuscript for whatever they may be worth to the user the score or more of the short curricula vitae I had collected before reaching this realization.

In any case, this encyclopedia should not be regarded as a "who's who" of American intelligence, i.e., the reader should not conclude that those persons to be found between its covers necessarily have, in my judgment, played a more important or significant role than those who may have been omitted. While I have tried to cover the truly giant figures, e.g., Dulles and Donovan, as well as a host of other important officials, covert operators, intelligence analysts, cryptologists, etc., I do not pretend to have compiled an absolutely comprehensive roll of such persons, nor even to know who all of them might be. At the same time, many others (e.g., the aforementioned "semi-famous") have been included among the peripheral entries simply because information regarding them was readily available. And I have been forced to omit a great many significant figures because I could locate little or nothing of the basic information one would wish to find in a curriculum vitae.

For all biographic entries I have tried to include as complete a c.v. as possible, encompassing not only the person's intelligence career but date and place of birth, education, and nonintelligence occupations as well. I have attempted to find a date of death for deceased subjects, but may have failed to do so for some people who outlived their own newsworthiness by so many years that they had long since been dropped from biographic annuals when they died quietly at an advanced age, escaping as well the notice of the major newspapers' obituary columns. The absence of a date of death in an entry, therefore, does not necessarily mean that I have evidence that the person still lives, but may simply mean that I have been unable to find any report of his or her death. However, a question mark in this item means that although I have not found the date of death, I do have some positive evidence that the person has in fact passed away.

The Wars of America

Among the core entries there are nine major articles discussing the role of intelligence in the American Revolution, the War of 1812, the Mexican War, the Civil War, the Spanish-American War, the First World War, the Second World War, the Korean War, and the Vietnam War. Each of these articles is prefixed by an overview of the general military history of the war. I have included these overviews contrary to the practice of many writers who have treated intelligence as though it had some sort of independent existence, like the smile that remained after the Cheshire Cat had vanished. Most of the popular literature, written to satisfy the general reader's taste for intrigue and adventure, makes no attempt to connect all the covert derring-do in any meaningful way with the great historical events that were the reason for it. To get beyond this level of "spying-as-entertainment," therefore, I have included the overviews of the major American wars as general contexts for the subsequent discussions of intelligence in those wars.

In attempting to recount the role of military intelligence in American wars, I find I have gone where, curiously, few military historians have ventured. Serious military historians and biographers seem seldom to address such matters as the nature, the source, or the reliability of the information upon which great decisions were made. Astonishingly, within the enormous bodies of literature on the strategy and tactics of the American Revolution or the Civil War, for example, there is scarcely a single systematic study of the relationship between command decision, on the one hand, and the intelligence available to the commanders, on the other. I do not claim even to have begun to fill this void with these entries. But in collecting and presenting all the relevant material I could find, I feel that I have at least identified the need for further research and analysis by qualified military historians and espionologists.

Covert Action Operations

I have prefaced each of the entries on important events in American intelligence history with some general background to the event, especially in the cases of U.S. covert action operations, about which a stupefying amount of misinformation is regularly published.* Covert action operations are foreign policy measures initiated by the policy-making elements within the executive branch of the federal government with the consent (and often at the initiative) of the President; they are not, as many would have it, adventures conceived and initiated by intelligence agencies or individual intelligence officers. Therefore a brief review of the foreign policy background of such an operation adds much to the comprehension of the whys and hows of the operation itself. In the light of such background material, even so ill-starred an undertaking as the Bay of Pigs invasion emerges as something more than the wanton, mindless wickedness of most accounts. Although a review of the long evolution of the Cuban operation does not alter the fact that it was, in the end, supreme folly, it can explain how reasonable and well-intentioned people happened to stumble down this particular primrose path. (I realize that in disturbing the fashionable view that all covert actions—indeed, all clandestine operations of any kind—are unmitigatedly stupid and evil, I invite the charge that I am acting as an apologist for such things. I shall cheerfully endure the calumny if I can help to improve the reader's understanding of what these incidents were all about.)

Cross-References

Some names and terms used within the text of an entry are themselves the subjects of entries elsewhere in the encyclopedia. I had originally intended to flag all such references through the typographic device of printing them in capital letters in order to alert the reader that more information on the subject was available elsewhere. However, I found that an absolutely consistent application of this convention seemed likely to annoy the eye and distract the reader more often than it would prove helpful in referring him or her to related information in the work. For example, if a person served in the U.S. Army as an infantryman during the Second World War, but had

---

*For example, a recent essay in the *New York Times Book Review* ("Whose Foreign Policy Is It Anyway?" by Sanford J. Ungar, December 21, 1986, p. 3) makes the erroneous assertion that "the CIA removed the democratically elected Prime Minister of Iran, Mohammed Mossadegh, in order to put the Shah back on his throne. . . ." As I note in the article on the Iran Coup, Mossadegh was not quite "democratically elected" to the post of prime minister; he was appointed to that office by the Shah on the advice of the Iranian parliament. The Shah requested his resignation shortly before the CIA coup when the mentally and politically unstable Mossadegh demanded the authority to govern without answering to Parliament. The Shah, by the way, was not "put back on his throne" by the CIA coup; he never formally left it.

no involvement in intelligence during that war, there is no obvious benefit to the reader in noting within his biographical entry that an article on intelligence in the Second World War may be found elsewhere in the work. But references to the Second World War in the biographic entry for, say, General William Donovan, ought to have such a cross-reference because his role as founder and director of the Office of Strategic Services is also discussed in the entry on the Second World War.

There are also many names and terms that are likely to be obscure to the general reader, who might therefore wish to pause and read through the cross-referenced exposition of certain terms. For example, the biographic entry for former CIA Director William J. Casey notes that he served on the President's Foreign Intelligence Advisory Board (PFIAB), and I think this ought to be cross-referenced even though the entry on the PFIAB does not mention Casey.

In general, then, I have tried to use the following criteria for cross-referencing names and terms within entries:

1   If additional information bearing on the specific subject under discussion may be found in another entry, the name or term is cross-referenced.
2   If some sort of parenthetical explanation of the meaning of a term appears necessary, or the identity of a person mentioned within any entry seems needed, the term or name is cross-referenced.

Otherwise, I have omitted cross-references. To supplement this arrangement, I have provided an index to the encyclopedia. Thus, the reader who, upon finding in a biographic entry that "Smith served in M.I.8, the codebreaking section of the Military Intelligence Division during the First World War," wishes to find all the other references to M.I.8 (for which there is not a separate entry), may do so through the index.

Coverage

Finally, I must acknowledge a sense of dissatisfaction with the comprehensiveness, or lack thereof, of this work as I release it for publication. There remains a host of topics in American intelligence and espionage, both recent and historical, that I have not been able to cover for one or another reason. For some omissions, including a number of important figures in current or recent intelligence events, I was not able to locate sufficient information for a useful entry. But for the majority of things I wish were in the book but are not, the shortage was not of information but of time and energy.

The historical aspects of American intelligence can be researched almost endlessly. For example, during the brief period required to draft this introduction, additional information received in response to research inquiries I made several months earlier caused me to stop and revise two biographical entries for personalities from the American Revolution and the Civil War, and to create an entirely new entry for a Revolutionary War agent on whom I previously had almost no information. Researching the history of American intelligence is obviously an open-ended activity.

Regarding more recent topics, the period during which I researched and wrote this book was marked by an extraordinary number of front-page news stories relating to American intelligence, including the defection and re-defection of Vitaly S. Yurchenko, a senior KGB officer; the discovery of the Walker family spy ring; the arrest and conviction of U.S. Navy counterintelligence specialist Jonathan Jay Pollard for selling classified information to Israeli Intelligence; the arrest, conviction, and suicide of Larry Wu-Tai Chin, who served for thirty years as a Chinese penetration of the CIA; the first known instance of an FBI agent (Richard W. Miller) working for Soviet Intelligence; Soviet penetration of American embassies in the Soviet bloc and elsewhere; and, of course, a seemingly endless series of disclosures related to the roles of the National Security Council and the CIA in secret arms sales to Iran and allegedly improper diversions of the profits therefrom to the anti-Communist forces in Nicaragua. None of these topics are covered in the text. Prudence might well dictate the omission of most of them anyway; an encyclopedia is not a newsmagazine, and the earliest accounts of such matters are the least reliable. But in any case, they have necessarily been omitted because it was impossible to keep up with the flood of information.

During this same period, while I labored to read and digest all the relevant literature, there appeared a bountiful crop of new books on American intelligence, including serious studies with newly disclosed information on such things as covert action, Anglo-American intelligence liaison, satellite reconnaissance, and other sophisticated collection methods. Although I have made use of several of them to update some of the entries upon which they bear, this exploitation has been incomplete. Given the rate at which these works are appearing, and the time required for the systematic study, analysis, and confirmation of the information contained in each of them, the task of reflecting the contents of one in all the related encyclopedia entries before yet another comes down the conveyor belt seems to be a race I cannot hope to win, and one in which I am destined to lose more and more ground as time goes by. Like Alice, I find it takes all the running I can do to stay in the same place.

The temptation to compose "just one more" entry to reflect some nugget of information turned up in the eleventh hour has long delayed completion of this work, sorely taxing and finally exhausting the patience of my publisher. But now an inviolable deadline has been imposed, and henceforth all such nuggets must be gathered aside for inclusion in whatever subsequent editions there may be.

In publishing something less than a completely comprehensive collection of information on American intelligence and espionage, I console myself with the advice of several persons who have examined the manuscript and say that, whatever material may have been omitted, the book as it stands will be a valuable resource to students of the subject. Although it cannot claim to be the last word as a reference work on American intelligence, I am encouraged to hope that knowledgeable people will find this encyclopedia to be, at least, the first word.

G. J. A. O'TOOLE

The Encyclopedia
of
American
Intelligence
and Espionage

A

A-2

(1) Assistant chief of staff, intelligence, of the U.S. Air Force; (2) the intelligence section of an Air Force general staff.

See AIR FORCE INTELLIGENCE.

ABEL, RUDOLF IVANOVICH (1903–November 16, 1971): Soviet intelligence officer

Born William Fisher, the son of Russian emigrés living in England, Abel was taken back to the Soviet Union by his father in 1921. According to his official Soviet biography (which contains so many falsehoods that it is a very dubious source), he became fluent in several languages while working with other Russian political emigrés who had returned to Russia. His official biography also states that between 1922 and 1926 he enrolled in the Young Communist League and served in the radio engineering corps of the Red Army; and in 1927 he joined the OGPU (United State Political Administration), the designation of the agency now known as the KGB.

Abel's official biography ends there, but according to a book allegedly written by a fellow Soviet intelligence officer, Gordon Lonsdale, but which is believed to have been ghostwritten by HAROLD A. R. PHILBY, he was a Soviet penetration agent during the SECOND WORLD WAR, and succeeded in becoming an officer in the Abwehr, the German military intelligence service. However, this and much else of what Lonsdale/Philby stated about Abel is thought to be a fabrication by Soviet intelligence intended to glamorize and enhance his image in the USSR.

In November 1948 Abel arrived in Canada, using the name and papers of Andrew Kayotis, a naturalized American citizen who had died while visiting his native Lithuania the year before. Abel's activities immediately afterward are unknown, but in 1950 he was living in New York City, using the identity of Emil R. Goldfus, the son of German immigrants, who had died in infancy some forty-seven years earlier. Little information is available regarding Abel's life and activities in New York from 1950 to 1953 apart from the leases he signed on the two apartments he lived in on the Upper West Side and a savings account he opened in a bank in that neighborhood. On the bank application, he listed his occupation as photographer. During this period he had social (and presumably professional) contact with Morris Cohen and Lona Cohen, two Soviet espionage agents then living in the neighborhood.

In 1953 Abel moved to Brooklyn Heights, where he rented an artist's studio. He represented himself to the artists occupying the other studios in the same building as Emil Goldfus, a retired photofinisher who now dabbled in painting, music, photography, and electronics. Abel left the Brooklyn studio in mid-1955, after telling his neighbors he was going to California to market a photographic device he had invented. In fact, he was returning to Moscow for a visist. He was back in Brooklyn in mid-1956.

In 1954 Abel had made contact with Reino Hayhanen, a Soviet intelligence officer living in the New York area under a pseudonym. Hayhanen had been sent by the KGB to serve as Abel's courier, servicing drops and operating a clandestine radio transmitter. Hayhanen drank heavily, embezzled official funds, and generally failed to provide the support Abel expected. In April 1957 Abel ordered him to return to Moscow. Hayhanen reached Paris, then decided to defect to the American intelligence representatives there. Two months later the evidence he supplied the FBI led to Abel's arrest and detention as an illegal alien and subsequent indictment on charges of espionage.

Abel was tried and convicted of espionage and two lesser counts—conspiring to obtain defense secrets, and failing to register as a foreign agent. His court appointed lawyer, JAMES B. DONOVAN, asked the judge not to inflict the death penalty on the possibility that Abel might be traded at some future time for an American intelligence officer arrested in the Soviet Union. The judge sentenced Abel to thirty years for espionage, plus ten and five years for the two lesser charges.

Abel was incarcerated in the federal penitentiary in Atlanta, Georgia, until 1962, when, through Donovan's intervention, he was exchanged for U-2 pilot FRANCIS GARY POWERS.

(Donovan, *Strangers on a Bridge*; Bernikow, *Abel*; Rositzke, *The KGB*; Lamphere, *The FBI-KGB War*.)

AGEE, PHILIP (July 19, 1935–): Clandestine Service officer

A native of Florida, Agee graduated from Notre Dame University in 1956 and joined the Central Intelligence Agency the following year. He was enrolled in the CIA's career officer training program, which included three years of service with the U.S. Air Force (one year of active duty, followed by two years of Air Force cover while serving in the CIA—a program devised to satisfy the trainee's military obligation with a minimum interruption of CIA training). He attended Air Force Officer Candidate School and was commissioned as a second lieutenant in 1958, then returned to the CIA training program in 1959.

In 1960 Agee completed training and was assigned to the Western Hemisphere Division of the Plans Directorate, as the CIA CLANDESTINE SERVICE was then called. Shortly thereafter he was assigned to the CIA station in Quito, Ecuador, and served there until 1964, when he was assigned to the station in Montevideo, Uruguay. In 1966 he returned to CIA headquarters in Washington, where he served in the Mexico Branch of the Western Hemisphere Division. In 1967 he was assigned to the Mexico City station.

Agee resigned from the CIA in 1969 and began writing a book about his career in the Agency. While working on the book, he lived in Paris and Havana. The book, *Inside the Company*, was published in 1975. It contained a detailed account of CIA covert activities in Latin America and listed the names of hundreds of Clandestine Service officers, agents, front organizations, and other CIA assets. Publication of the book forced the WH Division to close down many of its operations.

Agee subsequently edited the magazine *Counterspy* and a series of books entitled *Dirty Tricks*, which identified more U.S. intelligence personnel and operations.

(Agee, *Inside the Company*; *Political Profiles*.)

AGENT

An unclassified publication of the Central Intelligence Agency defines *agent* as "an individual, usually foreign, who acts under the direction of an intelligence agency or security service to obtain, or assist in obtaining, information for intelligence or counterintelligence purposes, and to perform intelligence functions." However, the Federal Bureau of Investigation, the U.S. Secret Service, and other federal law enforcement agencies use the term *special agent* as the title of a staff employee with investigative or other official responsibilities. Journalists and other laymen often use the term *agent* inaccurately, as in "CIA agent," to designate an *intelligence officer* or *case officer*.

The use of the term *agent* in American intelligence parlance was not common in the American Revolution. *Confidential correspondent* was the term used by HERCULES MULLIGAN's near contemporaries to designate his function as General Washington's secret intelligence agent in New York City during the Revolution. Maj. BENJAMIN TALLMADGE characterized his arrangement with the CULPER SPY RING as "a private correspondence with some persons in New York which lasted through the war." And British spy Dr. BENJAMIN CHURCH was found guilty by an American court-martial of carrying on a "criminal correspondence" with the enemy. *Correspondence* was also the term Sir Henry Clinton used to characterize the reports he received from his defector-in-place, BENEDICT ARNOLD. Of course, those working for the other side were (and continue to be) described simply as *spies*, and their activity as *spying*.

The connotation "secret intelligence work" for the term *secret correspondence*, was, of course, institutionalized in the name of the first American intelligence agency, the COMMITTEE OF SECRET CORRESPONDENCE.

Although the term *agent* seems to have been seldom used in an intelligence context during the Revolution, it was adopted thereafter. In his introduction to the 1831 edition of *The Spy*, James Fenimore Cooper recalls the novel's inspiration in a story related to him years before by John Jay, who during the Revolution "had occasion to employ an agent whose services differed but little from those of a common spy." Cooper never made explicit what that small difference might be, nor did he prefer *agent* to *spy* when titling his fictionalized version of Jay's story. In the "as-told-to" memoirs of ENOCH CROSBY (reportedly the real-life model for Cooper's protagonist), Crosby's amanuensis, H. L. Barnum, characterizes Crosby and others like him as *secret agents.*

The term *secret agent* had some currency in Civil War spying. Confederate spy HENRY T. HARRISON, for example, styled himself as such although he also used the more popular euphemism *scout.* *Detective* was commonly used by federal officials to designate their covert operators (see NATIONAL DETECTIVE BUREAU), perhaps because the first Union intelligence service was PINKERTON'S NATIONAL DETECTIVE AGENCY. However, after the war *detective* took on a slightly unsavory connotation because some private detective agencies recruited according to the formula that it takes a thief to catch one, and perhaps also because of the controversial part Pinkerton's and similar agencies played in industrial labor disputes. Whatever the reason, such organizations often designated their detectives as *operatives.*

When the U.S. Secret Service was established in 1865, its original rules specified that "the title of regular employees will be Operative, Secret Service. Temporary employees will be Assistant Operatives or Informants." In his 1898 account of his agency's work against the MONTREAL SPY RING, Secret Service Chief JOHN E. WILKIE refers to members of his staff as *operatives, agents,* or simply "men."

When the Justice Department began hiring personnel to investigate violations of federal law in the 1870s, such persons were called *special detectives, agents,* or *special agents. Special agent* was the term adopted by the Department's Bureau of Investigation when it was created in 1908, and the title was subsequently adopted by the Secret Service.

"Spies and agents" was one heading in the list of intelligence sources set down by Lt. Col. Walter C. Sweeney in his 1924 exposition on military intelligence, but he did not explain the difference, if any, between the two terms. The intelligence units of the armed services have rarely used the term *agent* as a job title for commissioned or enlisted personnel, although members of the Army's Counter Intelligence Corps (see ARMY INTELLIGENCE) were sometimes called *agents.*

In his official history of the Office of Strategic Services, KERMIT ROOSEVELT uses the term *agent* in reference to OSS SECRET INTELLIGENCE BRANCH officers who operated covertly overseas. The term is used in the same way by other OSS veterans in their memoirs and reminiscences. Roosevelt uses the term *sub-agent* to designate local persons who cooperated with and/or worked for OSS agents in the field. However, Becket's *Dictionary of Intelligence* quotes (but does not identify) OSS manuals that used the term *operative* to designate "an individual employed by and responsible to the OSS and assigned under special programs to field activity," and *agent* as "an individual recruited in the field who is employed or directed by an OSS operative or by a field substation." In other words, *operatives* were OSS staff employees, and *agents* were not (perhaps this schema was imposed from above within the OSS but was not honored by the people in the field). Becket says this was the origin of the CIA distinction between *agents* and *case officers.*

(Central Intelligence Agency, *Intelligence, the Acme of Skill;* O'Brien, *Hercules Mulligan, Confidential Correspondent of General Washington;* Bakeless, *Turncoats, Traitors and Heroes;* Pennypacker, *George Washington's Spies on Long Island and in New York;* Barnum, *The Spy Unmasked;* Horan, *The Pinkertons;* Bowan and Neal, *The United States Secret Service;* Sweeney, *Military Intelligence;* Roosevelt, *War Report of the OSS;* Becket, *Dictionary of Espionage.*)

AIR FORCE INTELLIGENCE

The First World War marked the first extensive use of aircraft in war, thereby creating the requirements for such related intelligence as technical information concerning the performance of enemy aircraft and the strength, location, and organization of enemy air forces (i.e., air order of battle). The first American intelligence unit to be concerned with such intelligence was the Air Intelligence Subsection (G2-A-7) of G-2, AEF, the Intelligence Section of General John J. Pershing's American Expeditionary Force in France (see ARMY INTELLIGENCE) during 1917–18. After the war this subsection—along with the AEF itself—ceased to exist. Thereafter the Military Intelligence Division (MID) of the War Department's General Staff took over responsibility for air intelligence.

The collection of foreign air intelligence became a major function of MID during the 1920s, a period of rapid advances in aviation and growth of military aviation. By February 1926 there were air attachés based at the American embassies in London, Paris, and Rome for the specific purpose of collecting technical information on the aeronautical advances being made in Western Europe. In August of that year an Air Section was created within MID to handle air intelligence.

Army Air Corps

Also in mid-1926 the old Army Air Service, which General Pershing had separated from the Signal Corps in 1917, became the Army Air Corps, a more autonomous organization under the newly created assistant secretary of war for air. This change brought with it bureaucratic pressures for corresponding autonomy in the field of air intelligence. An intelligence section was created within the Information Division of the Office of the Chief of the Air Corps (the Division itself dated from 1921, when it was part of the Office, Chief of the Air Service; the intelligence section was added in 1926).

A separate unit that collected technical intelligence on foreign aircraft had existed within the Airplane Engineering Department of the Air Service since 1917. This unit, the Foreign Data Section, became the Technical Data Section in 1927, and continued to maintain an existence separate from both MID and the Air Corps' Information Division.

The Air Corps achieved a further degree of autonomy in 1935 with the creation of the General Headquarters Air Force, a reorganization that shifted command of most Air Corps combat units from the Army's ground commanders to the new centralized headquarters. (Adding to the proliferation of air intelligence, the new GHQ Air Force also had its own small intelligence section—three officers and fourteen enlisted men.) The trend toward autonomy took another major step in 1941 when all of the Army's air units were combined into a single semiautonomous branch, the Army Air Forces. The AAF had its own general staff, the Air Staff, and the old Information Division of the Office of the Chief of the Air Corps became the Intelligence Division of the Air Staff, or A-2, following the same numerical format of other Army general staffs but using the prefix A, rather than G.

Since its establishment in 1926, the Information Division had been a rival of MID, and there had been a duplication of effort between the two intelligence units. When A-2 was established in 1941, the Army's adjutant general tried to eliminate this rivalry and duplication through a clear definition of responsibilities: the new unit was authorized to prepare studies, estimates, and surveys covering the technical and tactical needs of the AAF, but MID still retained primary responsibility for handling "general air intelligence activities." However, this delineation of responsibilities failed to resolve the problem, which had actually been exacerbated by the elevation of air intelligence to the status of a general staff division.

Second World War

With the approach of the SECOND WORLD WAR, A-2 acquired the additional task of identifying profitable potential targets within prospective enemy countries. This activity was carried out by an economic analysis section and led to the Strategic Target Objective Folder program, which was instituted during the war. Because strategic bombing became the principal role of the Army Air Forces during the war, target intelligence became the major activity of A-2 and the air intelligence staffs of subordinate Air Force commands. Aerial Reconnaissance by long-range, high-altitude photo-reconnaissance aircraft was the chief collection technique. However, historians regard the performance of A-2 during the war as less than satisfactory, partly because of the continuing jurisdictional dispute with G-2 and, in the Pacific, with Naval Intelligence as well. American air intelligence in the European Theater was assisted by the British, who had developed aerial reconnaissance techniques and had begun collecting European target intelligence long before the war.

U.S. Air Force

The establishment of the U.S. Air Force in 1947 as a separate armed service, coequal with the Army and Navy, ended the jurisdictional dispute between A-2 and G-2, and elevated Air Force Intelligence to the status of its rival (although the director of intelligence was subordinate to the Air Force deputy chief of staff, operations, and it was not until 1957 that this additional command echelon was removed and the post of Air Force assistant chief of staff, intelligence, was created). The Air Force Security Service (later the Air Force Security Command) was created in 1948 to handle Air Force *communications intelligence* and *communications security*. At about the same time, the Office of Special Investigations, a security and counterintelligence division, was established (see JOSEPH F. CARROLL). OSI was not made a part of Air Force Intelligence, however, but reports directly to the Air Force inspector general.

ELINT—electronic intelligence (see SIGINT)—became a major collection responsibility for Air Force Intelligence. Under a 1957 reorganization, an Electronics Intelligence Coordinating Group was created to operate a worldwide network of sensors and ELINT installations. The Directorate of Collection and Dissemination supervised collection activities—especially overhead reconnaissance—ran the air attaché system (the overseas assignment of Air Force officers to U.S. embassies), and served as a central reference and dissemination unit. The Directorate of Estimates produced a wide variety of finished air intelligence, and the Targets Directorate selected targets and compiled relevant intelligence pertaining to them.

During the late 1950s and early 1960s Air Force Intelligence became involved in a bureaucratic struggle with the Central Intelligence Agency over control of OVERHEAD RECONNAISSANCE as carried out by satellites and such high-performance aircraft as the U-2 and the SR-71. The conflict was eventually resolved in favor of the Air Force in the matter of airborne reconnaissance, but reconnaissance satellite operations came under the control of the NATIONAL RECONNAISSANCE OFFICE. This agency, which the under secretary of the Air Force usually directs, is supervised by a committee that includes the director of central intelligence.

Like the Army and Navy intelligence units, Air Force intelligence suffered a reduction in influence with the creation of the DEFENSE INTELLIGENCE AGENCY in 1961. In 1965 the three military branches lost their representation on the United States Intelligence Board (see NATIONAL FOREIGN INTELLIGENCE BOARD) in favor of a single seat on the Board held by the director of DIA.

Today's Air Force Intelligence

The Office of the Assistant Chief of Staff, Intelligence (OACSI), primarily a management organization, directs all intelligence collection and analysis within the Air Force. It consists of a Directorate of Estimates and a Directorate of Intelligence Plans and Systems.

The Air Force Intelligence Service (AFIS), which was established in 1972, is also commanded by the assistant chief of staff, intelligence (a major general), and is concerned with a broad spectrum of intelligence matters ranging from targets to escape and evasion. The AFIS includes a Directorate of Soviet Affairs and the Air Force Special Activities Center, a worldwide HUMINT (human intelligence, i.e., that collected by human agents) operation.

The Electronic Security Command is a separate command, not under the assistant chief of staff, intelligence. It conducts cryptographic, cryptanalytic, and electronic warfare functions for the Air Force, and maintains a large network of SIGINT facilities in the United States, Germany, Greece, Italy, the United Kingdom, Korea, Japan, the Philippines, and elsewhere around the world. It also operates under the direction of the NATIONAL SECURITY AGENCY for the purposes of strategic intelligence collection.

The Foreign Technology Division (FTD), part of the Air Force Systems Command, is the lineal descendant of the 1917 Foreign Data Section of the Airplane Engineering Division and the 1927 Technical Data Section. It has been based at Dayton, Ohio, at the present-day Wright Patterson Air Force Base, since shortly after the First World War, and, because of its highly specialized technological role, has always remained separate and distinct from the rest of Air Force Intelligence. In 1942 it became known as the Technical Data Laboratory; in 1945 as T-2, the intelligence division of the Air Technical Service Command; in 1951 the Air Technical Intelligence Center; and more recently by its present name. The FTD's major areas of intelligence activity include the prevention of technological surprise, transfer of foreign technology to enhance that of the United States, identification of weaknesses of foreign weapon systems, and interpretation of the intentions of foreign powers through analysis of the design and capabilities of their weapons systems. The FTD has primary responsibility for the analysis of TELINT from Soviet missile tests. The Division also carries out extensive biographic intelligence collection on Warsaw Pact scientists and engineers engaged in aerospace work.

The Air Force Technical Application Center at Patrick Air Force Base, Florida, is yet another member of today's Air Force intelligence complex. It operates the U.S. Atomic Energy Detection System, a worldwide network of sensor sites and installations that collects intelligence on foreign nuclear programs.

The major Air Force commands operate their own intelligence offices, producing the specialized intelligence required for their respective missions. Thus, for example, the Strategic Air Command is concerned with all aspects of strategic bomber and missile operations, the U.S. Air Force in Europe (USAFE) collects and produces intelligence on Soviet and Warsaw Pact armed forces, etc.

(Bidwell, *History of the Military Intelligence Division, Department of the Army General Staff*; Ransom, *Central Intelligence and National Security, The Intelligence Establishment*; MacCloskey, *The American Intelligence Community*; Richelson, *The U.S. Intelligence Community*; Hopple and Watson, *The Military Intelligence Community*.)

AIR PROPRIETARIES

Air operations are often an essential part of both SECRET INTELLIGENCE and COVERT ACTION operations, especially in the Third World, where road or rail transportation is limited or entirely lacking. In order to have on hand a pool of equipment and trained personnel for air operations, the CIA CLANDESTINE SERVICE has subsidized, purchased, or established airlines as PROPRIETARY COMPANIES. These airlines, which were private companies partially or entirely owned and controlled by the CIA, could also be used to provide commercial cover to agents and intelligence officers (see COVER). Within the agency organization, the air proprietaries came under the deputy director for support, although many of the air operations were supervised by the Clandestine Service.

Civil Air Transport

The first of the CIA's air proprietaries was Civil Air Transport, a Nationalist Chinese-registered airline formed in 1946 by former U.S. Army Air Corps Maj. Gen. Claire L. Chennault of Flying Tigers fame, and WHITING WILLAUER, a Washington lawyer and wartime lobbyist for Chinese Nationalist leader Chiang Kai-shek. CAT's pilots were drawn from a pool of American military pilots who remained in the Far East after the war in search of adventure. During the Chinese Civil War between the Nationalists and the Communists, CAT functioned as an unofficial auxiliary to the Nationalist Air Force, flying evacuation missions under the guns of the advancing Communist army, and occasionally flying combat missions.

The Civil War prevented CAT from realizing the profitable civilian air transport business in China that had been the hope of its founders. It was nearly bankrupt in 1949 when it attracted the attention of FRANK G. WISNER, then chief of the Office of Policy Coordination, as the CIA's covert action department was then called. Wisner, who expected shortly to undertake operations in the Far East, saw the potential value of CAT as a supplier of air support to the CIA in the region. He contracted with the airline to this end, underwrote it with an initial payment of $500,000, and assigned ALFRED T. COX, the CIA/OPC chief in China to work with Chennault and Willauer.

After the fall of mainland China to the Communists in December 1949, CAT, which had removed its headquarters to Taiwan, experienced further financial reversals. Wisner decided that CIA/OPC would purchase the airline in order to preserve it as an agency asset in the Far East. The transaction was carried out through a complex arrangement of intermediaries, dummy corporations, and exchanges of stock in order to conceal the CIA ownership of CAT. Essentially, CAT became a subsidiary of the Airdale

Corporation, a Delaware holding company whose directors were all employees of the CIA's Office of Finance. Chennault remained with the airline as chairman of the board, while Willauer stayed on as president. Cox became vice-president, and another CIA employee, an accountant from the Agency's Office of Finance, was made treasurer.

CAT was active during the Korean War, both in its cover role as a civilian carrier and in its essential function as a covert action support unit. In the former role it provided air charter service to the U.S. military forces, ferrying personnel and material between Japan and Korea. In the latter it was used by OPC to air-dispatch guerrillas and other agents into North Korea. The airline was also used in dispatching agents into mainland China and recovering them in OPC's Operation Tropic, the support of "third force" guerrillas (i.e., anti-Communists not affiliated with the Nationalist Chinese regime on Formosa) on the Chinese mainland.

CAT was part of Operation Paper, the CIA/OPC support of Nationalist Chinese guerrillas led by General Li Mi in northern Burma. The guerrillas were supposed to invade adjacent Chinese provinces; CAT evacuated them to Taiwan after the operation failed.

In 1953–54 CAT was used in overt non-CIA operations in which the U.S. government provided contract air service to the French forces in Indochina. CAT's planes airdropped supplies to the besieged French forces in Dien Bien Phu in 1954.

Medical and personal problems forced Willauer to leave CAT in 1953. He was succeeded by GEORGE A. DOOLE, JR., a veteran airline executive who was recruited by the CIA for the task. Cox left the airline for other CIA assignments in 1954.

During the INDONESIA REBELLION, a CIA-supported attempt to overthrow the regime of President Sukarno in 1958, CAT pilots flew combat air support for the rebels (see ALLEN L. POPE). CAT was used to dispatch and support CIA-trained guerrillas into Tibet in the TIBET OPERATION in 1958–61. The CIA later established another air proprietary, Air Ventures, Inc., which operated as a charter service in Nepal while providing air support to the anti-Communist Tibetans during the mid-1960s.

The Airdale Corporation, the Delaware holding company that owned CAT, changed its name to the Pacific Corporation in 1957. Pacific, of which Doole was president, also owned two other proprietaries— Air Asia, an aircraft maintenance company in Taiwan, and Civil Air Transport Company Limited. The latter company, created in 1955 as an entity distinct from CAT, took over CAT's regularly scheduled domestic (i.e., Taiwanese) and international airline routes, while CAT continued to operate the air transport contract part of the business and most of the covert air operations.

Air America

In 1959 CAT changed its name to Air America. It continued to support CIA operations in the Far East, especially in the SECRET WAR IN LAOS and the VIETNAM WAR. In Laos, Air America transports, STOL (short take-off and landing) aircraft, and helicopters provided logistical support to L'Armée Clandestine, the secret army of Laotian tribesmen whom the CIA recruited, organized, trained, and commanded to combat North Vietnamese and Pathet Lao forces in Laos. In Vietnam the airline flew a wide variety of missions, ranging from covert CIA air operations of the type conducted in Laos to overt air transportation under contract to other U.S. government agencies and the Republic of Vietnam.

The overt side of Air America's business in Southeast Asia was so profitable that it balanced the costly covert air operations, in effect making the proprietary virtually a no-cost asset. Insiders attribute the profitability of the company to the business talent of George Doole, Jr.

Southern Air Transport

In addition to his cover job of president of the Pacific Corporation, Doole was the CIA officer in charge of other Agency air proprietaries that were not established under the Pacific corporate umbrella. One of these was Southern Air Transport, a Miami-based cargo line that was operating air cargo service in Florida, the Bahamas, and the Caribbean at a loss before it was secretly purchased by the CIA in 1960. The Agency acquired the company on the assumption that covert action operations would be required in Latin America, and that SAT would serve in the same air support role that Air America played in the Far East. SAT became a profitable business under Doole's direction, through overt air transport contracts with other U.S. government agencies.

The Air Proprietaries Complex

During the 1950s and 1960s the CIA purchased or acquired an interest in a host of small airlines, air charter companies, and related businesses. Intermountain Aviation, based near Tucson, Arizona, was used to train Agency personnel and others (e.g., the Khamba tribesmen used in the TIBET OPERATION) in parachuting. Double-Chek Corporation, a Miami firm, was used as an intermediary to hire and pay the American pilots who flew combat missions in the

BAY OF PIGS INVASION. Caramar (Caribbean Marine Aero Corporation) hired Cuban exiles for the CIA to fly B-26 bombers against rebels in the Congo in 1964. Air Ethiopia, Air Jordan, and Iran Air were partially subsidized by the Agency.

By 1963 the complex of CIA-owned or -controlled airlines had become so large that the Agency established a management committee, the Executive Committee for Air Proprietary Operations (EXCOMAIR), to supervise and coordinate it. The Committee was chaired by CIA General Counsel LAWRENCE R. HOUSTON and was composed of representatives of the Clandestine Service, the Directorate of Support, and the director of central intelligence.

During the mid-1970s the CIA greatly reduced the size of the air proprietaries complex, having found that maintaining the cover of such a large and widespread establishment was not feasible. Air America, Southern Air Transport, Intermountain, and most or all of the others were sold to private buyers.

(Leary, *Perilous Missions;* Robbins, *Air America;* Marchetti and Marks, *The CIA and the Cult of Intelligence;* Marks, *The CIA's Corporate Shell Game.*)

ALAMO SCOUTS

A long-range ground reconnaissance unit of the Sixth Army in the Southwest Pacific Area during the Second World War. Established in November 1943, the Alamo Scouts numbered some three hundred men who took part in nearly one hundred missions. Missions ranged from pure reconnaissance to commando-style raids. The Scouts were infiltrated into Japanese-controlled areas, and recovered by means of seaplanes, submarines, and PT boats. In January 1945 the Scouts raided a Japanese prisoner-of-war camp on Luzon in the Philippines and freed more than five hundred Allied prisoners.

(Powe and Wilson, *The Evolution of American Military Intelligence.*)

ALBANIA OPERATION

Summary: In 1950–52 the Central Intelligence Agency and the British Secret Intelligence Service ran a joint covert action operation, code-named Valuable, aimed at overthrowing the Communist government of Albania. The operation failed because it was penetrated by Soviet intelligence.

Background: Only slightly larger than Massachusetts, the Balkan State of Albania lies on the eastern Adriatic coast, bounded by Greece to the east and Yugoslavia to the north and east. Traditionally Albania has had a tribal society made up of about

Members of the Alamo Scouts in training at Fergusson Island, New Guinea, in early 1944. Source: Department of Defense.

seventy percent Moslems, twenty percent Orthodox Christians, and ten percent Roman Catholics. In 1928 Ahmed Bey Zogu, the son of the most powerful Moslem clan chieftain in northern Albania, proclaimed Albania a kingdom and himself King Zog I. Zog's reign was corrupt and unpopular, and he was, in fact, the puppet of Italian dictator Benito Mussolini who had forced Albania to accept the status of an Italian client-state. In 1939, shortly before the outbreak of the Second World War, Zog and Mussolini had a falling out, and Zog fled into exile. He spent the war in England and later settled in Egypt as the guest of King Farouk, who was himself mostly of Albanian extraction.

Germany occupied Albania during the war, and the Albanian resistance was led by Enver Hoxha, a young schoolteacher and the founder of the Albanian Communist Party. After the war Hoxha formed a Communist government and established himself as head of state. During 1946–49 Albania and its Communist neighbor Yugoslavia provided aid and sanc-

tuary to the Communist insurgents who were waging a civil war in Greece.

In 1948 Marshal Tito of Yugoslavia broke with Stalin and the Kremlin over the issue of international Communism; Tito remained committed to Communist ideology, but he rejected Soviet hegemony and espoused a policy of Yugoslavian nationalism. He wished Yugoslavia to remain Communist but independent of Moscow.

Stalin responded, first, with an unsuccessful campaign of subversion aimed at overthrowing Tito, and then with purges in other Balkan states to prevent "deviationist" elements from following Tito's example. There was a series of show trials and executions of Communist Party officials whose loyalty to Moscow had come into question in Bulgaria, Romania, and Albania.

The CIA/SIS Operation

Late in 1949 foreign policy planners in the U.S. State and Defense departments took a new interest in Albania in light of the recent developments in the Balkans. Yugoslavia's alienation from Moscow denied the Soviets a land corridor to Albania, which would hinder their efforts to aid the Albanian regime in the event of an anti-Communist rebellion. American planners started to contemplate a covert action operation aimed at fomenting such a revolt. Defense strategists did not consider Albania to be of major military value, although an anti-Communist coup would block Soviet plans to build a naval base in the Albanian port of Valoa. The principal value of such an operation was seen as political, in that it would further weaken Soviet control in the Balkans and perhaps lead to a general anti-Soviet uprising in Eastern Europe.

The proposal for an Albania operation originated with the British Secret Intelligence Service. Britain, which considered the eastern Mediterranean a traditional British sphere of influence, had actually attempted a small-scale operation in 1947, recruiting about a dozen Albanian emigrés in Greece and Italy, training them in the techniques of sabotage and subversion, and parachuting them into the mountains of central Albania. The operation had dragged on since then without significant results. The British believed a larger campaign would succeed, but their domestic economic difficulties prevented them from pursuing such a campaign independently; they therefore proposed a joint Anglo-American operation to the State Department.

The Americans decided to go ahead with the project late in 1949, and it was given the code name Valuable and assigned to the Office of Policy Coordination—the newly created covert action department within the CIA (see CENTRAL INTELLIGENCE AGENCY). The day-to-day coordination of Valuable was to be carried out in Washington by the Special Policy Committee, a four-person board with representatives from the State Department, OPC, the British Foreign Office, and SIS. State's representative was ROBERT P. JOYCE, a foreign service officer who had served in the Office of Strategic Services and was an expert on both the Balkans and secret operations. OPC's representative was FRANKLIN A. LINDSAY, an OSS veteran who had fought with Tito's partisans in Yugoslavia and was now chief of OPC's East European Division. The man from the British Foreign Office was George Jellico, a veteran of the British commando outfit, the Special Air Service. The SIS representative was H.A.R. ("Kim") PHILBY, recently arrived in Washington to serve as liaison officer between the SIS and the CIA. As is now generally known, Philby was also a penetration agent who had been working for Soviet intelligence since before the Second World War.

Political control of the operation was the nub of a complex dispute between SIS and CIA and, within CIA, between OPC and its rival, the Office of Special Operations (see CENTRAL INTELLIGENCE AGENCY for a discussion of the rivalry between OPC, the covert action department, and OSO, the secret intelligence department of the CIA during its early years). The British, who had a close working liaison with the Greek intelligence and security services, proposed as political leader Abbas Kupi, an Albanian exile in Greece. However, the American planners feared that Kupi's presumed sympathy toward a Greek territorial claim to part of Albania would lead to conflict with other Albanian factions.

CIA/OSO, which had a similar close relationship with Italian security and intelligence, proposed that leadership be selected from among the many Albanian refugees in Italy. Most of those refugees, however, had been sympathetic to the old Italian-dominated regime of King Zog, and it was therefore feared that they might be just as divisive of Albanian unity as Abbas Kupi. CIA/OPC favored Hassan Dosti, an Albanian emigré living in New York City. Dosti was a young lawyer and the head of the Albanian National Council, a group sponsored by the National Committee for a Free Europe, an organization funded and controlled by the OPC for the specific purpose, among others, of providing political leadership to anti-Communist movements in Europe (see RADIO FREE EUROPE/RADIO LIBERTY).

Just how (or whether) this three-way dispute was resolved is obscure and rendered moot by the failure of Operation Valuable. The matter is worth noting,

nonetheless, because similar problems of complex exile politics arose in many subsequent CIA covert operations involving emigrés (see BAY OF PIGS INVASION).

The paramilitary part of Operation Valuable consisted of recruiting, training, and equipping Albanian emigrés and sending them into their homeland to wage a guerrilla war against the Communist regime of Enver Hoxha. Albanian leadership of this phase was recruited from among King Zog's Royal Guard, which had accompanied him into exile in Cairo. Capt. Zenel Shehu was appointed commander; his deputies were Capt. Nalil Sufa and Hamit Matjani (the latter, a leader of the anti-Nazi resistance, was called "The Tiger" and had been in and out of Albania several times since 1946). Under the covert auspices of the CIA and the SIS, the three formed the Committee of Free Albanians and began to recruit among the emigré groups in Egypt, Greece, and Italy.

The OPC officer assigned to run Valuable "on the ground" in the eastern Mediterranean was MICHAEL BURKE, an OSS veteran with experience operating behind German lines in Italy. Training camps were established in Cyprus and Malta, both still British colonies, and in Frankfurt, West Germany. The first of the emigré agents was sent into Albania in April 1950; more followed in the subsequent months. Some were air-dispatched, parachuting from C-47s flown by CIA crews out of a remote airstrip near Bari, an Adriatic seaport on the heel of the Italian boot about a hundred air miles from the Albanian coast. Other agents were infiltrated by sea, arriving off the coast by submarine and landing in rubber boats. Still others were sent in by land, across Albania's southern border with Greece.

When some of the first agents failed to report to overflying CIA aircraft by ground-to-air radio, Burke thought the new communication equipment used might have failed, or that they had simply become frightened and abandoned their mission. However, after some agents made their way back across the Greek-Albanian border, it became apparent that Valuable had been penetrated and that the Albanian militia had been waiting for most of the agents when they arrived.

Not realizing that the penetration had taken place at the highest level through the Soviet agent Philby, who was taking part in the day-to-day control of the operation in Washington, Burke and the other officers running Valuable on the ground in the eastern Mediterranean tried to remedy matters by tightening security at the training camps. This, of course, failed to stop the leak, and more agents were captured throughout 1951 and early 1952, including Captains

Shehu and Sufa, the Albanian leaders of the operation, who were shot.

Valuable was terminated in 1952, having failed to overthrow the Communist Albanian regime of Enver Hoxha. By some accounts it cost the lives of five hundred Albanian exiles.

(Page, Leitch, and Knightley, *The Philby Conspiracy*; Philby, *My Silent War*; Felix, *A Short Course in the Secret War*; Hunt, *Undercover*; Cookridge, *The Third Man*; Powers, *The Man Who Kept the Secrets*; Burke, *Outrageous Good Fortune*; Rositzke, *The CIA's Secret Operations*.)

ALBRECHT, RALPH GERHART (August 11, 1896–): lawyer, intelligence officer

A native of Jersey City, New Jersey, Albrecht graduated from the University of Pennsylvania in 1919 and from Harvard Law School in 1923, after which he practiced law in New York City.

In 1941 Albrecht was commissioned in the U.S. Naval Reserve and assigned to the OFFICE OF NAVAL INTELLIGENCE. As a result of his pre-war representation of American companies in their claims against Germany growing out of German sabotage in the FIRST WORLD WAR, he had acquired a knowledge of German intelligence. ONI made use of this background and had him organize a prisoner interrogation branch.

Albrecht's experiences in London in 1941 with British psychological warfare operations against Germany prompted him to propose to Captain ELLIS M. ZACHARIAS, deputy director of ONI, the formation of a psychological warfare branch within ONI. This proposal resulted in the Special Warfare Branch, Op-16-W. Albrecht, who spoke fluent German, was the voice of "Commander Robert Lee Norden," the fictitious character invented by LADISLAS FARAGO, chief of research and planning of the Special Warfare Branch. "Commander Norden" was spokesman for the U.S. Navy's "white" propaganda (see COVERT ACTION) radio broadcasts to the crewmen of German U-boats operating off the U.S. coasts.

In 1945 Albrecht was transferred to the Office of Strategic Services, where he served as assistant director. He served as a special assistant to the U.S. attorney general and associate trial counsel at the Nuremburg war crimes trials in 1945–46. Later he returned to the private practice of law.

(*Who's Who in America*, 37th ed.; Dorwart, *Conflict of Duty*; Zacharias, *Secret Missions*; Farago, *Burn After Reading*; Smith, *OSS*.)

ALDRICH, HARRY STARKEY (1895–): Army officer, intelligence officer

A native of Kalamazoo, Michigan, Aldrich graduated from the Michigan College of Mining in 1917. He served in the U.S. Army in the First World War and afterwards was with the Army in the Far East. He was an Army language officer at Peking, China, in 1928–32 and a member of Brig. Gen. John Magruder's American Military Mission to China in 1941.

Aldrich served in Army Intelligence during the Second World War and was assigned to the Office of Strategic Services in 1944. Appointed chief of the OSS SECRET INTELLIGENCE BRANCH in Cairo, he later took charge of all OSS operations in the Middle East.

(National Archives, OSS Files, "Prominent Persons in the OSS"; Cave Brown, *The Last Hero*; Smith, *OSS*.)

ALDRIDGE, EDWARD C., JR. (August 18, 1938–): business executive, government official, intelligence officer

A native of Houston, Texas, Aldridge graduated from Texas A & M in 1960 and earned an M.S. from the Georgia Institute of Technology in 1962. During 1962–67 he was manager of the missile and space division of Douglas Aircraft Company in St. Louis, Missouri. In 1967 he joined the Department of Defense and was director of the Strategic Defense Division until 1972, when he joined the LTV Aerospace Corporation as manager of advanced concepts. In 1973 he joined the Office of Management and Budget as a senior management associate, and the following year he rejoined the Defense Department as deputy assistant secretary. During 1977–81 he was vice president of the Strategic Systems Group.

In 1981 Aldridge was appointed under secretary of the Air Force and as such became the director of the NATIONAL RECONNAISSANCE OFFICE.

(*Who's Who in America*, 42nd ed.; Richelson, *The U.S. Intelligence Community*.)

ALLEN, GEORGE W. (ca. 1926–): intelligence officer

A native of Massachusetts, Allen served in the U.S. Navy during the Second World War. He graduated from the University of Utah and joined Army Intelligence as an intelligence analyst in 1949. During the 1950s he specialized in CURRENT INTELLIGENCE on Vietnam and the Far East.

In 1963 Allen transferred to the Central Intelligence Agency, where he was a senior analyst on Far Eastern matters in the Office of Current Intelligence. He served in Vietnam during 1964–66 as senior analyst at the CIA's Saigon station and was wounded when the U.S. embassy in Saigon was bombed in 1965. The following year he returned to CIA headquarters, where he was special assistant for Vietnam affairs to Director RICHARD M. HELMS. Allen retired in 1979 but continued to work as a contract consultant to the CIA.

Allen was a persuasive witness for the defense during the 1985 trial of Gen. William Westmoreland's unsuccessful libel suit against CBS News and former CIA intelligence analyst Samuel A. Adams. A CBS documentary had made assertions that the Army had deliberately fabricated low estimates of Viet Cong strength and Allen backed up these assertions, testifying that the Army estimates were not made "in good faith."

(N.Y. *Times,* January 23, 1985, p. B28.)

ALLEN, JAMES: balloonist, intelligence officer

At the outbreak of the Civil War Allen was a resident of Providence, Rhode Island, a member of the 1st Regiment of the Rhode Island State Militia, and a balloonist of four years' experience. He and Dr. William H. Helme, a dentist and fellow balloonist, traveled to Washington with two of Allen's balloons to offer their equipment and services to the U.S. Army (see RECONNAISSANCE BALLOONS). On June 9 they made a demonstration flight in Washington for the Army.

Helme apparently withdrew after the first demonstrations, but Allen remained and undertook some reconnaissance flights for the Army in northern Virginia shortly thereafter. Both of Allen's balloons were soon destroyed in mishaps, however, and Allen returned to Rhode Island in July 1861. In March he returned with his brother Ezra to serve as an aeronaut in the Army of the Potomac under THADDEUS S.C. LOWE.

Allen remained in the balloon corps for its duration, which included the Peninsula Campaign, and made many reconnaissance flights. After Lowe resigned in May 1863, Allen served as chief of the Corps until it was disbanded the following month.

(Bidwell, *History of the Military Intelligence Division, Department of the Army General Staff;* Glines, *The Compact History of the United States Air Force.*)

ALLIED GEOGRAPHICAL SECTION

This agency was established by Gen. CHARLES A. WILLOUGHBY, Gen. Douglas MacArthur's assistant chief of staff for intelligence, early in the SECOND WORLD WAR. The section was responsible for compiling, verifying, and integrating all geographical information needed for Allied military operations in New Guinea and the Southwest Pacific, areas that theretofore had largely been unmapped or poorly mapped.

(Spector, *Eagle Against the Sun;* Ind, *Allied Intelligence Bureau.*)

ALLIED INTELLIGENCE BUREAU

This agency coordinated and supported the intelligence and COVERT ACTION operations of American, British, Dutch, and Australian units in the Southwest Pacific Theater during the SECOND WORLD WAR. At the outbreak of the war in the Pacific, Gen. Douglas MacArthur had declined the use of the Office of Strategic Services to coordinate the various Allied clandestine assets in the Southwest Pacific on the grounds that control from OSS headquarters in Washington would be unwieldy and impractical. (It has also been suggested that MacArthur's refusal was prompted by his earlier opposition to the creation of the OSS, and to his intelligence staff's jealousy of its jurisdiction over the Southwest Pacific.) Instead he directed his G-2 (see ARMY INTELLIGENCE) section head, Maj. Gen. CHARLES A. WILLOUGHBY, to establish a means of coordinating the Allied units at the command level of MacArthur's Far East headquarters. In July 1942 Willoughby established the Allied Intelligence Bureau to "obtain and report information of the enemy in the Southwest Pacific Area, and in addition, where practical . . . weaken the enemy by sabotage and destruction of morale, and . . . render aid and assistance to local efforts in the same end in enemy-occupied territories." The Bureau was placed under joint U.S.-Australian control; it was directed by Col. C.G. Roberts, the head of Australian Military Intelligence, and his deputy, Lt. ALLISON IND of the U.S. Army. Ind also served as the Bureau's finance officer, an arrangement that gave MacArthur veto power over any of its operations.

The Allied Intelligence Bureau was headquartered in Melbourne, Australia. The units under the Bureau included British intelligence and covert action elements that had been operating out of Australia earlier in the war; the Netherlands Indies Forces Intelligence Service; an Australian propaganda service; and the Royal Australian Navy's Islands Coastwatching Service. The last-named was probably the single most valuable component of the Bureau.

The coastwatchers had been established in 1919 to

keep watch over Australia's vast unguarded coasts as well as the offshore islands placed under Australian mandate after the First World War. The watchers were, for the most part, planters, missionaries, or civil servants who reported regularly by radio on the situation in their local areas. As the Second World War approached, the coastwatchers were incorporated into Australian naval intelligence, and thence into the Allied Intelligence Bureau.

The coastwatchers remained on the Pacific islands that had been captured by the Japanese, and their radio reporting network stretched from Bougainville through the central Solomon Islands to Guadalcanal and Port Moresby, New Guinea. They reported on the extent of Japanese troop and naval movements. The information they supplied was considered critical to the Allied victories on Guadalcanal, the Solomons, and New Guinea. They also aided in the rescue of American air and naval crews stranded in Japanese territory. Lt. (jg.) John F. Kennedy and his crew were rescued after the sinking of PT-109 through the work of a coastwatcher.

In addition to running such secret intelligence operations as the coastwatchers, the Allied Intelligence Bureau carried out an extensive program of aerial reconnaissance; in support of a single campaign—the Ninth Australian Division's strike to recapture the rich Borneo oil fields in 1945—the Bureau conducted more than 150 reconnaissance flights.

Covert action teams of the Allied Intelligence Bureau carried out commando and sabotage raids in Japanese-occupied territory and supported local resistance groups, especially in the Philippines. The Bureau also initiated such innovative subversion techniques as infiltrating Islamic religious leaders from the Middle East into the Philippines, where they worked with their local coreligionists to foment a holy war against the Japanese.

After the war the Allied Intelligence Bureau was disbanded.

(Ind, *Allied Intelligence Bureau*; Spector, *Eagle Against the Sun*; Corson, *Armies of Ignorance*.)

ALLIED TRANSLATOR AND INTERPRETER SECTION

This agency was established by Gen. CHARLES A. WILLOUGHBY, Gen. Douglas MacArthur's chief of intelligence, late in 1942. Headed by Lt. Col. SIDNEY F. MASHBIR, the section was responsible for the translation of captured Japanese documents and the interrogation of Japanese prisoners of war.

ATIS was originally staffed by approximately forty multilingual officers and men of the Australian, Ca-

nadian, and British armies, in addition to White Russians, East Indies Netherlanders, and a handful of Americans. Later in the war it grew to a strength of nearly two thousand, largely nisei troops—Americans of Japanese descent—who risked death and reprisals against their relatives in Japan in case of capture.

ATIS translated some 350,000 Japanese documents and interrogated over 10,000 prisoners of war. It was described by Willoughby (in what surely was an overstatement) as "possibly the most important intelligence agency of the war."

(Spector, *Eagle Against the Sun*; Ind, *Allied Intelligence Bureau*; Mashbir, *I Was an American Spy*; Finnegan, *Military Intelligence*.)

ALSOP, JOHN DE KOVEN (August 4, 1915–): businessman, covert operations officer

A native of Avon, Connecticut, Alsop attended the Groton School and graduated from Yale University in 1937. From 1937 to 1942 he worked for the Wall Street investment firm of Smith, Barney.

In 1942 Alsop was commissioned in the U.S. Army and assigned to the Office of Strategic Services. He served in the OSS SPECIAL OPERATIONS BRANCH and took part in the JEDBURGH OPERATION, in which three-man Allied teams were parachuted behind German lines in France immediately after D-Day to coordinate the work of the French Resistance. He also served in the OSS in China. Discharged with the rank of captain in 1945, he was awarded the Bronze Star, the French croix de guerre, and other decorations.

After the war he joined the Mutual Insurance Company in Hartford, Connecticut, and has since held several senior positions with that company, including the presidency. He has been active in the Republican Party in Connecticut and, in 1962, was the unsuccessful Republican candidate for governor.

Alsop's brother STEWART ALSOP also served in the OSS.

(Smith, *OSS*; *Who's Who in the East*, v. 11.)

ALSOP, STEWART JOHONNOT OLIVER (May 17, 1914–May 26, 1974): journalist, covert operations officer

A native of Avon, Connecticut, Alsop graduated from the Groton School in 1932 and from Yale in 1936 and worked as an editor for Doubleday Doran in New York City. In 1942 he enlisted in the British Army and advanced to the rank of captain. In 1944

Japanese-American translators of the Allied Translator and Interpreter Section interrogating a Japanese prisoner of war in New Guinea. Source: Department of Defense.

he transferred to the U.S. Army and was assigned to the OSS SPECIAL OPERATIONS BRANCH. He took part in the JEDBURGH OPERATION, in which three-man Allied teams were parachuted behind German lines in France immediately after D-Day to coordinate the work of the French Resistance. (Alsop's brother JOHN ALSOP also served in the OSS.) After the war, he and his brother Joseph Alsop wrote a syndicated newspaper column. He became a senior editor of *Newsweek* and wrote several books, including *Sub Rosa* (with THOMAS BRADEN), an account of OSS operations.

Alsop's grandmother, Corinne Roosevelt Robinson, was a sister of Theodore Roosevelt.

(*Who Was Who in America*, v. 6.)

AMERASIA CASE

Established in 1936, *Amerasia* was a periodical of small circulation (about 1,700 copies) devoted to Asian affairs. Its editorial policy favored the wartime alliance between Chiang Kai-shek and the Chinese Communists for the purpose of fighting Japan, and seemed generally to favor the Communists.

Early in 1945 an intelligence analyst in the Research and Analysis Branch of the OFFICE OF STRATEGIC SERVICES came across an article in the January issue of the periodical on Anglo-American rivalry in Thailand that seemed to quote verbatim from a classified OSS report he remembered seeing. He reported the discovery to the OSS Office of Security, which placed the magazine's offices in New York City under surveillance. On the night of March 11, 1945 OSS investigators burglarized the offices and found a copy of the classified OSS report on Thailand. They also discovered that the magazine's files contained scores of documents belonging to the OSS, the Office of Naval Intelligence, Army Intelligence, and the State Department. The documents were classified, and some were stamped Top Secret (see SECURITY CLASSIFICATION SYSTEM).

The investigators reported their find to OSS Director WILLIAM J. DONOVAN, who informed the heads of the other agencies involved. The Federal Bureau of Investigation was called into the case.

The initial object of the FBI's surveillance was Philip J. Jaffe, the editor of *Amerasia*. Jaffe was a Russian-born American citizen; a successful greeting-card manufacturer; a friend of high-ranking American Communists; a longtime supporter of Communist front organizations, especially those that promoted Soviet foreign policy in China and Asia; and a frequent associate of employees of the Soviet consulate in New York City. Physical and electronic surveillance of Jaffe disclosed his association with several U.S. government employees who had access to the classified material found in his offices: Lt. Andrew Roth, an ONI officer; Emmanuel S. Larsen, a foreign service officer in the State Department's Office of Far Eastern Affairs; and John S. Service, a State Department expert on Far Eastern affairs.

On June 6, 1945 the FBI arrested Jaffe, Roth, Larsen, and Service; Mark Gayn, a free-lance writer; and Kate Mitchell, Jaffe's coeditor. All were charged with conspiracy to commit espionage, and several hundred classified government documents in the *Amerasia* files were seized as evidence.

The government was unable to prove that any of the defendants had given any of the classified information to the Soviet Union or any other foreign power (and indeed, Jaffe's publication of some of the material in his magazine was completely inconsistent with the classic methods of espionage). Furthermore, the evidence linking four of the others to the case was deemed insufficient for prosecution, leaving Jaffe and Larsen as the only defendants in the case. And the case was prejudiced by the fact that the OSS break-in was carried out without a warrant. The charges against Jaffe and Larsen were reduced to conspiracy to steal classified information, to which Jaffe pleaded guilty and was fined $2,500, and Larsen pleaded nolo contendere and was fined $500.

This somewhat anticlimactic conclusion notwithstanding, the *Amerasia* case provided ammunition for Sen. Joseph R. McCarthy of Wisconsin in 1950, when he began his campaign against purported Communists in the State Department and other government agencies. As a result, John S. Service, who had returned to the State Department, was subjected to several prolonged loyalty hearings, then dismissed by the department in 1951. He was reinstated in 1957 after a long court battle.

Larsen, one of the two people convicted of anything in the case, furnished its most surprising sequel in 1946 when he charged that the State Department was indeed honeycombed with Communists, although he claimed not to be one of them. His most astounding charge was that the government had

deliberately fumbled the case against Jaffe, who he implied had been guilty, unlike himself. Larsen's charges resulted in sensational press coverage but no substantial consequences.

The *Amerasia* case highlighted the deficient security precautions in force in the government to safeguard classified information. It seems to have had no other significant results.

(Smith, *OSS*; Seth, *Unmasked*; De Toledano, *J. Edgar Hoover*; Cook, *The FBI Nobody Knows*.)

AMERICAN BLACK CHAMBER

The Cipher Bureau, a code-breaking unit jointly run by the War and State departments from 1919 to 1929 (see CRYPTOLOGY, HERBERT O. YARDLEY). It was known informally as the Black Chamber, after the "black chambers" of Great Britain, France, and other European powers, which intercepted mail and broke codes in the eighteenth and nineteenth centuries.

(Yardley, *American Black Chamber*; Kahn, *The Codebreakers*.)

AMERICAN PROTECTIVE LEAGUE

A private organization of unpaid volunteers who, with U.S. government sanction, tried to catch enemy agents and domestic draft dodgers during the FIRST WORLD WAR; the League was the brainchild of Chicago billboard advertising executive Albert M. Briggs. In 1917, Briggs proposed to A. BRUCE BIELASKI, then chief of the Justice Department's Bureau of Investigation (later the FEDERAL BUREAU OF INVESTIGATION), the formation of a civilian auxiliary to aid the Bureau in countering German espionage and sabotage operations in the United States. At the time the Bureau had a staff of three hundred agents, far fewer than the number needed to keep track of the one million enemy aliens in the country while also carrying out the Bureau's other investigative responsibilities. Bielaski therefore accepted Briggs's proposal.

Bielaski's acceptance gave the League a quasi-official status, as did the issuance to each League member of a badge resembling a police shield and bearing the legend "American Protective League, Secret Service Division." After the United States entered the war, the League also became affiliated with the Army's Military Intelligence Division (see ARMY INTELLIGENCE) through the auspices of Major RALPH H. VAN DEMAN.

The goal of the League was to have an agent in

every American bank, business, and industrial plant to report on any disloyalty that employees might demonstrate. The league grew rapidly, reaching one hundred thousand within three months, and blossoming into a quarter-million would-be spy-catchers soon thereafter. It was soon too large for the Bureau of Investigation or the Army's Military Intelligence Division to manage or control.

The League accomplished little in the way of counterespionage but chalked up a deplorable record of illegal arrests, harrassment, wiretaps, and other violations of privacy and civil rights, as well as anti-labor activities. Although the government ordered the League to disband after the war, many of its local chapters continued their domestic spying and anti-labor activities under other names.

(Jensen, *The Price of Vigilance*; Corson, *Armies of Ignorance*; Whitehead, *The FBI Story*.)

AMERICAN REVOLUTION

Background: The causes of the American Revolution are so familiar there is no need to review them here. One of them bears mention, however, for it directly influenced the intelligence history of the Revolutionary War: the Stamp Act.

The Stamp Act was passed by the British Parliament in 1765 in order to raise revenue for the support of frontier garrisons protecting the American colonies from Indian attacks. It required the colonists to use tax stamps on all legal and commercial papers, pamphlets, newspapers, almanacs, cards, and dice. It established a revenue-collection bureaucracy in the colonies for the sale of the stamps and the enforcement of the law. Unlike earlier revenue measures, the Stamp Act fell more or less equally upon all of the colonies (earlier revenue measures, e.g., the Sugar Act, penalized the commercial colonies of New England, but rested lightly upon the agricultural colonies in the South). The result was that resentment became universal among the colonists. The Stamp Act, therefore, had the unintended effect of unifying colonial resistance to British rule.

Active resistance to the Stamp Act resulted in the establishment of a colonial secret society called the SONS OF LIBERTY, which was in fact a confederation of various political clubs and mercantile societies that had existed long before the Act was imposed. The Sons of Liberty used various means to prevent enforcement of the Act, e.g., rioting, destroying the stamps, and attacking stamp agents. Some chapters of the organization established mutual security pacts with their counterparts in the other colonies, vowing

to come to each other's aid should Britain resort to enforcement by military means.

The Sons of Liberty did not disband with the repeal of the Stamp Act in 1766. The organization continued to function as the Patriot underground during the decade that preceded the Revolution, giving rise to the more formalized shadow agencies of the COMMITTEES OF CORRESPONDENCE in 1772, and the Committees of Safety in 1775. This dissident infrastructure, well-established and in place at the outbreak of hostilities in 1775, functioned as an intelligence network just before the war and during its first months, and provided the clandestine assets from which the Continental Army's military secret service was organized in 1777.

The War: Hostilities commenced on April 19, 1775 when a British attempt to seize Patriot military stores precipitated the battles of Lexington and Concord. British-occupied Boston was subsequently invested by a force of New England militia. The force was taken over by the Continental Congress in June and became the nucleus of the Continental Army. Gen. GEORGE WASHINGTON was appointed Commander-in-Chief.

Cannon and other ordnance seized at Ticonderoga in May, when that fort was captured by New England militiamen, led by Ethan Allen and BENEDICT ARNOLD, were moved to Boston in December, when the frozen ground made possible transportation of the heavy pieces. Faced with this artillery, General Howe, the British commander in Boston, evacuated the city by sea, withdrawing his troops to Halifax, Nova Scotia, in March 1776.

Continental forces had invaded Canada the previous fall, capturing Montreal and investing Quebec. But the Americans were forced to withdraw when the British sent fresh troops and a relief expedition to the two cities in May 1776. The British then pressed southward into New York, but were fought to a standstill during the summer and fall by the retreating Continentals.

The British Hudson-Champlain Strategy

Meanwhile, General Howe, who had withdrawn from Boston to Halifax in March, took the offensive with an assault on New York in August and September 1776. His plan was to gain control of the Hudson River and so split the colonies in two. Washington foresaw this move and had already transferred his forces to Manhattan and Brooklyn, but he was overpowered by the British assault and forced to withdraw to White Plains and the Hudson Highlands near West Point. After establishing a stronghold in the Highlands, he withdrew most of his army through

New Jersey. His defensive plan was to keep inshore of Howe, moving when the British commander moved. Late in December he attacked the British at Trenton, and a few days later at Princeton, forcing Howe back to New Brunswick, New Jersey. He then established himself for the winter at Morristown.

In the late spring of 1777 the British resumed their campaign to bisect the colonies by taking control of the Hudson and Lake Champlain. In June Gen. John Burgoyne led a British force southward across Champlain, while a second column under Lt. Col. Barry St. Leger moved down the Mohawk Valley to join Burgoyne at Albany. The British campaign failed, however, after a series of setbacks and defeats: St. Leger at Fort Stanwix, New York, and Burgoyne at Bennington, Vermont, and Saratoga, New York.

Burgoyne's failure may have been due in part to lack of support by Howe, who was supposed to have proceeded up the Hudson from Manhattan to join the invading force. Instead, Howe moved his main force south by sea to the head of Chesapeake Bay and captured Philadelphia on September 26th. Washington, having failed to stop Howe, withdrew to Valley Forge for the winter.

In March 1778 Howe was replaced as British Commander-in-Chief by Gen. Henry Clinton. Soon thereafter Clinton evacuated the British force from Philadelphia and returned it to New York, fighting the major battle of Monmouth Court House while en route. The battle marked the last major action in the north.

The War Moves South

In the fall of 1778 Clinton sent an expedition south, which occupied Savannah and Augusta, Georgia. He and Lord Cornwallis led an expedition that captured Charleston, South Carolina, in May 1780. The British insured their control over the Carolinas two weeks later in their defeat and slaughter of a relief column of Virginia militia at Waxhaws in northern South Carolina. A Continental relief expedition under Gen. Horatio Gates was wiped out by Cornwallis at Camden, South Carolina, in August 1780.

The tide turned with the Continental victory at King's Mountain, South Carolina, in October 1780, followed by the victories at Cowpens in January 1781, and Guilford Court House, North Carolina, in March. Cornwallis withdrew to Wilmington, North Carolina, then moved the main body of his troops to Virginia.

The final act of the war was played when the American alliance with France, signed in February 1778, made itself felt. A French land and naval force under General Rochambeau arrived at Newport, Rhode Island, in the summer of 1780, and a second

naval squadron commanded by Admiral DeGrasse arrived early in 1781. The French forces, together with Washington's army, laid siege to Cornwallis at Yorktown, Virginia, and forced his surrender in October 1781. Although there were small engagements subsequent to Cornwallis's surrender, and the peace treaty that ended the war was not signed until 1783, Yorktown effectively marked the end of significant hostilities.

Intelligence: The Revolution was a war of divided loyalties. The two sides shared the same language, culture, customs, and—until 1776—even the same government. Whenever such ingredients are present—as in Civil War America or postwar Berlin—there is an abundance of potential espionage agents. Among the Patriots these potential agents were organized in such underground organizations as the Sons of Liberty and the Committees of Correspondence long before the war, and therefore some primitive secret intelligence networks (e.g., PAUL REVERE's Boston organization, "the Mechanics") were in place at the beginning of the war. No comparable pre-war Loyalist underground existed, but individual Tory agents (e.g., BENJAMIN CHURCH and JOSEPH GALLOWAY) were working for the British long before hostilities commenced.

Intelligence played an essential role in bringing about the battles of Lexington and Concord, which actually triggered the war. An unidentified Tory agent in Concord informed the British commander in Boston that the patriots had hidden military stores in the village, and thereby brought about the nocturnal British expedition intended to seize the supplies. And it was the Patriots' intelligence network in Boston that discovered the British preparations for that expedition, resulting in Paul Revere's famous ride.

Intelligence and Washington's Strategy

The Revolution was largely a war of movement waged over great distances, and so, timely intelligence regarding the location and strength of the enemy was vital to the commanders on both sides. When hostilities escalated into a full-scale war—i.e., in the summer of 1776, when the British invaded New York—military intelligence became even more important. In September Washington established KNOWLTON'S RANGERS, an intelligence and reconnaissance unit, as a step toward redressing the strategic imbalance between the British and Continental armies. (Creation of the unit is regarded as the birth of American military intelligence, and the inclusion of the year 1776 in the present-day logo of U.S. Army intelligence is a reference to it.)

The British force was larger and better trained and equipped than the Continentals. Moreover, the Royal Navy controlled the coastal waters, giving the British the advantage in speed and security in moving large bodies of troops. This superiority in strength and mobility put the strategic initiative into the hands of the British and forced a defensive strategy on Washington, viz., keeping the British between himself and the sea, and moving when they moved. Timely intelligence regarding British movements was obviously basic to this strategy.

Washington was so keenly aware of the necessity of good intelligence that he at first took personal charge of the matter of recruiting, training, and running secret intelligence agents. For example, JOHN HONEYMAN, an agent recruited by Washington and reporting directly to him, carried out a secret reconnaissance crucial to the American victory at the Battle of Trenton in December 1776. Washington also recruited Joshua Mersereau, whose family spy ring provided one of the first networks in British-occupied New York (see MERSEREAU SPY RING). However, Washington's secret intelligence requirements expanded so rapidly that he soon delegated the role of case officer to selected subordinates. Thus, from 1777 onward, Washington had what amounted to a formal secret service.

Many of Washington's officers ran secret intelligence networks for him. Col. ELIAS DAYTON took over the Mersereau ring and established other networks in New York. New York, which was the British stronghold in America from 1776 onwards, was a principal intelligence target of Washington, and he had many networks operating in Manhattan and Long Island at the same time. Nathaniel Sackett and Gen. Charles Scott ran two such organizations, and Maj. BENJAMIN TALLMADGE established one of the most effective New York networks, the CULPER SPY RING. During the brief (September 1777–June 1778) British occupation of Philadelphia, Washington received reports from the STAY BEHIND NETWORK established on his orders by Gen. Thomas Mifflin.

Washington was a master of military deception and counterintelligence, and he often misled the British by furnishing false information to their intelligence agents. When his greatly depleted army was wintering at Morristown, New Jersey, early in 1777, he discouraged General Howe from attacking by planting grossly inflated reports of his troop strength on two independent and unsuspecting British agents, and arranged to have it confirmed to Howe by a double agent. The following winter Washington executed an even more elaborate deception operation to convince the British commanders that he was preparing attacks on both Philadelphia and New

General Washington meeting with one of his agents—an early nineteenth-century illustration. Source: Author's collection.

York, when in fact his army, badly beaten at Brandywine and Germantown, was licking its wounds at Valley Forge.

In several instances, the Continentals' intelligence played the most crucial role in the eventual outcome of the war. For example, Washington was twice saved from British kidnapping and assassination attempts through information supplied by one of his New York agents, HERCULES MULLIGAN. And the French naval victory at the Battle of the Chesapeake Capes—which opened the way to the siege of Yorktown and the surrender of Cornwallis—was due in part to the French admiral's possession of the Royal Navy's signal code, an item collected a few days earlier by JAMES RIVINGTON, another of Washington's New York agents.

The climactic victory at Yorktown was itself due in large part to Washington's intelligence and deception operations. Through a calculated campaign of disinformation, Washington convinced Clinton that the object of his troop movements in New Jersey in

August 1781 was a planned attack on the British stronghold of New York City, thus precluding any possibility of Clinton reinforcing Cornwallis at Yorktown. And after the siege of Yorktown was in place, ciphered British dispatches intercepted by Washington's agents and decrypted by JAMES LOVELL disclosed Clinton's timetable for relieving Cornwallis by sea. The information alerted Admiral de Grasse, who forestalled the British relief attempt.

The importance of intelligence to the Patriots is also illustrated by their intelligence failures. Washington suffered a serious defeat, and nearly the loss of his army, because his basic intelligence about the terrain was inaccurate at the Battle of Brandywine Creek in September 1777. And, had Washington's intelligence been good enough to predict Clinton's route through New Jersey in June 1778, when the British commander was moving his army from Philadelphia to New York, the Continentals would have been able to attack it while in column and deal it a serious defeat.

Washington's espionage network in Philadelphia and New Jersey was good, but not good enough to learn the planned route. As it was, Washington knew on June 23rd that the British column had reached Bordentown, New Jersey, but, able only to guess at Clinton's subsequent route toward New York, he was forced to spread his troops over several possible routes. Consequently he could not initiate a major engagement, and could do no more than harass the British until they reached Monmouth on June 28th. Both the Americans and the British suffered heavy losses at Monmouth, and military historians regard the battle as a tactical draw. Had Washington been able to defeat the British force five days earlier as it marched out of Bordentown, such a victory, on the heels of the British surrender at Saratoga, would have ended the war.

British Intelligence

The British were not without their own intelligence assets in the colonies. The *Dictionary of American History* estimates that one-third of the population of the colonies was loyal to Great Britain during the Revolution, and many of the Loyalists were ready to serve the British as secret intelligence agents. However, the British government, refusing to see the shadows of coming events, failed to exploit these assets in any organized way before the Revolution, and therefore British commanders Howe and Clinton were forced to improvise ad hoc intelligence apparatuses as the need arose.

What the British lacked in foresight, however, they often made up for in good fortune. Thus, for example, the Paul Revere spy ring in pre-war Boston— perhaps the premier Patriot intelligence network— was penetrated by Dr. Benjamin Church, apparently a DEFECTOR-IN-PLACE from the American side, and a WALK-IN agent who required no special invitation from the British to serve as their agent. They were equally fortunate in having the services of CORTLAND SKINNER, the former colonial attorney general of New Jersey, who proved to be effective both as the commander of a Loyalist brigade and the chief of an extensive Tory underground.

British intelligence in the colonies was put on a more systematic footing by Maj. JOHN ANDRÉ, who became Gen. Henry Clinton's chief of intelligence in October 1779. André's organization extended into Vermont, New Hampshire, Rhode Island, Connecticut, New York, New Jersey, Pennsylvania, Maryland, and Delaware (Massachusetts was neglected because so few Tories remained there, and because the British planned no military operations in that state). After André's execution in October 1780, he was succeeded as Clinton's intelligence chief by OLIVER DE LANCEY, a New York Tory who had been educated in England and was a British officer before the Revolution. With the assistance of Maj. GEORGE BECKWITH he reorganized the British secret service in America and managed it until the end of the war.

A separate British intelligence operation was run out of Quebec by the British commander in Canada, Gen. FREDERICK HALDIMAND. Haldimand, who ran what is called the Northern Department of the British Secret Service, managed secret intelligence and covert action operations in the northern colonies, and undertook secret negotiations aimed at returning Vermont to British allegiance.

Some British army commanders (e.g., Burgoyne) employed Indians for scouting and reconnaissance, and it may be the British were at some disadvantage in recruiting poor or middle-class farmers for these tasks. The Loyalists came from every stratum of colonial society, but certain groups seem to have been especially well represented in their ranks: crown officials, clergymen, physicians, teachers, merchants, large landowners, and prosperous farmers. Many of the secret agents in the British service came from these groups. While the identities of relatively few of the Loyalist (or Patriot) agents are known, and therefore data do not exist to prove such a theory, it may be that an urban and professional bias of British intelligence assets in America resulted in a relative disadvantage in the area of combat intelligence, but worked to British advantage in political intelligence operations. In this regard it is worth noting that at the start of the Battle of Saratoga—the British defeat that marked the turning point in the war—Burgoyne lacked vital field intelligence because most of his Indian scouts had just deserted, and he was forced to fight in a condition of "tactical blindness." And it may also be significant to this hypothesis that the greatest British intelligence coup of the war was a political operation, viz., the defection of BENEDICT ARNOLD.

Intrigue in Europe

From the earliest days of the war it was apparent that some sort of military aid from one of Britain's traditional European opponents would be vital to achieving American independence. France was the most obvious potential benefactor; just a decade had passed since she had fought yet another in a series of wars (the French and Indian, or Seven Years, War) with Britain and lost her Canadian territory. It was only to be expected that she would now try to fish in the newly troubled American waters, perhaps in the hope of recovering what had been lost in the New World, or simply to make some mischief for the British.

Late in 1775 the French government sent a secret diplomatic agent, JULIEN ACHARD DE BONVOULOIR, to America to meet with the COMMITTEE OF SECRET CORRESPONDENCE, the Continental Congress's foreign relations agency, to discuss covert aid and political support. As a result of that meeting Bonvouloir made an optimistic report to the French foreign ministry of American resolution and prospects, and the Committee sent its secret agent, SILAS DEANE, to France. Deane, through the good offices of PIERRE AUGUSTIN CARON DE BEAUMARCHAIS, arranged to procure military supplies in exchange for American commodities such as rice and tobacco. Congress subsequently sent BENJAMIN FRANKLIN and Arthur Lee to France to join Deane in a diplomatic commission aimed at forming a military alliance with France.

The British had their own considerable intelligence resources in Europe, where their elaborate professional secret service had been in place since the days of Elizabeth I's intelligence chief, Sir Francis Walsingham, and was working efficiently at the time of the Revolution under the direction of WILLIAM EDEN. The American commissioners in France became a major intelligence target of Eden's secret service, which sought to monitor the development of Franco-American relations and, if possible, prevent an alliance.

Eden's apparatus in France included LORD STORMONT, the British ambassador to the French court; PAUL WENTWORTH, an American entrepreneur from New Hampshire; and EDWARD BANCROFT, the Massachusetts-born secretary of the American commission. Bancroft—physician, naturalist, and protégé of Franklin—was possibly the most valuable British agent of the Revolutionary War, since he was in a position to report not only on the confidential conversations of the American commission and the French Foreign Ministry but also on the dispatches and instructions exchanged between the commission and the Continental Congress.

Despite such an impressive penetration, the British were unable to derail the American commission, and a Franco-American military alliance was established in February 1778 (helped considerably by the encouraging news of the American victory at Saratoga a few months earlier). The British failure was largely due to the adroitness of Franklin as a diplomat and, perhaps, as an intelligence officer in his own right. Many writers and espionologists (e.g., ALLEN DULLES in his *Craft of Intelligence*) find it impossible to believe that the perspicacious Sage of Philadelphia was unaware of Bancroft's treachery, and some theorize that he exploited it pragmatically to manipulate the British government by controlling the information Bancroft reported. In any case, Franklin had his own intelligence sources in London among the many friends he had made for himself and his cause during his years as a colonial agent in England.

A separate secret service, run for the British Admiralty by Sir PHILIP STEPHENS, operated out of Rotterdam and reported on military cargoes sent from French ports to aid the Americans. This intelligence led to the interception of some of the shipments, but the British generally failed to interdict the French supply line.

During the final years of the war the British secret services concentrated on trying to disrupt the Franco-American alliance through such political ruses as offering (or seeming to offer) a separate peace with one side or the other. These efforts also failed, thanks again to Franklin's shrewdness and diplomatic ability.

Spanish Intelligence

Spain's interest in the American Revolution was similar to that of France, i.e., it presented an opportunity to take vengeance against the ancient enemy, England, and perhaps to recover territory lost to the English in earlier conflicts. Spain allied herself with France (but not with the United States) against Britain in 1779, and also made grants and loans to the U.S. government during the war.

Spain ran its own secret intelligence operations in North America from a base in Havana during the Revolution. Beginning in 1776 several agents, posing as merchants, were sent to Florida—territory Spain had lost to Great Britain—and Philadelphia, where the Continental Congress met.

The most important of the Spanish agents was Juan de Miralles, who served in the dual roles of intelligence agent and unofficial minister to the U.S. government in Pennsylvania and New Jersey from 1777 until his death in 1780. He established cordial relationships with the leaders of Congress, made arrangements for Spanish aid to the Patriots, and worked for Spanish entry into the war on the condition of the return of Florida to Spain. At the same time he reported back to Spain via Havana on current political and military developments in North America.

The diplomacy and espionage of Spanish Intelligence in North America was a factor in bringing Spain into the war, but is of much less importance to the conduct and outcome of the Revolution than the intelligence operations of the U.S. and Great Britain.

Triumph of the Amateurs

The intelligence history of the Revolution, like its military history, is a case of talented and dedicated amateurs going up against the experienced professionals of a major world power, and winning. Because it was a war of divided loyalties, both sides had serious problems of defections and penetrations, and neither side seemed particularly skilled in the counterintelligence techniques needed to deal with such problems. The British Army in America, while not completely devoid of military intelligence assets, seems not to have developed them sufficiently to offset the disadvantages of fighting in a foreign land that was home to its opponent. And although the British secret service had excellent political intelligence regarding American diplomatic initiatives with the French, this advantage did not enable Britain to disrupt the vital Franco-American alliance.

While it is idle to speculate on "alternate history," it nonetheless seems likely that, without Washington's military intelligence service to offset Britain's superior strength and mobility, and Franklin's intrigues and secret diplomacy that insured the crucial alliance with France, American independence might well have been lost.

(Boatner, *The Encyclopedia of the American Revolution*; *DAH*; Bakeless, *Turncoats, Traitors and Heroes*; Ford, *A Peculiar Service*; Van Doren, *Secret History of the American Revolution*; Auger, *Secret War of Independence*; Morris, *The Peacemakers*; Bendiner, *The Virgin Diplomats*; Schoenbrun, *Triumph in Paris*; Central Intelli-

gence Agency, *Intelligence in the War of Independence*; Bemis, "British Secret Service and the French-American Alliance"; Patrick, "The Secret Service of the American Revolution"; Cummins, "Spanish Espionage in the South During the American Revolution"; Thompson, "Intelligence at Yorktown"; Miller, *Origins of the American Revolution, Triumph of Freedom*; Wallace, *Appeal to Arms*; Flexner, *George Washington in the American Revolution*; Casey, *Where and How the War Was Fought*.)

AMORY, ROBERT (March 2, 1915–): lawyer, educator, intelligence officer

A native of Boston, Amory earned an A.B. and an LL.B from Harvard University in 1936 and 1938, respectively, and practiced law in New York City from 1938 to 1940. In 1941 he enlisted in the U.S. Army as a private and later saw action in New Guinea and the Philippines, rising to the rank of colonel and commanding an amphibian engineering regiment. He was discharged in 1946 and joined the staff of the Harvard Law School, where he was professor of law and accounting until 1952, when he joined the Central Intelligence Agency.

Amory served as the agency's deputy director for intelligence during ALLEN DULLES's term as director of central intelligence. He left the CIA in 1962, shortly after Dulles was succeeded by JOHN McCONE.

Amory was one of the few senior CIA officials who took no blame for the failure of the BAY OF PIGS INVASION, because the officers of the CIA CLANDESTINE SERVICE who mounted the invasion excluded him and the Intelligence Directorate from taking part in it.

Between 1962 and 1965 Amory was chief of the International Division of the Bureau of the Budget. From 1965 to 1972 he was a member of a Washington, D.C. law firm.

Amory is the brother of writer Cleveland Amory.

(*Who's Who in America*, 42nd ed.; Wyden, *The Bay of Pigs*.)

ANDERSON, RUDOLPH, JR. (1927–October 27, 1962): Air Force officer, reconnaissance pilot

A native of Spartanburg, South Carolina, Anderson attended Clemson Agricultural College, then worked briefly as a cost accountant before joining the U.S. Air Force in 1951. After completing pilot training, he was assigned to the 15th Tactical Reconnaissance Squadron in Korea, where he served from 1953 to 1955.

Anderson had reached the rank of major and was serving with the 408th Strategic Reconnaissance Wing on October 14, 1962, when he and Maj. RICHARD S. HEYSER flew the U-2 photoreconnaissance sorties over western Cuba that revealed the presence of Soviet offensive missiles on the island. This discovery marked the beginning of the CUBAN MISSILE CRISIS.

Anderson flew subsequent reconnaissance sorties over Cuba during the crisis, enabling American photointerpreters to monitor Soviet missile preparations there. He was on one such mission when he was shot down and killed by a Soviet surface-to-air missile.

Anderson was the only person killed in combat during the missile crisis that nearly led to a nuclear world war.

(Daniel and Hubbell, *Strike in the West;* Kennedy, *Thirteen Days.*)

ANDRÉ, JOHN (May 2, 1750–October 2, 1780): British army officer, intelligence officer

A native of London, England, André was the son of a Swiss merchant who settled in England. After studying mathematics and military drawing at the University of Geneva, he returned to London and worked in the family business. In January 1771 he bought a second lieutenant's commission in the Royal Welsh Fusiliers, and later that year a first lieutenancy in the Seventh Regiment of Foot. In 1772 he enrolled in the University of Göttingen to study mathematics. He sailed for America in 1774 to rejoin his regiment, which had been sent to Canada.

André was captured by Continental forces at St. John's, Ontario, in November 1775, but was freed in a prisoner exchange one year later. He was made a captain in the Twenty-sixth Regiment and was aide-de-camp to Gen. Charles Gray during the British occupation of Philadelphia. There he became acquainted with Elizabeth (Peggy) Shippen, a young Philadelphian of Tory sympathies who was shortly to become the wife of Gen. BENEDICT ARNOLD.

After the British evacuation of Philadelphia, André became aide-de-camp to Gen. Henry Clinton in New York City. In that capacity he was entrusted with Clinton's correspondence with British secret agents and informers. In effect, he was Clinton's intelligence officer and as such he became involved in the secret correspondence between Clinton and Benedict Arnold that began in May 1779. The following year, André, participating in negotiations with Arnold for the surrender of West Point, had a clandestine meeting with Arnold in Haverstraw, New York, on the

Maj. Rudolph Anderson, Jr. Source: U.S. Air Force.

night of September 21–22. Unable to rejoin the British sloop *Vulture,* in which he had traveled to Haverstraw, he attempted to return to New York by passing through the American lines in civilian clothes and bearing a pass signed by Arnold. He was captured near Tarrytown, New York, on September 23rd when, mistaking three American militiamen for British soldiers, he identified himself as a British officer. A search of his person turned up several military documents Arnold had given him. André was arrested and taken to the American command post at North Castle.

Maj. BENJAMIN TALLMADGE, suspecting that Arnold was involved with the captured British officer, prevented the local American commander from returning André to Arnold at West Point. Word of André's capture reached Arnold, however, and he fled to New York City. General Clinton rejected an American proposal to exchange Arnold for André.

André was taken to Tappan, New York, where he was tried by a military board, found guilty of spying, and sentenced to death. Washington refused to pardon André and rejected his request to be shot as a soldier rather than hanged as a spy. André was

Pen-and-ink self-portrait of Maj. John André, made just before his execution. Source: Yale University Art Gallery.

hanged at Tappan on October 2nd. In 1821 his remains were removed and interred in Westminster Abbey.

(Flexner, *The Traitor and the Spy*; Van Doren, *Secret History of the American Revolution*; Boatner, *Encyclopedia of the American Revolution*.)

ANDREWS, JAMES J. (ca. 1829?–June 7, 1862): Union secret service agent

Andrews's origins and early life are mysterious and obscure, and there is even some question regarding his true name. He arrived in Flemingsburg, Kentucky, in 1859, in search of a job as a schoolteacher. Although no such position was open, he settled in the town and worked as a house painter. He said that he was a native of Hancock County, Virginia, which he had left after suffering business and financial losses and a romantic disappointment.

In the summer of 1861, a few months after the outbreak of the Civil War, Andrews visited Louisville and there, apparently, was recruited to serve as a civilian agent in the secret service ALLAN PINKERTON had organized for the Department of the Ohio. He served as a scout and courier for Gen. William Nelson during military expeditions against the Confederate forces in eastern Kentucky late in 1861.

During the winter of 1861–62 Andrews undertook several secret intelligence missions behind Confederate lines for Gen. Don Carlos Buell, commander of the Army of the Ohio. He pretended to be a blockade runner, i.e., a smuggler who carried medical supplies and other contraband through the Union lines to sell to the Confederates. Andrews operated out of Louisville, and later Nashville, Tennessee, and penetrated as far south as Atlanta, Georgia.

In February 1862 Andrews proposed a paramilitary operation to General Buell. The plan was aimed at severing the rail line between Atlanta and Chattanooga (see ANDREWS'S RAID). Andrews and a party of Union troops in civilian clothes entered Confederate territory, hijacked a locomotive, and attempted to destroy railroad tracks and bridges between the two cities. The operation ultimately failed, and he and the others were captured by the Confederates. Andrews and seven of his men were hanged as spies.

In his account of the raid and the raiders, writer Charles O'Neill offers an interesting theory that Andrews was actually Andreas Johan Kars, a Finnish-born ex-officer of the Russian army who emigrated to the United States in 1850.

(Bryan, *The Spy in America*; Boatner, *Civil War Dictionary*; O'Neill, *Wild Train*.)

ANDREWS'S RAID

A Union paramilitary operation of the CIVIL WAR. In the spring of 1862 the Army of the Ohio (a territorial subdivision of the Union army consisting of some 115,000 men under the command of Gen. Don Carlos Buell) was advancing through Tennessee. The Third Division, under the command of Maj. Gen. Ormsby Mitchel, was located in the center of the state and was preparing to advance on Chattanooga. In February JAMES J. ANDREWS, a civilian employee of the Union Army and a secret service agent with experience in operating behind Confederate lines, proposed to lead a paramilitary mission into Georgia to cut the railroad line between Atlanta and Chattanooga, thus interdicting Confederate reinforcement of the latter city when Mitchel advanced. General Buell rejected the plan at first, but later consented on the advice of his chief of staff.

In early March Andrews and a team of eight volunteers from the Ohio Volunteer Infantry, a part of the Army of the Ohio, traveled disguised as civilians to Atlanta, where Andrews expected to find one of his agents, a railroad locomotive engineer who was prepared to steal a train and run it up the line toward Chattanooga. En route, Andrews and his men were to destroy rail and the railroad bridges. However, upon arrival in Atlanta, Andrews discovered that his agent had been conscripted into the Confederate army. Since neither Andrews nor any of his team could operate a locomotive, he cancelled the mission and returned to Union lines.

Andrews made a second attempt on April 7th. He selected twenty-five volunteers from the Ohio infantry for the job. All were enlisted men and seasoned combat veterans, and three of them had pre-war experience in operating railway locomotives. The men, dressed in civilian clothes and armed only with revolvers, set out on foot, singly or in groups of twos and threes, for Marietta, Georgia, where they were to rendezvous with Andrews at the Marietta Hotel. Their cover story, if questioned, was that they were Confederate soldiers who had escaped from a Union prison camp.

Andrews and twenty of his men met in Marietta; two others had been stopped by a Confederate patrol and, after telling their story, were actually pressed into service in the Confederate army. Two more simply disappeared, apparently having deserted, and another arrived in Marietta too late to join his comrades.

The group that assembled in Marietta for the operation consisted of: Pvts. WILSON BROWN, WILLIAM KNIGHT, and MARTIN J. HAWKINS, all of whom had been locomotive engineers in civilian life; Pvts. WILLIAM BENSINGER, ROBERT BUFFUM, JACOB PARROTT, JOHN R. PORTER, SAMUEL ROBERTSON, SAMUEL SLAVENS, JAMES SMITH, GEORGE D. WILSON, JOHN A. WILSON, JOHN WOLLAM, and MARK WOOD; Cpls. DANIEL DORSEY and WILLIAM H. REDDICK; Sgt. Maj. MARION A. ROSS; and Sgts. ELIHU MASON, WILLIAM PITTENGER, and JOHN M. SCOTT. At about 5:00 A.M. on April 12th Andrews and his men, posing as civilian passengers, boarded a train for Chattanooga.

Andrews's plan was to hijack the train and proceed north towards Chattanooga, destroying the railroad bridges in his wake. When the train stopped at Big Shanty (now Kennesaw) and the crew and passengers got off and went to breakfast, Andrews's men uncoupled the coaches from the locomotive—which was called "The General"—and three boxcars. Andrews and Pvt. Wilson Brown took over the locomotive cab while the remainder of the team boarded the boxcars. "The General" steamed northward out of the Big Shanty station, peppered by a hail of bullets fired by the startled Confederate guards.

Andrews stopped the train after a few miles in order to cut the telegraph wires and prevent word of the hijacking from being sent ahead. He stopped again at Cass Station, some twenty miles from Big Shanty, in order to take on fuel and water after having convinced the stationmaster that the train was on an urgent mission to deliver ammunition to the Confederates at Chattanooga. He was delayed again at the railroad junction at Kingston, five miles farther

"The General," the locomotive hijacked by Andrews's raiders. Source: Library of Congress.

on, where "The General" was forced to wait on a siding for more than an hour while southbound trains passed on the single track line.

The delay enabled William A. Fuller, the Confederate conductor of the stolen train, to gain in his pursuit, which had begun by handcar from Big Shanty to Etowah, a few miles north along the rail line. There he had commandeered a locomotive and a small party of Confederate troops, and the group proceeded thus to Kingston and beyond. Fuller's party overtook Andrews when the Union raiders stopped "The General" in order to tear up a stretch of track. The Yankees jumped back aboard their train and sped off with Fuller and the Confederate soldiers in hot pursuit. The chase continued for some ninety miles while Andrews's team made several unsuccessful attempts to derail the pursuing Confederate train. Eventually "The General" ran out of fuel and the raiders fled on foot, only to be captured within a few days and imprisoned at Chattanooga and Atlanta.

Andrews, Scott, Ross, George D. Wilson, Robertson, Slavens, and two others—Pvt. Philip Gephart Shadrach and William Campbell, a civilian—were tried, convicted of espionage, and hanged in the

Atlanta prison in June. The rest of the raiders remained in prison, but a group of them escaped the following October. Six were recaptured and were exchanged for six Confederate prisoners of war in March 1863. They were Bensinger, Buffum, Mason, Pittenger, Reddick, and Parrott. Each was awarded the Medal of Honor by Secretary of War Edwin Stanton. The medal had only recently been created, and the six were the first recipients of the decoration. The first medal was presented to Parrott, the youngest of the group.

Andrews's Raid has been celebrated in fiction, verse, radio shows, and at least thrice in heavily fictionalized film accounts: *The Railroad Raid* (1912); *The General*, a 1926 silent film starring Buster Keaton; and *Andrews' Raiders* in 1956 (later released for television as *The Great Locomotive Chase*.)

(Bryan, *The Spy in America*; Boatner, *Civil War Dictionary*; O'Neill, *Wild Train*.)

ANFUSO, VICTOR L. (March 10, 1905– December 28, 1966): jurist, U.S. congressman, intelligence officer

A native of Sicily, Italy, Anfuso moved to the United States in his youth. After graduating from St. Lawrence University with an LL.B. in 1927, he practiced law in New York City and was active in the Democratic Party.

During the Second World War Anfuso served in the OSS SECRET INTELLIGENCE BRANCH. His Sicilian background was of value to him in directing espionage operations in German-occupied Italy. In 1948 he was peripherally involved in an operation of the Central Intelligence Agency that prevented a Communist victory in the Italian elections (see ITALIAN ELECTION OPERATION).

Anfuso was elected to Congress from the Eighth Election District of New York, serving one term in 1951–52. In 1954 he was a magistrate of the City of New York. He was returned to Congress that year and served until 1958.

(Smith, *OSS: Who Was Who In America*, v. 4.)

ANGLETON, JAMES JESUS (1917–May 11, 1987): intelligence officer

A native of Boise, Idaho, Angleton grew up in Arizona and in Italy, where his father represented an American company. Angleton entered Yale University in 1937 and studied literature. While at Yale, he co-founded and edited a literary magazine, *Furioso*, which published some of the leading American poets of the day. After graduation from Yale he entered Harvard Law School.

In 1943 Angleton was recruited into the Office of Strategic Services by NORMAN HOLMES PEARSON, his former English instructor at Yale. Angleton served in the OSS COUNTER-ESPIONAGE BRANCH. He was sent to London to learn counterintelligence techniques from the British Secret Intelligence Service. There he met and befriended British intelligence officer (and Soviet penetration agent), HAROLD ("KIM") PHILBY.

Late in 1944 Angleton was placed in charge of OSS counterintelligence operations in Italy. After the war and the dissolution of the OSS he remained in its successor organization, the Strategic Services Unit, which became part of the Central Intelligence Group in 1946 (see CENTRAL INTELLIGENCE AGENCY). He was in the CIG when it was transformed into the CIA in September 1947.

During this transitional period Angleton continued to run counterintelligence operations in Italy, where he was the senior American intelligence officer. He worked closely with the Italian police and security services and with the Jewish underground, then actively engaged in Italy and elsewhere in Europe in transporting survivors of the Holocaust to Palestine. Through these sources he managed to acquire much valuable information and material. Among the items he sent back to Washington were the secret correspondence between Hitler and Mussolini, which was entered as evidence in the Nuremburg war crimes trials; the correspondence between Stalin and Tito that foreshadowed the latter's 1948 split with the Kremlin; and Soviet instructions to Italian Communists for supporting their comrades in the Greek civil war.

By 1949 Angleton returned to Washington and served on Staff C, as the CIA's counterintelligence staff was then known. In this capacity both he and his fellow CIA counterintelligence officer, WILLIAM K. HARVEY, had close professional and personal associations with Harold "Kim" Philby, who was then the British SIS liaison officer with the CIA and the Federal Bureau of Investigation in Washington. Although Angleton may have become suspicious of Philby based upon information supplied him about this time by an Israeli source, it apparently was Harvey who unmasked the Soviet agent.

Angleton became chief of the CIA's Counterintelligence Staff. Originally part of the Office of Special Operations, the Counterintelligence Staff became part of the Plans Directorate in 1952 when the agency's COVERT ACTION and SECRET INTELLIGENCE units were merged. The Staff was divided into several units: security, operations, research and analysis, liaison, and one or two others. The liaison unit worked with friendly foreign intelligence services on projects of common interest. Because of his long association with Israeli intelligence, dating back to his postwar days in Italy, Angleton took personal charge of liaison with the Israelis.

Among the accomplishments of Angleton and the Counterintelligence Staff was obtaining a copy of the Nikita Khrushchev secret 1956 speech before the Soviet Communist Party in which he denounced Stalin.

The nature of counterintelligence operations is labyrinthine: opposition agents are sometimes "turned" to become double agents, and double agents are on occasion transformed into triple agents, and suspected "moles" within one's own organization may be carefully cultivated and fed disinformation to mislead the other side. After long years working in such an environment, it is not surprising that Angleton developed a hyper-suspicious mental set in which he became convinced that a Soviet "mole" had penetrated the CIA, suspected the distinguished diplomat W. Averell Harriman of being a Soviet agent, and saw the Tito-Stalin split of 1948 and the Sino-Soviet rift of the early 1960s as nothing but charades designed to lure the West into a false sense of security. That such excessive suspiciousness may be an occupational hazard of counterintelligence work is indicated by the fact that a member of his staff compiled a body of circumstantial evidence suggesting that Angleton himself was a Soviet penetration agent.

Such seemingly paranoid behavior on Angleton's part dismayed WILLIAM E. COLBY after he became chief of the Clandestine Service in 1973. Colby reduced Angleton's power within the INTELLIGENCE COMMUNITY by relieving him of several important functions, e.g., liaison between the CIA and the Federal Bureau of Investigation, which had long been his exclusive province. He also forced the termination of the CIA's secret mail-opening operation, which had been inaugurated in 1955 by Angleton and run by him ever since.

Colby later wrote that he "couldn't absorb" Angleton's theories and became convinced that the counterintelligence chief's extreme suspicions "were actually hurting good clandestine operational officers." He therefore forced Angleton into retirement late in 1974. This move coincided with revelations in the press of Operation Chaos, a program established and run by Angleton at the request of President Lyndon Johnson to determine whether there was any foreign financing or manipulation of the domestic anti-Vietnam War movement (Angleton found none). The coincidence of Angleton's departure at this time gave rise to the erroneous impression that he had been

responsible for all of the "Family Jewels," the list of illegal or questionable activities engaged in by the CIA.

After his retirement Angleton served as chairman of the Security and Intelligence Fund, an organization that promotes public understanding of and support for a strong American intelligence community, and which has raised defense funds for former intelligence officers who have been sued for actions they performed in the course of their duties.

(Martin, *Wilderness of Mirrors*; Colby and Forbath, *Honorable Men*; *Political Profiles*; *New York Times Magazine*, June 25, 1978; obituary, *New York Times*, May 12, 1987, p. D31.)

ARMSTRONG, HAMILTON FISH (April 7, 1893–April 24, 1973): editor, author, foreign policy specialist, intelligence officer

A native of New York City, Armstrong graduated from Princeton University in 1916. He worked for the *New Republic* magazine until 1917, when he was commissioned a second lieutenant in the U.S. Army. He was appointed military attaché to the Serbian War Mission in the United States, and, in 1918 was assigned to the Military Intelligence Section of the General Staff (see ARMY INTELLIGENCE). He was sent to Belgrade, where he served as acting military attaché until he left the Army in July 1919.

Armstrong was one of the founding members of the Council on Foreign Relations in 1921, and he founded the Council's journal, *Foreign Affairs*. He served as managing editor of the journal until 1928, and was editor until 1972. He wrote and edited several books on foreign policy and collaborated with fellow Council member ALLEN W. DULLES on two books—*Can We Be Neutral?* (1936) and *Can We Stay Neutral?* (1939)—which dealt with the relationship of the United States to the war in Europe and argued against isolationism.

Armstrong held several ad hoc positions in the United States government, including the State Department. He was appointed special assistant to the American ambassador in London in 1944 and held the rank of minister, and was later a special advisor to Secretary of State Edward Stettinius.

Armstrong was one of the so-called "Princeton Consultants" to the Central Intelligence Agency's Board of National Estimate in the 1950s (see CENTRAL INTELLIGENCE AGENCY, NATIONAL INTELLIGENCE ESTIMATE). Deputy Director of Central Intelligence WILLIAM H. JACKSON recruited the consultants in order to correct what he regarded as an imbalance of academics on the Board. (The

Military intelligence emblem of the U.S. Army. Source: National Military Intelligence Association.

other Princeton Consultants were GEORGE F. KEN-NAN and Vannevar Bush. They met in the Princeton Gun Club, hence the name.)

(*Current Biography*, 1948, 1973; Karalekas, *History of the Central Intelligence Agency.*)

ARMY INTELLIGENCE

The intelligence components of the U.S. Army trace their lineage to KNOWLTON'S RANGERS, a reconnaissance and intelligence unit of the Continental Army in the AMERICAN REVOLUTION (it is for this reason the year 1776 appears in the present-day Army Intelligence logo). However, the Army has not maintained an intelligence service continuously throughout the two centuries of its history. The Army established intelligence units during the MEXICAN WAR and the CIVIL WAR, but they reported to individual field commands, and, like Knowlton's Rangers, they went out of existence upon the cessation of hostilities. There was no permanently established or national-level intelligence unit within the Army until 1885.

The Military Information Division

The Military Information Division of the War Department was established in October 1885 by Brig. Gen. R. C. Drum, the adjutant general, within the Reservations Division of the Miscellaneous Branch of his office. According to a tradition unsupported by contemporary records, Secretary of War William C. Endicott directed Drum to establish the Division after Drum had been unable to answer the secretary's request for some information regarding the armed forces of a certain foreign power.

The MID was charged with collecting "military data on our own and foreign services which would be available for the use of the War Department and the Army at large." The Army did not have a general staff at this time, and the new division was apparently intended to help the adjutant general's office fill this void by collecting information on such matters as "progress in the military arts," in addition to the narrower field of foreign military intelligence.

Initially the MID consisted of one officer, Maj. William J. Volkmar, and several civilian clerks, and was no more than a central reference service. The information filed and indexed by the staff came from open source literature, BASIC INTELLIGENCE (e.g., topographical studies) on the United States, Canada, and Mexico gathered by various War Department bureaus and field commands, and reports made by officers serving as observers with foreign armies and by other personnel who happened to travel abroad. The flow of information into the Division increased rapidly, however, and in 1889 it was established as a separate division reporting directly to the adjutant general.

Military Attaché System

Also in 1889 the Army established a system of military attachés to serve abroad at American embassies and legations. The first attachés were assigned to London, Paris, Vienna, Berlin, and St. Petersburg. This preoccupation with Europe, however, did not reflect a perceived military threat from that quarter; the likelihood of war with a European power seemed remote. The attachés were instructed to

> Examine into and report upon all matters of a military or technical character that may be of interest and value to any branch of the War Department and to the service at large. . . . Examine the military libraries, bookstores and publisher's lists in order to give early notice of any new or important publications or inventions or improvements in arms, or in any branch of the service; also give notice of such drawings, plans, etc.; which may be of importance and within your power to procure.

The theory and technology of warfare was advancing rapidly at this time, European powers were often in the lead, and the function of the attachés and the MID included "technology transfer" as much as foreign intelligence.

The staff and files of the MID grew rapidly. By 1894 the Division had amassed 30,000 index cards; by 1897 the staff had grown to eleven officers, plus clerks and messengers. In 1892 an attempt by Gen. A. W. Greely, the chief signal officer, to absorb the Division into the Signal Corps prompted the Army to examine thoroughly the role of the MID and conclude that "the duties of the information division are as broad as the military service and the art of war itself," and hence it must be a "general intelligence division." Thereafter the mission and role of the Division was enhanced, and its director was elevated to the status of assistant adjutant general.

The Spanish-American War

The Division had been collecting information on Cuba since 1892, and as the likelihood of war with Spain over the island increased, Cuba became the focus of MID attention. In April 1897 Maj. ARTHUR L. WAGNER was made director of the Division. Anticipating War Department intelligence requirements, Wagner obtained approval to send two of his staff, Lts. ANDREW S. ROWAN and HENRY H. WHITNEY, on covert reconnaissance missions to Cuba and Puerto Rico, respectively. Both returned with a wealth of valuable intelligence. (Rowan's mission was celebrated by Elbert Hubbard in his widely printed and notoriously inaccurate essay "A Message to Garcia.")

The Rowan mission, information supplied by the Cuban insurgents' political front organization in New York, and the basic intelligence collected and indexed by the MID over a period of years, enabled the Division to publish "Military Notes on Cuba"—a useful compendium of basic intelligence—in June 1898 and disseminate it to the offices of the expeditionary force that departed Tampa, Florida, for Santiago de Cuba on June 14th.

The MID of the Philippines

However, the MID had not anticipated that the Philippine Islands would also be a theater of the war with Spain, or that the U.S. Army would be required to fight a protracted counterinsurgency campaign in the Philippines immediately after the Spanish-American War. The Division had collected virtually no information on the Philippines, so to fill this intelligence void Gen. Elwell S. Otis, the American military governor of the Philippines and commander of the U.S. occupation forces, ordered the establishment of the Bureau of Insurgent Records as a unit in his Manila headquarters early in 1899. The Bureau, which maintained files on the Filipino insurgents fighting the American occupation, was enlarged and reorganized along the lines of the MID in December 1900, and its name was changed to the Military Information Division, Adjutant General's Office, Headquarters, Division of the Philippines.

Lt. Col. Joseph T. Dickman was put in charge of the new unit. Dickman was assisted by Captain RALPH VAN DEMAN, who had served in the War Department's MID during 1897–98. Dickman and Van Deman added a Map Section to the existing Insurgent Records Section, recruited Filipino undercover agents, and established liaison with the information officers attached to the 450 U.S. Army posts throughout the Philippines. The Division's job was tactical intelligence and counterintelligence. In June 1902 it became a branch of the War Department's MID, with which it had held close liaison since its creation.

The Army General Staff

The serious administrative problems that arose within the Army and the War Department during the Spanish-American War prompted President McKinley to appoint a postwar investigative commission headed by Maj. Gen. GRENVILLE M. DODGE, and this postmortem eventually led to the creation of an Army General Staff Corps in 1903. The General Staff was comprised of three divisions: the First Division handled such administrative matters as personnel management, training, and transportation; the Third Division was responsible for military education—including the newly created Army War College—war planning, engineering, and artillery; the Second Division was responsible for military information, i.e., intelligence, military attachés, and the central reference functions that had been the responsibility of the War Department's Military Information Division. In fact, the MID was removed from the Adjutant General's Office and became the General Staff's Second Division.

The Second Division—which was still known informally as the MID—had no responsibility for the making of war plans. War planning was the exclusive domain of the Third Division, and especially of the Army War College, which became the MID's principal customer. The planners in the College were dependent upon the MID's files, library, country studies, and attaché reports. Consequently the MID's offices were moved out of the State-War-Navy building near the White House to the War College's building on the outskirts of Washington.

Eventually the War College swallowed the MID completely. In June 1908 the General Staff was reorganized; the three divisions were dissolved in favor of two sections. The Third Division became the Second Section—and retained its informal designation, "the War College Division"—and the MID became the Military Information Committee of that section. The officers of the newly subordinated unit were assigned teaching duties as well as intelligence work. Eventually the MID records and personnel were dispersed throughout the War College Division.

The net effect of this reorganization was that the role and influence of the intelligence unit within the War Department was greatly diminished. This merger was, of course, accomplished over the unavailing protests of the MID chief, Lt. Col. T. W. Jones, and the other intelligence officers involved.

Although the MID had performed well in supporting the General Staff's planning for the Army's peacekeeping intervention in Cuba in 1906, and had provided important intelligence to the White House during the Japanese war scare of 1907, its intelligence activities declined after the 1908 reorganization. By the time a force under Gen. John J. Pershing was sent to guard the Mexican-American border in 1915, intelligence work within the General Staff had almost ceased completely. Pershing's subsequent pursuit of Pancho Villa into Mexico after the latter's raid on Columbus, New Mexico, was conducted without intelligence support from the MID, although Pershing established his own very effective field intelligence service under Maj. James A. Ryan.

In May 1915 Van Deman, who had then reached the rank of major, was assigned to the War College Division of the General Staff. Upon discovering the neglected state of military information, he began a campaign to revive the activity and restore the MID as a separate division of the General Staff. Van Deman was abetted in his efforts by the sympathetic chief of the War College Division, Gen. H. H. Macomb, and by the general spirit of preparedness urged by many in the government who considered American involvement in the war in Europe to be inevitable.

Although Chief of Staff Gen. Hugh L. Scott did not endorse Van Deman's proposals for a formal reestablishment of the MID, Macomb's successor, Brig. Gen. Joseph E. Kuhn, brought about a sort of de facto revival of the Division late in 1916 by cancelling the remainder of the War College course and assigning the officers of the War College Division to study the flow of intelligence coming from the military attachés and observers in Europe.

First World War

On May 3, 1917, less than a month after American entry into the FIRST WORLD WAR, General Kuhn established the Military Intelligence Section within the War College Division. Major Van Deman was appointed chief of the section and was given two officers and two clerks to staff it. From these modest beginnings the Section grew rapidly during the eighteen months of American involvement in the war, and swelled to 282 officers, 29 noncommissioned officers, and 948 civilian employees by the time the war ended. In August 1918 a new chief of staff, Gen. Peyton C. March, gave Van Deman's unit official status by establishing the Military Intelligence Division as a coequal part of the General Staff. This was only a formality, however, for Van Deman's unit had been functioning as a division of the General Staff from the time it was created.

The Military Intelligence Division was far more than the central reference service that the old Military Information Division had been. In addition to collecting, collating, and distributing military information and supervising the work of the military attachés abroad, the MID supervised the activities of intelligence officers attached to other Army commands, departments, and posts; ran secret intelligence and counterintelligence operations; and carried on liaison with the intelligence services of the Allies. Van Deman worked closely with Lt. Col. C. G. Dansey, a member of the British Secret Intelligence Service and part of the British Military Mission to Washington, and he based the structure of the MID very much on the organizational concepts used by the British. (Bidwell says this liaison brought the term "intelligence" into American usage, replacing the traditional "information," and also introduced "espionage" and "counterespionage" into Army Intelligence parlance.) Additional guidance from the British service was obtained through the American military attaché in London, Col. Stephen L. Slocum.

Following the British taxonomy of intelligence activities into positive and negative (i.e., collecting intelligence about the enemy, and denying him intelligence about oneself, respectively), Van Deman formed the MID into a Positive and a Negative branch. The Positive Branch consisted of M.I.2, Foreign Intelligence (collection, collation, and dissemination of foreign combat, economic, political, psychological, and geographical intelligence); M.I.5, Military Attachés (supervision of the work of the military attachés abroad); M.I.6, Translation (a translation service for the entire War Department); M.I.7, Graphic (maps and photographs); M.I.8, Cable and Telegraph (a cryptological unit—see HERBERT O. YARDLEY);

and M.I.9, Field Intelligence (training field intelligence officers for overseas duty).

The Negative Branch consisted of M.I.3, Counter-Espionage in the Military Service (organizing, instructing, and supervising counterespionage operations against enemy subversion within the American military); M.I.4, Counter-Espionage Among Civilian Population (working with the Justice Department, the SECRET SERVICE, STATE DEPARTMENT INTELLIGENCE, the unofficial organization of EMANUEL V. VOSKA, the AMERICAN PROTECTIVE LEAGUE, and other organizations to combat the subversion of German intelligence and other groups attempting to undermine the American war effort); M.I.10, Censorship (censorship of foreign postal matter, prisoner-of-war mail, military communications, official War Department announcements, the press, books, and motion pictures; also cooperation with the Post Office Department and the national Committee on Public Information, an official propaganda agency; M.I.11, Passports and Port Control (working closely with the Department of State and the Justice Department to keep track of persons of interest to intelligence agencies arriving in or departing from the United States); M.I.12, Graft and Fraud (investigating cases of misconduct arising from Army procurement of supplies).

In addition to the Positive and Negative branches, the MID had an administrative unit, M.I.1, which was concerned with the Section's personnel, office management, and the publication of such intelligence products as daily and weekly intelligence summaries, and training materials.

To coordinate its activities with local police, businessmen, and organizations, the MID established branch offices in Philadelphia, St. Louis, Seattle, Pittsburgh, New Orleans, and New York.

Despite the administrative problems that came with such explosive growth, the MID managed to carry out some important positive intelligence functions. Military attachés in the Netherlands, Italy, Switzerland, Norway, and Denmark obtained very useful information regarding the plans and operations of the Central Powers in Europe, and the attaché in Cuba procured the arrest and extradition to the United States of Dr. Walter von Scheele, a German agent who subsequently disclosed valuable military information in exchange for immunity from prosecution.

The major emphasis of the MID during the war was counterintelligence, however. This reflected the view held by Van Deman (and many other Americans both in the government and the private sector) that German subversion, sabotage, and espionage was the most immediate threat to the American war effort. During the two-and-a-half years prior to American entry into the war German agents carried out an elaborate program of sabotage and political warfare within the United States, ranging from economic operations aimed at fomenting labor unrest in factories supplying munitions to the Allies (see PAPEN, FRANZ VON), to the massive BLACK TOM EXPLOSION in New York Harbor. Van Deman and others expected that such subversion would be stepped up after the American declaration of war, and there was particular concern over the loyalty of pacifists, isolationists, German-Americans, and Anglophobic Irish-Americans, most of whom were thought to be inclined toward opposing the war effort for their own partisan reasons.

In August 1917 the Corps of Intelligence Police was formed as a special counterintelligence investigative unit within the MID. The Corps was created at the request of the headquarters of the American Expeditionary Force in France, which asked the MID for fifty French-speaking men in the grade of sergeant of infantry to assist in performing counterintelligence missions overseas. A few months later 250 more sergeants were added to the Corps to carry out counterintelligence investigations within the United States (principally in New York City, which was a center of both Allied shipping and German subversion).

Even the code-breaking unit, M.I.8, a part of the Positive Branch, devoted most of its energies to counterintelligence cases. It concentrated much effort on detecting invisible writing (see CRYPTOLOGY) and deciphering obscure foreign shorthand systems, both of which were employed by German agents, and it broke the cipher in a document that led to the espionage conviction of LOTHAR WITZKE.

American Expeditionary Force, France

Another reason the MID placed relatively less emphasis on positive intelligence during the war was the existence of a field intelligence unit within the staff of the American Expeditionary Force in France. When General Pershing sailed for France in May 1917 he brought along a complete general staff corps for the AEF consisting of five sections, G-1 through G-5. G-2, the Intelligence Section, was headed by (then) Maj. DENNIS E. NOLAN. It provided Pershing with a complete range of positive military intelligence data—enemy order of battle, maps and terrain studies, etc., and also performed counterintelligence and censorship. It had its own communication intelligence unit, the Radio Intelligence Section, which performed radio interception, traffic analysis, cryptanalysis, and even intercepted enemy field telephone and carrier-pigeon communications.

Army mobile radio direction-finding van near Verdun, France, 1918. Source: National Archives.

Coordination between the MID and the AEF's G-2 proved difficult. In an effort to resolve the problem, Van Deman was sent to France in June 1918 for a tour with Pershing's staff, and Col. MARLBOR-OUGH CHURCHILL of the AEF General Staff returned to Washington to take charge of the MID. This belated exchange of officers was beginning to solve the coordination problem when it was overtaken by events and the war ended.

Siberia and Northern Russia

In February 1918 the new Soviet government withdrew Russia from the war and the Allied coalition, and signed a separate peace treaty with Germany shortly thereafter. During the following summer the U.S. Army joined with Britain, France, and several other nations in intervening in the tangled and tumultuous situation that had developed in Siberia and

northern Russia. The American Expeditionary Force, Siberia, was commanded by Maj. Gen. William S. Graves and had its own general staff corps including a G-2 section drawn from the Philippine section of the MID. The AEF, Northern Russia, was part of a Allied force commanded by British Maj. Gen. Frederick C. Poole (shortly to be succeeded by Maj. Gen. Edmund Ironsides of the British Army). The American contingent included military attachés and other intelligence personnel.

Owing to personality clashes within the general staff corps of AEF, Siberia, its G-2 section did little effective intelligence work before the force was withdrawn. The American intelligence officers attached to the northern Russia force did better, however, collecting and disseminating useful intelligence regarding the political and military situation in the region, and running an extensive counterespionage organization. They also played a vital role in the international negotiations that took place while the force was in Russia.

The Paris Peace Conference

The MID played an active role in supporting the American Peace Commission at the PARIS PEACE CONFERENCE OF 1919. Gen. Tasker H. Bliss, a member of the Commission, assigned Colonel Van Deman the overall responsibility for the Commission's physical, personnel, and communications security. Major Yardley took charge of the latter area, devising the codes and ciphers to be used in communicating with Washington and with the Commission's agents in the field. Yardley also set up a cryptanalysis unit to read intercepted wireless traffic of other participants at the conference.

The MID chief Marlborough Churchill, who had reached the rank of brigadier general, went to Paris with the Commission in the capacity of its "General Military Liaison Coordinating Officer." Churchill was accompanied by a contingent of twenty officers from the MID.

Van Deman and many of the MID officers who accompanied Churchill to Paris served in the Commission's ad hoc intelligence service, which was managed by a committee chaired by foreign service officer Ellis L. Dresel. The intelligence service dispatched agents to European areas that were the subject of the Peace Conference's deliberations in order to provide President Woodrow Wilson and the other American peace commissioners with up-to-date information important to them.

G-2, War Department

With the coming of peace the MID shrank as suddenly as it had swelled upon American entry into the war, but it was not reduced to its pre-war size. As of June 1920 it still retained seventy-nine officers, four noncoms, and 159 civilian employees. The Cryptographic Bureau of M.I.8 was "spun off" as a separate unit jointly funded by both the War and State departments, and continued to be headed by Yardley, who had returned to civilian status (see AMERICAN BLACK CHAMBER, HERBERT O. YARDLEY).

In August 1920 General Churchill was succeeded by General Nolan as chief of the MID, and the following year General Pershing became chief of staff. Pershing reorganized the War Department General Staff along the lines of his general staff in the AEF, France—i.e., into five major divisions instead of the traditional four—and adopted the AEF short designations, G-1, G-2, etc. Thus the MID acquired the alternate designation of G-2, which it thereafter re-

tained (see G-2). One unhappy consequence of Pershing's reorganization was that the MID was now headed by a colonel, Congress having authorized only four general officers for the posts of assistant chiefs of staff. The MID thereby suffered a serious diminution of both status and effectiveness. The size of the division's staff and budget continued to shrink in the postwar era, bottoming out in 1936 at eighteen officers and forty-eight civilians.

The general staff structure of the War Department was copied within subordinate Army commands. The staff of every corps or area commander included an intelligence officer designated the "Assistant Chief of Staff for Military Intelligence," or "G-2." (A staff intelligence officer attached to a lower echelon was designated "S-2.") Although the duties of these officers, and their exact relationship to the MID remained ill-defined, the MID established some standardization of intelligence practices and procedures throughout the Army by issuing a series of publications and manuals for use by the G-2s and S-2s in the field.

Despite the continual erosion of staff and budget during the two decades following the First World War, the MID managed to maintain a program for the collection of significant foreign intelligence through military attachés, G-2s and S-2s of overseas commands (e.g., Hawaii and the Philippines), interviews with foreign travelers returning to the United States, confidential personal contacts with American businesses operating overseas, and a variety of public sources. Because Japan had been regarded as a potential adversary since before the First World War, the Far East was an area of special MID interest from the mid-1920s onward. With the resurgence of German militarism under Hitler in the mid-1930s, Germany and Europe also became the subjects of special attention by the MID foreign intelligence analysts.

Counterespionage and Countersubversion

The MID's wartime emphasis on domestic surveillance did not cease completely with the Armistice, however. Radical political groups, and even some labor organizations, were regarded in many quarters as a threat toward the violent overthrow of the government. Anticipating an Army role in countering riots and other public disorders, the MID worked out an arrangement for close liaison and the exchange of domestic political intelligence with the Justice Department's Bureau of Investigation (see FEDERAL BUREAU OF INVESTIGATION) in 1921. But some Army domestic intelligence operations were conducted without the prudent control of the MID. G-2s and S-2s of some subordinate commands, and some members of the Military Intelligence Reserve (a part of the Army's Officers Reserve Corps) on inactive duty initiated their own unofficial investigations of domestic political and labor groups, often employing heavy-handed or amateurish methods. The resultant public backlash caused the MID's legitimate countersubversion activities to be severely fettered. Counterintelligence remained neglected in the MID until 1939, when growing German and Japanese espionage and subversion in the United States and elsewhere in the western hemisphere created a political climate that permitted the Division to establish a Counterintelligence Branch.

Air Intelligence

The growth of military aviation in the period immediately following the First World War had intelligence implications that were soon appreciated by the MID. The airplane had largely replaced the balloon as an OVERHEAD RECONNAISSANCE platform during the war, and the science of photointerpretation had emerged. Now that the airplane was a potent weapon, there was a need for intelligence on foreign air forces. In 1926 an Air Section was created within the MID to deal with both of these aspects of military aviation. At about the same time, however, the old Army Air Service was given the new and more independent status of the Air Corps, and an Information Division was established within the Office of the Chief of the Air Corps (see AIR FORCE INTELLIGENCE). This Division—later re-designated as the Intelligence Division—duplicated much of the work of the MID's Air Section, and the resultant jurisdictional dispute went unresolved until the Second World War.

Communications Intelligence

The MID's Cipher Bureau—the "American Black Chamber"—which had been jointly funded by the War and State departments since 1919, was closed in 1929 after the new secretary of state, Henry L. Stimson, withdrew State Department support on ethical grounds ("Gentlemen do not read each other's mail"). Coincidentally, the War Department had decided a short time before to transfer all its communications intelligence activities to the supervision of the chief signal officer (i.e., the head of the Army Signal Corps). In July 1929 the Signal Intelligence Service was established within the Signal Corps, and WILLIAM FRIEDMAN was made its director (see CRYPTOLOGY, NATIONAL SECURITY AGENCY). The functions of the SIS were to create codes and ciphers for use by the Army, break foreign codes and ciphers,

and conduct training and research in cryptography. As international tensions increased during the mid- and late 1930s, the SIS was enlarged and its communications intelligence activities were stepped up. In 1940 Friedman broke "Purple," the Japanese diplomatic cipher, and by 1941 SIS and Navy cryptanalysts had broken a variety of other Japanese codes and ciphers. Although these breakthroughs did not prevent the PEARL HARBOR ATTACK, they were of enormous value to the subsequent American war effort.

Second World War

In February 1942, shortly after the American entry into the SECOND WORLD WAR, the War Department General Staff was reorganized and an attempt was made to separate the planning and policy functions of the MID from the operational responsibilities of collecting, analyzing, and disseminating intelligence. A Military Intelligence Service was created to carry out the latter activities, under the general supervision of the assistant chief of staff for intelligence (i.e., the head of the MID). This separation of functions was more theoretical than actual, however, because Maj. Gen. GEORGE V. STRONG, the MID chief, considered the new arrangement unworkable and undertook a de facto merging of the MID and the MIS.

The MID/MIS established and operated the Military Intelligence Training Center at Camp Ritchie, Maryland, along with other installations to train field intelligence officers for assignment overseas. It supervised the Counter Intelligence Corps within the United States (the Corps was the old Corps of Intelligence Police, which was enlarged and renamed in January 1942). The CIC conducted background investigations of government personnel, carried out counterintelligence investigations, and was responsible for the security of the Manhattan Project (see BORIS T. PASH, PEER DE SILVA).

A special analytical unit was established within MID/MIS to integrate the communications intelligence collected by SIS with collateral intelligence (see SPECIAL BRANCH).

Although the OFFICE OF STRATEGIC SERVICES had been given the responsibility for most foreign secret strategic (as opposed to combat) intelligence operations in Europe, General Strong—a severe critic of the OSS—established a separate secret intelligence unit within the MIS to collect strategic intelligence in Europe. This unit, headed by Col. JOHN V. GROMBACH, was apparently jointly supported by the War Department, the FBI, the State Department, and perhaps other government agencies. It was so well hid-

German agents with their radio equipment captured by the Army Counter Intelligence Corps in France during the Second World War. Source: Department of Defense.

den that even now little open source information is available regarding its operations. Even its official name has not been disclosed, and it is known to students of intelligence history simply as the GROMBACH ORGANIZATION.

In December 1944 the MID took over operational control of the Signal Intelligence Service, which by then was known as the Signal Security Agency, leaving administrative control with the Signal Corps. The Agency operated a far-flung network of collection sites—the Aleutians, Hawaii, Australia, India, and Ethiopia, and produced valuable communications intelligence.

Intelligence Overseas

While MID/MIS dealt with intelligence and counterintelligence operations within the continental United States, overseas intelligence activities were decentralized. No single Army unit or agency had overall responsibility for them. In the European and North African (and most other) theaters of the war, combat intelligence was the responsibility of the G-2s attached to the staffs of field commands down to the division level, the S-2s attached to lower command levels, and their respective Counter Intelligence Corps and Signal Intelligence Service detachments. The activities of field intelligence personnel were not at all limited to the sort of work generally associated with headquarters staffs. For example, CIC agents landed with the first waves of the 36th Infantry Division at Salerno and were among the first Allied troops to enter Rome. Often moving ahead of the regular front-line troops, they captured enemy documents and files before they could be destroyed, seized enemy agents and collaborators, and interrogated prisoners of war. In some instances they proceeded so far ahead of the general advance that they were in fact operating behind enemy lines, risking not only capture by the enemy but also the accidental "friendly fire'' of the advancing Allied armies. Signal intelligence detachments were also close to the front, and their interception of enemy tactical communications repeatedly frustrated German counterattacks. And tactical aerial reconnaissance became such a valuable combat intelligence tool in the European Theater of Operations that a new section, G-2 Air, was established at Army and Corps staff levels in 1944.

As the Allied armies advanced across France and up through Italy, the OSS of necessity joined with Army Intelligence in providing tactical intelligence support. (See OFFICE OF STRATEGIC SERVICES.)

The Southwest Pacific

In the Southwest Pacific Theater—generally, Australia, the Solomon Islands, New Guinea, the Netherlands East Indies, and the Philippines—General Douglas MacArthur created his own intelligence service. His umbrella organization was the ALLIED INTELLIGENCE BUREAU, a joint U.S.-Australian coordinating agency headed by MacArthur's G-2, Maj. Gen. CHARLES A. WILLOUGHBY. The ALLIED GEOGRAPHICAL SECTION, an agency established by Willoughby, provided basic geographic intelligence on uncharted or poorly mapped areas within the theater. Yet another agency, the ALLIED TRANSLATOR AND INTERPRETER SECTION (ATIS), translated captured Japanese documents and interrogated Japanese prisoners of war. The Counter Intelligence Corps was very active in the theater, so much so that MacArthur's CIC chief, Col. (later Brig. Gen.) Elliot R. Thorpe, established a counterintelligence school in Brisbane, Australia, in June 1943 to train CIC agents. As in Europe, the CIC performed a variety of tasks, including collecting combat intelligence in the field. Many of the CIC combat detachments were integrated with the ATIS prisoner interrogators, and were often among the first assault waves in the amphibious landings.

Communications intelligence was provided by the CENTRAL BUREAU, another joint Australian-American agency. The job of sifting the intelligence from the CB's intercepts belonged to a special section of the G-2 staff in MacArthur's headquarters.

Long-range ground reconnaissance was undertaken by the ALAMO SCOUTS, an elite unit under the command of the Sixth Army's G-2. The scouts carried out nearly one hundred missions, ranging from pure reconnaissance to commando raids.

The Postwar Period

The Army and the rest of the defense establishment were far more aware of the value of military intelligence at war's end than they had been at the beginning. Nonetheless, the abrupt reduction in military budgets led to a cutting back of intelligence activities in the Army. A reorganization of MID in 1944 had restored the MID/MIS separation that General Strong had resisted, and thereafter the MID was strictly limited to intelligence policy and planning matters and was completely divorced from operations. Except for signals intelligence and counterintelligence, MIS intelligence activity came to a nearly complete halt after V-J Day. The intelligence training center at Fort Ritchie, Maryland, was closed. All field radio intelligence units were abolished, and their assets were consolidated in the Signal Security Agency, which was renamed the Army Security Agency (ASA) in September 1945. Although the mission of the CIC was broadened to include some positive intelligence collection, this and the military attaché program comprised all of the Army's activity in the positive field. The creation of the U.S. Air Force as a separate military service in 1947 stripped away all of the Army's aerial reconnaissance functions. And the creation of the CENTRAL INTELLIGENCE AGENCY the same year led to the termination of MIS support for the Grombach Organization and forestalled any future Army expansion into the area of foreign secret intelligence activities.

Korean War

With the coming of the KOREAN WAR in June 1950, the Army was caught short of intelligence capability as a result of the recent cutbacks. Tactical CIC and ASA units were quickly transferred from Japan to support the Eighth Army in Korea, but the U.S. forces continued to suffer from a shortage of trained intelligence personnel until 1952. A lack of Korean and Chinese linguists reduced the role of prisoner-of-war interrogations as an intelligence source and heightened the importance of signals intelligence and aerial reconnaissance, but even in the two latter fields a shortage of trained personnel hampered operations. Photointerpreters were in especially short supply. Most of these difficulties were eventually overcome, but military intelligence never quite reached the level of effectiveness it had achieved during the Second World War when the cease-fire ended hostilities in Korea in 1953.

Department of Defense

The creation of the Department of Defense in 1947 and the subordination of the individual armed services to DOD prompted a series of reorganizations in Army Intelligence (and in the Navy and Air Force intelligence, as well) during the ensuing three decades. The general trend of these reorganizations was to consolidate strategic intelligence matters within the DOD and the Joint Chiefs of Staff, leaving Army Intelligence, NAVAL INTELLIGENCE, and Air Force intelligence with a set of sharply defined, service-specific intelligence tasks.

In 1949 the Armed Forces Security Agency was created as an agency of the Joint Chiefs of Staff. The new agency took over most of the strategic communications intelligence (COMINT) and communications security (COMSEC) functions of the Army Security Agency and its Navy and Air Force counterparts, leaving the ASA with only those field COMINT and COMSEC functions that could not practically be centralized. (In 1952 the AFSA was transformed into a civilian agency of the Defense Department, the NATIONAL SECURITY AGENCY.)

The role of Army intelligence was further narrowed with the creation of the DEFENSE INTELLIGENCE AGENCY in 1961. DIA took over such functions as establishing intelligence collection requirements, CURRENT INTELLIGENCE production, the military attaché system, and participation in the production of NATIONAL INTELLIGENCE ESTIMATES from Army intelligence and the other armed service intelligence components. This left the Army's assistant chief of staff for intelligence with such limited and specific responsibilities as intelligence training, internal Army security and counterintelligence, technical intelligence regarding tactical or ground-forces weapon systems, mapping, charting, geodesy, and combat intelligence.

Tactical intelligence support of major Army commands was provided through a decentralized system of MI (Military Intelligence) Groups. The MI Groups were composed of specialist staffs whose functions encompassed the full spectrum of military intelligence activities (except COMINT, which remained with separate ASA units): prisoner interrogation, photointerpretation, counterintelligence, order of battle, etc. At about this time military intelligence was established as a new branch of the Army, i.e., it became a distinct career specialty comparable to the infantry or artillery, and thereby the MI Groups and other Army intelligence components were able to attract and retain high-quality personnel who wished to make military intelligence their profession.

Vietnam War

The system of decentralized MI Groups and smaller MI units was known as the Military Intelligence Organization (MIO) concept. The MIO concept received its first practical test in the VIETNAM WAR, where it was found to be an effective means of providing combat intelligence support.

Such positive intelligence activities that remained after the creation of DIA were assigned to the Counter Intelligence Corps, which was redesignated the Intelligence Corps, later the U.S. Army Intelligence Command (USAINTC). Established as a major Army command in 1965, USAINTC was primarily responsible for counterintelligence within the continental United States. Because the urban riots of the late 1960s raised the real possibility that the Army would be used to quell domestic civil disorders, USAINTC began collecting domestic intelligence to support such operations. These collection activities were soon enlarged to include individuals active in the anti-war movement. When USAINTC's domestic surveillance activities were publicly disclosed in the early 1970s, public indignation and political reaction caused the Command's activities to be sharply curtailed. Even the task of routine personnel background investigations—comprising ninety percent of the command's activities—was withdrawn from USAINTC and assigned to a newly created Defense Department agency, the Defense Investigative Service. In 1974 USAINTC ceased to be a major Army command and was transformed into the U.S. Army Intelligence Agency, a field-operating agency under the assistant chief of staff for intelligence.

In 1975 Army intelligence underwent another major reorganization. The Army Security Agency was broken up and most of its units were integrated into the normal Army command structure. Those that remained were merged with the Army Intelligence Agency to form a new major Army command, the U.S. Army Intelligence and Security Command (INSCOM). At the tactical level, the ASA assets were merged with the MI Groups and other MI units. The new tactical intelligence support units were designated Combat Electronic Warfare and Intelligence (CEWI) units.

Today's Army Intelligence Organization

Today Army intelligence consists of a complex of agencies under the direction of the Office of the Assistant Chief of Staff for Intelligence (OACSI). The OACSI itself includes some general administrative and management activities plus four directorates. The Foreign Liaison Directorate conducts liaison with and renders assistance to the military intelligence services of U.S. allies and friends. The Foreign Intelligence Directorate produces current intelligence, long-range assessments, and technical intelligence, and establishes collection requirements. The Counterintelligence Directorate is involved in policy matters regarding a broad range of security and counterintelligence activities. The Intelligence Systems Directorate operates such major collection systems techniques as SIGINT, PHOTINT, and HUMINT (see -INT).

INSCOM remains the major operational agency, performing a wide range of functions: intelligence analysis, counterintelligence operations, and intelligence collection. The command also carries out SIGINT/COMSEC activities for the NATIONAL SECURITY AGENCY.

The U.S. Army Missile Intelligence Agency produces intelligence on foreign missile systems relating to the Army's mission, i.e., tactical missiles and—because of Army responsibilities in the U.S. ballistic missile defense program—strategic missiles.

The U.S. Army Foreign Science and Technology Center, which is subordinate to the Army Material Readiness and Development Command, produces foreign technical intelligence needed in U.S. Army planning and research and development activities.

Additionally, several other Army components—e.g., the Special Forces—engaged in paramilitary operations, irregular warfare, or counterterrorist action have some intelligence involvement as well.

(Bidwell, "History of the Military Intelligence Division, Department of the Army General Staff"; Powe and Wilson, *Evolution of American Military Intelligence*; Powe, "Emergence of the War Department Intelligence Agency"; Van Deman, *Memoirs*; Finnegan, *Military Intelligence*; Ransom, *The Intelligence Establishment*; Richelson, *The U.S. Intelligence Community*.)

ARNOLD, BENEDICT (January 14, 1741–June 14, 1801): army officer, defector

A native of Norwich, Connecticut, Arnold was the son of a distinguished New England family (a great-grandfather of the same name was governor of Rhode Island). At the age of fourteen he was apprenticed to a druggist, but twice ran away while still a teenager to serve in, and then desert from, the New York militia.

He completed his apprenticeship and, in 1762, opened a pharmacy and bookstore in New Haven, Connecticut. His business flourished and he became a successful merchant in the West Indian and Canadian trade. Arnold became a captain of the Connecticut militia in December 1774 and, in April 1775, on learning of the battles of Lexington and Concord, he assembled his men and led them to Cambridge, Massachusetts, to join the American forces.

Arnold was commissioned a colonel and, together with Ethan Allen, led an expedition that captured Fort Ticonderoga in northeastern New York and put the ordnance taken there into the hands of the American forces besieging the British at Boston. Immediately after the fall of Ticonderoga he sailed to the northern end of Lake Champlain and captured the British fort at St. John's, Ontario. However, despite these outstanding services, the Massachusetts authorities proved ungrateful and even failed to reimburse him for the personal funds he had expended on their behalf. His misfortune was compounded by the death of his wife during his absence from Connecticut.

These adverse circumstances did not discourage Arnold from proposing an attack on Canada to Gen. GEORGE WASHINGTON, who had recently been made commander-in-chief of the Continental armies. Washington consented, and Arnold planned and led an expedition against Quebec, laying siege to that city throughout the winter of 1775–76, but failing to capture it in an attack on December 31st. The arrival of British reinforcements in the spring forced him to withdraw, but he fought a successful rearguard action on Lake Champlain in October, which forestalled the British invasion of New York. However his services were again rewarded with ingratitude when the Continental Congress passed him over and promoted five officers junior to him to the rank of major general. (Arnold was by then a brigadier general, a rank to which he had been promoted during the Quebec siege.)

Arnold was dissuaded from resigning his commission by General Washington, and, in April 1777, he rushed to Danbury, Connecticut, upon learning of a British raid on that city. He rallied what American troops he could find there and harassed the numerically superior British force as it withdrew to Norwalk. This time Congress expressed its gratitude by promoting him to major general, but it did not make full amends for its earlier neglect by restoring his seniority to the five junior officers it had promoted over him. Furthermore, Arnold's enemies in Congress succeeded in making him the object of a politically motivated investigation into the minute details of his bookkeeping of Army accounts during the siege of Quebec. This time Arnold actually submitted his resignation to Congress, but withdrew it at the personal request of General Washington and upon receiving word that he was needed to resist a new British campaign in New York.

Arnold led a force of 800 men to lift the British siege of Fort Stanwix (near what today is Rome, New York), and he succeeded in sending the numerically superior British force in full flight back to Oswego. Soon thereafter he distinguished himself again at the battles of Freeman's Farm and Bemis Heights, and was severely wounded in the latter engagement.

Congress restored Arnold's seniority, and, after recovering from his wounds, he was placed in command of Philadelphia in June 1778, after the British forces that had occupied the city since September 1777 were evacuated. In April 1779 he married Margaret (Peggy) Shippen, the daughter of a wealthy Philadelphia merchant, and a young woman of Tory sympathies. He became embroiled in several quarrels with the Pennsylvania civil authorities and with Congress; charges were made that he had exploited his military position for private gain and used troops of the local militia as his personal servants. He demanded and received a court-martial to clear himself of the charges. In December 1779 the court exonerated him on most counts, but recommended a reprimand on two minor points.

Arnold's quarrels, grievances, his belief that he had been dealt with unjustly by Congress, and perhaps the influence of his Tory bride were factors that together prompted him to offer to sell military information to Sir Henry Clinton, the British commander-in-chief. The secret correspondence between Arnold and Clinton began in May 1779, a month after his marriage, and continued until December, when, apparently mollified by the belief that he would be fully cleared by the court-martial, he broke it off. He resumed the correspondence in May 1780, however, after receiving the mild reprimand written by General Washington regarding the two minor charges that had been sustained. The Arnold-Clinton correspondence was carried between Philadelphia and New York by JOSEPH STANSBURY, a Philadelphia Tory who served as courier; British secret agents SAMUEL WALLIS and JOHN RATTOON also carried some of the messages. Stansbury's New York contact was the Reverend JOHN ODELL, who passed along the letters to Clinton's aide-de-camp, Major JOHN ANDRÉ. Among the many items of military information Arnold furnished was word that a French expeditionary force of six thousand troops under General Rochambeau was expected to arrive shortly in Rhode Island, intelligence Clinton regarded as being of major strategic value.

In July 1780 Arnold was given command of the American fortress at West Point, including a large area covering outposts at Stony Point and Verplanks Point to the south, Fishkill to the north, and North Castle to the east. He proposed to Clinton the surrender of these strongholds to the British for a payment of £20,000. While he negotiated this deal with Clinton, he continued to supply the British commander with military information, sending it

Benedict Arnold. Source: Library of Congress.

by way of his wife in Philadelphia, who forwarded it to Clinton through Stansbury, Odell, and André.

Through Col. BEVERLY ROBINSON, a prominent Tory and British secret agent, André arranged to meet with Arnold to work out the final details of the surrender of West Point. The two met clandestinely in Haverstraw, New York, on the night of September 21–22, 1780. After the meeting André was unable to rejoin the British sloop *Vulture*, in which he had sailed up the Hudson River from New York to the meeting. Arnold made out passes that would permit André to cross the American lines at White Plains, and sent him back along that route to New York in the company of JOSHUA HETT SMITH, an American secret agent who was apparently unaware of the nature of André's mission. (Smith believed André was simply an eccentric merchant who enjoyed wearing a British officer's uniform.) It was now necessary for André to exchange his British uniform for civilian clothes in order to avoid discovery.

André was captured on the morning of September

Lt. Col. Turner Ashby. Source: National Archives.

23rd near Tarrytown, New York, when, mistaking three American militiamen for British soldiers, he declared himself to be a British officer. A search of his person turned up several military documents Arnold had given him: a summary of Continental Army strength, a report about the troops at West Point and the surrounding area, an estimate of the forces needed to garrison the defenses, a report about the ordnance on hand at West Point, an artillery deployment plan for defense of the stronghold, a copy of the minutes of a recent council of war held by General Washington, and Arnold's assessment of the weak points in the West Point defenses. André was arrested and taken to the American command post at North Castle.

Although Arnold was not implicated by the documents, his role in the affair was soon recognized by Maj. BENJAMIN TALLMADGE, who persuaded the American commander at North Castle not to send his prisoner back to Arnold at West Point. However, he did not prevent a report of André's capture from being sent to Arnold, and, upon learning of the development, the general fled to New York aboard the *Vulture.*

André was hanged as a spy after General Clinton rejected an American proposal that he be exchanged for Arnold. An attempt to kidnap Arnold by Sgt. Maj. John Champe of the Continental Army a few weeks later in New York did not succeed, although Champe was able to report to Washington that apparently no other American officers had been involved in Arnold's treason.

Arnold was given the rank of brigadier general in the British Army. He led marauding expeditions into Virginia in December 1780 and into Connecticut, where he burned New London in September 1781. In December 1781 he, his wife, and his son went to England. There he lived on a military pension and entered into several unsuccessful commercial ventures. One of these prompted him to move to Nova Scotia in 1787, but failure and local hostility caused him to return to England in 1791.

(Van Doren, *Secret History of the American Revolution;* Flexner, *The Traitor and the Spy;* Boatner, *Encyclopedia of the American Revolution;* Bakeless, *Turncoats, Traitors and Heroes.*)

ASHBY, TURNER (October 23, 1828–June 6, 1862): businessman, planter, Confederate army officer, and secret service agent

A native of Fauquier County, Virginia, Ashby was a prosperous grain dealer, planter, and local politician in the Shenandoah Valley of Virginia before the Civil War. When he heard of John Brown's raid in 1859 he raised a volunteer cavalry company and led it to Harper's Ferry, too late to engage Brown's men, who had already been captured by federal authorities. At the outbreak of the Civil War Ashby's cavalry company was merged with the 7th Virginia Cavalry. He was commissioned and promoted to lieutenant colonel in the Virginia militia in June 1861.

Ashby became a scout and secret intelligence agent for Gen. Thomas J. ("Stonewall") Jackson. His knowledge of horses enabled him to cross through Union lines in the guise of a veterinarian and enter Union army camps, where his expertise was very welcome. In this way he was able to observe Union military strength and movements, and his undercover reconnaissance trips took him as far north as Pennsylvania. Ashby organized an informal secret service that reported back to him on Union military movements in Virginia. BELLE BOYD may have been one of his agents.

Although Ashby's intelligence services for Jackson were of great value, he is better remembered as a cavalry commander. He was promoted to brigadier general in May 1862 and commanded a cavalry brigade during the Shenandoah Valley campaign of

May–June 1862. Ashby was killed in action in a rearguard action near Harrisonburg.

(*Who Was Who in America,* historical volume; Boatner, *Civil War Dictionary;* Bakeless, *Spies of the Confederacy;* Kane, *Spies for the Blue and Gray.*)

ASSET

1 Anything—a person, organization or object—useful to an intelligence service in performing covert operations.
2 A person or organization not under the direct control of an intelligence service but nonetheless useful to the service in performing covert operations.

The term is often used in the first sense as a concise reference to the total operational environment within a country, e.g., "British intelligence had few intelligence assets in Albania at the time," meaning few agents, sympathizers, safe-houses, arms caches, letter-drops, etc. In the second sense, the term is frequently used to distinguish between a person who will sometimes cooperate with the intelligence service in its covert operations and an AGENT working under the direction of a CASE OFFICER. For example, a journalist who may occasionally exchange information with an agent or case officer would be considered an asset in the second sense of the term.

AURELL, GEORGE EMANUEL (January 8, 1905–February 1970): diplomat, clandestine service officer

Although Aurell was born in Kobe, Japan, his parents were American citizens (his father had been in business in Japan). He attended Park College (1922–23) and Northwestern University (1923–24), and he earned a B.S. from Oklahoma State University in 1927. From 1927 to 1930 he was American vice-consul at Yokohama, Japan. He served in the U.S. Army in the Second World War, was awarded the Legion of Merit and the Bronze Star, and was discharged in the rank of lieutenant colonel. After the war he served as commercial manager on the Southwestern staff of General MacArthur in Tokyo.

Aurell served with the Central Intelligence Agency. In 1950 he was chief of the Office of Policy Coordination (as the CIA's COVERT ACTION unit was then known) in Japan. In 1953 he became chief of the Far Eastern Division of the CIA's Clandestine Service, succeeding LLOYD GEORGE in that position, and supported by DESMOND FITZGERALD, the deputy division chief. Aurell presided over the FE Division during the period when EDWARD LANSDALE was directing the Philippine counterinsurgency program against the Huk guerrillas and assisting Magsaysay in getting elected president of the Philippines.

In 1956 Aurell became chief of the CIA Manila station, having been succeeded by ALFRED ULMER as the FE Division chief. In 1959 he returned to Washington because of poor health, and JOHN RICHARDSON replaced him as Manila station chief. From 1962 to 1966 he served in Bangkok, Thailand.

(Smith, *Portrait of a Cold Warrior; Who Was Who,* vol. 5.; Leary, *Perilous Missions.*)

B

BABCOCK, JOHN C. (1836–November 19, 1908): architect, intelligence officer

A native of Warwick, Rhode Island, Babcock and his parents moved to Chicago in 1855. Trained as an architect, he was working as a well-paid ($1,000 per year) member of a large Chicago architectural firm at the outbreak of the Civil War. In August 1861 he enlisted as a private in the Sturgis Rifles, a Chicago unit that served as the personal guard of Gen. George B. McClellan, commander of the Division of the Potomac (later called the Army of the Potomac). In November 1861 Babcock was assigned to the intelligence service organized for McClellan by Allan Pinkerton, possibly working at first as a draftsman-mapmaker. After the Sturgis Rifles was disbanded in 1862 he was mustered out of the Army but remained with Pinkerton and the Army of the Potomac, officially listed as a civilian employee of the Topographical Department.

Babcock remained with the Army of the Potomac after Pinkerton departed in the wake of McClellan's removal from command in November 1862. In the absence of any other intelligence officer he served as a one-man secret service for McClellan's successor, Gen. Ambrose Burnside. In January 1863, when Burnside's successor, Gen. Joseph Hooker, established the Bureau of Military Information under (then) Col. George H. Sharpe, Babcock became Sharpe's deputy.

Babcock proved to be a talented intelligence officer, displaying particular skills as an interrogator and order-of-battle specialist. Soon after the Bureau began operating he produced an organization table of Lee's army that historian and espionologist Edwin C. Fishel has determined to be quite accurate. His estimates of Confederate troop strength proved to be far more accurate than those produced by Pinkerton for McClellan, and Fishel's research shows they were amazingly close to the true numbers.

Fishel notes that Babcock also operated as an agent in the field on at least one occasion. When the Confederates invaded Maryland and Pennsylvania in June 1863 with the Army of the Potomac in pursuit, Sharpe sent Babcock ahead to organize local espionage at Frederick, Maryland, a project he executed with considerable daring, since the town was already occupied by Southern soldiers.

Babcock became Gen. George Meade's intelligence officer in March 1864 when Sharpe was transferred to Grant's staff (Meade had succeeded Hooker as commander of the Army of the Potomac in June 1863). Babcock served in this capacity until the end of the war. He was present at Appomattox Court House, Virginia, on April 9, 1865, when Lee surrendered.

After the war Babcock settled in New York City and resumed his work as an architect. In 1868 he became one of the three founders of the New York Athletic Club. After his retirement he moved to Mount Vernon, New York.

(Fishel, "The Mythology of Civil War Intelligence"; Schmidt, "G-2, Army of the Potomac"; John C. Babcock file, Local History Department, Mount Vernon (New York) Public Library; obituaries, *New York Times*, November 21, 1908, p. 9, *New York Herald*, November 21, 1908, *Mount Vernon Argus*, November 21, 1908.)

BAGLEY, TENNENT HARRINGTON (November 11, 1925–): clandestine service officer

A native of Annapolis, Maryland, Bagley served in the U.S. Marine Corps in 1943–46, and was discharged in the rank of first lieutenant. He graduated from the University of Southern California in 1947 and studied at the University of Geneva, earning a degree in political science in 1948 and a doctorate in that subject in 1951.

Bagley served with the Central Intelligence Agency. He was political officer at the American embassy in Vienna, Austria, in 1951–52, and at Bern, Switzerland, in 1958–61. He was deputy chief of the Soviet Bloc Division of the CIA's Clandestine Services and later chief of the Agency's station in Brussels, Belgium.

(Agee, *Inside the Company; Who's Who in Government*, 1st ed.)

BAKELESS, JOHN EDWIN (December 30, 1894–August 8, 1978): author, intelligence officer, espionologist

A native of Carlisle, Pennsylvania, Bakeless earned a bachelor's degree from Williams College in 1918, a master's from Harvard University in 1920, and a Ph.D. from Harvard in 1936. Although he pursued a lifelong career in letters, he was an officer in the U.S. Army Reserve continuously from 1918 onwards, serving on active duty in both world wars. Between 1934 and 1940 he received special intelligence training, and in 1941 went on active duty in the rank of major. During the Second World War he was assistant military attaché in Turkey, and served as a

John C. Babcock with his horse "Gimlet." Source: Library of Congress.

Gen. Lafayette C. Baker. Source: Library of Congress.

member of the American Section of the Allied Control Commission for Bulgaria. He completed his active duty tour in the rank of colonel.

Among his many books is *Turncoats, Traitors and Heroes* (1959), an account of espionage during the American Revolution. He collaborated with his wife, author Katherine Little Bakeless, in a version of this book for young adult readers, *Spies of the Revolution* (1962). He is also the author of *Spies of the Confederacy* (1970).

(*Who Was Who in America*, vol. 7.)

BAKER, LAFAYETTE CURRY (October 13, 1826–July 3, 1868): intelligence and counterespionage officer

A native of Stafford, New York, Baker grew up in the adjoining town of Elba. At the age of thirteen he and his family moved to the Michigan wilderness near what is today the city of Lansing.

Baker left Michigan in 1848 and engaged in what he later vaguely described as "mechanical and mercantile pursuits" in New York, Philadelphia, and San Francisco. While living in San Francisco during 1853–61 he was a member of the Vigilance Committee, as the notorious local vigilante society was called.

At the outbreak of the Civil War Baker, who was visiting New York City, went to Washington to offer his services to the federal government. With the

recommendation of former New York Congressman Hiram Walbridge and Philadelphia Congressman William D. Kelley, Baker was introduced to the elderly Lt. Gen. Winfield Scott, then general-in-chief of the U.S. Army. Scott engaged Baker to undertake an espionage mission into Virginia in July 1861 to collect information regarding the strength and disposition of the Confederate forces at Manassas and elsewhere in the state. Baker returned safely from this mission, although he was arrested and imprisoned in Richmond for a time on suspicion of espionage.

On Scott's recommendation, Baker went to work as a detective for Secretary of War Simon Cameron, with the mission of catching blockade runners who were smuggling arms and ammunition to the Confederates. Shortly thereafter he was hired by Secretary of State William H. Seward to establish and run a counterespionage service for the Department of State. In February 1862 Baker's unit was transferred to the War Department, which now assumed the responsibility for counterespionage, and Baker began reporting to the new secretary of war, Edwin Stanton. Baker called his organization the NATIONAL DETECTIVE BUREAU, an unofficial designation. Baker's official title was provost marshal of the War Department.

Baker and his Bureau succeeded in catching Confederate spies, most notably BELLE BOYD and Wat Bowie. He went beyond his counterespionage charter to arrest such other offenders as Southern sympathizers, Army deserters, bounty jumpers, war profiteers, prostitutes, and corrupt government employees. He is said to have operated without regard for such constitutional niceties as due process or warrants for search or arrest. Reportedly, suspects were rounded up and thrown into the notorious Old Capitol prison, where Baker would often subject them to harsh or even brutal interrogation. However, such excesses, while often reported, are not well documented; Baker may have acquired a more fearsome reputation than the facts actually warrant.

In June 1863 Stanton commissioned Baker as a colonel in the U.S. Army and authorized him to raise a cavalry battalion for service in the District of Columbia. The First District of Columbia Cavalry—or "Baker's Rangers," as the unit was called—was a sort of mounted police and counterinsurgency outfit, which patrolled through Washington's Maryland and Virginia suburbs. The Rangers fought several engagements against John S. Moseby's Partisan Rangers, but failed to capture Moseby.

Immediately after the assassination of President Lincoln on April 14, 1865, Stanton summoned Baker, who was in New York City, to return to Washington

Lafayette Baker claims to have interviewed Confederate President Jefferson Davis while visiting Richmond undercover. Source: Author's collection.

and take part in the search for John Wilkes Booth (see LINCOLN CONSPIRACY). After ten days, during which federal troops searched the Maryland and Virginia countryside in vain, Baker sent his cousin, Luther Baker, to guide a troop of New York cavalry to the vicinity of the farm near Port Royal, Virginia, where the man whose remains were subsequently identified as those of Booth was then hiding. Baker's wonderful perspicacity in this matter (he explained it as the result of deduction from information supplied him by an unidentified "colored man"), his role supervising the disputed identification of the dead man as Booth, his secret disposal of the corpse, and his sharing in the reward for the capture of Booth ($3,700), have led students of the assassination to speculations about Baker ranging from fraud to complicity in the assassination conspiracy, although none of these theories has been proved.

Baker was promoted to the rank of brigadier general by Stanton immediately after the recovery of the

body supposed to be that of Booth. He assigned several of his detectives to protect President Andrew Johnson from assassins, but he soon ran afoul of the President when Johnson became convinced Baker was spying upon him.

Baker was released from the Army and government service in February 1866. About the same time he was indicted on charges of false imprisonment and extortion that arose from a complaint made by a woman—a friend of the President—whom he arrested after she visited the White House. While Baker was acquitted on the extortion charge, he was convicted on the false-imprisonment charge, but a sympathetic judge sentenced him to a fine of only $1.35.

After his departure from Washington Baker engaged in an unsuccessful hotel venture in Lansing, Michigan. The following year he published a melodramatic account of his service as chief of the National Detective Bureau; the book was ghost-written by a journalist named Phineas Headley. Baker returned to Washington in 1868 to present testimony (later proven to be false) implicating President Johnson in treasonable correspondence with the Confederacy during the Civil War.

(*DAB; Who Was Who in America*, historical volume; Mogelever, *Death to Traitors*; Corson, *Armies of Ignorance*; Baker, *History of the United States Secret Service*; Roscoe, *Web of Conspiracy*; Eisenschiml, *Why Was Lincoln Murdered?*)

BALTIMORE PLOT

In February 1861 a conspiracy was mounted by secessionists in Baltimore, Maryland, to assassinate President-elect Abraham Lincoln as he passed through that city en route to his inauguration in Washington.

In mid-January Samuel Morse Felton, president of the Philadelphia, Wilmington & Baltimore Railroad, engaged private detective ALLAN PINKERTON to investigate reports that in the event of war Maryland secessionists planned to destroy the railroad. (By one account Felton was advised by reformer and lecturer Dorothea Dix of a secessionist conspiracy to isolate Washington.) Pinkerton and a team of his agents, including TIMOTHY WEBSTER and Hattie Lawton, went to Maryland to investigate. They learned that at least three secessionist organizations—the National Volunteers, the Baltimore Guards, and the Palmetto Guards—were indeed planning violence of the sort suspected by Felton.

Assuming a pseudonym and disguised as a broker, Pinkerton cultivated a local secessionist named Luckett who introduced him to Cypriano Ferrandini (sometimes Fernandina or Ferrandina), an Italian immigrant who ran a barber shop in Barnum's Hotel. Ferrandini readily boasted to Pinkerton that he was organizing a plot to assassinate Lincoln and was prepared to do so himself, if necessary. One of Pinkerton's agents penetrated the conspiracy and was present when eight would-be assassins were selected by lot, although he was unable to observe which of those assembled actually drew the marked ballots. However, he did manage to learn the details of the planned ambush.

In his pre-inaugural tour from Springfield to Washington, Lincoln was due to stop in Philadelphia on Washington's birthday (February 22nd) in order to unfurl the new American flag (Kansas had been admitted to the Union on January 29th) at Independence Hall. He was due to travel on to Harrisburg, Pennsylvania, that night, then continue on to Washington the next day. His route, which had been published in the newspapers, called for him to take the Northern Central Railroad from Harrisburg to Baltimore, arriving at the Calvert Street depot in that city, from which point he would ride in an open carriage over a distance of about one mile to the depot of the Baltimore & Ohio Railroad, on which he would continue to Washington. The assassins' plans called for a diversion at the Calvert Street depot during which Lincoln would be shot. The killers would escape to Virginia aboard a steamer waiting in the Chesapeake Bay. The plotters foresaw no earnest effort by the Baltimore Police to apprehend them; Chief of Police George P. Kane was aware of the plan and was in sympathy with it.

While Pinkerton was learning of the assassination plan, Timothy Webster had infiltrated one of the local secessionist military organizations and discovered that the killing of Lincoln in Baltimore was to be the signal for a general uprising in Maryland. Telegraph lines were to be cut, bridges blown up, and railroad tracks destroyed to prevent federal troops from entering Baltimore and to cut off the nation's capital from communication with the North.

On February 21st Pinkerton called on Lincoln in Philadelphia and set the matter before him, urging that he forgo the flag-raising planned for the next day and the side trip to Harrisburg and proceed immediately to Washington, passing through Baltimore unannounced that night. However, the President-elect was unwilling to agree to the plan.

That same evening Lincoln was visited by Frederick W. Seward, who brought an urgent message from his father, Lincoln's designated secretary of state. William Seward's message enclosed a report from Gen. Winfield Scott warning of the Baltimore assassination plot. Lincoln questioned young Seward closely in an attempt to learn whether this new report was the result of an independent discovery, or was somehow merely an echo of Pinkerton's investigation.

In fact, the Scott report was the result of the action of New York City Police Superintendent John A. Kennedy, who had heard rumors of the Baltimore plot and sent one of his detectives, David S. Bookstaver, to Baltimore to verify it. Operating undercover and ignorant of Pinkerton's investigation, Bookstaver independently discovered the plot and went immediately to Washington where he reported it to an officer on General Scott's staff.

Convinced now that Scott's report corroborated Pinkerton's, Lincoln agreed to an alternative plan proposed by Pinkerton. After the scheduled Philadelphia flag-raising and Harrisburg speech, Lincoln would immediately return to Philadelphia aboard a special train, switch to an overnight train to Washington that would pass through Baltimore in the middle of the night and over the B&O tracks, thereby eliminating the mile-long carriage ride between depots. His unscheduled evening departure from Harrisburg would be made without fanfare, and the telegraph lines leading from the city would be cut to prevent word from being sent ahead.

The operation was executed flawlessly. Pinkerton agent KATE WARNE, posing as Lincoln's sister, booked two rear sleepers on the Washington train. Other Pinkerton detectives were posted along the tracks in Maryland with instructions to signal the train to pass if the way was clear. Lincoln arrived in Washington at 6:00 A.M. on the 23rd without mishap, although the press got wind of the affair and used it to ridicule the new President. The government took no action to prosecute the Baltimore plotters.

The Baltimore Plot failed, first of all, because Fernandini and his co-conspirators hadn't taken even minimum security precautions and, in fact, seemed inclined to advertise their plans. Pinkerton's investigation, leading to his discovery of the plot, was launched by accident and not as part of a systematic presidential security plan, but it is apparent that Lincoln would have received adequate warnings from other sources even if Pinkerton had not become involved.

Once the plot was made known to Lincoln, it was prevented because Pinkerton devised a thoroughly effective counterplan and Lincoln had the good sense to agree to it. Both of these elements were missing in April 1865 in the successful LINCOLN CONSPIRACY (Pinkerton was not in charge of security and was not even in Washington), and Lincoln had long since gotten into the habit of appearing in public without any security whatsoever. Ironically, Lincoln's disregard of the danger of assassination may have been a result of the ridicule he received after the Baltimore Plot.

(Sandburg, *Abraham Lincoln: The War Years*; Horan, *The Pinkertons*; Pinkerton, *Spy of the Rebellion*; Roscoe, *The Web of Conspiracy*.)

BANCROFT, EDWARD (January 9, 1744– September 8, 1821): naturalist and British intelligence agent

Bancroft is generally regarded as the British Secret Service's most valuable agent during the American Revolution. A native of Westfield, Massachusetts, at an early age he moved to Hartford, Connecticut, where his widowed mother married an innkeeper. Sometime in his early youth he became the protégé of PAUL WENTWORTH, who arranged for him to become the assistant to a doctor in Surinam in 1763. There he studied chemistry and such locally accessible subjects as tropical poisons.

After a brief visit to New England Bancroft went to London in 1769 and studied medicine at St. Bartholomew's Hospital. While there he published several works: *An Essay on the Natural History of Guiana . . . with an account of the Religion, Manners, and Customs of several Tribes of its Indian Inhabitants;* and *Remarks on the Review of the Controversy between Great Britain and her Colonies.* (He also published a novel, *Charles Wentworth,* in 1770, but apparently no copy has survived; it was said to have been an attack on Christianity.) It may have been his publications on the subjects of natural history and colonial politics that brought him to the attention of BENJAMIN FRANKLIN, who was then in London as the colonial agent of Pennsylvania, Georgia, and Massachusetts. Franklin became Bancroft's friend and mentor, introducing him to such men as the chemist Joseph Priestley. Franklin sponsored Bancroft's membership in the prestigious British Royal Society, to which he was elected a fellow in 1773. Bancroft completed his medical studies and became an M.D.

Franklin also recognized the young man's talent for espionage and used him as a spy in some of the many intrigues of colonial politics in which he was then involved. When Franklin was appointed American minister to France in 1775 he instructed his fellow minister, SILAS DEANE, to hire Bancroft as secretary to the American ministry at Passy, outside Paris. At the same time Bancroft's old friend and mentor, Paul Wentworth, recruited him to the British Secret Service.

Bancroft made the most of his situation in Passy to spy for the British. As the legation's secretary, he saw all official documents and dispatches. He was able to keep London informed of every shipload of French arms and supplies sent to the Americans, all secret diplomatic exchanges between the American ministers and the governments of France and other European powers, the instructions sent by Congress and the COMMITTEE OF SECRET CORRESPONDENCE to the American ministers, and Franklin's progress in securing a treaty with France to bring her into the war as an American ally. When the Treaties of Alliance and Commerce were signed at Versailles on February 6, 1778, Bancroft arranged to have copies of the documents in the hands of Lord North and King George III within forty-two hours. His regular means of communicating with Wentworth and LORD STORMONT was through a dead drop beneath a boxwood tree in the Tuileries Gardens. He would write his reports in invisible writing (see CRYPTOLOGY) between the lines of a putative love letter that he would leave in a bottle concealed in the drop.

Bancroft engaged in several subterfuges to preserve his cover. When Congress was tardy in paying his salary he threatened to quit his post. He often tried to throw suspicion on others, including BEAU-MARCHAIS's secretary, as well as loyal Americans in Paris. His cover seems to have been perfect. He accompanied John Paul Jones on some of the raids along the English Coast, and in 1779 he was sent on a secret mission by Franklin and the Marquis de Lafayette to Ireland to assess the possibility of fomenting a revolt among the Presbyterian Ulstermen who were sympathetic to the American Revolution (he reported that the time was not ripe and the project was scrapped).

In addition to spying in the American ministry, he recruited Franklin's colleague, Silas Deane, into the British Secret Service. The historian Julian P. Boyd has presented a persuasive circumstantial case that Dean's death in 1789 was not due to natural causes as has been supposed, but from a poison administered by Bancroft for the purpose of silencing a possible witness against himself.

Bancroft's role as a British agent apparently remained unknown during his lifetime. After the war he traveled to America and continued to report to the British Secret Service, suggesting that a counter-revolution could be effected by dividing the states over British trade, but apparently the plan was not adopted in London. He returned to England and pursued his scientific interests, specializing in the chemistry of dyes and publishing in 1794 *Experimental Researches concerning the Philosophy of Permanent Colours.*

Bancroft died at Margate in 1821. His role as a British spy was not disclosed until the 1880s, when the British government opened some of its official archives to American researcher B. F. Stephens. His grandson, a British general, was so distressed at learning of his grandfather's espionage role that he destroyed most of Bancroft's personal papers, which might have shed interesting light on some of the intelligence operations of the American Revolution.

(*DNB*; Einstein, *Divided Loyalties*; Bendiner, *The Virgin Diplomats*; Currey, *Code Number 72*; Bemis, "British Secret Service and the French-American Alliance"; Boyd, "Silas Deane: Death by a Kindly Teacher of Treason?")

BANGS, GEORGE HENRY (ca. 1831– September 12, 1883): journalist, detective, Union intelligence officer and secret service agent of the Civil War

Bangs's first job was as a reporter on a newspaper owned and edited by his father, and the experience aroused his interest in criminal investigation. In 1856

he joined the New York Police Department and was assigned to the force guarding the Crystal Palace, a large exhibition hall erected in 1852 for America's first World's Fair. While in that position he met ALLAN PINKERTON who recruited him as a private detective with PINKERTON'S NATIONAL DETECTIVE AGENCY (some accounts have Bangs joining Pinkerton's in 1853).

Bangs was one of the detectives Pinkerton brought to Cincinnati in May 1861 when he organized a secret service for Gen. George B. McClellan. Bangs was Pinkerton's chief assistant during his CIVIL WAR operations (May 1861–November 1862), and he undertook frequent clandestine missions into Confederate-held territory during this period.

After the war Bangs became general manager of Pinkerton's and held that position until his death.

(Obituary, *New York Times*, September 15, 1883, p. 8; Horan, *The Pinkertons*.)

BARMINE, ALEXANDER G. (1899–December 25, 1987): Soviet army officer, intelligence officer, and defector; U.S. intelligence officer and government official

A native of Byelorussia, Barmine fought in the civil wars that followed the Russian Revolution. He graduated from the Soviet General Staff College in 1923, later earning a master's degree in Farsi. He also became proficient in several other languages.

Barmine became a brigadier general in the Red Army and a senior officer of Soviet military intelligence. He headed the Soviet trade delegations to Paris and Milan from 1929 to 1932. In 1937 he was serving as Soviet chargé d'affaires in Athens when he defected to the West. His decision to defect was prompted by Stalin's purge of the Soviet military and a summons he received to return to Russia, probably to face imprisonment or execution.

For the next three years Barmine lived in Paris, occasionally writing articles for the *New York Times* on the excesses of Stalin's rule. In 1940 he moved to New York City. He enlisted in the U.S. Army in 1942 and was assigned to the Office of Strategic Services. He served in the OSS as a translator and an advisor on Soviet affairs. He was discharged in October 1944, reportedly because of an article he had written for *Reader's Digest* magazine that was critical of the Roosevelt administration's pro-Soviet policies.

Barmine wrote for several magazines after the war and became chief of the Russian Branch of the Voice of America. In 1964 he became the officer in charge of Soviet affairs for the United States Information

Agency. He became a special advisor to the Agency in 1969, a post he held until his retirement in 1972.

(Smith, *OSS;* Brook-Shepherd, *The Storm-Petrels;* obituary, *New York Times,* December 28, 1987, p. D13.)

BARNES, C. TRACY (ca. 1912–February 19, 1972): lawyer, covert operations officer

Barnes graduated from the Groton School, earned a bachelor's degree at Yale University, and graduated from the Harvard Law School. During the Second World War he was commissioned in the U.S. Army Air Forces and served in intelligence. He transferred to the OFFICE OF STRATEGIC SERVICES and was assigned to the Special Operations branch. He was a member of a JEDBURGH team and made several parachute jumps behind German lines in France. Later he worked closely with ALLEN DULLES in Bern, Switzerland. He became a close friend of Dulles who described him as the bravest man he had ever known. He was awarded the Silver Star and the French Croix de Guerre.

Following the war he practiced law in Providence, Rhode Island, and was president of the Urban League of Rhode Island. In 1950 he moved to Washington, D.C., where, during the Korean War, he served as counsel to the undersecretary of the Army and deputy director of the Psychological Strategy Board (see COVERT ACTION).

Recruited to the Central Intelligence Agency, he served in the Plans Directorate (see CIA CLANDESTINE SERVICE) under FRANK WISNER, and he was a principal figure in the GUATEMALA COUP of 1954. From 1954 to 1956 he was chief of the CIA base in Frankfurt, Germany. From 1957 to 1959 he was chief of station in London. In 1960 and 1961, as assistant to Deputy Director for Plans RICHARD BISSELL, he played a major role in planning and executing the BAY OF PIGS OPERATION. In 1961 he became chief of the Domestic Operations Division.

He retired from government service in 1968 and became a special assistant for community relations to Kingman Brewster, Jr., president of Yale University. He retired in 1970.

(Obituary, *New York Times,* February 20, 1972; Smith, *OSS;* Powers, *The Man Who Kept the Secrets;* Dulles, *The Secret Surrender.*)

BARNES, EARL WALTER (August 23, 1902–): Air Force officer, intelligence officer

A native of Alliance, Nebraska, Barnes graduated from the United States Military Academy in 1925 and from an Army flight school the following year. He advanced through grades to the rank of major general in 1948. During the Second World War he commanded the Thirteenth Air Force in the South Pacific.

During the late 1950s and the 1960s Barnes served on the Board of National Estimates (see NATIONAL INTELLIGENCE ESTIMATES) of the Central Intelligence Agency.

(*Who's Who in America,* v.28; Cline, *The CIA: Reality vs. Myth.*)

BARRETT, DAVID DEAN: Army officer, intelligence officer

Barrett, a Chinese linguist, was said to be so fluent in the language that he could tell jokes convincingly in Chinese to the Chinese—the only American so gifted. In the rank of U.S. Army captain he was assistant military attaché to (then) Col. Joseph W. Stilwell when the latter was military attaché in China and Thailand in 1935–39.

During the SECOND WORLD WAR Barrett, then a full colonel, was military attaché in China, and he later served as executive officer of a military school established at Kunming, China, to train Chiang Kai-shek's officers. In 1944 he was chief of the "Dixie Mission," a delegation of seventeen officers, including five from the Office of Strategic Services, sent to establish liaison with the Chinese Communists at Yenan, China. While in that capacity he became involved in Gen. Albert Wedemeyer's proposal to send American paratroops to north China to fight alongside the Chinese Communist guerrillas. When this plan was aborted for domestic American political reasons, Barrett was caught in the aftermath and, as a consequence, did not receive his scheduled promotion to brigadier general.

(Smith, *OSS;* Tuchman, *Stilwell and the American Experience in China.*)

BARRY, EDWARD BUTTEVANT (October 20, 1849–November 27, 1938): naval intelligence officer

Barry was born in New York City and graduated from the Naval Academy in 1869. Between 1894 and 1897 he served in the Office of Naval Intelligence. There, together with RICHARD WAINWRIGHT and WILLIAM WIRT KIMBALL, he helped devise the war plans that were executed by the United States during the SPANISH-AMERICAN WAR.

Barry was promoted to the rank of rear admiral in 1909.

(Dorwart, *The Office of Naval Intelligence; Who Was Who in America*, vol. 2.)

BASE

A unit of an intelligence service in a foreign country, subordinate to that service's local station. The base is managed by a chief of base, who reports to the local chief of station.

(De Silva, *Sub Rosa*)

BASIC INTELLIGENCE

Relatively static or slowly changing information about a country or geographical area, e.g., its history, geography, topology, climate, cultures, religions, system of government, politics, armed services, intelligence services, leaders and elites, communications, transportation systems (roads, railroads, airports, etc.), and economy. SHERMAN KENT wrote that it is "the groundwork which gives meaning to day-to-day change and . . . without which speculation into the future is likely to be meaningless." Basic intelligence is compiled in the form of encyclopedic collections such as the National Intelligence Surveys produced by the CIA INTELLIGENCE DIRECTORATE.

See also INTELLIGENCE TAXONOMY.

(Kent, *Strategic Intelligence for American World Policy*; Breckinridge, *The CIA and the U.S. Intelligence System*; Ransom, *The Intelligence Establishment*; Hopple and Watson, *The Military Intelligence Community*.)

BATES, DAVID HOMER (July 2, 1843–June 15, 1926): telegrapher, cryptanalyst

A native of Steubenville, Ohio, Bates attended the public schools there and in Pittsburgh, Pennsylvania. In March 1859 he went to work for the Pennsylvania Railroad in Pittsburgh as a telegrapher. In April 1861 he was recruited into the War Department by Andrew Carnegie, who had lately been supervisor of the Railroad's Pittsburgh division, and was then supervisor of the War Department's telegraph lines in the East.

CHARLES A. TINKER, ALBERT B. CHANDLER, and Bates were the self-styled "Sacred Three," the principal telegraphers in the War Department's telegraph office during the Civil War. In addition to sending and receiving telegrams, and enciphering and deciphering some of them, they were occasionally called upon to solve intercepted Confederate cryptograms, and they achieved some success in doing so (see WIRETAPPING AND COMMUNICATIONS INTELLIGENCE IN THE CIVIL WAR).

After the war Bates joined the Western Union Telegraph Company and remained there for many years. During the war he had been in almost daily contact with President Lincoln, and in 1907 he published *Lincoln in the Telegraph Office*, his reminiscences of his conversations with the President.

(Harlow, *Old Wires and New Waves*; Kahn, *The Codebreakers*; obituary, *New York Times*, June 16, 1926.)

BAUGHMAN, U(RBANUS) E(DMUND) (May 21, 1905–November 9, 1978): U.S. Secret Service chief

A native of Camden, New Jersey, Baughman joined the Secret Service as a clerk in 1927. In 1934 he was made an agent and he continued to advance in positions in New York City; Newark, New Jersey; and Washington, D.C. He was appointed chief of the Secret Service in 1948.

Baughman instituted several new management mechanisms in the Secret Service: a system of internal inspection, a management review committee, and a reorganization of the service's central office. He retired in 1961.

(*Who's Who in America*, v. 28; Bowen and Neal, *The United States Secret Service*; Youngblood, *20 Years in the Secret Service*.)

BAXTER, JAMES PHINNEY, 3RD (February 15, 1893–June 17, 1975): historian, educator, intelligence analyst

A native of Portland, Maine, and the son of an old New England family prominent in commerce and industry, Baxter attended Phillips Academy at Andover, Massachusetts. He graduated from Williams College in 1914 and worked for a year for the Industrial Finance Corporation in New York City. In 1921 he left the business world and joined the faculty of Colorado College as an instructor in history. He entered Harvard University a year later and earned a master's and doctorate in history in 1923 and 1926, respectively. In 1925 he joined the history faculty at Harvard, becoming a full professor in 1936. He also lectured at the Naval War College at Newport, Rhode Island, during this period. In 1937 he became president of Williams College, where he also taught diplomatic history.

In July 1941 Baxter was recruited by Col. WILLIAM J. DONOVAN to establish and organize the Research and Analysis Branch of the Office of the Coordinator of Information, the predecessor of the OFFICE OF STRATEGIC SERVICES. He served as chief of the OSS RESEARCH AND ANALYSIS BRANCH until

November 1942, when he was succeeded in that post by Prof. WILLIAM LANGER. Baxter served on a part-time basis as a deputy to Donovan until February 1943, when he left to join the Office of Scientific Research and Development. He remained with OSRD as the agency's historian until 1946, then returned to the presidency of Williams College. His history of OSRD, *Scientists Against Time*, won a Pulitzer Prize in 1946.

(*Current Biography*, 1947, 1975; Roosevelt, *War Report of the OSS*.)

BAY OF PIGS INVASION

Summary: During mid-1960 the Central Intelligence Agency, at the direction of President Eisenhower, undertook a major covert action operation aimed at overthrowing the Communist regime of Fidel Castro in Cuba. The operation was to culminate in a major paramilitary operation—an invasion of Cuba by a force of some 1,400 CIA-trained and -equipped anti-Castro Cuban exiles. The invasion, which was approved by President Kennedy soon after he took office, was carried out during April 15–19, 1961. It failed, and thereby marked the end of the emphasis on covert action that had prevailed in the CIA during the 1950s.

Background: After it gained its independence from Spain in 1898 as a consequence of the Spanish-American War, Cuba was governed by an honest but ineffectual administration under President Thomas Estrada Palma until 1908. Afterwards it suffered under a series of corrupt authoritarian regimes. From 1933 to 1944 these regimes were controlled, directly or otherwise, by Fulgencio Batista, a former Cuban Army sergeant. Batista returned to power through a coup d'etat in 1952, and thereafter ruled as virtually an absolute dictator.

The United States was Cuba's chief trading partner: it was the principal market for Cuban sugar—the country's major crop and the basis of its economy—and the main source of Cuban imports, especially food. American companies owned a large percentage of the Cuban farmland and most of the means of production. Consequently, American interests controlled the Cuban economy, a situation many Cubans resented deeply and one that fueled the fires of anti-Americanism in Cuba. American commercial interests made no objection to Batista's corrupt authoritarian regime, and he in turn protected those interests.

Fidel Castro

On July 26, 1953 a band of young, middle-class Cubans, led by Fidel Castro and his younger brother,

Raul, raided the Cuban Army's Moncada Barracks in Santiago de Cuba, while a coordinated attack was launched simultaneously against the barracks at nearby Bayamo. Castro, the son of a prosperous planter and, at the time, a twenty-five-year-old graduate of the University of Havana's law school, had been active in the more violent aspects of Latin American politics since his student days. The attacks on the Moncada and Bayamo barracks failed, and Castro fled into hiding in the mountains. He was captured several days later, but his life was spared through the intercession of the Roman Catholic bishop of Santiago. Castro was sentenced to fifteen years in prison, but was released eighteen months later under a general amnesty decreed by Batista.

After a period of exile in Mexico, Castro returned to Cuba in December 1956, leading an insurgent force of some eighty troops including the Argentine-born Ernesto "Che" Guevara. For the next two years Castro waged an increasingly effective guerrilla war against the Batista regime from his stronghold in the rugged Sierra Maestra mountains of Oriente Province in eastern Cuba. Aided by the corruption, low morale, and incompetent leadership of the Cuban Army, and the general dissatisfaction with Batista's rule, Castro succeeded in overthrowing the dictator and driving him into exile on January 1, 1959.

The U.S. and Castro

Official American attitudes toward Castro's revolution were ambivalent. In March 1958 the U.S. government had placed an embargo on arms shipments to Batista's government in tacit recognition that a civil war was being fought on the island, yet the U.S. Military Mission to Cuba continued to train Batista's troops. Earl E. T. Smith, the American ambassador to Cuba, was a staunch supporter of Batista, but senior officers in the State Department concerned with Latin American affairs regarded the Cuban dictator as a liability and, months before Castro came to power, they began to persuade Batista to step down in favor of some alternative to Castro. Indeed, Batista's decision to flee the country was made just two weeks after Ambassador Smith reluctantly told him that the United States could no longer support him and recommended that he abdicate.

The U.S. government granted official recognition to Castro's government just one week after Batista departed. Six American companies doing business in Cuba advanced $1.5 million in future taxes to the Cuban government to help Castro stabilize the country's economy. But a chill fell over this atmosphere of cautious goodwill within a month, when Castro's firing squads began executing hundreds of the Batista regime's police and military officials after what was in most cases a mockery of a trial. Several hundred were shot within a short time, prompting protests in Congress and the American press. Castro and his spokesman angrily replied that there had been no similar American denunciation of the brutalities of the Batista regime. (Batista had avoided international criticism by torturing and killing his enemies out of public view, while Castro courted publicity for his killings, staging show trials in the Havana sports arena and inviting the press to photograph the executions of Batista's henchmen.)

Tens of thousands of Cubans opposed to Castro left the country, and some 50,000 of them soon settled in Miami, Florida. Among the latter were former officials of the Batista government regarded as "criminals" by Castro, who demanded their return. The U.S. government, however, refused to comply. Relations with Castro declined further when some of the Cuban refugees carried out air raids against Cuban cane fields and other targets, apparently from airfields in Florida. One of the most notable of these air raids occurred on October 11, 1959, when Maj. Pedro Luis Diaz Lanz, former chief of the Cuban Air Force, dropped leaflets and—according to the Castro regime—bombs on Havana from a B-25 bomber. Diaz Lanz had already outraged Castro several months earlier when he defected to the United States and testified before the Senate Internal Security Subcommittee that Communists were taking over Cuba.

Castro and Communism

Castro's denials that his revolution was Communist were lent credence by his public quarrels with the Cuban Communist Party, which dated from the party's criticism of his 1953 attack on the Moncada Army Barracks (the Communists characterized Castro as a "petty bourgeois adventurist") and continued for almost a year after he came to power in 1959. (The Communist Party had been legalized by Batista in 1938 and supported him from 1940 to 1944). However, Castro's public hostility toward the Communists appeared to soften late in 1959, and at the same time he undertook a purge of the moderates and anti-Communists within his regime.

Communist control of the Castro regime was greatly strengthened by the appointment of Communists to the intelligence and internal security agencies. Maj. Ramiro Valdes became chief of the Cuban Army's G-2 (military intelligence service), and Maj. Manuel Pineiro became his deputy in charge of counterintelligence. Both men were communists and comrades of Castro since the 1953 Moncada raid. Under Valdez and Pineiro G-2 became a highly efficient political

secret police for the detection of counterrevolution. It was aided by the civilian Committees for the Defense of the Revolution, a nationwide network of informers headed by José Matar, a Communist.

Soviet involvement with Castro became overt early in 1960 with the official visit to Cuba of Anastas Mikoyan, the first deputy Soviet premier. The visit resulted in an agreement covering trade and economic aid, as well as the presence of Soviet "technicians" in Cuba. In May Soviet Premier Khrushchev announced that the Soviet Union would defend Cuba against "American aggression." In July Castro visited Czechoslovakia to purchase arms, and later visited Moscow, where he was warmly welcomed.

The decline of U.S.-Cuban relations was hastened by Castro's moves against American commercial interests in his country. In June 1959 he began a land reform program that involved expropriating the large landholdings of such American agricultural firms as the United Fruit Company, offering no other compensation than twenty-year notes for sums far less than market value. A year later he seized all other American property in Cuba, including banks, electric power companies, sugar refineries, hotels, rubber companies, and oil refineries. In retaliation the U.S. government cut off any further purchases of Cuban sugar under a preferential agreement that had been in effect for many years. Shortly thereafter, in October 1960, the U.S. banned all American exports to Cuba, except food and medical supplies. On January 3, 1961 the U.S. severed diplomatic relations with Cuba.

Early CIA Operations Against Castro: U.S. foreign policy makers began formally considering intervention in Cuba to remove the Castro regime as early as March 1960, when the NATIONAL SECURITY COUNCIL met to review the subject. Two months earlier, in January, the Central Intelligence Agency set up a task force to plan and manage anticipated COVERT ACTION against Castro. In early March the Agency produced a policy paper entitled "A Program of Covert Action Against the Castro Regime." The paper envisioned the creation of a unified anti-Castro Cuban exile organization, a propaganda campaign aimed at Cuba, the establishment of an underground to carry out secret intelligence and covert action operations, and the development of a paramilitary force outside Cuba to be sent to Cuba for guerrilla warfare. The basic concept underlying the paper was the premise that Castro could be overthrown using the same formula through which he had come to power, i.e., a guerrilla movement in the mountains that would spread to a disaffected Cuban populace. On March 17th President Eisenhower approved the CIA plan.

The CIA established a task force, i.e., an ad hoc project organization, to carry out the program. The Task Force came under RICHARD M. BISSELL, then director of the CIA CLANDESTINE SERVICE. As in the case of the GUATEMALA COUP six years earlier, J. C. KING and his Western Hemisphere Division were bypassed on the grounds that King was not adept at covert action operations. And, also as in the case of Guatemala, overall responsibility for the project was given to C. TRACY BARNES, who was now Bissell's assistant (although in practice Bissell stayed closely involved with the project for its duration, while Barnes appears to have played the ancillary role of liaison officer with the White House, the State Department, and the Joint Chiefs of Staff). Reporting directly to Barnes was the Task Force director, JACOB D. ESTERLINE, an Office of Strategic Services veteran with considerable paramilitary experience who served as CIA chief of station in Guatemala and Venezuela.

The Cuban Exile Political Front

Responsibility for creation of a Cuban exile political front organization fell to the Task Force's political action chief, GERRY DROLLER. Droller (whose pseudonym, "Frank Bender," turns up in most published accounts of the operation) was a German-born OSS veteran with experience in the CIA's European Division. The reason he was selected for this task remains obscure: he lacked experience in Latin American political affairs and did not speak Spanish.

E. HOWARD HUNT was assigned to work in the field with the Cuban exiles. In what seems a complex and ambiguous administrative arrangement, he reported directly to Barnes, but also to Esterline and Droller. Hunt spoke Spanish, had played an important role in the Guatemala coup, had served as chief of station in Mexico and Uruguay, and had held other senior positions in the Clandestine Service. With some justification he regarded himself as senior to and better qualified than Droller, and Barnes's acknowledgment of this fact may have been the reason for the awkward reporting arrangement.

From the hundreds of Cuban exile groups in the United States, all of which were competing for U.S. government support, Droller and Hunt selected five leaders to form a Cuban exile front organization, FRD (Frente Revolucionario Democratico). All five were both anti-Castro and anti-Batista in their politics. First among them was Manuel F. Artime Buesa, a founder and leader of the MRR (Movimiento de Recuperacion Revolucionaria), the anti-Castro underground in Cuba. Artime was a young physician and psychiatrist who had served with Castro in the mountains, but who had defected and formed the MRR after he discovered the Cuban leader's plan to make the country Communist.

In order to help conceal the official U.S. government connection with the Front, Hunt took the Cuban leaders to Mexico City, where he established offices for the organization. The Mexican government apparently considered the group unwelcome, however, and subjected it to close surveillance and other harassment. The decision was then reluctantly made to remove the group to Miami.

Propaganda Operations

The CIA Cuba Task Force's propaganda operations were assigned to DAVID A. PHILLIPS, a Spanish-speaking officer with extensive knowledge of Latin America who had worked for Hunt as a propaganda specialist in the Guatemala coup. Phillips, who reported directly to Esterline, was in charge of a broad range of anti-Castro propaganda activities, including Cuban exile groups—women, professionals, students, and workers—acting as propaganda fronts, and programs for radio propaganda and leaflets to be dropped over Cuba. Phillips's largest single propaganda operation was Radio Swan, an ostensibly commercial fifty-kilowatt broadcast frequency station based on Swan Island in the Caribbean off the coast of Honduras. The station broadcast programs taped in the CIA radio studios in Miami—news analysis, entertainment, and anti-Castro speeches by Cuban exiles. Phillips also bought time (through agents) on legitimate radio stations throughout the Caribbean, arranging to broadcast relatively innocuous material at first, and prepared to broadcast strong anti-Castro propaganda when required.

Paramilitary Operations

The task of recruiting and training a guerrilla force of Cuban exiles initially fell to a retired military officer from the CIA's Office of Training (in his memoir of the operation E. Howard Hunt describes him as a retired Marine officer and refers to him only as "Ned"). Small recruiting and training camps were set up in Florida and Louisiana. ROBERT K. DAVIS, the CIA chief of station in Guatemala and a veteran of the Guatemala coup, arranged with Guatemala President Miguel Ydigoras for a central Cuban training camp and an air base in his country. The camp, called Camp Trax, was established at Helvetia, a coffee plantation in the Sierra Madre mountains near Retalhuleu, a town about thirty miles from the country's Pacific coast. Young Cuban exiles were recruited in the United States by FRD, the exile front organization, and screened by CIA doctors, psychologists, and security officers before being sent to Camp Trax. The first of the recruits began arriving at Camp Trax in May. (On arriving at the camp each recruit was assigned a number, beginning with 2500. Recruit number 2506, Carlos Rodriguez Santana, was killed in a fall during training, and he was honored by his comrades who adopted his number as the designation of what subsequently became the invasion force, Brigade 2506.) The CIA's chief trainer in guerrilla warfare techniques at Camp Trax was NAPOLEON VALERIANO, a Filipino counterinsurgency expert who had served with EDWARD G. LANSDALE in the CIA's campaigns against Communist guerrillas in the Philippines and Vietnam.

An airstrip was constructed near Retalhuleu for air support of the operations—air dispatch of guerrillas into Cuba, air drops of supplies, and drops of propaganda leaflets. Several C-46 and C-54 transport planes—sanitized to conceal U.S. government ownership—were obtained. Experienced pilots were recruited from among the Cuban emigrés in Miami and sent to Retalhuleu for training.

CIA Invasion Plans: By summer of 1960 the CIA began to put into effect the plan that President Eisenhower had approved in March. The Cuban exile political front had been established under secret CIA aegis. Radio Swan had begun broadcasting in May. The CIA Task Force had made contact with the underground in Cuba and had begun airdropping supplies to it. And the guerrilla army in training at Camp Trax was continuing to grow in both size and readiness. However, this progress was accompanied by serious difficulties.

Personal and political differences were causing increased dissension among the FRD front leaders; one of the leaders resigned from the Front after failing to increase his control over it. Whatever ability Droller and Hunt may have had to resolve these differences were diminished by personal conflicts of their own; their quarrels eventually prompted Bissell to transfer Hunt back to CIA headquarters to work for Phillips in the Task Force's propaganda operation.

Emigré politics was also causing dissension among the Cuban troops at Camp Trax, especially during the later stages of the project when former soldiers in Batista's army were recruited; the situation had deteriorated to the point of a near-mutiny by January at which point the leaders of the dissidents were arrested and held in captivity in a remote jungle camp in northern Guatemala for the duration of the operation.

Underground operations within Cuba were less than effective. Castro's Coast Guard was scoring a high percentage of "kills" of Task Force maritime missions (infiltration and exfiltration of Cuba by small craft, usually speedboats). Airdrop missions to guerrillas in the Sierra Maestra and Escambray mountains seldom found the agreed-upon light signals from the ground designating their drop zones. The CIA Task Force officers blamed it on poor navigation by the Cubans. The Cuban aircrews resented the accusation. They suspected the CIA-controlled guerrilla units had been infiltrated by Castro's G-2. Ethnic friction between Cuban recruits and American air instructors reportedly combined with the airdrop failures to lower morale among the Cuban aircrews. Thirteen pilots quit and were interned for the duration of the operation.

Concurrent with these setbacks in the CIA's covert action operation against Castro, there were increasingly heavy shipments of Communist arms to Cuba, and evidence of increasingly effective control of the island's civilian population by Castro's G-2 and secret police. The National Security Council's 5412 Committee (see COVERT ACTION) began to doubt that Castro could be overthrown by guerrilla action alone.

The Invasion Plan

In the face of these adverse factors, Bissell, Barnes, and Esterline began to consider landing a small (200–300 man) infantry strike force on the Cuban coast to establish an enclave that would attract anti-Castro dissidents in the area and perhaps inspire a general uprising throughout the country. Such an enclave would also permit the establishment of an anti-Castro Cuban provisional government, which could then seek recognition from sympathetic nations and request overt military aid from the United States. Because such an amphibious landing could not succeed without air support, the Task Force managers also considered developing a combat air capability. Pending the 5412 Committee's final approval of the plan, Bissell went forward with some preparatory steps in the autumn of 1960.

"Ned," the former Marine officer who had been in charge of the Task Force's paramilitary operations, was replaced by Colonel JACK HAWKINS, then an officer on active duty with the Marine Corps. While serving with the ALLIED INTELLIGENCE BUREAU during the Second World War, Hawkins had led Filipino guerrillas against the Japanese. He and Esterline began to work out an operational plan for an amphibious landing in Cuba.

On November 4th they revised the training program at Camp Trax. Guerrilla training was to be deemphasized, and the number of recruits to be trained as guerrillas was to be cut to sixty. All other recruits were to be trained for conventional airborne and amphibious operations. In line with this change, Napoleon Valeriano was replaced as chief of training by an ex-Marine with more conventional combat experience.

Bissell brought in Air Force Col. Stanley W. Beerli to organize the combat air-support capability needed for an amphibious landing. Beerli had worked with Bissell before as commander of the CIA's U-2 reconnaissance aircraft detachment in Turkey (see OVERHEAD RECONNAISSANCE, FRANCIS GARY POWERS). He selected the World War II vintage B-26 light bomber to be the invasion's air support weapon, reasoning that so many of the aircraft had been sold as surplus to nations throughout the world that its use would not necessarily imply U.S. involvement in the operation. Further, Castro's air force, the FAR (Fuerza Aerea Revolucionaria, or Revolutionary Air Force), possessed several B-26 bombers, and the CIA plan called for the cover story that the invasion's air support consisted entirely of Cuban Air Force planes flown by pilots who had spontaneously decided to join the insurgents after the landings had begun.

Beerli procured a number of the bombers from the U.S. Air Force's "mothball" depot near Tucson, Arizona. CIA technicians sanitized them, removing all identifying numbers and insignia. Flight instructors experienced in flying the B-26 were recruited from the Alabama Air National Guard, which had until recently been equipped with the bomber.

To transport the invasion force to Cuba, the CIA task force made confidential arrangements with the Garcia Line, a Cuban shipping company with six freighters, owned by an anti-Castro Cuban family.

The Interregnum

Preparations for the proposed invasion went on during the U.S. presidential elections of November 1960. After the Kennedy victory, the Eisenhower administration and the 5412 Committee declined to give final approval to the invasion proposal, choosing instead to postpone the matter and leave it to the new administration to decide whether or not to go forward with it.

President-elect Kennedy was told of the Cuban project soon after the election (November 18th) by Allen Dulles and Bissell, and he was given a full briefing by Dulles on November 29th. Kennedy gave his tentative approval and told Dulles to continue preparations. On December 8th the CIA made a formal presentation of the plan to the 5412 Committee, and Hawkins, the new paramilitary chief, outlined an operation involving the amphibious landing of between 600 and 750 men on the Cuban coast,

preceded by the infiltration of small guerrilla teams, and supported by air strikes against military targets a day or so before the landings. The major target of the air strikes would be Castro's air force, which was estimated to be comprised of at least four T-33s (the trainer version of the Korean War vintage F-80 jet fighter), fifteen B-26s, and ten British Sea Furies (propeller-driven fighters). The destruction of those aircraft on the ground would free the invasion force from the danger of air attack during and after the landings. The objective of the landings would be to seize and hold a limited area on the coast, maintain a visible presence, provide a rallying point for the guerrillas in the mountains, and precipitate a general anti-Castro uprising throughout the country. The committee did not formally approve the plan at this meeting, but it apparently gave tacit approval to the continuing preparations.

The Trinidad Plan

Esterline and Hawkins developed a detailed operational plan for the invasion at about this time. Arrangements had been made by the CIA Task Force with Nicaraguan President Somoza to use Puerto Cabezas, a seaport on the Caribbean cost of Nicaragua, as the embarkation point for the Garcia Line's fleet of transports to carry the expedition to Cuba. The airfield at Puerto Cabezas—code-named "Happy Valley" by the Task Force—would be used to launch the air strikes in support of the invasion. A point on Cuba's southern coast near the city of Trinidad, about thirty miles east of Cienfuegos, was selected for the landing.

The Trinidad area offered several advantages: it lay at the foot of the Escambray Mountains, where many anti-Castro guerrillas were operating; if the invading force was unable to hold the area, it could join the guerrillas in the mountains; all of the land approaches to the area that Castro might use to attack crossed bridges that could be destroyed in advance; there were also indications that the population of Trinidad was strongly anti-Castro and therefore could be relied upon to support the invaders. And the location of Trinidad near the center of the southern coast offered the hope that the invasion force might break out to the north and cut the island in half.

On the negative side, the presence of guerrillas in the Escambray Mountains had drawn a large force of Castro's militia to the general area of south central Cuba, with about 5,000 of them encircling the mountains. But the most serious drawback to targeting Trinidad was the limitations of the local airfield, which could not accommodate B-26 aircraft. This meant all the invasion's air support would have to continue to originate in Central American bases, even after the landings—a situation that threatened the cover story that the planes were from Castro's air force and were flown by crews that had defected to join the invaders.

The detailed Trinidad Plan was presented to the new administration soon after President Kennedy was inaugurated. The secretaries of defense and state, and the attorney general (the President's brother, Robert) were briefed on January 22, 1961. Two days later the President was briefed. He withheld his approval for the plan, but authorized the CIA Task Force to continue the program of propaganda and guerrilla activities in Cuba that it had been conducting for the past nine months. Meanwhile, he ordered the Department of Defense and Joint Chiefs of Staff (JCS) to review the Trinidad Plan.

Review of the Trinidad Plan was carried out by a five-officer committee chaired by Brig. Gen. David W. Gray. The committee's report, which was approved by the Joint Chiefs and forwarded to the secretary of defense on February 3rd, was ambiguous. It gave the Trinidad Plan an overall "favorable assessment," if certain shortcomings were corrected, but warned that its "ultimate success" would depend upon a sizable popular uprising in Cuba, or a substantial follow-up (presumably an overt U.S. military intervention at the request of a provisional government-in-arms established by the Cuban invaders). But the committee also said the Plan had only a "fair chance of ultimate success." And after the failure of the invasion, Gray said he thought everyone understood that by "fair" he meant "not too good."

The Joint Chiefs sent a three-officer team to inspect Brigade 2506 at Camp Trax during February 24–27th. The team noted that the preparations there and at Puerto Cabezas were highly visible and estimated that the odds against achieving surprise in the operation were therefore "about 85 to 15." The JCS evaluators noted that if surprise were not achieved, the attack would fail.

In fact, at this point there was really no chance that the invasion would be a complete surprise to Castro. The *Nation,* the *New York Times,* and other publications had been running stories about the Guatemalan training base and the intense activity there since early January. The fact that a U.S.-backed force of Cubans was training there for an invasion of Cuba was well known throughout Latin America at least as early as October 30th, when a story to that effect appeared in the Guatemala City newspaper, *La Hora,* and therefore it seems very likely that Castro had learned at least that much through his own G-2 or the Soviet intelligence services by then. The fact that the Brigade's preparations had become public knowl-

edge was noted by the 5412 Committee when it met on December 8th. Nonetheless, the JCS team's assertion two months later that surprise was essential to the operation's success apparently failed to lead to the obvious conclusion that success was therefore impossible.

President Kennedy was faced with a dilemma of choosing between very unattractive alternatives. Secretary of State Dean Rusk, presidential assistant Arthur Schlesinger, Jr., and others advised against invading Cuba on the grounds of the adverse international political reaction likely to result even in the event that the operation was successful. And a careful reading of the advice furnished by the JCS made it clear that the military believed the invasion had little chance of succeeding. But if the invasion plans were canceled the disgruntled members of the brigade could be expected to make public that fact, which would in turn create the impression that the Kennedy administration was unwilling to resist Castro, thereby discouraging resistance to Castroism elsewhere in the western hemisphere, and laying Kennedy open to domestic political charges of being "soft" on Communism. (Arthur Schlesinger, Jr. quotes Kennedy as saying, "If we have to get rid of these 800 men [i.e., Brigade 2506], it is much better to dump them in Cuba than in the United States, especially if that is where they want to go.") And the decision could not be deferred: the brigade members were growing restive at Camp Trax, where the approaching rainy season would soon make further training impossible; the Guatemalan president had begun pressing the U.S. government to remove the Brigade from his country; and the Soviet Union was expected to equip Castro with MIG fighters and to train Cuban pilots to fly them within a few months, making the invasion impossible without the overt support of modern U.S. Air Force or Navy combat aircraft.

The Zapata Plan

Curiously, although the Brigade's preparations had become public knowledge and its U.S. sponsorship a matter of widespread inference, the Kennedy administration's chief concern regarding the Trinidad Plan now focused on the problem of *deniability,* i.e., whether the U.S. government could plausibly deny that it was involved in the operation. This concern translated into a rejection of the plan, primarily on the grounds that the airfield near Trinidad could not accommodate B-26 aircraft, and therefore the cover story that the Brigade's air support originated entirely within Cuba could not be maintained.

The President and the National Security Council

met on March 11th to consider the proposed invasion. After reviewing the Trinidad Plan Kennedy stated that although he was willing to go ahead with the overall invasion project, he could not endorse so "spectacular" an operation as Trinidad. He directed the CIA planners to come up with an alternate invasion site with an airfield capable of handling the B-26 bombers, and to plan a "quiet" landing, i.e., one that might be carried out at night, and which would not resemble a World War II amphibious assault. The CIA planners worked furiously for several days (a remarkably short span of time in which to reiterate the original planning process, which had taken months) and proposed several other landing sites. The alternative plans were presented to the JCS on March 14th.

Of the several alternative sites proposed by the CIA Task Force the JCS found the eastern area of the Zapata swamp, some twenty or thirty miles west of Cienfuegos and near the Bay of Pigs, the most feasible. Near the mouth of the bay, at Playa Giron, there was a 4,100-foot runway, adequate for the B-26 bombers. There were relatively few approaches through the marshy terrain Castro could use to send his forces against the invaders. And it was supposed the area was sparsely populated, with few troops nearby. On the other hand, the site was closer to Havana and its concentrations of troops and aircraft. And the marshes could also prevent the invaders from fleeing to the interior to operate as guerrillas if the invasion failed. Even if the invaders could make their way through the marshes, the Escambray Mountains lay more than fifty miles eastward, too far away to offer safety.

According to the Zapata Plan, there would be a small diversionary landing of 160 men on the eastern tip of Cuba two days before the main invasion. At the same time there would be limited air strikes against Castro's air force, supposedly the action of defecting pilots. The landings at Zapata would take place at night, in order to satisfy the President's requirement for a "quiet," or less "spectacular," operation. However, the size of the expeditionary force had grown from the 200–300 men in the initial plan proposed the previous summer, through the 600–750 men in the plan presented to the 5412 Committee in December, to more than 1,400 men between January and March. Of course, the increase in force improved the chances of success (and may have been in part dictated by the Zapata Plan, which called for landings at several different points), but it further complicated the problem of keeping the landings "quiet."

In detail, the plan called for seizing beaches along forty miles of the Cuba shore. An airborne force would be dropped some miles inland to take control of the roads Castro's forces would have to use to cross the Zapata swamps to reach the beachhead. The invaders were to hold the beachhead for three days, during which time they would be joined by some 500 guerrillas who were said to be in the vicinity. The leaders of the Cuban Revolutionary Council—the successor to the FRD, the exile front—were to be flown to the beachhead to establish a government-in-arms.

According to a CIA estimate, there were 2,500–3,000 people active in the anti-Castro underground within Cuba, and they were supported by some 20,000 sympathizers. It was further estimated that about twenty-five percent of the Cuban population would actively support a well-organized and well-armed force after it had established a beachhead in Cuba. Additionally, the CIA estimated that a much larger number of Cubans would rally to the invaders' cause after it became apparent that they would succeed in defeating Castro.

Although the JCS approved the Zapata Plan, it regarded it as even less likely to succeed than the Trinidad Plan. Chief of Naval Operations Adm. Arleigh Burke said that Zapata's chances of success were "less than fifty percent." But Bissell believed the Zapata Plan was actually superior to Trinidad in some important ways.

Concern within the White House and State Department continued to focus on the deniability of the operation, especially in regard to the matter of air support. President Kennedy continued to give his tentative approval to the invasion, but still retained the option to cancel it up to twenty-four hours before D-Day. During the final weeks several additional modifications were made to the Zapata plan, "pruning" it in the interests of deniability. Both Esterline, the Task Force chief, and Hawkins, the paramilitary chief, began to feel that this whittling away of the original plan would result in the invasion's failure, and both called on Bissell and threatened to resign. However, Bissell prevailed upon them to accept the changes and stay in their posts.

The decline in confidence within the CIA Task Force apparently did not spread to Camp Trax, where the morale of the members of Brigade 2506 was actually increasing as the prospect of overthrowing Castro seemed to draw near. It is clear that the leaders and men of the Brigade were unaware of the doubts and debates within the Kennedy administration, and they also were ignorant of the ground rule Kennedy established early on that no U.S. armed forces would be involved in the operation under any circumstances. Survivors of the Brigade later stated that the CIA personnel at Camp Trax had positively promised them that, if necessary, U.S. air and ground forces would be brought in to ensure the success of the undertaking. The CIA personnel in question denied this, but LYMAN B. KIRKPATRICK, the CIA inspector general who carried out a postmortem of the operation, wrote,

> Having reviewed this subject rather closely, I am quite convinced that the truth lies somewhere in between. It seems most likely that while the Americans didn't go so far as to say that United States forces would actually land in Cuba, it is only fair to suspect that in the excitement and emotional heat just before the landing they must certainly have been as encouraging as possible.

The process of reviewing, debating, and revising the invasion plans caused repeated slippages in the planned D-Day; the original target date of sometime in March gave way to April 5th, then April 10th, and finally April 17th. On April 12th Bissell presented a detailed timetable for the operation to the President, the National Security Council, and the JCS:

April 10 Brigade 2506 had begun arriving at Puerto Cabezas, Nicaragua, and started boarding transports. Boarding to be completed by April 12th.

April 11 First transport departed Puerto Cabezas. Last transport to depart by morning of April 13th.

April 14 Diversionary night landing in Oriente province (through early morning of April 15).

April 15 Eight B-26 bomber sorties to be flown from Puerto Cabezas against air force targets in Cuba at Havana, San Antonio de los Banos, and Santiago de Cuba. A ninth bomber to fly directly to Miami as an ostensible defection, the pilot to announce "cover story" that defecting pilots of Castro's air force had carried out the air strikes.

April 17 Main landings at the Zapata area before dawn. Transports to withdraw before daylight. Six B-26 bombers to be flown out of Puerto Cabezas against air base targets at Camaguey, Cienfuegos, San Antonio de los Banos, Havana, and Santa Clara. An additional air strike to be flown against Managua, an army base where overhead reconnaissance had detected forty heavy tanks. Two B-26 bombers and a liaison aircraft to land at seized airstrip at Playa Giron. Transports to return after dark to complete discharge of supplies.

April 24 Diversionary landing in Pinar del Rio province on western end of Cuba.

President Kennedy did not give final approval for the invasion at the April 12th meeting, even though the Brigade had boarded the transports, the first of which had already left Puerto Cabezas and was on its way to Cuba. He was informed that the final decision could not be postponed beyond midnight, April 14th.

Arthur Schlesinger, Jr. estimates that President Kennedy had made up his mind to go ahead with the invasion as of April 8th. However, considering Kennedy's concern with deniability, it is surprising that a series of articles appearing in the *New York Times* from April 7th through the 14th, disclosing the invasion preparations in detail, did not prompt him to change his mind. Schlesinger notes that hours before the April 14th decision deadline, Kennedy received an extremely optimistic report on the prospects of the operation from a Marine colonel who had been sent to Camp Trax to inspect the Brigade. How heavily this may have weighed in favor of the operation in the President's thinking is, of course, an imponderable. In any case, the midnight "no-go" deadline came and went without a White House decision to cancel the operation, and the President's tentative approval became final by default.

The Invasion: The diversionary landing in Oriente province, scheduled for the night of April 14–15, was aborted when adverse conditions were encountered at the landing site. Apparently the leaders of this expedition did not know their mission was diversionary—the information had been withheld for security reasons—and therefore did not understand the importance of going through with it on schedule.

The Preliminary Air Strikes

The preliminary air strikes against the three main Cuban airfields took place as planned on April 15th. One bomber was shot down, crashing in the sea near Havana. A second and third developed mechanical trouble after the attack and were forced to land at Key West and Grand Cayman Island, respectively. Reports from some of the returning aircrews indicated that about half of Castro's air force had been destroyed by the strikes, but post-attack overhead reconnaissance by U-2 flights showed that only five aircraft had been totally destroyed. At least two of Castro's B-26s, two of his Sea Furies, and three or four of his T-33s survived the attacks. In all, the attack consisted of single strikes by eight of the invasion's B-26s, less than an all-out air attack by the full Cuban exile air force, and less than what had been foreseen as necessary to destroy completely Castro's air force. The less-than-maximum effort was made in order to support the fiction that the strikes were entirely the work of defectors from Castro's air force, and not that of a U.S.-sponsored force originating beyond Cuban shores. The CIA Task Force planners had assigned the critical job of completing the destruction of Castro's air force to the B-26 attacks scheduled to coincide with the landings on the morning of April 17th.

The deception mission of a ninth B-26 took place as scheduled, the exile pilot landing his bomber at Miami International Airport shortly after the air strikes in Cuba. U.S. Immigration Service officials kept reporters away from the pilot but gave out his cover story, viz., that he and two other pilots of Castro's air force had defected, bombing targets in Cuba in the process. The commander of the U.S. Naval Air Station at Key West announced that the B-26 that had landed there was flown by another of the defectors.

Second Air Strikes Cancelled

Later on April 15th, at a meeting of the UN General Assembly's political committee, American UN Ambassador Adlai Stevenson responded to Cuban charges of U.S. involvement in the raids by presenting a photograph of the B-26 that had landed in Miami, pointing out its FAR markings, and reading a wire service report of the pilot's cover story. Stevenson, who had been incompletely briefed on the invasion plans, did not know of the deception flight and therefore believed the representations he was making to the UN were true. When he learned otherwise after the UN meeting he complained to Secretary of State Dean Rusk of what he foresaw as a loss of American credibility and his personal prestige in the international body. (By this time journalists of the New York, Miami, and Washington press had begun to call attention to discrepancies in the cover story of the deception flight, e.g., small but telling differences in detail between the B-26 in Miami and the B-26s flown by Castro's air force.)

Rusk and President Kennedy shared Stevenson's concern and felt that the additional air strikes scheduled for the morning of the invasion would compound the problem. At about 9:30 P.M., April 16—the eve of the landings—Kennedy, believing that the strikes were important but not vital, ordered them cancelled and specified that no further strikes be flown until they could fly (or appear to fly) from the airfield at Playa Giron, or in other words, after a beachhead had been secured. During the night of April 16–17 Bissell and CIA Deputy Director CHARLES P. CABELL appealed to Rusk and Kennedy to reinstate the air strikes; but apparently they failed to convey that they were vital to the success of the operation, so the cancellation remained in effect.

After receiving orders to cancel the air strikes on the Cuban airfields, the CIA air commanders at Puerto Cabezas revived their air support plan, scheduling the B-26s to fly continuous air support missions over the landing areas instead.

The Landings

Three landing sites had been selected by the CIA Task Force planners. Playa Giron, a beach just to the east of the mouth of the Bay of Pigs, was designated "Blue Beach" by the planners. It was to be the principal landing site because of its proximity to the airfield. "Red Beach" was the code name for the landing site on the northernmost end of the Bay, near Playa Larga, and about twenty miles northwest of Blue Beach. A third landing was to take place at "Green Beach," some twenty miles east of Blue Beach.

The Brigade's military commander was José Perez San Roman, a former Cuban army officer who once had led an unsuccessful mutiny against Batista. The invasion's political chief was Manuel Artime of the Cuban Revolutionary Council.

The transports arrived off the Bay of Pigs as scheduled on the night of April 16–17, and the landing commenced at Blue Beach at 1:15 A.M. Resistance by a small group of Castro's militiamen was quickly overcome. At about the same moment the Red Beach landings began and also encountered immediate but slight resistance. But, contrary to the Task Force's expectations, there were radio stations near both beaches and they were used by the militia to alert higher commands. Having lost the element of surprise, the invasion commanders cancelled the Green Beach landing, which would have involved sending the transports to that point after the Blue Beach landing was complete. The force scheduled to be landed at Green Beach went ashore at Blue Beach instead.

Unexpected coral reefs off Blue Beach caused difficulty and delay in landing the expedition's tanks and other heavy equipment. The reefs also forced the troops to wade through water to reach the shore, thereby damaging their radio equipment and permanently cutting communications between the Blue Beach force and the transports.

At Red Beach, the landing was slowed when the motors of two of the nine landing boats failed to work. Because the trip from the transport *Houston* to the beach took twenty minutes, the failure of the landing boats greatly delayed the disembarkation, and 180 troops were still aboard ship at dawn when Castro's air force attacked. The ship was struck at

6:30 A.M. and began sinking. Her skipper ran her aground on the west coast of the bay. Many of the survivors made their way south and were later rescued by the U.S. Navy.

The landing at Blue Beach was still in progress at dawn when Castro's air force attacked. In spite of the air attacks the landings were completed by 8:25 A.M. and the invaders advanced inland, but one of the transports, the *Rio Escondido,* carrying ten days' supply of ammunition and other needed supplies, as well as the expedition's communication center, was sunk. The loss of the communications center, together with the water damage to the Blue Beach force's radios, combined to make command and control of the operation very difficult thereafter.

The Brigade's airborne force was dropped near San Blas, ten miles northeast of Blue Beach, at 7:30 A.M. It took control of the crossroads there, and established outposts along the roads to the north and east. The paratroops were reinforced by troops from the Blue Beach landing. A second airborne force that was dropped north of Red Beach apparently was captured by Castro's forces before it could go into action.

The Brigade encountered strong resistance from Castro's ground forces, which were quickly rushed to the landing areas. The Red Beach force met Cuban militiamen four miles north of Playa Larga. By midafternoon Castro's tanks were brought into play, and his artillery was employed soon thereafter. The Blue Beach force and the airborne troops met a militia force approaching from the north, near San Blas, in the afternoon.

After the air attacks on the two transports, CIA Task Force commanders ordered the remainder of the invasion flotilla to put out to sea. Throughout the day there was heavy action in the air over the landing areas. The Brigade's B-26s maintained continuous air support by flying thirteen combat sorties during the day, but four of the planes were lost to Castro's T-33 jet trainers, each of which was armed with a pair of .50-caliber machine guns. The effectiveness of the armed T-33s against the B-26s and

The *Rio Escondido* on fire off Blue Beach after attack by Cuban aircraft on the morning of April 17, 1961. Source: Cuban photograph.

surface targets had not been anticipated by the invasion planners.

Although two of Castro's B-26s and two of his Sea Fury fighters were lost to anti-aircraft fire during the first day, his T-33s remained in operation. Because of the devastating effectiveness of the jets against the Brigade, President Kennedy was persuaded to authorize air strikes on the night of April 17–18 against the airfield at San Antonio de los Banos, where the T-33s were believed to be based. (Presumably the Brigade's possession of the airstrip at Playa Giron provided the necessary plausible cover for the flights.) Five B-26 sorties were flown, but weather and darkness prevented the pilots from locating their target, and none of the T-33s was destroyed.

The Second Day

During the night of April 17–18 the CIA carried out an electronic diversion off the coast of Pinar del Rio, the western tip of Cuba. A flotilla of small boats equipped with electronic gear, lights, and sound equipment created the illusion that a large force was landing. The "landing" was reported to Castro, who diverted some of his armored force to the area. However the illusion was exposed with the coming of daylight, and the diversion apparently had no significant effect on Castro's defense posture.

Also during the night of April 17–18 the invading force that had landed at Red Beach came under heavy attack by Castro's forces, including tanks. At 7:30 A.M. the expedition commanders ordered the exiles to retreat to Blue Beach and join the invading force there. The retreat was accomplished by the late morning.

Castro's militia and artillery attacked the Blue Beach/airborne contingent near San Blas during the night, and forced it back toward the town during the day (April 18th).

The Brigade's air support continued during April 18th, although some American civilian contract pilots were used to supplement the exiles, some of whom were exhausted from the nearly continuous combat duty during the past twenty-four hours, and some of whom simply refused to fly. During the afternoon six sorties were flown against a Castro column of tanks and vehicles approaching Blue Beach from the Red Beach area (along the coastal road on the eastern side of the Bay of Pigs). A large part of the column was destroyed.

The Third Day

The intense fighting of the two previous days left the invaders critically short of ammunition, although the extent of this shortage was apparently unknown to the CIA Task Force commanders (the damage to the communication equipment at Blue Beach, and the loss of the *Rio Escondido* with the expedition's communication center, denied the White House and CIA headquarters an accurate and updated picture of events on the beachhead throughout the operation). Efforts to resupply the beachhead from the sea on the morning of the second day were cancelled when it became apparent that the transports and landing craft would be sunk by Castro's planes. A small delivery of ammunition was made by one of the Brigade's C-46 cargo planes, which landed at Blue Beach before dawn. Three other C-46 supply flights were turned back by the presence of the enemy air force.

President Kennedy gave approval for U.S. Navy jet fighters to fly over the beachhead from 6:30 to 7:30 A.M. to provide defensive air cover for the Brigade's C-46 ammunition supply flights and their B-26 escorts. However, apparently through confusion in regard to the time standards in use by the CIA and the navy, the hour of air cover was flown before the Brigade's aircraft arrived over the beachhead. Consequently the supply flights were driven away, and two of the B-26s were shot down.

Hampered by the lack of ammunition, and facing a far superior force, the invaders fell back from San Blas toward Blue Beach. By nightfall they had ceased further resistance and attempted to disperse and make their way through Castro's lines into the interior of Cuba. A handful escaped by small boat to the safety of U.S. Navy warships offshore. The rest were rounded up by Castro's forces within the next two weeks.

One hundred and fourteen members of the Brigade died in the invasion, but Castro suffered far greater losses, estimated by a Cuban doctor to have been about 1,650 dead and two thousand wounded. Of the invaders 1,189 were captured by Castro's forces. The prisoners were released eighteen months later in exchange for $62 million worth of food and medicine provided by private American sources. The exchange was worked out through the good offices of JAMES B. DONOVAN, who conducted the negotiations with Castro at the unofficial request of Attorney General Robert Kennedy.

Causes of the Failure: Although the Bay of Pigs invasion has been subjected to innumerable postmortems, the reasons for its failure remain a matter of debate. The major points at issue can only be summarized here.

President Kennedy's cancellation of the follow-up air strikes is often presented as the fatal blow. Kennedy's apologists point out that, based on the results of the first air strikes, the follow-up strikes would probably have failed to destroy all of Castro's combat aircraft. Defenders of Kennedy's decision also argue that, even had the Brigade been able to achieve air superiority, it would nonetheless have fallen before the overwhelmingly superior strength of Castro's ground forces.

A CIA estimate that large numbers of Cubans would be likely to support the invasion and rise up against Castro is often given as a fatal false assumption underlying the operation. Allen Dulles, in his *Craft of Intelligence*, denies this, writing, "I know of no estimate that a spontaneous uprising of the un-armed population of Cuba would be touched off by *the landing*" (emphasis added). Richard Bissell told historian Hugh Thomas, "We did not expect the underground to play a large part." But the CIA Task Force planners did estimate that some twenty-five percent of the Cuban population would support the Brigade *after it had successfully established a beachhead or enclave on the island.* The JCS's evaluation of the Trinidad Plan (and presumably the Zapata Plan) as feasible was based on the assumption that the landing would *eventually* spark a general uprising. (Indeed, the belief that some 1,400 invaders could survive the resistance of a force ten to a hundred times larger must have rested on the assumption of either a general uprising or else overt aid by U.S. armed forces.)

The failure of any general uprising to materialize during the three days of battle following the landings was therefore not a cause of the operation's failure. However, it is worth nothing that, had the beachhead been held, the expected subsequent uprising might not have taken place. On April 15th, in the wake of the pre-invasion air strikes, Castro rounded up and incarcerated some 100,000 (Schlesinger said 200,000 in his account) Cubans who were regarded as potentially disloyal to the Castro regime, probably thereby neutralizing the ringleaders of the expected uprising.

The failure of the invasion to surprise Castro could not have come as a surprise to the planners. Even if more effective security measures had been enforced by the CIA Task Force managers, it seems unlikely that an invasion force of 1,400 exiles could have been recruited, trained, equipped, dispatched, and supported without alerting the defenders' counterintelligence services. It is difficult therefore to reconcile the JCS approval of the invasion plan with the JCS stipulation that surprise was necessary to success. It is even more difficult to comprehend the erosion of the original plan to comply with White House requirements for deniability. It appears that different participants in the invasion planning and manage-

ment process may have had different standards of security and deniability. There seems to have been no explicit analysis of the probable consequences of failure to meet those standards.

The failure of U.S. intelligence to assess correctly the effectiveness of Castro's air force—especially the superiority of the armed T-33s against the B-26s—has been ventured as an underlying cause of the invasion's failure. However, this assertion is equivalent to the theory that the cancellation of the follow-up strikes caused the failure, i.e., it rests upon the debatable assumption that, with air superiority, the invasion would have succeeded.

There seems to be general agreement that the ultimate cause of failure was the inadequacy of the organization managing the operation. Military writer Hanson Baldwin observed in the *New York Times* (August 1, 1961), "In effect, everybody had a hand in the Cuban venture and yet nobody was clearly in charge." The Taylor Commission, appointed by President Kennedy to analyze the reasons for the failure, found

> The Executive Branch of the government was not organizationally prepared to cope with this kind of paramilitary operation. There was no single authority short of the President capable of coordinating the actions of CIA, State, Defense, and USIA [United States Information Agency]. Top level direction was given through ad hoc meetings of senior officials without consideration of operational plans in writing and with no arrangement for recording conclusions and decisions reached.

This severe organizational limitation was most apparent during the early months of the new administration, and would probably have been less of a factor in an older, better established administration. In his analysis of the failure, CIA officer David Phillips lists the Eisenhower administration's decision to postpone the operation after the Kennedy election victory as one of the chief causes of the failure, and he cites the decision to abandon the Trinidad Plan for the Zapata Plan as yet another. Had Eisenhower gone ahead with the Trinidad Plan in the fall of 1960, the operation would certainly have had a far greater chance of success. Whether or not it would have in fact succeeded of course remains unknowable.

Another school of thought maintains that such large-scale covert action operations as the Bay of Pigs invasion usually have little chance of success in any case. Lyman B. Kirkpatrick, the CIA inspector general who conducted the Agency's postmortem of the operation, wrote

Finally, the most important lesson of all was that it is seldom possible to do something by irregular means that the United States is not prepared to do by diplomacy or direct military action.

Consequences of the Failure: The failure was a personal and political embarrassment for Kennedy and a humiliation for U.S. foreign policy. Soon after the invasion Castro completed the communization of Cuba and increased his ties to the Soviet Union (although some commentators say that the inevitable had only been hastened).

The affair was the largest single disaster in the history of the CIA, and there were major changes in the Agency as a result of the failure: Allen Dulles, Richard Bissell, and General CHARLES P. CABELL were forced into retirement. Dulles was succeeded by JOHN A. MCCONE, a director who increased the CIA's emphasis on technical intelligence collection, while Bissell was succeeded by RICHARD HELMS, who was inclined to place secret intelligence over covert action as the principal responsibility of the Clandestine Service.

The Bay of Pigs invasion seems to have marked the end of the "golden age of covert action" in the CIA, a period that began with the successful ITAL-IAN ELECTION OPERATION and included the early successes of the IRAN COUP and the GUATEMALA COUP. While the U.S. government did not abandon covert action as an instrument of American foreign policy, its earlier perception of covert action as the panacea to Soviet postwar expansionism was finally corrected as American policymakers became fully aware of the limitations of covert action.

(Agular, *Operation Zapata;* Wyden, *Bay of Pigs;* Johnson, et al., *The Bay of Pigs;* Hunt, *Give Us This Day;* Phillips, *The Night Watch;* Kirkpatrick, *The Real CIA;* Schlesinger, *A Thousand Days;* Thomas, *Cuba;* Wise and Ross, *The Invisible Government;* Blackstock, *The Strategy of Subversion;* Szulc and Meyer, *The Cuban Invasion.*)

BEALL, JOHN YATES (January 1, 1835–February 24, 1865): Confederate Army and Navy officer, secret service agent

A native of Jefferson County, Virginia, Beall attended the University of Virginia circa 1855–59 and studied law. In 1861 he joined the Stonewall Brigade, a Confederate unit trained and first led by (then) Col. Thomas J. ("Stonewall") Jackson. He was badly wounded in the Shenandoah campaign of 1862 and invalided out of the service.

While recuperating Beall conceived a plan to capture the U.S.S. *Michigan,* a Union gunboat guarding

John Yates Beall. Source: Author's collection.

Lake Erie, and the only armed vessel on the Great Lakes. The plan was rejected by Confederate Naval Secretary Stephen R. Mallory on the grounds that an operation in or near Canadian waters might jeopardize the cordial relations between Great Britain and the Confederacy and the construction of Confederate warships then in progress in British shipyards. Beall next proposed and was given permission to engage in privateering against Union vessels on Chesapeake Bay. He organized a small guerrilla force and began operations in April 1863.

Beall and his men cut the telegraph cable to the eastern shore of Virginia in July 1863, blew up the federal lighthouse on Smith Island in August, and by September had captured a small flotilla of sloops and fishing schooners. He captured the *Alliance,* a large supply sloop carrying supplies for the Union garrison at Port Royal, South Carolina, and he sent it to Richmond. In November Beall and his men were captured by the Maryland Volunteers. They were subsequently exchanged for Union prisoners of war.

After serving briefly in the Confederate Army engineers' corps, Beall renewed his plan to capture the

Michigan. He went to Toronto in September 1864 and set the proposal before JACOB THOMPSON, Confederate Commissioner and senior Confederate secret agent in Canada, and Captain THOMAS H. HINES, his associate. They approved the plan as part of a larger operation aimed at freeing Confederate prisoners of war held on Johnson's Island in Lake Erie (see NORTHWEST CONSPIRACY). In Hines's plan, the *Michigan* would be seized by a guerrilla team led by Beall and then be used to provide artillery support for a mass escape from the prison camp.

On September 18th Beall and a party of twenty-eight guerrillas disguised as passengers, hijacked the *Philo Parsons,* a large Lake Erie steamboat. He next stopped, boarded, and captured another steamboat, the *Island Queen.* After landing all of the captives from the two vessels on the American side of the lake, the Confederate agents proceeded to the vicinity of Johnson's Island where the *Michigan* was stationed.

According to Hines's plan, another Confederate agent who had befriended the commander of the *Michigan* would present a banquet for the captain and his officers in the ship's wardroom that evening, incapacitate them with drugged champagne, and then signal to Beall with a rocket to indicate that this part of the operation had been carried out. However, the plan was betrayed by Godfrey J. Hyams, an escaped Confederate prisoner of war who had joined the Confederate secret service in Canada. The Confederate agent assigned to stage the banquet was identified and arrested before he could carry out his task. When the signal rocket failed to appear, Beall's men aboard the *Philo Parsons* realized that the operation had been discovered, and they refused Beall's orders to proceed with the attempted capture of the gunboat. Beall had no alternative but to return to Canada after burning and scuttling the *Philo Parsons.*

In December 1864 Beall took part in a Confederate operation aimed at freeing several Confederate generals, colonels, and lieutenant colonels, prisoners of war, who were being transported by rail from Johnson's Island to Fort Lafayette in New York Harbor. The operation failed and Beall was arrested before he could return to Canada. He was convicted by a court-martial of espionage and violation of the laws of war, and sentenced to death. Despite appeals for clemency to President Lincoln from Governor John Andrew of Massachusetts, Representative Thaddeus Stevens of Pennsylvania, and other prominent Northerners, Beall was hanged at Fort Lafayette.

(*Who Was Who in America,* historical volume; Horan, *Confederate Agent.*)

Pierre Augustin Caron de Beaumarchais. Source: Library of Congress.

BEAUMARCHAIS, PIERRE AUGUSTIN CARON DE (January 24, 1732–May 18, 1799): lawyer, businessman, inventor, writer, French secret agent

Born Pierre Augustin Caron, the son of a French watchmaker, he was apprenticed to that trade. At an early age he invented the escapement, which is still used in most mechanical clocks and watches. Through his skill and audacity he became watchmaker to Louis XV and a court favorite, purchasing the title "de Beaumarchais" to add an aristocratic appendage to his name. Beaumarchais became a prosperous merchant, as well as a secret agent for Louis XV and, later, Louis XVI.

When the COMMITTEE OF SECRET CORRESPONDENCE sent SILAS DEANE to Paris to negotiate French aid for the AMERICAN REVOLUTION, the French Foreign Ministry employed Beaumarchais to handle the matter confidentially. Because France wanted to help the Americans, but was not yet ready to take the step of an open alliance (and hence war with Britain), Beaumarchais established a covert PROPRIETARY COMPANY, Hortalez & Cie, through which the United States purchased French military supplies in exchange for American commodities such as rice and tobacco. The firm was capitalized in the sum of three million livres, which was contributed in equal parts by loans from France, Spain, and Beaumarchais and his business associates.

Although Beaumarchais's operations were discovered and initially frustrated by British secret service officer, LORD STORMONT, they soon became effective. Eventually Hortalez was running a fleet of forty ships that carried arms to America. One historian has estimated that ninety percent of the military supplies used by the Continentals in the crucial victory at Saratoga came from such French sources. Soon after victory the French openly allied themselves with the United States, and the covert mechanism of Hortalez & Cie was no longer necessary.

Misstatements by Arthur Lee, one of the American diplomatic commissioners in France, confused the Continental Congress regarding whether or not America was supposed to repay France for the aid channeled through Hortalez & Cie (Lee apparently exploited the situation in order to accuse SILAS DEANE of profiteering and peculation.) This left Beaumarchais in the middle; as the proprietor of the company he was personally responsible for the loans. The covert and ostensibly private nature of Hortalez & Cie made it difficult for the French Foreign Ministry to clarify the matter without embarrassment. Although the French eventually did clarify it, Beaumarchais did not succeed in obtaining full payment during his lifetime and it remained for his heirs to pursue the matter with Congress.

This tangled situation proved to be only a trifling setback for Beaumarchais, who imported sugar and other products from the West Indies on the returning Hortalez ships, and so turned a tremendous profit. In fact the entire affair was little more than a minor episode in Beaumarchais's life.

Beaumarchais devoted some of the quieter moments of his life to writing *The Barber of Seville* and *The Marriage of Figaro*, the plays upon which the Rossini and Mozart operas are based. While undertaking to publish the complete works of Voltaire (a splendid piece of quixotism—two thirds of them were banned in France), he met two paper merchants, Etienne and Joseph de Montgolfier. He befriended the Montgolfier brothers and became a patron of their early experiments with passenger-carrying balloons, as well as an early advocate of aviation.

Beaumarchais has inspired several generations of biographers.

(Boatner, *Encyclopedia of the American Revolution;* Lemaitre, *Beaumarchais;* Grendel, *Beaumarchais;* Cox, *The Real Figaro.*)

BECKER, LOFTUS EUGENE (c. 1911–August 26, 1977): lawyer, intelligence officer

Becker graduated from Harvard University in 1932 and graduated magna cum laude from Harvard Law School where he was the editor of the Harvard Law Review. He practiced law in Washington, New York, and Paris, and served with the U.S. Army in Europe during the Second World War.

In 1951 Becker was recruited by General WALTER BEDELL SMITH, then director of the Central Intelligence Agency, to serve as the CIA's first deputy director for intelligence. Becker held that position until 1953, when he returned to the private practice of law. (He was succeeded as DDI by ROBERT AMORY.)

Becker interrupted his private law practice again in 1957–59, when he served as a legal advisor in the State Department.

(Cline, *The CIA: Reality vs. Myth;* obituary, *New York Times,* August 27, 1977, 24:6.)

BECKWITH, GEORGE (1753–1821): British army officer, intelligence officer

The son of a distinguished military family of Yorkshire, Beckwith was commissioned an ensign of the British Army's 37th regiment in 1771 and sent to America. He distinguished himself in several engagements in the AMERICAN REVOLUTION and led the British advance into Elizabethtown and New Brunswick (both New Jersey) in 1776. Promoted to the rank of captain, he worked with Major JOHN ANDRÉ in dealing with the American general and defector, BENEDICT ARNOLD, and handled many of the administrative details involved in Arnold's planned surrender of West Point.

In 1781, Beckwith, who had been promoted to the rank of major, helped to reorganize the British secret service in America. As aide to Sir Guy Carleton, then commander of the British forces, he was given full responsibility for British secret service operations. He continued to direct intelligence operations until the British evacuation of New York in 1783.

Beckwith's three-year tour as intelligence officer in New York gained him familiarity with its leading Loyalist families, and for that reason he was chosen by Lord Dorchester, the governor general of Canada, to serve as his secret agent in the United States in 1787. The British refused to establish diplomatic relations with the new nation immediately after the war, and instead relied upon secret agents to keep abreast of political and economic developments in America. To this purpose Beckwith made five extended visits to New York and Philadelphia between 1787 and 1792.

Beckwith's reports to Dorchester and the British secretary for foreign affairs revealed the prevalence of strong monarchical sentiment among upper-class Americans. Among those of decidedly pro-British leanings was Alexander Hamilton, who became the first U.S. secretary of treasury in 1789. Hamilton met frequently with Beckwith and provided the British agent with confidential information regarding the plans and policies of the administration of President Washington. Beckwith also played an important role in Hamilton's secret efforts to swing American foreign policy to a pro-British line.

Beckwith became governor of Bermuda in 1797, of St. Vincent in 1804, and of Barbados in 1808. Made a major general in 1798, he commanded British forces in the West Indies and South America. He was knighted in 1809 for taking Martinique. The following year he drove the French from Guadeloupe. He returned to England in 1814 and was promoted to full general. He commanded the British forces in Ireland from 1816 to 1820.

(Van Doren, *Secret History of the American Revolution;* Boyd, *Number 7, Alexander Hamilton's Secret Attempts to Control American Foreign Policy;* Boatner, *Encyclopedia of the American Revolution.*)

BEERS, COLWELL E.: intelligence officer

Beers served with the CIA CLANDESTINE SERVICE. During 1950–51 he was deputy to HANS V. TOFTE, the chief of COVERT ACTION in Japan and Korea for the CIA's Office of Policy Coordination. Beers was in charge of the CIA/OPC complex at the U.S. Naval Air Station at Atsugi, Japan, and training facilities at Chigasaki on Sagami Bay. He was subsequently chief of the Joint Technical Advisory Group (JTAG), the CIA cover organization in Japan that handled Operation Tropic. Tropic consisted of guerrilla operations on the Chinese mainlaind carried out by "third force" units, i.e., anti-Communist forces not allied with the Nationalist Chinese on Taiwan.

(Leary, *Perilous Missions.*)

BELL, JOHN S. (?–June 19, 1917): law enforcement officer, U.S. Secret Service chief

A native of New York City, Bell moved to Newark, New Jersey, at the age of eighteen. In 1884 he was made chief of police of Newark, and in 1885 he became chief of the New Jersey department of the U.S. SECRET SERVICE. In 1888 he was made chief of the Secret Service.

Bell was regarded as an honest and dedicated law enforcement officer. His frequent appeals to the Treasury Department for a larger staff of agents to deal with the growing problem of counterfeiting is said to have led to his dismissal in 1890.

(Bowen and Neal, *The United States Secret Service; New York Times* obituary, June 20, 1917, p.11.)

BENSINGER, WILLIAM (January 14, 1840–1920): soldier, Union secret agent

A native of Wayne County, Ohio, Bensinger and his parents moved to Hancock County circa. 1858. He received an elementary education in local schools in both locations. Four months after the opening of the Civil War, Bensinger enlisted as a private in the Ohio Volunteer Infantry, which was part of the Army of the Ohio.

In April 1862 Bensinger volunteered to take part in a paramilitary operation behind Confederate lines aimed at severing the rail line between Atlanta and Chattanooga (see ANDREWS'S RAID). He and a party of twenty other Union troops in civilian clothes led by JAMES J. ANDREWS hijacked a locomotive and attempted to destroy railroad tracks and bridges between the two cities. Bensinger was captured by Confederate troops and imprisoned (Andrews and seven of the others were hanged). He and five others escaped, were recaptured, and were exchanged for Confederate prisoners of war in March 1863. Bensinger and the others were awarded the newly created Medal of Honor by Secretary of War Edwin Stanton. They were the first soldiers to receive that decoration.

After the war Bensinger returned to Ohio and became a farmer in Deweyville.

(Bryan, *The Spy in America;* Boatner, *Civil War Dictionary;* O'Neill, *Wild Train.*)

BERDING, ANDREW HENRY (February 8, 1902–): journalist, counterintelligence officer

A native of Cincinnati, Berding received a B.A. degree from Xavier University in 1926. In 1928 he received a B.A. and M.A. in English literature from Oxford University. After leaving Oxford he became a correspondent for the Associated Press in Europe, and was AP bureau chief in Rome from 1933 to 1937. He returned to the United States and covered the State Department for AP until 1940, when he joined the staff of the *Buffalo Evening News.*

Berding joined the U.S. Army Air Corps after the start of the Second World War and was eventually assigned to the Office of Strategic Services, where he worked in the OSS COUNTER-ESPIONAGE

BRANCH. Berding became chief of counterespionage in Italy and, later, in Germany. He was discharged with the rank of lieutenant colonel in 1946, having been awarded the Bronze Star and the Legion of Merit.

After the war he collaborated with former Secretary of State Cordell Hull in writing Hull's memoirs. In 1948 he joined the Department of State and served in several capacities as information or press officer. In 1953 he became deputy director of the U.S. Information Agency, and in 1957 he was named assistant secretary of state for public affairs, the State Department's chief public relations advisor.

(*Current Biography,* 1960; Smith, *OSS.*)

BERG, MORRIS ("MOE") (March 2, 1902– May 30, 1972): baseball player, linguist, lawyer, intelligence officer

A native of New York City, Berg graduated from Princeton University in 1923. While in college he studied modern languages and played baseball, distinguishing himself in both activities. After graduation he signed on with the Brooklyn Dodgers as a first baseman. At the end of the baseball season he went to France for further language study. He subsequently was a catcher for the Chicago White Sox while attending Columbia Law School. He graduated in 1928, was admitted to the New York State bar, and joined the Wall Street law firm of Satterlee and Canfield. Nonetheless, he continued to play for the White Sox during the baseball season.

After an injury Berg was traded to the Cleveland Indians in 1931 and the following year to the Washington Senators, with whom he played until 1934. While in Washington his multilingual fluency and odd combination of vocations earned him frequent invitations to embassy dinners and parties, and he soon became very much the man about town in the nation's capital. It may have been during this period that his potential value as a secret intelligence agent came to the attention of the U.S. government. In any case, while on a tour of Japan with an American all-star baseball team in 1934, he made motion picture films of Tokyo that were subsequently used during the Second World War to plan (then) Lt. Col. James H. Doolittle's bomber raid on that city.

Berg played and coached for the Boston Red Sox until 1941, when he left baseball to undertake a tour of Latin America for the OFFICE OF COORDINATOR OF INTER-AMERICAN AFFAIRS, a U.S. government agency charged with countering Axis propaganda in Latin America. During the tour Berg met and conferred with many Latin American government officials, journalists, businessmen, etc., and through these discussions collected much useful political intelligence.

In 1943 Berg was recruited into the Office of Strategic Services as a civilian employee. Later that year he was sent on a secret mission to Yugoslavia to assess the rival partisan leaders, Draža Mihajlović and Joseph Broz Tito. Berg reported that Tito's force was stronger and appeared to have more popular support.

Berg apparently functioned as a special agent of OSS director, Gen. WILLIAM J. DONOVAN, working alone, rather than as part of the secret intelligence or operations units of the agency. From 1944 to 1945 he was deeply involved in an OSS project, code-named AZUSA, aimed at assessing Axis progress in developing nuclear weapons. He went to Rome two days after the city was liberated by American forces, in order to interview Italian scientists regarding Italian work on an atomic bomb. In Switzerland he managed to learn from a visiting German scientist that Germany was at least two years away from a successful bomb. He learned the exact whereabouts in Germany of Werner Heisenberg, chief of the German nuclear program, and other German scientists working in the program, information that enabled the Allies to pick them up promptly after V-E Day and remove them to England before they fell into the hands of Soviet forces. Additionally, Berg learned much about Axis progress in high-speed aeronautics and bacteriological warfare.

Berg remained with the Strategic Services Unit after the OSS was dissolved (see OFFICE OF STRATEGIC SERVICES), but resigned in October 1946. He was awarded the Medal for Merit, but inexplicably refused the honor.

In 1951 Berg worked as a contract employee of the Central Intelligence Agency, advising and consulting on foreign scientific programs, especially those of the Soviet Union and its East European satellites. Several years later he served on the staff of NATO's Advisory Group for Aeronautical Research and Development.

(Kaufman, Fitzgerald, and Sewell, *Moe Berg.*)

BERLE, ADOLF AUGUSTUS, JR. (January 29, 1895–February 17, 1971): lawyer, government official, diplomat, intelligence officer

A native of New York City, Berle graduated from Harvard in 1913 and earned an M.A. and a LL.B. from that institution in 1914 and 1916, respectively. He joined the law firm of Louis B. Brandeis in Boston, but left to enlist in the U.S. Army in 1917. He was commissioned as a second lieutenant and assigned to the Military Intelligence Division of the Army's General Staff (see ARMY INTELLIGENCE). He served in M.I.2, the Foreign Intelligence section. In the summer of 1918 he was loaned to the State Department for "special work in Santo Domingo." During 1919 he was a staff member of the American delegation to the PARIS PEACE CONFERENCE.

Berle returned to civilian life and the private practice of law. He was a member of several New York law firms and eventually founded the firm of Berle and Berle with his brother, specializing in corporate law and Latin American affairs. He became a professor of corporate law at Columbia University in 1927, a part-time post he held until 1964.

In 1933 Berle became a member of President Franklin D. Roosevelt's New Deal "brain trust." He served as special counsel for the Reconstruction Finance Corporation during 1933–38. In 1938 he became assistant secretary of state for Latin American Affairs. In that capacity he was the State Department official most immediately concerned with the activities of German intelligence in Latin America.

Berle represented the Department of State on the JOINT INTELLIGENCE COMMITTEE, which coordinated U.S. intelligence activities during the SECOND WORLD WAR. He played an important role in the assignment of Latin American counterintelligence jurisdiction to the FEDERAL BUREAU OF INVESTIGATION and the creation of the FBI's Special Intelligence Service, which carried out operations against German Intelligence in Latin America.

In the bureaucratic competition that marked U.S. intelligence during the war, Berle was a partisan of the FBI and Army intelligence and an adversary of WILLIAM J. DONOVAN and the Office of Strategic Services. He tried to sabotage the establishment of the OSS FOREIGN NATIONALITIES BRANCH in 1941, and played a major role in the dispute between J. EDGAR HOOVER and Donovan regarding the latter's use of WALLACE B. PHILLIPS's espionage network in Mexico.

Berle negotiated an agreement with President Juan Perón of Argentina under which the Argentinians would make a sincere effort to keep the Germans from using their neutral country as a base for subversion and espionage in the western hemisphere. He helped draft the Agreement of Chapultepec, which was signed by twenty Latin American countries in 1945, and which committed the signatories to the suppression of Axis subversion.

Berle returned to teaching, writing, and the private practice of law in 1944. He served briefly as U.S. ambassador to Brazil during 1945–46. President John F. Kennedy appointed him to chair two task forces to study the problems of Latin America and to devise new modes of American policy in the western hemisphere.

(*Encyclopedia of American Biography*; Bidwell, "History of the Military Intelligence Division, Department of the Army General Staff"; Troy, *Donovan and the CIA*; Jeffreys-Jones, *American Espionage*; Rout and Bratzel, *The Shadow War*.)

BERLIN TUNNEL

In the early 1950s the CIA and Britain's Secret Intelligence Service jointly undertook the secret construction of a tunnel between East and West Berlin for the purpose of tapping into the East German telephone and telegraph system. The Berlin tunnel project—code-named Gold—was the sequel to an SIS tunnel project—code-named Silver—that tapped Soviet communication lines in Vienna.

Project Gold was initiated after Carl Nelson of the CIA's Office of Communications discovered that the teletype encryption system then in use by both the Soviet Union and the West contained a flaw that permitted the system to be defeated by electronic means. After Nelson's discovery was used successfully to decipher Soviet teletype traffic intercepted by Silver, Project Gold was launched in Berlin under the overall direction of the CIA's Berlin base chief, WILLIAM KING HARVEY.

The East Berlin communication system was an especially tempting target because, due to the configuration of the communications network, most Eastern European telephone and teletype links were routed through the Berlin hub. For example, Soviet military communications between Moscow and Bucharest or Warsaw passed over the wires in East Berlin. This was confirmed when a CIA agent established a temporary tap in an East Berlin switching station, routing the intercepted signals to a listening post in West Berlin's central post office. This temporary tap was in danger of being discovered, however, so the tunnel project was undertaken to establish a permanent listening post.

The labor of Project Gold was divided between the CIA and SIS according to this agreement: the CIA would procure a site and dig a tunnel to a point directly below the buried communication lines; it would record all the intercepted signals; and it would process all the intercepted teletype traffic. MI6 would dig a vertical shaft up from the end of the tunnel to the buried lines, tap into the lines, and process the intercepted telephone communications.

The site selected for the tap was a point just beyond the Schoenefelder Chaussee, a major highway on the southern edge of Berlin. Charts of the Berlin communications system showed that the lines passed eighteen inches below a drainage ditch near the road. Aerial reconnaissance and soil analysis identified an area best suited for digging a tunnel. Construction began early in 1954.

It was necessary first to construct a large building at the West Berlin side of the planned tunnel to conceal the excavation and to house the equipment and personnel that would be needed when the intercept operations began. The true purpose of the structure was cleverly concealed through a double cover: the new building was announced as an Army warehouse, but a set of elaborate parabolic antennas was mounted on the roof to create the impression that it was in fact to be an ELINT listening post intended to intercept radio and radar signals from the nearby Soviet air base at Schoenfeld. Thus the East German border guards and Soviet intelligence officers believed they understood the reason for the barbed-wire fence and other strict security precautions around the building, and the mysterious comings and goings of U.S. Army personnel at all hours of the day and night.

The "warehouse" was completed in August 1954, and excavation of the tunnel was begun by sixteen Army sergeants under the command of combat engineer Lt. Col. Leslie Gross. Gross and his men had practiced by digging a 450-foot tunnel through similar soil at the Army's White Sands Missile Proving Ground in New Mexico while the Berlin building was being constructed.

They began the Berlin Tunnel by sinking a vertical shaft eighteen feet in diameter down to a depth of twenty feet. Next, a horizontal tunnel six and one-half feet high was dug in an eastward direction, toward the East German communications lines. Thus the roof of the tunnel was thirteen and a half feet below the surface.

Work continued round the clock, with three men digging while two hauled away the dirt and piled it in the twelve-foot-deep basement of the "warehouse." As the excavation progressed, circular-steel liner plates were moved into place to form a tube, and mortar was pumped into whatever spaces remained between the plates and the surrounding earth. The plates had been sprayed with a rubberized coating to muffle noise during emplacement. From the "warehouse" building above, a lookout watched the East German border guards through a telescope while digging went on and warned the excavation crew by a field telephone whenever one of the guards on control passed over the tunnel.

By February 25, 1955 the tunnel had reached a point directly below the targeted communications

lines. Thirty-one thousand tons of dirt had been removed to the "warehouse" basement to excavate the 1,476-foot tube. One hundred and twenty-five tons of steel plate had been bolted together to form the tunnel, and one thousand cubic yards of mortar had been pumped into the space around it.

Now the SIS team began burrowing upward toward the buried communication lines lying a dozen feet above. The earth was carefully scraped away, revealing three black, rubber-sheathed cables. A reinforced concrete roof was put in place above the lines to prevent the traffic passing overhead on the Schoenfelder Chaussee from breaking through the foot-and-a-half of earth above the top of the shaft. Nitrogen gas sealed inside the cables would be released when the SIS technicians cut into them to place the taps. To prevent the gas from escaping and alerting the East Germans, the last fifty feet of the tunnel was separated from the rest by a steel-and-concrete barrier and pressurized.

Each of the three cables contained 172 circuits, and each circuit carried at least 18 separate communication channels. Amplifiers in the tunnel boosted the intercepted signals and relayed them back to a bank of 150 tape recorders in the "warehouse." Tapes of the voice transmissions were flown to London where a team of White Russian emigrés translated them. The teletype tapes were sent to CIA headquarters in Washington, where special equipment was used to decipher them and they were then processed by a team of fifty German- and Russian-speaking translators.

During the winter of 1955–56 the tunnel was in danger of discovery because heat from the electronic equipment had warmed the surrounding earth, threatening to leave a telltale area of melted snow after the first snowfall. A cooling system was quickly installed in the tunnel to guard against the possibility.

On April 21, 1956, more than a year after the communications interception began, the tunnel was discovered by a Soviet maintenance crew, apparently by accident. The CIA and SIS personnel beat a hasty retreat, sealing the mid-tunnel barrier behind them.

It was not until September 1958 that all of the taped intercepts had been fully processed. Project Gold had yielded voluminous amounts of Soviet and Eastern European order of battle (i.e., military organization) intelligence, but otherwise little to justify the $25 to $30 million cost of the project. The reason for this surprising deficiency came to light in 1961 with the discovery that SIS agent George Blake was a Soviet penetration agent. Blake had taken part in the early CIA-SIS meetings in 1953 at which the tunnel

Lt. John B. Bernadou. Source: Author's collection.

was planned. Project Gold, it developed, had been known to Soviet intelligence from the start.

(Martin, *Wilderness of Mirrors*.)

BERNADOU, JOHN BAPTISTE (November 14, 1858–October 2, 1908): naval intelligence officer

A native of Philadelphia, Pennsylvania, Bernadou graduated from the U.S. Naval Academy in 1882 and was detailed to serve with a Smithsonian Institution expedition to Korea, which had only recently been opened to foreign visitors. As a result of his visit he concluded that the area was of importance to American strategic interests as a possible site for naval bases. While stationed at the American legation in Seoul in 1884 he saved the lives of a party of visiting Japanese officials, an act that earned him a reward from the Japanese government.

On his return from Asia in 1884 he was assigned to the Office of Naval Intelligence, where he served under ONI Chief Raymond Perry Rodgers. Bernadou functioned as a linguist, translating technical papers from French, German, Russian, Swedish, Spanish, and several other languages, and as an economic intelligence analyst. In the latter capacity he studied world supplies of nickel ore, which had recently become a major factor in the construction of steel warships. He also helped compile a survey of world seaports and coaling stations, and wrote papers on

such diverse subjects of ONI interest as international law, foreign policy, and the chemistry of smokeless gun powders.

Promoted to the rank of lieutenant in June 1896, Bernadou was given command of the torpedo boat *Winslow* in December 1897 and saw action during the Spanish-American War. On May 11, 1898 he was severely wounded in an action in the harbor of Cardenas, Cuba. He was later advanced ten places on the promotion list in recognition of his service in the war.

In 1906 he assumed the position of naval attaché at the U.S. embassies in Rome and Vienna. While in that capacity at the time of a Japanese war scare in 1907, he proposed to ONI that he would attempt to identify Japanese secret agents operating in Europe. However, the large sum he requested to underwrite this operation was refused on the grounds that war with Japan was not imminent.

While on duty in Europe, Bernadou became ill from lingering complications of his war wounds, and he died shortly after returning to the United States.

(Dorwart, *The Office of Naval Intelligence; Who Was Who in America*, vol. 1; *New York Times*, Oct 3, 1908, p. 9.)

BETTS, THOMAS JEFFRIES (June 14, 1894–): U.S. Army officer, intelligence officer

A native of Baltimore, Maryland, Betts graduated from the University of Virginia. In 1917 he was commissioned a second lieutenant in the U.S. Army, and advanced through grades to the rank of brigadier general in 1943.

Betts served in ARMY INTELLIGENCE. At the time of the PEARL HARBOR ATTACK in 1941, he was chief of the Situation Section of the Intelligence Branch within the office of the Army's assistant chief of staff for intelligence. That unit was concerned with worldwide CURRENT INTELLIGENCE for the Army and the Secretary of War.

During 1944–45 Betts was an intelligence officer at the Supreme Headquarters Allied Expeditionary Force in Europe, and in 1945 he served as director of intelligence for the U.S. Group Control Council for Germany. In 1946 he was chief intelligence officer for the Bikini nuclear weapons tests. During 1947–48 he was U.S. military attaché in Warsaw, Poland.

After his retirement from the Army, Betts served with the Central Intelligence Agency. During the early 1950s he was the Agency's senior representative in London, where, assisted by Dr. RAY S. CLINE, he worked out an exchange of FINISHED INTELLIGENCE with the British Secret Intelligence Service.

Betts was, by avocation, a writer. He published numerous short stories, articles, and poems.

Betts was awarded many decorations, including the Victory Medal, the Defense Medal, the Distinguished Service Medal, the Bronze Star, and the Purple Heart. Among his many foreign decorations were Commander, Order of the British Empire, and the Soviet Red Banner.

(*Who's Who in America;* v. 28; Cline, *CIA, Reality vs. Myth;* Wohlstetter, *Pearl Harbor: Warning and Decision.*)

BIELASKI, A(LEXANDER) BRUCE (April 2, 1883–February 19, 1964): lawyer, government official

A native of Montgomery County, Maryland, Bielaski earned an LL.B. from George Washington University in 1904. He joined the Department of Justice in 1905 and was assigned to its Bureau of Investigation (later the FEDERAL BUREAU OF INVESTIGATION) when it was established in 1908.

Bielaski became Bureau director in 1912, and served in that position until 1918, during which time the agency was responsible for investigating German subversive activities in the United States in the FIRST WORLD WAR. He was responsible for the Bureau's involvement with the AMERICAN PROTECTIVE LEAGUE during the war.

In 1925–26 Bielaski was special assistant to the United States Attorney General, in which capacity he prosecuted liquor smuggling rings. In 1929 he began a long association with the National Board of Fire Underwriters, an insurance industry group, and over the years he held a series of senior positions with that organization.

In 1922 Bielaski was kidnapped and held for ransom by bandits in Mexico. He escaped from them unaided after being held for three days.

(*Who Was Who in America,* v. 4; Corson, *Armies of Ignorance.*)

BIGELOW, JOHN (November 25, 1817– December 19, 1911): writer, journalist, government official, diplomat, intelligence officer

A native of New York State, Bigelow attended Trinity College in Hartford, Connecticut, and graduated from Union College in Schenectady, New York, in 1835. He was admitted to the New York bar in 1838 and was an inspector of Ossining Prison during 1845–46. He was an owner and editor of the *New York Evening Post* during 1849–61.

John Bigelow. Source: National Archives.

Shortly after the outbreak of the Civil War in 1861 Secretary of State William H. Seward sent Bigelow to Paris as consul general, with instructions to promote pro-Union propaganda in order to frustrate Confederate attempts to obtain French commercial or political cooperation. He proved skillful both as an overt spokesman for the Union cause and as a "gray propaganda" agent (see COVERT ACTION). Bigelow inspired many French books, pamphlets, and newspaper stories presenting the Northern side of the American conflict. He also developed contacts in the German and Austrian press in order to disseminate the Union viewpoint in those countries.

Bigelow worked closely with HENRY S. SANFORD, the U.S. minister to Belgium and chief of the American secret service in Europe, to thwart the efforts of the Confederate secret service to obtain French-built warships (see JAMES D. BULLOCH) and other military supplies. He procured some of the official papers of John Slidell, the Confederate diplomatic representative in France, bearing on these operations, and used them after the war (1888) to write *France and the Confederate Navy, 1862–68: An International Episode.* During 1865–66 he was the American minister to France.

Bigelow served as chairman of a New York State investigation commission in 1875, and was New York Secretary of State during 1875–77. He spent most of his postwar years writing, and his works include a biography of Benjamin Franklin, whose writings he collected, edited, and published.

(*DAB; Who Was Who in America*, v. 1; Case and Spencer, *The United States and France: Civil War Diplomacy;* Monaghan, *Diplomat in Carpet Slippers;* Owsley, "Henry Shelton Sanford and Federal Surveillance Abroad, 1861–1865"; Clapp, *Forgotten First Citizen.*)

BIRCH, JOHN (ca. 1918–August 25, 1945): clergyman, air force officer, intelligence officer

The son of American missionaries who had served in China, Birch was a fundamentalist Baptist clergyman in Macon, Georgia, before serving in the U.S. Army during the Second World War. Commissioned as an officer, he was assigned to intelligence duties in China because he was fluent in Chinese. He served as an intelligence officer with Gen. Claire Chennault's Fourteenth Air Force and reached the rank of captain before being transferred to the Office of Strategic Services in May 1945.

Shortly after VJ-Day, Birch led an OSS team from Sian, a town in northern China some 150 miles south of Yenan. His mission was to collect intelligence on local military conditions in an area occupied by both the Nationalist and Communist Chinese forces. On August 25, 1945 he was killed by Chinese Communist troops when he attempted to pass a Communist roadblock.

In 1958 Birch's name was appropriated by the founders of an ultra right-wing organization that described the OSS officer as "the first casualty in the Third World War between Communists and the ever-shrinking Free World." The John Birch Society not only campaigned against Communist subversion but it opposed social security and the income tax. Its founder accused President Eisenhower of being a Communist agent. Some of Birch's former comrades have stated that the distinction of having the organization named after him is an honor the OSS officer might have wished to forgo.

(Hymoff, *The OSS in World War II;* Smith, *OSS.*)

BISSELL, CLAYTON LAWRENCE (July 29, 1896–December 23, 1972): army officer, intelligence officer

A native of Kane, Pennsylvania, Bissell earned an LL.B. from the Valparaiso University Law School in 1917. That same year he enlisted as a private in the Aviation Section of the U.S. Army Signal Corps. He attended various service schools and earned a commission in the Army. In 1921 he made an official trip to England, France, Germany, Italy, and Holland to study aviation progress in those countries. From 1921 to 1924 he was an assistant to Gen. Billy Mitchell and took part in the first round-the-world flight. He served in China in 1941–42 and commanded the Tenth Army Air Force in 1942–43.

In 1943 Bissell was chief of Army Air Force Intelligence. In 1944 he became assistant chief of staff for intelligence (G-2; see ARMY INTELLIGENCE), and served in that capacity until the end of the war. While G-2 he opposed the proposals of General WILLIAM J. DONOVAN to transform the Office of Strategic Services into a peacetime central intelligence agency (see CENTRAL INTELLIGENCE AGENCY), which he saw as a threat to the autonomy of Army Intelligence.

From 1946 to 1948 Bissell was military air attaché at the American embassy in London. He retired in the rank of major general. Among his many decorations are the Distinguished Service Cross, the Distinguished Service Medal, the Silver Star, and the Distinguished Flying Cross.

(*Who Was Who in America*, v. 5; Troy, *Donovan and the CIA.*)

BISSELL, RICHARD MERVIN, JR. (September 18, 1909–): economist, intelligence officer

The son of a wealthy insurance company executive, Bissell was born in Hartford, Connecticut, where he spent the first nine years of his life in a house that his father bought from Mark Twain. (The house is now a museum open to the public.) He attended the Groton School, the London School of Economics, and received a Ph.D. from Yale University in 1932. He taught economics at Yale until 1941. During World War II he worked in Washington as an economist for the Department of Commerce and other government agencies.

In 1952 Bissell joined the Central Intelligence Agency and was assigned to the CIA CLANDESTINE SERVICE. In 1954 he was made special assistant for planning and coordination, which meant that he was in charge of developing the U-2 project for OVERHEAD RECONNAISSANCE. Bissell is generally credited with responsibility for the swift development and successful operation of the U-2 aircraft and the reconnaissance program. Later he managed the development of the CIA reconnaissance satellite program with equal success.

The Black Tom railroad terminal after the explosion of July 30, 1916. Source: National Archives.

In 1958 Bissell was made deputy director for plans (i.e., chief of the Clandestine Service), and as such was in charge of all covert operations of the CIA. By 1961 he had been tentatively selected by President Kennedy to be ALLEN DULLES's successor as director of the CIA. However, Bissell was responsible for organizing and carrying out the BAY OF PIGS INVASION, and after the failure of that operation his prospects for promotion to the director's office disappeared. He resigned from the CIA in 1962. President Kennedy awarded him the Medal of Freedom.

Bissell served as president of the Institute for Defense Analysis, a nonprofit Pentagon "think tank" from 1962 to 1964, and later as an executive with United Aircraft Corporation in Connecticut.

(*Who's Who in America*, 43rd. ed.; Mosley, *Dulles*; Wyden, *Bay of Pigs*; Powers, *The Man Who Kept the Secrets*.)

BLACK PROPAGANDA

A forgery that is made to appear to have originated with a source other than the true one. It usually takes the form of a document purporting to have originated with an adversary government or organization, and intended to discredit or frustrate that adversary. For example, Czechoslovakian intelligence once circulated several forged "U.S. government" documents that appeared to disclose an American conspiracy to overthrow Latin American governments.

Another example of black propaganda might be a phony "letter from home" alleging some disturbing situation on the home front and actually sent by a psychological warfare unit to a soldier of an opposing army.

See COVERT ACTION.

(Blackstock, *Agents of Deceit*; Smith, *Portrait of a Cold Warrior*; Becket, *Dictionary of Espionage*.)

BLACK TOM EXPLOSION

At 2:08 A.M. on July 30, 1916 more than two million pounds of munitions stored on Black Tom Island in New York harbor exploded. The series of explosions shattered windows throughout New York City and were heard as far away as Philadelphia. The explo-

Lt. Victor Blue. Source: Author's collection.

sions and the resultant fire did some $14 million in damage and killed three men and a child.

The munitions, which exploded while in storage at the Black Tom Terminal of the Lehigh Valley Railroad, were awaiting shipment to Russia for use against Germany in the First World War, which the United States had not yet entered. The incident was suspected to be one of sabotage by German agents. Although considerable evidence was later adduced implicating LOTHAR WITZKE and KURT JAHNKE, both German Secret Service agents, German responsibility for the explosion was never proved.

(Landau, *The Enemy Within*.)

BLAKE, JOHN FRANCIS (July 10, 1922–): government official, intelligence officer

A native of San Francisco, California, Blake graduated from the University of San Francisco in 1943. He was commissioned as an officer in the U.S. Army and assigned to the Office of Strategic Services. After the war he continued with the OSS and its successor agencies and was one of the "charter members" of the CENTRAL INTELLIGENCE AGENCY.

During 1974–79 Blake was the CIA's deputy director for administration. Between July 1977 and February 1978 he was also acting deputy director of central intelligence.

Blake retired from the CIA in 1979 and served as president and executive director of the Association of Former Intelligence Officers during 1979–80. In 1981 he became staff director of the U.S. Senate Select Committee on Intelligence.

Blake is an adjunct professor at the DEFENSE INTELLIGENCE COLLEGE and vice-president of Electronic Warfare Associates, a Virginia firm.

(*Who's Who in America*, 42nd edition; Cline, *The CIA: Reality vs. Myth*.)

BLUE, VICTOR (December 6, 1865–January 22, 1928): naval officer

A native of Richmond County, North Carolina, Blue graduated from the Naval Academy in 1887. During the SPANISH-AMERICAN WAR he carried out three missions behind the lines in Spanish-occupied Cuba. On May 31 and June 1, 1898, he carried out a liaison mission, contacting Cuban insurgent Gen. Maximo Gomez. During June 11–13 he landed on the southeast coast of Cuba and, guided by insurgents, traveled to a point from which he could observe the bay of Santiago de Cuba. The purpose of this mission was to investigate reports that some of the Spanish squadron believed to be blockaded in the bay by the American fleet was actually elsewhere; a U.S. invasion force of 16,000 troops aboard thirty-eight transports was waiting at Port Tampa for Blue's reconnaissance before sailing for Cuba. Blue carried out his mission successfully, reporting that all the Spanish ships were in the bay. On June 25–27 he again ventured past Spanish lines to observe the current positions of the Spanish ships in the bay as part of a planned torpedo attack that was never carried out. For these instances of what Adm. William T. Sampson described as "extraordinary heroism," he was advanced five places on the Navy's promotion list.

Blue advanced to the rank of rear admiral and commanded the battleship *Texas* during World War I. He retired in 1920.

(O'Toole, *The Spanish War*; DAB; Bryan, *The Spy in America*.)

BLUM, PAUL: businessman, intelligence officer

Blum, an American, lived in Japan for many years before the SECOND WORLD WAR. During the war he served with the OFFICE OF STRATEGIC SER-

VICES. He was assigned to the Secret Intelligence Branch in Switzerland, where he worked closely with ALLEN W. DULLES, serving as both his counterintelligence aide and his Far Eastern specialist. Blum played a central role in the negotiations between Dulles and German SS Gen. Karl Wolff, which resulted in the surrender of all German and Fascist forces in northern Italy shortly before V-E Day in 1944.

Blum later served with the Central Intelligence Agency in Switzerland.

(Smith, *OSS*; Mosley, *Dulles*.)

BLUM, ROBERT (March 12, 1911–July 9, 1965): foreign affairs specialist, intelligence officer

A native of San Francisco, Blum graduated from the University of California at Berkeley in 1930 and earned a Ph.D. from that institution in 1936. From 1937 to 1942 he was a research assistant and instructor in international relations at Yale University.

Blum joined the Office of Strategic Services in 1942 and was assigned to the OSS COUNTER-ESPIONAGE BRANCH. He was a member of the team headed by NORMAN HOLMES PEARSON that was sent to London in 1942 to serve as liaison with the counterintelligence section of the British Secret Intelligence Service and to learn the techniques of counterintelligence. Blum subsequently served in Paris with the OSS.

Blum was executive secretary of the Greenwood Foundation during 1946–47, was a member of the staff of the Office of the Secretary of Defense in 1947–49, and served with the Economic Cooperation Administration (the Marshall Plan agency) in France in 1949–50.

During 1950–51, Blum was chief of the U.S. Special Technical and Economic Mission to Cambodia, Laos, and Vietnam, an organization affiliated with the Central Intelligence Agency. While in this post he openly opposed French colonialism in Southeast Asia, and he was pessimistic about the achievement of American goals in the region.

In 1952–53 Blum was assistant deputy for economic affairs of the U.S. special representative in Europe. In 1953 he was chief of staff of the President's Commission on International Information Activities. From 1953 to 1962 he served as president of the Asia Foundation, an organization created and funded by the CIA as a cover for "gray propaganda" and other COVERT ACTION operations in the Far East.

After leaving the Asia Foundation, Blum held the position of director of China policy studies for the Council on Foreign Relations.

(*Who Was Who in America*, v. 4; Smith, *OSS*; Leary, *Perilous Missions*; Smith, *Portrait of a Cold Warrior*.)

BONVOULOIR, JULIEN ACHARD DE (1749–April 18, 1783): French secret service agent

A native of Normandy, France, Bonvouloir claimed to have served as an officer in the French army in Santo Domingo (now the Dominican Republic and Haiti) before visiting the British colonies in America in 1774. The following year he was in London, where he reported to the French ambassador, the Compte de Guines, on the situation in America, stated that he had developed sources of information there, and offered to return to America on behalf of the French foreign ministry.

Bonvouloir's proposal came at an opportune moment. The French foreign minister, Count de Vergennes, was aware that the COMMITTEE OF SECRET CORRESPONDENCE was making inquiries regarding the possibility of French political and material support for the AMERICAN REVOLUTION and he required extensive political intelligence regarding the situation in America in order to consider the possibility of a Franco-American alliance against Great Britain.

In September 1775 Bonvouloir, posing as an Antwerp merchant on a private commercial errand, sailed for America. He arrived in Philadelphia late in December and met with BENJAMIN FRANKLIN and other members of the Committee of Secret Correspondence. On the instructions of the French foreign ministry he disclaimed any official connection with the French government, but stated that he had powerful friends at court and that, as an American sympathizer, he would be pleased to serve as an unofficial channel between the Committee and these powerful friends. Franklin understood that this was a pose and the reason for it. With the necessary preliminaries out of the way, he and Bonvouloir proceeded to explore the conditions of a French alliance.

The French objective was to weaken Great Britain, which had recently bested her in the Seven Years War. To this end she would be willing to open her ports to American ships, sell the Americans arms in exchange for agricultural commodities, and even send two military engineers to advise on the construction of fortifications. France had no designs on getting back Canada, nor did she wish to entangle America in political or military ties, Bonvouloir assured Franklin. However, she must be assured that there was a real commitment to independence among the English colonists in America, and that they stood a reasonable chance of winning it. Franklin, undismayed by resistance from Loyalists and the fact that Gen. GEORGE WASHINGTON's small, ill-equipped army was nearly out of gunpowder, convinced Bonvouloir that American patriotism was unanimous, Washington's troop strength was growing, and the war was going splendidly. The French agent sent a glowing report back to the foreign ministry.

Bonvoulouir's visit prompted the Committee to send its own agent, SILAS DEANE, to France in order to pursue further the matter of French aid. On Bonvouloir's return to France he was given a commission in the French army and subsequently served in India.

(Boatner, *Encyclopedia of the American Revolution*; Auger, *The Secret War of Independence*.)

BOWIE, BEVERLY MUMFORD (1914– November 15, 1958): writer, magazine editor, intelligence officer

A native of Richmond, Virginia, Bowie attended the Solebury School in New Hope, Pennsylvania, and graduated magna cum laude from Harvard University in 1935. He worked for *Newsweek,* and later moved to Washington, D.C. to work for the U.S. Department of Agriculture as an economist (his major area of study at Harvard). In 1939 he joined the staff of Senator Sheridan Downey of California.

In 1942 Bowie was commissioned an ensign in the U.S. Naval Reserve and assigned to the Office of Strategic Services. He served in the OSS RESEARCH AND ANALYSIS BRANCH and saw duty in Africa and Italy. In 1944 he took part in an OSS-Air Force operation in which some 1,700 American airmen held as prisoners of war in Romania were rescued and evacuated. He parachuted into Bucharest and helped establish an OSS intelligence station there shortly before the advancing Red Army arrived in the city.

Bowie remained with the Research and Analysis Branch when it was transferred to the State Department after the war, in 1945. In 1946 he returned to Senator Downey's staff, and the following year published a novel, *Operation Bughouse,* a humorous account of his OSS experiences.

In 1950 he joined the staff of *Pathfinder* magazine and became associate editor. In 1951 he joined the *National Geographic* magazine and was assistant editor at the time of his death.

(*New York Times* obituary, November 16, 1958, p. 88; Cave Brown, *The Last Hero,* Cline, *The CIA: Reality vs. Myth.*)

BOWIE, ROBERT RICHARDSON (August 24, 1909–): lawyer, educator, foreign affairs specialist, government official, intelligence officer

A native of Baltimore, Maryland, Bowie graduated from Princeton University in 1931 and earned an LL. B. degree from Harvard University in 1934. He practiced law in Baltimore and was assistant director of the Maryland Legislative Council. During 1941–42 he was assistant attorney general of Maryland. He served in the U.S. Army during 1942–46. Bowie was professor of law at Harvard University from 1945–55, during which period he also served as general counsel to the U.S. high commissioner for Germany in 1950–51 and as the director of the Policy Planning Staff of the State Department in 1953–55. In the latter capacity he took part in planning the IRAN COUP of the Central Intelligence Agency.

Bowie was assistant secretary of state for policy planning during 1955–57. In 1957 he became professor of international affairs and director of the Center of International Affairs at Harvard University. He was a counselor in the State Department in 1966–68.

Bowie served with the CIA as deputy director for intelligence from 1977–79.

(*Who's Who in America,* 37th edition; Roosevelt, *Countercoup.*)

BOWSER, MARY ELIZABETH: Union secret service agent(?)

Bowser was born a slave in the Richmond, Virginia, household of John Van Lew, the father of ELIZABETH VAN LEW, who was to become the central figure in the Richmond Underground during the Civil War. Bowser and the other household slaves were freed by Miss Van Lew during the early 1850s, after the death of her father. Through Van Lew's sponsorship she attended school in the North, and she was living in Philadelphia at the outbreak of the Civil War.

Most popular accounts of Miss Van Lew's wartime espionage for the Union claim that she brought Bowser back to Richmond to work as one of her agents, and sent her to work as a maid in the household of Confederate President Jefferson Davis. This would have made her one of the highest-placed espionage agents of the Civil War. However, the facts of Bowser's supposed secret service are poorly documented. The earliest published account about it may be the single paragraph in Beymer's 1912 book on Civil War spies, *On Hazardous Service.* Beymer writes, "What she was able to learn, how long she remained behind

Jefferson Davis's dining-chair, and what became of the girl ere the war ended are questions to which Time has effaced the answers."

Some historians suspect the Bowser story is just one of the many romantic myths about Civil War spying. It should be noted, however, that Van Lew went to great pains to eradicate much of the official record of the Richmond Underground in order to protect herself and her associates from the former Confederates' postwar vengeance, and while the evidence supporting the Bowser story is meager, even less is known of many of the other members of the spy ring.

Dannett states that Bowser kept a wartime diary that is now in private hands, but does not offer further details.

(Beymer, *On Hazardous Service*; Corson, *Armies of Ignorance*; Kane, *Spies for the Blue and Gray*; Dannett, *Profiles of Negro Womanhood*.)

BOYD, (ISA)BELLE (May 9, 1843–June 11, 1900): actress, Confederate secret agent

A native of Bunker Hill, Virginia (now West Virginia), Boyd attended Mount Washington Female College in Baltimore during 1855–59. The daughter of an ardently secessionist family, she shot at (and later said she killed) a reportedly rowdy Union soldier who invaded her home when Federal troops occupied Martinsburg in July 1861. (She was eighteen at the time.) In spite of this incident, many of the young Union officers were disposed to fraternize with her and, according to her memoirs, inadvertently disclosed information of military value that she promptly transmitted to the Confederate forces.

The true extent and importance of Boyd's secret intelligence work is lost in the romantic mythology of CIVIL WAR espionage, and she may have been the quintessence of what Civil War historian and espionologist Edwin C. Fishel calls "the magnolia blossom school of Civil War history." Curtis C. Davis, who has made a detailed study of Boyd, regards her as "the Civil War's most overrated spy." However, one of her biographers, Louis A. Sigaud, considers her memoirs—the principal source regarding her intelligence work—as essentially sound, if somewhat embellished in detail.

Boyd seems to have reported some of her information through Lt. Col. TURNER ASHBY, Confederate cavalryman and Gen. Thomas J. ("Stonewall") Jackson's secret agent. Completely indifferent to the disciplines of TRADECRAFT, she was twice arrested by federal authorities during 1861–62. Chivalry prevailed over counterespionage, however, and the

teenage girl was admonished and released on both occasions. The incidents made her something of a celebrity, and *Leslie's Weekly*, a popular northern magazine, dubbed her "the Cleopatra of the Secession." The Associated Press had also termed her "an accomplished prostitute" (although the evidence indicates she was no more than an accomplished flirt); nonetheless the allegation so outraged her that she granted an interview to the *New York Tribune*, in which she denied it while freely admitting to her role as Rebel spy and courier.

In spite of the publicity attending her admissions, Boyd continued to function as a Confederate secret agent. She claimed that she managed to overhear in its entirety a conference between Gen. James Shields and his officers in mid-May 1862 in which Shields detailed his plans to remove most of his troops from Front Royal, Virginia, in order to support other units of the Army of the Potomac in the Shenandoah campaign. She recounted that, immediately upon the conclusion of this conference, she once again managed to talk her way through the Union lines and deliver the information to Colonel Ashby, much to the military advantage of Stonewall Jackson.

A short time later, when Jackson advanced on Front Royal, she crossed battlefields to bring him an updated report on Union strength and disposition around the town. Immediately thereafter Jackson overran the town and drove the Union forces across the Potomac. Boyd's part in this engagement is the most famous of her exploits, and the information she furnished Jackson is often characterized as crucial to the battle's outcome. But as historian Fishel points out, Boyd's report only confirmed what Jackson had established in two weeks spent diligently gathering intelligence from a variety of sources, including his cavalry, other agents, and Union prisoners of war and deserters.

In July 1862 federal authorities again arrested Boyd after she entrusted one of her reports to General Jackson to a courier who happened to be a Union agent. She was imprisoned in the Old Capitol prison in Washington and was released in a prisoner exchange after several months. Returning to Martinsburg, she was arrested, imprisoned, and released once again in 1863. In 1864 she traveled to England as a courier with dispatches for the Confederate agents there. Her mission was temporarily interrupted when the U.S. Navy captured her ship. Continuing on her mission to London, she was followed there by Ens. Samuel Hardinge, the naval officer who had been in charge of the prize crew that had taken charge of the Confederate ship. Hardinge, enamored of Boyd, had abandoned his naval career to press his suit of the Confederate agent. They were married in Piccadilly in August 1864 (Boyd later recalled that Hardinge had turned over the U.S. Naval signal code book to her as proof of his love). Hardinge returned alone to the United States shortly thereafter, possibly on an errand for the Confederate secret service. He was charged with spying by the federal authorities and imprisoned. After the war he rejoined her in England, but soon died of illnesses contracted in prison.

Boyd published her wartime memoirs and pursued a theatrical career, making her debut in *Lady of Lyons* in Manchester in 1866. After a successful two-year tour on the English stage, she returned to America where she continued to appear as an actress for about ten years. In later life she lectured on her wartime experiences. She twice remarried and had several children.

(*Who Was Who in America*, historical volume; Davis, "The Civil War's Most Over-Rated Spy," "The Pet of the Confederacy Still? Fresh Findings about Belle Boyd"; Fishel, "The Mythology of Civil War Intelligence"; Bakeless, *Spies of the Confederacy*; Kane, *Spies for the Blue and Gray*.)

BRADEN, THOMAS WARDELL (February 22, 1918–): journalist, intelligence officer

A native of Greene, Iowa, Braden graduated from Dartmouth University in 1940. He served with the British army in Africa and Italy during 1941–44 before transferring to the U.S. Army and the Office of Strategic Services. He took part in the JEDBURGH OPERATION in which Allied teams parachuted into France immediately after D-Day to establish liaison with the French Resistance.

Braden taught English at Dartmouth from 1946 to 1948, then was the executive secretary of the Museum of Modern Art in New York City. In 1951 he was recruited by ALLEN DULLES to serve with the Central Intelligence Agency.

Between 1951 and 1954 Braden served as chief of the International Organizations Division of the CIA CLANDESTINE SERVICE. The function of this division was to provide covert support of the non-Communist political left around the world through financial aid to trade unions, political parties, and international organizations of students and journalists. This program was initially undertaken at Braden's suggestion.

Braden resigned from the CIA in 1954 to work as a journalist. He is the author of several books, including the autobiographical *Eight is Enough,* upon which a successful television situation comedy was based.

(*Who's Who in America*, 43rd. ed.; Smith, *OSS*; Meyer, *Facing Reality*.)

BRELIS, (CONSTANTINE) DEAN (April 1, 1924,–): journalist, novelist, educator, paramilitary officer

A native of Newport, Rhode Island, Brelis joined the U.S. Army in 1942 as an enlisted man. He served with Detachment 101 of the Office of Strategic Services, the guerrilla group that operated behind Japanese lines in Burma and China. He was given a battlefield commission as a second lieutenant. He was discharged in 1945, having been awarded a Bronze Star and other decorations.

Brelis worked as a reporter for the *Boston Globe* from 1946 to 1949, and received an A.B. from Harvard University in 1949. He worked as a journalist for Time-Life, Inc. from 1949 to 1954, and was an instructor at Harvard and Radcliffe College from 1958 to 1963. In 1963 he joined the National Broadcasting Company as a foreign correspondent. He moved to the Columbia Broadcasting System in 1970.

Brelis collaborated with WILLIAM R. PEERS in writing *Behind the Burma Road* (1963), a history of Detachment 101.

(*Contemporary Authors*, vol. 9R.)

BRENNAN, EARL: legislator, diplomat, lobbyist, intelligence officer

Brennan, an American, was educated in Italy as a boy. He served as a Republican member of the New Hampshire legislature. He returned to Italy as a member of the State Department's consular service and served on the staff of the American embassy in Rome during the first years of the Fascist regime. In that capacity he became well-acquainted with the Italian secret police, the powerful Italian Masonic Order, high-ranking Fascist officials, and Benito Mussolini himself.

In January 1942 OSS officer DAVID BRUCE, recognizing the potential intelligence value of Brennan's Italian connections, recruited Brennan into the Office of the Coordinator of Information, the predecessor of the Office of Strategic Services. Brennan served in the Secret Intelligence Branch of the OSS, running espionage operations into Italy and Sicily.

During the 1960s Brennan was a registered foreign agent in Washington representing dissident Haitian groups opposed to the Duvalier regime in their homeland.

(Smith, *OSS*.)

BRINTON, (CLARENCE) CRANE (February 2, 1898–September 7, 1958): historian, intelligence analyst

A native of Winsted, Connecticut, Brinton graduated from Harvard University in 1919 and received a Ph.D. from Oxford University in 1923. He became a member of the history faculty of Harvard in 1923 and taught there until 1942, when he joined the Office of Strategic Services.

Brinton served as an intelligence analyst in the OSS RESEARCH AND ANALYSIS BRANCH in London and France. After the war he returned to Harvard.

Brinton's pre-war historical studies focused on the French Revolution, and he enlarged the scope of his research in *The Anatomy of Revolution*, published in 1938. This work attempted to identify the dynamics common to the French, English, American, and Russian revolutions. By some accounts the book was used as a blueprint for coups d'etat initiated by covert action officers of the Central Intelligence Agency in the early 1950s. Brinton's fellow historian and OSS veteran, KERMIT ROOSEVELT, reportedly considered *Anatomy* so germane to such endeavors that he made it required reading for his staff prior to the IRAN COUP.

(*Current Biography*, 1959, 1968; Copeland, *The Game of Nations*; Smith, *OSS*.)

BRODIE, BERNARD (May 20, 1910– November 24, 1978): military and naval theorist, psychological warfare officer

A native of Chicago, Brodie earned a Ph. B. and a Ph. D. from the University of Chicago in 1932 and 1940, respectively. In 1940 and 1941 he was a fellow at the Princeton Institute for Advanced Study. He taught at Dartmouth College from 1941 to 1943, when he was commissioned in the U.S. Naval Reserve and assigned to the Office of Naval Intelligence. He served as naval advisor in Op-16-W, the Special Warfare Branch, which was engaged in psychological warfare.

After the war he taught international relations at Yale University (1945–51), was a senior staff member of the Rand Corporation (1951–66), and was a professor at the University of California (1966–78). He wrote several books on military affairs, including *Sea Power in the Machine Age*, *A Guide to Naval Strategy*, and *Strategy in the Missile Age*. His colleague in the ONI Special Warfare Branch, LADISLAS FARAGO, regarded him as "the outstanding and most lucid American expert on strategy in political scientific terms."

(*Who Was Who in America*, vol. 7; Farago, *Burn After Reading*.)

BROE, WILLIAM V. (ca. 1910–): intelligence officer

Broe served in the CIA CLANDESTINE SERVICE. During a period including 1964 he was chief of the CIA's Tokyo Station. From about 1966 until 1972 he was chief of the Western Hemisphere Division.

Broe was involved in the 1970 affair in which the International Telephone and Telegraph Corporation sought to prevent Marxist candidate Salvatore Allende from taking office as president of Chile. Former CIA director JOHN A. MCCONE, then a director at ITT, expressed his concern over Chilean developments to Director of Central Intelligence RICHARD HELMS, who sent Broe to meet with ITT president Harold Geneen to discuss the matter. Geneen proposed that ITT furnish $1 million for the CIA to funnel into the campaign of an Allende opponent. Broe refused the offer on behalf of CIA, but he subsequently sought ITT's cooperation in an abortive CIA plan to mount an economic destabilization COVERT ACTION operation against Allende.

Broe was succeeded by THEODORE G. SHACKLEY as chief of the Western Hemisphere Division in 1972. Broe became the CIA inspector general and subsequently retired from the Agency.

(Sampson, *The Sovereign State of ITT*; Powers, *The Man Who Kept the Secrets*; Agee, *Inside the Company: CIA Diary*.)

BROSS, JOHN ADAMS (January 17, 1911–): covert operations officer, intelligence officer

A native of Chicago, Bross attended the Chicago Latin School and the Groton School. He earned an A.B. and an LL.B. from Harvard University in 1933 and 1936, respectively. He practiced law in New York City from 1936 to 1942, when he was recruited into the Office of Strategic Services by WILLIAM J. DONOVAN.

Bross, assigned to the OSS SPECIAL OPERATIONS BRANCH, was one of the first OSS officers to be trained in covert operations by the British Special Operations Executive. He participated in the JEDBURGH OPERATION, in which three-man teams parachuted into German-occupied France to coordinate the operations of the French Resistance with the Allied D-Day landings. Bross left the OSS in 1946 with the rank of lieutenant colonel, having been awarded the Legion of Merit, the Bronze Star, the Order of the British Empire, and the King Christian X Medal of Liberation.

Bross returned to the practice of law in New York between 1946 and 1949, when he became assistant general counsel to the U.S. High Commissioner to Germany. In 1951 he joined the Central Intelligence Agency and was assigned to the Office of Policy Coordination, the name then used for the COVERT ACTION arm of the agency. He became chief of the OPC's Eastern European Division, and later was a senior officer in the CIA CLANDESTINE SERVICE. From 1963 to 1971 he was deputy to the director of central intelligence for programs evaluation, and he served as head of the NATIONAL INTELLIGENCE PROGRAMS EVALUATION STAFF (NIPE), an interagency management panel. He retired in 1971.

(Smith, *OSS*; Powers, *The Man Who Kept the Secrets*; *Who's Who in America*, 43rd ed.)

BROWN, SPENCER KELLOGG (ca. 1843–September 25, 1863): schoolteacher, soldier, sailor, Union secret service agent

A native of New York State, Brown moved with his parents and sisters to the Kansas Territory in 1855. The family was of anti-slavery sympathies in the Border War that was fought in Kansas in the late 1850s, and it suffered at the hands of the pro-slavery forces.

Largely self-educated, Brown obtained a job as school-teacher in Missouri after leaving home, but he was forced to abandon it and flee when local slavery advocates suspected that he was related to radical abolitionist John Brown. He subsequently changed his name to Spencer Kellogg to avoid a repetition of the incident.

In January 1861 Brown enlisted (as Kellogg) as a private in the U.S. Army. After the outbreak of the CIVIL WAR he served as a scout (i.e., a secret service agent) for the Union Army in Missouri. He was successful in this capacity, and in September Maj. Gen. John C. Fremont appointed him a first lieutenant and assigned him to recruit the "Lyon Legion," a body of scouts to be attached to the Twelfth Missouri Volunteers. However, Fremont was transferred before Brown's commission was confirmed.

Brown, whose enlistment had expired when Fremont applied for his commission, next enlisted in the Union Navy and was assigned to the U.S.S. *Essex*, an ironclad gunboat operating on the Mississippi River. In January 1862 he proposed to the ship's commander, Captain William D. Porter, that he and another crewman go ashore in Confederate territory disguised as deserters in order to reconnoiter enemy fortifications along the river. Porter consented, and Brown and his comrade set out on their mission.

The pair worked as laborers for the Confederate Engineering Corps, which gave them the opportunity to observe the fortifications along the river south of Columbus, Kentucky. Before they could return to Union territory and report the information they had gathered, however, Brown was arrested by the Confederate authorities on suspicion of espionage. Although he allayed their suspicions, he was released only on the condition that he enlist in the Confederate Army.

Shortly before he was due to be sworn in, Brown escaped and returned to Union lines with the military information he had initially gathered, plus additional information he had collected regarding Corinth and Iuka, Mississippi, and Memphis and Fort Pillow, Tennessee, places he had reconnoitered during his captivity. He arrived at the headquarters of General Ulysses S. Grant on April 7, 1862, the morning of the second day of the Battle of Shiloh.

Upon returning to the *Essex*, Brown was made a petty officer by Porter. In August 1862 he undertook a special mission to sink a ferryboat the Confederates were using to supply their besieged garrison at Port Hudson, Louisiana. Commanding a transport and a force of forty men, he succeeded in sinking the boat. However, during the action he and four of his men landed in Confederate territory in a small boat and were taken prisoner.

Brown was taken to Jackson, Mississippi, where he was recognized by a Confederate engineer who had known him during his intelligence mission in Kentucky. He was charged with espionage and imprisoned in Selma, Alabama; later in Montgomery; and finally in the Richmond, Virginia, prison called Castle Thunder. There he was tried and found guilty of espionage for his earlier mission, despite a provision in the rules of war, recognized by both sides, that ended his liability for such prosecution with his return to his own lines.

He was sentenced to death and was hanged.

(Smith, ed., *Spencer Kellogg Brown*; Bryan, *The Spy in America*; Kane, *Spies for the Blue and Gray*.)

BROWN, WILSON W. (ca. 1840–ca. 1912): businessman, soldier, Union secret agent

A native of Dowling, Ohio, Brown was a locomotive engineer with the Mobile and Ohio Railroad before the Civil War. In 1861 he enlisted as a private in the Ohio Volunteer Infantry, which was part of the Army of the Ohio. In April 1862 he volunteered to take part in a paramilitary operation behind Confederate lines aimed at severing the rail line between Atlanta and Chattanooga (see ANDREWS'S RAID). He and a party of twenty other Union troops in civilian clothes, led by JAMES J. ANDREWS, hijacked a locomotive and attempted to destroy railroad tracks and bridges between the two cities. He was captured by Confederate troops and imprisoned (Andrews and seven of the others were hanged). He and several others escaped. Brown made his way back to his regiment.

After the war Brown was a sales agent in Dowling, Ohio.

(Bryan, *The Spy in America*; Boatner, *Civil War Dictionary*; O'Neill, *Wild Train*.)

BRUCE, DAVID KIRKPATRICK ESTE (February 12, 1898–December 5, 1977): diplomat, intelligence officer

A native of Baltimore, Maryland, Bruce attended the Gilman School in that city. He enrolled in Princeton University but left in his sophomore year to serve as an artilleryman in the First World War. Following his discharge from the Army he studied law at the University of Virginia and the University of Maryland, and practiced law in Baltimore. He entered politics in 1924 and served one term in the House of Delegates of the Maryland Legislature. The following year he joined the State Department as a foreign service officer. During 1926–28 he served as vice-consul in Rome.

In 1928 Bruce left the foreign service and pursued business interests in New York City. Establishing his residence in Virginia, he was elected to the Virginia House of Delegates in 1940. In 1941 he joined the Office of Strategic Services and become chief of the OSS SECRET INTELLIGENCE BRANCH.

Bruce was commissioned in the rank of colonel in the U.S. Army Air Corps. From 1943 to 1945 he was assigned to London, where he served as director of all OSS activities in the European Theatre of Activities.

After the war Bruce served with the American Red Cross, and in 1947 and 1948 he was assistant secretary of commerce. For most of the rest of his life he held important diplomatic posts, including those of U.S. ambassador to England, France, and Germany; U.S. representative to the Vietnam Peace Talks in Paris; chief of the U.S. Liaison Office in Peking; and U.S. ambassador to NATO.

(*Current Biography*, 1949; *Who Was Who in America*, vol. 7; Smith, *OSS*.)

BRYAN, JOSEPH, 3RD (April 30, 1904–): writer, intelligence officer

A native of Richmond, Virginia, Bryan graduated from Princeton University in 1927. He worked as a reporter and editorial writer for the *Richmond News Leader* and *Chicago Journal* during 1928–31, and was associate editor of *Parade* magazine in 1931–32. He was managing editor of *Town and Country* during 1933–37, and associate editor of the *Saturday Evening Post* in 1937–40. In 1940 he became a free-lance writer.

Between 1927 and 1964 Bryan belonged, successively, to the U.S. Army Reserve, Naval Reserve, and Air Force Reserve, reaching the rank of colonel in the Air Force Reserve. During the early 1950s he worked for the Central Intelligence Agency as chief of the Political and Psychological Warfare Staff of the Office of Policy Coordination, as the CIA's COVERT ACTION department was then called (see CENTRAL INTELLIGENCE AGENCY).

Bryan's articles have appeared in many national magazines, including *Reader's Digest*, *McCall's*, and *Holiday*. He collaborated with Adm. William F. Halsey on the latter's autobiography, and is the author of several other books, including a dual biography of the Duke and Duchess of Windsor.

(*Contemporary Authors*, New Revision Series, v. 11; Hunt, *Undercover*.)

BUCHER, LLOYD M. (September 1, 1927–): naval officer

Bucher was born in Pocatello, Idaho. After the death of his mother he was raised by his grandparents in California, but later was placed in orphanages in Idaho. In 1941 he was transferred to Boy's Town in Omaha, Nebraska. In 1946 he graduated from Boy's Town and enlisted in the U.S. Navy.

Bucher rose through the naval ranks, was commissioned, and reached the rank of commander by 1967, when he was given command of the U.S.S. *Pueblo*, a coastal freighter converted for use by the Navy as a SIGINT platform. He was in command of the ship on January 23, 1968 when it was captured by North Korean forces in internal waters (see PUEBLO INCIDENT).

Bucher and his surviving officers, crewmen, and two civilian Navy employees were released eleven months later. A court of inquiry investigating the circumstances of the seizure of the *Pueblo* recommended that he be tried by a general court-martial for alleged offenses connected with the loss of the ship. However, the secretary of the navy directed that all charges against Bucher and other officers of the *Pueblo* be dropped.

Bucher subsequently retired from the Navy.

(Bucher, *Bucher: My Story*.)

BUCKINGHAM, BENJAMIN HORR (February 11, 1848–January 16, 1906): naval intelligence officer

A native of Canton, Ohio, Buckingham graduated from the Naval Academy in 1869. His first intelligence mission involved a tour of Korea, Siberia, and Russia, which resulted in a very detailed report of these lands, published in 1883 by the Office of Naval Intelligence. In November 1885 he was assigned as the first permanent naval attaché to continental Europe, accredited to the American embassies in Paris, Berlin, and St. Petersburg. He met with foreign naval officers, government officials, industrialists, and other potential sources of information, toured shipyards and naval bases, and thus acquired information of considerable value about European naval matters.

Buckingham advanced to the rank of lieutenant commander in 1896. Poor health forced him to retire from the Navy in October 1898.

(Dorwart, *The Office of Naval Intelligence; National Cyclopedia of American Biography*, vol. 34.)

BUCKLEY, WILLIAM FRANK, JR. (November 24, 1925–): editor, newspaper columnist, political activist, television personality, novelist, intelligence officer

A native of New York City, Buckley spent his early childhood in France and England where he attended private schools. He studied at the University of Mexico in 1943 and served in the U.S. Army in 1944–46, reaching the rank of second lieutenant.

Buckley graduated from Yale University in 1950 and the following year published *God and Man at Yale*, an assault on what he saw as the anti-religious and politically liberal bias of the Yale faculty. Soon after his graduation he joined the Central Intelligence Agency and served in the Office of Policy Coordination, as the COVERT ACTION unit of the CIA was then known (see CENTRAL INTELLIGENCE AGENCY). He served in Mexico City for a year. According to E. HOWARD HUNT, who was then chief of the CIA/OPC station in Mexico and later Buckley's lifelong friend, Buckley's assignments included helping Eudocio Ravines, a Chilean ex-Marxist, write an anti-Communist book and translate it into English for publication in the United States.

Buckley left the CIA after his year in Mexico and embarked upon a long and distinguished career as the foremost intellectual spokesman for political conservatism in America. He founded the *National Review*, wrote several books attacking liberalism and expounding the conservative point of view, hosted a television interview program, wrote a syndicated newspaper column, and founded the New York Conservative Party, on whose ticket he ran unsuccessfully for mayor of New York City in 1965. His brother James is the former Conservative Party senator from New York.

Since 1976 Buckley has written a series of commercially successful spy novels centering on the exploits of a fictional CIA officer, Blackford Oakes.

(*Current Biography*, 1982; *Who's Who in America*, 42nd edition; Hunt, *Undercover*.)

BUFFUM, ROBERT (ca. 1830–June 20, 1871): soldier, Union secret agent

A native of Massachusetts, Buffum emigrated to Kansas circa 1836 and fought on the anti-slavery side in the Border War in that territory in the late 1850s. Shortly after the outbreak of the Civil War, he enlisted as a private in the Ohio Volunteer Infantry, which was part of the Army of the Ohio.

In April 1862 Buffum volunteered to take part in a paramilitary operation behind Confederate lines aimed at severing the rail line between Atlanta and Chattanooga (see ANDREWS'S RAID). He and a party of twenty other Union troops in civilian clothes, led by JAMES J. ANDREWS, hijacked a locomotive and attempted to destroy railroad tracks and bridges between the two cities. He was captured by Confederate troops and imprisoned (Andrews and seven of the others were hanged). He and five others escaped, were recaptured, and exchanged for Confederate prisoners of war in March 1863. Buffum and the others were awarded the newly created Medal of Honor by Secretary of War Edwin Stanton, the first Americans to receive that decoration.

After the war Buffum killed a man in Orange County, New York, over what he regarded as disrespect for the memory of President Lincoln. He was sentenced to life imprisonment and sent to a hospital for the criminally insane, where he killed himself.

(Bryan, *The Spy in America*; Boatner, *Civil War Dictionary*; O'Neill, *Wild Train*.)

BULL, HAROLD ROE (January 6, 1893–November 1, 1976): army officer, intelligence officer

A native of Springfield, Massachusetts, Bull graduated from the United States Military Academy in 1914. He served in France with the Allied Expeditionary Force during the First World War. Later he served in Hawaii, taught at the Infantry School, and served on the War Department's General Staff.

At the outbreak of the Second World War, Bull was professor of military science and tactics at the Culver Military Academy in Culver, Indiana. During the war he served with the War Department General Staff, with the Allied Forces Headquarters in North Africa, as commander of the Third Corps, and as General Eisenhower's assistant chief of staff in London. He was the Army's chief of civil defense during 1947–58 as well as commandant of the National War College.

During the early 1950s Bull served on the Board of National Estimates of the Central Intelligence Agency (see NATIONAL INTELLIGENCE ESTIMATE). His objectivity and skill in handling evidence on military subjects won him respect as an outstanding contributor to the Board.

(*Who's Who in America*, v.24; *New York Times*, November 5, 1976, p. A23; Cline, *The CIA: Reality vs. Myth*.)

BULLOCH, JAMES DUNWODY (June 25, 1823–January 7, 1901): naval officer and Confederate secret service agent

Born near Savannah, Georgia, Bulloch entered the U.S. Navy in 1839 and saw sea duty aboard several ships. From 1849 to 1851 he served with the Coast Survey, then commanded the *Georgia* on mail service. He left the Navy with the rank of lieutenant and was master of a private mail and passenger steamship when the Civil War began. On May 9, 1861 he was commissioned as an agent of the Confederate Navy and sent to England to obtain arms and arrange for the purchase and construction of warships. Despite the efforts of HENRY SHELTON SANFORD, chief of the Northern secret service in Europe, Bulloch succeeded in departing England in command of the *Fingal* with a cargo of arms and ammunition, and in running the blockade of Savannah.

He returned to England in 1862 and arranged for the Confederate acquisition of several cruisers, including the *Florida* and *Alabama* (the latter destined for a spectacular career raiding Northern shipping). He made arrangements for the acquisition of two powerful ironclad men-of-war known as the "Laird Rams," from the shipbuilding firm of that name, but Sanford forced the British authorities to block the sale. Further pressure brought on the British by the U.S. government forced Bulloch to move his operations to Paris in 1863, where he continued to function as chief of the Confederate secret service in Europe for the duration of the war. After the war he entered the mercantile business in Liverpool, England.

James D. Bulloch. Source: Author's collection.

Bulloch lived to see his nephew, Theodore Roosevelt, elected vice-president of the United States in 1900. His half-sister, Martha Bulloch, was Roosevelt's mother.

(Bulloch, *The Secret Service of the Confederate States in Europe*; Monaghan, *Diplomat in Carpet Slippers*; Owsley, "Henry Shelton Sanford and Federal Surveillance Abroad"; *WAMB*).

BUNCHE, RALPH JOHNSON (August 7, 1904–December 9, 1971): anthropologist, educator, diplomat, intelligence analyst

A native of Detroit, Michigan, Bunche graduated from UCLA in 1927, and received master's and doctorate degrees from Harvard in 1928 and 1934, respectively. He taught political science at UCLA, Howard University, and Swarthmore College. In 1941 he joined the OSS RESEARCH AND ANALYSIS BRANCH as senior social science analyst in charge of research on Africa and other colonial areas. He served as deputy chief, then chief, of the Branch's Near East-Africa section. Between 1944 and 1947 he served with the Department of State. Later he was a professor of government at Harvard University, and held a wide variety of diplomatic positions with the U.S. government and the United Nations. In 1950 he was awarded the Nobel Peace Prize.

BUNDY, WILLIAM PUTNAM (September 24, 1917–): foreign policy and defense specialist, intelligence officer

A native of Washington, D.C., Bundy grew up in Boston, attended the Groton School, graduated from Yale University in 1939, and earned a master's degree in history from Harvard University in 1940. After serving in the U.S. Army Signal Corps during the Second World War (he was discharged with the rank of major after having been awarded the Legion of Merit and a British decoration), he returned to Harvard and earned a law degree in 1947. He was admitted to the Washington, D.C., bar and practiced law for three years. In 1951 he joined the Central Intelligence Agency.

Bundy became an intelligence analyst in the CIA's Office of National Estimates (see NATIONAL INTELLIGENCE ESTIMATE). In 1953 he was made special assistant to the deputy director for intelligence, ROBERT AMORY. In the course of a background check for a special security clearance required for the new position, the Federal Bureau of Investigation turned up the fact that he had years before contributed to a fund for the defense of Alger Hiss (Bundy had already disclosed this before joining the CIA. See WHITTAKER CHAMBERS for background on the Hiss case.) This information found its way into the hands of Senator Joseph McCarthy, who promptly included the CIA in his search for Communists within the U.S. government. (McCarthy's appetite was undoubtedly whetted by the fact that Bundy was the son-in-law of his bête noire, former Secretary of State Dean Acheson.) McCarthy's attack on Bundy was thwarted by the resolute opposition of ALLEN DULLES, but the incident had a chilling effect on the liberal atmosphere that had previously prevailed within the CIA. The new self-scrutiny that ensued within the Agency led to the expulsion of some CIA employees and the unpleasant inquisition of others (see CORD MEYER).

In 1960 Bundy took a leave of absence from the CIA to serve on President Eisenhower's Commission on National Goals, and in 1961 President Kennedy appointed him deputy to the assistant secretary of defense for international security affairs. Bundy succeeded to the assistant secretary post in 1963. In 1964 President Johnson appointed him assistant secretary of state for far eastern affairs. In that capacity he became one of the principal architects of and spokes-

men for the Johnson administration's policies in Southeast Asia.

Bundy's brother, McGeorge Bundy, also served in the Johnson administration and, as special assistant to the President for national security, he also played a major role in formulating American policy in Southeast Asia.

(*Current Biography*, 1964; Mosley, *Dulles*; Smith, *OSS*.)

BUREAU OF INTELLIGENCE AND RESEARCH (INR)

The intelligence component of the Department of State. Commonly referred to as "INR" within the government, the Bureau was established in 1957 as a successor to earlier intelligence organizations in the State Department (see STATE DEPARTMENT INTELLIGENCE).

Since 1963 the director of INR has held the rank of assistant secretary of state. The Bureau is located entirely in Washington, has no overseas stations or bases, and conducts no covert operations. It receives reports from U.S. diplomats abroad, raw and finished intelligence from the Central Intelligence Agency and other member agencies of the INTELLIGENCE COMMUNITY, but its own intelligence collection activity is limited to open sources, e.g., the press. It is responsible for disseminating intelligence to the appropriate units of the State Department, producing finished political and economic intelligence bearing directly on the formulation of foreign policy, producing CURRENT INTELLIGENCE for use by the Department and the White House, and coordinating with the CIA such matters as State Department COVER for CIA operations and personnel overseas. The Bureau takes part in the production of NATIONAL INTELLIGENCE ESTIMATEs, and the director represents the State Department on the NATIONAL FOREIGN INTELLIGENCE BOARD.

The second ranking officer in INR is the deputy assistant secretary for intelligence and research, who is responsible for the Office of the Executive Director—the general administrative element of the Bureau—and the Office of Intelligence Support, the branch of the Bureau that receives, processes, and disseminates intelligence.

There are three major organizational divisions of INR, each the responsibility of a deputy assistant secretary: Coordination, Current Analysis, and Assessments and Research. Coordination involves such matters as official cover for personnel of other U.S. intelligence agencies, proposals from other agencies for covert operations abroad, liaison with the representatives of some foreign intelligence services, and requests for biographical and other data originating outside of the State Department.

Current Analysis is primarily concerned with producing intelligence with an immediate bearing on foreign policy making. The organization is comprised of six offices corresponding to major geographical areas, and a seventh that specializes in politico-military analysis.

Assessments and Research is concerned with longer range analytical studies concerning political, economic, demographic, and other trends expected to have important foreign policy implications.

(Ransom, *The Intelligence Establishment*; Richelson, *The U.S. Intelligence Community*; Hilsman, *To Move a Nation*.)

BUREAU OF MILITARY INFORMATION

The intelligence service of the federal forces in the eastern theater of the Civil War (i.e., the Army of the Potomac and, after Grant took command, the conglomerate of forces known as the Armies Operating Against Richmond) during 1863–65. After President Lincoln dismissed Gen. George B. McClellan from the command of the Army of the Potomac in November 1862, Allan Pinkerton's tenure as the Army's intelligence chief came to an end. He departed, taking his force of private detectives and secret agents with him. Only JOHN C. BABCOCK remained, serving as a one-man secret service for McClellan's successor, Gen. Ambrose Burnside.

Gen. Joseph Hooker, who replaced Burnside in January 1863, appointed Col. GEORGE H. SHARPE

Bureau of Military Information, Army of the Potomac. Left to right: Gen. George H. Sharpe, John C. Babcock, unidentified man, and Col. John McEntee. Source: Library of Congress.

as his deputy provost marshal and put him in charge of reestablishing an intelligence service for the Army of the Potomac. The unit was known as the Bureau of Military Information. Under Sharpe, the Bureau became an effective positive intelligence agency (see INTELLIGENCE TAXONOMY) and grew to a strength of seventy scouts and agents, retaining that strength for the duration of the war. Babcock served as Sharpe's deputy, and Capt. John McEntee was Sharpe's principal assistant.

The Bureau was soon functioning as a truly modern intelligence service, collecting information from all possible sources—prisoners of war, Confederate deserters and refugees, Southern newspapers (see NEWSPAPERS IN THE CIVIL WAR), the Army of the Potomac's balloon corps (see RECONNAISSANCE BALLOONS), Signal Corps observation posts, communication intercepts (see WIRETAPPING AND COMMUNICATIONS INTELLIGENCE IN THE CIVIL WAR), liaison with other commands, as well as from the spies and informers who worked for the Bureau behind Confederate lines. The Bureau collated, analyzed, and digested this flow of information, and produced an intelligence product that was reliable and easily understood by Hooker and the other commanders.

One of the first major tests of the Bureau came in the Chancellorsville Campaign (April–May, 1863), when Hooker successfully enveloped Lee's army at Fredericksburg, one of the most brilliant strategic coups of the war. Historians have credited the success to good planning, but Fishel discovered that intelligence provided by the Bureau of Military Information probably was the basis of Hooker's march to the enemy rear.

In June 1863, when Gen. Robert E. Lee made his second attempt to take the war into the North, the Bureau's scouts and other sources located and followed the individual components of the Confederate force as it crossed the Potomac and advanced into Pennsylvania, and they provided Sharpe, Hooker, and Gen. George Meade (who replaced Hooker as commander of the Army of the Potomac on June 28th) detailed reports of Confederate strengths, dispositions, and movements of troops before and during the Battle of Gettysburg (July 1–3, 1863).

After Gettysburg, Sharpe's Bureau became well known and highly regarded by other Union commanders. In October Gen. William S. Rosecrans, commander of the Army of the Cumberland, asked Meade to have the Bureau keep him informed of all Confederate movements in the Tennessee combat area. And when Gen. Ulysses S. Grant took overall command of the Union Army in March 1864, he arranged for Sharpe to join his staff (Babcock became

Meade's intelligence officer). The Bureau continued to function as a unit, however, serving both Meade and Grant (the latter had taken the field with the Army of the Potomac).

When Grant began his siege of Petersburg and Richmond in the final phase of the war, the Bureau took over direction of the Union espionage network run by ELIZABETH VAN LEW in Richmond.

After the war the Bureau of Military Information was dissolved.

(Fishel, "The Mythology of Civil War Intelligence"; Schmidt, "G-2, Army of the Potomac"; Bidwell, "History of the Military Intelligence Division, Department of the Army General Staff.")

BURKE, MICHAEL (June 8, 1918–February 5, 1987): sports and television executive, covert operations officer

Burke was born in Enfield, Connecticut, but while he was still an infant his father moved the family to his native County Galway, Ireland. Burke spent his boyhood in Galway, but the family returned to Connecticut several years later and settled in Hartford. He attended Kingswood Prep school in West Hartford, graduating in 1935, and in 1939 he graduated from the University of Pennsylvania. He worked for an insurance company as a marine cargo inspector on the New York waterfront until 1942, when he was commissioned an ensign in the U.S. Naval Reserve and assigned to the Office of Strategic Services.

Burke was placed in the OSS SPECIAL OPERATIONS BRANCH. In 1943 he took part in an operation, code-named MacGregor, in which an advance undercover team led by JOHN M. SHAHEEN infiltrated German-held Italy in an attempt to persuade the anti-Nazi commander of the Italian Navy to surrender his fleet when the Allies landed in Salerno. The MacGregor project failed to achieve its original objective because, unknown to the OSS, negotiations between the Italian admiral and the Allies were already under way. However, Burke and his teammates were successful in achieving a secondary objective: they smuggled a group of Italian weapons specialists out of Italy and back to Washington. The group included Italian scientist Dr. Carlo Calosi and Adm. Eugenio Minisini, both of whom had been instrumental in the development of the Italian SIC torpedo, a very deadly magnetic-activated device developed at the Italian torpedo works at Baia. Calosi, Minisini, and the rest of the exfiltrated Italian team were turned over to Dr. STANLEY LOVELL of the OSS RESEARCH AND DEVELOPMENT BRANCH, who arranged to have them work at the U.S. Navy's torpedo station at Newport, Rhode Island, to develop countermeasures against the SIC torpedo.

The following year Burke was a member of a JED-BURGH OPERATION team that parachuted into the Vosges Mountains of German-occupied France to coordinate the work of the French Resistance with the Allied landings at Normandy. He was awarded the Navy Cross, the Silver Star, and the French Medaille de la Resistance for his service in the OSS.

COREY FORD and Alistair MacBain chronicled Burke's OSS adventures in *Cloak and Dagger,* their 1946 book on the OSS. The book was made into a motion picture of the same title. Gary Cooper played Burke, who served as technical advisor on the production. Burke remained in Hollywood for several years as a screenwriter for Warner Brothers.

Burke was one of the veteran OSS covert operations officers recruited by the recently created Central Intelligence Agency in 1949. He was assigned to the Eastern European Division of the Office of Policy Coordination (as the Agency's COVERT ACTION group was then called). Together with division chief FRANK LINDSAY and his deputy, JOHN BROSS, Burke participated in the ALBANIA OPERATION, an unsuccessful attempt to overthrow the Communist regime of Enver Hoxha in Albania.

Burke left the CIA in 1954 and was hired by HENRY RINGLING NORTH, an OSS veteran and fellow member of the MacGregor team, to manage his family's Ringling Brothers Barnum and Bailey Circus. In 1956 Burke was hired by Columbia Broadcasting System president Frank Stanton to serve as president of CBS's European branch. In 1962 Burke was made vice-president of development at CBS, and brought about the network's acquisition of several nonbroadcasting businesses, including the New York Yankees baseball team in 1964. Burke became president and chairman of the board of the Yankees in 1966 and held that position until 1973, when he became president of Madison Square Garden Center. He retired in 1981.

(Burke, *Outrageous Good Fortune; Current Biography,* 1972; *Who's Who in America,* 42nd ed.; Smith, *OSS;* Hymoff, *The OSS in World War II;* Lovell, *Of Spies and Stratagems;* obituary, *New York Times,* February 7, 1987, p. 10.)

BURNHAM, JAMES (November 22, 1905–July 28, 1987): journalist, writer, intelligence officer

A native of Chicago, Illinois, Burnham graduated from Princeton University in 1927 and earned a B.A. and M.A. from Oxford University in 1929 and 1932, respectively. From 1929 to 1953 he was a professor of philosophy at New York University. He was a prominent American Communist of the Trotskyist faction, editing the Trotskyist journal *New International.* In 1940 he broke with Communism and gradually moved to the political right.

Burnham's knowledge of domestic and foreign Communist organizations and his extensive contacts in Europe were of value to the Central Intelligence Agency, to which he served as a consultant during the early 1950s. He advised the Office of Policy Coordination, as the Agency's COVERT ACTION unit was then called (see CENTRAL INTELLIGENCE AGENCY), on a wide variety of matters.

In 1955 Burnham joined the staff of the *National Review,* the conservative periodical founded by WILLIAM F. BUCKLEY, as one of the original members of its editorial board. During his long association with the magazine he was a regular contributor to its pages.

(*Political Profiles: Eisenhower Years;* Hunt, *Undercover;* obituary, *New York Times,* July 30, 1987.)

BUSH, GEORGE HERBERT WALKER (June 12, 1924–): businessman, diplomat, congressman, vice-president of the United States, intelligence officer

A native of Milton, Massachusetts, Bush served in the U.S. Navy as a naval aviator during the Second World War. He was discharged with the rank of lieutenant (jg.), having been awarded the Distinguished Flying Cross and three Air Medals.

Bush graduated from Yale University in 1948. He was co-founder and director of the Zapata Petroleum Corporation in 1953–59 and president of the Zapata Off Shore Corporation in 1956–64. He served as congressman from the Seventh District of Texas in the 90th and 91st Congresses. He was U.S. ambassador to the United Nations in 1971–72; chairman of the Republican National Committee in 1973–74; and chief of the U.S. Liaison Office in Peking, China, in 1974–75.

In January 1976 President Gerald Ford appointed Bush director of central intelligence, to succeed WILLIAM E. COLBY in that position. He is credited with helping to institute reforms in the Central Intelligence Agency begun by Colby, and restoring the morale and public confidence in the Agency following the adverse publicity resulting from the congressional investigations of the intelligence community. Bush left the post of DCI in January 1977 when President Jimmy Carter appointed Adm. STANSFIELD TURNER to succeed him.

George Bush—oil portrait by C.L. MacNelly. Source: Central Intelligence Agency.

Bush was Ronald Reagan's running mate and was elected vice-president of the United States in 1980 and reelected to that office in 1984.

(*Who's Who in America,* 42nd ed.; Cline, *CIA: Reality vs. Myth.*)

BUXTON, G. EDWARD (May 13, 1880–March 15, 1949): journalist, manufacturer, intelligence officer

A native of Kansas City, Missouri, Buxton graduated from Brown University in 1902, worked briefly as a reporter for the *Providence* (Rhode Island) *Journal,* and received an LL.B. degree from Harvard University in 1906. During the First World War he served initially as a correspondent in France, Germany, and Belgium, and later as an infantry officer, receiving a Purple Heart and other decorations.

After the war Buxton worked as an executive in the textile industry, and was prominent in the Republican Party in Rhode Island. Early in 1942 Gen. WILLIAM J. DONOVAN recruited him to serve as his assistant director in the Office of Strategic Services. As Donovan's second in command, he was responsible for the central administrative staff of OSS. In July 1945 he resigned because of illness. After the Second World War he sat on the boards of directors of Fruit of the Loom, Inc. and several other companies.

(Roosevelt, *War Report of the OSS; Who Was Who in America,* vol. 2.)

C

CABELL, CHARLES PEARRE (October 11, 1903–May 25, 1971): air force officer, intelligence officer

A native of Dallas, Texas, Cabell graduated from the U.S. Military Academy in 1925 and from the Army Air Corps pilot training program in 1931. After commanding a combat wing of the Eighth Air Force in Europe, he held several air intelligence posts in 1944 and 1945. He had already been director of air force intelligence in 1948 and served with the Joint Chiefs of Staff, when President Eisenhower appointed him deputy director of the CIA in 1953 on the recommendation of Gen. WALTER BEDELL SMITH. According to some accounts, the appointment was made in order to offset and balance the administrative weaknesses of the new director of the agency, ALLEN DULLES. Cabell served as DDCI throughout Dulles's term as director. He was forced out in 1962 as part of the top-level ''house-cleaning'' following the BAY OF PIGS INVASION.

General Cabell was awarded the Distinguished Intelligence Medal upon his retirement from the CIA. He had earlier been awarded the Distinguished Service Medal, the Distinguished Flying Cross, the Legion of Merit and the Bronze Star.

(*Who Was Who in America*, v.6; Corson, *Armies of Ignorance*.)

CALDWELL, WILLIAM B.: intelligence officer

Caldwell, who served in the Federal Bureau of Investigation as a special agent during 1941–46, was one of the FBI agents with a background in Latin American intelligence work recruited by J. C. KING into the Central Intelligence Agency in the late 1940s.

Caldwell served in the Western Hemisphere Division of the CIA CLANDESTINE SERVICE and was

Gen. Charles P. Cabell. Source: U.S. Air Force.

chief of station in Havana in 1959 when Fidel Castro came to power. He was subsequently transferred to the Far East Division and served as deputy chief of the Manila station.

(Smith, *Portrait of a Cold Warrior*.)

CARACRISTI, ANN Z. (February 1, 1921–): journalist, cryptologist, intelligence officer

A native of Bronxville, New York, Caracristi graduated from Russell Sage College in 1942 and went to work as a cryptanalyst for the Army Security Agency (see ARMY INTELLIGENCE) the same year. After the war she worked briefly as a journalist before returning to the ASA. She remained with the Agency when it was merged into the Armed Forces Security Agency in 1949 and continued with the successor NATIONAL SECURITY AGENCY in 1952. In 1959 she became chief of NSA's Office of SIGINT research.

In 1972 Caracristi became deputy chief of NSA's A Group, which is responsible for all cryptanalysis of the Soviet Union and its satellite countries. She became chief of the unit in 1975. In 1980 she was appointed deputy director of the NSA, the senior civilian post in that agency. She held the post until her retirement in 1982.

(*Who's Who in America*, 37th ed.; Bamford, *The Puzzle Palace*.)

CARLUCCI, FRANK CHARLES, 3RD (October 18, 1930–): diplomat, government official, intelligence officer

A native of Scranton, Pennsylvania, Carlucci graduated from Princeton University in 1952. During 1952–54 he served in the U.S. Naval Reserve and was discharged with the rank of lieutenant (jg.). He did postgraduate work at the Harvard University School of Business Administration in 1956.

Carlucci joined the U.S. Department of State as a foreign service officer in 1956. He served as vice-consul and economic officer in Johannesburg, South Africa, during 1957–59; was second secretary and political officer in Kinshasa, Congo (now Zaire), in 1960–62; was officer in charge of Congolese political affairs, 1962–64; served as consul general in Zanzibar (Tanzania) in 1964–65; and as counselor for political affairs in Rio de Janeiro, Brazil, in 1965–69.

Carlucci was appointed assistant director for operations in the Office of Economic Opportunity in 1969, and served as director of operations in 1970–71. He served in the Office of Management and Budget as associate director and deputy director in 1971–72, and was under secretary of health, educa-

tion and welfare in 1974–75. During 1975–78 he was U.S. ambassador to Portugal.

In 1978 Carlucci was invited to assume the post of deputy director of central intelligence by Central Intelligence Agency Director Adm. STANSFIELD TURNER. Turner who had had serious differences with the two previous incumbents, E. HENRY KNOCHE and JOHN F. BLAKE, wanted someone for the job who was not a veteran intelligence officer, and hoped that an "outsider" like Carlucci could help him institute his program for administrative reform within the Agency. Carlucci accepted the position and became DDCI in February 1978.

During his tenure Carlucci succeeded in increasing the centralization of Agency management and putting through other changes ordered by Turner, but before Turner's entire program could be accomplished, the newly inaugurated President Reagan replaced Turner and Carlucci with WILLIAM J. CASEY and Adm. BOBBY R. INMAN in January and February, 1981, respectively.

After leaving the CIA Carlucci was appointed deputy secretary of defense. In December 1986 President Reagan appointed him assistant to the President for national security affairs. In 1987 Carlucci became secretary of defense.

(*Who's Who in America*, 42nd ed.; Turner, *Secrecy and Democracy*.)

CARRINGTON, HENRY BEEBEE (March 2, 1824–October 26, 1912): lawyer, writer, Army officer, intelligence officer

A native of Wallingford, Connecticut, Carrington graduated from Yale University in 1845. He taught at the Irving Institute at Tarrytown, New York, and later at the New Haven Collegiate Institute.

He studied at the Yale Law School and, in 1848, moved to Columbus, Ohio, where he practiced law and was active in the local Republican Party. In 1857 he was asked by his friend, Gov. Salmon P. Chase, to reorganize the Ohio state militia. His success in this task led to his appointment as adjutant general. At the outbreak of the Civil War Carrington's swift action in organizing the militia in response to President Lincoln's call for troops, and in dispatching his units to West Virginia, was instrumental in keeping that state from joining the Confederacy. Shortly afterward he was commissioned as a colonel in the 18th U.S. Infantry and placed in command of the Army camp near Columbus.

He was promoted to brigadier general of volunteers in 1862 and placed in charge of recruitment in Indiana. While in that position he was requested by

Gov. Oliver P. Morton of Indiana also to undertake an investigation of the subversive activities of the Copperheads, as the anti-war wing of the Democratic Party was called. Carrington organized a small staff for this purpose and obtained evidence leading to several federal indictments. Convinced by this preliminary work that the subversion was more widespread and serious than had first been suspected, he recruited a Union soldier and clerk from the Tennessee provost marshal's office, FELIX A. STIDGER, to work undercover and penetrate the KNIGHTS OF THE GOLDEN CIRCLE, a Copperhead secret society.

From Stidger's reports during the spring and summer of 1864, Carrington learned of the NORTHWEST CONSPIRACY, an ambitious COVERT ACTION operation. Through it Confederate secret service agents based in Canada planned to use the Sons of Liberty (the successor organization to the Knights of the Golden Circle) to foment revolution, overthrow the governments of Indiana, Illinois, and Ohio, and split those states off from the Union to form a Northwest Confederacy that would be allied with the Confederacy against the Union. The intelligence Carrington supplied to the local authorities and Washington resulted in measures that thwarted this conspiracy and led to the arrest of the conspirators.

Carrington presided over a military court that tried and convicted the conspirators, but the U.S. Supreme Court overruled his decisions in a landmark case (*Ex parte Milligan*, 1866). The Court held that President Lincoln, who had authorized Carrington to try the conspirators, did not have the power to establish military tribunals to try civilians except in an actual theater of war where civil courts were no longer functioning.

After the war Carrington rejoined his regular Army regiment and served in the Western territories. He was severely wounded in the Red Cloud War, and later established friendly relations with the Indians. He subsequently taught military science at Wabash College and negotiated a treaty with the Flathead Indians of Montana in 1889.

While teaching at Tarrytown, New York, after his graduation from Yale in 1845, Carrington had met and befriended Washington Irving, who encouraged his interest and research in the American Revolution. Carrington never abandoned this early interest, and, in 1876, published *Battles of the American Revolution*. He also wrote a biography of George Washington and several other books on such varied subjects as the American Indians, Russia, and the mineral resources of Indiana.

(*DAB*; Boatner, *Civil War Dictionary*; Horan, *Confederate Agent*.)

Gen. Henry B. Carrington. Source: National Archives.

CARROLL, JOSEPH FRANCIS (March 19, 1910–): FBI agent, security specialist, Air Force officer, DIA director

A native of Chicago, Illinois, Carroll graduated from St. Mary's College in 1933 and from Loyola University law school in 1940.

Carroll joined the Federal Bureau of Investigation in 1940, served as a special agent in Tennessee, Illinois, and Washington, D.C., and became administrative assistant to FBI director J. EDGAR HOOVER in 1947. That same year Hoover lent Carroll to the newly established U.S. Air Force to organize and direct an Air Force security and investigation division. In order to serve in this capacity, Carroll was given a temporary commission of colonel in the Air Force Reserve.

Carroll established and organized the Air Force's Office of Special Investigations (see AIR FORCE INTELLIGENCE), serving as its first director. He was promoted to the temporary rank of major general in 1950, and later that year was made Air Force deputy inspector general for security. He also directed the Office of the Provost Marshal and continued to head the Office of Special Investigations. In 1954 he was granted the permanent rank of brigadier general in the regular Air Force.

In 1958 Carroll was made deputy commander of the United States Air Forces in Europe, and the following year became chief of staff for Europe. In 1960 he was promoted to the rank of lieutenant general and made inspector general of the Air Force, and in September of that year he led the investigation of the defection to the USSR of two cryptologists from the NATIONAL SECURITY AGENCY, WILLIAM H. MARTIN and BERNON F. MITCHELL.

In 1961 Carroll was made director of the newly established DEFENSE INTELLIGENCE AGENCY. He held that post until his retirement in 1968.

(*Current Biography*, 1962; *Who's Who in America*, 37th ed.)

CARTER, JOHN FRANKLIN, JR. (April 27, 1897–November 27, 1967): journalist, writer, diplomat, intelligence officer

A native of Fall River, Massachusetts, Franklin attended St. Mark's School in Southboro, Massachusetts, and graduated from Yale University in 1920. He was employed by the U.S. Department of State and served at the American embassies in Rome and Constantinople (Istanbul) in 1918–19. He was the private secretary to the American ambassador in Rome during 1920–21. In 1922 he worked as the Rome correspondent for the *London Daily Chronicle,* and the following year he joined the staff of the *New York Times.*

In 1928 Carter left the *Times* to rejoin the State Department, serving as an economics specialist in the Western Europe Division. After a tour with State's Far Eastern Division he resigned from the State Department in 1932 to work as a free-lance writer and journalist, and as Washington correspondent for *Liberty* magazine.

Beginning in 1923 Carter published a series of books on politics, government, and foreign affairs. His 1934 work, *The New Dealers,* was favorable to the administration of President Franklin Delano Roosevelt, to whom Carter became a close friend and confidant. After a tour as a senior official with the Department of Agriculture in 1934–36, he began a syndicated daily newspaper column, "We the People," under the pseudonym Jay Franklin.

Sometime shortly before the Second World War, Carter began to run a small quasi-official intelligence service for President Roosevelt. Carter continued to run the service during the war and sought to establish it as a permanent peacetime intelligence agency. General WILLIAM J. DONOVAN had a similar proposal through which he hoped to establish the Office of Strategic Services as the country's postwar central intelligence agency (see CENTRAL INTELLIGENCE AGENCY); Carter warned Roosevelt against Donovan, alleging that the OSS had been "penetrated" by British intelligence. After President Truman succeeded Roosevelt, he dismissed Carter's proposal and dispensed with the services of Carter's intelligence network.

Carter continued writing his newspaper column until 1948. He was a prolific author of both fiction and nonfiction books, written under his own name and several pseudonyms. During the 1930s, under the pseudonym "Diplomat," he wrote seven book-length mystery stories with diplomatic or Washington settings, among them *Murder in the State Department* and *The Brain Trust Murder.*

(*Current Biography*, 1941, 1968; Troy, *Donovan and the CIA.*)

CARTER, MARSHALL SYLVESTER (September 16, 1909–): Army officer, intelligence officer

A native of Fort Monroe, Virginia, Carter graduated from the U.S. Military Academy in 1931 and earned an M.S. degree from the Massachusetts Institute of Technology in 1936. He was attached to the War Department General Staff between 1942 and 1945, and served in China in 1945. From 1947 to 1949, he was a special assistant to the Secretary of State and went on to become minister at the U.S. embassy in London in 1949–50.

Carter served tours in Japan, Alaska, Korea, and the continental United States until 1962 when he was appointed deputy director of the Central Intelligence Agency. He served in that capacity during JOHN MCCONE's term as director of central intelligence. In 1965 he left the CIA to become director of the NATIONAL SECURITY AGENCY. He held that position until 1969, when he retired with the rank of lieutenant general. Under Carter the NSA established an identity of its own and a degree of independence from the Department of Defense.

Carter's decorations include the Distinguished Intelligence Medal, the Distinguished Service Medal, the Legion of Merit, and the Bronze Star.

(*Who's Who in America*, 42nd ed.; Bamford, *The Puzzle Palace.*)

CARVER, GEORGE A., JR. (ca. 1930–): intelligence officer

Carver spent his childhood in China, where his father was chairman of the English Department of the University of Shanghai. He graduated from Yale University. In 1962 he joined the Central Intelligence Agency and served in the Far East Division. From 1966 to 1973 he was the special assistant to the director for Vietnamese affairs. In this capacity he was pessimistic regarding United States involvement in the VIET-NAM WAR. Two assessments of the military and political situation prepared under his supervision in August 1966 and May 1967 seemed to suggest that the war was unwinnable and was being clumsily prosecuted, and that the bombing of North Vietnam was having little effect on the Communists ability to fight the war. However, Carver's pessimism later diminished, and in 1967 he found himself at odds with most other CIA analysts studying the question.

In the CIA-Army Intelligence dispute in 1967 regarding the Vietcong and North Vietnamese troop strength figures to be used in a NATIONAL INTELLIGENCE ESTIMATE, Carver tended to adopt the Army view that the local Vietcong self-defense forces did not represent a significant component of Communist strength. In 1984 he testified as a witness for the plaintiff in a libel suit filed by Gen. William Westmoreland against both CBS and former CIA analyst Samuel A. Adams over a CBS documentary about this controversy.

Carver retired from the CIA in 1979. He has since been a senior fellow at Georgetown University's Center for Strategic and International Studies, and is the president of C&S Associates, a consulting firm he founded.

(Powers, *The Man Who Kept the Secrets*; Halberstam, *The Best and the Brightest*; *New York Times*, November 9, 1984, p B6.)

CASE OFFICER

An unclassified publication of the CENTRAL INTELLIGENCE AGENCY defines the term as "A professional employee of an intelligence organization who is responsible for providing direction to an agent."

See also, AGENT, STATION, and CIA CLANDESTINE SERVICE.

(Central Intelligence Agency, *Intelligence: The Acme of Skill*.)

CASEY, WILLIAM JOSEPH (March 13, 1913– May 6, 1987): lawyer, businessman, government official, intelligence officer

A native of New York City, Casey graduated from Fordham University in 1934 and earned an LL.B. from St. John's University Law School in 1937. During the Second World War he joined the U.S. Navy and was commissioned. After a period of serving as

William J. Casey—photograph by Everett Raymond Kinstler. Source: Central Intelligence Agency.

reviewer of procurement contracts in Washington, he managed to be assigned to the Office of Strategic Services. He organized the OSS headquarters secretariat, which served as a personal staff to OSS Director WILLIAM J. DONOVAN, then was sent to London to organize a similar unit for DAVID K.E. BRUCE, chief of the OSS in the European Theater of Operations. During the final two years of the war he was chief of the OSS SECRET INTELLIGENCE BRANCH in the European Theater, in which capacity he was responsible for OSS intelligence penetrations of Germany.

After the war Casey taught tax law at New York University and at the Practicing Law Institute in New York. He collaborated with tax specialist Jacob K. Lasser in writing several books on tax management and financial planning, and wrote several books on investment management. He also practiced law in New York City and Washington, D.C.

Casey was active in Republican politics, unsuccessfully seeking the Republican nomination for a seat in the House of Representatives in 1966. He took part in Richard Nixon's presidential campaign in 1968, and in 1971 President Nixon appointed him chairman of the Securities and Exchange Commission. In 1973 he was appointed undersecretary of state for economic affairs, and in 1974 he was made president and chairman of the Export-Import Bank.

In 1976 President Ford appointed Casey to the PRESIDENT'S FOREIGN INTELLIGENCE ADVISORY BOARD. During 1980 he was manager of Ronald Reagan's presidential campaign. In 1981 President Reagan appointed him director of the CENTRAL INTELLIGENCE AGENCY.

As director of Central Intelligence Casey was often a controversial figure on Capitol Hill, where there were frequent demands for his resignation. He was highly regarded by President Reagan, however, and is said to have had more influence on policymaking than most previous DCIs. Although a firm believer in the judicious use of COVERT ACTION (which had been resumed during his tenure, in such places as Afghanistan and Central America), he also took an active interest and personal involvement in the production of NATIONAL INTELLIGENCE ESTIMATES and other FINISHED INTELLIGENCE. He was highly esteemed within the CIA and the INTELLIGENCE COMMUNITY, and he did much to restore the morale and prestige of the Agency, which had been badly damaged during the term of Adm. STANSFIELD TURNER. He was considered a superior DCI by many CIA insiders, especially his former colleagues in the OSS.

In January 1987 Casey, then recovering from surgery to remove a brain tumor, resigned from his position as DCI because of his poor health. He was succeeded by WILLIAM H. WEBSTER.

A voracious reader with a special interest in history, Casey was the author of a book on the battlefields of the American Revolution, *Where and How the War Was Fought.*

(*Current Biography,* 1972; *Who's Who in America,* 42nd ed.; Persico, *Piercing the Reich;* Cline, *The CIA: Reality vs. Myth; New York Times,* February 3, 1987, p. 1.)

CASTLEMAN, JOHN BRECKINRIDGE (June 30, 1841–May 23, 1918): Confederate army officer and secret service agent

A native of Fayette County, Kentucky, Castleman was attending Transylvania College at Lexington when the CIVIL WAR began. He enlisted in the Confederate Army and was commissioned as a captain in the Kentucky cavalry of (then) Col. John Hunt Morgan (the unit better known as Morgan's Raiders). Castleman was one of several officers of that unit who went to Canada in 1864 to serve under Capt. THOMAS H. HINES in the operation known as the

NORTHWEST CONSPIRACY. He was second in command under Hines.

Castleman led the party of Confederate guerrillas who burned several Union transports at St. Louis, Missouri in September 1864, and he was captured shortly thereafter in Mattoon, Illinois by federal detectives working for Brig. Gen. HENRY B. CARRINGTON. Due to the intercession of his brother-in-law, Judge Samuel M. Breckinridge (a Kentuckian loyal to the Union), President Lincoln ordered that Castleman not be hanged. Instead he was imprisoned in solitary confinement for nine months, and then released and exiled to Canada.

After the war Castleman toured England, Scotland, and Ireland with JACOB THOMPSON. He returned to the United States after President Andrew Johnson declared an amnesty and, in 1868, graduated from the University of Louisville with an LL.B. He was associated with the Royal Insurance Company of Liverpool, England, from 1869 to 1902. He lived in Louisville, Kentucky, where he was active in Democratic politics. In 1898 Castleman was commissioned a brigadier general in the U.S. Volunteers and served in Puerto Rico during the Spanish-American War. After the war he served as adjutant general of Kentucky and he commanded state troops during the insurrection in Kentucky that followed the assassination of Governor Goebel in 1900.

In 1917 Castleman published *Active Service,* a memoir of his military career.

(*Who Was Who in America,* v.1; Horan, *Confederate Agent.*)

CENTRAL BUREAU

A joint Australian-American communications intelligence unit under the command of the U.S. Army's chief signal officer in the Southwest Pacific Theater during the SECOND WORLD WAR. The CB was established in August 1942 and included personnel of the Australian Special Wireless Group, the Royal Australian Air Force, and the U.S. Signal Intelligence Service (see ARMY INTELLIGENCE). The CB was under Brig. Gen. Spencer B. Akin, General MacArthur's chief signal officer. There were three assistant directors, Lt. Col. ABRAHAM SINKOV of SIS, Maj. A. W. Sandford of the SWG, and Wing Commander Roy Booth of the RAAF. The CB had a direct radio link with SIS headquarters in Arlington, Virginia, and Sinkov was eventually placed in overall charge of the unit.

CB detachments were assigned to all field units for operations and rapid reporting including, for a short period, the flagships of Admirals Halsey and Spruance. The COMINT collected by the CB was analyzed by a special G-2 section of MacArthur's General Headquarters.

(Powe and Wilson, *The Evolution of American Military Intelligence;* Lewin, *The American Magic;* Kahn, *The Codebreakers.*)

CENTRAL INTELLIGENCE AGENCY

General: The CIA is a part of the Executive Branch of the federal government. It reports to the President through the NATIONAL SECURITY COUNCIL (NSC). Established by the NATIONAL SECURITY ACT OF 1947, it has primary responsibility for the clandestine collection of foreign intelligence, coordination of national intelligence, and such clandestine activities as COVERT ACTION. The CIA has primary responsibilities for conducting counterintelligence abroad, and for the research and development of technical collection systems (e.g., reconnaissance satellites). It is responsible for the production of political, military, economic, biographic, sociological, and scientific and technical intelligence to meet the needs of national policymakers.

The director of central intelligence (DCI) is also the chairman of the NATIONAL FOREIGN INTELLIGENCE BOARD, a body composed of the chiefs of all other intelligence components of the federal government that, in effect, serves as a board of directors of the INTELLIGENCE COMMUNITY. The CIA supports the DCI in this function.

The CIA consists of four major directorates (i.e., major divisions, each of which is headed by a deputy director): the CIA ADMINISTRATION DIRECTORATE, the CIA CLANDESTINE SERVICE, the CIA INTELLIGENCE DIRECTORATE, and the CIA SCIENCE AND TECHNOLOGY DIRECTORATE.

Background: The seed of the Central Intelligence Agency was planted in 1943 by Gen. WILLIAM J. DONOVAN; he hoped to preserve from post-World War II demobilization the intelligence and operations apparatus he had assembled within the OFFICE OF STRATEGIC SERVICES during the war and establish it as a permanent government institution. At the request of Gen. WALTER BEDELL SMITH he wrote a report in September 1943 on the possible permanent integration of the OSS into the military establishment as a "Fourth Arm," with status equivalent to that of the Army, Navy, and Air Force. No action was immediately taken on this proposal, but in November 1944 Donovan sent a memorandum to President Roosevelt in reply to the latter's request for his suggestions regarding a postwar intelligence service.

Donovan's memorandum proposed a central intel-

Emblem of the Central Intelligence Agency. Source: Central Intelligence Agency.

ligence service reporting directly to the President. The director, whom the president would appoint, would be "advised and assisted" by an advisory board consisting of the secretaries of state, war, and the Navy, and "such other members as the President may subsequently appoint." The agency would coordinate the functions of all government intelligence components, as well as collect, evaluate, and disseminate intelligence within the government. It would be authorized to conduct "subversive operations abroad," and to perform "such other functions and duties relating to intelligence as the President from time to time may direct." It would not "conflict with or limit necessary intelligence functions within the Army, Navy, Department of State and other agencies." (In other words, the proposed agency would provide strategic national intelligence to the White House, but would not interfere in military intelligence or other specialized types of intelligence collected and used by subordinate government agencies.) It would have no police or law enforcement functions. In time of war the agency's operations would be coordinated with the military and be subject to the control of the Joint Chiefs of Staff and the commanders of the war theaters involved.

Donovan's Plan Sabotaged

Donovan's plan received a generally unfavorable and antagonistic reaction from the intelligence components of the State, War, and Navy departments, the Joint Chiefs of Staff, and the Federal Bureau of Investigation; each department was jealous of its own intelligence domain and saw the proposed central agency as an encroachment. The Joint Chiefs of Staff (JCS) responded with a counterproposal that, while endorsing the idea of a central intelligence service, provided for greater participation and control by the War and Navy departments. In February 1945, while the proposals were still under consideration, a series of newspaper reports appeared in Washington, New York, and Chicago describing the Donovan and JCS plans in great detail and characterizing them as a New Deal plot to create an "American Gestapo."

The furor resulting from the disclosure and newspaper charges caused President Roosevelt to hold the matter in abeyance for several months. He took up the Donovan proposal again in April, directing Donovan to obtain the consensus of the various government intelligence components regarding his proposed central agency in order to go forward with the plan. The President died a few days later, before any further action was taken.

The OSS Dissolved

On coming into office, President Truman showed little interest in any of the existing plans for a postwar central intelligence service, and became even less enthusiastic under the impact of the budget-cutting mood that followed the surrender of Japan in August 1945. On September 20, 1945 he signed an executive order terminating the OSS as of the following October 1st.

The OSS RESEARCH AND ANALYSIS BRANCH and the Presentation Branch (an audiovisual briefing unit) were transferred to the State Department where they formed the Interim Research and Intelligence Service, headed by Col. ALFRED MCCORMACK (see STATE DEPARTMENT INTELLIGENCE). The OSS SECRET INTELLIGENCE BRANCH, the OSS COUNTER-ESPIONAGE BRANCH, and all other remaining OSS elements not yet demobilized were transferred to the Army as the Strategic Services Unit, commanded by Gen. JOHN MAGRUDER. Donovan was relieved from active duty and he returned to private life and the practice of law.

Truman's Program

President Truman also transferred to the State Department the remnants of the Office of War Information, the OFFICE OF THE COORDINATOR OF INTER-AMERICAN AFFAIRS, and the Foreign Economic Administration, all of which had some propaganda or intelligence functions. He directed Secretary of State James F. Byrnes to "take the lead in developing a comprehensive and coordinated foreign intelligence program," which, he said, "should be done through the creation of an interdepartmental group, heading up under the State Department." However, this arrangement proved unworkable be-

cause of several political and bureaucratic obstacles (see STATE DEPARTMENT INTELLIGENCE).

The failure of the State Department to "take the lead," as Truman had directed, left the way open for the military services to do so. As part of a larger plan for the integration of the Army, Navy, and Air Force within a single government department, a proposal for a central intelligence service was drafted by Rear Adm. SIDNEY SOUERS and others in the Navy. The Navy plan was a revised version of the plan offered by the Joint Chiefs of Staff, i.e., a central agency for the coordination of intelligence, but under the control of the State, War, and Navy departments, which would also retain their own respective intelligence services.

The Central Intelligence Group

On January 22, 1946 President Truman signed a presidential directive establishing a central intelligence service much along the lines of the Navy proposal. The directive set up the National Intelligence Authority (NIA), a body comprised of the secretaries of state, war, and the Navy, plus the President's personal representative, Adm. William D. Leahy. The NIA was to "plan, develop and coordinate . . . all Federal foreign intelligence activities." The directive also established, as the NIA's operating arm, the Central Intelligence Group (CIG), a quasi-agency consisting initially of a small staff of intelligence analysts who were to coordinate intelligence gathered throughout the government. Funds and staff for the CIG were provided by the State, War, and Navy departments; the CIG had no budget of its own.

Truman's directive also established the post of director of central intelligence (DCI) who would be appointed by the President, be responsible to the NIA, and sit as a nonvoting member of the NIA. The DCI was not to be, strictly speaking, the director of the CIG. Rather, in the vague and confusing language of the directive, the CIG was to function "under [his] direction." Truman offered the director's job to Admiral Souers, who reluctantly accepted it with the stipulation that he would be free to resign and return to civilian life after six months, which, in fact, he did.

Souers was succeeded as DCI in June 1946 by Lt. Gen. HOYT S. VANDENBERG, whose personal prestige and connections (his uncle was a powerful Republican senator from Michigan) enabled him to make considerable progress in expanding the power of the CIG. He succeeded in securing a new presidential directive that enhanced the executive authority of the DCI. Under Vandenberg the CIG acquired its own budget; established the Office of Research and Evaluation (which was soon renamed the Office of Reports and Estimates), which began to conduct intelligence research and analysis; and took over the Strategic Services Unit (SSU) from the War Department. The SSU's skeletal remnants of the OSS wartime secret intelligence and counterespionage apparatus in Europe and Asia became the Office of Special Operations of the CIG. The OSS FOREIGN NATIONALITIES BRANCH became the Domestic Contact Service of the CIG. And the CIG acquired the FOREIGN BROADCAST INFORMATION SERVICE, formerly a part of the Federal Communications Commission, which had monitored Axis propaganda broadcasts during the war.

Despite these substantial gains, the CIG still remained something less than the central intelligence agency of Donovan's original conception. It was still, in the words of its general counsel, LAWRENCE R. HOUSTON, "a step-child of three separate departments," rather than "an integrated organization." At Vandenberg's insistence, Houston, his associate, John S. Warner, and Walter L. Pforzheimer, head of the CIG's Legislative Liaison Branch, prepared a draft bill for the statutory establishment of a central intelligence agency by Congress and submitted it to the White House. However, the Truman administration showed little or no enthusiasm, and no immediate action was taken on the proposed bill.

The National Security Act of 1947

In May 1947 Vandenberg moved on to the post of Air Force Chief of Staff and was followed as DCI by Rear Adm. ROSCOE H. HILLENKOETTER. Before leaving the CIG, however, Vandenberg succeeded in having the White House incorporate the central intelligence agency legislation within a bill for the unification of the armed services. The unification bill, the National Security Act of 1947, created the Department of Defense, which united the Army, Navy, and Air Force under a single cabinet-level officer, the secretary of defense. The Act also created the National Security Council, a coordination and policy planning body consisting of the President, the vice-president, and the secretaries of state and defense.

The Act established the Central Intelligence Agency under the National Security Council and made the director of central intelligence the head of the Agency. It stipulated that, in the event the DCI was selected from among the commissioned officers of the armed services, he would be freed from any obligation of obedience to the military and would exercise no military command function while serving as DCI. The Act defined the duties of the CIA as:

1 to advise the National Security Council in matters concerning such intelligence activities of the Government departments and agencies as relate to national security;

2 to make recommendations to the President through the National Security Council for the coordination of such intelligence activities of the departments and agencies of the Government as relate to national security;

3 to correlate and evaluate intelligence relating to the national security, and provide for the dissemination of such intelligence within the Government using where appropriate existing agencies and facilities: *Provided,* That the Agency shall have no police, subpena [sic], law-enforcement powers, or internal-security functions: *Provided further,* That the departments and other agencies of the Government shall continue to collect, evaluate, correlate, and disseminate departmental intelligence: *And provided further,* That the Director of Central Intelligence shall be responsible for protecting intelligence sources and methods from unauthorized disclosure;

4 to perform, for the benefit of the existing intelligence agencies, such additional services of common concern as the National Security Council determines can be more efficiently accomplished centrally;

5 to perform such other functions and duties related to intelligence affecting the national security as the National Security Council may from time to time direct.

The National Security Act was passed by Congress and was signed by President Truman on July 26, 1947. The Central Intelligence Agency came into existence formally on September 18, 1947.

The Cold War

The CIA came into being at one of the most tense moments of the postwar period, when the primary focus of American foreign policy concern was Soviet expansion in Europe. Six months earlier, in March 1947, President Truman had announced the Truman Doctrine, a policy whereby the United States would help non-Communist nations resist Communist takeover "by armed minorities or by outside pressure." The United States had sent financial aid to Greece and Turkey to help those countries combat Communist insurgency, but throughout Eastern Europe the presence of Soviet occupation forces facilitated gains by local Communist political parties. In September 1947, the same month the CIA began operations, the Soviet government established the Com-

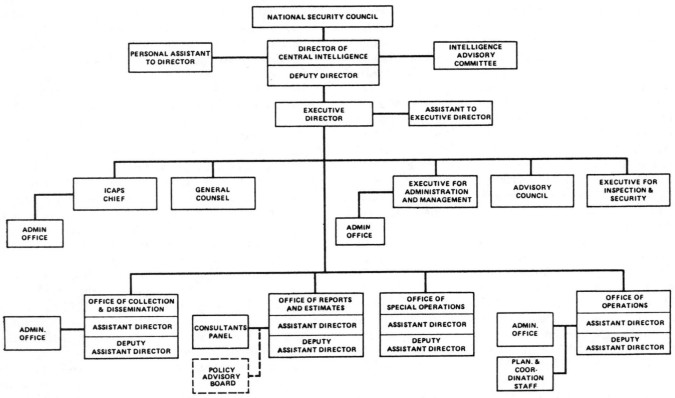

CIA organization, 1947. Source: Report of Senate Select Committee Investigating the Intelligence Community, 1976.

munist Information Bureau, or Cominform, to coordinate the activities of the local Communist parties throughout Europe. Six months later Communists staged a coup d'etat in Czechoslovakia, establishing a Soviet puppet regime in that country.

It is a measure of the tension of the times that in March 1948 Gen. Lucius D. Clay, the U.S. commander in Germany, where American and Soviet forces faced each other, cabled Washington that war might come "with dramatic suddenness" at any moment. Ten days later, a CIA intelligence estimate (containing contributions from the departments of State, Army, Navy, and Air Force) could only assure the President that war was not probable within the next sixty days.

History: At the outset the CIA was nothing more than the CIG without the awkward and unworkable management scheme that had made it "the stepchild of three separate departments." The new agency's secret intelligence apparatus still consisted of nothing but the skeletal remnants of the OSS Secret Intelligence and Counter-Espionage branches. These units formed the Office of Special Operations of the CIA. The OSO comprised a small collection of overseas assets, administered by PHILIP HORTON in

France, RICHARD HELMS in Germany, ALFRED ULMER in Austria, JAMES ANGLETON in Italy, ALBERT SEITZ in the Balkans, and JAMES KELLIS in China. In July 1949 the CIA took over responsibility for ARMY INTELLIGENCE for the Gehlen Organization, the surviving portion of German wartime military intelligence commanded by Gen. Reinhard Gehlen, which still maintained extensive assets in Eastern Europe.

Intelligence Analysis

The fledgling CIA's research and analysis was centered in the Office of Reports and Estimates (ORE), which consisted of a staff of analysts specialized by geographical area and a staff of editors who compiled the CIA's intelligence publications. Much of ORE's activity was directed into preparing a daily current intelligence report for the President. The daily report was compiled and written by R. JACK SMITH. RAY S. CLINE, then an analyst with ORE's Global Survey Division (headed by LUDWELL LEE MONTAGUE), produced a monthly report for the National Security Council entitled, "Estimate of the World Situation," a compilation of items selected from the daily reports and others supplied by the regional desks of ORE. The few NATIONAL INTELLIGENCE ESTIMATES that were prepared were done by the Global Survey Division (a three-man staff consisting of Cline, Montague, and Deforest Van Slick) and coordinated through the Intelligence Advisory Committee (see NATIONAL FOREIGN INTELLIGENCE BOARD), a body made up the chiefs of the armed services intelligence units, the State Department's Office of Intelligence and Research, and representatives of the Federal Bureau of Investigation and the Atomic Energy Commission. The production of national estimates was a slow and cumbersome process; the first estimate on the USSR took two years to complete. The early national estimates were criticized for tending to focus on short-term, narrowly defined problems and for being too noncommittal or containing too many dissenting footnotes (the last two defects resulted from the difficulty in achieving a consensus of the member agencies of the Intelligence Advisory Committee).

The CIA came under criticism in Congress and elsewhere in April 1948 after Communist-inspired rioting in Bogotá, Colombia, disrupted the Ninth Inter-American Conference, a diplomatic meeting of western hemisphere nations attended by an American delegation headed by Secretary of State George C. Marshall. However, in defense of the CIA, Adm. Hillenkoetter made public CIA dispatches forecasting the incident weeks in advance and charged that the warnings had been withheld from Marshall by State Department personnel.

Hillenkoetter again defended the CIA two years later against charges that it had failed to forecast the North Korean invasion of South Korea in June 1950 (see KOREAN WAR). He pointed out that the Agency had been accurately reporting for almost a year that the North Koreans were building their military strength to the point where they were capable of such an attack. But apparently the CIA reports had not been sufficiently emphatic to alert the National Security Council to the danger.

The Bedell Smith Reforms

This intelligence failure, and a general displeasure with the CIA's performance under Hillenkoetter, led President Truman to replace him with Gen. WALTER BEDELL SMITH in October 1950. Smith immediately implemented the recommendations of a management study that had been made of the CIA for the National Security Council a year earlier by ALLEN DULLES, WILLIAM H. JACKSON, and Matthias F. Correa, all Wall Street lawyers. To ensure the study's findings

were put in effect, Smith recruited Jackson to serve as his deputy director of central intelligence.

Smith and Jackson persuaded WILLIAM LANGER, the eminent historian who had been chief of the OSS RESEARCH AND ANALYSIS BRANCH, to take a year's leave of absence from Harvard University to establish the CIA Office of National Estimates (see NATIONAL INTELLIGENCE ESTIMATE). ONE, replacing the piecemeal approach to intelligence that the CIA had been following, became the single authoritative source of intelligence advice to the president.

Langer brought in a number of prestigious academics to serve in ONE. To balance what he feared might be an overly academic approach to intelligence, Jackson arranged for a panel of outside consultants to review draft intelligence estimates. The panel consisted of GEORGE F. KENNAN, a veteran foreign service officer and State Department Soviet expert who was then with the Institute for Advanced Studies; HAMILTON FISH ARMSTRONG, a founding member of the Council on Foreign Relations and editor of the Council's publication, *Foreign Affairs;* and atomic scientist Vannevar Bush. The panel, which met in the Gun Club at Princeton University, was informally known within the Agency as "the Princeton Consultants."

Smith and Jackson also put in effect the management study's recommendations regarding the Office of Research and Evaluation, which it was felt had become an organization without a clear focus. In attempting to satisfy a broad miscellany of requirements from other agencies for political, economic, scientific, and technical intelligence, ORE had diluted the substance of the FINISHED INTELLIGENCE it produced. The office was reorganized; political intelligence was left to STATE DEPARTMENT INTELLIGENCE, and the Office of Research and Reports— the unit's new designation—was made to concentrate on BASIC INTELLIGENCE and economic intelligence. ORR consisted of a Basic Intelligence Division, which was responsible for coordinating and producing the National Intelligence Surveys; a Map Division, which took over the files and many of the personnel of the Map Division of the old OSS RESEARCH AND ANALYSIS BRANCH; and the Economic Research Area (ERA).

MAX MILLIKAN, an economist from the Massachusetts Institute of Technology, was recruited to serve as assistant director of ORR, and to organize the ERA. Under Millikan, economic intelligence became the focus of the Agency's intelligence research and analysis activity. This marked a significant departure from the CIA's earlier charter, which limited its analysis to the coordination of materials supplied by other government agencies. The work of ERA had a major impact on strategic and military analysis of the Soviet Union during the 1950s and put the CIA firmly in the business of intelligence production.

Covert Action

Smith next turned his attention to the problem of COVERT ACTION. At the time, this was an anomalous function of the CIA performed by the Office of Policy Coordination, an organization protected by the secrecy mechanisms of the Agency but which operated independently of the direct control of the director of central intelligence.

This situation had been created in the winter of 1947–48 when the National Security Council ordered the CIA to undertake a program of psychological and political operations aimed at preventing a Communist victory in the Italian national elections scheduled for April 1948 (see ITALIAN ELECTION OPERATION). This program, carried out by an ad hoc unit established within the Agency's Office of Special Operations, was such a resounding success that it inspired exaggerated hopes within the Agency, the State Department, and the National Security Council, hopes that a broad program of covert action might be an effective solution to the pressing problem of Soviet expansionism throughout the world. Therefore the National Security Council issued a directive on June 18, 1948 establishing a permanent covert action agency.

The Office of Policy Coordination

The agency, which formally came into being on September 1, 1948, was called the Office of Policy Coordination (OPC). Its specific mission was to weaken Soviet control over both its own population and the nations of Eastern Europe, to weaken pro-Soviet regimes and Communist parties throughout Europe and Asia, and to advance the interests of anti-Communist political parties, governments, and leaders.

Though its budget and staff positions were lumped within the secret budget of the CIA, the OPC was a separate administrative entity. Its director reported to the secretaries of State and Defense, bypassing the director of central intelligence. The relationship between OPC and CIA was complex and unusual. In theory, at least, OPC was not to initiate any specific proposals for covert action; these were to originate within the CIA, where foreign intelligence specialists were presumed to know when and where such operations were likely to be effective. The CIA would send its proposals to a special panel of State and Defense officials for approval, after which they would

be given to OPC for action. This cumbersome arrangement reflected some uncertainty regarding the CIA's legal authority for covert action, and it insured that the responsibility for such action remained at the level of the National Security Council and not with a subordinate agency.

The director of OPC was FRANK G. WISNER who had served with the OSS as chief of secret intelligence activities in Turkey and Romania during the war. The State Department officer with primary responsibility for supervising OPC was GEORGE F. KENNAN, veteran foreign service officer, Soviet affairs specialist, and at the time chairman of State's Policy Planning Committee. Kennan had, in fact, written the proposal to the NSC that resulted in the creation of OPC.

Soviet testing of a nuclear weapon in 1949 and the fall of China to the Communists the same year heightened the tense cold war atmosphere in the Truman administration. In April 1950 the National Security Council issued directive NSC 68, which called for the United States to take the lead in opposing the expansion of international Communism through, inter alia, covert action. The formalization of covert action as a permanent instrument of American foreign policy increased the importance of OPC and spurred the growth of its staff and budget.

The Clandestine Service

By the time Bedell Smith took office as director of central intelligence in 1950, OPC had a staff of several hundred persons and was growing rapidly; it had a budget in excess of $4.7 million; and it had initiated a great number of psychological, political, economic, and paramilitary projects worldwide (e.g., RADIO FREE EUROPE/RADIO LIBERTY). All of this was regarded with dismay by the secret intelligence officers of OSO, who viewed the new organization with a combination of bureaucratic envy and professional skepticism toward such a heavy investment in covert action. The professional staff of OSO consisted largely of OSS veterans who had persevered through the lean years of 1945–47, shunted from OSS to the State Department, to SSU, and to CIG, with no assurance that there was ever to be a career intelligence service. They resented OPC, which had filled its ranks from outside CIA, largely with other OSS veterans who had returned to civilian life and been lured back to government service with salaries considerably more generous than those paid the OSO staff. Furthermore, the secret intelligence professionals of OSO viewed the more swashbuckling and spectacular business of covert action with mistrust, doubting its essential soundness, and fearing that it could jeopardize their own covert intelligence collection operations within many of the OPC-targeted countries.

Smith recognized OPC as an administrative problem of major proportions and lost no time in bringing it under his direct control; within a week of taking office he dissolved the cumbersome State-Defense supervisory mechanism and declared that henceforth the director of OPC would report to the DCI. Soon thereafter he created the post of deputy director for plans to supervise both the OPC and the OSO, and thereby established the CIA CLANDESTINE SERVICE, the directorate responsible for all Agency covert operations. In January Smith recruited the first incumbent to fill this post, ALLEN W. DULLES. The OPC-OSO rivalry continued to present management problems, however, which were not resolved until August 1952 when the two organizations were merged.

The Korean War

The KOREAN WAR brought a period of rapid growth to the CIA. Senior and middle-level officials throughout the government demanded information from the ORR, with the result that that office grew from a staff of 461 in July 1951 to 766 persons by February 1953. The full CIA INTELLIGENCE DIRECTORATE—consisting at the time of ORR and ONE, plus the Office of Current Intelligence, the Office of Scientific Intelligence, the Office of Operations (a unit that collected information from open sources), and the Office of Collection and Dissemination (a reference library and dissemination service)—swelled to about three thousand persons during this period.

The Rise of Covert Action

The Clandestine Service enjoyed an even greater growth, most of which took place within OPC, which blossomed from a modest 302 people in 1949 to a force of 2,812 staff employees and 3,142 overseas contract personnel by the time it merged with OSO in 1952. OPC took an active role in Korea, where its Far East Division undertook such projects as the establishment of an escape-and-evasion network to assist American airmen brought down in enemy territory, training and equipping Korean guerrillas for irregular warfare operations in North Korea, and Operation Tropic, the support of "third force" Chinese (i.e., anti-Communists not affiliated with the Nationalist Chinese regime on Formosa) in guerrilla operations on the Chinese mainland (see HANS V. TOFTE).

The Clandestine Service by no means limited its covert action operations to Korea and the Far East; by 1952 it had personnel at forty-seven overseas stations. One of its earliest successes was achieved in the Philippines where Col. EDWARD G. LANSDALE, the OPC station chief, and his assistant, GABRIEL L. KAPLAN, helped the Filipino armed forces thwart the attempt by Communist Huk guerrillas to overthrow the government during the early 1950s. Lansdale and Kaplan also used the CIA's covert assets to assist the Philippines in conducting honest elections, and thereby helped Defense Minister Ramon Magsaysay achieve the presidency in 1953.

Also in 1953, the Clandestine Service staged a coup d'etat in Iran, toppling Prime Minister Mohammed Mossadegh, who had seized power with the help of the Iranian Communist Party, and restoring the Shah and his appointed government to power (see IRAN COUP). The following year it overthrew Guatemalan President Jacobo Arbenz Guzman, a leftist reformer believed to have been under Communist influence, and installed a military junta in Guatemala headed by Col. Carlos Castillo Armas (see GUATEMALA COUP).

Not all such covert action operations were successful, however. During 1950–52 the Clandestine Service worked with the Freedom and Independence movement, an ostensibly anti-Soviet underground organization in Poland, better known as WIN from its Polish initials. The Clandestine Service airdropped money, arms, ammunition, and radios to WIN, unaware that it had been penetrated by the Polish security police. WIN was completely under Communist control when the Polish government disclosed the deception in December 1952 in order to embarrass the U.S. government. And anti-Communist and anti-Soviet groups in the Ukraine and the Baltic states, which were supported on a limited basis by the Clandestine Service, also proved to be of no practical value in countering Soviet expansion and were eventually wiped out by Soviet security forces. But the most serious Clandestine Service covert action failure of this period was the joint Anglo-American operation aimed at overthrowing the Communist government of Albania (see ALBANIA OPERATION), which was penetrated in Washington by Soviet mole HAROLD ("KIM") PHILBY.

Despite these failures, the Clandestine Service successes in the Philippines, Iran, and Guatemala seemed to fulfill the expectations implicit in NSC 68 that covert action could be the panacea needed to contain Soviet expansionism. Within the Clandestine Service covert action had become ascendent over secret intelligence collection; with the merger of the OPC and OSO in 1952, former OPC chief Wisner succeeded Dulles as deputy director for plans—i.e., chief of the Clandestine Service—while OSO veteran RICHARD M. HELMS was relegated to the number two position as Wisner's deputy.

The Dulles Era

The advent of the Eisenhower administration in 1953 marked the beginning of a new period in CIA history. Eisenhower moved Bedell Smith to the State Department as under secretary of state and appointed Allen Dulles to succeed him as DCI. Dulles's brother, John Foster Dulles, was the new Secretary of State. The relationship of the Dulles brothers had the effect of short-circuiting the official government chain of command and made the Agency, in fact if not in theory, an extension of the Cabinet and an integral element in American foreign policy making.

Allen Dulles preferred to leave the day-to-day administration of the CIA to his deputy, Gen. CHARLES P. CABELL, and involve himself directly in the activities of the Clandestine Service. The personal and informal channel that linked Clandestine Service Chief Wisner and Allen Dulles with the secretary of state and the President facilitated the approval of covert projects that otherwise would have had to run the bureaucratic gauntlet of the State Department and the NSC. This situation further facilitated the use of covert action, an instrument already much in favor in the government.

CIA covert action received an additional endorsement in the 1954 report of the Doolittle Committee, a panel chaired by Gen. James Doolittle, which had been commissioned by President Eisenhower to study the work of the Clandestine Service. The report stated that the CIA must build a covert action service "more ruthless" and more effective than that of America's adversaries.

The limitations of covert action began to become apparent during the late 1950s, however. Red Sox/Red Cap, an operation aimed at fomenting anti-Soviet revolts in Eastern Europe using CIA-trained emigrés from the Soviet bloc, misfired when it was overtaken by the spontaneous anti-Soviet uprising in Hungary in October 1956. Forced to act prematurely, the Red Sox/Red Cap agents in Hungary met the same fate as the other Hungarian freedom fighters when Soviet armed forces crushed the revolt. The idea of activating Red Sox/Red Cap in Czechoslovakia was given some consideration, but President Eisenhower terminated the operation on the recommendation of Gen. LUCIAN K. TRUSCOTT, who advised the President on covert action matters.

The failure of Red Sox/Red Cap was an institutional disaster for the CIA Clandestine Service and a personal one for Wisner, for whom it seemed to precipitate the breakdown that eventually caused his death. This failure was followed by the failure of a Clandestine Service plan to overthrow President Sukarno of Indonesia in 1958 (see INDONESIA REBELLION).

The following year Chinese Communist armed forces crushed an uprising in Tibet launched by Tibetan guerrillas trained and equipped by the CIA as part of a Clandestine Service covert action program that had been under way since 1953 (see TIBET OPERATION). The spectacular failure of the BAY OF PIGS INVASION in April 1961 capped this series of disasters and marked the end of both the "golden age of covert action" in the CIA and the Dulles era.

Technical Collection

After the development of nuclear weapons by the USSR in 1949, intelligence about the Soviet capability to deliver nuclear strikes on Western targets became a CIA objective of the highest priority. Beginning in September 1949 the CIA Office of Special Operations dispatched secret intelligence agents by land, sea, and air into the Soviet Union—to destinations ranging from the Baltic coast to Sakhalin in the Sea of Japan—to report whatever military preparations they could observe. The agents were Soviet emigrés who had been recruited by the CIA in Western Europe, and trained and equipped there for their missions before being sent back to their homeland. Their reports—usually transmitted to the CIA by clandestine radio—were valuable in that they confirmed that the USSR was not preparing to launch an immediate full-scale nuclear attack on the West, but they could not provide a detailed picture of Soviet developments in nuclear weaponry and long-range delivery systems. Furthermore, the agents found it impossible to evade detection and apprehension by Soviet counterintelligence services for any protracted period; sooner or later most were caught, while others simply stopped reporting. The program was terminated in 1954, its results deemed no longer sufficient to justify the human costs involved.

Overhead Reconnaissance

Aerial reconnaissance of the Soviet Union offered an alternative means of early warning. Beginning in the late 1940s the U.S. Air Force made flights along the Soviet borders and, occasionally, over the USSR in an effort to observe military activities. The border flights provided no reconnaissance of the deep interior of the USSR, of course, and the overflights were in constant danger of interception. During 1955–56 the CIA and the Air Force sent unmanned high-altitude balloons equipped with cameras drifting from Western Europe across the Soviet Union to the vicinity of Japan, where they were recovered. Although the program—known as the MOBY DICK PROGRAM—produced useful results, its effectiveness was limited because the balloons were subject to the vagaries of high-altitude winds and sometimes did not pass over targets of intelligence interest.

In 1956 the CIA began reconnaissance flights over Soviet territory using the U-2 reconnaissance aircraft. The Lockheed Aircraft Company had developed the U-2 for the Clandestine Service in order to meet the special requirements for an aircraft that could fly at altitudes above the limits of possible Soviet interception (see OVERHEAD RECONNAISSANCE). The specially developed cameras carried by the U-2 made ground photographs of exceptional detail, even from the plane's extreme operational altitudes. The U-2 program yielded highly valuable strategic military intelligence on the USSR until it was terminated following the shooting down of FRANCIS GARY POWERS in May 1960. But with the introduction of reconnaissance satellites in August 1960 the supply of such intelligence resumed.

Developed jointly by the CIA and the Air Force, the DISCOVERER RECONNAISSANCE SATELLITE and its successor systems proved even more effective than the U-2 because they could cover larger areas in less time than the aircraft, because they could be used without danger of interception and were therefore used more often, and because they employed more advanced photographic and other technology. Overhead reconnaissance soon became a major—and probably the most important—source of strategic intelligence about the USSR, Eastern Europe, and China. In 1958 the Photographic Intelligence Center was established as a unit of the CIA Intelligence Directorate, and was headed by ARTHUR LUNDAHL, a photographic intelligence specialist who had played a key role in the development of the photographic equipment used by the U-2. In 1961 the Center, renamed the NATIONAL PHOTOGRAPHIC INTERPRETATION CENTER, was made a "service of common concern," providing photointerpretation services to the entire INTELLIGENCE COMMUNITY. Management of the strategic reconnaissance programs became a community function, as opposed to a purely CIA activity, and came under the National Reconnaissance Executive Committee, an interagency panel (see NATIONAL RECONNAISSANCE OFFICE).

The 1960s

JOHN A. MCCONE, who succeeded Dulles as DCI after the latter was forced into retirement in November 1961 following the Bay of Pigs failure, was by his background predisposed to manage the technological enterprise that intelligence had lately become. As the importance of overhead photography grew, so did that of the electronic intelligence collected by the NATIONAL SECURITY AGENCY, becoming a second major source of the strategic intelligence coordinated and produced by the CIA. Furthermore, the sheer volume of data gathered by these technical collection systems presented a problem in correlation and analysis that could only be solved by technical means, i.e., computers and electronic data processing. And because the capabilities of the Soviet and Chinese scientific establishments had become an increasingly important factor in national intelligence, the very substance of much of the information collected and processed by the Agency had taken on a scientific and technical character.

Responding to the important new role of technology in intelligence, McCone established the Directorate for Science and Technology in August 1963. This became the fourth major branch of the CIA structure, joining the Clandestine Service, the Intelligence Directorate, and the Support Directorate. Rather than appoint an intelligence professional without a technical background to the new post of deputy director for science and technology, he recruited Dr. ALBERT D. WHEELON, an aerospace engineer, for the job (see also HERBERT SCOVILLE).

The S&T Directorate consisted of the Office of Scientific Intelligence, a unit that had been part of the Intelligence Directorate and that was concerned with basic scientific research conducted by foreign countries; the Data Processing Staff, a computer services group; the Office of ELINT, an electronic intelligence unit that had been part of the Clandestine Service; the Development Projects Division, the Clandestine Service unit that had been responsible for developing the U-2 and other overhead reconnaissance systems; the Office of Research and Development, a newly created unit charged with employing new technologies in the INTELLIGENCE CYCLE; and the Foreign Missile and Space Analysis Center, a unit established to keep track of foreign missile and space programs.

Intelligence Production

McCone enlarged the CIA's intelligence production role by paving the way with a series of agreements between the Agency and the State and Defense departments. In March 1965 he obtained the consent of Secretary of State Dean Rusk to expand ORR's economic research programs beyond the Sino-Soviet bloc, to which they had been limited by agreement since 1951. This new charter to produce economic intelligence on a worldwide basis permitted ORR to study such important national intelligence matters as the growing economic strength of Japan and Western

Europe, and the vulnerability of emerging Third World nations to Soviet economic penetration. Reflecting this new emphasis on economic intelligence production, the Economic Research Area of ORR became the separate Office of Economic Research in 1967.

At the same time, the remainder of ORR, consisting of its strategic and military intelligence components, was combined with the Military Division of the Office of Current Intelligence to form the Office of Strategic Research. The creation of OSR reflected the Agency's enlarged role in strategic analysis, an area that had been jealously guarded by the armed services, in part for reasons of professional expertise, and in part because of the direct connection between assessments of foreign military threats and the armed services' budgets. Secretary of Defense Robert McNamara's mistrust of the objectivity and quality of service-produced military estimates led him to look to the CIA in these matters. At the Secretary's request, the Agency began to make comparative assessments of Soviet and American military programs and to participate with the Defense Intelligence Agency in exercises in long-term Soviet force projections. The Agency also received primary responsibility for assessing the cost and resource impact of foreign military and space programs.

Cuban Crises

The CIA played a crucial role in the Kennedy administration's management of the CUBAN MISSILE CRISIS in October 1962. Although the Agency's Board of National Estimates had mistakenly forecast a month before the crisis that Soviet Premier Khrushchev would not install offensive nuclear missiles in Cuba, McCone took a contrary view and personally advised the President of his suspicions. After U-2 reconnaissance flights (made at the urging of the Defense Intelligence Agency) revealed that the Soviets were indeed installing such missiles, the Intelligence Directorate under Dr. RAY S. CLINE coordinated the full capabilities of the intelligence community—including overhead reconnaissance of both the USSR and Cuba, supplemented by human agents in both places—to keep the administration apprised of the developing situation. During the crisis, however, the Board of National Estimates again failed to forecast Soviet actions correctly, predicting erroneously that only an American invasion of Cuba would persuade the Soviets to withdraw the missiles. But despite the Board's failure to predict Soviet behavior in this case, the CIA's performance during the crisis enhanced the Agency's prestige within the government and rehabilitated its relations with the Kennedy administration, relations which had been damaged by the failure of the Bay of Pigs Invasion.

The CIA was not equally successful in its covert action operations aimed at removing Fidel Castro from power and toppling his government. This program, which antedated the Bay of Pigs Invasion and continued long after the failure of that operation, was conducted by the Clandestine Service and consisted of a variety of covert action techniques, including paramilitary, sabotage, and propaganda activities (see MONGOOSE). Proceeding on what apparently was a misunderstanding of orders received from the Kennedy White House, Clandestine Service director RICHARD BISSELL and Office of Security director SHEFFIELD EDWARDS undertook the assassination of Castro through a variety of intermediaries, including American underworld figures John Rosselli and Salvatore Giancana (see ROBERT A. MAHEU, WILLIAM K. HARVEY). These unsuccessful assassination plots continued until 1965, when they were discontinued.

Other Assassination Plots

During the 1960s and early 1970s the Clandestine Service was involved in several other assassination plots. In 1960 LAWRENCE R. DEVLIN, the CIA chief of station in the Congo (now Zaire), and another CIA officer were asked by their superiors to assassinate Patrice Lumumba, a Congolese political leader. However, a United States Senate committee that investigated the matter in 1975 found that Lumumba's murder by Congolese rivals in 1961 apparently was not the result of the CIA plot.

The Senate committee's investigation of the involvement of the CIA in several other political assassinations around the world found that it had furnished weapons and other aid to the conspirators responsible for the deaths of President Rafael Trujillo of the Dominican Republic in 1961 and Gen. René Schneider of Chile in 1970. However the committee also found that there was no conclusive evidence that the Agency had caused the Trujillo killing, and that the Agency had withdrawn its support of the Chilean conspirators prior to the Schneider killing.

Assassination was ruled out of CIA covert action operations by the directives of RICHARD M. HELMS and WILLIAM E. COLBY in 1972 and 1973, respectively. President Reagan's Executive Order No. 12333 of December 1981 states: "No person employed by or acting on behalf of the United States Government shall engage in, or conspire to engage in, assassination."

Africa and Southeast Asia

The relinquishment of their African colonies by several European powers during 1960 led U.S. policy-makers to anticipate Soviet encroachment on the newly independent African states. Consequently the CIA presence in Africa was enlarged during this period; during 1959–63 the number of CIA stations in Africa increased by 55.5 percent. The Clandestine Service was especially active in the Congo (Zaire), where it provided assistance in the form of air support and paramilitary aid to President Joseph Mobutu in suppressing a Communist-led revolt in 1964 (see LAWRENCE R. DEVLIN, AIR PROPRIETARIES).

During the 1960s paramilitary operations became the predominant form of covert action employed by the Clandestine Service, surpassing covert psychological and political operations in budgetary allocations by 1967. This paramilitary emphasis was in response to directives from the Kennedy administration to develop an unconventional warfare capability that could be used to counter Communist guerrilla activities around the world in a manner less likely to provoke a major Soviet-American military confrontation than would conventional warfare.

By far the largest paramilitary operations of the Clandestine Service were in Southeast Asia, where the Agency's large-scale involvement began in 1962 with programs in Laos and Vietnam (see VIETNAM WAR). In Laos the Communist Pathet Lao forces were receiving increasing support from North Vietnam and the USSR, in violation of the Geneva Agreement in 1954 that officially neutralized the country. To counter the growing power of the Pathet Lao without openly confronting the Communists on their Agreement violations, the Eisenhower and Kennedy administrations used the CIA to recruit, train, arm, and supply the Meo tribesmen of Laos both for guerrilla operations and conventional warfare against the Communists. This force, known as L'Armée Clandestine, or Secret Army, grew from a few hundred troops in the late 1950s to 30,000 or 40,000 men by 1973, when the United States withdrew its military presence in Southeast Asia (see SECRET WAR IN LAOS).

In Vietnam the CIA began in the mid-1950s by helping the South Vietnamese government organize police forces and paramilitary units (see EDWARD LANSDALE). After 1965 the program escalated to full-scale paramilitary assistance to South Vietnam. The Agency's programs were directed both at North Vietnam and at countering the Vietcong insurgency in the South.

In Southeast Asia, remarks former CIA officer HARRY ROSITZKE, "the CIA became an all-purpose instrument of action like the Office of Strategic Services during the war with Germany and Japan." The Agency's paramilitary operations in the region grew too large to remain covert. Rositzke notes that CIA station chiefs in Saigon became semipublic figures, and other CIA officers were often cited by name in news reports. In the opinion of former CIA official Dr. Ray S. Cline, the emphasis on paramilitary activity in Southeast Asia diverted the CIA from its more basic tasks: "Much useful work was done, but the covert action pressures on the CIA distorted its overall effort. . . ."

Southeast Asia also loomed large in the Agency's intelligence analysis and production, of course. One major focus of study was the order of battle, i.e., the actual strength of Vietcong and North Vietnamese forces. In 1967 a major dispute arose between the Army's command in Vietnam and some CIA analysts over the actual number of enemy troops; the Army estimated the figure to be 270,000, while the Agency concluded the correct number was at least twice as large. The discrepancy was due in part to such complex issues as whether the local Vietcong defense forces should be regarded as an important component of Communist strength. The ensuing controversy was highly charged by the gloomy implications of the CIA estimate, the credibility of the Army's claims to progress in winning the war, the domestic political implications if those claims were unfounded, and President Johnson's clear preference for good news. In any event the CIA deferred to the Army's estimate, but later revised it upward in the wake of the Communist Tet offensive of 1968. In general, CIA intelligence analysis regarding Southeast Asia tended to be pessimistic about the long-term prospects for military success (see GEORGE A. CARVER).

Raborn and Helms

The high regard in which President Kennedy held the CIA during the final year of his presidency was not fully shared by President Johnson. McCone resigned in 1965, reportedly because Johnson did not accord him the stature and access he had enjoyed under Kennedy, and Johnson appointed Adm. WILLIAM F. RABORN to succeed McCone because, by some accounts, the President preferred to control the Agency through an "outsider," rather than promote a veteran CIA "insider" to the post. Raborn's tenure was brief, however, and after his resignation in 1965 the President seemed content to let veteran Clandestine Service officer RICHARD M. HELMS succeed him.

Under Helms the CIA rose in Johnson's esteem,

partly as a result of the Agency's accurate prediction in May 1967 that the Israelis would defeat the Arabs in the Six Day War, which occurred the following month. However, the preoccupation of Johnson and his administration with Southeast Asia at the expense of other foreign policy concerns put Helms in a less-than-ideal position as the government's chief intelligence officer and tended to distort the overall functioning of the Agency.

Helms's tenure as DCI lasted through the first term of the Nixon administration, a period during which the Agency's role in foreign policy making was considerably reduced by the President's national security advisor, Henry Kissinger, a knowledgeable and opinionated student of foreign affairs. The Agency's prestige was further diminished by President Nixon's antipathy toward the CIA and its intelligence analysts, whom he regarded as having a liberal academic orientation. Nixon was not equally indifferent to the Agency's Clandestine Service, however, and in 1970 he and Kissinger directed Helms to undertake an effort to prevent the Chilean president-elect, Marxist Salvatore Allende, from taking office. (The operation proved unsuccessful.)

Schlesinger and Colby

Nixon did not reappoint Helms as DCI after the presidential elections of 1972, reportedly because Helms had resisted the president's attempts to involve the CIA in the Watergate affair as a means of sidetracking the FBI investigation of the case. In February 1973 Helms was succeeded by JAMES R. SCHLESINGER, an economist then serving as chairman of the Atomic Energy Commission. Schlesinger, who had conducted a management study of the INTELLIGENCE COMMUNITY while serving with the Bureau of the Budget in 1971, was reportedly suggested by Henry Kissinger.

Unlike most of his predecessors, Schlesinger brought to the job a strong sense of the DCI's role as manager of the whole intelligence community, as opposed to the narrower function of simply heading the CIA. As a former director of strategic studies for the Rand Corporation, a former assistant director of the Office of Management and Budget, and an "outsider" without institutional loyalties to the CIA or any other intelligence agency, he was well-suited to deal with the diverse, manifold, complex, and enormous interagency activity that intelligence had become during the 1960s. He was, perhaps, hostile to the CIA "old guard," the OSS veterans and other "charter members" of the Agency who retained the professional orientation of the Dulles era. He agreed with the

diminished emphasis on covert action, which in any case had been in decline since the late 1960s.

In May 1973, when the resignation of Attorney General Richard Kleindienst over involvement in the Watergate affair precipitated a reshuffling of the Nixon Cabinet, Schlesinger was appointed secretary of defense after only four months as DCI. However, many of the management and administrative changes he had begun were continued by his successor, WILLIAM E. COLBY. Although he had spent most of his long intelligence career in the OSS and the Clandestine Service, Colby had acquired a broader orientation during his two years as the Agency's executive director-comptroller and had worked closely with Schlesinger in that capacity (and, briefly, as director of the Clandestine Service) to implement the latter's policies.

The Schlesinger-Colby administrations put a series of major changes into effect in the Agency and the intelligence community at large. They strengthened and enlarged the role of the INTELLIGENCE COMMUNITY STAFF, which assists the DCI in his role as community manager in regard to budgetary matters, separating it from the CIA, adding non-Agency personnel to it, and elevating it to the status of a separate bureaucratic entity within the government. They reduced the size of the CIA by seven percent, making most of the cuts in the Clandestine Service through the enforced retirement of many of the OSS veterans and "charter members." Colby implemented Schlesinger's plan to abolish the Board of National Estimates and the Office of National Estimates, which they believed had become increasingly isolated from other analytical components and irrelevant to the foreign policy-making process. Colby established a new system for the production of national intelligence estimates: a group of twelve National Intelligence Officers, senior experts in such subjects as China, Soviet affairs, Europe, Latin America, or strategic weaponry, would serve as special consultants to the DCI. In 1974 he established the Office of Political Research within the Intelligence Directorate; the Office conducts long-term, in-depth political intelligence analysis.

Schlesinger and Colby also dispensed with many of the CIA's trappings of pseudo-secrecy and clandestine mystique that had contributed nothing to the Agency's security but often made it appear ridiculous to outsiders, and which eroded the respect of many staff employees for serious and legitimate security measures. They changed the title of the chief of the Clandestine Service from the deliberately obscure and misleading "Deputy Director for Plans" to the more accurate and descriptive "Deputy Director for Operations," and they erected a sign identifying the

CIA headquarters exit from the George Washington Parkway in Langley, Virginia, where there had previously been only a small sign for the Agency's diminutive neighbor, the Bureau of Public Roads.

The Family Jewels

Colby spent much of his tenure as DCI responding to official investigations of the Agency and the intelligence community. These probes were the indirect result of an internal investigation that Schlesinger initiated in 1973 after learning of the CIA's assistance to E. HOWARD HUNT in connection with Hunt's illegal entry and search of a psychiatrist's office while he was employed by the Nixon White House. Concerned about possible CIA involvement in other improper activities, Schlesinger and Colby conducted a complete review of all the Agency's activities since the time it was established that were possible violations of its charter or otherwise "questionable." The result was a list of nearly seven hundred such activities, which became known as the "Family Jewels."

Included on the Family Jewels list were such items as Project HT/LINGUAL, the opening of selected mail between the United States and two Communist countries by the Clandestine Service's counterintelligence staff during 1953–73; MH/CHAOS, the joint CIA-FBI infiltration of the anti-Vietnam War movement in the United States on the orders of President Johnson to determine whether the movement was financed or manipulated by foreign powers; MK/ULTRA, a research and development program sponsored by the Clandestine Service's Technical Services Division to explore the use of drugs, hypnotism, and other psychological techniques in covert operations (see TRUTH DRUGS), a program that resulted in the death of one CIA officer who had been given LSD without his knowledge; ZR/RIFLE, a Clandestine Service program to develop a capability for disabling foreign leaders through a variety of means, including assassination (see WILLIAM K. HARVEY); the several assassination plots in which the Agency was involved; and an assortment of wiretappings, buggings, and break-ins carried out within the United States by the CIA's Office of Security without appropriate warrants.

Colby, with Schlesinger's concurrence, decided to turn over the Family Jewels list to the Congressional committees responsible for oversight of the CIA. Some of the items on the list eventually fell into the hands of a *New York Times* investigative reporter, and in December 1974 the *Times* published an exposé of the Agency's infiltration of anti-war groups. The disclosure led to further investigations and exposés, and, in the mood of distrust of government that followed the Watergate affair, public indignation and outcry.

The Rockefeller Commission

In January 1975 President Ford appointed a commission headed by former Vice-President Nelson Rockefeller to investigate the CIA's domestic intelligence activities. The Rockefeller Commission's report, published in June 1975, found that "the great majority of the CIA's domestic activities comply with its statutory authority," but some fell within a "doubtful area" between legal authorization and activities "specifically prohibited" by the Agency's charter, while a few "were plainly unlawful and constituted improper invasions upon the rights of Americans." The Commission recommended several remedies in the form of revisions to the Agency's statutory charter and presidential directives to clarify and limit domestic CIA activities, and the strengthening of supervision and control of the Agency by Congress and the PRESIDENT'S FOREIGN INTELLIGENCE ADVISORY BOARD.

Congressional Investigations

At about the same time that the Rockefeller Commission was beginning its investigation in January 1975, the U.S. Senate established the Select Committee to Study Government Operations with Respect to Intelligence Activities, under the chairmanship of Sen. Frank Church, an Idaho Democrat. The charter of the Church Committee, much broader than that of the Commission, included the full intelligence community and its activities, foreign as well as domestic. It was authorized to investigate "the extent, if any, to which illegal, improper, or unethical activities were engaged in by any agency of the Federal Government." Within a month the House followed suit with its own Select Committee under Representative Lucien N. Nedzi, a Michigan Democrat.

The Church Committee's investigation continued through 1975 and into early 1976, assembled a large collection of classified intelligence documents, and in both closed and open sessions took testimony from Colby, former DCI's, and a large number of other intelligence officers. Some CIA officials considered the Committee a mechanism contrived to further Senator Church's plans to run for the presidency in 1976. Others saw it as an "inquisition," and feared that the very survival of the Agency was in jeopardy. However, Colby, who bore the brunt of the investigation for the CIA, later recalled he was relieved to find that "despite some sanctimonious hyperbole about the failure of CIA to reflect the highest standards of American life, the [Committee's] final report in general was a comprehensive and serious review of the history and present status of American intelligence, with its faults shown as an aspect of the nation's historical experience in the Cold War. . . ," and, although he did not agree with all of the report's conclusions and recommendations, he "welcomed its repudiation of the image of CIA as a 'rogue elephant'. . . ."

The House investigation was not held in similar regard, however. After several months of quarrelling in the House over Representative Nedzi's perceived sympathies toward the CIA and the intelligence community, the House Committee was scrapped and succeeded by a second one headed by Rep. Otis Pike, a New York Democrat. The Pike Committee was less committed to the security of the classified information it received than was the Church Committee, and its staff was the source of many leaks to the press. The text of the Committee's final report was passed to a reporter and printed in the *Village Voice*, a New York weekly newspaper, in its editions of February 16th and 23rd, 1976. Pike then admitted that he had had inadequate control of the Committee staff. The Committee's investigations had no constructive results and, in Colby's view, were "a thoroughgoing waste of time and money."

The Church Committee's recommendations were embodied in President Carter's Executive Order No. 12063 of January 1978, which sought to clarify the boundaries of intelligence activities, establish effective oversight, and specify the authority and responsibility of the DCI. No legislation resulted from the Committee's investigation because the matter became mired in acrimonious debate in Congress. However, the investigations did prompt Congress to revamp and strengthen its mechanisms for overseeing the CIA and the intelligence community. In May 1976 the Senate established a permanent Senate Select Committee on Intelligence, and the House followed suit in July of the following year.

The congressional investigations created serious internal problems for the CIA. The press leaks of sensitive information, especially regarding the secret cooperation the Agency had received from many foreign nationals, damaged the sensitive liaison arrangements between the Clandestine Service and the intelligence and security services of many friendly foreign powers. These countries had lost confidence in the CIA's ability to protect their secrets (a problem that was greatly exacerbated by the disclosures made by renegade former Clandestine Service officer PHILIP AGEE in his book, *Inside the Company*, at the height of the investigations). Morale was seriously damaged. The public disclosure of the Agency's past misdeeds, actual and alleged, resulted in personal embarrassment to many staff employees, most of whom had no knowledge of any of the Family Jewels, but who were nonetheless presumed to be aware of all of them by acquaintances and even friends and family. "What shall I tell my children?" became a common lament among those whose children were of a generation already antipathetic toward their parents' government service in the wake of Vietnam and Watergate.

For much the same reason the Agency began to encounter difficulty in recruiting young people for careers in intelligence and in obtaining the same cooperation it had enjoyed in the past from the American business and academic communities. To many CIA staffers the assassination of RICHARD S. WELCH, chief of the Clandestine Service's station in Athens, in December 1975—a tragedy some blamed on the sort of disclosures that had accompanied the investigations—was the nadir of a thoroughly dismal period of the Agency's history.

Colby's effectiveness as DCI was impaired by the public clamor arising from the congressional investigations, and in January 1976 President Ford appointed GEORGE BUSH to succeed him in the post. A prominent Republican who had served in Congress, as ambassador to the United Nations, and as chief of the American Liaison Office in Peking, Bush had no ties to the CIA or the intelligence community, and thus held the public image of an "outsider" who would keep close rein on the Agency. To the CIA insiders it came as a pleasant surprise to discover Bush's commitment to and talents for restoring the Agency's battered morale and rehabilitating its public prestige. He appointed veteran intelligence analyst E. HENRY KNOCHE to serve as his deputy as well as his guide to the unfamiliar world of the Agency, and left the day-to-day management of the CIA to him.

Intelligence research and analysis in the CIA remained generally unaffected by the tumultuous affairs of the Family Jewels, the Rockefeller Commission, and the congressional investigations, but several other external developments exerted considerable influence. The reduction and termination of American military involvement in Southeast Asia during the early 1970s shifted focus away from that area of the world, which had occupied so much intelligence attention only a few years before. The foreign policy initiatives of the Nixon administration—detente with the Soviet Union, opening of relations with Communist China, strategic arms limitations—resulted in new and different intelligence requirements. Because of the Arab embargo on oil shipments to the United States that followed the Arab-Israeli war of October

1973, the continuing use of oil by the Arabs as a foreign policy instrument, and the growing use of terrorism by the Palestinians and other Islamic political groups, intelligence analysts allocated more attention to the Middle East. Kissinger's disdain for the CIA's intelligence product continued, and his elevation to the rank of Secretary of State in 1973 (while simultaneously retaining his position as national security advisor to the President until 1975) further reduced the Agency's influence on the foreign policy-making process.

The Soviet Estimates

CIA intelligence output also received a serious setback as the result of the agency's substantial underestimate of Soviet military spending in a January 1975 National Intelligence Estimate. Gen. Daniel O. Graham, the director of the Defense Intelligence Agency, pointed out the error, which arose from an economic intelligence technique the CIA had developed during the 1950s for estimating the cost of military procurements to the Soviet economy through an analogy with similar procurements by the United States. Since the evidence supported the DIA position that this method yielded a greatly underestimated assessment of Soviet military expenditures, it followed that the CIA had been making the same overly optimistic estimates of Soviet intentions for many years (see also GEORGE J. KEEGAN).

The discovery of the CIA's error reinforced the suspicions of those (e.g., the armed services, the Nixon administration, and former DCI Schlesinger) who believed the Agency's Intelligence Directorate had an "arms control bias," i.e., tended to downplay the threat of Soviet strategic strength and belligerency. In August 1975, George W. Anderson, then chairman of the PRESIDENT'S FOREIGN INTELLIGENCE ADVISORY BOARD, proposed to President Ford that there should be a "competitive analysis" of Soviet strategic strength and intentions. Ford agreed, and the following year the "A Team/B Team" exercise was conducted in which a panel of outside experts, the B Team, worked in parallel with and independent of the CIA analysts, the A Team, in drafting the 1976 national intelligence estimate of the Soviet threat. A liaison officer provided the B Team with the same intelligence data the A Team was given. The exercise was supervised and coordinated by the NATIONAL SECURITY COUNCIL.

The B Team was chaired by Dr. Richard E. Pipes, professor of Russian history at Harvard University, and included Gen. Daniel O. Graham, Paul Nitze, and several other individuals highly knowledgeable in the areas of Soviet history, foreign policy, and

military power. As expected, the B Team's findings differed greatly from those of the A Team, most notably in the matter of the accuracy of Soviet missiles, a critical factor in estimating their potential effectiveness against hardened (i.e., reinforced, and therefore less vulnerable) American Minuteman missile silos in a first-strike scenario. The B Team argued that the accuracy of the Soviet missiles could not be determined by American intelligence and that therefore there was no basis for the CIA's position that the weapons were less accurate than comparable American missiles. And if the Soviet missiles were more accurate than the CIA said, then the Minuteman missiles would soon be vulnerable to a Soviet first strike. Moving from the particular to the general, the B Team reviewed past Soviet policy and strategic programs and argued that, contrary to the view long held by the CIA, the Soviets intended to develop a first-strike, "war-winning" capability.

What impact, if any, the B Team's report may have had on the CIA's national intelligence estimates or American defense policies remains obscure. The matter reached its climax in late December 1976, during the transition between the outgoing administration of President Ford and the new administration of President Carter, who was not strongly disposed to adopt a hawkish view of Soviet intentions. The substance of the B Team study and the attendant controversy over CIA estimates was made public, and there ensued a public discussion of the matter, including a Senate study. Such discussion must, at the very least, have brought many fundamental assumptions held by the CIA estimators under a new searching scrutiny, both within and outside of the Agency. Subsequent unclassified CIA reports on the Soviet economy projected a considerable increase in military spending, and by early 1979 a draft national intelligence estimate being prepared by the CIA foresaw a "drastic improvement" in Soviet missile accuracy in the early 1980s and the possibility that the Soviets could neutralize the Minuteman missile by the mid-1980s.

The Carter-Turner Years

In January 1977 President Carter, in one of the first acts of his administration, replaced Bush as DCI. This was the first instance in which the post of DCI was treated as a political job subject to the vagaries of national partisan politics, rather than as a highly sensitive national security position above the political arena. Carter's disgust with some of the more sensational recent revelations about the CIA had become well-known during the campaign, and he demonstrated his hostile attitude toward the Agency by his first choice for the new DCI: Theodore Sorensen, a former special counsel to President Kennedy, whose nomination to the intelligence post was challenged in the Senate because he had been a conscientious objector to military service. Carter's ultimate choice was Adm. STANSFIELD TURNER, his Annapolis classmate and an able naval officer lacking any experience in intelligence.

In style as well as substance, Turner was very much the "outsider" sent by the new president to take a firm hand in correcting the CIA, which both men declared to be a "disgrace." The Clandestine Service was the principal object of Turner's early attentions, and in October 1977, nine months after taking office, he abolished 850 positions within that directorate, a measure that involved the forced early retirement of 147 officers and the outright discharge of another seventeen. This major reduction in force, which was carried out abruptly, and in a coldly impersonal manner, was seen in the Agency and throughout the government as a purge of the leadership of the Clandestine Service. It did indeed mark the end of an era, removing virtually all the OSS veterans and other "charter members" who had served in the Agency since its earliest years.

Turner's purge of the Clandestine Service was a perfect expression of the views of the President regarding covert operations, which he viewed as "dirty tricks" and as dishonorable. Soon after taking office Carter abolished the PRESIDENT'S FOREIGN INTELLIGENCE ADVISORY BOARD because of that panel's record of support for covert actions and the Clandestine Service (the PFIAB was restored by President Reagan).

Turner replaced E. Henry Knoch, the veteran CIA official who had run the Agency for George Bush as his second in command, with FRANK C. CARLUCCI, another "outsider," and he isolated himself from the old Agency hands by surrounding himself with Navy cronies, most of whom had no intelligence background. Turner's adversarial style of management inspired widespread resentment in the Agency, stopped the healing of injured CIA morale that Bush had begun, and reportedly earned for him the distinction of being the most disliked DCI in the Agency's history.

Though Turner was antipathetic to the Clandestine Service and all its works, he proved quite able at managing the overhead reconnaissance and other technical intelligence collection activities of the CIA and the intelligence community. Indeed, in the wake of the congressional investigations and the new involvement of congresspersons and their staffs in intelligence oversight, technical collection seemed the only still viable mode of intelligence activity. The problem of leaks aside, however, in Turner's view technical systems had wrought so radical a change in the business of intelligence collection that human agents had to be relegated to a supplemental role, filling in the few "missing pieces" that could not be obtained by technical means. Turner's emphasis on the mechanization of intelligence was similar to that practiced by John McCone in the immediate post-Bay of Pigs years. (However, expenditures for technical collection systems, as well as for all other intelligence activities, were cut drastically by the Carter administration.)

Turner found that the replacement by Schlesinger and Colby of the CIA's Board of National Estimates and Office of National Estimates with a system of National Intelligence Officers had not achieved the intended goal of making National Intelligence Estimates more relevant to policymakers' needs, and in fact had worked to the contrary. He therefore established the National Intelligence Council, a body similar in concept to ONE (but an intelligence community rather than an Agency unit); some veteran intelligence analysts praised him for making this change. Further, he took a personal hand in the estimate production process, unlike most of his predecessors, and even wrote some of the estimates himself. Nonetheless, under Turner the NIE's did not recover their former importance in foreign policy making.

Turner's tenure as DCI ended along with the Carter presidency, which did not survive the domestic political consequences of the Iran hostage crisis and the disastrous failure of the American attempt to rescue the captives. The administration's failure to anticipate the embassy takeover by the Islamic militants and the inability to employ irregular warfare to release the hostages was viewed by many CIA traditionalists as an ironic rebuttal of the Carter-Turner intelligence policies.

Turner's hirings, firings, and promotions, as well as the organizational changes he made during his directorship, combined to produce a very different CIA from the one he inherited from George Bush; it was not an organization that the incoming administration of President Reagan viewed with admiration. In fact, the dissatisfaction of the president-elect's transition team with the CIA extended well beyond the tenure of Stansfield Turner and focused on a series of supposed intelligence failures extending far back into the 1960s. Once again CIA intelligence analysts were criticized as having a liberal academic view of the world and an "arms control bias" in assessing the Soviet strategic threat. Much of the criticism was really an expression of the Reagan people's antipathy toward the foreign policy initiatives

Director of Central Intelligence Command Responsibilities

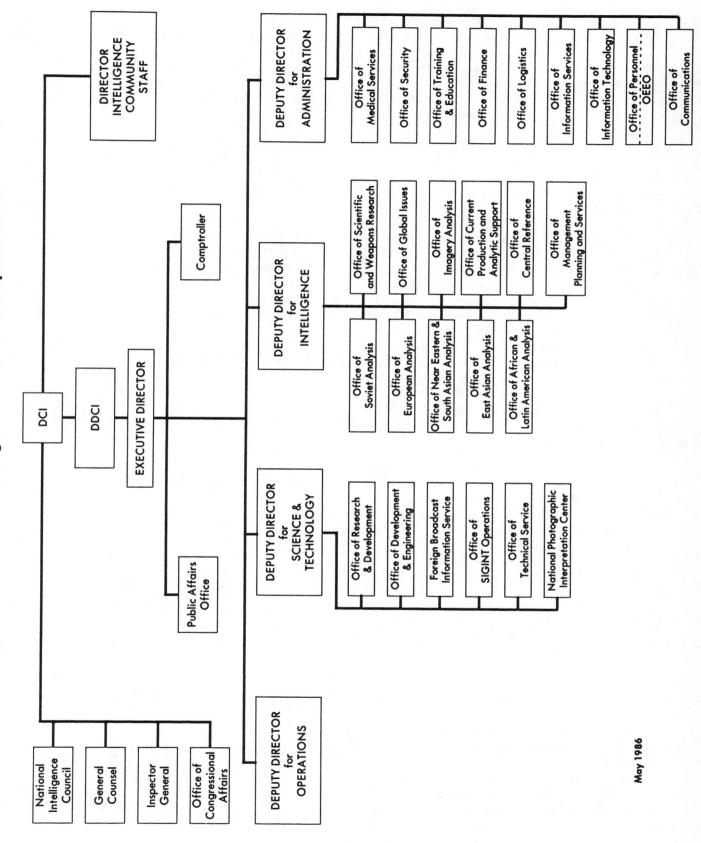

DCI

DDCI

EXECUTIVE DIRECTOR

National Intelligence Council

General Counsel

Inspector General

Office of Congressional Affairs

Public Affairs Office

Comptroller

DIRECTOR INTELLIGENCE COMMUNITY STAFF

DEPUTY DIRECTOR for OPERATIONS

DEPUTY DIRECTOR for SCIENCE & TECHNOLOGY
- Office of Research & Development
- Office of Development & Engineering
- Foreign Broadcast Information Service
- Office of SIGINT Operations
- Office of Technical Service
- National Photographic Interpretation Center

DEPUTY DIRECTOR for INTELLIGENCE
- Office of Scientific and Weapons Research
- Office of Global Issues
- Office of Imagery Analysis
- Office of Current Production and Analytic Support
- Office of Central Reference
- Office of Management Planning and Services
- Office of Soviet Analysis
- Office of European Analysis
- Office of Near Eastern & South Asian Analysis
- Office of East Asian Analysis
- Office of African & Latin American Analysis

DEPUTY DIRECTOR for ADMINISTRATION
- Office of Medical Services
- Office of Security
- Office of Training & Education
- Office of Finance
- Office of Logistics
- Office of Information Services
- Office of Information Technology
- Office of Personnel / OEEO
- Office of Communications

May 1986

of previous administrations, e.g., detente with the USSR and the SALT agreements, and seemed to impute to the Agency a degree of influence over policymaking it had not in fact enjoyed since the Dulles era. Some of its other discontents were more specific and germane, however, e.g., the reduction of satellite photoreconnaissance capability as a budget-cutting measure by Carter and Turner, several recent instances in which a few CIA employees and contractors had sold highly classified Agency information to Soviet Intelligence, and the "probable general penetration of the CIA and high-level intelligence posts throughout the government" by Soviet agents, a very grave allegation.

Several draconian remedies were considered by the Reagan transition team, including the dismemberment of the CIA into three separate organizations for counterintelligence, intelligence analysis and production, and covert operations. In the event, however, President Reagan kept the Agency intact and gave the task of bringing it into line with his administration's policies to his new DCI, WILLIAM J. CASEY.

Casey did not fit neatly into either of the categories of "insider" or "outsider." An OSS veteran who was chief of the OSS Secret Intelligence Branch in the European Theater, he did not remain in intelligence or government service immediately after the war, but instead became a very successful businessman and a prominent and active Republican. During the early 1970s he served on a presidential commission headed by ROBERT D. MURPHY that reviewed the functioning of the intelligence community in foreign policymaking, and in 1976 Casey was appointed to the PFIAB by President Ford. His political views and foreign policy orientation were quite close to those of Reagan (whose presidential campaign he managed in 1980), and he enjoyed entrée to the Oval Office that had not been enjoyed by any DCI since John McCone in the Kennedy administration. Reagan elevated Casey to Cabinet rank, making him the first DCI to be given that status within the government.

Casey's personal prestige within the Reagan administration restored the status lost by the Agency during the Carter-Turner years. He held his own during a series of conflicts with Congress that inevitably arose when the recently imposed congressional oversight mechanisms met their first serious tests as the Agency undertook new and large covert operations in Central America and the Middle East.

Casey worked at improving the overall competence of the CIA, especially in intelligence analysis and production, one of the areas that was severely criticized by the Reagan transition team. He took a strong personal hand in the production of National Intelligence Estimates. His 1986 appointment of ROBERT

M. GATES, who formerly served in the concurrent posts of deputy director of intelligence and chairman of the National Intelligence Council, as deputy director of central intelligence, was a reflection of the emphasis Casey put on intelligence production. Under Casey, the Intelligence Directorate was reorganized into a group of geographically oriented units to focus more sharply on the USSR, Europe, the Near East, and South Asia, East Asia, and Africa and Latin America. Scientific intelligence, moved into the Science and Technology Directorate when the latter was established in 1963, was returned to the Intelligence Directorate, where it is now the Office of Scientific and Weapons Research. The Intelligence Directorate also contains the current intelligence unit and several support groups, e.g., the Office of Central Reference. The Office of Global Issues, a development of the Office of Political Research, that Colby established in 1974 to conduct long-term political intelligence analysis, is also retained in the new Directorate organization.

Casey took a stronger role than most DCIs in managing the intelligence community, a function he fulfilled to a great extent through the budgetary activities of the Intelligence Community Staff, which he reorganized, enlarged, and strengthened.

When Casey resigned due to grave illness in January 1987 and was succeeded by William H. Webster, the CIA appeared to be entering another period of crisis and congressional attack as a consequence of alleged unauthorized support of the anti-Sandinista contra forces in Nicaragua, and the Agency's part in the secret arms sales to Iran.

(Troy, *Donovan and the CIA*; Karalekas, *History of the Central Intelligence Agency*; Cline, *The CIA: Reality vs. Myth*; Ranelagh, *The Agency*; Breckinridge, *The CIA and the U.S. Intelligence System*; Colby and Forbath, *Honorable Men*; Turner, *Secrecy and Democracy*; Powers, *The Man Who Kept the Secrets*; Rositzke, *The CIA's Secret Operations*; Corson, *Armies of Ignorance*; Kirkpatrick, *The Real CIA*; Prados, *The Soviet Estimate*; Ransom, *The Intelligence Establishment*; Richelson, *The U.S. Intelligence Community*; Central Intelligence Agency, *Fact Book on Intelligence*; *Intelligence: The Acme of Skill*.)

CHADWICK, FRENCH ENSOR (February 29, 1844–January 27, 1919): naval officer

A native of Morgantown, West Virginia (then Virginia), Chadwick graduated from the Naval Academy in 1864 and saw action in the Civil War. In 1879 Lt. Comdr. Chadwick toured Europe and compiled a report on foreign systems of naval training for the

Office of Naval Intelligence. In 1882 ONI assigned him as naval attaché in London, in which position he served until 1884. He amassed a large volume of valuable information on European navies during this period. In 1892 he was made chief of ONI, a post he held for one year. In 1898 he served on the Naval Court of Inquiry that investigated the destruction of the battleship *Maine* in Havana harbor. He commanded the cruiser *New York* during the Spanish-American war; a decade later he published a definitive history of that war.

Chadwick was a sailor-scholar with a great gift for collecting and analyzing openly available military and naval information. He typified the role of ONI during the period prior to the Spanish-American War.

(Dorwart, *Office of Naval Intelligence; DAB.*)

CHALET RECONNAISSANCE SATELLITE

A successor to the RHYOLITE RECONNAISSANCE SATELLITE, the Chalet is an orbital surveillance platform designed to follow a geosynchronous orbit, i.e., making one orbital revolution every twenty-four hours and, therefore, remaining fixed above one point on the surface of the earth. It is equipped with a very large antenna for intercepting foreign telemetry and other SIGINT data. It was first launched in 1978.

(*New York Times*, January 13, 1985, Section 6, p. 54; *Newsweek*, January 31, 1983.)

CHAMBERLIN, STEPHEN J. (December 23, 1889–October 23, 1971): Army officer, intelligence officer

A native of Spring Hill, Kansas, Chamberlin graduated from the U.S. Military Academy in 1912. In 1912–17 he served in California, on the Mexican border, and in the Philippines. He subsequently served in a variety of Army staff positions. During the Second World War he was chief of staff for the Army in Australia (1942), and G-3 (assistant chief of staff for training and organization) for the Southwest Pacific in 1942–45. In 1946–48 he was chief of ARMY INTELLIGENCE. He retired with the rank of lieutenant general.

Among the many decorations awarded Chamberlin were the Distinguished Service Medal, the Silver Star, and the French croix de guerre.

(*Who Was Who in America*, v. 5.)

CHAMBERS, WASHINGTON IRVING (April 4, 1856–September 23, 1934): naval intelligence officer

A native of Kingston, New York, Chambers graduated from the Naval Academy in 1876 and served with the Office of Naval Intelligence between 1883–84 and 1885–88. In October 1884 he was selected by the Secretary of the Navy to make a confidential reconnaissance of Panama and Nicaragua, both of which were then being considered as possible sites for a canal across the Central American isthmus. He taught at the Naval War College from 1892 to 1894. In December 1908 he was promoted to the rank of captain. He retired from the Navy in 1913.

Chambers played an important role in the early development of aviation in the U.S. Navy and is known as "the Father of Naval Aviation."

(Dorwart, *Office of Naval Intelligence; Who Was Who in America*, vol. 4; *National Cyclopedia of American Biography*, vol. 25.)

CHAMBERS, (DAVID) WHITTAKER (April 1, 1901–July 9, 1961): journalist, Soviet secret intelligence agent

A native of Philadelphia, Pennsylvania, Chambers enrolled at Columbia University in 1920. He was expelled from Columbia in 1923 for having written and published a play deemed offensive to the Christian religion. He went to Europe and traveled briefly in Germany, Belgium, and France. Upon his return he was readmitted to Columbia. He supported himself through part-time work in the public library, but he was accused of stealing books and discharged. He joined the Communist Party in 1924. Soon thereafter he began writing for the Party's newspaper, the *Daily Worker*, and shortly after became editor of that publication.

In 1932 Chambers became a secret agent of Soviet intelligence, according to his own account given many years later. He stated that he worked as a courier for Col. Boris Bykov, who was a senior Soviet military intelligence officer living in New York City in the 1930s, and that he had serviced a network of Soviet agents highly placed within the administration of President Franklin D. Roosevelt.

In 1937, Chambers said, he experienced an ideological conversion from Communism and he quit the Party the following year. He worked for the National Research Project of the federal Works Progress Administration, and eventually secured an editorial position with *Time* magazine. In September 1939 he approached ADOLF A. BERLE, JR., then assistant secretary of state for Latin American affairs, and asserted that several senior government officials were members of the Communist Party, although he did not disclose his own role as a Soviet espionage agent. Among the officials Chambers named was Alger Hiss, a Harvard Law School graduate who had served as secretary to Supreme Court Justice Oliver Wendell Holmes, and who was at that time an official in the Far Eastern Division of the State Department. Berle made an official report of Chambers' allegations, but no action was taken.

Chambers repeated his charges to the Federal Bureau of Investigation on several occasions, but again did not disclose his own role as a Soviet courier. The FBI followed up the reports, but apparently did not develop a case against any of the people Chambers had named. (FBI counterespionage specialist ROBERT J. LAMPHERE notes that Chambers did not begin cooperating actively with the Bureau until late 1948, and had earlier lied to the FBI when he denied knowing Gerhart Eisler, a senior Soviet intelligence officer in the United States.)

In August 1948 the House Committee on Un-American Activities subpoenaed Chambers to testify at its "Hearings Regarding Communist Espionage in the United States Government." In his testimony, Chambers recounted his Communist Party affiliation and his activities in "an underground organization of the United States Communist Party," which, he said, included former Assistant Secretary of the Treasury Harry Dexter White and Alger Hiss (the latter had by then played a major role in the creation of the United Nations and had since become president of the Carnegie Endowment for International Peace).

Both White and Hiss appeared before the Committee at their own request to deny Chambers's allegations (White died of a heart attack three days after testifying). Hiss also denied knowing anyone by the name of "Whittaker Chambers," but he later identified Chambers as a man he had known as George Crosley, a free-lance journalist to whom he had subleased an apartment and lent money a dozen years earlier.

Hiss challenged Chambers to repeat his accusations outside of the Committee, where he would not be protected from legal action by official privilege. Chambers did so and Hiss filed suit for slander. During pretrial discovery hearings, Chambers produced as evidence in his defense a cache of classified State Department documents from 1938 that, he said, he had received from Hiss. Some of the documents were in Hiss's handwriting; others were retyped copies. Chambers said he had kept the documents to counter threats of Soviet retaliation against him. He subsequently produced and handed over to the HUAC five roles of microfilm, two of which contained classified State Department documents initialed by Hiss. Because Chambers said he had secreted the film in a hollow pumpkin the film became known as the "Pumpkin Papers."

Both Chambers and Hiss testified to their contradictory versions of events before a grand jury in December. On December 15th the grand jury indicted Hiss on two counts of perjury for his denials that he had seen Chambers after January 1, 1937 and that he had given government documents to Chambers. No charge of espionage was made because the statute of limitations had expired.

The case against Hiss consisted largely of Chambers's testimony, the physical evidence of the documents and film, and the testimony of FBI experts who had matched some of the retyped State Department material to a typewriter that had been owned by Hiss. His first trial ended with a hung jury, but he was convicted of perjury after his second trial in January 1950. Hiss served forty-four months in prison. Thereafter he continued to insist upon his innocence.

Chambers resigned from his position with *Time* soon after his HUAC testimony in 1948. He published his confessional autobiography, *Witness*, in 1952. He became an active anti-Communist and was welcomed as a repentant sinner by many on the political right, including WILLIAM F. BUCKLEY. Chambers wrote for Buckley's *National Review* during 1957–58. He was enrolled in Western Maryland College as an undergraduate at the time of his death.

In 1984 President Ronald Reagan awarded Chambers a posthumous Medal of Freedom.

(*Political Profiles*, The Truman Years; Weinstein, *Perjury: This Hiss-Chambers Case*; Cooke, *A Generation on Trial*; Lamphere, *The FBI-KGB War*.)

CHANDLER, ALBERT BROWN (August 20, 1840–February 2, 1923): telegrapher, businessman, cryptanalyst

A native of West Randolph, Vermont, Chandler became a telegrapher and messenger in his hometown. In 1859 Chandler joined the Cleveland and Pittsburgh Railroad, and advanced to the position of freight agent in Manchester, Pennsylvania. On June 1, 1863 he joined the War Department's Military Telegraph Service and was assigned to the Department's telegraph office in Washington.

Chandler, CHARLES A. TINKER, and DAVID H. BATES were the self-styled "Sacred Three," the principal telegraphers in the War Department's telegraph office during the Civil War. In addition to sending and receiving telegrams, and enciphering and deciphering some of them, they were occasionally called upon to solve intercepted Confederate cryptograms, and they achieved some success in doing so (see WIRETAPPING AND COMMUNICATIONS INTELLIGENCE IN THE CIVIL WAR).

After the war Chandler worked for the Western Union Telegraph Company and other telegraph companies. He became president of the Postal Telegraph Cable Company.

(*National Cyclopedia of American Biography*, v. 3; *Who Was Who in America*, v. 1; Kahn, *The Codebreakers*; Harlow, *Old Wires and New Waves*.)

CHARYK, JOSEPH VINCENT (September 9, 1920–): engineer, businessman, intelligence officer

A native of Alberta, Canada, Charyk graduated from the University of Alberta in 1942 and earned an M.S. and Ph.D. from the California Institute of Technology in 1943 and 1946, respectively. He became a U.S. citizen in 1948. He taught at Cal Tech and worked at the school's Jet Propulsion Laboratory during 1945–46. During 1946–55 he was on the faculty of Princeton University, and he worked in senior technical management positions for Lockheed Aircraft Corporation and other aerospace firms during 1955–59.

In 1959 Charyk became assistant secretary of the Air Force for research and development, and in 1960 he became under secretary of the Air Force. When the NATIONAL RECONNAISSANCE OFFICE was created in August 1960, Charyk became its first director, while also continuing in the post of Air Force under secretary (Charyk began the tradition whereby the under secretary also serves as the NRO director).

In 1963 Charyk left the Air Force and the NRO to become president and a director of the Communications Satellite Corporation. He has remained in that post since then, and also has held other senior positions in private high technology firms.

(*Who's Who in America*, 42nd ed.; Richelson, *The U.S. Intelligence Community*.)

CHEATHAM, BENJAMIN FRANKLIN (October 20, 1820–September 4, 1886): farmer, government official, Army officer, intelligence officer

A native of Nashville, Tennessee, Cheatham served in the Tennessee Volunteers in the Mexican War and attained the rank of colonel. After a brief prospecting trip to California during the Gold Rush of 1849, he returned to Tennessee and became a major general in the state militia.

Albert B. Chandler in Army uniform during the Civil War. Source: National Archives.

At the outbreak of the Civil War Cheatham was commissioned a brigadier general in the Confederate Army. In mid-1862 he took over the task of organizing a secret service for the Army of Tennessee from Col. J. STODDARD JOHNSON. Because he had spent most of his life in Tennessee Cheatham was better able than Johnson to recruit local people to serve as agents. He organized the unit that became known as COLEMAN'S SCOUTS and put Capt. HENRY B. SHAW in charge of it.

Cheatham commanded a division and later a corps in the Army of Tennessee. He was promoted to major general in March 1862, and was wounded in the Battle of Stones River (December 30, 1862–January 3, 1863). After the war he farmed in Tennessee and served four years as the state's superintendent of prisons. In 1885 President Grover Cleveland appointed Cheatham postmaster of Nashville.

(*WAMB; Who Was Who in America*, historical volume; Bakeless, *Spies of the Confederacy*.)

CHILD, JULIA MCWILLIAMS (August 15, 1912–): author, chef, OSS employee

A native of Pasadena, California, Child graduated from Smith College in 1934 and worked in the advertising department of W.&J. Sloane in New York City from 1939 to 1940. Between 1941 and 1945 she served with the Office of Strategic Services in Washington, D.C., Ceylon, and China. While with Detachment 202, the OSS unit in China, she served as secretary to OSS officer Paul Child, whom she later married.

Julia Child later became famous as the author of books on cooking and cuisine, and as television's "French Chef."

(*Who's Who in America*, 42nd ed.; Hunt, *Undercover*.)

CHURCH, BENJAMIN (August 24, 1734–?): physician, Continental army surgeon, British double agent

A native of Newport, Rhode Island, Church attended the Boston Latin School during 1745–50, and graduated from Harvard in 1754. He studied medicine at the London Medical College, married an Englishwoman, and returned to America. About 1768 he settled in Raynham, Massachusetts, where he practiced medicine.

Church was active in colonial politics and was a member of the Boston COMMITTEE OF CORRESPONDENCE. He was also a member of PAUL REVERE's Boston spy ring. However, his true allegiance was to the British and he worked as a British espionage agent from circa 1774, reporting to Thomas Hutchinson, the royal governor of Massachusetts, and his successor Gen. Thomas Gage, the British commander-in-chief.

According to Van Doren, Church's report to Gage that the Americans had military stores at Concord led to the British expedition that resulted in the Battles of Lexington and Concord in April 1775. A few days later Church went to Boston and met with Gage, apparently to establish arrangements for future reporting, and he covered this meeting by claiming to his American compatriots that he had been arrested while on the medical mission to Boston, taken before the British commander, and later released. A month later he informed Gage of the American plans to fortify Bunker Hill.

Although he had become an object of the suspicions of Revere and others, Church was made chief of the first Continental Army Hospital in Cambridge, Massachusetts, in July 1775. He was finally discovered in September of that year when an enciphered letter he had attempted to send to the British by means of his mistress fell into American hands. Under interrogation by Gen. GEORGE WASHINGTON, the woman disclosed that she had been acting as a courier for Church, who was then arrested.

Church's home was searched, but apparently all incriminating documents had been removed by an accomplice (Van Doren suggests it may have been BENJAMIN THOMPSON). Nonetheless, he was convicted by a council of war of carrying on a criminal correspondence with the British. Because of an oversight the Continental Army did not have the legal authority to hang a spy; Church was therefore imprisoned. He was subsequently permitted to go into exile, by some accounts to the West Indies. He departed from Boston on a schooner and was presumed lost at sea when neither he nor the vessel were ever heard from again. The date of this fateful voyage seems a matter of uncertainty. *Who Was Who in America* gives it as 1776; Van Doren puts it in the latter part of 1777; Bakeless says it was 1780.

(*Who Was Who in America*, historical volume; Boatner, *Encyclopedia of the American Revolution*; Van Doren, *Secret History of the American Revolution*; Bakeless, *Turncoats, Traitors and Heroes*.)

CHURCHILL, MARLBOROUGH (August 11, 1878–July 9, 1942): Army officer, intelligence officer

A native of Andover, Massachusetts, Churchill graduated from Harvard in 1900. He was commissioned as a second lieutenant in the U.S. Army in 1901. In 1917, by then a colonel, he was assigned to the general staff of the American Expeditionary Force in France.

In June 1918 Churchill succeeded Col. RALPH VAN DEMAN as the chief of the Military Intelligence Division of the Department of the Army's General Staff (see ARMY INTELLIGENCE). Soon thereafter he was promoted to the temporary rank of brigadier general. He continued in the position of assistant chief of staff and director of military intelligence until September 1920, when he was succeeded by Brig. Gen. DENNIS E. NOLAN.

Churchill served as "General Military Liaison Coordination Officer" of the American Peace Commission at the PARIS PEACE CONFERENCE OF 1919, heading a contingent of twenty intelligence officers from MID.

Together with HERBERT O. YARDLEY, Churchill was instrumental in establishing the joint State and War departments' Cipher Bureau (see AMERICAN BLACK CHAMBER).

Churchill held many decorations, including the Distinguished Service Medal, the French Legion of Honor, and the British Companion of the Bath.

(Bidwell, "History of the Military Intelligence Division, Department of the Army General Staff"; *Who's Who in America*, v. 2.)

CIA ADMINISTRATION DIRECTORATE

That part of the CIA responsible for the Agency's personnel administration, training, finance, security, communications, computer services, medical services, and the logistical support of overseas operations. The Administration Directorate is headed by the deputy director for administration, and the abbreviation DDA is commonly used to designate the Directorate as well as the deputy director.

The Directorate was established in 1950 by CIA Director WALTER BEDELL SMITH when he consolidated all the management functions required by the rapidly growing Agency and placed them under the newly created post of deputy director for support. The organization was designated the Support Directorate until the mid-1970s, and the initials DDS were used to refer both to the Directorate and the deputy director. A short time thereafter, the organization became known as the Management and Support Directorate, and then received its current name. Since then the initials DDA have been used.

Though the Directorate performs most of the same administrative functions as other government bureaucracies, its tasks are often more complex because of the sensitive and clandestine nature of the CIA. As presently constituted, the Directorate consists of the Office of Medical Services, which provides cleared medical personnel when such are needed to treat Agency employees; the Office of Security, which is responsible for the security of Agency installations, security investigations, the security clearance of personnel, and related functions; the Office of Training and Education; the Office of Finance, which necessarily deals in many foreign currencies and must fulfill special security requirements while doing so; the Office of Logistics, which supports the many unique and demanding needs of the CIA CLANDESTINE SERVICE overseas; the Office of Information Services, a computer and data processing service unit once part of the CIA SCIENCE AND TECHNOLOGY DIRECTORATE; the Office of Personnel; and the Office of Communications, which provides secure communications for CIA facilities overseas and in the United States.

Deputy Director for Administration	Dates
Murray McConnel	1950–51
Walter Wolf	1951–53
Lawrence White	1953–65
Robert Bannerman	1965–71
John Coffey	1971–73
Harold Brownman	1973–74
JOHN BLAKE	1974–79
Donald Wortman	1979–81

Gen. Marlborough Churchill. Source: National Archives.

Max Hugel	1981
Harry Fitzwater	1981–

(Karalekas, *History of the Central Intelligence Agency*; Ranelagh, *The Agency*; Richelson, *The U.S. Intelligence Community*.)

CIA CLANDESTINE SERVICE

Synonymous with the CIA Operations Directorate, the term refers to that part of the CIA that conducts secret intelligence collection, covert action, and other clandestine operations.

The Clandestine Service was established as such in January 1951 by CIA Director WALTER BEDELL SMITH when he placed both the Office of Special Operations (OSO)—the CIA's secret intelligence unit—and the Office of Policy Coordination (OPC)—the covert action unit—under the newly created post of deputy director for plans (DDP). The DDP post was filled by the newly recruited ALLEN W. DULLES. The reason why Dulles was given a title that implied that planning was his primary function remains obscure.

In August 1952 OPC and OSO were merged. The new unit became known as the Plans Directorate, a name obviously derived from the title of the deputy director in charge of it. Thereafter, until the unit was renamed the Operations Directorate in 1973, it was referred to as "the DDP" and, alternatively, "the Clandestine Service." Since 1973 it has been called the DDO (after the new title of its chief: deputy director for operations) or the Operations Directorate, though the term "Clandestine Service" has survived as an alternate name. That term has generally been used throughout this work instead of "DDP," "Plans Directorate," "DDO," or "Operations Directorate," though all five terms refer to the same unit.

There are six geographic area divisions within the Clandestine Service, corresponding to the Soviet bloc, Western Europe, the western hemisphere, East Asia, the Near East, and Africa. Each area division is subdivided into "country desks," one for each of the countries within the area in which there is a Clandestine Service station. There is, furthermore, the Special Operations Division, which is concerned with covert paramilitary operations; the Foreign Resources Division, which conducts clandestine operational activities within the United States against foreign targets; and the Domestic Collection Division, which openly collects intelligence from Americans who have traveled abroad.

There are several functional staffs within the Clandestine Service concerned with such specialized functions as counterintelligence, cover, foreign intelligence, and covert action.

Deputy Director for Plans/Operations	Dates
ALLEN DULLES	1951
KILBOURNE JOHNSTON	1951–52
FRANK WISNER	1952–58
RICHARD BISSELL	1958–62
RICHARD HELMS	1962–65
DESMOND FITZGERALD	1965–67
THOMAS KARAMESSINES	1967–73
WILLIAM COLBY	1973
William Nelson	1973–76
William Wells	1976–78
JOHN MCMAHON	1978–81
Max Hugel	1981
John Stein	1981–84
Clare George	1984–

(Karalekas, *History of the Central Intelligence Agency;* Breckinridge, *The CIA and the U.S. Intelligence System;* Ranelagh, *The Agency;* Richelson, *The U.S. Intelligence Community.*)

CIA INTELLIGENCE DIRECTORATE

That part of the CIA that produces finished national intelligence. The Intelligence Directorate is headed by the deputy director for intelligence, and the abbreviation DDI is commonly used to designate the Directorate as well as the deputy director.

The Directorate was established in January 1952 by CIA Director WALTER BEDELL SMITH when he placed all of the Agency's intelligence production offices under the newly created post of deputy director for intelligence. These included the Office of National Estimates, the Office of Research and Reports, the Office of Scientific Intelligence, the Office of Current Intelligence, the Office of Operations (which collected openly available information), and the Office of Collection and Dissemination (a central reference and distribution unit).

As presently constituted, the Directorate consists of five production offices oriented to the geographic areas of the USSR, Europe, the Near East and South Asia, East Asia, and Africa and Latin America; plus the Office of Scientific and Weapons Research; the Office of Global Issues, which conducts long-term, in-depth political intelligence analysis; the Office of Current Production and Analytic Support; the Office of Central Reference; and the Office of Planning and Management Services.

Deputy Director for Intelligence	Dates
LOFTUS BECKER	1952–53
ROBERT AMORY	1953–62
RAY S. CLINE	1962–66
R. JACK SMITH	1966–71
Edward Proctor	1971–76
Sayre Stevens	1976–77
ROBERT BOWIE	1977–79
Bruce Clarke	1979–82
ROBERT GATES	1982–86
Richard J. Kerr	1986–

(Karalekas, *History of the Central Intelligence Agency;* Central Intelligence Agency, *Fact Book on Intelligence;* Ranelagh, *The Agency.*)

CIA SCIENCE AND TECHNOLOGY DIRECTORATE

That part of the CIA responsible for collecting and processing information gathered by technical collection systems, e.g., OVERHEAD RECONNAISSANCE, and for developing advanced technology for use in collection and processing. The Directorate is headed by the deputy director for science and technology, and the abbreviation DDS&T is commonly used to designate the Directorate as well as the deputy director.

In 1962 CIA Director JOHN A. MCCONE established the Research Directorate in an attempt to consolidate and integrate the Agency's scientific and technical functions (see HERBERT SCOVILLE). Because of bureaucratic resistance, however, this attempt was frustrated. In August 1963 McCone again tried to accomplish this end through the establishment of the Science and Technology Directorate, and was successful. The S&T Directorate consisted of the Office of Scientific Intelligence, a unit formerly in the INTELLIGENCE DIRECTORATE that was concerned with basic scientific research in foreign countries; the Data Processing Staff, a computer services group; the Office of ELINT, an electronic intelligence unit that had been part of the CIA CLANDESTINE SERVICE; the Development Projects Division, the Clandestine Service unit that had been responsible for developing the U-2 and other overhead reconnaissance systems; the Office of Research and Development, a newly created unit charged with employing new technologies in the INTELLIGENCE CYCLE; and the Foreign Missile and Space Analysis Center, a unit established to keep track of the missile and space programs of foreign powers.

As presently constituted, the S&T Directorate no longer includes the Office of Scientific Intelligence, which was recently moved back to the Intelligence Directorate. The FOREIGN BROADCAST INFORMATION SERVICE and the NATIONAL PHOTOGRAPHIC INTERPRETATION CENTER, both long under the deputy director for intelligence, are now in the S&T Directorate. The scope of the Office of ELINT apparently has been enlarged, and the unit is now the Office of SIGINT. The Development Projects Division has become the Office of Development and Engineering. The Technical Services Division of the Clandestine Service has been moved into the S&T Directorate, where it is now the Office of Technical Service. The Office of Research and Development remains in the Directorate.

Deputy Director for Science and Technology	Dates
ALBERT WHEELON	1963–67
CARL DUCKETT	1967–76
Leslie Dirks	1976–82
Evans Hineman	1982–

(Karalekas, *History of the Central Intelligence Agency;* Central Intelligence Agency, *Fact Book on Intelligence;* Ranelagh, *The Agency.*)

CIVIL WAR

Background: The ultimate causes of the American Civil War are well known. The immediate events that triggered the war began with the election of Abraham Lincoln in November 1860. This prompted the seces-

sion of South Carolina in December, followed during the next few weeks by Mississippi, Florida, Alabama, Georgia, Louisiana, and Texas. In February 1861 delegates from the states that had seceded met in Montgomery, Alabama, to form the government of the Confederate States of America.

The outgoing administration of President James Buchanan did not acknowledge the Confederate government, but it also took pains to avoid a confrontation with it during Buchanan's remaining weeks in office. The points of immediate contention were Fort Sumter at Charleston, South Carolina, and Fort Pickens at Pensacola, Florida, which were claimed by the Confederacy but remained in federal hands. Although Confederate batteries fired on and drove off a merchant ship carrying supplies and reinforcements to Fort Sumter in January, Buchanan took no action and Sumter remained under a virtual state of siege.

Soon after his inauguration in March, President Lincoln ordered a naval squadron to Charleston to relieve Fort Sumter, simultaneously notifying the governor of South Carolina of his intention, and thereby forcing the Confederacy either to acquiesce or accept the political liability of initiating hostilities. The Confederate government chose the latter course, demanded the surrender of Sumter, and, after the commander of the federal garrison refused, fired on it on April 12th, thereby precipitating the war.

The War: Fort Sumter fell on April 14th. There followed an uneasy period of several months without any significant combat, during which time both North and South worked to put armies in the field. President Lincoln's call for the state militias to be mobilized triggered the secession of Virginia, Arkansas, Tennessee, and North Carolina. With the lines now drawn, both sides began to prepare for action and devise national strategies.

At the outset both the Union and Confederacy were inclined to some degree to passive strategies. The South had already achieved its objective, for the moment: secession from the Union and the establishment of the Confederate States of America. Moreover, it hoped for aid and perhaps active military intervention on its behalf by England and/or France, both heavily dependent on Southern cotton and both ready, for important economic and geopolitical reasons, to see the United States fragmented (Britain proclaimed her neutrality on May 13th, thereby recognizing the belligerency of the Confederacy). Southern optimists found reasons to hope the North would prefer to accept the new status quo, rather than fight a major war to recover the seceded states.

The Anaconda Plan

For its part, the North found reasons to hope for recovery of the Confederate states without bloodshed. Within a week of the fall of Fort Sumter the U.S. Navy began a blockade of the South that soon extended 3,550 miles from Virginia to Texas. This, and a federal prohibition against trade with the rebellious states, was aimed at the economic strangulation of the South and the interdiction of aid, military and otherwise, from Europe. Gen. Winfield Scott, general-in-chief of the Army, formulated the Anaconda Plan (as it was somewhat derisively dubbed by his detractors), which called for continuing the blockade, dividing the Confederacy physically and economically through the control of the Mississippi River, and insuring the security of the national government at Washington through military control of northern Virginia. With the South thus isolated and divided, Scott hoped that Unionist sentiment in the Confederacy would eventually prevail, and that the rebellious states would return to the Union peacefully.

Northern Advantages

Northern optimism was encouraged by the overwhelming military and strategic advantages held by the North over the Confederacy. The population of the North—the pool of potential military manpower—was more than double that of the South. The North had a larger arsenal with which to arm its forces, and enormous superiority in the industrial capacity to produce more of the same. The North had more miles of railroad, more rolling stock, and a greater population of horses and mules, the motive power of armies of the time. Even in agriculture, the North outstripped the South in production capacity. And the Union possessed a navy, albeit a deteriorated one, and industrial capacity the South did not have, to build additional modern warships.

This material superiority failed to compel the hoped-for bloodless Northern victory, however, or bring about a swift military defeat of the South. The first major battle of the war took place on July 21, 1861 at Bull Run, when a federal force attempted to flank the Confederate stronghold at the strategic railroad junction of Manassas, Virginia, some twenty-five miles southwest of Washington. The Confederates used their interior lines of communication—including in this case a railroad line linking Manassas with points to the west—to concentrate their forces, outnumber the federals in the field, and send them fleeing back to Washington in disarray.

With its defeat at the First Battle of Bull Run, the North began to realize that a long and bloody struggle lay ahead. The Anaconda Plan—originally the foundation of Northern hopes for a bloodless victory—now became the basis of the North's more aggressive strategy. Geography dictated the overall structure of the war. The South, destined by the objectives, strengths, and strategies of both sides to be the major war zone, was divided by natural features into three theaters of operations: the Eastern, between the Atlantic and the Appalachian Mountains; the Western, between the mountains and the Mississippi; and the Trans-Mississippi, those territories west of the great river (the last-named, although the scene of much fighting, never assumed a major strategic importance to either side).

The Defensive Orientation

The commanders of both sides had in common their military education at West Point (many who faced each other in civil war had been classmates) and their professional experience in the MEXICAN WAR and the long period thereafter, when the main job of the Army was to prepare to defend the nation against aggression from beyond its shores and borders and to protect settlements from Indian attack on the western frontier. Military science as taught at West Point during the three decades before the war had stressed engineering and the use of fortifications, an emphasis seemingly consistent with the defensive role of the Army, but one that tended to neglect the study of the tactics and strategy of mobile offensive warfare. Thus, at the outbreak of the war, the commanders of neither North nor South were well prepared by training or experience (except for the brief Mexican experience) to wage offensive war. This predisposition toward fortifications and defensive tactics was further encouraged by observation of the effects of rifled muskets and artillery, a Civil War innovation in the American military experience. Rifling greatly increased the range and accuracy of such weapons, with devastating results when used to defend against traditional frontal attacks.

The American inadequacy in waging offensive war did more to handicap the Union, since the war aims of the Confederacy were, at least at the outset, consistent with a defensive posture. It soon became clear that the South, although militarily and economically weaker than the North, was nonetheless strong enough to hope to sustain its independence.

The North Takes the Offensive

The North at last came to grips with the problem and took the offensive early in 1862. In the West,

Union forces under Generals Halleck and Grant moved southward and took control of the Mississippi Valley down almost to Vicksburg, Mississippi, while an amphibious force under Adm. David Farragut and Gen. Benjamin Butler captured New Orleans. These two strokes nearly accomplished the division of the Confederacy as envisioned in Scott's Anaconda Plan.

Also in the spring of 1862, the Union launched a major campaign in the East aimed at capturing the Confederate capital, Richmond. The Army of the Potomac—the main Union fighting force of the Eastern theater, commanded by Gen. George B. McClellan, who had succeeded Scott as general-in-chief of the Union forces—was transported by water from Washington to Fort Monroe, Virginia, at the tip of the peninsula formed by the York and James rivers. But McClellan's advance up the peninsula toward Richmond bogged down when he spent a month laying siege to Yorktown, thereby permitting the Confederates to concentrate their forces between the federals and Richmond and frustrate the Union plan.

Incidental to the Peninsula Campaign was the ascendancy of Gen. Robert E. Lee, who succeeded Gen. Joseph E. Johnston in the overall command of Confederate forces in Virginia after Johnston was wounded. Lee was convinced that the South would eventually lose if it maintained its purely defensive strategy and allowed the Union to keep the initiative to choose the time and place of battle. Gen. Thomas J. "Stonewall" Jackson, the Confederate commander in the Shenandoah Valley, shared Lee's view. Jackson believed that concentrated attacks on vital Northern points would be far more effective than spreading defensive forces thinly along a frontier, and that the best means of defense was an offensive strategy.

Lee's Offensive Strategy

After McClellan's withdrawal from the peninsula, Lee persuaded Confederate President Jefferson Davis to approve his plan for a bold offensive strike through Maryland and into Pennsylvania. Lee's plan called for the capture of Harrisburg, Pennsylvania, a move that would cut the North's major east-west railroad link. In September he crossed the Potomac River into Maryland and encountered McClellan's reorganized Army of the Potomac at Sharpsburg, near Antietam Creek. One of the bloodiest battles of the war ensued and was fought to a standoff. Lee, having lost more than a quarter of his army, withdrew across the Potomac to Virginia. McClellan, having suffered even greater casualties, did not pursue him.

McClellan's failures at offensive warfare prompted President Lincoln to replace him as commander of the Army of the Potomac after Antietam (he had

already lost his job as general-in-chief). His successor, Gen. Ambrose Burnside, enjoyed only a brief tenure because of his poor judgment in attacking a well-entrenched Confederate force under Lee at Fredericksburg, Virginia, in December. Gen. Joseph Hooker, the next commander of the Army of the Potomac, also failed to push past the Rappahannock River into southern Virginia; when he attempted to flank the Confederate stronghold at Fredericksburg early in May 1863, he encountered Lee at Chancellorsville. Resorting to defensive tactics, he left the initiative to Lee, thereby bringing about another Union defeat. The battle proved costly to Lee, however; he lost the skillful and aggressive Gen. "Stonewall" Jackson, who fell victim to accidental friendly fire.

Still convinced that the Confederacy must take the offensive if it was to survive, Lee undertook a second invasion of the North in June, advancing up the Shenandoah Valley through Virginia, across the Potomac River and Maryland, and into Pennsylvania, where he met the Army of the Potomac—now commanded by Gen. George Meade—at Gettysburg on July 1st. After three days of fighting and enormous losses on both sides, Lee was turned back and he retreated into Virginia. Like McClellan after Antietam, Meade failed to pursue the retreating Confederates.

The failure of Lee's second invasion of the North coincided with a Confederate defeat in the West: Vicksburg, Mississippi, fell to General Grant on July 4th, after a two-month siege. The fall of Vicksburg, the last Confederate stronghold on the Mississippi River, meant that the Union had gained control of the entire length of the river, thereby dividing the Confederacy as envisioned in Scott's Anaconda Plan.

A War of Attrition

Having countered Confederate moves to take the war into the North, and having completed the isolation of the Confederacy, the Union only had to destroy the South's will and capacity to persist in rebellion (the Confederacy had failed in its diplomatic campaign to enlist Britain or France as an ally, and President Lincoln's Emancipation Proclamation of September 1862 made it politically impossible for Britain to intervene on behalf of the Confederacy). In March 1864 Lincoln appointed, as his new general-in-chief of the Union armies, Gen. Ulysses S. Grant, who had demonstrated his capacity for offensive warfare in the West. For the next twelve months, Grant fought a war of attrition, pushing Lee back to Richmond and laying siege to Petersburg, a vital Confederate railroad center and the key to the defense of Richmond. During the same period, Gen.

William T. Sherman marched southward from Tennessee, captured Atlanta, and left a wide swath of destruction across Georgia all the way to the coastal city of Savannah. He next turned north, leaving yet more devastation in his wake, as he marched through the Carolinas to join Grant in Virginia.

The numerical superiority of the North proved decisive. Early in April 1865 Petersburg fell to Grant, followed almost immediately by the fall of Richmond. Lee was unable to break out of the fast-closing Union trap to join forces with General Johnston in the Carolinas. On April 9th he surrendered his army to Grant at Appomattox, Virginia. Johnston surrendered the remaining Confederate forces to Sherman on April 26th, thereby bringing an end to the war.

Intelligence in the War: Although the war had been foreseen for years, neither side had made any prewar intelligence preparations. In fact, intelligence seems to have been the least of the concerns of both Union and Confederate commanders, at least at the outset of hostilities. There were some reasons for complacency: both sides had good BASIC INTELLIGENCE of the geography and topography of the war zones (although McClellan was surprised to find the Warwick River in his path as he advanced up the James Peninsula); the commanders on both sides knew each other—and each other's command styles— well, having served together in the same army for years, and in some cases having been classmates at West Point (Jefferson Davis had graduated from West Point, served as chairman of the U.S. Senate Military Affairs Committee, and was President Franklin Pierce's secretary of war before becoming president of the Confederate States); and the military assets of both sides—fortifications, arsenals, warships, railroad lines, etc.—were well known to both.

But the participants were soon to discover that they were fighting a war that would at times move at a swifter pace than they had ever experienced or heard of. Military railroads and telegraph were to have their first extensive use in this war. An army could be moved in hours across distances that generals customarily measured in days of marching. A commander's orders could be transmitted over hundreds of miles in no time at all. A strategic or tactical situation could change with a rapidity previously unknown in warfare, and timely military intelligence was to become a precious advantage.

The Confederates, forced to take a defensive posture, desperately needed to know well in advance where the Union's blows were going to fall so that they would have time to concentrate their numerically inferior forces to defend those points. And the Northern general invading Southern territory needed to know not only what lay ahead but what was on his flank and to his rear, if he was not to be caught in a Confederate trap.

These factors, so obvious in hindsight, were not equally clear to the participants at the time, however. Scott, the first Union general-in-chief, had relied heavily on intelligence during the MEXICAN WAR (see MEXICAN SPY COMPANY), but little that he did in the Civil War suggested that he felt it very important in fighting the Confederacy. Scott's successor, McClellan, showed some concern about intelligence, but his interest seemed to focus entirely on Confederate troop strength and ORDER OF BATTLE, and these were grossly overestimated by his intelligence chief, ALLAN PINKERTON, who thus encouraged that same military hesitancy that led President Lincoln to dismiss McClellan.

Contrary to what is widely and popularly held (see CIVIL WAR ESPIONAGE MYTHOLOGY), the Confederate leaders showed no more understanding of the value of intelligence than did the federals. Throughout the war Gen. Robert E. Lee never established a formal military intelligence function within the staff of the Army of Northern Virginia. He relied instead on his cavalry under Gen. J.E.B. Stuart to serve as "the eyes of the army," a policy that brought him to the brink of disaster on the eve of the Battle of Gettysburg (see HENRY T. HARRISON). Lee's neglect of intelligence was usually compensated, however, by an almost preternatural gift for reaching the right assessment of a tactical situation with little or no facts to work from. As Civil War historian Edwin C. Fishel says, "He understood the art of war much better than the art of military intelligence."

The "Secret Services"

Although it is widely believed that the Union and the Confederacy each had a "Secret Service," i.e., a single agency operating at the national level with central responsibility for all military and other intelligence, such was never the case. Contrary to myth, Pinkerton's detective force served only McClellan in his capacity as commander of the Army of the Potomac. The detective force of Col. LAFAYETTE C. BAKER (see NATIONAL DETECTIVE BUREAU) is mistakenly believed to have been both a centralized intelligence and counterintelligence agency of the War Department, as well as the embryonic stage of the United States SECRET SERVICE, but it was neither. Baker and his detective staff were concerned almost exclusively with counterintelligence (i.e., spy-catching) and law enforcement, and their activities were nearly always limited to the greater Washington area.

The CONFEDERATE SECRET SERVICE was a national-level intelligence agency, headquartered at the Confederate seat of government in Richmond. The full scope of its responsibilities and activities remain unknown in the absence of its records, which disappeared at the fall of Richmond, but it was definitely not a centralized military intelligence agency serving all the Confederate forces in the field. Military intelligence was a matter left to the individual Confederate field commander to deal with (or ignore) as he saw fit. The Union army followed the same policy.

There were no standardized procedures. Intelligence—the term actually used was *military information*—was the responsibility of the provost marshal in many cases, but sometimes it was assigned to the adjutant of the command, the signal officer, the chief of staff, or even the commanding general himself. Union Gen. GRENVILLE M. DODGE, for example, took personal charge of intelligence, supervising the work of his chief of scouts, L. A. NARON and the secret service Naron headed. And the nucleus of COLEMAN'S SCOUTS, the secret service of the Confederate Army of Tennessee, was established by Gen. BENJAMIN F. CHEATHAM, although the organization was developed and run by Capt. HENRY B. SHAW (also known as "E. C. Coleman").

The term *scout* was often a euphemism for *spy*. The essential distinction between scouting and spying depended upon whether the person making a reconnaissance of enemy territory and forces did so in the uniform of his own side, in civilian clothing, or in enemy uniform. Many scouts, e.g., JOHN C. BABCOCK, were actually civilians and therefore not entitled to wear a uniform in any case. In practice a scout's choice of attire was dictated by necessity, which usually meant civilian clothing or enemy uniform when operating behind enemy lines.

By far the most professional of the many Civil War "secret services" was the BUREAU OF MILITARY INFORMATION, established by Col. GEORGE H. SHARPE at the behest of Gen. Joseph Hooker when he became commander of the Union's Army of the Potomac in January 1863. Only in March 1864, when Sharpe became General-in-Chief Grant's intelligence officer, and Grant located his headquarters with that of the Army of the Potomac, did the Bureau begin to resemble the sort of army-wide G-2 popularly believed to have existed throughout the war.

Sources

Like the American Revolution, the Civil War was a war of divided loyalties between people who shared the same language and customs, but who often disagreed with their next-door neighbors on the political issues that led to the war. So there was an abundance of volunteers on both sides, ready, willing, and able to spy. The secret agent of the Civil War was the occasional civilian informant who happened to be in the right place at the right time to provide information to a commander; the full-time civilian volunteer spy, e.g., ELIZABETH VAN LEW; and the enlisted or commissioned soldier who agreed to exchange his uniform for mufti and serve behind enemy lines, e.g., HENRY T. HARRISON, SAMUEL DAVIS, or SPENCER K. BROWN.

The role of secret agents, and especially the contributions and importance of certain individual agents, has been greatly exaggerated in the popular literature of the Civil War (see CIVIL WAR ESPIONAGE MYTHOLOGY.) Although secret agents provided crucial intelligence, they were by no means the only, or even the principal, intelligence source in the war. Reconnaissance by cavalry was an important means of obtaining information, and, as previously noted, this was the principal means employed by General Lee. Surprisingly, signal intercepts and aerial reconnaissance were also employed to collect intelligence (see WIRETAPPING AND COMMUNICATIONS INTELLIGENCE IN THE CIVIL WAR, RECONNAISSANCE BALLOONS). The signal towers and other elevated points used by signalmen to communicate by semaphore also provided vantage points for important observation of enemy movements. Prisoners of war, deserters, and refugees brought important information from behind enemy lines, and the skillful interrogation of such people was a major intelligence procedure (apparently the Civil War marked the introduction of TRUTH DRUGS in interrogation, although these seem to have been used on a very limited basis). And newspapers, although filled with errors and disinformation, were exploited as an intelligence source, especially by the Confederacy (see NEWSPAPERS IN THE CIVIL WAR).

Covert Action and Irregular Warfare

The Civil War saw the full range of special operations—paramilitary, psychological, political and economic. One of the most noted paramilitary operations, ANDREWS'S RAID, was mounted by Union forces in support of Gen. Ormsby Mitchel's planned attack on Chattanooga, Tennessee, in 1862. Although there was extensive SUBVERSION IN THE CONFEDERACY, which encouraged desertion and draft-dodging and which Northern commanders may have exploited for secret intelligence operations, the U.S. government failed to make much use of Unionist sentiment in the South for the purpose of subversive warfare.

Most irregular warfare was waged by the Confederates, who made repeated attempts to exploit the Copperheads, i.e., the pro-secession, anti-Washington sentiment in the border states (see KNIGHTS OF THE GOLDEN CIRCLE), and promote various forms of subversion in the North. One of the earliest of such operations was actually mounted before the war, apparently without the authorization or knowledge of the Confederate leaders. Its object was the assassination of President-elect Lincoln before he could take office (see BALTIMORE PLOT).

Although the Confederates established a network of secret intelligence agents and saboteurs in Kentucky and Indiana in 1862 (see THOMAS H. HINES), and Gen. John Hunt Morgan hoped to provoke an uprising by the Copperheads when he led raiding parties into Indiana and Ohio in 1863, subversion in the border states did not yield the expected results and failed to frustrate the Union's major objective in the Western theater of the war, i.e., dividing the Confederacy through control of the Mississippi.

The Confederates increased their emphasis on covert action in 1864, prompted in part by the very unfavorable strategic situation of the South following the Battle of Gettysburg and the fall of Vicksburg in the previous year, and in part by the growing war-weariness in the North, which promised to crystallize during the national election campaigns in the late summer and fall. JACOB THOMPSON, one of the most ambitious Confederate covert operators, was sent to Toronto, Canada, where he mounted economic and psychological operations against the Union and was in overall command of the NORTHWEST CONSPIRACY, a massive covert operation aimed at separating several border states from the Union and establishing them as a Northwest Confederacy, which would then ally itself with the South against the Union.

Although the Northwest Conspiracy resulted in the burning of federal warehouses at Mattoon, Illinois; the burning of several federal military transports at St. Louis, Missouri; the robbery of banks in a Vermont border town (see ST. ALBANS RAID); the burning of several public buildings in New York City; and the hijacking of two steamboats on Lake Erie (see JOHN Y. BEALL), it failed to achieve its two major objectives: the mass release of Confederate prisoners of war held in Illinois and Ohio, and the inciting of a general uprising in the Northwest among the Copperheads. These failures were due in large part to Union counterintelligence, which penetrated the highest councils of the Copperhead Sons of Liberty (see FELIX A. STIDGER and HENRY B. CARRINGTON).

Covert Operations Abroad

The Confederacy sent a series of diplomatic agents to Europe in quest of recognition, aid, and intervention, while the U.S. government worked through its diplomatic missions to thwart any such developments. Both sides conducted "gray" propaganda operations aimed at winning the European public and governments to their respective causes. Henry Hotze and Edwin De Leon, the chief Confederate propagandists, were responsible for such publications as the *Index*, a weekly newspaper published in London and ostensibly of British origin, which employed celebrated British writers to present the Confederate case. The Union side was ably presented, both overtly and covertly, by JOHN BIGELOW, the American consul general in Paris, who developed sympathetic press contacts in France, Germany, Austria, and England.

Confederate propaganda was also disseminated by Comdr. MATTHEW F. MAURY of the Confederate Navy, whose international reputation for his work in navigation, oceanography, and meteorology lent dignity to his efforts to win European hearts and minds to the Confederate cause (one of the doors thus opened to Maury was that of Napoleon III, to whom the scientist proposed an alliance between France and the Confederacy).

In addition to carrying on propaganda and secret diplomacy, Maury was involved with JAMES D. BULLOCH, often characterized as chief of the Confederate Secret Service in Europe. Whether or not Bulloch actually reported to the organization known as the Confederate Secret Service, he was the Confederate Navy's chief agent in Europe, and his principal task was the procurement of warships for the Confederacy, an operation that could not be undertaken openly without embarrassing British and French claims of neutrality.

Working against Bulloch was HENRY S. SANFORD, the U.S. minister to Belgium, and the head of an intelligence network with agents in European textile mills, factories, shipyards, ports, and postal and telegraph offices. Sanford's organization gathered information on Bulloch's procurement activities, which the American ambassador then turned over to the government of the countries involved (principally Great Britain), thereby forcing those governments to step in and stop the sale or construction of the Confederate warships. Sanford's efforts notwithstanding, Bulloch procured several cruisers, including the *Florida* and the *Alabama*, for the Confederacy, before he was forced to move his operations from England to France in 1863.

Enter the Intelligence Professional

After the Napoleonic wars (1796–1815), the Civil War was the longest and most widespread conflict of the nineteenth century; some historians see it as qualitatively different from previous wars and, with its sustained mobilization and deployment of mass armies and its employment of newly developed military technologies, more like a twentieth-century war. It is not surprising, then, that the war marked the first American use of systematic military intelligence methods, the use of such modern collection techniques as aerial reconnaissance and signal intercepts, and the establishment of intelligence as a distinct organizational and functional element within an army. What is surprising is that the intelligence lessons of the war were immediately forgotten with the cessation of hostilities, and that twenty years were to elapse before the military services established anything like permanent intelligence units (see ARMY INTELLIGENCE, NAVAL INTELLIGENCE). In this regard it is worth noting that intelligence had not been a part of the American military tradition at the outbreak of the war, and most of the important figures in Civil War military intelligence—e.g., Allan Pinkerton, George H. Sharpe, Grenville M. Dodge, WILLIAM NORRIS, Benjamin F. Cheatham—were not West Point graduates or professional soldiers, but civilians who quickly returned to civilian life after the war.

Intelligence and the Course of the War

It is surprising that no comprehensive assessment of the contribution of secret operations to the outcome of the Civil War has ever been made. What is available in the way of a published record seems to suggest that these operations came to very little. Certainly the covert action operations of both the North and South cannot be demonstrated to have altered the course of events. The Northwest Conspiracy and Andrews's raid were utter failures. Confederate propaganda and secret diplomacy in Europe did not accomplish its purpose of winning an English or French alliance, and the role of federal countermeasures in frustrating those efforts remains imponderable. As regards espionage, the memoirs of a score or so of self-proclaimed spies carefully avoid, for the most part, the matter of exactly what information was obtained by all the derring-do, thereby inviting the suspicion that there were few espionage successes and that intelligence had little effect on the decisions taken by political and military leaders.

There were a great many truly decisive secret service activities in the realm of military intelligence, however, but most of them remain obscure, yet to be extracted from the archives and from the papers of the commanders and their intelligence officers and agents. The after-action reports and the postwar writings of the generals usually avoided the subject of intelligence; where they touched on it they preferred to attribute their decisions to information from overt sources, such as reconnaissance, captured dispatches, or prisoner interrogation. Such sources often did provide critical information, but their contribution has not been examined systematically. According to Fishel, who has studied the relationship of federal intelligence to the marches and battles, there is an "intelligence explanation" of each campaign—one or more important intelligence successes, or equally important intelligence failures, which played a significant part in the outcome of events.

Our real knowledge of Civil War intelligence and espionage remains sketchy. Only a score or so of truly important intelligence operatives are known: those few spy memorists who actually performed deeds comparable to those they claimed, and a small assortment of others turned up by serious historians and espionologists who have examined the extant records. But hundreds of other secret service operators remain unknown because no systematic and comprehensive study of the records has ever been done for this purpose. From payrolls and other administrative records, Fishel has identified some 4,200 Union and Confederate spies, scouts, detectives, guides, and informers, and he has to date discovered evidence of important or interesting activities by about two hundred of these operators (a full account of most of these activities remains to be established through analysis of other records). It is likely that a careful examination of the remaining 4,000 operatives would turn up at least several hundred additional significant individuals and cases.

Thus, Civil War intelligence and espionage remain a largely unknown area a century and a quarter after the event, and will continue to do so until relevant archival materials bearing on it have been fully studied.

(Fishel, "The Mythology of Civil War Intelligence"; Schmidt, "G-2, Army of the Potomac"; Canan, "Confederate Military Intelligence"; Gaddy, "William Norris and the Confederate Signal and Secret Service"; Owsley, "Henry Shelton Sanford and Federal Surveillance Abroad"; Horan, *Confederate Agent*; Bakeless, *Spies of the Confederacy*; Miller, ed., *Soldier Life and the Secret Service*; Bulloch, *The Secret Service of the Confederate States in Europe*; Time-Life Books, *The Civil War: Spies, Scouts and Raiders*; Boatner, *Civil War Dictionary*; Symonds, A Battlefield Atlas of the Civil War;

Weigley, "American Strategy from Its Beginnings through the First World War.")

CIVIL WAR ESPIONAGE MYTHOLOGY

Intelligence history is often elusive, obscure, or misleading, but seldom does it achieve the level of mendacity found in the espionage literature of the CIVIL WAR. And rare is the body of folklore that has achieved such wholesale acceptance by both popular and scholarly writers. Much of what has been published consists of popular accounts based ultimately upon the often exaggerated (and sometimes wholly fictional) memoirs of some two dozen men and women who claimed that they were in the "secret service" of either the Union or the Confederacy. Thus the literature of Civil War intelligence is journalistic rather than scholarly, and has grown more through the repetition and amplification of unverified (and often unverifiable) anecdotes or legends than through systematic research.

The "Secret Service" Myth

The propensity of ALLAN PINKERTON and LAFAYETTE C. BAKER to refer to their respective wartime organizations as the "United States Secret Service" has misled many readers into believing that a) that was the official designation of one or both of those organizations; b) one or the other was a centralized, national-level intelligence agency of the Union during the war; and c) they were the embryonic form of the U.S. Treasury Department agency of that name that today protects the President of the United States and enforces the laws against counterfeiting (see SECRET SERVICE (U.S.)). All three of these beliefs are false.

Pinkerton's organization had no official designation (at first he headed his reports, "Headquarters City Guard," later "Headquarters, Army of the Potomac"). It was limited to intelligence (and some counterintelligence, i.e., spy-catching) work for Gen. George B. McClellan when he was commander of the Army of the Potomac (1861–62). Baker was provost marshal of the War Department and his activities were primarily counterintelligence and law enforcement in the greater Washington area. Although he sometimes called his detective force "the NATIONAL DETECTIVE BUREAU," as well as many other impressive-sounding variations of that name (and in his memoirs even referred to it as "the United States Secret Service"), the unit had no official designation.

Intelligence and counterespionage were never centralized by either the Union or the Confederacy. The U.S. Secret Service was created after the Civil War,

in 1865; neither Pinkerton nor Baker was ever associated with it.

Pinkerton's Failure

Civil War historians generally agree that McClellan's excessive caution and his resultant failure as a commanding general were largely due to gross overestimates of Confederate troop numbers made by Pinkerton, and that Pinkerton was therefore incompetent. However, historian and espionologist Edwin C. Fishel questions the validity of this explanation (see ALLAN PINKERTON). Fishel also has pointed out that the designation of Pinkerton as incompetent overlooks his impressive performance in counterespionage, beginning with the roundup of Rose O'Neal Greenhow and her Confederate spy ring. During and immediately after the period in which Pinkerton was active in counterespionage in Washington, the Confederates' intelligence from the federal capital was of low quality and Gen. Robert E. Lee complained of the inability to get spies into the city.

Magnolia Blossoms and Crinolines

Victorian social attitudes and mores tended to protect women from searches, intensive interrogation, and the harsher consequences of unsuccessful espionage during the Civil War. Both North and South exploited the situation by employing female informers, couriers, and secret intelligence agents. The few who went public with accounts of their wartime experiences enjoyed large audiences for their books and lectures. These melodramatic memoirs exaggerated considerably their authors' real roles, and in one case (that of S. EMMA EDMONDS) may have been wholly invented (while on the other hand, ELIZABETH VAN LEW, one of the most important agents of the war, never published or lectured afterwards). The effect has been to create a distorted picture of the conduct of intelligence operations during the war, and in some cases has led to completely erroneous versions of certain events.

One of the most notable of such instances was the information supplied by Confederate secret agent ROSE GREENHOW and the role it played in the South's victory at the First Battle of Bull Run. According to a tradition buttressed by statements made by Gen. Pierre Beauregard, the Confederate commander in that battle, Greenhow's information warned him of the impending federal attack and thereby saved the day. However, records of dispatches received and sent by Beauregard reveal that he had ignored Greenhow's information, and that his actions that day were based on tactical intelligence gathered on the battlefield.

A similar piece of folklore concerns the contribution of Confederate agent BELLE BOYD to Gen. Thomas J. ("Stonewall") Jackson's success at Front Royal, Virginia. Although Boyd's famous sortie across the battlefield to advise Jackson that the Federals were only lightly defending Front Royal is credited as crucial to the Confederate commander's decision to capture the town, the record shows that he had already learned this information through a variety of less romantic intelligence methods.

Agents and Other Sources

Flamboyant accounts of Civil War spying, and the ease with which the spy-memoirist achieved the status of folk hero, have created the impression that agents and informers were the only intelligence sources

employed in the war. Although agents were one of the most important sources available, other types of information were collected by both sides. Cavalry reconnaissance, interrogation of prisoners and deserters, espionage, scouts, signal intercepts (see WIRETAPPING AND COMMUNICATIONS INTELLIGENCE IN THE CIVIL WAR), refugees, and newspapers (see NEWSPAPERS IN THE CIVIL WAR) all were important intelligence sources.

Indeed, one can measure the failure of Civil War spy literature to reflect the significant realities of intelligence in the conflict by considering what it omits. There is, for example, scarcely a reference to the BUREAU OF MILITARY INFORMATION, which served the Union's Eastern armies under Hooker, Meade, and Grant—by far the most modern and professional intelligence service of the war—or its chief, Col. GEORGE H. SHARPE. And the period's literature is marked by another curious lack—one

Lafayette Baker claimed to have encountered Belle Boyd (pictured) while working undercover behind Confederate lines. Source: Author's collection.

that can be found in much other intelligence and military history: rarely do the chroniclers of the spies' daring deeds detail just what crucial datum they obtained and furnished their masters, or what part this piece of information may have played in the command decisions of the war.

(Fishel, "The Mythology of Civil War Intelligence"; Davis, "Companions of Crisis: The Spy Memoir As a Social Document.")

CLINE, RAY STEINER (June 4, 1918–): educator, historian, intelligence officer

A native of Anderson, Illinois, Cline attended Harvard University, receiving his A.B. in 1939, his M.A. in 1941, and his Ph.D. in 1949. He also studied at Oxford University in 1939–40.

In 1941 Cline was selected for a three-year term as a Junior Fellow in Harvard's Society of Fellows, but after America's entry into the Second World War he left Harvard and joined the U.S. Navy's Office of Naval Communications (see NAVAL INTELLIGENCE), serving as a civilian cryptanalyst from August 1942 to April 1943. In June 1943 he joined the Office of Strategic Services and was assigned to the Current Intelligence Staff of the OSS RESEARCH AND ANALYSIS BRANCH, where he worked as an intelligence analyst and eventually became chief of current intelligence.

Cline stayed with the OSS through the war and until it was dissolved in October 1945. In 1946 he joined the Operations Division of the War Department General Staff, and subsequently the Office of Military History of the U.S. Army, where he worked on the official history of the Army in the war. He was the author of the volume entitled *Washington Command Post*, a study of the military planning and strategic organization of forces by the War Department's General Staff.

Cline completed his work for the Army in 1949. He was then recruited into the Central Intelligence Agency by R. JACK SMITH and LUDWELL LEE MONTAGUE, both of the Office of Reports and Estimates, the research and analysis unit of the recently established CIA. In 1950 he worked with WILLIAM LANGER, SHERMAN KENT, and others to establish the process by which national estimates were made. He served as chief of the Estimates Staff of the Office of National Estimates, and participated in the drafting of many of the early national estimates (see NATIONAL INTELLIGENCE ESTIMATE).

In October 1951 Cline was sent to London where he served as liaison between the Office of National Estimates and British intelligence. In 1953 he returned to CIA headquarters and became the staff officer in charge of estimates of Soviet capabilities and intentions. In 1954 he helped introduce the use of computerized war games in preparing net estimates (i.e., estimates of the potential threat posed by foreign military capabilities).

In 1955 Cline was made chief of the Sino-Soviet area analytical staff of the Office of Current Intelligence and became the Agency's senior analyst for current intelligence on the USSR, Eastern Europe, the People's Republic of China, North Korea, and North Vietnam. In 1958 he transferred to the CIA CLANDESTINE SERVICE and became chief of the Agency's Taiwan station.

In 1962 Cline returned to CIA headquarters to succeed ROBERT AMORY as deputy director for intelligence, i.e., chief of the CIA INTELLIGENCE DIRECTORATE. In 1966 he requested an overseas assignment and was made special coordinator and adviser to the U.S. ambassador to West Germany (Marchetti and Marks say Cline was "head [of] agency operations in West Germany"; Powers says he was chief of station in Frankfurt, West Germany, which is essentially the same thing).

In 1969 Cline left the CIA and became director of the State Department's BUREAU OF INTELLIGENCE AND RESEARCH, remaining in that position until his retirement in 1973. Since then he has taught at Georgetown University's School of Foreign Service and done research at the Center for Strategic and International Studies, where he is director of world power studies. He is also president of the National Intelligence Study Center in Washington, D.C.

(Cline, *The CIA: Reality vs. Myth; Who's Who in America*, 42nd ed.; Smith, *OSS*; Marchetti and Marks, *The CIA and the Cult of Intelligence*; Powers, *The Man Who Kept the Secrets*.)

CLOVER, RICHARDSON (July 11, 1846– October 14, 1919): naval intelligence officer

A native of Hagerstown, Maryland, Clover graduated from the U.S. Naval Academy in 1867, and went on to serve in various Navy stations and departments. In November 1897 he was made chief of the Office of Naval Intelligence. During the tense weeks between the destruction of the U.S.S. *Maine* and the outbreak of the SPANISH-AMERICAN WAR, he served on the Naval War Board and supervised ONI's efforts to acquire warships, material, and strategic intelligence in Europe. After war was declared he sought a combat command, and on May 1 was given command of the gunboat *Bancroft*, which was part of the naval force that escorted the Fifth Army Corps to Santiago and supported the amphibious landings at Daiquiri and Siboney.

In October 1898 Clover returned to ONI and headed it during one of the most important periods in its history. Flush with the naval successes of the recent war, the Navy was able to persuade Congress to elevate ONI to the status of a permanent, formally organized office within the Bureau of Navigation, and to increase its size and budget. Clover supervised the reorganization of ONI, establishing six divisions charged with the specific subject areas of ordnance, personnel, communications, steam engineering, ship card indexing, and attaché correspondence.

Between 1900 and 1903 Clover served as naval attaché in London. He was promoted to the rank of rear admiral in 1907 and retired from the Navy in 1908.

(Dorwart, *The Office of Naval Intelligence; Who Was Who in America*, vol. 1.)

COFFIN, WILLIAM SLOAN, JR. (June 1, 1924–): clergyman, covert operations officer

A native of New York City, Coffin moved to Carmel, California, when he was nine years of age, and attended public schools there. In 1938 he studied the piano briefly in Paris, France, and the following year he entered the Phillips Academy in Andover, Massachusetts. After graduating in 1942 he studied at Yale University Music School for a year and then entered the U.S. Army.

Because of his fluency in French Coffin was assigned to Army Intelligence as a liaison officer with the French army in Europe during the Second World War. Later, after learning Russian, he became a liaison officer with the Soviet army. He was discharged with the rank of captain in 1947 and returned to Yale, where he received a degree in government in 1949.

Shortly before his graduation from Yale Coffin was recruited by the Central Intelligence Agency (his brother-in-law, FRANK LINDSAY, was at the time chief of the Eastern European Division of the CIA's covert operations department, the Office of Policy Coordination). However, before going on active duty with the CIA, he opted instead to follow a career in the ministry, and entered the Union Theological Seminary.

When the Korean War broke out in June 1950, Coffin decided to leave the seminary and serve in the CIA. He recalled in his memoirs that this decision was based in part on a strong, personal anti-Stalinist sentiment resulting from his participation, while in the Army, in the forced repatriation of Russian prisoners of war who had fought against the Stalin re-

gime under Gen. Andrey Vlasov, a former Soviet officer. These Russians, whom he had come to understand and like, faced death or other severe punishment in Russia, and he had seen three of them commit suicide rather than return to their native land. The experience left him with "a burden of guilt" that was a factor in his volunteering for the CIA.

After receiving training in covert operations he was assigned to the Eastern European Division of the Office of Policy Coordination and sent to Germany in November 1950. From then until June 1953 he worked as a case officer, recruiting and training anti-Soviet Russian emigrés to be infiltrated into the Soviet Union. In his memoirs he later described these operations as "a spectacular failure." Apparently all of the agents infiltrated were captured, having been betrayed either by HAROLD "KIM" PHILBY, who was the liaison officer between British intelligence and the CIA during part of this period, or by a Soviet agent within the operation in Germany.

Upon leaving the CIA Coffin entered the Yale University Divinity School and earned a bachelor of divinity degree in 1956. After serving a year as chaplain at Phillips Academy at Andover, and another year as chaplain at Williams College, he became chaplain at Yale University. Later he served as an advisor to the Peace Corps and was the first director of the Corps' field training center in Puerto Rico.

During the 1960s he became active in the civil rights and anti-war movements. Because he and Dr. Benjamin Spock encouraged young men to destroy their draft cards they were convicted in 1968 of conspiracy to aid and abet disobedience to the Selective Service Act, but the convictions were overturned.

In 1976 Coffin left the chaplaincy at Yale and a year later became the senior minister of Riverside Church in New York City. In December 1979 he was one of four American clergymen who visited the American hostages in Iran and spent Christmas with them.

(Coffin, *Once To Every Man; Current Biography*, 1980.)

COLBY, WILLIAM EGAN (January 4, 1920–): lawyer, intelligence officer, director of Central Intelligence

The son of a career Army officer, Colby was born in St. Paul, Minnesota, and raised on Army posts in Panama, China, and the United States. He graduated from Princeton University in 1940 and enrolled in Columbia University Law School. In 1941 he interrupted his law studies to serve in the U.S. Army, in which he was commissioned a second lieutenant.

Colby was trained in the field artillery and then

William E. Colby—oil portrait by Lloyd Embry. Source: Central Intelligence Agency.

attended the Army's parachute school at Fort Benning, Georgia. An injury sustained in a practice jump sidelined him when his unit was shipped overseas. In 1943 he was assigned to the OSS SPECIAL OPERATIONS BRANCH. After commando training in Scotland and England, he participated in the JEDBURGH OPERATION, in which three-men teams were parachuted into France immediately after the Normandy landings to coordinate the French Resistance with the Allied advance. After several weeks behind German lines, he returned to London, where he was given command of an OSS OPERATIONAL GROUP of Norwegian-Americans scheduled to be parachuted into Norway. He led the group during the several months that it carried out sabotage and other paramilitary operations in German-occupied Norway, and he was there when Germany surrendered in May 1945. He was discharged with the rank of major and awarded a Bronze Star, a Silver Star, the French Croix de Guerre, and the Norwegian St. Olaf's Medal for his wartime service.

After the war Colby returned to Columbia Law School and received an LL.B. in 1947. He went to work for the Wall Street law firm of former OSS Director WILLIAM J. DONOVAN, and also did volunteer legal work for the Legal Aid Society and the American Civil Liberties Union. In 1949 he left Donovan's firm to join the legal staff of the National Labor Relations Board in Washington. When the Korean War broke out in 1950, he was recruited into the Central Intelligence Agency by his former commanding officer in the OSS.

Colby was assigned to the Office of Policy Coordination, as the CIA's covert action department was then called. He was attached to the Scandinavian branch of OPC's Western European Division and sent to Stockholm under State Department cover. His job was to establish STAY-BEHIND NETS, networks of indigenous agents who would remain in Scandinavia in the event of a Communist takeover or Soviet occupation, for the purposes of espionage and sabotage.

In 1953 Colby was transferred to the CIA's Rome station where he took charge of a large-scale political operation aimed at supporting the center democratic political parties and candidates in Italy against the Italian Communists. After the 1958 Italian elections, in which the Communists were again prevented from coming to power, he was assigned to the Far Eastern Division of the Plans Directorate, as the CIA's Clandestine Service was then called.

In 1959 Colby was sent to Saigon, where he served as liaison between the CIA and the Diem government (see VIETNAM WAR). In 1960 he was made chief of the Saigon station. His work emphasized the sort of rural development operation that had been used successfully by Gen. EDWARD G. LANSDALE against the Huk guerrillas in the Philippines a decade earlier. In 1962 he returned to Washington, and JOHN RICHARDSON succeeded him as chief of the Saigon station.

Colby was appointed deputy chief of the Far East Division of the Plans Directorate and shortly became chief. He remained in that capacity until 1967, a period in which the CIA was heavily involved in countering Communist insurgency in Laos and elsewhere in Southeast Asia (see SECRET WAR IN LAOS).

In 1968, while being groomed for the position of chief of the Soviet and East European Division, Colby was specifically requested by President Johnson to return to Vietnam to head the Civil Operations and Rural Development Support (CORDS) program of the State Department. To do this, he went through the formality of taking a leave of absence without pay from the CIA and joining the State Department. He was given the diplomatic rank of ambassador to facilitate the work in Vietnam.

The CORDs program included the controversial Phoenix program, which was aimed at identifying the leaders and officers of the Vietcong—the so-called "Vietcong infrastructure"—and arresting, incarcerating, or otherwise neutralizing them. Colby later denied, in sworn testimony before Congress, charges that this program included the systematic assassination of members of the Vietcong.

In 1971 the illness of one of his children forced Colby to resign his CORDS post and return to Washington. Rejoining the CIA, he became the Agency's executive director-comptroller, a management post immediately below that of deputy director of central intelligence. In this position he revised and streamlined the CIA's budgeting procedures.

In 1973 Colby succeeded THOMAS KARAMESSINES as deputy director for Plans, i.e., chief of the CIA CLANDESTINE SERVICE. Under Colby (and his boss, CIA Director JAMES R. SCHLESINGER) the size and role of the Plans Directorate was reduced and covert action was deemphasized. Colby ordered that the quasi-euphemistic name of the organization be changed to the Operations Directorate. He reduced the power of Counterintelligence Staff chief JAMES J. ANGLETON, stripping Angleton of several long-held functions, such as liaison between the CIA and the Federal Bureau of Investigation. Colby also terminated the CIA's mail-opening operation, which had been carried out by Angleton's staff since 1952.

The disclosure in 1973 of the CIA's support of E. HOWARD HUNT in planning the illegal entry of a Los Angeles psychiatrist's office in an attempt to obtain derogatory information regarding Daniel Ellsberg (an operation Colby hadn't known about) prompted Schlesinger and Colby to compile the so-called "Family Jewels" list. Examination of the collective CIA conscience resulted in a list of nearly seven hundred CIA activities that were possible violations of the Agency's charter or were otherwise "questionable."

In May 1973, when Attorney General Richard Kleindienst's resignation over involvement in the Watergate affair precipitated a reshuffling of the Nixon administration, CIA Director Schlesinger was moved to the position of Secretary of Defense, and Colby succeeded him as director of central intelligence.

One of Colby's first acts as DCI was to abolish the Board of National Estimates (see NATIONAL INTELLIGENCE ESTIMATE), a move that had been planned but not carried out by Schlesinger. Colby later explained that he had sensed in the Board "an ivory-tower mentality" that had isolated it from the national policy-making process. He replaced the Board with twelve National Intelligence Officers (sometimes nicknamed "the Wise Men," although one of Colby's appointees happened to be a woman). These senior experts in such subjects as China, Soviet affairs, Europe, Latin America, and strategic weaponry served as special consultants to the director of central intelligence. Colby also revised the format of the CIA's daily intelligence reports to the President and other senior administration officials, adopting the headline, summary, and detailed-report format of a newspaper (and even adopting the journalistic name, *National Intelligence Daily*), all in the interest of seeing that the CIA's intelligence product reached the highest administration officials.

Convinced that James Angleton's labyrinthine approach to counterintelligence was hampering the collection of positive secret intelligence, and that Angleton's role as liaison with the Israeli secret service was also not in the interest of the CIA's intelligence objectives, Colby removed Angleton from his post as chief of the Counterintelligence Staff. Angleton's retirement, coincident with press revelations of the CIA's surveillance of American anti-war dissidents and other items from the Agency's "Family Jewels," created the impression that he had been made a scapegoat for all these matters and had been forced out of the Agency in disgrace. In his memoirs, written after his own retirement from the Agency, Colby attempted to correct this impression.

Much of Colby's tenure as DCI was occupied with the task of responding to official inquiries into the CIA's questionable activities. These included the Rockefeller Commission, the Senate committee investigation led by Sen. Frank Church, and the House committee investigation led by Rep. Otis Pike. Colby is generally regarded as having performed well in the role of apologist for the CIA, minimizing the damage done to the Agency by these investigations and disclosures.

However, because of Colby's reluctance to turn some classified documents over to the Pike Committee, the Committee threatened to charge him with contempt of Congress. This, and the disclosure that the CIA had (years before Colby was its director), disobeyed a presidential directive to destroy its supply of deadly poisons, created a public furor and caused President Ford to request his resignation late in 1975. Ford offered him the post of ambassador to NATO, which Colby declined. He was succeeded as DCI by GEORGE BUSH in January 1976. Since then he has practiced law in Washington, D.C.

In addition to the awards and decorations he earned in the Second World War, Colby holds the Distinguished Intelligence Medal, the Intelligence Medal of Merit, and the Career Intelligence Medal.

(Colby and Forbath, *Honorable Men*; Cline, *The CIA: Reality vs. Myth*; *Who's Who in America*, 42nd ed.)

COLEMAN'S SCOUTS

The Scouts were the secret service of the Confederate Army of Tennessee in the Civil War.

When Gen. Braxton Bragg succeeded Gen. Pierre G. Beauregard as commander of the Army of Tennessee in June 1862 he directed Col. J. STODDARD JOHNSTON to organize an intelligence service. Johnston established some agent networks in Tennessee and Kentucky, but soon turned them over to Gen. BENJAMIN F. CHEATHAM, who, unlike Johnston, was a native of Tennessee and hence better acquainted with the local populace and countryside.

Cheatham built Johnston's network into a more comprehensive and effective secret service and put it under the command of Capt. HENRY B. SHAW in April 1863. Shaw, who had lived in Nashville and owned a Mississippi steamboat before the war, was a veteran secret agent who had worked for Gens. Nathan B. Forrest and Joseph Wheeler in Tennessee. When he took over the unit Shaw adopted the pseudonym "E. C. Coleman" (sometimes "Colman"), and the secret service became known as Coleman's Scouts.

The Scouts consisted of at least forty-five, and perhaps more, Confederate soldiers from various commands who were familiar with the Tennessee–Kentucky area and acquainted with its people, and who were ready to volunteer for the very hazardous duty of operating out of uniform behind Union lines. At least eleven of them, including Shaw himself and the tragic SAMUEL DAVIS, were eventually captured by the Union counterespionage services.

Coleman's Scouts achieved a number of notable successes. At Chickamauga General Bragg received full information on Union strength as a result of the Scouts' work. They continued to operate for the duration of the war, and were commanded by one Alexander Greig, or Gregg, after Shaw was captured in November 1863. They provided accurate and detailed reports of General Sherman's movements in Georgia to Confederate Gen. Joseph E. Johnston. The unit remained in service even after General Lee's surrender at Appomattox Court House, and disbanded only after Johnston surrendered on April 26, 1865.

(Bakeless, *Spies of the Confederacy*; Bryan, *The Spy in America*.)

COMMITTEE OF SECRET CORRESPONDENCE

On November 29, 1775 the Continental Congress appointed a secret committee "for the sole purpose of Corresponding with our friends in Great Britain, Ireland and other parts of the world." The object of this correspondence was to collect political intelligence regarding the extent of English and European sympathy toward the AMERICAN REVOLUTION. The Committee (which is sometimes confused with the SECRET COMMITTEE), was dominated by BENJAMIN FRANKLIN, the only member with experience in foreign affairs, and also included John Jay.

Arthur Lee, of the Lee family of Virginia, who was practicing law in London at the time, became the Committee's first European agent. Franklin also corresponded with two of his trusted friends in Europe, Dr. Jacques Barbeu-Dubourg in Paris, and Charles W.F. Dumas in the Hague, asking them to sound out the possibility of an alliance with the United States.

As a result of Lee's efforts, the French ambassador in London dispatched a secret agent, JULIEN ACHARD DE BONVOULOIR, to America to study the situation there with respect to covert aid and political support. Achard de Bonvouloir met with Franklin and other members of the Committee, with the outcome that the Committee sent its own secret agent, SILAS DEANE, to France in March 1776 to carry out negotiations in the matter. Deane was also to represent the Secret Committee in regard to the procurement of arms and munitions. Deane's mission resulted in the creation of a dummy corporation, Hortalez & Cie (see PIERRE AUGUSTIN CARON DE BEAUMARCHAIS), through which the United States purchased French military supplies in exchange for commodities such as rice and tobacco.

After the Continental Congress dispatched a diplomatic commission—Franklin, Deane, and Lee—to France in September 1776, the Committee of Secret Correspondence was renamed the Committee on Foreign Affairs. It was thus the premier U.S. government agency for both foreign intelligence and diplomatic representation, and so may be regarded as the ultimate precursor of both the State Department and the Central Intelligence Agency.

Congressional dissatisfaction with the Committee's performance led to its dissolution in January 1781 and the creation of the post of executive secretary of Foreign Affairs.

(Boatner, *Encyclopedia of the American Revolution*; Auger, *The Secret War of Independence*.)

COMMITTEE ON FOREIGN INTELLIGENCE (CFI)

The CFI is a three-person body created by an executive order of President Ford in February 1976. It is composed of the deputy assistant to the President for national security affairs, the deputy secretary of defense for intelligence, and the director of central intelligence (DCI), who is the Committee's chairman. In the language of the executive order, the Committee is empowered to "control budget preparation and resource allocation for the National Foreign Intelligence Program, i.e., all U.S. foreign intelligence collection activities." This authority enables the DCI to enforce all the other coordinating powers he holds—in theory—within the INTELLIGENCE COMMUNITY.

(Cline, *The CIA, Reality vs. Myth.*)

COMMITTEES OF CORRESPONDENCE

The organized infrastructure of Patriot dissidents in the colonies just before the AMERICAN REVOLUTION.

The committees were closely allied with the older organization known as the SONS OF LIBERTY, but were more formally constituted, in some cases as standing committees of the colonial assemblies or provincial congresses. Like the Sons, the committees were a means of unifying Patriot sentiment through an intercolonial communication network.

The first committee was established in Boston in 1772, largely through the urging of Sam Adams. At about the same time committees were established in Virginia. Soon hundreds of local and county committees were organized throughout the colonies to tie together rural Patriots with their brethren in the towns and cities.

The committees disseminated Patriot propaganda and marshaled public opinion against the British. They sometimes exercised judicial, legislative, and executive functions, becoming, in effect, a Patriot shadow government or underground. The communication network provided by the committees was instrumental in the convening of the Continental Congresses.

In 1775 the Committees of Safety were organized as a direct outgrowth of the Committees of Correspondence. The initial function of the Committees of Safety was military: to mobilize the militia and seize military stores. Later, supported by the Second Continental Congress, they took over other basic governmental functions.

The Patriot underground, comprised of the Sons of Liberty and the committees, was the beginning of American intelligence. Most of the early Patriot secret intelligence networks of the Revolution (e.g., PAUL REVERE's Boston spy ring) and singleton agents (e.g., HERCULES MULLIGAN) came from this un-

derground. When General WASHINGTON took command of the Continental Army in 1775 he made contact with the various Committees of Safety for the purpose of receiving military intelligence from their members. Washington recruited many of these individuals when he and his intelligence officers organized the first formal intelligence networks in 1777.

(Boatner, *Encyclopedia of the American Revolution; DAH*; Miller, *Sam Adams: Pioneer in Propaganda*; Davidson, *Propaganda and the American Revolution.*)

CONEIN, LUCIEN: covert operations officer

At the age of seventeen, Conein left his home in Missouri to join the French foreign legion. After American entry into the Second World War he was transferred to the Office of Strategic Services and assigned to the OSS SPECIAL OPERATIONS BRANCH. He was a member of the JEDBURGH OPERATION, in which three-man teams of Allied agents parachuted into German occupied France to coordinate the operations of the French resistance with the Allied landings at Normandy. Later in 1944 he parachuted into French Indochina and served as liaison officer to a French guerrilla unit fighting the Japanese occupation forces. He made the acquaintance of Vietnamese including Ho Chi Minh, Vo Nguyen Giap, and Duong Van Minh, who were to play a major role decades later when America became involved in the VIETNAM WAR. Conein led a daring raid against a Japanese divisional headquarters at Lang Son on the Chinese border.

After the war Conein served in the Central Intelligence Agency. In July 1954 he arrived in Vietnam to become the second member of a CIA covert operations team headed by Col. EDWARD LANSDALE. He remained in Vietnam with the CIA throughout the 1950s and 1960s. In 1963, because of his long friendship with General Minh, he became liaison between the U.S. embassy in Saigon and the group of Vietnamese generals who overthrew the Diem regime. After the coup he was assigned to Washington, but he soon returned to Vietnam as part of a team of counterinsurgency specialists that included Daniel Ellsberg, the Defense Department analyst who later disclosed the Pentagon Papers.

Conein retired from the CIA in 1968 and briefly pursued a war-surplus trading venture in Vietnam. In 1971 Conein's knowledge of the Diem coup and his acquaintanceship with Daniel Ellsberg attracted the attention of Conein's former OSS and CIA colleague, E. HOWARD HUNT, who was then working with the White House investigations unit known as "the Plumbers." Conein provided little information helpful to the Plumbers' project of discrediting Ellsberg, but Hunt managed to dupe Conein with some forged cables that seemed to implicate the Kennedy administration in the Diem coup. The unwitting Conein repeated the contents of the bogus cables in an interview he gave for an NBC documentary about Vietnam.

In 1973 Conein was appointed chief of the Special Operations Branch of the Drug Enforcement Agency, and he soon recruited twelve former CIA covert operations officers to serve under him. Apparently the function of this branch was to conduct covert operations outside the United States against persons involved in international drug traffic. According to the *Washington Post*, some unnamed DEA officials have claimed that these covert operations included assassination, a charge denied by Conein and his superiors at DEA. Conein admitted to a Senate investigating committee in 1975 that a private manufacturer of assassination devices had briefed him on his wares in 1974, but he denied that he or the DEA had purchased any of them.

Conein is one of the most flamboyant and colorful figures in the recent history of American intelligence. In 1975 he caused a furor by stating to a reporter from the *Washington Post* that, while in France with the OSS, he had joined "the Corsican Brotherhood," an international organized crime group similar to the Sicilian Mafia, and that he continued to hold membership in this group. The remark aroused much dismay in the DEA and the Justice Department and resulted in a reprimand. The claim itself, apparently without foundation, was an example of Conein's deadpan sense of humor.

(Smith, *OSS*; Hymoff, *The OSS in World War II*; Hunt, *Undercover*; Colby and Forbath, *Honorable Men*; *Washington Post*, June 13, 1976, p. C1; February 9, 1977, p. B15.)

CONFEDERATE SECRET SERVICE

The exact functions and history of the Confederate agency sometimes known as "the Signal and Secret Service Bureau" are obscure because its official records were lost (by some accounts they were destroyed when the Confederate government fled Richmond in early April 1865). What is known of it has been assembled by historians from such fragmentary sources as dispatches, personal correspondence, and memoirs, etc.

The Confederate Signal Bureau was a unit established within the Adjutant and Inspector General's office of the Confederate War Department in May 1862, which supervised the Confederate Army Signal Corps. Official Confederate records sometimes refer to the "Signal & Secret Service Bureau," and one extant printed letterhead used by Maj. (later Col.) William Norris, the chief of the Signal Bureau, reads "War Department, Secret Service Bureau, Richmond, Va." Although this has caused some confusion among historians, there is now no question that the Signal Bureau and the Secret Service Bureau were two functional parts of a single agency.

There is also no question that Norris's Signal Bureau operated a system of secure communications—involving semaphore, courier, and other techniques—for the Confederate War Department, was responsible for the manufacture and procurement of signal and cipher apparatus, trained and assigned signal personnel to armies in the field, and performed other tasks normally associated with communications. (The picture is even further confused by the existence of the Independent Signal Corps, which performed some of these same functions along the James and Appomattox rivers in Virginia.)

The "secret service" part of Norris's Bureau was responsible for, among other things, secret and secure communications with Confederate agents in the North, Canada, and Europe, and may have taken a hand in recruiting and directing those agents. The Bureau operated a service known as the Secret Line, an "underground railroad" linking the Confederate government in Richmond with way stations, agents, "safe houses," Potomac ferrymen, and Southern sympathizers in the North. The Secret Line transported agents and others to and from the North. It also procured files of the latest Northern newspapers (see NEWSPAPERS IN THE CIVIL WAR), and delivered books and small parcels from the North to the Confederate leaders. And it collected and reported information about Union military movements on the Potomac and in the tidewater region of Virginia.

The Secret Service Bureau was involved in the Northwest Conspiracy, at least to the extent of providing secret and secure communications between Richmond and the Conspiracy leaders in the North and Canada. It is not clear from available records whether individual Confederate secret agents of the Conspiracy were administratively members of the Bureau.

Historian and espionologist Edwin C. Fishel points out that the inclusion of the phrase "secret service" in the name of the bureau has occasionally given rise to the mistaken notion that it was the central intelligence service of the Confederacy with a nationwide area of responsibility. Fishel notes that "it *was* the signal and secret-service arm of the [Confederate] War Department," but that this does not mean the agency was a nationwide or army-wide intelligence service. Whatever the full extent of the Signal and Secret Service Bureau's operations, it is clear that it had no central intelligence function or nationwide jurisdiction. Although the Bureau collected military intelligence in those areas in which the Secret Line operated, it did not serve as a "national level" coordinating agency for Confederate intelligence collection. Confederate military intelligence was handled on an individual basis by commanders in the field, and was collected by such diverse organizations as Coleman's Scouts, which had no connection with the Bureau.

(Gaddy, "William Norris and the Confederate Signal and Secret Service"; Fishel, "The Mythology of Civil War Intelligence"; Canan, "Confederate Military Intelligence"; Taylor, "The Signal and Secret Service of the Confederate States.")

COON, CARLETON STEVENS (June 23, 1904–June 3, 1981): anthropologist, intelligence officer

A native of Wakefield, Massachusetts, Coon graduated magna cum laude from Harvard University in 1925 and earned master's and doctoral degrees from Harvard in 1928. Between 1925 and 1934 he did field work in anthropology in North Africa, the Balkans, Ethiopia, and Arabia. In 1934 he joined the faculty of Harvard.

In 1942 Coon joined the Office of Strategic Services with the rank of major, U.S. Army, and served as a covert operations officer. He was immediately assigned to North Africa with the mission of enlisting the aid of the Riff tribes of Morocco in the Allied North Africa landings. Later he helped organize the Corps Franc d'Afrique, a military unit consisting of recently liberated French Algerians that was based near Algiers. When former Vichy French Adm. Jean Darlan was assassinated by a member of Coon's Corps Franc unit in December 1942, and circumstantial evidence was produced that pointed to Coon, his OSS superiors hastily transferred him to Tunisia.

Coon's OSS adventures continued almost without pause. In September 1943, while preparing to parachute into Albania, he was summoned by Gen. WILLIAM J. DONOVAN and sent to lead a commando-style landing in Corsica. A month later he was put in charge of Operation Audry, a program to infiltrate OSS agents into Yugoslavia and supply the Yugoslavian guerrillas.

In 1945 Coon was awarded the Legion of Merit. He returned to his anthropology post at Harvard and pursued a career as one of America's most distinguished scholars.

(*Who Was Who in America*, vol. 7; Smith, *OSS*; Cave Brown, *The Last Hero*; Coon, *A North Africa Story*.)

COOPER, CHESTER L. (January 13, 1917–): foreign affairs specialist, intelligence officer

A native of Boston, Massachusetts, Cooper attended Massachusetts Institute of Technology, New York University, and Columbia University, and holds a Ph.D. from American University.

During the Second World War he served in the U.S. Army and was assigned to the Office of Strategic Services. He served in OSS Detachment 101 in the China-Burma-India Theater. After the war he remained in the Strategic Services Unit and became a member of the staff of the Central Intelligence Agency when it was created in 1947.

In 1953–55 Cooper was assigned to the National Security Council as staff assistant, and in 1955–58 he was attached to the United States embassy in London as liaison officer. From 1958 to 1963 he served as chief of the estimates staff of the CIA's Office of National Estimates. During the CUBAN MISSILE CRISIS of 1962 he was sent to London by RAY S. CLINE, deputy director for intelligence, to brief Prime Minister Macmillan and other members of the British government on the situation in Cuba and American intentions in the crisis.

In 1963–64 Cooper was special deputy to Deputy Director Cline for liaison with the National Security Council. In 1964 he left the CIA to become senior member of the staff of presidential national security advisor McGeorge Bundy. In this capacity he carried out a variety of sensitive, high-level missions in pursuit of a negotiated settlement to the VIETNAM WAR.

In 1967 Cooper joined the Institute for Defense Analysis, a private, nonprofit "think tank" that provides consultation to the Department of Defense. He later became director of the Washington office of the Institute for Energy Analysis.

Cooper's greatest expertise in intelligence and foreign policy is in the area of Asian affairs, and he has attended, as an advisor to the head of the American delegation, virtually every major international conference dealing with Asian problems since the Far East conference of 1954. He was also closely involved in the Suez crisis of 1956, functioning as the sole American contact with the British government. He is the author of several books on foreign affairs, including *The Lost Crusade: America in Vietnam* (1970), and *Suez, 1956*.

(*Contemporary Authors*, v.29R; Cooper, *Lost Crusade* (biographical sketch of author); Cline, *The CIA: Reality vs. Myth*.)

COOPER, MERIAN C. (October 24, 1893– April 1973): motion-picture producer/director, intelligence officer

A native of Jacksonville, Florida, Cooper attended the U.S. Naval Academy from 1911 to 1914. He served in the U.S. Army during the First World War as a combat pilot in France. After the war he went into moviemaking as writer, director, and producer. His most famous film was the 1933 *King Kong,* which he coauthored and coproduced.

In 1942 Cooper was commissioned as a colonel in the U.S. Army Air Corps and assigned to intelligence (A-2). He served briefly as a part-time advisor to Gen. WILLIAM J. DONOVAN in establishing the Visual Presentation Branch of the Office of the Coordinator of Information, the predecessor agency to the Office of Strategic Services. Shortly thereafter he became chief of staff of the China Air Task Force under Gen. Claire L. Chennault.

After the war he teamed up with OSS veteran JOHN FORD and produced several Western films starring John Wayne.

(Roosevelt, *War Report of the OSS; Who Was Who in America,* vol. 6.)

COPELAND, MILES (July 16, 1916–): jazz musician, writer, management consultant, intelligence officer

A native of Birmingham, Alabama, Copeland was a jazz arranger for big bands in the 1930s. In 1940 he enlisted in the U.S. Army to play in Glen Miller's orchestra, and was assigned to the Office of Strategic Services during the Second World War. Serving in the Counterespionage Branch under the alias of "Major Lincoln," he negotiated with the German Army's Paris command on behalf of ALLEN DULLES.

After the war Copeland remained with the War Department as an intelligence officer and subsequently served with the Central Intelligence Agency. In 1947–50 he was political attaché at the United States embassy in Damascus, Syria. He later served in several foreign service posts, specializing in Middle East and African matters. In 1957 he joined the private consulting firm of KERMIT ROOSEVELT and has also held senior positions in other private firms in the United States and Europe. He has written several books, including some on foreign intelligence matters.

(*Contemporary Authors,* v. 29R; Copeland, *Without Cloak or Dagger.*)

CORVO, MAX (ca. 1920–): intelligence officer

Corvo was serving as a private in the U.S. Army during the Second World War when he was assigned to the Office of Strategic Services, commissioned, and assigned to the OSS SECRET INTELLIGENCE BRANCH. He recruited a dozen Sicilian-Americans from the Italian communities of Hartford and Middletown, Connecticut, into a Secret Intelligence unit that operated in North Africa, Sicily, and Italy. Corvo achieved the rank of major. After the war he returned to civilian life and published a weekly newspaper in Middletown.

(Smith, *OSS:* Cave Brown, *The Last Hero.*)

COUNTERINTELLIGENCE and COUNTERESPIONAGE

These two terms are widely used by both intelligence professionals and the general public to designate a variety of related but distinct activities and ideas. The usage of the two terms, which are sometimes synonyms and at other times mutually exclusive nouns, falls into three general categories:

   a) catching spies or other covert operators;

   b) depriving foreign governments of information by frustrating the efforts of their intelligence services to collect it;

   c) collecting intelligence on the activities of foreign intelligence services, in order to assess the intentions and policies of their governments; or, in other words, inferring the plans of a foreign government from the questions it asks its spies to answer.

GEORGE WASHINGTON's deception of the British by permitting their agents to collect false information regarding his strength and intentions is an example of b.

Had the American intelligence services recognized the significance of the Japanese service's request for detailed reports on American ships at Pearl Harbor (see PEARL HARBOR ATTACK) it would have been a happy example of c.

Whether counterespionage or counterintelligence, or both, mean a, b, or c, or some combination of them, depends on who is using the word(s). For example, ALLEN DULLES wrote that operations aimed at "find[ing] out what the intelligence services of hostile countries are after, how they are proceeding and what kind of people they are using and who they are . . . belong to the field of counterespionage and the information derived from them is called counterintelligence." But former CIA officer PEER DE SILVA says that counterintelligence is "essentially the same" as counterespionage, which he defines as "efforts made by one intelligence service to contain or frustrate the espionage efforts of a hostile intelligence service." Espionologist LADISLAS FARAGO distinguishes between the two, however, defining counterintelligence as "the organized effort to protect specific data that might be of value to an opponent's own intelligence organization," and counterespionage as spy-catching.

An unclassified publication of the Central Intelligence Agency defines counterintelligence as "intelligence activity intended to detect, counteract, and/or prevent espionage and other foreign clandestine intelligence activities, sabotage, international terrorist activities or assassinations conducted for or on behalf of foreign powers. Counterintelligence also refers to the information derived from such activity."

(Dulles, *The Craft of Intelligence;* De Silva, *Sub Rosa;* Farago, *War of Wits;* Central Intelligence Agency, *Intelligence: The Acme of Skill.*)

COVER

A fabrication intended to conceal intelligence activity.

The term often refers to the purported affiliation of an intelligence officer or agent with some organization other than the intelligence service for which he works. Cover may sometimes involve a fabricated identity, i.e., the assumption by the officer or agent of an alias and a personal background that has either been invented or acquired from a real person. A cover story may be devised to conceal an operation, e.g., the Central Intelligence Agency's U-2 reconnaissance flights of the 1950s were represented to be meteorological research by the U.S. National Advisory Committee for Aeronautics. The full details of a cover story, e.g., a fabricated personal history, comprise what is called a *legend.*

The term *notional* refers to the fabricated details of a cover legend. For example, the person to whom the covert operator ostensibly reports is his notional supervisor; the duties associated with his cover job are his notional duties, etc. He may even take a notional business trip to one destination to cover travel to another place in the line of duty.

Sometimes personnel may be placed under cover without any serious expectation that their true roles or affiliations will be concealed from close scrutiny, but in order to satisfy the formal or political requirements of some situation, e.g., to enable a host government to claim ignorance of their intelligence activity. Such "fig leaf" cover is called *light cover.* Light cover is usually accomplished through a fabricated affiliation with some government agency other than an intelligence service, e.g., the diplomatic service,

and is therefore called *official cover.* Official cover provided by the diplomatic service usually has the added advantage of giving the bearer diplomatic immunity; in the event that the officer or agent is apprehended by the local authorities while conducting illegal intelligence activities, he or she will be declared *persona non grata* and expelled from the country instead of being prosecuted (such a person is said to have been *p.n.g.-ed* in intelligence jargon).

Cover that is intended to withstand close scrutiny and conceal a person's intelligence role is called *deep cover.* It is often achieved by fabricating an affiliation with a private or ostensibly private organization such as a business firm or foundation. Such cover is called *commercial cover* or *nonofficial cover.* Some deep cover agents, e.g., the Soviet intelligence officer RUDOLF ABEL, assume a completely false identity, often of a nationality different from their own.

In order for a cover legend to withstand close scrutiny, arrangements must be made for the organization providing the cover to cooperate in the fabrication and to respond convincingly to inquiries about the individual. To make such arrangements is to *backstop* the cover legend.

Often a commercial company or other organization is created by an intelligence service for the purpose of providing nonofficial cover for its personnel. Such a fabricated organization is called a *proprietary* or a *devised facility.* Becket says the Federal Bureau of Investigation uses the term *notional organization* in reference to dummy organizations created by the Bureau for several covert purposes, e.g., dissemination of *gray propaganda.*

JOSEPH BURKHOLDER SMITH distinguishes between *cover for status* and *cover for action.* He defines the former as "a tradecraft term meaning some occupation or activity that gives a person a viable ostensible reason for being in a country when his real reason for being there is his espionage or other illegal clandestine activity," and the latter as "an activity that explains by some believable story, other than the truth, why a spy sees the people he does, is surrounded by the accoutrements he possesses, lives the way he does, and so forth." Thus, for example, an intelligence officer in a foreign country whose status cover is that of an official of the American embassy might take an ostensible personal shopping trip (action cover) to a distant city in order to meet an agent.

(Breckinridge, *The CIA and the U.S. Intelligence System;* Rositzke, *The CIA's Secret Operations;* Felix, *A Short Course in the Secret War;* Smith, *Portrait of a Cold Warrior;* Becket, *Dictionary of Espionage.*)

COVERT ACTION

Covert action is the attempt to influence the internal affairs of other nations through secret means. It is the collective term for all those adversarial activities directed at a foreign government or organization that go beyond the accepted measures of diplomacy, but which fall short of open warfare. The term is approximately synonymous with subversion. Stated in terms of the formulation of Clausewitz, who said that "War is . . . a continuation of political relations . . . by other means," covert action can be thought of as a third option lying between politics and war. Because the advent of nuclear weapons has made all-out war impractical as a means of advancing national goals or settling international conflicts, covert action has been increasingly employed by East, West, and the Third World since 1945. It is the principal form of engagement in the cold war.

Covert action is generally regarded as embracing four different types of operations:

Psychological operations, or propaganda: The objective of psychological operations is to influence public opinion within a target country. Propaganda is subdivided into "white," "black," and "gray." "White propaganda," which does not fall within the category of covert action, consists of openly avowed propaganda efforts, such as the broadcasts of Radio Moscow or the Voice of America.

"Gray propaganda," which does fall in the category of covert action, is secretly sponsored in order to appear to have originated from some independent source. For example, RADIO FREE EUROPE and RADIO LIBERTY had funds secretly supplied by the CIA, allowing these stations to operate as though they were not controlled by the U.S. government. Press reports "planted" with cooperating journalists is yet another example of "gray propaganda."

"Black propaganda" is a counterfeit, made to appear as if it had originated with the adversary government or organization, and intended to discredit that adversary or frustrate his operations. For example, in 1964 the Czechoslovakian intelligence service mounted a black propaganda operation intended to persuade the public in several Latin American nations that the United States was undertaking a series of coups against their governments. The Czech operation involved the forgery of a United States Information Agency press release, a letter allegedly written by J. EDGAR HOOVER, and other documents that seemed to substantiate the purported American conspiracy.

Political Operations: Such operations are aimed at influencing the political process within a target country, either through advancing the power of favored politicians or parties, or frustrating their opponents, or both. Political operations may be mounted to keep a friendly regime in office or to oust an unfriendly regime. The CIA's covert supplying of funds and technical aid to the anti-Communist candidates in the Italian elections of 1948 is an example of a political operation (see ITALIAN ELECTION OPERATION).

Political operations are not limited to intervention in peaceful proceedings such as elections or parliamentary votes, but also include such measures as the provision of anti-terrorist training and equipment to a country's national police force, or sabotage training to an insurgent group. Covert sponsorship or support of such actions as coups d'etat and assassinations is a political operation. The CIA-inspired IRAN COUP of 1953 is an example of one such operation.

Paramilitary Operations: Such operations involve recruiting, training, equipping, advising, or commanding guerrilla, commando, or other irregular forces, generally composed of nationals of the target country. The work of the OSS SPECIAL OPERATIONS BRANCH with resistance groups in Europe during the Second World War is an example of a paramilitary operation. Other examples: the failed ALBANIA OPERATION and the BAY OF PIGS INVASION.

Economic Operations: Such operations are aimed at destabilizing a regime through an attack on the national economy (see, for example, the gold price manipulation of Confederate agent JACOB THOMPSON during the Civil War.)

Most large covert-action operations do not fall neatly into one of these categories, however, but tend to overlap two or more of them. Thus, the GUATEMALA COUP was a combined psychological, political, and paramilitary operation.

Covert action has been known to American history since the AMERICAN REVOLUTION, when France covertly supplied arms and other military aid to the American rebels during 1776–78, before she entered into a formal alliance with the United States and open war against England (see HORTALEZ & CIE). Although irregular military operations had been undertaken in wartime (e.g., ANDREWS'S RAID) covert action was rare in peacetime during the nineteenth and early twentieth centuries. One instance was the American support of a revolution that established the Republic of Panama in 1903 and paved the way for the construction of the Panama Canal.

In 1948, however, with the creation of the Office of Policy Coordination (see CENTRAL INTELLIGENCE AGENCY), covert action was institutionalized as an instrument of U.S. foreign policy. During the 1950s such successful covert operations as the

IRAN COUP and the GUATEMALA COUP enhanced the role of covert action in American policy. Covert action was further encouraged by the 1954 report of the Doolittle Committee (see CENTRAL INTELLIGENCE AGENCY), which stated that

Hitherto acceptable norms of human conduct do not apply. If the United States is to survive, long-standing American concepts of "fair play" must be reconsidered. We must . . . learn to subvert, sabotage and destroy our enemies by more clever, more sophisticated and more effective methods than those used against us. . . .

However, the failures of several CIA covert-action operations, including the INDONESIA OPERATION and the BAY OF PIGS INVASION, prompted a reappraisal of covert action and a reduction of its role in American policy. Nonetheless, covert action continues to be a major weapon in the American cold-war arsenal.

Beginning in 1948, the covert-action operations of the Office of Policy Coordination came under the joint supervision of the State and Defense departments. This arrangement was discontinued in 1951, at the request of CIA Director WALTER BEDELL SMITH, and the Psychological Strategy Board, a subcommittee of the NATIONAL SECURITY COUNCIL, assumed supervision. In 1953 this arrangement in turn was scrapped in favor of the Operations Coordinating Board, which consisted of the under secretary of state, the deputy secretary of defense, the special assistant to the President for cold war affairs, and the director of the Mutual Security Administration (the foreign aid program).

In 1955 the covert-action oversight mechanism was again revised by two NSC policy directives, NSC 5412/1 and NSC 5412/2, which established a group of "designated representatives" of the President and the secretaries of state and defense to review and approve covert-action projects. This group was known as the "5412 Committee" and later as the "Special Group." During the Kennedy administration, the initiation of large-scale paramilitary operations resulted in the creation of two additional oversight bodies, the Special Group on Counterinsurgency—called the Special Group (CI)—and the Special Group (Augmented). The latter was responsible for supervising only one operation, MONGOOSE, which was aimed at the overthrow of the government of Cuban president Fidel Castro.

Under the Johnson administration the Special Group was renamed the "303 Committee," although the actual oversight of covert-action operations tended to be carried out through President Johnson's "Tuesday Lunches," attended by the President, the director of central intelligence, the secretary of defense, the President's national security advisor, the chairman of the Joint Chiefs of Staff, and the presidential press secretary. The review process was again revised by the Nixon administration in 1970, when the Special Group became the "40 Committee" after National Security Decision Memorandum 40, which specified the new oversight procedures.

The Hughes-Ryan Amendment to the Foreign Assistance Act of 1974 required that members of eight congressional committees be briefed in advance on any CIA covert-action operation. This proved unworkable because of press leaks, and was revised as part of the Intelligence Authorization Act for Fiscal Year 1981 (which became law in 1980), which reduced the number of committees to be briefed to two.

The term SPECIAL ACTIVITIES has lately been introduced as a synonym for covert action.

(Karalekas, *History of the Central Intelligence Agency*; Cline, *The CIA, Reality vs. Myth*; Rositzke, *The CIA's Secret Operations*; Bittman, *The Deception Game*; Felix, *A Short Course in the Secret War*; Jordan and Taylor, *American National Security*; Blackstock, *The Strategy of Subversion*.)

COX, ALFRED T. (ca. 1915–July 1973): intelligence officer

Cox was raised in New York City and graduated from DeWitt Clinton High School. In 1936, after serving three years as an enlisted man in the U.S. Army, he enrolled at Lehigh University, where he studied civil engineering. After his graduation in 1940 he worked for the Dravo Corporation of Pittsburgh, Pennsylvania.

Cox, an officer in the U.S. Army Reserve, went on active duty early in 1942, took paratroop training at Fort Benning, and volunteered for the Office of Strategic Services. He played a major role in the development of the OSS OPERATIONAL GROUPS, which he described as "highly trained, bilingual officers and soldiers who operated in small, hard-hitting guerrilla bands behind enemy lines."

Cox led an operational group that parachuted behind German lines in southern France, ahead of the advancing Allied invasion forces in August 1944. The group destroyed bridges and power lines and ambushed German columns. In March 1945 he was sent to China where he organized and trained Chinese commando units.

Cox was discharged in 1946 and held several civilian jobs. In 1949 he was recruited by FRANK G. WISNER into the Office of Policy Coordination, as

Enoch Crosby. Source: Library of Congress.

CRITCHFIELD, JAMES H: Army officer, businessman, intelligence officer

Critchfield was an officer in the U.S. Army during the Second World War. After the war he joined the Central Intelligence Agency and was the CIA's liaison officer with the Gehlen Organization (the intelligence service of former Wehrmacht intelligence officer Gen. Reinhard Gehlen), from 1950 to 1955. From 1956 to 1961 he was chief of the East European Division of the CIA CLANDESTINE SERVICE. From 1961 to 1971 he served as chief of the Near East Division. Later he was the chief intelligence officer for energy. Critchfield retired from the CIA and, since 1975, he has been president of Tetra Tech International, a subsidiary of Honeywell, Inc. The Sultanate of Oman employs Tetra Tech to help manage several Omani government agencies as well as in the development of the province of Masandam on the Strait of Hormuz. Critchfield is one of the closest American advisors to Sultan Qaboos bin Said, the ruler of Oman.

(Powers, *The Man Who Kept the Secrets; New York Times*, March 26, 1985, p.A8.)

CROSBY, ENOCH (January 4, 1750–1835): tradesman, soldier, government official, counterespionage agent

A native of Harwich, Massachusetts, Crosby was raised in Putnam County, New York, a few miles west of Danbury, Connecticut. After serving an apprenticeship he worked as a shoemaker in Danbury, and there enlisted in the local militia regiment in 1775 soon after the battle of Lexington.

The unit in which Crosby served took part in the invasion of Canada and the occupation of Montreal in November 1775. His enlistment having expired shortly thereafter, he returned to Danbury and resumed his civilian trade.

In September 1776 Crosby decided to reenlist, and he set out for Manhattan, where Gen. GEORGE WASHINGTON's forces had retreated after the Battle of Long Island. While passing through Westchester County he fell in with a stranger who happened to be a Tory and mistook Crosby for the same. Crosby accepted the man's invitation and spent several days as his guest, during which time he learned of a group of local Tories who were forming a Loyalist unit and planned to join the British forces.

Crosby went immediately to White Plains and reported what he had discovered to the local Committee of Safety (see COMMITTEES OF CORRESPONDENCE). He agreed to work for the Committee in

the COVERT ACTION department of the Central Intelligence Agency was then called. In October of that year he was sent to Hong Kong to take charge of CIA/OPC operations in China, which was then in the last phase of the civil war that led to Communist rule on the Chinese mainland. During the final months of 1949 he was in contact with the few remaining Nationalist Chinese groups on the mainland, trying to organize anti-Communist guerrilla forces. The project proved to have been begun too late, however.

Cox continued to run covert operations in the Far East during the KOREAN WAR. He was instrumental in CIA's purchase of Civil Air Transport, an airline operating in the Far East (see AIR PROPRIETARIES). In 1952 he was assigned to manage CAT and was responsible for Operation Squaw, in which CAT aircraft flew into combat zones in Vietnam to supply the French forces fighting the Communist Viet Minh insurgents, and Squaw II, in which the airline dropped supplies to the besieged French troops at Dien Bien Phu in 1954.

Cox left CAT and the Far East in 1954. He served at CIA headquarters as a specialist in counterinsurgency theory. After his retirement he worked as a CIA contract employee on a history of CIA operations.

(Leary, *Perilous Missions.*)

an undercover capacity to aid in the arrest of the Tories. Subsequently he was taken to Fishkill, New York, as a "prisoner" along with the arrested Tories, and while being held there he agreed to continue working undercover as an agent of the Committee for Detecting and Defeating Conspiracies, a six-member counterespionage and countersubversion panel that included John Jay.

Using his civilian trade as cover, Crosby posed as an itinerant shoemaker, traveling through the towns and villages of Westchester, Putnam, and Dutchess counties and surrounding areas. Professing Tory sympathies, he repeatedly penetrated Loyalist groups and was instrumental in their arrest. After several months of such operations and a series of contrived "escapes" from the American authorities in order to continue his work, he came under suspicion by the Westchester Tories. The Committee therefore sent him to Albany, where he was unknown. After a period of service in Albany and Claverack, New York, he ended his secret service in May 1777.

While Crosby was living with his brother in Highland, New York, their home was invaded by a Tory gang bent on vengeance and he was severely beaten and left for dead. He recovered, however, and served several enlistments with the Continental Army.

After the war Crosby became a farmer near Carmel, New York. He was justice of the peace in the town of Southeast, deputy sheriff of Putnam County, and deacon in the local Presbyterian church.

Years after the war, John Jay told Crosby's story, without identifying him by name, to James Fenimore Cooper, and Cooper is said to have modeled Harvey Birch, the hero of his novel, *The Spy*, on Crosby.

(Barnum, *The Spy Unmasked*; Bakeless, *Turncoats, Traitors and Heroes*.)

CRYPTOLOGY

Language and Concepts: *Cryptology* is the study of secret communication. It embraces both *cryptography* and *cryptanalysis;* the former refers to the methods used to try to render a message unintelligible to unauthorized persons (yet intelligible to the recipient), while the latter refers to the methods unauthorized persons employ in trying to make sense of the message once they have intercepted it. The message in its intelligible form is called the *plaintext*. A message sent without benefit of cryptology is called *cleartext* and is said to be sent *in clear*.

The methods used to render a message unintelligible fall into two general categories: *ciphers* and *codes*. In the film *2001*, the name of the villainous computer,

HAL, seems to have been a filmmaker's inside joke; HAL translates into IBM when each letter is replaced by its immediate alphabetical successor. This transformation is an example of a cipher (a very simple one called a Caesar cipher after an early user, Julius Caesar).

Codes are lists of words, numbers, or other symbols that are used to replace the plaintext in the message. For example, in the code used by the CULPER SPY RING in Revolutionary New York, 728 meant Long Island, 341 meant January, and 711 meant Gen. George Washington. The Zip code system used by the U.S. Postal Service is another example of a code (although not a secret code, of course).

Generally speaking, a code requires the use of a special dictionary—a code book—to translate between the plaintext and the coded message, while a cipher involves some procedure whereby letters are substituted or rearranged in order to translate between the plaintext message and its enciphered counterpart.

The great American cryptologist WILLIAM F. FRIEDMAN explained the difference between code and cipher in this way:

In code systems, the units or symbols to be translated can be of different lengths: a letter, a syllable, a word, a sentence, or just a string of letters or numbers is agreed to stand for a particular word or a whole phrase in the message (for example, "A cat may look at a King" might be agreed to mean "Oil Shares steady," or "JAZYN" to be the code sign for "Come home—all is forgiven—Mother"). In contrast, the units in cipher systems are of uniform length and bear a uniform relationship to the units of plain text. Usually one letter in the cipher corresponds to one letter in the message, though in some systems groups of two or even three letters are used in a cipher to stand for one letter in the message.

Cryptosystem is a more general term, which encompasses both code and cipher.

To transform a plaintext message into code is to *encode* it; the reverse is to *decode* it. To transform a plaintext message into cipher is to *encipher* it; the reverse is to *decipher* it. The plaintext, after encoding, becomes the *codetext*; after enciphering it is the *ciphertext*.

A *cryptogram* is a message consisting of codetext or ciphertext.

Encrypt and *decrypt* are more general terms that encompass encode and encipher, and decode and decipher, respectively. Purists insist upon the distinction between decrypting, which they say is done only by an authorized recipient of the message, and *cryptanalyzing,* the work of an unauthorized third

Encrypted letter from Benedict Arnold to Sir Henry Clinton of July 15, 1780 offering to turn over West Point to the British for 20,000 pounds. Source: William L. Clements Library.

Arnold's letter of July 15, 1780 as decrypted by Jonathan Odell. Source: William L. Clements Library.

party who has intercepted the message. *Break*, *solve*, and *crack* are often used as informal synonyms for the awkward and stridulous *cryptanalyze*, and *code-breaking* is a common, informal synonym for cryptanalysis (even if the cryptosystem broken happens to be a cipher).

Decrypt, decode, and decipher are sometimes also used as nouns, designating the end result of the decryption, or the cryptanalysis, process.

A message that has been encoded may then be enciphered for additional security. This process is known as *superencipherment*. Code that has been enciphered is called *encicode* (enciphered code); code that has not been enciphered, or that has been enciphered and later deciphered, is called *placode* (plain code).

In addition to the use of cryptosystems to render a message unintelligible, there are techniques that conceal the very existence of the message from unauthorized persons. Such concealment techniques do not properly fall within the field of cryptography, but belong to *steganography*, the art of concealed writing, which is a separate branch of cryptology. Nevertheless, some steganographic techniques are inaccur-

ately called *concealment ciphers*. One of the earliest forms of the concealment cipher was the so-called "puncture cipher," which consisted of punching inconspicuous holes with a pin under certain letters in a newspaper, pamphlet, or other piece of printed matter in order to form the words of the message.

Secret writing or *invisible writing* is the most common steganographic method. It consists of writing the message in *invisible ink* (called *white ink* and *sympathetic ink* in Revolutionary times), often between the visible lines of a letter or printed page. The recipient develops the secret writing by some chemical or physical method (e.g., by brushing a developing chemical on the paper, or by heating it).

Other steganographic methods include the *microdot*, the photographic reduction of a printed message to a pinhead-sized dot that can be concealed within the dot over an "i" on a typed or printed page; and *burst transmission*, the high-speed radio transmission of a prerecorded message, usually at a precise, preestablished moment, which is completed in so short an interval that it escapes detection by unfriendly radio monitors.

Steganography is mainly employed by espionage

agents and other covert operators whose open use of cryptosystems would compromise their cover (in practice, of course, agent communications are often encrypted as well as concealed, in case the concealment fails).

American Cryptology: Codes, ciphers, and secret writing were widely used by both sides during the AMERICAN REVOLUTION. General Washington used a combination of code and secret writing to communicate with his agents (the invisible ink he used was prepared by John Jay's brother, Sir James Jay). British case officers PAUL WENTWORTH and LORD STORMONT used secret writing to communicate with their penetration agent, EDWARD BANCROFT, in the American mission to France. And American defector BENEDICT ARNOLD used a dictionary code—i.e., a system in which page and line number indicate the location of the word in a dictionary—to communicate with his British case officer, JOHN ANDRÉ.

The British had a cryptanalysis unit—the Deciphering Branch of the Post Office—since the early eighteenth century, and it may be presumed that British intelligence made use of it when encrypted American correspondence was intercepted. The United States had no equivalent organization, although it was common for educated people of the time to dabble in both cryptography and cryptanalysis. Both BENJAMIN FRANKLIN and Thomas Jefferson devised cipher systems, and the latter invented an enciphering/deciphering device, the "wheel cypher," which was so effective it continued to be used by the U.S. Army and Navy well into the twentieth century.

American defector-in-place Dr. BENJAMIN CHURCH was detected when one of his enciphered messages to the British was intercepted and delivered to General Washington. The message was deciphered (i.e., cryptanalyzed) by Elbridge Gerry, a Massachusetts official, and Col. Elisha Porter of the Massachusetts militia, working together, and independently by the Reverend Samuel West. Both decrypts agreed exactly and revealed the degree of Church's treason.

One of the most important American cryptanalysts of the Revolution was JAMES LOVELL, a member of the Continental Congress. Among the many intercepted British cryptograms Lovell succeeded in solv-

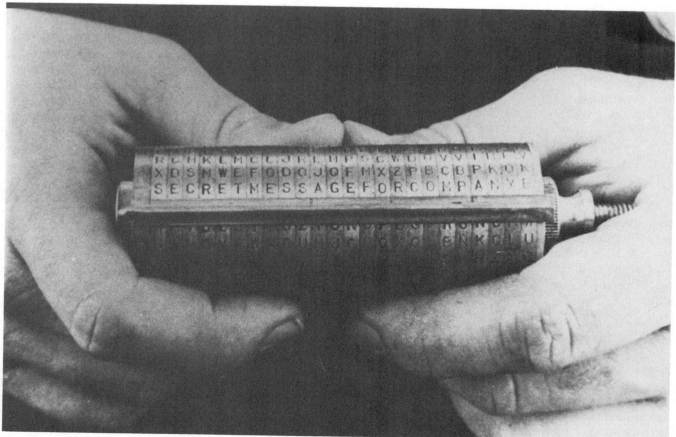

The M-94 cipher device, adopted by the U.S. Army in 1923, was based on an invention of Thomas Jefferson. Source: George Marshall Foundation.

Confederate cipher disk. Source: The Museum of the Confederacy.

ing were several messages passed between Lord Cornwallis and Sir Henry Clinton at the time of the climactic Yorktown campaign. The messages disclosed Clinton's timetable for relieving Cornwallis by sea after the siege of Yorktown was in place, and enabled Washington to alert French Admiral de Grasse, who forestalled the British relief attempt. (De Grasse had benefited from another American intelligence coup a few weeks earlier during the Battle of the Chesapeake Capes when possession of the Royal Navy's signal code enabled him to anticipate British maneuvering; but this was a matter of espionage, not cryptanalysis; the code had been stolen by JAMES RIVINGTON, one of Washington's New York agents.)

No notable feats of American cryptography or cryptanalysis are recorded for the WAR OF 1812 or the MEXICAN WAR, although both were marked by major failures in American communications security: vital military information was sent in clear and intercepted by the enemy in at least two major incidents, which may reflect a decline in official American interest in cryptology during the early nineteenth century.

The Gold Bug

Though official interest may have fallen off, there was widespread popular interest in cryptography in America at this time, due in no small part to the work of Edgar Allan Poe. While writing for a Philadelphia newspaper in 1839, Poe challenged his read-

ers to write to him in cipher and promised to solve all entries. He managed to solve almost all of them, a feat due as much to the simplicity of the ciphers used by his readers as to his own moderate talent as a cryptanalyst. However, the stunt boosted popular interest in cryptology in America and earned Poe a somewhat exaggerated reputation as a code-breaker. Inspired by the popularity of the subject, Poe repeated his challenge a year later, after he had become editor of *Graham's Magazine,* and also published "A Few Words on Secret Writing," an expository essay on elementary cryptology. He subsequently constructed an ingenious short story, "The Gold Bug," around the theme of cryptanalysis. The tale became firmly established in American literature and undoubtedly has been the childhood inspiration of generations of American code-breakers.

The Civil War

The extensive use of the telegraph and semaphore communication by the armies of both sides during the CIVIL WAR gave cryptography and cryptanalysis an importance it had not theretofore enjoyed in American military intelligence (see WIRETAPPING AND COMMUNICATIONS INTELLIGENCE IN THE CIVIL WAR). Early in the war ANSON STAGER devised a word-transposition cipher, in which the message to be encoded was written as a series of lines across a rectangular grid; the words were selected from the grid according to a pattern of vertical and/or diagonal lines cross the grid, and then reassembled in a scrambled and unintelligible order. This system was used by the U.S. War Department's Military Telegraph service throughout the war, apparently with great security against Confederate code-breaking efforts.

The Confederates, less able cryptographers than the Federals, made regular use of the Vigenere cipher, a moderately complex cryptosystem, but one easily solved by serious cryptanalysts, of which the Union's Military Telegraph service had several, including the self-styled "Sacred Three," DAVID HOMER BATES, ALBERT B. CHANDLER, and CHARLES A. TINKER. Bates, Chandler, and Tinker were telegraphers who doubled as cryptanalysts with considerable success whenever intercepted or captured Confederate cryptograms were presented to them. The Union armies in the field also had a high-degree of cryptanalytic know-how.

The growth of the telegraph as a major means of communication for business and government after the Civil War prompted the development of cryptosystems to protect privacy. Cryptology became so bound up with public life that it played an important part in the presidential elections of 1876 and 1880. In 1878 the *New York Tribune* solved several encrypted telegrams that Democratic politicians had exchanged during the dispute following the Hayes-Tilden election two years earlier (the election was so close that Congress created an Electoral Commission to settle the matter). The decrypted telegrams revealed that the Democrats had attempted to buy the election, a revelation that counted in the Republicans' favor in the 1880 elections and helped elect their candidate, James A. Garfield.

Cryptanalysis played no part in 1898 in the American victory in the SPANISH-AMERICAN WAR (although crucial communications intelligence was furnished the Signal Corps by an American agent in the Havana cable office; see MARTIN L. HELLINGS). Cryptology was, in fact, sadly neglected in official circles at the turn of the century, but enjoyed a renascence after 1912, when HERBERT O. YARDLEY joined the State Department as a telegrapher and code clerk.

First World War

During the FIRST WORLD WAR Yardley established and headed M.I.8, the cryptological section of the Military Intelligence Division (see ARMY INTELLIGENCE), which compiled codes for use by the Army, established secure communications with military attachés and intelligence officers overseas, developed chemicals for reading secret writing, and solved intercepted foreign codes and ciphers. Its staff was capable of reading more than thirty shorthand systems.

The First World War was fought soon after radio came into use as an alternative to telegraph and cable in international and military communication. Radio increased opportunities for message interception, and therefore increased efforts in making and breaking cryptosystems (and, in fact, American entry into the war was encouraged by the British interception and cryptanalysis of the ZIMMERMANN TELEGRAM, which had been dispatched by both cable and wireless). In addition to Yardley's M.I.8, the U.S. Army had a Radio Intelligence Section, an element of the Gen. John J. Pershing's intelligence staff in France, which solved intercepted German communications.

After the war M.I.8 became a jointly funded unit of the War and State departments, known officially as the Cipher Bureau, and unofficially as the AMERICAN BLACK CHAMBER. During the Bureau's ten years of existence (1919–29), its small staff solved more than 45,000 telegrams in the cryptosystems of more than twenty foreign governments, and gave American negotiators an invaluable advantage in international arms limitations talks during 1921–22 (see HERBERT O. YARDLEY).

In 1924 the U.S. Navy established the Code and Signal Section of the Office of Naval Communications (see NAVAL INTELLIGENCE), which later acquired the alternate designation, Op-20-G. Under the command of its founder, Laurence F. Safford, Op-20-G focused on Japanese cryptosystems with great success, and was the principal source of naval intelligence on Japan between the wars.

The joint State-War Cipher Bureau was dissolved in 1929, after Secretary of State Henry L. Stimson withdrew State Department financial support for the unit. Coincidentally, the Army established the Signal Intelligence Service of the Signal Corps under WILLIAM F. FRIEDMAN. The SIS created cryptosystems for use by the Army, broke foreign cryptosystems, and carried out training and research in cryptology. The unit also focused on Japan as that country became increasingly aggressive during the 1930s. In 1940 an SIS team under Friedman broke ''Purple,'' a machine cipher that was the most secure Japanese diplomatic cryptosystem. SIS worked closely with the Navy's Op-20-G on the Japanese intelligence target, and by 1941 cryptanalysts of the two units had broken a variety of other Japanese codes and ciphers.

Second World War

Although the Army and Navy cryptanalysts were reading much of the Japanese diplomatic and military traffic in the months before December 1941, this information was poorly analyzed and disseminated within the U.S. government, and therefore failed to avert the PEARL HARBOR ATTACK. However, Navy cryptanalytic activities played a major role in winning the war in the Pacific. The Fleet Radio Unit, Pacific (FRUPAC) at Pearl Harbor, headed by veteran cryptanalyst and Japanese linguist Lt. Comdr. JOSEPH ROCHEFORT, and later by Capt. William B. Goggins, played a crucial part in the American victory at MIDWAY, was instrumental in the YAMAMOTO INTERCEPTION, supplied the American submarine fleet with the intelligence needed to destroy Japan's merchant marine in the Pacific, and guided the American amphibious advance across the western Pacific through the Japanese-held islands (see also CENTRAL BUREAU).

Cryptanalysis was also important in the war in Europe, but most strategic communications intelligence in this zone was the result of British codebreaking (see SPECIAL BRANCH, TELFORD TAYLOR).

National Security Agency

In 1949 the Armed Forces Security Agency was created as an agency of the Joint Chiefs of Staff and took over most of the strategic communications intelligence functions of the SIS (which by then had become the Army Security Agency) and Op-20-G, as well as the corresponding functions of AIR FORCE INTELLIGENCE. In 1952 the AFSA was transformed into the NATIONAL SECURITY AGENCY, a civilian agency of the Defense Department. Since then, the NSA has become the premier American cryptologic agency.

(Kahn, *The Codebreakers*; Pratt, *Secret and Urgent*; Weber, *United States Diplomatic Codes and Ciphers, 1775–1938*; Bamford, *The Puzzle Palace*; Lewin, *American Magic*.)

CUBAN MISSILE CRISIS

Summary: On October 15, 1962, United States intelligence agencies discovered that the Soviet Union was installing offensive nuclear missiles in Cuba. Had they become operational, the missiles would have been capable of reaching targets in most of the continental United States. Such a development would have constituted a qualitative increase in the Soviet strategic threat: it would have roughly doubled the nuclear megatonnage the Soviets could target on the United States; outflanked the U.S. defensive system, which was designed to resist a Soviet attack over the North Pole, not one from south of the continental United States; and drastically cut the warning time available to U.S. commanders in the event of an attack. Furthermore, it would have enhanced Soviet prestige in the western hemisphere and diminished that of the United States, in addition to creating a domestic political problem for President Kennedy's administration, which was already vulnerable on the subject of Cuba as a result of the failed BAY OF PIGS INVASION.

On the evening of October 22 Kennedy made a televised address to the nation in which he reported the situation and announced a quarantine of Cuba, i.e., a naval blockade to exclude shipments of offensive weapons to the island. He also stated that the United States would regard any nuclear missile launched from Cuba as a Soviet attack on the United States and would respond with a retaliatory attack against the Soviet Union.

The U.S. armed forces went from DEFCON (Defense Condition) 5—peacetime alert—to DEFCON 2, just short of the status of war. Five of eight divisions of the Army Strategic Reserve were placed on alert;

the First Armored Division was sent from Texas to Georgia, and a command post for an invasion of Cuba was established in Florida. Polaris missile submarines left their base in Scotland and took up stations within range of the Soviet Union. Some of the nuclear-equipped bombers of the Strategic Air Command were dispersed to civilian airfields. SAC increased its airborne alert, i.e., the portion of the nuclear bomber force kept in the air at all times.

The crisis was resolved on October 28 when Soviet Premier Khrushchev agreed to withdraw the missiles in return for an American pledge not to invade Cuba.

The role of American intelligence in the affair was, first, to detect the presence of the missiles in Cuba; second, to monitor Soviet progress on the missile sites during the crisis; third, to forecast Soviet responses to possible American actions during the crisis; and, fourth, to insure Soviet compliance with the agreement to remove the missiles. Some commentators have questioned the effectiveness of American intelligence in performing the first of these functions, charging that clear evidence of Soviet intentions was available long before the intelligence community detected the presence of the missiles. Others maintain the intelligence agencies sounded the warning almost as soon as could reasonably be expected.

The Soviet Buildup: The Soviet Union had been supplying conventional arms to Cuba since the summer of 1960, but the pace of shipments dropped off early in 1962. Apparently, the Soviets decided to export long-range nuclear missiles to Cuba in the spring or summer of 1962. The arms buildup was scheduled to take place in two phases. During the first phase sophisticated defensive weapons would be introduced: twenty-four batteries of SA-2 SAMs (surface-to-air missiles), forty-two MIG-21 fighter planes, short-range harbor defense missiles, and coastal patrol boats armed with ship-to-ship missiles. During the second phase offensive weapons would be introduced: forty-eight MRBMs (Medium Range Ballistic Missiles, i.e., with a range of 1,100 nautical miles), twenty-four IRBMs (Intermediate Range Ballistic Missiles, i.e., with a range of 2,200 nautical miles), and forty-two IL-28 bombers, capable of delivering nuclear payloads over a round-trip range of six hundred nautical miles.

There were to be four offensive missile sites in Cuba. The MRBM sites were to be at San Cristobal, fifty miles south of Havana, and Sagua la Grande, 135 miles east of Havana. Because the MRBM the Soviets were using was mobile, little more was required in the way of preparing the sites than construction of facilities for the storage of rocket propellents and warheads, and a dirt road leading to a flat piece of ground large enough to accommodate two large vehicles: a trailer to carry the missile and an erector to raise it to launching position. With those preparations made, MRBMs could be trucked in and made ready to fire within seventy-two hours.

The IRBMS were to be installed at Guanajay, near Havana, and at Remedios, in central Cuba, about fifty miles southeast of the MRBM installation at Sagua la Grande. These sites required more elaborate preparations: launch rings, flash deflectors, storage bunkers, control buildings, etc.

In order to assemble, operate, and defend these weapons, the Soviet Union sent some 22,000 soldiers and technicians to Cuba.

The buildup began in July and the first of the offensive missiles (MRBMs) arrived at the Cuban port of Mariel on September 8th aboard the Soviet freighter *Omsk.* Another shipment of MRBMs arrived in Mariel aboard the *Poltava.* Throughout September and the first half of October additional MRBMs, plus missile trailers, erector vehicles, radar vans, and other related material and equipment arrived in Cuba. On October 24th, the date the American quarantine of the island took effect, eighteen more Soviet cargo ships were at sea, en route to Cuban ports.

Preparation of the missile sites proceeded at a pace later described by American analysts as "remark-able." Some of the MRBMs had been delivered to the San Cristobal site, though they had not yet been readied for firing on October 14th, when an Air Force U-2 photographed them. None of the IRBMs had arrived in Cuba before the quarantine was put in effect.

Intelligence Sources: In addition to the general worldwide sources of information regarding Soviet capabilities and information, American intelligence agencies had four sources of information specific to the situation in Cuba:

1 Maritime intelligence, i.e., reports, photographs, and other data concerning cargo shipments from Soviet, East European, and other ports to Cuba.
2 Refugee reports, i.e., information obtained by interviewing refugees who had recently left Cuba.
3 Secret intelligence, i.e., information collected by espionage agents in Cuba and reported to American intelligence.
4 Aerial photography by U-2 and other photo-reconnaissance aircraft overflying Cuba.

Soviet Secrecy, Deception, and Disinformation: The Soviets successfully concealed the character of the Cuban buildup through a careful program

Soviet ship *Volgoles* leaving Cuba with Soviet missiles, November 9, 1962. Source: U.S. Navy.

U-2 photograph of Medium Range Ballistic Missile site at San Cristobal, Cuba, taken on October 14, 1962. Missile trailers and erectors can be seen in the cleared area to the right of the center of the picture. Vehicles are parked in a row in a second clearing to the left. Source: Central Intelligence Agency.

of deception in Moscow and Washington, while maintaining the utmost secrecy in Cuba.

The Soviets evacuated all Cuban civilians from the port of Mariel in order to prevent observation of the cargo being unloaded. Cubans were also excluded from the missile sites. At the Mariel wharves, trucks were lowered into the holds of the Russian ships, loaded, covered with tarpaulins, then hoisted out again. The trips from the port to the construction sites were made at night. The Soviet military personnel sent to operate and protect the missile sites wore civilian clothing.

The Soviets, who of course realized that American intelligence would inevitably discover that some sort of large Soviet military buildup was under way in Cuba, sought to mislead the U.S. government on the question of offensive missiles. On September 4th Soviet Premier Khrushchev sent the Soviet ambassador in Washington to Attorney General Robert Kennedy with a confidential message promising that he would create no trouble for the United States during the fall election campaign. On September 6th he reiterated this point in a message to presidential

counsel Theodore Sorensen: "Nothing will be undertaken before the American congressional elections that could complicate the international situation or aggravate the tension in the relations between our two countries. . . ." Another message relayed by way of yet another Soviet official with access to the White House was more explicit: "No missile capable of reaching the United States would be placed in Cuba." On September 11th Tass, speaking for the Soviet government, stated that Soviet nuclear weapons were so powerful "there is no need to search for sites for them beyond the boundaries of the Soviet Union." On October 16th—the day after U.S. intelligence had discovered the missiles—Khrushchev told the American ambassador in Moscow that Soviet purposes in Cuba were wholly defensive. Two days later Soviet Foreign Minister Andrei Gromyko visited the White House and assured President Kennedy that Soviet aid to Cuba was "by no means offensive."

The Emerging Intelligence Picture: American intelligence became aware of the Soviet buildup almost as soon as it began in mid-July. On August 23rd the Central Intelligence Agency's Office of Current Intelligence issued a report on "Recent Soviet Military Aid to Cuba." It reported that twenty shiploads of Soviet arms had reached Cuba, and that the cargoes included transportation, electronic, and construction equipment, such as communication vans, radar vans, trucks, and mobile generator units. Five more ships were en route from Black Sea ports. There was construction under way at two sites near Matanzas in western Cuba. Between three thousand and five thousand Soviet-bloc military technicians and other personnel had arrived on the island. The intelligence community also knew that crates had been observed aboard the Soviet ships and intelligence analysts suspected they contained SAM (i.e., defensive surface-to-air) missiles. A U-2 flight over Cuba on August 29th confirmed the presence of SAMs, positively identifying two SAM sites, and pinpointing six other locations that might also have surface-to-air missile installations.

On August 22nd CIA Director JOHN MCCONE told President Kennedy he suspected the Soviets were introducing offensive missiles into Cuba, a theory he had advanced to Kennedy a few days earlier in the form of a memorandum. Apparently he failed to persuade the President.

McCone suspected that the SAMs were in Cuba to protect offensive missile sites from aerial photography or air strikes. His suspicions may have been enhanced by reports from P.L. THYRAUD DE VOSJOLI, the chief of the French foreign intelligence service in Washington, who had passed on to Mc-

Cone reports of offensive missiles he had received while visiting Cuba in July or August. Whatever the basis for his suspicions, they were not shared by the professional intelligence analysts in the CIA, such as SHERMAN KENT and other members of the Board of National Estimate.

Refugee and Agent Reports

CIA officers interviewing Cuban refugees in Opa Locka, Florida, also heard reports of offensive missiles in Cuba, but they had been hearing similar reports ever since Fidel Castro came to power in Cuba and allied himself with the Soviet Union. The file of such reports for the year 1959 alone was five inches thick. Thus, such information was received with much skepticism at CIA headquarters.

In the middle of the night of September 12th, a CIA subagent observed a truck convoy proceeding in a westerly direction from a secure port area near Havana. His report, which reached CIA headquarters on September 21st, described the trailers as twenty meters long (approximately sixty feet—about the length of the MRBM) and carrying loads concealed by canvas tarpaulins. However, CIA analysts doubted the accuracy of the subagent's estimate of length, and theorized that the trailers actually contained SAMs, which are about ten meters long. A second nighttime trailer convoy was sighted on September 17th, but this report did not reach Washington until October 3rd.

Later in September a report was received from Cuba relating that Fidel Castro's personal pilot had been overheard boasting that Cuba now had long-range missiles and no longer need fear the United States. This, of course, fell far short of constituting hard evidence.

Maritime Intelligence

American intelligence received one early indication of MRBMs in August or early September, but it was overlooked. The maritime intelligence reports indicated that two of the ships employed in the arms buildup, the *Omsk* and the *Poltava* (i.e., the two ships carrying the first of the MRBMs), had exceptionally large hatches. Normally used for carrying lumber, they had been diverted to the Cuban project. Further, photographs of the two ships en route to Cuba showed them riding high in the water, an indication that they were carrying "space-consuming" cargo, i.e., objects of low density, such as missiles. However, intelligence failed to recognize that these two vessels had been selected specifically because their large hatches would accommodate the MRBMs, and assumed they

were being used simply because the Soviet Union was hard pressed to find enough ships to use in the buildup.

Overhead Reconnaissance

American U-2s overflew Cuba on September 5th, 17th, 26th, and 29th, and October 5th and 7th. These flights collected information on SAM sites, coastal defense missiles, MIG fighters, missile-equipped patrol boats, and IL-28 bombers. However, the effectiveness of these reconnaissance flights was hindered by political considerations. On August 30th a U-2 strayed over the Soviet Union—Sakhalin Island in the Sea of Japan—without adverse incident. Then on September 9th a U-2 flown by the Chinese Nationalists was shot down by SAM missiles over the Chinese mainland. The State Department feared that, in the wake of these incidents, the downing of a U-2 over Cuba would produce the same sort of political crisis that arose two years earlier when the U-2 flown by FRANCIS GARY POWERS was shot down. Consequently COMOR (Committee on Overhead Reconnaissance—see NATIONAL FOREIGN INTELLIGENCE BOARD) agreed to modify the U-2 flight plans. Rather than flying the length of the island of Cuba, the planes would fly along the Cuban territorial limit, photographing the island obliquely, and occasionally "dip into" Cuban airspace at selected points. It was also decided to concentrate surveillance on the eastern part of Cuba, rather than the western end where the SAM sites were concentrated (and where the offensive missiles were located).

The National Intelligence Estimate

On September 18th the Board of National Estimates released a special national intelligence estimate, SNIE 85-3-6, "The Military Buildup in Cuba." The estimate reviewed the evidence to date and addressed the question of offensive nuclear missiles. It judged that the Soviets were unlikely to deploy such weapons in Cuba, citing the facts that they had never placed them in Eastern European satellites, that to place them in Cuba would create serious command and control problems for Moscow, and that the introduction of a large number of Soviet military personnel on the island would be a political liability in Latin America. The document also theorized that the Soviets "would almost certainly estimate that [putting nuclear missiles in Cuba] could not be done without provoking a dangerous U.S. reaction."

Because the estimate concluded that the idea of the Soviets putting offensive weapons in Cuba was irrational and inconsistent with their policy, it is worth noting that, decades after the event, experts on the Soviet Union continue to disagree in their assessments of the exact motives, objectives, and expectations of the Soviet Union in the affair. Even though it was totally wrong, the national intelligence estimate still seems to make sense in retrospect. At the time, this American model of Soviet policymaking provided the context within which positive intelligence reports on Cuba were interpreted.

CIA director John McCone, however, remained unconvinced by the estimate and suspicious of the Soviet buildup. During September he was on his honeymoon on the French Riviera, but he sent a series of telegrams to CIA headquarters—later dubbed "the honeymoon telegrams"—urging that the possibility of offensive missiles be given more consideration. Because President Kennedy had already heard McCone on this subject, and because McCone had offered no evidence not already available within the intelligence community, and perhaps because McCone had no training or experience as a professional intelligence officer, these telegrams were not circulated beyond the CIA or incorporated into the estimate in the form of a dissenting footnote.

The Missiles Discovered

However, McCone was not the only one in the intelligence community to have suspicions. Col. John Ralph Wright, Jr. of the Defense Intelligence Agency had analyzed the pattern of SAM sites in recent U-2 photographs of western Cuba and noted a similarity with clusters of SAM sites that protected offensive missile sites in the Soviet Union (information that had been obtained by U-2 overflights of Soviet territory prior to the Powers incident of May 1960). He projected the geometrical shape formed by the sites on a map of Cuba and found it centered on San Cristobal. By September 27th he had convinced DIA Director Gen. JOSEPH CARROLL to call for a U-2 flight to photograph the area. The CIA was persuaded to share Wright's suspicions by September 29th, and John McCone persuaded COMOR to order a flight at a meeting on October 4th. The actual flight plan was approved on October 9th. The flight received presidential approval the following day, but was thereafter delayed for several days by forecasts of bad weather over western Cuba.

On October 14th a U-2 flown by Maj. RICHARD S. HEYSER of the U.S. Air Force 4080th Strategic Reconnaissance Wing photographed the San Cristobal area. Within twenty-four hours photointerpreters at the NATIONAL PHOTOGRAPHIC INTERPRETATION CENTER had analyzed the films and identified the MRBM sites.

Intelligence During the Crisis: Aerial reconnaissance of Cuba became nearly continuous after the initial discovery on October 15th. By October 22nd the Air Force had flown nearly twenty U-2 sorties over the island. On October 17th the MRBM sites at Sagua la Grande were discovered, along with the construction in progress on the IRBM sites at Remedios and Guanajay.

After President Kennedy's public confrontation of the Soviets on October 22, low-level photoreconnaissance flights were begun by the Air Force, using the RF-101 Voodoo aircraft, and the Navy, using the RF-81 Crusaders. The high-altitude U-2 flights also continued. By October 24th NPIC photointerpreters and intelligence analysts had identified four 1,200-man Soviet battle groups in four locations throughout Cuba; these were equipped with thirty-five to forty tanks and Frog tactical missiles capable of using nuclear warheads. Analysts revised the estimate of total Soviet-bloc manpower on the island upward to 22,000 men.

The increased aerial surveillance disclosed that the missile sites were not in as advanced a state of readiness as had initially been supposed, but that Soviet crews were now working around the clock to complete them. Both the Board of National Estimate and the Office of Current Intelligence (CIA) agreed that the IRBM sites could not be made ready before December 1st. The OCI also raised some question as to whether the nuclear warheads for any of the missiles had yet been delivered to Cuba.

The continued aerial reconnaissance of Cuba, vital to American decision-making during the crisis, cost the life of one U.S. Air Force pilot, Maj. RUDOLPH ANDERSON, JR., who was shot down over Cuba on October 27th, the day before the crisis was resolved.

On October 19th, three days before Kennedy went public with the crisis, the CIA's Board of National Estimate released a special national intelligence estimate, SNIE 11-18-62, which tried to assess Soviet motives for introducing the missiles into Cuba and forecast Soviet responses to American actions. The estimate forecast that the Soviets would neither use the missiles, if and when they were made ready, nor withdraw them if confronted by the United States. While it discounted the possibility that the missiles had been intended as bargaining chips, it theorized that the Soviets would propose negotiations on the general question of foreign bases if confronted by the United States. The estimate seemed to imply that American military action would be the only means of removing the missiles.

A second special estimate, SNIE-19-62, released on October 20th, forecast that the Soviets would be less likely to retaliate to a swift American invasion of

Cuba than to "more limited forms of military action against Cuba." Furthermore, it suggested that such an invasion, rather than limited action, would dissuade the Soviets from "opening new theaters of conflict."

Although these two estimates seemed to argue for an invasion, and John McCone (back in Washington to take part in managing the crisis) advocated air strikes against the missile sites, President Kennedy chose the less drastic option of the quarantine. In the event, the first estimate was proved wrong when the Soviets agreed to withdraw the missiles in return for nothing more than an American pledge not to invade Cuba.

U-2 reconnaissance flights over Cuba during December and January confirmed that the Soviets had withdrawn the missiles and IL-28 bombers, and had destroyed the missile sites.

Intelligence Performance: Some commentators have characterized the Cuban Missile Crisis as an "intelligence failure" and have compared it with the American failure to anticipate the PEARL HARBOR ATTACK. In both cases intelligence suffered from an overabundance of information that made it difficult to distinguish the relevant "signals" from the irrelevant "noise." In both cases individual indications and evidence tended to be misinterpreted in the context of an erroneous overall view—in the Pearl Harbor case, the belief that the Japanese did not have the capability to attack the fleet in Pearl Harbor, but intended only to launch a campaign in Southeast Asia; in the Cuban case, the belief that Soviet foreign policy would not permit the deployment of nuclear missiles beyond Soviet borders.

However, while Pearl Harbor was a total intelligence failure, the Cuban crisis was only a slightly tarnished success. A failure on the scale of the Pearl Harbor debacle would have meant that the U.S. government did not learn of the missiles until they were fully operational. But, in fact, American intelligence discovered the missiles shortly after they had been delivered to San Cristobal, the first of the MRBM sites. Even if intelligence analysts had paid more attention to the early indications and photographed San Cristobal in mid-September, there would not yet have been missiles to be seen in the photographs. Without such positive and conclusive evidence, the refugee and agent reports and the maritime intelligence would not have provided a basis for action by the President or the National Security Council.

The most serious intelligence failure of the Cuban Missile Crisis seems to lie in the area of analyzing and forecasting Soviet foreign and strategic policy-making. Both the initial estimate that the Soviet leaders would not install the missiles in Cuba and the

Director of Central Intelligence John McCone (left) arriving at the White House. Source: Central Intelligence Agency.

subsequent estimate that they could not be persuaded to remove them proved false. However, these failures may be attributed to the limit of the state of the art of intelligence estimating, and they are mirrored by the failure of the counterpart estimators in the Kremlin to forecast accurately the American response to the inevitable discovery of the missiles.

(Prados, *The Soviet Estimate;* Allison, *Essence of Decision;* Hilsman, *To Move a Nation;* Abel, *The Missile Crisis;* Divine, *The Cuban Missile Crisis;* Kennedy, *Thirteen Days;* Daniel and Hubbell, *Strike in the West;* Wohlstetter, "Cuba and Pearl Harbor: Hindsight and Foresight.")

CULPER SPY RING

An American secret intelligence network in New York City and Long Island during the AMERICAN REVOLUTION.

The Culper Ring was established by Maj. BENJAMIN TALLMADGE in August 1778 in order to provide Gen. GEORGE WASHINGTON with military intelligence regarding the British force under Gen. Henry Clinton, which had recently withdrawn from Philadelphia to occupy New York City. Tallmadge recruited ABRAHAM WOODHULL, a farmer of Setauket on Long Island, to serve as the chief of the ring.

Woodhull's principal agent was ROBERT TOWNSEND, a dry-goods dealer in New York, and a part-time writer for JAMES RIVINGTON's Tory newspaper, *The Royal Gazette*. Woodhull collected intelligence directly through his dry-goods business and newspaper work, and indirectly through the coffee shop he owned jointly with Rivington, and a boarding house (frequented by the British) owned by his sister and her husband, Amos Underhill. Rivington eventually became a member of the ring, and New York tailor and intelligence agent HERCULES MULLIGAN may also have taken part in the operation.

In their reports to Washington, Woodhull was designated by the pseudonym "Samuel Culper, Sr.," and Townsend was "Samuel Culper, Jr."

Townsend passed his information to Woodhull through Austin Roe, a Setauket tavern keeper whose business frequently brought him to New York City. Roe would leave Townsend's reports in a dead drop on Woodhull's farm. Townsend sometimes passed on his reports directly to Woodhull, either when the latter could visit the city without attracting attention, or when Townsend traveled to Long Island on the pretext of business or visiting his father (who lived in Oyster Bay). Townsend and Woodhull concealed their written reports to General Washington through the use of an invisible ink (see CRYPTOLOGY) developed for Washington by Sir James Jay (brother of John Jay). Additional security was later added in the form of a numerical communication code in which, for example, Washington was "711," Long Island "728," Setauket "729," Woodhull "722," Townsend "723," etc. Townsend's common-law wife, who was a member of the ring and died aboard a prison ship after being arrested by the British, was "355." She is otherwise unknown to history.

Upon receiving a report from Townsend, Woodhull would dispatch the document across Long Island Sound through Caleb Brewster, a Setauket blacksmith and boatman, who handed it either to Tallmadge or one of his couriers. From there the report was carried swiftly to Washington's headquarters.

The Culper Spy Ring operated successfully and without detection throughout the war. Among the valuable items of intelligence it supplied to General Washington were the warning that the British planned to counterfeit American currency, and word that British commander Clinton was preparing to lead a large force out of New York to attack Rochambeau's army, which had recently landed at Newport, Rhode Island. Washington used this latter intelligence to his advantage by arranging for Clinton's own secret service to obtain some false papers suggesting that Washington planned to attack lightly defended New York in Clinton's absence. The ruse worked, and Clinton abandoned his plan to attack the French.

(Ford, *A Peculiar Service*; Pennypacker, *George Washington's Spies*; Bakeless, *Turncoats, Traitors and Heroes*; Bryan, *The Spy in America*.)

CUMMINGS, SAMUEL (February 7, 1927–): businessman, intelligence officer

A native of Pennsylvania, Cummings served in the U.S. Army during 1945–46 and graduated from George Washington University in 1949. During his Army and college years he pursued an early interest in firearms as a hobby and became expert in the identification of weapons of foreign manufacture. This expertise led to his recruitment by the Central Intelligence Agency in 1950.

Cummings served in the CIA's Office of Scientific Intelligence where he helped keep track of the disposition of surplus weapons from the Second World War, many of which were turning up on the Communist side in the Korean War. During 1951–52 the CIA sent him to Europe where, posing as a Hollywood film producer collecting theatrical props for war films, he bought captured German weapons that were to be used to arm the Nationalist Chinese on Taiwan. In 1952 he was sent to Costa Rica to buy up a large quantity of small arms and ammunition declared surplus by the government of that country.

Cummings left the CIA in 1952 and established the International Armament Corporation, or Interarms (sometimes called Interarmco). His business flourished and he became the largest private arms dealer in the world.

Cummings, who lives in Monaco and Switzerland, became a British citizen in 1972 to resolve a complex problem involving his children's nationality.

(Brogan and Zarca, *Deadly Business*.)

CURRENT INTELLIGENCE

Information about current or recent events of intelligence interest. If *basic intelligence* may be thought of as corresponding to an encyclopedia, current intelligence is the daily newspaper or weekly newsmagazine. A dictionary published by the Joint Chiefs of Staff defines it as "intelligence of all types and forms of intermediate interest, which usually is disseminated without delays necessary to complete evaluations of interpretations." Veteran naval intelligence officer E. Luther Johnson writes that it "covers all topics from political to technical intelligence. From the point of view of time, it encompasses ongoing events, usually beginning at the present time and reaching back, from a practical standpoint, to whatever earlier studies exist about a topic under consideration. . . ."

The daily intelligence reports published for the President and other senior officials by the Office of Current Production and Analytic Support of the CIA INTELLIGENCE DIRECTORATE are examples of current intelligence. When he took office in 1973 CIA Director WILLIAM E. COLBY emphasized the "daily newspaper" quality of these reports by giving them a journalistic format and the name *National Intelligence Daily*.

(Hopple and Watson, *The Military Intelligence Community*; Ransom, *The Intelligence Establishment*.)

CUSHMAN, PAULINE (June 10, 1833– December 2, 1893): actress, Union secret agent

A native of New Orleans, Cushman was born Harriet Wood. She was raised in Grand Rapids, Michigan, and left home at age eighteen to follow a career on the stage, assuming the stage name Pauline Cushman. She married Charles Dickenson, a fellow actor and musician, who joined the U.S. Army to play in a military band at the outbreak of the Civil War. After his illness and death she resumed her theatrical career.

In March 1863, while appearing in a production of *The Seven Sisters* at Wood's Theater in Louisville, Kentucky, Cushman was approached by two paroled Confederate officers who offered to pay her if she would toast the Southern cause from the stage. When she reported the proposition to the local Union military authorities, she was asked to comply with the Confederates' request as a ruse to unmask Confederate sympathizers in the audience and to establish her cover as a Confederate sympathizer in order to carry out future tasks in the Union secret service.

After Cushman staged the incident in the theater she was fired by the manager and arrested by Union troops. She was quickly released and subsequently approached by Confederate sympathizers in the Louisville area. Through these contacts she was able to work as a Union counterespionage agent, discovering local Confederate espionage, guerrilla, and smuggling operations. She resumed her acting career

Pauline Cushman. Source: Library of Congress.

in Nashville, Tennessee and continued her counterespionage activities in that area.

While in Nashville in May 1863 Cushman was asked by military intelligence officers of the Northern Army of the Cumberland to undertake an espionage mission behind Confederate lines to collect positive intelligence on the Confederate Army of Tennessee, commanded by Gen. Braxton Bragg. She was dispatched to Confederate territory through the expedient of a staged "public expulsion" from the North of a group of female Confederate sympathizers. She performed her intelligence assignment through a series of amorous contacts with Confederate officers, but was discovered and apprehended while trying to return to the North, and brought before General Bragg in Shelbyville, Tennessee. She was tried on charges of espionage by a military court. Stolen military papers found among her possessions sealed the case against her, and she was found guilty and sentenced to death. However, the Confederates left her in Shelbyville when they withdrew from the town under a Union advance, and she was repatriated to the North.

Cushman delivered the information she had collected to the Union military intelligence officials and was thanked and rewarded for her secret services, which necessarily ceased at that point. She returned to the stage and, billed as "the Spy of the Cumberland," also lectured on her intelligence experiences.

She remarried twice and died a suicide in San Francisco.

(*Who Was Who*, historical volume; Kane, *Spies for the Blue and Gray*; Boatner, *Civil War Dictionary*.)

CUSHMAN, ROBERT EVERTON, JR.
(December 24, 1914–January 2, 1985): marine officer, intelligence officer

A native of St. Paul, Minnesota, Cushman graduated from the U.S. Naval Academy in 1935 and was commissioned a second lieutenant of marines. He served in Shanghai, China, and several other posts during the next few years. In June 1941, having advanced to captain, he was given command of the marine detachment aboard the battleship U.S.S. *Pennsylvania*, and was aboard her at Pearl Harbor during the Japanese attack in December. During the war, he served with heroism and distinction on Bougainville, Guam and Iwo Jima, earning the Bronze Star, the Legion of Merit, and the Navy Cross.

After a post-war tour at Quantico, Virginia, and another with the Office of Naval Research, Cushman was assigned to the Central Intelligence Agency in 1949. He served in the Office of Policy Coordination, as the CIA's COVERT ACTION department was then known. Promoted to the rank of colonel in 1950, he left the Agency in 1951.

After several subsequent assignments and a promotion to brigadier general, Cushman was named assistant for national security affairs to Vice-President Nixon in 1957. In that capacity he had a peripheral involvement in the early planning for the BAY OF PIGS INVASION.

Cushman later commanded the Third Marine Division on Okinawa (1961–62), served as assistant chief of staff of the Marine Corps (1962–64), and commanded Camp Pendleton, California (1964–67). In April 1967 he was named commander of the Third Marine Amphibious Force in South Vietnam.

In April 1969 President Nixon appointed Cushman deputy director of central intelligence, the second highest post in the CIA. While in that position he agreed to the telephone request of a White House aide to provide technical assistance to former CIA officer E. HOWARD HUNT (Cushman later recalled that the aide was John Ehrlichman, but Ehrlichman denied that he had been the caller). Unbeknown to Cushman, the assistance Hunt requested was used to burglarize the office of Daniel Ellsberg's psychiatrist in order to collect possible derogatory information on the former Defense Department analyst who had leaked the Pentagon Papers to the press. Cushman terminated the assistance after Hunt's subsequent requests raised suspicion within the CIA.

Cushman left the CIA in January 1972 to become commandant of the Marine Corps. He held that post until his retirement in 1975.

(*WAMB*; obituary, *New York Times*, January 4, 1985, p. B4; House of Representatives, *Inquiry into the Alleged Involvement of the Central Intelligence Agency in the Watergate and Ellsberg Matters*, October 23, 1973.)

D

DARRAGH, LYDIA: American secret agent (?)

Born Lydia Barrington in Dublin, Ireland, Darragh was the wife of William Darragh, a Philadelphia schoolteacher during the American Revolution. According to a tradition passed down by her descendants, but not otherwise substantiated, she served as a secret intelligence agent for Gen. GEORGE WASHINGTON in Philadelphia during the British occupation of that city. According to this account she availed herself of the opportunity offered when Gen. William Howe, the British commander, appropriated some rooms in her house for his conference room and personal apartment. Darragh purportedly eavesdropped on Howe and reported what she heard to Washington, using her fourteen-year-old son as courier. In one instance, she purportedly warned Washington of an impending British surprise night attack on his positions at Whitemarsh, Pennsylvania, planned for December 4–5, 1777.

Washington was indeed forewarned of the British attack, and Howe, having lost the advantage of surprise, returned to Philadelphia after a few skirmishes with the Continentals. But certain historians call into question whether Darragh was one of the several sources of Washington's warning on this—or any—occasion.

(Bakeless, *Turncoats, Traitors and Heroes*; Bryan, *The Spy in America*.)

DAVIS, CHARLES HENRY (August 18, 1845– December 27, 1921): naval officer

The son of a distinguished naval officer of the same name, Davis was born in Cambridge, Massachusetts and graduated from the Naval Academy in 1864. After ten years of routine assignments he spent two years in astronomical and geodetic work at the Naval Observatory, then three years in a series of expeditions to various corners of the globe to perfect a technique of establishing exact longitudes through the use of submarine telegraph cables.

In 1889 he was appointed chief of the Office of Naval Intelligence, a role he hoped to broaden through his close association with his brother-in-law, Rep. Henry Cabot Lodge of Massachusetts, a leading civilian navalist and a member of the House Committee on Naval Affairs. Davis's plan depended on a close and intimate association with Secretary of the Navy Benjamin F. Tracy, but it was thwarted when ONI was transferred to the direct supervision of the assistant secretary, James Russell Soley. A Harvard-educated lawyer who had taught history and law at the Naval Academy and was something of a naval intelligence buff himself, Soley kept a tight reign on the ONI and stood as an obstacle between Davis and Tracy. Davis's ambitions were further frustrated by his reputation as a querulous and moody officer who damaged the morale of ONI.

Davis's tour as ONI chief included a crisis late in 1891: a war with Chile threatened to erupt after a Valparaiso mob killed two crewmen from the cruiser *Baltimore*, then visiting the port. Davis served on an informal crisis team with Soley and Commodore William F. Folger, and ONI was able to provide some minimal intelligence support to the war planning and preparations. Fortunately the situation was defused through diplomatic action.

Davis left ONI without regret in 1892. He was promoted to the rank of rear admiral in 1904.

(Dorwart, *The Office of Naval Intelligence; DAB*.)

DAVIS, ROBERT KENDALL (ca. 1918–): intelligence officer

Davis served in the Federal Bureau of Investigation as a special agent during 1941–46. Fluent in Spanish, Davis was assigned to the FBI's Special Intelligence Service, the unit that operated in Latin America during the SECOND WORLD WAR. He was one of the FBI/SIS agents recruited into the CENTRAL INTELLIGENCE AGENCY by J.C. KING during the late 1940s to serve in the Western Hemisphere Division of the CIA's Clandestine Service.

Davis was in charge of logistics for the CIA's GUATEMALA COUP in 1954. He was chief of station in Guatemala in 1961 and made the arrangements to establish the CIA training bases in that country for the anti-Castro Cuban emigrés who took part in the BAY OF PIGS INVASION.

Davis later served as chief of the CIA station in Lima, Peru.

(Wyden, *The Bay of Pigs;* Wise and Ross, *The Invisible Government;* Agee, *Inside the Company.*)

DAVIS, SAMUEL (October 6, 1844–November 27, 1863): Confederate secret agent

A native of Rutherford County, Tennessee, Davis grew up on his father's small farm and received little formal education. After Tennessee seceded from the Union shortly after the outbreak of the Civil War, he enlisted in the Rutherford Rifles, which soon thereafter became part of the 1st Tennessee Infantry. He served through the campaign in West Virginia and in most of the engagements under Gen. Braxton Bragg in Tennessee.

After the Battle of Stones River (December 30, 1862–January 3, 1863) Davis was detailed to COLEMAN'S SCOUTS, Bragg's elite reconnaissance and secret service unit commanded by Capt. HENRY B. SHAW. Shortly after the Battle of Chickamauga (September 19–20, 1863) he was sent undercover through Union lines to ascertain the strength of Federal units between Nashville and Decatur, Alabama, and to purchase U.S. Army pistols on the black market in Nashville. He completed the mission successfully.

In late October or early November Shaw led a small team of his agents, including Davis, on another covert reconnaissance mission into the Union-held territory around Nashville. This sortie was accomplished without mishap and, on November 10th, Davis was sent into the area again. Davis rendezvoused with Shaw near Union-held Pulaski, Tennes-

see, on November 19, 1863 and received intelligence reports and dispatches he was to carry back to General Bragg. Davis also met with local Confederate agents who turned over to him an assortment of valuable documents, including detailed drawings of the fortifications at Nashville and other Union strongholds in Tennessee. While en route back to Confederate lines he was stopped by two men in Confederate uniform who were in fact agents of L.A. NARON, General Dodge's Chief of Scouts (i.e., intelligence and counterespionage).

After Davis produced a Confederate pass he was arrested, brought to Naron and searched. The incriminating documents were discovered and Davis was taken to Dodge, who proposed to spare the agent's life if he would disclose the sources of the documents he had been carrying, the identities of other Confederate secret service agents and informers, and the routes they used to cross the Union lines. Davis resolutely refused to provide any of this information and was court-martialed and sentenced to death.

At the time of Davis's capture, Shaw, too, had been taken prisoner, although his captors did not appreciate who he was. Had Davis disclosed Shaw's identity, the latter would have been tried and executed. However, contrary to several accounts, Davis apparently was unaware of Shaw's capture, so this was not a factor in his refusal to cooperate with Dodge.

Davis was given several days to think over Dodge's proposition, and an officer sent by Dodge made a last effort to persuade him as he stood on the scaffold. Nonetheless Davis remained resolute until the end, declaring that he would prefer to "die a thousand times," rather than "betray a friend."

Those who have dubbed Davis "the Nathan Hale of the Confederacy" are quick to add that, unlike Davis, Hale had no choice but to become a martyr.

(Bakeless, *Spies of the Confederacy; National Cyclopedia of American Biography,* v.8.; Kane, *Spies for the Blue and Gray.*)

DAYTON, ELIAS (May 1, 1737–October 22, 1807): Army officer, merchant, Continental congressman, intelligence officer

A native of Elizabethtown (now Elizabeth), New Jersey, Dayton was apprenticed as a mechanic before joining the New Jersey militia. He was commissioned a lieutenant in March 1756, fought in the French and Indian (Seven Years) War, and was promoted to captain in 1760. Afterward he opened a general store in Elizabethtown, and became a member of the local

Committee of Safety (see COMMITTEES OF COR-RESPONDENCE) in 1774.

Dayton had an active military career during the American Revolution. He was commissioned a colonel in the Continental Army in January 1776 and took part in the capture of a British transport ship, the *Blue Mountain Valley*, that month. He led his regiment against the Indian allies of the British in New York State, fought at Brandywine, Germantown, Monmouth, and Yorktown, as well as in lesser battles and skirmishes. He was promoted to brigadier general in January 1783 on the recommendation of Gen. GEORGE WASHINGTON.

In addition to commanding a Continental regiment, Dayton also ran an extensive secret intelligence apparatus in Staten Island and Manhattan for Washington. He took over management of the MERSEREAU SPY RING circa 1777. Some of his networks are believed to have penetrated the British Army.

After the war Dayton returned to his business and was a state legislator and a major general of the New Jersey militia. He represented New Jersey in the Continental Congress during 1787–88.

(Boatner, *Encyclopedia of the American Revolution*; Bakeless, *Turncoats, Traitors and Heroes; Who Was Who in America*, historical volume.)

DE LANCEY, OLIVER (the younger) (1749–1822): British army officer and intelligence officer

A native of New York City, De Lancey was the son of a prominent and politically powerful colonial family in that city. Educated in England, he entered the British army in 1766 and was promoted to the rank of captain in May 1773. He saw action during the American Revolution in New York, Pennsylvania, New Jersey, and South Carolina. He was promoted to the rank of major and served as deputy quartermaster general in Gen. Henry Clinton's expedition against Charleston, South Carolina, in 1780.

De Lancey succeeded Maj. JOHN ANDRÉ as Clinton's adjutant general and chief intelligence officer after André was captured and hanged by Gen. GEORGE WASHINGTON in 1780. Aided by Maj. GEORGE BECKWITH, he reorganized the British secret service in America. He was the CASE OFFICER for WILLIAM HERON, the British agent and double traitor, and he used Heron in an unsuccessful attempt to engineer the defection of American Gen. Samuel H. Parsons. He made a similar unsuccessful attempt to defect American Gen. John Sullivan. When the Continental Army mutinied in Pennsylvania in January 1781, De Lancey tried several unsuccessful schemes to induce the mutineers to defect to the British side.

In May 1781 De Lancey became adjutant general of the British army in America and was promoted to lieutenant colonel. After the war he continued his military career and rose to the rank of full general. After retiring he served in Parliament.

(Boatner, *Encyclopedia of the American Revolution*; Van Doren, *Secret History of the American Revolution*; Bakeless, *Turncoats, Traitors and Heroes*.)

DE SILVA, PEER (June 26, 1917–): Army officer, intelligence officer

A native of San Francisco, California, de Silva enlisted as a private in the U.S. Army in 1936 and was later admitted to the U.S. Military Academy. After graduation he was commissioned a second lieutenant in 1941. He was assigned to Army intelligence and attended the Army's Advanced CIC (Counter Intelligence Corps) school in 1942.

De Silva was assigned to security on the Manhattan Project, the secret wartime program that developed the first nuclear weapons. He served on the project in San Francisco and later Los Alamos, where he was in charge of security. He also had the special assignment of guarding the project's director, J. Robert Oppenheimer, and was among the first to raise questions regarding Oppenheimer as a security risk. In 1945 he was given the task of transporting the bomb that was to be used against Nagasaki, to the Pacific island of Tinian where it was assembled and loaded aboard a B-29 bomber.

After the war de Silva, then a lieutenant colonel, applied for and received a transfer to the War Department's Strategic Services Unit, which was all that remained of the espionage and counterespionage branches of the Office of Strategic Services when the OSS was dissolved in September 1945. After several months working in counterespionage and security he was detached from the SSU in order to take part in a War Department program for the study of the Soviet Union.

As part of this program de Silva studied the Russian language at Columbia University during 1946–47, and attended a U.S. Army school taught by anti-Soviet Russian emigrés in Oberammergau (later Regensburg), Germany during 1947–48. He further broadened his knowledge of Russian and the Soviet Union during 1948–49 when he served as a diplomatic courier between the American embassies in Moscow and Helsinki, Finland.

In December 1949 de Silva was assigned to detached service with the Central Intelligence Agency.

He served as deputy to the chief of the CIA base in Pullach, West Germany, which was the liaison unit between the Agency and the Gehlen Organization, the West German intelligence service subsidized by the CIA. In addition to his liaison duties he worked with Gehlen's officers and agents in collecting intelligence regarding the Soviet occupation zone of Germany and running agent networks within the Soviet zone.

In April 1951 de Silva's tour at Pullach was complete and he was transferred to CIA headquarters in Washington. He was assistant to Eric Timm, the chief of the Foreign Intelligence Staff of the Office of Special Operations, as the SECRET INTELLIGENCE unit of the CIA was then known. Later that year he was appointed chief of operations within the Soviet Russia Division of OSO. In that capacity he participated in the program then under way in which Ukrainian and other emigrés from the Soviet Union were recruited to work as agents in their homeland. However, this program proved generally ineffective; virtually all of the agents were either captured or otherwise neutralized soon after arriving in the USSR, and de Silva was instrumental in bringing it to an end.

In September 1953 de Silva resigned from the U.S. Army in order to remain with the CIA as a civilian employee (the alternative being a non-CIA assignment with the Army). In 1955 he was transferred to the East European Division of the Clandestine Service and sent to Vienna as deputy chief of the CIA station there. The following year he became chief of the station.

In August 1959 de Silva left the Vienna post to become chief of station in Seoul, Korea. The assignment actually involved reopening the CIA's Korean station, which had been closed several years earlier as a result of an incident in which a yacht carrying Korean President Syngman Rhee and his guests was fired on when it approached a CIA training base on an offshore island in the Yellow Sea. De Silva's task was to reestablish the liaison with the Korean security and intelligence services, which had been severed when Rhee ordered the CIA out of Korea following the shooting incident.

De Silva left Korea in July 1962 to become chief of station in Hong Kong, a post he later described as a "rest and recreation" assignment after his tour in Seoul, which had encompassed the decline of the corrupt administration of the near-senile Rhee, and a violent coup d'etat by the Korean army. From Hong Kong de Silva ran intelligence operations into mainland China, attempting, among other things, to collect information on the Chinese nuclear program.

In December 1963 de Silva was appointed chief of the Saigon station, which was the largest CIA station at that time. His immediate tasks were to cement relations with the American ambassador to Vietnam, Henry Cabot Lodge, who had demanded the departure of de Silva's predecessor, JOHN RICHARDSON, and to establish liaison with the new South Vietnamese regime, which had come to power only a few months earlier in a coup d'etat that involved the assassinations of President Ngo Dinh Diem. He was successful in both missions. Besides the usual duties of running agent operations into North Vietnam, he established a program to train the Vietnamese national police in humane methods of prisoner interrogation, and he initiated the People's Action Teams. The teams were made up of armed Vietnamese volunteer units that defended their villages and localities against the Vietcong, while at the same time teaching their fellows useful farming skills and indoctrinating them in anti-Vietcong political theory.

In March 1965 de Silva was seriously wounded when the Vietcong detonated a car bomb outside the American embassy. The incident cost him the sight in his left eye. Because of his physical condition he was ordered to leave Saigon and return to CIA headquarters in Washington in June 1965.

De Silva was appointed to the newly created post of special assistant for Vietnam affairs to the director of central intelligence, then Adm. WILLIAM RABORN. In 1966 he was "lent" by the CIA to Graham Martin, the American ambassador to Thailand, to serve as his advisor on counterinsurgency. In 1968 he returned to CIA headquarters, where he was appointed director of the Office of Training, and a year later he was made chief of the San Francisco base of the CIA CLANDESTINE SERVICE's Domestic Operations Division. During 1971–72 he was chief of station in Canberra, Australia. De Silva retired from the CIA in January 1973.

(De Silva, *Sub Rosa;* Cullum, *Biographical Register of the Officers and Graduates of the U.S. Military Academy at West Point . . . ,* v.8; Stern and Green, *The Oppenheimer Case.*)

DEAK, NICHOLAS LOUIS (October 8, 1905– November 18, 1985): banker, economist, covert operations officer

A native of Hateg, Hungary, Deak graduated from the Academy of World Trade in Vienna in 1925 and earned a Ph.D. in Economics and Finance from the University of Neuchatel (Switzerland) in 1929. From 1930 to 1935 he worked for the Royal Hungarian Trade Institute. He was manager of the Hungarian and Romanian subsidiaries of the British Overseas

Bank from 1935 to 1937, and he served with the Economics Department of the League of Nations in Geneva from 1937 to 1939.

Deak moved to the United States in 1939 and taught at the Perkiomen College Preparatory School. In 1941 and 1942 he taught economics at the City College of New York. In 1942 he joined the U.S. Army and was assigned to the OSS SPECIAL OPERATIONS BRANCH.

Deak served in Syria, Egypt, Italy, Malaya, and Singapore. He was to be part of a 1943 operation—planned but never executed—in which men would parachute into Romania and, disguised as firemen, sabotage the Ploesti oil fields. In the fall of 1945 he headed a Special Operations team working with the French against the Vietminh guerrillas in Vietnam. He was discharged with the rank of major.

After the war Deak returned to international finance. He became president of Deak and Co., the largest foreign currency exchange firm in the United States, Canada, and the Far East, and held controlling interests in Swiss and Austrian banks. In 1974–75 he served as president of the Veterans of the OSS.

Deak was murdered at his office by a mentally disturbed client in 1985.

(Smith, *OSS; Who's Who in America*, 42nd ed; *New York Times*, November 19, 1985, p. 1.)

DEANE, SILAS (December 24, 1737– September 23, 1789): lawyer, Continental congressman, diplomatic agent, defector (?)

A native of Groton, Connecticut, Deane graduated from Yale in 1758 and earned an A.M. degree from that institution in 1763. He was admitted to the Connecticut bar in 1761. A leader of the Revolutionary movement in Connecticut, he was secretary of that colony's COMMITTEE OF CORRESPONDENCE in 1773, and a delegate to the first and second Continental Congresses in 1774–76.

In April 1776 Deane was sent to France by the Continental Congress as an agent of the COMMITTEE OF SECRET CORRESPONDENCE, representing the SECRET COMMITTEE and the Commercial Committee, as well. He explored the possibility of a French alliance and worked with PIERRE AUGUSTIN CARON DE BEAUMARCHAIS to arrange for the dispatch of French military aid to the Americans through the cover corporation, HORTALEZ & CIE. In September 1776 he was appointed one of the three American diplomatic commissioners to France (BENJAMIN FRANKLIN and Arthur Lee were the others).

After the Franco-American alliance was signed in 1778, Deane was recalled to America to answer charges

Silas Deane. Source: Library of Congress.

made by Lee and others that he had engaged in profiteering in collusion with Beaumarchais. Although the basis of these charges arose out of the confusion resulting from Lee's misstatement that the French aid had been given without expectation of repayment, the Congress did not fully exonerate him. He returned to France in 1780 to collect documentary evidence supporting his innocence, but apparently became alienated from the American cause.

In 1781 Deane apparently cooperated with British intelligence in the persons of EDWARD BANCROFT and PAUL WENTWORTH, although historians debate the degree and character of his culpability. He wrote several letters to influential Americans stating his failing confidence in the American cause and urging some accommodation with Britain short of independence. These letters came into British hands, were reviewed by Lord North and the King, and then forwarded to Gen. Henry Clinton, the British commander in New York, with instructions to have them published with the cover story that they had been intercepted while en route to the addresses. The letters were duly published in *The Royal Gazette*, the Tory newspaper published by JAMES RIVINGTON.

The publication of the letters caused Deane to be accused of treason. He became an exile, living in Ghent, Belgium, and in England. In 1789 he decided to move to Canada, but he died aboard ship while still in British waters, the apparent victim of an overdose of laudanum. However, historian Julian P. Boyd has made an interesting circumstantial case that Deane may have been poisoned by Bancroft to prevent him from disclosing what he knew of Bancroft's employment by the British secret service.

(Boyd, "Silas Deane: Death by a Kindly Teacher of Treason"; *Who Was Who in America*, historical volume; Boatner, *Encyclopedia of the American Revolution*; Van Doren, *Secret History of the American Revolution*; Davidson and Lytle, *After the Fact*.)

DEFECTOR-IN-PLACE

A member of an organization of intelligence interest—e.g., the armed services, the government, an intelligence service—who transfers his or her allegiance to another country, generally an adversary of his own, but who remains in his original post, serving as a PENETRATION AGENT. OLEG V. PENKOVSKY, for example, was a defector-in-place who served as a penetration agent within Soviet intelligence for the British and American intelligence services. BENEDICT ARNOLD was a defector-in-place within the Continental Army until he was discovered and fled to British-occupied New York City (see also *mole*).

DEFENSE INTELLIGENCE AGENCY

An agency of the Department of Defense, the DIA was established in August 1961 by Secretary of Defense Robert S. McNamara. It was intended to provide a single military voice (rather than the three individual voices of the Army, Navy, and Air Force intelligence services) in the development of NATIONAL INTELLIGENCE ESTIMATES; to eliminate redundancy in the military intelligence services by consolidating the duplicated activities within a single agency; to supervise and coordinate the work of those intelligence services; and to produce CURRENT INTELLIGENCE for use by the senior officials of the Defense Department. In general, the DIA was created to take over all the armed services' intelligence activities except signal intelligence (see SIGINT), OVERHEAD RECONNAISSANCE (the responsibility of the NATIONAL SECURITY AGENCY and the NATIONAL RECONNAISSANCE OFFICE, respectively), and those activities specific to a particular branch of the armed services.

In the case of ARMY INTELLIGENCE, the DIA took over such functions as establishing intelligence collection requirements and current intelligence pro-

duction, leaving the Army's assistant chief of staff for intelligence (G-2) with such limited and specific tasks as intelligence training of Army personnel, internal Army security and counterintelligence, technical intelligence regarding tactical or ground forces weapons systems, mapping, charting, geodesy, and combat intelligence. A similar realignment of responsibilities was made in NAVAL INTELLIGENCE and AIR FORCE INTELLIGENCE.

The DIA was established on a recommendation of a Joint Study Group appointed in 1959 under the Eisenhower administration. The United States Intelligence Board (see NATIONAL FOREIGN INTELLIGENCE BOARD) had set up this group to study the organization and functioning of the INTELLIGENCE COMMUNITY. According to several accounts, the decision to establish the agency grew directly from the so-called "missile gap" controversy of the 1950s in which the three armed services intelligence units reached widely disparate estimates regarding the strength and character of the Soviet missile threat, estimates that were believed to have been made for self-serving purposes, i.e., each unit emphasized the role of the armed service it belonged to in countering the threat. Whatever role this controversy played, the decision to establish DIA seems in any case to have evolved from the 1947 decision to subordinate the individual armed services within the newly created Department of Defense, and the trend toward government centralization that reached its peak during the Kennedy administration.

In 1965 the United States Intelligence Board was reorganized; the three seats previously held by the Army, Navy, and Air Force were eliminated in favor of a single seat held by the director of DIA. However the heads of the three armed services' intelligence units continued to attend USIB (and today's National Foreign Intelligence Board) meetings as nonvoting participants.

The director of the DIA reports to the secretary of defense through the Joint Chiefs of Staff. He is the chief intelligence officer to both the secretary and the Joint Chiefs, as well as commander of the Defense Attaché System in which military, naval, and air attachés serve overseas at U.S. embassies (the attachés of the three armed services have been reporting through DIA since 1965).

The DIA has undergone several reorganizations during its relatively brief existence. Today it consists of five major directorates: Management and Operations, Resources and Systems, Intelligence and External Affairs, Foreign Intelligence, and JCS Support.

(Corson, *Armies of Ignorance*; Richelson, *The U.S. Intelligence Community*; Kirkpatrick, *The Real CIA, The*

U.S. Intelligence Community; Ransom, *The Intelligence Establishment*; MacCloskey, *The American Intelligence Community*.)

DEFENSE INTELLIGENCE COLLEGE

An accredited, degree-granting institution operated and controlled by the DEFENSE INTELLIGENCE AGENCY under the direction of the Joint Chiefs of Staff. The college was established in 1962 as the Defense Intelligence School through a merger of the Naval Intelligence School's postgraduate curriculum and the Army's Strategic Intelligence School. In 1983 it became the Defense Intelligence College and became fully accredited by the Middle States Association of Colleges and Schools.

Students at the Defense Intelligence College come from the four military services, the Defense Intelligence Agency, the Central Intelligence Agency, the National Security Agency, the Federal Bureau of Investigation, and other government agencies (e.g., the Library of Congress). Courses range in length from two days to a twelve-month program leading to the degree of Master of Science of Strategic Intelligence, unique to the College. The College's resident faculty consists of some fifty military officers and civilians and is augmented by adjunct professors qualified by knowledge of and/or experience in the field of intelligence.

(Keesing, "The Defense Intelligence College.")

DEFENSE SPECIAL MISSILE AND ASTRONAUTICS CENTER

According to espionologist James Bamford, the DEFSMAC is a strategic early-warning center located at the NATIONAL SECURITY AGENCY headquarters at Ford Meade, Maryland. Established in 1966, the DEFSMAC processes the input from a variety of SIGINT and other sensors in order to detect imminent threats to the United States in the form of foreign missiles, aircraft, or other overt military activities. Indications intelligence produced by DEFSMAC is transmitted to the White House Situation Room, the National Military Command Center at the Pentagon, alternate national command posts, and such subordinate command centers as the North American Air Defense Command headquarters in Colorado.

See also DEFENSE SUPPORT SATELLITES, VELA RECONNAISSANCE SATELLITE, MIDAS EARLY WARNING SATELLITE.

(Bamford, *The Puzzle Palace*.)

Emblem of the Defense Intelligence College. Source: Defense Intelligence College.

DEFENSE SUPPORT SATELLITES

A set of three reconnaissance satellites (see OVERHEAD RECONNAISSANCE) stationed in geosynchronous orbits over selected points on the surface of the earth. The satellites are equipped with infrared sensors to detect foreign missile launches. They may be the successors to the MIDAS EARLY WARNING SATELLITE.

(*New York Times*, February 24, 1986, p. B6.)

DENIED AREA

A country or geographical area in which the local security or counterintelligence services effectively prevent Westerners from traveling freely, communicating with local citizens, or collecting information, even of a general nature, without official approval. These restrictions obviously constrain secret intelligence operations within the area, especially the development of sources among the populace. U.S. intelligence services regard the USSR, the Soviet East European bloc, such Soviet client states as North Korea, Vietnam, and Cuba, and some non-Communist Third World countries as denied areas.

(Breckinridge, *The CIA and the U.S. Intelligence System*; Copeland, *Without Cloak or Dagger*.)

DERIABIN, PETER (February 13, 1921–): Soviet intelligence officer and defector

A native of the Soviet Union, Deriabin taught school before the outbreak of the Second World War. He served in the Red Army in the battle of Stalingrad and later was wounded. In 1945 he joined the NKVD (the People's Committee for Internal Affairs), one of several predecessors to the KGB. He served in Siberia during 1945–47, and at MVD headquarters in Moscow during 1947–53 (the NKVD became the MVD, Ministry of Internal Affairs, in 1946), reaching the rank of major.

In 1953 Deriabin was assigned to Vienna, Austria. A few months later, in 1954, he defected to the Central Intelligence Agency and was given political asylum in the United States. He was kept "under wraps" until 1959 while he was extensively debriefed on Soviet intelligence sources and methods.

Deriabin exposed the presence of a Soviet intelligence officer, Vladimir Pavlichenko, who was working in the Public Information Office of the United Nations in New York. Among the other information Deriabin supplied was the presence of two Soviet agents—known to him only by the code names PETER and PAUL—within the Gehlen Organization, the West German intelligence service subsidized by the CIA, and the fact that one of his former colleagues, Soviet intelligence officer Anatoli Golitsin, was a likely candidate for recruitment by the CIA. The former disclosure contributed to the eventual apprehension in 1961 of Heinze Felfe, a Soviet penetration agent within the West German BND (Federal Intelligence Service), as the Gehlen Organization was known after 1956. American intelligence officers recalled the tip about Golitsin when the Russian approached the CIA station chief in Helsinki, Finland, in 1961 as a WALK-IN and defected to the United States.

Deriabin was the highest ranking Soviet intelligence officer to defect to the West as of 1954 and so provided the CIA with an unprecedented insight into the workings of Soviet intelligence. His autobiographical book, *The Secret World* (written in collaboration with Frank Gibney, a professional writer, and published in 1959), was described in a CIA report in 1965 as "probably the most authoritative public account of KGB organization and activity."

Deriabin worked for the CIA, where he translated from the Russian the documents published as the book, *The Penkovskiy Papers* (see OLEG PENKOVSKY).

(Wise and Ross, *The Espionage Establishment*; Martin, *Wilderness of Mirrors*; Deriabin, *The Secret World*.)

DESPRES, EMILE (September 21, 1909–April 1973): economist, intelligence analyst

A native of Chicago, Illinois, Despres graduated from Harvard University in 1930. From 1930 to 1937 he was a specialist in foreign exchange with the Federal Reserve Bank in New York City. During 1939–41 he was an economic advisor to the Board of Governors of the Federal Reserve.

Despres served with the Office of Strategic Services from 1941 to 1944. He was director of the Economics Division of the OSS RESEARCH AND ANALYSIS BRANCH and also served as a member of the Board of Analysts and an alternate member of the Joint Intelligence Staff of the Joint Chiefs of Staff. During 1945–46 he acted as advisor on German economic affairs to the State Department.

From 1946 to 1961 Despres was a member of the faculty of Williams College. From 1961 to 1973 he was professor of economics at Stanford University.

(Cline, *CIA, Reality vs. Myth; Who Was Who in America*, v. 5.)

DESTABILIZE

To overthrow, e.g., a government, through COVERT ACTION. The entry of this term into the professional intelligence lexicon is another example of life imitating art in the language of intelligence (see MOLE). Rep. Michael Harrington of Massachusetts coined the term in 1974 in a letter summarizing the secret testimony of WILLIAM E. COLBY before the House Armed Forces CIA subcommittee regarding the CIA operations in Chile (see RICHARD M. HELMS, WILLIAM V. BROE). In fact Colby had not actually used the term. Nonetheless, when the letter was leaked and became the basis of a *New York Times* story, the reporter also attributed the term, within quotation marks, to Colby. Colby's denial that he had ever used the term, which was published in the letters column of the *Times*, failed to put to rest the belief that he had, and that it was a common CIA term. It proved so apt a locution that it was soon adopted in many quarters, including within the CIA itself.

(Phillips, *The Night Watch.*)

DEUEL, WALLACE RANKING (June 14, 1905–): journalist, intelligence officer

A native of Chicago, Deuel graduated from the University of Illinois in 1926 and taught political science and international law at the American University in Beirut from 1926 to 1929. In 1929 he joined the staff of the *Chicago Daily News*, where he was, successively, an editorial writer, assistant to the foreign editor, in charge of the New York cable office, and correspondent in Washington, Rome, and Berlin.

In 1941 Deuel joined the Office of the Coordinator of Information, the predecessor of the Office of Strategic Services. He became a special assistant to OSS Director WILLIAM J. DONOVAN. After the war he remained with the OSS for a brief period to begin an official history of the agency, a project that was completed by KERMIT ROOSEVELT.

(*Who's Who in America*, v. 24; Roosevelt, *War Report of the OSS*.)

DEVISED FACILITY

A term used in the CIA CLANDESTINE SERVICE to denote a PROPRIETARY COMPANY or other organization (e.g., the Committee for a Free Europe—see RADIO FREE EUROPE/RADIO LIBERTY) established to provide COVER for a SECRET INTELLIGENCE or COVERT ACTION operation.

(Breckinridge, *The CIA and the U.S. Intelligence System*.)

DEVLIN, LAWRENCE RAYMOND (June 18, 1922–): intelligence officer

A native of New Hampshire, Devlin served in the U.S. Army during 1942–46 and was discharged with the rank of major. He graduated from San Diego State College in 1947 and earned an M.A. from Harvard University in 1949. He worked as an editor in a publishing house in 1950–53, and as a political affairs analyst for the U.S. Department of the Army during 1953–57.

Devlin then served in the CIA CLANDESTINE SERVICE. During 1957–60 he was a political officer at the American embassy in Brussels, Belgium. During 1960–63 he was the CIA chief of station at Leopoldville (now Kinshasa) in the Congo (now Zaire). In that capacity he was a principal figure in the CIA's unsuccessful attempt to assassinate Congolese leader Patrice Lumumba (see CENTRAL INTELLIGENCE AGENCY). When he testified regarding this operation before the Church Committee he used the pseudonym "Victor Hedgman."

After serving at CIA headquarters in Washington during 1963–65, Devlin did a second tour in the Congo during 1965–67. He was reputedly instrumental in establishing Joseph Mobutu as president of the Congo.

During 1968–70 Devlin served in Vientiane, Laos, from where he ran the CIA's paramilitary program in that country (see SECRET WAR IN LAOS). He returned to Washington and CIA headquarters in 1970 and became chief of the Africa Division of the Clandestine Service.

Devlin retired from the CIA in 1974 and afterward represented the business interests of an American financier in the Congo, where it was reported that Devlin was the only American to retain entrée with President Mobutu.

(*Who's Who in Government*, 1st ed.; Stockwell, *In Search of Enemies*; Kwitny, *Endless Enemies*; Powers, *The Man Who Kept the Secrets*; U.S. Senate, *Alleged Assassination Plots Involving Foreign Leaders*.)

DISCOVERER RECONNAISSANCE SATELLITE

The Discoverer program was begun in 1956 under the joint sponsorship of the Central Intelligence Agency and the U.S. Air Force. It was aimed at developing an orbital reconnaissance platform that could carry long-range, high-resolution cameras for overhead photography, and which had the capability to de-orbit so that the photographs thus made could be recovered.

The *Discoverer* satellite was a modified Agena rocket, built by the Lockheed Aircraft Corporation. It was 19.2 feet long, five feet in diameter, and carried a camera and an on-board film processor built by Eastman Kodak, plus a capsule to carry the film back to earth. A Thor rocket was used as a first stage to launch the *Discoverer*, and the Agena carried it into an orbit ranging from one hundred to several hundred miles altitude. When its reconnaissance mission was complete, a retro-rocket, fired on a radio command from a ground station, de-orbited the capsule, which deployed a parachute on re-entering the atmosphere. The capsule was recovered in mid-air by an Air Force C-119 or C-130 transport carrying special trapeze-like equipment built by the All-American Engineering Company. The recovery zone was an area of the Pacific Ocean near Hawaii; in case the midair "snatch" failed, the floating capsule could be recovered from the water.

After a series of initial failures, *Discoverer 13* was successfully recovered on August 11, 1960. Subsequent Discoverer satellites were improved by increased booster thrust—permitting heavier photographic systems to be used—and other refinements. The program marked the resumption of OVERHEAD RECONNAISSANCE of Soviet strategic sites, which had been interrupted by the termination of the U-2 flights over Soviet territory after the shooting down of FRANCIS GARY POWERS in May 1960. It ushered

Lockheed Agena spacecraft used to orbit the Discoverer Reconnaissance Satellite. Source: U.S. Air Force.

in the reconnaissance satellite as a principal means of intelligence collection.

The Discoverer series was in use throughout the 1960s. It was augmented by the SAMOS RECONNAISSANCE SATELLITE and other reconnaissance satellites during that period, and replaced by the more advanced KH-9 RECONNAISSANCE SATELLITE in the early 1970s.

(Klass, *Secret Sentries in Space;* Greenwood, "Reconnaissance and Arms Control.")

DODGE, GRENVILLE MELLEN (April 12, 1831–January 3, 1916): engineer, railroad builder, businessman, Army officer, intelligence officer

A native of Danvers, Massachusetts, Dodge graduated from Norwich University in 1851. Trained as a civil engineer, he went west and worked as a surveyor for the Illinois Central Railroad, and later for the Mississippi & Missouri Railroad in Iowa. He settled in Iowa City and, from 1855 to 1861, was engaged in railroad construction, while at the same time being involved in banking and other commercial ventures.

Dodge organized a unit of the Iowa militia in 1856 and, after the outbreak of the Civil War, he was commissioned a colonel and led Iowa troops in Missouri during 1861–62. In March 1862 he was commissioned a brigadier general in the Army of the Tennessee. He commanded a division in the Vicksburg campaign (October 1862–July 1863) and the Atlanta campaign (May–September, 1864). Promoted to major general in June 1864, he was severely wounded in August of that year near Atlanta, but returned to duty in December to take command of the Department of Missouri.

As a Civil War commander, Dodge is best known for his prodigious feats of bridge and railroad construction for the Army. In the Atlanta campaign, for example, he rebuilt a 710-foot bridge across the Chattanooga River in three days. However, espionologists know him to have been one of the more important Union intelligence officers of the Civil War (Bakeless rates him as one of the three best intelligence officers in the Union Army).

Late in 1862, while taking part in the Vicksburg campaign, Dodge began establishing a network of secret service agents throughout the Confederacy. One of the best of them, PHILIP HENSON, became a successful double agent for Dodge, operating deep in Mississippi and Georgia for two years and making frequent trips back to Union territory to report his observations.

Dodge's secret service consisted of about a hundred such agents operating from Tennessee to Richmond and south to the Gulf of Mexico. Run by Dodge's chief of scouts, L.A. NARON, the organization was primarily concerned with positive intelligence (see INTELLIGENCE TAXONOMY), but also performed a counterespionage function. Dodge and Naron first detected the operations of COLEMAN'S SCOUTS, the elite secret service unit of Confederate Gen. Braxton Bragg, and made a major effort to roll it up. Dodge managed to capture several of its members, including the unfortunate SAMUEL DAVIS, and even its leader, Capt. HENRY B. SHAW (although he remained ignorant of Shaw's importance), but he failed to neutralize the organization, which continued to operate through the final days of the war.

The intelligence unit Dodge organized also functioned for the duration of the war, even after Dodge took command of the Department of Missouri. He resigned from the Army in May 1866. Afterward he served a term (1866–68) in Congress as a representative from Iowa, and became chief engineer of the Union Pacific Railroad. He was responsible for most of the construction of the railroad line across the Great Plains and Rocky Mountains from Omaha, Nebraska, to Promontory Point, Utah, where the tracks joined those of the Central Pacific, establishing the first American transcontinental railroad link in 1870. He continued to work in the railroad industry, built lines in the United States, Mexico, and Cuba, and served as president or chairman of the board of several railroads.

After the Spanish-American War, President William McKinley appointed Dodge chairman of a commission to investigate the management of the War Department during the war. The report of the Dodge Commission led to many of the management reforms that were initiated in the Army under Secretary of War Elihu Root.

(*DAB; The National Cyclopedia of American Biography,* v. 16; *WAMB;* Bakeless, *Spies of the Confederacy;* Kane, *Spies for the Blue and Gray.*)

Gen. Grenville M. Dodge. Source: Library of Congress.

DOERING, OTTO ("Ole") C., JR. (1904–): lawyer, intelligence officer

A native of Wilmette, Illinois and the son of a prominent Chicago family, Doering earned an LL.B. from Cornell University in 1927 and went to work for the law firm of Cravath, de Gersdorff, Swaine, and Wood. In 1929 he joined Donovan, Leisure, Newton, and Lumbard, the Wall Street law firm of WILLIAM J. DONOVAN. He became a partner in the firm in 1935 and was Donovan's lifelong friend.

In 1941 Doering assisted the Military Affairs Committee of the U.S. House of Representatives in an inquiry into the status of American national defense. In 1942 he was an advisor to the Remington Arms Company. Later that year Donovan brought him into the Office of the Coordinator of Information, the predecessor to the OFFICE OF STRATEGIC SERVICES.

Doering served as chief of the agency's Secretariat, which functioned as Donovan's personal staff. Later Doering held the positions of OSS general counsel, executive officer, and assistant director. Throughout his service with the OSS Doering was, in fact, Donovan's chief of staff. Doering's organizational and administrative talents complemented Donovan's rather more mercurial operating methods, and he became known as "the glue that held the OSS together."

After the war Doering returned to the practice of law with Donovan's firm.

(Cave Brown, *The Last Hero;* Ford, *Donovan of OSS;* Troy, *Donovan and the CIA;* Office of Strategic Services, "Prominent Persons in the OSS.")

DONOVAN, JAMES BRITT (February 29, 1916–January 19, 1970): lawyer, intelligence officer

A native of New York City, Donovan graduated from Fordham University in 1937 and earned an LL.B. from Harvard University in 1940. He practiced law in New York City until 1942, when he became associate general counsel of the U.S. Office of Scientific Research and Development in Washington, D.C., an agency that worked closely with the Office of Strategic Services, providing the OSS with scientific and technical expertise. In 1943 he was commissioned in the U.S. Naval Reserve and assigned to OSS, where he served as general counsel. (Donovan was not related to OSS Director WILLIAM J. DONOVAN.)

In May 1945 Donovan joined the staff of the U.S. chief prosecutor at the Nuremburg war crimes trial. As associate prosecutor, he was in charge of all visual evidence, including captured enemy photographs and motion pictures.

Donovan returned to civilian life in 1946 and became general counsel for the National Bureau of Casualty Underwriters. In 1951 he joined in forming the law firm of Watters, Cowen & Donovan and commenced the private practice of law, while continuing to serve with the Casualty Underwriters.

In 1957 Donovan became defense counsel for Soviet intelligence officer RUDOLPH IVANOVICH ABEL, then under indictment for failing to register as a Soviet agent and for conspiracy to commit espionage. Although Abel was convicted, Donovan argued successfully that his client be spared a death sentence on the grounds that he might someday be exchanged for an American convicted of spying in the USSR. Abel was sentenced to thirty years in prison. Donovan's plea proved prophetic, and in 1962 he arranged the exchange of Abel for CIA pilot FRANCIS GARY POWERS. Later that year he performed a similar service when, as representative of the families of the Cuban troops captured by Fidel Castro's forces in the BAY OF PIGS INVASION, he negotiated with Castro for their release in exchange for food and medical supplies.

Donovan was president of the New York Board of Education from 1963 to 1965, and president of Pratt Institute from 1968 to 1970. He was decorated with the Legion of Merit and the Distinguished Service medal for intelligence.

(Donovan, *Strangers on a Bridge; Who Was Who in America*, vol. 5; *Current Biography*, 1961; Johnson et al., *The Bay of Pigs*.)

DONOVAN, WILLIAM ("Wild Bill") JOSEPH (January 1, 1883–February 8, 1959): lawyer, public official, Army officer, intelligence officer, "the Father of American Intelligence"

A native of Buffalo, New York, Donovan graduated from Columbia University in 1905 and Columbia Law School in 1907. He practiced law in Buffalo and, in 1912, he organized a cavalry troop in the New York National Guard. He saw service with this troop on the Mexican border in 1916.

During the First World War he served in France with the U.S. Army's 165th Infantry, the former "Fighting 69th." Wounded three times, he received numerous decorations, including the Medal of Honor, and was discharged with the rank of colonel. During the next two decades he alternated private law practice with a variety of official and quasi-official government assignments. He was U.S. district attorney for western New York, assistant U.S. attorney general, and a member of several federal commissions and delegations. He was active in the Republican Party at both the New York State and national levels and made two unsuccessful bids for elected office: lieutenant governor and governor of New York State in 1922 and 1932, respectively. In 1929 he founded the Wall Street law firm of Donovan, Leisure, Newton, and Lumbard and became active in corporate law.

A man of enormous energy and wide-ranging interests, Donovan did not limit himself to domestic affairs. While honeymooning in Japan in 1919, he undertook a two-month secret mission to Siberia at the request of the United States government to report on the anti-Bolshevik movement of the White Russians led by Adm. Alexander Kolchak. In the ensuing years he made frequent business trips to England and the Continent, and in 1935 he went to Rome, Egypt, and Ethiopia on an unofficial mission for the War Department to observe the Italian campaign against Ethiopia. During the next few years he made several trips to Europe to observe and report on the Spanish civil war and other military matters in Czechoslovakia, the Balkans, and Italy.

After the outbreak of the Second World War in 1939, Donovan's intimate familiarity with European military affairs brought him into frequent close contact with President Franklin Roosevelt and his Cabinet. In 1940 Roosevelt sent him on a confidential fact-finding mission to England to report on Britain's ability to survive German attack. A few months later the President sent him on another mission to England and the Mediterranean to assess the military and political situation. Donovan estimated that Britain had the will to survive if given American aid, and he urged that aid be given.

While in England Donovan met with Churchill and other British cabinet ministers and senior officials, including Col. Stewart Menzies, the head of the British Secret Intelligence Service. He also became well-acquainted with WILLIAM S. STEPHENSON, then chief of SIS in the United States, and his conversations with Stephenson persuaded him that the United States needed a centralized agency to control all foreign intelligence activities, including psychological warfare and other forms of COVERT ACTION.

Six months before the PEARL HARBOR ATTACK, Donovan proposed to Roosevelt that a "Service of Strategic Information" be created for this purpose. The President agreed to a step somewhat short of this: he created the post of coordinator of information—in effect, the President's chief intelligence officer—and authorized the expenditure of the President's secret funds to "employ necessary personnel and make provision for the necessary supplies, facilities and services" (see OFFICE OF STRATEGIC SERVICES). Roosevelt appointed Donovan to the post.

Donovan rapidly built up his staff and his Office of the Coordinator of Information became, in fact if not in theory, the agency he had proposed. In June 1942, after much friction with the Federal Bureau of Investigation and other rival government intelligence agencies, Donovan and his staff were transferred to the jurisdiction of the newly created Joint Chiefs of Staff and formally established as the OFFICE OF STRATEGIC SERVICES.

Donovan's management style—informal, innovative, and hyperactive—might be summed up in his standard response to the imaginative proposals made by his staff: "Sure, let's give it a try." The agency he created was composed of scholars who specialized in history, economics, and social science; corporate lawyers, bankers, and other businessmen with a flair for foreign intrigue; and adventurers with a talent for irregular military operations. They were for the most part amateurs, in the sense that they had little or no experience as professional soldiers, intelligence officers, or foreign service officers. The OSS was later characterized as "a remarkable institution, half cops-and-robbers and half faculty meeting."

The OSS chalked up a remarkable record of accomplishments during the war (see OFFICE OF STRATEGIC SERVICES), and Donovan tried to make it a permanent branch of the postwar government. Although he was not immediately successful in effecting this, his specific proposal was adopted three

Gen. William J. Donovan during the Second World War. Source: U.S. Army.

years later in the establishment of the CENTRAL INTELLIGENCE AGENCY.

After the war Donovan retired from active duty with the rank of major general and served briefly as aide to the U.S. chief prosecutor at the Nuremburg war crimes trials. He returned to the private practice of law with his Wall Street firm until 1953, when President Eisenhower appointed him ambassador to Thailand. He served in that post for just over a year, during which time he was instrumental in removing the CIA-backed forces of General Li Mi from the country (see KOREAN WAR), and in increasing by one-third the number of American military advisors assigned to Thailand to assist in countering Communist insurgency in Southeast Asia.

In his role as elder statesman of the American intelligence community, Donovan urged a program of vigorous covert action to counter Soviet expansion in the late 1940s and 1950s.

(Troy, *Donovan and the CIA;* Cave Brown, *The Last Hero;* Ford, *Donovan of the OSS;* Leary, *Perilous Missions; Current Biography,* 1953; *Who Was Who in America,* vol. 3; *WAMB.*)

DOOLE, GEORGE ARNTZEN, JR. (August 12, 1909–March 9, 1985): aviator, businessman, intelligence officer

A native of Quincy, Illinois, Doole graduated from the University of Illinois in 1931. He enlisted in the U.S. Army Air Corps as an aviation cadet and, after successfully completing flight training, was commissioned as a second lieutenant. He served in flying status in Hawaii, France, and the Panama Canal Zone. After leaving the Army in 1934 he joined Pan American World Airways as a flight mechanic and apprentice pilot. He flew for Pan Am in Texas, Mexico, and Central America, learning all aspects of the airline business. He took a leave of absence in 1939 to attend Harvard Business School and earn an M.B.A. degree. Returning to Pan Am he flew in Colombia. He served in the Army Air Force during the Second World War. After the war he was Pan Am's regional director for the Middle East and Asia.

A colonel in the Air Force Reserve, Doole was called to active duty during the Korean War in 1951. He served in Air Force Intelligence as chief of estimates for the Middle East under Gen. CHARLES P. CABELL (whom Doole had known during his service in the Air Corps in the 1930s). In July 1953 Cabell, then deputy director of central intelligence, faced management problems in the CIA's clandestine Far East air service, Civil Air Transport (see AIR PROPRIETARIES). He recruited Doole to the Central Intelligence Agency to take charge of the troubled airline.

Doole became a senior officer of the CIA, in charge of the Agency's vast complex of air proprietaries around the world. His cover was the presidency of the Pacific Corporation, the Delaware holding company of which Civil Air Transport, Air America, and other CIA air proprietaries were subsidiaries. He was also chief executive of Air America and Air Asia. Through his business and management skills the proprietaries flourished and even turned a handsome profit.

Doole retired from the CIA in 1971 and became active in his family business, Arntzen Enterprises, which has interests in air operations throughout the world.

(*Who's Who in America,* 37th ed.; Leary, *Perilous Missions;* Robbins, *Air America;* Marchetti and Marks,

The CIA and the Cult of Intelligence; New York Times, December 30, 1985, p. B8.)

DORSEY, DANIEL ALLEN (ca. 1840–ca. 1916): schoolteacher, soldier, Union secret service agent

Dorsey was a native of Ohio who spent part of his childhood in Virginia. He taught school in Fairfield County, Ohio, before the Civil War. In 1861 he enlisted in the Ohio Volunteer Infantry, a part of the Army of the Ohio. He had attained the rank of corporal by April 1862, when he volunteered to take part in a paramilitary operation behind Confederate lines aimed at severing the rail line between Atlanta and Chattanooga (see ANDREWS'S RAID). He and a party of twenty other Union troops in civilian clothes and led by JAMES J. ANDREWS hijacked a locomotive and attempted to destroy railroad tracks and bridges between the two cities. Dorsey was captured by Confederate troops and imprisoned (Andrews and seven of the others were hanged). He and several others escaped. Dorsey made his way to Union lines in Kentucky.

After the war Dorsey lived in Kearney, Nebraska.

(Bryan, *The Spy in America;* Boatner, *Civil War Dictionary;* O'Neill, *Wild Train.*)

DOSTERT, LEON EMILE (May 14, 1904–September 2, 1971): linguist, intelligence officer

A native of Longwy, France, Dostert studied at Occidental College in Los Angeles, California, in 1924–26. He earned a B.S., a Ph.B., and an M.A. from Georgetown University in 1928, 1930, and 1931, respectively, and taught French at Georgetown from 1926 to 1941. In 1939–40 he was an attaché at the French embassy in Washington. He became an American citizen in 1941.

Dostert was commissioned a major in the U.S. Army and assigned to the Office of Strategic Services in 1942. He served first on the French desk of the OSS SECRET INTELLIGENCE BRANCH, then later as liaison officer to French Gen. Henri Giraud and as interpreter for General Eisenhower. After the war he acted as chief of the language division at the Nuremburg war crimes trials. He was discharged with the rank of colonel in 1946, having been awarded the Legion of Merit, the Bronze Star and the French Legion of Honor and croix de guerre.

Dostert directed the simultaneous interpretation division of the United Nations in 1946–47. From 1963 to 1971 he was on the faculty of Occidental College where he became professor emeritus of languages and linguistics. He also frequently served as a language consultant to the U.S. government, foreign governments, and private corporations.

(Smith, *OSS*; *Who Was Who in America*, v. 5.)

DOUBLE AGENT

According to veteran CIA CLANDESTINE SERVICE officer PEER DE SILVA, the term means "An intelligence agent who, for whatever reason, while appearing to work for his original intelligence service, is actually working for a hostile intelligence service. Such an intelligence agent has been 'doubled.' "

Note that the term refers to an AGENT, not to a CASE OFFICER or other official. A double agent is often not a citizen of either the country he purports to serve or the country he truly serves, but a native of the country in which the two intelligence services happen to be operating. He is usually not a staff employee of any intelligence service, but simply a person in a position to serve a foreign intelligence service.

The distinction is important because double agents are very often confused by journalists and other laymen with PENETRATION AGENTS and DEFECTORS-IN-PLACE, e.g., HAROLD A.R. PHILBY, a Soviet penetration agent of British intelligence, is often erroneously described as a double agent.

In his official history of the Office of Strategic Services, KERMIT ROOSEVELT presented a restricted definition of the term in the context of OSS wartime operations: ". . . captured agents who would be persuaded to continue their activities for the enemy, ostensibly in good faith but acting at the direction of X-2 [the OSS COUNTER-ESPIONAGE BRANCH]. . . . A second standardized form of double agent operation would be the case of an agent recruited by X-2 and infiltrated into enemy territory to induce the enemy to employ him as an agent and return him to Allied territory."

(De Silva, *Sub Rosa*; Roosevelt, *War Report of the OSS*.)

DOUGLASS, KINGMAN (April 16, 1896– October 8, 1971): businessman, intelligence officer

A native of Oak Park, Illinois, Douglass graduated from Yale University in 1918 and pursued a career in investment banking. During the Second World War he served in the U.S. Army Air Force as a senior intelligence liaison officer with the British Air Ministry, and later was with the Allied Intelligence Group in the Pacific Theater.

After the war Douglass served with the Central Intelligence Group (see CENTRAL INTELLIGENCE AGENCY). He was appointed assistant director and acting deputy director of central intelligence by Adm. SIDNEY W. SOUERS in March 1946. He held those positions until July 1946, when he transferred to the CIG's Office of Special Operations. He resigned from the CIG in September 1946, but returned to the CIA to serve as assistant director, current intelligence, from January 1951 until July 1952.

Douglass returned to private business after his service with the CIA.

(Central Intelligence Agency, *Directors and Deputy Directors of Central Intelligence*.)

DOWNES, DONALD C. (1903–): schoolteacher, intelligence officer

A native of Baltimore, Maryland, Downes attended Phillips Exeter Academy, graduated from Yale University, and taught at a prep school in Massachusetts. Prior to the American entry into the Second World War he worked as an agent for the Office of Naval Intelligence in the Balkans and the Middle East, and for the British Secret Intelligence Service in the United States, where he investigated links between German agents and some members of the isolationist America First Committee. He also served as SIS contact with prominent emigrés from Axis-occupied nations who were members of the Free World Association, a refugee group.

In 1942 Downes joined the Office of the Coordinator of Information, the predecessor of the Office of Strategic Services. He served as a member of ALLEN W. DULLES's intelligence staff in New York City, working with ARTHUR J. GOLDBERG on the Labor Desk of the OSS SECRET INTELLIGENCE BRANCH. Downes's mission to Mexico City in March 1942 to obtain a list of potential intelligence "assets" in Spain led to a bitter bureaucratic controversy between WILLIAM J. DONOVAN and the heads of other U.S. agencies with intelligence jurisdiction in Latin America (the FEDERAL BUREAU OF INVESTIGATION and the OFFICE OF THE COORDINATOR OF INTER-AMERICAN AFFAIRS). This dispute arose despite the fact that Downes had obtained FBI permission before making the journey.

Downes organized a group of Spanish and Basque exiles and American leftists who had fought against Franco in the Spanish civil war. During July–November 1942, Downes planned, and he and some of his agents executed, a series of four burglaries of the

Spanish embassy in Washington, D.C. for the purpose of photographing the Spanish diplomatic cipher and related periodic key changes in order to help assess Spanish intentions regarding an alliance with the Axis powers. During the fourth break-in, however, Downes and his people were interrupted and arrested by FBI agents in a move reportedly regarded by Donovan as a further and extreme example of Hoover's animosity toward the OSS.

Shortly thereafter, Downes and his group were sent to Algiers to help counter the threat of Spanish cooperation with Germany and the possibility that Germany might be permitted to use Spanish Morocco as a base of operations against the Allied forces in North Africa. However, Downes's group was initially used by Col. WILLIAM EDDY for combat intelligence missions in Tunisia. In 1943 Downes sent his agents into Spanish Morocco and even into metropolitan Spain to collect intelligence on German operations there as well as on Spanish military preparations.

In September 1943 Downes and a team of seventy-five Italian agents and American officers he had organized landed with the U.S. invasion force at Salerno, Italy, to carry out combat intelligence missions. A few weeks later, Downes and Donovan had a dispute over the OSS's new policy for Italian operations—Donovan ordered OSS personnel to work with or recruit only Italians loyal to King Victor Emmanuel III, a policy Downes regarded as both dishonorable and unworkable—and other Italian matters. As a result Donovan transferred Downes out of OSS/Italy.

In 1944 Downes was assigned to the White House where he wrote special intelligence reports. In 1953 he published a book about his OSS experiences.

(Smith, *OSS*; Cave Brown, *The Last Hero*; Tompkins, *A Spy in Rome*; Downes, *The Scarlet Thread*.)

DOWNES, EDWARD OLIN DAVENPORT (August 12, 1911–): music historian, intelligence analyst

A native of Boston, Downes studied at Columbia University, the Manhattan School of Music, and the universities of Paris and Munich. He wrote for the *New York Post* and the *Boston Evening Transcript* as music critic between 1936 and 1941. In 1943 he joined the Office of Strategic Services and worked as an intelligence analyst and editor on the Current Intelligence Staff of the OSS RESEARCH AND ANALYSIS BRANCH. After the transfer of the R&A Branch to the State Department in 1946 he returned to his career as music critic and historian. He has taught music history at Wellesley College and the University of Minnesota, and was assistant music critic for the *New York Times* from 1955 through 1958. Downes has been commentator for many classical music and operatic radio broadcasts, and hosts the "First Hearing" series on New York City classical music station, WQXR.

(*Who's Who in America*, 42nd ed.; Cline, *The CIA: Reality vs. Myth.*)

DOWNEY, JOHN THOMAS (ca. 1930–): intelligence officer

Downey grew up in New Britain, Connecticut, attended the Choate School, and graduated from Yale University in 1951. In June 1951 he joined the Central Intelligence Agency and served in the Office of Policy Coordination, as the CIA's COVERT ACTION unit was then called. After three months of training at Fort Benning, Georgia, he was assigned to the Far East Division of CIA/OPC.

Downey was stationed at the CIA/OPC complex at the U.S. Naval Air Station at Atsugi, Japan. He took part in Operation Tropic, CIA-supported guerrilla operations on the Chinese mainland carried out by "third force" units, i.e., anti-Communist forces not allied with the Nationalist Chinese on Taiwan. One of Downey's first assignments was to establish an agent network in the Manchurian province of Kirin. Early in 1952 he selected four Chinese who had been trained at a CIA installation on Saipan and formed them into "Team Wen" (named after team leader Chang Tsai-wen, a twenty-eight-year-old native of Kirin). The team was parachuted into Kirin in July 1952.

On November 29, 1952 Downey and fellow CIA/OPC officer, RICHARD G. FECTEAU, were aboard a Civil Air Transport (see AIR PROPRIETARIES) DC-3 sent to Kirin to recover a Chinese agent who had been working with Team Wen. The recovery was to be effected by the "skyhook snatch" technique, in which a low- and slow-flying aircraft hooked a wire line on the ground to which the agent was strapped, lifting him from the ground and into the airplane. In the midst of this maneuver the plane was hit by gunfire from Communist troops on the ground, who, according to one account of the incident, had been alerted by a double agent operating within Team Wen.

The aircraft crashed, killing the CAT pilot and copilot. Downey and Fecteau were taken prisoner and charged with espionage. Downey was sentenced to life in prison; Fecteau was given a twenty-year sentence. The U.S. government officially denied that the two men were CIA officers on an intelligence mission, stating instead that they were civilian employees of the U.S. Army who had been on a routine flight between Korea and Japan.

Personal appeals to the Chinese Communist government by the mothers of the two men in 1958 failed to bring about their release. Fecteau was released after serving nineteen years in December 1971, two months before President Richard Nixon's trip to Peking. Downey was released in March 1973 after a public acknowledgment by President Nixon that Downey was in fact a CIA officer.

(Leary, *Perilous Missions;* Wise and Ross, *The Invisible Government; New York Times,* March 10, 1973.)

DROLLER, GERRY: intelligence officer

A native of Germany, Droller served with the Office of Strategic Services during the Second World War, distinguishing himself through service in German-occupied France, where he organized resistance groups. He later served in the Central Intelligence Agency and became an officer on the Swiss desk of the CIA CLANDESTINE SERVICE.

In 1960 Droller was appointed political action chief of the operation that became known as the BAY OF PIGS INVASION. Droller, whose pseudonym for the operation was "Frank Bender," worked with E. HOWARD HUNT in Miami to organize anti-Communist Cuban exiles and help form a Cuban government-in-exile that could be installed in Cuba after the anticipated fall of the Castro regime. Droller knew little about Latin America and spoke no Spanish. These deficiencies, together with his reputedly abrasive manner, created difficulties in his assignment, and his differences with Hunt led to the latter's reassignment to CIA Headquarters and the propaganda aspects of the Cuban operation.

Despite his association with the Bay of Pigs failure, Droller was promoted to special assistant to J.C. KING, chief of the Western Hemisphere Division of the Clandestine Service. During the mid-1960s he was chief of the WH branch responsible for covert operations within the so-called *"Cono Sur,"* or southern cone of South America—Uruguay, Paraguay, Argentina, and Chile. He was later chief of the Covert Action Staff of the Western Hemisphere Division.

(Wyden, *Bay of Pigs;* Phillips, *The Night Watch;* Smith, *Portrait of a Cold Warrior;* Agee, *Inside the Company.*)

DUCKETT, CARL E.: intelligence officer

Duckett, a professional intelligence officer, succeeded ALBERT D. WHEELON as deputy director for science and technology in the Central Intelligence Agency

in 1966. He continued in that post until his retirement in the mid-1970s. He was awarded the Distinguished Intelligence Medal.

(Alsop, *The Center;* Colby and Forbath, *Honorable Men.*)

DUER, WILLIAM (March 18, 1747–May 7, 1799): Army officer, Continental congressman, banker, businessman, intelligence officer

A native of Devonshire, England, Duer attended Eton College, was commissioned in the British army, and served as aide-de-camp to Lord Clive in India. In 1773 he settled in New York where he became a leading Whig in the political prelude to the American Revolution. He became a member of the New York Committee of Safety (see COMMITTEES OF CORRESPONDENCE), deputy adjutant general of the New York militia, a delegate to the Continental Congress, and a member of the Congress's Board of War.

Duer served on the Committee for Detecting and Defeating Conspiracies, a New York counterintelligence unit. He and his colleague Nathaniel Sackett were particularly effective in catching British spies. They also ran their own agents, one of whom was ENOCH CROSBY.

Through marriage and several postwar commercial ventures, Duer became wealthy. He served as assistant secretary of the Treasury under Alexander Hamilton. However, imprudent land speculation and a suit by the government over irregularities in his Treasury accounts led to his arrest and imprisonment for debt. He was in debtor's prison at the time of his death.

(*Who Was Who in America,* historical volume; Boatner, *Encyclopedia of the American Revolution;* Bakeless, *Turncoats, Traitors and Heroes;* Barnum, *The Spy Unmasked;* Central Intelligence Agency, *Intelligence in the War of Independence.*)

DULLES, ALLEN WELSH (April 7, 1893– January 29, 1969): lawyer, foreign service officer, intelligence officer

A native of Watertown, New York, Dulles attended school in Auburn, New York, and the École Alsatienne in Paris, France. He graduated from Princeton University in 1914, and, after traveling in the Far East taught English for one year in Allahabad, India. He then returned to Princeton and earned an M.A. degree in 1916.

Dulles's maternal grandfather, John W. Foster, was secretary of state in the administration of Benjamin Harrison; his father's uncle, John Welsh, was the

Allen W. Dulles—oil portrait by Garner Cox. Source: Central Intelligence Agency.

American minister in London during 1877–79; and an uncle by marriage (who had married one of John W. Foster's daughters), Robert M. Lansing, had been President Woodrow Wilson's secretary of state. In 1916 Dulles followed this family tradition of foreign service and joined the diplomatic corps.

In May 1916 he was appointed third secretary in the American embassy in Vienna. The following year, after the United States declared war on Germany and Austria, the embassy in Vienna was closed and he was sent to the embassy in Bern, Switzerland, where he was given intelligence duties. Neutral Switzerland was an active zone of international intrigue in the war years, and it was during this period that an episode supposedly occurred that Dulles was often to recount later: One afternoon while he was duty officer in the otherwise deserted embassy he received a telephone call from Vladimir Ilyich Lenin, then an obscure Russian exile living in Switzerland. Lenin told Dulles that he urgently wished to speak to someone in the American legation when he arrived in Bern later that afternoon. Dulles, who was due to go

off duty soon, had a date with a young woman, and he rejected the Russian's plea, telling Lenin that no one could see him before the following morning. The next morning Lenin did not come to the embassy but was aboard a train on his historic and fateful return to Russia.

This, at least, was the tale Dulles often recounted years later as a cautionary tale to young intelligence officers who might be tempted to put personal matters ahead of duty. However, efforts to verify the anecdote have led some to doubt that it actually happened.

Dulles served with the American delegation to the PARIS PEACE CONFERENCE OF 1919 (as did his brother, John Foster Dulles). He helped draw the frontiers of the newly created country of Czechoslovakia, and worked on political problems related to the Russian Revolution and the peace settlement in Central Europe. Subsequently he was first secretary in the American embassy in Berlin. From October 1920 to April 1922 he served with the American Commission in Constantinople (Istanbul), after which he returned to Washington to become chief of the State Department's Near Eastern Affairs Division.

During this period, Dulles was also a delegate to the Geneva conferences on arms traffic (1925) and disarmament (1926). He also studied law at George Washington University and received an LL.B. in 1926.

That year Dulles resigned from the State Department and joined the New York law firm of Sullivan and Cromwell, of which his brother, John Foster Dulles, was the senior partner. The firm handled many cases involving large corporate clients and international law, e.g., land lease matters in Central America for the United Fruit Company and munitions export control disputes for the Du Pont Corporation. Dulles's official involvement in international affairs did not entirely cease; he was legal advisor to the American delegation to the Three Power Naval Conference in 1927, and to the delegations to the Geneva disarmament conferences of 1932 and 1933. In 1938 Dulles unsuccessfully sought the Republican nomination for a congressional seat from New York, and in 1940 he took an active role in the presidential campaign of Republican candidate Wendell Willkie.

In 1941 Dulles was sent to Bolivia on a confidential assignment by the U.S. government to neutralize German influence in the Bolivian air lines. Early in 1942 he joined the Office of the Coordinator of Information, the predecessor to the Office of Strategic Services. As chief of the OSS's New York City office he developed a staff of specialists in German and European affairs, including refugees from Germany and Nazi-occupied Europe, and maintained liaison with the British Security Coordination, the American department of the British Secret Intelligence Service located in New York City (see WILLIAM STEPHENSON).

In November 1942 he returned to Bern, Switzerland, to establish an OSS station there. He arrived in the country forty-eight hours before the German occupation of Vichy France effectively isolated nationals of Allied countries within Switzerland. He remained in Switzerland throughout the duration of the war, running agent operations into Germany and Nazi-occupied Europe. Among the accomplishments of Dulles and his Bern staff were:

> Early reports of the Nazi missile development program on the island of Peenemünde in the Baltic Sea, where concealed factories were producing V-1 and V-2 missiles (the resulting Allied air raids on the factories delayed the missile program).
> Penetration of the Abwehr, the German military intelligence service, through Hans Berndt Gisevius, an Abwehr officer opposed to Hitler.
> Contact with the anti-Nazi German underground, which was plotting to assassinate Hitler.
> Detection of the fact that German intelligence had broken the diplomatic code used by the U.S. legation in Bern, information that enabled the legation to change codes before highly confidential messages were intercepted.
> Acquisition of some 1,600 German secret documents concerning the German secret service in Spain, Switzerland, Sweden, and England.
> Negotiations with SS General Karl Wolff that led to the surrender of all German and Italian Fascist forces in northern Italy shortly before VE-Day.

After VE-Day Dulles was chief of the OSS station in Wiesbaden, Germany. He left that post in November 1945 and returned to the practice of law with Sullivan and Cromwell, but he retained his active involvement in matters of intelligence and foreign policy. In 1946 he became president of the Council on Foreign Relations, a private organization to which he had belonged since the 1920s. The Council, an influential group of private citizens with a special interest in American foreign policy, had long been recognized as the quasi-official general staff of the U.S. foreign policy-making machinery. Dulles was foreign policy advisor to Thomas E. Dewey during the latter's unsuccessful candidacy for the presidency in 1948. He also served as a consultant to HOYT S. VANDENBERG and ROSCOE H. HILLENKOETTER during their terms as directors of central intelligence (1946–50).

In 1948 Dulles, WILLIAM H. JACKSON, and Matthias F. Correa—all Wall Street lawyers—carried out a study of the American intelligence establishment for the NATIONAL SECURITY COUNCIL. The study recommended a number of reforms, and after WALTER BEDELL SMITH became director of central intelligence in 1950, he invited Dulles to join the CIA to help implement these recommendations. Dulles accepted the invitation in January 1951 and became the deputy director responsible for two rivaling branches, the Office of Special Operations (CIA's SECRET INTELLIGENCE unit) and the Office of Policy Coordination (the COVERT ACTION component). He began the bureaucratic process that eventually led to the merger of these two units into the single Agency component, the Plans Directorate (see CIA CLANDESTINE SERVICE), ending the rivalry that had been disruptive to CIA covert operations. In August 1951 he became deputy director of central intelligence. After Smith's departure from the Agency in 1953, Dulles became its new director.

Dulles stepped into the position of DCI at about the same time that his brother, John Foster Dulles, was selected by President Eisenhower to be secretary of state. Throughout most of the Eisenhower years (i.e., until the death of John Foster Dulles in 1959) this unusual situation tended to bypass the established lines of bureaucratic oversight between the White House and the CIA.

Dulles's personal prestige and connections enhanced the image and role of the CIA within the government, though he was sometimes criticized as an indiscreet promoter of the Agency. His personal power enabled him to resist an attempt by Sen. Joseph McCarthy in 1953 to extend his hunt for purported Communists into the CIA (see WILLIAM P. BUNDY), and Dulles is regarded as the first Eisenhower administration official to stand up to the senator.

As DCI Dulles was known within the Agency as "the great white case officer," a reference to his involvement in the details of covert operations (he worked closely with his Clandestine Service chief, FRANK G. WISNER, often conceiving ideas for covert projects and involving himself in their "micromanagement") and his neglect of the administrative details of running a government agency. He was, in fact, regarded as a poor administrator, but he was ably supported in the day-to-day details of running the Agency by his deputy, Gen. CHARLES P. CABELL.

COVERT ACTION took precedence over intelligence during Dulles's term as DCI, a period that saw the IRAN COUP, the GUATEMALA COUP, and other similar programs and operations. However this was more a reflection of the emphasis in policy of Dulles's brother, the secretary of state, and perhaps an overestimation by other members of the National Security Council of the effectiveness of covert action as a means of halting Soviet expansion.

Secret intelligence operations were also promoted during Dulles's administration, which saw the development of the U-2 RECONNAISSANCE AIRCRAFT and the beginning of dramatic innovation in the use of technical means of intelligence collection. However, Dulles had little interest in the more prosaic processes of intelligence analysis and production and was generally content to leave that area to his deputy director for intelligence, ROBERT AMORY.

The most serious of Dulles's shortcomings may have been his failure to assert and exercise the role of the DCI as the government's chief intelligence officer and coordinator of the activities of the other member agencies of the INTELLIGENCE COMMUNITY.

Dulles's tenure as DCI came to an end in 1961 as a direct consequence of the failure of the BAY OF PIGS INVASION. This ill-conceived operation represented the final extreme of the emphasis on covert action that marked the Dulles era at CIA. Although he was not responsible for conceiving it, and apparently did not involve himself closely in the "micro-management" of it, his policy of segregating the Clandestine Service from the Intelligence Directorate, where those who did not believe an invasion of Cuba would prompt a general anti-Castro uprising remained officially ignorant of the planned operation, contributed to bringing about the disaster.

As a consequence of the failure, Dulles resigned as DCI in September 1961. He returned to the practice of law with Sullivan and Cromwell. In 1964 he served on the Warren Commission, which investigated the assassination of President Kennedy.

Dulles held many awards and decorations, including the Medal for Merit, the Medal of Freedom, the National Security Medal and the French Legion of Honor. He was the author of several books on foreign affairs and intelligence, the first of which, a short history of the Boer War, he wrote at the age of eight. It was privately printed by his doting grandfather, former Secretary of State John W. Foster.

(*Who Was Who in America*, v. 5; *Current Biography*, 1949, 1969; Mosley, *Dulles*; Persico, *Piercing the Reich*; Dulles, *The Craft of Intelligence, The Secret Surrender*; Karalekas, *History of the Central Intelligence Agency*.)

E

EC-121 INCIDENT

On April 14, 1969 a U.S. Navy EC-121 (a SIGINT reconnaissance version of the four-engine, propeller-driven Lockheed Constellation airliner) was shot down by two North Korean Mig fighters over international waters of the Sea of Japan some ninety miles off the coast of North Korea. The aircraft was on a SIGINT mission out of Atsugi Air Base in Japan and was to have made several passes parallel to the North Korean coast and no closer than fifty nautical miles from it before proceeding to Osan Air Base in the Republic of Korea. Thirty Navy personnel and one Marine were aboard. Apparently all were lost.

Caught off balance and preoccupied with the Vietnam War and other events in Southeast Asia, the Nixon administration failed to make any substantial response to the incident beyond protecting subsequent ELINT flights in the area with fighter escorts.

(Kissinger, *White House Years;* Nixon, *Memoirs;* Bamford, *The Puzzle Palace.*)

EDDY, WILLIAM ALFRED (March 9, 1896–1962): Marine officer, educator, scholar, diplomat, intelligence officer

Eddy was born in Sidon, Syria, the son of American missionaries. He graduated from Princeton Univer-

Lockheed EC-121 SIGINT reconnaissance aircraft. Source: U.S. Air Force.

sity in 1917, and was commissioned a lieutenant in the U.S. Marine Corps. He served as an intelligence officer with the Allied Expeditionary Force in France in the FIRST WORLD WAR, and was wounded in the battle of Belleau Woods. He was discharged with the rank of captain.

After the war Eddy returned to Princeton and earned an A.M. and a Ph.D. in 1921 and 1922, respectively. In 1923 he published a critical study of *Gulliver's Travels*. That same year he joined the faculty of the American University in Cairo, Egypt, and he served as chairman of the Department of English until 1928, when he became an assistant professor of English at Dartmouth College. In 1936 he became president of Hobart College and William Smith College in Geneva, New York.

Eddy resigned the presidency of the two colleges in 1942 to return to active duty as a Marine officer. He was promoted to the rank of major (and soon advanced to full colonel) and assigned to the Office of the Coordinator of Information, the predecessor of the Office of Strategic Services. Because of his fluency in Arabic and his familiarity with the Middle East, he was sent to French North Africa, ostensibly as naval attaché to American Ambassador ROBERT D. MURPHY, but in fact as Murphy's collaborator in a covert operation to pave the way for the Allied invasion of North Africa.

Eddy established a clandestine radio network across North Africa, with stations at Tangier, Casablanca, Algiers, Tunis, and Oran; organized a SECRET INTELLIGENCE network among the desert tribesmen, Islamic clergymen, and others living in the region; penetrated the Spanish consulate in French Morocco with two agents who supplied the OSS with copies of German cables passing through the code room; and collected other important intelligence. Eddy also fed disinformation to German intelligence regarding Allied invasion plans, which led the German Navy to divert its ships to Dakar, several thousand miles away on the western coast of Africa, a move that left the North African coast undefended.

In 1944 Eddy was sent to Saudi Arabia as U.S. envoy extraordinary and minister plenipotentiary. He remained there until 1946, when he was made chief of a special diplomatic mission to Yemen. Later that year he returned to Washington to succeed Col. ALFRED MCCORMACK as chief of the State Department's Interim Research and Intelligence Service, the postwar remnant of the OSS's Research and Analysis Branch (see STATE DEPARTMENT INTELLIGENCE). His assignment was, in effect, to dismantle this unit, dividing it up among the various geographical desks within State.

In 1947 Eddy left the government to become a consultant on Arab government relations to the Arabian-American Oil Company. He remained in that position until 1957, and also served as an officer of the American Friends of the Middle East, an organization funded by the Central Intelligence Agency.

Eddy was awarded the Distinguished Service Cross, the Navy Cross, two Purple Hearts, two Silver Stars, the Legion of Merit, and the Army Commendation Ribbon.

(Smith, *OSS*; Ford, *Donovan of OSS: Who's Who in America*, v. 32.)

EDEN, WILLIAM (April 3, 1744–May 28, 1814): British lawyer, government official, diplomat, intelligence officer

The third son of an English baronet, Eden attended Eton and earned a B.A. and an M.A. from Christ Church, Oxford, in 1765 and 1768, respectively. He practiced law in London. In 1772 he was appointed under secretary of state.

Shortly before the AMERICAN REVOLUTION Eden became chief of the British secret service in Europe. He recruited PAUL WENTWORTH, an American-born adventurer, and sent him to France to obtain intelligence regarding BENJAMIN FRANKLIN and the other American commissioners charged by the Continental Congress with obtaining French aid and alliance.

Eden was relieved of his secret service responsibilities in 1778 so that he might serve with the Carlisle Commission, a five-member delegation headed by the Earl of Carlisle, which was sent to America in a fruitless attempt to achieve peace. Eden may have been involved in the Commission's secret service activities in America, which included an approach by a British agent to Continental Congressman Richard Henry Lee for some unknown objective (the agent was arrested, later released and sent back to England).

Eden served as a member of Parliament and held a variety of governmental and diplomatic posts. In 1789 he undertook a commercial mission to the United States. He was created a peer of Great Britain as Lord Auckland in 1793.

Eden was an ancestor of British Prime Minister Sir Anthony Eden.

(*DNB*; Boatner, *Encyclopedia of the American Revolution*; Schoenbrun, *Triumph in Paris*; Bendiner, *The Virgin Diplomats*; Currey, *Code Number 72*.)

EDMONDS, S(ARAH) EMMA E(VELYN) (December 1841–September 5, 1898): nurse, male impersonator, Union soldier and secret service agent (?)

Born Sarah Edmondson in New Brunswick, Canada, Edmonds left home in 1856, worked briefly as a milliner, then, disguised as a man, she became a traveling book salesman. She moved to the United States where, as "Frank Thompson," she continued to travel for a Hartford, Connecticut, publisher.

At Detroit, Michigan, in May 1861, still in the guise of Thompson, Edmonds enlisted as a private in the Second Michigan Infantry to serve as a male nurse. She served in that unit until April 1863 when she deserted at Lebanon, Kentucky. Resuming her true sex and identity, she lived in Oberlin, Ohio, where she wrote *Nurse and Spy in the Union Army: The Adventures and Experiences of a Woman in Hospitals, Camps, and Battle-Fields*. The book, which was published the following year by the Hartford company for which she had worked as a salesman, was a bestseller. It purported to be a true account of her service as both Army nurse and Union secret service agent, but is one of the most dubious and unverifiable of its genre (see CIVIL WAR ESPIONAGE MYTHOLOGY).

According to *Nurse and Spy*, Edmonds saw service in uniform at both battles of Bull Run, and at the battles of Antietam and Fredericksburg. She asserts that she volunteered to serve as a spy sometime in 1862 and was summoned to Gen. George B. McClellan's headquarters where she was personally interviewed by McClellan and two other generals she identifies only as "M." and "H." After being tested in her knowledge of firearms and given a phrenological examination, she was sworn into the secret service. Next she dyed her skin black and donned a wig of "real negro wool," crossed the Confederate lines and entered Yorktown, Virginia, in the guise of a Negro laborer, and crossed back into Union territory a short time later with details of the Confederate fortifications. It was the first of eleven secret missions she claimed she made during the war.

Even granting that some of the more patently preposterous elements of Edmonds's story might have been literary embellishments, one still cannot overlook crucial internal evidence that suggests the tale was totally untrue. While it is barely plausible that McClellan might have personally recruited a spy, and that he might have convened a board of his generals to help him do so, it is doubtful that he would have undertaken this without the involvement of ALLAN

S. Emma Edmonds. Source: Author's collection.

PINKERTON, his secret service chief, or GEORGE BANGS, Pinkerton's deputy. Edmonds makes no reference to Pinkerton (or his nom de guerre, E.J. Allen), Bangs, or to any of the other Pinkerton agents who served in McClellan's secret service (see PINKERTON'S NATIONAL DETECTIVE AGENCY).

Edmonds's claim to have been Private "Frank Thompson" is valid, however, for Congress awarded her a pension in 1886, and she was admitted to the Grand Army of the Republic, a Civil War veterans association, as its only woman member. In later years she abandoned her claim to having been a Union spy, but she implied her motive was a newly found distaste for the "mean deception necessarily practiced by a spy," rather than the falsehood of her earlier claims.

Despite the dubious character of Edmonds's espionage memoirs, her story is often accepted at face value and repeated by authors of accounts of Civil War spying.

Edmonds married Linus H. Seelye in 1863.

(Dannett, *She Rode with the Generals*; Bryan, *The Spy in America*; Edmonds, *Nurse and Spy in the Union Army*; Buranelli and Buranelli, *Spy/Counterspy*.)

EDWARDS, SHEFFIELD (?–1975): intelligence officer

Edwards was director of the Office of Security of the Central Intelligence Agency during the 1950s and early 1960s. He was an early proponent of the use of the polygraph in clearing CIA personnel (see LIE DETECTION).

In 1953 he was involved in the investigation of CIA officer WILLIAM P. BUNDY, as a result of the FBI charges instigated by Sen. Joseph McCarthy that Bundy was disloyal. After investigating Bundy, Edwards reported to CIA Director ALLEN W. DULLES that the charges were unfounded, which enabled Dulles to keep McCarthy from extending his search for purported Communists in government to the CIA.

Edwards was a principal figure in the early (1960) attempts by the CIA to assassinate Fidel Castro (see CENTRAL INTELLIGENCE AGENCY, WILLIAM K. HARVEY). He was the CIA officer who suggested the use of the Mafia to achieve that end, and he approached former FBI agent ROBERT A. MAHEU to act as a "cut out" between the CIA and the Mafia. Edwards and Maheu had earlier worked together in support of a CIA "black propaganda" (see COVERT ACTION) operation involving the production of a bogus pornographic film purportedly featuring Indonesian President Sukarno.

Edwards also authorized Maheu to install an audio surveillance device in the hotel room of comedian Dan Rowan in order to determine whether Rowan had learned of the assassination plan from singer Phyllis McGuire, a close friend of Salvatore Giancana, the Mafia figure Maheu had selected for the assassination plan.

(Powers, *The Man Who Kept the Secrets*; U.S. Senate, *Alleged Assassination Plots Involving Foreign Leaders*; Copeland, *Without Cloak or Dagger*; Martin, *Wilderness of Mirrors*.)

EIFLER, CARL FREDERICH (1906–): law enforcement officer, government official, clergyman, intelligence officer

Eifler joined the Los Angeles Police Department before he was twenty years old. He later served as a chief inspector in the U.S. Border Patrol on the Mexican border. At the time of the PEARL HARBOR ATTACK he was deputy director of U.S. Customs in Honolulu. A captain in the U.S. Army Reserve, he was called to active duty with the Thirty-Fifth Infantry Regiment in Hawaii.

Eifler was a licensed pilot, an exceptional marksman, had boxed professionally, and was skilled in jujitsu, but it was his long acquaintance with Gen. Joseph Stilwell, commander of American forces in the China-Burma-India theater that attracted the attention of Col. WILLIAM J. DONOVAN. Donovan, director of the Office of the Coordinator of Information, the predecessor to the Office of Strategic Services, was searching for a way to establish a paramilitary unit of his agency in Asia in the face of Stilwell's opposition to the plan.

Donovan arranged for Eifler's transfer to COI so that he could establish and command the agency's paramilitary Detachment 101 (the first of its kind, but assigned the three-digit designation in the belief that a smaller number would be less prestigious). In May 1942 Eifler, who had been promoted to the rank of major, and his twenty-five officers and enlisted men departed for India.

Eifler's acquaintance with Stilwell was not at first sufficient to overcome the general's distrust of paramilitary operations, and Detachment 101 languished in New Delhi for several weeks. However, the requirements of an upcoming offensive aimed at retaking northern Burma from the Japanese persuaded Stilwell to change his mind. In September he dispatched Eifler and his group with the imperative, "The next thing I want to hear out of you are some loud booms from behind the Jap lines."

Eifler and Detachment 101 were soon operating behind enemy lines in Burma, sabotaging Japanese communications and supply lines and providing tactical support to American air and ground forces. Eifler's group trained and equipped the Kachin tribesmen of Burma as guerrilla fighters and led them against the Japanese very effectively.

Eifler was relieved of command of Detachment 101 late in 1943 because of injuries he sustained in the crash of a two-seater L-5 reconnaissance aircraft. He was discharged with the rank of colonel. Detachment 101 contained to operate in Burma under the command of Lt. Col. WILLIAM R. PEERS.

After the war Eifler earned a D.D. degree and became a Protestant minister in California.

(Smith, *OSS*; Hymoff, *The OSS in World War II*; Ford, *Donovan of the OSS*; Alsop and Braden, *Sub Rosa*.)

ELLICOTT, JOHN MORRIS (September 4, 1859–September 16, 1955): naval officer

A native of St. Inigoes, Maryland, Ellicott graduated from the U.S. Naval Academy in 1883. He served with the Office of Naval Intelligence during 1888–91. In 1897 when the Naval War College was studying the strategic problem of Japanese interest in the Hawaiian Islands (which the United States was then on the point of annexing), he carried out a reconnaissance of the islands; RICHARD WAINWRIGHT used the information Ellicott gathered in the ONI position paper he wrote stressing the strategic importance of Hawaii to the United States.

Ellicott served aboard the *Baltimore* at the battle of Manila Bay (May 1, 1898) and throughout the Spanish-American War. After the war he compiled information on possible sites for a U.S. naval base in the Philippines, and this work earned him an assignment to the Naval War College (1900–01). In 1901 he published an article in the *Proceedings* of the U.S. Naval Institute, "Naval Reconnaissance in Time of Peace," which called for reform of naval intelligence procedures.

A prolific writer, Ellicott published several books (including a novel), short stories, essays, and professional papers. He reached the rank of captain and retired in 1912, but was recalled to active duty during 1918–22.

(Dorwart, *The Office of Naval Intelligence; Who Was Who in America,* vol. 3.)

ENGLISH, GEORGE BETHUNE (March 7, 1787–September 20, 1828): journalist, Marine Corps officer, secret agent

A native of Cambridge, Massachusetts, English graduated from Harvard in 1807. He studied theology, wrote a tract against Christianity, and edited a rural newspaper before being commissioned a lieutenant in the U.S. Marine Corps through the good offices of John Quincy Adams.

English served in the Marine Corps in the Mediterranean and resigned at Alexandria, Egypt. He converted to Islam and served as an artillery officer in the Turkish army. After conspicuous service in campaigns in the Sudan during 1820–21, he returned to the United States.

In 1823 English proposed to Secretary of State John Quincy Adams that he return to Turkey as a secret agent in order to discover how the Turks might regard a proposal for a commercial treaty with the United States and American trade on the Black Sea. Adams agreed, English returned to Turkey, resumed his Muslim identity, secretly obtained a copy of the commercial treaty between Turkey and France (which he sent back to Adams), and arranged the prelimi-

naries for further negotiations between the United States and Turkey.

(*Who Was Who in America,* historical volume; Wriston, *Executive Agents in American Foreign Relations.*)

ERICKSON, ERIC SIEGFRIED (1889–1983): businessman, intelligence agent

A native of Brooklyn, New York, Erickson worked in the Texas oil fields after graduating from high school, and gradually worked his way up to assistant superintendent of the Standard Oil refinery in Bayonne, New Jersey. At age twenty-eight he enrolled as a freshman at Cornell University and earned an engineering degree in 1921, after taking a brief leave to serve as a U.S. Army officer during the First World War.

Erickson spent several years in the Far East as a salesman, first for Standard Oil, and later for Texas Oil. Subsequently he became managing director of the Texas Oil operations in Sweden, his parents' native country. While in Sweden in the 1920s, he left Texas Oil and started his own oil import company. Having made a permanent home in Sweden, he became a Swedish citizen in 1936.

In 1939 Erickson was recruited by Laurence Steinhardt, the U.S. ambassador to the USSR, to serve as an intelligence agent for the United States in the event of American involvement in the Second World War. As an established European oilman who spoke German fluently, Erickson was in an excellent position to visit Germany regularly and do business with the Nazi government, a cover which would enable him to collect vital intelligence on the German oil industry.

Between 1941 and 1944 Erickson made more than thirty trips into Germany; he was accepted as an ardent Nazi sympathizer and befriended Hermann Göring and Heinrich Himmler. His reports to Allied intelligence provided an accurate and up-to-date picture throughout the war of German oil resources and enabled Allied air forces to bomb the European oil installations that were vital to the Nazi war machine.

Erickson's ostensible Nazi collaboration cost him most of his friends, but this was remedied after the war when his true role was revealed and President Harry S. Truman honored him with an invitation to the White House. He returned to his oil business and later retired to live on the French Mediterranean cost.

Erickson's wartime exploits were reported in a 1958 book by Alexander Klein, *The Counterfeit Traitor.* This was made into a film of the same name in 1962; William Holden played the role of Erickson.

(Klein, *The Counterfeit Traitor*; obituary, *New York Times*, January 25, 1983, p. D25.)

ESPIONAGE ACTS

In the wake of a two-year sabotage campaign by German Intelligence during the FIRST WORLD WAR, marked by a series of fires and explosions at munitions plants, storage facilities, and aboard cargo ships, Congress passed, and the President signed into law, the Espionage Act of 1917. The Act authorized heavy punishment for anyone engaged in espionage, interfering with the armed forces or shipping, violating American neutrality laws, and for a variety of related offenses. The following year the Sedition Act was added, providing similar punishment for anyone who should, during wartime, "utter, print, write, or publish any disloyal, profane, scurrilous, or abusive language" about the flag, the armed forces, or the government.

Some 1,500 persons were prosecuted under the acts during the war; most of them had simply written or spoken against American involvement in it.

The law was further strengthened by the Espionage and Sabotage Act of 1954, which authorized the death penalty or life imprisonment for espionage or sabotage in peacetime as well as during wartime. The Act required agents of foreign governments to register with the U.S. government. It also suspended the statute of limitations for treason. The scope of the Act was broadened in 1958 to cover Americans engaged in espionage against the U.S. while overseas.

ESPIONOLOGY

The study of the history, organization, and methods of intelligence. An *espionologist* is one who makes such studies, while *espionological* is the quality of being related to such studies.

Not found in dictionaries, the word espionology is a neologism coined by the author of this work to fill a vacuum. Noting that the term "intelligencer" was beginning to be used in print in reference to students of intelligence matters, he anticipated that the horrendous "intelligenceology" would soon make its debut if it were not somehow preempted. Seeing his duty, he did it.

Some may object that the term espionology rests upon too narrow a base—espionage, the secret and usually illegal collection of intelligence by human agents, which has become a progressively smaller part of modern intelligence activity. However, the word espionage has a much broader etymological foundation than its current narrow meaning might suggest. As a descendant of the Latin *specere*—to look—it is part of the English branch of a large linguistic family which includes *aspect, prospect, speculate, circumspect, expect, inspect, perspicacious,* and *suspicion* (and, of course, *spy* and *espy*), all of which are very much at home in the world of intelligence.

Linguistic purists may object to appending the Grecian "ology" to this Latin root. The author argues in reply that this admixture symbolizes the international character of intelligence and espionage, and he therefore hopes that this coinage proves *auspicious* (yet another of *specere*'s English descendants).

ESTERLINE, JACOB D: intelligence officer

Esterline attended the University of Pennsylvania and served in the Office of Strategic Services during the Second World War. He was a member of Detachment 101, the OSS paramilitary unit that operated behind Japanese lines in Burma and China. After the war he worked as an accountant, then joined the CIA CLANDESTINE SERVICE. He was chief of a CIA paramilitary training center in Georgia and later served in the Western Hemisphere Division, where he was a Cuban Desk Officer. He became chief of the Agency's station in Guatemala, preceding ROBERT K. DAVIS in that post. During 1957–60 he was chief of station in Caracas, Venezuela.

In 1960 Esterline became project director for the operation that was later to become known as the BAY OF PIGS INVASION. He and Col. JACK HAWKINS, a Marine officer assigned to the CIA for the Cuban project, together worked out the plans for the operation. However, Esterline was not able to implement these plans exactly as they were formulated, and when higher levels within the government decreed alterations in the operation, he and Hawkins threatened to resign. Persuaded by Deputy Director for Plans RICHARD M. BISSELL to remain with the project despite his misgivings, Esterline became a helpless witness to the disaster from the vantage of the CIA's Washington command post. Afterward, on his own initiative, he went to Miami to comfort and apologize to the relatives of the Cubans killed or captured in the operation.

Esterline subsequently served as deputy chief of the Western Hemisphere Division. In 1972, when he was chief of the Miami station of the Clandestine Service's Domestic Operations Division, he became involved peripherally in the Watergate affair after learning of some of the activities of E. HOWARD HUNT in the Miami area. However, once CIA headquarters advised him that Hunt had left the CIA and was working for the White House, he did not pursue the matter further.

(Powers, *The Man Who Kept the Secrets;* Wyden, *Bay of Pigs;* Agee, *Inside the Company;* Phillips, *The Night Watch;* Peers and Brelis, *Behind the Burma Road.*)

EVANS, ALLAN (July 2, 1903–August 22, 1970): intelligence officer

A native of London, England, Evans moved to the United States in 1916. He attended the Loomis School in 1918–20 and graduated from Harvard University in 1924. He earned an M.A. and a Ph.D. from Harvard in 1925 and 1931, respectively. He was an instructor in German at Harvard during 1925–28 and an assistant instructor in history during 1927–38. He became an American citizen in 1939.

In 1942 Evans joined the Office of Strategic Services and served in the OSS RESEARCH AND ANALYSIS BRANCH as chief of the London office. When the OSS was dissolved in 1945 he was one of the intelligence analysts who were transferred to the State Department. He served as director of State's Office of Coordination and Liaison during 1946–47, and became director of State's Office of Intelligence Research in 1947 (see STATE DEPARTMENT INTELLIGENCE). He held that post until the State Department created the BUREAU OF INTELLIGENCE AND RESEARCH (INR) in 1959, when he became special assistant to the director of that agency. From 1961 to 1970 he was deputy director of research of INR.

(*Who Was Who in America*, v. 5).

F

FAHS, CHARLES BURTON (September 22, 1908–): orientalist, educator, diplomat, intelligence officer

A native of New York City, Fahs graduated from Northwestern University in 1929 and earned an M.A. and a Ph.D. from that institution in 1931 and 1933, respectively. He attended the University of Berlin during 1929–30, the Ecole Nationale des Langues Orientales Vivantes during 1933–34, Kyoto Imperial University during 1934–35, and Tokyo Imperial University during 1935–36.

Fahs taught Oriental Affairs at Pomona College and Claremont College during 1936–40. He was visiting professor at the College of Chinese Studies in Peking during 1940–41. In 1941 he became an intelligence analyst with the Office of the Coordinator of Information, the predecessor to the Office of Strategic Services. He served in the OSS until 1945 and was chief of the Far East Division of the OSS RESEARCH AND ANALYSIS BRANCH. Transferred along with a number of other OSS intelligence analysts to the State Department in 1945, he served as acting chief of State's Far East research division until 1946 (see STATE DEPARTMENT INTELLIGENCE).

Fahs held the position of director of humanities with the Rockefeller Foundation from 1946 to 1962. He then joined the foreign service and, from 1962 to 1967, he served at the American embassy in Tokyo as minister for cultural affairs. During 1967–68 he was a visiting professor at Muhlenberg College in Allentown, Pennsylvania. In 1968 he joined the faculty of Miami University in Oxford, Ohio, where he was director of international programs and professor of government.

(*Who's Who in America*, 37th ed.)

FAIRBANK, JOHN KING (May 24, 1907–): historian, sinologist, intelligence officer

A native of Huron, South Dakota, Fairbank graduated from Harvard University in 1929 and received a Ph.D. from Oxford University in 1936. He joined the history faculty of Harvard in 1936 but in 1941 left to serve as an intelligence analyst with the Office of the Coordinator of Information, the predecessor to the Office of Strategic Services.

In 1942 Fairbank was sent to Chunking, China, where he was chief of the local office of the OSS RESEARCH AND ANALYSIS BRANCH and special assistant to the American ambassador to China. He returned to Washington in 1943 and served with the Office of War Information, the wartime "white propaganda" agency (see COVERT ACTION) during 1944–45. Fairbank was director of the U.S. Information Service in China during 1945–46. In 1946 he returned to Harvard.

Fairbank was one of the American China specialists whom Senator Joseph McCarthy accused of sympathizing with the Chinese Communists during his search for purported Communists and Communist sympathizers in government in the 1950s. In 1959 Fairbank founded the East Asian Research Center at Harvard and served as its director until 1972. He is the author of several books on East Asia and served as chairman of the Council on East Asian Studies during 1973–77.

(Smith, *OSS; Who's Who in America,* 42nd ed.)

FARAGO, LADISLAS (September 21, 1906–October 15, 1980): journalist, espionologist, psychological warfare officer

A native of Csurgo, Hungary, Farago graduated from the Academy of Commerce and Consular Affairs in Budapest in 1926. He worked as a reporter for the *New York Times* in Berlin and for the Associated Press in Ethiopia and moved to the United States before the Second World War.

His book *German Psychological Warfare* (1940) attracted the attention of Lt. Comm. Cecil H. Coggins, a Navy doctor connected with the Office of Naval Intelligence. Coggins recruited Farago to serve as chief of research and planning for the newly organized Op-16-W, the Special Warfare Branch of ONI. The function of Op-16-W was psychological warfare. Farago invented "Comm. Robert Lee Norden," a fictitous character who served as spokesman for the Navy's "white" propaganda radio broadcasts to the crewmen of German U-boats operating off the U.S. coasts. The Norden broadcasts proved extremely effective in undermining the morale of the U-boat crews. Farago also prepared a comprehensive study of Japanese history for Capt. ELLIS M. ZACHARIAS, deputy director of ONI, which was used to great effect in formulating propaganda aimed at inspiring a Japanese surrender. This project, however, was cut short by the dropping of nuclear weapons on Hiroshima and Nagasaki.

Farago served with ONI until 1946. Between 1950 and 1952 he worked for RADIO FREE EUROPE. He is the author of numerous books on the history of espionage in the Second World War, including *War of Wits* (1954), *Burn After Reading* (1961), *The Broken Seal* (1967), and *The Game of the Foxes* (1971). He also wrote *Patton: Ordeal and Triumph* (1964), from which a popular motion picture was made.

(*Who Was Who in America,* vol. 7; Farago, *Burn After Reading;* Zacharias, *Secret Missions.*)

FARLEY, WILLIAM DOWNES (?–June 9, 1863): Confederate Army officer and scout

A native of South Carolina, Farley attended the University of Virginia. At the outbreak of the Civil War he enlisted as a private in the South Carolina regiment commanded by (then) Col. Maxcy Gregg. He was soon commissioned a lieutenant. Later he served

with the rank of captain as an aide to Gen. Milledge Bonham in Virginia.

While on a scouting mission in uniform near Dranesville, Virginia, in November 1861, Farley was captured by Union troops and imprisoned in Washington's Old Capitol Prison for several months; he was then released in a prisoner exchange.

On his return to the Confederate Army Farley served as a scout. He was assigned to the staff of Gen. J.E.B. Stuart, and he became Stuart's chief of scouts. Farley was killed at the battle of Brandy Station (Fleetwood Hill), Virginia, in the first and largest cavalry engagement of the war.

Freeman rates Farley as the best of the scouts.

(Freeman, *Lee's Lieutenants;* Bakeless, *Spies of the Confederacy.*)

FECTEAU, RICHARD GEORGE (ca. 1927–): intelligence officer

Fecteau lived in Lynn, Massachusetts, and attended Boston University before joining the Central Intelligence Agency in 1952. After only five months with the Agency he was sent to the Far East and, on November 29th, he accompanied fellow CIA officer, JOHN T. DOWNEY, on a flight over the Chinese mainland in a DC-3 operated by Civil Air Transport, a CIA-owned airline (see AIR PROPRIETARIES).

The flight was on a mission to the Manchurian province of Kirin to recover a Chinese agent who had been working with CIA-supported anti-Communist guerrillas. The recovery method was to be the "skyhook snatch" technique, in which a low- and slow-flying aircraft hooked onto a wire line to which the agent was strapped, lifting him from the ground and into the airplane. In the midst of executing this maneuver the plane was hit by gunfire from Communist troops on the ground.

The aircraft crashed, killing the CAT pilot and copilot. Fecteau and Downey were taken prisoner and charged with espionage. Downey was sentenced to life in prison; Fecteau was given a twenty-year sentence. The U.S. government officially denied that the two men were CIA officers on an intelligence mission, stating instead that they were civilian employees of the U.S. Army who had been on a routine flight between Korea and Japan.

Personal appeals to the Chinese Communist government by the mothers of the two men in 1958 failed to secure their release. Fecteau was finally released after serving nineteen years in December 1971, two months before President Richard Nixon's trip to Peking. Downey was released in March 1973 after a public acknowledgment by President Nixon that Downey was in fact a CIA officer.

(Leary, *Perilous Missions*; Wise and Ross, *The Invisible Government*.)

FEDERAL BUREAU OF INVESTIGATION

Background: Under the law that created the Department of Justice in 1870, the attorney general of the United States became the head of the new department and was given full authority over U.S. attorneys and federal marshals. The Department had no detective unit, however, and was required to obtain detectives from outside the Department for cases requiring extensive investigation. Detectives were usually borrowed from the U.S. Secret Service on a case-by-case basis. Others were hired from private agencies, especially the PINKERTON'S NATIONAL DETECTIVE AGENCY, until 1892, when the Pinkertons' involvement in the bloody Homestead strike prompted Congress to prohibit the federal government from hiring private detectives. Thereafter the Justice Department was forced to rely exclusively on the Secret Service for detective personnel.

In 1908 the use of Secret Service agents by the Justice Department became a political issue, and Congress attached an amendment to the Justice Department's appropriations bill forbidding it to borrow Secret Service agents during the ensuing fiscal year. President Theodore Roosevelt thereupon directed Attorney General Charles J. Bonaparte (the American-born grandson of Napoleon I's youngest brother, Jerome) to establish a detective force within the Justice Department. Bonaparte transferred nine Secret Service agents to the Justice payroll, and put them under the supervision of his chief examiner, Stanley W. Finch. Fourteen Justice department investigative employees were also transferred to the new division, which was christened the Bureau of Investigation by Bonaparte's successor, Attorney General George W. Wickersham, in 1909.

Intelligence in the Bureau of Investigation: The Bureau had no counterintelligence or countersubversion function during the first few years of its existence, but was concerned entirely with investigation of criminal matters. When German Intelligence began a COVERT ACTION campaign of sabotage and subversion within the United States prior to American entry into the FIRST WORLD WAR, the task of investigating the incidents was given to the Secret Service, which had handled domestic counterintelligence during the SPANISH-AMERICAN WAR. However, on July 1, 1916 Congress authorized the Bureau to conduct counterintelligence investigations for the Department of State.

With American entry into the war in April 1917, the Bureau's counterintelligence role was greatly enlarged to include monitoring some one million registered "enemy" aliens in the United States (i.e., nationals of Germany or Austria-Hungary who happened to be living in the United States, and who were for the most part immigrants awaiting American citizenship), enforcement of the new draft-registration law and ESPIONAGE ACTS, and investigation of the rash of (mostly groundless) reports of German spies and saboteurs made by a newly spy-conscious public. The Bureau's staff—expanded by one-third from three hundred to four hundred agents—was still insufficient to deal with this burgeoning workload. Bureau director A. BRUCE BIELASKI unwisely accepted the offer of the AMERICAN PROTECTIVE LEAGUE to serve as an unpaid volunteer auxiliary force. The league was a loosely organized group of a quarter of a million citizens, most of whom had no more qualification for counterintelligence work than an ardent desire to play spy-catcher. Elevated to the quasi-official status conferred upon them by the Bureau's sponsorship, the League soon achieved a deplorable record of illegal arrests, harassment, wiretaps, and other violations of privacy and civil rights.

General Intelligence Division

In 1919, in the wake of a wave of bombings by radical political groups aimed at a number of prominent persons and senior government officials (including himself), Attorney General A. Mitchell Palmer created the General Intelligence Division of the Justice Department. The GID was to be a central reference facility and intelligence research and analysis service concerned with the subversive groups and individuals investigated by the Bureau: Communists, anarchists, and radical labor organizations such as the International Workers of the World. To head the GID, Palmer appointed J. EDGAR HOOVER, a young (twenty-four) Justice Department law clerk. For most practical purposes, however, the new division was controlled by WILLIAM J. FLYNN, who had been chief of the Secret Service during the war, and had been named to succeed A. Bruce Bielaski as head of the Bureau of Investigation in 1919.

The wartime Sedition Act (see ESPIONAGE ACTS) empowered the Secretary of Labor to deport aliens who were anarchists or who advocated the violent overthrow of the government. Invoking the Act, and using intelligence produced by the GID, Attorney General Palmer directed the Bureau to round up thousands of aliens suspected of anarchist or revolutionary beliefs. The Bureau began the dragnet, known to history as the Palmer Raids, in November 1919. It culminated in raids in thirty-three cities on January 2, 1920, resulting in the arrest of some four thousand people and the eventual deportation of some six hundred of them. The Bureau's heavy-handed methods, through which several thousand innocent persons were arrested and detained, became a political issue and reflected unfavorably on the Bureau.

Public and official concern with anarchism and subversion continued, however, fueled by a number of incidents, the most notable of which was a Wall Street bombing in September 1920 that killed thirty-eight people and wounded hundreds of others. The Bureau and the GID continued to focus attention on radical political groups and other organizations, e.g., labor organizations believed to be involved in radical politics. The Army's Military Intelligence Division (see ARMY INTELLIGENCE) and the Office of NAVAL INTELLIGENCE had similar concerns, especially regarding counterintelligence within the armed services, and worked closely with the Bureau and the GID. Public hostility toward domestic intelligence activities by the armed services was very intense, however, and therefore the Bureau of Investigations remained the primary agency for countersubversion.

Under Director William J. Burns, formerly the famous head of a private detective agency, the Bureau became involved in the scandals during the administration of President Warren G. Harding (1921–23). Several disreputable or corrupt persons became Bureau agents (see, for example, GASTON B. MEANS). When President Calvin Coolidge's new Attorney General, Harlan Fiske Stone, took office in 1924, he accepted Burns's resignation and, on the recommendation of Secretary of Commerce Herbert Hoover, appointed J. Edgar Hoover (no relation) to the directorship. Hoover, who had been assistant director of the Bureau since 1921, undertook a general housecleaning, ridding the Bureau of the corrupt employees of the Harding years, establishing new policies to ensure the professionalism and integrity of the staff, and transforming the Bureau into a highly effective law enforcement agency.

The Federal Bureau of Investigation: Although Stone abolished the GID and directed Hoover to focus the Bureau's attention on federal criminal investigations, counterintelligence was not entirely neglected. The Bureau continued to have responsibility for enforcement of the espionage laws, for example. The Bureau's countersubversion role was restored in 1937 by President Franklin D. Roosevelt (under whose administration the agency had been rechristened the Federal Bureau of Investigation in 1935). Roosevelt authorized the FBI to investigate subversive activities carried on by Communists, Fascists, and the agents of foreign governments within the United States.

Second World War

With the approach of the SECOND WORLD WAR the FBI's investigation of espionage cases increased dramatically, jumping from an average of thirty-five cases per year during 1933–37 to 634 cases in 1938. By 1939 six separate federal agencies were investigating such cases, and President Roosevelt instructed his Cabinet that henceforth only the FBI, the Army's Military Intelligence Division, and the Office of Naval Intelligence were to handle espionage and counterespionage matters. Furthermore, he ordered the heads of the three agencies to form a committee to coordinate their activities in these matters. The committee thus formed agreed that the FBI would have responsibility for counterintelligence involving civilians within the United States and territories, except the Canal Zone, Guam and Samoa, and the Philippine Islands, and cases of espionage "directed from foreign countries," as requested, by the Army, Navy, or State Department. In 1940 President Roosevelt made the FBI responsible for positive non-military foreign intelligence throughout the western hemisphere. In response to this, Hoover established the Special Intelligence Service within the FBI (a recent study by Rout and Bratzel of U.S. counterespionage in Latin America during the Second World War suggests that Hoover anticipated the President's order and had already put a covert intelligence apparatus in place in Latin America). At about this time, and with the President's consent, Hoover established a working liaison with British intelligence through WILLIAM STEPHENSON, the chief of British intelligence in the western hemisphere.

Domestic Counterintelligence

The FBI was highly effective in its counterintelligence role during the Second World War. In his history of the FBI (endorsed in a foreword by J. Edgar Hoover), Whitehead states that the Bureau investigated 19,649 cases of suspected sabotage during the war and found "not a single case of enemy directed sabotage." But in his study of German wartime operations in the United States and Great Britain, Farago challenges this conclusion and states that German documents show "the Abwehr was in the sabotage business in the United States on a substantial scale throughout the war." In any case, German sabotage in the United States seems to have been less effective, less widespread, and less spectacular than during the First World War.

The success of the FBI's counterintelligence activity against German intelligence owes much to the loyalty of WILLIAM G. SEBOLD, a German-American recruited by German intelligence, who volunteered to work as a double agent for the FBI. Through Sebold the Bureau was able to roll up thirty-three German agents and so neutralize the entire German apparatus in the United States in 1940. Apparently German intelligence was unable to reestablish an effective secret intelligence or covert action apparatus within the United States during the war, although it tried; the FBI continued to turn up German agents in America occasionally after 1940 (see, for example, PASTORIUS).

The FBI did not repeat its First World War mistake of sanctioning an amateur "auxiliary" counterintelligence group. Hoover declined the offers of groups and individuals including the American Legion and motion-picture producer Cecil B. De Mille to augment the Bureau's special agents with untrained volunteers.

Latin America

Equally effective and even more extensive were the operations of the FBI's Special Intelligence Service in Latin America. Some agents operated under official cover as "legal attachés" at American embassies throughout the region, while others used such commercial cover as salesmen, stockbrokers, or journalists. One of the earliest (May 1941) achievements of FBI/SIS was the detection of a plot by pro-Nazi Bolivians to overthrow the pro-British government of Bolivia and replace it with a German-leaning government that would cut off the country's export of strategically important tungsten ore to the United States. With the help of British intelligence the FBI obtained proof of the conspiracy, and the U.S. government was able to thwart it.

The FBI carried out extensive operations against German subversion in Mexico, Brazil, Chile, and Argentina, as well as in Central America and the Carribean. Working wherever possible with the local authorities, the Bureau conducted investigations leading to the arrest of more than four hundred Axis espionage agents, saboteurs, and propagandists and the shutting down of twenty-four clandestine radio transmitters. Additionally, the Bureau's work slowed the flow of strategic supplies from Latin America to the Axis powers.

The Special Intelligence Service operated from July 1, 1940 until March 31, 1947. Although Hoover hoped to give the SIS a worldwide role after the war, he failed to obtain President Truman's approval for the move. In 1947 Truman transferred jurisdiction for secret intelligence operations in Latin America from the FBI to the Central Intelligence Group (see CENTRAL INTELLIGENCE AGENCY). Many of the FBI agents who had served in Latin America with the SIS were recruited to the CIG and later the CIA by J. C. KING, who had worked with them in his capacity as U.S. military attaché in Argentina during the war. Some of the SIS veterans remained in the Western Hemisphere Division of the CIA CLANDESTINE SERVICE until as late as the 1970s.

The termination of the SIS did not end the FBI's overseas presence, however. FBI agents continued to be assigned to American embassies as legal attachés. Their function was to serve as liaison with foreign national police forces and to deal with American citizens who fell afoul of the local laws. Additionally, the legal attachés collected foreign intelligence through their local contacts. Though this function was ended in the early 1970s, the Bureau continues to keep legal attachés abroad for the other purposes to the present day.

THE COLD WAR

Domestic counterintelligence remained a major part of the FBI's activity during the late 1940s and 1950s. Its principal adversaries in this field were the Soviet intelligence services and their surrogates, the intelligence services of the Warsaw Pact countries. The FBI took a major role in such celebrated and controversial cases as those of the Rosenbergs and Alger Hiss, and a host of other cases that were less publicized but more clear-cut.

The FBI also deeply penetrated the tanks of the American Communist Party, the Ku Klux Klan, and other radical political groups. In 1956 the Bureau undertook a program called Cointelpro ("counterintelligence program") against the Communist Party. The program, more covert action than counterintelligence, aimed at disrupting the Party through a variety of deception tactics similar to black propaganda: anonymous or fictitious letters discrediting Party members in the eyes of their comrades, forgeries and rumors with a similar objective, and a variety of related tactics. The Cointelpro operation proved highly effective in undermining the American Communist Party and rendering it virtually impotent.

The success of Cointelpro against the Communist Party encouraged the Bureau to extend it to racist hate groups, both white and black, and to radical leftist political groups. During the civil rights and anti-war movements of the 1960s, the program was directed at the New Left and included a broad program of infiltration of dissident groups, as well as wiretapping, electronic surveillance, mail openings, break-ins, and other disruptive operations against them.

In March 1971, some one thousand documents bearing on the Cointel program were stolen from the Bureau's offices in Media, Pennsylvania. Anticipating the negative public reaction that would follow the release of these papers, the Bureau terminated the program. Publication of the documents did indeed produce intense public indignation and severely damaged the image of the FBI.

The death of J. Edgar Hoover in May 1972 marked the end of an era for the FBI, which had been an extension of his personality for nearly half a century. (Congress has since passed a law limiting the FBI director's term to a maximum of ten years.) Hoover was succeeded by L. Patrick Gray, a retired naval officer. Gray soon fell victim to the Watergate affair and resigned under a cloud that same year. Gray was succeeded by Clarence M. Kelley, a former FBI agent. He served as director until 1977 when President Jimmy Carter appointed William H. Webster to the post. Webster, a former federal judge, emphasized the investigation of white-collar crime and political corruption, recruited members of minority groups, and steered clear of such excesses as Cointelpro. Under Webster the FBI has reclaimed much of its lost prestige.

While the FBI now emphasizes federal law enforcement, it continues to serve as the premier federal agency in matters of counterintelligence within the United States and is an active member of the INTELLIGENCE COMMUNITY. Additionally, the Bureau has the limited positive foreign intelligence role specified by President Ronald Reagan in his Executive Order 12333 of December 4, 1981, which permits the Bureau to:

> Conduct within the United States, when requested by the officials of the intelligence community designated by the President, activities undertaken to collect foreign intelligence or support foreign intelligence collection requirements of other agencies within the intelligence community.

(Whitehead, *The FBI Story*; Overstreet and Overstreet, *The FBI in Our Open Society*; Cook, *The FBI Nobody Knows*; Tully, *The FBI's Most Famous Cases*; Donner, *The Age of Surveillance*; Rout and Bratzel, *The Shadow War*; Farago, *The Game of the Foxes*; Richelson, *The U.S. Intelligence Community*; Ungar, *FBI*.)

FINISHED INTELLIGENCE

"The final product of the intelligence system, intended for the upper reaches of government, is known as 'finished intelligence.' "—Breckenridge, *The CIA and the U.S. Intelligence System*.

See also INTELLIGENCE CYCLE, INTELLIGENCE TAXONOMY.

FIRST WORLD WAR

The War: When the war began in Europe in August 1914 with Germany and Austria-Hungary—the Central Powers—fighting against Britain, France, and Russia—the Allies—President Woodrow Wilson resolved to maintain America's traditional policy of neutrality in the affairs of the Old World. Unwilling to restrict her foreign trade, the United States claimed the rights to use the sea-lanes with impunity, to trade with the belligerents of either side as well as with the neutral European nations, and to protect the safety of American passengers traveling on ships of the belligerent nations. These rights were denied by both the Allies and the Central Powers. The British stopped, searched, and escorted American vessels into British ports to prevent trade with Germany or even with neutral nations that might transship American goods to the enemy. Germany, unable to blockade British or French ports, resorted to submarine warfare to interdict transatlantic shipping. On May 7, 1915 a German U-boat sank the British liner *Lusitania*; 128 of the 1,200 passengers lost in the disaster were American citizens.

The anti-German feeling created in the United States by the *Lusitania* incident was abetted by a skillful British propaganda campaign, incidents of German sabotage and subversion in the United States, and widespread sympathy for America's historic ally, France. Anglophilic and anti-German sentiments among American policymakers tilted U.S. policy even further to the Allied side. Nonetheless, American support for the Allies was broadly opposed by German-Americans, Anglophobic Irish-Americans, pacifists, and isolationists, and President Wilson was reelected in 1916 with the platform slogan, "He kept us out of war."

America Enters the War

Wilson sought to mediate a negotiated peace, but was unsuccessful. In January 1917 Germany resumed unrestricted submarine warfare, which she had suspended in September 1915 in the wake of the *Lusitania* sinking. Anti-German sentiment in the United States was further inflamed by the publication of the ZIMMERMANN TELEGRAM, evidence that Germany was attempting to enlist Mexico against the United States. German U-boats sank three American merchant ships in mid-March; two weeks later Wil-

The sinking of the *Lusitania* by a German submarine with the loss of 128 American lives in May 1917 created a wave of anti-German and pro-war sentiment in the United States. Source: Author's collection.

son asked Congress for a declaration of war against Germany, and war was declared four days thereafter.

Troops of the American Expeditionary Force under Gen. John J. Pershing began arriving in France in June 1917. After a short period of training they were sent to reinforce the British and French along the Western Front, two parallel lines of trenches and barbed wire stretching several hundred miles from Ostend on the English channel to the Swiss border near Basel. This front had remained essentially static since the two sides fought to a standstill in 1915, moving only a few yards one way or the other at the cost of enormous casualties whenever either side mounted a major offensive. On the Eastern Front, Russia and the Central Powers faced each other across a line stretching from the Baltic Sea to Romania, and

German and Austrian forces had pushed some hundred miles eastward during 1914–1917.

The American entry into the war on the Allied side was partially offset by the withdrawal of Russia from the war in February 1918, as an aftermath of the Communist revolution in that country several months earlier. The Central Powers were thereby able to transfer hundreds of thousands of troops from the Eastern Front to counter the American buildup on the Western Front. Germany launched a major spring offensive in 1918 aimed at breaking through the Western Front and capturing Paris and the French channel ports, hoping thus to forestall the arrival of further American reinforcements and supplies, and so bring the war to a swift end.

The German drive came within fifty-six miles of Paris before being halted and turned back by an

American counteroffensive. In mid-July, after months of bitter fighting and a series of massive German offensives and Allied counteroffensives, the Germans began to retreat and the Allies went on the offensive. By November Germany faced the prospect of having the Western Front pushed within her national borders, and agreed to an armistice. She was subsequently forced to agree to the peace terms dictated by the Allies at the PARIS PEACE CONFERENCE OF 1919.

Intelligence during American Neutrality: The American intelligence history of the war can be divided into two separate phases: the period of American neutrality (August 1914–April 1917) and the period of American belligerency (April 1917–November 1918). During the first phase American intelligence was concerned almost exclusively with countering German sabotage and subversion within the United States and the western hemisphere.

German Covert Action in the Western Hemisphere

Before the war Germany had established one of the most extensive intelligence services in the world, but its assets were concentrated in Europe; only one part-time agent operated in the United States. German war plans assumed that victory would be won after a short but decisive campaign through Belgium and northern France, and the need for covert operations in the United States became apparent only when this swift victory failed to materialize. Faced with the prospect of a protracted war, Germany realized that her survival might depend on denying American material support to the Allies. German intelligence was therefore directed to undertake a major campaign of sabotage and subversion within the United States.

The German COVERT ACTION campaign in the western hemisphere was under the overall supervision of Count Johann von Bernstorff, the German ambassador to Washington. Initially, implementation of the campaign was the responsibility of Dr. Heinrich Albert, the German commercial attaché; Capt. FRANZ VON PAPEN, the military attaché; and Capt. Karl Boy-Ed, the naval attaché; all of whom worked out of their respective offices in New York City, a major port for munitions shipments to the Allies; and Franz von Bopp, the German consul general in San Francisco, who was responsible for operations on the West Coast. Dr. Konstantin Dumba, the ambassador to Washington from Austria-Hungary, also participated in the apparatus, apparently working under von Bernstorff's direction.

Count Johann von Bernstorff, German ambassador to Washington, had overall responsibility for German covert action operations in the United States during 1914–17. Source: Author's collection.

The first task of the German covert action organization was to recruit agents to carry out the actual sabotage and subversion. They found an abundance of candidates among resident German aliens and German-Americans, as well as Irish-Americans and other ethnic and political groups whose aims coincided with German war objectives. For example, von Papen recruited Paul Koenig, chief of security for the Atlas Line (a subsidiary of the German-owned Hamburg-American steamship line), and he put his private detective force at the service of the German organization. KURT JAHNKE, a German-born private detective, went to work for von Bopp as a saboteur on the West Coast. Others, such as LOTHAR WITZKE, a German naval cadet who escaped from internment in Chile and made his way to the United States, volunteered their services. This improvised secret service was soon augmented by professional agents sent from Germany, e.g., Capt.. FRANZ VON RINTELEN, Capt. Erich von Steinmetz, MARIA DE VICTORIA, and demolition expert Robert Fay.

Capt. Karl Boy-Ed (foreground), German naval attaché in Washington during the First World War, helped direct the sabotage campaign in the United States. Source: Author's collection.

German Covert Action

The German campaign included all four types of covert action: political, psychological, economic, and paramilitary, and had as its first priority cutting off the flow of munitions to the Allies from American suppliers. Von Papen and Albert bought up large quantities of munitions and such strategic materials as chlorine and carbolic acid in order to prevent them from being sold to the Allies, bought up machine tools in order to deny such equipment to American munitions makers, and established a dummy munitions company that offered inflated wages in order to cause labor unrest in competing plants, as well as accepting, and later defaulting on, contracts to supply munitions to the Allies. Fomenting labor unrest in munitions plants was also the primary task of a network run by Austrian ambassador Dumba.

Even with the support of the German treasury, however, these economic operations failed to have an appreciable effect on the American munitions industry's capacity to produce and export supplies to the Allies, and therefore the German organization resorted increasingly to sabotage during 1915–16. Explosive and incendiary bombs were placed in munitions plants, storage facilities, and aboard cargo ships carrying munitions bound for Allied ports. The most spectacular sabotage incident was the BLACK TOM EXPLOSION on July 30, 1916, in which some two million pounds of munitions awaiting shipment to Russia were destroyed. (German involvement was suspected but not proved in the explosion of the Hercules Powder Company plant at Eddystone, Pennsylvania, on April 10, 1917, which took 112 lives.)

In addition to facilities for producing, storing, and shipping munitions, the German sabotage operation also targeted an assortment of other facilities, all more or less related to American material support to the Allies. There were at least two unsuccessful plots to blow up the Welland Canal, which links Lake Ontario and Lake Erie, and a failed attempt to blow up a Canadian Pacific Railway tunnel in British Columbia. The international railroad bridge at Vanceboro, Maine, was blown up in January 1915, and an attempt was made to blow up the Elephant-Butte Dam on the Rio Grande in 1917.

The German covert action campaign included some ambitious political operations. One was aimed at fomenting a revolution in Mexico in order to restore former President Victoriano Huerta to power, a move calculated to instigate a war between Mexico and the United States (this was in line with a long-standing German contingency plan to exploit American concern with political instability in Mexico, where Germany had established a considerable and influential presence, in order to keep the United States too busy with events on her southern border to be able to interfere in the European war). The plan failed when it was penetrated by agents of British intelligence. Even more ambitious was the German plot to create a rebellion in the Punjab—thus diverting British arms from the war to secure the Indian colony—by organizing, arming, and supporting Sikh emigrés and students living in the United States and Canada. This, too, failed, apparently falling apart of its own weight.

Somewhat more effective were the German political and psychological operations aimed at winning sympathy for the Central Powers and keeping the United States from active participation in the war on the Allied side. Dr. Albert, the German commercial attaché, hired William Bayard Hale, an American public relations man, as a propagandist. Albert also inspired and subsidized pro-German books, subsidized *The Fatherland*, a newspaper edited by German-American writer and dramatist George Sylvester Viereck, and secretly purchased a major New York daily newspaper, the *Mail and Express*. The German political/psychological apparatus worked closely with (and sometimes even created) such isolationist, pacifist, or anti-British political action organizations as the American Truth Society, American Women for Strict Neutrality, the American Humanity League, and the Arms Embargo Conference, which agitated against American support for the Allies.

British Intelligence and Covert Action in America

British intelligence in America had a twofold task during the period of American neutrality: to counter German sabotage operations, and to bring the United States into the war on the Allied side. Like the Germans, the British ran their American organization under the official cover of their legation in Washington. Although the British ambassador, Sir Cecil Spring-Rice, certainly was aware of British covert operations run from the embassy, the extent of his participation in them is obscure. These activities seem to have been, at the beginning of the war, the responsibility of Comdr. Guy Gaunt, the British naval attaché. Gaunt later shared the responsibility with WILLIAM WISEMAN, who appeared on the scene ostensibly as a representative of the Purchasing Commission of the British Ministry of Munitions early in 1916. Wiseman was an officer of the British Secret Intelligence Service, while Gaunt reported to the British Naval Intelligence Department.

British covert operations in America were greatly abetted when, on August 5, 1914, the day after Britain went to war, a British ship cut the submarine telegraph cable that linked Germany directly to the western hemisphere. Along with the subsequent severance of an alternate transatlantic cable route via West Africa and Brazil this put Britain in control of all wire service dispatches from Europe to the United States, which was of enormous advantage to the British propaganda war against the Germans in America. More important, it forced the German Foreign Office and Secret Service to communicate with their American representatives and agents by means of wireless, which was more easily intercepted by British intelligence. By mid-1915 "Room 40, Old Building," the British Naval Intelligence Department's cryptanalysis unit, had acquired several German cryptosystems and was intercepting and reading most of the German diplomatic and intelligence traffic.

Dr. Konstantin Dumba, Austrian ambassador to Washington, was involved in the German sabotage campaign in the United States during 1914–17. Source: Author's collection.

Commander Gaunt passed along selected items of the intelligence product of Room 40's COMINT operations to Col. Edward M. House, President Wilson's close friend and advisor. The material was first SANITIZED to conceal the method that had been employed to collect it. Other items were delivered to the American embassy in London, where Adm. William R. Hall, director of British Naval Intelligence, presented them to Edward Bell, the American foreign service officer responsible for liaison with British intelligence, or directly to Walter H. Page, the American ambassador. In this way British intelligence was able both to help American law enforcement and counterintelligence work against the German sabotage and subversion campaigns and to expose German secret diplomatic moves inimical to American interests, and thereby encourage anti-German sentiment within the Wilson administration. The climax of this operation was the so-called ZIMMERMANN TELEGRAM affair in February 1917: the British delivered to Wilson the contents of a German diplomatic dispatch that revealed Germany's attempt finally to play its "Mexico card" by promising Mexico the return of the territories it lost to the United States in the MEXICAN WAR in exchange for a military alliance against the United States.

In addition to the judicious use of its COMINT to influence American policy and actions, British intelligence sponsored human counterintelligence operations against the German apparatus in America through the medium of the intelligence service organized among Czech and Slovak emigrés in America by EMANUEL V. VOSKA. Because many of Voska's agents spoke perfect German, they were able to pass as Germans and penetrate the German and Austrian legations. Gaunt and Wiseman arranged for Voska to work closely with U.S. law enforcement and counterintelligence to frustrate German subversion. This alliance led to the exposure and disruption of the German plans for a Mexican revolution.

Voska's organization also cooperated with British propaganda efforts in the United States by feeding inside information on German subversion to the press, especially the *Providence Journal,* which was edited by Australian-born and English-educated John R. Rathom, a press asset of Commander Gaunt. Rathom arranged for the simultaneous publication of his exposés by the influential *New York Times.*

U.S. Intelligence

At the outbreak of the war in 1914 the United States had only the most rudimentary positive foreign intelligence organization, and virtually no national counterintelligence unit. The Department of State had no formal intelligence component, but continued to handle intelligence as it always had done: either as a routine part of diplomatic reporting, or as an ad hoc project when some particular need arose.

The Office of NAVAL INTELLIGENCE had been concerned about the German naval threat since at least 1900, and in 1911 had developed War Plan Black, a detailed scenario for a war with Germany. However, Japan had loomed as a larger threat in the view of ONI, especially after the Japanese war scare in 1907–08, and somewhat greater attention was directed toward Japan during the years immediately before the war.

ARMY INTELLIGENCE was in an even worse state of unpreparedness in 1914. The Military Intelligence Division of the War Department's General Staff had been abolished in 1908 and its staff scattered throughout the War College Division, in effect liquidating the Army's intelligence service. Perhaps the best illustration of the Army's difficulties in preparing for the war is the 1915 incident in which President Wilson, learning from the newspapers that the General Staff was making a German contingency war plan,

angrily ordered a halt to the planning and even considered transferring the entire General Staff Corps out of Washington.

At this time Mexico was America's most pressing foreign policy problem, and eighty percent of the U.S. Army had been sent to guard the Mexican border (or cross it in pursuit of Pancho Villa). As late as 1916, virtually the only Army intelligence activity even indirectly related to the war in Europe was the field intelligence units that supported the troops on the Mexican border; they were collecting, among other things, intelligence on the considerable German presence in Mexico. Because Mexico was a key element in Germany's strategy toward the United States, German officers were serving in the Mexican army, and a sizable colony of German businessmen and diplomatic personnel provided cover for clandestine activities in the country. However, neither the Army's field intelligence units nor the General Staff's War College Division had the staff capability to exploit the collected material to obtain useful strategic intelligence.

The American Counterintelligence Program

The Bureau of Investigation, forerunner of the FEDERAL BUREAU OF INVESTIGATION, had been established in 1908 to provide investigative support to the Department of Justice's law enforcement activities. However, since there were no federal (or state) espionage laws to enforce in 1914, the Bureau had no counterintelligence unit.

Although the prime role of the Secret Service was to protect the President and enforce the laws against counterfeiting along with other laws involving the Treasury Department, it had been called upon by presidents from time to time to investigate other matters. During the SPANISH-AMERICAN WAR it was responsible for domestic counterintelligence (see MONTREAL SPY RING). On May 14, 1915 (one week after the sinking of the *Lusitania*) President Wilson ordered his secretary of the treasury to use the Secret Service to put the personnel of the German and Austrian legations under surveillance. Within a week the Secret Service had tapped the telephone lines of the German and Austrian embassies in Washington, and the offices of von Papen, Boy-Ed, and Albert in New York City.

Because of the critical foreign policy aspect of this newly instituted American counterintelligence operation, overall coordination became the responsibility of the Department of State in the person of Counselor Frank R. Polk, the second-ranking officer in the Department. Polk carried on liaison with British intelligence and the Secret Service, passing along to Secret Service Chief WILLIAM J. FLYNN the items he received from Gaunt, Wiseman, and the London embassy, and providing the British with the results of the Secret Service's surveillance. Polk was also responsible for coordinating positive intelligence for the Department (see STATE DEPARTMENT INTELLIGENCE).

In addition to wiretapping, the Secret Service conducted physical surveillance of the German attachés, and on July 24, 1915 an alert agent recovered a briefcase Albert inadvertently left behind when he got off an elevated train in New York City. The contents of the briefcase disclosed many of the most important German economic operations, e.g., the dummy munitions company that had been established to disrupt arms sales to the Allies. Since none of these economic operations were actually illegal, the U.S. government could take no official action based on the evidence, but the secretary of the treasury leaked the documents to the *New York World*, thereby striking a propaganda counterblow against the German organization and neutralizing the effectiveness of the exposed operations.

On September 1, 1915 the British authorities arrested James F. J. Archibald in England on the basis of information supplied by Voska's organization in the United States. Archibald was an American newspaperman serving as a courier for German intelligence. Among the papers British intelligence took from Archibald and released to the press were documents revealing Dumba's labor-agitation operations, some of them implicating von Papen as well. Shortly thereafter the U.S. government declared Dumba persona non grata and expelled him.

On October 24, 1915 Secret Service agents, acting on information supplied by the New York City Police Department's Bomb Squad, arrested Robert Fay, a German intelligence demolitions expert, in New Jersey. Although Fay refused to implicate von Papen, circumstantial evidence linked him to the German military attaché's office.

On December 9, 1915 the U.S. government declared both von Papen and Boy-Ed personae non grata. Von Papen departed for Germany on December 21 under an American safe-conduct pass permitting him to travel through Britain en route home. When his ship reached Falmouth British intelligence searched his luggage and seized a mass of documents, including check stubs and other documents linking him to several German agents and saboteurs who had already been identified by Secret Service investigations.

Von Papen was succeeded both as military attaché and case officer by his assistant, Wolf von Igel. On April 18, 1916 agents of the Department of Justice raided von Igel's New York office at the very moment he was preparing to ship the contents of a large safe—the complete records of von Papen's sabotage and subversion operation—to the German embassy in Washington for safekeeping (a coincidence that prompts some historians to speculate that the agents who planned the raid had access to information obtained either through British intelligence radio intercepts or the Secret Service's wiretapping). The seventy pounds of papers were confiscated by the Justice Department and yielded a complete picture—down to agents' names, addresses, and telephone numbers—of the von Papen-von Igel apparatus.

The von Igel raid did not enable U.S. counterintelligence to roll up the entire German sabotage organization in America, however, because in the twenty months since war had broken out in Europe German intelligence had established extensive assets independent of the official cover provided by the German legation. The fires and explosions in plants, storage facilities, and cargo ships continued unabated (the massive Black Tom blast occurred on July 30th, more than three months after the von Igel raid).

The counterintelligence role of the Bureau of Investigation was established on July 1, 1916, when Congress authorized it to conduct investigations on behalf of the State Department.

Intelligence During American Belligerency: The American declaration of war against Germany on April 6, 1917 brought Army and Navy intelligence the support that had been lacking for so long. Within a month the Military Intelligence Section, a separate intelligence unit, was established within the War College Division of the Army's General Staff under Maj. RALPH VAN DEMAN. The newly created Section received a massive infusion of personnel—civilian employees and reservists, as well as regular army officers—as did the Office of Naval Intelligence.

The sudden enrichment of the military and naval intelligence services came too late in the war for them to make a corresponding increase in their output of positive strategic intelligence. Positive intelligence regarding the Central Powers and other European nations was already well-covered by the British and French intelligence services in any case, and the Wilson administration continued to receive most of its strategic intelligence from the British through the established channels of Wiseman, Gaunt, and the London embassy. The formal alliance between the United States and Britain led to even closer cooperation between the State Department and British intelligence, manifest in such functions as a joint Anglo-American secret intelligence mission in revolutionary Russia (see W. SOMERSET

MAUGHAM). The American military and naval attachés in Europe were, for the most part, reduced to the role of liaison officers with their Allied counterparts.

American Intelligence Overseas

Field or tactical intelligence for the American forces in Europe was another matter, and both the Army and Navy swiftly established intelligence units within their respective headquarters staffs in France and England. The General Staff of Gen. John J. Pershing's American Expeditionary Force in France established G-2, the intelligence section, under Maj. DENNIS E. NOLAN. G-2 furnished a complete range of positive military intelligence products—enemy order of battle, maps and terrain studies, etc.—as well as such negative intelligence services as field counterintelligence and censorship. G-2 also ran a highly effective communications intelligence unit, the Radio Intelligence Section, which performed radio interception, traffic analysis, and cryptanalysis in the field, and even intercepted enemy field telephone and carrier-pigeon communications. Vice Adm. William S. Sims, commander of U.S. naval forces in Europe, established an intelligence unit within his headquarters staff under Comdr. John V. Babcock.

G-2 units were also included in the general staffs of the American Expeditionary Forces sent to Siberia and northern Russia during 1918–19.

Domestic Counterintelligence

Back in the United States, ONI and Van Deman's Military Intelligence Section concentrated on counterintelligence and countersubversion, areas which appeared to be of critical importance in light of the two-year record of fires, explosions, strikes, propaganda, and political agitation of the German covert action campaign in America. The Military Intelligence Section established a very extensive Negative Branch, which was concerned with such matters as counterespionage within both the Army and the civilian population; censorship of foreign mail, military information, etc.; monitoring persons of intelligence interest traveling to or from foreign countries; and investigating cases of graft and fraud arising from Army procurement of war material. M.I.8, the Section's cryptanalysis unit (see HERBERT O. YARDLEY), nominally a part of the Positive Branch, devoted much of its resources to counterintelligence cases. Additionally, the Section established a Corps of Intelligence Police to serve as counterintelligence agents both at home and abroad.

ONI also focused on counterintelligence, both at home and in Latin America. The Aids for Information, a network of counterintelligence officers, worked within the various naval districts of the United States, while other ONI agents traveled undercover through Cuba, Mexico, Guatemala, and South America on the lookout for suspected German submarine bases and wireless stations.

Domestic counterintelligence became the primary responsibility of the Justice Department's Bureau of Investigation soon after the declaration of war, and its staff was increased from three hundred agents to four hundred soon after the declaration of war. Even this one-third expansion of the Bureau's force proved inadequate to meet its enormous workload, which included monitoring some one million registered "enemy" aliens in the United States (i.e., nationals of the Central Powers nations who happened to be living in the United States, and who were for the most part immigrants awaiting American citizenship), enforcing the new draft-registration law and ESPIONAGE ACTS, and investigating the rash of (mostly groundless) reports of German spies and saboteurs made by a newly spy-conscious public.

The American Protective League

To augment his meager agent staff in the face of this escalating workload, Bureau director A. BRUCE BIELASKI imprudently accepted the offer of the AMERICAN PROTECTIVE LEAGUE to act as an unpaid volunteer auxiliary force. The League was a loosely organized group of a quarter of a million citizens, most of whom had no more qualification for counterintelligence than an ardent desire to play spy-catcher. Elevated to quasi-official status by the Bureau's sponsorship, the League soon achieved a deplorable record of illegal arrests, harassment, wiretaps, and other violations of privacy and civil rights. Unfortunately the Bureau was not alone in its cooperation with the League. Both the Army's Military Intelligence Section and the ONI worked closely with the League in the domestic counterintelligence field.

Germany's Mexican-based Operations

The spy-mania that spawned the League and focused the energies of Army and Navy intelligence on "the enemy within" was not entirely unfounded, of course. With the departure of von Bernstorff and the rest of the German legation from Washington, the German espionage and sabotage organization did not close up shop and go home. Instead it transferred its base of operations to Mexico City where it came under the general direction of Heinrich von Eckardt, the German ambassador to Mexico. Mexican-based

German agents such as LOTHAR WITZKE crossed and recrossed the U.S. border to carry out sabotage, espionage, and subversive activities under the operational direction of KURT JAHNKE, the chief of German Naval Intelligence in America.

Germany's Mexican-based apparatus was soon penetrated by the U.S. and British intelligence services, however. The Army's Military Intelligence Section recruited Paul Bernardo Altendorf, an Austrian Pole living in Mexico; Altendorf succeeded in infiltrating the German apparatus. William Neuhoffer, a German-American working for the Justice Department's Bureau of Investigation, went to Mexico posing as a draft-dodger and was also accepted into the German organization. William Gleaves, a black Canadian working for British Naval Intelligence, also penetrated the Mexican-based network. There may have been other penetrations; these three became known when they capped their counterintelligence activities with the arrest and conviction of Lothar Witzke, one of the Black Tom saboteurs and the only German agent sentenced to death in the United States (but later pardoned) during the war.

The Inquiry

One sign of America's growing intelligence sophistication was President Wilson's creation of a small BASIC INTELLIGENCE organization shortly after American entry into the war. Known as "the Inquiry," the group was established by presidential advisor Col. Edward M. House and consisted of a panel of experts—mostly college professors who specialized in history, economics, geography, and ethnography—who were asked to study the problems of the postwar peace that Wilson anticipated (see PARIS PEACE CONFERENCE OF 1919).

Consequences: While earlier American wars prompted temporary concern with intelligence and ad hoc measures to provide needed intelligence apparatus, U.S. involvement in the First World War brought about a permanent American intelligence establishment. After the war the Congress created the post of under secretary of state, thereby institutionalizing the intelligence coordination function that the Department's counselor, Frank Polk, had performed during the war. The Military Intelligence Division became a formal part of the War Department's General Staff, and G-2 units became fixed elements of all staffs down to the division level. Within the Navy, the creation of the post of chief of naval operations (CNO) in 1915, and the subordination of ONI and the War Plans Division to the CNO, elevated intelligence to a general staff level within the Navy, and integrated it into the Navy's war planning activities.

The establishment of the Inquiry in 1917; its subsequent transformation into the Territorial, Economic, and Political Intelligence Division of the American Peace Commission at Versailles; and the other intelligence components of the Commission (see PARIS PEACE CONFERENCE OF 1919) represented the first effort to institutionalize a mechanism whereby strategic national intelligence could be put in the service of American foreign policy. Although this apparatus was dissolved at the end of the conference, the lessons learned were not forgotten, and many of the participants later played a role in forming the American intelligence establishment in the SECOND WORLD WAR.

The war saw the first widespread military use of the wireless. Consequently communications intelligence played a major role. In this area radio interception, direction finding, and traffic analysis were combined with the much older techniques of cryptanalysis. M.I.8., the communication intelligence unit of the Military Intelligence Section, was born, and continued its existence as the joint War-State Cipher Bureau after the war (see AMERICAN BLACK CHAMBER, HERBERT O. YARDLEY). The Office of Naval Communications was created and shortly gave birth (1924) to the Navy's own communications intelligence service, Op-20-G (see NAVAL INTELLIGENCE). The introduction of radio COMINT marked the beginning of the new era of high technology in intelligence.

The massive German campaign of sabotage and subversion affected American intelligence in both positive and negative ways. The FBI was given a permanent counterintelligence role, and Army and Navy intelligence developed extensive institutional experience in counterintelligence. However, the great emphasis on counterintelligence within the Army and Navy may have created a functional imbalance in those departments' intelligence activities during the period between the wars that was detrimental to their positive intelligence activities. And the official encouragement of the American Protective League created a Frankenstein's monster of vigilantism that continued to affect American public affairs adversely well into the 1950s.

(Landau, *The Enemy Within*; Tuchman, *The Zimmermann Telegram*; Jeffreys-Jones, *American Espionage*; Jones and Hollister, *The German Secret Service in America, 1914–1918*; Fowler, *British-American Relations, 1917–1918*; Bernstorff, *My Three Years in America*; Whitehead, *The FBI Story*; Millis, *Road to War*; Rintelen, *The*

Dark Invader; Katz, *The Secret War in Mexico*; Papen, *Memoirs*.)

FITZGERALD, DESMOND (ca. 1910–July 23, 1967): lawyer, intelligence officer

A native of New York City, FitzGerald attended St. Mark's School at Southboro, Massachusetts, graduated from Harvard University in 1932 and from Harvard Law School in 1935. He practiced law in New York City until enlisting as a private in the U.S. Army in the Second World War.

FitzGerald was assigned to the Office of Strategic Services, serving in the China-Burma-India theater. He was a liaison officer with the Chinese army in Burma and China and rose to the rank of major. His decorations included the Bronze Star and the Burma and China ribbons. After the war he returned to the practice of law in New York and was active in reform politics in that city.

FitzGerald joined the Central Intelligence Agency in 1951 and became deputy chief of the Far East Division of the Office of Policy Coordination, as the CIA's Clandestine Service department was then known. He served under Col. RICHARD STILWELL, LLOYD GEORGE, and GEORGE AURELL during their respective tenures as chiefs of the FE Division, and worked closely with Col. EDWARD LANSDALE during the latter's covert campaign to bring about the election of Ramon Magsaysay as president of the Philippines. FitzGerald recruited fellow New Yorker GABRIEL KAPLAN into the CIA's FE Division to go to the Philippines and work with Lansdale in CIA-sponsored community development programs.

FitzGerald subsequently became chief of the China Command, a field group based in Japan, which managed the Agency's Chinese operations. He later served as chief of political and paramilitary warfare on the Covert Action staff of the Plans Directorate, as the CIA's Clandestine Service was then called. In that capacity he advised against CIA support for the ill-fated INDONESIA REBELLION. In 1958 he became chief of the FE Division. In 1963 he was put in charge of the Special Affairs Staff, a CIA task force set up to remove Fidel Castro and his regime in Cuba. The operation, known by the code name MONGOOSE, involved several unsuccessful attempts to assassinate Castro.

In 1964 FigzGerald was made chief of the Western Hemisphere Division of the Plans Directorate. In June 1966 he succeeded RICHARD HELMS as deputy director for plans, i.e., chief of CIA CLANDESTINE SERVICE. As DDP, FitzGerald collected intelligence that enabled the Agency to furnish President Johnson with an accurate prediction of the Six Day War be-tween the Arabs and Israelis in June 1967. FitzGerald died of a heart attack while playing tennis a few weeks later. President Johnson posthumously awarded him the National Security Medal.

(Smith, *Portrait of a Cold Warrior*; Alsop, *The Center*; Powers, *The Man Who Kept the Secrets*; Phillips, *The Night Watch*; New York Times, September 3, 1939, section II, p. 1; obituary, *New York Times*, July 24, 1967, p. 27; *New York Times*, September 16, 1967, p. 68.)

FLORES, THOMAS JOHN, JR. (March 12, 1923–): Clandestine Service officer

A native of Illinois, Flores served in the U.S. Army in 1940–46 and was discharged with the rank of captain. He graduated from Georgetown University in 1950 and went on to serve with the Central Intelligence Agency. He was attached to the Department of State in San José, Costa Rica in 1953–57. In 1960–63 he was assigned to Montevideo, Uruguay, where he acted as CIA chief of station. Later he became chief of the Cuban Branch of the CIA CLANDESTINE SERVICE in Washington. In 1967 Flores was assigned to Caracas, Venezuela.

(Agee, *Inside the Company*; *Who's Who in Government*, 1st ed.)

FLYNN, WILLIAM JAMES (November 18, 1867–October 13, 1928): law enforcement officer, government official

A native of New York City, Flynn was educated in the public schools. He joined the SECRET SERVICE in 1897 and served in that organization continuously until 1917, except for a period of eight months in 1910–11 when he was on detached service with the New York City Police Department to reorganize the Detective Bureau. From 1912 to 1917 he was chief of the Secret Service.

In September 1918 he was appointed chief of the secret service of the U.S. Railroad Administration, an agency that was formed to run the American railroads on an emergency basis during the First World War, and that was terminated in 1920.

In July 1919 Flynn was appointed director of the Bureau of Investigation of the Justice Department (see FEDERAL BUREAU OF INVESTIGATION). In August 1921 he was dismissed by President Warren G. Harding's attorney general, Harry M. Daugherty, who appointed William J. Burns as his successor.

(*Who Was Who in America*, v. 1; Whitehead, *The FBI Story*.)

FORD, COREY (April 29, 1902–July 27, 1969): writer, humorist, espionologist, OSS officer

A native of New York City, Ford attended Columbia University, where he was editor of the campus humor magazine. After graduating in 1923 he wrote humorous pieces, often including literary parodies, for popular magazines. He was one of the group of humorists of the 1920s and 1930s that included Robert Benchley, James Thurber, Frank Sullivan, Ring Lardner, Don Marquis, and Dorothy Parker.

During the Second World War Ford was commissioned a colonel in the U.S. Army Air Corps and served as a liaison officer with the Office of Strategic Services. After the war he collaborated with Alistair MacBain on *Cloak and Dagger,* a book about the OSS. The book, which included an account of the experiences of MICHAEL BURKE, was made into a motion picture. Ford also wrote a history of espionage in the American Revolution (*A Peculiar Service,* 1965) and a biography of OSS director, Gen. WILLIAM J. DONOVAN (*Donovan of the OSS,* 1970). An enthusiastic outdoorsman, he became an associate editor and columnist for *Field and Stream* magazine.

(*Who Was Who in America,* vol. 5; obituary, *New York Times,* July 28, 1969.)

FORD, FRANKLIN LEWIS (December 26, 1920–): historian, educator, intelligence officer

A native of Waukegan, Illinois, Ford graduated from the University of Minnesota in 1942. He served in the U.S. Army during 1943–46 and was assigned to the Office of Strategic Services. He served as an intelligence analyst in the OSS RESEARCH AND ANALYSIS BRANCH in France and Germany.

After the war Ford earned an M.A. and Ph.D. from Harvard University. He taught at Bennington College during 1949–52 and joined the faculty of Harvard University in 1953. He was dean of the Harvard Faculty of Arts and Sciences during 1962–70. Since 1968 he has been McLean Professor of Ancient and Modern History.

(Smith, *OSS; Who's Who in America,* 42nd ed.)

FORD, JOHN (February 1, 1895–August 31, 1973): filmmaker, naval officer, intelligence officer

A native of Cape Elizabeth, Maine, Ford was born Sean O'Feeney (sometimes written as the Gaelic O'Fearna). He was raised in Portland, Maine, where he attended local schools. In 1914, after attending

William J. Flynn. Source: Library of Congress.

the University of Maine for a short time, he followed his brother Francis to Hollywood. He changed his name to John Ford and was employed by motion-picture studios as a property man. He learned film-making by performing a variety of jobs in the motion-picture industry, and after a year became an assistant director. By 1919 he was directing feature films for Fox Studios. He received major recognition in 1935 when his film *The Informer* won the Academy Award for best direction and was a critical and popular success.

Ford held a commission as lieutenant commander in the U.S. Naval Reserve, and in 1940 he began assembling a reserve unit composed of some 200 experienced Hollywood filmmakers. In October 1941 Ford and his unit were assigned to the Office of the Coordinator of Information, the predecessor to the Office of Strategic Services. This assignment was at the suggestion of MERIAN C. COOPER, the filmmaker best known for creating and directing the original 1933 version of *King Kong.* Cooper was then serving as special assistant to Col. WILLIAM J. DONOVAN, the coordinator of information.

Ford and thirty of his men from the reserve unit

John Ford, while serving in the Office of Strategic Services. Source: National Archives.

became the Field Photographic Division of the COI, later the Field Photographic Unit of the OSS SECRET INTELLIGENCE BRANCH, and yet later (after January 1943) the OSS Field Photographic Branch. Ford's initial job was to produce U.S. documentary films and among the first were documentaries on defense preparations in Panama and Iceland, the first Atlantic convoys to Europe, and a historical account of the PEARL HARBOR ATTACK.

The charter of Ford's unit was later expanded to include the production of OSS training films and documentary records of OSS activities in the field. Among the latter were documentaries on the activities of OSS Detachment 101, the paramilitary unit that operated behind Japanese lines in Burma and China; the missions carried out by the OSS SPECIAL OPERATIONS BRANCH and the OSS OPERATIONAL GROUPS in France, the Balkans, and Italy; and the Normandy landings in June 1944. The unit also accompanied the Allied advance across Europe during 1944–45, filming installations, topography, and combat operations; the newly filmed footage was used immediately for purposes of combat intelligence. This activity was soon institutionalized as the OSS Intelligence Photographic Documentation Project, aimed at establishing a worldwide basic photographic intelligence file of areas and installations of strategic importance.

Ford received several decorations for his wartime service, including the Legion of Merit, the Purple Heart, and the Air Medal. He also received Academy Awards for two of the documentaries he made while with the OSS, *December 7th* and *Midway*.

Ford was discharged with the rank of captain and later served with the rank of rear admiral during the KOREAN WAR. He returned to filmmaking and is perhaps best remembered for the many western films he made starring John Wayne.

(*Who's Who in America*, 37th ed; *Current Biography*, 1941, 1973; Roosevelt, *War Report of the OSS*; Troy, *Donovan and the CIA*.)

FOREIGN BROADCAST INFORMATION SERVICE (FBIS)

In 1939, Hadley Cantril, a Princeton University psychologist and public opinion researcher, and his colleagues established the Princeton Listening Center in order to study Nazi radio propaganda. This pioneering project in propaganda research was taken over by the Federal Communications Commission in 1941 because of its potential value as an open source of intelligence on the Axis powers. As a unit of the FCC staffed by editors, translators, and information analysts, the Listening Center became the Foreign Broadcast Monitoring Service. Liaison was established with a similar service operated by the British Broadcasting Service. The two services exchanged information and divided radio station coverage: the BBC unit concentrated on European stations, while the FCC service covered the rest of the world. The service proved its worth during the war, translating hundreds of thousands of words daily, summarizing them, and disseminating the product to intelligence analysts who gleaned valuable information from the transcripts.

After the war the unit was transferred to the War Department and later became part of the Central Intelligence Group (see CENTRAL INTELLIGENCE AGENCY). The CIA has since operated the Foreign Broadcast Information Service, as it is now known, as "a service of common concern" (in the words of the NATIONAL SECURITY ACT of 1947) for the INTELLIGENCE COMMUNITY, other components of the government, and even journalists and the general public. The scope of FBIS activity has been extended beyond radio broadcasts to include foreign television, newspapers, magazines, and technical, scientific, military, and economic journals—in short, virtually all open sources of information in areas of U.S. foreign intelligence interest.

Liaison and cooperation between the FBIS and the BBC has continued to the present day.

(Troy, *Donovan and the CIA*; Cline, *CIA: Reality vs. Myth*; Meyer, *Facing Reality*; Childs and Whitton, eds., *Propaganda by Short Wave*.)

FORGAN, JAMES RUSSELL (March 12, 1900– January 31, 1974): investment banker, intelligence officer

A native of Evanston, Illinois, Forgan graduated from St. Mark's Preparatory School in Southboro, Massachusetts, in 1918, and from Princeton University in 1922. He worked his way up as clerk, cashier, and vice-president of several Chicago banks until 1927 when he became a vice-president of the investment firm of Brokaw & Company. In 1931 he became a partner in Glore, Forgan & Company in Chicago and New York City.

Forgan was a close friend of ALLEN DULLES. During the SECOND WORLD WAR he was commissioned a lieutenant colonel in the U.S. Army and assigned to the Office of Strategic Services. He was attached to the OSS European headquarters in London, and in 1945 he succeeded DAVID K. E. BRUCE as chief of OSS in the European Theater of Operations. After the war he returned to his banking business.

Among the many decorations Forgan was awarded were the Distinguished Service Medal, the Legion of Merit, the Legion of Honor, the French croix de guerre and the Order of the British Empire. He was also given the Gen. William J. Donovan award of the Veterans of the OSS.

(*Who Was Who in America*, v. 6; Smith, *OSS*.)

FOULK, GEORGE CLAYTON (October 30, 1856–August 6, 1893): naval officer, diplomat

A native of Marietta, Pennsylvania, Foulk graduated third in his class from the U.S. Naval Academy in 1876. After serving with the Asiatic Squadron for several years, he and two other young officers carried out a reconnaissance of Siberia and Russia. In November 1883 he was appointed naval attaché to the newly opened U.S. legation in Seoul, Korea. Apparently his assignment there was more than routine; although he reported through the Office of Naval Intelligence, his orders came directly from President Chester A. Arthur and Secretary of State Frederick Freylinghuysen. In 1885 he was made chargé d'affaires of the Seoul legation.

Foulk performed creditably in a delicate position complicated by court intrigue and the hostility of the Chinese government, which had designs on Korea. In 1887 he was recalled by Washington on the demands of the Chinese government and the Korean Foreign Office, then under Chinese influence.

Foulk, who had married a Japanese, resigned his

James R. Forgan, while serving in the OSS. Source: National Archives.

diplomatic commission and moved to Yokohama, Japan, where he was employed by the American Trading Company. In 1890 he left that position to join the faculty of Doshisha College in Kyoto, where he taught mathematics until his death.

(Dorwart, *The Office of Naval Intelligence; DAB.*)

FRANKEL, SAMUEL BENJAMIN (July 14, 1905–): naval officer, intelligence officer

A native of Cincinnati, Ohio, Frankel graduated from the U.S. Naval Academy in 1929. He served on cruisers and destroyers in American and Far Eastern waters, and later with the Office of Naval Intelligence. In 1936 Frankel and two other junior grade lieutenants were sent to Riga, Latvia, for two years to study the Russian language, a consequence of the recent diplomatic recognition of the Soviet Union by the Roosevelt administration. While there the three collected information about the Soviet Union until the U.S. State Department complained that their intelligence activities might jeopardize Soviet-American relations.

Frankel was assistant naval attaché in Murmansk, USSR, during 1941–44, and naval attaché in China during 1948–50 (he spoke Chinese, in addition to Russian). In 1961 he became deputy director of ONI. During 1961–64 he was chief of staff of the Defense Intelligence Agency. Retiring from the Navy in 1964,

Benjamin Franklin. Source: Library of Congress.

Frankel joined the System Development Corporation where he served as a department manager until his retirement in 1970.

(*Who's Who in America*, 37th ed; Dorwart, *Conflict of Duty*.)

FRANKLIN, BENJAMIN (January 17, 1706– April 17, 1790): printer, scientist, inventor, writer, publisher, government official, diplomat, statesman, intelligence officer

A native of Boston, Franklin was apprenticed as a printer to his brother, James, before moving to Philadelphia in 1723. There he pursued the printing trade and at the age of twenty-four became owner and publisher of the *Pennsylvania Gazette*. In 1732 he began writing and publishing *Poor Richard's Almanack*. He became active in public life, organizing a debating club (which eventually became the American Philosophical Society), establishing a circulating library, a fire company, and an academy, and helping to form a militia. His inventions (e.g., the Franklin stove, bifocal eyeglasses) and his scientific research (e.g., the discovery of the electrical nature of lightning) made him famous in Europe as well as in America.

Franklin was active in colonial government and held the posts of clerk of the Pennsylvania Assembly (1736–51), deputy postmaster at Philadelphia (1737–53), and, jointly with William Hunter, postmaster general of the colonies (1753–74). He went to England on behalf of the Pennsylvania Assembly in 1757 and subsequently became the colonial agent in London for Pennsylvania, Georgia, and Massachusetts. He was instrumental in securing repeal of the Stamp Act in 1766.

Shortly after his return to Philadelphia in 1775 Franklin was chosen a member of the Second Continental Congress and appointed first postmaster general of the United States. He helped draft the Declaration of Independence and was a signer. He became the dominant member of the Continental Congress's foreign policy and foreign intelligence arm, the COMMITTEE OF SECRET CORRESPONDENCE, and was instrumental in sending SILAS DEANE to France in 1776 to negotiate for French military aid.

In September 1776 Franklin, Deane, and Arthur Lee were appointed members of a diplomatic commission to France. He arrived in France in December and remained there throughout the war, serving, in effect, as the American ambassador (in September 1778, Congress appointed him American minister plenipotentiary, making him the sole American representative in France). He played a crucial role in securing an alliance with the French and in preserving it during the war.

Franklin and his fellow commissioners became prime targets of British intelligence as soon as they arrived in France, and the British quickly recruited Franklin's friend and protégé, EDWARD BANCROFT, the secretary of the American ministry. Franklin's apparent failure to perceive Bancroft's treachery is offered by one historian, Cecil B. Currey, as evidence that Franklin was himself a British agent; the theory has gained little currency among other historians who cite Franklin's crucial role in the vital French alliance. ALLEN DULLES, in his study of the craft of intelligence, speculates that Franklin was aware of Bancroft's double role, but suggests that Franklin exploited it to play back disinformation to the British. And during 1777 Franklin may actually have wanted Britain to be well-informed on his progress toward a French alliance, which he might have seen as an inducement to the British to sign an early peace with the Americans.

Dulles follows espionologist Bakeless in believing that Franklin had an extensive intelligence service of his own in England, including some highly placed sources within the government. Franklin did indeed have many powerful friends in England, people he knew from his long years as a colonial agent in

London. And he secretly corresponded with many of them, including Cabinet ministers and opposition political leaders, during the war.

Franklin's influential contacts enabled him to elicit unofficial British peace overtures during the war. A master of intrigue himself, he perceived that most such early feelers were simply attempts to drive a wedge between France and the United States and so end the vital alliance. He was also aware that he and his fellow commissioners were the object of close surveillance by the French secret service, which was on the alert for any sign pointing to such a separate peace. His shrewdness, wit, and good humor enabled him to steer a steady course through this labyrinthine situation and preserve American interests.

Franklin summed up his policy for dealing with such problems in a reply to a friend who had warned him that he was "surrounded by spies":

> I have long observ'd one Rule which prevents any Inconvenience from such Practices. It is simply this, to be concern'd in no Affairs that I should blush to have made publick, and to do nothing but what Spies may see & welcome. When a Man's Actions are just and honourable, the more they are known, the more his Reputation is increas'd and establish'd. If I was sure, therefore that my Valet de Place was a Spy, as probably he is, I think I should not discharge him for that, if in other Respects I lik'd him.

In 1781 Congress appointed Franklin one of three American commissioners authorized to negotiate a peace treaty with Britain. He guided these delicate negotiations to a successful conclusion in September 1783.

Franklin returned to Philadelphia in 1785 and was soon chosen president of the Pennsylvania Executive Council, a post in which he served until 1788. He was a member of the Constitutional Convention in May 1787 and was instrumental in bringing about the Convention's unanimous adoption of the Constitution.

(Van Doren, *Benjamin Franklin*; Boatner, *Encyclopedia of the American Revolution*; Morris, *The Peacemakers*; Shoenbrun, *Triumph in Paris*; Auger, *The Secret War of Independence*; Bendiner, *The Virgin Diplomats*; Bakeless, *Turncoats, Traitors and Heroes*; Dulles, *The Craft of Intelligence*; Currey, *Code Number 72*.)

FREEDOM COMPANY OF THE PHILIPPINES

Col. EDWARD G. LANSDALE of the Far Eastern Division of the CIA CLANDESTINE SERVICE estab-

lished this organization in November 1954. The purpose of the Freedom Company was to provide cover for Filipinos who had helped defeat the Communist Huk guerrillas by working on CIA-sponsored community development programs in the Philippines, and who were to perform a similar function in Vietnam.

Lansdale used the Freedom Company to assist in establishing the Diem regime in Vietnam. The company helped write the constitution of Vietnam, train the Vietnamese president's Guard Battalion, and organize the Vietnamese Veterans Legion. The Company also ran the CIA-funded Operation Brotherhood, which resettled Vietnamese refugees from the Communist north.

In 1957 the Freedom Company was transformed into a profit-making firm, the Eastern Construction Company, which no longer received direct support from the CIA, but which retained close ties to the Agency.

See VIETNAM WAR.

(Smith, *Portrait of a Cold Warrior*; Lansdale, *In the Midst of Wars*; New York Times, *The Pentagon Papers*.)

FRIEDMAN, WILLIAM FREDERICK (September 24, 1891–November 12, 1969): geneticist, cryptologist

Born in Kishinev, Russia, Friedman was the son of a Romanian linguist who emigrated with his family to the United States in 1893, at which time the child's given name was changed from Wolfe to William. The family settled in Pittsburgh, Pennsylvania.

Friedman graduated from Cornell University in 1914 and did graduate work in genetics there in 1914–15. George Fabyan, owner of Riverbank Laboratories in Geneva, Illinois, hired him to work as an agricultural geneticist.

Fabyan was a wealthy textile merchant who maintained Riverbank in order to dabble in several fields of interest to him—acoustics, chemistry, genetics, and cryptology. His interest in the latter arose from his belief that Francis Bacon was the actual author of Shakespeare's plays, and that proof of this thesis was somehow enciphered in the original folios and manuscripts attributed to Shakespeare.

Through his work in cryptography at Riverbank, Friedman discovered that he possessed considerable talent in the subject. Fabyan put him to work on the Shakespeare project and, by 1917, Friedman was director of the Riverbank Cipher Department as well as the Genetics Department. While at Riverbank he met and married Elizabeth Smith, one of the cryptologists working on the project; Elizabeth and

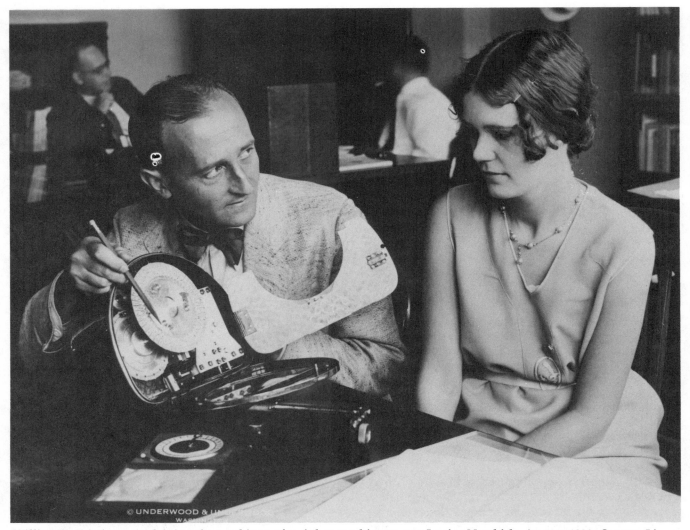

William F. Friedman explaining the workings of a cipher machine to one Louise Newkirk, August 1930. Source: Library of Congress.

William Friedman were destined to become two of America's leading code-breakers.

Because Riverbank was, at the time, the only cryptological center in the United States, it was enlisted to assist the federal government during the First World War. Friedman broke a cipher used by Indian revolutionaries who were attempting to purchase arms illegally in the United States for use in overthrowing British rule in their homeland. He also demonstrated to the British the penetrability of their cipher system, which they believed could not be broken.

Shortly after America's entry into the war, the U.S. Army sent a class of four officers to Riverbank to receive a cram course in cryptanalysis from Freidman. The course was so successful that several sub-sequent groups, one numbering sixty officers, were sent to Riverbank for the same training. In June 1918 Freidman was commissioned a first lieutenant in Army Intelligence and sent to France, where he solved German military ciphers.

Before leaving for France, Friedman wrote a series of seven technical monographs for use in training student cryptanalysts, and he added an eighth when he returned to Riverbank after the war. These documents are now regarded as a landmark in the history of cryptology. One of the series, *The Index of Coincidence and Its Applications in Cryptography*, introduced sophisticated statistical methods into cryptography and, in effect, transformed cryptography from a special art into a branch of applied statistics. Friedman regarded *The Index of Coincidence* as his greatest single contribution to the field of cryptology, and students of the subject describe it as a monumental development.

Friedman and his wife left Riverbank in 1920 and, on January 1, 1921 he began a six-month contract with the U.S. Signal Corps to devise cryptosystems. At the end of that period he became a permanent employee of the War Department. After a period of teaching a course in military codes and ciphers for the Signal Corps, he became the Corps' chief cryptanalyst (Friedman coined the word *cryptanalysis*—now well-established—to distinguish cipher-breaking from *decipherment*, the authorized conversion of cryptograms to plaintext. See CRYPTOLOGY).

During the next several years he became well-known because of his patents for several cipher machines, his cryptanalysis of some messages in the Teapot Dome scandal, and his involvement in the cryptological aspects of several other public affairs. By 1929 he was widely recognized as one of the world's leading authorities on cryptology and he was invited to write the article on Codes and Ciphers in the *Encyclopedia Britannica*.

In 1929 the Signal Intelligence Service was established within the Signal Corps (see ARMY INTELLIGENCE, CRYPTOLOGY) and Friedman was made its director. The function of the SIS was to create codes and ciphers for use by the Army, break foreign codes and ciphers, and conduct training and research in cryptology. Friedman recruited a small staff of linguists and mathematicians into the Service.

In August 1940 Friedman and his staff managed to break PURPLE, the War Departments' code word for the extremely difficult cipher that the Japanese Foreign Office put into use a year earlier (see PEARL HARBOR ATTACK). The enormous mental effort took its toll, and he was hospitalized with a nervous breakdown a few months later. Although Friedman later returned only to limited duty, he remained chief cryptologist and director of the SIS, and continued in this capacity when the agency became part of the Army Security Agency in 1945 (see ARMY INTELLIGENCE).

In 1947, with the liquidation of the War Department and the creation of the Department of Defense, he became cryptologist for the new Department. When the Defense Department's cryptological operations were moved into the newly created NATIONAL SECURITY AGENCY in 1952, he went along and became the NSA's chief technical consultant and special assistant to the director. He retired in 1955, but continued to serve as a consultant to NSA. He was awarded the Medal for Merit, the National Security Medal, and the War Department's Exceptional Service Award.

In 1956 Congress awarded Friedman $100,000 as compensation for the royalties he had not been able to earn on his cryptological patents because of security considerations. In 1957 William and Elizabeth Friedman published *The Shakespearean Ciphers Examined*, in which they analyzed in depth Fabyan's theory that Bacon was the author of Shakespeare's plays—which had originally brought them together, both in marriage and their careers in cryptography—and found it without serious merit.

(Kahn, *The Codebreakers*; Bamford, *The Puzzle Palace*; *Who Was Who in America*, v.5; Clark, *The Man Who Broke Purple*.)

G

G-2

1) The assistant chief of staff for intelligence in the general staff of the Department of the Army; 2) the military intelligence unit(s) of the U.S. Army; 3) chief of intelligence in the general staff of an Army command level of division or higher.

The term was introduced in 1917 to designate the intelligence division of the general staff of Gen. John J. Pershing's American Expeditionary Force in France. After Pershing's general staff structure was adopted by the War Department in 1920, G-2 became the shorthand designation of the assistant chief of staff for intelligence, and also an alternate designation for the Department's Military Intelligence Division (see ARMY INTELLIGENCE). Because the general staffs of subordinate command levels down to the division followed the same structure, intelligence officers attached to such staffs also came to be designated G-2s.

The term G-2 was commonly used to designate the entire Army intelligence organization from the 1920s onward, but it has fallen into relative disuse in recent years, probably because of the more complex arrangement of intelligence components within the Army since the 1960s.

At times the term has been adopted by some foreign countries, e.g., Cuba and Ireland, to designate their military intelligence services.

See also S-2.

GADE, JOHN ALLYNE (February 10, 1875–August 16, 1955): architect, banker, diplomat, naval officer, intelligence officer

A native of Cambridge, Massachusetts, Gade attended schools in Norway, Germany, and France. He graduated from Harvard University in 1896, practiced architecture in New York City for fifteen years, and during 1916–17, was active in war relief work.

Gade was an officer in the U.S. Naval Reserve as well as a friend of Franklin D. Roosevelt, then the assistant secretary of the Navy. He attained the rank of captain in the Reserve and during 1917–19, he served as naval attaché with the U.S. legation in Copenhagen, Denmark (his brother, Horace Upton Gade, was naval attaché in Norway at the same time). Gade established close ties with the intelligence services of the other Allies and studied their methods of espionage and counterespionage. In 1919 he represented the U.S. State Department in the Baltic provinces. While in that position he urged the Navy to appoint a permanent peacetime naval attaché to Scandinavia, from which vantage point the officer might "observe Russian conditions and report upon and counteract Bolshevism, as well as study the Russian press."

Gade resigned from government service and entered the Wall Street banking firm of White, Weld and Company, but he continued to concern himself with questions of intelligence. In 1929 he offered officers of ONI and ARMY INTELLIGENCE a critical analysis of what he described as the "foreign information service" of the United States. He compared it to the European intelligence services he had studied and concluded that "we were amateurs where they were past masters," and that the United States had failed to profit from its experience in the FIRST WORLD WAR. One of Gade's chief criticisms of the American system was the rivalry between the competing intelligence components of the Army, the Navy, and the State Department, and he proposed "some sort of a central Intelligence Agency" reporting directly to the president.

While different in detail, Gade's plan for a central intelligence agency was similar in concept to the proposals offered by Gen. WILLIAM J. DONOVAN fifteen years later, proposals that eventually evolved into the charter of the CENTRAL INTELLIGENCE AGENCY. Thomas F. Troy, author of an official CIA internal history of the early days of the Agency, credits Gade with being the first to pinpoint the defects of the pre-1941 American intelligence system and to propose a central intelligence agency. Gade proved to be too far ahead of his time, however, and his proposal was ignored and buried in the files of ONI.

In 1938 Gade returned to active duty in the Navy and served as naval attaché at the American embassy in Brussels and the U.S. legation in Lisbon. He retired from active duty in 1940. He was awarded the Navy Cross and other decorations.

Gade published an account of his experiences as a naval attaché, *All My Born Days*, in 1942.

(*Who Was Who in America*, v. 3; *Who's Who in New York*, 8th ed. (1924); Dorwart, *The Office of Naval Intelligence, Conflict of Duty*; Troy, *Donovan and the CIA*.)

GALLOWAY, DONALD: Army officer, intelligence officer

During the late 1940s Colonel Galloway was deputy director, and later director, of the Office of Special Operations, the SECRET INTELLIGENCE unit of the CENTRAL INTELLIGENCE AGENCY. He was brought into the Agency by then Director of Central Intelligence HOYT S. VANDENBERG.

(Powers, *The Man Who Kept the Secrets*.)

GALLOWAY, JOSEPH (1731–August 29, 1803): lawyer, legislator, government official, British secret agent, intelligence officer

A native of West River, Maryland, Galloway studied law at Princeton and earned an LL.D. from that institution. He served in the Pennsylvania Assembly and was speaker of that body during 1766–75. As a delegate to the First Continental Congress in 1774, Galloway proposed what became known as "Galloway's Plan of Union," a compromise plan to resolve American grievances against Britain by giving the colonies something approaching dominion status (the plan was defeated by a single vote).

Galloway began working as a British secret agent in 1774, while serving in the Continental Congress. He sent his information to London through William Franklin, the Tory son of BENJAMIN FRANKLIN.

Joseph Galloway. Source: Author's collection.

He may have been one of the spies who provided the British with plans showing the location of the underwater obstacles the Americans had placed in the Delaware River near Philadelphia.

Having aroused the suspicion of the Patriots, Galloway sought the protection of British Gen. William Howe and subsequently ran a secret intelligence service for him. He secured military maps of Pennsylvania and collected intelligence he later claimed was instrumental to the British victory at the Battle of Brandywine (September 11, 1777).

During the British occupation of Philadelphia (September 1777–June 1778) Galloway was appointed superintendent of police and of the port. He continued to operate his secret service, which, he later stated, consisted of "upwards of 80 Spies," and obtained valuable intelligence on American recruiting, strength, troop positions, and hospitals, as well as inside information of the proceedings of the Continental Congress. He acquired detailed information on American fortifications at Valley Forge and provided Adm. Richard Howe with navigational information regarding the Delaware River. He also entertained plans at various times to kidnap several New Jersey officials

Robert M. Gates. Source: Central Intelligence Agency.

and even the entire Continental Congress, although none of these daring schemes was ever attempted.

After the British evacuation of Philadelphia, Galloway went to London as a spokesman for the American Loyalists. He charged General Howe with incompetence in testimony before the House of Commons, and published pamphlets to the same effect. For his part, Howe claimed that Galloway's intelligence services had been incompetent and of little value.

Galloway's petition to return to America in 1793 was rejected. He remained in England for the rest of his life.

(Bakeless, *Turncoats, Traitors and Heroes*; Van Doren, *Secret History of the American Revolution*; Boatner, *Encyclopedia of the American Revolution*; *Who Was Who in America*, historical volume.)

GARDNER, JOHN WILLIAM (October 8, 1912–): psychologist, government official, public advocate, OSS psychological assessment officer

A native of Los Angeles, Gardner received a bachelor's and master's degree from Stanford University in 1935 and 1936, respectively, and a Ph.D. from the University of California in 1938. He taught psychology at the University of California, Connecticut College, and Mount Holyoke College between 1936 and 1942, when he became head of the Latin-American section of the FOREIGN BROADCAST INFORMATION SERVICE of the Federal Communications Commission. In 1943 he received a commission as a first lieutenant in the U.S. Marine Corps and was assigned to the OFFICE OF STRATEGIC SERVICES. He assisted Harvard psychologist HENRY MURRAY in setting up the OSS's West Coast psychological assessment program at the Capistrano Beach Club in San Clemente, California. He also served in the Mediterranean and European theaters of war.

After the war Gardner held various prestigious positions, including president of the Carnegie Corporation from 1955 to 1965, and secretary of health, education and welfare, from 1965 to 1968. Later he was chairman of the Urban Coalition (1968–70) and founder and president of the public interest organization Common Cause (1970–77). He has also held various teaching positions.

(*Who's Who in America*, 42nd. ed.; Marks, *The Search for the "Manchurian Candidate"*; Roosevelt, *War Report of the OSS*.)

GATES, ROBERT MICHAEL (September 25, 1943–): intelligence officer

A native of Wichita, Kansas, Gates graduated from the College of William and Mary in 1965 and earned a master's degree in history from Indiana University in 1966. That same year he joined the Central Intelligence Agency, where he served successively as a current intelligence analyst, a member of the staff of the special assistant to the director of central intelligence for Strategic Arms Limitations, and as one of two assistant national intelligence officers for strategic programs.

In 1974 Gates earned a doctorate in Russian and Soviet history from Georgetown University. That same year he was assigned to the NATIONAL SECURITY COUNCIL staff, a position he held for six years. He subsequently was appointed to a series of administrative positions and served as national intelligence officer for the Soviet Union prior to his appointment as deputy director for intelligence in 1982. In September 1983 he was made, concurrent with his position as DDI, chairman of the National Intelligence Council, the body that produces the NATIONAL INTELLIGENCE ESTIMATES.

In April 1986 Gates was appointed deputy director of central intelligence, succeeding John N. McMahon in that post. In February 1987 President Ronald Reagan nominated Gates to succeed WILLIAM J. CASEY as director of central intelligence. However, Gates's knowledge of the Reagan administration's secret overtures to Iran, and congressional pique over the administration's failure to inform Congress of that matter, prompted doubts that Gates's appointment would be confirmed. Although Gates was confident of receiving confirmation, he asked that his nomination as DCI be withdrawn in order to protect the intelligence community from the negative effects of a prolonged political debate over the matter in the Senate. He continued to serve as DDCI under WILLIAM WEBSTER.

Gates holds the Intelligence Medal of Merit and the Arthur S. Fleming Award.

(Central Intelligence Agency, *Fact Book on Intelligence; New York Times*, February 3, 1987, p. A12.)

GEORGE, LLOYD: intelligence officer.

An American intelligence officer who worked with the Thai resistance during the Second World War, George became chief of the Far East Division of the Office of Special Operations of the CENTRAL INTELLIGENCE AGENCY (OSO was the designation given to the Strategic Services Unit when it became part of the Central Intelligence Group in 1946—see CENTRAL INTELLIGENCE AGENCY). With the merger of the OSO and the Office of Policy Coordination to form the CIA's Plans Directorate in 1952, George became chief of the Far East Division of Plans, and as such he was responsible for both SECRET INTELLIGENCE and COVERT ACTION in the Far East. During the mid-1950s George was deputy chief, and later chief, of the CIA's North Asia Command, a component headquartered near Tokyo, Japan, and responsible for the Agency's covert operations in Japan, Korea, Taiwan, Okinawa, Hong Kong, the Chinese mainland, and the Philippines.

(Smith, *Portrait of a Cold Warrior;* Hunt, *Undercover.*)

GIROSI, MARCELLO: journalist, filmmaker, intelligence officer

Girosi was a prominent Italian-American journalist in New York City in 1943 when his family connections with the Italian navy came to the attention of the Office of Strategic Services. Girosi's brother, Adm. Massimo Girosi, was a member of the Italian navy's Supreme Command, and another brother, Cesare, was a commander in the Italian navy (their father had been an admiral). OSS officer JOHN SHAHEEN thought Marcello Girosi could be prevailed on to approach Admiral Girosi with a proposal to surrender the Italian navy to the Allies (since the Girosis were royalists, it was hoped the admiral might be antipathetic to Mussolini).

Girosi was recruited into the OSS and assigned to the operation, which had been given the code name Project MacGregor (the MacGregor team also included MICHAEL BURKE, JOHN RINGLING NORTH, and PETER TOMKINS). The operation was overtaken by events, however. Unknown to Shaheen, surrender negotiations between the Italian naval command and the Allies were already under way, and the navy surrendered before the MacGregor operation could be carried out.

However, the MacGregor team achieved a secondary objective: they smuggled a group of Italian weapons specialists out of Italy and back to Washington. The Italians helped the U.S. Navy develop countermeasures against a particularly deadly torpedo they had developed.

After the war Girosi became a motion-picture producer and made several Italian and American movies starring Sophia Loren.

(Roosevelt, *War Report of the OSS;* Smith, *OSS;* Burke, *Outrageous Good Fortune.*)

GITTINGER, JOHN (ca. 1917–): psychologist, intelligence officer

A native of Oklahoma, Gittinger served in the U.S. Navy as a lieutenant commander during the SECOND WORLD WAR. He worked as a high school guidance counselor and earned a master's degree in psychology. About 1947 he became director of psychological services at the state hospital in Norman, Oklahoma. There he had the opportunity to observe and test a large number of vagrants and itinerants, and the data he collected was the basis for a theory relating different types of human personality to apparently trivial individual characteristics, e.g., how a person held or smoked a cigarette. By observing a wide range of such personal habits, he was able to make an indirect assessment of a subject's personality. He named this technique the Psychological Assessment System.

In 1950 Gittinger joined the Central Intelligence Agency. He became chief of the assessment staff of the Technical Services Division of the CIA CLANDESTINE SERVICE. He and his staff carried out psychological assessments of potential agents and defectors, and advised CIA case officers as to the likely response a recruitment overture would elicit. They also made psychological assessments of recruits to friendly foreign intelligence services that the CIA helped to establish, and a variety of other individuals of interest to Agency covert operations. The personality assessments they made of foreign leaders (e.g., Ferdinand Marcos of the Philippines, the Shah of Iran) were used as an element of positive intelligence.

During the 1950s Gittinger and his staff worked under cover of the Society for Human Ecology, a CIA-funded organization in New York City. In 1962 they moved to Washington and operated as Psychological Assessment Associates, a CIA-proprietary firm. Both of these organizations also funded external research projects to expand and refine Gittinger's system.

Gittinger retired from the CIA in 1973, but continued to work as a contract employee of the Agency for a few years.

(Marks, *The Search for the "Manchurian Candidate"*.)

GLAVIN, EDWARD F.J. (ca. 1903–July 25, 1984): Army officer, educator, intelligence officer

A native of New York City, Glavin graduated from the U.S. Military Academy in 1927 and later earned a degree from Balliol College at Oxford University. He served as military attaché at the American embassy in London, as a regimental adjutant on Governors Island in New York, and after being promoted to the rank of colonel, he was serving as public relations officer for the First Army and Eastern Defense Command in 1943 when he was assigned to the Office of Strategic Services.

Gen. WILLIAM J. DONOVAN appointed Glavin Mediterranean Theater commander, in part as a way of muting Army criticism of previous OSS mismanagement of its activities in Italy. Besides handling such delicate matters of inter-service politics, Glavin organized and directed COVERT OPERATIONS in Africa, France, Italy, and the Balkans. For his part in negotiating the surrender of German forces in northern Italy on May 2, 1945 he was awarded the Distinguished Service Medal.

After the war Glavin served as an Army public information officer and as director of the Army's education programs in Germany. After his retirement from the Army in 1955 he took a master's degree in educational administration at Columbia University and subsequently headed the development offices at New York University and Pennsylvania Military College, and an international management studies program at Syracuse University. He retired in 1973 as assistant to the president of the New York State University College in Plattsburgh, New York.

(Brown, *The Last Hero*; obituary, *New York Times*, July 28, 1984, p. 8.)

GLEASON, SARELL EVERETT (March 14, 1905–November 20, 1974): historian, national security official, intelligence officer

A native of Brooklyn, New York, Gleason earned bachelor's, master's, and doctoral degrees at Harvard University in 1927, 1928, and 1934, respectively, and spent a year pursuing postgraduate studies at the University of Paris in 1931. He taught history at Harvard until 1938, when he became an associate professor of history at Amherst College. In 1943 he joined the Office of Strategic Services and headed the Current Intelligence Staff of the OSS RESEARCH AND ANALYSIS BRANCH. Later he was assigned to a staff responsible for liaison with the Joint Chiefs of Staff.

After the war Gleason served as historian with both the State Department and the Council on Foreign Relations. He was deputy executive secretary of the National Security Council from 1950 to 1959, and cultural attaché at the American embassy in London from 1959 to 1961.

(*Who Was Who in America*, vol. 6; Cline, *The CIA: Reality vs. Myth*.)

GODDARD, GEORGE WILLIAM (June 15, 1889–?): Air Force officer, intelligence officer

A native of Tunbridge Wells, England, Goddard enlisted as a private in the Aviation Section of the U.S. Army Signal Corps in 1917. The following year he attended the Officer's School in Aerial Photography at Cornell University's U.S. School of Military Aeronautics. After graduation he was commissioned a second lieutenant and attended pilot training school.

In 1919 Goddard was made chief of aerial photographic research for the Army. He specialized in the field of aerial photoreconnaissance from this time until his retirement as a brigadier general in the U.S. Air Force in 1953. He pioneered most of the developments in that field during that period, including night photography; color, infrared, high-altitude, and stereoscopic photography; aerial mapping and photogrammetry. He developed special cameras for aerial reconnaissance, including the long-focal-length lens cameras introduced in the SECOND WORLD WAR and used extensively in OVERHEAD RECONNAISSANCE since then.

After his retirement Goddard served as assistant to the president of the Itek Corporation, a leading private firm in the field of aerial photography.

Among his many awards and decorations, Goddard held the Legion of Merit, Distinguished Service Medal, and the French croix de guerre.

(*Who's Who in America*, v. 34; Infield, *Unarmed and Unafraid*; Powe and Wilson, *The Evolution of American Military Intelligence*.)

GODFREY, EDWIN DREXEL, JR. (June 14, 1921–): political scientist, intelligence analyst

A native of New York City, Godfrey graduated from Williams College in 1944. He served in the U.S. Army from 1942 to 1945, and returned to Williams as an instructor in political science in 1946–47. He was an assistant instructor in political science at Princeton University in 1947–50, and he received an M.A. and Ph.D. from Princeton in 1950 and 1953, respectively.

Godfrey held the post of assistant professor at Williams College from 1951 to 1957. In 1957 he joined the Central Intelligence Agency and served in the CIA INTELLIGENCE DIRECTORATE. For several years he was director of the Office of Current Intelligence. He left the CIA in 1970 and has since been director of the Masters of Public Administration Program of Rutgers University in Newark, New Jersey.

Godfrey is the author of two books on French politics, *The Politics of the Non-Communist Left in Post War France* (1954), and *The Government of France* (3rd ed., 1968).

(*Who's Who in America*, 37th ed.; biographical sketch, *Foreign Affairs*, April 1978.)

GOIRAN, ROGER: intelligence officer

Goiran served in the CIA CLANDESTINE SERVICE. He was chief of station in Teheran and Brussels. During the mid-1960s he was chief of the Western Europe Division of the Clandestine Service. While in that position he undertook an encyclopedic study of high-level Soviet political penetration in Europe, identifying local Soviet agents and their KGB case officers.

(Hunt, *Undercover*.)

GOLDBERG, ARTHUR JOSEPH (August 8, 1908–): attorney, diplomat, secretary of labor, U.S. Supreme Court justice, intelligence officer

A native of Chicago, Goldberg received his bachelor's and law degrees from Northwestern University in 1929 and 1930, respectively. He practiced law in Chicago until 1942, when he was commissioned a captain in the U.S. Army and assigned to the Office of Strategic Services. He became chief of the Labor Division of the OSS SECRET INTELLIGENCE BRANCH, rising to the rank of major.

After the war Goldberg returned to the practice of law and served as general counsel to the AFL-CIO and the United Steelworkers. He was secretary of labor in 1961 and 1962. In 1962 President Kennedy appointed him a justice of the U.S. Supreme Court. In 1965 he stepped down to accept the post of U.S. ambassador to the United Nations, a post he held until 1968. He has since practiced law and held various teaching positions and public offices, including U.S. ambassador-at-large.

(*Who's Who in America*, 42nd ed.; Smith, *OSS*.)

GOMEZ, RUDOLPH E. (May 27, 1915–): Clandestine Service officer

A native of Arizona, Gomez joined the Federal Housing Administration as an auditor in 1935. In 1941–42 he was a censor for the War Department, and in 1942–45 he served as a customs officer for the Treasury Department.

In 1946 Gomez joined the Department of State as a foreign service officer and later served with the Central Intelligence Agency. In 1946–48 he was assigned to Lisbon, Portugal, and in 1950–52 he served in Havana, Cuba. He was assigned to Buenos Aires in 1952–57.

Gomez was deputy chief of the Western Hemisphere Division of the CIA CLANDESTINE SERVICE. In 1960–65 he was assigned to Santiago, Chile, where he was chief of the CIA's station. In 1969 he returned to Lisbon, where he served as chief of station.

(Agee, *Inside the Company*; *Who's Who in Government*, 1st ed.)

GOODFELLOW, MILLARD PRESTON (May 22, 1892–September 5, 1973): newspaper publisher, covert operations officer

A native of Brooklyn, New York, Goodfellow attended the New York University School of Journalism and worked as a reporter on the *Brooklyn Eagle* and then on the *Brooklyn Times* and the *New York Evening Mail*. He served in a variety of capacities from copy editor to city editor. During the FIRST WORLD WAR he served as a second lieutenant in the U.S. Army Signal Corps. Later he was a special correspondent for the *New York Times* on the Mexican border.

About 1919 he returned to the *Eagle*, this time to work on the business side of the newspaper as circulation manager and later advertising manager. He was publisher of the paper from 1932 to 1938.

Prior to American entry into the Second World War, Goodfellow was commissioned a major in Army Intelligence and in August 1941 was assigned to serve as liaison officer with the Office of the Coordinator of Information (COI), the predecessor to the Office of Strategic Services. In January 1942 he was assigned the task of organizing and directing COI's Special Operations Branch (see OSS SPECIAL OPERATIONS BRANCH).

Goodfellow and DAVID K.E. BRUCE, then head of COI's Secret Intelligence Branch, were sent to a training school set up by the British Secret Intelligence Service near Toronto, Canada, to learn the techniques of SECRET INTELLIGENCE and COVERT ACTION. When COI became the OSS, Goodfellow was made deputy director for operations, responsible for the operations branches of the agency.

One of the most notable developments in Goodfellow's service in the OSS was his friendship with Korean expatriate Syngman Rhee, then head of the Korean provisional government in exile. Rhee, who had been rebuffed by the State Department as having no real standing in Korea, received a significant boost to his status in Washington as a result of Goodfellow's sponsorship.

After the Japanese surrender, Goodfellow was sent to Korea, which had been placed under joint Soviet and U.S. occupation, pending establishment of a democratic government. There he served as a political advisor to the U.S. occupation command, and when U.S.-Soviet negotiations did not lead to the formation of a satisfactory Korean government, he recommended the formation of a separate government in South Korea.

After the war Goodfellow pursued a variety of business interests, including publishing the *Pocatello* (Idaho) *Tribune*, and serving as president of Overseas Reconstruction, Inc., a Washington firm with business dealings in Latin America, Southeast Asia, and the Middle East.

(*Who's Who in America*, v. 36; obituary, *New York Times*, September 6, 1973, p. 40; Smith, *OSS*; Corson, *Armies of Ignorance*; Roosevelt, *War Report of the OSS*; Hymoff, *The OSS in World War II*.)

GOUGELMAN, TUCKER (?–1976): intelligence officer

Gougelman saw combat as a Marine officer during the Korean War, was wounded and lost a foot. He later served with the CIA CLANDESTINE SERVICE.

During the early 1960s he was chief of the CIA maritime base at Danang, Vietnam, from which agents were dispatched to and recovered from North Vietnam by swift patrol boats.

After his retirement he lived in Bangkok, Thailand, but he returned to Vietnam shortly before the North Vietnamese victory in 1975 to help Vietnamese friends and former associates escape from the country. He was captured by the Vietcong and held prisoner for a year, during which time he was interrogated by the Soviet KGB and other intelligence organizations. He died while in captivity and his remains were turned over to the United States government in 1977.

(De Silva, *Sub Rosa*; Snepp, *Decent Interval*.)

GRAYMAIL

The threat by defendants in espionage or national security-related cases to disclose classified information in the course of their legal defense. Graymail is regarded as a major reason why there were no successful espionage prosecutions in the United States from 1966 to 1975.

In 1980 Congress passed the Classified Information Procedures Act—better known as "the graymail statute"—to counter this practice. The Act permits private evidentiary hearings, requires the defense to prove the classified material is relevant to the case, and allows a judge to prevent full disclosure of classified documents at the trial by, for example, having them summarized.

Although the graymail statute has facilitated the convictions of several intelligence-connected defendants, U.S. intelligence agencies are still sometimes reluctant to prosecute especially sensitive national security cases.

(*Time*, November 19, 1984, p. 115; Becket, *Dictionary of Espionage*; Goulden, *The Death Merchant*.)

GREENHOW, ROSE O'NEAL (1817?–October 1, 1864): Confederate espionage agent

Greenhow was born Rose O'Neale (the family name was shortened to O'Neal while she was a child), the daughter of a prosperous planter of Port Tobacco, Maryland, who died soon after her birth. The family moved to Poolesville, a town in Montgomery County, Maryland, some twenty-five miles northwest of Washington, D.C. In her early teens she and her sisters went to live with their aunt who ran the Old Capitol boardinghouse in Washington on Capitol Hill that was the home away from home of many senators and congressmen (the boardinghouse derived its name from its original function—as the meeting place of Congress while the Capitol was being rebuilt after its destruction by the British in 1814). She was schooled in the social graces and received a basic education in local schools. Her knowledge of, and interest in, politics resulted from her close acquaintance with Sen. John C. Calhoun of South Carolina, who often stayed at her aunt's boardinghouse when Congress was in session. She also became acquainted with many other political figures of the time who stopped or dined at the Old Capitol while in Washington. O'Neal was a favorite of Dolley Madison, then the reigning *grande dame* of the nation's capital, and as she grew to maturity she became well established in Washington society.

In 1835 Rose O'Neal married Robert Greenhow, a prominent Virginia lawyer who worked as a linguist for the Department of State. Her husband's official duties brought her into a broader social circle and she displayed considerable talent for political intrigue. Her influence with James Buchanan, who served as secretary of state in 1845–49, raised eyebrows and stirred up some gossip. When the Oregon Territory became a matter of controversy between Britain and the United States, she was suspected by some of being in the pay of the English legation as a spy, and her husband was not assigned to translate related documents supplied by American agents in Mexico. In 1849 she was involved in a plot by Venezuelan adventurer Gen. Narcisco Lopez to wrest Cuba from Spain and attach it to the United States. The plan, which intended to make Cuba a slaveholding state, was supported by Southern politicians, with whom she sympathized politically.

In 1850 Greenhow accompanied her husband to San Francisco where he had gone to settle land-claim disputes arising from the recent war with Mexico. They lived in San Francisco until 1854 when Robert died as a result of injuries received in a fall while Rose was visiting Washington. After returning briefly to San Francisco to settle their affairs, she moved back to Washington. With the inauguration of her friend and confidant, James Buchanan, a bachelor, as President in 1857, her influence in Washington rose to a new height. She had, in fact, worked to achieve Buchanan's election, traveling to California in 1856 to help organize support for him there.

During Buchanan's administration (1857–61) Greenhow became increasingly embroiled in secessionist politics, then the principal issue in Washington and the country. She used all her influence in behalf of the Southern cause and reportedly even had an adulterous affair with Sen. Henry Wilson, an ardent antislavery Republican from Massachusetts, to further secessionist interests. And she engaged in what was at least a passionate flirtation with Democratic Sen. Joseph Lane of Oregon in the hope of influencing the 1860 Democratic presidential ticket.

Shortly after the outbreak of the Civil War, Greenhow was approached by Col. THOMAS JORDAN, an Army Officer who had chosen the Confederate side and was soon to resign his commission in the U.S. Army, join the Confederates, and become Gen. P.G.T. Beauregard's adjutant general. Jordan cautiously proposed that Greenhow serve in Washington as a Confederate espionage agent, and she accepted. He supplied her with a simple cipher and communication instructions.

Greenhow's extensive connections in Washington's social and official circles, her resourcefulness, and her considerable charm enabled her to gather military intelligence and pass it on to Jordan. She worked in cooperation with other Confederate agents in Washington, chief among whom were William T. Smithson, a prominent banker; Michael Thompson, a lawyer; and Aaron Van Camp, a dentist.

According to tradition, Greenhow's greatest contribution to the Confederate cause was the intelligence she supplied regarding Union movements and plans just prior to the first Bull Run campaign. According to popularly accepted accounts, she had seen, early in July 1861, the War Department orders to Gen. Irwin McDowell to attack Beauregard and drive him from the important railroad junction at Manassas, Virginia, and she reported this by courier to Jordan, informing him that the advance was scheduled for mid-July. The popular accounts also say that on July 16 a Confederate courier Jordan had sent to Greenhow for additional information returned with word from her that the attack was to begin that day, and she had also given him the detailed route McDowell's force planned to follow from Alexandria, Virginia, to Manassas. The following day, according to these accounts, Greenhow reported to Jordan that the Union forces planned to cut the Manassas Gap Railroad line to prevent Beauregard from receiving reinforcements.

The traditional view, held by Greenhow's biographers and some historians, and based on the gallant Beauregard's own account, is that it was this intelligence that enabled the Confederate commander to thwart the Union plan and win a major victory for the Confederacy at Bull Run. However, this account has been called into question by historian and espionologist Edwin C. Fishel, who points out a host of improbabilities and impossibilities in the story (e.g., she would had to have known details of the plan before McDowell had actually decided upon them, in order to have reported them to Jordan at the time she is supposed to have done so) and suggests that Greenhow's reports were not the basis of Beauregard's tactics; that it was tactical intelligence collected on the battlefield, i.e., visual observation of movements of the Union force, upon which the Confederate general actually based his decisive actions. Fishel believes Greenhow probably did deliver some solid information to Jordan, e.g., that the Union commanders were planning to take the initiative in Virginia, and the fact that the advance had actually begun. But he finds that these facts have been embellished by many writers to the point that Greenhow's contribution has been greatly exaggerated.

Greenhow had never made a secret of her secessionist allegiance, and she did not pretend to have had a change of heart to disguise her espionage operations. Furthermore, apart from the training she received from Jordan in cryptography and communications, she knew nothing of intelligence TRADE-CRAFT, and pursued the information she sought rather openly and brazenly. Consequently she soon came under suspicion by Thomas A. Scott, the acting assistant secretary of war, who assigned ALLAN PINKERTON to watch Greenhow's Washington home. Working in the slightly comical manner of a private detective in a divorce case, Pinkerton easily established that Greenhow was receiving military information, and he identified one of the Army officers who was giving it to her. He later rounded up many of Greenhow's comrades in Jordan's Washington espionage network.

Greenhow was arrested and confined to her home, which the government then used to house other woman prisoners. However, since she continued to try to communicate with the Confederacy the Federals imprisoned her in the Old Capitol boarding-house where she had spent her adolescence, which had since been converted into a prison. She remained there from January to June 1862, when she was released and sent through the lines to Richmond where she was warmly received and paid a fee of $2,500 for the secret services she had rendered the Confederacy.

In August 1863 she traveled to Europe. She was presented to Napoleon III and Queen Victoria, both of whom were sympathetic to the Southern cause, and she published an account of her experiences, *My Imprisonment and the First Year of Abolition Rule at Washington,* which was both a financial success and an effective piece of Confederate propaganda.

In August 1864 she departed Europe, carrying dispatches from Confederate secret agents abroad. The ship on which she was traveling ran aground in a storm while attempting to run the Union blockade outside Wilmington, North Carolina. Greenhow was drowned while attempting to land in a small boat, and she was buried with Confederate military honors.

(Ross, *Rebel Rose;* Kane, *Spies for the Blue and Gray;* Stern, *Secret Missions of the Civil War;* Boatner, *Civil War Dictionary;* Fishel, "The Mythology of Civil War Intelligence"; Beymer, *On Hazardous Service.*)

GRENFELL, GEORGE ST. LEGER (May 30, 1808–1868?): British soldier of fortune and Confederate agent

A native of Penzance, Cornwall, Grenfell was the black sheep of an aristocratic English family. As a young man, he joined a French cavalry regiment in Algeria, only to convert to Islam and fight against the French on the Arab side. Later he fought the Riff pirates off the Morocco coast and served with Garibaldi in South America. Still later he obtained a regular commission in the British army. He served during the Sepoy Rebellion in India and in the Crimean War, attaining the rank of lieutenant colonel. He came to the United States and in June 1862 he joined Morgan's Raiders. He served with the Confederate cavalry under Gens. John Morgan, Joseph Wheeler, and J.E.B. Stuart and was noted for his reckless bravery.

In 1864 he was recruited by Lt. THOMAS HINES to participate in the NORTHWEST CONSPIRACY. Grenfell's job was to lead an attack on Camp Douglas near Chicago to release the thousands of Confederate prisoners of war held there. Assuming the cover of an English sportsman, he scouted the site and prepared for the attack. However, the operation was betrayed, and Grenfell was arrested, tried, and sentenced to death. His sentence was commuted to life imprisonment and he was sent to Fort Jefferson, "the American Devil's Island" in the Dry Tortugas. There he befriended fellow prisoner Dr. Samuel Mudd, who had been sentenced to life for his alleged part in the LINCOLN CONSPIRACY. Grenfell and Mudd performed heroic service during the yellow fever epidemic at the prison. On March 8, 1868 Grenfell and several other prisoners escaped from Fort Jefferson in a small boat during a severe storm. No trace of the fugitives or their boat was ever found, and Grenfell was presumed lost at sea, despite persistent reports that he had been seen in Florida, Cuba, Brazil, and Paraguay.

(Carter, *The Riddle of Dr. Mudd;* Horan, *Confederate Agent;* Starr, *Colonel Grenfell's Wars.*)

GROMBACH, JOHN V. (January 2, 1901–?): Army officer, athlete and sportswriter, motion-picture writer and producer, businessman, intelligence officer

A native of New Orleans, Louisiana, Grombach attended the Virginia Military Institute and graduated from the U.S. Military Academy in 1923. From 1923 to 1925 he was a military police and prison officer on Governors Island, New York, except for a period in 1924 when he was acting junior military attaché in Paris, France. From 1923 until 1926 he was also head coach of the Second Corps (all service) football team. In 1926–28 he was assistant provost marshal in the Panama Canal Zone.

In 1928 Grombach resigned from the Army to become a motion-picture and radio writer and producer. He worked for a subsidiary of Columbia Broadcasting, and later formed his own production company.

Grombach was recalled to active duty by the Army in 1941 and was assigned to ARMY INTELLIGENCE with the rank of colonel. In 1942 he established and became chief of what was subsequently known as the GROMBACH ORGANIZATION, apparently a joint secret intelligence activity of the War Department, the Federal Bureau of Investigation, the Federal Communication Commission, the State Department, and other government agencies with intelligence or counterespionage functions. This unit conducted secret intelligence operations in Europe that were regarded as an infringement on the jurisdiction of the Office of Strategic Services by OSS Director WILLIAM J. DONOVAN and his assistant, G. EDWARD BUXTON. However, the OSS withheld protest in the hope of encouraging a favorable White House response to Donovan's plan for a postwar central intelligence agency (see CENTRAL INTELLIGENCE AGENCY). Grombach himself remained adamantly opposed to investing the new CIA with any secret intelligence functions and testified to that effect in congressional hearings on the National Security Act of 1947, which set up the Agency.

In 1942—the same year he established the Grombach Organization—Grombach also became president of Industrial Reports, Inc., although it is not clear from available open sources whether or how these two organizations were related. Grombach remained president of Industrial Reports until about the time of his death in the early 1980s. From January 1, 1947 onward he was also president of the Universal Service Corporation, a firm colocated with Industrial Reports at Grombach's Manhattan offices.

Grombach described himself in a 1973 consultants directory as a private consultant in the fields of international sales promotion, public and government relations, and security and industrial intelligence. It is not clear from available open sources whether he was involved in the post-1947 activities of the Grombach Organization.

In his youth Grombach was an accomplished boxer and fencer. He was intercollegiate heavyweight boxing champion in 1922, Army champion in 1924, and a member of the U.S. Olympic boxing team in Paris in 1924. He was a member of the U.S. international fencing teams in London (1926) and Paris (1937), and National Open (Masters) épée champion in 1950. He was a member of the U.S. Olympic Games Committee in 1956, 1960, 1964, and 1968, and secretary general of the International Fencing Federation in 1960–64. He wrote several books and magazine articles on sports, and was a radio sports commentator.

Grombach was awarded the Legion of Merit and the Army Commendation Medal.

(*Who's Who in America,* v. 28 and the 42nd ed.; Troy, *Donovan and the CIA; Who's Who in Consulting,* 2nd ed.; U.S. House of Representatives, *Hearing Before the Committee on Expenditures in the Executive Departments . . . on H.R. 2319 . . . June 27, 1947.*)

GROMBACH ORGANIZATION

A secret intelligence agency affiliated with ARMY INTELLIGENCE during the SECOND WORLD WAR, and with the CENTRAL INTELLIGENCE AGENCY during the early 1950s. Thereafter it had no affiliation with the U.S. government. Open source information regarding this organization is sketchy, sparse, fragmentary, and sometimes contradictory.

The Grombach Organization was established by Col. JOHN V. GROMBACH in mid-1942 at the behest of Maj. Gen. GEORGE V. STRONG, the Army's assistant chief of staff for intelligence. Strong was one of the most dedicated opponents of the OFFICE OF STRATEGIC SERVICES and wished to institute a rival intelligence collection service.

Perhaps in order to hide the existence of the organization from OSS, on whose bureaucratic jurisdiction it trespassed, Grombach resorted to some very irregular administrative methods in setting up the unit. In the words of LYMAN B. KIRKPATRICK, who, as CIA secret intelligence chief in the mid-1950s had occasion to study the Grombach Organization's origins, it was

one of the most unusual organizations in the history of the federal government. It was developed completely outside of the normal governmental structure, used all of the normal cover and communications facilities normally operated by intelligence organizations, and yet never was under any control from Washington.

In his biographic entry in *Who's Who in America*, Grombach describes his Second World War duties with the War Department's Military Intelligence Service as "chief, liaison br. between War Department and State Department, FBI., FCC., etc." perhaps suggesting that the Grombach Organization was a joint activity of several federal agencies with intelligence interests.

The Grombach Organization conducted secret intelligence operations in Europe from 1942 until at least 1947. The only account of any of these operations seems to be that of James G. McCargar, who, writing under the pseudonym of "Christopher Felix," related his work as a case officer for the organization in Budapest during 1946–47 in *A Short Course in the Secret War* (1963).

In 1947 Colonel Grombach and his organization waged a bitter and unsuccessful campaign against efforts by the Central Intelligence Group (see CENTRAL INTELLIGENCE AGENCY) to absorb them and their secret intelligence function. Grombach also tried at about that time to prevent the establishment of the CIA. Failing in that, he tried (without success) to influence the appointment of the CIA director. Kirkpatrick writes that, at this time, the Grombach Organization was being supported by subsidies from "other government departments," presumably such agencies as the State Department and the FBI, which apparently had participated in the organization from its inception.

According to Kirkpatrick, after Gen. WALTER BEDELL SMITH became CIA director in September 1950, "the men running [the Grombach] organization came in and said they wanted to work with and for the CIA." It is not clear from available sources whether Grombach was still involved with the unit at this time, or whether he had in fact returned to civilian life in 1947, as indicated in his *Who's Who* curriculum vitae. However, it may be noted that he continued through this period and until about the time of his death in the early 1980s as president of Industrial Reports, Inc., a position he assumed in 1942, i.e., when he first established the Grombach Organization. What connection, if any, may have existed between Industrial Reports and the Grombach Organization is not available in the open literature.

In response to the Grombach Organization's offer, the CIA decided to subsidize the unit on a trial basis. According to Kirkpatrick, who was then involved as director of the Office of Special Operations, the CIA's secret intelligence department, the Organization proved extremely difficult to deal with because it mistrusted the CIA and refused to disclose its sources of information.

Kirkpatrick writes that the Grombach Organization continued to maintain this adversarial relationship with the Agency, and that many of the sources it was using were nothing more than PAPER MILLS run by emigrés and exiles who who had no useful information to impart. He further states that the Organization made false allegations to the Red-hunting Sen. Joseph McCarthy that a dozen CIA employees were security risks. Kirkpatrick says that the Organization had proposed to work for Senator McCarthy in his search for Communists in the federal government.

The CIA terminated its subsidy of the Grombach Organization about this time, i.e., in the mid-1950s. What became of it thereafter cannot be determined from the open record, but it may be worth noting that in 1973 Grombach described his Industrial Reports, Inc., as providing consulting services in the fields of "security and industrial intelligence," suggesting that the Grombach Organization may have continued to operate exclusively in the private sector.

(Troy, *Donovan and the CIA*; Constantinides, *Intelligence and Espionage: An Analytical Bibliography*; Kirkpatrick, *The Real CIA*; Felix, *A Short Course in the Secret War*; *Who's Who in Consulting*, 2nd ed.; *Who's Who in America*, 42nd ed.)

GUATEMALA COUP

Summary: In June 1954 the Central Intelligence Agency and the State Department staged a coup d'etat in Guatemala, overthrowing President Jacobo Árbenz Guzman, a leftist reformer believed to have been under Communist influence, and installed a military junta headed by Col. Carlos Castillo Armas.
Background: In 1944 a coalition of independent businessmen, intellectuals, and army officers overthrew Guatemala's dictator Jorge Ubico and ended the tradition of oligarchic rule in that country. Juan Jose Arévalo, a leftist educator and a leader of the revolt, acceded to power and undertook a program of social and economic reform aimed at bettering the lot of the poor and middle class. This program was continued by Arévalo's successor, Jacobo Árbenz Guzman, an army officer who had played a prominent role in ousting Ubico. When Árbenz was elected president in 1950, he stepped up the reform program, especially regarding land reform and the reduction of the power of foreign interests in Guatemala. He soon alienated American commercial interests when

he signed a law expropriating much of the land held by the American-owned United Fruit Company.

In his confrontation with United Fruit, Árbenz received the enthusiastic support of the Guatemalan Labor Party, as the Communist party of Guatemala called itself. Unlike Arévalo, who had been strongly anti-Communist, Árbenz readily accepted the support of the Communists and regarded them as an integral part of his political coalition. Although he installed none in his Cabinet, he appointed several Communists to sub-Cabinet posts. Communists were best represented within the government's National Agrarian Department, the agency directly involved in the expropriation of United Fruit's landholdings.

Árbenz's campaign against United Fruit also had the support of many moderate Guatemalans. The size, power, and U.S. ownership of the company made it a popular target of ordinary Guatemalans, despite the fact that it had invested $60 million dollars in the country; constructed Guatemala's railroad, telegraph, and telephone systems; created nearly 40,000 jobs; and paid wages several times higher than those of other Guatemalan employers. These benevolences notwithstanding, many Guatemalans saw United Fruit's control of the national economy as an obstacle to progress and industrialization.

Árbenz's actions alarmed American foreign policy-makers, who, as early as 1952, considered undertaking a COVERT ACTION operation to remove Árbenz from power. At the behest of the United Fruit Company, President Truman authorized the CIA to provide weapons to Nicaraguan President Anastasio Somoza Garcia, who had volunteered to lead an expedition against the Árbenz regime. However, the project, called Operation Fortune, was canceled after Under Secretary of State DAVID K.E. BRUCE learned of it and, together with Secretary of State Dean Acheson, dissuaded Truman from it.

Acheson left office with the inauguration of President Eisenhower in 1953. His successor, John Foster Dulles, was much more positively disposed toward overthrowing Árbenz. It is notable that Dulles—and other senior U.S. foreign policy-makers—had strong private ties to the United Fruit Company. Dulles's law firm of Sullivan and Cromwell had represented the company for many years, and Dulles is said to have personally negotiated the 1936 contract that was the basis of the company's operations in Guatemala. However, the imputation that Dulles may have been personally interested in the Guatemalan situation should be regarded in the light of his uncompromising anti-Communism, and the likelihood that he considered Árbenz's expropriation of American-owned land an integral part of the Guatemalan president's accommodation with the Communists.

American policy-makers cited the frequent suspension of constitutional guarantees and the censorship of the press by both Árbenz and his predecessor as further evidence of a Communist threat in Guatemala. While such criticism was undoubtedly made partly for its propaganda value, the similarity between recent developments in Guatemala and the early stages of the recent Soviet takeovers in Eastern Europe was probably a source of true concern within the Eisenhower administration. Although the actual potential for a Communist coup in Guatemala in 1954 remains a subject of historical debate, there seems little question that Dulles and other American foreign policy-makers perceived it as a real danger.

On March 29, 1953, soon after Dulles took office, a group of anti-Communist Guatemalan army officers seized the provincial capital of Salma. The Guatemalan government quickly crushed the uprising and discovered that it had been undertaken by United Fruit, Nicaragua, the Dominican Republic, El Salvador, and Honduras. (In *Bitter Fruit*, their account of the Guatemala Coup, authors Schlesinger and Kinzer say that the abortive rebellion was instigated and supported by the CIA.)

The failure of this operation did not persuade the Eisenhower administration to cease its efforts to unseat Árbenz. In August 1953 an ad hoc subcommittee of the Operations Coordinating board (see COVERT ACTION) approved a new CIA plan for a coup d'etat against Árbenz.

The CIA/State Coup: The CIA and the State Department jointly worked out a plan for a covert action operation—dubbed Operation Success—to overthrow Árbenz and replace him with an anti-Communist regime. The plan was developed by RAYMOND G. LEDDY, the State Department's specialist on Central America and Panama; C. TRACY BARNES, special assistant to CIA CLANDESTINE SERVICE chief FRANK G. WISNER; and J.C. KING, chief of the Clandestine Service's Western Hemisphere Division.

The joint CIA/State Department plan involved launching a psychological campaign to end the Guatemalan army's support for Árbenz; providing paramilitary support for Col. Carlos Castillo Armas, a former Guatemalan army officer and a leader of an anti-Árbenz faction; and putting economic and diplomatic pressure on Árbenz and his administration to stand aside and permit Castillo Armas to take power. (Castillo Armas was selected to receive U.S. support after an earlier candidate, lawyer, and coffee planter Juan Cordova Cerna, became seriously ill.)

Within the State Department, the principal officers

responsible for Operation Success were Leddy and John E. Peurifoy, the recently appointed U.S. ambassador to Guatemala. Peurifoy, who had served as ambassador to Greece, had been selected for the job because of his reputation as an aggressive anti-Communist and a man of action. He was a self-described advocate of "big stick" foreign policy, and his assignment to the Guatemala post was a calculated act of intimidation of Árbenz.

Within the CIA, overall responsibility for Operation Success rested with C. Tracy Barnes. Because ALLEN DULLES and Wisner regarded Western Hemisphere Division chief J.C. King as diffident and inept in matters of covert action, he was largely bypassed for this operation, and an ad hoc task force was established directly under Barnes. Col. Albert Haney, the chief of station in South Korea, was recalled to serve as the task force commander. E. HOWARD HUNT was made chief of the operation's propaganda and political action staff. Hunt selected as his assistant DAVID A. PHILLIPS, an officer with a background in writing and acting who had an extensive knowledge of Latin America. CIA Director Dulles took a close personal interest in the operation and assigned his recently hired special assistant, RICHARD M. BISSELL, to track and facilitate its progress.

Haney established a headquarters for the operation on a U.S. Marine air base at Opa-Locka, Florida. With the cooperation of President Somoza he established several support installations in Nicaragua: two training bases for Castillo Armas's Guatemalan exile "army" of some 300 men; an airstrip at Puerto Cabezas on the Atlantic Coast (which was used again seven years later in the BAY OF PIGS INVASION); and clandestine radio stations that were to broadcast propaganda over the same wavelengths used by Guatemalan radio transmitters. Other stations were set up for the same purpose in Honduras through the good offices of WHITING WILLAUER, then U.S. ambassador to that country.

The CIA provided some thirty Second World War aircraft—fighters, light bombers, and transports. Some of these were piloted and maintained by employees of Civil Air Transport, one of the Agency's AIR PROPRIETARIES, while others were manned by American pilots and crewmen recruited in Central America as contract employees for Operation Success.

Despite the paramilitary preparations, the operation's planners hoped to achieve their aim without resorting to arms. In January 1954 they began a combined propaganda and economic program aimed at precipitating Árbenz's downfall or resignation, but Árbenz responded with a propaganda campaign of

his own. An effort to bribe Árbenz to resign also failed.

The Guatemalan situation seemed to take on a new urgency in mid-April when U.S. intelligence sources learned of the departure of a Swedish freighter, the *Alfhem*, from the Polish port of Szczecin, apparently carrying a load of Czechoslovakian arms and bound, they suspected, for Guatemala. The ship arrived at the Guatemalan port of Puerto Barrios on May 15th and unloaded its cargo, which was indeed some 2,000 tons of small arms and artillery from Czechoslovakia. The following day the U.S. Intelligence Advisory Committee (see NATIONAL FOREIGN INTELLIGENCE BOARD) met and made a quick estimate that the arms would enable Guatemala to crush her neighbors and posed a threat to the Panama Canal. On May 17th the NATIONAL SECURITY COUNCIL authorized the execution of the paramilitary part of Operation Success.

On May 1 the radio propaganda part of Operation Success had begun to be put into effect. The CIA's radio transmitters in Nicaragua and Honduras went on the air as the "Voice of Liberation," a dissident station claiming to be based in the Guatemalan countryside. The station's broadcasts were aimed at women, soldiers, workers, and young people, and were calculated to intimidate Communists and their sympathizers, and to encourage neutrals and anti-Communists to rally to Castillo Armas's insurgent movement.

On June 18th Castillo Armas led his "Army of Liberation"—a force of some three hundred troops—across the border from Honduras, and stopped six miles inside Guatemala at the town of Esquipulas. Earlier that day, P-47 fighter-bombers of the CIA's air force bombed the Pacific port of San José. A C-47 dropped propaganda leaflets on the capital, Guatemala City. Fighters and bombers attacked other targets in the country.

During the next several days, Castillo Armas and his tiny army remained bivouacked at Esquipulas while the CIA's "Voice of Liberation" radio station broadcasts reported that he was marching toward the capital at the head of a column of several thousand troops. The air strikes continued, attacking fuel depots, ammunition dumps, radio transmitters, and other targets throughout the country, including Guatemala City. The primary mission of the air strikes was not military but psychological, and their success is indicated by the nickname they were given by the Guatemalans—*"sulfatos,"* i.e., laxatives, for the effect they presumably had on the Guatemalan army and the Árbenz government. Indeed, in some cases the planes dropped only smoke bombs, and during one nighttime raid on Guatemala City, the sounds of exploding bombs actually came from a tape played through a public-address system on the roof of the American embassy.

The combined psychological assaults of the air strikes, the propaganda broadcasts and leaflets, and Ambassador Peurifoy's meetings with Guatemalan army commanders all had their effect by June 27. Árbenz stepped down and relinquished the reins of government to Col. Carlos Enrique Diaz, the army chief of staff. Two days later, after continued psychological pressure by Peurifoy, the radio broadcast, and the air strikes, Diaz stepped down in favor of a military junta. The junta quickly accepted Castillo Armas as its leader. In August the other members of the junta resigned, and on September 1, 1954 Castillo Armas became president.

The Guatemala coup was successful in that it removed whatever danger of a Communist takeover Árbenz may have presented. In March 1956, after twenty months of inept and unpopular rule, Castillo Armas was assassinated by one of his bodyguards. Thereafter Guatemala returned to the authoritarian oligarchic rule that existed before 1944, although subsequent governments have not been as cooperative as before 1944 either with the U.S. government or American commercial interests.

Coming as it did on the heels of the successful IRAN COUP of 1953, the success of the Guatemala coup had a profound effect on the CIA and American foreign policy-makers in that it seemed to confirm the superlative effectiveness of covert action operations as a means of countering Soviet expansionism. When the Bay of Pigs invasion was planned several years later, many of the same CIA personnel and the same techniques were used. Some students of intelligence history believe the success of the Guatemala coup led to the unrealistic optimism that brought about the Bay of Pigs disaster.

(Cook, *The Declassified Eisenhower;* Schlesinger and Kinzer, *Bitter Fruit;* Corson, *Armies of Ignorance;* Phillips, *The Night Watch;* Hunt, *Undercover;* Wise and Ross, *The Invisible Government;* Rositzke, *CIA's Secret Operations.*)

GURFEIN, MURRAY IRWIN (November 17, 1907–December 18, 1979): attorney, government official, jurist, intelligence officer

A native of New York City, Gurfein attended Columbia University and graduated from Harvard University Law School in 1930. He served as assistant U.S. attorney for the Southern District of New York from 1931 to 1933, as chief assistant to Gov. Thomas E. Dewey's investigation of organized crime in 1935–38, and as assistant district attorney of New York County from 1938 to 1942. While in the latter position in 1942, he helped arrange an alliance between the Office of NAVAL INTELLIGENCE and the Mafia in New York City; in exchange for the release on parole of Charles "Lucky" Luciano (a.k.a. Salvatore Lucania), who was serving a thirty-five-year sentence in New York State for white slavery, the Mafia would conduct sabotage and other operations in Sicily in support of the Allied landings there, as well as assisting in ONI counterespionage operations on the New York waterfront.

Gurfein was commissioned as a major in the U.S. Army in 1942 and assigned to the OFFICE OF STRATEGIC SERVICES. He played a major role in the OSS's so-called K Project, an unsuccessful operation aimed at prying Bulgaria from its alliance with the Axis powers and allying it with the United States.

Gurfein was later promoted to lieutenant colonel. He served as chief of intelligence of the Psychological Warfare Division of the Supreme Headquarters Allied Expeditionary Force (SHAEF) in Europe. After the war he served as assistant to the U.S. chief counsel at the Nuremburg trials.

Gurfein practiced law from 1946 until 1971, when he was appointed a federal judge in the Southern District of New York. Shortly after his appointment he rendered a decision against the government's attempt to suppress publication of the "Pentagon Papers" by the *New York Times.*

(*Who's Who in America,* 37th ed.; Campbell, *The Luciano Project;* Smith, *OSS;* Cave Brown, *The Last Hero;* Jeffreys-Jones, *American Espionage.*)

H

A duplicate of the statue of Nathan Hale by Bela Lyon Pratt at CIA headquarters, Langley, Virginia. The original statue stands at Yale University in front of Connecticut Hall, in which Hale roomed as an undergraduate in 1769–73. Source: Central Intelligence Agency.

HALE, NATHAN (June 6, 1755–September 22, 1776): schoolteacher, Army officer, intelligence agent

A native of Coventry, Connecticut, Hale was one of twelve children. He was outstanding at both athletics and scholarship, and entered Yale at the age of 14. He graduated in 1773 and became a schoolteacher. On July 6, 1775 he was commissioned a lieutenant in the Seventh Connecticut militia, and soon joined the Continental Army and served in the Nineteenth Continental Regiment during the siege of Boston. On January 1, 1776 he was promoted to the rank of captain. Arriving in New York City with his regiment on April 30th, 1776, he was soon selected by Lt. Col. Thomas Knowlton to lead a company of his famed rangers (see KNOWLTON'S RANGERS).

Late in June British Gen. William Howe, having evacuated Boston and marched to Halifax, arrived with his troops in New York Bay by sea and occupied Staten Island (see AMERICAN REVOLUTION). On August 27th the American forces under General Washington were beaten on Long Island, and retreated to Manhattan where they prepared to take a stand. Washington was badly in need of information on British strength and intentions and asked his commanders to find a spy who would undertake a mission behind British lines on Long Island. When no candidates were produced, Washington asked Lt. Col. Knowlton to find a volunteer among his ranger officers, and Captain Hale was the only one to step forward. When a brother officer tried to dissuade him on the theory that espionage was a dishonorable

The hanging of Nathan Hale, September 22, 1776. Source: Library of Congress.

trade, Hale is said to have replied, "Every kind of service, necessary to the public good, becomes honorable by being necessary."

Hale had no training in even the basic techniques of espionage, and was personally ill-suited for the role of spy. He was, first of all, far from inconspicuous in appearance, being above average height and having a face that had been scarred by exploding gunpowder. Worse, his cousin Samuel Hale was a Tory and the British army's deputy commissary of prisoners, and happened to be with General Howe on Staten Island at that moment. To make matters even worse, the Americans failed to arrange a cover story to account for Hale's absence from his command and, in fact, his mission was common knowledge among many of the rangers. The possibility that the British might have their own spy in the American camp seems not to have occurred to anyone.

Hale left Manhattan on or about September 12 (the exact date is disputed by historians) and traveled two or three days along the Westchester and Connecticut shores in search of a means of crossing Long Island Sound. At Norwalk he found the master of a sloop who was willing to take him across the Sound. He landed at Huntington on the north shore of Long Island, exchanged his uniform for civilian clothes, and arranged for his companion, Sgt. Stephen Hempstead, to wait across Long Island Sound at Norwalk, Connecticut, from which he would return to exfiltrate him at a preestablished time. Adopting the guise of a Dutch schoolmaster, he started west toward the British lines.

Before he could complete his mission, the British made a successful landing at Kip's Bay on the east side of Manhattan on September 15th and pushed Washington back to Harlem Heights, north of what is today West 127th Street. Hale followed the British, passed within their lines, collected detailed and current information on their strength and disposition, and attempted to get back to the American lines. However, on the night of September 21st he was captured by the British, charged with espionage and taken before General Howe who ordered him hanged. The cause of his betrayal is unknown. Some accounts, without any evidence, say he was recognized and denounced by his Tory cousin. Others claim he was caught off guard when he mistook a boat from the British warship *Halifax* as American confederates coming to exfiltrate him. It may be significant that he had been stationed in New York City for the previous five months, and his identity as an officer in the Continental Army must have been common knowledge. His complete lack of training in espionage tradecraft makes almost any theory plausible.

Hale was hanged the next morning. According to General Howe's aide-de-camp, the scholar-turned-spy uttered as his final words a paraphrase of a line from Addison's *Cato*: "I only regret that I have but one life to lose for my country."

The place of Hale's execution was in front of the British artillery park near the Dove Tavern, which stood near today's intersection of Sixty-sixth Street and Third Avenue.

(Bakeless, *Turncoats, Traitors and Heroes*; Boatner, *Encyclopedia of the American Revolution*; Thompson, "Sleuthing the Trail of Nathan Hale"; Ford, *A Peculiar Service*.)

HALL, ROGER WOLCOTT (May 20, 1919–): writer, sports announcer, covert operations officer

A native of Baltimore, Maryland, Hall graduated from the University of Virginia in 1941. That same year, he joined the U.S. Army. He was commissioned a second lieutenant and, in 1943, he was transferred to the OFFICE OF STRATEGIC SERVICES and assigned to the Special Operations Branch. He took part in the operation, code-named Jedburgh, in which three-man teams of allied covert operations officers parachuted into German-occupied France to coordinate the operations of the French Resistance with the Allied landings at Normandy. Later he was part of an OSS Operational Group in Norway led by Maj. WILLIAM COLBY, although his section had not yet been dropped into the country when the Germans surrendered. Hall wrote a frequently humorous book about his OSS experiences. After the war he worked as a sports announcer for a Baltimore radio station, and as a free-lance writer and journalist.

(*Contemporary authors*; Hall, *You're Stepping on My Cloak and Dagger*.)

HALPERIN, MAURICE: educator, political scientist, intelligence analyst

Halperin was educated at Harvard University and the University of Paris, receiving a doctorate from the latter institution in 1931. He served as an intelligence analyst in the OSS RESEARCH AND ANALYSIS BRANCH and was chief of the Latin American Division.

In 1953 Halperin was dismissed from the faculty of Boston University after J. EDGAR HOOVER told a congressional committee that he had been a Communist agent while in the OSS. Halperin moved to Mexico in 1958, spent three years on the faculty of the Soviet Academy of Sciences in Moscow, and taught at the University of Havana during 1962–68. He was later professor of political science at Simon Fraser University in Vancouver, British Columbia. In 1972 he published a historical and political analysis of the Cuban regime of Fidel Castro.

(Smith, *OSS*.)

HARRISON, HENRY THOMAS (ca. 1832–?): Confederate officer, scout, and secret agent

Harrison may be the agent of that surname who performed the most decisive piece of spying of the Civil War.

Harrison's name and his most important exploit first appeared in the literature in a recollection of the battle of Gettysburg published in the *Century* magazine in the 1880s by former Confederate Gen. James Longstreet. Longstreet recounted a meeting with Harrison on the night of June 28, 1863 near Chambersburg, Pennsylvania, where the general was commanding a corps of the Army of Northern Virginia during Lee's second invasion of the North. At that moment Lee had heard nothing from Gen. J.E.B. Stuart, his cavalry commander and "the eyes of the Army," for several days; Stuart was raiding far to the east of Lee's army and therefore had not performed his usual reconnaissance function. Harrison informed Longstreet that the federal Army of the Potomac, which Longstreet believed to be in Virginia, had crossed into Maryland, was located near Frederick, less than fifty miles to the southeast, and was marching northward. This information, immediately conveyed to General Lee, was vital: because the Confederate force was strung out along a line some eighty miles long in its northward advance through Pennsylvania, it was likely to be defeated piecemeal in a series of attacks by a concentrated Union force. Worse, Lee had just ordered elements of his army to advance across the Susquehanna River, further diffusing his strength. He immediately ordered his army to concentrate near Gettysburg (and so set the stage for the famous battle) and thereby saved it from complete annihilation. This move, prompted by Harrison's intelligence, is credited with preventing the complete destruction of Lee's army.

Accounts of Harrison's role in the Gettysburg campaign appeared in the memoirs of several members of Longstreet's staff many years later, but none gave his full name or much other information concerning him beyond the facts that he was paid $150 per month for his espionage services, which apparently had been extensive well before Gettysburg, and that he had worked directly for Confederate Secretary of War James A. Seddon before being assigned to Longstreet. In 1970 historian and espionologist John Bakeless made the plausible and well-documented (but apparently mistaken) case that Harrison was James Harrison, a Shakespearean actor. In 1981 Dr. Meriwether Stuart, a student of Civil War espionage, made a careful study of the actor's career and showed that he had been appearing in Richmond at a time when Harrison, the secret agent, was known to have been at Franklin, Virginia, nearly a hundred miles away. Stuart therefore concluded that the actor and the secret agent were two different Harrisons. The mystery may have finally been solved by historian James O. Hall, who located the secret agent's granddaughter, who provided her ancestor's given names and enough additional data to enable Hall to locate Confederate records confirming the intelligence role of Henry Thomas Harrison.

According to various documents unearthed by Hall, Harrison was a native of Yazoo County, Mississippi. In 1861 he served as a Confederate scout—apparently with the rank of second lieutenant—in Virginia. He seems next to have served as a scout and secret agent for Gen. THOMAS JORDAN in Mississippi during 1862. Early in 1863 he was transferred to Virginia, where, operating behind Union lines, he worked directly for Secretary of War Seddon. Later in the spring of that year he served as a scout in North Carolina for Gen. D.H. Hill, but after attracting the attention of federal authorities in the area, he was transferred to the service of General Longstreet in Virginia. It was while working for Longstreet that he may have rendered the memorable service to Lee on the eve of the Battle of Gettysburg.

Records of Harrison's career after Gettysburg are sketchy. Apparently Longstreet cashiered him and returned him to Secretary Seddon in September as the result of an incident in which Harrison, while somewhat drunk one night, appeared in an amateur theatrical production of *Othello* in Richmond (this apparently isolated venture into the theater was the key that led Bakeless to his mistaken conclusion that the secret agent was a professional actor). Some days later Harrison, then in Washington, married a young woman from Fairfax County, Virginia, whom he may have encountered during his scouting days in Virginia in 1861. Harrison seems to have continued serving as a Confederate secret agent. In April 1864 he went on a mysterious mission that took him to New York City.

According to the family history supplied by his granddaughter, Harrison briefly served the French-

William K. Harvey. Source: Official FBI photograph.

backed Emperor Maximilian in Mexico after the war. He went to search for gold in the Montana Territory in 1866, disappeared, and was presumed dead until 1900, when he turned up in Fairfax County, Virginia, made an unsuccessful effort to visit his two daughters (both by then married women in their mid-thirties), and then disappeared once and for all.

(Hall, "The Spy Harrison"; Stuart, "Of Spies and Borrowed Names"; Bakeless, *Spies of the Confederacy*.)

HARVEY, WILLIAM KING (September 13, 1915–June 9, 1976): intelligence officer

A native of Danville, Indiana, Harvey earned a law degree from Indiana University in 1937 and practiced law in Maysville, Kentucky. In 1940 he joined the FBI and, after serving briefly in the Pittsburgh field office, he was transferred to Washington, where he was assigned to counterespionage work against Soviet espionage networks within the United States. In this capacity he worked with Elizabeth Bentley, a former Soviet agent who cooperated with the FBI.

In 1947 Director J. EDGAR HOOVER ordered

Harvey transferred to duty in Indianapolis as punishment for a minor infraction of Bureau rules. Harvey resigned and was hired by the newly formed Central Intelligence Agency, then in great need of officers with experience in working against Soviet intelligence. He was assigned to Staff C, as the CIA's counterintelligence staff was then designated.

Harvey's professional and social life brought him into contact with HAROLD A.R. PHILBY, the first secretary of the British embassy in Washington. An intelligence officer of MI6, Philby was functioning as liaison between British intelligence and the CIA, while he was in fact serving as a penetration agent for Soviet intelligence. Harvey is credited with having unmasked Philby as a Soviet "mole" in June 1951.

In 1952 Harvey was made chief of the CIA base in Berlin. There he supervised Project Gold, the construction of a tunnel from West Berlin to East Berlin, which enabled the CIA and British intelligence to tap into the East German and Soviet telephone and teletype networks. The operation earned Harvey the Distinguished Intelligence Medal (see BERLIN TUNNEL).

In 1959 Harvey was assigned to CIA headquarters in Washington, where he was made Chief of Staff D, a communications intercept group. In early 1961 he took over responsibility for the Agency's "Executive Action" program. The program was aimed at developing various means of disabling foreign leaders, including assassination.

In November 1961, seven months after the abortive Bay of Pigs invasion, Harvey was ordered to explore the possibility of employing the Executive Action program against Fidel Castro and other Cuban leaders. (Beginning in 1960 there had been several earlier efforts mounted by the CIA to assassinate Castro; see CENTRAL INTELLIGENCE AGENCY.) In April 1962 Harvey contacted John Rosselli, a Mafia figure who had once been a member of the Al Capone gang, and obtained his cooperation in the Castro plan. Rosselli was to arrange for Cubans in Havana who were associated with the Mafia to carry out the proposed assassination. Harvey, on behalf of the CIA, would provide weapons and other material support for the plan. After Rosselli's assassination arrangements failed several times, Harvey terminated the CIA's association with the Mafia figure in mid-February 1963.

The attempts to assassinate Castro were part of a larger enterprise code-named MONGOOSE, which was a campaign of COVERT ACTION against Cuba mounted after the Bay of Pigs invasion. MONGOOSE, also involving the infiltration of agents into Cuba on missions of propaganda and sabotage, was conducted by a specially organized department of the CIA, Task Force W. Harvey was chief of Task Force W during 1961–63, but the failure of the operation to realize significant results led to his reassignment. In 1963 he was made chief of the CIA station in Rome, Italy.

Harvey's tour as Rome station chief achieved no more success than his previous assignment, and in fact was said to have brought about a decline in relations between the Agency and its Italian counterpart services. His stay in Rome was further complicated by health and personal problems—he had long had a drinking problem that now apparently worsened, and he suffered a heart attack. He was recalled to Washington and placed in charge of the Special Services Unit, a group charged with devising countermeasures to electronic surveillance.

Harvey resigned from the CIA in 1969 and took a job as an editor with the Bobbs-Merrill Publishing Company in Indianapolis. He was working in that capacity when he died from heart disease eight years later.

(U.S. Senate, *Alleged Assassination Plots Involving Foreign Leaders*; Martin, *Wilderness of Mirrors*; Hinckle and Turner, *The Fish is Red*; *Who's Who in America*, v. 34.)

HASKELL, JOHN HENRY FARRELL (December 5, 1903–): Army officer, businessman, government official, intelligence officer

A native of Fort Leavenworth, Kansas, Haskell attended the Brooklyn Polytechnical School in 1917–19, and was a student in Sainte-Croix, France in 1919–20. He graduated from the U.S. Military Academy in 1925 and served as a second lieutenant in the U.S. Army Corps of Engineers during that year.

Haskell resigned from the Army and joined the National City Company, a New York City banking firm, in 1925, remaining with the firm until 1931. In 1939 he became a vice-president of the New York Stock Exchange.

Haskell was a member of the New York National Guard from 1925 to 1940. In 1940 he returned to active duty with the Army and graduated from the Command and General Staff School in 1941. He served as chief of staff with the Twenty-seventh Division in the Pacific in 1942, and was acting director of civil affairs in the War Department during 1942–43.

In 1943 Haskell was assigned to the Office of Strategic Services. (Haskell's father had been the commanding officer of OSS Director WILLIAM J. DONOVAN during the First World War, and Haskell's brother, JOSEPH HASKELL, was chief of OSS Special

Operations in London.) Haskell served in several posts with the OSS in the Middle East, Russia, and the European Theater, and was chief of OSS/Italy.

During 1944–45 Haskell served with the Twelfth Army group and was wounded in action in Germany. He retired from the Army in 1946, having been awarded the Legion of Merit, Bronze Star, Purple Heart, the French croix de guerre, and several other foreign decorations. He returned to the vice-presidency of the New York Stock Exchange. During 1948–49 he also served as chief of the Marshall Plan mission to Sweden.

Haskell left the New York Stock Exchange in 1955 to become U.S. defense advisor to NATO, a post he held until 1960. From 1960 to 1968 he was the Paris representative of the Bankers Trust Company.

(*Who's Who in America*, 37th ed.; Smith, *OSS*.)

HASKELL, JOSEPH FARRELL (July 1, 1908–): Army officer, businessman, intelligence officer

A native of Omaha, Nebraska, Haskell graduated from the U.S. Military Academy in 1930. He served on various posts in the United States and the Philippines during 1930–41. He was assistant chief of staff for intelligence (see ARMY INTELLIGENCE) of the Seventh Corps during 1941–42, and during 1943 served with the chief of staff to the Supreme Allied Command in London, England.

In 1943 he was transferred to the Office of Strategic Services at the request of OSS Director Gen. WILLIAM J. DONOVAN (Haskell's father had been Donovan's commander during the First World War, and Haskell's brother, JOHN HASKELL, was chief of OSS/Italy). Donovan made Haskell chief of the OSS SPECIAL OPERATIONS BRANCH in London, knowing that the officer's reputation within the Army's European Theater command would enhance the OSS's respectability in American and British military circles in London. As a direct consequence of Haskell's appointment, the Special Operations Executive (the British counterpart of the OSS SO Branch) suggested a merger of the two groups in London, and a joint unit was formed under Haskell and British Brig. Gen. Eric T. Mockler-Ferryman.

During 1944–45 Haskell commanded a company of the Seventh Armored Division. He was assistant chief of staff at the headquarters of the Army Forces of the Middle Pacific during 1945–46, and served on the War Department General Staff in 1946. He retired with the rank of colonel in 1946, having been awarded the Silver Star, Legion of Merit, Bronze Star, the French Legion of Honor and croix de guerre, and several other foreign decorations.

Haskell joined the National Distillers and Chemical Corporation in New York City in 1946 and was vice-president for industrial relations of that firm from 1957 to 1963. Subsequently he was chairman of Haskell and Stern Associates, a management consulting firm.

(*Who's Who in America*, 42nd ed.; Smith, *OSS*.)

HAWKINS, JACK: Marine officer

Hawkins served in the U.S. Marines and was assigned to the ALLIED INTELLIGENCE BUREAU during the Second World War. While in the AIB he operated in the Japanese-occupied Philippines as a leader of Filipino guerrillas. He also saw combat on Iwo Jima and during the KOREAN WAR.

In 1960 Hawkins, then a colonel, was lent to the Central Intelligence Agency to advise on preparations for the operation later known as the BAY OF PIGS INVASION. He collaborated with JACOB D. ESTERLINE, the project director, in working out the plans for the operation, and, like Esterline, had serious misgivings when these plans were revised by higher levels within the government. Hawkins was CIA headquarters chief of paramilitary operations for the project.

(Wyden, *Bay of Pigs*.)

HAWKINS, MARTIN JONES (ca. 1830– January 1886): railroad engineer, soldier, Union secret service agent

Before the CIVIL WAR, Hawkins had worked in the South as a railroad engineer and a circus performer. In 1861 he enlisted in the Ohio Volunteer Infantry, which was part of the Army of the Ohio. In April 1862 he volunteered to take part in a paramilitary operation behind Confederate lines aimed at severing the rail line between Atlanta and Chattanooga (see ANDREWS'S RAID). He and a party of twenty other Union troops in civilian clothes and led by JAMES J. ANDREWS hijacked a locomotive and attempted to destroy railroad tracks and bridges between the two cities. He was captured by Confederate troops and imprisoned (Andrews and seven of the others were hanged). He and several others escaped. Hawkins made his way to Federal lines in Kentucky.

After the war Hawkins settled in Quincy, Illinois, where he worked at a variety of engineering jobs.

(Bryan, *The Spy in America*; Boatner, *Civil War Dictionary*; O'Neill, *Wild Train*.)

HAYDEN, STERLING (March 26, 1916–May 23, 1986): actor, intelligence officer

Best known by his screen name, Hayden was born Sterling Relyea Walter in Montclair, New Jersey. After working as a merchant seaman and fisherman, he made his film debut in 1940. Through his friendship with a son of WILLIAM J. DONOVAN, he joined the Office of Strategic Services after having been commissioned a captain in the U.S. Marine Corps. His nautical background led to his assignment to the OSS MARITIME UNIT and eventually to the command of the OSS base at Monopoli, a small port on the Adriatic in southeast Italy. He commanded a fleet of fourteen schooners that ran arms and supplies through the German blockade to the Yugoslavian partisans. Later he served with the OSS First Army Detachment in Germany. He was awarded the Silver Star.

Hayden resumed his motion-picture career after the war and starred as a leading man in the late 1940s and 1950s. Later in his career he appeared in character roles.

(Smith, *OSS*; Hymoff, *The OSS in World War II*; *Who's Who in America*, 42nd ed., obituary, *New York Times*, May 24, 1986, p. 28.)

HAYHANEN, REINO (May 14, 1920–1961?): Soviet intelligence officer and defector

A native of Kaskisarri, a village near Leningrad, USSR, Hayhanen graduated from a teachers college in 1939, taught school for three months, then was drafted into the NKVD (People's Commissariat for Internal Affairs, as the Soviet intelligence agency now known as the KGB was then designated). Because he spoke Finnish he was assigned as an interpreter in Finland during the Soviet invasion of that country during 1939–40. In 1940 he was sent to the Karelian Republic of the USSR, where he carried out counterespionage work and, in 1943, became a member of the Communist Party. In 1948 he was sent to Estonia for a year of espionage training, including learning English. At the completion of this course he was promoted to the rank of major and informed that he would be sent to the United States.

As preparation for this assignment he was given the identity of Eugene Nicoli Maki, a native American of Finnish extraction who visited Finland with his parents in 1927 and disappeared. Hayhanen was sent to Finland to establish his identity as Maki and obtain a U.S. passport. He arrived in Finland in 1950 and lived in the country for two and a half years, then applied for and received a U.S. passport. About the same time he married Hannah Kurikka, a Soviet citizen who may have been unaware of his intelligence role.

Hayhanen went to Moscow in July 1952 for additional training in espionage tradecraft. In October he arrived in New York City and later sent for his wife. They lived in several locations in the greater New York area before purchasing a house in a secluded region near Peekskill, New York, a spot he selected as suitable for the operation of a clandestine radio transmitter.

In 1954 Hayhanen was contacted by RUDOLF ABEL, a Soviet deep cover agent in New York City, and the intelligence officer Hayhanen had been sent to assist as courier and communications officer. However, Hayhanen, who had a serious drinking problem, failed to meet Abel's expectations, and Abel ordered him back to Moscow in 1957. Hayhanen got as far as Paris, then defected to the American intelligence representatives there. His disclosures to the FBI and his testimony led to the arrest and conviction of Abel on espionage charges. Hayhanen also turned in ROY A. RHODES, a U.S. Army sergeant who had worked for Soviet intelligence while serving on the staff of the American military attaché at the U.S. embassy in Moscow.

Hayhanen was granted political asylum in the United States. In 1961 spokesmen for the Central Intelligence Agency reportedly advised the producers of a television documentary in which he had recently appeared that he had died. According to some accounts he was killed in an automobile accident; according to others he died of natural causes, perhaps as a result of habitual and excessive drinking.

(Bernikow, *Abel*; Donovan, *Strangers on a Bridge*.)

HEADLEY, JOHN WILLIAM (ca. 1840–November 6, 1930): businessman, government official, Confederate Army officer, secret agent

A native of Hopkins County in western Kentucky, Headley enlisted in the First Kentucky Cavalry Regiment in 1861 and soon was promoted to first sergeant. He served under Gen. Nathan Bedford Forrest and was among the several hundred Confederate troops who escaped with Forrest from Fort Donelson, Tennessee, when that installation was captured by Gen. Ulysses S. Grant in February 1862. Soon thereafter Headley began working as a secret agent for Gen. Braxton Bragg.

In 1863 Headley was commissioned as a lieutenant in the Confederate cavalry, serving both as cavalryman and secret agent under Gen. John Hunt Morgan in the unit known as Morgan's Raiders. In 1864 he went to Canada to serve in an undercover capacity under Capt. THOMAS H. HINES and to take part in the NORTHWEST CONSPIRACY, a covert action operation aimed at fomenting rebellion in several Northern states through subversion and sabotage.

Headley was second in command, under Col. Robert Martin, of a phase of the Northwest Conspiracy that involved an attempt to burn a large part of New York City on November 25, 1864. In January 1865 he took part in an abortive attempt to kidnap Vice-President-elect Andrew Johnson.

Headley was arrested by Union troops after the war but quickly escaped. He settled in Louisville, Kentucky, where he went into the tobacco business and local politics. In 1891 he was appointed secretary of state of Kentucky, a post he held until 1896. In 1906 he published his war memoirs.

Headley married Mary Overall, a Confederate secret agent he had known during the war. In later life he and his wife followed their children to Los Angeles, California, where he lived out his last years.

(Headley, *Confederate Operations in Canada and New York* and biographic material prepared by the Time-Life editors to accompany the Time-Life reprint edition; Horan, *Confederate Agent.*)

HECKSCHER, HENRY (1910–): intelligence officer

A native of Germany, Heckscher moved to the United States before the Second World War and became an American citizen. He served in the Office of Strategic Services, and remained in the Strategic Services Unit, which preserved the OSS's assets after that agency was dissolved in 1945. He continued with the SSU and the Central Intelligence Group (see CENTRAL INTELLIGENCE AGENCY) and so was one of the charter members of the CIA. By 1953 he was chief of the CIA base in Berlin.

The following year Heckscher was serving in Guatemala, where he played an important role in the GUATEMALA COUP. During the late 1950s he was chief of station in Vientiane, Laos. During the late 1960s and early 1970s he was chief of station in Chile, where he helped draft one of the early CIA plans aimed at preventing Salvatore Allende from taking power. He was outspoken in his estimate that the special COVERT ACTION operation ordered against Allende by President Nixon would fail. After his tour as chief of station in Chile he retired from the CIA.

(Powers, *The Man Who Kept the Secrets;* Phillips, *The Night Watch.*)

John W. Headley. Source: Author's collection.

HECKSHER, AUGUST (September 16, 1913–): journalist, educator, foundation executive, public administrator, intelligence officer

A native of Huntington, New York, Hecksher graduated from St. Paul's School in Concord, New Hampshire, in 1932, and from Yale University in 1936. He attended Yale Law School in 1937, then studied government at Harvard University where he earned an M.A. in 1939. He taught American government and political theory at Yale from 1939 to 1941.

During 1941 to 1945, Hecksher served as a civilian employee of the Office of the Coordinator of Information and its successor, the Office of Strategic Services. He served in the OSS FOREIGN NATIONALITIES BRANCH and the OSS RESEARCH AND ANALYSIS BRANCH, and saw duty in North Africa.

After the war Hecksher edited the *Citizen Advertiser* in Auburn, New York, until 1948, when he moved to New York City to become chief editorial writer for the *New York Herald Tribune*. He was with the *Tribune* until 1956. The following year he became director of the Twentieth Century Fund. He later served as administrator of recreation and cultural affairs and commissioner of parks in New York City.

(*Current Biography*, 1958; *Who's Who in America*, 37th ed.; Smith, *OSS*.)

HEIDSIECK, CHARLES: vintner, businessman, supposed Confederate agent and courier

A native of France, Heidsieck was a member of the famous champagne producing family. He happened to be in New Orleans on business at the outbreak of the Civil War. He is said to have volunteered to work as a courier for the Confederate secret service, and to have posed as a bartender aboard Mississippi steamboats in order to carry secret dispatches through Union lines. It is further asserted that, when captured by the Federal authorities he escaped hanging through the intervention of the Lincoln administration.

(Davis, *Our Incredible Civil War*.)

HELLINGS, MARTIN L. (1841–September 16, 1908): telegraph manager, intelligence officer

Hellings was born near Jenkintown, Pennsylvania. During the Civil War he served two years in Company G, Seventh Regiment, Pennsylvania Reserve Corps, and received an honorable discharge after being wounded at Antietam. He learned telegraphy, was hired by the Western Union Telegraph Company, and eventually was sent to Key West, Florida, to manage the International Ocean Telegraph Company, a Western Union subsidiary that operated the submarine telegraph cables between Havana, Key West, and the Florida mainland. He married the daughter of William Curry, a local merchant said to be one of the richest men in Florida, and in addition to his work for Western Union, he was taken into his wife's family's business. His short but important intelligence career began in 1897, shortly before the outbreak of the SPANISH-AMERICAN WAR.

In December the U.S.S. *Maine* was stationed at the Key West Naval Base in response to heightened Spanish-American tensions and growing concern over American lives and property in Cuba. The battleship's captain, CHARLES D. SIGSBEE, was an old acquaintance of Hellings and had done some favors for Hellings and the telegraph company twenty years earlier. Hellings now agreed to return those favors by assisting Sigsbee in some confidential arrangements related to his mission at Key West. Hellings apparently arranged with Florida railroad and steam-

ship magnate H.B. Plant to have the officers of one of Plant's ships, the *Olivette*, carry confidential messages between Sigsbee and the American consul general at Havana. Hellings also furnished Sigsbee with information obtained by the Western Union telegraphers in Havana, most notably Domingo Villaverde. These services became even more valuable late in January 1898 when the *Maine* was sent to Havana. On the night of February 15, 1898, Villaverde circumvented the Spanish military censor at Havana to telegraph Hellings that the *Maine* had blown up in the harbor, and Hellings notified the American naval authorities at Key West.

When war was declared in April, Hellings's Cuban intelligence network became an integral part of the U.S. Army Signal Corps, and Hellings was commissioned a captain in the Volunteer Signal Corps. The Havana-to-Key West cable remained open by the mutual consent of the Spanish and American authorities, and Villaverde continued to report clandestinely from Havana to Hellings and the other Signal Corps officers at Key West. The information was promptly relayed to Washington and the White House.

The most valuable information Hellings received from Villaverde came over the wire on May 19th. It was a report that a Spanish squadron of four cruisers and two torpedo boat destroyers under Adm. Pascual Cervera y Topete had arrived at the port of Santiago de Cuba on the southeast coast of the island. The location of Cervera's squadron had been a major source of concern in Washington and along the Eastern Seaboard, and failure to pinpoint it was hamstringing American plans for an invasion of Cuba. The information enabled the U.S. Navy to blockade the squadron at Santiago, thus neutralizing a major element of Spanish military strength, a development that led to the land-and-sea battles of Santiago, the decisive turning points of the war.

Hellings was killed by a railroad train while crossing the tracks near Devon, Pennsylvania, in 1908.

(O'Toole, *The Spanish War*, "Our Man in Havana.")

HELLIWELL, PAUL LIONEL EDWARD (September 17, 1913–ca. 1980): lawyer, banker, intelligence officer

A native of Brooklyn, New York, Helliwell graduated from the University of Florida in 1937 and was awarded a J.D. by the same school in 1939. He practiced law in Miami until 1941 when he was commissioned in the U.S. Army and assigned to Army Intelligence. He was subsequently assigned to the Office of Strategic Services.

Helliwell served in the OSS SECRET INTELLI-

GENCE BRANCH and headed the SI Branch in Kunming, China. He was also responsible for intelligence operations in French Indochina and, early in 1945, he had several contacts with Vietnamese Communist leader Ho Chi Minh, who was then fighting the Japanese in Indochina. He presented Ho with some token revolvers and ammunition in gratitude for the rescue of downed American fliers, but he declined to furnish other arms that Ho might have used against the French (see VIETNAM WAR).

Discharged from the Army and OSS in 1946 with the rank of colonel, Helliwell was awarded the Legion of Merit and several other decorations. He subsequently served in the Central Intelligence Agency as an aide to FRANK G. WISNER in the Office of Policy Coordination (see CENTRAL INTELLIGENCE AGENCY). Helliwell had become well-acquainted with Gen. Claire Chennault during his service in China, and Chennault contacted him in 1949 regarding the proposed use by the CIA of Civil Air Transport, a China-based airline in which the general was interested. Helliwell's recommendation to Wisner in this matter resulted in the CIA subsidy and eventual acquisition of CAT (see AIR PROPRIETARIES).

Helliwell returned to the private practice of law in Miami in 1952 and was involved in banking and insurance in Florida. He served for a time as consul general in Miami for the government of Thailand.

(*Who Was Who in America*, v. 7; Smith, *OSS*; Leary, *Perilous Missions*.)

Richard M. Helms—oil portrait by William F. Draper. Source: Central Intelligence Agency.

HELMS, RICHARD MCGARRAH (May 30, 1913–): journalist, intelligence officer

A native of St. David's, Pennsylvania, Helms spent some of his boyhood in Europe, where he attended schools in Germany and Switzerland and became fluent in German and French. He graduated from Williams College in 1935 and pursued a career in journalism. He went to Europe as a correspondent for United Press, covered the 1936 Olympic games in Berlin and interviewed, among other celebrities, Adolf Hitler. Upon returning to the United States, he joined the staff of the *Indianapolis Times* and became the newspaper's national advertising director.

In 1942 Helms joined the U.S. Navy and, after a sixty-day training course at Harvard University, was commissioned as a lieutenant. After a year of serving in antisubmarine operations with the Navy's Eastern Sea Frontier command in New York City, he was assigned to the Office of Strategic Services. OSS trained Helms in intelligence TRADECRAFT and as-

signed him to the OSS SECRET INTELLIGENCE BRANCH.

Helms served in Washington, London, Paris, and Luxembourg, running espionage operations against Germany. After VE-Day he was assigned to Berlin, and he stayed on in Germany with the Strategic Services Unit, the caretaker outfit that preserved OSS assets after it was dissolved in September 1945. His job was to preserve the skeletal agent networks in those countries left over from OSS wartime espionage operations, and to carry out liaison with Allied intelligence services in the area. He remained with SSU when it was transferred to the newly created Central Intelligence Group in 1946 (see CENTRAL INTELLIGENCE AGENCY) and renamed the Office of Special Operations, the SECRET INTELLIGENCE department of CIG. He was discharged from the Navy with the rank of lieutenant commander and became a civilian employee of CIG. Returning to Washington, Helms was chief of Foreign Division M of CIG/OSO, which was responsible for secret intelligence operations in Germany, Austria, and Switzerland. He remained in OSO after the CIG was established as the Central Intelligence Agency in September 1947.

In November 1951 Helms succeeded LYMAN G. KIRKPATRICK to the position of deputy assistant director for operations, the number two position in OSO. Kirkpatrick had been promoted to assistant director for operations, but when he was stricken with polio and hospitalized in July 1952, Helms moved into his post. It was at this same time that OSO was merged with the Office of Policy Coordination, the COVERT ACTION department of CIA, to form the CIA CLANDESTINE SERVICE (then designated the Plans Directorate). Helms became the number two man in the new and larger unit, serving under FRANK G. WISNER, the deputy director for plans (i.e., the chief of the Clandestine Service).

Under Wisner and his successor, RICHARD M. BISSELL, the Clandestine Service emphasized covert action—e.g., the IRAN COUP and the GUATEMALA COUP—but Helms was both distrustful of and skeptical about such operations, which was characteristic of the professional secret intelligence officers who had previously served in the OSS. From its earliest beginnings in 1960 he had serious misgivings about the operation that became known as the BAY OF PIGS INVASION, and he managed to completely distance himself from it, in effect running the rest of the Clandestine Service for Bissell while Bissell involved himself entirely in the Cuban operation. Perhaps because he was thus not held responsible in any way for the failure of the operation, he was appointed to succeed Bissell as chief of the Clandestine Service after the latter was forced to resign in its wake in February 1962.

Despite his distaste for covert action operations he inherited many of them along with the position of Clandestine Service chief. Perhaps the one such operation least to his taste was the ongoing effort to remove Fidel Castro from power in Cuba by any means, including assassination. Pressure from the Kennedy administration on the CIA to accomplish this task actually increased after the Bay of Pigs invasion (although Helms testified before the Church Committee that he had never specifically discussed assassination with the President).

After JOHN A. MCCONE resigned as CIA director in April 1965 he reportedly recommended Helms as his successor. However, President Lyndon Johnson appointed Vice Adm. WILLIAM F. RABORN to that post and made Helms deputy director of central intelligence, the number two post in the Agency. When Raborn resigned after his short tenure in June 1966, Johnson appointed Helms CIA director.

Helms secured his position and that of the CIA in Johnson's esteem in May 1967 when he delivered a special NATIONAL INTELLIGENCE ESTIMATE to the White House accurately predicting an Israeli victory in the anticipated Six Day War. Appropriately, this estimate benefited from information furnished by the secret intelligence operators of the Clandestine Service (see DESMOND FITZGERALD).

Helms's tenure as DCI included the period of greatest U.S. involvement in the VIETNAM WAR, and while Helms, as a professional intelligence officer, was skeptical of prospects for American success in Vietnam, he was not outspoken in this view within the Johnson administration, nor did he support CIA intelligence analyst Samuel A. Adams in his emphatic rejection of Army intelligence estimates of Vietcong and North Vietnamese troop strength. Like ALLEN W. DULLES, another former Clandestine Service chief who became CIA director, Helms had little disposition to exercise his role as the government's chief intelligence officer and leader of the INTELLIGENCE COMMUNITY, and he remained oriented toward covert intelligence operations.

Helms was reappointed CIA director by President Nixon in 1969. Nixon's national security advisor, Henry Kissinger, a knowledgeable and opinionated student of foreign affairs, reduced the importance of the CIA within the administration. Nixon himself distrusted the CIA and disliked what he regarded as the liberal academic intellectual orientation of the Agency's intelligence analysts.

On Nixon's and Kissinger's specific orders, Helms directed the CIA to undertake an effort to overthrow the Chilean government of Marxist Salvatore Allende (see WILLIAM B. BROE). The operation failed, however.

In 1972 Helms resisted an attempt by Nixon to involve the CIA in the Watergate affair as a means of sidetracking the FBI investigation of that matter. Apparently because of this refusal, Nixon did not reappoint Helms as CIA director. Helms left the Agency in February 1973 to accept the position of U.S. ambassador to Iran, a post he held until 1976.

In 1973 Helms, while testifying under oath before the Senate Foreign Relations Committee during the confirmation hearings for his appointment to the Iran post, denied that the CIA had tried to overthrow the government of Chile. As he later explained, "I found myself in a position of conflict. I had sworn my oath to protect certain secrets. I didn't want to lie. I didn't want to mislead the Senate. I was simply trying to find my way through a very difficult situation in which I found myself."

In 1977 Helms was charged with perjury with regard to his testimony, pleaded guilty, and was given a fine and a suspended jail sentence.

Since 1977 Helms has worked as a business consultant on international matters.

(*Current Biography*, 1967; *Who's Who in America*, 42nd ed.; Powers, *The Man Who Kept the Secrets*; Karalekas, *History of the Central Intelligence Agency*.)

HENRY, JOHN (or JAMES): British secret intelligence agent of the early 1800s

Henry's origin and background are obscure—there is even some question regarding his first name: by some accounts he was a native of Ireland who became an American citizen, served as an artillery officer in the U.S. Army, resigned his commission, and studied law in Montreal. Sometime circa 1808 Henry offered his services as a secret intelligence agent to Sir James Craig, the governor-general of Canada. Henry proposed to travel through New England to assess local public opinion regarding Great Britain, and to identify those Americans who harbored pro-British sympathies and would continue to be pro-British even in the event of a war between the United States and Britain.

Sir James accepted Henry's offer and the latter carried out his mission, discovering considerable pro-British sentiment among the Federalists of New England (who, in fact, had taken no pains to hide it). He duly reported his findings to Sir James, and returned to Canada after several months to present the governor-general with a bill for his intelligence services, which he valued in the sum of $160,000. This sumptuous figure may have seemed even more surprising to Sir James, who had until then labored under the misapprehension that Henry expected no other reward for his work than the satisfaction of having rendered signal services to the Crown.

This misunderstanding eventually (in 1812) led Henry to disclose his secret mission to President James Madison, who spent $50,000 of public funds to purchase documents from Henry purporting to prove that the New England Federalists (Madison's political foes) were ready to secede from the Union and rejoin Great Britain. By the time Madison discovered that the Henry papers contained nothing but warmed-over editorials from New England newspapers, the British agent was safety out of the country.

The fact that the British had sent a secret intelligence agent into the United States was disclosed, and it inflamed anti-British public opinion on the eve of the WAR OF 1812. Henry went to England and apparently resumed his cloak-and-dagger career in 1820, when he was sent to Italy by certain British political interests to turn up derogatory material regarding Caroline Amelia, queen of Britain's George IV.

(Bryan, *The Spy in America*; Ind, *A Short History of Espionage*; Beirne, *The War of 1812*.)

HENSON, PHILIP (1827–?): newspaper publisher, Union double agent of the Civil War

A native of what was then Indian territory and is now northeast Alabama, Henson lost his father at an early age and made his living through a variety of jobs. As a young man he lived in Kansas, New Mexico, Georgia, and other parts of the South, and eventually settled in Rienzi, Mississippi, where he worked as a store clerk.

After the outbreak of the Civil War Henson obtained a job as a slave overseer on a local plantation, a position that made him exempt from conscription into the Confederate Army. When Union forces advanced into Mississippi in 1862 Henson, along with most of his neighbors, took an oath of loyalty to the Union. Shortly thereafter he was recruited into the secret service of the Army of the Mississippi by General Rosecrans's chief of police, WILLIAM TRUESDAIL. Later he worked for Gen. GRENVILLE M. DODGE, and it is likely he reported to Dodge's secret service chief, L.A. NARON.

Although Henson's secret service is supported by General Dodge's postwar testimonials in his behalf, most of the details of his exploits are supported only by Henson's own ghostwritten memoirs. The following is a summary of Henson's account.

Henson proved to be an effective secret service agent, abetted by his Southern accent, a wide circle of friends and acquaintances ready to assert (sincerely and mistakenly) that he was a loyal Confederate, and an excellent memory that made it unnecessary to carry incriminating notes and reports. Late in 1862 he was arrested by Confederate troops near Columbus, Mississippi, while on a covert reconnaissance mission. He was taken before Gen. Daniel Ruggles, whom he soon convinced of his putative loyalty. Ruggles recruited Henson to work for him as a scout (i.e., a spy), an arrangement that enabled him thereafter to pass easily in either direction through the Confederate lines.

Henson later worked as a secret agent for Confederate Gens. Samuel Gholson and Samuel Ferguson, while he continued to serve Dodge (probably through Naron). He used the classic method of the double agent, delivering intelligence of small value to the enemy to protect himself, while he furnished important information to his true employer.

In 1864 Henson, while on a protracted covert reconnaissance in Mississippi, was arrested by the Confederates as a spy and taken before Gen. Nathan B. Forrest, but his Confederate bona fides was confirmed by General Gholson, who happened to be present. Forrest then dispatched Henson to Georgia on assignment to hunt out Union spies for Gen. Leonidas Polk. Henson took the opportunity to collect intelligence on Confederate forces in the area. Later, Polk dispatched him into Union territory on a covert reconnaissance mission. Polk's pass enabled him to pass easily through the Confederate lines and deliver his report to Dodge.

Henson pushed his luck a bit too far shortly thereafter. In May 1864, while on yet another reconnaissance for Dodge in Confederate territory, he was arrested on a charge of draft-dodging that quickly escalated into suspicion of espionage. Because he carried no notes or other incriminating material, the case against him was flimsy and circumstantial. The Confederates were unwilling to try and hang a man who might well be innocent, but equally unwilling to release him to (possibly) commit more mischief. In the event he spent many miserable months in prisons in Mobile, Alabama, and Meridian, Mississippi. In February 1865 his captors resolved their dilemma by permitting him to enlist in the Confederate Army, which was then in dire need of manpower. Possibly with the assistance of other Union secret service agents working for Dodge, he escaped from a troop train and made his way back to Dodge's headquarters in Mississippi.

After the war Henson returned to Mississippi and published a pro-Republican newspaper.

(Kane, *Spies for the Blue and Gray.*)

HEPPNER, RICHARD PINKERTON (1908–): lawyer, government official, intelligence officer

A native of New York City, Heppner graduated from Princeton University in 1932 and from Columbia Law School in 1935. He served on the staff of the attorney general of New York State, and in 1936 joined the New York law firm of Wiley, Wilcox and Sheffield. In 1938 he joined the law firm of WILLIAM J. DONOVAN, Donovan, Leisure, Newton and Lumbard.

Heppner was an officer in the U.S. Army Reserve and he went on active duty in 1941 to serve as special assistant to Donovan, then director of the Office of Coordinator of Information, the predecessor to the Office of Strategic Services. In 1942 he went to London and attended the Combined Operations Training Center (i.e., the commando school) at Inverary, Scot-

land. Promoted to the rank of major, he served as assistant to William Phillips, chief of OSS/London and former ambassador, on the latter's Presidential mission to India in 1942–43.

In 1944 Heppner was promoted to the rank of colonel and sent to China to take charge of OSS/China. He remained in that post until the end of the war.

Heppner rejoined the Donovan law firm after the war. He served as deputy assistant secretary of defense for International Security Affairs during the Eisenhower administration.

(Office of Strategic Services, OSS File, "Prominent Persons in the OSS"; Smith, *OSS.*)

HERBERT, RAYFORD W.: intelligence officer

Herbert was one of the former special agents of the Federal Bureau of Investigation who joined the Central Intelligence Agency in the late 1940s. He served in the Western Hemisphere Division of the CIA CLANDESTINE SERVICE as deputy to J.C. KING, the long-time chief of the Western Hemisphere Division.

(Corson, *The Armies of Ignorance;* Smith, *Portrait of a Cold Warrior.*)

HERON, WILLIAM (1742–January 8, 1819): government official, American and British secret agent

A native of Cork, Ireland, Heron was educated at Trinity College in Dublin before emigrating to America. He settled in Reading, Connecticut, and was elected to the Connecticut Assembly in 1778. Little is known of his life before the American Revolution.

Sometime circa 1780 Heron undertook his double role as spy for both the Americans and the British. He exploited his friendship with his Reading neighbor, Gen. Samuel H. Parsons of the Continental Army, to obtain a pass through American lines in order to enter British-occupied Manhattan on personal business. While making this trip he was entrusted by Gen. BENEDICT ARNOLD, then in command of the American stronghold at West Point, with a letter addressed to "John Anderson," a pseudonym of Arnold's British CASE OFFICER, Maj. JOHN ANDRÉ. Suspicious of Arnold, Heron did not believe the letter but turned it over to Parsons. Although the letter was innocently worded and did not disclose Arnold's treachery, Heron's action insured Parsons's confidence in him after Arnold's defection became known.

The position of trust Heron thus achieved enabled

him to play a treacherous game in which he made repeated visits to Manhattan, where he reported to British intelligence officer, Maj. OLIVER DE LANCEY, on American military matters he had learned through Parsons's incautious talk. He also misrepresented Parsons to the British as a disaffected American officer similar to Arnold, and obtained money under the pretense that he could engineer Parsons's defection. Heron maintained his standing with Parsons and other American officials by delivering to them intelligence on British military matters gathered during his visits to Manhattan.

Heron was an opportunist, loyal only to himself. While he was playing his double game, he continued to serve in the Connecticut Assembly, serving several terms until 1796. His treason, unsuspected during his lifetime, remained unknown until 1882, when material from British archives was released to an American historian.

(Bakeless, *Turncoats, Traitors and Heroes;* Bryan, *The Spy in America;* Van Doren, *Secret History of the American Revolution; Who Was Who in America,* historical volume.)

HEYSER, RICHARD S. (1927–): Air Force officer, reconnaissance pilot

A native of Battle Creek, Michigan, Heyser attended the University of Florida before joining the U.S. Air Force in 1951. After completing pilot training he served in Japan in 1953 and 1954.

Heyser had reached the rank of major and was serving with the 4080th Strategic Reconnaissance Wing when, on October 14, 1962, he and Maj. RUDOLPH ANDERSON, JR. flew two U-2 photoreconnaissance sorties of western Cuba. Heyser's cameras photographed sites near San Cristobal, where preparations were under way to install Soviet offensive missiles. The discovery precipitated the CUBAN MISSILE CRISIS. Heyser and Anderson flew subsequent photoreconnaissance missions over Cuba during the crisis, enabling American photointerpreters to monitor the progress of Soviet missile preparations.

(Daniel and Hubbell, *Strike in the West;* Prados, *The Soviet Estimate.*)

HILLENKOETTER, ROSCOE HENRY (May 8, 1897–June 18, 1982): naval officer, intelligence officer, director of central intelligence

A native of St. Louis, Missouri, Hillenkoetter graduated from the U.S. Naval Academy in 1919. He served in a variety of sea and shore assignments,

Rear Adm. Roscoe H. Hillenkoetter—oil portrait by Comis. Source: Central Intelligence Agency.

including a tour aboard a submarine, and also taught modern languages at the Naval Academy.

In 1933 Hillenkoetter was assigned to the Office of Naval Intelligence and served a two-year tour as assistant naval attaché at the American Embassy in Paris, France. He was made a diplomatic courier so that he was free to wander about Europe observing military conditions. His usual courier route took him to Berlin, Warsaw, Moscow, and Prague. After a two-and-a-half year hiatus during which he served aboard the U.S.S. *Maryland,* he returned to Paris and his assistant naval attaché assignment, with the additional role as assistant naval attaché for Madrid and Lisbon. During his frequent trips to Spain he helped evacuate Americans who had become involved in the Spanish civil war.

In 1940 Hillenkoetter was relieved of his Madrid and Lisbon duties and made naval attaché in Paris. He was thus on hand to observe and report on the German takeover of Paris in June 1940. After the American diplomatic staff was relocated to Vichy in unoccupied France, he worked closely with the French underground and made frequent trips to North Africa to report on German military activities there.

In November 1941 Hillenkoetter was assigned to the U.S.S. *West Virginia* as executive officer. He was wounded when the ship was sunk during the PEARL HARBOR ATTACK. From September 1942 to March 1943 he was the officer in charge of intelligence on the staff of Pacific commander Admiral Nimitz. He commanded the U.S.S. *Dixie* until 1944 when he was given shore duty in the Bureau of Naval Personnel.

After the war Hillenkoetter commanded the U.S.S. *Missouri* on a cruise to Turkey, Greece, Italy, and North Africa. In 1946 he returned to the post of naval attaché in Paris.

In May 1947 Hillenkoetter was appointed director of the Central Intelligence Group (see CENTRAL INTELLIGENCE AGENCY). He remained in this post while the CIG became the CIA later that year, and served until 1950, when he was succeeded by Gen. WALTER BEDELL SMITH.

Hillenkoetter subsequently commanded the Seventh Task Force in Formosan waters, and the Third Naval District. He retired in 1957 with the rank of vice admiral and later served in senior executive positions with several private corporations.

Among the many decorations awarded Hillenkoetter were the Purple Heart, the Bronze Star, the Legion of Merit, and the Greek Order of the Phoenix.

(*Current Biography*, 1950; *WAMB*; Dorwart, *Conflict of Duty*.)

HILSMAN, ROGER, JR. (November 23, 1919–): government official, educator, national security specialist, intelligence and covert operations officer

The son of a career Army officer, Hilsman was born in Waco, Texas, and grew up on Army posts in the midwest, California, and the Philippines. He graduated from the U.S. Military Academy in 1943 and, with the rank of second lieutenant, joined Merrill's Marauders, an elite, regiment-sized unit of volunteer jungle fighters operating in the China-Burma-India theater under the leadership of famed Brig. Gen. Frank D. Merrill.

After recovering from wounds sustained in combat with the Japanese, Hilsman transferred to the OFFICE OF STRATEGIC SERVICES and was assigned to Detachment 101, the contingent of the OSS Special Operations Branch fighting in the China-Burma-India theater. He commanded a guerrilla battalion of Kachin (Burmese tribesmen) jungle fighters for a year,

operating behind enemy lines. After the defeat of Japan, he was part of an OSS rescue team that parachuted into Manchuria to search for American prisoners of war still held by the Japanese in the chaotic situation prevailing in the area immediately after the war. The OSS team found Gen. Jonathan M. Wainwright and several other high-ranking officers among the prisoners held at Sian. At Hoten, Captain Hilsman found an American officer who had been a prisoner of the Japanese since shortly after the fall of Corregidor in May 1942—Col. Roger Hilsman, Sr., his father.

After the war, Hilsman, then a major, remained with the OSS and its postwar incarnations, the Strategic Services Unit, the Central Intelligence Group, and the CENTRAL INTELLIGENCE AGENCY. He was, first, assistant chief for Far East intelligence operations, and then special assistant to the executive officer of the CIA. In 1947 he left the CIA and entered Yale University, earning a master's degree in international relations in 1950 and a doctorate in the same field the following year. During the Korean War he worked as a planning officer with the American forces of NATO.

In 1953 Hilsman joined the Center for International Studies at Princeton University, where he taught for three years. In 1956 he became chief of the foreign affairs division of the Library of Congress's Legislative Reference Service, and in 1958 he took the position of deputy director of the Service. During this period he published several books on strategic intelligence and military policy.

In February 1961 President Kennedy appointed Hilsman director of the State Department's BUREAU OF INTELLIGENCE AND RESEARCH. Hilsman did not act simply as the administrator of a large government bureaucracy; he took an active role in the collection and analysis of intelligence, serving as an intelligence advisor to the secretary of state and the President. His firsthand experience with guerrilla operations in Southeast Asia was of particular value during a period when the United States was attempting to deal with the growing problem of insurgency in the area. He played a very active role during the CUBAN MISSILE CRISIS, communicating with Soviet officials and briefing congressional and other government officials on developments.

In 1963 Hilsman succeeded W. Averell Harriman as assistant secretary of state for Far Eastern affairs. He held this post until February 1964, when he resigned and joined the public law and government faculty of Columbia University.

(*Current Biography*, 1964; Ford, *Donovan of the OSS*; Hilsman, *To Move a Nation*.)

HINES, THOMAS HENRY (ca. 1841–1898): lawyer, jurist, Confederate army officer, and secret agent

Hines resigned from the faculty of the Masonic University in La Grange, Kentucky, at the outbreak of the Civil War to lead Buckner's Guides, a small volunteer unit of Confederate cavalry. He and the unit served under Gen. Albert S. Johnston in Kentucky during the first months of the war, carrying out guerrilla raids on Union forces and military installations. He was commissioned a lieutenant in November 1861. On December 31 he and ten men carried out a successful raid on the Union garrison at Borah's Ferry, Kentucky.

Hines was forced to disband Buckner's Guides after the Confederate withdrawal from Kentucky and the death of General Johnston in the Shiloh campaign of April 1862. In May he enlisted as a private in the Kentucky cavalry of (then) Col. John Hunt Morgan (the unit was better known as Morgan's Raiders). He was commissioned a captain the following month and resumed leading guerrilla raids into Kentucky, as he had done while commanding Buckner's Guides. At the same time he made frequent lone, covert trips into Kentucky in civilian disguise to meet with the state leaders of the Copperheads, as the Northern anti-war Democrats were called (see KNIGHTS OF THE GOLDEN CIRCLE). He organized networks of intelligence agents and saboteurs among the Copperheads.

In July 1863 Hines took part in Morgan's Ohio raid, a mission in which (then) General Morgan led some 2,400 cavalry troopers across the Ohio River into Indiana and Ohio. The operation was planned on the assumption that Copperhead sentiment in the area was so strong that the local militia would change sides. Morgan and Hines also hoped to release and arm a large number of Confederate prisoners of war held near Indianapolis. Their hope was nothing less than to bring the state of Indiana into the Confederacy. The Copperhead support failed to materialize, however, and the militia did not join with Morgan's Raiders, but fought against them. The expedition was routed and Federal troops captured Hines at Buffington, Ohio, on July 19th. The rest of the force, including General Morgan, was captured a week later.

Hines, Morgan, and the other captives were incarcerated in the prisoner-of-war camp on Johnson's Island near Sandusky, Ohio. As punishment for an attempted escape, they were sent to the Ohio State Penitentiary at Columbus. In November 1863 Hines engineered their escape from that prison, and they made their way back through Confederate lines.

In March 1864 Confederate Secretary of War James

Thomas H. Hines. Source: Author's collection.

A. Seddon commissioned Hines as the military commander of what became known as the NORTHWEST CONSPIRACY, a Confederate COVERT ACTION operation aimed at bringing about the secession of Ohio, Indiana, and Illinois from the Union. The plan called for the use of the Knights of the Golden Circle to inflame Copperhead sentiment in these states, foment revolution, and overthrow the state governments. At the same time, tens of thousands of Confederate prisoners of war held in camps within these states would be freed and armed to take part in the uprising. Confederate troops covertly based in Canada would cross the border into these states, while other Southern troops would land on the Maine coast and march across that state, burning farms and towns along the path of the advance.

Hines went to Toronto, Canada, in April 1864 to establish a headquarters for the operation. He worked with JACOB THOMPSON, the Confederate commissioner and chief secret agent in Canada, who was in overall charge of the operation. The date set for the uprising was August 29th, to coincide with the opening of the Democratic National Convention in Chicago. However, Union counterintelligence had penetrated the operation (see FELIX A. STIDGER) and the authorities were alerted. The Copperheads refused to go ahead with the plan, and the operation was aborted.

Hines made a second attempt on November 8th, Election Day. This operation was planned to include New York City, where Hines's agents were to seize control of the city and take over the U.S. Sub-Treasury on Wall Street. This operation, too, fell victim to Union counterintelligence, and some of Hines's lieutenants were arrested on November 6th. Hines himself managed to escape to the Confederacy. In December he was again sent to Canada to continue guerrilla warfare against the North, but he soon returned to Kentucky to attempt to organize a new guerrilla force there. After the defeat of the Confederacy he set out for Canada once more. In Detroit, two days after the assassination of President Lincoln, Hines was mistaken by a mob for John Wilkes Booth, whom he closely resembled, and he only escaped alive to Canada by hijacking a ferryboat.

He remained in Toronto after the war, studying French at the University of Toronto, and law under former Chief Justice of the Kentucky Court of Appeals, Joshua Bullitt, who was also living in that city as an expatriate at the time. In 1866, after an amnesty had been declared, he returned to Kentucky where he was admitted to the bar and practiced law in Bowling Green. In 1875 he was elected chief justice of the state's Court of Appeals.

(Horan, *Confederate Agent*; Bryan, *The Spy in America*; McMaster, *Our House Divided*.)

HITCH, CHARLES JOHNSTON (January 9, 1910–): economist, educator, intelligence analyst

A native of Boonville, Missouri, Hitch earned an A.A. from the Kemper Mill School in 1929, a B.A. from the University of Arizona in 1931, and studied at Harvard University in 1931–32. He attended Oxford University as a Rhodes scholar, earning a B.A. and an M.A. in 1934 and 1938, respectively. He taught at Oxford from 1935 until 1943, when he was commissioned as a first lieutenant in the U.S. Army and assigned to the Office of Strategic Services.

Hitch served in the OSS RESEARCH AND ANALYSIS BRANCH as an economic intelligence analyst. After the war he resumed teaching at Oxford and was a visiting professor at the University of São Paulo, Brazil. In 1948 he joined the Rand Corporation where he served as chief of the economics division until 1961, when he joined the Department of Defense.

Hitch assisted Secretary of Defense Robert McNamara in installing a new budget planning system in the Pentagon. In 1965 he joined the University of California and later became president of the university.

(Cline, *The CIA, Reality vs. Myth*; *Who's Who in America*, 37th ed.)

HOLBORN, HAJO (May 12, 1902–1969): historian, intelligence analyst

A native of Berlin, Germany, Holborn received a Ph.D. from the University of Berlin in 1924. From 1926 to 1931 he was assistant professor of history at the University of Heidelberg, and professor of history at the School of Politics in Berlin in 1931–34. In 1934 he moved to the United States and joined the faculty of Yale University.

In 1943 Holborn joined the Office of Strategic Services, where he served as an intelligence analyst in the OSS RESEARCH AND ANALYSIS BRANCH. After the war in Europe, he served as an advisor to the American occupation forces in Germany and a consultant to the Department of State. He returned to Yale in 1949.

(*Who's Who in America*, v. 28; Smith, *OSS*.)

HONEYMAN, JOHN (ca. 1730–ca. 1823): tradesman, farmer, American double agent

A native of Ireland, Honeyman emigrated to America and served in the British army during the French and Indian (Seven Years) War. He settled in Philadelphia and worked as a weaver.

In 1775 Honeyman volunteered his services as a secret agent to Gen. GEORGE WASHINGTON. He proposed to pose as a Loyalist butcher in order to pass freely within British-controlled areas and observe British military strength and movements. Washington accepted the proposal, and Honeyman soon moved to Griggstown, a village a few miles southwest of New Brunswick, New Jersey, where he began his imposture.

In December 1776 Honeyman contrived to be arrested as a suspected Tory spy by pickets of Washington's forces posted in Pennsylvania, just across the Delaware River from Trenton. Honeyman was taken to Washington, to whom he reported on what he had just observed of the British force occupying Trenton. The information he supplied was of great value to the American commander in planning his attack on Trenton a few days later (see AMERICAN REVOLUTION).

To maintain Honeyman's cover as a Loyalist and suspected British spy, Washington had him confined to the guardhouse, but also contrived to permit him to escape so that he could return to Trenton and participate in a deception operation in support of the coming American attack. When Honeyman made his way back to Trenton, he reported to the British commander that the Continental forces were in a state of hopeless disorganization and were on the brink of mutiny. This misinformation may have contributed to the commander's complacency and his subsequent disregard of reports from local Tory farmers that Washington's forces were preparing to move. In any event, the attack on the morning of December 26th came as a complete surprise.

Honeyman's cover as a Tory and British spy was so complete that it was necessary for Washington to order the protection of his wife and children from Patriot zealots in Griggstown. Honeyman's subsequent secret services for Washington, if any, have not been recorded. After the war he moved to Lamington, New Jersey, where he was a prosperous farmer.

Accounts of Honeyman's secret service were passed down as oral tradition to his descendants and verified by local historians in the nineteenth century. His exploit is memorialized by a plaque and stone marker in Washington Crossing State Park near Trenton.

(Falkner, "A Spy for Washington"; Bakeless, *Turncoats, Traitors and Heroes*.)

HOOD, WILLIAM J. (1920–): intelligence officer

Hood served in Army Intelligence during the Second World War, then transferred to the Office of Strategic Services. He served in the OSS COUNTER-ESPIONAGE BRANCH in London, and later in OSS/Switzerland under ALLEN W. DULLES. After the war he served in the Central Intelligence Agency. He was a senior aide to JAMES J. ANGLETON, chief of the Counterintelligence Staff of the CIA CLANDESTINE SERVICE. For a time Hood was chief of operations in the Western Hemisphere Division of the Clandestine Service.

Hood retired from the CIA in 1975 and has since written and published an account of Pyotr Popov, a Soviet military intelligence officer and DEFECTOR-IN-PLACE who worked for the CIA. He is also the author of a novel, *Spy Wednesday* (1986).

(Hood, *Mole*; Martin, *Wilderness of Mirrors*; Agee, *Inside the Company*.)

HOOVER, CALVIN BRYCE (April 14, 1897–June 23, 1974): economist, educator, intelligence officer

A native of Berwick, Illinois, Hoover served in the U.S. Army in France during the First World War. He graduated from Monmouth College in Monmouth, Illinois, in 1922, and was awarded a Ph.D. from the University of Wisconsin in 1925, and he joined the economics faculty of Duke University that year.

Hoover spent 1929–30 in the Soviet Union, studying the Soviet economic system, and in 1931 he published *The Economic Life of Soviet Russia*. He was on hand to witness Hitler's rise to power in Germany in 1932–33, and published *Germany Enters the Third Reich* in 1933. He was an early and emphatic critic of both the Soviet and Nazi regimes.

Hoover served as advisor to several federal agencies during the New Deal. In 1941 he joined the Office of the Coordinator of Information, and he remained with that agency when it became the Office of Strategic Services in 1942. He served in the OSS RESEARCH AND ANALYSIS BRANCH, and later in the OSS SECRET INTELLIGENCE BRANCH. In the latter unit he was responsible for espionage operations in Sweden, and he used this opportunity to direct some operations against the Soviets. He left the OSS in 1945 and was awarded the Medal of Freedom.

After the war Hoover served in several advisory posts in the federal government and was a member of the Board of National Estimates (see NATIONAL INTELLIGENCE ESTIMATE) of the Central Intelligence Agency.

(*Who Was Who in America*, v. 6; *Contemporary Authors*, Permanent Series, v.1; Smith, *OSS*; Cline: *The CIA, Reality vs. Myth*.)

HOOVER, J(OHN) EDGAR (January 1, 1895–May 2, 1972): government official, intelligence officer

A native of Washington, D.C., Hoover worked as a messenger and clerk in the Library of Congress while attending George Washington University at night. He earned an LL.B. in 1916 and an LL.M. in 1917.

Hoover joined the Department of Justice in 1917. In 1919 he was made special assistant to the attorney general and put in charge of the newly created General Intelligence Division, a unit established to collect intelligence on radical political groups and individuals suspected of involvment in a wave of bombings and other subversion (see FEDERAL BUREAU OF INVESTIGATION). In 1921 he was made assistant director of the Bureau of Investigation, as the FBI was then called.

Hoover served in the assistant directorship during the Harding administration (1921–23), although he was not involved in the corruption that was rampant in the Bureau and the Justice Department during those years. In 1924, when Harlan Stone, the new attorney general appointed by President Calvin Coolidge, was searching for someone to take charge of the Bureau and clean it up, Secretary of Commerce Herbert Hoover (no relation) recommended J. Edgar Hoover for the job.

Hoover held the post of FBI director for the rest of his life—forty-eight years. The Bureau, which he reformed and transformed into a highly effective law enforcement and counterintelligence agency, became an extension of his own personality, and his biography after 1924 is almost indistinguishable from the history of the FBI.

Hoover apparently aspired to no other post than director of the FBI. His long tenure in the job was the result of his excellent performance, his talent for carefully managing his own public image and that of the Bureau, and, according to many accounts, the files of potentially damaging material he maintained about almost everyone with the power to replace him (President Lyndon Johnson, in explanation of why he kept Hoover on as FBI director, reportedly said, "I'd rather have him inside the tent pissing out than outside the tent pissing in."—*Time*, February 10, 1975, p. 16).

Contrary to legend, Hoover was only fairly adept in competing with rival intelligence services for bureaucratic jurisdiction. While he won his struggle with WILLIAM J. DONOVAN and the Office of Strategic Services for intelligence jurisdiction in Latin America during the SECOND WORLD WAR, he failed in his attempt to acquire worldwide intelligence responsibility for the FBI's Special Intelligence Services after the war, and lost all but the Bureau's domestic counterintelligence role to the Central Intelligence Agency.

Hoover ran the FBI in very much the style of a stern paterfamilias presiding over an extended family, and with the passage of decades he became increasingly eccentric, puritanical, intolerant, and defensive (for example, it is reported that because he distrusted people with moist palms, new agents were advised to dry their palms with a hankerchief before entering the director's office for an introductory handshake). He distrusted the patriotism of those holding views different from his own, and equated any criticism of himself or the Bureau with anti-Americanism or Communism. Toward the end of his life and career, the more notorious manifestations of these traits obscured his past accomplishments and the fair-mindedness that marked his earlier years. His virulent hatred of the Rev. Martin Luther King, Jr. is well-known, for example, but few know that Hoover was virtually the only voice in the Roosevelt administration to speak out against the internment of Japanese and Japanese-Americans during the Second World War, an injustice that was warmly endorsed by such famous humanitarians as Earl Warren, then governor of California.

Hoover seems to have inspired no moderate sentiments toward himself. Those with whom he dealt responded with either fawning adulation or bitter hatred. For this reason, together with his compulsive secretiveness and public-image management, his life-long celibacy, and the destruction of all his personal files by his loyal secretary after his death, he seems destined to remain one of the most enigmatic figures of his time.

(*Who Was Who in America*, v. 5; *Current Biography*, 1950; De Toledano, *J. Edgar Hoover: The Man in His Time*; Cook, *The FBI Nobody Knows*.)

HORTALEZ & CIE

A French covert PROPRIETARY COMPANY (full name: Roderigue Hortalez et Cie.) established by PIERRE AUGUSTIN CARON DE BEAUMARCHAIS in 1776 as a conduit for French military aid to the AMERICAN REVOLUTION. It continued to operate until the French-American alliance, signed in February 1778, made covert aid unnecessary. (See also COMMITTEE OF SECRET CORRESPONDENCE, SILAS DEANE.)

(Boatner, *Encyclopedia of the American Revolution*.)

HORTON, JOHN R. (ca. 1920–): intelligence officer

Horton joined the Central Intelligence Agency in 1948 and worked in the Western Hemisphere Division of the CIA CLANDESTINE SERVICE. He served as chief of station in Montevideo, Uruguay, and later as chief of station in Mexico City. He retired from the CIA in 1975.

In May 1983 Horton was hired out of retirement as a contract employee by the CIA to serve as a national intelligence officer for Latin America (see NATIONAL INTELLIGENCE ESTIMATE). He coordinated a study of political, economic, military, and diplomatic conditions in Mexico, and while involved in this study became embroiled in a dispute with CIA Director WILLIAM J. CASEY.

According to newspaper interviews given by Horton, Casey pressured him to revise the study so as to support foreign policies of the Reagan administration. Specifically, it was reported that Casey wished the study to find that Mexico's internal problems constituted a threat to its stability and to the overall security of Central America and the United States. When Horton refused to make the revisions, Casey had the report rewritten by another intelligence analyst, and Horton resigned in protest in May 1984.

(*New York Times*, September 28, 1984, p. A1; Agee, *Inside the Company.*)

HORTON, PHILIP: editor, intelligence officer

A former English instructor at Harvard University, Horton served in the Office of Strategic Services as an assistant to JOHN C. WILEY, one of the founders of the OSS FOREIGN NATIONALITIES BRANCH. He later served in the Central Intelligence Agency and in 1947 was the first chief of the Paris station of the CIA's Office of Special Operations. He subsequently left the CIA and, from 1949 until 1968, was executive editor of the *Reporter* magazine.

(Smith, *OSS*.)

HOUSTON, LAWRENCE REID: lawyer, intelligence officer

Houston graduated from Harvard in 1935 and earned an LL.B. from the Virginia Law School in 1939. He was one of the many Wall Street lawyers recruited by WILLIAM J. DONOVAN into the Office of Strategic Services during the Second World War. He joined the OSS in 1944, served in the OSS SECRET INTELLIGENCE BRANCH and was deputy to Col. HARRY S. ALDRICH, the chief of OSS operations in the Middle East.

After the war Houston was general counsel of the Central Intelligence Group. In 1946 he, his deputy John S. Warner, and CIG legislative counsel Walter L. Pforzheimer drafted the legislation that eventually created the CENTRAL INTELLIGENCE AGENCY. Houston was one of the chief midwives in the birth of the Agency.

Houston served as CIA general counsel until his retirement in 1973. His tenure in the post extended over most of the first three decades of the Agency's history, during which time he dealt with the countless unprecedented legal questions arising from the introduction of a secret intelligence agency within the American system of law and government. Virtually unknown to the public, he came to be highly respected within governmental circles and especially within the CIA.

Houston holds the Intelligence Medal of Merit, the Distinguished Intelligence Medal, and the Civil Service League Award.

(Smith, *OSS*; Troy, *Donovan and the CIA*.)

HOWLAND, WESTON (July 3, 1895–): manufacturer, businessman, intelligence officer

A native of New Bedford, Massachusetts, Howland graduated from Haverford College in Pennsylvania in 1917. He worked for several Massachusetts textile mills and became president of Warwick Mills in 1932.

In 1942 Howland left Warwick Mills to serve with the Office of Strategic Services. He became chief of the OSS Office of Security.

(*Who's Who in America*, v. 24; Burke, *Outrageous Good Fortune*.)

HUGHES, H(ENRY) STUART (May 7, 1916–): historian, intelligence officer

A native of New York City, Hughes is the grandson of U.S. Supreme Court Justice Charles Evans Hughes. He graduated from Amherst College in 1937, and received an M.A. and a Ph.D. from Harvard University in 1938 and 1940, respectively.

Hughes enlisted in the U.S. Army in 1941 and later was assigned to the Office of Strategic Services. He served in the OSS RESEARCH AND ANALYSIS BRANCH in North Africa and Italy. After the war he stayed with the R&A Branch when it was transferred to the State Department as the Interim Research and Intelligence Service (see STATE DEPARTMENT INTELLIGENCE). He became chief of the European research division.

Hughes left the State Department in 1948 and joined the history faculty of Harvard University. He has taught history and political science at Stanford University and, since 1975, has been professor of history at the University of California at San Diego.

(Smith, *OSS*; *Who's Who in America*, 43rd ed.)

HUGHES, JOHN CHAMBERS (October 3, 1891–May 1971): businessman, diplomat, intelligence officer

A native of Louisville, Kentucky, Hughes graduated in 1914 from Princeton University, where he was a classmate of ALLEN W. DULLES. He pursued a career in textile manufacturing in New York. During the Second World War he served in the Office of Strategic Services as chief of the OSS New York office. During 1953–55 he was U.S. ambassador to NATO. He later served as chairman of the board of the Free Europe Committee, the CIA-sponsored organization that operated RADIO FREE EUROPE and Radio Liberty.

(Smith, *OSS; Who Was Who in America*, v. 5.)

HUNT, E(VERETTE) HOWARD (October 9, 1918–): writer, intelligence officer

A native of Hamburg, New York, Hunt graduated from Brown University in 1940. He joined the U.S. Naval Reserve and served aboard a destroyer during 1941, but was invalided out of the service in 1942 after a shipboard injury. He worked as a screenwriter and editor of documentary and training films during 1942–43 and as a war correspondent for *Life* magazine in 1943. Later that year he enlisted in the U.S. Army Air Corps and was commissioned a second lieutenant after attending Officer Candidate School.

Hunt was assigned to the Office of Strategic Services and served in Detachment 202, the OSS OPERATIONAL GROUP in China. He was discharged with the rank of first lieutenant in 1946. After working as a free-lance screenwriter in Hollywood during 1947–48 he joined the Economic Cooperation Administration (the Marshall Plan agency) and served in Europe during 1948–49. In 1949 he was recruited into the Central Intelligence Agency by FRANK G. WISNER, director of the Office of Policy Coordination, as the CIA's COVERT ACTION unit was then known.

Hunt served as the CIA/OPC chief of station in Mexico City during 1950–52, and he became deputy chief of the station in 1953 after the merger of OPC and the Office of Special Operations created the CIA CLANDESTINE SERVICE in August 1952 (see CENTRAL INTELLIGENCE AGENCY). In 1953 he returned to CIA headquarters in Washington to serve as chief of the Southeast Europe Division of the Clandestine Service, but he was soon transferred to the Western Hemisphere Division when the CIA received authorization for the Agency's GUATEMALA COUP.

Hunt served as deputy to C. TRACY BARNES, the officer in overall charge of the operation. Hunt was responsible for planning the political and propaganda aspects of the operation, a task in which he was assisted by DAVID ATLEE PHILLIPS. Having completed his work before the operation was executed in June 1954, Hunt was sent to Tokyo as chief of covert operations for the North Asia Command, a Clandestine Service department responsible for activities in North and South Korea, Japan, the Chinese mainland, Taiwan, Okinawa, Hong Kong, and the Philippines.

In 1956 Hunt left Tokyo and became chief of station in Montevideo, Uruguay, and he remained at this post until March 1960 when he was invited to participate in the operation that became known as the BAY OF PIGS INVASION. The operation was regarded by the Clandestine Service planners as something of a repeat of the Guatemala Coup, and many of the officers who had taken part in the latter operation were asked to participate in it.

Hunt reported to C. TRACY BARNES, who was in overall charge of the Cuban operation, and also to JACOB ESTERLINE, the project chief. Hunt's job was to work with anti-Castro Cuban exiles and help form a government-in-exile that could be installed in Cuba after the anticipated fall of the Castro regime. He was assisted in this by CIA contract employee Bernard L. Barker, who had worked for the Agency in Cuba during the 1950s. Hunt's advocacy of the right wing of the Cuban emigration group in general, and of Manuel Artime, leader of the Movement of Revolutionary Recovery, in particular, led to strained relations between Hunt and GERRY DROLLER, the political action chief of the operation. This situation resulted in Hunt's reassignment to work with David Atlee Phillips in the operation's propaganda department. After the failure of the Cuban invasion Hunt was retained by CIA director ALLEN W. DULLES to serve as his assistant, and Hunt helped him respond to the several ensuing investigations of the operation.

Hunt was next assigned to the newly formed Domestic Operations Division, which was headed by C. Tracy Barnes. Hunt's principal job was to handle CIA's covert subsidization of certain books and news services (see FREDERICK A. PRAEGER). Late in 1963 he was nominated as deputy chief of the Madrid station, but the appointment was vetoed by the U.S. ambassador to Spain, Robert Woodward, who had come to dislike him while serving as ambassador to Uruguay during Hunt's tour as chief of station in that country.

During his service with the CIA Hunt had continued to write fiction as an avocation. While with the Domestic Operations Division he began a series of spy novels centered on the character "Peter Ward," a fictitious CIA officer, and written under the pen name "David St. John." According to Hunt, the fact that the true identity of David St. John was available through the copyright registry in the Library of Congress created a security problem for the CIA, but Hunt says he got around this problem by resigning as a staff employee of the CIA, rejoining the Agency as a contract employee, and leaving the United States for "a period of time." Hunt moved to Madrid in 1965, where he carried out a political action assignment. He returned to the United States in 1966 and was assigned to the Western European Division of the Clandestine Service.

Hunt retired from the CIA in 1970 and was employed by Robert R. Mullen & Co., a Washington public relations firm that had been associated with the CIA. In 1971 he was hired as a part-time propaganda consultant to the Nixon administration, responsible initially for investigating and researching the role of the Kennedy administration in enlarging American involvement in the Vietnam War. This job eventually involved him in the White House Special Investigative Unit, the so-called Plumbers, and the several escapades collectively known as the Watergate affair.

Hunt was indicted and pleaded guilty to charges of wiretapping, burglary, and conspiracy in connection with the break-in at the Democratic national headquarters in June 1972. He subsequently served several years in federal penitentiaries. Since his release in 1977 he has resumed his writing career.

(Hunt, *Undercover, Give Us This Day; Who's Who in America*, 42nd ed.; Phillips, *The Night Watch*; Wyden, *The Bay of Pigs*; Schlesinger and Kinzer, *Bitter Fruit*.)

I

IND, ALLISON (November 23, 1903–April 16, 1974): Army officer, writer, espionologist, intelligence officer

A native of Lead, South Dakota, Ind graduated from the University of Michigan in 1926. In 1926–34 he was a reporter, movie critic, and columnist for the *Ann Arbor* (Michigan) *Daily News*. Ind enlisted in the U.S. Army Reserve in 1930 and was assigned to Army Intelligence. He went on active duty in 1940.

Ind served in Air Corps intelligence until May 1942, when he transferred to the intelligence section of Gen. Douglas MacArthur's headquarters in Melbourne, Australia. In July of that year he co-founded the ALLIED INTELLIGENCE BUREAU, which coordinated and supported all Allied intelligence and COVERT ACTION operations in the Southwest Pacific theater. He served as deputy director of the Bureau throughout the war and remained in the Army until 1960, when he retired with the rank of colonel.

Ind was also a prolific writer of both fiction and non-fiction under his own name as well as pseudonyms ("Phil Stanley", "Richard Wallace"). He wrote an account of the Allied Intelligence Bureau and *A Short History of Espionage*, which he later expanded into *A History of Modern Espionage*. He was working on a book of codes and ciphers at the time of his death.

(*Contemporary Authors*, Permanent Series, v. 1; Ind, *Allied Intelligence Bureau*.)

INDONESIA REBELLION

Summary: In 1958 the Central Intelligence Agency supported a rebellion in the Indonesian army in Sumatra with the intention of overthrowing President Sukarno, whom U.S. policymakers viewed as sympathetic and cooperative toward domestic Communists and the Soviet Union. The rebellion failed.

Background and Discussion: Since the former Netherlands East Indies was established as the independent republic of Indonesia in 1945, it was led by President Sukarno. Controversy within the Indonesian government over Sukarno's policies and personal style led to the resignation of several senior officials, including the vice-president, in December 1956. In the wake of this split, many regional councils in the country adopted an autonomous, if not rebellious, attitude toward the central government. The Banteng Council of Central Sumatra was particularly active and, after many nationally known political leaders joined, it issued an ultimatum demanding reforms within the central government. When this ultimatum was rejected, the Council and a coalition of other dissident leaders formed the Revolutionary Republic of Indonesia on February 15, 1958.

The dissidents had the active cooperation of Lt. Col. Achmad Hussein, the Indonesian army commander in central Sumatra, and Col. Maludin Simbolon, the commander in northern Sumatra, as well as other army commanders throughout the country. In April 1957 Hussein made contact through an intermediary with the CIA station in Djakarta to sound out the possibility of American aid to an all-out rebellion against the Sukarno government.

At the time U.S. foreign policy-makers—especially Secretary of State John Foster Dulles—were disturbed by overtures Sukarno had made to the Soviet Union and his apparent intention of bringing about greater representation of the Indonesian Communist Party within his government. The Eisenhower administration had, in fact, already considered some sort of COVERT ACTION against Sukarno, but was frustrated by the lack of CIA assets within Indonesia. The administration therefore decided to aid the rebels through the CIA, although DESMOND FITZGERALD, then chief of political and paramilitary warfare for the CIA CLANDESTINE SERVICE, had doubts about the abilities of the rebels and advised against CIA involvement.

The CIA furnished arms to the rebels, as well as three paramilitary advisors (one of whom was the later legendary ANTHONY A. POE). The Agency also supplied air support in the form of B-26 bombers flown by pilots of Civil Air Transport (see AIR PROPRIETARIES). Nonetheless, the insurgents were unable to overcome the concerted force of Sukarno's loyal military forces.

On May 18, 1958 one of the CAT pilots, ALLEN LAWRENCE POPE, was shot down near Ambon in the Celebes, after accidentally bombing a church and killing much of the congregation. Pope was taken prisoner, and the potential disclosure of his links with the CIA forced the Eisenhower administration to terminate paramilitary aid to the insurgents.

The insurgents continued to fight a guerrilla war against the central government, but were eventually crushed two and a half years later. Religious, political, and personal disunity among the insurgents contributed to the defeat.

The operation marked a major setback to advocates of covert action within the CIA and the U.S. government. And it was a personal setback for ALFRED C. ULMER, who, as chief of the Far East Division of the Clandestine Service, was the CIA officer with overall responsibility for the operation. Ulmer was shortly replaced in that post by FitzGerald.

(Powers, *The Man Who Kept the Secrets*; Smith, *Portrait of a Cold Warrior*; Cline, *The CIA: Reality vs. Myth*; Special Operations Research Office, *U.S. Army Area Handbook for Indonesia*.)

INMAN, BOBBY RAY (April 4, 1931–): naval officer, intelligence officer

A native of Rhonesboro, Texas, Inman enlisted in the Navy after graduating from the University of Texas in 1950 and was commissioned an ensign in 1952. He advanced through grades rapidly and served in various intelligence capacities. In 1965–67 he was assistant naval attaché in Stockholm.

In 1971–72 Inman attended the National War College. The following year he became executive assistant and senior aide to the vice chief of naval operations. In 1973–74 he held the position of assistant

chief of staff for intelligence on the staff of the commander-in-chief of the U.S. Pacific Fleet; his specific job was chief of the Current Intelligence Branch at Pacific Fleet headquarters in Hawaii. In 1974–76 he was director of Naval Intelligence. In 1976–77 he served as vice director of plans, operations and support of the Defense Intelligence Agency. In 1977–81 he was director of the National Security Agency. In 1981 Inman was advanced to the rank of admiral—a rare achievement for an officer who did not graduate from the U.S. Naval Academy—and appointed deputy director of the Central Intelligence Agency.

Inman is representative of a "new breed" of senior intelligence officers, people who entered government service after the Second World War, and who are more oriented toward technical intelligence collection and analysis than covert operations.

Inman resigned from the CIA in April 1982 in a policy debate within the Reagan administration, reportedly over the reorganization of counterintelligence operations. He has since pursued a career in private industry.

Inman's first name—Bobby, not Robert—was reportedly proposed by his grandfather.

(*New York Times*, February 2, 1981, p. A14; April 22, 1982, pp. 1, 27; *Who's Who in America*, 42nd ed.; Bamford, *The Puzzle Palace*.)

-INT

Since the Second World War, the suffix -INT, which stands for "intelligence," has been employed in the construction of abbreviated compound words in official U.S. intelligence usage. Examples are SIGINT (signals intelligence), COMINT (communications intelligence), ELINT (electronics intelligence), RADINT (radar intelligence), TELINT (telemetry intelligence), PHOTINT (photographic intelligence), and HUMINT (human intelligence).

INTELLIGENCE

1) Information about an adversary useful in dealing with him; 2) an organization or activity concerned with such information.

The *Oxford English Dictionary* offers examples of the use of the word in the sense of "communications of spies, secret or private agents, etc." as early as the sixteenth century, and instances in which it has been used to mean "the agency for obtaining secret information; the staff of persons so employed, secret service," from the seventeenth century.

The word was frequently used in the sense of 1) during the American Revolution ("The necessity of procuring good intelligence is apparent and need not be further urged . . . ," GEORGE WASHINGTON to ELIAS DAYTON, July 26, 1777). However, the word was also officially used in a different sense in the name of the Continental Congress's Committee of Intelligence, which was charged with the publication of reports covering the "state of the armies and navies of the United States." Here the word appears to have had its older and more common meaning of information-in-general.

After the Revolutionary War *intelligence* fell into relative disuse in the American military establishment, remaining so throughout the nineteenth century. During that time the word was generally used in the United States to mean information of any kind, often with the connotation of "news." Fishel notes that, although Gen. Philip Sheridan used the term "intelligence community" in his memoirs (1888), "intelligence" had no specific military meaning during the Civil War. "Military information" was used to denote information concerning the enemy, and the agency or activity collecting it was described as *secret service*.

When the U.S. Navy established an Office of Intelligence within its Bureau of Navigation in 1882 (see NAVAL INTELLIGENCE), it intended the unit to collect and compile any naval information of potential use to the service. At the time the Navy was attempting to recover from the long period of neglect it suffered after the Civil War, and hoped to overtake the more advanced navies of Europe. The word "intelligence" in the unit's name had the meaning of information-in-general, and was consistent with the organization's primary mission of technology transfer. It was only a decade later that ONI began to focus primarily on the threat presented by foreign sea power.

When the U.S. Army created a counterpart to ONI in 1885, it was called the Division of Military Information. The term "information" predominated in Army usage until the early twentieth century. Bidwell credits liaison between ARMY INTELLIGENCE and BRITISH INTELLIGENCE during the FIRST WORLD WAR as the reason the Army officially adopted the terms *intelligence, espionage,* and *counterespionage*.

After the First World War the term *intelligence* remained firmly established in Army, Navy, and State Department official usage. However, when President Franklin Roosevelt appointed Col. WILLIAM J. DONOVAN to head the prototype agency of the OFFICE OF STRATEGIC SERVICES in 1941, he designated him "Coordinator of Information," authorizing him "to collect and analyze all information and data, which may bear upon national security. . . ."

The revival of "information" was brief; when the OSS was created in 1942 the organization adopted *intelligence* to describe the information it collected regarding the Axis powers. The term has remained in use since then, especially since the creation of the Central Intelligence Agency in 1947.

(Fishel, "The Mythology of Civil War Intelligence"; Bidwell, "History of the Military Intelligence Division, Department of the Army General Staff.")

INTELLIGENCE COMMUNITY

Government and the media have come to use this term to designate all those federal agencies with some role in foreign intelligence. It includes the CENTRAL INTELLIGENCE AGENCY, the DEFENSE INTELLIGENCE AGENCY, the NATIONAL SECURITY AGENCY, the BUREAU OF INTELLIGENCE AND RESEARCH of the State Department, the intelligence and security components of the armed services, counterespionage elements of the FEDERAL BUREAU OF INVESTIGATION, and government units responsible for reconnaissance operations (see NATIONAL RECONNAISSANCE OFFICE). Several other agencies with a peripheral role in intelligence are also considered to be part of the intelligence community: the Department of the Treasury, which overtly collects and produces intelligence related to U.S. foreign economic policy, and also has responsibility for the SECRET SERVICE; the Department of Energy, which overtly collects information on foreign energy matters; and the Drug Enforcement Agency, which collects and produces intelligence on the foreign and domestic aspects of narcotics trafficking.

(Cline, *The CIA, Reality vs. Myth;* Jordan and Taylor, *American National Security.*)

INTELLIGENCE COMMUNITY STAFF

The IC Staff was established early in 1972 by RICHARD M. HELMS, then director of central intelligence. The staff was created to replace the NATIONAL INTELLIGENCE PROGRAMS EVALUATION (NIPE) office, and it was the result of recommendations made in a study of the INTELLIGENCE COMMUNITY by JAMES R. SCHLESINGER, then assistant director of the Bureau of the Budget. The purpose of the staff is to assist the DCI in his role as manager of the community in regard to budgetary matters, the allocation of resources to intelligence objectives, the relative costs and effectiveness of all U.S. intelligence activities, and other management matters of common concern to U.S. intelligence agencies.

At first composed entirely of CIA members, the IC Staff was later enlarged to include representatives of other intelligence agencies. In 1976 President Gerald Ford directed that the Staff have its own funding, separate from that of the CIA, as well as its own building, and an increased number of full-time employees (rather than staffers "lent" or detailed to it). In effect Ford's directive established the IC Staff as a separate bureaucratic entity within the government, thus emphasizing that its function is to support the director of central intelligence in his role as chief of the intelligence community, rather than as director of the CENTRAL INTELLIGENCE AGENCY.

(Colby, *Honorable Men*; Karalekas, *History of the Central Intelligence Agency*; Turner, *Secrecy and Democracy*.)

INTELLIGENCE CYCLE

The overall process by which information—or "raw intelligence"—is collected, transformed into finished intelligence, and placed in the hands of policymakers. The cycle consists of five steps:

1. **Planning and Direction:** The management of the cycle, including the identification of the intelligence-collection requirements that guide the collectors (i.e., agents, ELINT sensors, photoreconnaissance satellites, etc.). This step is initiated by requests or other requirements for intelligence on specific subjects by the President, the NATIONAL SECURITY COUNCIL, or other major departments or agencies of the federal government.

2. **Collection:** The gathering of raw data relevant to the intelligence requirements. Sources may range from openly available materials, e.g., newspapers, through human agents, to technical collection systems.

3. **Processing:** The transformation of the collected data into a more usable form, e.g., the translation or decryption of intercepted message traffic, the photointerpretation of overhead reconnaissance photographs, or the computer analysis of numerical economic data.

4. **Production and Analysis:** The construction of complete (or at least larger) pictures (figuratively, and sometimes literally) from the fragments of information that have been collected and processed; the

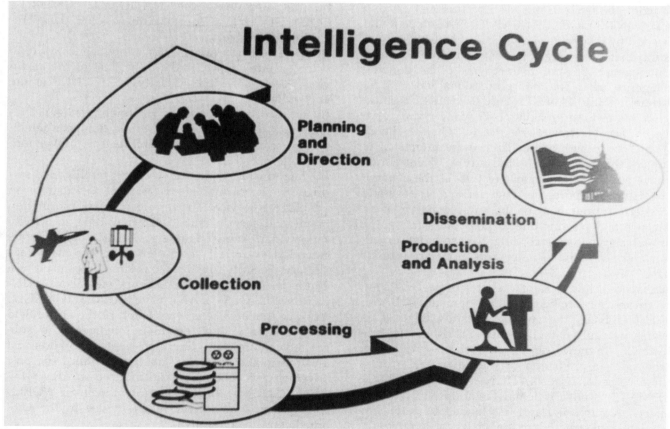

The Intelligence Cycle. Source: Central Intelligence Agency.

transformation of facts into knowledge, a process that proceeds from the specific toward the general.

5. Dissemination: The delivery of finished intelligence to the policymakers and others who need it, through publications, briefings, and other modes of communication.

(Central Intelligence Agency, *Intelligence: The Acme of Skill, Fact Book on Intelligence*; Breckinridge, *The CIA and the U.S. Intelligence System*.)

INTELLIGENCE OVERSIGHT BOARD (IOB)

The IOB is a panel of three eminent private citizens who regularly review reports from the inspectors general and general counsels of United States intelligence agencies concerning activities of those agencies that raise questions of legality or propriety. It was created by President Ford in 1976 in the wake of disclosures of such questionable activities by the CENTRAL INTELLIGENCE AGENCY and other intelligence agencies.

(Cline, *The CIA, Reality vs. Myth*.)

INTELLIGENCE TAXONOMY

The word *intelligence* as it is used professionally within the U.S. INTELLIGENCE COMMUNITY can be found preceded by a bewildering variety of adjectives, suggesting that there might be almost unlimited kinds of intelligence. Several distinct ways of categorizing intelligence are in common professional use:

By time: SHERMAN KENT devised this classification in his ground-breaking 1949 work, *Strategic Intelligence for American World Policy*. "On the theory that the consumers of intelligence are interested in things of the past, present and future," Kent wrote, "I have adopted the element of time as the element of overruling importance. This permits an easy and consistent arrangement of the subject matter of intelligence and permits one to postpone cataloguing this subject matter according to use-to-be-served, consumer, etc. until a later and more appropriate stage."

Thus, according to Kent's schema of past, present, and future, all intelligence is fundamentally BASIC INTELLIGENCE, the cumulative knowledge of an adversary acquired in the past; CURRENT INTELLIGENCE, or news of the adversary; or *estimative intelligence*, or prediction of the adversary's future course of action (see NATIONAL INTELLIGENCE ESTIMATE). Kent's schema was adopted by the intelligence community and has tended to define the organizational structure of the analytical components of U.S. intelligence agencies.

By substance: The particular aspect of the adversary to which the intelligence relates, e.g., military intelligence, political intelligence, economic intelligence, geographic intelligence, biographic intelligence, transportation intelligence, or scientific intelligence.

By source: The means used to collect the intelligence, e.g., electronic intelligence, communications intelligence, signals intelligence, human intelligence, photographic intelligence, etc. (see -INT). Special intelligence connotes an especially sensitive source, and is usually synonymous with communications intelligence. SECRET INTELLIGENCE, a term now infrequently used, usually means human intelligence collected by clandestine or covert means, i.e., through espionage; overt intelligence comes from openly available sources, e.g., the media, or official publications.

By use: The military or government function supported by the intelligence, e.g., strategic intelligence, tactical intelligence, operational intelligence, and indications or warning intelligence.

By user: Departmental intelligence pertains to the mission of some government department, e.g., military intelligence of an adversary's ground forces would be departmental intelligence to be used by the U.S. Army; while national intelligence is that used by the President, the NATIONAL SECURITY COUNCIL, etc., in formulating national policy regarding that adversary.

By stage of processing: "Raw" intelligence, or unevaluated intelligence, is the basic grist of the *intelligence cycle* mill; FINISHED INTELLIGENCE is the end product of the cycle.

By nationality of adversary: Foreign intelligence relates to a foreign adversary, while domestic intelligence pertains to such internal threats as subversion, sabotage, etc.

By relationship to the adversary's intelligence service: Negative intelligence is used to frustrate an adversary's service. The term can mean information about that service, but it also may refer to activity rather than knowledge, e.g., security precautions intended to protect one's own secrets from the adversary. Security intelligence is sometimes used as a synonym for negative intelligence (see also COUNTERINTELLIGENCE AND COUNTERESPIONAGE). Positive intelligence is what is left of the entire field of intelligence after negative intelligence is subtracted, according to Sherman Kent, who adds that this formulation is really "not too helpful." The positive/negative schema was introduced to ARMY INTELLIGENCE by the British during the FIRST WORLD WAR, but is no longer much in use in the U.S. intelligence community.

All of these schema, which are simply different

ways of slicing up the overall field of intelligence, are not at all mutually exclusive. For example, the report of a public appearance and speech by a foreign head of state would be: current, political, overt, unevaluated, foreign, positive intelligence, and might also be indications and national intelligence as well.

(Kent, *Strategic Intelligence for American World Policy*; Hopple and Watson, *The Military Intelligence Community*; Ransom, *The Intelligence Establishment*; Breckinridge, *The CIA and the U.S. Intelligence System*.)

IRAN COUP

Summary: In August 1953 the CENTRAL INTELLIGENCE AGENCY staged a coup d'etat in Iran, toppling Prime Minister Mohammed Mossadegh, much of whose political power came from the Iranian Communist Party (the Tudeh), and restoring the Shah, Mohammed Reza Pahlevi, and his appointed government to power.

Background: During the Second World War British, American, and Soviet forces occupied Iran for strategic reasons. They forced the Iranian ruler, Shah Reza Khan, to abdicate because they believed him to be pro-Nazi, and installed his twenty-three-year-old son, Mohammed Reza Pahlevi, in his place.

At the Teheran Conference, President Roosevelt, Prime Minister Churchill, and Premier Stalin agreed that their respective forces would be withdrawn from Iran within six months after the end of hostilities. Britain and the United States made good on this pledge late in 1945, but the Soviet forces stayed on in the oil-rich northern Iranian province of Azerbaijan and tried to inspire a revolt that they hoped would lead to the secession of the province and its annexation by the USSR. However, after diplomatic pressure and a show of military force by the United States, the Soviets left the country in 1946.

In 1951, after the assassination of the Iranian prime minister, General Razmara, the Shah came under heavy political pressure to appoint as Razmara's successor Dr. Mohammed Mossadegh, a seventy-year-old member of the Majlis, the Iranian legislature. Mossadegh was a European-educated landowner who had served in the Majlis since 1915. Westerners considered him unreasonable, demagogic, and xenophobic, and he had also earned a reputation for eccentric public behavior, e.g., giving press conferences from his bed, appearing in public in his pajamas, and breaking into weeping fits in the middle of his speeches. The Shah, nonetheless, yielded to the pressure and appointed Mossadegh prime minister in May 1951.

Mossadegh's bête noire was the Anglo-Iranian Oil Company, which had obtained exclusive rights to Iranian oil in 1909. Although Iran earned half of its government revenues from royalties paid to it by Anglo-Iranian, the company was earning nearly five times the amount from Iran's oil, and the company was paying even more to the British government in taxes than it was paying to Iran. This very inequitable arrangement was equally unpopular with Mossadegh, the Shah, and most Iranians, irrespective of their political positions.

On the same day he was appointed prime minister, Mossadegh presented a bill to the Majlis calling for the nationalization of the Anglo-Iranian Oil Company. It was immediately and unanimously passed, and the following day signed into law by the Shah.

In retaliation for the move, Anglo-Iranian withdrew all its personnel from the country, leaving Iran without the technical expertise and manpower to operate the pumps, pipelines, and refineries. The company also declared its proprietary rights to any oil that might be taken from the fields and threatened legal action against any foreign parties that might purchase Iranian oil. The two moves were completely effective. Other oil-producing countries moved in to fill the vacuum left in the world market by the shutoff of Iranian oil, and Iran was deprived of virtually all its foreign trade and government revenue. A major economic crisis soon followed.

Faced with the crisis, Mossadegh, in July 1952, demanded the authority to govern for six months without recourse to Parliament and that the powers of minister of war be handed over to him as well. The Shah refused and demanded Mossadegh's resignation. The prime minister resigned, and rioting, inspired by Mossadegh's party, the National Front, immediately ensued. The Iranian Communist Party allied itself with Mossadegh and joined in the rioting. After five days the Shah was forced to reappoint Mossadegh. In October Mossadegh broke off diplomatic relations with Great Britain.

The CIA Coup: In November 1952, representatives of the Anglo-Iranian Oil Company approached KERMIT ROOSEVELT, a senior CIA covert operations officer who specialized in Middle Eastern affairs, proposed that the United States join in an operation to overthrow Mossadegh, and presented him with a detailed plan for a coup d'etat. They made it clear that they were also speaking on behalf of the British government (a majority stockholder in Anglo-Iranian), and that the proposal had the approval of Prime Minister Winston Churchill and his foreign minister, Anthony Eden. Roosevelt responded that in his estimation President Truman would not agree to CIA participation in the operation and suggested waiting to make the proposal until after President-elect Eisenhower had been inaugurated in January 1953. This was done, and as Roosevelt predicted, Eisenhower and his secretary of state, John Foster Dulles, proved receptive to the idea.

Meanwhile the situation in Iran worsened. In February the Shah announced his plan to abdicate. The announcement set off new rioting between pro-Shah and pro-Mossadegh factions, and once again the Communist Tudeh party was prominent among the latter. However, the extent of his support persuaded the Shah to change his mind and remain on the throne. At the same time, the instability of the situation and the growing alliance between Mossadegh and the Communists heightened fears in Washington that Iran would follow Eastern Europe down the now-familiar path to Soviet dominion. Support for the British-CIA proposal for a coup took on a new sense of urgency.

On June 25, 1953 Roosevelt presented his twenty-two-page revision of the British operational plan in a meeting with Secretary of State John Foster Dulles, Under Secretary of State Gen. WALTER BEDELL SMITH, CIA Director ALLEN DULLES, ROBERT RICHARDSON BOWIE (then head of the State Department's policy planning staff), ROBERT D. MURPHY (then Deputy Under Secretary for Political Affairs), and several other officials. Roosevelt's plan—code-named Ajax—was based on the (correct) assumptions that the Shah wished to replace Mossadegh with a prime minister friendly to the West and opposed to the Communists, and that the majority of the Iranian public and armed forces would support the Shah against Mossadegh. The plan detailed the precise means to be used in marshaling support for the Shah and encouraging him to take the desired steps.

The plan was approved and Roosevelt went to Iran, entering the country surreptitiously in order to avoid alerting the Mossadegh regime that an operation might be underway. Working with the staff of the CIA base in Teheran, he organized the necessary preparations. H. NORMAN SCHWARZKOPF, who had served as chief of the Imperial Iranian Gendarmerie during the Allied occupation of Iran during the war, acted as intermediary between Roosevelt and the Shah, but on Schwarzkopf's advice, Roosevelt later made direct, covert contact with the Shah and obtained his agreement to the specific steps of the Ajax operation.

On August 9th the Shah flew to his summer palace on the Caspian Sea. There he signed decrees removing Mossadegh from office and appointing in his place Gen. Fazollah Zahedi, a Shah loyalist. At midnight on August 14th Col. Nematollah Nassiry, chief of the Palace Guard, drove up to the prime minister's residence at the head of a column of tanks and presented the decrees to a servant. He was immediately arrested by forces under the command of Gen. Tazhi Riahi, the Iranian chief of staff and a Mossadegh loyalist. The following morning Mossadegh made a radio broadcast announcing that there had been an attempted coup inspired by foreign elements and that he therefore was taking complete control of the government. Troops loyal to Mossadegh began searching Teheran for General Zahedi, but the general remained safely out of sight in a hideout arranged by Roosevelt. Meanwhile the Shah fled the country to await the outcome of the attempted coup.

Two days of rioting by the Tudeh followed, but when the American ambassador threatened to evacuate all Americans from Iran, Mossadegh ordered his police to restore order. The police, who had been trained by General Schwarzkopf and were for the most part partisans of the Shah, crushed the Communist rioting with enthusiam, but they were not equally zealous on August 19th, when pro-Shah demonstrators led by agitators paid by Roosevelt began marching through the streets of Iran. At a psychologically critical moment, Roosevelt, who had been orchestrating events from a basement command post, produced General Zahedi. Zahedi, leading the pro-Shah anti-Mossadegh mob plus a column of tanks and loyalist troops, marched on Mossadegh's residence. A two-hour battle ensued. When it was over Mossadegh was in hiding, his supporters under arrest, and Zahedi had assumed the post of prime minister. The Shah quickly returned to Iran and resumed his throne.

Mossadegh was convicted of treason and sentenced to three years of house arrest in his home village, in addition to an indefinite term of exile in that village. He remained there for the rest of his life. Colonel Nassiry was promoted to brigadier general. Prime Minister Zahedi restored diplomatic relations with the British. An international consortium of Western oil companies signed a twenty-five-year pact with Iran for its oil, with more favorable terms for Iran than those of the old Anglo-Iranian agreement. Forty percent of the oil went to Anglo-Iranian, forty percent to a group of American oil companies, Royal Dutch Shell got fourteen percent, and the Compagnie Française des Petroles got six percent. The United States granted Iran $45 million in immediate economic aid. Iran remained a staunch American ally until the Shah was deposed in 1979.

The Iran coup was the first major covert operation carried out by the CIA after the ad hoc ITALIAN ELECTION OPERATION in 1948. It succeeded because it was based upon a thorough and accurate assessment of the political situation in the country, followed by skillfull political action. In this instance the CIA operators acted as catalysts to bring about a development which could possibly have happened without external encouragement. No paramilitary operations were employed. The success of the Iran coup and that of the Guatemala coup the following year encouraged the CIA to attempt similar operations elsewhere in the world during the next few years (e.g., the INDONESIA REBELLION, the TIBET OPERATION, the BAY OF PIGS INVASION). However, those operations were not equally successful.

(Roosevelt, *Countercoup;* Ambrose, *Ike's Spies;* Mosely, *Power Play.*)

ITALIAN ELECTION OPERATION

Summary: In 1948 the CENTRAL INTELLIGENCE AGENCY conducted a covert political operation in Italy aimed at defeating the Communist candidates in the national elections and keeping the Christian Democrats in power. The operation, which was a success, was the first COVERT ACTION operation of the newly established CIA.

Background: The winter and spring of 1948 was one of the most tense periods in the cold war. In February the Communists staged a coup d'etat in Czechoslovakia. In March Gen. Lucius Clay, the chief of United States occupation forces in Europe, cabled Washington that he believed a war with the Soviet Union might "come with dramatic suddenness."

Throughout the winter of 1947–48 the NATIONAL SECURITY COUNCIL viewed with apprehension the Italian national elections scheduled for April 18, 1948. It was feared that the presence of a Communist government in neighboring Yugoslavia, the continuing civil war between the Communists and the nationalists in Greece, and recent Soviet expansion in Eastern Europe might intimidate Italian voters, enabling the Italian Communist Party to gain a majority of parliamentary seats and, hence, control of the Italian government. Washington feared the result would be Soviet control of the eastern Mediterranean and that it would lead to a Communist victory in France.

The CIA Operation: In December 1947 the National Security Council authorized a campaign of covert psychological warfare, i.e., "black propaganda" against the Italian Communists in order to influence the elections. This task originally assigned to the Department of State, was reassigned to the CIA after Secretary of State George Marshall protested that the exposure of such an operation conducted by the State Department would be a disastrous embarrassment for American foreign policy.

The CIA—only three months old—was involved exclusively in intelligence operations at this time, and had no capability for psychological warfare or any other type of covert action. On December 22, 1947 the Agency established the Special Procedures Group within its secret intelligence branch, the Office of Special Operations, in order to carry out the Italian election operation and other psychological warfare projects.

In January 1948 Secretary of Defense James V. Forrestal proposed to CIA Director Adm. Roscoe Hillenkoetter that the Agency enlarge the Italian election operation to include the massive infusion of secret funds to the Christian Democrats and other centrist politicians in order to insure a Communist defeat. Hillenkoetter consulted with CIA General Counsel LAWRENCE HOUSTON, who advised that the law establishing the CIA did not authorize such an operation. Nonetheless, Hillenkoetter agreed to the project.

The CIA station in Rome, in reply to an inquiry from headquarters, estimated that the operation would cost at least $10 million, a sum that exceeded the unvouchered funds then available to the CIA. Hillenkoetter and Forrestal turned to Secretary of the Treasury John W. Snyder, who agreed to make available the Economic Stabilization Fund for the project. The Fund had been established during the Second World War out of confiscated Axis assets and was intended to be used to check swings in the value of American and other currencies. By funding the operation in this way, the CIA avoided having to make the Bureau of the Budget aware of the Italian election operation. Secretary Snyder also provided the support of the Internal Revenue Service in laundering the money and transferring it to CIA-controlled accounts in Italy.

Use of the funds was patterned on certain practices common to local American elections: they were spent to provide "walking around money" to help get out the vote, and for the printing and distribution of pamphlets, posters, and other campaign paraphernalia. By some unsubstantiated accounts, some of the money was also used to bribe election officials and to carry out other underhanded measures.

According to Secretary Forrestal's diary, he was informed by the Italian ambassador to Washington that a similar operation was being conducted by the Soviet Union, and that the aid Moscow was giving the Italian Communists was in excess of $30 million, or three times the American investment.

The American covert financial aid program was carried out in parallel with the CIA's black propaganda campaign (see COVERT ACTION), which involved the planting of news stories and an inspired campaign of letter-writing by Italian-Americans to friends and relatives in Italy, urging them to vote against the Communists.

When the elections were held on April 18th, the Christian Democrats won 307 of 574 parliamentary seats, thus excluding the Italian Communists from any role in the government. The CIA's operation was regarded as crucial to this victory.

The success of the first American postwar covert-action operation brought covert action into favor in Washington as a third option lying between conven- tional diplomatic relations and open military force. It led to the formation of the Office of Policy Coordina- tion, the original covert-action department within the CIA, and spurred the frequent use of covert action by the United States government in the 1950s and after.

(Corson, *Armies of Ignorance*; Braden, "The Birth of the CIA"; Cline, *The CIA: Reality vs. Myth*; Karalekas, *History of the Central Intelligence Agency*.)

J

J-2

1) The assistant chief of staff, intelligence, of a joint military command; 2) the intelligence section of the general staff of a joint command. (A joint command involves two or more armed services, e.g., the Army, Navy, and Air Force.)

See G-2, S-2.

JACKSON, C(HARLES) D(OUGLAS) (March 16, 1902–September 19, 1964): publishing executive, psychological warfare officer, national security specialist

A native of New York City, Jackson graduated from Princeton University in 1924, ran his father's business for several years, and joined Time, Inc. in 1931. He was a vice-president of Time in 1940 when he took a leave of absence to organize the Council for Democracy, an anti-isolationist propaganda group.

In 1942–43 Jackson was special assistant to the U.S. ambassador in Ankara, Turkey. In 1943 he became deputy chief of psychological warfare for the Air Force, and in 1944 joined General Eisenhower's staff, and helped organize psychological warfare operations in support of the D-Day landings in Normandy.

Jackson returned to Time, Inc. after the war, but in 1951 he left again to serve as president of the Free Europe Committee, the Central Intelligence Agency front organization that set up and operated RADIO FREE EUROPE and Radio Liberty. Shortly after taking office in 1953, President Eisenhower appointed Jackson his special assistant for cold war planning, a psychological warfare position. Jackson helped draft Eisenhower's first major foreign policy declaration in

March 1953, a response to Soviet peace propaganda following the death of Stalin.

Eisenhower ignored much of Jackson's political advice, including his recommendations that the American public be fully informed of the facts of nuclear warfare, and that the president take a strong stand against Sen. Joseph R. McCarthy's inquisitorial crusade. As the result of the latter advice, Jackson became one of McCarthy's targets.

Jackson resigned from the White House staff in 1954 and returned to Time, Inc. From 1960 to 1964 he was publisher of *Life* magazine.

(*Political Profiles, Eisenhower Years; Who Was Who in America*, v. 4.)

JACKSON, WILLIAM HARDING (March 25, 1901–September 28, 1971): lawyer, banker, intelligence officer

A native of Nashville, Tennessee, Jackson graduated from St. Mark's School in Southborough, Massachusetts, in 1920, from Princeton University in 1924, and from Harvard Law School in 1928. He worked for the New York law firm of Cadwalader, Wickersham and Taft until 1930, when he moved to the Wall Street law firm of Carter, Ledyard and Milburn. In 1934 he was made a partner in Carter, Ledyard.

Jackson was commissioned a captain in the U.S. Army in 1942 and assigned to the Army Air Force Intelligence School at Harrisburg, Pennsylvania. He served briefly with the Office of Strategic Services and in January 1944 was assigned to the intelligence staff of the U.S. Military Headquarters in London, England. He became assistant deputy to Gen. Omar

Bradley. He was discharged from the Army in August 1945 with the rank of colonel.

Jackson returned to Carter, Ledyard, but left in 1947 to join the investment banking firm of J.H. Whitney and Company as a partner. He continued to take an interest in foreign policy and intelligence matters, and was a member of the Council on Foreign Relations, which was headed at that time by ALLEN W. DULLES. In 1948 Jackson, Dulles, and Matthias Correa, another Wall Street lawyer, were commissioned by the NATIONAL SECURITY COUNCIL to undertake a study of the U.S. intelligence establishment. The study, which focused on the CENTRAL INTELLIGENCE AGENCY, enumerated the problems in the Agency's execution of both its intelligence and operational missions, and made recommendations for reorganization.

When Gen. WALTER BEDELL SMITH became director of central intelligence in 1950, he invited Jackson to become deputy director of central intelligence and help implement the recommendations of the Dulles-Jackson-Correa study (he also brought Dulles into the CIA for the same purpose). Jackson accepted and became DDCI in October 1950.

Chief among the CIA's management problems was the rivalry between the Office of Special Operations and the Office of Policy Coordination, the Agency's departments of SECRET INTELLIGENCE and COVERT ACTION, respectively (OPC was headed by FRANK G. WISNER, who had been a partner in Jackson's old law firm, Carter, Ledyard). Jackson attempted to solve this problem by putting both OSO and OPC under one senior CIA officer, the newly created deputy director for Plans (a position filled by Dulles) who would take charge of the Agency's Clandestine Service. The problem was only partially corrected by this, however, and was not fully resolved until OSO and OPC were merged in 1952.

Among Jackson's other innovations was the creation of the so-called "Princeton consultants," a panel composed of GEORGE F. KENNAN, HAMILTON FISH ARMSTRONG, and scientist Vannevar Bush, which reviewed drafts of NATIONAL INTELLIGENCE ESTIMATES. Jackson believed the panel would offset what he saw as an imbalance of academics on the Board of National Estimates.

Jackson also brought economist MAX MILLIKAN into the CIA to serve as assistant director of the Office of Research and Reports, the Agency's economic intelligence unit.

Jackson left the post of deputy director in August 1951 (he was succeeded by Dulles), but continued to serve as a consultant to the CIA. He returned to the Whitney Law firm, staying there until his retirement in 1956.

In 1955 Jackson served as special assistant to Secretary of State John Foster Dulles. The following year he was a special assistant to President Eisenhower.

(*Current Biography*, 1951, 1971; *Who Was Who in America*, v. 5; Karalekas, *History of the Central Intelligence Agency*; Cline, *The CIA, Reality vs. Myth*.)

JAHNKE, KURT (1882–): German and Japanese secret agent and intelligence officer

A native of Germany, Jahnke emigrated to America some years before the FIRST WORLD WAR and served in the U.S. Border Patrol (Landau says he served in the U.S. Marines). His duties brought him into contact with Chinese groups in San Francisco, and he subsequently established himself in the lucrative business of shipping the bodies of Chinese dead to their homeland for burial. He became well-connected in extremely influential Chinese circles (e.g., the family of Sun Yat-sen).

During the First World War Jahnke worked for German intelligence in the United States and Mexico. Under cover of a job as a private detective in San Francisco he worked as a saboteur for Franz von Bopp, the German consul general in that city. By May 1916 he had become director of von Bopp's sabotage activities. He worked closely with LOTHAR WITZKE and is believed to have been involved with Witzke in the BLACK TOM EXPLOSION.

In 1916 Jahnke was assigned to the German legation in Mexico, which was a major base of German COVERT ACTION against the United States and Canada. From there he directed sabotage and incited dock strikes in the United States. In 1917 he was appointed chief of German naval intelligence in North America.

After the war Jahnke went to China, where he worked for Dr. Sun Yat-sen and various Chinese warlords. He trained Chinese intelligence agents at the Whampoa Military Academy and also worked for Japanese intelligence in Manchuria. Returning to Germany, he joined the personal staff of Nazi leader Rudolf Hess and worked for Reinhard Heydrich, the chief of the SD (Sicherheitdienst, the security service), and for SD foreign intelligence chief (and later Heydrich's successor), Walter Schellenberg. He served as a liaison between SD and Japanese intelligence.

Jahnke was also in contact with Richard Sorge, the Soviet secret intelligence agent in Japan, although Sorge apparently cooperated with Jahnke without the knowledge and consent of Soviet intelligence.

After Rudolf Hess's apparent defection to Britain in 1941, Jahnke, as a close associate of Hess, fell from the good graces of Hitler, Heydrich, and other Nazi leaders, although he continued to work for Schellenberg. In 1942 the Gestapo charged him with being an agent of British intelligence. Although the charge was never proved, Jahnke remained under Gestapo surveillance and was forced to end his work for the SD. He was banished to his estate near Stralsund in Pomerania where he was captured by Soviet forces in 1945. Nothing was heard of him thereafter.

(Landau, *The Enemy Within*; Schellenberg, *The Labyrinth*; Farago, *The Game of the Foxes*.)

JANTZEN, ROBERT JOHN (May 24, 1915–): clandestine service officer

A native of New York, Jantzen graduated from the University of Buffalo in 1937 and after serving in the U.S. Naval Reserve in 1942–46, was discharged with the rank of lieutenant commander. In 1946 he joined the Department of State as a foreign service officer and later served with the Central Intelligence Agency.

Jantzen was assigned to the American embassy in Calcutta, India, in 1947–48. From 1948 to 1957 he was assigned to Singapore, where he was chief of the CIA's station. In 1958–69 he served in Bangkok as chief of station. In 1969 he was assigned to Ottawa, Canada.

(Smith, *Portrait of a Cold Warrior*; *Who's Who in Government*, 1st ed.)

JEDBURGH OPERATION

Jedburgh was the code name of a joint operation carried out by the OSS SPECIAL OPERATIONS BRANCH of the Office of Strategic Services, the British SPECIAL OPERATIONS EXECUTIVE, and the Free French forces. The operation, which was coordinated with the Allied D-Day landings at Normandy in June 1944, involved parachuting three-man teams into occupied France to coordinate the guerrilla operations of the French Resistance with the invading force.

The three-man Jedburgh teams consisted of two officers and one enlisted radio operator. In the original concept, each team was to be composed of an American, a Briton, and a Frenchman. However, because of availability of qualified manpower, there was preponderance of American and British personnel.

Among the OSS/Jedburgh personnel who later achieved prominence were WILLIAM COLBY, STEWART ALSOP, JOHN ALSOP, THOMAS BRADEN, MICHAEL BURKE, LUCIEN CONEIN, and SERGE OBOLENSKY.

The Jedburgh operation took its code name from the village of Jedburgh, on the Jed River in Roxburghshire, Scotland, where the teams were trained.

(Cave Brown, *The Secret War Report of the OSS*; Smith, *OSS*.)

JOHNSON, C(LARENCE) L(EONARD) ("KELLY") (February 27, 1910–): aeronautical engineer, designer of the U-2 and SR-71 reconnaissance aircraft

A native of Ishpeming, Michigan, Johnson graduated from the University of Michigan in 1932 and earned an M.S. from that institution in 1933. That same year he joined the Lockheed Aircraft Corporation in Burbank, California. In 1938 he was made chief engineer.

At Lockheed, Johnson established the "Skunk Works," a development plant housed in unoccupied hangers and an old distillery (the name was borrowed from the comic strip, *Li'l Abner*). Under Johnson, the "Skunk Works" developed the legendary P-38 Lightning fighter plane of the Second World War, the P-80—the first American jet fighter plane—the Constellation airliner, and the F-104 jet fighter.

In the spring of 1954 Johnson began development of the U-2 reconnaissance plane for the U.S. Air Force and the Central Intelligence Agency (see U-2, OVERHEAD RECONNAISSANCE). The first model of the aircraft was flown on August 1, 1955, and delivery to the CIA began shortly thereafter. This rapid drawing-board-to-production-line process is considered phenomenal in the aerospace industry.

In 1959 Johnson began work on what was eventually to be designated the SR-71. An early version of this high-speed, high-altitude reconnaissance aircraft flew in 1962. The operational model was put into reconnaissance service by the U.S. Air Force two years later.

Johnson was awarded the Medal of Freedom by President Lyndon Johnson in 1964 in recognition of the importance to national security of his engineering achievements. He also holds the National Medal of Science and numerous other awards for his achievements in aircraft design and engineering.

(*Current Biography*, 1968; *Who's Who in America*, 37th ed.; Gunston, *Spy Planes*.)

JOHNSTON, J(OSIAH) STODDARD (February 10, 1833–October 4, 1913): lawyer, journalist, government official, Confederate army officer, and intelligence officer

A native of New Orleans, Louisiana, Johnston was orphaned at the age of five and raised by maternal relatives in Kentucky. He graduated from Yale Uni-

A Jedburgh team preparing to parachute into German-occupied France. Source: National Archives.

versity in 1853 and earned an LL.B. from the University of Louisville in 1854. He was a cotton planter and farmer in Arkansas and Kentucky during 1855–62.

In 1862 Johnston, a nephew of Confederate Gen. A.S. Johnston, was commissioned a colonel in the Confederate Army and served on the staff of Gen. Braxton Bragg, then commander of the Army of Tennessee. One of his first tasks for Bragg was to organize a secret service, a network of amateur but effective agents in Tennessee and Kentucky. Johnston's organization was enlarged by Gen. BENJAMIN F. CHEATHAM, who was a Tennessee native and therefore better acquainted with the local people and countryside. The unit eventually became known as COLEMAN'S SCOUTS.

Johnston served as Bragg's intelligence officer until the end of the Chattanooga campaign, i.e., November 1863. He later served on the staffs of Gens. Simon B. Buckner and John C. Breckinridge.

After the war Johnston practiced law at Helena, Arkansas, until 1867, when he became editor of the *Frankfort* (Kentucky) *Yeoman*. He was active in Democratic politics in Kentucky, and served as the secretary or chairman of the state party during 1868–88. He was Kentucky's adjutant general in 1871, secretary of state during 1875–79, and an unsuccessful candidate for the Democratic gubernatorial nomination in 1875. Johnston wrote histories of Louisville and Kentucky, and was associate editor of the *Louisville Courier-Journal* during 1903–08.

(*Who Was Who in America*, v. 1; Bakeless, *Spies of the Confederacy*; Bryan, *The Spy in America*.)

JOHNSTON, KILBOURNE ("PAT"): Army officer, intelligence officer

Johnston was the son of Gen. Hugh Johnson, head of the National Recovery Administration during the 1930s, but he elected to spell his name differently. A retired U.S. Army colonel, he served with the Central Intelligence Agency. He succeeded ALLEN W. DULLES as deputy director for plans (i.e., chief of the CIA CLANDESTINE SERVICE) in August 1951, and he held that post until the following August, when he was succeeded by FRANK G. WISNER.

(Powers, *The Man Who Kept the Secrets*; Leary, *Perilous Missions*.)

JOINT INTELLIGENCE COMMITTEE

An agency of the U.S. Joint Chiefs of Staff that functioned during the SECOND WORLD WAR. The JIC, which was established in March 1942, synthesized intelligence received from all sources for use by the Joint Chiefs of Staff. It also represented the Joint Chiefs on the Combined Intelligence Committee, an Anglo-American intelligence-coordinating body. The JIC consisted of representatives of the Military Intelligence Division (see ARMY INTELLIGENCE); the Office of NAVAL INTELLIGENCE; the assistant chief of the Air Staff, Intelligence (see AIR FORCE INTELLIGENCE); the Department of State; the Foreign Economic Administration; and the OFFICE OF STRATEGIC SERVICES. Much of the JIC's work was done by specialized subcommittees, e.g., Technical Industrial Intelligence, Topographical Studies, Joint Studies Publication, Archives, Weekly Summary Editorial Board, Publications Review, and other subcommittees.

At the end of the war the Joint Chiefs decided to continue to use JIC to coordinate interdepartmental military intelligence requirements.

(Ransom, *The Intelligence Establishment*; Troy, *Donovan and the CIA*; Corson, *Armies of Ignorance*.)

JOLIS, ALBERT E. (ca. 1912–): jeweler, intelligence officer

A native of England, Jolis became an American citizen. His family had been in the diamond business for generations, and through his family's enterprises he became familiar with anti-Communist labor leaders in Europe. This background brought him to the attention of ARTHUR GOLDBERG, then chief of the Labor Section of the OSS SECRET INTELLIGENCE BRANCH.

Goldberg arranged for Jolis to be transferred from the U.S. Army military police to the OSS to serve in his Section. Jolis served in the unit both in North Africa and in London. After the Allied liberation of Paris in 1944 he was sent there as assistant chief of the Secret Intelligence Branch in that city. From there he successfully sent a Russian-born agent to penetrate the SD (Sicherheitsdienst, the SS security service) headquarters in Berlin. Jolis's agent arranged the defection of several high-level ethnic Russians who had been working for the SD. Jolis met them in Switzerland and arranged for their debriefing regarding SD operations.

After the war Jolis returned to the jewelry business and became the Paris representative of Diamond Distributors, Inc.

(Smith, *OSS*; Persico, *Piercing the Reich*.)

JONES, GEOFFREY M.T. (ca. 1919–): businessman, intelligence officer

Jones graduated from Princeton University and served in the Office of Strategic Services. As a member of the OSS SPECIAL OPERATIONS BRANCH he operated behind German lines in France, organizing and leading French resistance fighters.

Jones served briefly with the Central Intelligence Agency. He left the CIA in 1948 and became a public relations executive. During the early 1980s he served a term as president of Veterans of OSS, the OSS alumni organization.

(Smith, *OSS*; Cline, *The CIA: Reality vs. Myth*.)

JORDAN, THOMAS (September 30, 1819– November 27, 1895): Army officer, newspaper editor, Confederate intelligence officer

A native of Luray, Virginia, Jordan graduated from the U.S. Military Academy in 1840. He fought in the Seminole War and the Mexican War, and fought Indians in the Pacific Northwest during 1850–60. He resigned from the U.S. Army in May 1861 and, commissioned a lieutenant colonel in the Confederate Army, he was assigned the post of adjutant-general to Gen. G. T. Beauregard.

Before leaving Washington to assume his post in the Confederacy, Jordan recruited several women of secessionist sympathies to work as secret intelligence agents. The best-known of these was ROSE O'NEAL GREENHOW, a prominent widow with extensive connections in Washington's social and official circles. Jordan served as Greenhow's CASE OFFICER, providing her with a cipher and other paraphernalia and instruction in intelligence TRADECRAFT. The

Gen. Thomas Jordan. Source: National Archives.

information she furnished him contributed greatly to General Beauregard's victory at the first Battle of Bull Run.

Jordan was Beauregard's chief of staff at Shiloh, in the Corinth campaign, and the operations around Charleston. He remained in that post until the end of the war.

In 1866 he was editor of the *Memphis* (Tennessee) *Appeal*. He favored the American annexation of Cuba for military and economic reasons, and he went to Cuba in 1869 to serve as chief of staff and later commander of the Cuban insurgents fighting for independence from Spain in the first year of what would be known as the Ten Years War. After some insurgent defeats, he fled Cuba in an open boat and returned to the United States. He later moved to New York City and founded and edited a newspaper, the *Financial and Mining Record of New York*.

Jordan wrote many books and articles about the Civil War, including a notorious attack on Jefferson Davis in the October 1865 *Harper's Magazine*.

(*Who Was Who in America*, historical volume; Horan, *The Pinkertons*; Ross, *Rebel Rose*; Boatner, *Civil War Dictionary*; Eliot, *West Point in the Confederacy*.)

JOYCE, ROBERT PRATHER (October 17, 1902–February 8, 1984): foreign service officer, intelligence officer

A native of Los Angeles, California, Joyce graduated from Yale University in 1926 and studied at the Free School of Political Science in 1926–27. He entered the U.S. Foreign Service in 1928 and served in Shanghai, Bolivia, Panama, and Yugoslavia. From 1941 to 1943 he was first secretary of the American embassy in Havana, Cuba.

In 1943 Joyce left the Foreign Service to serve as a civilian employee of the Office of Strategic Services. He was assigned to Cairo and later to Bari, Italy, where he was in charge of the Secret Intelligence Branch for the Balkans. In 1944 he became Gen. WILLIAM J. DONOVAN's political officer at the Allied Forces Mediterranean headquarters in Caserta, Italy. The following year he succeeded ALLEN W. DULLES as chief of the OSS station in Bern, Switzerland.

Joyce joined the Foreign Service in 1947 and was assigned to Trieste, Italy, as American political advisor to the commander of the British-U.S. Zone of the then occupied city. In 1948 he returned to Washington and served on the State Department's Policy Planning Staff. He was a member of the four-person Special Policy Committee, the joint Anglo-American board that planned and coordinated the ALBANIA OPERATION.

In 1952 Joyce was assigned to Paris, France, where he served as counselor at the American embassy. He acted in the same capacity in Rio de Janeiro in 1956–57. In 1957 he became special assistant to the director of the BUREAU OF INTELLIGENCE AND RESEARCH, and then acting director of the Bureau in the following year.

From 1959 until his retirement in 1962 he was consul general at Genoa, Italy.

(obituary, *Foreign Service Journal*, May 1984; *Who's Who in America*, v. 28; Cave Brown, *The Last Hero*; Smith, *OSS*; Philby, *My Silent War*.)

K

KAMPILES, WILLIAM: intelligence officer

Kampiles joined the Central Intelligence Agency in March 1977 and was assigned as a watch officer to work in the Agency's Operations Center, which monitors worldwide events around the clock. His several requests for transfers to the CIA CLANDESTINE SERVICE were denied, and he had frequent conflicts with his supervisors. He resigned from the CIA in November 1977, taking with him a copy of a manual for the KH-11 RECONNAISSANCE SATELLITE that he had found among the reference materials in the Center. He sold the document to Soviet intelligence for $3,000 and was apprehended by U.S. counterespionage authorities.

Kampiles claimed he had sold the manual in order to gain the confidence of the Soviets, and that he intended to return to the CIA to serve as a double agent for the Agency. His explanation was not accepted. He was tried, convicted of espionage, and sentenced to forty years in prison.

(Turner, *Secrecy and Democracy*.)

KAPLAN, GABRIEL LOUIS (September 14, 1901–September 17, 1968): lawyer, covert operations officer

A native of New York City, Kaplan attended Swarthmore College and Columbia University and earned a law degree from New York University in 1925. He practiced law in New York City and was active in New York Republican politics. From 1942 to 1946 he was a personnel officer in the U.S. Army Air Corps, holding the rank of lieutenant colonel. He was awarded the Legion of Merit for his service in the Southwest Pacific.

In 1952 Kaplan was recruited into the Central Intelligence Agency by DESMOND FITZGERALD, then deputy chief of the Far Eastern Division of the Office of Policy Coordination, as the COVERT ACTION department of the CIA was then called. FitzGerald, who himself had been involved in reform politics in New York City, knew Kaplan personally and believed his political skills were applicable to the Far East. FitzGerald recruited Kaplan to go to the Philippines to help Gen. EDWARD LANSDALE insure the election of Ramon Magsaysay. Kaplan's job was simply to instruct the Filipinos in the practical means of conducting elections to insure that they were free and honest.

Kaplan's initial cover in the Philippines was the Committee for Free Asia (later known as the Asia Foundation), but this proved unsatisfactory to Kaplan's operations. In order to provide Kaplan with the necessary cover, the CIA arranged with friendly and influential persons, including former U.S. ambassador to the Philippines Myron Cowan, and financier and philanthropist Cummins Catherwood, to form the Catherwood Foundation. The Foundation sponsored a group of prestigious Americans who called themselves the Committee for Philippine Action in Development, Reconstruction and Education. The committee's acronym, COMPADRE, is a word with special significance in the Philippines.

In his days in New York politics, Kaplan had learned to work with veterans groups, chambers of commerce, Rotary Clubs, and similar organizations, and in the Philippines he recruited Filipinos with similar talent for dealing with corresponding groups in that country. The result was the founding of the National Movement for Free Elections (NAMFREL), a Filipino organization (funded by the CIA) that taught such practical matters as ballot thumbprinting, voter identification, and other methods to prevent cheating and insure an honest election. A second organization, the Magsaysay for President Movement, promoted the idea that Magsaysay was a national figure, rather than simply a partisan candidate, and sought to insure a broad nonpartisan base of support for him.

The result of Kaplan's efforts was an honest election and a landslide victory for Magsaysay in 1953.

Kaplan stayed on in Manila until 1958, moving the COMPADRE operation into the area of community development, i.e., the development of local and national mechanisms for self-help and self-government. Community centers equipped with libraries, public-address systems, learning aids, and some agricultural equipment were established throughout the islands. Programs were established to train villagers in modern methods of agriculture, health, road building, communications, and education. The centers became the foci of local self-government in which citizen committees were elected to serve as a communication link with the national government in Manila. The COMPADRE program was successful in establishing these democratic institutions as a counter to the continuing threat of Communist insurgency in the Philippines.

After his return to the United States in 1958, Kaplan retired from the CIA, but continued as a consultant to the Far East Division of the CIA CLANDESTINE SERVICE. He founded the Community Development Counselling Service in Arlington, Virginia, which provided consulting services to public and private groups in underdeveloped countries throughout Latin America and the Far East.

(Smith, *Portrait of a Cold Warrior*; *National Cyclopedia of American Biography*, vols. 53, 54.)

KARAMESSINES, THOMAS H. (ca. 1916–1978): lawyer, intelligence officer

The son of a Greek immigrant, Karamessines graduated from Columbia University and Columbia Law School. He served as an assistant to Thomas E. Dewey, the "racket-busting" New York district attorney, circa 1940. After America's entry into the Second World War he entered the U.S. Army as a private. His knowledge of Greek language and history led to his transfer to the Office of Strategic Services.

Karamessines was commissioned and rose to the rank of major. He served in the OSS COUNTER-

ESPIONAGE BRANCH (X-2), and with the OSS mission in Greece. He joined the Central Intelligence Agency at the time of its establishment in 1947 and served in the CIA CLANDESTINE SERVICE. He was a case officer, reportedly without peer in the matter of secret intelligence tradecraft. He served as chief of station in several European capitals, including Athens, Vienna, and Rome.

In 1962 Clandestine Service chief RICHARD M. HELMS appointed Karamessines his chief of operations. He was assistant deputy director for plans (i.e., number two man in the Clandestine Service) under DESMOND FITZGERALD, and he succeeded FitzGerald in the top position after his death in July 1967.

Under Karamessines the Clandestine Service mounted an operation in 1970 aimed at overthrowing the Chilean government of Marxist Salvatore Allende. The operation, which did not succeed, was launched on the specific orders of President Nixon.

When Nixon declined to reappoint Helms as director of central intelligence in 1973, Karamessines elected to retire from the CIA. He left the Agency in March 1973.

(Alsop, *The Center*; Smith, *OSS*; Phillips, *The Night Watch*; Meyer, *Facing Reality*; Powers, *The Man Who Kept the Secrets*.)

KARLOW, SERGE PETER: linguist, intelligence officer

The multilingual son of a distinguished voice coach, Karlow was commissioned as a lieutenant in the U.S. Navy shortly after graduating from college. He served in the Office of the Coordinator of Information and its successor agency, the Office of Strategic Services. He was a member of the COI's Oral Intelligence Branch, which interviewed European refugees arriving in New York City during 1941–42 in order to obtain intelligence regarding the situation in their homelands.

The OI Branch was dissolved in mid-1942 and Karlow was transferred to another component of the OSS Intelligence Services. After the war and the liquidation of the OSS he remained with the Strategic Services Unit and was with SSU when it became part of the Central Intelligence Group (see CENTRAL INTELLIGENCE AGENCY). Karlow was executive officer of the SSU's History Project, which produced an official history of the OSS (see KERMIT ROOSEVELT). He served with the CIA CLANDESTINE SERVICE in Germany in the early 1950s. He later worked as a private consultant.

(Roosevelt, *War Report of the OSS*; Persico, *Piercing the Reich*; Ranelagh, *The Agency*.)

KEEGAN, GEORGE JOSEPH, JR. (July 4, 1921–): Air Force officer, intelligence officer

A native of Houlton, Maine, Keegan graduated from Harvard University in 1944. He was commissioned a second lieutenant in the U.S. Air Force and advanced through grades to the rank of major general. He received an M.A. from George Washington University in 1965 and also studied at the National War College that year.

Keegan served in Air Force Intelligence. He was chief of intelligence for the Seventh Air Force in the Vietnam War during 1967–69, and chief of intelligence for the U.S. Pacific Command in Hawaii during 1969–70. During 1970–71 he was deputy chief of plans and operations for the Air Force Logistics Command. In 1971 he became chief of Air Force Intelligence in Washington, D.C.

Keegan enlarged the size and scope of Air Force Intelligence to such an extent that he reportedly incited the bureaucratic jealousy of the Central Intelligence Agency. For his part Keegan was disdainful of the CIA intelligence analysis, especially in the area of military intelligence estimates.

In 1974 Keegan was especially critical of a NATIONAL INTELLIGENCE ESTIMATE that attributed only benevolent and conciliatory motives to the Soviet Union in its detente with the United States, and denied that the Soviets were seeking to use the easing of East-West relations as a means of achieving strategic advantage. Keegan and his staff wrote a rebuttal of the estimate, citing published Soviet statements that indicated the Soviets intended to cause the United States to decelerate its defense programs, to acquire high technology from the United States, and to shift the balance of strategic power in favor of the Soviet Union. Keegan's arguments led to an independent reassessment of the estimate and the discovery that the CIA had greatly underestimated Soviet military expenditures.

Keegan also strongly supported Air Force Intelligence research, which led to the discovery that the Soviet Union was developing powerful particle-beam weapons intended for antiballistic missile use and space warfare.

Keegan retired from the Air Force in January 1977. He became founder and president of the Institute for Strategic Affairs and co-chairman of the Coalition for Peace through Strength, both private organizations engaged in the study of strategic matters.

Among the decorations awarded to Keegan are the Distinguished Service Medal, the Legion of Merit, and Air Medal, and the Distinguished Flying Cross.

(*Who's Who in America*, 42nd ed.; Canan, *War in Space*.)

KELLERMAN, HENRY JOSEPH (January 12, 1910–): foreign service officer, intelligence analyst

A native of Berlin, Germany, Kellerman attended the University of Freiburg and the University of Heidelberg before earning a law degree from the University of Berlin in 1937. He attended Johns Hopkins University in 1937–38 and received a diploma from the Columbia University School of Social Work in 1941.

In 1942–44 Kellerman served as a propaganda analyst with the Foreign Broadcast Intelligence Service. In 1944–45 he was an intelligence analyst with the Office of Strategic Services. In 1945 he acted as chief of research for the U.S. chief prosecutor at the Nuremburg war crimes trials.

Later in 1945 he joined the Department of State as a research analyst in the BUREAU OF INTELLIGENCE AND RESEARCH. He has since held a variety of foreign posts. In 1956–61 he was U.S. representative to UNESCO in Paris.

(Smith, *OSS*; *Who's Who in America*, 37th ed.)

KELLEY, ROBERT FRANCIS (February 13, 1894–1975): foreign service officer, intelligence officer

A native of Somerville, Massachusetts, Kelley graduated from Harvard University in 1915 and earned an A.M. from that institution in 1917. During 1915–16 he pursued postgraduate studies at the University of Paris.

Kelley was commissioned as a second lieutenant in the U.S. Army in October 1917, rose to the rank of captain, and served in Army Intelligence. He was assistant military attaché in Denmark and Finland, and military observer in the Baltic states. He resigned from the Army in 1922.

Kelley joined the State Department and was vice consul in Calcutta, India, in 1923. In 1925 he became assistant chief of State's Division of East European Affairs, moving up to the position of chief of the Division the following year. Under Kelley the Division focused on Soviet affairs (it was commonly known as "the Russian Division" within State). Kelley, who spoke Russian, established a State Department training program in which foreign service officers studied Russian language, culture, and history in Europe (GEORGE F. KENNAN was one of the alumni of this program). Kelley assembled the best library on the Soviet Union in the United States, and compiled voluminous files of materials collected from every possible source on every aspect of Soviet life. His subordinate, Raymond L. Murphy, compiled special files on Soviet propaganda and espionage agents working in the United States.

In 1937 Kelley and the East European division became the target of what Kennan later described as "a curious purge." The Division was abolished, its library sent to the Library of Congress, its special files destroyed, and its staff reassigned. Kelley was exiled to the U.S. embassy in Ankara, Turkey, where he served for many years as counselor, then retired. According to Kennan, Kelley and his Division were regarded by some in the State Department as taking Russia "too seriously," and Kelley's sharply critical stance regarding Soviet policy may have been seen by Joseph E. Davies, the new American ambassador to Moscow, as potentially harmful to Soviet-American relations. Others have theorized that the abolition of the Division reflected covert Soviet influence within the Roosevelt administration.

(*Who's Who in America*, v. 24; Kennan, *Memoirs (1925–1950)*; *"Ah, Sweet Intrigue"*; *"For Your Information."*)

KELLIS, JAMES: educator, intelligence officer

An American of Greek descent, Kellis was educated in Cairo, Egypt. He served in the OSS SPECIAL OPERATIONS BRANCH in German-occupied Greece, where, in 1944, he led Greek resistance fighters in the sabotage of railroad bridges used by the Nazis to carry strategic materials from Turkey to Germany. The following year he led an OSS team into Peking, China, where he received the surrender of the entire Japanese General Staff for North China.

After the war and the liquidation of the OSS in September 1945, Kellis stayed on in China with the Strategic Services Unit, the caretaker agency that maintained OSS wartime assets (see CENTRAL INTELLIGENCE AGENCY). He served in the Far East with the Central Intelligence Agency until 1954.

Kellis later became a professor of political science at a Connecticut college.

(Smith, *OSS*; Hymoff, *The OSS in World War II*; Cave Brown, *The Last Hero*.)

KENNAN, GEORGE FROST (February 16, 1904–): historian, Soviet expert, diplomat

A native of Milwaukee, Wisconsin, Kennan graduated from Princeton University in 1925 and entered the U.S. Foreign Service the following year. He served as vice consul in Geneva, Hamburg, and Berlin. In 1928 and 1929 he served in Estonia, Latvia, and Lithuania, countries that were regarded as "listening posts" for the Soviet Union, with which the United States did not have diplomatic relations.

In 1929 Kennan began studying the Russian language, literature, history, and politics under a program established by the State Department in anticipation of establishing relations with Moscow. When relations were established in 1933, he was assigned to the American embassy in Moscow as third secretary. Except for an interval as consul and second secretary in Vienna in 1935, he remained in Moscow until 1937, rising to the post of second secretary. After a year in Washington he was assigned to Prague, where he remained in the post of second secretary of the legation until the outbreak of the Second World War in September 1939. He was then assigned to Berlin. After the United States entered the war in December 1941, he was interned in Germany and repatriated five months later. He served as counselor of the American legation in Lisbon in 1942–43. In 1944 he was again assigned to Moscow where he served as minister-counselor until 1946.

A long dispatch Kennan filed from Moscow in 1946 in which he analyzed the reasons for Soviet postwar truculence and intransigence brought him to the attention of Secretary of the Navy James V. Forrestal. Forrestal arranged to have Kennan return to Washington and serve on the faculty of the newly created National War College. After a year in that position, he was appointed chairman of the State Department's newly established Policy Planning Committee. The Committee was to analyze and forecast general trends in world affairs and conduct long-range planning of American foreign policy. The post of chairman was, in effect, that of American diplomatic chief of staff.

Writing under the cryptonym "Mr. X," Kennan published an article in the July 1947 number of the journal *Foreign Affairs* entitled "The Sources of Soviet Conduct." The thesis of the article was that Soviet postwar expansion in Europe was not motivated by the desire for a buffer zone to enhance Russian security, but rather by a commitment to the ideology of Marxism and Leninism that saw conflict between socialism and capitalism as inevitable and made it a duty for the USSR to subvert or conquer the capitalist West. The article prescribed a policy of "containment" of Soviet expansion, i.e., a long-term program of countering such expansion until internal Soviet events brought about a moderation in the USSR's foreign policy. Although Kennan later disowned the more militaristic interpretations of his thesis, the article was generally seen as a call to arms against

Soviet aggression and served to crystallize an unspoken view held by many in the West that a policy of massive rearmament was needed to counter Soviet expansion. The result was the "Containment Doctrine" that formed the basis of American Soviet policy during the late 1940s and the early 1950s. Kennan's article is therefore regarded as a significant milestone in the progress of the cold war.

Kennan was instrumental in the adoption of peacetime COVERT ACTION operations by the U.S. government and the establishment of a covert-action unit within the CENTRAL INTELLIGENCE AGENCY. After the success of the ITALIAN ELECTION OPERATION in 1948, in which the CIA undertook a covert-action operation to insure that the Christian Democrats succeeded over the Communists in the Italian elections, Kennan proposed to the NATIONAL SECURITY COUNCIL the establishment of a unit to be called the Special Studies Group within his Policy Planning Staff in the State Department. The unit was to be a permanent mechanism for such covert-action operations. The NSC endorsed the idea, but established the unit—which was called the Office of Policy Coordination—within the CIA. However, the director of OPC did not report to the director of central intelligence, but to a two-person board representing the State and Defense departments. Kennan was the State Department representative on this board until 1950, when he took a leave of absence from the government to do research at the Institute for Advanced Studies at Princeton, New Jersey.

Kennan returned to government service and Moscow in May 1952 when he was appointed ambassador to the USSR. However he was declared persona non grata by the Soviets the following October, ostensibly because of critical comments he made in a visit to Berlin regarding Soviet treatment of Western diplomats. Kennan returned to the Institute for Advanced Study in 1953. In 1957–58 he took a leave of absence to teach at Oxford University.

Kennan is the author of numerous books and articles in the fields of history and foreign relations. His book *Russia Leaves the War* was awarded the Pulitzer Prize for history for 1957.

(*Current Biography*, 1947, 1959; Kennan, *Memoirs*; Karalekas, *History of the Central Intelligence Agency*.)

KENT, SHERMAN (December 1, 1903–March 11, 1986): historian, intelligence officer

A native of Chicago, Kent earned a Ph.B. and a Ph.D. from Yale University in 1926 and 1933, respectively. He taught history at Yale from 1928 onward (with a brief hiatus in 1931–32), and was an assistant professor in 1941 when he joined the Office of the Coordinator of Information, the predecessor of the Office of Strategic Services. He was assigned to the OSS RESEARCH AND ANALYSIS BRANCH under WILLIAM LANGER and headed the African Section from 1941 to 1943, and the Europe Africa Division from 1943 to 1945. In 1945, when the R&A Branch was transferred to the State Department and became the Office of Research and Intelligence (see STATE DEPARTMENT INTELLIGENCE), he went along, and he served as its director in 1946. He also became a member of the resident civilian staff of the National War College.

In 1947 Kent returned to Yale as a full professor of history. In 1948 he published *Strategic Intelligence for American World Policy*, a highly regarded study of the INTELLIGENCE CYCLE and its role in the formulation of foreign policy. The book stressed the role of the intelligence analyst as "a specialty of the very highest order," and argued that it was a profession quite distinct from those of the diplomat and military officer (to whom intelligence analysis had largely been relegated prior to the SECOND WORLD WAR).

In 1950 William Langer, who was then on a leave of absence from Harvard University to organize the Board of National Estimates of the CENTRAL INTELLIGENCE AGENCY, persuaded Kent to return to Washington to serve on the Board. Kent served as Langer's deputy and, after Langer returned to Harvard, he became director of the Board (see NATIONAL INTELLIGENCE ESTIMATE).

Kent's eighteen-year tenure as director of the Board of National Estimates was distinguished by frequent successes. Despite his impressive academic background, Kent was regarded by intelligence professionals as an intensely practical person, far from the stereotypical ivory tower scholar. His attitude in this regard may be epitomized in what has come to be known in intelligence circles as "Kent's Law of Coups," which states: "Those coups d'etat known about in advance don't take place."

In 1961 Kent and the Board of National Estimate (like most CIA units outside of the CIA CLANDESTINE SERVICE) were not informed in advance of the BAY OF PIGS INVASION. However, in a paper on the political situation in Cuba, Kent accurately estimated that the Cuban people would either be unwilling or unable to overthrow the Castro regime. This estimate, of course, directly contradicted one of the principle false assumptions on which the invasion plan was based viz., that the landing of the exiles would eventually inspire a spontaneous uprising in Cuba. Unfortunately, the estimate was not heeded.

Kent was not equally prescient in every case, however. In 1962, for example, the Board of National

Estimate advised that it was unlikely that the Soviet Union would introduce offensive missiles into Cuba (see CUBAN MISSILE CRISIS). However, the Board's reasoning—that the USSR had never installed such weapons even in its satellite countries, that a missile base in Cuba would present the Soviets with serious command and control problems, and that the necessary introduction of large numbers of Soviet personnel into Cuba would be a political liability for the Russians in Latin America—seems, in retrospect, very reasonable, even if entirely mistaken.

Kent retired from the Board and the CIA in 1968. He was succeeded by his deputy, ABBOTT SMITH. In 1967 he was awarded the President's Award for Distinguished Federal Service.

In addition to several scholarly works in history, Kent wrote and published some children's stories.

(*Contemporary Authors*, v. 53; *Who's Who in America*, v. 34; Cline, *The CIA: Reality vs. Myth*; Smith, *OSS*; Prados, *The Soviet Estimate*; Kirkpatrick, *The U.S. Intelligence Community*; obituary, *New York Times*, March 15, 1986, p. 10).

KENT, TYLER GATEWOOD (1911–): linguist, foreign service officer

Kent was born in Newchang, Manchuria, where his father was the American consul. He attended St. Albans preparatory school, graduated from Princeton University in 1932, and later studied at the Sorbonne, the University of Madrid, and George Washington University. He became an accomplished linguist, fluent in French, German, Greek, Italian, Spanish, and Russian.

Kent joined the State Department in 1934 as a clerk in the foreign service, and was assigned to the American embassy in Moscow. In July 1939 he became a code and cipher clerk. The following September he was transferred to London, working in the same capacity.

Kent removed official State Department documents from the Moscow and London embassies, including copies of confidential messages between Roosevelt and Winston Churchill. He later said he acted because he believed these documents proved that the foreign policy of President Franklin Roosevelt's administration was contrary to the interests of the American people. Soon after his arrival in London he turned over many of these documents to Anna Wycoff, the daughter of a White Russian, anti-Bolshevik emigré. Possibly without Kent's knowledge or consent, Wycoff turned over the documents to an Italian diplomat. The Italian government passed them on to the German ambassador to Rome, who sent them to German intelligence.

British intelligence intercepted the German ambassador's reports to Berlin and so discovered the leak and eventually its source in the American embassy in London. Kent was arrested, confidential documents were found in his apartment, and he admitted his part in the affair, which he maintained was aimed only at bringing the papers to the attention of the U.S. Congress in order to prevent America's involvement in the war. Lacking proof that he had turned over the information to a foreign government, the British government tried him for something less than espionage. He was convicted and sentenced to seven years imprisonment. In 1945 he was deported to the United States, where he sought and found obscurity.

Kent claimed to have developed an intense animosity toward Communism during his tour in Moscow, and he apparently was a Fascist sympathizer. Although these factors are generally understood to be the motives of his theft of the documents, some historians and espionologists have noted several anomalies in his case and speculated that he may actually have been entrapped by Soviet intelligence while in Moscow and subsequently have been acting under Soviet control. British intelligence reportedly reclassified Kent as a Soviet agent after the war.

(Farago, *The Game of the Foxes*; Kahn, *The Codebreakers*; Peake, "The Putative Spy.")

KH-8 RECONNAISSANCE SATELLITE

The KH-8 Close Look satellite is an orbital surveillance platform designed to obtain detailed, high-resolution photographs of ground features and objects of special interest that have been singled out in large-area photographs previously made by other reconnaissance satellites. The KH-8 can drop as low as seventy miles altitude for a "close look" at the intelligence target. Its cameras reportedly can distinguish items on the ground six inches across. The satellite can remain in orbit for up to six months, depending on its consumption of film and fuel.

(*New York Times*, January 15, 1985, Section 6, p. 52; *Newsweek*, January 31, 1983.)

KH-9 RECONNAISSANCE SATELLITE

The KH-9 "Big Bird" is an orbital surveillance platform that carries high-resolution cameras in a north-south polar orbit ranging in altitude from 103 to 167 miles. It remains in orbit up to nine months, returning images to the ground either by de-orbiting film in recoverable pods or by transmitting television-like pictures to a ground receiving station. The video is sent via a twenty-foot antenna unfurled from the body of the satellite after it achieves orbit. An area surveillance camera—made by Eastman Kodak—is used to identify surface features of interest, which are then rephotographed by the KH-9's high-resolution camera—built by Perkin-Elmer Corporation—that reportedly can resolve detail of less than a foot from an altitude of one hundred miles. The KH-9 is believed also to carry SIDE-LOOKING AIRCRAFT RADAR, capable of resolving useful detail from distances in excess of 100 miles.

The KH-9, which is a modified Agena rocket, ten feet in diameter, fifty feet long, and weighing fifteen tons, is launched into orbit by a Titan 3D booster. The first KH-9 was placed in orbit June 15, 1971.

(*New York Times*, January 13, 1985, Section 6, p. 52; *Newsweek*, January 31, 1983; Klass, *Secret Sentries in Space*; Greenwood, "Reconnaissance and Arms Control.")

KH-11 RECONNAISSANCE SATELLITE

The KH-11 Digital Imaging Reconnaissance satellite is a long-lived (i.e., remaining in orbit for up to two years) surveillance platform that relays its pictures to earth, providing a quick (a matter of hours) response to requirements for photographs of an area of intelligence interest. Developed for the NATIONAL RECONNAISSANCE OFFICE by TRW, Inc., the KH-11 reportedly stands six stories tall and weighs fifteen tons. It orbits the earth in a north-south polar orbit at altitudes ranging between 170 and 320 miles, and has an orbital period of ninety-two minutes.

The KH-11's cameras are activated by radio command from ground installations. The photographs are converted to digital form and transmitted by way of a second, relay satellite to the Mission Ground Site at Fort Belvoir, Virginia.

The KH-11 reportedly also collects SIGINT data.

The first KH-11 was launched into orbit on December 19, 1976.

(*New York Times*, January 13, 1985, Section 6, page 52; Bamford, *The Puzzle Palace*; *Newsweek*, January 31, 1983, p. 20.)

KH-12 RECONNAISSANCE SATELLITE

The KH-12 is an orbital surveillance platform said to have the ability to detect objects on the ground that are less than six inches across. The satellite can descend to a low orbit for a "close look" at intelligence targets, and therefore may be a longer-lived version of the KH-8 RECONNAISSANCE SATELLITE. The first KH-12 was scheduled for launch in 1986 from the space shuttle, but may have been delayed as a consequence of the space shuttle *Challenger* disaster of January 1986. Reportedly, a planned fleet of four satellites would permit coverage of any designated area on the surface of the earth within twenty minutes of receiving a command from a ground station.

(*New York Times*, February 24, 1986, p. B6.)

KIMBALL, WILLIAM WIRT (January 9, 1848–January 26, 1930): naval officer

A native of Paris, Maine, Kimball graduated from the U.S. Naval Academy in 1869. Endowed with an interest in and aptitude for mechanical engineering, he became an expert in torpedoes and contributed to the development of machine guns. After a variety of assignments at sea and ashore, he took part in the landing of U.S. forces in Panama in April-May 1885 to protect American interests during an insurrection there. As a consequence of this episode he wrote a special intelligence report on French progress on the Panama Canal, a document that reflected his interest in the use of intelligence in developing naval war plans.

Kimball served with the Office of Naval Intelligence from 1894 to 1897, during which time he took part in the joint ONI-Naval War College war-gaming exercises that led to plans for the SPANISH-AMERICAN WAR. The so-called "Kimball Plan," completed in June 1897, called for a naval blockade of Cuba and the attack and blockade of Manila. These were the two most significant features of American strategy when the war was fought a year later. Assistant Secretary of the Navy Theodore Roosevelt was impressed with Kimball's plan and got the Navy ready to put it into effect as war approached early in 1898. Roosevelt praised Kimball for having done "invaluable work . . . in formulating and preparing plans of action for the war with Spain."

Kimball was promoted to the rank of rear admiral in 1908 and commanded the Nicaraguan Expeditionary Squadron in 1909–10, when the U.S. intervened in a revolution in that country. During this intervention he coordinated intelligence collection and applied the findings to strategic war plans for the area so effectively that the State Department used the results in formulating policy.

In addition to his intelligence work and other naval duties, Kimball was instrumental in the development of the submarine, working closely with inventor John P. Holland.

Kimball retired in January 1910, while he was still in command of the Nicaraguan Expeditionary Squadron, but he remained in service until the squadron was withdrawn in April of that year. During the First World War he was recalled to active duty.

(*DAB*; Dorwart, *The Office of Naval Intelligence*.)

KING, J(OSEPH) C(ALDWELL) (October 5, 1900–1975): Army officer, businessman, clandestine service officer

A native of New York State, King graduated from the U.S. Military Academy in 1923 and was commissioned as a second lieutenant. He served in the infantry until 1924. In 1924–25 he studied diplomacy at the L'École Libre des Sciences Politiques in Paris, France.

In 1925–26 King worked as general manager of King Mines and San Bernabe Mines in Durango, Mexico. In 1926–27 he traveled and studied in Spain, Germany, and the Far East. In 1927 he became vice-president of the King Chemical Company in Bound Brook, New Jersey. In 1930 he joined the Latin American Department of Johnson and Johnson, the pharmaceutical company.

During the Second World War King returned to active duty with the U.S. Army and served in Argentina as American military attaché. In this capacity he was involved with the intelligence operations run in Latin America during the war by the FEDERAL BUREAU OF INVESTIGATION.

King's wartime activities led to his appointment as chief of the Western Hemisphere Division of the CIA CLANDESTINE SERVICE when the CIA was formed in 1947. He recruited many of the FBI agents with whom he had worked in Latin America to staff the Division. His acquaintanceship with Latin American police officials and the executives and security officers of many American companies doing business in Latin America proved useful in his position, but he was regarded within the Agency as having little flair for sophisticated political or propaganda operations. He was also cautious in his attitude toward paramilitary operations, and his conservatism in such matters caused him to be edged aside in the planning and execution of the GUATEMALA COUP and the BAY OF PIGS INVASION, both of which were managed by C. TRACY BARNES.

King remained in his position as chief of the WH Division during his entire period of service with the CIA, reportedly setting a record in that regard. He retired from the CIA in 1964 and was succeeded by DESMOND FITZGERALD as WH Chief.

(Cullum, *Biographical Register of the Officers and Graduates of the U.S. Military Academy at West Point*

. . . , v. 6; Smith, *Portrait of a Cold Warrior*; Powers, *The Man Who Kept the Secrets*.)

KINTNER, WILLIAM ROSCOE (April 21, 1915–): Army officer, diplomat, political scientist, covert operations officer

A native of Lock Haven, Pennsylvania, Kintner graduated from the U.S. Military Academy in 1940. After ten years of service as an Army officer he was assigned to the Central Intelligence Agency in 1950 as a member of the senior staff of the Office of Policy Coordination, as the COVERT ACTION department of the CIA was then called. He left the CIA in 1952 and commanded an infantry battalion in Korea. In 1954 he became a member of the planning staff of the NATIONAL SECURITY COUNCIL. He retired from the Army with the rank of colonel in 1961, having been awarded the Legion of Merit and the Bronze Star, and became deputy director of the Foreign Policy Research Institute of the University of Pennsylvania and professor of political science at the university's Wharton School.

From 1973 to 1975 Kintner was U.S. ambassador to Thailand. He is the author of several books on Communist subversion and issues of military and foreign policy, including *The Front is Everywhere* (1950).

(*Who's Who in America*, 42nd ed.)

KIRKPATRICK, LYMAN BICKFORD, JR. (July 15, 1916–): intelligence officer

A native of Rochester, New York, Kirkpatrick graduated from Princeton University in 1938, and wrote and did editorial work for the Bureau of National Affairs and U.S. News, Washington, D.C. publishers, from 1938 until 1942. In 1942 he was recruited by Gen. WILLIAM J. DONOVAN into the Office of the Coordinator of Information, the predecessor organization to the Office of Strategic Services. Later that year he transferred to the newly formed OSS and served in Europe until 1945, reaching the rank of major.

In 1947 Kirkpatrick joined the newly formed Central Intelligence Agency. He served as a division chief from 1947 to 1950, assistant director for special operations from 1950 to 1953, inspector general from 1953 to 1961, and executive director until his retirement in 1965.

In 1961, after the BAY OF PIGS INVASION, Kirkpatrick wrote a scathing critique of the operation, a document that became famous in intelligence circles despite having been suppressed within the CIA.

Kirkpatrick is regarded by many CIA insiders as

the man likely to have succeeded ALLEN DULLES as director of the agency had his career not been seriously hampered by paralysis following a polio attack in 1952.

Kirkpatrick was awarded the Distinguished Intelligence Medal in 1965.

After his retirement from the CIA, Kirkpatrick joined the faculty of Brown University where he taught political science. He has also taught at the Navy War College (1971–72) and the DEFENSE INTELLIGENCE COLLEGE (1975–77).

(*Who's Who in America*, 42nd ed.; Kirkpatrick, *The Real CIA*; Wyden, *Bay of Pigs*; Powers, *The Man Who Kept the Secrets*.)

KNIGHT, WILLIAM J. (1837–ca. 1916): mechanic, soldier, Union secret agent

A native of Wayne County, Ohio, Knight worked as a railroad shop hand and mechanic before the Civil War. In 1861 he enlisted in the Ohio Volunteer Infantry, which was part of the Army of the Ohio. In April 1862 he volunteered to take part in a paramilitary operation behind Confederate lines aimed at severing the rail line between Atlanta and Chattanooga (see ANDREWS'S RAID). He and a party of twenty other Union troops in civilian clothes and led by JAMES J. ANDREWS hijacked a locomotive and attempted to destroy railroad tracks and bridges between the two cities. He was captured by Confederate troops and imprisoned (Andrews and seven of the others were hanged). He and several others escaped. Knight made his way back to his regiment.

After the war Knight worked as an engineer in Minnesota for several years, then became chief engineer of a wood-processing plant in Stryker, Ohio.

(Bryan, *The Spy in America*; Boatner, *Civil War Dictionary*; O'Neill, *Wild Train*.)

KNIGHTS OF THE GOLDEN CIRCLE

This organization, founded in 1854, was a secret society dedicated to the promotion of pro-slavery policies and the American acquisition of Mexico. It may have had its roots in the earlier Southern Rights Clubs, activist associations that aggressively pursued Southern political and economic unity and the protection of the institution of slavery.

The Knights were founded by George W. L. Bickley, a bogus physician of Cincinnati, Ohio, who furnished the organization with all the trappings of a secret society, e.g., secret handshakes and other recognition signs, arcane symbols, mysterious rituals, and elaborate titles. Bickley found an abundant supply of eager recruits throughout the South, and had soon established a network of "castles," as the local lodges were called, south of the Mason-Dixon Line. By 1860 the organization was also well-established in the North, especially in Indiana, Illinois, and Ohio. As the Civil War approached the Knights became closely identified with the Copperheads, as the Peace Democrats were called.

When the war broke out the Knights in the North became, in effect, a Confederate fifth column. They engaged in subversion, sabotage, and other illegal activities aimed at damaging the Northern war effort. Men of military age were recruited to go south and join the Confederate Army; the homes of men who had gone off to fight for the North were burned. The Knights smuggled guns into Missouri to arm Quantrill's Confederate irregular force in Kansas and Missouri. In Illinois, General Grant was forced to disband a unit of the state militia because it was virtually a branch of the Knights. In Kentucky, where the Knights were particularly strong, the organization served as an intelligence service for the Confederate cavalry of Gen. John Hunt Morgan (the unit known as Morgan's Raiders).

In 1863 Bickley was arrested and imprisoned in the federal penitentiary at Columbus, Ohio. About the same time the Knights merged with the Corps de Belgique, a similar organization popular in Missouri, and became the Order of the American Knights. In 1864 the group again changed its name to the Sons of Liberty. Former Ohio Democratic Congressman Clement L. Vallandingham became the supreme commander.

In 1862 Gov. Oliver P. Morton of Indiana became seriously concerned about the threat posed by the Knights in his state, and requested Brig. Gen. HENRY B. CARRINGTON to investigate the organization. Carrington sent Union secret service agent FELIX A. STIDGER to penetrate their ranks in May 1863. Stidger became a top official in the Sons of Liberty and his intelligence reports to Carrington kept the federal authorities apprised of the progress of the NORTHWEST CONSPIRACY, a plan whereby Confederate secret service agents based in Canada were to use the Sons of Liberty to foment revolt and overthrow the governments of Indiana, Illinois, and Ohio in the summer or fall of 1864. (Also see THOMAS HENRY HINES.) Stidger's work, together with other penetrations and defections, helped to thwart the conspiracy and led to the arrest, trial, and conviction of much of the leadership of the Sons of Liberty in September 1864.

During the war the membership of the Knights/Sons reportedly numbered in the tens or even hundreds of thousands. The size of the organization probably worked against its effectiveness as a subversive agency, first, by diluting it with large numbers of members with limited commitment to its goals, and, second, by vastly increasing the chances of defection or penetration. Although the Knights did manage to inflict substantial damage on the Union war effort in the early months of the war, by 1864 they seemed to be almost completely ineffective in carrying out their part in the Northwest Conspiracy.

In his recent revisionist study of the Knights and related groups, historian Frank L. Klement concludes that the Knights were a far smaller and less dangerous group than has traditionally been supposed.

(*DAH*; Boatner, *Civil War Dictionary*; McMaster, *Our House Divided*; Horan, *Confederate Agent*; Klement, *Dark Lanterns*.)

KNOCHE, E(NNO) HENRY (January 14, 1925–): intelligence officer

A native of Charleston, West Virginia, Knoche graduated from Washington and Jefferson College in 1946. He served as a naval officer in the Second World War and the Korean War.

Knoche joined the Central Intelligence Agency and for many years was an intelligence analyst in the CIA INTELLIGENCE DIRECTORATE. He was director of the FOREIGN BROADCAST INFORMATION SERVICE in 1972, and director of the Office of Strategic Research in 1973. During the tenure of WILLIAM E. COLBY as director of Central Intelligence (1973–75), Knoche helped Colby deal with the complex problems associated with the CIA's responses to the congressional investigations of the INTELLIGENCE COMMUNITY.

In July 1976 CIA Director GEORGE BUSH appointed Knoche deputy director of central intelligence, the number two official in the CIA, and the person concerned with much of the day-to-day management of the Agency. Knoche also served as acting director of central intelligence during the interregnum of January–March 1977, after Bush left the post of DCI and before STANSFIELD TURNER assumed it.

Turner differed with Knoche on matters of management policy, and these differences led him to replace Knoche in July 1977 with JOHN F. BLAKE, who served as acting deputy director of central intelligence until February 1978, when FRANK C. CARLUCCI became the permanent DDCI.

Knoche, who retired from the CIA concurrent with stepping down from the DDCI post, thereafter pursued private business interests.

(Central Intelligence Agency, *Directors and Deputy Directors of Central Intelligence*; Cline, *The CIA: Reality vs. Myth*; Ranelagh, *The Agency*; Turner, *Secrecy and Democracy*.)

KNOWLTON'S RANGERS

The first intelligence and reconnaissance unit of the U.S. Army during the AMERICAN REVOLUTION. Nicknamed "Congress's Own," it was established in 1776 by Gen. GEORGE WASHINGTON after the need for such a unit became apparent during the battle of Long Island (creation of the unit is regarded as the birth of American military intelligence, and the year 1776 in the present-day logo of U.S. Army Intelligence is a reference to it). It consisted of one hundred thirty men and twenty officers, all hand-picked volunteers, and was commanded by Lt. Col. Thomas Knowlton who had served in a similar unit led by Col. Israel Putnam during the French and Indian (Seven Years) War. The unit's mission included supplying forward reconnaissance, scouting enemy outposts, collecting intelligence, and performing other secret duties "either by water or land, by night or day." One of Knowlton's company commanders was Capt. NATHAN HALE.

(Ford, *A Peculiar Service*; Bidwell, "History of the Military Intelligence Division, Department of the Army General Staff"; Powe and Wilson, *The Evolution of American Military Intelligence*.)

KOMER, ROBERT WILLIAM (February 23, 1922–): national security specialist, government official, intelligence officer

A native of Chicago, Komer graduated from Harvard in 1942 and received an M.B.A. from that university in 1947. During 1942–46 he served in the U.S. Army; he was awarded a Bronze Star, and discharged with the rank of first lieutenant.

Komer joined the Central Intelligence Agency in 1947 and worked as an intelligence analyst. He served in the Office of National Estimates (see NATIONAL INTELLIGENCE ESTIMATE) and left the CIA in 1956. Komer, an expert on Vietnam and Southeast Asia, served on the National Security Council staff from 1961 to 1965 and was a deputy special assistant, then special assistant, to President Lyndon Johnson during 1965–67. In 1967–68 he was deputy to the commander of the U.S. Military Advisory Command in Vietnam (USMACV) for the CORDS program (CORDS—Civil Operations and Rural Development Support—was a State Department program aimed at eliminating popular support for the Vietcong in the countryside; see VIETNAM WAR).

Komer served as U.S. ambassador to Turkey in 1968–69. He was a social science researcher for the Rand Corporation from 1969 to 1977. From 1977 to 1979 he was the advisor on NATO affairs to the Secretary of Defense and from 1979 to 1981 he held the position of undersecretary of Defense for policy. Since 1981 he has been a member of the faculty of George Washington University.

(Cline, *CIA: Reality vs. Myth; Who's Who in America*, 43rd ed.)

KOREAN WAR

Background: From 1910 until the end of the Second World War, Korea was part of the Japanese empire. On August 8, 1945, two days after U.S. Air Forces dropped an atomic bomb on Hiroshima, and six days before Japan surrendered, the Soviet Union declared war on Japan and launched a large-scale (and generally unopposed) invasion of Japanese Manchuria, southern Sakhalin, the Kurile Islands, and Korea. On the pretext that there had been no formal capitulation of the Japanese forces in the area, the Soviets continued to advance down the Korean peninsula for several days after Japan surrendered and only halted when they encountered the northward advance of American occupation forces at the thirty-eighth parallel of north latitude. This line became the demarcation line between the American and Soviet zones of trusteeship. The Soviets established a puppet regime in their zone, the Democratic People's Republic of North Korea, and resisted efforts by the United Nations to hold nationwide Korean elections aimed at unifying the country and establishing it as a single sovereign nation. The UN then established the Republic of Korea in the southern zone, and in 1949 the American occupation forces withdrew.

Exploiting the vulnerability of the new and inexperienced government of the ROK, the North Koreans undertook a campaign of subversion in the south. In early June the North Korean government reversed its past position, called for nationwide elections, and requested UN supervision of the process. Apparently this was a cover for the final preparations in the Communists' plan for an invasion of South Korea, which they launched on June 25, 1950.

The War: The North Korean invasion force consisted of some 100,000 troops supported by Soviet-made tanks and artillery. Faced with only token resistance by the South Korean army and five hundred American military advisors, the invaders swept southward. President Harry S. Truman immediately ordered U.S. air and naval forces in East Asia to go to the aid of South Korea. Two days after the invasion began the Truman administration took advantage of a Soviet boycott of the UN Security Council to introduce a resolution giving official UN sanction to his action, and in the absence of a Soviet veto the resolution was passed. The Security Council resolution appealed to UN member nations to join the United States in resisting the North Korean aggression; ultimately the U.S. and ROK forces were joined by substantial or token military contingents from Australia, Belgium, Canada, Colombia, Ethiopia, France, Great Britain, Greece, Luxembourg, the Netherlands, New Zealand, the Philippines, South Africa, Thailand, and Turkey.

Inchon Landing

North Korea retained the military initiative during July and August, while the US/UN forces under Gen. Douglas MacArthur assembled in a five-hundred-square-mile area around the port of Pusan in the southeast corner of the Korean peninsula. On September 15th, however, MacArthur executed a bold counterstroke, landing a powerful Marine and Army force at Inchon, a port on the central west coast of Korea, twenty-five miles west of the South Korean capital, Seoul. The amphibious force pressed eastward, capturing Seoul by September 29th and threatening the North Korean lines of communication to the south. At the same time a second US/UN force struck northward from Pusan. By the end of the month all North Korean forces had been driven from the south, except some small remnants of the invading force that withdrew to the mountains to conduct guerrilla operations.

The Chinese Invasion

South Korean troops of the US/UN command crossed the 38th parallel into North Korea on October 1st, meeting little resistance as they advanced northward. On October 3rd Communist China warned that it would intervene militarily if non-Korean UN forces entered North Korea. Notwithstanding this, the UN General Assembly on October 7th voted for the restoration of peace and security throughout Korea, thereby giving tacit approval to the entry of UN international forces into North Korea. The U.S. First Marine Division landed at Wonsan on the northeast coast on October 26, and the Army's Seventh Division landed at Iwon, eighty miles farther north, three days later. By then most North Korean resistance had ended and the North Korean army had completely disintegrated and scattered. However, the US/UN forces began to encounter small units of Chinese "volunteers" late in October, and on November 25th, as the US/UN advance approached the Manchurian border, the Chinese launched a massive counterattack with some two hundred thousand troops. To avoid a direct confrontation with the United States, China continued to maintain the fiction that the thoroughly trained and equipped Chinese regular forces in Korea were "volunteers" fighting on their own initiative.

The US/UN northward advance had been divided by terrain, roads, and overconfidence into two columns separated by a gap that widened to eighty miles as the forces approached the Manchurian border. The Chinese drove into this gap and flanked the two overextended US/UN columns. The US/UN forces withdrew under the force of the Chinese onslaught, and by early January 1951 the Chinese had pushed south of the thirty-eighth parallel, retaken Seoul, and driven the US/UN forces into the southern third of the Korean peninsula. However, the US/UN counterattacked in the spring, and by June had retaken most of South Korea.

The Static War

The Chinese intervention led to a change in the overall US/UN strategy and objectives. The Truman administration was unwilling either to introduce nuclear weapons into the conflict or to strike north of the Yalu River into China. Instead, the administration chose to seek a negotiated settlement to reestablish the status quo antebellum. However, General MacArthur believed that no satisfactory conclusion of the war could be reached without carrying the war into China, and after he publicly stated this belief, Truman replaced him as commander in April 1951. Peace negotiations commenced in Panmunjom, a Korean village near the thirty-eighth parallel, the following October and dragged on for more than twenty-two months while fighting continued, casualties mounted, and the front between the two forces remained essentially static. On July 27, 1953 the UN and North Korea signed an armistice establishing a boundary and demilitarized zone at approximately the thirty-eighth parallel, i.e., at the pre-war demarcation line.

Intelligence in the War: Although more than three decades have passed since the hostilities, no comprehensive unclassified assessment of the role of intelligence in the Korean War has been published. However, enough fragmentary information is available to provide a broad general outline of the matter.

Warnings and Indications Intelligence

The North Korean invasion of the south that triggered the war came as a complete surprise to U.S. policymakers. Five days before the invasion Dean Rusk, then assistant secretary of state for Far Eastern affairs, testified before the House Committee on Foreign Affairs that "We see no present indications that the [North Koreans] have any intention of fighting a major war for that purpose [i.e., taking over South Korea]."

Immediately after the North Korean invasion, the CENTRAL INTELLIGENCE AGENCY was called to account by the Truman administration, Congress, and the media to explain why it had failed to provide advance warning of the attack. In fact, the CIA had few intelligence assets in Korea or Japan because General MacArthur, the commander of U.S. forces in the Far East, had excluded it from the area in much the same way he had excluded the Office of Strategic Services from the Southwest Pacific during the SECOND WORLD WAR, preferring to rely on his own chief of intelligence, Gen. CHARLES WILLOUGHBY. In May 1950, a month before the North Korean invasion, MacArthur relented slightly and consented to a modest CIA presence in Japan, but the Agency personnel assigned to that country were not due to arrive until July. The CIA, therefore, was reduced to relying largely upon intelligence from Willoughby's staff in order to form its estimates of the Korean situation. Despite this handicap, the CIA was held responsible in the matter, and Director ROSCOE HILLENKOETTER was called before the Senate Appropriations Committee on June 26th, the day after the attack.

Hillenkoetter had told the *New York Times* the day before that the CIA had been aware that ". . . conditions existed in Korea which could have meant an invasion this week or the next." In his testimony before the Senate committee, Hillenkoetter stated that the Agency had warned the President, the secretary of state, and the secretary of defense on June 19th that North Korean forces were about to invade the south, and that he was unable to explain why this warning had not been acted upon. This was flatly denied by the two Cabinet officials in their testimony before the same committee. The CIA had, in fact, sent an estimate to the State and Defense Departments and the White House on June 14th stating that North Korea was *capable* of invading South Korea at any time and capturing Seoul in ten to twelve days. But the estimate did not warn that the North Koreans *intended* to do so.

However, in his memoir of the Korean War, Gen. Matthew Ridgway cites a report from a CIA unit—presumably one of the few Agency assets in the Far East—to the Far East Command headquarters in Tokyo on June 19th, the day Hillenkoetter says he warned the administration:

Only six days before the [North Koreans] crossed the border in force a Central Intelligence field agency reported "extensive troop movements" north of the 38th parallel, together with "evacuation of all residents from the Northern side of the parallel to a depth of two kilometers; suspension of civilian freight service from Wonsan to Chorwon and reservation of this line for transporting military supplies only; movements of armed units to border areas; and movement of large shipments of ordnance and ammunition to border areas." How anyone could have read this report and not anticipated an attack is hard to fathom. Yet this report was not used as a basis for *any* conclusion by G-2 at General Headquarters in Tokyo and it was forwarded to Washington in routine fashion with no indication of urgency. Later GHQ was to disclaim all responsibility for failure to interpret these almost classic preparations and to insist that it had "forwarded all the facts" to Washington.

It is not clear from the unclassified record whether this same report may have reached CIA headquarters in Washington by a different channel on June 19th and may have thus been the basis for Hillenkoetter's claim that the CIA warned State, Defense, and the White House. For his part, General Willoughby recalled that he had reported often and accurately on the situation in Korea in the months before the war, and that in any case Korea was the responsibility of the intelligence staff of the Korea Military Advisory Group—the American advisory group with the ROK army—and not that of the Far East Command. (In fact, Secretary of State Dean Acheson had publicly declared in January 1950 that South Korea was not within the world perimeter that the United States was committed to defend, a statement that some say encouraged the Communist attack.) However, Goulden states that General Willoughby's intelligence staff dismissed indications that an invasion was imminent. Goulden also characterizes Willoughby's intelligence as, in general, unreliable information based upon "dribbles of second- and thirdhand information from low-level defectors, refugees, and the few Western diplomats stationed in Pyongyang."

The North Koreans had been building their military capability along the border for a year, a fact that had been frequently noted in CIA intelligence analysis. The Agency and other members of the INTELLIGENCE COMMUNITY had become increasingly concerned over North Korean intentions in the months before the invasion, and on April 12, 1950 the Watch Committee, an interagency group responsible for warnings and indications intelligence, met to consider a report from Willoughby's staff that stated that "the North Korean People's Army will invade South Korea in June of 1950." For reasons still obscure,

however, this assessment failed to prompt the Joint Chiefs of Staff's Armed Forces Security Agency (see NATIONAL SECURITY AGENCY) to make North Korea a priority target for communications intelligence collection, perhaps the means most likely to have revealed the Communists' intentions. (The Far East Command's report is noted in Bamford's account. The generally poor quality of Willoughby's intelligence reports—if Goulden's characterization of them is valid—may be the reason this accurate assessment of North Korean intentions was ignored by the Watch Committee.)

Increased COMINT collection might not have disclosed the invasion plan, however. Corson states that the North Koreans executed a "communications deception plan" aimed at disguising their preparations. He writes that "the North Koreans had made a conscious effort not to increase the volume of their radio traffic and had disguised tactical orders and instructions in innocuous administrative messages. In essence, this produced a kind of 'radio silence,' but one which left confirmation of the North Koreans' intentions and timetable to human rather than communications sources."

One factor in the intelligence failure was, paradoxically, the obvious success of Communist subversion in South Korea and the instability of the ROK government of Syngman Rhee. The North Koreans' call for nationwide Korean elections in early June, a reversal of a position they had consistently held for several years, suggested that they expected to achieve their objective through nonmilitary means. On May 17th, even before the call for elections had been made, a monthly CIA "Review of the World Situation" forecast that if Rhee lost ground in the South Korean elections that month it "would considerably lessen the chances for Communist exploitation in South Korea." Of course, the North Korean request for UN-supervised elections was merely a deception to cover the final invasion preparations.

Veteran senior CIA officer LYMAN KIRKPATRICK sums up the failure this way:

> . . . like any military force anxious to achieve surprise, [the North Koreans] had drawn out their buildup over a long period of time in order not to arouse suspicion. If proper military security were observed, only a very few senior officers would know of the date and time of the attack. Like the Battle of the Bulge, advance warning could have come only from an intelligence penetration—an agent—in the highest levels of the North Korean army, or from a communications slip, and there were neither of these.

No thorough, unclassified postmortem of the initial Korean War intelligence failure, along the lines of

Roberta Wohlstetter's analysis of the PEARL HARBOR ATTACK, has yet been written. Such a study may well find that the failure to foresee the Korean invasion shares many of the same causes of the Pearl Harbor failure, e.g., a failure to distinguish between relevant and irrelevant items in the flow of intelligence reports, a failure to analyze and integrate the available intelligence properly, and misinterpretation of the facts in the light of a prior and erroneous conclusion regarding enemy intentions.

Chinese Intervention Forecasts

The task of forecasting the likelihood of Chinese military intervention after the UN forces entered North Korea in October 1950 was compounded by the problem of forecasting General MacArthur's actions. President Truman recalled that the general ignored the orders of the Joint Chiefs of Staff that he should not place non-Korean units near the Manchurian border, in consideration of the Chinese threat to intervene if such forces even entered North Korea. On October 20th the CIA reported to Truman that the Chinese would move far enough into Korea to safeguard their hydroelectric plants on the Yalu River, the Korea-Manchuria border, a forecast that may have seemed to imply that this would be the limit of Chinese interest and intervention. Corson states that the CIA warned of large-scale Chinese troop movements toward Korea in August, and that Hillenkoetter (who left the post of DCI in September) warned Truman that MacArthur's drive to the Manchurian border "was likely to induce a major Chinese response." He also states that DCI WALTER BEDELL SMITH (Hillenkoetter's successor) warned MacArthur of the presence of eleven Chinese combat divisions of which the general was unaware. However, Goulden says the CIA equivocated and that the Agency's reports in early autumn "were so contradictory as to be meaningless," warning of possible Chinese or even Soviet intervention while simultaneously insisting that no real evidence had been found to support such forecasts.

Whatever the extent of the strategic intelligence warning of Chinese intervention, it obviously was insufficient to persuade Truman and the Joint Chiefs of Staff to halt MacArthur's northward advance, or at least insist that he use only ROK troops in North Korea. The failure of the US/UN forces to detect the Chinese invasion force until they encountered it, and the vulnerable disposition of US/UN forces near the Yalu River, were undeniable field intelligence and command failures for which MacArthur and his staff must be held responsible. (General Ridgway, who succeeded MacArthur as supreme commander of the US/UN forces, recalled that "[The] wholly human failing of discounting or ignoring all unwelcome facts seemed developed beyond average in MacArthur's nature.")

Aerial Reconnaissance

Due to cutbacks made after the SECOND WORLD WAR, ARMY INTELLIGENCE was caught short by the Korean War. Tactical Counter Intelligence Corps and Army Security Agency units were quickly transferred from Japan to Korea at the outbreak of hostilities, but the U.S. forces continued to suffer from a shortage of trained intelligence personnel until 1952. A lack of Korean and Chinese linguists reduced the role of prisoner-of-war interrogation as an intelligence source and increased the importance of signals intelligence and aerial reconnaissance, but even in the latter fields a shortage of trained personnel hampered operations.

Infield states that forty-four percent of all intelligence used by US/UN ground forces during the war came from aerial reconnaissance. Aerial photography was certainly a more important source of intelligence than it had been in any earlier war. The war also marked the introduction of aerial color photography, a development based on the work of aerial reconnaissance pioneer Gen. GEORGE W. GODDARD, that greatly aided the photointerpreter in distinguishing between natural backgrounds and camouflaged equipment and installations. The film also recorded and emphasized the subtle color changes in grass over which men and vehicles had recently passed, thereby enabling photointerpreters to trace enemy troop movements. Stereoscopic color aerial photography was also used in combat for the first time; the technique aided photointerpretation and was also of great value in briefing paratroops on the terrain of drop zones. The panoramic camera, which provides a horizon-to-horizon picture of the terrain below, was yet another innovation of the war.

Aerial photoreconnaissance played an important role in the Inchon landings in September 1950. One serious drawback to the planned landing site was the unusually large drop in the water level in Inchon harbor during low tide, a factor that limited to only a few hours the period during which landing craft could be beached there on the planned D-Day of September 15th, and which made the location of underwater obstacles a matter of crucial importance. A series of photoreconnaissance missions flown at wave-top altitude over Inchon harbor at various tidal stages produced precise tidal information, and stereoscopic photographs enabled photointerpreters to determine the height of underwater obstacles to within two inches.

The Air Force and Navy also used aerial photoreconnaissance in support of their strategic bombing operations, in collecting intelligence that was used in compiling target folders, and in making post-strike damage assessment. Oblique photographs taken by aircraft flying along the Yalu River were the principal source of intelligence on troop and equipment movements on the Chinese side of the border. Navy reconnaissance aircraft maintained regular and frequent surveillance of the Formosa Strait area, permitting the Seventh Fleet to operate in Korean waters while continuing to protect Taiwan against the possibility of major Communist Chinese military or naval action. But the largest single function of aerial reconnaissance was the collection of enemy ORDER OF BATTLE intelligence—the identification, location, strength, equipment, and movements of the North Korean and Chinese enemy.

The demand for aerial reconnaissance by the US/UN ground forces far outstripped the Air Force's ability to supply it, especially early in the war. Besides the shortage of trained personnel and facilities, there were severe organizational problems in the processing and dissemination of intelligence. There was, for example, often a complete lack of coordination between the work of the photointerpreters and other intelligence analysts, so that much of the first group's time was wasted in discovering through photoanalysis information that had already been collected by other means. And there was little coordination between the ground commanders' planning of military operations and their prospective requirements for the Air Force's photoreconnaissance service, with the result that facilities and personnel were used inefficiently. The solving of these management and administrative problems during the war was in itself an advance in the integration of tactical aerial reconnaissance into the INTELLIGENCE CYCLE.

Covert Action

MacArthur's intelligence failure regarding the Chinese invasion weakened his hand in keeping the CIA out of Japan and Korea. In January 1951 CIA Director Smith met with MacArthur in Tokyo to discuss an increased Agency presence in the area (Corson states that Smith "laid down the new intelligence law to MacArthur"). As a result the CIA soon took on a larger role in the war.

COVERT ACTION rather than SECRET INTELLIGENCE was the CIA's principal function in the war zone. In July 1950, after MacArthur had reluctantly agreed that May to a modest CIA presence in Japan, a small contingent from the Agency's Office of Policy Coordination (see CIA CLANDESTINE SERVICE) headed by HANS V. TOFTE and GEORGE E. AURELL arrived in Tokyo. Tofte established six CIA installations in Japan, the major one at Atsugi Naval Air Station, fifty miles south of Tokyo. His most immediate task was to work with the Air Force Office of Special Investigations (see AIR FORCE INTELLIGENCE) to establish an escape-and-evasion network in North Korea to assist American airmen brought down behind Communist lines. By the end of 1950 the network was in place. The CIA/OPC contingent had grown to one thousand men by this time, an expansion MacArthur and Willoughby probably permitted because covert action did not compete with any function of the Far East Command's G-2 staff.

As the war became static in mid-1951, and was being fought along a generally stable main line of resistance, the CIA effort focused on guerrilla warfare. The CIA/OPC group recruited and trained Koreans to fight in irregular units behind Communist lines. Between April and December 1951 it sent forty-four guerrilla teams and attached intelligence units into North Korea. The teams operated from Antung in the west to Rashin and Yuki in the northeast, harassing the Communist lines of communications and supply from China. These operations were so effective that the Chinese believed fifty thousand troops were operating north of the thirty-eighth parallel, while in fact only 1,200 CIA/OPC guerrillas carried out the operations.

Covert Operations Against China

Covert action also provided a means of striking against China without entering into a direct military confrontation with that country, a response that mirrored the Chinese army's own sub-rosa involvement in the war. CIA/OPC ran Operation Tropic, a program of support for so-called "third force" elements within China, i.e., anti-Communists not affiliated with Chiang Kai-shek's Nationalist Chinese government on Taiwan. Tropic got under way in 1951 with the recruitment of Chinese agents in Hong Kong and their training in guerrilla warfare at CIA bases on Saipan and in Japan. These agents were to infiltrate the Chinese mainland and organize and lead the third force dissidents. In the spring of 1952 CIA/OPC began infiltrating the Tropic agents into China by airdrop, using aircraft of Civil Air Transport (see AIR PROPRIETARIES). Although no unclassified assessment of the effectiveness of Tropic is available, veteran CIA intelligence officer HARRY ROSITZKE implies that it was a failure. The project was terminated in 1953; it may have been concluded as a result of the Chinese capture of CIA/OPC officers JOHN T. DOWNEY and RICHARD G. FECTEAU while attempting to exfiltrate a Tropic agent by air in November 1952.

Yet another CIA/OPC operation against China, codenamed Paper, involved the scattered remnants of Chiang Kai-shek's army that fled into Burma after the Nationalists were defeated by the Communists in 1949. General Li Mi led one of the largest contingents of the refugee army in Burma, which consisted of some four thousand troops. Operation Paper was intended to equip and support Li Mi's army in order to harass the Chinese and divert their armed forces from Korea. The operation began in February 1951 with the delivery of arms and supplies to Li Mi in Burma through the CIA PROPRIETARY COMPANY, the SEA SUPPLY COMPANY. In May the Li Mi force, supported by airdrops of supplies by Civil Air Transport, entered the Yunnan province of China and advanced sixty miles before Chinese troops inflicted heavy casualties and turned them back. The Li Mi army tried again two months later with the same results. Another unsuccessful attempt was made in the summer of 1952.

Operation Paper failed to divert Chinese troops from Korea, and it greatly damaged American relations with Burma after the defeated Li Mi army turned to banditry and drug-trading in that country. The situation was resolved by WILLIAM J. DONOVAN, then ambassador to Thailand, who negotiated and managed the evacuation of the Li Mi force to Taiwan in 1953–54.

Consequences: The Korean War had several important effects on the CIA. The Agency's failure to warn of the North Korean invasion led to the appointment of Gen. Walter Bedell Smith as director of Central Intelligence, and the reforms and reorganization instituted by Smith changed the shape of the Agency and defined it for the next quarter of a century. The war also established the CIA's jurisdiction in East Asia, from which it had been excluded by General MacArthur. And the CIA grew greatly both in size and influence during the war.

The growth of CIA covert-action activities worldwide during the war led the Agency to recruit many of the veterans of the OSS SPECIAL OPERATIONS BRANCH who had returned to civilian life after the Second World War. Many of these recruits, e.g., WILLIAM E. COLBY, THOMAS BRADEN, JOHN A. BROSS, JACOB D. ESTERLINE, MICHAEL BURKE, FRANKLIN LINDSAY, and ALFRED T. COX, brought with them the swashbuckling spirit of OSS special operations that was to predominate in the CIA during the 1950s, and some of them remained in the Agency

and continued to be a major influence during the next several decades.

The failure of the communications intelligence activities of the Armed Forces Security Agency to forecast the North Korean invasion led to the appointment of the presidential Brownell Committee to investigate COMINT services, which in turn resulted in the establishment of the NATIONAL SECURITY AGENCY in 1952.

Aerial reconnaissance, which had emerged as a major method of intelligence collection during the Second World War, received even greater emphasis in Korea, and this accelerated the development of its technology and methodology.

As a nonwar—it was officially designated a UN "police action"—the Korean War was the first conflict in which American military operations were constrained by the need to avoid escalation into a general nuclear conflict. This placed new and unprecedented demands on the intelligence services, e.g., the requirement to conduct intelligence collection and covert-action operations against Communist China while no formal state of war existed with that country. This blurring of the distinction between war and peace—a fundamental characteristic of the cold war—permanently enlarged the peacetime role of all American intelligence services.

(*DAH*; Ridgway, *The Korean War*; Paige, *The Korean Decision*; Corson, *Armies of Ignorance*; Goulden, *Korea*; Kirkpatrick, *The Real CIA*; Truman, *Memoirs*, v. 2; Rositzke, *The CIA's Secret Operations*; Leary, *Perilous Missions*; Karalekas, *History of the Central Intelligence Agency*; Powe and Wilson, *Evolution of American Military Intelligence*; Infield, *Unarmed and Unafraid*; Bamford, *The Puzzle Palace*.)

KULLBACK, SOLOMON (April 3, 1907–): mathematician, cryptologist

A native of New York City, Kullback graduated from the City College of New York in 1927, received an M.A. in mathematics from Columbia University in 1929, and a Ph.D. in the same subject from George Washington University in 1934. He was one of the four junior cryptologists hired by WILLIAM F. FRIEDMAN to serve in the newly established Signal Intelligence Service (see CRYPTOLOGY, NATIONAL SECURITY AGENCY) in 1930.

During the SECOND WORLD WAR Kullback headed the Cryptanalytic Branch of the Signal Intelligence Service. After the war he went along when the Service became part of the Armed Forces Security Agency, and remained when the AFSA became the

National Security Agency in 1952. He was chief of the NSA's Office of Research and Development until he retired from government service in 1962.

Kullback was a member of the faculty of George Washington University while serving in the government, and he continued teaching at the university until 1974, when he joined the faculty of Florida State University. In 1976 he taught at Stanford University. He continues to consult in the field of cryptology.

(Kahn, *The Codebreakers*; Bamford, *The Puzzle Palace*; *Who's Who in America*, 43rd ed.)

L

LA MOUNTAIN, JOHN (1830–February 14, 1870): balloonist

A native of Wayne County, New York, La Mountain began experimenting with balloons in the 1850s. In 1859 he and fellow balloonist JOHN WISE set a distance record with an 804-mile flight from St. Louis, Missouri, to Henderson, New York.

In May 1861 La Mountain offered his two balloons, his hydrogen gas generator, and his services to Gen. Benjamin F. Butler, the commander of the Union's Army of Virginia (see RECONNAISSANCE BALLOONS). Butler accepted and found La Mountain's reconnaissance flights over his headquarters at Fort Monroe to be extremely useful. The fort, which stands near Hampton, Virginia, on the Chesapeake Bay, was almost completely surrounded by Confederate troops, and thus Butler's forces were unable to occupy any advanced point from which to reconnoiter the area.

La Mountain made his first ascent for Butler during the evening of July 25, 1861. During subsequent ascents, sometimes accompanied by Butler, he was able to discover hidden Confederate installations and accurately assess enemy strength. He put to rest reports that the Confederates were massing for a major assault on Fort Monroe. While working for Butler La Mountain pioneered reconnaissance ascents from the decks of ships, a technique that enabled him to extend the range of his observations in the area.

In September 1861 La Mountain was transferred to the Army of the Potomac and worked for Gen. William B. Franklin. He made a series of spectacular free ascents in which he drifted over the Confederate lines, carried out his reconnaissance, then ascended to higher altitude where he found an opposite wind to ride back to safety. However, his quarrels with THADDEUS S. C. LOWE, chief of the Army of the Potomac's balloon corps, led to his dismissal in February 1862.

La Mountain shared with his fellow Civil War balloonists a proficiency in operating the craft, but from the point of view of military intelligence he is said to have an additional asset—a special talent for observing and accurately estimating enemy strength from his airborne vantage point.

(*Who Was Who in America,* historical volume; Bidwell, "History of the Military Intelligence Division, Department of the Army General Staff"; MacCloskey, *From Gasbags to Spaceships;* Glines, *The Compact History of the United States Air Force.*)

LAMPHERE, ROBERT JOSEPH (February 14, 1918–): businessman, intelligence officer

A native of Wardner, Idaho, Lamphere attended the University of Idaho during 1936–40, and completed his law studies at the National Law School in Washington, D.C., earning an LL.B. from the latter institution in 1941. He then joined the Federal Bureau of Investigation and was trained as a special agent.

Lamphere served in the FBI's Birmingham, Alabama, office for seven months, and was then transferred to New York City, where he investigated Selective Service Act violations during the next three and a half years. In early 1945 he was assigned to the Bureau's Soviet Espionage Squad in New York. He took a major part in the investigation and prosecution of Gerhart Eisler, an Austrian-born officer of Soviet intelligence who had carried out espionage activities in the United States during the 1940s.

In the fall of 1947 Lamphere was promoted to a supervisory position within the Espionage Section at FBI headquarters in Washington. His first assignment there was to set up counterintelligence coverage on Soviet bloc intelligence services operating within the United States. He soon took an interest in a file of enciphered messages that the Bureau had accumulated during 1944–45. The messages had been exchanged between the Soviet consulate in New York City and Soviet intelligence headquarters in Moscow, but U.S. cryptanalysts had been unable to decipher them. Lamphere enlisted the help of a cryptanalyst of the Army Security Agency (see ARMY INTELLIGENCE, NATIONAL SECURITY AGENCY) who had some success in reading the messages.

The deciphered messages led Lamphere to discover Judith Coplin, a political analyst in the Justice Department's Foreign Agents Registrations section who was working for Soviet intelligence. He linked Coplin to her Soviet CASE OFFICER, Valentin Gubitchev, a Soviet employee of the United Nations Secretariat, and the FBI arrested both. They were tried and convicted on several charges, including conspiracy to commit espionage. Each was sentenced to fifteen years imprisonment, but Gubitchev's sentence was suspended and he was expelled from the United States, and Coplin's conviction was overturned on technical legal grounds.

Using more intelligence gained from the deciphered messages, Lamphere discovered that the British mission to the Manhattan Project (the wartime nuclear weapons development program) had been penetrated by a Soviet agent in 1944. The agent was Klaus Fuchs, a German-born physicist and a Communist. The discovery of Fuchs led Lamphere and his associates in the Espionage Section to the Soviet intelligence network led by Julius Rosenberg that had been operating in the United States during the Second World War (see ROSENBERG CASE).

Lamphere resigned from the FBI in 1955 and joined the Veterans Administration, where he worked in investigations and rose to the rank of deputy administrator. In 1961 he left the government to join the John Hancock Mutual Life Insurance Company in Boston, Massachusetts, and became a senior vice-president of the company in 1976.

(Lamphere and Shachtman, *The FBI-KGB War*; *Who's Who in America*, 42nd ed.)

LANGER, WILLIAM LEONARD (March 16, 1896–December 26, 1977): historian, educator, intelligence analyst

A native of Boston, Langer received his A.B., his A.M., his Ph.D., and his LL.D degrees from Harvard University in 1915, 1920, 1923, and 1945, respectively. He joined the history faculty of Harvard in 1927, specialized in recent German history, and was Coolidge professor of history in 1941 when he was recruited by the Office of the Coordinator of Information, the predecessor agency to the Office of Strategic Services.

Early in 1942 Langer succeeded JAMES PHINNEY BAXTER III as chief of the OSS RESEARCH AND ANALYSIS BRANCH, and he continued in that capacity throughout the war. (Langer's brother, psychologist Walter Langer, also served in the OSS.) After the war the R&A Branch was transferred to the Department of State (see STATE DEPARTMENT INTELLIGENCE), where Langer served as a special assistant for intelligence to the secretary of state. His group became the embryo of State Department's BUREAU OF INTELLIGENCE AND RESEARCH. He returned to Harvard after 1946.

In 1950 Gen. WALTER BEDELL SMITH, the director of the CENTRAL INTELLIGENCE AGENCY, persuaded Langer to take a year's leave of absence from Harvard to return to government service in Washington in order to form a unit within CIA for the production of NATIONAL INTELLIGENCE ESTIMATES. Langer organized a two-tier structure: an Office of National Estimates, the support staff that assembled and summarized information in preparation of a draft estimate; and a Board of National Estimates, a small panel that negotiated the language of the final estimate among the interested intelligence agencies. In 1951, with the national estimates machinery in place and working, he returned once again to Harvard.

Langer served as a member of the PRESIDENT'S FOREIGN INTELLIGENCE ADVISORY BOARD between 1961 and 1969.

(Roosevelt, *War Report of the OSS*; Cline, *The CIA: Reality vs. Myth*; *Who Was Who in America*, v. 7; Prados, *The Soviet Estimate*.)

LANSDALE, EDWARD GEARY (February 6, 1908–February 23, 1987): Air Force officer, intelligence officer

A native of Detroit, Michigan, Lansdale attended the University of California at Los Angeles and worked for an advertising agency in San Francisco. During the Second World War he served in the Office of Strategic Services and in Army Intelligence. He was commissioned as a lieutenant in 1943 and advanced to the rank of major, becoming chief of the Intelligence Division of the staff of the G-2, Armed Forces/Western Pacific. In that capacity he served in the Philippines, where he remained until 1948 as deputy chief of G-2. He became an expert on the Philippines, which became independent of the United States in 1946.

In 1947 Lansdale transferred to the newly established U.S. Air Force and was commissioned as a captain. Late in 1948 he returned to the United States where he was an instructor at the Air Force Strategic Intelligence School in Denver, Colorado. The following year he was assigned to staff work in Washington.

Lansdale served with the Central Intelligence Agency as a member of the Far East Division of the Office of Policy Coordination, as the Agency's COVERT ACTION unit was then known. In September 1950 he was sent to the Philippines under cover of the Joint U.S. Military Advisory Group, a unit that was helping the government of the Philippines resist the efforts of the Communist Huk guerrillas to overthrow the government.

Lansdale was chief of the Manila station of CIA/OPC during 1951–54. He worked closely with the Philippine defense minister, Raymond Magsaysay, in developing counterinsurgency techniques to combat the Huks. These techniques ranged from psychological warfare—e.g., exploiting the susperstitions of Filipino peasants—to activities of the sort later carried out by the Peace Corps—e.g., establishment of community centers throughout the islands where modern methods of agriculture, health, road building, and communications were taught. In the latter area he was ably assisted by CIA officer GABRIEL L. KAPLAN.

Lansdale's anti-Huk program was successful in ending the guerrilla war against the Philippine government. He was the model for "Col. Edwin B. Hillandale" in William J. Lederer's and Eugene Burdick's *The Ugly American;* Hillandale was the Good American who charmed the natives of a fictitious Far Eastern country by learning their customs and language, thus helping to defeat the local Communist rebels, and this was indeed the spirit of Lansdale's work in the Philippines.

Magsaysay's prestige among his countrymen was greatly enhanced as a result of the victory over the Huks, and Lansdale threw the CIA's support behind him as a candidate for president of the country in the 1953 elections. Lansdale and Kaplan introduced such practical means of insuring an honest election

as ballot thumbprinting and voter identification. They also organized the Magsaysay for President Movement, which promoted the idea that Magsaysay was a national figure, rather than simply another partisan candidate, hoping thus to insure a broad, nonpartisan base of support for him. The result was a landslide victory for Magsaysay.

After the French defeat at Dien Bien Phu in 1954, Lansdale was sent to Vietnam to try to repeat in that country what he had accomplished in the Philippines, i.e., the selection and promotion of a strong national leader to lead the democratic forces in Vietnam against the Communist insurgents, and the defeat of the insurgents through the use of the psychological warfare and community development techniques that he and Kaplan had developed in the Philippines (see VIETNAM WAR). Lansdale operated under cover of the U.S. Saigon Military Mission, an entity created for his mission. He brought along a number of Filipino advisors to help in the project. They operated under the aegis of the FREEDOM COMPANY OF THE PHILIPPINES, a sort of Filipino precursor of the Peace Corps that was established and funded by the CIA to assist Lansdale.

The national leader Lansdale chose for the United States to support was Ngo Dinh Diem, the prime minister of the government of Emperor Bao Dai, whom the French had installed as national leader as they prepared to withdraw from Vietnam. Through the Freedom Company, Lansdale helped write the constitution of the Republic of Vietnam, train Diem's presidential guard, and organize the Vietnamese Veterans Legion, a group that was supposed to be a focus of political support for Diem. However, Lansdale soon discovered that Vietnam was not the Philippines and, more important, Diem was not Magsaysay. Specifically, Diem was not disposed to tolerate a loyal opposition, a policy that tended to force his political opponents into the arms of the Communist insurgents.

Although Lansdale was the staunchest of Diem's American supporters, and he thwarted early efforts by some American advisors to replace the Vietnamese president, he eventually realized that Diem's policies were disastrous. In 1956 Lansdale traveled to Washington in an effort to convince President Eisenhower and Secretary of State John Foster Dulles, that they should pressure Diem into making democratic reforms in Vietnam. When he failed to accomplish this he requested and received a transfer from Vietnam.

In November 1961, in the wake of the failure of the BAY OF PIGS INVASION, President Kennedy appointed Lansdale, who was no longer serving with the CIA, as chief of operations of Operation MON-

GOOSE, one of a series of unsuccessful COVERT ACTION operations aimed at toppling the regime of Fidel Castro in Cuba. Lansdale was to coordinate the CIA's MONGOOSE operations with those of the Departments of State and Defense. Although Lansdale envisioned MONGOOSE as an essentially political operation in which anti-Castro elements would be planted and nurtured in Cuba, it also included assassination as one of the possible means of removing Castro and other Cuban Communist leaders. MONGOOSE was abandoned following the CUBAN MISSILE CRISIS of October 1962.

Lansdale retired from the Air Force with the rank of major general in 1963. In 1965–68 he was in Vietnam again, serving as special assistant to the American ambassador. However he had little influence on policymaking during this period.

(*Who's Who in America*, 37th ed.; *Political Profiles: The Eisenhower Years*; Lansdale, *In the Midst of Wars*; Smith, *Portrait of a Cold Warrior*; Halberstam, *The Best and the Brightest*; Senate, U.S. *Alleged Assassination Plots Involving Foreign Leaders*; Rositzke, *The CIA's Secret Operations*; obituary, *New York Times*, February 24, 1987, p. A1.)

LAYTON, EDWIN THOMAS (April 7, 1903–April 14, 1984): naval officer, intelligence officer

A native of Nauvoo, Illinois, Layton graduated from the U.S. Naval Academy in 1924. During 1929–32 he was naval attaché at the American embassy in Tokyo, where he studied the Japanese language. He was assistant naval attaché in Peking, China, in 1932–33. In 1937–39 he was again assigned to Tokyo as assistant naval attaché.

At the time of the PEARL HARBOR ATTACK, Layton, then a lieutenant commander, was fleet intelligence officer for the Pacific Fleet, headquartered in Hawaii (he had held the post exactly one year to the day on December 7, 1941). He later testified before the joint congressional committee that investigated the circumstances of the attack that he had had access to all the intelligence available at Pearl Harbor at the time. This information did not include the crucial COMINT information and other intelligence held in Washington that should have alerted the government to the impending attack at Pearl.

Layton held the Pacific Fleet intelligence post until 1946. He advanced through grades to the rank of rear admiral. In 1948–50 he was director of the U.S. Naval Intelligence School in Washington, D.C. He served as chief intelligence officer of the Pacific Command and the Pacific Fleet during the Korean War.

Rear Adm. Edwin T. Layton. Source: U.S. Navy.

Layton was awarded the Distinguished Service Medal and other decorations. The Edwin T. Layton Chair of Naval Intelligence was established in his honor at the Naval War College in Newport, Rhode Island.

(*Who's Who in America*, v. 28; Wohlstetter, *Pearl Harbor: Warning and Decision*; Holmes, *Double-Edged Secrets*; obituary, *Foreign Intelligence Literary Scene*, August 1984; Layton, *"And I Was There."*)

LEDDY, RAYMOND GREGORY (December 18, 1912–March 5, 1976): FBI agent, foreign service officer, national security specialist

A native of New York City, Leddy graduated from Holy Cross College in 1933 and from Fordham University Law School in 1936. After practicing law in New York City, he joined the Federal Bureau of Investigation in 1938. In 1940 he was assigned to the American embassy in Madrid as legal attaché, and he served there until 1942. In 1942 he went to Havana and served as legal attaché at the American embassy there until 1944. In 1943 he transferred from the FBI to the Foreign Service.

Leddy returned to Madrid in 1944, serving once

again as attaché until 1945. After a two-year assignment in Washington he was assigned to Caracas, Venezuela, where he served as second secretary, then as first secretary of the American embassy.

From 1952 to 1955 Leddy was the State Department's officer in charge of Central America and Panama. His wartime service with the FBI in Spain and Cuba had brought him into close association with many of the former FBI agents who staffed the Western Hemisphere Division of the CIA CLANDESTINE SERVICE. He played a major role in planning the CIA's GUATEMALA COUP in 1954.

Leddy was assigned to the National War College in 1956 and later to the American embassies in Buenos Aires and Mexico City. From 1968 until his retirement from the State Department in 1970 he was career minister with the U.S. Army's Southern Command in the Panama Canal Zone. From 1970 to 1973 he was deputy assistant secretary of defense for inter-American affairs. Leddy lectured on "The Third World and Its Implications for United States Security Interests" at the Army War College in Carlisle, Pennsylvania from 1973 to 1975.

(obituary, *New York Times*, March 9, 1976, p. 36; *Who's Who in America*, v. 28; Corson, *Armies of Ignorance*.)

LEE'S LOST ORDER

After its victory at the second battle of Bull Run, Gen. Robert E. Lee's Army of Northern Virginia crossed the Potomac into Maryland with the object of capturing Harrisburg, Pennsylvania, thus severing the North's major east-west railroad link (see CIVIL WAR). To safeguard his line of supply through northern Virginia, Lee planned to reduce the Federal garrison at Harper's Ferry, West Virginia. To accomplish this he issued Special Order No. 191 on September 9, 1862, dividing his army into four parts; three of the elements were to converge on Harper's Ferry, while the fourth advanced to the vicinity of Hagerstown, Maryland.

The Confederate force was bivouacked near Frederick, Maryland, when Lee issued his order. Four days later a copy of the order, wrapped around three cigars, was found by a Union soldier in a nearby field. The order was delivered to Gen. George McClellan, the Union commander, who recognized its authenticity and importance. This accidental discovery was one of the most important intelligence coups of the war, giving McClellan an unprecedented military advantage. Although some of the Confederate's movements deviated significantly from Lee's order, historian and espionologist Edwin C. Fishel

has found that Union espionage uncovered these variations, thereby preserving the advantage gained by McClellan through the original discovery.

McClellan sent his cavalry to monitor the Confederate progress in executing Lee's order, while at the same time cautiously moving his army toward the divided Confederate force. Lee's own reconnaissance discovered the Union advance, and he hastily reunited his force at a defensive position behind Antietam Creek, near Sharpsburg, Maryland. The two forces clashed on September 17th, which was the bloodiest day of the war, ending in a narrow technical victory for McClellan in that his army held the field and the Confederates turned back to Virginia.

Although it was long believed that Lee had regrouped his army after being informed by a Southern sympathizer that McClellan had acquired a copy of his order, a recent study by Stephen W. Sears concludes that Lee only learned of the intelligence coup months later, when it became public.

(Sears, *Landscape Turned Red*.)

LEWIS, PRYCE (ca. 1828–?): salesman, detective, Union secret service agent of the Civil War

A native of England, Lewis had worked as a book salesman before he was recruited by ALLAN PINKERTON to work as a detective for PINKERTON'S NATIONAL DETECTIVE AGENCY circa 1853. Accounts of his Civil War exploits seem to rest entirely on his own memoirs and those of Pinkerton, both of which may have been rather embellished.

Lewis was in Jackson, Mississippi, investigating a murder case, when the Civil War began. Making his way back to Pinkerton's headquarters in Chicago, he took the opportunity to observe Confederate military preparations and activities in the South and prepared a detailed report on what he had seen. Pinkerton turned the document over to the War Department and to Gen. George B. McClellan, for whom he was now operating a secret service.

Lewis's talent for collecting military intelligence prompted Pinkerton to send him into western Virginia, an area of particular interest to McClellan. Lewis's upper-class English accent, his polished manner, and his quick wit, enabled him to pass himself off as "Lord Tracy," a young English peer on a combined cotton-buying and pleasure trip to America. Riding in an elegant coach driven by his "footman" (another Pinkerton agent), carrying a stock of champagne, port, and fine cigars, and wearing a costume that included a silk top hat and Pinkerton's gold watch and diamond ring, Lewis set out on his mission late in June 1861.

The first test of Lewis's cover appeared on the road to Charleston in the person of Confederate Col. George Patton (whose grandson and namesake was a distinguished general in the Second World War). Patton was deceived so completely that he treated Lewis to a guided tour of the Confederate fortifications at the junction of the Coal and Kanawha rivers, one of the chief entrances to Virginia.

Lewis spent nineteen days touring western Virginia, conducting a secret reconnaissance of the area while maintaining his Englishman cover. In one town he impressed the populace by delivering an impromptu lecture on his experiences in the Crimean War and the probability that Great Britain would soon throw in with the Confederacy. He returned to Cincinnati in July with a wealth of military intelligence for McClellan.

Pinkerton next sent Lewis to Baltimore to take part in the Agency's penetration operation against the secessionists in that city. About the same time he took part in the investigation of Confederate secret service agent ROSE O'NEAL GREENHOW.

In February 1862 Pinkerton sent Lewis and JOHN SCULLY to Richmond to make contact with Pinkerton agent TIMOTHY WEBSTER, who was operating in the Confederate capital as a penetration agent and had not been heard from for some time. Lewis and Scully were recognized as Pinkerton agents and arrested by the Confederate authorities. To save his own life Scully betrayed Webster. Seeing that the damage had been done, Lewis confirmed Scully's story. Webster was hanged. Lewis and Scully were incarcerated in Castle Thunder, the Confederate prison in Richmond, until September 1863, when they were released in an exchange of prisoners of war.

After his return to Washington Lewis was given a job as bailiff in the Old Capitol Prison.

(Horan and Swiggett, *The Pinkerton Story;* Horan, *The Pinkertons.*)

LIAISON AND UNILATERAL OPERATIONS

A distinction is made by the CIA CLANDESTINE SERVICE between two general types of operations conducted from a CIA station overseas. Liaison operations, as the term implies, are those carried out in cooperation with the intelligence or security services of the host government. Unilateral operations are those involving contact with persons or organizations within the host country, but not connected with, and sometimes in opposition to, the host government.

Recalling his tour as chief of the CIA's Saigon station during 1960–62, WILLIAM E. COLBY writes that liaison operations "involved primarily the exchange, coordination and analysis of information about the Communist apparatus and its activities in both the north and in the south, the interrogation of refugees from the north and of Vietcong cadre captured in the south, and the development of better techniques for the collection of intelligence on the Communists. . . ." The job of CIA officers engaged in unilateral operations, Colby recalls, was "to establish and maintain connections with the whole array of political factions working openly or subversively in South Vietnam, from the fanatic religious sects and bandit gangs on the extreme right to the liberal groups on the left. . . ."

Colby notes that liaison officers required only light cover to do their job, while unilateral officers needed deep cover (see COVER.)

(Colby and Forbath, *Honorable Men.*)

LIBERTY INCIDENT

On June 8, 1967 the U.S.S. *Liberty*, a freighter converted for use by the U.S. Navy and the National Security Agency as a SIGINT platform, was cruising in international waters some fourteen miles off the Sinai Peninsula in the Mediterranean Sea. The Six Day War between Israel on one side and Egypt, Jordan, and Syria on the other, was then in progress, and the *Liberty*'s mission apparently was to monitor Arab communications during the conflict. At 2:00 P.M. local time the ship was attacked by Israeli jet fighters with rockets, napalm, and machine-gun fire. Twenty-four minutes later the *Liberty* was attacked by three Israeli torpedo boats and was hit by machine-gun fire and a torpedo.

The attack continued for two hours, leaving thirty-four American officers and crewmen dead, 171 wounded, and the *Liberty* severely damaged. The government of Israel apologized for the incident, paid reparations to the U.S. government and the survivors, and explained that the attacking forces had mistaken the 10,680-ton, 455-foot *Liberty* for the 2,640-ton, 275-foot Egyptian transport *El Quseir*. Many students of the incident have voiced skepticism regarding the Israeli explanation and have theorized that the Israelis deliberately launched the attack in order to conceal the supposed fact that the Six Day War had been started by Israel, and not by Egypt, evidence of which might have been discovered through the *Liberty*'s SIGINT collection activities. However, the Israeli explanation was officially accepted by the U.S. government.

(Bamford, *The Puzzle Palace*; Ennes, *Assault on the "Liberty."*)

LIE DETECTION

Background: Because the essence of espionage is deception, techniques for the detection of deception are fundamental to counterintelligence and counterespionage. Lie detection is a skill based on the commonly observed fact that the act of lying is often accompanied by observable changes in the behavior or physiology of the subject. Shifting of the gaze, changes in inflection of the voice, hesitancy, and other behavior are commonly held to be outward signs of possible deception. Formalized psychological theories of deceptive behavior maintain that the act of deception is accompanied by one or more emotional responses such as guilt, anxiety, or fear, which in turn produce faint but detectable changes in certain physiological processes, such as in the rates of pulse or respiration. Since the turn of the century a body of practical experience by police interrogators has indicated that the use of sensitive instruments to observe and measure such physiological changes during interrogation can be useful in the detection of deception.

In 1895 the Italian criminologist Cesare Lombroso found that measurements of the pulse rate and blood pressure of suspects under interrogation helped to identify guilty individuals. Another Italian investigator, Vittorio Benussi, reported in 1914 that changes in the respiration rate seemed related to deception. In 1915 American criminal lawyer William Moulton Marston conducted a series of experiments at Harvard University that demonstrated a correlation between systolic blood pressure and deception. In 1921 John A. Larson, a Berkeley, California, police officer with psychological training, constructed a device to make a continuous recording of blood pressure, pulse rate, and respiration during interrogation, and this device was further refined by Larson's associate, Leonard Keeler, who developed a prototype of the instrument since known as the polygraph.

The Polygraph: A person taking a polygraph test is seated in a quiet room with the polygraph examiner. A corrugated rubber tube is stretched across his chest to measure the rate and depth of his breathing. A blood pressure cuff of the type used by physicians is placed round his upper arm and inflated so as to impede but not quite block circulation; the cuff picks up changes in pulse and blood pressure. A pair of small electrodes are attached to the subject's fingers or the palm of his hand; a small electric current flowing between them measures a variable known as the galvanic skin response (GSR), an electrical change in the skin that seems affected by the subject's emotional states.

Prior to the test the polygraph examiner will review with the subject the questions he intends to ask. Then the examiner proceeds to ask the questions in the same sequence, pausing ten or fifteen seconds between each to permit the physiological responses to be recorded on the moving chart of the polygraph.

The essence of the technique consists of comparing the polygraph changes accompanying the answers to different types of questions: control questions to measure the level of response to general, guilt-related issues ("Have you ever in your life stolen anything?"); irrelevant questions to measure the subject's general level of anxiety ("Are you wearing a white shirt?"); and relevant questions bearing directly on the matter under investigation ("Have you ever worked for a foreign intelligence service?").

Obviously there is a large element of subjective judgment involved in such a procedure. The emotional responses registered on the polygraph can be the result of many psychological factors or individual associations other than deception (curiously, the polygraph and similar devices are most reliable in confirming the truth of a subject's answer, since the absence of any response is considered to be a highly reliable indication of truthfulness).

The effectiveness of the polygraph technique has been obscured by controversy. Those who find the polygraph offensive, unethical, or dangerous to civil liberties sometimes seem to conclude that because the technique is repugnant to them it therefore must also be ineffective. Polygraph proponents, for their part, often make absurd and meaningless claims for the accuracy of the instrument. To further confound the situation, many completely unqualified and untrained people equip themselves with a polygraph instrument and pretend to be polygraph examiners.

Because a polygraph is an instrument intended to aid a human interrogator, statements regarding its exact numerical accuracy are as meaningless as estimates of the top speed of a bicycle or discussions about the ability of a grand piano to produce a concerto. Although experiments have been conducted in an attempt to measure "the effectiveness of the polygraph," these have in fact been application of the technique to artificially contrived situations comparable to parlor games. The applicability of such results to the real world of criminal investigation, counterespionage, or counterintelligence has not been demonstrated and is highly questionable. Attempts to quantify the effectiveness or accuracy of the polygraph tend to foster the myth that the instrument, and not the interrogator, is the "lie detector."

The polygraph and similar instruments have been found useful as investigative aids by police and counterintelligence and counterespionage agents. Beyond that, little that is meaningful can be said regarding the technique's effectiveness.

The Polygraph in Intelligence: In intelligence work, the polygraph is used in three different ways. First, it is used as an employee screening device just as in nonintelligence organizations. Job applicants are examined regarding the truthfulness of the personal background information they have supplied, and in regard to personal characteristics or history that might have an adverse effect upon their performance. A preemployment polygraph examination by an intelligence agency might include questions regarding alcohol and drug use, sexual preference and liaisons, personal finances, and other matters considered as possible openings for blackmail, bribery, or other means of coercion.

Secondly, employees of intelligence agencies may be required to take routine polygraph examinations from time to time in which they will be questioned about possible unauthorized disclosures to journalists or others. Here the chief function of the polygraph is deterrence. When President Nixon ordered John Ehrlichman to institute the mass polygraph testing of government employees to locate the source of certain press leaks in July 1969, he said, "I don't know anything about polygraphs, and I don't know how accurate they are, but I know they'll scare the hell out of people."

The third role of the polygraph is directly related to counterespionage and counterintelligence. Here the objective is to insure, for example, that an individual who is being recruited as an indigenous agent or a defector-in-place is not in fact a DOUBLE AGENT or a PENETRATION AGENT. In short, the aim is to make sure the individual is not working for the other side, and to confirm that whatever information he is furnishing is true to the best of his knowledge.

When the polygraph is used in this way, the examiner must consider the possibility that the subject has been schooled in "polygraph countermeasures," techniques for defeating a polygraph examination. If the subject is in fact a double or penetration agent, the polygraph examination becomes a subtle game of wits.

Drugs have been employed to mask the physiological responses measured by the polygraph, but for a drug to be effective for this purpose it must also be undetectable in a blood or urine test. Hypnotism has been tried as a polygraph countermeasure, but with uncertain results. Flexing the leg or back muscles or the anal sphincter while responding truthfully to control or irrelevant questions can heighten the po-

lygraph response and consequently disguise the emotional response to relevant questions. However, as a "counter-countermeasure" against such tricks some polygraph examiners use a special chair that will detect the subject's slightest bodily movement.

One of the most effective polygraph countermeasures is based on the discovery that intense mental effort will produce transient physiological changes similar to those resulting from deception. Intelligence agents have defeated the polygraph test through the strategem of, say, mentally dividing or multiplying a pair of large numbers immediately after giving a truthful answer to a control or irrelevant question. The effect is the same as that of muscle flexing, but without the telltale bodily movement.

The Psychological Stress Evaluator: The polygraph has remained basically unchanged since 1921. Its usefulness in intelligence applications is restricted by two limitations in the use of the instrument: the subject must consent and cooperate with the examiners; and, therefore, the subject must be aware the examination is being given. For many years intelligence services have sought for a new instrument that would transcend these limitations. In 1970 three veterans of U.S. Army Intelligence—Allan Bell, Jr., Charles McQuiston, and Wilson Ford—discovered that the emotional responses accompanying deception produced certain inaudible changes in the human voice, and that such changes could be detected with a special instrument they constructed called a Psychological Stress Evaluator (PSE).

The PSE is based on a phenomenon known as physiological microtremor, a normal condition of the human body. The contraction of a voluntary muscle is known to be accompanied by tremors of the muscle in the form of minute oscillations having a frequency of ten cycles per second. These tremors are too faint to be visible by the naked eye, but can be detected with special laboratory equipment.

Microtremor affects the voice through the oscillation of the muscles used to stretch the vocal cords. The effect is analogous to plucking a guitar string, then twisting the tuning key back and forth, resulting in an alternately rising and falling note. Again, the effect is too faint to be audible, but can be detected with the PSE.

The application of microtremor to lie detection is based on the discovery that the oscillation attenuates and even vanishes during states of anxiety of the kind associated with deception. The PSE is thus able to perform the same function as the polygraph, but without the necessity of physically attaching the instrument to the subject. The instrument can be used over a telephone or other voice communication channel, and even on a sound recording. However, like

John Wilkes Booth. Source: Library of Congress.

the polygraph, the PSE is strictly a device for observing physiological changes during interrogation. It is an investigative aid, not a "lie detector."

(Smith, "The Polygraph," *Scientific American*; Marks, *The Search for the "Manchurian Candidate"*.)

LINCOLN CONSPIRACY

Summary: At about 10:30 P.M., April 14, 1865 President Abraham Lincoln was shot and mortally wounded while attending a performance of *Our American Cousin* at Ford's Theater in Washington, D.C. The assassin was identified by scores of eyewitnesses as JOHN WILKES BOOTH, a prominent actor and member of a distinguished theatrical family. At about the same moment that Lincoln was shot, Secretary of State William Seward was assaulted in the bedroom of his Washington home by a knife-wielding attacker; Seward survived, although he was seriously wounded.

Booth escaped but was reportedly killed by Union troops on a farm near Port Conway, Virginia, on April 26th. Scores of people suspected of having conspired with Booth in the assassination were arrested. The eight who were charged and brought to trial during May 9th–June 30th were:

Mary Eugenia Surratt, a thirty-nine-year-old widow who ran a Washington boardinghouse frequented by Booth.

Samuel Alexander Mudd, a thirty-two-year-old physician of Bryantown, Maryland, who sheltered Booth on the night of the assassination and treated a leg injury he sustained during his escape from Ford's Theater.

David Herold, a twenty-one-year-old drugstore clerk who accompanied and assisted Booth during his escape.

Lewis Payne, a twenty-year-old Confederate veteran from Alabama who was identified as Secretary Seward's assailant.

George Andrew Atzerodt, a thirty-three-year-old German-born coachmaker and boatman of Port Tobacco, Maryland.

Edward Spangler, about forty years of age, a carpenter and stagehand at Ford's Theater.

Samuel Bland Arnold, a twenty-eight-year-old Confederate veteran from Baltimore.

Michael O'Laughlin, a twenty-seven-year-old Confederate veteran and Baltimore feed store clerk.

The official indictment also named Mrs. Surratt's son, John H. Surratt, as well as Jefferson Davis, JACOB THOMPSON, and several other Confederate leaders as co-conspirators, none of whom were in federal custody. The government attempted to prove not only that the eight defendants in the dock were guilty but that they were part of a larger conspiracy involving the Confederate secret service.

All eight defendants were found guilty. Mrs. Surratt, Atzerodt, Herold, and Payne were sentenced to hang; the sentences were carried out on July 7th. Mudd, Arnold, and O'Laughlin were sentenced to life imprisonment at hard labor. Spangler was sentenced to six years imprisonment. The four were incarcerated at the federal prison at Fort Jefferson in the Dry Tortugas. Mudd, Spangler, and Arnold were pardoned by President Andrew Johnson in 1868. O'Laughlin died of yellow fever while in prison.

John Surratt was apprehended in November 1866 in Alexandria, Egypt, where he had fled after having been identified while serving in the Vatican as a papal Zouave. He was returned to Washington and was brought to trial before a civil court, but the jury could not reach a verdict. He was again brought to trial the following year, but the charges were dropped on a legal technicality.

No legal action was ever taken against Jefferson Davis or the other Confederates alleged to have been involved in the conspiracy. The theory of high-level

Confederate involvement gradually fell into disrepute, while alternate theories have since been propounded, some implicating Secretary of War Edwin Stanton and others implicating Vice-President Johnson in the assassination. The whole truth of the Lincoln assassination has thus far eluded historical accounts because:

1   The military trial of the conspirators was orchestrated by Secretary Stanton and the other Radical Republicans in the government for the primary purpose of justifying the harsh postwar measures he favored (including the hanging of Jefferson Davis and other Confederate leaders), rather than establishing the truth. The government's case involved distortions, suppressed evidence, and outright perjury, and the basic rights of the accused to present an adequate defense were denied.
2   The assassination was again made to serve partisan political purposes in 1868, when the Radical Republicans, seeking grounds for the impeachment of President Andrew Johnson, further confused the record in an effort to implicate Johnson in the plot.
3   The official War Department records documenting the investigation of the conspiracy were withheld by the government until the 1930s, some even longer (perhaps to protect the privacy of surviving witnesses). While a few talented amateurs have made fascinating discoveries, an exhaustive review of these records remains to be published.

Theory of a Confederate conspiracy: Booth, Atzerodt, and John Surratt were definitely involved with the Confederate secret service, and there is evidence that the other defendants may also have had such connections. The Confederate leaders may have known of an earlier conspiracy by Booth and some of the others to kidnap Lincoln and exchange him for Confederate prisoners of war, but there is no evidence they were aware of Booth's decision to kill Lincoln after the kidnap plan was thwarted. Many students of the case believe that only Atzerodt, Payne, and Herold were aware of Booth's assassination plan.

One piece of evidence was offered at the trial suggesting a direct connection between Booth and Confederate Secretary of State Judah Benjamin—a Vigenere cipher tablet found in Booth's trunk identical to one found in Benjamin's office. In fact, the Vigenere was a familiar cipher device used throughout the Confederacy. (see CRYPTOLOGY).

Theory of Andrew Johnson's involvement: Although there was abundant rumor and hearsay evidence implicating Johnson, the single piece of tangible evidence offered to link him to the crime is one of Booth's calling cards. Generations of historians have repeated the story that Booth brought the card to Johnson's hotel on the afternoon before the assassination, when the assassin tried to call on the vice-president, and that it was left in Johnson's mailbox when the desk clerk determined that Johnson was not in. However, a careful reading of the statement of the desk clerk, the only person to give testimony on the incident, reveals that the calling card was found in the mailbox of Colonel Browning, Johnson's secretary, that the clerk did not recall receiving it or putting it there, and that he would not have recognized Booth had he seen him. In other words, there is no evidence linking Johnson to the assassination.

Theory of a Federal conspiracy: In the 1930s amateur historian Otto Eisenschiml was given access to the War Department's files on the assassination. Eisenschiml subsequently published two books implying that the assassination conspiracy had involved persons in the federal government, particularly Secretary of War Stanton. The theory has since been elaborated by other researchers. Some of the major points of the theory are listed here:

• According to his sister, Booth may have been a double agent, crossing Union lines with a pass signed by General Grant.

• The War Department learned in advance of Booth's conspiracy to kidnap Lincoln, but took no action against him and the other conspirators at the time.

• John Parker, the bodyguard assigned to Lincoln the night of the assassination, left his post during the evening and went to a nearby bar. Nevertheless, no action was ever taken against him for this dereliction.

• Lincoln's request that Stanton assign Maj. Thomas Eckert as his bodyguard that night was refused by the Secretary of War.

• Although scores of eyewitnesses identified Booth as the assassin immediately after the shooting, the War Department did not put out a bulletin identifying him until many hours later. Booth's escape route across the Anacostia River into Maryland was the only one not immediately sealed by the government, and reports that Booth had fled in that direction were ignored until the following day. The military telegraph lines running out of Washington were mysteriously out of order for several hours after the assassination, and the interruption seems never to have been investigated. All of this has been interpreted to mean that the government aided Booth's escape.

• Dr. Mudd, who may not have known Booth's identity and who claimed to be unaware of the crime, was prosecuted, while other Confederate sympathizers in Maryland and Virginia who aided Booth's escape were never charged by the government, despite having been identified in the War Department's investigation.

• The man, alleged to have been Booth, who was killed by Union troops near Port Conway, Virginia, may have been someone else. Disparities in accounts of the incident and the official identification of the body, leave room to believe that Booth may have escaped, perhaps with government cooperation.

Innocent explanations may be found for many of these circumstances when and if a thorough review of the official records is undertaken. However, the time is probably long since past when a full and accurate account of the Lincoln assassination conspiracy can be expected.

(Eisenschiml, *Why Was Lincoln Murdered?*, *In the Shadow of Lincoln's Death*; Roscoe, *The Web of Conspiracy*; Bryan, *The Great American Myth*.)

LINDSAY, FRANKLIN ANTHONY (March 12, 1916–): businessman, covert operations officer

A native of Kenton, Ohio, Lindsay graduated from Stanford University in 1938 and worked for the U.S. Steel Corporation in 1938–39. In 1940 he joined the U.S. Army and later was assigned to the Office of Strategic Services. He served for a year and a half behind enemy lines in southern Austria and with Tito's partisans in Yugoslavia. In 1945 he was chief of the U.S. Military Mission to Yugoslavia. He was discharged from the Army with the rank of lieutenant colonel and awarded the Legion of Merit.

Lindsay did postgraduate work at Harvard University in 1946 and was executive assistant to Bernard Baruch, the U.S. representative to the United Nations Atomic Energy Commission in 1946. During 1947–48 Lindsay served as a consultant to the U.S. House of Representatives Committee on Foreign Aid, which studied the feasibility of the proposed Marshall Plan. He was with the Economic Cooperation Administration in Paris in 1948–49 as an assistant to Averell Harriman. In 1949 he joined the Central Intelligence Agency.

Lindsay was assigned to the Office of Policy Coordination, then the CIA's department responsible for COVERT ACTION, and became chief of the OPC's Eastern European Division. Under his leadership the EE Division carried out a program of infiltrating Russian and East European emigrés into their native lands to work as agents. (In 1950 Lindsay helped recruit his brother-in-law, WILLIAM SLOAN COFFIN, JR., who participated in this operation.) He was also involved in the planning and execution of the

joint Anglo-American ALBANIA OPERATION of 1949–50 in which a force of some 500 Albanian emigrés were recruited, trained, equipped, and sent into Albania with the objective of overthrowing the Communist government there. (The operation failed when it was betrayed by Soviet penetration agent HAROLD ("KIM") PHILBY, who was then serving in Washington as the liaison officer from the British Secret Intelligence Service to the CIA.)

Lindsay left the CIA in 1953. Since 1961 he has been with the Itek Corporation in several senior posts.

(*Who's Who in America*, 42nd ed.; Powers, *The Man Who Kept the Secrets*; Coffin, *Once to Every Man*; Philby, *My Silent War*.)

LINEBARGER, PAUL MYRON ANTHONY (July 11, 1913–August 6, 1966): writer, Far East specialist, psychological warfare officer

A native of Milwaukee, Linebarger attended schools in Hawaii, Germany, and China. He received an A.B. from George Washington University in 1933 and a Ph.D. from Johns Hopkins University in 1936.

From 1930 to 1936 Linebarger was private secretary to his father, who had been legal advisor to the Chinese revolutionary leader, Sun Yat-sen, and who subsequently served as advisor to the Nationalist government of China in Nanking and Washington. The younger Linebarger taught and tutored at Harvard University in 1936–37 and at Duke University in 1937–45.

Linebarger participated in the formation of the Office of War Information in 1942 (see OFFICE OF STRATEGIC SERVICES), where he served as a Far Eastern Specialist on the Operation Planning and Intelligence Board. He was commissioned as a second lieutenant in the U.S. Army in 1942 and advanced to the rank of major during his service as a psychological warfare officer in China. He was awarded the Bronze Star.

In 1945 Linebarger joined the faculty of Johns Hopkins, where as a professor of Asian politics he lectured in the School of Advanced International Studies. He was visiting professor of international relations at the University of Pennsylvania in 1954–55, and at the Australian National University in 1957.

Linebarger was regarded as one of the foremost experts in psychological warfare and propaganda and he served as a consultant on these subjects to the Central Intelligence Agency and the Department of Defense. He taught courses for CIA employees and advised Col. EDWARD G. LANSDALE on counterinsurgency operations against the Huk guerrillas in the Philippines.

(Smith, *Portrait of a Cold Warrior; Who Was Who in America,* v. 4.)

LORD, WALTER (October 8, 1917–): author, historian, OSS officer

A native of Baltimore, Maryland, Lord graduated from Princeton University in 1939 and received an LL.B. from Yale University in 1946. From 1941 to 1942 he served with the Office of the Coordinator of Information and from 1942 to 1945 with the Office of Strategic Services. After the war he was a consultant to the OSS History Project of the War Department's Strategic Services Unit.

He is the author of many widely read narrative histories, e.g., *A Night to Remember, Day of Infamy, The Dawn's Early Light.*

(Roosevelt, *War Report of the O.S.S.; Who's Who in America,* 42nd ed.)

LOVELL, JAMES (October 31, 1737–July 14, 1814): schoolteacher, government official, cryptologist

A native of Boston, Massachusetts, Lovell graduated from Harvard in 1756. He taught school in Boston where he was master of the North Grammar School from 1757 until 1775, when the school was closed by the British and Lovell was arrested as an American spy. He was taken to Halifax, Nova Scotia, by the British when they evacuated Boston in 1775, but was exchanged for a British officer in November 1776.

Soon after his release Lovell was sent to the Continental Congress, where he represented Massachusetts from 1777 to 1782. He served on the Committee on Foreign Affairs (see COMMITTEE OF SECRET CORRESPONDENCE). He was sharply critical of Gen. GEORGE WASHINGTON and BENJAMIN FRANKLIN, and schemed unsuccessfully to be sent to France to replace Franklin. He was one of the Continental Congressmen who joined with Arthur Lee in accusing SILAS DEANE of profiteering in France.

Lovell was an accomplished linguist and mathematician, and had a good knowledge of CRYPTOLOGY. Washington put his talents as a cryptanalyst to good use on several occasions when encrypted British dispatches were intercepted. During the Yorktown campaign Lovell solved several messages between Lord Cornwallis and Sir Henry Clinton that disclosed Clinton's timetable for relieving Cornwallis by sea after the siege of Yorktown was in place. This

enabled Washington to alert French Admiral de Grasse, who thwarted the British plan.

In 1782 Lovell resigned from Congress and returned to Boston to become tax collector. He was state customs collector for Massachusetts in 1788, and in 1789 was appointed naval officer for Boston and Charlestown.

Kahn calls Lovell the Father of American Cryptanalysis.

(*Who Was Who in America,* historical volume; Boatner, *Encyclopedia of the American Revolution;* Kahn, *The Codebreakers.*)

LOVELL, STANLEY PLATT (August 29, 1890– January 4, 1976): chemist, technical support specialist

A native of Brockton, Massachusetts, Lovell graduated from Cornell University in 1912 and then worked for several chemical companies, first as a chemist and later as an executive. He pioneered the application of organic chemistry to shoemaking, orthopedic surgery, and clothing manufacture.

In 1942 Lovell went to Washington to take a wartime post with the government's Office of Scientific Research and Development. Soon afterward he was recruited by WILLIAM DONOVAN to serve in the Office of Strategic Services as director of research and development (i.e. Chief of the OSS RESEARCH AND DEVELOPMENT BRANCH).

According to Lovell, Donovan told him, "I need every subtle device and every underhanded trick to use against the Germans and the Japanese. . . . You will have to invent all of them, Lovell. . . ." Lovell drew upon his own background as a chemist to devise ways to use everything from itching powder to plastic explosives for sabotage, assassination, psychological warfare, and the other irregular forms of combat practiced by the OSS. When a project went beyond the limits of his own expertise, he drew upon a special group of distinguished scientists, appealing, as he put it, to "the 'Peck's Bad Boy' beneath the surface" with the exhortation, "Throw all your normal law-abiding concepts out the window. Here's a chance to raise merry hell. Come help me raise it."

Lovell and his research and development group printed perfect forgeries of foreign currency, passports, and other papers. They developed a silent and flashless .22 caliber pistol; a high explosive, called "Aunt Jemima," that looked exactly like wheat flour, could be mixed with milk or water, kneaded into dough and baked into bread, and then used to destroy a bridge; a barometric bomb that could be set to destroy an aircraft when it reached some preset

Thaddeus S.C. Lowe. Source: Library of Congress.

altitude; a high explosive that looked exactly like coal, to be used in blowing up locomotives; a capsule botulinus toxin so powerful that "the lethal dose . . . gelatine coating and all . . . was less than the size of the head of a common pin"; and other similar equipment and materials.

Lovell supervised the development of several substances intended either to kill or blind Adolf Hitler, or to imbalance his endocrine system so that he would develop pronounced and embarrassing female sex characteristics. However, no opportunity to expose Hitler to these substances was ever found.

Lovell and his group also worked on TRUTH DRUGS. They attempted to find a substance that could be administered without the subject's knowledge, induce the subject to become talkative and speak the truth as he knew it, would not be habit-forming or harmful, and would leave the subject without memory of his covert interrogation. After experimenting with many substances the researchers found that a drug called tetrahydrocannabinol acetate seemed to meet some of the requirements. However, the drug apparently was seldom used operationally by the OSS during World War II.

After the war Lovell returned to private industry and served as a director of several companies in Massachusetts. He was awarded the Presidential Medal for Merit in 1948 in recognition of his OSS service.

(Lovell, *Of Spies and Stratagems*; Cave Brown, *The Last Hero*; *Who Was Who in America*, v. 6.)

LOWE, THADDEUS SOBIESKI CONSTANTINE (August 20, 1832–January 16, 1913): inventor, balloonist

A native of Jefferson Mills, New Hampshire, Lowe was educated in local schools and pursued special studies in chemistry. In 1856 he became interested in ballooning, a field in which there had already been considerable development and experimentation in the United States. He made his first ascent from Ottowa, Canada, in 1858.

Lowe's dream was to cross the Atlantic Ocean by balloon, and as preparation he undertook a long-distance flight from Cincinnati, Ohio, on April 20, 1861. The winds carried his craft, the *Enterprise*, on a nine-hour flight that ended with a landing at Unionville, South Carolina. The Civil War was, at that moment, only eight days old, and he was immediately jailed as a Union spy. He talked his way out of this predicament and was given a safe-conduct pass back to Cincinnati.

In June Lowe went to Washington to propose the use of balloons by the U.S. Army in the war. He demonstrated the capabilities of the craft to President Lincoln and, in August 1861, was hired as a civilian employee of the Army of the Potomac. He became the "chief aeronaut" of the balloon corps, which consisted of seven balloons and attendant gas generators, telegraph sets, wagons, and other ground equipment; nine civilian balloonists; and ground crews drawn from the enlisted ranks.

Lowe and his balloon corps were involved in the entirety of the Peninsula campaign, but the usefulness of reconnaissance balloons was a matter of controversy among Union Army officers, and Lowe resigned in May 1863. The balloon corps was disbanded a month later (for a more detailed account of Lowe's Civil War activities see RECONNAISSANCE BALLOONS).

After the war Lowe sold a military signalling system he had invented to the Brazilian government. He became interested in refrigeration and is credited with the first commercial process for ice-making. He also developed improvements in the manufacture of illuminating gas and coke, and invented equipment for use in industrial metallurgy. He spent his last years in California where he established an astronomical observatory atop Mount Lowe, near Mount Wilson, in the Sierra Madre range.

(*DAB; Who Was Who in America,* v. 1; Glines, *Compact History of the United States Air Force.*)

LUNDAHL, ARTHUR CHARLES (April 1, 1915–): photogrammetrist, geologist, intelligence officer

A native of Chicago, Lundahl studied geology at the University of Chicago, earning a B.S. in 1939 and an M.S. in 1942. He served in the Office of Naval Intelligence from 1942 to 1946, and was discharged with the rank of captain.

Lundahl became a civilian employee and chief engineer of the U.S. Navy Photo Interpretation Center in Anacostia, Maryland, in 1946, and remained until 1953 when he was recruited to the Central Intelligence Agency to head a small photointerpretation office within the CIA Intelligence Directorate.

Lundahl played a key role in the development of the U-2 and reconnaissance satellite programs (see OVERHEAD RECONNAISSANCE). He supervised the development of the cameras, lenses, and films that were used in these programs.

In 1958 Lundahl became the director of the CIA's Photographic Intelligence Center, which was formed through a merger of his photointerpretation unit and a statistical analysis division from the Office of Current Intelligence. In 1961 this was made a "service of common concern" to the INTELLIGENCE COMMUNITY and was re-named the NATIONAL PHOTOGRAPHIC INTERPRETATION CENTER (NPIC).

Lundahl holds many awards and honors, including the U.S. Navy intelligence award for national defense.

(*Who's Who in America,* 37th ed.; Cline, *The CIA, Reality vs. Myth;* Prados, *The Soviet Estimate.*)

M

MACGREGOR, CLARK (July 12, 1922–): lawyer, congressman, businessman, intelligence officer

A native of Minneapolis, Minnesota, MacGregor served as a second lieutenant in the U.S. Army during 1942–45. He was assigned to the Office of Strategic Services and served in Detachment 101, the guerrilla unit that operated behind Japanese lines in Burma and China. He was awarded the Bronze Star and the Legion of Merit.

MacGregor graduated from Dartmouth College in 1946 and from the University of Minnesota Law School in 1948. He practiced law in Minneapolis until 1961, and he represented the third congressional district of Minnesota in the Eighty-seventh through Ninety-first Congresses (1961–1971). During 1971–72 he was counsel to President Nixon for congressional affairs, and he directed the Nixon reelection campaign in 1972.

Since 1972 he has been a vice-president of United Technologies Corporation.

(Smith, *OSS; Who's Who in America*, 42nd ed.)

MACOMBER, WILLIAM BUTTS, JR. (March 28, 1921–): diplomat, intelligence officer

A native of Rochester, New York, Macomber attended the Phillips Andover Academy and graduated from Yale University in 1943. He was commissioned as a lieutenant in the U.S. Marine Corps and assigned to the Office of Strategic Services. He served in the OSS SPECIAL OPERATIONS BRANCH and took part in Operation JEDBURGH as a member of a team parachuted behind enemy lines in France to coordinate the Allied landings with the French Resistance.

After the war Macomber returned to Yale and received an M.A. degree in 1947. Next he attended Harvard University and received an LL.B. in 1949, and then he earned an M.A. from the University of Chicago in 1951.

From 1951 to 1953 Macomber served with the Central Intelligence Agency. In 1953–54 he was a special assistant for intelligence at the Department of State. Subsequently he served as administrative assistant to Sen. John Sherman Cooper, special assistant to Undersecretary of State Herbert Hoover, Jr., and special assistant to Secretary of State John Foster Dulles. From 1957 to 1962 he was assistant secretary of state for congressional relations. From 1961 to 1964 he was ambassador extraordinary and plenipotentiary to Jordan. He has since served in several other senior posts in the State Department, and was ambassador to Turkey during 1973–78.

(*Who's Who in America*, 42nd ed.; Smith, *OSS.*)

MADDOX, WILLIAM PERCY (November 21, 1901–September 27, 1972): journalist, political scientist, foreign service officer, intelligence officer

A native of Princess Anne, Maryland, Maddox graduated from St. John's College at Annapolis, Maryland, in 1921. After working for a year as a reporter for the *Baltimore Evening Sun*, he was awarded a Rhodes scholarship and attended Oxford University where he received a B.A. in 1925. While at Oxford he worked as a correspondent for the *New York Herald Tribune*.

In 1925 Maddox joined the political science faculty of the University of Oregon. In 1928–29 he was an acting associate professor of government at the University of Virginia. In 1931 he earned a master's degree from Harvard University. He taught at Harvard and Radcliffe until 1936, earning a Ph.D. from Harvard in 1933. He served on the political science faculties of Princeton University and the University of Pennsylvania, and in 1941–42 worked for the Council on Foreign Relations and the Foreign Policy Association.

In 1942 Maddox was commissioned as a major in the U.S. Army and assigned to the Office of Strategic Services. He served as chief of the OSS SECRET INTELLIGENCE BRANCH in London from 1942 to 1944, during which time he developed a close working relationship between the SI Branch and the British Secret Intelligence Service. In 1944 he took charge of SI activities in the Mediterranean theater at Caserta, Italy. In 1945 he was discharged with the rank of colonel, having been awarded the Legion of Merit, the Order of the British Empire, the French Legion of Honor, and the Polish Polonia Restituta.

In 1946 Maddox joined the State Department. The following year he was made director of State's new Foreign Service Institute. From 1949 to 1965 he served at American embassies in Lisbon, Trinidad, South Africa, and Singapore, and was a staff advisor to the U.S. Arms Control and Disarmament Agency.

After his retirement from government service Maddox served in several capacities with Pratt Institute, Brooklyn, New York, including acting president in 1967–68.

(Smith, *OSS*; *Current Biography*, 1947; *Who Was Who in America*, v. 5.)

MAGIC

The compartmentation code assigned to Japanese diplomatic traffic that was intercepted by American intelligence as a result of the breaking of Purple, the Japanese diplomatic code, in 1940. The distribution list for MAGIC material was limited to the President, the secretary of state, secretary of war, and secretary of the Navy, and a small, select group of senior military officers and White House advisors.

See CRYPTOLOGY, PEARL HARBOR ATTACK.

MAGRUDER, JOHN (June 3, 1887–April 30, 1958): Army officer, intelligence officer

The son of a distinguished old Virginia military family, Magruder was born in Woodstock, Virginia. He received a B.S. from the Virginia Military Institute in 1909 and was commissioned as a second lieutenant in the U.S. Army in 1910. After service in the Philippines and in France during the First World War, he was assigned to the U.S. embassy in Peking, China, in 1920, serving as assistant military attaché until 1924 and as military attaché until 1930.

Magruder attended the Army's Command and General Staff School during 1926 and the Army War College in 1931. Between 1932 and 1935 he was the commandant of his alma mater, Virginia Military Institute; and from 1935 to 1938 he served as military attaché at the U.S. embassy in Bern, Switzerland. He became chief of the Intelligence Branch of the War Department General Staff in 1938 and served in that office until 1941.

In 1941 and 1942 Magruder was chief of the U.S. Military Mission to China. He joined the OFFICE OF STRATEGIC SERVICES in mid-1942 and became deputy director of intelligence services in January 1943. After the war, when the OSS was dissolved, he was made director of the Strategic Services Unit, the branch of the War Department that inherited the residual files and personnel of the OSS. Early in 1946 he resigned in protest against the dismemberment of the foreign intelligence apparatus and the dispersal of its "expensively trained, handpicked personnel."

(Smith, *OSS*; Cline, *The CIA, Reality vs. Myth*; *Who Was Who in America*, v. 3.)

MAHEU, ROBERT A.: law enforcement officer, businessman, private detective, intelligence agent

Maheu served as a special agent of the Federal Bureau of Investigation during 1940–47. In 1954 he established the firm of Robert Maheu & Associates in Washington, D.C. He was paid a monthly retainer of $500 by the Central Intelligence Agency and worked for the CIA's Office of Security on assignments that a staff employee of the Agency later described as covert operations in which the CIA "didn't want to have an Agency person or government person get caught." Maheu's case officer was James O'Connell, a former special agent of the FBI who was the operational support chief of the CIA's Office of Security.

During 1954–55 Maheu cooperated with the CIA in sabotaging a contract between the government of Saudi Arabia and Greek shipping magnate Aristotle Onassis, which would have given Onassis virtual control of all oil shipments from Arabia. Maheu learned the terms of the contract through an electronic listening device he planted in Onassis's hotel room, and publicized them in a Rome newspaper he had purchased with Agency funds. The publicity caused the Saudi government to terminate the contract.

Maheu also worked with Office of Security Director SHEFFIELD EDWARDS in a "black propaganda" (see COVERT ACTION) operation involving the production of a bogus pornographic film purportedly featuring Indonesian President Sukarno.

The CIA ended its monthly retainer to Maheu after his private investigative business became more lucrative (in the late 1950s he acquired billionaire Howard Hughes as a client), but continued to hire him when needed. In 1960, when Clandestine Service chief RICHARD M. BISSELL asked Edwards to find someone to assassinate Fidel Castro, Edwards contacted Maheu through his case officer, James O'Connell, and asked him to locate a candidate for the assignment. Maheu solicited underworld figure John Rosselli and proposed a plan in which Rosselli would arrange for Cuban emigrés to carry out the operation. Rosselli was to be paid $150,000 for his services. Maheu introduced Rosselli to O'Connell and subsequently served as the intermediary between the two.

Rosselli recruited another organized crime figure, Salvatore Giancana, to participate in the operation. Subsequently Maheu suspected that Giancana had discussed his involvement with his close friend, singer Phyllis McGuire, and that McGuire, in turn, might have disclosed the information to comedian Dan Rowan. Perhaps in order to investigate the possibility, Maheu hired a private investigator who installed a tap on the telephone in Rowan's Las Vegas hotel room (according to other accounts the line was tapped in order to satisfy Giancana, then busy with the operation in Miami, that McGuire and Rowan were not enjoying an amorous liaison in Las Vegas). In any case, Edwards had given his approval to the tap, and when it was discovered, the private detective was arrested, and Edwards was forced to intervene with the Justice Department to prevent prosecution of the detective.

The assassination operation was abandoned after the failure of an attempt to poison Castro. When it was subsequently reactivated by WILLIAM K. HARVEY in 1962, Maheu was not included as intermediary between the CIA and Rosselli.

During the 1960s Maheu became more closely associated with his client, Howard Hughes, and eventually became Hughes's trusted lieutenant. However, Hughes broke with Maheu in 1970, after which time Maheu pursued other business ventures.

(Senate, U.S., *Alleged Assassination Plots Involving Foreign Leaders;* Wise, *The American Police State;* Martin, *Wilderness of Mirrors;* Wyden, *The Bay of Pigs.*)

MARCUSE, HERBERT (July 19, 1898–July 31, 1979): philosopher, university professor, intelligence analyst

A native of Berlin, Germany, Marcuse studied at the University of Berlin and received a Ph.D. in philosophy, magna cum laude, from the University of Freiburg in 1922. He left Germany in 1933 when Hitler came to power, taught at Geneva, Switzerland, for a year, then came to the United States where he took a post as lecturer at Columbia University. He became an American citizen in 1940.

In 1941 Marcuse joined the Research and Analysis Branch of the Office of the Coordinator of Information, the predecessor to the Office of Strategic Services, and he remained in the OSS throughout the war. He was an intelligence analyst in the German Section of the OSS RESEARCH AND ANALYSIS BRANCH, serving under his colleague, Franz Neumann.

After the war, when the R & A Branch was transferred to the State Department (see STATE DEPARTMENT INTELLIGENCE), Marcuse went along. He became chief of the Central European Section, supervising the production of intelligence studies for the State Department and the Central Intelligence Agency.

In 1951 Marcuse left the State Department to become a research fellow with the Russian Institute at Columbia University, and the following year he lectured at the Russian Research Center at Harvard University. In 1954 he joined the faculty of Brandeis University as professor of politics and philosophy, and in 1965 he left Brandeis to become professor of philosophy at the University of California at San Diego.

Marcuse's political philosophy melded the thought of Marx and Freud into an indictment of American society. During the late 1960s he became an intellectual leader of the New Left.

(*Current Biography,* 1969; *Who's Who in America,* 37th ed.; Smith, *OSS;* obituary, *New York Times,* July 31, 1979, p. 1.)

MARINE CORPS INTELLIGENCE

The U.S. Marine Corps maintains a small intelligence service distinct from the components of NAVAL INTELLIGENCE (the Corps comes under the Department of the Navy). According to an unclassified government publication, Marine Corps intelligence

focuses on providing responsive intelligence support to Marine Corps tactical commanders, primarily in the amphibious warfare mission area, but also across the full spectrum of Marine Corps worldwide contingency missions. Marine Corps intelligence coordinates closely with and receives extensive support from other Service, theater, and national agencies but, particularly, Naval Intelligence elements, both at the Fleet and National levels.

Marine Corps intelligence consists of the Office of the Director of Intelligence, within which there are five branches: Counterintelligence, Intelligence Plans and Estimates, Intelligence Management, Signals Intelligence and Electronic Warfare, and National Intelligence Affairs.

(Central Intelligence Agency, *Intelligence, the Acme of Skill*; Richelson, *The U.S. Intelligence Community*.)

MARTIN, EDWIN McCAMMON (May 21, 1908–): economist, foreign service officer and diplomat, intelligence officer

A native of Dayton, Ohio, Martin graduated from Northwestern University in 1929 and did postgraduate work there in 1929–35. He worked as an economist for the Central Statistics Board in 1935–38 and for the Bureau of Labor Statistics in 1938–40. From 1940 to 1944 he served with the War Production Board.

Martin joined the Office of Strategic Services in 1944 and served as deputy director of the Far Eastern section of the OSS RESEARCH AND ANALYSIS BRANCH. From 1945 to 1947 he was chief of the Division of Japanese and Korean Economic Affairs of the State Department.

Martin continued to serve in a series of senior positions in the State Department, including assistant secretary of state for economic affairs (1960–62) and assistant secretary of state for inter-American affairs (1962–64). From 1964 to 1968 he was U.S. ambassador to Argentina. He later served in Paris, France, with the Organization for European Cooperation and Development.

(*Who's Who in America*, 37th ed.)

MARTIN, ROBERT (?–April 18, 1900): businessman, Confederate Army officer and secret agent

Martin served as a colonel in the Confederate cavalry under Gen. John Hunt Morgan (the unit known as Morgan's Raiders). He was chief of scouts for Gen. John C. Breckinridge at Shiloh in April 1862. In 1864 he went to Canada to serve under Capt. THOMAS H. HINES and take part in the NORTHWEST CON-

Robert M. Martin. Source: Author's collection.

SPIRACY, a COVERT ACTION operation aimed at fomenting rebellion in several Northern states through subversion and sabotage. He led a party of Confederate guerrillas that attempted to burn a large part of New York City on November 25, 1864. In December he participated in an abortive attempt to derail a train near Buffalo, New York, and free a number of Confederate prisoners of war aboard it. In January 1865 he took part in an abortive attempt to kidnap Vice President-elect Andrew Johnson.

After the war Martin settled in Evansville, Indiana, where he was in the tobacco warehouse business. In 1874 he moved to New York City and became manager of tobacco inspections for the David Dowes Company. In 1887 he moved to Louisville, Kentucky, continuing to work in the tobacco business. He died in Brooklyn, New York, where he had gone for special treatment for an old lung wound.

(Horan, *Confederate Agent*; Stern, *Secret Missions of the Civil War*.)

MARTIN, WILLIAM H. (May 27, 1931–): cryptologist, defector

A native of Columbus, Georgia, Martin was raised in the state of Washington. His exceptional intelligence was recognized in high school and Martin was encouraged to finish school in three years. After attending Central Washington University for a year, he enlisted in the U.S. Navy. Because of his mathematics background he was assigned to cryptographic duties with the Navy Security Group. He served in Alaska and later at the Navy's communication intercept station at Kamiseya, Japan.

After his discharge in 1954, Martin remained in Japan where he worked as a civilian employee of the Army Security Agency (see ARMY INTELLIGENCE). After a year he returned to the United States and enrolled in the University of Washington, where he studied mathematics. After graduation in 1957 he joined the National Security Agency and worked as a cryptologist in the Office of Research and Development.

In 1960 Martin and his NSA associate, BERNON F. MITCHELL, with whom he had served in the Navy, defected to the Soviet Union, where they disclosed to the Soviet government highly classified information regarding the NSA and American electronic intelligence operations.

Martin changed his name to Sokolovsky, became a Soviet citizen, and married a Russian woman. He reportedly is disillusioned with life in the Soviet Union.

(Bamford, *The Puzzle Palace*.)

MASHBIR, SIDNEY FORRESTER (ca. 1892–): Army officer, intelligence officer

Mashbir was a captain in the Arizona National Guard in 1916 when he was sent into northern Mexico by Gen. Frederick Funston to investigate reports of Japanese military activity in the area.

(In 1907 Japanese-American relations were troubled over the treatment of the Japanese in California, and there was a Japanese war scare in the United States. The following year the State Department received unconfirmed reports that Mexico had secretly leased Magdalena Bay, on the Pacific Coast of Baja California, to Japan for a naval base. In 1911 the Japanese fleet visited Mexico and Grand Admiral Yashiro spoke publicly about a Mexican-Japanese military alliance against the United States. All of these were still recent events in 1916 when Pancho Villa raided border towns in Arizona, and they contributed to the sense in Washington that there was a threat from south of the border at the same time that the country was being drawn into the war in Europe.)

In the guise of a civilian prospector, Mashbir traversed the desert of the Mexican state of Sonora and discovered evidence that a large force of Japanese troops had landed from a warship in the Gulf of California in what apparently was a training and reconnaissance mission. However, Mashbir's report of his discovery apparently resulted in no concern or policy actions in Washington.

Mashbir was commissioned a captain in the U.S. Army in June 1917 and placed in charge of counterespionage and counterintelligence in the Army's Eastern Department. In that capacity he was instrumental in detecting and arresting agents of German Intelligence in the Army. In June 1920 he was sent to Tokyo, Japan, as assistant military attaché.

While serving in Japan Mashbir learned the Japanese language and became acquainted with many leading Japanese businessmen and industrialists. At the request of the U.S. naval attaché in Tokyo, he drew up the so-called M-Plan, a comprehensive plan for a secret intelligence network in Japan to be activated in the event of a Japanese-American war. However, no action was taken by the Office of Naval Intelligence, and the network was not established.

In 1923 Mashbir resigned his commission and accepted an offer of employment with a Japanese engineering firm. He was made responsible for importing American agricultural and industrial machinery, such as tractors, hydroelectric equipment, etc. for the firm. This change of careers was, in fact, an unofficial intelligence mission he undertook with the knowledge and consent of his immediate superiors in Army Intelligence, and of which (then) Lt. ELLIS M. ZACHARIAS and others in ONI were also aware.

Mashbir's clandestine mission in Japan soon came to an abrupt end when the Japanese earthquake of September 1923 destroyed the firm employing him. He returned to the United States, but was prevented from regaining his Army commission by a recently promulgated bureaucratic injunction against reinstatement of officers who had resigned. His former superiors in Army Intelligence were unable to secure an exception for him, since disclosure of his Japanese assignment would have created diplomatic difficulties for the United States. However, he enrolled in the Army's Military Intelligence Reserve and attained the rank of lieutenant colonel.

In 1937, when the possibility of a war with Japan had become very tangible, Zacharias and ONI Director Capt. William D. Puleston, sent him to Japan to explore the possibility of establishing the secret intelligence network he had designed in his 1921 "M-Plan." Mashbir discovered that it was far too late to attempt such an undertaking, but returned to the United States with some valuable political intelligence. Army Intelligence, which was unaware of ONI's sponsorship of Mashbir's visit, became suspi-

Col. Sidney Mashbir, second from left, interpreting during Japanese surrender negotiations at the end of the Second World War. Source: Department of Defense.

cious of him and opened a file on him as a possible Axis sympathizer or agent.

After American entry into the Second World War, Mashbir applied for active duty in the Army and was assigned to the post of lieutenant colonel in charge of the Intelligence Branch of the Chief Signal Officer. Apparently this assignment was a means of keeping him under surveillance by Army Intelligence, which continued to regard him as a possible Japanese agent because of his 1937 visit to Japan. Eventually the matter was cleared up by Zacharias, who made ONI's file on Mashbir available to the Army.

In September 1942 Mashbir was detailed to the headquarters of Gen. Douglas MacArthur's Far East Command in Australia. There he served under MacArthur's chief of intelligence, Maj. Gen. CHARLES A. WILLOUGHBY, and established the ALLIED TRANSLATOR AND INTERPRETER SECTION, which he headed throughout the war.

(Mashbir, *I Was an American Spy*; Zacharias, *Secret Missions*; Ind, *A Short History of Espionage*; Finnegan, *Military Intelligence*.)

MASON, ELIHU H.: soldier, Union secret agent of the Civil War

Sergeant Mason of the Third Division, Army of the Ohio, volunteered to take part in a paramilitary operation behind Confederate lines aimed at severing the rail line between Atlanta and Chattanooga in April 1862 (see ANDREWS'S RAID). Dressed in civilian clothes, he and a party of twenty other Union troops led by JAMES J. ANDREWS hijacked a locomotive and attempted to destroy railroad tracks and bridges between the two cities. He was captured by Confederate troops and imprisoned. Though Andrews and six of the others were hanged, Mason and five others escaped, were recaptured, and exchanged for Confederate prisoners of war in March 1863. Mason and the other five were awarded the newly created Medal of Honor by Secretary of War Edwin Stanton. They were the first to receive that decoration.

(Bryan, *The Spy in America*; Boatner, *Civil War Dictionary*; O'Neill, *Wild Train*.)

Matthew Fontaine Maury. Source: U.S. Navy.

MAUGHAM, WILLIAM SOMERSET (January 25, 1874–December 15, 1965): author, British and American intelligence agent

Born in the British embassy in Paris, Maugham attended King's School at Canterbury and the University of Heidelberg. After completing medical training at St. Thomas's Hospital in London, he followed a literary career and achieved success in 1897 with his first novel, *Liza of Lambeth*. His fluency in French (which was his first language) and other languages led to his recruitment by the British Secret Intelligence Service in 1915. Using his well-established role as writer as his cover, he ran an agent network from Switzerland during the First World War. In 1917, at the request of family friend SIR WILLIAM WISEMAN, he undertook an intelligence mission to Russia for the U.S. State Department. Russia was, at the time, in the unsettled phase of Kerensky's provisional government, and the purpose of Maugham's mission was to assess the political situation and to conduct an anti-German propaganda campaign in Russia. Maugham, who was known to the State Department only by the pseudonyms "S" and "So-

merville," sailed from the West Coast late in July and traveled to Petrograd by way of Tokyo and the Trans-Siberian Railroad, arriving at his destination in September. With the help of EMANUEL VOSKA he made contact with Czech patriot Thomas Masaryk, who planned to help establish an anti-German propaganda operation. During September and October Maugham accurately assessed the political situation in Russia and saw that the Kerensky government would soon fall to the Bolsheviks. He left Russia to report to American and British officials in London in November. He was there on November 7th when his forecast was confirmed.

Maugham recounted some of his intelligence experiences in fictionalized form in a series of short stories published as *Ashenden: or The British Agent* in 1928.

(Fowler, *British-American Relations, 1917–1918*; Jeffreys-Jones, *American Espionage*.)

MAURY, JOHN MINOR (April 24, 1912–): lawyer, Marine Corps officer, intelligence officer

A native of Charlottesville, Virginia, Maury earned an LL.B. from the University of Virginia in 1936 and did postgraduate study at the Russian Institute of Cornell University in 1943.

Maury was the assistant commonwealth attorney for Albermarle County, Virginia, during 1936–40. He served with the U.S. Marine Corps Reserve during 1940–46, and he was chief of the U.S. Military Mission to Murmansk, USSR, in 1944–46. He joined the Central Intelligence Group in 1946 and continued with that organization after it became the Central Intelligence Agency in 1947. He served with the CIA in various posts and locations. During 1952–53 he was assigned to the National War College as lecturer in Soviet Affairs. He was chief of the Soviet Division of the CIA CLANDESTINE SERVICE during the early 1960s, and chief of station in Greece. He became the Agency's legislative counsel in 1968, and retired in the mid-1970s.

(*Who's Who in Government*, 1st ed.; Ranelagh, *The Agency*.)

MAURY, MATTHEW FONTAINE (January 14, 1806–February 1, 1873): Navy officer, oceanographer, Confederate secret agent

A native of Fredericksburg, Virginia, Maury grew up on a farm near Franklin, Tennessee. In 1825 he entered the Navy as a midshipman and rose to the rank of lieutenant in 1836, the same year in which he published a major work on navigation. An accident left him lame and unfit for sea duty, but in 1842 he was appointed superintendent of the Depot of Charts and Instruments. In 1844 he was made director of the Naval Observatory in Washington, D.C. Within a few years he had achieved an international reputation for his work in navigation, oceonography, and meteorology.

In 1861, after the secession of Virginia, Maury resigned from the U.S. Navy and accepted a commission as commander in the Confederate Navy. He spent the first year of the Civil War developing torpedoes and mines for use in coastal, river, and harbor defenses. In 1862 he was sent to Europe to serve under Confederate secret service chief JAMES DUNWODY BULLOCH. There he assisted Bulloch in the procurement of warships for the Confederacy and continued his researches in underwater ordnance, but his principal value was that of propaganda agent. Maury's international reputation as a scientist opened European doors, permitting him to plead the Confederate cause. He became involved with Napoleon III's plan to put Maximilian of Austria on the Mexican throne, a scheme that initially envisioned an alliance between France and the Confederacy and the restoration of California to Mexico. However, by the time Maximilian was prepared to go to Mexico, the fortunes of the Confederacy were waning and Napoleon lost interest in that part of the plan.

After the fall of Fort Fisher, North Carolina, in January 1865, Maury went to Havana and worked with Confederate agents there on a plan to breach the Union's blockade at Galveston, Texas, through the use of electrically detonated torpedoes and mines. However, word of General Lee's surrender reached him at Havana before this operation could be mounted.

After the war Maury went to Mexico where he was appointed imperial commissioner of immigration by Maximilian. He tried to establish a colony of Confederate exiles in that country, but little came of this enterprise, and Maury returned to England in 1866. After President Andrew Johnson declared an unqualified amnesty to all Confederates in 1868, Maury returned to the United States to accept a post as professor of meterology at the Virginia Military Institute.

(Bulloch, *The Secret Service of the Confederate States in Europe*; WAMB; Stern, *The Confederate Navy*.)

MCCLELLAND, HAROLD MARK (November 4, 1893–November 1965): Army officer, intelligence officer

A native of Tiffin, Iowa, McClelland graduated from Kansas State College in 1916. He was commissioned a second lieutenant in the U.S. Army in 1917 and graduated from the Army Flying School the following year.

McClelland advanced through grades to the rank of brigadier general in 1942. From 1942 to 1946 he was the air communications officer of the Army Air Forces. After the war he served as commanding general of the Airways and Air Communications Service, and deputy commander of services of the Military Air Transport Service.

After his retirement from the Air Force McClelland served with the Central Intelligence Agency. During the 1950s he managed the Agency's communication facilities between CIA headquarters and the overseas stations.

(*Who Was Who in America*, v. 4; Cline, *CIA, Reality vs. Myth*.)

MCCONE, JOHN ALEX (January 4, 1902–): businessman, government official, intelligence officer

A native of San Francisco, McCone graduated from the University of California at Berkeley in 1922. He joined the Llewellyn Iron Works in Los Angeles as a riveter and boilermaker and, by 1933, had worked his way up to the position of executive vice-president and director of the company, which by then had become the Consolidated Steel Corporation.

In 1937 McCone formed the Bechtel-McCone Company, which designed and built petroleum refineries and power plants. During the Second World War he was involved in shipbuilding and aircraft production. After the war he branched out into shipping in the Pacific and Far East.

McCone served on a presidential commission on air defense in 1947, and the following year he served as a special assistant to Secretary of Defense James V. Forrestal. During 1950–51, when he held the position of under secretary of the Air Force, he urged a larger Air Force share of the Defense budget and the inauguration of a major missile development program. From 1958 to 1960 he was chairman of the Atomic Energy Commission.

In 1961 President Kennedy selected McCone to succeed ALLEN W. DULLES, who had been forced to resign as director of the Central Intelligence Agency in the wake of the failure of the BAY OF PIGS INVASION. Although he lacked any training or experience in the field, McCone demonstrated considerable native ability in intelligence work. Content to leave clandestine operations in the hands of RICHARD M. HELMS, then chief of the CIA CLANDESTINE SERVICE, he concentrated on carrying out

John A. McCone—oil portrait by William F. Draper.
Source: Central Intelligence Agency.

his function as the government's principal foreign intelligence officer and coordinator of all American intelligence activities. He gave special emphasis to technical intelligence collection, especially the reconnaissance satellite programs that were just then becoming a major intelligence source (see OVERHEAD RECONNAISSANCE). He took a personal interest in intelligence analysis, and paid close attention to the substance as well as the management of that area.

McCone disagreed with a national estimate issued by the Board of National Estimate on September 18, 1962, which forecast that the Soviet Union would not install offensive missiles in Cuba. His conclusion was based on an assessment that the purpose of Soviet surface-to-air missiles recently installed in western Cuba was to protect planned offensive missile sites. About this time he was on the French Riviera on a honeymoon with his second wife, but he sent several cables—later dubbed the "honeymoon cables"—to CIA headquarters urging that the possibility of offensive missiles be considered. In the event, he was proved correct by subsequent aerial reconnaissance

in mid-October and other intelligence information. McCone returned to Washington on October 17th to supervise CIA activities during the CUBAN MISSILE CRISIS, and to participate in the National Security Council deliberations on American moves to end the crisis.

McCone, regarded by many intelligence professionals as one of the most effective directors of central intelligence, is credited with rehabilitating the CIA's prestige after the Bay of Pigs debacle, leading the Agency's outstanding performance during the Cuban Missile Crisis, and enlarging the role and influence of the Agency on U.S. strategic policy planning. However, President Johnson did not accord him the stature and access he had enjoyed under President Kennedy, and this prompted him to resign in 1965.

McCone returned to his private business interests, but served as a consultant to the CIA. He became a director of International Telephone and Telegraph Company, and in 1970 was involved in ITT's proposal to provide funds to the CIA for a COVERT ACTION operation aimed at preventing Marxist Salvatore Allende from coming to power in Chile.

(*Who's Who in America*, 37th ed.; *Current Biography*, 1959; Cline, *The CIA: Reality vs. Myth*; Prados, *The Soviet Estimate*; Karalekas, *History of the Central Intelligence Agency*; Martin, *Wilderness of Mirrors*; Sampson, *The Sovereign State of ITT*.)

MCCORD, JAMES WALTER, JR. (July 26, 1924?–): security officer

The details of McCord's life prior to his June 1972 arrest in the offices of the Democratic National Committee in the Watergate building are inconsistently documented and obscure. The information offered here was compiled from the sources listed at the end of this article.

A native of Waurika, Oklahoma, McCord joined the Federal Bureau of Investigation in 1942 and served in "radio intelligence." Late in 1943 he left the Bureau and served two years in the U.S. Army Air Corps. After two years in the service he enrolled at the University of Texas and subsequently graduated. In 1948 he returned to the FBI as a special agent in San Francisco and San Diego. In 1951 he left the Bureau again and joined the Central Intelligence Agency.

McCord served in the CIA's Office of Security and, by some accounts, took part in the 1961 BAY OF PIGS INVASION, served in Europe in 1962–64 as the Agency's senior security officer there, and ultimately became chief of the CIA's physical security division.

McCord retired from the CIA in 1970 (October 9, 1918, the date of birth he gave the police at the time of his arrest, may therefore be the correct one; the date listed above is from his bail records), and established his own security firm the following year in Rockville, Maryland. He was active in church and community affairs and taught a course in industrial security at Montgomery County Community College.

Early in 1972 McCord went to work for the Republican National Committee and the Committee to Re-Elect the President. As an expert in audio surveillance, he became involved in the use of covert electronic-listening devices in the Watergate offices of the Democratic Party. He was arrested with six other men during the July 17th break-in at those offices.

McCord and the others were indicted and convicted of burglary and other charges related to the break-in. Just prior to his sentencing in March 1973 he disclosed to the authorities that White House counsel John Dean, 3rd, presidential aides H.R. Haldeman and Charles Colson, and former Attorney General John Mitchell had been involved in the break-in conspiracy. McCord's revelations led to the subsequent investigations of the Nixon administration and the crimes and improprieties collectively known as the Watergate affair.

McCord was sentenced to one-to-five-years imprisonment for his Watergate role. His sentence was subsequently shortened and he was released in the late summer of 1975.

(Lukas, *Nightmare*; *New York Times*, *The Watergate Hearings*; *Political Profiles*.)

MCCORMACK, ALFRED (January 13, 1901– July 11, 1956): lawyer, Army intelligence officer

A native of Brooklyn, New York, McCormack graduated from Princeton University in 1921 and earned an LL.B. from Columbia Law School in 1925. In 1925–26 he was law clerk to U.S. Supreme Court Justice Harlan F. Stone. In 1926 he joined a New York City law firm and later became a partner.

In 1942 he was commissioned a colonel in the U.S. Army and assigned to the Military Intelligence Division of the War Department (see ARMY INTELLIGENCE), where he served initially as deputy chief of the SPECIAL BRANCH. The Special Branch was, in fact, created in response to a study that Secretary of War Henry Stimson requested McCormack to make of the military's communication intelligence operations immediately after the PEARL HARBOR ATTACK. McCormack is credited with building up a highly efficient evaluation and analysis group for handling communications intelligence. In 1944 he

was made director of intelligence of the Military Intelligence Service.

In 1945, when the OSS RESEARCH AND ANALYSIS BRANCH of the Office of Strategic Services was transferred to the State Department after the termination of OSS (see STATE DEPARTMENT INTELLIGENCE), McCormack was assigned to State to manage the group. However, the resistance of the veteran career foreign service officers to the inclusion of the newcomers within their ranks, and the opposition of Army Intelligence and the Office of Naval Intelligence to the new State Department unit, impelled McCormack to resign and return to the private practice of law in 1946. He was awarded the Distinguished Service Medal and the Order of the British Empire for his wartime service.

(*Who Was Who in America*, v. 3; Bamford, *The Puzzle Palace*; Cline, *The CIA, Reality vs. Myth*; Braden, "The Birth of the CIA.")

MCCOY, FRANK ROSS (October 29, 1874– June 4, 1954): Army officer, diplomat, intelligence officer

A native of Lewiston, Pennsylvania, McCoy graduated from the U.S. Military Academy in 1897 and saw action in Cuba in the Spanish-American War and in the Philippines during the Philippine Insurrection. While in the Philippines in 1905, he commanded the expedition that tracked down and killed the Moro terrorist Datu Ali.

McCoy served as aide-de-camp to Maj. Gen. Leonard Wood in Cuba and the Philippines. Later he was assistant to President Theodore Roosevelt, and to Secretary of War William Howard Taft during the second intervention in Cuba. While attached to the General Staff in 1911–1914, he undertook a secret mission to Colombia concerning possible routes for a canal across the Central American isthmus. In 1915–16 he commanded a cavalry patrol against Mexican bandits, and in 1917 he served as military attaché in Mexico. He served in France in the First World War, commanding an infantry brigade.

McCoy was chief of staff of the American Mission to Armenia in 1919, and of a special mission to the Philippines in 1921. In 1921–25 he served as assistant to the American governor-general of the Philippines, and he commanded American relief efforts following the Japanese earthquake of September 1923. In 1928 he was appointed by President Coolidge to supervise the presidential election in Nicaragua. That same year he was a delegate to the Pan-American conference. In 1929 he led a commission investigating a dispute between Bolivia and Paraguay. In 1932 he was the

American member of the League of Nations commission investigating Japanese actions in Manchuria. He retired from the army in 1938 with the rank of major general.

In 1941 McCoy was appointed to the special commission led by U.S. Supreme Court Justice Owen J. Roberts to investigate the PEARL HARBOR ATTACK. Later he headed a military commission appointed to try Nazi spies and saboteurs. He served on the Board of Analysts of the OSS RESEARCH AND ANALYSIS BRANCH. Gen. WILLIAM J. DONOVAN, who had served under McCoy in France in the First World War and had subsequently become his close friend, recommended to President Franklin Roosevelt that, in the event of his death or incapacity, McCoy should succeed him as chief of the Office of Strategic Services.

During 1945–49 McCoy was a member and first chairman of the Far Eastern Commission, appointed by President Truman to oversee the American occupation of Japan.

From 1939 to 1946 McCoy was president of the Foreign Policy Association.

(*WAMB; Who Was Who in America*, v. 3; Roosevelt, *War Report of the OSS*; Cave Brown, *The Last Hero*.)

MCENTEE, JOHN (ca. 1835–December 20, 1903): businessman, government official, Army officer, intelligence officer

McEntee was a resident of Kingston, New York, before the Civil War. In 1861 he enlisted in the Twentieth New York Regiment, a volunteer unit raised in the Kingston area, rose to the rank of sergeant, and was later commissioned as a second lieutenant. He was promoted to captain in October 1863.

From 1863 until the end of the Civil War, McEntee served under GEORGE H. SHARPE and his deputy, John C. Babcock, as the third-ranking member of the BUREAU OF MILITARY INFORMATION, the intelligence service Sharpe organized for the Army of the Potomac.

According to historian and espionologist Edwin C. Fishel, McEntee was usually given the assignment whenever intelligence projects away from Army headquarters were called for, e.g., commanding a detachment of the Bureau's enlisted men serving as scouts (or, when they could penetrate enemy lines, as spies). One such mission during the early stages of the Gettysburg campaign was critically important to discovering enemy movements. McEntee also conducted liaison with the Army's cavalry corps and with Union forces in the Shenandoah Valley.

McEntee took part in the Kilpatrick-Dahlgren raid,

an unsuccessful attempt to release Union prisoners of war held in Richmond, Virginia, during February 28–March 4, 1864. He was promoted to lieutenant colonel in 1864 and was brevetted colonel in February 1865. Immediately after the war he served in the Provost Marshal's Department in Richmond, and in June 1865 was appointed provost judge of Richmond. He served in that post until 1866.

McEntee subsequently worked in the New York Customs House. For many years he managed a large foundry and boiler factory in Kingston.

(obituary, *New York Times*, December 21, 1903; Stuart, "Colonel Ulric Dahlgren and Richmond's Union Underground, April 1864.")

MCKAY, DONALD COPE (February 14, 1902–): historian, intelligence officer

A native of Salt Lake City, Utah, McKay graduated from Stanford University in 1926 and received an A.M. and a Ph.D. from Harvard University in 1927 and 1932, respectively. He taught history at Harvard and was associate professor when he left in 1941 to join the Office of the Coordinator of Information, the predecessor of Office of Strategic Services. He was assigned to the OSS RESEARCH AND ANALYSIS BRANCH and served on the Board of Analysts. After the war he returned to the history faculty at Harvard.

(Cline, *The CIA: Reality vs. Myth; Who's Who in America*, v. 28.)

MCMAHON, JOHN N. (July 3, 1929–): intelligence officer

A native of East Norwalk, Connecticut, McMahon graduated from Holy Cross College in 1951. He joined the Central Intelligence Agency in September of that year and served overseas. In 1957 he was on active duty with the U.S. Army and underwent basic training. Thereafter he returned to the CIA and in 1959 was assigned to the U-2 program (see OVERHEAD RECONNAISSANCE, U-2 RECONNAISSANCE AIRCRAFT).

In 1965 McMahon was appointed deputy director for the Agency's reconnaissance research and development program. In 1971 he was made director of the Office of Electronic Intelligence, and later became director of the Office of Technical Service. In August 1974 he became associate deputy director for administration. In May 1976 he was made associate deputy to the director of central intelligence for the intelligence community.

In January 1978 DCI STANSFIELD TURNER made McMahon deputy director for operations (i.e., head of the CIA CLANDESTINE SERVICE). Although most of McMahon's experience was in activities other than covert operations, Turner appointed him because, as he later explained, he wished to place the Clandestine Service under an officer with broad CIA experience, instead of a career covert operator.

McMahon held the DDO post until April 1981, when he became director for national foreign assessment (a short-lived term then in use for the deputy director of intelligence; see CIA INTELLIGENCE DIRECTORATE). In January 1982 he became executive director of the Agency, and the following June was promoted to deputy director of central intelligence, the second highest post in the CIA. He resigned from that post and retired in March 1986 for personal reasons. He was succeeded by ROBERT M. GATES.

McMahon has been described in the press as "a generalist with intimate knowledge of the agency's inner workings," who "is popular with the oversight committees." He holds a CIA Certificate of Distinction, the Intelligence Medal of Merit, two Distinguished Intelligence Medals, and the Intelligence Distinguished Service Medal.

(Central Intelligence Agency, *Fact Book on Intelligence; New York Times,* January 20, 1985, Section 6, p. 26; March 5, 1986, p. B8.)

John N. McMahon. Source: Central Intelligence Agency.

MEANS, GASTON BULLOCK (July 11, 1879–December 12, 1938): detective, law enforcement officer, swindler, German intelligence agent

A native of Blackwelder's Spring, North Carolina, Means attended the University of North Carolina from 1898 to 1901. He worked as a textile salesman from 1904 to 1914, when he became an intelligence agent for Capt. Karl Boy-Ed, the German naval attaché in Washington. Means reported to Boy-Ed on Allied munitions purchasing and shipping. At the same time, Means was hired as a detective by the William J. Burns International Detective Agency.

Means severed his relations with Boy-Ed after American entry into the First World War, but continued with the Burns Agency. In 1917 a North Carolina jury acquitted him of the charge of embezzling a large amount of money from and murdering a rich widow.

In 1921, when William J. Burns of the Burns Detective Agency was appointed chief of the Justice Department's Bureau of Investigation (as the FEDERAL BUREAU OF INVESTIGATION was then called) he brought along Means to serve as a special agent. Means was suspended in 1922 for forging a will, but Burns managed to keep him in the Bureau by listing

him as a paid informer. In 1924 the Bureau severed all ties with Means on the orders of the new director, J. EDGAR HOOVER.

In 1925 Means was convicted of extortion and of withdrawing liquor from government warehouses. He served two years in a federal penitentiary. In 1932 he extorted $104,000 from a wealthy Washington, D.C., woman, who believed she was paying a ransom for the recovery of the kidnapped son of Charles Lindbergh. Means was convicted of grand larceny and sentenced to fifteen years. He died in prison.

(Who Was Who in America, historical volume; Whitehead, *The FBI Story.*)

MEEKER, LEONARD CARPENTER (April 4, 1916–): lawyer, diplomat, intelligence analyst

A native of Montclair, New Jersey, Meeker graduated from the Deerfield Academy in 1933 and from Amherst College in 1937. He earned an LL.B. from Harvard University in 1940 and joined the U.S. Treasury Department the same year. In 1941 he moved to the Justice Department.

During the Second World War Meeker served in the OSS RESEARCH AND ANALYSIS BRANCH.

Working with ARTHUR SCHLESINGER, JR. and RAY S. CLINE, he edited a weekly current intelligence bulletin produced by the R&A Branch.

In 1946 Meeker joined the State Department's Office of Legal Advisor. He continued in that Office, becoming the Department's legal advisor in 1965. In 1969 he was appointed U.S. ambassador to Romania.

(*Who's Who in America*, 42nd. ed.; Smith, *OSS*.)

MERSEREAU SPY RING

A Patriot secret intelligence network of the AMERICAN REVOLUTION that operated in Staten Island and New York.

The network began operations circa mid-1776 when Gen. GEORGE WASHINGTON recruited Joshua Mersereau, a Patriot refugee from Staten Island, to serve as a secret intelligence agent. Mersereau sent his son, John LaGrange Mersereau, back to Staten Island to collect information regarding the British army there and in Manhattan. The younger Mersereau operated for eighteen months, after which time he was forced to stop and escape because he had fallen under British suspicion. He was succeeded by his brother Paul, who continued to report to Washington from Staten Island. Joshua Mersereau's brother John also served as a secret agent in the network, as did several other persons who were not members of the Mersereau family. The network eventually became part of the extensive SECRET INTELLIGENCE apparatus run by Col. ELIAS DAYTON.

In addition to collecting positive intelligence, the Mersereau ring also fed disinformation to British intelligence in support of some of Washington's deception operations.

(Bakeless, *Turncoats, Traitors and Heroes*.)

MEXICAN SPY COMPANY

In March 1847, in the last and decisive campaign of the MEXICAN WAR, a force of some ten thousand American troops led by Gen. Winfield Scott landed at Vera Cruz and advanced on Mexico City, capturing the capital in September. To provide intelligence, scouting, and other activities in support of the American advance, Col. Ethan Allen Hitchcock of Scott's staff organized a company of Mexicans willing to serve the U.S. Army. The unit initially consisted of five scouts, but it grew rapidly to a force of one hundred (some accounts put the figure at two hundred) and became known as the "Mexican Spy Company."

The company was nominally led by one Captain Spooner, an American officer from Virginia, but the actual leader was Manuel Dominguez, a bandit from the town of Puebla with a grudge against the Mexican government (by one account Dominguez had been an honest weaver until he was robbed by a Mexican officer). Most of the members of the Mexican Spy Company had previously belonged to Dominguez's bandit gang.

The Mexican Spy Company provided Scott with vital BASIC INTELLIGENCE regarding the terrain, roads, strongholds, etc., along the route of the American advance. It helped counter the threat from Mexican guerrillas harassing the American advance. While Mexico City was under siege the Company sent espionage agents through Mexican lines and into the capital to gather essential information about the city's defenses.

Dominguez remained faithful to the Americans despite repeated inducements by the Mexican commander to "turn" him and make him a double agent. After the war sixty-two members of the Mexican Spy Company and thirty of their dependents were evacuated to New Orleans.

(Bidwell, "History of the Military Intelligence Division, Department of the Army General Staff;" Bryan, *The Spy in America*; Bauer, *The Mexican War*; Campbell, "Ethan Allen Hitchcock.")

MEXICAN WAR

Background: United States annexation of Texas in 1844 caused Mexico to break off diplomatic relations with Washington. In July 1845 President James K. Polk sent an Army detachment under Gen. Zachary Taylor to the southern border of Texas to protect against a possible Mexican assault. In the meantime Polk sent an American emissary to Mexico in a bid to renew diplomatic relations and to negotiate Mexican acquiescence in the matter of Texas, and the sale of New Mexico (including what is now Arizona) and California to the United States. The Mexican president, while refusing to consider the American overtures, was nonetheless overthrown by a militant faction of his countrymen on the grounds that he had had treasonable dealings with the United States.

In response to the Mexican refusal Polk ordered General Taylor to advance to the Rio Grande, thus placing the Army in disputed territory long claimed by both Texas and Mexico. On April 25, 1846 American and Mexican forces clashed in a skirmish north of the Rio Grande and American casualties resulted. The incident was adopted as a casus belli by Polk, who took the position that Mexican forces had invaded U.S. territory (i.e., the disputed zone) and "shed American blood upon the American soil." Congress declared war on Mexico on May 13th.

The War: General Taylor drove a numerically superior Mexican force from the city of Matamoros and advanced southwestward, capturing Monterrey in the state of Nuevo Leon on September 25, 1846. Meanwhile American naval units blockaded Mexican ports on both the Pacific coast and the Gulf of Mexico. An expeditionary force sent from Fort Leavenworth under the command of Col. Stephen W. Kearney occupied Santa Fe on August 18th. Kearney then led part of this force on to California, where American and Mexican forces had been fighting around Los Angeles and San Diego. By January 1847 most active Mexican resistance in California was brought to an end.

In February 1847 a Mexican relief expedition under Gen. Antonio López de Santa Ana attacked the American forces occupying northern Mexico. Santa Ana was defeated by a numerically inferior American force under General Taylor at Buena Vista, near the town of Saltillo, on February 22–23. In March, an American force under Gen. Winfield Scott landed on the Mexican coast three miles south of Vera Cruz and captured the city on March 29th. Thereafter Scott advanced toward the Mexican capital, overcoming enemy resistance at Cerro Gordo in April, and Contreras and Churubusco in August. In September he captured Mexico City, in effect concluding the war, although minor engagements between Mexican and American forces continued through the early months of 1848. A military armistice was declared on February 29, 1848. On March 10th the Senate ratified the Treaty of Guadalupe Hidalgo, officially ending the war. According to its terms, Mexico relinquished all claims to Texas above the Rio Grande and ceded New Mexico (including what is now Arizona, Utah, Nevada and parts of Wyoming and Colorado) and California to the United States. The U.S. agreed to pay Mexico $15 million and assume the claims of American citizens against the Mexican government.

Intelligence Operations: Despite the long period of tension preceding the opening of hostilities, the U.S. War Department had drawn up no war plans, and therefore no intelligence requirements had been defined. Gen. Zachary Taylor seemed especially impervious to the need for even BASIC INTELLIGENCE and failed to take advantage of his long period of encampment in southeast Texas to collect information regarding terrain, routes for advance, etc. The best source of such information available in the War Department at the opening of hostilities was the personal journal written thirty years earlier by Lt. Zebulon M. Pike during his travels in Texas and northern Mexico.

During the war the American commanders han-

dled combat intelligence as an ad hoc matter in the absence of any formal intelligence staff. Cavalry played a major role in collecting intelligence, and engineering officers carried out technical reconnaissance missions to gather data to be used in planning attacks against fortified positions. General Scott's advance from Vera Cruz to Mexico City was greatly facilitated by the MEXICAN SPY COMPANY, which performed intelligence and security missions and carried out operations against Mexican guerrillas.

Apparently the Mexican forces also lacked any formal intelligence-gathering function, although their basic intelligence was excellent because they were fighting on completely familiar terrain. The Mexicans also profited by the American failure to establish secure communications, and they achieved one of the most important intelligence coups of the war when they intercepted a dispatch from General Scott to General Taylor in January 1847, detailing the projected amphibious landing at Vera Cruz and directing Taylor to detach the bulk of his regular force for use in the operation. The information was apparently crucial to General Santa Ana's decision to counterattack Taylor in northern Mexico the following month, and could well have resulted in a major American reversal had the Mexicans succeeded in winning the closely contested Battle of Buena Vista.

The Mexican War taught the U.S. Army and the War Department valuable lessons in several areas, including military intelligence. However, these lessons were quickly forgotten after the termination of hostilities.

(Bauer, *The Mexican War;* Bryan, *The Spy in America;* Bidwell, "History of the Military Intelligence Division, Department of the Army General Staff.")

MEYER, CORD (November 10, 1920–): political activist, writer, intelligence officer

A native of Washington, D.C., Meyer was raised in Europe and New York City. He graduated from St. Paul's School in Concord, New Hampshire, in 1939, and from Yale University in 1942. Meyer enlisted in the U.S. Marine Corps Reserve and was commissioned as a second lieutenant in 1943. He saw combat in the Pacific and received a wound on Guam that cost him his left eye. Awarded the Purple Heart, the Bronze Star, and a Navy Unit Citation, Meyer was discharged with the rank of captain. His twin brother, Quentin, who also served in the Marine Corps in the Pacific, was killed on Okinawa.

While recovering from his wounds, Meyer wrote a series of articles for the *Atlantic Monthly* proposing the establishment of a world governmental organization. After the establishment of the United Nations in 1945 he published an article criticizing what he regarded as the shortcomings of the UN, including the Security Council veto and the weakness of the UN's enforcement powers in the International Court of Justice. In 1947 he was a principal in the creation of the United World Federalists, a group dedicated to transforming the UN into a true world government, complete with authority over its individual member nations. He became president of the United World Federalists, and a vice-president of the World Movement for a World Federal Government, an international organization with similar aims. He published a book, *Peace or Anarchy*, in 1947 putting forth the world federalist viewpoint. During this same period he was also active in the American Veterans Committee, especially in working to keep Communists from taking control of it.

Meyer's experience with Communists in the AVC, and his growing belief that Stalin would never agree to the commitments required to transform the UN into a world government, undermined his faith in the world federalist program and he resigned from the United World Federalists in 1949. He returned to Harvard University where he had earlier held a fellowship for postgraduate study in international relations. While at Harvard he began research on a book (never completed) on the history of the cold war. While researching the book, he became further convinced of Stalin's duplicity and aware of the threat posed by the Soviet Union. After receiving a Ph.D. from Harvard he was recruited into the Central Intelligence Agency by ALLEN W. DULLES, then chief of the CIA CLANDESTINE SERVICE.

Meyer first served in the Office of Policy Coordination, as the CIA's COVERT ACTION department was then called. He worked in the International Organizations Division, which had been established in 1951 by THOMAS W. BRADEN to provide covert support of the non-Communist left around the world through financial aid to trade unions, political parties, and international organizations of students and journalists. The Division also supervised and supported RADIO FREE EUROPE and RADIO LIBERTY, the Agency's radio propaganda organizations in Europe.

In 1953 Meyer was suspended by the CIA as the result of a report on him prepared and forwarded to the Agency by the Federal Bureau of Investigation. The report consisted of an assortment of allegations against Meyer, ranging from the unanswerable statement, made by an unidentified informant who had met Meyer once, that he must be a Communist; to the undeniable fact that Meyer had associated with Cass Canfield, the chairman of the board of the publishing house of Harper and Brothers, and polit-

ically a moderate Democrat. In the political climate of Washington in 1953 (the influence of Sen. Joseph R. McCarthy was growing), the acting director of the CIA, Gen. CHARLES P. CABELL (Dulles, then director, was out of the country at the time), felt he had no alternative but to suspend Meyer and force him to make a formal response to the charges.

Meyer retained a lawyer, wrote a detailed "political autobiography," explaining the development of his political views, and collected sworn affidavits from a number of influential friends attesting to his loyalty. He submitted these to a two-man panel composed of CIA General Counsel LAWRENCE R. HOUSTON and SHEFFIELD EDWARDS, the director of security. On the basis of Meyer's defense, Houston and Edwards recommended that he be reinstated. He returned to the Agency after the two-month period needed to clear up the matter.

By some accounts the ordeal altered Meyer's political personality, transforming him from a peace-oriented liberal into a fanatical cold warrior, "more Catholic than the Pope." In his memoirs Meyer disdained "this simplistic demonology . . . the convenient theory that from a humane Dr. Jekyll I had been transformed by exposure to the Agency's influence into an evil Mr. Hyde."

In 1954 Meyer succeeded Braden as chief of the International Organizations Division. When the Division merged with the Clandestine Service's Covert Action Staff in March 1962, he became chief of that staff, responsible both for international operations and for guiding the area divisions of the Clandestine Service in the conduct of covert action.

Meyer's role in the CIA came to public attention in 1967 when *Ramparts* magazine published an exposé of the CIA's covert support of the National Student Association. The disclosure of the CIA's role brought attacks from the left, which was disturbed by the Agency's secret manipulation of the student group, and from the right, which was outraged that government funds had been used to support an organization actively opposing American involvement in Vietnam. In his memoirs Meyer noted a similarity between this situation and his days in the United World Federalists, which had also been the target of both ends of the political spectrum.

In July 1967 Meyer was appointed assistant deputy director for plans (i.e., the number two man in the Clandestine Service) under THOMAS H. KARAMESSINES. He held the post until 1973 when he was made chief of the CIA's London station. He held that sensitive post, which included liaison with the British intelligence and security services, until July 1976, a period that was filled with the many sensational disclosures of the presidential commissions and

Japanese cruiser after battle of Midway. Source: National Archives.

congressional committees investigating the U.S. intelligence community (see CENTRAL INTELLIGENCE AGENCY). Meyer's tasks included reassuring the British that the "flap" in Washington would not endanger their own sensitive sources.

When he returned from the London post, Meyer served as a special assistant to CIA Deputy Director E. HENRY KNOCHE, reviewing the INTELLIGENCE COMMUNITY's provisions for warning of attacks on the United States and for handling major international crises. He retired from the CIA at the end of 1977 and has since written a syndicated newspaper column.

Meyer's short story "Waves of Darkness," a fictionalized account of his wounding on Guam, won the O. Henry Prize for the best first-published story of 1946, and the MGM Atlantic Prize.

(*Current Biography*, 1948; Meyer, *Facing Reality;* Powers, *The Man Who Kept the Secrets.*)

MIDAS EARLY WARNING SATELLITE

The MIDAS (MIssile Detection And Surveillance) program was undertaken in the late 1950s to provide early warning of a missile attack launched from the Soviet Union. Detection of missile launches was to be accomplished by equipping a satellite with infrared sensors that would register the thermal radiation given off by the flame of a rocket launch. Difficulties with these sensors caused delays and eventually the abandonment of the MIDAS program. More sophisticated launch-detecting systems reportedly were developed during the 1970s and placed in geosynchronous orbits in sight of Soviet ICBM installations.

(Klass, *Secret Sentries in Space.*)

MIDWAY, BATTLE OF

Summary: Midway, an island lying 1,400 miles northwest of Honolulu, has been United States territory since 1867 and was of strategic importance during the SECOND WORLD WAR. Early in June 1942 a Japanese armada under Adm. Isoroku Yamamoto advanced on Midway with the object of capturing it and thus gaining control of the western Pacific. The U.S. Navy had obtained advance knowledge of the Japanese plan through communications intercepts and cryptanalysis, and was therefore able to mount a surprise attack on the Japanese fleet. The ensuing battle, involving carrier-based planes and submarines of both fleets, took place during June 3–6, and was a major American victory and the turning point of the naval war in the Pacific.

Background and Discussion: In the wake of his successful PEARL HARBOR ATTACK, Yamamoto planned to secure control of the western Pacific by capturing strategically located Midway. He also anticipated that the United States, in an effort to regain the island, would counterattack with the remainder of the Pacific Fleet. Because the Pacific Fleet was far smaller than his own, and would have to engage him at a time and place of his own choosing, he expected to destroy it and thus consolidate Japanese control of the western Pacific.

Yamamoto's plan called for an operation involving two hundred ships to be assembled in Hiroshima Bay for the attack. A diversionary assault on the Aleutians was planned. Consequently a large volume of Japanese radio traffic was generated as the logistical arrangements for the operation were made. This traffic, sent in the Japanese naval cipher, was intercepted by U.S. Navy listening posts in the Pacific and sent to the Navy's cryptanalytical unit in Hawaii, the Combat Intelligence Unit of the 14th Naval District (see NAVAL INTELLIGENCE).

The Unit, under the leadership of Lt. Comdr. JOSEPH J. ROCHEFORT, broke the Japanese cipher and read the messages. However, the target of the planned attack remained unknown because the Japanese had referred to it in terms of a pair of map coordinates, "AF," in their radio messages. Although Rochefort's unit suspected that AF meant Midway, some doubt remained. The matter was settled when Rochefort arranged to have a radio message sent in clear stating that the freshwater distillation plant on Midway had broken down. This message was intercepted by the Japanese, and soon thereafter Rochefort's unit intercepted and deciphered a Japanese message reporting that "AF" was short of fresh water.

With the complete Japanese battle plan for Midway in his possession, Adm. Chester Nimitz ordered his three aircraft carriers to a point 350 miles northeast of Midway, where they could wait undetected to launch a surprise attack on the flank of the numerically larger Japanese fleet. Nimitz did indeed take Yamamoto by surprise on the morning of June 3rd. In the ensuing battle Yamamoto lost three of his aircraft carriers; one American carrier, the *Yorktown*, was sunk. The Japanese called off the operation against Midway and withdrew. The operation ended the Japanese threat against Hawaii and the West Coast

and forced Yamamoto to take the defensive for the rest of the war.

(Kahn, *The Codebreakers*; Holmes, *Double-Edged Secrets*; Potter, "The Crypt of the Cryptanalysts.")

MILER, NEWTON S.: intelligence officer

Miler served in the U.S. Navy during the Second World War, then joined the Strategic Services Unit, the caretaker unit that was created to take charge of the assets of the Office of Strategic Services after the OSS was dissolved in September 1945. He remained with that organization after it became part first of the Central Intelligence Group and then, in 1947, of the CENTRAL INTELLIGENCE AGENCY (see CENTRAL INTELLIGENCE AGENCY). He served in the CIA CLANDESTINE SERVICE and was a chief of an overseas station of the CIA. He later served on the Counterintelligence Staff of the Clandestine Service and became chief of counterintelligence operations under CI chief JAMES J. ANGLETON.

After CIA Director WILLIAM E. COLBY forced Angleton to retire in December 1974, Miler also retired. Since his retirement he has been active in improving public understanding of intelligence, especially among college students, through his lectures and writings.

(Martin, *Wilderness of Mirrors*.)

MILES, MILTON EDWARD (April 6, 1900–March 25, 1961): Navy officer, intelligence officer

A native of Jerome, Arizona, Miles enlisted in the U.S. Navy as an apprentice seaman in 1917. He was appointed to the U.S. Naval Academy, graduated in 1922, and was assigned to the Navy's China station at Hong Kong, where he served until 1927. He took a postgraduate course in electrical engineering at the Naval Academy during 1927–28, and earned an M.S. in the same subject from Columbia University in 1929. He served several tours at sea and ashore as an engineering officer, and commanded the destroyer U.S.S. *John D. Edwards*. In 1939 he was assigned to the Interior Control Board, a naval engineering unit.

In April 1942 Miles was sent to Chunking, China, as a naval observer with secret orders to establish weather stations and a system of coastwatchers to support the Pacific Fleet and prepare for amphibious landings three or four years thereafter. Working with Nationalist Chinese General Tai Li, he organized a force of Chinese guerrillas that was trained and equipped by the U.S. Navy. This organization even-

tually was known as the SINO-AMERICAN COOP-
ERATIVE ORGANIZATION (SACO), of which Tai
Li was director and Miles deputy director. Miles was
commander of the U.S. Naval Group China, which
consisted of the American trainers and advisors in
SACO. He was also briefly coordinator of OSS activ-
ities in China during 1943, until OSS Director WIL-
LIAM J. DONOVAN had a falling out with him and
Tai Li and withdrew OSS support from SACO.

After the war Miles, who had advanced to the rank
of rear admiral, commanded cruiser divisions of the
Atlantic Fleet, the Naval Department in the Panama
Canal Zone, and the Third Naval District. He retired from the Navy with the rank of vice admiral in
1958.

Miles's decorations included the Distinguished
Service Medal, the Purple Heart, the Legion of Merit,
the Chinese Order of Cloud and Banner, and the
Mexican Order of the Aztec Eagle.

(*Who Was Who in America*, v. 4; obituary, *New York
Times*, March 26, 1961, p. 93; Miles, *A Different Kind
of War*.)

MILES, SHERMAN (December 5, 1882–?), Army officer, intelligence officer

A native of Washington, D.C., Miles was the son of
Nelson A. Miles, the commanding general of the
U.S. Army during the Spanish-American War. He
graduated from the U.S. Military Academy in 1905.
Commissioned as a second lieutenant in the U.S.
Army, he served in the cavalry, the coastal artillery,
and the field artillery. During 1912–40 he served
several times on the Army's General Staff and as
military attaché in Europe, including service as mili-
tary attaché in Russia during the First World War.
Miles was operations officer (G-3) of the Army's
Hawaiian Department from 1929 to 1932, and during
1934–38 he was chief of the Projects Section of the
War Plans Division. Promoted to brigadier general in
1939, he became assistant chief of staff for intelligence
(G-2; see ARMY INTELLIGENCE) on May 1, 1940.
He held that post until January 30, 1942, a period
that included the PEARL HARBOR ATTACK.

Miles was one of the U.S. government officials
who received MAGIC, the intelligence material that
became available after WILLIAM F. FREIDMAN broke
the Japanese diplomatic cipher. Like other senior
American intelligence officers, he was aware of the
increasing likelihood of a Japanese attack on U.S.
forces toward the end of 1941, but was unable to
foresee the possibility that the Japanese would strike
as far east as Hawaii.

Gen. Sherman Miles as a young officer. Source: National Archives.

Miles was one of the principal witnesses to give
testimony before the Senate investigation of the intelligence failure of the PEARL HARBOR attack, and
he was often unfairly made to look like a fool under
the senators' cross-examination.

Miles retired with the rank of major general.

(*Who's Who in America*, v. 23; Wohlstetter, *Pearl
Harbor: Warning and Decision*.)

MILLIKAN, MAX FRANKLIN (December 12, 1913–December 14, 1969): economist, intelligence officer

A native of Chicago, Millikan studied at the California Institute of Technology during 1931–33 and graduated from Yale University in 1935. He studied at
Cambridge University during 1935–36, and was an
instructor in economics at Yale during 1938–41. After
he received a Ph.D. from Yale in 1941 he stayed on
as an assistant professor.

Millikan took a leave of absence from Yale in 1942
to work for the U.S. Office of Price Administration
(the wartime rationing agency), and later the War
Shipping Administration. In 1946 he was an eco-

nomic intelligence analyst in the State Department. In 1949 he joined the economics faculty of the Massachusetts Institute of Technology.

Millikan took a leave of absence from MIT in January 1951 to serve with the CENTRAL INTELLIGENCE AGENCY, which had then begun to focus its research and analysis in the area of economic intelligence. WILLIAM H. JACKSON, the deputy director of central intelligence, recruited Millikan and appointed him assistant director of the Office of Research and Reports. Millikan's mandate to conduct economic intelligence research and analysis marked a significant departure from the CIA's earlier charter of limiting its intelligence activities to the coordination of information supplied by other government intelligence agencies. Millikan's work had a major impact on strategic and military analysis of the Soviet Union during the 1950s and put the CIA firmly in the business of intelligence production.

Millikan left the CIA and returned to MIT in 1953, having first arranged for an ongoing consultancy arrangement between the Agency and MIT's Center for International Studies. Millikan directed the Center until his death in 1969.

Millikan was the son of Robert A. Millikan, the Nobel Prize-winning physicist who discovered the electron.

(*Who Was Who in America*, v. 5; Karalekas, *History of the Central Intelligence Agency*; Cline, *The CIA, Reality vs. Myth*.)

MITCHELL, BERNON F. (March 11, 1929–): cryptologist, defector

A native of San Francisco, Mitchell was raised in Eureka, California, studied for a year and a half at the California Institute of Technology, and enlisted in the U.S. Navy. He was assigned to the Navy communications intercept station at Kamiseya, Japan. In 1954, after being discharged from the Navy, he enrolled at Stanford University where he studied mathematics. After graduation in 1957 he joined the NATIONAL SECURITY AGENCY and worked as a cryptologist in the Office of Research and Development.

In 1960 Mitchell and his NSA associate, WILLIAM H. MARTIN, with whom he had served in the Navy, defected to the Soviet Union, where they disclosed to the Soviet government highly classified information regarding the NSA and American electronic intelligence operations.

Mitchell became a Soviet citizen and works as a computer specialist in Leningrad. He reportedly has made several unsuccessful attempts to return to the United States.

(Bamford, *The Puzzle Palace*.)

MOBY DICK PROGRAM

Moby Dick was the code name of a program sponsored by the Central Intelligence Agency and carried out by the U.S. Air Force to develop high-altitude balloons for OVERHEAD RECONNAISSANCE. The program, which was the result of a study carried out by the Rand Corporation in 1946, was undertaken by the Air Force's Cambridge Research Center and Wright Air Development Center in 1951. It involved the use of very large polyethylene balloons carrying a six hundred-pound gondola that contained a camera and control instrumentation. The balloons, which carried an automatic ballasting system that enabled them to maintain a constant altitude, ascended to altitudes between 50,000 and 100,000 feet, where they were carried westward by the wind. A transmitter on board sent out a radio signal every two minutes, permitting the balloons to be tracked from ground stations and airborne aircraft. After about three days—the time needed for the balloon to drift across the Soviet Union and/or China—the balloons would descend to 28,000 feet, at which altitude the gondola would be jettisoned and parachuted to earth. The descending gondola would then be recovered by an aircraft, either in midair during the descent or on the surface.

The MOBY DICK balloons were test-flown across the United States from launch points at Tillamook, Oregon; Vernalis, California; and Edwards Air Force Base, California. The tests, which were conducted during 1951–52, provided useful and unprecedented meteorological data to the Air Force Weather Service and the U.S. Weather Bureau.

The operational balloon reconnaissance program, which was designated WS-119L, was transferred to the Air Force Atmospheric Devices Laboratory in 1953. Difficulties in the midair recovery technique and other remaining technical problems were solved by August 1955.

Balloon overflights of the Soviet Union began in November 1955. The balloons were launched in Western Europe and recovered in the vicinity of Japan. The flights continued through the spring of 1956 and produced excellent results, although some balloons suffered from the vagaries of the wind and failed to pass over areas of intelligence interest, and others descended prematurely, fell into Soviet hands, and elicited diplomatic protests.

The balloon program was discontinued in mid-1956

when the first U-2 RECONNAISSANCE AIRCRAFT flights over the Soviet Union were begun. The camera and recovery equipment developed in the MOBY DICK/WS-119L program were used in the DISCOVERER RECONNAISSANCE SATELLITE several years later.

(Rostow, *Open Skies*; Prados, *The Soviet Estimate*.)

MOLE

A PENETRATION AGENT. The adoption of this term by American intelligence professionals during the 1970s may either be an instance of life imitating art—the term was used by John Le Carré in several of his spy novels—or else another instance of British intelligence jargon finding its way into American professional usage. WILLIAM HOOD notes that the term was used by Karl Marx, but in the context of politics rather than intelligence. Intelligence bibliophile Walter Pforzheimer has established an ancient and illustrious pedigree for the espionage sense of the word, which he found in Sir Francis Bacon's 1622 history of King Henry VII:

Hee was carefull and liberall to obtaine good Intelligence from all parts abroad. . . . He had such Moles perpetually working and casting to undermine him.

See DESTABILIZE.

(Safire, *On Language*; Hood, *Mole*.)

MONGOOSE

The code name of one of a series of COVERT ACTION operations ordered by President Kennedy and conducted by the CIA CLANDESTINE SERVICE that were aimed at toppling the regime of Fidel Castro in Cuba. Operation MONGOOSE was launched in the fall of 1961, in the wake of the BAY OF PIGS INVASION failure.

MONGOOSE was conceived by presidential assistant Richard Goodwin, Attorney General Robert Kennedy, and Air Force Gen. EDWARD G. LANSDALE (whose assignment to the CIA had ended some years before). They envisioned an elaborate program, including psychological warfare, sabotage, paramilitary operations, and the use of the U.S. armed forces in support of a Cuban uprising against Castro. Much of the MONGOOSE concept originated with Lansdale, who believed the key to success was to have "the [Cuban] people themselves overthrow the Castro regime rather than [the] U.S. engineer efforts from outside Cuba." According to one of the participants, Robert Kennedy characterized the operation as hav-

ing "the top priority of the U.S. Government—no time, money, effort or manpower is to be spared."

A special oversight mechanism for the operation was established at the level of the NATIONAL SECURITY COUNCIL. Called the Special Group (Augmented) (SGA), it consisted of the regular members of the Special Group, which oversaw all covert action operations, augmented by Attorney General Kennedy and Gen. Maxwell Taylor. Lansdale was appointed chief of operations of MONGOOSE. WILLIAM K. HARVEY of the CIA Clandestine Service was made chief of Task Force W, a CIA unit established especially for the operation.

Although Attorney General Kennedy and the rest of the SGA managed and monitored Operation MONGOOSE in the most minute detail, there is some question as to whether the President was aware of Harvey's efforts to arrange the assassination of Castro through organized crime figure John Rosselli. In the event the assassination plot failed, the operation did not achieve any significant sabotage in Cuba, and it apparently was limited to intelligence gathering.

MONGOOSE was terminated after the CUBAN MISSILE CRISIS of October 1962, although the CIA subsequently undertook additional unsuccessful attempts to assassinate Castro.

(See also, CENTRAL INTELLIGENCE AGENCY, SHEFFIELD EDWARDS, ROBERT MAHEU.)

(U.S. Senate, *Alleged Assassination Plots Involving Foreign Leaders*; Corson, *Armies of Ignorance*; Ranelagh, *The Agency*.)

MONTAGUE FOX AFFAIR

In June 1780, while the soldiers of George III were trying to suppress the revolution in Britain's American colonies, there was rioting in London over an issue unrelated to the war. Lord George Gordon had called a mass meeting in St. George's fields to protest the government's easing of the harsh anti-Catholic laws. The meeting turned into a riot and an angry mob of some sixty thousand Protestants rampaged through London, burning buildings, overturning carriages, and laying siege to Parliament. After eight days of rioting, order was finally restored. Some English observers suspected that the riots had been secretly instigated by the Americans or their French allies, although no conclusive evidence of this was ever produced.

Less than a week after the riots a man—apparently English—presented himself at the embassies of Spain and France at the Hague. He went by the name Montague Fox and claimed to have been personally involved in the riots, and to have sacked the Admiralty building and the home of Lord Sandwich, the First Lord of the Admiralty. He offered to sell British naval plans and other secret documents he claimed to have stolen in the rioting. In addition, he proposed that he be supplied with four thousand guns to start an uprising against the British government in Cornwall.

"Fox" was referred to the French foreign minister, Compte de Vergennes, who received him at Versailles and heard his proposals. Vergennes was reserved and wary, suspecting that the overture might be a trap by the British to implicate France in the recent riots. "Fox" next visited the American minister plenipotentiary, BENJAMIN FRANKLIN. Franklin also was wary of the man and expressed doubt as to the feasibility of the proposed Cornish uprising. The stranger's credibility was not enhanced by his failure to produce any of the purported British documents, which he claimed were still hidden safely somewhere in England.

The French were not prepared to dismiss "Fox" completely; they gave him some money and asked to see the documents. He made a trip to England and returned with an assortment of papers allegedly stolen from Sandwich and the Admiralty. Some proved genuine, but of minor value; others were suspect; still others were obvious frauds. "Fox" dropped out of sight for six months, turning up next in Hanover, where he called himself "M. Montagu," allegedly a British naval officer ready to sell his services as a spy to the French legation. His offer was declined, and he disappeared. Nothing more was heard from him.

(Morris, *The Peacemakers*.)

MONTAGUE, LUDWELL LEE: historian, Army officer, intelligence officer

A colonel in Army intelligence, Montague served as executive secretary of the JOINT INTELLIGENCE COMMITTEE during the Second World War (the JIC was an interagency body, composed of representatives from the armed services intelligence components, the State Department, the Foreign Economic Administration, and the Office of Strategic Services). He was the author of a report highly critical of Gen. WILLIAM J. DONOVAN's 1944 proposal for a postwar central intelligence agency (see CENTRAL INTELLIGENCE AGENCY). However, Montague later claimed that the CIA had its origins not in Donovan's proposal but in a plan he had worked out while serving on the JIC (a claim disputed by other knowledgeable students of the Agency's origins).

Montague later served in the State Department as a civilian, and in 1946 was one of the first senior intelligence analysts assigned by State to the newly established Central Intelligence Group. He headed the CIG's Central Reports Staff, which produced the Daily Summary of intelligence for President Truman, and later a Weekly Summary. Later he was chief of the CIG's Office of Reports and Estimates, an enlarged version of the CRS that also produced intelligence estimates.

Montague remained with the CIG when it became the CIA in 1947. He assisted WILLIAM L. LANGER in establishing the Office of National Estimates, and he served for many years as a member of the Board of National Estimates (see NATIONAL INTELLIGENCE ESTIMATE). He retired from the Agency in the 1970s.

Apart from his intelligence duties, Montague was the author of historical works, including a history of the relations between the United States and Haiti.

(Troy, *Donovan and the CIA*; Cline, *The CIA, Reality vs. Myth*; Karalekas, *History of the Central Intelligence Agency*.)

MONTGOMERY, BENJAMIN FRANKLIN (July 5, 1853–July 7, 1926): telegrapher, intelligence officer

A native of Petersburg, Virginia, Montgomery was educated at the Kelley Academy in Virginia. After working for the Western Union, the Franklin, and the Atlantic telegraph companies, he joined the U.S. Army Signal Corps in 1875 and served at the headquarters of the chief signal officer during 1875–77. In March 1877 he was assigned to detached duty at the White House, where he took charge of the newly established telegraph office under President Rutherford B. Hayes. In 1878 he declined a commission in the Signal Corps in order to remain at the White House as a civilian employee.

Montgomery became a permanent White House fixture for the next twenty-three years, serving Presidents Hayes, Garfield, Arthur, Cleveland, Harrison, McKinley, and Theodore Roosevelt in the capacity of executive clerk and acting assistant presidential secretary.

As the president's communication officer, Montgomery was often called upon to operate what amounted to a White House command post. During the railroad strikes of 1877, when rioting broke out in Baltimore, Pittsburgh, Chicago, and St. Louis, he kept President Hayes in constant touch with the commanders of the federal troops dispatched to quell the disorders. He performed the same duty during other major civil disorders and natural disasters, such as the Johnstown flood and the Galveston hurricane.

Under McKinley, Montgomery was appointed chief intelligence officer, the White House official responsible for receiving the intelligence reports made by the Cuban agents of Capt. MARTIN LUTHER HELLINGS, reports that proved critical in the conduct of the SPANISH-AMERICAN WAR. During that war Montgomery was also responsible for the White House Operating Room, the prototype of later national military command posts.

In August 1898 Montgomery was commissioned as a lieutenant colonel in the Signal Corps and he was put in charge of the White House Telegraph and Cipher Bureau shortly after the war when that office was made a formal and permanent part of the Executive Office.

In 1905 Montgomery was transferred to duty in California. Two years later he retired and moved to New York City, where he lived until his death.

(O'Toole, *The Spanish War; Who Was Who in America*, v. 1; *Telegraph Age*, June 1, 1902; obituary, *New York Times*, July 9, 1926, 19:6.)

Benjamin F. Montgomery. Source: National Archives.

MONTREAL SPY RING

At the outbreak of the SPANISH-AMERICAN WAR in 1898, Lt. Ramon Carranza, formerly naval attaché at the Spanish embassy in Washington, established an intelligence station in the Windsor Hotel in Montreal. Before the war the Spanish legation had spied upon the Cuban emigrés in the U.S. through the services of the PINKERTON NATIONAL DETECTIVE AGENCY, and Carranza now turned to a Canadian private detective agency to recruit agents for work in the United States. The detective agency provided him with Frank Mellor, a former Canadian artilleryman, who undertook to organize a spy ring. According to the plan, Mellor would recruit other veterans of the Canadian Army who would go to the United States, enlist in the Army, and when they landed in Cuba or the Philippines, they would cross the Spanish lines, surrender, identify themselves as Carranza's agents (by a distinctive ring each was issued) and report American military plans. But Mellor was a pugnacious man with an unsavory background and he proved unsuited to the delicate task Carranza had entrusted to him. One of his recruits, an Englishman, reported the scheme to the British consul in Kingston, Ontario, and the U.S. State Department was informed by the British government. The matter was passed on to the SECRET SERVICE, which already knew of Carranza's operation. Mellor was himself arrested by the Secret Service a short

time later when he tried to enlist in the Army at Tampa, Florida.

Secret Service chief JOHN E. WILKIE had discovered the operation when he sent a team of agents to follow Carranza to Canada at the outbreak of the war. One of the agents took a room near Carranza's in the Windsor Hotel and overheard a conversation between the Spanish officer and George Downing, a young English-born naturalized American citizen who had served as a petty officer aboard the U.S.S. *Brooklyn*. The agent heard Carranza recruit Downing for espionage in Washington, D.C.

Downing was followed and placed under surveillance. He visited the Navy Department in Washington, where he apparently knew his way around, and subsequently tried to mail a report to a cover address in Montreal. The letter was intercepted by the Secret Service and found to contain information regarding naval preparations. Downing was picked up and held. Two days later he was found hanging in his cell, apparently a suicide.

Carranza had meanwhile transferred his station from the hotel to a rented house. Since he had taken only a two-month lease, he was not surprised when the rental agent sent around three prospective tenants to view the place. They were in fact a pair of American actors and Secret Service agent Ralph Redfern, who had been watching the house from his rented rooms across the street. While the three were being shown through the house Redfern managed to steal an unmailed letter Carranza had written to his cousin, an admiral in the Spanish navy. The letter contained explicit references to Carranza's espionage operation, which of course violated Canadian neutrality. Disclosure of this evidence to the British and Canadian authorities put the Spanish operation out of business.

Although Carranza had committed some serious indiscretions that ultimately led to his exposure, he managed to collect some valuable information regarding American military movements and pass it along to the Spanish authorities in Havana before he was stopped.

(Jeffreys-Jones, "The Montreal Spy Ring of 1898 and the Origins of 'Domestic' Surveillance in the United States"; O'Toole, *The Spanish War*.)

MOODY, JAMES (1744–April 6, 1809): British army officer and intelligence agent

A native of New Jersey, Moody was a farmer at the outbreak of the American Revolution. A Tory, he objected to a New Jersey law requiring an oath of allegiance to the American side. He enlisted in a British loyalist brigade under command of Gen. CORTLAND SKINNER in 1777 and the New Jersey government gave orders to have him arrested on sight. The following year his property was confiscated by the state of New Jersey.

Moody took part in a guerrilla raid through New Jersey in June 1779. In November of that year he went under cover to spy on Gen. GEORGE WASHINGTON's forces. The following month he went on a reconnaissance mission across New Jersey and into Pennsylvania to observe the forces under Gen. John Sullivan. On his return trip he managed to examine the ration books of the Continental Army in Morris County, New Jersey, which enabled him to make a precise estimate of American strength. On the same excursion he spied on General Gates's forces at Pompton, New Jersey, and rescued a fellow British spy who was awaiting execution in an American jail.

Moody's abortive attempt to kidnap New Jersey Governor William Livingston led the governor to put a price on his head, but the droll Moody replied in kind by offering two hundred guineas for the governor, whom he described as "an incorrigible rebel," or one hundred guineas for Livingston's ears and nose, which Moody said were "too well known to be mistaken" (the unfortunate Livingston was reportedly overendowed in these organs).

Moody was captured at Englishtown, New Jersey, by Gen. Anthony Wayne's troops in 1780 and imprisoned at West Point. Later, he was transferred to General Washington's headquarters, from which he managed to escape.

In March 1781 he captured a pouch of General Washington's secret dispatches near Haverstraw, New York, and delivered them to the British forces in New York City. He was subsequently successful in stealing other American dispatches, but his attempt to steal the papers of the Continental Congress at Philadelphia in November 1781 failed and led to the capture and execution of his brother and fellow spy, John Moody. Moody narrowly escaped capture himself and made his way back to New York City.

Moody, who had been commissioned an ensign in the British army in 1779, was promoted to lieutenant in 1781. He went to England in 1782 and was granted a pension of one hundred pounds per year. In 1786 he moved to Novia Scotia, where he became a colonel in the local militia.

(Bakeless, *Turncoats, Traitors and Heroes; Who Was Who in America*, historical volume.)

MORGAN, HENRY STURGIS (October 24, 1900–): banker, intelligence officer

Although Morgan was born in London, England, his parents were American (his father was financier J. Pierpont Morgan). He attended Groton School and, after graduating from Harvard University in 1923, he worked in the family business, J.P. Morgan & Co., becoming a partner in 1928. In 1935 he became treasurer of Morgan Stanley & Co. In 1941 he was commissioned a commander in the U.S. Naval Reserve and was assigned to the Office of Strategic Services, where he served as chief of the OSS CENSORSHIP AND DOCUMENTS BRANCH. He returned to civilian life in 1945.

Morgan's brother, JUNIUS SPENCER MORGAN, also served in the OSS, in the Special Funds Branch.

(Smith, *OSS; Who's Who in America*, v. 34.)

MORGAN, JUNIUS SPENCER (March 15, 1892–October 1960): banker, intelligence officer

A native of New York City, Morgan was the son of financier J. Pierpont Morgan. He graduated from Harvard University in 1914 and joined the family business, J.P. Morgan & Co., in 1915. In 1942 he was commissioned a lieutenant commander in the U.S. Naval Reserve. The following year he was assigned to the Office of Strategic Services and served in the

OSS SPECIAL FUNDS BRANCH in London. He was discharged in 1944 with the rank of captain and resumed his position as director of J.P. Morgan & Co.

Morgan's younger brother, HENRY S. MORGAN, also served in the OSS, as chief of the Censorship and Documents Branch.

(Smith, *OSS*; *Who Was Who in America*, v. 4.)

MORGAN, WILLIAM J. : psychologist, intelligence officer

Morgan earned a Ph.D. in psychology at Yale University and worked as a professional psychologist before enlisting in the U.S. Army as a private in 1942. After completing Officer Candidate School and being commissioned as a second lieutenant in September 1943 he was assigned to the Office of Strategic Services.

Morgan served as a psychological testing officer at the British-run intelligence training center at Pemberley, England. He subsequently served in the OSS SPECIAL OPERATIONS BRANCH. In August 1944 he parachuted behind German lines in France, organized and trained a band of 550 French resistance fighters, and led them in action against the Germans.

After the war Morgan served with the Central Intelligence Agency. He was chief of the CIA's training staff during 1947–49, and chief of the psychological assessment staff during 1949–52.

In 1959 Morgan published *The OSS and I*, a memoir of his wartime experiences in the OSS.

(Smith, *OSS*; Morgan, *The OSS and I*.)

MULLIGAN, HERCULES (September 25, 1740–March 4, 1825): tailor, haberdasher, secret agent

A native of Coleraine, County Antrim, Ireland, Mulligan was brought to America by his parents when he was about six years old. The Mulligan family had Whig leanings in the politics of New York City before the American Revolution, and Mulligan was active in such patriotic organizations as the SONS OF LIBERTY and the New York Committee of Correspondence. He owned a tailor shop and haberdashery on Queen (now Pearl) Street.

In 1772 Mulligan befriended the young Alexander Hamilton when the latter lived in the Mulligan home after arriving in New York from the West Indies. Through Hamilton, Mulligan became a "confidential correspondent" (i.e., a secret intelligence agent) for Gen. GEORGE WASHINGTON, following the occupation of the city by the British during the war.

As a tailor to many of the British officers in New York, he was well-situated to pick up useful bits of military intelligence. Hercules's brother, Hugh, a member of a New York banking firm that dealt with the British occupation forces, was also a valuable source of information and useful introductions. And some British officers were billeted in Mulligan's home on Queen Street, where they may have revealed bits of military information in casual conversation.

In April 1777 Mulligan informed Washington of General Howe's planned expedition to Delaware. Information he obtained and reported to Washington is credited with having foiled a British plan to kidnap the general, and on another occasion he successfully warned Washington of a British plan to assassinate him in Connecticut. According to George Washington Custis, a grandson of Martha Washington, Mulligan "conveyed to the American Commander the most important information during the occupancy of New York by the British army."

Although Mulligan and ABRAHAM WOODHULL were aware of each other's espionage activities on behalf of General Washington, it is not clear whether Mulligan was a member of Woodhull's CULPER SPY RING.

Mulligan was arrested several times by the British authorities, and he has the distinction of having been accused of espionage and treason by BENEDICT ARNOLD after the American defector fled to New York City. Nothing was ever proved against Mulligan and he was released each time.

Washington entered New York City to observe the departure of the British on the first Evacuation Day, November 25, 1783. The following morning his first stop was Mulligan's tailor shop, where he breakfasted with Mulligan and his family, then ordered a complete civilian wardrobe from his former secret agent. Thereafter Mulligan's shop boasted the title: "Clothier to Genl. Washington."

Mulligan prospered after the war and became one of New York's leading citizens. He retired from business in 1820. Between 1784 and 1787 he was a vestryman of Trinity Church, where he is buried near the grave of his friend, Alexander Hamilton.

(O'Brien, *Hercules Mulligan, In Old New York*; Ford, *A Peculiar Service*; Bakeless, *Turncoats, Traitors and Heroes*.)

MURPHY, DAVID E. (June 23, 1921–): intelligence officer

A native of New York, Murphy graduated from the Cortland State Teachers College in 1942 and served in the U.S. Army during 1942–46. In 1946 he joined the Department of the Army as a civilian employee and served in Army Intelligence. He served in Korea during the Korean War.

Murphy joined the Central Intelligence Agency sometime during the 1950s and served in the CIA CLANDESTINE SERVICE. He was chief of the CIA base in Munich, and later chief of the Soviet branch in Berlin (he speaks fluent Russian). He was chief of the Soviet Bloc Division during the 1960s, and in 1968 became chief of station in Paris.

According to one published account (Martin, *Wilderness of Mirrors*), Murphy was one of the Clandestine Service officers who aroused the suspicions of JAMES J. ANGLETON, and Murphy was given the Paris station assignment only after a long and intensive investigation established that these suspicions were unfounded. However, Angleton reportedly warned the head of French intelligence that the new CIA station chief was a Soviet agent. Though he doesn't give the names, former CIA Director WILLIAM E. COLBY was apparently referring to this case in his memoirs, *Honorable Men*. Colby recalls that the head of "a friendly liaison service" took him aside and asked about the report, which he had gotten from CIA counterintelligence, that the local CIA station chief was a Soviet agent. Colby says he reviewed the files, conducted his own investigation, and assured the foreign official that he had complete trust in the station chief in question.

Murphy served in the Paris post through the early 1970s.

(*Who's Who in Government*, 1st ed.; Agee and Wolf, *Dirty Work*; Martin, *Wilderness of Mirrors*; Colby and Forbath, *Honorable Men*.)

MURPHY, JAMES RUSSELL (January 8, 1905–): lawyer, counterespionage officer

A native of Piedmont, Missouri, Murphy earned an LL.B. from George Washington University in 1931. He practiced law in Washington, D.C., and Virginia until 1941, when he joined the Office of the Coordinator of Information, the predecessor agency to the Office of Strategic Services. In 1943 he was made chief of the OSS COUNTER-ESPIONAGE BRANCH, and he served in that capacity until 1946 when he returned to the practice of law. Since 1951 he has been a member of the Washington law firm of Cross, Murphy and Smith. In recognition of his service with the OSS he received several decorations, including the Medal of Merit, the Medal of Freedom, the Legion of Honor, the French croix de guerre, the War Cross, and the Italian Merito di Guerra.

One of the junior counterintelligence officers who

served under Murphy and became his protege was JAMES J. ANGLETON, later chief of the Counterintelligence Staff of the Central Intelligence Agency.

(*Who's Who in America*, 42nd ed.; Cave Brown, *The Last Hero*.)

MURPHY, ROBERT DANIEL (October 28, 1894–): foreign service officer, diplomat, intelligence officer

A native of Milwaukee, Wisconsin, Murphy attended Marquette Academy and Marquette University before joining the Post Office Department in Washington, D.C. in 1916. He worked as a postal clerk and the following year, transferred to the foreign service. He served as a consular clerk in the American embassy in Bern, Switzerland, in 1917–19, and then returned to Washington, D.C., where he served as assistant chief of revenue agents in the Treasury Department while attending evening law classes at George Washington University. In 1920 he was awarded an LL.B. degree and admitted to the District of Columbia bar.

Murphy rejoined the foreign service and during the next few years served as vice-consul in Zurich and Munich, and consul at Seville. From 1926 to 1930 he worked for the State Department in Washington, D.C. (he returned to George Washington University and earned an LL.M. in 1928), and then was made consul at Paris. He had risen to the rank of counselor of the embassy when the German troops arrived in the city during the early months of the Second World War. Subsequently he served as charge d'affaires at Vichy.

In November 1940 Murphy was sent to French North Africa as President Franklin Roosevelt's special representative. There he directed the work of twelve American "vice-consuls," who were in fact espionage agents of Army and Navy Intelligence. The group produced intelligence that was of great value to American strategic planning when the U.S. became involved in the war.

In 1942 Murphy was joined by Col. WILLIAM EDDY of the Office of the Coordinator of Information (see OFFICE OF STRATEGIC SERVICES), and the two jointly planned intelligence and subversion in support of the scheduled Allied landings in North Africa. Murphy was placed in charge of all OSS activities in North Africa and, in November, he launched the COVERT ACTION operation that was to prepare the way for the invasion. The objective of the operation was to forestall all Vichy French resistance to the landings and so achieve a bloodless victory. However, errors in identifying the assigned landing points disrupted the coordination between the invading Allied armies and the underground activities. Murphy managed to repair some of the resulting damage by striking a bargain with Vichy collaborator Adm. Jean Darlan, who agreed to order a cease-fire in exchange for a promise of political authority in North Africa. Murphy was later criticized for making this concession, but the arrangement was approved by Secretary of State Cordell Hull, and Murphy was awarded the Distinguished Service Medal in December 1942.

Murphy subsequently conducted negotiations for the entrance of French West Africa into the war on the Allied side, and in 1943 participated in negotiations for an armistice in Italy. From 1944 to 1949 he was political advisor to the American military government in Germany. He later served as ambassador to Belgium and Japan and in several high-level posts in the State Department. After his retirement from government service he was chairman of the board of Corning Glass and director of the Corning Glass Works.

During the early 1970s Murphy was appointed head of a presidential commission to study the government's foreign policy-making organization. In its report, completed in 1975, the Murphy Commission recommended, among other things, strengthening the mechanisms for outside oversight of intelligence agencies and their activities. President Ford appointed Murphy to serve on the newly created INTELLIGENCE OVERSIGHT BOARD.

(*Current Biography*, 1958; Smith, *OSS*; Murphy, *Diplomat Among Warriors*; *Who's Who in America*, 37th ed.)

MURRAY, HENRY ALEXANDER (May 13, 1893–June 23, 1988): psychologist, intelligence officer

A native of New York City, Murray attended the Groton School in 1906–11, graduated from Harvard University in 1915, and earned an M.D. from Columbia Medical School in 1919, an M.A. from Columbia in 1920, and a Ph.D. from Cambridge University in 1928. After serving internships at the Presbyterian Hospital in 1920–22 and the Rockefeller Institute for Medical Research in 1922–24, he joined the faculty of Harvard University, where he taught psychology and served as director of the Harvard Psychological Clinic (1928–43).

In 1943 Murray was commissioned as a major in the U.S. Army Medical Corps and assigned to the Office of Strategic Services. He had been recruited by OSS director Gen. WILLIAM J. DONOVAN because of his work in the assessment of personality.

"The whole nature of the functions of the OSS were particularly inviting to psychopathic characters," Murray once remarked. "It involved sensation, intrigue, the idea of being a mysterious man with secret knowledge." Murray's job was to devise tests and screening procedures to try to keep such people out of the OSS. He and his colleagues, including Dr. JOHN W. GARDNER, set up the OSS's psychological assessment program. After the war their techniques were documented in a book, *Assessment of Men*, by the OSS Assessment Staff (New York: Rinehart, 1948). This work formed a basis for later research in psychological assessment by the Central Intelligence Agency.

Murray was discharged with the rank of lieutenant colonel in 1946 and returned to his teaching post at Harvard.

(*Who's Who in America*, v. 28; Marks, *The Search for the "Manchurian Candidate"*; Smith, *OSS*.)

N

NARON, L.A.: Union secret agent and intelligence officer

A native of Alabama, Naron was a Union loyalist who served the North in the Civil War. Because his home was in Chickasaw County, Alabama, General Sherman gave him the nickname "Chickasaw," which he thereafter adopted as a nom de guerre.

As "Captain Chickasaw," Naron served under Gen. GRENVILLE M. DODGE. During the early part of 1863 he undertook a secret mission in Alabama and Mississippi, the details of which are unknown. Afterward he served as Dodge's chief of scouts and ran the secret service organization Dodge had established. Naron also performed a counterespionage function, and it was he who arrested Confederate agent SAMUEL DAVIS.

Naron apparently lost his taste for intelligence work. He retired well before the end of the war and went to live with his family in Illinois. Apparently no record of Naron's full name has survived. In extant records he is sometimes styled "L.H. Naron" or "L.O. Naron."

(Bakeless, *Spies of the Confederacy*.)

NATIONAL DETECTIVE BUREAU

A Union counterespionage agency of the CIVIL WAR.

Officially, no such agency existed within the U.S. government during the Civil War. The name refers to a staff of detectives and counterespionage officers headed by LAFAYETTE C. BAKER, provost marshal of the War Department from circa February 1862 until circa February 1866. Baker's unit was involved almost exclusively in counterespionage and criminal inves-tigation, and its activities were for the most part centered in the Washington area, where it was head-quartered in a building at 217 Pennsylvania Avenue. Baker's unit succeeded in arresting Confederate espionage agents (see BELLE BOYD), blockade runners, corrupt government officials, and other law-breakers. The unit did have a small field office in New York City, however, and some of its agents operated as far away as Canada. It played a minor role in penetrating the NORTHWEST CONSPIRACY.

Without any official authorization, Baker some-times used stationery with the printed letterhead "National Detective Police Department." In 1867 he published a highly exaggerated memoir of his war-time service entitled *History of the United States Secret Service*, and this title has led some writers into the mistaken belief that Baker's unit was the forerunner of the SECRET SERVICE (which, in fact, was not established until after the war in 1865, and has always been a division of the Treasury Department).

Baker and others have made reference to the unit by a variety of other names:

Bureau of Detective Service
Bureau of Secret Service
National Detective Police
National Executive Police
National Secret Service Bureau of the United States
United States Secret Service Bureau

To add to the perplexity, Baker's staff of detectives is also sometimes confused with his First District of Columbia Cavalry, or "Baker's Rangers," a cavalry battalion raised and commanded by Baker, which served as a sort of mounted police and mobile coun-terinsurgency force in the Washington area.

The legend that Baker was the master spy-catcher

A Confederate agent shot while trying to escape from Baker's men. Source: Author's collection.

of the Civil War, and that he ran a vast, national-level agency called "the secret service," has become part of the CIVIL WAR ESPIONAGE MYTHOLOGY.

(Fishel, "The Mythology of Civil War Intelligence"; Mogelever, *Death to Traitors*; Baker, *History of the United States Secret Service*; Corson, *Armies of Ignorance*.)

NATIONAL FOREIGN INTELLIGENCE BOARD

The NFIB, which is chaired by the director of central intelligence, consists of the directors of the DEFENSE INTELLIGENCE AGENCY, the NATIONAL SECURITY AGENCY, the State Department's BUREAU OF INTELLIGENCE AND RESEARCH (INR), and other federal agencies with a foreign intelligence role. It functions as an advisory body to the director of central intelligence, and it provides a means of coordinating the activities of the represented agencies. It is, in a sense, the "board of directors" of the INTELLIGENCE COMMUNITY.

The NFIB's main tasks are the discussion and final approval of NATIONAL INTELLIGENCE ESTIMATEs before they are passed on to the NATIONAL SECURITY COUNCIL, and the establishment of intelligence-collection requirements and priorities.

The NFIB has existed in various forms, and under various names, since the Central Intelligence Group (CIG) was created in 1946 (see CENTRAL INTELLIGENCE AGENCY). It was then called the Intelligence Advisory Board and was composed of the chiefs of ARMY INTELLIGENCE, the Office of Naval Intelligence, AIR FORCE INTELLIGENCE, and STATE DEPARTMENT INTELLIGENCE. Because the Central Intelligence Group was not a true agency and, therefore, had no budget, its people, money, and facilities were provided by the member agencies of the Intelligence Advisory Board, and the Board therefore acted as an executive committee over the CIG.

With the creation of the Central Intelligence Agency in September 1947, the Board was replaced by the Intelligence Advisory Committee, which at first played an advisory role to the NATIONAL SECURITY COUNCIL and in effect supervised the director of central intelligence. After Gen. WALTER BEDELL SMITH became DCI, however, he succeeded in reducing the Committee's powers. Thereafter it functioned as a mechanism to coordinate the work of the CIA with the other intelligence agencies, and as a final step in the production of National Intelligence Estimates. The Committee was enlarged to include a representative of the Joint Chiefs of Staff, and also representatives of the Federal Bureau of Investigation and the Atomic Energy Commission, who participated when estimates involved questions of U.S. internal security or the Soviet nuclear program, respectively.

In 1958 the Intelligence Advisory Committee was merged with the United States Communications Intelligence Board to form the United States Intelligence Board (USIB). In 1965 the representatives of the Army, Navy, and Air Force intelligence agencies were replaced on the Board by a single representative of the DEFENSE INTELLIGENCE AGENCY, in order to redress the imbalance favoring the intelligence viewpoints of the Department of Defense. However, the National Security Agency, which is also a component of the Department of Defense, continued to have its own representative of the USIB. The Board, then, was made up of the directors of the DIA, the NSA, State's INR, representatives of the FBI and the AEC, and the deputy director of central intelligence. As chairman of the Board, the director of central intelligence acted in the capacity of the government's senior intelligence officer, rather than solely as a representative of the CIA.

With the growth of the intelligence community, more than a dozen USIB subcommittees were created to coordinate the work of intelligence agencies. The Committee on Overhead Reconnaissance (COMOR), for example, was created in 1960 to coordinate intelligence-collection requirements for the development and operation of OVERHEAD RECONNAISSANCE systems (COMOR was succeeded in 1967 by COMIREX—the Committee on Imagery Requirements and Exploitation).

In 1977 CIA Director STANSFIELD TURNER endorsed the action inaugurated by his predecessor, GEORGE BUSH, to replace the USIB with a body known as the National Foreign Intelligence Board. The NFIB has the same functions as the USIB and for all practical purposes the two bodies are the same. The CIA's deputy director for the INTELLIGENCE COMMUNITY STAFF was made a member of the NFIB.

(Karalekas, "History of the Central Intelligence Agency"; Cline, *The CIA, Reality vs. Myth*; Kirkpatrick, *The Real CIA*; Prados, *The Soviet Estimate*.)

NATIONAL INTELLIGENCE ESTIMATE

The NIE is the highest form of finished national intelligence (see FINISHED INTELLIGENCE). It is intended to reflect the consensus of the INTELLIGENCE COMMUNITY regarding some issue of major importance to national security, and it attempts to forecast the future development of present military, political, or economic situations so as to identify the implications for national policymakers. Dr. RAY S. CLINE, a former head of the CIA INTELLIGENCE DIRECTORATE, describes NIEs as "papers setting forth probable situations or occurrences that would make a major difference to our national security or our foreign policy."

An NIE is an attempt to answer a question, e.g., What level of strategic nuclear capability will the USSR have achieved five years from the present, and how will it relate to Soviet intentions toward the West? The question may be posed by the President, the director of central intelligence, a member of the NATIONAL SECURITY COUNCIL, or some other senior government official. Most NIEs relate to issues of continuing concern, e.g., Soviet strategic capabilities, and are produced or updated annually or biannually, or on some other regular schedule. A Special National Intelligence Estimate (SNIE) is produced when some unforeseen development, e.g., the Berlin crisis or the CUBAN MISSILE CRISIS, requires an immediate ad hoc study of some situation.

A national estimate that assesses a foreign nation's intentions or future policies is called a *straight estimate*. An estimate of the consequences of a hypothetical change in U.S. policy is a *general estimate*. General estimates are always initiated by a senior policymaker, i.e., they never originate in the intelligence community. A *net estimate* is a comparative analysis of a foreign nation's capability and probable intentions, and the corresponding U.S. capability to respond, e.g., a projection of Soviet strategic missile defenses in terms of their capability to stop a U.S. retaliatory strike. Because net estimates involve extensive computerized war gaming, they are usually produced through a different organizational mechanism than are other national estimates.

An NIE is forwarded to the National Security Council over the signature of the director of central intelligence acting in his capacity as the government's chief intelligence officer (as opposed to his narrower responsibilities as head of the CENTRAL INTELLIGENCE AGENCY). The DCI may indeed have taken a major hand in writing the document, but most NIEs are the result of a process of deliberation and negotiation by analysts from the agencies repre-

sented on the NATIONAL FOREIGN INTELLI-
GENCE BOARD.

The Board of National Estimate

The concept of a national estimate based on all
available sources of information, coordinated with all
departments and agencies of the government having
an intelligence function, but produced by a centralized unit, was introduced by CIA Director WALTER
BEDELL SMITH shortly after he took office in 1950.
He recruited Harvard historian and former director
of the OSS RESEARCH AND ANALYSIS BRANCH
WILLIAM LANGER to organize a unit within the
Agency for the production of NIEs. Langer organized
a two-tier structure within the CIA Intelligence Directorate: an Office of National Estimates (ONE), a
support staff that assembled and summarized the
information needed to prepare a draft NIE; and a
Board of National Estimates (BNE), a panel of twelve
senior specialists—former armed services officers,
foreign service officers, academics, and others—whose
function was to negotiate the final wording of the
NIE among the interested intelligence agencies.

Langer recruited former Yale historian and OSS
intelligence analyst SHERMAN KENT to serve as his
deputy and as a member of the BNE. When Langer
returned to Harvard in 1951, Kent became chairman
of the BNE and was largely responsible for its functioning until his retirement in 1968.

The BNE system worked thusly: One member of
the Board was given overall responsibility for producing a draft NIE. Given the original question that
prompted the NIE, he and the rest of the Board set
out first to identify the "terms of reference," i.e., to
analyze the problem in order to identify the subsidiary questions that must first be answered. The political aspects of a problem were likely to be passed
on to the Department of State; military aspects would
go to the Defense Intelligence Agency or one of the
armed services' intelligence components; etc.

The resulting staff studies were compiled and integrated by analysts in ONE under the guidance of
the Board member responsible for the draft NIE, who
would then take the major role in coordinating the
views of the other Board members in the production
of the draft. When complete, the draft was forwarded
to the United States Intelligence Board (USIB; see
NATIONAL FOREIGN INTELLIGENCE BOARD),
whose members shaped the final NIE by a process
of negotiation aimed at achieving a compromise among
the parochial viewpoints and biases of the various
member agencies, e.g., the historical tendency of the
State Department to underplay Soviet malevolence,
and that of the Defense Department to enlarge the

Soviet strategic threat. Where consensus proved impossible, the dissenting USIB member could "take a
footnote," i.e., record his contrary view as a footnote
to the main text of the NIE. After approval by the
DCI in his capacity as chairman of the USIB, the NIE
would be forwarded to the NSC.

The National Intelligence Officers

By the early 1970s the BNE was perceived by some
in government to have become "ingrown" or stag-
nant, partly because members tended to serve long
tenures on the Board, with the consequence that
turnover of viewpoints and backgrounds was low.
Members were seen as being increasingly out of
touch with the changing environment of the intelligence community. NIEs were beginning to have little
or no role in national security policymaking, a trend
many observers attributed to Henry Kissinger's disdain for much finished intelligence. Kissinger, a
knowledgeable and opinionated student of foreign
affairs, was President Nixon's assistant for national
security affairs at the time, and later was concurrently
secretary of state.

In 1973 CIA Director WILLIAM E. COLBY abolished the BNE and the ONE, and established a new
system for the production of NIEs: a group of twelve
national intelligence officers (NIOs) who were senior
experts in such subjects as China, Soviet affairs,
Europe, Latin America, strategic weaponry, general
purpose forces, or warning and indications. These
NIOs reported directly to the DCI, thereby emphasizing his role as the officer ultimately responsible
for the content of the NIE. Colby recalled,

> I told the eleven men and one woman whom I chose
> for the jobs [of NIOs] that they were to put them-
> selves in my chair as DCI for their subject of special-
> ization. They were to have no more staff than one
> assistant and a secretary so that they could identify
> totally with my position and not develop a role of
> their own. They were chosen from the intelligence
> community and private life as well as from CIA. . . .

The NIO system was modified by Adm. STANS-
FIELD TURNER during his tenure as DCI. He reconstituted the individual NIOs into a body known as
the National Intelligence Council (NIC), which reports directly to the DCI. The NIC is a body similar
to the BNE, with a chairman and a vice chairman,
and a set of formal operational procedures, but it is
not a part of the CIA Intelligence Directorate; it is
separate and distinct from the CIA as an agency.

The decline of the role of the CIA in the production
of draft NIEs came at a time when the Agency's long-

held view on Soviet strategic nuclear capabilities and intentions (viz., that the USSR was not seeking to develop a first-strike "war-winning" capability) was receiving close scrutiny and serious challenge by others in the intelligence community (especially Air Force Maj. Gen. GEORGE J. KEEGAN and Air Force Intelligence). (See CIA, "The Soviet Estimates.")

Some critics, such as former DDI Dr. Ray S. Cline, see the separation of the NIE mechanism from the CIA Intelligence Directorate as a step in the wrong direction. Cline writes,

> The estimates unit, whatever its name, can be better staffed and is less likely to become isolated [and] rigid in its views, if it is an integral part of the CIA analytical services. It would also be more likely, in my view, to be protected from White House political pressure.

The NIE mechanism, wherever it is located, continues to produce only draft estimates. The National Foreign Intelligence Board, successor to the USIB, continues to negotiate the final language of the NIE and approve it. In this regard it is worth noting that when the USIB was reconstituted as the NFIB in 1977, the deputy director of central intelligence was given a seat. Thus it may be said that the CIA, in the persons of the DCI and the DDCI, has a greater weight than other intelligence agencies in the final approval of NIEs, although its role in drafting them has been reduced.

(Ransom, *The Intelligence Establishment*; Karalekas, *History of the Central Intelligence Agency*; Breckinridge, *The CIA and the U.S. Intelligence System*; Cline, *The CIA, Reality vs. Myth*; Richelson, *The U.S. Intelligence Community*; Colby and Forbath, *Honorable Men*; Turner, *Secrecy and Democracy*; Prados, *The Soviet Estimate*.)

NATIONAL INTELLIGENCE PROGRAMS EVALUATION (NIPE)

The NIPE office was established in 1963 by JOHN A. MCCONE, then director of central intelligence, for the purpose of assisting the DCI in his role as chief of the INTELLIGENCE COMMUNITY. It had three major responsibilities: reviewing and evaluating intelligence community programs; compiling a list of all U.S. intelligence activities for the purpose of analyzing their relative costs and effectiveness; and evaluating the results of actions taken by the U.S. Intelligence Board (see NATIONAL FOREIGN INTELLIGENCE BOARD) to achieve American intelligence objectives.

Veteran intelligence officer JOHN A. BROSS was made head of the NIPE office, a post he held until his retirement in 1971. In 1972 the NIPE office was replaced by the INTELLIGENCE COMMUNITY STAFF.

(Cline, *CIA, Reality vs. Myth*; Karalekas, *History of the Central Intelligence Agency*.)

NATIONAL PHOTOGRAPHIC INTERPRETATION CENTER (NPIC)

NPIC, which is housed in the old Naval Gun Factory in southwest Washington, D.C., is a centralized facility for photointerpretation and imagery analysis within the INTELLIGENCE COMMUNITY. The CIA runs it as a "service of common concern" (in the language of the NATIONAL SECURITY ACT of 1947, which established the CENTRAL INTELLIGENCE AGENCY and authorized it to provide such services).

NPIC was established in 1961 as a successor to the Photographic Intelligence Center, which had existed as a component of the CIA INTELLIGENCE DIRECTORATE since 1958. Directed by ARTHUR LUNDAHL, NPIC worked closely with intelligence components of the Department of Defense in gleaning intelligence from photographs made by reconnaissance aircraft and satellites.

NPIC was a subordinate unit of the CIAs Intelligence Directorate until the mid-1970s, when CIA Director WILLIAM COLBY brought it under the aegis of the CIA's SCIENCE AND TECHNOLOGY DIRECTORATE.

(Prados, *The Soviet Estimate*; Klass, *Secret Sentries in Space*; Cline, *CIA, Reality vs. Myth*.)

NATIONAL RECONNAISSANCE OFFICE

Reportedly, the U.S. government does not publicly acknowledge the existence of a government agency known as "the National Reconnaissance Office," but references to and discussions of such an agency have appeared in a variety of newspapers, magazines, and books, some of which are generally reliable. The information contained in this entry, and references to the National Reconnaissance Office appearing in other entries in this work, are based entirely on the published sources listed at the end of this entry.

The National Reconnaissance Office (NRO) is an agency of the Defense Department that was created in 1960 by President Eisenhower and the National Security Agency to manage the OVERHEAD RECONNAISSANCE and other reconnaissance operations of the U.S. INTELLIGENCE COMMUNITY. The NRO was initially placed under the under secretary of the Air Force, but later the National Reconnaissance Executive Committee (EXCOMM)—a panel composed of the director of central intelligence, the secretary of defense, and a representative of the White House—was created to supervise it. More recently, EXCOMM has reportedly been enlarged to include representatives of the Navy and other government agencies. By tradition, the director of the NRO usually is the under secretary of the Air Force. The first NRO director was Under Secretary JOSEPH V. CHARYK; since 1981 EDWARD C. ALDRIDGE has been Air Force under secretary and NRO director.

The NRO receives lists of intelligence targets agreed upon by the Committee on Imagery Requirements and Exploitation (COMIREX) and carries out the aircraft or satellite mission necessary to observe the targets and collect the required data. In the case of satellite missions, the NRO calculates the orbital parameters and related information and transmits it to the SATELLITE CONTROL FACILITY for use during the mission. In the case of reconnaissance aircraft or ship missions, the NRO produces a Joint Reconnaissance Schedule, which is submitted for national level approval.

An unofficial report published in 1974 stated that the annual budget of the NRO was then more than $1.5 billion. A 1985 newspaper report put the then current NRO budget at $2.5 billion. Still another recent estimate puts it in "the $3 to $4 billion range."

(*New York Times*, January 13, 1985, Section 6, pp. 39, 50, 52–54; October 20, 1985, Section 1, p. 19; Richelson, *The U.S. Intelligence Community*; Bamford, *The Puzzle Palace*; Prados, *The Soviet Estimate*; Marchetti and Marks, *The CIA and the Cult of Intelligence*.)

NATIONAL SECURITY ACT OF 1947

A law that, among other things, created the CENTRAL INTELLIGENCE AGENCY. The act established the Agency officially on September 18, 1947, put it under the direction of the National Security Council (also created by the Act), and defined the duties of the CIA and its director. It has been interpreted as giving the CIA legal authority to carry out COVERT ACTION. The act was signed into law by President Truman on July 26, 1947.

See CENTRAL INTELLIGENCE AGENCY.

NATIONAL SECURITY AGENCY

General: Officially described as "a separately organized agency within the Department of Defense," NSA is said to be "within but not a part of the Defense Department." Established by presidential order in 1952, the Agency has two principal func-

tions: conducting signals intelligence (SIGINT) operations and activities, and ensuring the communications security (COMSEC) of eighteen federal agencies involved in national security matters.

NSA headquarters is located at Fort Meade, Maryland, midway between Washington and Baltimore. In addition to the massive compound at Fort Meade, other elements of the headquarters are located nearby, adjacent to Baltimore's Friendship Airport.

The director of NSA (DIRNSA) reports to the secretary of defense and represents the Agency on the NATIONAL FOREIGN INTELLIGENCE BOARD. In addition to his role as head of NSA, he is simultaneously chief of the armed forces' Central Security Service, which supervises and directs the Service Cryptologic Agencies (SCAs), i.e., the cryptologic and signals intelligence components of the armed services.

Background: In 1949 Secretary of Defense Louis Johnson tried to consolidate most Defense Department strategic communications intelligence and communication security activities within a single new agency, the Armed Forces Security Agency (AFSA), under the Joint Chiefs of Staff (see ARMY INTELLIGENCE, NAVAL INTELLIGENCE). Johnson also established the Armed Forces Security Agency Council, a panel of officers from the three armed services, which in effect controlled the new agency. The United States Communications Intelligence Board—a body consisting of representatives of the intelligence components of the armed services, the State Department, and the FBI—worked with the Council to direct the COMINT activities of AFSA. This cumbersome management machinery defeated the original purpose of the AFSA, and the agency never achieved the intended consolidation.

The ineffectiveness of AFSA in meeting U.S. national communications intelligence requirements was highlighted by the failure of AFSA to produce COMINT forecasting the KOREAN WAR in June 1950 and the subsequent poor performance of the Agency during the war. These deficiencies prompted the Truman administration to appoint a committee in December 1951 under George A. Brownell—attorney, diplomat, and government official—to study the COMINT problem. The Brownell Committee recommended, inter alia, that AFSA be moved from the jurisdiction of the Joint Chiefs of Staff and placed directly under the secretary of defense. Strengthening the position of the director of AFSA and removing him from the interservice rivalries of the existing management mechanism would, the Committee said, eliminate the weaknesses and inefficiencies that had plagued AFSA.

President Truman accepted the Brownell Committee's plan and transformed it into a presidential directive dated October 24, 1952. The directive added one detail: it changed the name of the AFSA to the National Security Agency.

History: The directive that established NSA was classified, and the existence of the Agency remained classified information as well until 1957 when it was acknowledged in the *United States Government Organization Manual* with the terse statement that it is "an element of the Department of Defense" that "performs highly specialized technical and coordinating functions relating to the national security." NSA continued to maintain as low a profile as is possible for an agency that is several times the size—in staff, budget, and Washington headquarters physical plant—of the CIA. Its reticence was abetted by the nature of its activities, which are less potentially spectacular than covert action, are more remote from the controversy of the policymaking arena than finished national intelligence, and are beyond the technical literacy of most investigative journalists.

Although two of its employees, WILLIAM H. MARTIN and BERNON F. MITCHELL, defected to the Soviet Union in 1960, and others have sold highly classified COMINT data to Soviet intelligence, NSA has not been the subject of domestically published exposés by disaffected former employees. Former DIRNSAs and other Agency officials have not published their memoirs or cooperated with biographers. For these reasons, nothing approaching a comprehensive account of NSA since its creation has yet been published. However, some general outlines of the Agency's history are apparent from the several published studies listed at the end of this entry.

Size and Growth

One consistent thread in NSA's history has been its prodigious growth. In 1956 the Agency had nearly 9,000 employees. In 1967 Kahn estimated that there might be more than 12,500 NSA employees in Washington and at least an additional thousand stationed overseas. In 1985 Richelson estimated that the number of Washington employees was somewhere between 20,000 and 24,000. The NSA budget was reportedly in the neighborhood of half a billion dollars in 1960, and twice that in 1966. In 1985 Richelson reported various estimates of the figure as $1.2 billion, $3 billion, and $10 billion. Richelson further estimated that, when combined with the Central Security Service, i.e., the armed forces cryptologic activities controlled by the DIRNSA, the personnel figure is somewhere between 50,000 and 60,000, and the budget is in the $5 to $10 billion range. Whatever the precise figures, NSA is clearly the largest member agency of the INTELLIGENCE COMMUNITY. (NSA's

growth as an organization has been matched by the growth of its now truly enormous headquarters complex at and around Fort Meade, Maryland.)

Along with the burgeoning of its bureaucratic bulk, there has been an attendant growth in the scope of NSA's SIGINT coverage and the volume of its intelligence product. This growth, in turn, has been driven by the increasing use, worldwide, of microwave telecommunications, telemetry, radar, and other signal-emitting equipment by foreign governments and armed services, and the Agency's increasing technical capability to intercept and process such signals. During the 1950s NSA began constructing a network of intercept stations in West Germany, Japan, South Korea, Turkey, and other sites around the periphery of the USSR and Communist China, as well as in Hawaii, Okinawa, and the continental United States. In addition to eavesdropping on foreign radio and telecommunications, these stations intercept the electronic emissions of radars and aircraft, missile telemetry, communications from Soviet spacecraft, and a large variety of other sources of electromagnetic signals. (It is reported that in the early 1970s NSA managed to intercept the radio-telephone conversations of senior Soviet officials traveling around Moscow in their limousines.) The Agency has continued to enlarge this network, which collects signals intelligence on a virtually unlimited spectrum of targets ranging from the Soviet strategic missile program to the economies of Third World countries.

SIGINT Platforms

To its network of ground intercept stations, NSA has added a large number of supplementary SIGINT platforms in the air and on (and under) the sea. These airborne and seaborne platforms are in continuous operation along the borders of DENIED AREAS and other locations of major intelligence interest, and occasionally come to public notice as the result of hostile foreign action or other misadventure (see EC-121 INCIDENT, LIBERTY INCIDENT, PUEBLO INCIDENT, and RB-47 INCIDENT).

In addition to ships and aircraft, satellites such as the RHYOLITE RECONNAISSANCE SATELLITE and the CHALET RECONNAISSANCE SATELLITE collect SIGINT for NSA, and SIGINT collection packages are also sent into orbit aboard photoreconnaissance satellites such as the KH-11 RECONNAISSANCE SATELLITE.

A Civilian Agency

Another trend has been the increasingly civilian character of NSA. Although the Agency was established as a civilian component of the Department of Defense in 1952, it was then, in the words of one senior Army officer, "about 99 percent military," but by 1971, the officer estimated, fewer than five percent of the two thousand most senior positions in the Agency were filled by military personnel. Although the DIRNSA is always a senior military officer, the day-to-day management of NSA is the job of the deputy director (D/DIRNSA), and since 1956 that post has been held by a civilian. One D/DIRNSA, Dr. LOUIS W. TORDELLA, held the post for sixteen years (1958–74), spanning the tours of the five generals and two admirals who served as DIRNSAs during the same period. The DIRNSA is usually a senior officer with little or no specific background in COMINT or COMSEC, but the D/DIRNSA is typically a professional cryptologist who has risen through the civilian ranks of NSA.

The increasingly civilian character of NSA is the result of yet another historical trend, the increasing use of high technology in the Agency's operations and the consequent reliance upon the civilian scientific manpower pool to staff the Agency. Computer processing is so important to modern cryptanalysis that NSA has often been the driving force in advancing the state of the art in such technologies as multicomputer processing, teleprocessing, mass data storage, and advanced computer programming techniques. Mathematics, physics, electrical engineering, signal processing, and telecommunications are some of the other disciplines essential to the functions of NSA, and the Agency has often had to pioneer in these fields to meet its needs, rather than simply to procure and apply available "off the shelf" equipment or techniques. Thus NSA has come to be almost as much a center of science and technology as it is an intelligence agency.

The Private Sector

NSA sharpens its technological edge through continuous contact with the American scientific community. The NSA Scientific Advisory Board is a panel of experts from industry and academia that seeks to ensure that NSA is aware of the latest scientific and technical developments potentially of use to the Agency's mission. Under contract to NSA, the Communications Research Division of the Institute for Defense Analysis, a private think tank, draws upon some of American's most outstanding mathematicians and scientists to conduct research in cryptology and other fields of interest to NSA. And the Agency's technical proficiency is further nourished by the migration to and from its employment of scientists and engineers from the private sector.

In recent years NSA's relations with the private scientific sector have taken on an added dimension. With the "microchip revolution" that has made computers and other electronic information processing devices ubiquitous throughout the industrialized world, especially in such privacy-sensitive areas as banking and commerce, there has been an unprecedented demand in the private sector for equipment and techniques to secure communications and data. Since in this sphere the private sector utilizes the same national pool of talent and know-how that the Agency relies upon, and since private know-how cannot readily be made subject to export controls, NSA may soon be faced with foreign communications security measures quite as advanced as its own communications intelligence methods. Several skirmishes with private inventors and researchers in recent years do not yet seem to have defined clearly the NSA's legal authority over this perplexing problem.

On the other hand, NSA's own COMSEC role has lately been enlarged in order to assist private data banks—whether or not they may contain classified data—in protecting against unauthorized access. The Agency's Computer Security Technical Evaluation Center cooperates with private organizations by evaluating upon request their safeguards against such attacks. Bamford speculates that the Center may be intended to serve the additional purpose of encouraging the private sector to share its security innovations with the Agency.

Organization: There are three major components of NSA: the Office of Signals Intelligence Operations, the Office of Research and Engineering, and the Office of Communications Security.

Formerly known as the Office of Production, the Office of Signals Intelligence Operations performs the entire spectrum of signals intelligence, from intercept to cryptanalysis, traffic analysis, and analysis of unencrypted intercepts. The office is composed of three geographically oriented intelligence production groups: A Group, responsible for the Soviet Union and the Soviet bloc; B Group, responsible for China, Korea, Vietnam, and the rest of Communist Asia; and G Group, responsible for all other countries.

The Office of Communications Security—also known as "the S Organization"—implements COMSEC policy set forth by the NATIONAL SECURITY COUNCIL's U.S. Communications Security Committee. The Office produces the cryptographic equipment and establishes the communications security procedures for eighteen federal agencies involved in national security matters, including the Central Intelligence Agency, Department of Defense, Department of State, and the Federal Bureau of Investigation.

The Office of Research and Engineering is responsible for developing the equipment and techniques for signal interception, cryptanalysis, and secure communications. The Office's Mathematical Research Techniques Division applies mathematics to cryptanalysis. The Intercept Equipment Division develops SIGINT sensor devices. And the Cryptographic Equipment Division develops the encryption devices that are produced by the Office of Communications Security.

Other NSA Components

In addition to these three principal suborganizations, there is the Office of Telecommunications and Computer Services, a support unit; the Office of Installations and Logistics, which is responsible for NSA installations worldwide; and the Office of Administration. The Office of Plans and Policy serves as the DIRNSA's staff.

NSA's Office of Programs and Resources is the means by which the DIRNSA manages the Central Security Service (CSS) and the Consolidated Cryptologic Program. These constitute the mechanism by which the director supervises and directs the Service Cryptologic Agencies—the signals intelligence components of the Army Intelligence and Security Command, the Air Force Electronic Security Command, and the Navy Security Group Command—which operate NSA's worldwide network of intercept stations and platforms.

(Bamford, *The Puzzle Palace*; Kahn, *The Codebreakers*; Richelson, *The U.S. Intelligence Community*.)

NATIONAL SECURITY COUNCIL

A part of the Executive Office of the President of the United States, the NSC was established by the National Security Act of 1947 "to advise the President with respect to the integration of domestic, foreign and military policies relating to the national security so as to enable the military services and other departments and agencies of the Government to cooperate more effectively in matters involving the national security." A publication of the Central Intelligence Agency says, "The NSC is the highest Executive Branch entity providing review of, guidance for, and direction to the conduct of all national foreign intelligence and counterintelligence activities."

By law, the NSC consists of the President, the vice-president, the secretary of state, and the secretary of defense. The director of central intelligence (DCI) and the chairman of the Joint Chiefs of Staff participate in the NSC as advisors. The assistant to the President for national security affairs, the secretary

of the treasury, and the director of the Office of Management and Budget are also regular participants in NSC meetings, and other government officials may be present by invitation.

The NSC staff consists of several dozen people from various civilian agencies of the government, the armed services, and some individuals on leave from colleges, universities, and private institutions having a national security role. It is headed by the assistant to the President for national security affairs.

President Reagan established the Senior Interagency Group (SIG) as a committee of the NSC to advise and assist the NSC. The SIG is made up of the DCI, the assistant to the President for national security affairs, the deputy secretary of state, the deputy secretary of defense, the chairman of the Joint Chiefs of Staff, the deputy attorney general, the director of the Federal Bureau of Investigation, and the director of the National Security Agency. The chairmanship of this panel depends upon the substance of its agenda, e.g., when it meets to consider intelligence policy and activities it becomes the SIG (Intelligence) and is chaired by the DCI. The SIG (Intelligence) ensures the coordination of important intelligence policy issues requiring interagency attention, and monitors the execution of previously approved policies and decisions. Individual intelligence policy issues are handled by a corresponding Interagency Group (IG). The IGs were established to assist the SIG (Intelligence).

President Reagan also created the Special Situations Group (SSG) under the vice-president to deal with national security crises. The SSG is supported by the Crisis Pre-Planning Group, a working level group within the NSC staff and headed by the deputy to the assistant to the president for national security affairs.

Because the NSC is part of the Executive Office of the President, it has traditionally been regarded as not subject to congressional oversight. For this reason President Reagan and other presidents have occasionally employed the NSC staff in tasks and missions that lie outside the advisory activities of the NSC to avoid the risk of public disclosure that could result from their execution by other agencies of the government.

(Breckinridge, *The CIA and the U.S. Intelligence System*; Central Intelligence Agency, *Intelligence, The Acme of Skill, Fact Book on Intelligence*; New York Times, November 11, 1986, p. A10.)

NATIONAL SECURITY COUNCIL INTELLIGENCE DIRECTIVE (NSCID)

NSCIDs (pronounced "en-skids") are executive orders issued by the NATIONAL SECURITY COUN-

CIL with the authority of the President of the United States, which define and specify the scope, functions, authority, and responsibility of such agencies as the Central Intelligence Agency and the National Security Agency. NSCIDs are often augmented by DCIDs (director of central intelligence directive), which make more specific the policies and procedures prescribed in a NSCID.

NSCIDs and DCIDs are classified and not available to the public.

(Karalekas, *History of the Central Intelligence Agency*.)

NATSIOS, NICHOLAS ANDREW (July 31, 1920–): intelligence officer

A native of Lowell, Massachusetts, Natsios attended Lowell Technology Institute during 1939–40. He served in the U.S. Army during 1943–47, during which period he was assigned to the Office of Strategic Services. He served with the OSS in Italy and was commanding officer of the U.S. Occupation Forces in Milan, Italy, during 1945–47. He was discharged with the rank of captain. In 1948 he graduated from Ohio State University.

Natsios served with the Central Intelligence Agency as an officer of the CIA CLANDESTINE SERVICE. He served with the CIA in Greece from 1948 until 1956 when he became chief of the CIA's Saigon station. He was chief of station in Vietnam until 1960, when he was succeeded by WILLIAM E. COLBY. He was subsequently CIA chief of station in Paris (1960–62), Seoul, Korea (1962–65), Argentina (1965–69), the Netherlands (1969–72), and Iran (1972–74).

After his retirement from the CIA Natsios was a management consultant and a member of the faculty of the Fletcher Graduate School of Law and Diplomacy. He holds the Distinguished Service Medal, the Medal of Merit, the Bronze Star, and several foreign decorations.

(*Who's Who in America*, 42nd ed.; Powers, *The Man Who Kept the Secrets*; Colby *Honorable Men*.)

NAVAL INTELLIGENCE

Early History: Information about foreign and enemy naval matters has been important to national security since the earliest days of the Republic. Because the Royal Navy's control of American coastal waters during the AMERICAN REVOLUTION gave the British ground forces the advantage of superior mobility, much of Gen. GEORGE WASHINGTON's intelligence service was concerned with the movements of the British fleet. The theft of the Royal Navy's signal code by Washington's secret agent

JAMES RIVINGTON may have been an important factor in the events leading to the climactic American victory at Yorktown in 1781. And secret agents in European and West Indian seaports provided intelligence necessary to American privateering and arms-smuggling.

Intelligence regarding the Royal Navy was crucial to U.S. Naval operations aimed at lifting the British blockade of the Eastern Seaboard during the WAR OF 1812. Even in the Mexican War, which was fought almost entirely on land, intelligence collected by a naval surgeon, Dr. William Maxwell Wood, while on an espionage mission in Mexico just prior to the war, proved useful to the U.S. Army after the outbreak of hostilities.

During the Civil War the U.S. Navy established the Commission of Conference, a temporary advisory board that collected information to assist Secretary of the Navy Gideon Wells in planning war operations. Most of the work of Confederate secret service officer JAMES D. BULLOCH in Europe during the Civil War involved obtaining warships for the Confederate Navy, and therefore much of the activity of HENRY S. SANFORD, chief of the Union secret service in Europe, was directed toward frustrating his efforts. And the U.S. Navy required intelligence of Confederate fortifications to carry out its coastal and river operations at home; SPENCER K. BROWN, a seaman from the U.S.S. *Essex*, was hanged by the Confederates for gathering such information about fortifications on the Mississippi in Kentucky.

Despite this long tradition of intelligence activity, the U.S. Navy did not begin any systematic intelligence collection until the late 1860s. Early collection activities focused on hydrographic and other basic intelligence of Latin America and the Pacific regions, and technical intelligence on advances in naval warfare by the European sea powers.

Naval technology advanced rapidly in the decades following the Civil War. Europe was making progress in steam power, armored warships, breech-loading guns, long-range rifled artillery, and other areas while the U.S. Navy marked time with a fleet of obsolete, decaying hulks left over from the war. In 1873 a group of American naval officers founded the U.S. Naval Institute, a semi-official organization dedicated to the study of naval matters, especially the new naval technology. In the absence of a general staff within the U.S. Navy, the Institute was the only organized body that concerned itself with, among other things, naval intelligence.

The Office of Naval Intelligence

The War of the Pacific (1879–82) between Chile, on one side, and Bolivia and Peru on the other, was fought with modern warships built in European ship-yards, and thus brought modern naval warfare to the western hemisphere. The demonstrated fact that Chile now possessed a fleet superior to that of the United States, and the prospect of European inter-vention in Latin American affairs, prompted the U.S. Congress to authorize the modernization and expan-sion of the Navy. In March 1882, as part of the New Navy program, the Office of Intelligence—or, as it shortly became known, the Office of Naval Intelli-gence (ONI)—was established within the Navy's Bu-reau of Navigation.

The first chief of ONI was Lt. Theodorus Bailey Myers Mason, an active member of the Naval Insti-tute, and an officer who had already spent much time abroad studying the navies of Europe. His staff consisted of more than a dozen young naval officers. Mason was directed to collect and compile informa-tion on fourteen categories of naval intelligence, ranging from descriptions of foreign warships to data on coastal defenses.

The Bureau of Navigation ordered that each naval commander appoint a shipboard intelligence officer to gather information while in foreign ports and report it to ONI. By 1887 several ships were equipped with cameras and complete photographic outfits to photograph such objects of intelligence interest as foreign coastal defense batteries. The State Depart-ment furnished consular reports on foreign ports, trade, and merchant shipping.

Naval attachés at American embassies in Europe comprised a major source of information on advances in naval technology. Naval officers had been sent to Europe as roving attachés to study such matters as developments in ordnance from the beginning of the Franco-Prussian War in 1870. The first naval attaché to serve under the auspices of ONI was Lt. Comdr. FRENCH ENSOR CHADWICK who was sent to Lon-don in 1882 to serve as a sort of attaché-at-large in Britain and Europe. Chadwick, a scholarly officer who had already spent time in Europe gathering information for the Navy, proved to be an assiduous student of all things nautical and the source of a copious flow of books, journals, blueprints, reports and every other form of information on European naval matters. After a few years he was joined by Lts. BENJAMIN H. BUCKINGHAM and Nathan Sar-gent, who were sent to Europe to help Chadwick cover his beat, which stretched as far east as St. Petersburg, and as far south as Italy.

It should be noted that the term *intelligence*, as used in the United States in the nineteenth century, denoted information-in-general, rather than the nar-rower sense of "information useful in dealing with an adversary" it acquired later (see INTELLIGENCE).

Thus one task of ONI—perhaps the major one—during the first decade or so of its existence was "technology transfer," i.e., procuring information on the state of the art of naval warfare to be used by the Navy as it pursued its program of expansion and modernization. Secondarily, ONI was expected to promote that program by disseminating news of Eu-ropean naval progress to officers, congressmen, and the general public.

War Planning

Intelligence in the modern sense of the word re-ceived greater emphasis in the 1890s as the Navy began to engage in war-gaming and war planning. These activities were the province of the Naval War College, which had been established in 1884 at New-port, Rhode Island, as part of the naval revitalization program. The purpose of the College was to train seasoned naval officers in advanced strategy and tactics within the context of the new naval technol-ogy. Naval history, which had been the principal study at the College during its first years, proved to be of limited use in the study of modern naval war-fare—so great were the differences in parameters between the age of steam and the age of fighting sail. Naval war-gaming was introduced into the College's curriculum by Lt. William McCarty Little in 1887. Beginning in 1894 war-gaming and planning became the chief activity at the College, and each new class was assigned a major strategic problem, e.g., war between the United States and Great Britain.

These problems were more than pure academic exercise; in the absence of a general staff, the College represented the only permanently established war-planning activity in the Navy. The exercises were done in earnest; the scenarios selected were based upon contingencies that appeared likely in light of U.S. foreign relations of the day, and the College worked closely with ONI to insure that the gaming and planning incorporated the most up-to-date and accurate information on the foreign fleets involved. As a result intelligence in the modern sense of the word came into sharp focus, and ONI began to work toward some very specific intelligence-collection re-quirements.

Lt. Comdr. RICHARD WAINWRIGHT, chief of ONI during 1896–97, emphasized war planning as a joint ONI-Naval War College activity. One of the earliest joint planning exercises conducted at the College under his auspices was addressed to a war between the United States and Spain over the Span-ish colony of Cuba. In 1896 Lt. WILLIAM W. KIM-BALL, an ONI officer on detached duty at the Col-lege, worked out a comprehensive Spanish war plan designed to "liberate Cuba from Spanish rule." This plan led to successive versions worked out by the War College staff and an ad hoc Navy Department board; the refined plan was adopted as the Navy's official plan as the likelihood of war with Spain increased in mid-1897, and was, in fact, used when the SPANISH-AMERICAN WAR commenced in April 1898.

The Spanish-American War

Until 1898 ONI had generally restricted its collection activities to the abundant material available in open publications and information voluntarily furnished by host nations to American naval attachés abroad. But the Spanish-American War marked the first time ONI embarked on secret intelligence-collection operations.

Two young ensigns, William H. Buck and Harry H. Ward, were sent to Europe posing as wealthy tourists. They cruised aboard yachts in the Atlantic and Mediterranean to watch for Spanish fleet movements. The naval attaché in Berlin sent Edward Breck, a young naval officer who had attended Heidelberg University, to Spain posing as a German physician on vacation. But the most extensive secret intelligence operations were run by Lts. WILLIAM S. SIMS and John C. Colwell, the naval attachés in Paris and London, respectively. Sims and Colwell ran networks of paid agents extending from the Canary Islands to Port Said and even reaching into the Spanish naval base at Cadiz and the Spanish embassy in London. In addition to these collection activities, the two attachés used their agents for strategic deception, i.e., planting disinformation with Spanish agents to mislead Madrid regarding American plans.

The ONI's performance in the war, and the public enthusiasm over the Navy's role in the American victory over Spain, prompted Congress to establish ONI by law as a formal part of the Bureau of Navigation in 1899. Previously it had existed only as the creature of an executive order of the secretary of the Navy. The legislation gave ONI a new permanence and a larger claim on the Navy budget. Armed with this increased support, ONI chief Lt. Comdr. RICHARDSON CLOVER was able to establish a permanent civilian staff, and to reorganize the Office into six divisions charged with the specific subject areas of ordnance, personnel, communications, steam engineering, ship card indexing, and attaché correspondence.

In March 1900 the secretary of the Navy established the General Board, an advisory panel that provided a mechanism for the coordination of Navy policy and planning, though it lacked the management functions of a true general staff. The Board consisted of eleven officers, including the president of the Naval War College and the chief of ONI, and so provided an efficient medium for the development, adoption, and promulgation of naval war plans.

Germany and Japan

The expansion of ONI came at a time when the United States found itself abruptly thrust into the role of a world naval power, with overseas territories in the Caribbean and the Pacific. With this role came new adversarial relationships with other large naval powers, especially Germany and Japan, both of which had colonial aspirations in Asia, the Pacific, and Latin America, and were thus competitors with the United States in those areas.

Germany was the special concern of Capt. CHARLES D. SIGSBEE, who served as chief of ONI during 1900–03. He reflected the views of many other American navalists of the period—e.g., Alfred T. Mahan and Theodore Roosevelt—in the light of German-American confrontations in Samoa in 1889 and the Philippines in 1898, Germany's use of force against Haiti in 1897 and Venezuela in 1902, the Kaiser's undisguised aspirations for overseas colonies and naval bases, and the rapid expansion of the German navy. Sigsbee's concern extended to the activities of German agents and naval attachés in the United States and the large number of German-Americans serving as enlisted men in the U.S. Navy; he emphasized counterintelligence as much as positive collection in response to the perceived German naval threat.

Japan's victorious emergence from the Russo-Japanese War in 1905 as a major naval power with dominion over Korea and part of China temporarily overshadowed the German threat in the minds of American navalists. American possessions in the Pacific, especially the Philippines, seemed a potential bone of contention as Japan pushed ahead with her plans for territorial expansion in the Far East. Japan became the principal intelligence-collection target of ONI. The Navy assigned officers to Japan to learn the language, which presented an unusually difficult obstacle to the analysis and evaluation of the Japanese material that was being collected. Some war planning for a Japanese-American conflict was begun in 1906 and stepped up during the Japanese war scare in 1907–08. Reports that Japan had secretly leased Magdalena Bay, on the Pacific coast of Baja California, from Mexico to use as a naval base, and the unstable political situation in Mexico, prompted ONI to make a secret reconnaissance of seaports on the eastern coast of Mexico. By 1912 ONI had completed War Plan Orange, a detailed plan for an all-out war with Japan.

Japan did not completely eclipse Germany as an object of ONI interest during this period. The construction of the Panama Canal, begun in 1904 and completed in 1914, focused attention on Central America and the Caribbean, where Germany was still regarded as the principal naval threat. Collection of intelligence on German naval progress continued and War Plan Black, the detailed scenario for a war with Germany, was begun in 1911.

First World War

The advent of the FIRST WORLD WAR introduced new functions to ONI: domestic counterintelligence and countersubversion. During the two-and-a-half years prior to American entry into the war, German agents carried on an elaborate program of sabotage and political warfare within the United States, ranging from economic operations aimed at fomenting labor unrest in factories supplying munitions to the Allies (see FRANZ VON PAPEN) to the massive BLACK TOM EXPLOSION in New York Harbor. In response ONI organized a force of counterintelligence officers known as "Aids for Information." The Aids were assigned to the various Naval Districts within the United States, where they collaborated with such other official and semiofficial countersubversion agencies as the SECRET SERVICE, the Justice Department, the Military Intelligence Division (see ARMY INTELLIGENCE), and the AMERICAN PROTECTIVE LEAGUE to establish networks of local informants in ports, shipyards, and factories doing business with the Navy.

The ONI was also concerned with reports of German penetration of Latin America and the Caribbean. Rumors of secret German submarine bases and wireless stations in Mexico and elsewhere in the region prompted ONI to increase its surveillance of these areas. Large American companies operating in Latin American—e.g., Wells Fargo, Standard Oil, American Tobacco, and United Fruit—agreed to collect intelligence for the Navy through their corporate resources.

As part of the preparedness movement occurring within the American military establishment during the first years of the war, the Navy created the position of chief of naval operations. The CNO and his staff were responsible for operation of the fleet and the preparation of war plans (although they lacked the authority of a true Navy general staff). ONI was transferred from the Bureau of Navigation to the new Office of Operations. A War Plans Division was also established under the CNO.

With American entry into the war in April 1917 ONI was forced to grow explosively to keep pace with the new demands for intelligence. Director of Naval Intelligence Capt. Roger Welles turned to volunteers and naval reservists to fill vacancies. Most of the domestic counterintelligence slots were filled by such recruits, who usually lacked experience in either naval procedures or intelligence operations, and consequently ONI's domestic surveillance activity was often marked by overzealousness, amateurism, and abuses of civil rights. Individuals came under suspicion and were even dismissed from their jobs for simply looking or speaking like Germans or for somehow being associated with Germans. Soon the circle of suspicion grew to include pacifists, Jews, those involved in organized labor or radical politics, and others representing unfamiliar backgrounds or viewpoints.

Positive naval intelligence collection in Europe during 1917–18 by ONI was relatively meager. As the belligerent nations tightened internal security during the first years of the war, ONI's naval attaché network in Europe became much less effective as a means of collection. As latecomers to the war, the attachés were unable to organize much in the way of effective secret intelligence networks during the year-and-a-half of American involvement, and therefore were forced to rely upon their counterparts in the Allied intelligence services.

The American naval officer in most need of good positive intelligence was Vice Adm. William S. Sims, commander of all U.S. naval forces in Europe. The Navy's contribution to the war consisted—aside from a battleship division serving with the British Grand Fleet—in convoy-escort, minelaying, and antisubmarine duty. Sims, who had become very familiar with intelligence work during the Spanish-American war, established an effective intelligence unit within the staff of his headquarters in London. Under Sims's aide and personal friend, Comdr. John V. Babcock, the unit expanded and became, in effect, a second ONI, collaborating closely with British naval intelligence.

ONI's wartime positive collection activities were much more ambitious elsewhere in the world. In Latin America and the Far East the agency established elaborate networks of paid agents and informers. ONI agents traveled through Mexico, Guatemala, and South America disguised as agricultural surveyors, miners, and lumbermen, in search of suspected German submarine bases and wireless stations. The naval attaché in Havana organized an agent network in Cuba and frustrated German intelligence operations on the island. ONI also investigated the continuing reports of Japanese activity in the western hemisphere (see SIDNEY F. MASHBIR). A buyer for Bonwit Teller & Company, the curator of mammals of the American Museum of Natural History, and other Americans traveling in East Asia reported on Japanese activities in the region, while the naval attachés in Tokyo and Peking attempted to set up indigenous agent networks.

Naval Intelligence Between the World Wars

Postwar demobilization caused an abrupt shrinkage of ONI; the Washington office alone had numbered 306 officers as of November 1918, but it shrank to forty-two within eight months. Sharp cuts in the budget forced ONI to dissolve much of the overseas secret intelligence apparatus it had constructed during the war. The Five-Power Naval Treaty of 1922, by which the United States, Britain, France, Japan, and Italy agreed to limit the size of their navies, created a climate of complacency in the United States public and government regarding foreign naval threats and the importance of a strong U.S. Navy. And ONI, the principal means of verifying foreign compliance with the treaty, continued to suffer from the same general state of neglect afflicting the Navy as a whole.

Despite this adverse climate, ONI continued to focus its limited resources on Japan, which was still regarded as the principal threat to American interests in the western hemisphere and the Pacific. Japan had taken advantage of the First World War to seize the German-owned Caroline, Marshall, and Mariana island chains and retained them after the war as League of Nations mandates. Standing astride the American route to the Philippines, the Japanese mandates were of great strategic value in the Pacific, and ONI established as a major intelligence requirement information on the extent of Japanese naval bases and airstrips. For their part, the Japanese resisted all American attempts to obtain this information and instituted the strictest secrecy regarding their development of the islands. The possible fortification of these islands, Japan's designs on China, and a growing Japanese militarism made Japan ONI's primary foreign intelligence target. American anxiety increased further after Japan's invasion of Manchuria in 1931.

ONI stepped up its naval attaché program in Japan, assigning such officers as ELLIS ZACHARIAS, EDWIN LAYTON, and JOSEPH ROCHEFORT to Tokyo where they became fluent in Japanese, learned about the country, and collected as much information as possible on Japanese naval and military matters. However, efforts to establish indigenous secret intelligence networks in Japan met with little success (see, for example, SIDNEY F. MASHBIR).

Communications intelligence proved a more profitable source on Japanese naval matters. Radio intercepts and cryptanalysis were the province of the Code and Signal Section, which was part of the Navy's Office of Naval Communications (ONC was a unit of the Office of the Chief of Naval Operations). In January 1924 Lt. Laurance F. Safford was ordered to establish the Research Desk, a radio intelligence unit within the Section. By 1926 ONC had radio intercept stations on Guam, in the Philippines, and at Shanghai. Mobile intercept platforms were installed on the destroyer U.S.S. *McCormick* and later the cruiser U.S.S. *Marblehead*. Both ships cruised the western Pacific in 1927–28, intercepting Japanese radio traffic and monitoring Japanese naval maneuvers.

Breaking the Japanese code and cipher systems was a major objective of the Code and Signal Section. It received a head start in 1920 when an ONI team broke into a Japanese consulate in the United States and photographed the fleet code then in use by the Japanese navy. Subsequent break-ins during the next several years at Japanese government offices in New York City yielded photocopies of the No. 1 Imperial Japanese Secret Code, as well as a wealth of technical details on Japanese warships, aircraft, and ordnance. These materials greatly aided the cryptanalysts of the Code and Signal Section in understanding the underlying principles of Japanese naval cryptography. By 1926 the Navy code-breakers were able to read some of the intercepted Japanese ciphered radio messages. By 1930 their ability had increased to the point that they reaped a rich naval intelligence harvest by eavesdropping on the Japanese grand fleet maneuvers held that year.

The disclosure by HERBERT O. YARDLEY in 1931 of American success in breaking Japanese codes and ciphers impelled the Japanese to modify and improve their cryptosystems. This proved to be only a temporary setback, however, for the Code and Signal Section—now designated Op-20-G (i.e., the G section of Op-20, which was the Office of Naval Communications, the twentieth division of the Office of the Chief of Naval Operations; by the same nomenclature the War Plans Division was Op-12 and ONI was Op-16)—had become increasingly capable, and continued to solve Japanese codes and ciphers during the 1930s and throughout the SECOND WORLD WAR. These successes were the reward of the Navy's long-term program, begun in 1922, to develop a cadre of specialists in Japanese language, military and naval affairs, and cryptosystems. Rochefort, Layton, and Zacharias were only three of sixty-six Navy and Marine Corps officers who went through this program, which included a three-year stint in Tokyo to learn the language, and subsequent tours with ONI and the Office of Naval Communications.

Communications intelligence was the major source of information on Japan during the 1930s, a fact that prompted an ONI attempt to acquire the Op-20-G unit from ONC in 1930. This bureaucratic tug-of-war disrupted the flow of the COMINT product from ONC to ONI until the dispute was settled—in ONC's favor—in 1933. Despite this three-year gap, ONI and the War Plans Division continued to update War Plan Orange, the detailed plan for a war with Japan that it had first issued in 1912. The plan received a major overhaul in 1931–32 to reflect such new circumstances as the erosion of U.S. naval superiority in the Pacific as a result of the London Naval Treaty of 1930, which limited the size and number of American warships, and the Japanese invasion of Manchuria in 1931.

ONI did not completely ignore Europe, of course, and its attention was increasingly directed to that area with the growth of Nazism and Fascism during the 1930s. Capt. ROSCOE H. HILLENKOETTER, the naval attaché in Paris, was given the additional job of diplomatic courier for the State Department, a task that required extensive travel in Europe and thereby provided opportunities to observe military and naval developments. Yet another job, assistant naval attaché in Madrid and Lisbon, gave him a chance to observe the civil war in Spain.

A naval attaché was briefly assigned to the American legation in Moscow after diplomatic relations were established with the USSR in 1933, but the Soviet secretiveness proved so unrelenting that virtually no useful intelligence could be obtained, and the attaché's office was closed in 1935. SAMUEL B. FRANKEL and two other junior lieutenants were sent on a two-year assignment to study the Russian language in Latvia in 1936. They also collected intelligence on the Soviet Union until the State Department protested to ONI about their activities. ONI's files on the Soviet Union remained skimpy.

ONI continued to take an interest in Latin America between the wars. Early in the 1920s Mexico, still in the throes of political unrest, was an object of special interest. So seriously did ONI take the potential for south-of-the-border trouble that War Plan Green, a plan for war with Mexico, was frequently updated. Of course, Central America, with the vital Panama Canal and Nicaragua, where the U.S. had intervened, remained another major focus of attention. Naval attachés were assigned to the large U.S. naval missions to Peru and Brazil. ONI interest in Latin America sharply increased in 1938 upon evidence of

Japanese and German espionage and subversion in the region, and naval attaché offices were established in every major Latin America capital.

Domestic counterintelligence and countersubversion received due ONI attention after the First World War. Japanese agents replaced Germans as the principal objects of interest, but, like Army Intelligence, ONI also maintained surveillance on Communists, pacifists, labor leaders, civil-rights advocates, and others outside the American ideological mainstream, lumping all of them pretty much together. Counterintelligence was administered through a system of district intelligence officers, each of whom reported to his respective naval district commandant, as well as acting under the general management and control of ONI. Many of the DIOs accepted the enthusiastic volunteer assistance of the same sort of private vigilante groups that had worked with ONI and other government security agencies during the war. Once again amateurism gave rise to abuses.

Second World War

For naval intelligence, the period of 1939–41, between the advent of the Second World War in Europe and American entry into the war, was marked by bureaucratic squabbling over jurisdiction among ONI, ONC, and the War Plans Division. Adm. Richmond K. Turner, director of the War Plans Division, succeeded in wresting from ONI the responsibility for the production of all finished strategic intelligence, while Capt. Alan G. Kirk, director of ONI, was unable to recover any of the communications intelligence responsibilities his office had lost to ONC several years earlier. ONI's prestige was further damaged when it was forced to bear much of the Navy's share of blame for the PEARL HARBOR ATTACK.

The situation was aggravated shortly thereafter when Adm. Ernest J. King, named to the newly created post of commander and chief of the Navy (which combined the roles of chief of naval operations and commander-in-chief of the fleet), established an intelligence division within his staff, taking away even more of ONI's rapidly dwindling positive intelligence role. Left with little more than the tasks of negative intelligence, ONI was reduced almost completely to the role of a counterintelligence and security agency, a situation that persisted throughout most of the war. Even in the counterintelligence area ONI was not entirely free from jurisdictional conflicts. Its extensive attaché network in Latin American was strictly limited by the presidentially proclaimed primacy of the FEDERAL BUREAU OF INVESTIGATION's Special Intelligence Service in western hemisphere intelligence operations.

Although most of ONI's domestic counterintelligence and security work consisted of the routine of plant inspection, censorship, port and shipyard security, the organization occasionally rose to a special occasion, as it did in enlisting the help of Charles "Lucky" Luciano and several other Mafia leaders to secure the New York waterfront against Axis espionage and sabotage, and to obtain positive intelligence in support of the invasion of Sicily (Gov. Thomas E. Dewey commuted the sentences of Luciano and several of the other mafiosi and deported them to Italy as part of ONI's quid pro quo).

Communications intelligence continued to be of primary importance to the Navy. Op-20-G, the ONC's Code and Signal Section, was headed by Comdr. Laurence Safford, who had commanded the unit almost continuously since its establishment in 1924. The Section had expanded and now consisted of three subsections: GX, which conducted interception and direction-finding; GY, which did the cryptanalysis; and GZ, which translated and disseminated the intercepts. Op-20-G worked closely with Col. WILLIAM F. FRIEDMAN's Signal Intelligence Service (see ARMY INTELLIGENCE), sharing intercepted material and dividing up cryptanalysis duties to prevent a duplication of effort. By December 1941 the two units were processing Japanese diplomatic traffic on an alternate day basis and disseminating the MAGIC intelligence to the White House and other selected senior officials. During the war Op-20-G and SIS operated under a gentleman's agreement whereby the former transferred to the SIS its entire interest and capacity in all cryptanalytic fields other than Japanese naval and related ciphers.

Although the MAGIC material failed to avert the Pearl Harbor disaster, naval communications intelligence played a vital part in winning the war in the Pacific. There Navy COMINT activities were centered in the Fleet Radio Unit, Pacific (FRUPAC), at Pearl Harbor. Originally headed by veteran cryptanalyst and Japanese linguist Lt. Comdr. Joseph Rochefort, and later by Capt. William B. Goggins, FRUPAC played a crucial role in the American victory at MIDWAY, was instrumental in the YAMAMOTO INTERCEPTION, supplied the American submarine fleet with the intelligence needed to destroy the Japanese merchant marine in the Pacific, and guided the American amphibious advance across the western Pacific through the Japanese-held islands. FRUPAC's activities were supplemented by another Navy COMINT unit under Comdr. Rudolph J. Fabian at Gen. Douglas MacArthur's headquarters in Melbourne, Australia.

Although very much a Naval intelligence stepchild, ONI managed to perform some useful positive intelligence and COVERT ACTION tasks during the war. Capt. ELLIS ZACHARIAS served two tours with ONI in this period. During the first tour the aggressive officer served as deputy director of ONI and pushed the organization into the field of OPERATIONAL INTELLIGENCE, a term approximately equivalent to the Army's *combat intelligence* or *tactical intelligence* (but one with a completely different meaning in other intelligence usage). Zacharias defined the term as "everything a commander might need to take his ships into combat or to conduct amphibious warfare." Departing from ONI's traditional focus on the static information used in long-term strategic planning, he put a new emphasis on the collection and processing of the kind of "short shelf-life" intelligence—e.g., enemy ship movements—which is enormously valuable in the rapidly shifting situation within a war theater. He established a program whereby candidates were trained at an Advanced Naval Intelligence School in New York and later assigned to operational intelligence posts with the fleet.

Zacharias also established Op-16-W, the Special Warfare Branch of ONI, which conducted psychological warfare operations. The most successful of Op-16-W's campaigns was directed against German U-boat crews and consisted of a series of radio propaganda broadcasts by "Commander Norden," who was in fact German-speaking Comdr. RALPH G. ALBRECHT.

These achievements notwithstanding, ONI was generally a neglected and unpopular element of the U.S. Navy during the war, a situation dramatically illustrated by the fact that between 1940 and 1945 it had no fewer than seven directors.

Postwar Naval Intelligence

To the general effects of postwar demobilization on naval intelligence was added ONC's loss in 1949 of much of its communications intelligence role to the newly established Armed Forces Security Agency. AFSA, a unit reporting to the Joint Chiefs of Staff, took over many of the strategic communications intelligence and communications functions of Op-20-G and its Army and Air Force counterparts. The Navy was left with only those COMINT and COMSEC functions that could not practically be centralized. (In 1952 AFSA was transformed into a civilian agency, the NATIONAL SECURITY AGENCY.)

ONI was rehabilitated to the extent that the director of naval intelligence was also an assistant chief of naval operations, reporting through the vice chief of naval operations, but also directly responsible to the secretary of the Navy for such things as apprising naval planners and policymakers of the war-making capabilities and intentions of foreign nations, supplying the information needed for naval plans and operations, and coordinating the Navy's role within the INTELLIGENCE COMMUNITY. This last-named task was accomplished through the seat on the United States Intelligence Board (see NATIONAL FOREIGN INTELLIGENCE BOARD) held by the director of naval intelligence, but ONI lost both the task and the seat when the directors of ONI, Army Intelligence, and Air Force Intelligence were replaced on the Board by a single representative of the Defense Department, the director of the DEFENSE INTELLIGENCE AGENCY.

Ballistic Missile Submarines

As the importance of submarine-launched ballistic missiles in the postwar strategic threat to the United States grows, naval intelligence has been paying increased attention to foreign submarines, especially those of the USSR. Much of the intelligence regarding foreign submarine operations is collected by means of acoustic intelligence (ACOUSTINT), i.e., interceptions by a network of submerged hydrophones of telltale sounds made by a submarine or other ship and transmitted through the water. The Navy began work on its Sound Surveillance System (SOSUS) in 1950 and established its first hydrophone array off the East Coast of the United States in 1954. During the ensuing decades additional SOSUS networks have been installed along the West Coast and at various strategic locations and "choke points" around the world through which submarines must pass while on extended cruises (e.g., the Strait of Gibraltar). Data from this worldwide system of underwater sensors are transmitted to the Acoustic Research Center at Moffit Naval Air Station in California where they are integrated with data from other sources to provide a "real-time" submarine tracking capability.

Today's Naval Intelligence Organization

Naval intelligence has become a complex structure under the ultimate command of the assistant chief of naval operations for intelligence, who is also the director of the Office of Naval Intelligence. ONI has become the supervisory organization that manages this complex.

Subordinate to the director of naval intelligence are two deputy directors, respectively in charge of the Naval Intelligence Command and the Naval Security Group Command. The latter, which is the organizational descendant of Op-20-G, is responsible for naval signals intelligence and communications security. The Naval Intelligence Command is responsible for the rest of a broad spectrum of intelligence and counterintelligence operations.

Intelligence support to naval commands is furnished by the Fleet Intelligence Centers and the Fleet Ocean Surveillance Information Centers (FOSICs). There are two Fleet Intelligence Centers, one at Norfolk, Virginia, which covers Europe and the Atlantic, and another at Pearl Harbor, which supports the Pacific Fleet. The FOSICs, which maintain a "real-time" picture of naval movements within each of their areas of responsibility, are located at Rota, Spain; Norfolk, Virginia; London; Hawaii; San Francisco; and Japan.

(Dorwart, *The Office of Naval Intelligence, Conflict of Duty*; Layton, *"And I Was There"*; Holmes, *Double-Edged Secrets*; Zacharias, *Secret Missions*; Ransom, *The Intelligence Establishment*; Bamford, *The Puzzle Palace*; Lewin, *The American Magic*; Richelson, *The U.S. Intelligence Community*; Nicolosi, "The Spirit of McCarty Little"; Green, "The First Sixty Years of the Office of Naval Intelligence"; Campbell, *The Luciano Project*.)

NEWSPAPERS IN THE CIVIL WAR

Northern Newspapers and Confederate Intelligence: Quite naturally the Northern press gave extensive coverage to the war, typically devoting about one-third of their daily column space to war news. The smaller papers got their news from their Washington bureaus, from the Associated Press wire service, or from other papers, but many of the big-city papers sent special correspondents into the field to travel with the Army and make eyewitness reports of operations. There were more than 150 such "specials," as they were called, reporting the war news for Northern papers during the war.

The papers carried reports of battles; battlefield maps; lists of the killed, wounded, and missing; and sometimes word of military plans, troop movements, troop strengths, and other information of potential intelligence value to the Confederates. The Confederate commanders and intelligence officers were quick to recognize the usefulness of the Northern papers as intelligence sources. One of the major functions of the CONFEDERATE SECRET SERVICE Bureau was the securing of complete files of Northern newspapers for the government leaders in Richmond, and it accomplished the task with considerable efficiency. Baltimore morning papers sometimes reached the desk of President Jefferson Davis by the following evening, while the Secret Service got the New York papers to the Confederate capital only one day late. When conditions made it impractical to pass the bulky packages of newsprint through the Union lines,

Headquarters of the *New York Herald* in the field, 1863. Source: Library of Congress.

the Bureau dispatched agents to the North to search the papers for useful political or military intelligence, extract it, and digest it in the form of concise reports that were then more easily carried to Richmond by courier (see, for example, FRANKLIN STRINGFEL-LOW).

Individual Confederate military commanders also exploited the Northern papers as an intelligence source, of course, and one of the tasks of their "scout," or secret service, units was to obtain the publications. Sometimes the papers were obtained overtly through an informal exchange of newspapers between the two sides under a flag of truce. This practice was officially frowned upon, however, and Union Gen. Joseph Hooker, who may have believed the Confederates were receiving the better part of the intelligence bargain, did his best to end such exchanges.

Union Censorship

Whether or not the U.S. government knew the extent to which Confederate intelligence was actually exploiting the Northern press as a source, it recognized the potential dangers involved and made several attempts to stem the flow of military intelligence into the newspapers. In April 1861 all telegraph lines running out of Washington were placed under the censorship of the State Department. In August 1861 the War Department ordered that information regarding Army movements—past, present, or future—could not be telegraphed from Washington, "except after actual hostilities." Violators of the order were liable under the Department's Article 57 to the death penalty. In February the War Department took over all responsibility for telegraph and newspaper censorship. However, inconsistencies in the application of censorship rules led to an investigation by the House Judiciary Committee, which reported in March 1862 that the censorship was being used by the government to stifle legitimate discussion and criticism of the war effort.

Throughout the war both the War Department and the Army continued to struggle with the newspaper problem. The ambiguity of the Department's rules confused both censors and reporters, and though a few reporters were briefly jailed and a few papers were temporarily suspended, censorship remained generally ineffective. Moreover, an insidious quid pro quo often existed between journalist and officer or official, exactly as in more recent times, in which public officials gave favorable treatment to correspondents who treated them favorably in the press. Unwise disclosures were the price officials paid for a good press, all to the benefit of Confederate intelligence.

However, the Confederates soon found that the Northern newspapers were not to be relied upon completely as intelligence sources. Much of the reporting was inaccurate, some of it was invention, and the headings "IMPORTANT—IF TRUE" or "RUMORS AND SPECULATIONS," while common, were not always placed over reports of dubious authenticity. Nonetheless, the Northern papers remained a valuable intelligence source for the Confederates throughout the war.

Southern Newspapers and Union Intelligence: Southern newspapers carried less news of potential intelligence value than did their Northern counterparts, for these reasons:

1 Only about five percent of American paper mills were in the South. Consequently there was a shortage of newsprint, and therefore fewer papers and fewer pages.
2 Southern newspapers suffered from the same shortage of manpower that afflicted the Confederate Army, industry, and agriculture. Papers often suspended publication when their printers or editors were conscripted into the Army.
3 Confederate press censorship was far more effective than that of the Union. Reporters were generally excluded from the fronts, and the enforcement of censorship was more consistent. Censorship was loosened after the first two years of the war as a result of the efforts of the Press Association of the Confederate States of America, a cooperative wire service established in 1863, but it still remained more stringent than that imposed in the North.

These factors notwithstanding, potentially damaging disclosures of military information in the Southern press were not unknown. However, the actual damage done by such disclosures was probably small, since it is unlikely that Union intelligence paid very close attention to what was generally a poor intelligence source.

Like their Northern counterparts, the Southern papers frequently printed rumors, distortions, and other factual errors, further diminishing their value as an intelligence source.

(Bidwell, "History of the Military Intelligence Division, Department of the Army General Staff"; Andrews, *The North Reports the Civil War, The South Reports the Civil War*; Bakeless, *Spies of the Confederacy*; Fishel, "The Mythology of Civil War Intelligence"; Canan, "Confederate Military Intelligence.")

NIBLACK, ALBERT PARKER (July 25, 1859–August 20, 1929): Navy officer

A native of Vincennes, Indiana, Niblack graduated from the U.S. Naval Academy in 1880. After a two-year tour in the South Pacific he was assigned to the Coast and Geodetic Survey during 1884–86 to do survey and exploration work in Alaska. During 1893–96 he lectured on signaling and naval tactics at the Naval War College. Later he was naval attaché in Rome, Vienna, and Berlin.

As the Spanish-American War approached, Niblack's intelligence reports from Berlin emphasized the potential threat of the growing German navy, German imperialistic designs, and the possibility that unrest in Cuba and elsewhere in Latin America might tempt the Kaiser into a Caribbean adventure, themes that had already been taken up by Admiral Mahan, Theodore Roosevelt, and other American expansionists. Niblack's zeal in collecting German naval intelligence was apparently unlimited; he reportedly once rifled Kaiser Wilhelm's desk in search of battleship plans.

In the days immediately preceding the Spanish-American War, Niblack was successful in procuring torpedo components and other war material in Germany.

During the war Niblack served aboard the *Topeka* in the Cuban blockade and saw action at Nipe Bay on the northern coast of Cuba. In November 1898 he was assigned to the *Olympia*, then at Manila, and took part in a basic intelligence survey of the Philippine island of Luzon.

Niblack later served in China during the Boxer Rebellion, and commanded a regiment of seamen in the American occupation of Vera Cruz, Mexico, in 1914. During the First World War he was promoted to rear admiral and commanded U.S. naval forces in the western Mediterranean.

In May 1919 he was made chief of the Office of NAVAL INTELLIGENCE and held that post until September 1920. The aging officer neither desired the job nor executed it especially well. Whatever cloak-and-dagger panache he may have exhibited during his days as naval attaché in Berlin was apparently gone; now he forswore "anything savoring of 'gum-shoe' methods," although such methods played an increasing part in ONI procedure during the First World War period. He also resisted the emphasis on counterespionage then popular among government intelligence services during this time of red scares and anarchist threats. Instead he focused on collecting STRATEGIC INTELLIGENCE on the growing threat of Japan in the Pacific.

After his tour as director of ONI, Niblack was assigned to London as military attaché, and there he seems to have regained his taste for the clandestine side of intelligence. He had already begun to organize a network of European agents to collect intelligence on Germany, Russia, and Japan, when the undertaking was quashed by Acting Secretary of the Navy Theodore Roosevelt, Jr.

In January 1921 Niblack was promoted to the rank of vice admiral in charge of U.S. naval forces in Europe, and in July 1922 he was given command of the Sixth Naval District. He retired from the Navy in July 1923.

(Dorwart, *The Office of Naval Intelligence, Conflict of Duty; Cyclopedia of American Biography,* v. 28.)

NOLAN, DENNIS EDWARD (April 22, 1872– February 24, 1953): Army officer, intelligence officer

A native of Akron, Ohio, Nolan graduated from the U.S. Military Academy in 1896. He served in the Spanish-American War and in the Philippines before being assigned to the War Department's General Staff. In 1917 he was assigned to the General Staff Corps of Gen. John J. Pershing's American Expeditionary Force in the FIRST WORLD WAR.

Nolan, then a major, was made chief of the AEF's G-2 section, Pershing's intelligence service (see ARMY INTELLIGENCE). In addition to keeping Pershing, his general staff, and subordinate commanders aware of the situation on the western front, Nolan felt strongly that he and his section should watch the enemy on the Russian, Macedonian, and Italian fronts, a position that conflicted with the jurisdiction of the Military Intelligence Division of the War Department. Nolan overcame this opposition, and his section operated with a great degree of independence of the higher-echelon MID in Washington. He was made a temporary colonel in August 1917, and a temporary brigadier general in August 1918.

After the war Nolan became director of the War Department's Military Intelligence Division, a post he held from September 1920 to August 1921. He was given the permanent rank of brigadier general

Gen. Dennis E. Nolan. Source: Library of Congress.

in March 1921, and achieved the rank of major general in 1925. He retired from the Army in 1936 and was an official of the 1939 New York World's Fair. He was later active in public affairs in New York City.

Nolan held several decorations including the Distinguished Service Medal, the Distinguished Service Cross, and the French croix de guerre.

(*Who Was Who in America,* v. 3; Bidwell, "History of the Military Intelligence Division, Department of the Army General Staff.")

NORRIS, WILLIAM (December 6, 1820– December 29, 1896): lawyer, businessman, Confederate army officer and intelligence officer

A native of Baltimore County, Maryland, Norris graduated from Yale College in 1840. He moved to New Orleans where he practiced law. In 1849 he went to California and served as judge advocate for the U.S. Navy's Pacific Squadron. He returned to Maryland in 1852, and in 1858 he established the Baltimore Mechanical Bakery.

Norris, who held strongly secessionist sympathies, moved to Richmond, Virginia, and offered his services to the Confederacy soon after the beginning of the Civil War. He served as a civilian aide on the staff of Brig. Gen. John Magruder, the commander of Confederate forces on the Virginia Peninsula, and he established a semaphore signaling system for Magruder on the peninsula and across the James River. Norris was commissioned a captain in the Confederate Army in either 1861 or 1862; the date of his commission is now uncertain.

In May 1862 the Signal Bureau was established as a semiautonomous office within the adjutant and inspector general's office of the Confederate War Department. Norris was promoted to major and placed in charge of it. He was also chief of the War Department's Secret Service Bureau, an organic part of the Signal Bureau (see CONFEDERATE SECRET SERVICE).

In his capacity as chief of the signal and secret services, Norris was responsible for maintaining secret and secure communications between the Confederate government in Richmond and its agents in the North and in foreign countries. He was also responsible for collecting intelligence on Union military movements along the Potomac, transporting secret agents and other persons on official business to and from the North, and procuring files of current Northern newspapers and other open source materials. The full extent of his intelligence responsibilities and operations are unknown because the official records of his organization(s) were lost (by some accounts they were destroyed when the Confederate government fled Richmond in early April 1865). However, it is clear that he was *not* responsible for all Confederate military intelligence, which was generally the province of the individual field commanders (see CIVIL WAR).

Norris was frequently absent from Richmond during the war, often for long periods, during which the Signal Bureau was managed by a deputy. While it may be supposed that the official reasons for the absences—e.g., inspection of Signal Corps facilities in the field—may have concealed Secret Service Bureau activities, there are insufficient extant records to confirm such supposition.

Norris left Richmond with the Confederate leaders in early April 1865. His connection with the Signal and Secret Service Bureau apparently ended at about that time, and on April 25th he was made Commissioner of Exchange (of prisoners of war) and was promoted to the rank of colonel.

After the war Norris returned to Maryland where he lived out his life in apparently diminished financial circumstances. He failed to realize plans to go abroad and serve in the armies of Chile and Egypt. Most of his personal papers—perhaps including records or memoirs of his wartime service—were lost when his home was destroyed by a fire in 1890.

(Gaddy, "William Norris and the Confederate Signal and Secret Service.")

NORTH, HENRY RINGLING (ca. 1909–): businessman, intelligence officer

North, the brother of circus impresario, John Ringling North, attended Yale University and served in the Office of Strategic Services. He served as finance officer in a small OSS unit attached to the U.S. Seventh Army in Europe. In 1943 he took part in Operation MacGregor, which was originally aimed at bringing about the surrender of the Italian navy, and which actually resulted in the defection of several Italian naval weapons specialists (see JOHN SHAHEEN, MICHAEL BURKE, MARCELLO GIROSI).

After the war North became vice-president and part owner of the Ringling Brothers Barnum and Bailey Circus.

(Smith, *OSS;* Hymoff, *The OSS in World War II;* Burke, *Outrageous Good Fortune.*)

NORTHWEST CONSPIRACY

Summary: In March 1864 the leaders of the Confederacy, in the face of serious military setbacks and a dwindling supply of manpower, authorized a major COVERT ACTION operation aimed at turning the tide of the Civil War in favor of the South. The plan was aimed at separating Indiana, Illinois, and Ohio (and perhaps several other states) from the United States and thereby removing them from the war. The Confederate planners hoped further to establish a Northwestern Confederacy that would ally itself with the Confederate States against the Union. They had their eyes on the North's upcoming presidential campaign and election, hoping that a successful operation would prompt the Democrats to nominate a peace candidate who would be swept into office by an electorate demoralized by the sudden and dramatic Confederate gains.

The basic plan of the operation, which was managed from a Confederate secret service headquarters in Toronto, Canada, was to exploit anti-war sentiment in the North, coordinate it with Confederate paramilitary operations to release and arm tens of thousands of Confederate prisoners of war, and overthrow the governments of several Northern states.

The conspirators set a date for the uprising and then postponed it several times. Actual attempts to carry out the operation on August 29th and November 8th failed, and many of the conspirators were arrested. The operation failed because of poor security (there were several important defectors from among the conspirators' ranks), penetration by Northern counterintelligence, and, perhaps most of all, because the anti-war, anti-Washington sentiment in the target states was far less widespread than the Confederate planners had estimated.

Background: During the Civil War, popular support of President Lincoln and the war effort was by no means unanimous throughout the North. Ideology or family ties predisposed some toward the Confederacy, while others resented such wartime measures as the suspension of habeas corpus, the embargo on trade with the Confederate states, and the military draft. Geographically, disaffection toward the war was concentrated in the Northwest (today's Midwest), especially Indiana, Illinois, and Ohio. Politically, the dissent movement was organized through the Copperheads, as the peace wing of the Democratic Party was called.

The leader of the Copperheads was Clement L. Vallandingham, a Democratic congressman from Ohio who had often argued against the use of military force to preserve the Union before his defeat in the elections of 1862. In 1863 he was arrested for making a speech considered treasonable by the military authorities in Ohio and was deported to the Confederacy.

Closely allied with the Copperheads were the KNIGHTS OF THE GOLDEN CIRCLE, a secret society that had been formed in 1854 by George W.L. Bickley, a bogus Cincinnati physician, and which was dedicated to the support of pro-slavery policies and the promotion of the American conquest of Mexico. After the outbreak of the Civil War the Knights conducted terrorist raids and other illegal activities throughout the Northwest, e.g., recruiting men for the Confederate Army, burning the homes of men who joined the Union Army, and running guns into Missouri to arm Confederate raiders. The secret organization was so ubiquitous that Gen. Ulysses Grant had to disband a unit of the Illinois militia because it was virtually a branch of the Knights.

From the earliest months of the war, the Confederate leaders gave careful attention to the prospect of exploiting the Copperheads and the Knights of the Golden Circle. Gen. John Hunt Morgan of Morgan's Raiders fame, apparently was one of the first to try to make use of the groups. During 1862 he assigned one of his officers, Capt. THOMAS H. HINES, to establish an underground network of secret intelligence agents and saboteurs among the Copperheads of Kentucky. In July 1863 Morgan led a force of some 2,400 raiders into Indiana with the expectation or hope that the local militia would switch sides and join him, overthrowing the Indiana state government and bringing the state into the Confederacy. However, Copperhead sentiment in the area proved insufficient, the militia remained loyal, and Morgan was captured and imprisoned. He and a group of his officers were freed in November 1863 in a prison break engineered by Captain Hines.

The Operation: Most of the documentary records of the Northwest Conspiracy were destroyed or lost with the fall of Richmond, so many of the details of the operation are unknown. The idea for the operation was first suggested to Confederate President Jefferson Davis in 1862, and he reportedly approved of it in principle. Certainly the desperate straits of the Confederacy in the spring of 1864 was a factor in the decision to go ahead with the plan. The draft riots that occurred in New York City, Vermont, New Hampshire, Indiana, and Ohio the previous summer may have struck the Confederate leadership as evidence of substantial anti-war or anti-Washington sentiment in the North, and therefore encouragement for the plan. And the upcoming presidential campaign and elections of 1864 certainly influenced the timing of the operation. In any case, the decision to go ahead with the Northwest operation seems to have been made in the winter or early spring of 1864.

In April Confederate President Jefferson Davis sent two Confederate commissioners—JACOB THOMPSON and Clement C. Clay—to Canada to carry out the operation. There they joined a third commissioner, James P. Holcombe and Capt. Thomas Hines, who had been commissioned as military commander of the operation. Serving under Hines were several other veterans of Morgan's Raiders: JOHN B. CASTLEMAN, ROBERT MARTIN, JOHN W. HEADLEY, BENNETT H. YOUNG, GEORGE ST. LEGER GRENFEL, and others. In June Thompson and Hines met with Vallandingham, who had traveled to Canada after his deportation to the Confederacy. They learned from him that while there were some 300,000 Copperheads in Illinois, Indiana, Ohio, Kentucky, and New York, by no means all of them could be counted on to support a Northwest Conspiracy, and a large number would endorse nothing more radical than political pressure on Washington to negotiate an end to the war. However, Vallandingham was now supreme commander of a secret society called the Sons of Liberty, which was in fact the latest name of the Knights of the Golden Circle. Vallandingham assured the Confederates that the Sons were prepared to take part in a general uprising, and Thompson gave the Sons funds for that purpose.

The initial plan worked out by Thompson and Hines called for the capture of Camp Douglas, a prisoner-of-war camp near Chicago in which 30,000 Confederates were being held. Hines had rounded up a sizable number of escaped POWs in Canada and was forming them into units that would take over Douglas.

Simultaneously with the assault on the camp near Chicago, a force of 3,000 Sons of Liberty would march on the Rock Island Federal Prison—situated on an island in the Mississippi River between Rock Island, Illinois, and Davenport, Iowa—and release the 7,000 POWs held there. Other Sons would take over the state houses of Indiana, Ohio, and Illinois.

The Confederate prisoners, armed and released, plus the Sons of Liberty would constitute an army of 50,000, enough to secure the conspirators' control of the three states. A diversionary attack by regular Confederate forces in Kentucky and Missouri would keep the Union troops busy elsewhere while the conspirators consolidated their gains.

The plan was subsequently extended. Two more prisoner-of-war camps—Camp Chase near Columbus, Ohio, and Camp Morton at Indianapolis—were added to the list of initial targets. The Federal arsenals at Indianapolis, Springfield, Chicago, and Columbus would be seized to arm the released POWs.

An even more ambitious move was devised to divert Union attention from the planned uprisings in the Northwest—an amphibious invasion of the state of Maine. During May, June, and July, fifty Confederate engineers and topographers, disguised as artists who had come to paint and sketch the picturesque shore, toured the Maine cost in order to survey it for BASIC INTELLIGENCE to support the invasion. The armed Confederate steamers *Tallahassee* and *Florida* were to shell and burn the coastal cities, while a force of five thousand troops would land and fan out in five columns. Led by scouts from the local chapter of the Sons of Liberty, they would march across the state, sacking and burning government property and military installations.

The Fourth of July was set as the date of the Northwest uprising. It was later rescheduled for July 18th, and then once more for July 20th. The problem was the Sons of Liberty, who began to show reluctance as the date for the operation approached. Finally the conspirators decided on August 29th, which was to be the opening of the Democratic National Convention in Chicago. The presence of large numbers of Copperheads in the city offered additional assurance of the operation's success. However, the leaders of the Sons of Liberty again failed to set the machinery of the conspiracy in motion. They were further intimidated by the arrival in Chicago late in August of 3,000 Federal troops, summoned by Col. Benjamin Sweet, the commandant of Camp Douglas. Sweet had received word from an informer, an unidentified Confederate major in Canada, of the conspirators' plans to seize Camps Douglas and Morton.

Soon after the failure on August 29th, most of the leaders of the Sons of Liberty were rounded up and jailed by the Federal authorities. The organization had been penetrated by FELIX A. STIDGER, a Union secret agent working for Brig. Gen. HENRY B. CARRINGTON, the military commander of Indianapolis. Stidger, an enlisted man, had gone undercover in May 1863, posing as an ardent Copperhead. He was accepted into the Order of the American Knights, an earlier name of the Sons of Liberty, and rose to the rank of grand secretary of the organization in Indiana. Stidger's reports had kept Carrington informed of the progress of the Conspiracy during the summer of 1864, and his testimony at the trial of the Indiana Sons of Liberty helped convict them.

During September and October the Confederate secret agents of the Conspiracy undertook fragmentary paramilitary operations throughout the region. In September a raiding party led by Hines burned Federal warehouses at Mattoon, Illinois, while another party led by Capt. John B. Castleman burned several military transports at St. Louis, Missouri.

On September 18th Confederate Navy officer JOHN Y. BEALL and a party of twenty-eight guerrillas hijacked two Lake Erie steamboats and attempted to capture the U.S.S. *Michigan,* the only Union war vessel on the Great Lakes. However, the operation was betrayed to the Federal authorities by Godfrey Hyams, an escaped Confederate POW turned informer. Beall's failure to take the gunboat prevented him from accomplishing the objective of the mission, the release of the Confederate POWs held at the prison camp on Johnson's Island near Sandusky, Ohio.

On October 19th Lt. BENNETT H. YOUNG led a party of thirty raiders who robbed a bank in the Vermont border town of St. Albans (see ST. ALBANS RAID). The operation forced Washington to send troops to protect the Canadian border.

In November Hines made one final attempt to bring off the original plan of a general uprising in the Northwest. He had the support of Charles Walsh, the only leader of the Sons of Liberty not then in prison, who assured Hines that this time the members of that secret organization would do their duty. The targets now included New York, Missouri, and Iowa, as well as Illinois, Indiana, and Ohio. The date set for the operation was November 8th, Election Day.

Once again, however, the operation was betrayed. The prisoners at Camp Douglas had been alerted to the planned jailbreak by the conspirators, and informers among them disclosed this to the prison commandant, Colonel Sweet. Also, the NATIONAL DETECTIVE BUREAU was keeping the Confederates in Canada under surveillance at this point. Federal troops were rushed to Chicago and local citizens were recruited into a Home Guard to protect the city. Several of the leaders of the Conspiracy, including Walsh, were rounded up. Hines barely managed to escape back to Canada. News of the Chicago arrests intimidated the conspirators elsewhere. The planned uprising in New York City was forestalled by the arrival of Union Gen. Benjamin Butler with 10,000 troops and the declaration of a state of martial law in the city.

However, the New York conspirators, led by Lt. John W. Headley, attempted to burn down the city several weeks later, on November 25th. They managed to set fires in the Astor House, Barnum's Museum, and several hotels and theaters, but the Sons of Liberty again failed to rise to the occasion, and no general uprising ensued. Headley and his fellow arsonists escaped to Canada.

The last gasp of the Northwest Conspiracy took place in December, when John Beall and several other Confederate secret service agents tried to derail a train carrying prisoners of war from Johnson's Island to Fort Lafayette in New York harbor. This operation failed, too, and Beall was arrested, convicted of espionage, and hanged.

(Horan, *Confederate Agent*; Stern, *Secret Missions of the Civil War*; Bryan, *The Spy in America*; Corson, *Armies of Ignorance*; McMaster, *Our House Divided*; Boatner, *The Civil War Dictionary*; DAH.)

NOTH, ERNST ERICH (February 25, 1909–): scholar, psychological warfare officer

A native of Berlin, Germany, Noth earned a Ph.D. from the Johann Wolfgang Goethe University in Frankfurt in 1933 and did postgraduate work at the Sorbonne in 1934–35. He moved to the United States in 1941 and worked for the National Broadcasting Company from 1942 to 1944. In 1944 he went to work for the Office of Naval Intelligence, where he served as German desk officer in Op-16-W, the Special Warfare Branch, which conducted psychological warfare and propaganda operations.

Noth returned to NBC in 1945 and later taught modern and classical languages at the University of Oklahoma and Marquette University.

(Farago, *Burn After Reading*; Who's Who in America, 37th ed.)

O

OBOLENSKY, SERGE (October 3, 1890–): businessman, Army officer, intelligence officer

A member of Czarist royalty, Obolensky was born in Tsarkoe Selo (now Pushkin), Russia. His full title was Prince Serge Platonovich Obolensky-Neledinsky-Meletsky. He studied agriculture at St. Petersburg University and political economy at Oxford University. At the outbreak of the First World War he broke off his studies and returned to Russia to enlist as a private in the Imperial army. He saw action as a cavalryman in East Prussia and Latvia, reached the rank of major, and was awarded the crosses of St. George, St. Stanislav, and St. Ann.

After the Bolshevik Revolution in 1917, Obolensky fought with the White Russian forces in the Crimea. Later he fled Russia and moved to England, where he worked for a manufacturer of agricultural machinery and a brokerage house. In 1926 he moved to the United States and worked in banking and real estate.

In 1941 Obolensky enlisted in the New York State Guard as a private, after having been rejected by the U.S. Army. He was commissioned as a captain in 1942 and his unit was soon federalized. Obolensky was assigned to the Office of Strategic Services with the rank of major. He served with the OSS OPERATIONAL GROUPS, the commandos trained to operate in uniform behind enemy lines. When he parachuted into Sardinia in 1943 as leader of a four-man liaison team, he was, at age fifty-two, the oldest combat paratrooper in the Army. In 1944 he parachuted into occupied France and led an operational group fighting behind German lines for a month.

At the time of his discharge in 1945, Obolensky held the rank of lieutenant colonel and had been awarded the Bronze Star and the French croix de guerre. After the war he worked in the hotel and public relations businesses.

(*Who's Who in America*, 37th ed.; *Current Biography*, 1959; Smith, *OSS*.)

O'CONNOR, RODERICK LADEW (August 10, 1921–): lawyer, foreign service officer, corporation executive, clandestine services officer

A native of New York City, O'Connor attended St. Paul's School and graduated from Yale University in 1943. From 1943 to 1945 he served as a navigator in the U.S. Army Air Corps and was discharged with the rank of first lieutenant. He returned to Yale, earned a law degree in 1947, and practiced law in New York City from 1947 to 1949, when he became legislative assistant to then Sen. John Foster Dulles.

O'Connor joined the Central Intelligence Agency in 1950 and was assigned to the Eastern European Division of the Office of Policy Coordination, as the Agency's COVERT ACTION group was then called. He worked in West Germany with WILLIAM SLOAN COFFIN, JR. as a case officer, recruiting and training anti-Soviet Russian emigrés to be infiltrated into the Soviet Union as CIA agents.

In 1953 O'Connor joined the Department of State as a special assistant to Secretary of State John Foster Dulles. He remained with the State Department and served in various foreign service positions until 1959, when he became a vice-president of the Ciba Corporation. In 1969 he returned to the Department of

State to become assistant administrator of the Agency for International Development (AID).

(*Who's Who in American*, 37th ed.; Mosley, *Dulles*; Coffin, *Once to Every Man*.)

ODELL, JONATHAN (September 25, 1737– November 25, 1818): clergyman, physician, writer, poet, British secret agent and propagandist

A native of Newark, New Jersey, Odell graduated from the College of New Jersey (now Princeton University) in 1759. He studied medicine and became a surgeon in the British army, serving in the West Indies. He went to England, studied for the ministry, and was ordained in January 1767. In July of that year he moved to Burlington, New Jersey, where he became minister of St. Anne's (Anglican) Church.

Odell was loyal to the English Crown in the American Revolution and, at the outbreak of hostilities, he left St. Anne's to become chaplain to a Loyalist regiment in Pennsylvania. He spent most of the war in New York City working as a British propagandist, writing bitterly satirical sketches, verses, and essays lampooning the American revolutionists. He also worked as a British secret agent and played a part in the communication channel between BENEDICT ARNOLD and Sir Henry Clinton.

Odell was assistant secretary to the board of directors of the Associated Loyalists, a Tory group, and in July 1783 he became assistant secretary to Sir Guy Carleton, the British commander-in-chief. After the war he went to England, and then in 1784 he moved to New Brunswick, Canada, where he was rewarded with the post of registrar and clerk of the province, a well-paid and prestigious post. He remained in the job for twenty-eight years, then turned it over to his son.

(*Who Was Who in America*, historical volume; Boatner, *Encyclopedia of the American Revolution*; Van Doren, *Secret History of the American Revolution*.)

ODOM, WILLIAM ELDRIDGE (June 23, 1932–): Army officer, intelligence officer

A native of Cookeville, Tennessee, Odom graduated from the U.S. Military Academy in 1954. He earned an M.A. and a Ph.D. from Columbia University in 1962 and 1970, respectively.

From 1964 to 1966 Odom was a member of the U.S. Military Liaison Mission to Soviet Forces in Germany. In 1966–69, and again in 1974–76, he was assistant to the associate professor of government at the U.S. Military Academy. From 1972 to 1974 he was assistant Army attaché at the U.S. embassy in Moscow. He was a national security staff member at the White House from 1977 to 1981.

In 1981 Odom became assistant chief of staff for intelligence, Department of the Army (see ARMY INTELLIGENCE). In 1982 he was promoted to the rank of major general and in 1985 he was made director of the National Security Agency.

Odom holds the Defense Distinguished Medal and the Legion of Merit.

(*Who's Who in America*, 43rd ed.; *New York Times*, April 21, 1985, p. 36.)

OFFICE OF STRATEGIC SERVICES

(Also see entry headings prefixed "OSS . . .") During World War II the OSS existed as a civilian agency of the U.S. government for the centralized command of intelligence, propaganda, sabotage, subversion, and a variety of other clandestine activities that were in support of the war effort but did not readily fall into the traditional American military structure. It has been called "America's first central intelligence agency," and many of its personnel carried their wartime experiences in the OSS over into the postwar CENTRAL INTELLIGENCE AGENCY, where they exerted a powerful influence in molding the form and functions of the organization. National security specialist McGeorge Bundy has observed about the role and character of the OSS:

> The first great center of [geographic] area studies in the United States was not located in any university, but in Washington, during the Second World War, in the Office of Strategic Services . . . , a remarkable institution, half cops-and-robbers and half faculty meeting.

Origins

In July 1940 President Franklin Roosevelt sent WILLIAM J. DONOVAN, a Wall Street lawyer and World War I Medal of Honor winner, on a confidential and unofficial fact-finding mission to England to assess the morale, readiness, and outlook of British resistance to Hitler, and to identify the means by which the United States (then not yet at war and, in principle, neutral) might furnish aid to Britain and her allies in the war with Germany. In December of the same year Roosevelt sent Donovan on another such trip, which included visits to the battle zones of the Mediterranean area. During his visits to England Donovan established high-level contact with the British Secret Intelligence Service, and established a close association with WILLIAM S. STEPHENSON, chief of British Security Coordination in New York City (i.e., chief of SIS operations in the western hemisphere).

Stephenson persuaded Donovan that the United States, in anticipation of probable American involvement in the war, should establish a central agency, reporting directly to the President, for the control of all foreign intelligence and COVERT ACTION operations. Donovan proposed the agency to Roosevelt and prepared a detailed memorandum on the subject at the President's request. On July 11, 1941 Roosevelt signed a directive establishing the position of coordinator of information, who would be authorized to

> . . . collect and analyze all information and data, which may bear upon national security; to correlate such information and data, and to make such information and data available to the President and to such departments and officials of the Government as the President may determine; and to carry out, when requested by the President, such supplementary activities as may facilitate the securing of information important for national security not now available to the government.

Roosevelt appointed Donovan to the post and authorized him to spend the President's secret funds to "employ necessary personnel and make provision for the necessary supplies, facilities and services." Armed with this authorization, Donovan quickly built his Office of the Coordinator of Information (or the COI, as it was soon called) into a large quasi-agency, with a budget of $10 million.

The COI

The COI was divided into four major functional branches: Secret Intelligence, which conducted covert intelligence collection; Research and Analysis, which produced finished intelligence; the Foreign Information Service, which produced "white propaganda" (i.e., propaganda officially attributed to the government); and Special Operations, which carried out COVERT ACTION operations.

With the cooperation of the celebrated poet Archibald MacLeish, then Librarian of Congress, a Division of Special Information was set up within the Library of Congress to furnish BASIC INTELLIGENCE on world areas of interest to the COI. Within the Research and Analysis Branch of COI an impressive assortment of scholars worked under historian JAMES PHINNEY BAXTER III on the collection and analysis of intelligence. The Oral Intelligence Unit, under New England newspaperman G. EDWARD BUXTON, interviewed foreign travelers arriving in

New York City in order to obtain current reports on areas of interest. A Foreign Nationalities Branch collected foreign political intelligence from emigré groups within the United States. Other units of COI studied special operations and guerrilla warfare.

In London, a staff headed by New York lawyer William D. Whitney maintained liaison with the SIS and the other British secret services, while Sir William Stephenson performed a counterpart function in New York and Washington. Indeed, COI's relationship with the British services was closer than its liaison with other U.S. intelligence agencies, a fact illustrated most dramatically by the omission of Donovan and the COI from the distribution of MAGIC cryptanalytical intercepts (see PEARL HARBOR ATTACK).

Donovan and the COI were soon embroiled in the rivalries, jealousies, and intramural warfare that seem inevitably to arise among intelligence services. Chief among the COI's antagonists was J. EDGAR HOOVER, whose FEDERAL BUREAU OF INVESTIGATION then held the exclusive charter to conduct undercover operations in the western hemisphere, most especially including Latin America. Other adversaries included the State Department, Army Intelligence, and the Joint Chiefs of Staff.

The OSS

Following Pearl Harbor and the American entry into the war, the COI and the military intelligence services were forced to work together more closely. Inevitably the agency was moved from its position of direct subordination to the President and placed under the jurisdiction of the newly formed Joint Chiefs of Staff. The Foreign Information Service was split off as a separate entity, and renamed the Office of War Information. By President Roosevelt's executive order of June 13, 1942 the Office of the Coordinator of Information now became the Office of Strategic Services.

Administration

Col. G. EDWARD BUXTON, OSS, assistant director, managed a central administrative staff, which included the Office of the General Counsel, the Special Relations Office, the Planning Group, Personnel, and Security.

JAMES B. DONOVAN, was general counsel, the most important office of the administrative staff because of the curious and unprecedented legal status of the OSS, its personnel, and its operations within the traditional context of American law. Among the special legal problems it handled were those related to cover and covert OSS PROPRIETARY CORPORA-

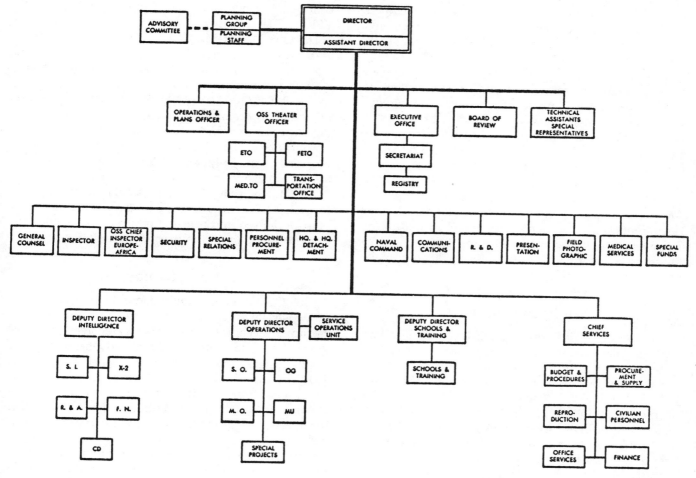

26 MAY 1944

OSS organization, May 1944. Source: National Archives.

TIONS, the normal personal legal affairs of OSS personnel working undercover, and the control of the unvouchered funds expended on clandestine operations. The general counsel's office also compiled all information collected by the OSS regarding war crimes, and a War Crimes Branch was established in 1945 and subsequently transferred to the American prosecutor's office at the Nuremburg trials.

The Special Relations Office was of comparable importance. It established liaison with other government agencies and departments, and with embassies, legations, and missions of foreign governments in Washington. Its main responsibility was liaison with the State Department regarding OSS agents working overseas under State cover.

The Planning Group was set up to coordinate OSS covert action operations with those of the military, i.e., the Joint Chiefs of Staff. It consisted of nine members: one appointed by the secretary of state,

two appointed by the Army, two appointed by the Navy, and four, including the group's chairman, appointed by Donovan.

The Personnel Office handled routine personnel administration, plus such special problems as obtaining draft deferments for OSS employees. The physical security of OSS offices and buildings and the background checking of OSS employees was the responsibility of the Security Office.

Technical Services

The OSS COMMUNICATIONS BRANCH was responsible for rapid and secure communication with agents in the field. It established a network of fixed and mobile relay stations linking all of the agency's far-flung operations with OSS headquarters in Washington; ran the Message Center, the Washington hub of the OSS communications network; and developed electronic surveillance equipment for use in the field.

The OSS SPECIAL FUNDS BRANCH dealt with the peculiar fiscal requirements of clandestine activity: the procurement of national currencies to be used by OSS agents in foreign countries; the evasion of Axis counterespionage efforts to trap OSS agents through marked money, special notes, or recorded serial numbers; and the aging of new paper money to avoid attracting attention to the agent who spent it.

The OSS RESEARCH AND DEVELOPMENT BRANCH developed special weapons and equipment for paramilitary operations; counterfeited identity documents; outfitted agents for travel in neutral or enemy territory; and collected and disseminated to other units information on all types of equipment used in OSS activities.

Intelligence Service

The OSS branches responsible for the collection, analysis, production, and dissemination of intelligence, and for counterespionage, were grouped under the deputy director for intelligence, Brig. Gen. JOHN MAGRUDER. They were:

The OSS RESEARCH AND ANALYSIS BRANCH, which produced finished intelligence in the form of daily and weekly current intelligence reports, intelligence estimates, and special studies.

The OSS SECRET INTELLIGENCE BRANCH, which carried out espionage, i.e., clandestine intelligence-collection operations, in the field.

The OSS COUNTER-ESPIONAGE BRANCH, which undertook operations against the Axis intelligence services.

The OSS FOREIGN NATIONALITIES BRANCH, which collected political intelligence from foreign emigré groups within the United States.

The OSS CENSORSHIP AND DOCUMENTS BRANCH, which collected and compiled intelligence through the interception of mail and other private communications for security purposes.

Operations

The OSS branches responsible for sabotage, psychological warfare, paramilitary operations, and all other forms of COVERT ACTION were grouped under the deputy director for operations, M. PRESTON GOODFELLOW. They were:

The OSS SPECIAL OPERATIONS BRANCH, which carried out sabotage and other physical subversion in enemy territory.

The OSS MORALE OPERATIONS BRANCH, which conducted "black" and "gray" propaganda (see COVERT ACTION) operations.

The OSS MARITIME UNIT, which infiltrated agents and supplied resistance groups by sea, conducted maritime sabotage, and developed equipment and devices to facilitate such operations.

The OSS SPECIAL PROJECTS OFFICE, which conducted a variety of miscellaneous operations involving either enemy or Allied secret weapons.

The OSS OPERATIONAL GROUPS, which were platoons of specially trained paramilitary troops who fought alongside local resistance groups.

A Field Experimental Unit, similar to the Special Projects Office, was formed to carry out operations of a specialized and unusual nature, but it came into existence too late in the war to see action.

Accomplishments

The OSS did not single-handedly win the war. However, by V-J Day it had chalked up an impressive record of accomplishment. An extensive OSS program of espionage, sabotage, and subversion in North Africa insured the success of the Allied landings in 1942. Teams of the Special Operations Branch were infiltrated by parachute or rubber boat into German-occupied countries throughout Europe to work with local resistance groups, training and equipping them, fighting alongside them in a guerrilla war against the Germans, and coordinating their operations with those of the Allies after the invasions of France and Italy began.

The Operational Groups fought behind enemy lines in Europe and Southeast Asia. The OGs had an effectiveness completely disproportionate to their small size. In Greece alone they killed or wounded at least 1,400 of the enemy while taking only twenty-five casualties themselves, and they succeeded in tying up large formations of the Wehrmacht for more than eighteen months. And OSS operations in Brittany after the Normandy landings kept German infantry engaged and denied General Rommel the armor he needed to launch a strategic counterattack during the first critical weeks of the invasion. This last accomplishment earned the gratitude and admiration of even the usually hostile Army G-2 (see ARMY INTELLIGENCE). The chief of G-2 estimated that the operation had saved ten or twelve thousand Allied lives and added in a report to Supreme Allied Headquarters, "You can be satisfied that the OSS has already paid for its budget in this theater."

The Secret Intelligence Branch operated networks of espionage agents worldwide. SI agents in Europe sent detailed reports to London that enabled the Allied air forces to pinpoint bombing targets. The small SI station in Bern, Switzerland, run by former diplomat and Wall Street lawyer ALLEN DULLES, learned about the German V-1 and V-2 missile programs while they were still in the development stage, and also learned that they were being developed at Peenemünde, which immediately became a target for Allied bombers. The station also found out about the plot by some German generals to assassinate Hitler ten days before the attempt was made. Another OSS agent reporting to the station discovered that German intelligence had broken the code used by the American legation in Bern, and communicated this information before highly confidential messages could be intercepted. Yet another source produced some 1,600 German secret documents bearing on the German intelligence operations in Spain, Switzerland, Sweden, and England. Negotiations in Switzerland between Allen Dulles and SS Gen. Karl Wolff led to the surrender of all German and Italian Fascist forces in northern Italy shortly before V-E Day.

Intelligence reports from OSS agents in France supplied most of the information U.S. Seventh Army commander Gen. Alexander M. Patch needed to take the calculated risk of invading southern France with only three American divisions and a small Allied airborne force in August 1944. OSS agents continued to operate in occupied territory as Patch's force advanced through France: the agents found the hole in the German lines through which the Seventh Army dashed 150 miles around the Germans' left flank, from Lyon to Besançon and on to Vesoul, and they located the only remaining Panzer division standing in the way of the American advance and targeted it for destruction by an air strike.

An OSS agent in Germany, wearing a Wehrmacht uniform, located the 166th Panzer Division, combat intelligence that enabled the U.S. Ninth Army to cross the Rhine in March 1945 with little fear of armored opposition. An OSS detachment in Italy supplied the American command with reports that prevented a surprise German counterattack after the Anzio landings of January 1944.

OSS commandos of Detachment 101 parachuted into northern Burma and led the Kachin tribesmen in a guerrilla war against the Japanese. The same group rescued Gen. Jonathan M. Wainwright from a Japanese prison camp in August 1945. Other OSS agents fought in China and supplied the air forces of Gen. Claire Chennault with target intelligence. Still others operated in Thailand and Indochina.

While these specific missions certainly contributed in a large way to the Allied victory, the OSS had an even more profound and long-term influence on American intelligence policy. First among these was the concept of a single, high-level agency for the coordination of national intelligence, an idea that led directly to the establishment of the CENTRAL INTELLIGENCE AGENCY three years after the end of the war. Second was the recognition of intelligence work as a distinct professional specialty, on a par with the military and diplomatic professions. And the third was the acceptance of COVERT ACTION as an effective third option in international relations, lying between diplomacy and open military action.

And, of course, the OSS provided a pool of veterans from which were drawn the individuals who founded and ran the CIA during its first three decades.

Termination

On September 20, 1945 President Truman terminated the OSS. The Research and Analysis Branch was transferred to the State Department, where it became the embryo of State's BUREAU OF INTELLIGENCE AND RESEARCH (see STATE DEPARTMENT INTELLIGENCE). The rest of OSS, including the remnants of the Secret Intelligence Branch and the Counter-Espionage Branch, was transferred to the War Department, where it became the Strategic Services Unit (SSU). There followed a brief bureaucratic struggle between the State Department and the armed services for the control of the national intelligence function. The SSU languished as an unwanted stepchild of the Army for several months, while such OSS veterans as RICHARD HELMS and JAMES ANGLETON remained in Europe and tried to hold together the agent networks and other apparatus that had been established during the war. Early in 1946 the Central Intelligence Group (CIG) was established under the National Intelligence Authority, a joint State-Army-Navy panel. The SSU was transferred into the CIG, where it became known as the Office of Special Operations. Finally, with the National Security Act of July 1947, the CIG became the the independent CENTRAL INTELLIGENCE AGENCY.

(Roosevelt, *War Report of the OSS*; Cave Brown, *Secret War Report of the OSS*; Smith, *OSS*; Troy, *Donovan and the CIA*; Persico, *Piercing the Reich*; Lovell, *Of Spies and Stratagems*; Downes, *The Scarlet Thread*; Dulles, *The Secret Surrender*; Cline, *CIA: Reality vs. Myth*; Ransom, *The Intelligence Establishment*; Hymoff, *The OSS in World War II*.)

OFFICE OF THE COORDINATOR OF INTER-AMERICAN AFFAIRS

A U.S. government psychological warfare agency of the SECOND WORLD WAR established to counter

Axis economic penetration and propaganda within Latin America.

The organization was proposed to the administration of President Franklin Roosevelt in June 1940 by Nelson A. Rockefeller, who was concerned about the growing Nazi threat in Latin America. Established as an Executive Office agency the following August, it was initially called the Office for the Coordination of Commercial and Cultural Relations Between the American Republics. Rockefeller was appointed the agency's director. The name was changed in July 1941 to the Office of the Coordination of Inter-American Affairs. It was the first American psychological warfare agency of the SECOND WORLD WAR (except for a cultural affairs division in the State Department, established in 1939).

The OCIAA conducted propaganda operations along the following lines:

1 Improving American news service to Latin America.
2 Conducting public opinion surveys in the region.
3 Coordinating motion-picture and newsreel presentations for Spanish audiences.
4 Organizing and subsidizing private committees of local pro-U.S. citizens in major South American cities.
5 Coordinating other cultural and commercial activities in Latin America.

The activities of the OCIAA eventually overlapped those of other government agencies with propaganda responsibilities, most notably the Office of the Coordinator of Information, the predecessor of the Office of Strategic Services. A personal rivalry resulted between Rockefeller and OCI Director WILLIAM J. DONOVAN, which was eventually resolved in Rockefeller's favor by Roosevelt, with the result that OCI/OSS was excluded from conducting psychological warfare operations in Latin America.

The OCIAA continued to operate throughout the war. It was abolished by President Truman on August 31, 1945. Some elements of the agency were then transferred to the State Department.

(Troy, *Donovan and the CIA*; Bidwell, "History of the Military Intelligence Division, Department of the Army General Staff.")

O'GARA, JOHN EDWARD (c. 1896–March 1, 1973): corporate executive, intelligence officer

A native of Hanover, New Hampshire, O'Gara graduated from Dartmouth College in 1917. After serving as an ensign in the U.S. Navy in the First World War, he returned to Dartmouth and earned a master's degree in commercial science in 1920. In 1922 he joined the management methods department of R. H. Macy & Co., the New York City department store. By 1932 he had become assistant general manager of Macy's. In 1935 he became executive vice-president and general manager of the store.

During the Second World War O'Gara took military leave from Macy's to serve with the rank of colonel in the U.S. Army. In 1944 he was assigned to the Office of Strategic Services, where he served as deputy director for personnel and as inspector general.

O'Gara returned to Macy's after the war, but again took leave in 1948 to serve as deputy assistant secretary of state for economic affairs. In 1950 he left Macy's to join the Central Intelligence Agency. He held several senior posts with the CIA until his retirement in 1961.

(obituary, *New York Times*, March 2, 1973, p. 38; Smith, *OSS*; Cline, *CIA: Reality vs. Myth*.)

O'GARA, JOHN FRANCIS (July 30, 1918–): intelligence officer

A native of Providence, Rhode Island, O'Gara graduated cum laude from Providence College in 1940. He served in the U.S. Army from 1942 to 1946 and was discharged with the rank of captain. He joined the Department of the Army as a civilian employee in 1946, serving as an intelligence analyst and a technical consultant in the Office of the Chief of Staff for Intelligence (see ARMY INTELLIGENCE). From 1961 to 1970 he served as assistant director of special intelligence in the Office of the Director of Defense Research and Engineering.

(*Who's Who in America*, 37th ed.)

OPEN CODE

A code concealed within an apparently innocuous message. The message is some form of open communication that may be read by an unauthorized person. The open code appears to be part of the innocuous message, but in fact conveys some secret information to an authorized recipient. The so-called winds code that the Japanese established before the PEARL HARBOR ATTACK was an example of an open code; the sentence "East wind rain" in the daily Japanese shortwave broadcast weather report was to signify that the Japanese embassy in Washington was to destroy its sensitive documents.

There are three types of open code: the jargon code, the null cipher, and the geometrical system.

The jargon code disguises words and phrases as

innocuous technical jargon. For example, in the Second World War a Japanese agent used dolls to represent American warships in her communications. Thus, her letter stating that "a broken doll in a hulu grass skirt will have all damages repaired by the first week in February" really meant that the American light cruiser *Honolulu* would be repaired by that date. The "winds code" mentioned above is another example of jargon code.

In a null cipher, only certain letters or words of the open text are significant, e.g., the hidden message consists of every fifth word, or the first letter of every word, etc.

Similar to the null cipher is the geometrical system, which uses a template, grill, or other device that, when placed over the innocuous text, reveals only those words that make up the hidden message.

The open code is a combination of cryptographic and steganographic techniques (see CRYPTOLOGY).

(Kahn, *The Codebreakers*.)

OPERATIONAL INTELLIGENCE

1) In CIA CLANDESTINE SERVICE usage, information used for the planning, execution, and control of SECRET INTELLIGENCE or COVERT ACTION operations. WILLIAM E. COLBY defines it as "the information necessary to identify potential agents, their tastes, their attitudes, and people who had access to them and through whom we could work. . . ." Breckinridge says, "Operational Intelligence reporting (Ops Intell) is for internal operational management only. It addresses the details of activity and environment in areas in which clandestine operations are being conducted." HARRY ROSITZKE cites as an example of operational intelligence the information needed to produce forged documents for agents operating within the USSR: "Knowledge of the personnel and history of Soviet military units destroyed with their records during the war, of bombed-out factories and houses, of city and town birth records that had burned . . . [which] helped guarantee that false birth dates and addresses as well as nonexistent landlords and employers could not be checked out in a police investigation."

2) In the Second World War NAVAL INTELLIGENCE usage, as defined by Adm. ELLIS M. ZACHARIAS, "material for the commanders in combat zones, information of immediate value for action," or, in other words, approximately the same as the Army's *combat intelligence* or TACTICAL INTELLIGENCE.

(Colby, *Honorable Men*; Breckinridge, *The CIA and the U.S. Intelligence System*; Rositzke, *The CIA's Secret Operations*.)

ORDER OF BATTLE

"A tabular compilation by unit showing organization, commanders, movements, and other details over an extended time."—*Webster's Third New International Dictionary of the English Language, Unabridged.*

In his 1924 exposition of military intelligence, Lt. Col. Walter C. Sweeney characterized it as "every class of information which pertains to the strength, composition, organization, location and disposition of enemy units."

Order of battle (OB) intelligence is a detailed and comprehensive picture of all or part of the armed forces of an actual or potential adversary, including both people and equipment. It is the most fundamental and important military intelligence that a commander needs to plan and/or fight a battle, a campaign, or a war. It is the "who," "where," "what," "how many," and "how much" of the opposing force.

(Sweeney, *Military Intelligence: A New Weapon in War*.)

OSS CENSORSHIP AND DOCUMENTS BRANCH

The wartime power of the government to censor mail and other private communications for the purposes of security also yielded positive intelligence that was passed on to the OFFICE OF STRATEGIC SERVICES. The principal function of the OSS Censorship and Documents Branch (CD) was to collect and compile such information, disseminate it to analysts in the OSS RESEARCH AND DEVELOPMENT BRANCH and the OSS SECRET INTELLIGENCE BRANCH, and facilitate its use for authenticating the cover of agents in the field.

The CD Branch was headed by banker HENRY S. MORGAN, son of financier J. P. Morgan (Henry's brother, JUNIUS S. MORGAN was with the OSS SPECIAL FUNDS BRANCH in London). From the War Department's Office of Censorship, the Censorship Division of the CD Branch received postal intercepts, cable intercepts, summaries of intercepted telephone conversations, reports of interviews with foreign travelers, and other similar information. Information from these sources that could aid in the formulation of agent's cover stories, or in the preparation of authentic-seeming counterfeit identification documents (e.g., copies of foreign passports, visas, driver's licenses), was passed on to the CD Branch Document Intelligence Division. The division served as a consultant to the cover experts of the operating branches and to the Research and Development

Branch, which was responsible for the manufacture of counterfeit identification documents.

In March 1944 the Radio Intelligence Division, which had been part of the OSS COMMUNICATIONS BRANCH, was transferred to the CD Branch. The Division, which operated under an OSS cover corporation called the FBQ Company, Inc., operated two radio listening posts, one at Bellmore, Long Island, and the other at Reseda, California. The two installations intercepted commercial, press, and diplomatic communications traffic and translated it from any of a half-dozen languages. Apparently the Division was originally intended to assume a cryptanalysis function, but this plan was effectively thwarted by Gen. GEORGE V. STRONG, chief of Army Intelligence, who wished the military to keep its code-breaking monopoly.

(Roosevelt, *War Report of the OSS*; Cave Brown, *The Last Hero*.)

OSS COMMUNICATIONS BRANCH

In the fall of 1942 the Communications Branch was established to meet the special requirements of the OFFICE OF STRATEGIC SERVICES for rapid and secure communication with agents in the field. Portable sending and receiving sets were developed for agent use, and a network of fixed and mobile relay stations was established to link all of the agency's far-flung operations with OSS headquarters in Washington.

Because of the highly specialized nature of agent communications, the Communications Branch recruited and trained its own technical personnel and conducted its own research, development, and engineering of communications equipment.

The electronic technology of the era was based on the vacuum tube. The home radio receiver in those days was a substantial piece of furniture commanding the living room. Solid-state microcircuitry was known only to readers of science fiction. In such a context, the technical achievements of the Communications Branch were remarkable. They included the famous "suitcase radio," the SSTR-1 transmitter-receiver-power supply, which could be packed into a small suitcase, or, if necessary, three small packages; a smaller, shorter-range radio, the SSTR-3, which could be fitted into a case 8 x 10 x 2 inches, batteries included; an air-to-ground system (code-named "Joan-Eleanor") that relayed communications to and from agents in the field through a wire recorder carried in a plane flying over the area in which the agent operated, and not detectable by enemy direction-finding equipment on the ground.

The Communications Branch also developed electronic surveillance equipment for use in the field, including a miniaturized wiretap that did not require direct physical connection to the telephone lines being tapped, and a tiny, supersensitive microphone for use as a "bug." Another ingenious device developed was a remote, radio-controlled switch, which could be used to detonate mines or flares to light targets for night bombers.

Included in the Communications Branch was the Message Center, the hub of the OSS communications network. There incoming and outgoing teletype traffic was enciphered and deciphered, paraphrased for security reasons, logged, disseminated, and filed.

(Roosevelt, *War Report of the OSS*; Persico, *Piercing the Reich*.)

OSS COUNTER-ESPIONAGE (X-2) BRANCH

The counter-espionage function in the OFFICE OF STRATEGIC SERVICES also included counterintelligence (i.e., in addition to spy-catching, it included such things as penetration of enemy intelligence services, disinformation, etc. See COUNTERINTELLIGENCE AND COUNTERESPIONAGE). The need for some such function was obvious, even before the Office of the Coordinator of Information had been transformed into the OSS, but it was equally obvious that an effective counterespionage/counter intelligence operation depends upon a vast body of files, dossiers, and other biographical records that can only be compiled over a period of many years. To meet this need, the OSS turned to the British Security Service and Secret Intelligence Service, which had assembled exactly this kind of data base relating to the Axis intelligence services over a period of more than a decade. (One of the British counterintelligence officers who trained their OSS counterparts in the tricks of the trade was HAROLD "KIM" PHILBY, and one of his students was future CIA counterintelligence chief JAMES J. ANGLETON. Also see NORMAN HOLMES PEARSON.)

The counterespionage/counterintelligence function began as a division within the OSS SECRET INTELLIGENCE BRANCH, but the rapid growth of its staff and responsibilities required that it be made a separate branch within the intelligence service in June 1943. Headed by Washington lawyer JAMES MURPHY, the branch was known as the Counter-Espionage Branch, and also by the more mysterious and cryptic designation, X-2. (The X-2 designation was borrowed from a unit of the British MI-5, the XX-Committee, also known as the Double-Cross Committee, which specialized in "turning" captured German agents and running them as DOUBLE AGENTS against German Intelligence.)

The separation of X-2 from other OSS units was also dictated by the special, sensitive nature of counterespionage/counterintelligence operations, and by the concern of the British intelligence services to limit access to and maintain tight control of the files they had furnished to OSS.

The heart of X-2 was the Registry, which kept the centralized collection of records of foreign, enemy, or potential enemy personnel, organizations, relationships, and known plans. By the end of the war, the Registry had indexed some 80,000 documents and reports, plus another 10,000 cables, producing a card file of some 400,000 entries.

The Watch List Unit intercepted and examined the mail and other communications of known or suspected enemy agents. The Insurance Intelligence Section, a unit staffed by six insurance experts, focused on Axis intelligence operations that were operated under the cover of legitimate insurance companies, and unexpectedly came up with some of the most valuable positive military intelligence on the Far East. The Enemy Intelligence Organization Section produced studies of Axis intelligence service to be used in operational planning and for the information of OSS agents in the field.

Late in the war X-2 learned that German intelligence was making plans for postwar Nazi subversion, in case of a Hitler defeat, and, to finance these planned operations was looting European jewels, paintings, objets d'art, and other items of small bulk and large value. In response to such information, X-2 established the Art Looting Investigating Unit. The unit's work helped the British and United States governments in trying to recover and return these treasures to their rightful owners after the war, but the principal X-2 interest in the matter was to identify the Nazi agents involved in order to neutralize their postwar plans.

Operating in the field, X-2 agents worked to penetrate foreign or enemy intelligence services, usually by means of double agents who either were captured enemy agents forced to work for X-2 and against their former services, or else agents recruited by X-2 and infiltrated into enemy territory in the hope that they would be recruited by the enemy service and sent back to Allied territory. In his official history of the OSS, KERMIT ROOSEVELT wrote a classic and concise description of counterintelligence operations:

Such operations naturally required the utmost delicacy in handling. The two basic types of operation . . . were subject to an infinity of variations and adaptations, depending upon the particular circumstances. On occasion operations involving controlled agents became extremely complicated. The enemy, of course, engaged in the same types of activity. Thus an enemy agent might be infiltrated into Allied territory to seek employment as an agent. His objective would be to return to enemy territory, ostensibly working for an Allied service, but actually operating for the enemy. Such an agent might be tripled, if his real purpose were discovered when he sought employment with the Allies.

Another variation would be a captured agent who might agree to be doubled, that is, to continue ostensibly operating his radio or other channel of communication for the enemy while under Allied control. If the enemy realized that such an agent had been "turned," he might try to feed the Allies deceptive material. . . . However, if it were realized that the enemy was aware of Allied control, the agent might be quadrupled in an intricate operation of deception and counter-deception. On occasion the operation might become too complicated, whereupon it would be dropped. . . .

There were infinite variations in methods of manipulating agents. They depended solely upon imagination, ingenuity and judgement. The value of success in such operations was, of course, great. Control of the enemy's intelligence instruments provided an important channel of deception; examination of the enemy's intelligence questionnaires to agents gave an indication of what he wished to know, and thereby provided a basis for deducing his plans and intentions.

(Roosevelt, *War Report of the OSS;* Smith, *OSS;* Persico, *Piercing the Reich.*)

OSS FOREIGN NATIONALITIES BRANCH

The function of the Foreign Nationalities Branch (FN) of the OFFICE OF STRATEGIC SERVICES was to obtain political intelligence regarding foreign countries from emigré groups within the United States. Specifically, the Branch established contact with influential political refugees and leaders of emigré groups, and studied the foreign-language press.

The Branch was originally established in December 1941 as part of the OSS's predecessor, the Office of the Coordinator of Information, by the distinguished diplomats JOHN C. WILEY and DEWITT C. POOLE. Poole headed the branch from its inception until the end of the war.

The Branch consisted of some fifty regular OSS employees augmented by 100 volunteer readers of the foreign press. The latter worked at universities throughout the country and were directed from Princeton University. Field representatives worked in New York, Boston, Seattle, Chicago, Cleveland, and Detroit, and in two cities in Wisconsin. Eager to avoid the stigma of "government spies" among the emigrés, many of whom had learned to distrust such agents in their native countries, the FN representatives usually did not disguise their employment by the government and were authorized to identify their agency as the OSS, if necessary.

The FN Branch issued periodic "Bulletins," each covering recent developments in a particular foreign nationality area; "Specials," which dealt with secret or sensitive matters and often included interviews with important emigré figures; and "News Notes," which focused on unusual stories not covered elsewhere, as well as significant changes of editorial opinion in the foreign-language press.

The Branch's output was not limited to political intelligence. One of its early reports was a comprehensive survey of military, naval, and air installations in Greece, which proved to be of considerable value to Army Intelligence. Other accomplishments of the Branch included obtaining the official details of a secret treaty concluded between the Czechoslovak government-in-exile and the USSR in July 1941, a matter that had theretofore only been rumored.

(Roosevelt, *War Report of the OSS*; Smith, *OSS*.)

OSS MARITIME UNIT

The Maritime Unit Branch (MU) of the OFFICE OF STRATEGIC SERVICES had four principal functions: infiltration of agents of other branches into enemy territory by sea; supply of resistance groups and others by sea; maritime sabotage; and development of special equipment and devices to facilitate the first three functions.

The unit was originally a part of the Special Operations Branch, a condition that reflected the failure of OSS to comprehend, at first, the full potential of maritime operations. Only in June 1943 did the unit achieve branch status. Nonetheless, the MU Branch accomplished much. It developed an inflatable surfboard with an electric motor that could drive it at five knots for fifteen miles, a collapsible kayak, underwater breathing devices, compasses and watches for use underwater, and a portable depth gauge. Underwater swimming training sites were established in California at Camp Pendleton; Catalina Island; and in Nassau, in the Bahamas. Experiments in which swimmers developed ways to enter protected harbors for the purpose of sabotage were conducted at Guantanamo Bay, Cuba.

The MU Branch was successful in smuggling supplies through the German Adriatic blockade to the Yugoslavian partisans (see STERLING HAYDEN). The branch's major accomplishments were in the area of infiltrating and supplying agents, a method that was particularly effective from Corsica toward north Italy and southern France, from bases in the Aegean Islands and southern Italy toward Greece, Albania, and Yugoslavia, and in the Far East. The maritime supply service operated by MU in the eastern Mediterranean was also successful. Underwater swimming groups were effective in the Pacific toward the close of the war.

Despite its late start, MU was able to demonstrate the effectiveness of clandestine maritime entry and attack and to develop new and valuable maritime devices and equipment.

(Roosevelt, *War Report of the OSS*.)

OSS MORALE OPERATIONS BRANCH

The Morale Operations Branch (MO) of the OFFICE OF STRATEGIC SERVICES was responsible for "gray" and "black" propaganda (see COVERT ACTION) and other psychological warfare operations aimed at inciting dissension, confusion, and disorder within the Axis countries and promoting subversion against the Axis governments.

From the date of its establishment, January 3, 1943, the MO Branch was plagued by several bureaucratic difficulties. The Office of War Information, the operation in charge of "white" propaganda which had been split off from the Office of the Coordinator of Information when that agency was transformed into the OSS in June 1942, was jealous of its jurisdiction in propaganda operations and met MO with a combination of suspicion and hostility. This interagency squabbling caused OSS to waste a great deal of time repeatedly redefining the role of the MO Branch in an effort to achieve a modus vivendi with OWI. To compound the difficulties further, the other operations branches of OSS also viewed MO with suspicion, regarded its proposed operations as dangerous to the security of other covert action operations, and considered them to be of doubtful effectiveness in any case. One consequence of all this was an inclination among the MO staff to seek transfers to other branches, and a consequent lack of continuity and personnel. In short, the MO Branch was soon a stepchild.

Despite such obstacles, the MO Branch achieved a few accomplishments. There was, for example, its contribution to the MUZAC Project, which consisted of broadcasts to the German army from "Soldatensender West," a powerful radio station run by the British. MO translated the lyrics of American popular songs into German and produced recordings of them by German-speaking vocalists for broadcast by the station. Some of the songs had no propaganda content, but were intended entirely to attract and hold a German audience, while others were satirical and attacked the Nazi leaders, or promoted war-weariness and defeatism.

The MO Branch also spread mischievous rumors, sometimes with unexpected effect. An MO-inspired story said that Mussolini had applied to Switzerland for asylum in case of an Allied invasion of Italy, but that the Swiss government had turned him down. The rumor came full circle, returning to Washington as a report cabled to the State Department by the U.S. minister in Bern, who urged that the information be treated with the utmost secrecy.

Since the effect of such propaganda operations is usually difficult, if not impossible, to measure, the contribution of the MO Branch to the OSS mission is debatable. However, one unequivocal accomplishment of the unit was to introduce covert propaganda into the American clandestine arsenal.

(Roosevelt, *War Report of the OSS*.)

OSS OPERATIONAL GROUPS

The Operational Groups (OGs) of the OFFICE OF STRATEGIC SERVICES were highly trained, foreign-language-speaking soldiers skilled in sabotage, small arms, and parachuting, who were intended to be used in small groups behind enemy lines to harass the enemy. The OG troops were similar to the personnel of the OSS SPECIAL OPERATIONS BRANCH (SO) in both their skills and training, as well as in their activities. However, the emphasis of SO was liaison with local resistance groups; that of OG was combat. Special Operations sent small teams—fewer than a half-dozen agents—behind enemy lines to train resistance groups and coordinate their operations; OGs operated in larger units—platoons of thirty to forty men—and fought alongside the local resistance guerrillas. The SO agents worked undercover, while the OGs fought in U.S. Army uniform. The OGs were approximately the American counterpart of the British Commandos and the prototype of the U.S. Special Forces ("Green Berets").

The Operational Groups were formed as a branch reporting to the OSS deputy director for operations, but in November 1944 they became the separate Operational Group Command, identified within U.S. Army tables of organization as the 2671st Special Reconnaissance Battalion.

Operational Groups operated behind the lines in every theater of the war, but were especially useful in disrupting enemy transport and logistics in Italy and France during the last year of the war, when the German forces were retreating. (Future CIA Director WILLIAM E. COLBY led a thirty-man OG of Norwegian-Americans into Norway in March 1945.)

See also ALFRED T. COX.

(Roosevelt, *War Report of the OSS*; Ford, *Donovan of the OSS*; Hymoff, *The OSS in World War II*.)

OSS RESEARCH AND ANALYSIS BRANCH

The Research and Analysis Branch (R&A) of the OFFICE OF STRATEGIC SERVICES was originally established and organized by Williams College historian and president JAMES P. BAXTER, 3RD, as part of the OSS's predecessor, the Office of the Coordinator of Information. Baxter remained in charge of the unit until November 1942, when he was succeeded by Harvard historian Professor WILLIAM L. LANGER.

The Branch was composed of scholars and specialists from many fields, including economics, geography, political science, and history. The employment of these scholars and specialists marked an innovation in intelligence analysis, a field previously monopolized by diplomats and military officers.

The Branch produced three general categories of intelligence report: the comprehensive regional study and appraisal, which was a complete area survey that included a detailed analysis of terrain, climate, transport, resources, and the social, governmental, and economic structure of the region; specialized studies of one or more economic, political, or geographical factors in a region; and foreign policy studies to support the development of American foreign policy in a given area.

Within the Branch there were four area divisions: Europe-Africa, Far East, USSR, and Latin America. Each of these was further divided into economic, political, and geographic subdivisions. A Current Intelligence Staff, headed by Amherst College historian SARELL E. GLEASON, worked closely with the regional divisions, producing timely reports, especially political intelligence, for key OSS officers and others. The staff produced the Daily Intelligence Summary and the Political Intelligence Weekly. The staff also operated the OSS War Room to facilitate integration of OSS plans with projected military and naval operations.

The Central Information Division (CID) was the central reference library for the Research and Analysis Branch and the other branches of the intelligence service. The CID library was divided into a Biographical Records Section, which compiled some 100,000 documented biographies of foreign persons of intelligence interest, and a Pictorial Records Section, which amassed a collection of some 227,000 photographs of enemy or occupied countries. The indexes to these collections grew to more than 400,000 cards.

The Map Division of the Research and Analysis Branch consisted of four sections: Cartography, Map Intelligence, Topographic Models, and Special Photography. The Cartography Section produced maps for Research and Analysis Branch intelligence studies that were, in the words of the OSS historian, "no mere illustrations, but were integral parts of the studies, many maps constituting intelligence reports in themselves." The Map Intelligence Section collected foreign maps from agents at overseas outposts. From road maps and tourist guides to highly specialized geological and resource studies, surveys, installation plans, and technical transportation and telecommunications charts, the Section built up one of the largest foreign map collections in the country, comprising approximately 500,000 items, all filed, indexed, and catalogued for ready reference.

Much of the Branch's work was with openly available foreign periodicals and publications. Research and Analysis Branch outposts overseas, from London to Chunking, provided headquarters with a steady flow of such materials, as did the OSS field offices in New York and San Francisco.

After the OSS was dissolved in September 1945 the Research and Analysis Branch was transferred to the State Department, where it became the Interim Research and Intelligence Service, headed by Col. ALFRED MCCORMACK. The IRIS went through two further incarnations in the next six months—the Office of Research and Intelligence, and the Office of Coordination and Liaison—and most of its analysts were transferred to the individual geographic area offices of the State Department (see STATE DEPARTMENT INTELLIGENCE).

Some of the scholars who worked as intelligence analysts in the OSS Research and Analysis Branch were destined for future fame. Among these were CRANE BRINTON, RALPH BUNCHE, RAY S. CLINE, EDWARD DOWNES, AUGUST HECKSHER, SHERMAN KENT, HERBERT MARCUSE, WALT W. ROSTOW, ARTHUR SCHLESINGER, JR., and R. JACK SMITH.

(Roosevelt, *War Report of the OSS*; Troy, *Donovan and the CIA*.)

OSS RESEARCH AND DEVELOPMENT BRANCH

Although some units of the OFFICE OF STRATEGIC SERVICES with highly specialized technical needs, such as the OSS COMMUNICATIONS BRANCH, conducted their own research and development, a Research and Development Branch was established to support less specialized units. The Branch was headed by businessman-chemist STANLEY P. LOVELL, who worked closely with such wartime government science bodies as the National Defense Research Committee and the Office of Scientific Research and Development. Through such intermediaries Lovell was able to tap the full resources of American scientific manpower, inviting his colleagues to collaborate with the exhortation, "Here's a chance to raise merry hell. Come help me raise it."

The Branch developed special weapons and equipment for paramilitary operations, e.g., a pocket incendiary device that was capable of starting nine simultaneous fires at a pre-established time; the limpet mine, which could be attached to a ship's hull by a frogman; a silenced, flashless .22 caliber automatic pistol; a silenced M-3 .45 caliber submachine gun; "Aunt Jemima," a high-explosive that looked exactly like wheat flour and could be mixed with milk or water, baked into bread, then used to destroy a bridge; and a large assortment of other weapons of sabotage and assassination.

The Branch also provided a large variety of items required to support agent cover. Using intelligence supplied by the OSS CENSORSHIP AND DOCUMENTS BRANCH, it counterfeited identity documents and outfitted agents for travel in neutral or enemy territory. "The enormity of [the latter] task," KERMIT ROOSEVELT notes in his official history of the OSS,

is indicated when it is realized that each agent had to be equipped with clothing sewn exactly as it would have been sewn if it were made in the local area for which he [i.e., the agent] was destined; his eyeglasses, dental work, toothbrush, razor, brief case, traveling bag, shoes, and every item of wearing apparel or accessory had to be microscopically accurate. Upon such details the life of the agent and, consequently, the success of his mission might depend.

And if the agent were nonetheless apprehended by the enemy, the branch developed the "L" tablet, which "produced death rapidly," and was "to be self-administered in the event of capture." The OSS pharmacists also developed the "K" tablet, which "was designed to insure that the person to whom it was to be administered would be knocked out for a reasonable period of time," as well as the "TD" tablet, "designed to insure that the subject would respond favorably to interrogation." (See TRUTH DRUGS.)

The Branch also collected and disseminated to other

OSS units information on all types of equipment, developed within or without the agency, which would be of use in the agency's activities.

(Roosevelt, *War Report of the OSS*; Lovell, *Of Spies and Strategems*; Cave Brown, *The Last Hero*.)

OSS SECRET INTELLIGENCE BRANCH

The Secret Intelligence (SI) Branch of the OFFICE OF STRATEGIC SERVICES was originally established within the OSS predecessor agency, the Office of the Coordinator of Information. It was initially headed by DAVID K. E. BRUCE, who remained in charge of it until 1943. The major function of the Branch was the collection of intelligence by clandestine means. (Originally the Branch also had the functions of counter-espionage and counterintelligence, but this part of the unit was spun off as the OSS COUNTER-ESPIONAGE BRANCH in June 1943.) Because the special nature of secret intelligence operations required flexibility and resourcefulness, the Branch was much less bureaucratically rigid than most other departments of OSS.

Geographic Desks were grouped into four divisions: Europe, Africa, Middle East, and Far East. The SI station in Madrid was staffed by some fifty agents who ran more than a thousand subagents in occupied France. A similar situation existed in Scandinavia. A small SI contingent in Bern, Switzerland, under ALLEN DULLES, operated successful networks in Italy and Germany.

The Branch's Reporting Board served as the link between the collectors and the consumers of the information acquired by SI, notifying agents in the field of the specific intelligence requirements of the analysts in Washington, and seeing to the prompt dissemination of information arriving from the field to those in need of it. The Board also served a management control function in evaluating the performance of agents in terms of the intelligence they produced.

The Labor Section of the branch was established to enlist the support of international labor for the collection of secret intelligence (and for sabotage and subversion as well). It was headed by ARTHUR GOLDBERG, future secretary of labor, U.S. Supreme Court justice, and U.S. ambassador to the United Nations. One of the section's most important operations was the Ship Observer Unit, which worked with the maritime unions of the United States and neutral countries to secure strategic information about military, naval, economic, and political conditions in enemy, occupied, and neutral countries. The Unit was also used to transport OSS agents, providing them cover as seamen or ship's officers, and to recruit agents and informants from among neutral merchant fleets.

Another unit of the Labor Section operated under the cover of a private, nongovernmental agency, the Office of European Labor Research (OELR), which was, in fact, a staff of German and Austrian emigré labor leaders serving as OSS contract employees. Operating out of its New York City offices, the OELR collected information on the European labor situation and related economic problems, as well as the status of resistance groups. The organization also helped to recruit agents within foreign labor organizations and served as a trusted intermediary between OSS and foreign labor leaders.

The Technical Section of the SI Branch provided scientific and technical expertise to the intelligence collection activities of the other sections. This was essential in such matters as the German V-1 and V-2 missile programs and the German nuclear weapons development program, because those field agents in a position to collect intelligence on such projects rarely had the requisite technical background to understand what they were looking at. The Technical Section developed "indicators" for use by such agents: characteristics that could be used by nontechnical personnel to help them recognize installations, equipment, and devices of interest. When agent reports on such objectives were received, the section interpreted and analyzed the raw information and produced finished scientific intelligence. In tracking the progress of German nuclear weapons development, the branch worked closely with Gen. Leslie R. Groves, chief of the U.S. nuclear program, known as the Manhattan Project (also see MORRIS BERG and BORIS T. PASH for related operations against the German nuclear program).

When the OSS was dissolved in September 1945 the Branch became part of the War Department's Strategic Services Unit (see CENTRAL INTELLIGENCE AGENCY).

In addition to Allen Dulles, two other future directors of the CENTRAL INTELLIGENCE AGENCY served in the SI Branch—RICHARD HELMS and WILLIAM CASEY. Some other CIA intelligence officers who began their careers in the Branch were PAUL BLUM, PAUL HELLIWELL, LAWRENCE R. HOUSTON, KERMIT ROOSEVELT, HANS V. TOFTE, ALFRED C. ULMER, and FRANK G. WISNER.

(Smith, *OSS*; Roosevelt, *War Report of the OSS*; Persico, *Piercing the Reich*; Troy, *Donovan and the OSS*.)

OSS SPECIAL FUNDS BRANCH

The Special Funds Branch of the OFFICE OF STRATEGIC SERVICES dealt with the peculiar fiscal prob-

Wireless telegraphy training at OSS training center in Jedburgh, Scotland. Source: National Archives.

lems posed by covert operations. It undertook the financing of such operations through unvouchered funds made available by the President and Congress. Such funds were needed to maintain cover, whether of a corporation, a training installation, a recruiting office, or an agent or group of agents in enemy or enemy-occupied territory. Unvouchered funds were essential to the most secret operations of the OSS.

Every dollar, pound, franc, reichsmark, guilder, or any other unit of the eighty currencies OSS spent around the world had to be "laundered" so that it could not be traced back to the agency or the U.S. government. The safety of OSS agents and the success of their operations depended upon the security of the currency used. The procurement of currency for use in undercover operations was subject to the most stringent security precautions.

The Axis counterespionage services understood this well and attempted to use monetary methods to catch OSS agents—marking money, recording serial numbers, and issuing special notes. This cat-and-mouse game sometimes required curious measures, e.g., it was discovered that one of the best ways to age new bills and avoid detection was to scatter them about

the floor of a room in which people were carrying on routine duties over a period of hours.

(Roosevelt, *War Report of the OSS.*)

OSS SPECIAL OPERATIONS BRANCH

The task of the Special Operations Branch (SO) of the OFFICE OF STRATEGIC SERVICES, was to carry out physical COVERT ACTION against the enemy. The principal activities were sabotage in enemy and enemy-occupied countries, and support and supply of resistance groups in those countries. Because it was necessary to coordinate special operations with conventional military operations in the same theater of war, the activities of the SO Branch were placed under the command of the local theater commander. SO Branch operations were also closely coordinated with the British counterpart organization, the Special Operations Executive. The headquarters staff of the SO Branch in Washington, which reached a peak of forty-five persons in 1944, was primarily responsible for recruiting, training, and supply.

The SO Branch achieved a notable early success in support of the Allied landings in North Africa in November 1942. At about the same time, OSS Detachment 101, a group of about twenty OSS agents attached to the India-Burma command of Gen. Joseph W. Stillwell, infiltrated an area near the borders of Burma, China, and Thailand to establish a guerrilla force of Kachin tribesmen to harass the Japanese. OSS Detachment 202 operated in China and Indochina. SO teams infiltrated France, the Low Countries, Italy, and the Balkans, and Norway to work with the local resistance groups against the German armies of occupation. In support of the Normandy landings of June 1944, the SO Branch mounted the JEDBURGH OPERATION in which three-man teams were parachuted into France to coordinate the French resistance with the Allied invasion force.

The SO Branch was the first organization in American history specifically charged with carrying out such activities as physical subversion, sabotage, and paramilitary operations. It innovated in blending such techniques as lock-picking, forging, and secret communications with the more conventional methods of waging war. Many veterans of the branch, e.g., WILLIAM COLBY, MICHAEL BURKE, LUCIEN CONEIN, THOMAS BRADEN, C. TRACY BARNES, JOHN BROSS, ALFRED T. COX, GERRY DROLLER, JACOB D. ESTERLINE, DESMOND FITZGERALD, E. HOWARD HUNT, FRANKLIN LINDSAY, and WILLIAM R. PEERS later served in the CIA CLANDESTINE SERVICE.

(Roosevelt, *War Report of the OSS*; Smith, *OSS.*)

OSS SPECIAL PROJECTS OFFICE

The Special Projects Office of the OFFICE OF STRA-TEGIC SERVICES was established at the end of 1943 to undertake projects that did not fall within the charter of any other OSS branch, and that overlapped geographic theater boundaries. The unit grew out of an operation code-named MacGregor, which was aimed at the subversion of the Italian fleet (see MI-CHAEL BURKE, JOHN SHAHEEN, HENRY RIN-GLING NORTH, MARCEL GIROSI). Although Italy capitulated while the project was in progress, the operation had been notably successful in obtaining personnel, equipment, and intelligence related to Italian secret weapons, especially radio-controlled glider bombs and torpedoes.

In April 1944 the unit launched a project, code-named Simmons, aimed at obtaining intelligence on a new German guided missile that had been observed and photographed during test flights from the German missile test station at Peenemünde. The unit planned a joint operation with the French Resistance and the Air Force to bomb a Portes des Valence (France) storehouse believed to contain some of the missiles, followed by a search of the ruins by members of the Resistance posing as firemen. However, the plan was thwarted, first by weather, then by the German evacuation of the area immediately after D-Day. A Special Projects officer in Cairo eventually obtained the desired intelligence on the missile from a German officer willing to deal with the OSS.

Special Projects also carried on a project, code-named Javaman, involving the modification of small air-sea rescue boats for use in harbor sabotage. The boats, disguised as ordinary craft, were in fact unmanned floating bombs, controlled by radio from an aircraft, and aimed by the use of television (this was probably the first proposed use of television for military purposes). The Javaman project was overtaken by events; before the boats could be put into operational use, the war ended.

(Roosevelt, *War Report of the OSS*; Lovell, *Of Spies and Stratagems*; Burks, *Outrageous Good Fortune*.)

OVER-THE-FENCE MISSION

In current U.S. intelligence jargon, a mission involving an illegal border crossing. When an agent is illegally infiltrated into a country by sea, the term "over-the-beach mission" may be used.

(Generous, *Vietnam: The Secret War*.)

OVERHEAD RECONNAISSANCE

Aircraft have been used for reconnaissance since the French Revolutionary Wars in 1794 when a French officer observed the battle of Fleurus from a balloon. Tethered observation balloons, a familiar reconnaissance technique during the nineteenth century, were employed by American forces in the CIVIL WAR and the SPANISH-AMERICAN WAR (see RECONNAIS-SANCE BALLOONS). During the 1890s the U.S. Army experimented with cameras carried by very large kites for aerial photoreconnaissance. Airplanes replaced balloons and kites in reconnaissance during the FIRST WORLD WAR, and the techniques of aerial reconnaissance were highly developed during the SECOND WORLD WAR. Until the 1950s such operations were conducted by regular uniformed armed-services personnel in wartime. With the advent of the cold war, however, aerial reconnaissance was added to the inventory of covert intelligence collection techniques. Nonuniformed covert intelligence personnel flew unmarked or falsely marked aircraft over countries with which no state of war existed. With the advent of reconnaissance satellites in the late 1950s, the term *overhead reconnaissance* came into use to designate intelligence collection from either aircraft or spacecraft.

The Cold War

Following the Soviet acquisition of nuclear weapons in 1949, American intelligence officers needed both early-warning intelligence and, during the 1950s and thereafter, a method of monitoring Soviet nuclear and missile development and deployment. This was the origin of modern American overhead reconnaissance. Human agents sent into the USSR by the CENTRAL INTELLIGENCE AGENCY's Office of Special Operations during 1949–54 provided a degree of early warning—i.e., the assurance that the Soviet Union was not preparing an imminent surprise attack on the West—but they reported virtually no useful scientific and technical intelligence on the Soviet research and development programs.

Aerial photography as a means of collecting intelligence on the Soviet Union began in the late 1940s. Photographs were taken by reconnaissance aircraft flying along the borders of the USSR, but most of the interior of the country was beyond the reach of this technique. Some use was made of a "piggyback" jet reconnaissance plane that was carried to the Soviet border by an RB-50 (i.e., an advanced reconnaissance version of the four-engine, propeller-driven, Second World War B-29 bomber), released for a swift dash to an intelligence target deep inside the country, and

Preparation of an aerial photoreconnaissance mission over France during the First World War. Pilot and observer plan the flight while a ground crewman installs the aerial camera in the Sopwith biplane. Source: National Archives.

returned to the "mother" craft before Soviet air defense could react. But this technique proved unacceptably hazardous and, owing to the limited range of the jet aircraft, inadequate for deep-penetration reconnaissance within the Soviet borders.

In 1946 the Rand Corporation proposed the use of both unmanned high-altitude balloons and artificial satellites for overhead reconnaissance of the USSR. In 1951 the U.S. Air Force and the CIA undertook the MOBY DICK PROGRAM to develop the balloons and related equipment and techniques for reconnaissance operations. The balloon system was perfected in August 1955, and unmanned balloon reconnaissance flights over the Soviet Union were carried out with good results from November 1955 through the spring of 1956, after which the program was termi-

nated and replaced by the U-2 RECONNAISSANCE AIRCRAFT program.

The U-2

The U-2 program had its origins in the Surprise Attack Panel, a body appointed by President Eisenhower in 1954 to study ways of reducing the possibility of a surprise attack on the United States. The Panel was chaired by Dr. James R. Killian, president of the Massachusetts Institute of Technology. Edward Land, president of the Polaroid Corporation and the inventor of the Polaroid camera, chaired the panel subcommittee concerned with intelligence matters.

The Land subcommittee studied the possibility of

reconnaissance overflights of the Soviet Union by very high-altitude aircraft that could operate above the effective ceiling of Soviet interceptors, and which would be equipped with special cameras capable of collecting useful intelligence from such heights. Something of the sort had already been undertaken using the RB-57, a modified Canberra twin-jet bomber that then held a world altitude record. The plane had been used for several joint Anglo-American overflights of the USSR, but even its high altitude proved inadequate for evading Soviet interceptors; a Royal Air Force RB-57 had nearly been shot down over the Ukraine in July 1953. The Land subcommittee recommended the development of a plane especially for overhead reconnaissance that could fly well above Soviet interceptors and surface-to-air missiles. Specifically, they endorsed the design that Lockheed Aircraft Corporation had already begun work on for such a reconnaissance aircraft. The plane, which came to be designated the U-2, was the brainchild of Lockheed's chief designer, C. L. ("Kelly") JOHNSON, and was developed at the company's Burbank, California, facility (nicknamed the "Skunk Works").

President Eisenhower approved the U-2 program in December 1954. For the purpose of secrecy the CIA took charge of the program and funded it out of its Contingency Reserve Fund, money held for such unanticipated expenditures. RICHARD M. BISSELL, special assistant to the director of central intelligence for planning and coordination, managed the program. The first U-2 was test-flown on August 1, 1955, less than eighteen months after Johnson began designing it, and only eight months after the government decision to go ahead with the program. Lockheed delivered twenty-two of the aircraft to the CIA during the first half of 1956.

The U-2B (the first production model) had an operational ceiling of 85,000 feet (well beyond the operational capability of Soviet interceptors of the time) and a range of more than 3,000 miles. Subsequent models had even higher operational ceilings and longer ranges. Photographic expert ARTHUR LUNDAHL, chief of the CIA's Photographic Intelligence Division, designed a special aerial camera for the U-2. The camera, scanning continuously through seven apertures, was able to record a 125-mile-long strip of land on a single piece of film, resolving detail so precisely that golf balls could be identified on a green from an altitude of 55,000 feet. The aircraft was also equipped with a "black box" for the collection of ELINT data, e.g., radar and radio signals emanating from the territory over which it flew.

U-2 Reconnaissance Flights over the USSR

Pilots and ground crews were recruited from the U.S. Air Force. The military personnel were "sheep-dipped," i.e., they went through the technical formality of resigning from the Air Force or being discharged, were enrolled as "civilian" employees of the CIA, and were assigned cover. Two U-2 squadrons were deployed at Air Force bases at Wiesbaden, Germany, and Adana, Turkey. A third squadron was established at Atsugi, Japan, in 1957. British intelligence took a part in the project and it became a joint Anglo-American program. Several RAF pilots—suitably "sheepdipped"—were trained to fly the U-2. Either the President of the United States or the prime minister of Great Britain could authorize overflights by any of the American and British pilots.

In July 1955, while the U-2 was still in development, President Eisenhower, participating in an East-West summit conference in Geneva, Switzerland, made his "open skies" proposal to the Soviet Union. According to the proposal, the United States and the USSR, as a step toward mutual disarmament, would permit unrestricted aerial photoreconnaissance of their respective countries, and even provide the other side with the facilities (e.g., use of air bases) for such flights. The Soviets rejected the proposal. Almost exactly one year later, the United States began its unilateral overhead reconnaissance of the USSR.

The first flight took place on July 1, 1956 and passed over Moscow, Leningrad, and the Baltic seacoast. Six flights were made over Soviet territory during July before the program was temporarily suspended, apparently as the result of Soviet protests to the United States. The overflights were later resumed, but on a much reduced schedule, and the U-2 was primarily used for reconnaissance flights along the Soviet borders. Very few flights were made over Soviet territory from early 1958 to April 1960. In all, only twenty or thirty U-2 penetrations of Soviet airspace reportedly took place in this period.

Collection guidance—i.e., the selection of intelligence targets for the U-2—was provided by a board called the Ad Hoc Requirements Committee, composed of representatives of the CIA, the State Department, and the military services' intelligence components. The Committee also coordinated clearance for the flights with the government departments involved, and obtained White House approval.

The final U-2 mission was flown on May 1, 1960, when the Soviets shot down a U-2 piloted by FRANCIS GARY POWERS near Sverdlovsk in the USSR. Powers had been on a 3,800-mile reconnaissance

U-2 photograph of Soviet space-vehicle launch site in south central USSR. The triangular pit is used to divert the hot rocket exhaust away from the launching pad. Source: Central Intelligence Agency.

mission, reportedly between Peshawar, Pakistan, and Bodo, Norway. While no additional flights over the Soviet Union were authorized, the U-2 continued to be used in the reconnaissance of other DENIED AREAS. The aircraft played a crucial role in providing advance warning of the CUBAN MISSILE CRISIS.

The use of U-2s continued during the 1960s and 1970s. Its latest evolutionary form, the TR-1, has a range of 4,000 miles and carries a variety of sophisticated electronic reconnaissance systems in addition to its cameras.

Many other types of aircraft have also been used in aerial reconnaissance. Anticipating advances in Soviet air defenses, U-2 designer C. L. Johnson began work on the SR-71 RECONNAISSANCE AIRCRAFT in 1959. The SR-71, which first flew in 1962, evades interception through a combination of high altitude and very high speed (i.e., over 2,000 miles per hour). The plane apparently has been used for reconnaissance in Southeast Asia and elsewhere; but it is not primarily intended to overfly the USSR. That task was inherited by another successor to the U-2, the reconnaissance satellite.

Reconnaissance Satellites

The Air Force and the CIA began studying other alternatives to the U-2 for overhead reconnaissance of the USSR in the mid-1950s. The reconnaissance satellite concept, which had been proposed in the 1946 Rand Corporation study, seemed the most promising. Essentially, the idea involved using an artificial earth satellite as an orbital platform for a long-range, high resolution camera, plus some means for recovering the photographic images thus made.

Two parallel programs were undertaken. The DISCOVERER RECONNAISSANCE SATELLITE program was begun in 1956. The Discoverer satellite was a modified version of the Agena rocket (already in use), which was placed in orbit by a Thor booster. The camera aboard the Agena was basically the same one that had been developed for the MOBY DICK high-altitude reconnaissance balloon program. A capsule carrying the exposed film was de-orbited into the atmosphere, then parachuted, to be recovered in midair using the equipment and techniques developed for recovering the MOBY DICK gondolas. The first successful Discoverer capsule was recovered on August 11, 1960 (i.e., three months after the ill-fated Powers U-2 flight).

The SAMOS RECONNAISSANCE SATELLITE was developed at the same time as the Discoverer program (SAMOS: Satellite And Missile Observation System). The first successful SAMOS satellite was placed in orbit on January 31, 1961. The essential difference between the two is that photographs taken by the SAMOS cameras were scanned by a television camera aboard the spacecraft and transmitted back to earth by a radio signal.

The two photographic recovery techniques complemented each other. Images recovered from the Discoverer were sharper and more detailed, while the SAMOS pictures could be had more quickly, and the SAMOS could remain in orbit and send back pictures over a long period of time.

Polar Orbits and Advanced Sensors

Both the Discoverer and SAMOS (and most subsequent reconnaissance satellites) were typically placed in polar orbit (i.e., an orbit passing over the north and south polar regions) enabling them to pass over every part of the earth. With a period (the time required for one complete circuit of the earth) of ninety minutes, a satellite will follow successive ground tracks separated by 22.5 degrees of longitude (equivalent to 1,100 miles at latitude 45 degrees, and 1,565 miles at the equator) due to the rotation of the earth. Thus, for example, a satellite in such an orbit and

The SR-71 reconnaissance aircraft was designed to be less vulnerable to interception than was the U-2. Source: Lockheed Aircraft.

passing over Boston during one circuit, would pass over Minneapolis on the next, and Spokane, Washington, on the next. Because ninety minutes is evenly divisible into the earth's rotation period (1,440 minutes), a satellite in such an orbit would follow the same ground track day after day. By selecting an orbit of slightly longer duration, however, the tracks will be made to shift slightly to the west each day; a slightly shorter period will shift the tracks slightly to the east, and this is what is generally done with reconnaissance satellites.

Cameras with focal lengths of one hundred inches, two hundred inches, and longer (compressed through folded optics for ease of packaging within the satellite) were found to achieve resolution at altitudes of one hundred miles equal or superior to that obtained by the U-2 camera at one-tenth those altitudes. "Black boxes" for the collection of ELINT data were also placed aboard the satellites.

To achieve a polar orbit a satellite must be launched either due north or south. This prohibited the use of Cape Canaveral for launching reconnaissance satellites because the areas immediately to the north and south of the Cape were populated and in danger of debris from an aborted launch. Instead of the Cape, Point Arguello, adjacent to Vandenburg Air Force Base on the California coast about 150 miles north of Los Angeles, was chosen. Reconnaissance satellites are usually launched southward from Point Arguello.

Advances in photography greatly enhanced the quality of information derived from overhead reconnaissance. Infrared sensors—which may be used to produce images even in total darkness—highlight the temperature difference between an object and its surroundings, and this data is often extremely useful. For example, a building that appears to be a barracks in a conventional photograph may be revealed to be a factory or a power plant. The water used by a nuclear submarine to cool its reactors and then exhausted in the submarine's wake, might be sufficiently warmer than the surrounding water to show up on an infrared scanner. The technique of "multispectral photography"—the simultaneous photography of the same scene using several different narrow portions of the visible and infrared spectra—can also disclose significant information invisible to conventional photography.

Management and Control

Management of the U.S. overhead reconnaissance programs and other reconnaissance operations (e.g., seaborne ELINT reconnaissance) was placed under the NATIONAL RECONNAISSANCE OFFICE in 1961. The NRO, an agency of the Department of Defense,

receives lists of reconnaissance targets from the Committee on Imagery Requirements and Exploitation, a panel of the NATIONAL FOREIGN INTELLIGENCE BOARD. These lists, which make up the collective reconnaissance interests of the INTELLIGENCE COMMUNITY, are then assigned to specific satellite missions. Control of the actual mission—i.e., launch, operation of the cameras, recovery of the images—is accomplished by the SATELLITE CONTROL FACILITY, a worldwide command and control system centered in a command post in Sunnyvale, California.

The analysis and interpretation of photographs obtained through overhead reconnaissance has become a highly specialized field. The CIA's Photographic Intelligence Division was formed in 1953 under ARTHUR LUNDAHL as part of the CIA INTELLIGENCE DIRECTORATE. In 1961 it became the NATIONAL PHOTOGRAPHIC INTERPRETATION CENTER (NPIC), operated jointly by the CIA and the Department of Defense as a "service of common concern" (in the words of the NATIONAL SECURITY ACT of 1947, which established the CIA) for the intelligence community.

Second and Third Generation Satellites

The first U.S. reconnaissance satellites, which were used during the 1960s, were succeeded by a family of second and third generation satellites during the 1970s and 1980s. The KH (Keyhole) satellites provide capabilities that were lacking in the earlier vehicles. The KH-8 RECONNAISSANCE SATELLITE can drop from its normal orbit to a lower one for a closer look at a target of interest. The KH-9 RECONNAISSANCE SATELLITE can remain in orbit for months, returning images to the ground by both the capsule and video methods. THE KH-11 RECONNAISSANCE SATELLITE, perhaps the most advanced of the series, can remain in orbit for up to two years, sending back high-quality images through a more advanced video technique known as *digital imaging*, in which the analog video signal is converted to digital form to reduce loss of detail during transmission to a ground station.

In addition to the KH series, there is the RHYOLITE RECONNAISSANCE SATELLITE, which occupies a geosynchronous orbit, i.e., its period of rotation is twenty-four hours, permitting it to remain in a fixed relative position over one spot on the surface of the earth, where it monitors foreign microwave communications and telemetry, and relays the intercepted signals back to earth. The CHALET RECONNAISSANCE SATELLITE is the successor to the Rhyolite. The VELA RECONNAISSANCE SATELLITE is positioned in orbit to watch for nuclear detonations and verify Soviet compliance with nuclear test-ban treaties. The MIDAS EARLY WARNING SATELLITE and its successors watch for the launch of intercontinental missiles from the Soviet Union.

Overhead reconnaissance has become one of the most important intelligence collection techniques (if not *the* most important) in use by the U.S. intelligence community. The ability to verify compliance to treaty agreements by such techniques has become a premise basic to all arms-limitation negotiations with the Soviet Union.

(Klass, *Secret Sentries in Space;* Taylor and Mondey, *Spies in the Sky;* Prados, *The Soviet Estimate;* Mosley, *Dulles;* Richelson, *The U.S. Intelligence Community;* Bamford, *The Puzzle Palace;* Rostow, *Open Skies; New York Times,* January 15, 1985, Section 6; *Newsweek,* January 31, 1983).

P

PADOVER, SAUL KUSSIEL (April 13, 1905– February 22, 1981): historian, educator, government official, intelligence officer

A native of Austria, Padover moved to Detroit, Michigan, in 1920. He graduated from Wayne State University in 1928, did postgraduate work at Yale University, and earned a master's and a doctorate degree from the University of Chicago in 1930 and 1932, respectively. He was a research associate at the University of California in 1933–36. From 1938 to 1943 he was assistant to U.S. Secretary of the Interior Harold L. Ickes.

In 1943–44 Padover was in London, England, as a political intelligence analyst for the U.S. Federal Communication Commission's Foreign Broadcast Monitoring Service (see FOREIGN BROADCAST INFORMATION SERVICE). In 1944 he was commissioned as a lieutenant colonel in the U.S. Army and assigned to the Office of Strategies Services. He was attached to the Psychological Warfare Division of the Supreme Headquarters Allied Expeditionary Force (SHAEF). Shortly after D-Day he landed at Normandy and joined the Allied advance. Working with a small OSS unit he interrogated German civilians, obtaining information upon which the American Military Government in Germany subsequently based its denazification policies. He was awarded the Bronze Star and the French Legion of Honor.

Padover returned to civilian life in 1946. He joined the faculty of the New School for Social Research in New York City in 1949 and was subsequently the dean of the School of Politics. The author of a number of scholarly books, he was a widely recognized authority on the political thought of Thomas Jefferson.

(*Current Biography*, 1952; *Who's Who in America*, 37th ed.; Lerner, *Sykewar*; Padover, *Experiment in Germany*; obituary, *New York Times*, February 24, 1981, p. B12.)

PAPEN, FRANZ VON (October 29, 1879–May 2, 1969): German diplomat, government official, secret service officer

A native of Werl, Germany, von Papen attended military schools, was commissioned as a lieutenant in the German army, and commanded a cavalry battalion. His marriage to the daughter of a wealthy ceramics manufacturer elevated his social status and brought him a transfer to a better regiment, a promotion to the rank of captain, and an assignment to the General Staff. In 1913 he was appointed military attaché at the German embassy in Washington, D.C., and the German legation in Mexico City. After the beginning of the FIRST WORLD WAR in 1914, von Papen opened offices at 60 Wall Street in New York City. These offices, under the cover name of the Bureau of the Military Attaché, were actually the New York station of the Intelligence Department of the German War Office.

Espionage was not von Papen's primary task; the United States had not yet entered the war. Von Papen was to aid the German war effort in several other ways. One assignment was to obtain large numbers of bogus non-German passports (mostly of American issue) to enable German aliens living in the United States and Latin America to return home through the Allied blockade and serve in the German armed forces.

Von Papen's principal job, however, was to prevent American manufacturers from supplying arms and ammunition to the Allies. During the first months of his assignment he achieved a degree of success in this through the skillful employment of economic COVERT ACTION. He bought up large quantities of such strategic materials as chlorine and carbolic acid in order to prevent the Allies from buying them. He established the Bridgeport Projectile Company, a munitions firm ostensibly owned by British interests, which was to make preemptive purchases of machine tools that might otherwise be used by other American munitions makers. The company also accepted and then defaulted on contracts to deliver munitions to the Allies, bought large preemptive options far into the future on gunpowder and other explosives, and caused labor unrest in neighboring munitions plants by driving up the local wage scale.

Von Papen also engaged in less sophisticated forms of sabotage, arranging through an intermediary to have bombs made and planted in cargo ships carrying war supplies to the Allies. He gave serious consideration to a plan to blow up the Welland Ship Canal, which links Lake Ontario and Lake Erie, but abandoned the idea when he realized the Canal was too well guarded. He was generally cautious in his pursuit of such ventures, and consequently had a serious quarrel with FRANZ VON RINTELEN, a less discreet German saboteur.

Von Papen's operation suffered a serious setback in July 1915, however, when a U.S. Secret Service agent who had been following Dr. Heinrich Albert, von Papen's principal assistant, took possession of a briefcase Albert lost while riding the Sixth Avenue elevated. The briefcase was packed with documents that disclosed many of von Papen's operations, including the Bridgeport Projectile Company, but it contained no information on such criminal activities as the bombs. Secretary of the Treasury William G. McAdoo quietly leaked the documents to the *New York World*, with fatal effects on the Bridgeport Projectile Company and some of the other schemes.

The next reversal came in September, when an American journalist serving as a German courier was seized by the British. Among the documents he was carrying was a letter from von Papen to his wife containing some highly insulting references to Americans. Naturally the British arranged for publication of the letter and savored the angry reaction in the United States. Hard on the heels of this incident came the arrest of Robert Fay, a German-born demolition specialist who had constructed bombs for von Papen. Although Fay did not implicate von Papen, the renewed public outcry against the German attaché prompted the State Department to declare him persona non grata and demand his recall (Capt. Karl

Capt. Franz von Papen. Source: Author's collection.

Boy-Ed, a German naval attaché and intelligence officer, was simultaneously expelled).

Von Papen returned to Germany in December 1915 and was promoted to the rank of major. After a short period on the Western Front during the Somme offensive he became chief of staff of the Fourth Turkish Army in Palestine, where he was nearly captured by British forces.

From 1921 to 1931 he was a member of the Prussian Diet. In 1932 he was appointed chancellor of Germany by President von Hindenburg, but he resigned after several months in the face of Nazi pressure. He subsequently struck a political deal with the Nazis and, when asked to form a government by Hindenburg, became vice chancellor (Adolf Hitler was chancellor). However, he was forced out of that post in 1934 after some squabbling with Nazi officials. He was appointed special envoy to Austria and he negotiated an agreement between Nazi Germany and Austria in 1936.

In 1939 von Papen was made ambassador to Turkey. He served in that post until 1944, during which time he ran secret intelligence operations against the Allies. His most notable accomplishment was the penetration of the British embassy through the British ambassador's Albanian valet, Elyeza Bazna, better known to espionologists by his code name, "Cicero." Among the information von Papen obtained from Bazna were records of all the wartime conferences between President Franklin Roosevelt and Prime Minister Winston Churchill.

Von Papen was acquitted of war crimes by the Nuremburg tribunal, but was sentenced to a jail term by a German denazification court in 1947. He was released in 1949.

(*Current Biography*, 1941, 1969; Papen, *Memoirs*; Landau, *The Enemy Within*.)

PAPER MILL

A group or individual offering information purporting to come from a reliable, well-placed, confidential source, but which in fact comes from rumors, speculations, analysis of openly available material, or invention. (". . . a large number of their so-called intelligence sources were nothing but 'paper mills.' These 'paper mills' were organizations of refugees or emigrés producing alleged intelligence reports from interrogating other refugees or emigrés or from the 'cocktail circuit.' They were worthless and unreliable and most frequently dedicated to selling a point of view."—Kirkpatrick, *The Real CIA*.)

The motive of many paper mills is monetary.

PARIS PEACE CONFERENCE OF 1919

American participation in the Peace Conference that ended the FIRST WORLD WAR marked one of the earliest and most ambitious efforts to integrate systematic intelligence activities with the formulation of American foreign policy. It may be seen as a watershed in the evolution of national-level intelligence in American policymaking. Many members of the staff that accompanied the American peace commissioners to the conference played important roles in the evolution of American intelligence during the following half-century.

Shortly after American entry into the war in April 1917, President Woodrow Wilson asked his advisor Col. Edward M. House to establish a group to study the problems of peacemaking that would arise after the war. The result was the Inquiry, a panel of experts—mostly college professors who specialized in history, economics, geography, and ethnography—who compiled an extensive library of basic intelligence for use by the American peace commissioners. The director of the Inquiry was Dr. Sidney E. Mezes, president of the College of the City of New York; his executive officer was Dr. Isaiah Bowman, director of the American Geographical Society. Liaison between the Inquiry and the Political Intelligence Department of the British Foreign Office was established in 1918 by WILLIAM WISEMAN, the Washington representative of British intelligence.

When President Wilson led the American Peace Commission to Paris he took with him the Inquiry, which then numbered some forty persons, including clerical staff. The group became an integral part of the Commission staff and was designated the Territorial, Economic and Political Intelligence Division.

General MARLBOROUGH CHURCHILL, chief of the Army's Military Intelligence Division (see ARMY INTELLIGENCE), led a group of twenty MID intelligence officers who provided support to the Commission. The Commission's security and counterespionage functions were handled by a small unit from MID headed by Col. RALPH VAN DEMAN. Maj. HERBERT O. YARDLEY established a small cryptological unit that insured the Commission's communication security, and also intercepted and read the communications of the other participants in the peace conference.

The Commission had an extensive current intelligence-collection operation involving agents and couriers operating throughout Europe. A committee chaired by U.S. foreign service officer Ellis L. Dresel, and including Van Deman and other representatives of Army intelligence, met daily to debrief agents and couriers returning from critical European sectors. Additionally, Commission staffers gathered intelligence while participating in various ad hoc Allied investigative missions sent to particularly troublesome areas where disorders had occurred.

Although the Commission's intelligence apparatus was dissolved at the close of the Peace Conference, many of the participants remembered the lessons they had learned regarding the importance of national intelligence. The Commission staff included ALLEN W. DULLES (and his brother, John Foster Dulles), and WHITNEY H. SHEPARDSON, both of whom later played important roles in the Office of Strategic Services and the Central Intelligence Agency. Many of the alumni of the Commission staff were founders or charter members of the Council on Foreign Relations (which, indeed, was conceived in Paris in May 1919 by Shepardson, Colonel House, General Tasker Bliss, and other members of the American delegation). This organization went on to contribute much to the American understanding of intelligence as an instrument of foreign policy.

Some of the staff of the American Peace Commission to the Paris Peace Conference of 1919. Col. Ralph Van Deman is seated second from the left. The man standing directly behind Van Deman may be Allen W. Dulles. Source: National Archives.

(Bidwell, "History of Military Intelligence Division, Department of the Army General Staff"; Fowler, *British-American Relations, 1917–1918;* U.S. Department of State, *Papers Relating to the Foreign Relations of the United States: The Paris Peace Conference, 1919,* v. 11.)

PARROTT, JACOB (ca. 1844–ca. 1912): soldier, Union secret agent

Parrott lived in Hardin County, Ohio, before the Civil War. In 1861 he enlisted as a private in the Ohio Volunteer Infantry, which was part of the Army of the Ohio. In April 1862 he volunteered to take part in a paramilitary operation behind Confederate lines aimed at severing the rail line between Atlanta and Chattanooga (see ANDREWS'S RAID). He and a party of twenty other Union troops in civilian clothes and led by JAMES J. ANDREWS hijacked a locomotive and attempted to destroy railroad tracks and bridges between the two cities. He was captured by Confederate troops and imprisoned (Andrews and seven of the others were hanged). He and five others escaped, were recaptured, and exchanged for Confederate prisoners of war in March 1863. Parrott and the other five were awarded the newly created Medal of Honor by Secretary of War Edwin Stanton. Parrott, being the youngest of the six, was awarded the Medal first, thus becoming the first person to receive the Medal of Honor.

After the war Parrott became a prosperous contractor and gravel bank operator in Kenton, Ohio.

(Bryan, *The Spy in America;* Boatner, *Civil War Dictionary;* O'Neill, *Wild Train.*)

PASH, BORIS T.: Army officer, intelligence officer

The son of a Russian immigrant, Pash had served as a relief worker in Russia before teaching school in California. In 1940 he joined the U.S. Army and was commissioned as an officer. He served in the Counter Intelligence Corps (see ARMY INTELLIGENCE), and after several weeks of training in investigative techniques by the Federal Bureau of Investigation, he

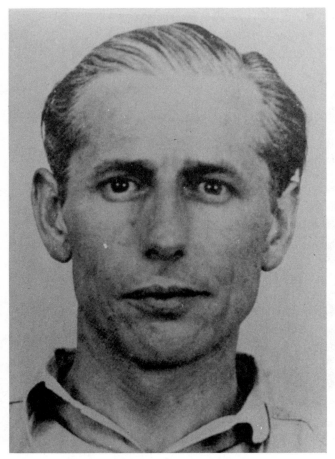

George J. Dasch, one of the two team leaders of the Pastorius operation. Source: Official FBI photograph.

became chief of counterintelligence for the Ninth Army Corps, an assignment that included responsibility for security at the West Coast facilities of the Manhattan Project (the wartime program that developed the first nuclear weapons). While investigating reports of a Soviet effort to penetrate the Project's Berkeley Radiation Laboratory, he became suspicious of Dr. J. Robert Oppenheimer and was among the first to raise questions regarding Oppenheimer as a security risk.

In November 1943 Pash was given command of the Alsos Mission, a team that was to advance with the Allied front-line troops in Europe, investigate the progress of the German nuclear weapons program, and seize the German nuclear facilities and personnel. He succeeded in capturing the German laboratories and nuclear material in April 1944, and took into American custody German nuclear scientists Otto Hahn and Werner Heisenberg, thus preventing their seizure by Soviet forces.

Assigned to the Central Intelligence Agency in March 1949, Pash served in the Office of Policy Co-

ordination, as the Agency's COVERT ACTION department was then called. He was chief of Program Branch 7 (PB/7), a unit that planned such operations as promoting defections from Communist countries and facilitating the escape of political refugees, and handled any other covert action not specifically assigned to some other component of CIA/OPC. According to both E. HOWARD HUNT and Pash's deputy, PB/7 was also responsible for carrying out assassination and kidnapping when so instructed by higher authority within the Agency; Pash, however, testified to a Senate committee that these activities were not part of the Branch's charter. All sources agree that the Branch had never actually carried out an assassination under Pash.

Pash left the CIA in January 1952, although he subsequently worked with the Agency on several projects. He was later chief of counterintelligence for the Sixth Army in San Francisco.

In 1969 Pash published *The Alsos Mission*, an account of the operation he led against the German nuclear program.

(Stern, *The Oppenheimer Case*; Corson, *The Armies of Ignorance*; Wyden, *Day One*.)

PASTORIUS

Operation Pastorius was the code name of a German military intelligence sabotage operation in the United States during the Second World War. The main object of the operation was to cripple American aircraft production by destroying aluminum plants in Pennsylvania, New York, Illinois, and Tennessee. A secondary objective was the destruction of bridges and water-supply facilities in the New York City area.

Operation Pastorius was planned and managed by Lt. Walter Kappe, an intelligence officer who had worked in the United States before the war as a propaganda specialist for the German-American Bund. He selected eight Germans who had also lived and worked in the United States and then returned to Germany to carry out the mission.

In June 1942, after a short period of training in Germany, the eight were sent to the United States in a pair of submarines. Four landed near Amagansett, Long Island, about one hundred miles east of New York City, on the night of June 12–13. The other four landed on Ponte Vedra Beach, twenty-five miles southeast of Jacksonville, Florida, on the night of June 16–17.

The operation was terminated by the leader of the New York City team, George John Dasch, then 39, who had lived in the United States from 1922 to 1941, working as a waiter and serving in the U.S. Army

Air Corps before returning to Germany. With the consent of Ernest Peter Burger, another member of the New York City team, Dasch turned himself in to the Federal Bureau of Investigation and disclosed the full details of the operation, including the whereabouts of the other seven saboteurs.

On July 2, 1942 President Franklin Roosevelt appointed a secret military commission to try the case against the eight men. All were found guilty of violating the laws of war on August 8; six were sentenced to death and executed that day. Dasch received a thirty-year sentence, and Burger was imprisoned for life. The sentences were commuted by President Truman in 1948, and Dasch and Burger were deported to Germany.

(Reader's Digest, *Secrets and Spies;* Farago, *The Game of the Foxes.*)

PEARL HARBOR ATTACK

Summary: At 7:55 A.M. local time on December 7, 1941, a force of Japanese carrier-based fighters, bombers, and torpedo aircraft attacked the U.S. Naval Base at Pearl Harbor and the Army air bases at nearby Hickam and Wheeler fields on the Hawaiian island of Oahu. No state of war existed between Japan and the United States and the attack caught the U.S. government by surprise. Some ninety-four American ships—most of the Pacific Fleet—were at Pearl Harbor at that moment; only the Fleet's three aircraft carriers happened to be elsewhere. Eighteen ships, including seven of the Fleet's eight battleships, were either sunk or so severely damaged as to be inoperable. One hundred eighty-eight aircraft were destroyed. Two thousand, four hundred and three Americans were killed; 1,178 were wounded. It was the worst single military defeat in American history, and it marked the entry of the United States into the SECOND WORLD WAR.

The Pearl Harbor attack was also a major intelligence failure, by far the worst in American history. Ironically, American military and political intelligence collection regarding Japan during the weeks, months, and years before the event was excellent. American cryptanalysts had broken the several Japanese diplomatic and consular cryptosystems, and in the years preceding the attack the U.S. Army and Navy COMINT units read many hundreds of highly informative Japanese messages. All of the information needed to support the conclusion that an attack was imminent was available to the top executive level of the U.S. government in Washington, D.C. Nonetheless, American intelligence failed, for several reasons, to anticipate the attack, and Army and Navy forces at

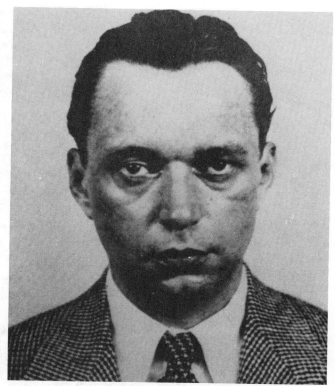

Ernest P. Burger, a member of one of the Pastorius teams. Source: Official FBI photograph.

Pearl Harbor were not put on a high state of alert. The Pacific Fleet was not dispersed as a precaution, and most of the Fleet's capital ships were concentrated in Pearl Harbor, increasing enormously the disastrous consequences of the surprise attack.

The lack of American preparedness for Pearl Harbor was examined by a presidential board of inquiry immediately after the event, and by a congressional investigation after the war. The failure to anticipate the attack, despite the abundant information available, has since been used as a case study by historians and students of intelligence.

The Pearl Harbor attack was frequently cited by those advocating a peacetime American intelligence service, and was a powerful influence in the creation of the CENTRAL INTELLIGENCE AGENCY in 1947. In 1955 the Hoover Commission noted, "The CIA may well attribute its existence to the surprise attack on Pearl Harbor and to the postwar investigation into the part Intelligence or lack of Intelligence played in the failure of our military forces to receive adequate and prompt warning of the impending Japanese attack."

Strategic and Diplomatic Background: The possibility of a Japanese-American war was anticipated as early as the 1890s when advocates of American sea

Official U. S. Navy Photograph

Explosion of ammunition magazines aboard the destroyer U.S.S. *Shaw* after it was it by a Japanese bomb during the Pearl Harbor attack. Source: National Archives.

power and expansion in the Pacific foresaw possible conflict with Japan over the Hawaiian Islands and the Philippines. Japan emerged from the Russo-Japanese War in 1905 as a major naval power with dominion over Korea and part of China. American opposition to Japanese territorial designs on China and other areas in the western Pacific in the ensuing three decades resulted in a gradual deterioration of Japanese-American relations.

In 1937 Japan increased her military presence in China and escalated hostilities against the Chinese. Japan's stated objective was the establishment of "A New Order in East Asia," the integration of China, Japan, and part of Manchuria under Japanese control. The Sino-Japanese war continued into 1940, when Japan signed an alliance with the Axis powers.

The U.S. government began embargoing the export of scrap iron and other strategic materials to Japan and, in July 1941, froze Japan's financial assets and credit in the United States. Great Britain and the Netherlands followed suit, thus effectively cutting off Japan's ability to purchase rubber, scrap iron, and petroleum. The action created a crisis for Japan.

During the latter part of 1941 the Japanese ambassador to Washington and the American secretary of state conducted negotiations aimed at resolving the crisis. The Japanese hoped to have their assets released and their credit restored; the United States sought to have Japan withdraw her troops from China as well as from Indochina, where the Japanese had wrested permission to build airfields from the weak French Vichy government.

The failure of the Japanese government to achieve its aims in the negotiations forced the Japanese premier to resign on October 18. He was succeeded by the more hawkish former war minister, Hideki Tojo. The negotiations, though deadlocked, were still in progress on December 7th, when the Japanese attacked Pearl Harbor.

Intelligence Sources: In August 1940, a team headed by WILLIAM F. FRIEDMAN, the chief cryptanalyst of the Army's Signal Intelligence Service (see CRYPTOLOGY, NATIONAL SECURITY AGENCY, ARMY

INTELLIGENCE) broke "Purple," the cryptosystem the Japanese used for their most important diplomatic communications. The achievement enabled SIS and the Navy's COMINT unit, Op-20-G (see NAVAL INTELLIGENCE), to read the highest-level Japanese diplomatic traffic between Washington and Tokyo, including all reports and instructions regarding the negotiations between the two governments late in 1941, and also the diplomatic communications between Tokyo and the Japanese embassies in such critical spots as Berlin and Rome. Thus the U.S. government had a source of comprehensive and reliable information on the most sensitive matters of Japanese foreign policy during a fifteen-month period prior to the Pearl Harbor attack. This breakthrough led to the establishment of a system of compartmentation to protect the intelligence and its source; the code word MAGIC was used to flag the compartmented material (see SECURITY CLASSIFICATION SYSTEM). The MAGIC material was held very closely within the government, distributed only to the President and the secretaries of state, war, and the Navy, and a small, select group of senior military officers and White House advisors.

In addition to the Purple material, SIS and Op-20-G were also reading cryptosystems used by Japanese agents in major American and foreign ports. Thus American intelligence analysts were in a position to know what installations, warships, military units, and other intelligence targets were of interest to the Japanese, and also the accuracy of the information supplied by Japanese secret intelligence agents. This information was available to the same U.S. government officials who had access to Purple decrypts.

Traffic analysis of Japanese naval and military radio communications—e.g., routine messages to and from warships—enabled American analysts to keep close track of the position of Japanese ships and other units most of the time. This provided a third source of intelligence to the U.S. government.

The American ambassador and the embassy staff in Tokyo provided highly reliable economic and political analysis to Washington, although this source became less valuable as Japanese censorship increased during 1941. Reports by American newspaper correspondents in Japan and elsewhere in the Far East regarding military and political developments was very accurate, although this open source also dried up in the last few weeks before the war. The editorial tone of the Japanese press offered a reliable index of the direction of Japanese policy in 1940–41.

Indications of Japanese Plans, Preparations, and Intentions: The Pearl Harbor Attack was planned by Adm. Isoroku Yamamoto about a year before the event. In January 1941 reports of the plan reached the American ambassador in Tokyo from a source in the Peruvian embassy in Tokyo. The ambassador and intelligence officers in Washington dismissed the report as fantastic, in part because of technical difficulties in using air-launched torpedoes in the relatively shallow waters of Pearl Harbor. In fact, higher Japanese military authorities had not accepted Yamamoto's plan at that time, having rejected it for much the same reason that Washington discounted the intelligence report. The plan was not adopted by the Japanese until May, and later that year the Japanese devised a torpedo to overcome the shallow-water difficulties of the harbor.

On September 24, 1941, Tokyo sent a message to a Japanese espionage agent in Honolulu asking him to provide detailed reports on the types and classes of naval ships at anchor or tied up at wharves, buoys, and in docks at Pearl Harbor, giving their exact positions and noting "when two or more vessels [are] along side the same wharf." This message was decrypted and translated on October 9th. Subsequent messages from Tokyo to the Honolulu agent requesting similar information during November and the first week of December were also intercepted before the Japanese attack. Army and Navy intelligence interpretations of these messages ranged from the possibility of a sabotage bomb plot to a Japanese effort to simplify their agent communications. There was no suspicion that the requests were intended to obtain target information for an air strike.

Throughout November 1941 U.S. Army and Navy intelligence noted increased Japanese military activity in China and Indochina, including the gathering of a strong naval force for operations off Southeast Asia, Palau, and the Marshall Islands. By November 27th Army intelligence reported that a large Japanese task force had been assembled in the area and estimated that the objective was Thailand and Indochina. On November 1st and again on December 1st, U.S. Navy COMINT units noted wholesale changes in Japanese ship call signs. These changes, which intelligence analysts associated with the expected Japanese move in Southeast Asia, frustrated the reconstruction of traffic patterns by American radio traffic-analysis units, thus creating uncertainty regarding the location of elements of the Japanese fleet. This uncertainty further obscured the location of the Japanese aircraft carriers, which had in fact departed the Kurile Islands in northern Japan on the Pearl Harbor mission on November 25th, and which were now proceeding under radio silence. When American listening posts failed to detect any radio transmissions from the carriers, Navy intelligence interpreted this to mean that they had switched to the short-range frequencies the Japanese navy used only in home waters.

(The possibility that the carriers were communicating on a special radio frequency was raised long after the attack by the report of a former Navy enlisted man assigned to Navy intelligence in San Francisco at the time. He recalled plotting the bearings of intercepted transmissions on about December 2nd, and fixing their origin within an area some hundreds of miles wide, north of Hawaii and just east of the international date line. Many students of the Pearl Harbor attack have expressed extreme skepticism regarding this story, however, and surviving Japanese communications officers who took part in the attack state unequivocally that absolute radio silence was maintained, even to the extent that the transmitter keys were sealed. In any case, if such intercepts were made and plotted by Navy listening posts, Navy intelligence apparently failed to associate them with the "missing" carriers.)

A message sent by the Japanese foreign minister to his ambassador in Washington on November 5th specified November 25th as the absolute deadline for the negotiations to result in an agreement with the United States. Subsequent messages on November 11th and 15th reiterated the urgency of concluding an agreement by the 25th. On November 22nd, in response to a request for more time from the Japanese ambassador, the Foreign Ministry agreed to delay the deadline until the 29th, but warned that no additional delays would be possible and that "after that things are automatically going to happen." Other messages sent from Tokyo to the ambassador during November reiterated the theme that the Japanese government was making its final effort to achieve an agreement with the United States and that a failure to do so would result in grave consequences. Frequent references were made to the possibility of war with the United States. All of these messages were intercepted by U.S. Army and Navy intelligence, decrypted within twenty-four hours, and distributed to all those officials on the MAGIC distribution list.

A Japanese special envoy arrived in Washington on November 15th to assist in the negotiations. When the deadline of November 29th came and went without the desired agreement, Tokyo sent several messages to the Japanese ambassador and the special envoy stating that although negotiations had been "de facto ruptured," the Japanese delegation should continue the talks "to prevent the United States from becoming unduly suspicious." During the first week in December Tokyo sent instructions to its Washington embassy to begin destroying its codes, a clear indication that the breaking of diplomatic relations

was imminent. These messages were also promptly decrypted and distributed to the MAGIC list.

On December 2nd Navy intelligence intercepted a message from Tokyo to a Japanese espionage agent in Honolulu requesting "day by day" reports of the American warships in Pearl Harbor, which information was characterized as of "the utmost importance," and ordering the agent to report "whether or not there are any observation balloons above Pearl Harbor or if there are any indications that they will be sent up," and "whether or not the warships are provided with anti-torpedo nets." However, because of the workload and insufficient manpower, this highly suggestive message was not deciphered until December 23rd.

Finally, Navy intelligence intercepted a long Japanese message from Tokyo to the ambassador in Washington on December 6–7. Most of this fourteen-part message was a recapitulation of the Japanese position in the negotiations, but the final part instructed the ambassador to break off negotiations with the Americans. A follow-up message specifically ordered that formal notice of the break was to be delivered to the U.S. government at precisely 1:00 P.M. Washington time (or 7:30 A.M. Hawaii time, some twenty-five minutes before the attack began). This was intercepted at 4:30 A.M., and promptly decrypted and translated. At 5:00 A.M. yet another message was intercepted. This one instructed the Japanese ambassador to destroy all remaining codes, cipher equipment, and secret documents at the embassy. It too was promptly decrypted, translated, and distributed.

(Another intelligence indicator frequently mentioned in the literature of Pearl Harbor is the so-called "winds code." This was an OPEN CODE established by encrypted Tokyo dispatches of November 19th to the Japanese embassies in Washington, London, and Moscow. It provided for the possibility that Japanese communications with those embassies might be cut off during a crisis. In that case a message disguised as a weather report would be included in the Japanese daily shortwave news broadcast and would be a signal for the respective embassy to destroy its codes and ciphers. The November 19 dispatches were intercepted by American intelligence, but the frequent claims that the code "East wind rain"—the pre-established signal to the Washington embassy—was broadcast and intercepted shortly before the attack have never been substantiated, and they are contradicted by the fact that there was no such rupture in the Japanese diplomatic communication link with the Washington embassy as would have caused Tokyo to resort to

Photograph of Pearl Harbor during attack, taken from Japanese aircraft (arrow points to cruiser U.S.S. *Phoenix*).
Source: Naval Historical Center.

the winds code. In any case, most historians now agree that, had such a message been heard, it would have added no significant information that was not already available in the MAGIC intercepts of the last-minute Japanese diplomatic traffic.)

The Intelligence Failure: Decades after the event, official American and Allied documents bearing on the circumstances of the attack continue to be unearthed and released to scholars. Even some personal recollections of "insiders" claiming to offer new revelations are made public from time to time. However, since none of these recently released documents have added significant new information, presumably all of the relevant details of the American intelligence failure are now a matter of public record.

During the final week of November 1941 the U.S. government realized that a Japanese attack against American territory was a significant possibility. The MAGIC intercepts had revealed the Japanese deadline of November 29th; the American policymakers

therefore knew that their decision not to seek a compromise with Japan would lead to an immediate crisis. Intelligence of Japanese military preparations in the Far East made it apparent that Japan was able to act immediately after the negotiations were broken off. However, this latter intelligence did not include the fact that Japan was capable of striking as far to the east as Hawaii, something American planners believed to be technically impossible.

On November 24th the Navy sent a "war warning" message to the fleet commanders in the Pacific and Far East alerting them to the possibility of a surprise attack "in any direction including [an] attack on [the] Philippines or Guam." A second warning message on November 27th warned of a possible "amphibious expedition against either the Philippines, Thai or Kra Peninsula or possibly Borneo." Similar warnings were sent to Army commanders.

Although the political intelligence showed that a Japanese strike against the United States was a real possibility, the available military intelligence suggested that Japan's first hostile move would be an attack against Allied territory in Southeast Asia. Intelligence analysts had tentatively forecast Japan's D-Day for a southeastern campaign as November 30th. When this failed to materialize the date was revised to December 7th. Although the analysts also recognized the possibility that the expected campaign might include the Philippines and Guam, these apparently were not considered likely targets.

There were relatively few intelligence indications that Hawaii might be an initial Japanese target, and these were either discounted (the report obtained in January 1941 from the source in the Peruvian embassy in Tokyo), or misinterpreted (the intercepted intelligence requirements messages from Tokyo to Honolulu during September-November 1941, requesting positions of ships in Pearl Harbor).

Viewed with the benefit of hindsight, however, the indications that Pearl Harbor was to be attacked have seemed so clear to some historians that they have established a small revisionist school that holds that President Franklin Roosevelt was fully aware of the impending attack on Pearl Harbor, but deliberately withheld warning to the Pacific Fleet so that the magnitude of the Japanese offense would overcome domestic isolationist resistance to American involvement in the war. However, most students of the event do not subscribe to this theory, instead attributing the debacle to the inefficiencies of the intelligence bureaucracy and the limitations of intelligence analysis as practiced in 1941. Among the reasons they offer to explain the failure are the following:

1. The significant information indicating an attack on Pearl Harbor was lost within an enormous mass of irrelevant intelligence data. For example, the intercepted Japanese instructions to espionage agents in Honolulu requesting data on American warships in Pearl Harbor were similar to intercepted information requests to Japanese agents in the Philippines, the Panama Canal Zone, and the West Coast of the United States. The frequency of requests concerning Pearl Harbor increased during the last few weeks before the attack, but this would only have been apparent through a careful numerical analysis, and that was not done.
2. Army and Navy cryptologic manpower was inadequate to handle the volume of intercepted Japanese traffic. The very suggestive request from Tokyo to a Japanese agent in Honolulu for reports as to whether the warships in Pearl Harbor were protected by torpedo nets was intercepted five days before the attack, but was not deciphered until three weeks later.
3. Japanese security and counterintelligence was good. Knowledge of the Pearl Harbor operation was held on a strict need-to-know basis, and disinformation—e.g., false radio traffic to disguise the locations of certain warships, false war plans disseminated to some Japanese commanders—helped confuse American intelligence.
4. American intelligence analysts were misled by the erroneous or partial conclusions they had already reached, which led them to ignore conflicting evidence they subsequently saw. The correct estimate that Japan would launch a major operation in Southeast Asia in early December led them to ignore the possibility that Japan would also undertake another major operation at the same time. Perhaps more important, the belief that Japan was incapable of projecting her military force as far east as Hawaii caused the analysts to ignore or misinterpret the radio silence of the aircraft carriers (and perhaps the mysterious radio signals that may have originated from the carrier task force north of Hawaii in early December).
5. The U.S. government failed to employ its existing capability for centralized intelligence coordination and analysis. Although the Office of the Coordinator of Information (see OFFICE OF STRATEGIC SERVICES) had been created for the purpose of analyzing and integrating information from the wide variety of intelligence sources available to the government, neither the director of the COI, WILLIAM J. DONOVAN, nor any of his subordinates was on the MAGIC distribution list. Others within the Army and Navy command structures—e.g., the commander of the Pacific Fleet at Pearl Harbor—who might have gone to an increased condition of readiness had they been aware of the intercepted Japanese diplomatic traffic, were also excluded from knowledge of most of the MAGIC material. In the interest of protecting the security of the MAGIC source (and through bungling and intraservice politics as well), distribution of the information overlooked some key agencies and individuals.
6. Finally, the U.S. government dealt with national security issues on an ad hoc basis at the time, and had no formal mechanisms, such as the NATIONAL SECURITY COUNCIL and the Joint Chiefs of Staff, to insure adequate handling of crisis situations. Neither did it have any sort of formal, around-the-clock national security com-

mand posts to insure continuous twenty-four-hour monitoring of worldwide events that might affect national security.

(Wohlstetter, *Pearl Harbor: Warning and Decision*; Layton, "And I Was There"; Prange, *At Dawn We Slept: Pearl Harbor*; Costello, "Remember Pearl Harbor"; Ransom, *The Intelligence Establishment*; Lord, *Day of Infamy*.)

PEARSON, NORMAN HOLMES (April 13, 1909–November 6, 1975): educator, editor, intelligence officer

A native of Gardner, Massachusetts, Pearson attended Phillips Academy at Andover, Massachusetts, in 1927–28 and graduated from Yale University in 1932. He did his graduate study at the University of Berlin in 1933 and attended Magdalen College, Oxford University, on a Rhodes scholarship. He earned a B.A. and M.A. at Oxford in 1934 and 1941, respectively. In 1941 he was awarded a Ph.D. by Yale University, and he served as an instructor in English literature at Yale until 1942.

At Oxford Pearson had become acquainted with several senior British intelligence officials, and for this reason he was recruited into the Office of Strategic Services in 1942 to act as liaison officer with the counterintelligence section of the British Secret Intelligence Service. Pearson, who had been crippled by polio, served as a civilian employee of the OSS. He and his OSS colleagues, Hubert Will, ROBERT BLUM, and Dana Durand, learned the techniques of counterintelligence from their British counterparts, including HAROLD "KIM" PHILBY. Pearson served as chief of the OSS COUNTER-ESPIONAGE BRANCH in London. In 1943 Pearson recruited his former student and fellow poet JAMES J. ANGLETON into the OSS Counter-Espionage Branch.

Pearson was awarded the U.S. Medal of Freedom as well as several foreign decorations in recognition of his wartime service. In 1946 he returned to the faculty of Yale and became one of its most distinguished students of English and American literature.

(*Who Was Who in America*, v. 6; *Contemporary Authors*, Permanent Series, v. 1; Smith, *OSS*; Cave Brown, *The Last Hero*; Philby, *My Silent War*; Martin, *Wilderness of Mirrors*.)

PEERS, WILLIAM RAYMOND (June 14, 1914–): Army officer, intelligence officer

A native of Stuart, Iowa, Peers attended the University of California at Los Angeles in 1933–37 and was commissioned as a second lieutenant in the U.S. Army in 1938. He was assigned to the Office of Strategic Services and served in Detachment 101, the OSS OPERATIONAL GROUP that conducted paramilitary operations behind Japanese lines in Burma and China. In 1944 he became commander of the detachment, and in 1945 he was OSS deputy director for the China theater.

From 1946 to 1949 Peers was an intelligence instructor at the Army's Command and General Staff College, Fort Leavenworth, Kansas. In 1950 he was assigned to the Central Intelligence Agency, where he served as director of training until 1951. From 1951 to 1952 he held the post of chief of the CIA's station on Taiwan. In that capacity he trained Nationalist Chinese commandos for covert raids against the Communist mainland.

In 1952 Peers left the CIA and subsequently held a wide variety of Army command and staff positions, advancing to the rank of lieutenant general in 1968 while serving in Vietnam. He directed the Army's investigation of the My Lai massacre in Vietnam.

Peers was awarded a large number of decorations, including the Distinguished Service Medal, the Legion of Merit, the Silver Star, and Bronze Star.

Peers collaborated with DEAN BRELIS in writing *Behind the Burma Road* (1963), a history of OSS Detachment 101.

(*Who's Who in America*, 37th ed.; Smith, *OSS*.)

PENETRATION AGENT (sometimes simply penetration)

A member of an organization of intelligence interest—e.g., an opposition intelligence service, a foreign military service, a foreign government—who reports on that organization for an adversary's intelligence service. While some penetration agents are sent to obtain employment with their target organization, most high-level penetrations are DEFECTORS-IN-PLACE. OLEG V. PENKOVSKY was an Anglo-American penetration of Soviet military intelligence, while HAROLD A.R. "KIM" PHILBY was a Soviet penetration of British intelligence. The penetration agent is distinguished from the DOUBLE AGENT.

See also MOLE, AGENT.

PENKOVSKY, OLEG VLADIMIROVICH (April 23, 1919–May 16, 1963?): Soviet army officer, intelligence officer, defector-in-place

A native of Ordzhonikidze, USSR, Penkovsky was the son of a civil servant of the Czarist government who was killed soon after his son's birth while fighting with the White Russian army against the Bolsheviks in the Russian civil war.

Penkovsky was raised by his mother in Ordzhonikidze. After finishing the tenth grade he entered a military school at Kiev where he studied artillery and joined the Komsomol, the Communist youth organization. In 1937 he joined the Soviet army. He served as an artillery officer during the Second World War and was severely wounded in 1944. During the war he was befriended by Gen. Sergey Varentsov, who arranged for him to attend the prestigious Frunze Military Academy after the war. In 1945 Penkovsky married the daughter of Gen. Dimitri Gapanovich, another wartime friend and a powerful member of the Soviet elite.

After graduation from the Frunze Academy in 1948 Penkovsky held staff positions in Moscow for about a year. In 1949 he accepted an invitation to transfer to the GRU, i.e., Soviet military intelligence. During 1949–53 he attended the Military Diplomatic Academy, where he studied intelligence and espionage. He served in the Middle Eastern department at GRU headquarters in Moscow until mid-1955 when he was assigned to Turkey as assistant military attaché.

While serving in Turkey Penkovsky became involved in a contretemps with his superior, the Soviet military attaché, over the latter's heavy-handed espionage methods. As a result both men were disciplined; Penkovsky was recalled to a desk job in Moscow in 1958. Dissatisfied with the GRU and hoping to transfer back to artillery, he enlisted the aid of General Varentsov in obtaining an appointment to the Dzershinsky Military Artillery Engineering Academy, where he studied missile technology during 1958–59. After graduation, however, he was not permitted to return to the artillery, but was sent back to the GRU to be assigned to India as military attaché. This assignment was abruptly cancelled before he could depart for New Delhi because the GRU discovered that Penkovsky's father had been loyal to the White Russians, information Penkovsky had never tried to conceal, but which nonetheless apparently had escaped official notice during his career.

The fact that Penkovsky had never known his father was taken into consideration by the GRU in assessing the implications of his "counterrevolutionary ancestry," and he was therefore not dismissed from the intelligence service. Instead he was given a senior desk officer position in the Moscow headquarters. In November 1960, the matter of his father apparently completely forgotten, he was made a senior officer in the Special Group of the GRU's Third Directorate, which collects scientific and technical intelligence on the United States, Canada, Great Britain, and Latin America. As part of this new assignment he was made deputy chief of the Foreign Department of the State Committee for Coordination of Scientific Research, ostensibly an organization for the dissemination of scientific information within the USSR but actually a cover for the GRU's foreign scientific intelligence-collection activities.

At about the time Penkovsky was given this new post, he apparently decided to work against the USSR and for the West. His initial approach to the U.S. embassy in Moscow was ignored because American intelligence officials suspected it was a Soviet provocation. He next approached British intelligence, hoping the British would help him in arranging contact with the Americans. The British assigned Greville Wynne, a British engineer and businessman, to work with him, establishing liaison with him in his capacity with the State Committee for the Coordination of Scientific Research.

In April 1961 Penkovsky visited London as head of a delegation of Soviet scientists and engineers under the auspices of the State Committee. During his sixteen days in Britain he met secretly at night with a team of British and American intelligence officers for extensive debriefings. He returned to Moscow in May, and during the next eighteen months he continued to function as a defector-in-place, passing information to the British and Americans through Western case officers and couriers, and visiting his contacts during several subsequent trips to the West.

The information Penkovsky supplied British intelligence and the Central Intelligence Agency included classified documents relating to Soviet strategic planning and capabilities. Dr. RAY S. CLINE, CIA deputy director for intelligence at the time, describes the information he provided on Soviet missiles as "invaluable to U.S. intelligence analysts during the Cuba missile crisis of the summer and fall of 1962," and characterizes Penkovsky as "the most successful CIA secret agent of the late Dulles–early McCone era."

Penkovsky declined repeated suggestions by his Western contacts that he end his dangerous work and come to live in the West. He eventually came under Soviet suspicion (Cline suggests it may have been as a result of the aid he furnished that proved so vital during the CUBAN MISSILE CRISIS). He was arrested on October 22, 1962 in the midst of that crisis. Wynne was arrested a week or so later in Hungary, where he was visiting on business. Both were tried on charges of espionage in May 1963. Penkovsky was sentenced to death; according to an official Soviet announcement he was shot on May 16, 1963. Wynne was given a prison sentence and in April 1964 was traded to the British for Soviet agent Gordon Lonsdale.

In his memoirs Wynne wrote that Penkovsky had

not been executed in May 1963, but held for further interrogation in a remote village and subsequently took his own life.

In 1965 *The Penkovskiy Papers* by Oleg Penkovskiy (a different transliteration of the Cyrillic characters of his name) and Frank Gibney was published. Gibney is a veteran journalist who collaborated with Soviet defector PETER DERIABIN on the latter's memoirs in 1959. Several critics questioned the authenticity of the book, which purported to be a collection of materials written or furnished by Penkovsky, and suggested that it might have been inspired by the CIA. In 1976 the U.S. Senate committee that had investigated the INTELLIGENCE COMMUNITY disclosed that the CIA did indeed have a hand in the preparation of the book, but that it had been based on authentic documents furnished to the West by Penkovsky.

(Penkovskiy and Gibney, *The Penkovskiy Papers;* Wynne, *Contact on Gorky Street;* Cline, *The CIA: Reality vs. Myth;* Karalekas, *History of the Central Intelligence Agency.*)

PENROSE, STEPHEN (March 19, 1908–December 9, 1954): educator, intelligence officer

A native of Walla Walla, Washington, Penrose graduated from Whitman College in 1928 and received a Ph.D from Columbia University in 1934. He taught physics at the American University of Beirut from 1928 to 1931, and philosophy and psychology at Whitman College from 1934 to 1937. He then moved to Rockford College, teaching philosophy and psychology and serving as dean of men until 1938, when he became assistant director of the Near East College Association in New York City. In 1942 he joined the Office of Strategic Services and was made chief of the OSS SECRET INTELLIGENCE BRANCH for the Near East. He was decorated with the Bronze Star. After the war he served briefly as an assistant to the secretary of defense. From 1948 until his death he was president of the American University of Beirut.

(*Who Was Who in America*, v. 3; Smith, *OSS;* Cave Brown, *Secret War Report of the OSS.*)

PHENIX, SPENCER (October 30, 1890–October 15, 1986): attorney, government official, intelligence officer

A native of New Britain, Connecticut, Phenix graduated from Phillips Exeter Academy in 1908 and from Harvard University in 1912. During 1912–17 he worked in municipal finance and administration in Boston and New York City. He served as a captain in the U.S. Army during 1918. He was a member of the staff of the Central Bureau of Planning and Statistics in Washington, D.C., and also worked with the Emergency Fleet Corporation during 1919–20. In 1921 he was on the staff of the New York State Legislative Commission to Investigate the Affairs of the City of New York.

In 1922 Phenix joined the U.S. Department of State as an assistant to Under Secretary of State Frank B. Kellogg, the official responsible for intelligence (see STATE DEPARTMENT INTELLIGENCE). He also served as a consultant to the secretary of state. He left the State Department in 1928 and, having graduated from George Washington University Law School in 1926, joined the New York City law firm of Lee, Higginson and Company. He was with the firm until 1938, then pursued business and banking activities in South America and Europe during 1938–41.

In 1942 Phenix joined the Office of Strategic Services. He served in the OSS SECRET INTELLIGENCE BRANCH and was assigned to the New York office of the OSS, where he was a close associate of ALLEN W. DULLES. He later served overseas with the OSS. During 1947–48 he was attached to the staff of the U.S. Military Government of Germany in Berlin and Frankfurt. During 1949 he was with the U.S. Economic Cooperation Administration (the Marshall Plan agency) in Greece.

From 1950 to 1954 Phenix was vice-president and treasurer of the Committee for a Free Europe, the organization formed and funded by the Office of Policy Coordination of the Central Intelligence Agency to work with East European emigrés and carry out psychological warfare against the Soviet Union's East European satellite countries (see RADIO FREE EUROPE/RADIO LIBERTY).

During 1956–58 he was the U.S. member of the mixed board for parole and clemency applications of German war criminals in Allied custody. In 1958 he served as U.S. member on international commissions concerned with property rights and interests in Germany and German external debts. He subsequently served on a commission that dealt with similar problems growing out of German actions in the war.

Phenix was a member of the Council on Foreign Relations.

(*Who's Who in America*, v. 32; Jeffreys-Jones, *American Espionage;* obituary, *New York Times*, October 24, 1968, p. 39.)

PHILBY, HAROLD ADRIAN RUSSELL (KIM) (January 1, 1912–): British intelligence officer, Soviet penetration agent

Philby was born in Amballa, India, the son of an Indian Civil Service officer. He attended Trinity College, Cambridge from 1929 to 1933, during which time he joined a Communist cell then active at the university and agreed to work for the Soviet secret service.

Posing as a journalist (actually accredited to the *London Times*), Philby worked as a Soviet agent in Spain during the civil war in that country. His cover was so effective that he was awarded the Spanish Red Cross of Military Merit by General Franco himself in appreciation of his sympathetic coverage of the Falangist side of the war.

In 1939 Philby was sent by the *Times* to cover the first fighting of World War II in France. In 1940 he was recruited by the British Secret Intelligence Service and he thereafter served as a Soviet penetration agent, or "mole," within British intelligence.

Philby's value to Soviet intelligence increased with every promotion he received within SIS. In 1944 he was made chief of the SIS's Russian desk, a particularly sensitive position for a Soviet "mole." In 1949 he reached the peak of his double career when he was sent to Washington to serve as liaison officer between SIS on the one hand and the CIA and FBI on the other.

Philby quickly formed close professional and social associations with the most important men in CIA, including ALLEN DULLES, FRANK WISNER, JAMES ANGLETON, and WILLIAM HARVEY (whom Philby, for some inexplicable reason, referred to as "William J. Howard" in his memoirs). He served on a four-member British-American committee to organize and carry out the ALBANIA OPERATION—an attempt to overthrow the Communist government of Albania. Their plan was to recruit, train, and equip a force of some 500 Albanian emigrés and send them into their native land in April 1950. Philby's betrayal of the Albania Operation to Soviet intelligence resulted in its failure. Several hundred men were killed in combat or captured and executed. The remainder escaped to Greece, where the operation had been launched.

Through his close association with CIA counterintelligence officers and with the FBI, Philby learned of British suspicions of Donald Maclean, a Soviet agent in the British Foreign Office. Philby dispatched his friend and fellow Soviet agent Guy Burgess, the second secretary of the British embassy in Washington, to London to warn Maclean. The defection of Burgess and Maclean to the Soviet Union one step ahead of British counterespionage focused suspicion on Philby. William Harvey of the CIA was the first to state his suspicions.

Philby was recalled to London in 1951 and he remained there under the shadow of suspicion for several years. Nonetheless, no action was taken against him, and he continued with the SIS. His good fortune in escaping punishment seems to have been the result either of British upper-class loyalty toward one of their own, or else fear that a full exposure of his double role would reflect badly on the SIS. In any case, Philby was eventually assigned to Beirut, Lebanon, where he remained until 1963, when he followed Burgess and Maclean to Moscow. He has since served in an administrative role with the KGB.

(Philby, *My Silent War*; Page, Leitch, and Knightley. *The Philby Conspiracy*; Martin, *Wilderness of Mirrors*.)

PHILLIPS, DAVID ATLEE (October 31, 1922–July 7, 1988): writer, actor, newspaperman, lecturer, intelligence officer

A native of Fort Worth, Texas, Phillips attended William and Mary College during 1940–41 and Texas Christian University during 1941–42. After a brief career as an actor he was inducted into the U.S. Army in 1943 and served as a bomber aircrew member in Europe. He was shot down over German-occupied territory and interned as a prisoner of war. After a year he escaped and made his way to the American forces advancing across Germany.

After his discharge in 1945 Phillips again worked briefly as an actor and then as a radio announcer, while he tried to launch a career as a playwright. He moved to Chile, where he continued to write, attended the University of Chile during 1948–49, and in 1949 became the publisher of the English-language *South Pacific Mail* and the proprietor of a commercial printing service.

In 1950 Phillips was recruited by the Central Intelligence Agency as a contract employee. He worked as a part-time agent of the CIA CLANDESTINE SERVICE in Chile, and he soon became a CIA CASE OFFICER. He left Chile in 1954 and served as assistant to E. HOWARD HUNT during the CIA's GUATEMALA COUP. He was responsible for the operation's black propaganda (see COVERT ACTION) radio, "the Voice of Liberation." Posing as a dissident station transmitting from within Guatemala, the Voice of Liberation broadcast material calculated to intimidate the Communists and Communist sympathizers in the country, while causing neutrals and anti-Communists to rally to the CIA-backed insurgent movement of Castillo Armas.

After his work in Guatemela, Phillips was made a permanent staff employee of the CIA. He served at Agency headquarters as a staff specialist in psychological warfare during 1955. His next assignment was Cuba, where he served under deep (i.e., nonofficial) cover through 1956. Early in 1957 he was transferred to Lebanon, where he was based for the next year and a half, posing as an American businessman.

Late in 1958 Phillips resigned from the CIA in order to carry on a public relations business in Cuba, although he continued to serve as a part-time contract employee of the Agency. When the Castro regime came to power in Cuba his business languished, although he continued to work for the CIA in Havana until 1960 when the danger of operating in Cuba without official cover became too great.

In March 1960 Phillips returned to the CIA as a staff officer and was assigned to the task force then being assembled to carry out a covert action program aimed at toppling the Castro regime in Cuba (the program that evolved into the BAY OF PIGS INVASION). He was responsible for the Task Force's propaganda operations, including radio propaganda.

Phillips remained with the Cuban project through the failure of the invasion in April 1961. Afterward he was assigned to the CIA station in Mexico City, where he served under official cover and was a senior covert action officer. In 1965 he became chief of station in Santo Domingo, the Dominican Republic, a position he held during the U.S. military intervention in that country that year, and in which he continued until 1967.

In 1968 Phillips returned to CIA headquarters to become chief of the Cuban Operations Group of the Clandestine Service's Western Hemisphere Division. The Group managed CIA espionage operations in Cuba and collected intelligence on Cuban military intervention and subversion around the world.

During 1970–72 Phillips was chief of station in Brazil. He served as chief of station in Caracas, Venezuela, in 1972. In mid-1973 he returned to CIA headquarters to succeed THEODORE G. SHACKLEY, JR. as chief of the Western Hemisphere Division.

In 1975 Phillips took early retirement from the CIA in order to be free to answer, as a private citizen, the many false charges that were being made at the time against the Agency and the INTELLIGENCE COMMUNITY. To this end he embarked on a program of lecturing on the subject of American intelligence, founded the Association of Former Intelligence Officers, and wrote *The Night Watch* (1977), his professional memoirs. He has since written several other books, including a spy novel and a book for young adults, *Careers in Secret Operations: How to Be a Federal Intelligence Officer.*

Phillips was awarded the Purple Heart and the Air Medal for his service in the Second World War.

(*Who's Who in America*, 42nd ed.; Phillips, *The Night Watch*.)

PHILLIPS, WALLACE BANTA (March 30, 1886–April 14, 1952): businessman, intelligence officer

A native of New York City, Phillips was educated at the Sorbonne. In 1913 he joined the Pyrene Co. Ltd., a London petrochemical and rubber company.

Phillips served in U.S. Army Intelligence in France in 1917–19, after which he returned to the Pyrene Co. He established a private intelligence service for commercial clients, which was headquartered in London, and which, he claimed, "had on its payroll no less than seven ex-Prime Ministers," and the reports of which had "wide circulation among influential American, British, and Continental financial and commercial companies."

In 1939 Rear Adm. Walter S. Anderson, the director of the Office of Naval Intelligence, hired Phillips to establish and operate a SECRET INTELLIGENCE unit within ONI. The unit, known as the K Organization, consisted of networks of agents in Europe, the Middle East, North Africa, and Mexico. The value of the K Organization to ONI is obscure, but the fact that Admiral Anderson permitted Phillips to offer the unit to Gen. WILLIAM J. DONOVAN in 1941, suggests he did not value it highly. He proposed it be made part of the office of the Coordinator of Information, the predecessor of the OFFICE OF STRATEGIC SERVICES. Donovan accepted the proposal, and the K Organization became the Special Information Service of the COI, with Phillips as its director.

The inclusion of Phillips's Mexican agents in the transfer created a bureaucratic problem for Donovan. J. EDGAR HOOVER regarded Latin America as the exclusive intelligence jurisdiction of the FEDERAL BUREAU OF INVESTIGATION, and although he had negotiated an exception with ONI in the case of Phillips's Mexican apparatus, he did not regard this agreement as transferable to the COI, which he saw as a serious rival to the Bureau. In fact, COI's responsibility for the Mexican agents was a temporary arrangement, which was to continue only until ONI could appoint a replacement for Phillips, at which time the agents were to return to Navy jurisdiction. This was just how the dispute was resolved.

Although Phillips's Special Information Service was the embryo of the OSS SECRET INTELLIGENCE BRANCH, Phillips himself did not long remain Donovan's secret intelligence chief. Phillips, regarded as a "loner," was distrusted by the British Secret Intelligence Service, which was at that time working closely with COI. Consequently Phillips was eased out and succeeded by DAVID K. E. BRUCE.

Phillips left the OSS in 1943 and returned to his business interests in London.

(*Who Was Who in America*, v. 3; Troy, *Donovan and the CIA*; Cave Brown, *The Last Hero*; Dorwart, *Conflict of Duty*.)

PINKERTON, ALLAN (August 25, 1819–July 1, 1884): detective, intelligence officer

A native of Glasgow, Scotland, Pinkerton was apprenticed to a cooper (barrel-maker) at the age of twelve. When he was eighteen and a journeyman cooper, he became active in the violent wing of the Chartists, a political movement aimed at democratic political and social reforms. In 1842 he fled Scotland to avoid arrest, emigrated to Canada and, shortly thereafter, to the United States. He settled in Dundee, Illinois, a Scottish settlement in the northwest environs of Chicago, where he established himself as a cooper.

Pinkerton's incidental involvement in the apprehension of some local counterfeiters earned him a reputation as an amateur sleuth and the post of deputy sheriff, first of rural Kane County, and later of Cook County, Illinois. He moved to Chicago and, in circa 1849, became that city's first detective. Some time in the early 1850s Pinkerton established the North-Western Police Agency, one of the first private detective agencies in the world. Contracts to provide security for the Illinois Central and other railroads enabled the agency to grow and expand geographically, and the name was changed to PINKERTON'S NATIONAL DETECTIVE AGENCY.

During the 1850s Pinkerton, a rabid abolitionist and friend of John Brown, was active in smuggling escaped slaves to Canada. Pinkerton later implied that he had planned to free John Brown after the latter was captured at Harper's Ferry, but had been thwarted by federal vigilance.

In January 1861 Pinkerton and his agency were hired by the Philadelphia, Wilmington & Baltimore Railroad to investigate reports that Maryland secessionists planned to destroy the railroad in the event of war. This investigation led to Pinkerton discovering and thwarting the BALTIMORE PLOT to assassinate President-elect Lincoln en route to his inauguration. In April he wrote to Lincoln and offered the cream of his agents as a federal secret service. Lincoln summoned him to Washington to discuss the idea, but without result.

In May 1861 Pinkerton was asked by Gen. George B. McClellan to organize a secret service for the Department of the Ohio, which he commanded (before the war McClellan had been vice-president of the Illinois Central Railroad, one of Pinkerton's largest clients). Pinkerton agreed, and in July 1861, when McClellan was placed in charge of the Army of the Potomac, Pinkerton and his detectives went along with him.

Operating under the pseudonym of "E. J. Allen," Pinkerton remained McClellan's secret service chief until the general was relieved of his command in November 1862 following Antietam. He performed two functions: chief of military intelligence and chief of counterespionage. His background in crime detection contributed to his success in the latter field; among his accomplishments was breaking up the Washington spy ring organized by Col. THOMAS JORDAN and the arrest of ROSE O'NEAL GREENHOW.

The scope of Pinkerton's positive intelligence service was quite narrow. Civil War historian and espionologist Edwin C. Fishel has found that Pinkerton's bureau had only two principal positive intelligence functions: running secret agents into Richmond and elsewhere in Virginia, and interrogating prisoners of war, deserters, and refugees. By contrast, Pinkerton's successor, GEORGE H. SHARPE, ran a greatly expanded positive intelligence operation, similar to modern intelligence services (see BUREAU OF MILITARY INFORMATION).

Pinkerton's Civil War service is chiefly known for his grossly inflated estimates of Lee's Army of Northern Virginia. He overrated enemy numbers by factors of two, three, and even four. By the time Lee reached his top strength of 88,000, Pinkerton was crediting him with 200,000—about twice the size of McClellan's own Army of the Potomac. There is a consensus among historians that these estimates contributed heavily to McClellan's excessive caution, the quality that caused President Lincoln eventually to dismiss him. Writers have blamed Pinkerton's inflated estimates on incompetence, alleging credulity on the part of his interrogators and spies, and attributing that failing to their lack of military background. Fishel, however, has pointed out that Pinkerton "worked for a general who did not really use intelligence except to justify his dislike of fighting." The possibility that the overestimates were fashioned to McClellan's liking are examined by Fishel in a work now in progress on Union intelligence.

Pinkerton ceased to work in military intelligence after McClellan's dismissal, but he continued to work for the War Department, investigating war-related claims against the government, frauds, and peculations for the duration of the war.

After the war Pinkerton returned his agency to its civilian practice. It flourished in the period of industrialization and economic growth of the postwar "Gilded Age."

(Horan and Swiggett, *The Pinkerton Story;* Horan, *The Pinkertons;* Fishel, "The Mythology of Civil War Intelligence"; Schmidt, "G-2, Army of the Potomac"; Bidwell, "History of the Military Intelligence Division, Department of the Army General Staff"; Morn, *"The Eye That Never Sleeps".*)

PINKERTON's NATIONAL DETECTIVE AGENCY

One of the first private detective agencies in the world, Pinkerton's was established in the early 1850s by Allan Pinkerton and was initially called the North-Western Police Agency. Contracts to provide security services to the Illinois Central and other railroads enlarged the size and scope of the business before the Civil War. An investigation into reported secessionist sabotage plans against the Philadelphia, Wilmington & Baltimore Railroad led Pinkerton's detectives to discover and thwart a conspiracy to assassinate President-elect Lincoln en route to his inauguration in February 1861 (see BALTIMORE PLOT).

In May 1861 Pinkerton put himself and his detectives (see GEORGE BANGS, TIMOTHY WEBSTER, KATE WARNE, PRYCE LEWIS, and JOHN SCULLY) at the service of Gen. George B. McClellan, then commander of the Department of the Ohio. In effect, the agency became McClellan's secret service, and it went along with him when he was placed in command of the Army of the Potomac in July 1861. The agency was effective at counterespionage (see ROSE O'NEAL GREENHOW), a function similar to its usual crime detection role. However, Pinkerton grossly overestimated the strength of Lee's Army of Northern Virginia by factors of two, three, and even four (see ALLAN PINKERTON).

After McClellan was relieved as commander of the Army of the Potomac in November 1862, Pinkerton and most of his agents ceased secret service work, although one, JOHN C. BABCOCK stayed on with the Army of the Potomac as a scout and a one-man secret service of McClellan's successor, Gen. Ambrose Burnside (see BUREAU OF MILITARY INFORMATION).

After the war the agency returned to its private police operations and flourished in the postwar period of economic growth and industrialization. Following the death of Allan Pinkerton in 1884, the management of the agency was taken over by his sons, William A. and Robert A. Pinkerton. Because its operations, unlike official police departments, were nationwide (and even occasionally worldwide), it became a de facto national police agency. It was the first American police organization to maintain centralized criminal records on a national and international basis. In 1897, under the auspices of the International Association of Chiefs of Police, the agency established the National Bureau of Criminal Identification, a centralized criminal records center. In 1924 the collection was turned over to the Identification Division of the Federal Bureau of Investigation.

During the late nineteenth and early twentieth centuries, the agency's anti-labor operations on behalf of large industrial clients became famous and unpopular. After the agency's involvement in the bloody Homestead strike in Pennsylvania in 1892, Congress passed the "Pinkerton Law," which prohibited the federal government from hiring private detective agencies.

Between 1895 and 1898 Pinkerton's worked for the Spanish government to thwart the efforts of Cuban emigrés and their American sympathizers to launch military expeditions from American territory against the Spanish colonial forces in Cuba. Apparently the agency's service to Spain was terminated in April 1898, with the outbreak of the Spanish-American War.

In 1914 the French government hired Pinkerton's to investigate a ring of German espionage and sabotage agents operating in New Orleans. A Pinkerton agent penetrated the organization, prevented the bombing of a French ship, and later brought about the arrest of the principal saboteur, who was detained for the duration of the FIRST WORLD WAR. However, after the United States entered the war the U.S. government was unreceptive to William Pinkerton's overtures to put the agency to work as a centralized intelligence and counterespionage service.

In recent years the agency, now called Pinkerton's Inc., has become primarily a private guard service, and it no longer handles labor cases. The agency's logo during its earlier years was a human eye above the motto "We never sleep," and it is believed this symbol led to the term "private eye."

(Horan and Swiggett, *The Pinkerton Story;* Horan, *The Pinkertons;* Schmidt, "G-2, Army of the Potomac"; Bidwell, "History of the Military Intelligence Division, Department of the Army General Staff"; Morn, *"The Eye That Never Sleeps."*)

Allan Pinkerton (seated, right) and staff while serving with the Army of the Potomac, October 1862. Standing, left to right: George H. Bangs, John C. Babcock, and Augustus K. Littlefield, all Pinkerton operatives. Seated at Pinkerton's right is William Moore, private secretary to Secretary of War Edwin M. Stanton. Source: Library of Congress.

PITTENGER, WILLIAM M.E. (January 31, 1840–1905): schoolteacher, clergyman, soldier, Union secret service agent

A native of Jefferson County, Ohio, Pittenger attended local schools while growing up on his parents' farm. At age sixteen he obtained a teacher's certificate and began teaching school in Ohio, and later in Illinois. He was reading law at the outbreak of the Civil War.

Putting aside his plans to become a lawyer, he enlisted in the Ohio Volunteer Infantry, which was part of the Army of the Ohio. He saw action at the battle of Bull Run in July 1861, and had achieved the rank of corporal by April 1862, when he volunteered to take part in a paramilitary operation behind Con-federate lines aimed at severing the rail line between Atlanta and Chattanooga (see ANDREWS'S RAID). He and a party of twenty other Union troops in civilian clothes, led by JAMES J. ANDREWS, hijacked a locomotive and attempted to destroy railroad tracks and bridges between the two cities. He was captured by Confederate troops and imprisoned (Andrews and seven of the others were hanged). He and five others escaped, were recaptured, and were exchanged for Confederate prisoners of war in March 1863. Pittenger and the other five were awarded the newly created Medal of Honor by Secretary of War Edwin Stanton. They were the first to receive the decoration.

Pittenger returned to civilian life and attended the Scientific School at Princeton, New Jersey, and the School of Elocution and Oratory at Philadelphia,

Pennsylvania. He became a minister of the Methodist Episcopal Church and settled in Haddonfield, New Jersey. He wrote *Daring and Suffering,* an 1864 account of his wartime adventures, and *The Great Locomotive Chase,* another book on the episode, in 1889. He also wrote several works on preaching and public speaking.

When Pittenger was captured by the Confederates during the war he was a witness for the prosecution in the trial of Andrews and the other seven who were hanged. Many years later some of the other surviving members of the raid gave voice to long-held suspicions that Pittenger had made a deal with the Confederates to save his own life at the expense of his comrades. These charges resulted in a long and bitter controversy in which he was repeatedly forced to defend his actions.

(*Who Was Who in America,* v. 1; Bryan, *The Spy in America;* Boatner, *Civil War Dictionary;* O'Neill, *Wild Train.*)

POE, ANTHONY A. (ca. 1924–): paramilitary specialist and intelligence officer

Poe was born Anthony A. Poshepny in Hungary. A refugee from the Nazis, he became a U.S. citizen, served as an enlisted man in the U.S. Marines, saw action and was wounded on Iwo Jima. He remained in Asia after the war and served with the CIA CLANDESTINE SERVICE. In the late 1950s Poe recruited and trained the Khamba (Tibetan) tribesmen who took part in the Agency's TIBET OPERATION. During the 1960s he served in Southeast Asia. He fought with the anti-Sihanouk mercenaries against the Communist forces in Cambodia and later took part in the SECRET WAR IN LAOS. In Laos he trained and led the Meo and Yau tribesmen of the Agency's Armée Clandestine against the North Vietnamese and Pathet Lao forces in the country. He also sent teams of Yau guerrillas into mainland China on COVERT ACTION and intelligence missions.

Poe operated under the commercial cover of Continental Air Service, an American firm that cooperated with the CIA. When he was exposed as a CIA officer in the press he transferred his operations to Thailand.

Poe operated with an independent and individualistic style reminiscent to some of a Chinese warlord. He became the subject of bizarre and fearsome legends.

(Robbins, *Air America;* Branfman, "The President's Secret Army.")

POLGAR, THOMAS (July 24, 1922–): intelligence officer

A native of Budapest, Hungary, Polgar came to the United States in 1938, earned a B.A. degree from the Gaines School in New York City in 1942, and became a naturalized citizen in 1943. He had acquired some facility in French, Greek, Spanish, and German during his early life in Europe; and after he was drafted into the U.S. Army, this linguistic ability led to his assignment to the Office of Strategic Services. Trained as a counterespionage agent, Polgar was dropped behind German lines in Europe, and operated in Berlin during the closing days of the war.

After the war Polgar remained with the OSS and with its subsequent incarnations, the Strategic Services Unit, the Central Intelligence Group and, finally, the CENTRAL INTELLIGENCE AGENCY. He became a principal assistant to Gen. LUCIAN TRUSCOTT, chief of the CIA's West German station, where he served until 1954. He was assigned to the American embassy in Vienna, from 1961 to 1970, when he became chief of the CIA's station in Buenos Aires, Argentina.

Polgar's successful handling of an airliner hijacking at Buenos Aires brought about his assignment as chief of station in Saigon, a post he held until the American evacuation in 1975.

Polgar became chief of the Agency's Mexico City station in 1976. He retired from the CIA in 1981 and has since worked as a writer for the *Miami Herald,* and as a consultant to the Department of Defense.

(Snepp, *Decent Interval;* Agee and Wolf, *Dirty Work; Who's Who in America,* 37th ed.)

POOLE, DEWITT CLINTON (October 28, 1885–September 3, 1952): diplomat, educator, intelligence officer

A native of Vancouver Barracks, Washington, Poole graduated from the University of Wisconsin in 1906, and earned a master of diplomacy from George Washington University in 1910. He entered the Foreign Service in December 1910, serving as a vice-consul at Berlin (1911–14) and Paris (1914–15); in 1918 and 1919 he served in Moscow as consul, special assistant to the ambassador and charge d'affaires. Later Poole held the posts of chief of the State Department's Division of Russian Affairs, consul general at Cape Town, and counselor at the American embassy in Berlin (1926–30). He resigned from the Foreign Service in 1930 to become director of the School of Public Affairs at Princeton University, where he was also a member of the Institute for Advanced Study.

In 1941 JOHN C. WILEY recruited Poole to the Office of the Coordinator of Information (predecessor to the Office of Strategic Services) to help establish a unit to obtain intelligence from groups of foreign nationals and the foreign language press in the United States. Wiley, with Poole's recommendations, oversaw formation of the Foreign Nationalities Branch, which was retained when the COI became the OSS in 1942 (see OSS FOREIGN NATIONALITIES BRANCH). Poole stayed on to become chief of the Branch and served in that capacity until the end of the war.

Poole left the OSS in 1945 and was visiting lecturer on international politics at Harvard in 1946 and 1947. Between 1949 and 1951 he was president of the National Committee for a Free Europe, the organization funded by the Central Intelligence Agency to sponsor RADIO FREE EUROPE.

(Roosevelt, *War Report of the OSS*; Smith, *OSS*; *Who Was Who in America*, v. 3.)

POPE, ALLEN LAWRENCE (1929–): aviator, paramilitary operator

Pope attended the University of Florida. An Air Force pilot, he flew combat missions in the Korean War. He worked for an airline in Texas before becoming a pilot with Civil Air Transport, the CIA-owned airline that operated in the Far East during the 1950s (see AIR PROPRIETARIES). During the operation in which CAT dropped supplies to the besieged French troops in Dien Bien Phu, he flew fifty-seven airdrop missions to the fortress, which was surrounded by Vietminh anti-aircraft positions.

During the INDONESIA REBELLION in 1958, Pope was one of the CAT pilots who flew B-26 bombers in support of the CIA-supported rebels. On the morning of May 18th, a Sunday, while flying a combat mission against loyalist Indonesian troops near Ambon in the Celebes, Pope mistook a church for a military target, bombed it, and killed most of the congregation. He was shot down, captured, tried, and sentenced to death.

Pope was not executed, but held in prison in Jakarta, and the American government negotiated with the Indonesians for his release. President Kennedy tried to obtain his release after taking office in 1961, and Robert Kennedy succeeded in doing so in July 1962.

Within a few months of his release Pope joined Southern Air Transport of Miami, Florida, another CIA-owned airline.

(Smith, *Portrait of a Cold Warrior*; Marchetti and Marks, *The CIA and the Cult of Intelligence*; Leary, *Perilous Missions*; Hilsman, *To Move a Nation*; Robbins, *Air America*.)

PORTER, JOHN REED (ca. 1841–ca. 1907): businessman, soldier, Union secret agent

Porter lived in Wood County, Ohio, before the Civil War. In 1861 he enlisted in the Ohio Volunteer Infantry, which was part of the Army of the Ohio. In April 1862 he volunteered to take part in a paramilitary operation behind Confederate lines aimed at severing the rail line between Atlanta and Chattanooga (see ANDREWS'S RAID). He and a party of twenty other Union troops in civilian clothes, led by JAMES J. ANDREWS, hijacked a locomotive and attempted to destroy railroad tracks and bridges between the two cities. He was captured by Confederate troops and imprisoned (Andrews and seven of the others were hanged). He and several others escaped.

After the war he helped his father run the family's general store in McComb, Ohio.

(Bryan, *The Spy in America*; Boatner, *Civil War Dictionary*; O'Neill, *Wild Train*.)

POSSONY, STEFAN THOMAS (March 15, 1913–): political scientist, foreign affairs specialist, psychological warfare specialist

A native of Vienna, Austria, Possony received a Ph.D. from the University of Vienna in 1933. He came to the United States in 1940 and became an American citizen in 1945. He was a member of the Institute for Advanced Study at Princeton, New Jersey, during 1941–43. In 1943 the Office of Naval Intelligence employed Possony as a psychological warfare expert. He was head of the German Desk of Op-16-W, the Special Warfare Branch of ONI. He wrote more than 250 scripts for the "Commander Norden" propaganda broadcasts aimed at German submariners (see RALPH G. ALBRECHT).

In 1946 Possony became a professor in the graduate school at Georgetown University, and at the same time was employed by the U.S. Air Force. He continued with both organizations until 1961, when he became director of the international political studies program of Stanford University's Hoover Institution.

He is the author of many books on military and foreign affairs.

(*Who's Who in America*, 37th ed.; Zacharias, *Secret Missions*; Farago, *Burn After Reading*.)

POTTS, JAMES M. (September 9, 1921–): intelligence officer

A native of Louisiana, Potts graduated from Yale University in 1942. During 1946–49 he worked for CARE, the international relief agency. He did graduate work at Columbia University, earning an M.A. in 1951.

Potts served with the Central Intelligence Agency. During 1951–60 he was an analyst and plans officer with the Department of the Army. In November 1960 he became deputy chief of the CIA station in Athens, Greece, a position he held until 1964. In February 1968 he returned to Greece as CIA chief of station, remaining in that position until August 1972.

In 1972 Potts was deputy chief, under LAWRENCE R. DEVLIN, of the Africa Division of the CIA CLANDESTINE SERVICE. He succeeded Devlin in that post in 1974, remaining in it until 1976, the period that included the beginning of the Agency's operations in Angola.

(Ray, et al., *Dirty Work 2*; Stockwell, *In Search of Enemies*.)

POWERS, FRANCIS GARY (August 17, 1929– August 1, 1977): Air Force officer, CIA reconnaissance pilot

Powers was a native of Burdine, Kentucky. He graduated from Milligan College in Tennessee in 1950, enlisted in the Air Force, went through the aviation cadet program and was commissioned as a second lieutenant in December 1952. He was assigned to the Strategic Air Command, an assignment that required him to have a top secret clearance. His high clearance level was one of the reasons he was recruited by the Central Intelligence Agency in January 1956 for the U-2 program (see OVERHEAD RECONNAISSANCE).

By arrangement with the Air Force, he was SHEEP-DIPPED, i.e., he resigned his commission and became a civilian employee of the CIA. He was sent to an isolated CIA training base in southern Nevada called Watertown, where he learned to fly the high-altitude reconnaissance aircraft. Completing his training in August 1956, he was assigned to the CIA's U-2 squadron at Incerlik Air Force Base at Adana, Turkey. The group was informally known as "Detachment 10-10," and operated undercover as the Weather Observational Squadron of the National Advisory Committee for Aeronautics (NACA), a civilian agency that was the predecessor of the National Aeronautics and Space Administration (NASA).

Powers flew his first mission over the Soviet Union in November 1956 and flew subsequent missions at irregular intervals during 1957 through 1959. During this period the Soviet government was aware of the overflights and had quietly protested them to the United States through diplomatic channels. However, to avoid the embarrassing admission that the Soviet Air Force was unable to intercept the high-altitude aircraft, the Soviets did not make their protests public and the flights continued. But by 1960 the Soviet Air Force apparently had improved its interception capability, and on May 1st Powers was shot down over Sverdlovsk while on a 3,800-mile flight reportedly from Peshawar, Pakistan, to Bodo, Norway.

Powers was held in Moscow's Lubyanka Prison and given a well-publicized trial in the Hall of Columns on August 17th. On August 19th he was sentenced to ten years' imprisonment. However, he served only about twenty months of this sentence, and on February 10, 1962 he was exchanged for Soviet intelligence officer RUDOLF IVANOVICH ABEL.

Upon his return to the United States Powers worked for a time for the CIA, then later as an engineering test pilot for Lockheed aircraft. He was flying as a helicopter traffic reporter for a California radio station when he was killed in a crash near Encino.

(Powers, *Operation Overflight*.)

PRAEGER, FREDERICK AMOS (September 16, 1915–): publisher, intelligence officer

A native of Vienna, Austria, Praeger attended the University of Vienna from 1933 to 1938, but studied at the Sorbonne during 1934. He moved to the United States in 1938 and held various jobs until 1942 when he enlisted in the U.S. Army as a private.

Praeger was assigned to Army intelligence and he taught Germany army organization and tactics. Later he was assigned to an intelligence unit of the Sixth Armored Division and participated in five European campaigns. He was given a battlefield commission of second lieutenant and was awarded the Bronze Star for his wartime service.

At the end of the war Praeger was in charge of the German and Austrian desk of the G-2 division at General Eisenhower's headquarters. He was discharged in 1946 but remained in Germany as a civilian employee of the American Military Government.

In 1950 Praeger founded Frederick A. Praeger, Inc., a publishing house that specialized in works on international relations, Russian history, the USSR, world Communism, military science, and art. In 1957 he published *The New Class*, a critique of Communism by Milovan Djilas, the former vice-premier of Yugoslavia. In 1967 Praeger stated that some "fifteen or sixteen" of the books published by his firm in the late 1950s had been done at the suggestion of the Central Intelligence Agency.

Praeger sold his publishing firm in 1968. Since 1975 he has been president of Westview Press in Boulder, Colorado.

(*Who's Who in America*, 41st ed.; *Current Biography*, 1959; *New York Times*, February 24, 1967, p. 16.)

PRESIDENT'S FOREIGN INTELLIGENCE ADVISORY BOARD (PFIAB)

The PFIAB is a panel of prominent private citizens that advises the President of the United States on matters concerning the management of the INTELLIGENCE COMMUNITY. It was created in February 1956 by President Eisenhower on the recommendation of the Hoover Commission. It was originally known as the President's Board of Consultants on Foreign Intelligence Activities and consisted of eight members and a small staff. Dr. James R. Killian, Jr., the president of the Massachusetts Institute of Technology, was the Board's first chairman.

The Board was automatically dissolved at the end of Eisenhower's presidency, and President Kennedy reestablished it only after the failure of the BAY OF PIGS INVASION. It was then renamed the President's Foreign Intelligence Advisory Board, and was chaired by Gen. James Doolittle. Clark Clifford chaired the PFIAB during the administration of President Lyndon Johnson. He was succeeded by Gen. Maxwell Taylor during the Nixon administration, and Adm. George Anderson and, later, Leo Cherne, during the Ford administration. President Carter abolished the PFIAB soon after taking office, but it was reestablished by President Reagan, who appointed Anne Armstrong to chair it.

The PFIAB meets approximately once every two months in Washington and receives briefings from the Central Intelligence Agency on CURRENT INTELLIGENCE collection and NATIONAL INTELLIGENCE ESTIMATES. The Board rarely concerns itself with COVERT ACTION operations, except for postmortems on notable failures. It is credited with stimulating the development of the U-2 RECONNAISSANCE AIRCRAFT, the SR-71 RECONNAISSANCE AIRCRAFT, and the reconnaissance satellite programs (see OVERHEAD RECONNAISSANCE). It encouraged CIA Director JOHN A. MCCONE to established the CIA SCIENCE AND TECHNOLOGY DIRECTORATE, and proposed the idea, adopted by Director GEORGE BUSH, of the so-called "A-Team/B-Team" exercise in which National Intelligence Estimates of Soviet strategic strength received independent review by a panel of experts outside the CIA.

Over the years membership of the PFIAB has grown to twenty-two.

(Marchetti and Marks, *The CIA and the Cult of Intelligence*; Ransom, *The Intelligence Establishment*; Cline, *The CIA: Reality vs. Myth*.)

PROPRIETARY COMPANY; OFTEN SIMPLY PROPRIETARY

A commercial corporation secretly owned by an intelligence agency that provides *nonofficial cover* for the that agency's operations and personnel.

See also AIR PROPRIETARIES, WESTERN ENTERPRISES, SEA SUPPLY COMPANY, DEVISED FACILITY, COVER.

(Breckinridge, *The CIA and the U.S. Intelligence System*; Marks, *The CIA's Corporate Shell Game*.)

PROVOCATION, ALSO PROVOCATION AGENT

An intelligence agent who seeks to plant false information on an opposition intelligence service. The *provocation* may pose as a WALK-IN or defector, and the purpose of his mission may simply be to embarrass the opposition service by enticing one of its CASE OFFICERS into exposing himself. He may also seek to learn the intelligence requirements, i.e., the subjects of intelligence interest, of the opposition service. Or his purpose may be to mislead the opposition regarding some important element of STRATEGIC INTELLIGENCE, to protect a PENETRATION AGENT who has come under suspicion, or to sow doubt, dissension, and suspicion within the opposition service in order to hamstring it.

PUEBLO INCIDENT

Summary: On January 23, 1968, the U.S.S. *Pueblo*, a small (970 tons) coastal freighter converted for use by the U.S. Navy as a SIGINT platform, was cruising off the eastern coast of North Korea. Although the *Pueblo* was beyond the twelve-mile territorial limit claimed by North Korea, she was challenged by two North Korean submarine chasers and four North Korean torpedo boats. North Korean jet fighter planes buzzed the ship and fired warning shots. When she refused to be boarded, the North Koran vessels fired on her, wounding four of the *Pueblo*'s crewmen, one fatally. The *Pueblo* was very lightly armed and capable of a speed of little more than thirteen knots—far

U.S.S. *Pueblo*. Source: U.S. Navy.

slower than the North Korean vessels—and therefore was forced to surrender.

The *Pueblo*'s captain, Comdr. LLOYD M. BUCHER, the five other officers, seventy-five enlisted men, and two civilian employees of the NAVY SECURITY GROUP, were taken prisoner and held in North Korea for eleven months.

Background and Discussion: The cruise of the *Pueblo* was part of a joint NATIONAL SECURITY AGENCY Naval Security Service operation code-named Clickbeetle, aimed at collecting SIGINT from Soviet and North Korean naval units and other intelligence targets in or near the northern Pacific Ocean, the East China Sea, and the Sea of Japan. Clickbeetle had been in progress for three years at the time of the *Pueblo* incident; the earlier cruises had been made by the U.S.S. *Banner*, a converted coastal freighter similar to the *Pueblo*. The *Pueblo* departed on its ill-fated cruise from the Japanese port of Yokosuka on January 5, 1968.

Clickbeetle and similar U.S. seaborne SIGINT operations had been inspired by similar operations conducted for many years by Soviet trawlers near American territorial waters or naval units. Such operations are not a violation of international law. However, there had been a sharp increase in border incidents along the thirty-eighth parallel in Korea in the weeks before the *Pueblo* incident, and two days before the incident, a force of thirty-one North Korean commandos had infiltrated Seoul in an unsuccessful attempt to assassinate the South Korean president. Shortly before the *Pueblo* left Yokosuka, the NSA sent a warning message regarding the cruise to the Joint Chiefs of Staff, noting recent belligerent actions by the North Koreans, and specifically actions in international waters. However, this message was sidetracked and failed to result in any precautionary action.

In his memoirs of his presidency, President Lyndon Johnson theorized that the *Pueblo* incident was a Communist feint, designed to force south Korea to withdraw its troops from Vietnam, and so help insure the success of the North Vietnamese Tet offensive that began eight days later (see VIETNAM WAR).

(Johnson, *The Vantage Point*; Bamford, *The Puzzle Palace*; Bucher, *My Story*; Brandt, *The Last Voyage of the USS Pueblo*; Armbrister, *A Matter of Accountability*.)

Q

QUINN, WILLIAM WILSON (November 1, 1907–): Army officer, businessman, intelligence officer

A native of Crisfield, Maryland, Quinn attended St. John's College in Annapolis, Maryland, during 1927–29, and graduated from the U.S. Military Academy in 1933. He commanded an infantry company, then was provost marshal of Manila, the Philippine Islands, during 1937–38. He attended the infantry school at Ford Benning, Georgia, during 1938–39, and the Command and General Staff School at Fort Leavenworth, Kansas, in 1941.

Quinn served in Army Intelligence and was G-2 of the Fourth Corps during 1943–44. In 1944–45 he was G-2 of the Seventh Army. When the German forces had been driven from southern France he met frequently with ALLEN W. DULLES, chief of the OSS SECRET INTELLIGENCE BRANCH station in Switzerland, to receive the latest intelligence Dulles had regarding the situation in Germany. Quinn worked closely with OSS agents (mostly German prisoners of war who agreed to work for the Allies) whom Dulles sent into Germany.

Quinn's close association with OSS secret intelligence and counterespionage operations during the war stood him in good stead when he took command of the Strategic Services Unit (the caretaker organization established to maintain OSS assets after the OSS was dissolved) in April 1946. He remained chief of the unit after it was absorbed into the Central Intelligence Group as the Office of Special Operations later in 1946 (see CENTRAL INTELLIGENCE AGENCY).

Quinn left CIG/OSO in 1947. He was G-2 with the Army's Tenth Corps during the Inchon landing of 1950 in the KOREAN WAR, and later commanded the Seventeenth Infantry Regiment of the Seventh Infantry Division in Korea. During 1953–55 he was chief of the Army section of the Joint U.S. Military Advisory Group in Greece.

Quinn had several infantry command assignments during 1955–57, and was chief of the Army's Public Information Division during 1960–61. In 1961 Quinn, then a lieutenant general, was made deputy director of the newly established DEFENSE INTELLIGENCE AGENCY. He left the DIA post in 1964 to take command of the Seventh U.S. Army in Germany, and retired in 1966.

After his retirement Quinn served as vice-president of the Martin Marietta Corporation until 1972. Thereafter he was president of Quinn Associates in Washington, D.C.

Among Quinn's many decorations and awards are the Distinguished Service Medal, the Silver Star, Legion of Merit, Air Medal, Purple Heart, and the French croix de guerre.

(*Who's Who in America*, 42nd ed.; Troy, *Donovan and the CIA*; Braden, "The Birth of the CIA"; Dulles, *The Secret Surrender*.)

QUINTANILLA, MARIA ALINE GRIFFITH Y DEXTER (May 22, 1921–): writer, intelligence officer

A native of Pearl River, New York, Maria Aline Griffith graduated from the College of Mount St.

Vincent in 1941 and shortly thereafter was recruited into the Office of Strategic Services. She participated in covert operations in Madrid during the war. After the war she met and married a Spanish nobelman.

She has written several books and worked as the Spanish representative of *Vogue* magazine.

(*Contemporary Authors*, v. 11–12R; Gannett Westchester Newspapers, May 10, 1983.)

R

RABORN, WILLIAM FRANCIS, JR. (June 8, 1905–): Navy officer, intelligence officer

A native of Decatur, Texas, Raborn grew up in Marlow, Oklahoma, and graduated from the U.S. Naval Academy in 1928. He became a naval aviator and established the Aviation Gunnery School at Barbers Point, Pearl Harbor, where he served from 1940 to 1942. During the Second World War he served aboard the aircraft carrier U.S.S. *Hancock* in several campaigns including Iwo Jima and Okinawa. He was awarded a Silver Star for his actions when the *Hancock* was hit in a Kamikaze attack.

After the war Raborn served several tours of duty in the research and development of guided missiles. In 1955 he was chosen to head the Polaris missile development program. He retired in 1963 with the rank of vice admiral and joined the Aerojet-General Corporation as vice-president for management. In 1965 President Johnson appointed him director of the CENTRAL INTELLIGENCE AGENCY, a post he took over from JOHN MCCONE.

The appointment as director of central intelligence of an individual with no intelligence experience and a minimal background in foreign affairs baffled and irritated professional CIA intelligence officers. Reports of Raborn's alleged gaffes and blunders soon made the rounds in Washington and found their way into the media. Raborn resigned in 1966 and was succeeded by his deputy director of central intelligence, RICHARD HELMS.

Although CIA insiders regarded Raborn's brief tenure as DCI as undistinguished, he is credited with instituting a centralized Operations Center in CIA, and with bringing about closer cooperation between the CIA CLANDESTINE SERVICE and the CIA INTELLIGENCE DIRECTORATE.

Raborn's decorations and awards include the Distinguished Service Medal and the National Security Medal.

(*Who's Who in America*, 37th ed.; Cline, *The CIA: Reality vs. Myth*; Powers, *The Man Who Kept the Secrets*.)

RADINT

Radar intelligence (see -INT). The term applies to intelligence collected through the use of radar. For example, foreign missile tests might be observed by tracking the test vehicle by radar; strategic installations might be observed by air- or spaceborne SIDE-LOOKING AIRCRAFT RADAR.

RADIO FREE EUROPE/RADIO LIBERTY (RFE/RL)

Summary: In 1950 and 1951, respectively, RFE and RL were covertly founded by the CIA CLANDESTINE SERVICE as a psychological COVERT ACTION operation. Based in Munich, West Germany, RFE and RL broadcast to Eastern Europe and the Soviet Union, respectively, carrying news, information, and entertainment otherwise denied to the radio audiences by the local Communist authorities. CIA sponsorship of the two radio stations was widely rumored during the 1960s and was publicly confirmed by Sen. Clifford Case in 1971. CIA support was terminated in 1973, after which the stations were openly funded by the U.S. government through the congressionally chartered Board for International Broadcasting.

Background: While serving as deputy assistant secretary of state for occupied countries FRANK G. WISNER had worked on the problems posed by the large number of refugees in Germany, Austria, and Trieste—Russians and East Europeans who had fled to the West. The refugees were strongly anti-Soviet and, of course, intimately familiar with the languages and society of their native lands. When Wisner became director of the newly created Office of Policy Coordination in 1948 (see CENTRAL INTELLIGENCE AGENCY, CIA CLANDESTINE SERVICE) he enlisted the aid of the refugees in the CIA/OPC's program of COVERT ACTION against the Soviet Union and its East European satellites. To carry out this plan he asked the assistance of veteran diplomat Joseph C. Grew and educator and former foreign service officer DEWITT CLINTON POOLE. Poole had headed the OSS FOREIGN NATIONALITIES BRANCH, a unit that had worked with political refugees in the United States during the war. Poole's wartime experience and contacts were directly applicable to what Wisner had in mind. With OPC funds and direction, Poole and Grew formed the National Committee for a Free Europe in June 1949 to provide a cover for CIA/OPC's refugee operations. Poole became president of the committee, and Grew served as chairman of its board of directors.

Poole and Grew enlisted the aid of *Fortune* publisher C.D. JACKSON to round up a roster of prominent Americans ready to lend their names to the Committee's letterhead (the original Committee included foreign service official and lawyer ADOLPH BERLE; newspaperman Mark Ethridge; and ALLEN DULLES, among others). Jackson, who had been General Eisenhower's chief of psychological warfare during the preparations for the D-Day landings, persuaded the general to take a more active part in the Committee. Eisenhower and Gen. Lucius Clay organized the Crusade for Freedom, ostensibly a drive to raise funds for the Committee from businesses and private individuals, and in reality a cover for the fact that the Committee's money came from the CIA.

The Committee worked to organize anti-Communist emigrés in both the United States and Europe. Its stated goals were "to keep alive the hope of freedom in the countries of Eastern Europe dominated by Russia . . . to preserve such exiled leaders of those satellite countries as have found asylum in the United States for the day of liberation, [and] to help rededicate Americans to their heritage of freedom."

The Committee's headquarters were located in midtown Manhattan. Its Intellectual Cooperation Division was set up in Washington, with the help of the Library of Congress, as a center where refugee scholars studied economic and political developments in their homelands. The Division also had a Mid-European Studies Center in New York City that received some support from New York University and the Carnegie Endowment for International Peace. The Division established the Free University in Exile in Strasbourg, France, to educate refugee youths for the day when it was hoped they could return to their native lands and assume leadership.

The Committee's American Contacts Division served as a lecture bureau for emigré leaders touring the United States. Under the National Councils Division, refugee groups were established for each of the Soviet satellite nations. The National Councils were to be virtual governments-in-exile, ready to be put in place whenever the satellite nation was liberated from Soviet grasp.

The Committee was also used to provide cover for a psychological warfare operation—radio propaganda directed against the Soviet-controlled governments of the East European satellites. Plans were made for a battery of powerful radio transmitters to be established in West Germany, operating under the name Radio Free Europe, a division of the Committee. The first of these, a shortwave station with a signal that carried across Eastern Europe, was opened near Frankfurt in July 1950. The following May a broadcast-band station was put into operation in Munich; its signal was beamed at Czechoslovakia. Eventually a complex of radio transmitters broadcast programs in the native languages to Bulgaria, Czechoslovakia, Hungary, Poland, and Romania.

The RFE stations broadcast talks by exiles, personal messages, replies to mail from listeners in the satellites, the names of Communist secret police agents and informers working undercover in the target countries, news items embarrassing to or derogatory of the Communist government, and American jazz and other popular music banned in Eastern Europe. Uninhibited by an overt connection to the U.S. government, RFE was able to denounce the Soviet Union and Communism in the harshest terms without causing diplomatic embarrassment to the U.S. government, which could deny that it had control over or responsibility for the RFE operation.

In parallel with the Committee for a Free Europe, CIA/OPC established the Committee for the Liberation of the Peoples of Russia in 1951, an organization of refugees from the Soviet Union. The Committee subsidized the Munich-based Institute for the Study of the USSR, which published, inter alia, *Who's Who in the USSR*, and established Radio Liberation, which broadcast news, information, and features in Russian and the languages of other Soviet ethnic groups to the USSR. In 1959 the station's name was changed to Radio Liberty.

Supervision of the refugee committees and the stations became the responsibility of the International Organizations Division of the CIA's Clandestine Service (See THOMAS W. BRADEN, CORD MEYER) after that Division was established in 1951, and was moved to the Covert Action Staff when the Division was merged with the Staff in 1962. As the prospect of successful uprisings against the Communist regimes in Eastern Europe dimmed during the 1950s, the role of the refugee committees in CIA COVERT ACTION diminished correspondingly; but the stations, which were achieving increasing success among their intended audiences, continued to operate and expand.

RFE eventually grew to 1,600 employees; RL to one thousand. The news and editorial staff of both operations collected and indexed a large volume of information through analysis of the Soviet and East European press, interviews with travelers and recent emigrés from the Communist countries, and from similar sources. The value of this vast information resource was recognized by CIA intelligence analysts, who systematically exploited it for material collateral to their other sources on the USSR and East Europe.

The stations attracted wide listenership because they filled a demand for accurate and uncensored world and national news that was otherwise unavailable within the Soviet bloc. Precisely because their credibility was their most appealing feature, the CIA refrained from using the stations to spread disinformation. Factual information was found to be the most effective method of psychological warfare in this instance, and the radios were a *gray propaganda* (see COVERT ACTION) operation only in the sense that their official American sponsorship—about $36 million per year—was concealed.

One measure of the radios' success was the campaign mounted against them by the Soviet and East European Communist authorities. In addition to attempting to jam the stations' signals by electronic means, the Communists undertook a variety of sabotage operations against them, including the apparent assassination of two RL employees, poisoning the food in the RFE cafeteria, infiltrating the stations' staffs with PENETRATION AGENTS, and intimidating some of the refugee employees by taking reprisals against relatives living in Soviet-controlled territory.

Some commentators have criticized the role of RFE during the Hungarian uprising against the Soviets in 1956, charging the station with having encouraged the Hungarians in the false hope of U.S. intervention on their behalf, or even of having provoked the uprising. Several independent reviews (e.g., one by an ad hoc commission of the West German government, and another by the Council of Europe) of tapes of the RFE broadcasts beamed at Hungary during the crisis have contradicted this assertion while finding that the tone and some of the remarks made during the broadcasts could have been misinterpreted. When the Czechoslovakian regime of Alexander Dubcek undertook a program of liberalization and independence of Moscow twelve years later, the RFE followed an especially cautious and circumspect editorial policy in order to forestall a similar situation. This, of course, became irrelevant to events after the Soviets invaded Czechoslovakia and arrested the government.

The Hungarian affair highlighted the question of the stations' sponsorship. During the early 1960s speculations regarding the CIA's role frequently appeared in books, magazine articles, and newspaper reports, and soon became a matter of widespread rumor. In 1971 Sen. Clifford Case publicly disclosed that the two stations were funded by the CIA, and introduced legislation to fund them by direct appropriation, thereby bringing them under open congressional oversight. CIA sponsorship and control of the stations was ended in December 1973 when Congress passed such a bill and established the Board for International Broadcasting to take over budgetary control and policy guidance of the stations. The Board consists of five members appointed by the President for three-year terms with the advice and consent of the Senate, as well as the chief executives of RFE and RL, who have nonvoting status. The Board receives its policy direction from the Department of State and reports annually to both the President and Congress.

(Meyer, *Facing Reality;* Karalekas, *History of the Central Intelligence Agency;* "Dewitt Clinton Poole," *Current Biography,* 1950; Cook, *The Declassified Eisenhower;* Wise and Ross, *The Invisible Government; New York Times,* January 24, 1971, p. 1, November 20, 1971, p. 8, February 21, 1972, p. 1, March 31, 1972, p. 27; August 22, 1972, p. 25.)

RATTOON, JOHN: British secret agent and courier

During the American Revolution, Rattoon, a resident of South Amboy, New Jersey, carried some of the treasonous correspondence of BENEDICT ARNOLD and Sir Henry Clinton between New York City and Philadelphia. Rattoon's role in the Arnold affair was never suspected during his liftime, which he lived out in South Amboy.

(Van Doren, *Secret History of the American Revolution.*)

RB-47 INCIDENT

On July 1, 1960 a U.S. Air Force RB-47 (a reconnaissance version of the B-47 medium-range strategic jet bomber) was shot down by a Soviet fighter plane over international waters while on a *ferret* ELINT mission over the Barents Sea. Four of the six crew members, including Maj. Willard G. Palm, were killed. Capt. Freeman B. Olmstead, the copilot, and Capt. John R. McKone, the navigator, survived and were captured by the Soviets.

Despite U.S. protests, Olmstead and McKone were incarcerated in the KGB's infamous Lubyanka Prison in Moscow, accused of spying, and subjected to intense interrogation. The two officers were released on January 21, 1961, ostensibly as a Soviet gesture of goodwill to the newly inaugurated President John Kennedy, but in fact as part of a spy exchange. Soviet secret intelligence agents Igor Y. Melekh and Willie Hirsch, who had been arrested on espionage charges by the Federal Bureau of Investigation and were awaiting trial, were released by federal authorities in April 1961 as the American part of the bargain.

The body of Major Palm was also returned and buried in Arlington National Cemetery.

(Cookridge, *Spy Trade;* Wise and Ross, *The Espionage Establishment.*)

RC-135 RECONNAISSANCE AIRCRAFT

The RC-135 is the reconnaissance version of the C-135, which is the military version of the Boeing 707 airliner. There are a number of different versions of the RC-135; most are equipped with a SIDE LOOKING AIRCRAFT RADAR. A variety of other SIGINT sensors are also commonly included in the reconnaissance accessories of the aircraft.

(Gunston, *Spy Planes.*)

READ, CONYERS (April 25, 1881–December 23, 1959): historian, intelligence analyst

A native of Philadelphia, Pennsylvania, Read earned an A.B., an A.M., and a Ph.D. from Harvard University in 1903, 1904, and 1908, respectively, and a B.Litt from Oxford University in 1909. He taught history at Princeton University and the University of Chicago, and became professor of English history at the University of Pennsylvania in 1934. Between 1941 and 1945 he served with the Office of Strategic Services as an intelligence analyst in the OSS RESEARCH AND ANALYSIS BRANCH. After the war he returned to the University of Pennsylvania.

(Cline: *The CIA Reality vs. Myth; Who Was Who in America,* vol. 3.)

RECONNAISSANCE BALLOONS

Balloons had been used in Europe for military reconnaissance since 1794, but American military commanders first considered them for use in 1840 in the Seminole War, when Col. John H. Sherburne of the U.S. Army proposed that scouts could locate Indian camps by ascending at night and noting the positions of their campfires. The plan was approved by the War Department but rejected by Gen. W.K. Armistead, the Army commander in Florida.

The military use of balloons was next proposed seven years later during the Mexican War, but the suggested use was the aerial bombardment of Vera Cruz, not reconnaissance. However, Vera Cruz was taken by American forces before the plan could mature.

The Civil War

By the beginning of the Civil War ballooning had become a field of considerable interest and experimentation in the United States, and several leading balloonists (the contemporary term was "aeronaut") immediately proposed the military use of the aircraft to the federal government. The first balloonist to receive serious attention was James Allen who made an officially sponsored demonstration ascent in Washington on June 9, 1861. However, Allen's fleet of two balloons was destroyed in mishaps before it could be put into actual reconnaissance use.

Balloonist Thaddeus S. C. Lowe soon made a much more impressive demonstration of the balloon's reconnaissance potential. On June 18th he ascended above Washington and sent a telegraph report of what he observed down a wire suspended from the balloon, and through the War Department's telegraph system to President Lincoln in the White House. In staging the event Lowe achieved several firsts: first electrical communication from an aircraft to the ground, first such communication to a President of the United States, and first "real-time" transmission of reconnaissance data from an airborne platform.

On June 22nd Lowe ascended above Arlington, Virginia, to observe the Confederate forces and made several more such ascents in the next two days near Falls Church, Virginia. The intelligence benefits of the ascents were impressive. Lincoln was so favorably impressed by Lowe's demonstrations that he recommended him to Gen. Winfield Scott, then general in chief of the Army. However, Scott's resistance to Lowe's ideas delayed any action on them until August.

In the meantime, JOHN WISE, the balloonist who had proposed the Vera Cruz bombing, was hired by the Army of the Potomac's Bureau of Topographical Engineers in July 1861. He made his first successful reconnaissance ascents on July 24th. He observed Confederate detachments reconnoitering the Washington defenses and located an artillery emplacement five miles from the city (on a free, i.e., untethered, ascent over the Confederate lines that same day, Lowe acquired even more useful intelligence and the return trip earned Lowe yet another first—the first American flier to be fired on by mistake by friendly troops). However, two days later Wise's balloon was inadvertently released without anyone aboard while being towed to an advance position, and Union troops shot it down to prevent its falling into Confederate hands. Wise was severely upbraided by Maj. Amiel W. Whipple, chief of the Topographical Engineers, and he resigned soon afterward.

JOHN LA MOUNTAIN, another pioneer American balloonist, put his craft in the service of Maj. Gen. Benjamin F. Butler, commander of the Union Army's Department of Virginia. Butler was in great need of the aerial reconnaissance La Mountain provided because Fortress Monroe, his headquarters on Chesapeake Bay near Hampton, Virginia, was almost completely surrounded by Confederate forces, and his forces could not occupy an advance position from which to reconnoiter the enemy. La Mountain began making his ascents for Butler on July 25, 1861. He discovered a hidden Confederate camp. By counting the number of tents, La Mountain was able to contradict earlier reports that there were several thousand enemy troops concentrated around Fortress Monroe preparing to attack that stronghold. La Mountain was a pioneer in the practice of ascending over water from the deck of a ship. On the evening of August 10, 1861 he made such a flight, accompanied by General Butler, from the tug *Adriatic*.

The Balloon Corps

In August Thaddeus Lowe became a civilian employee of the Army of the Potomac's Bureau of Topographical Engineers. He manufactured a large reconnaissance balloon, christened the *Union*, from which he directed artillery fire (another first) against Confederate positions at Falls Church, Virginia, on September 24th. The effectiveness of the *Union* prompted the Army to have Lowe procure six additional balloons: the *Intrepid*, a large craft the size of the *Union*; two medium-sized balloons, the *Constitution* and the *United States*; and two small ones, the *Eagle* and the

Excelsior. Together with the *Washington*, a medium-sized craft, these balloons formed the fleet of the balloon corps, which was in active service until June 1863. Lowe, who now styled himself "chief aeronaut," hired a staff of nine civilian balloonists to operate this fleet, including James Allen and his brother Ezra. La Mountain was transferred to the Army of the Potomac after General Butler was transferred from his command at Fortress Monroe, but La Mountain quarreled with Lowe and was consequently dismissed from the service in February 1862.

Lowe's balloons represented the contemporary state of the art. The balloon envelopes were made of gored sections of pongee, a type of silk, sewn together in double thicknesses. The envelope was enclosed in a rope net from which the observer's car was suspended. The envelope was filled with hydrogen gas, which was produced by the action of sulfuric acid on iron filings in a wagon-borne gas generator. The hot gas produced by the reaction was passed through water-cooled copper pipes to lower its temperature, and through lime filters for purification. The generator wagons were part of the balloon train, the convoy of wagons that carried the balloon, ropes, telegraph equipment, gas filters, etc., to the place from which the craft made its ascent. (Operation of the balloon train and the ground equipment was the work of Army enlisted men detailed to the balloon corps.) In Washington, which boasted gaslights, the balloons were sometimes filled from illuminating gas mains (illuminating gas of the period was coal gas, a mixture of hydrogen and other gasses). In the case of free flight, ascent was achieved by releasing ballast bags hung from the car; descent was accomplished by releasing some of the gas through a valve at the top of the envelope, which the observer in the car could work with a rope. Captive flights, which were more commonly used in Civil War reconnaissance, ascended or descended as the tether rope was unreeled or reeled in.

When inflated, Lowe's balloons towered several stories above the ground and the larger models could carry several passengers. Altitudes of one thousand feet or more were achieved easily; ascents of as much as twenty thousand feet had been made as early as 1850, and the altitude of a tethered balloon was limited only by the length of rope available. Brig. Gen. Fitz-John Porter, commander of a division of the Army of the Potomac, was an especially enthusiastic balloonist and made over one hundred flights together with Lowe. (Porter made one harrowing solo flight; while he was aboard and waiting for Lowe to join him, the balloon broke free of its tether and drifted over the Confederate lines near Yorktown. Amid a hail of enemy bullets he resourcefully cut loose enough ballast to ascend out of rifle range, then made a careful study of the Confederate positions through his telescope. After he drifted back over friendly territory he brought the craft to earth, guided by instructions Lowe shouted to him from below through a megaphone.)

The balloon corps operated during the entire Peninsula campaign (March–July, 1862) and afterward, but with varying degrees of effectiveness as an intelligence organization. Lowe provided critical intelligence just before the battle of Fair Oaks (Vir-

ginia, May 31–June 1, 1862), when he spotted a large concentration of Confederate troops preparing to attack. General Porter was, of course, an enthusiastic advocate of the unit, as was McClellan himself, and Gen. John Sedgwick, a corps commander in the Chancellorsville campaign, stated that Lowe had furnished full and frequent reports of enemy movements that could not have been obtained any other way. Other officers were not as fully convinced of the balloons' usefulness, however. Major Gen. Daniel Butterfield, Hooker's chief of staff, regarded them

Inflation of the Army of the Potomac's balloon *Intrepid* to reconnoiter the area of Fair Oaks, Virginia, during the Peninsula campaign in 1862. The two crates seen in the center, left, are gas generators. Source: Library of Congress.

as worthless, and the inability of the sluggish balloon trains to move rapidly when necessary was recognized by all as a serious drawback. Yet one of the most significant testimonials to the balloons' effectiveness came from Confederate Gen. E. P. Alexander, who recalled that, even if the balloons had collected no useful intelligence, they severely complicated the movements of Confederate forces trying to avoid observation. As early as September 1861 Confederate Gen. Pierre G. T. Beauregard found it necessary to instruct his troops to take special precautions against the observation balloons, and to adopt deceptive measures and camouflage whenever possible.

Opinion as to the military worth of the balloons probably depended on whether or not an officer had been willing to make an ascent himself. A telegraphic report by a civilian aeronaut could not have been nearly as useful to a commander as an actual look at the battlefield from the balloon's vantage point. No reconnaissance photographs were made by the balloonists, probably because of the difficulty of lugging cameras and darkroom equipment along in the already overburdened and unwieldy balloon trains.

The effectiveness of the balloon corps must also have been hampered by the severe administrative difficulties under which it operated. Between June 1861 and June 1863 it was under three different branches of the Army: the Topographic Engineers, the Quartermaster Corps, and the Corps of Engineers. A stepchild, the balloon corps was often neglected in the matter of logistics and even pay. Lowe was frequently forced to pay for supplies and services out of his own pocket, then try to obtain reimbursement from the Army. (However, it is also noted that there is some evidence Lowe padded his expense reports and indulged in other forms of peculation.) On occasion, the wagons, teams, and drivers that had been assigned to the Corps were withdrawn by the Army Quartermaster for uses regarded as more important. Lowe might have fared better in such cases had he and his aeronauts been commissioned officers, rather than civilian employees of the Army.

In April 1863 the balloon corps was transferred to the Corps of Engineers. The Army of the Potomac's chief engineer, perhaps reflecting the opinion of General Butterfield, then chief of staff, cut Lowe's pay from $10 per day to $6. Lowe resigned in protest and was succeeded in May by James Allen, but the Army disbanded the balloon corps the following month.

Confederate Balloons

Although the Confederate Army was aware of the usefulness of balloons, it lacked the materials and expertise to use them as extensively as the Army of the Potomac did. One Confederate balloon was flown by Capt. E. P. Bryan shortly before the withdrawal from Yorktown in May 1862. Unlike Lowe's craft, Bryan's balloon envelope was made from varnished cotton and inflated with hot air from a fire of pine knots and turpentine. Bryan used signal flags to report to the ground.

Another balloon was used by the Confederates during the Seven Days' battles. This one had a silken envelope and was inflated with illuminating gas in Richmond, then tied to an engine of the York River Railroad and moved to the front where the reconnaissance ascent was made. According to legend, the envelope of this makeshift craft consisted of "the last silk dresses in the Confederacy," which ostensibly had been sacrificed to the Southern cause by the ladies of Richmond. Lt. Gen. James Longstreet many years later described its capture by Union troops as "the meanest trick of the war and one I have never yet forgiven."

Spanish-American War

American forces made no further military reconnaissance use of balloons for thirty years after the balloon corps was disbanded. At the outbreak of the SPANISH-AMERICAN WAR in April 1898, the Army possessed only one balloon and balloon train, both of which were under the administration of the Signal Corps. The balloon was essentially the same as those used by Lowe in the Civil War, although it had benefited from some more recent technological innovations, e.g., the air-to-ground telegraph had been replaced by a telephone.

In April the balloon train and its commander, Lieutenant Colonel Joseph E. Maxfield, were ordered from Fort Logan, Colorado, to Sandy Hook, New Jersey (near the entrance to New York harbor). The balloon was supposed to provide early warning of the approach of the Spanish squadron of Admiral Pascual Cevera y Topete, which the military feared was en route to the East Coast of the United States for the purpose of bombarding major coastal cities. After Cervera was discovered and blockaded in the harbor of Santiago-de-Cuba late in May, Maxfield and the balloon train were ordered to Tampa, Florida, where they embarked with General Rufus Shafter's Cuban invasion force.

Maxfield and the balloon played an important role in the Santiago Campaign. On June 30 he made several ascents with Cuban General Demetrio Castillo and Lieutenant Colonel George McC. Derby, Shafter's chief engineering officer, to survey the Spanish positions east of Santiago and the terrain beyond the

American lines. Derby, whose Army maps of the area were rather sketchy, found the reconnaissance to be of great value.

The following day, July 1, Maxfield and Derby ascended once again to observe the complex military operations undertaken that morning against the San Juan Heights and the fortress of El Caney. Derby's early reports were of considerable value to Shafter, whom illness had forced to remain several miles to the rear, but later in the day, after Derby had ordered the balloon brought almost to the front, it drew withering fire from the Spanish lines. Maxfield and Derby were unhurt, but the balloon served as a range marker of the narrow jungle road along which most of the American force was crowded. The ensuing Spanish fire was so intense that the American troops, unable to retreat from it, were prompted to the historic charges up San Juan Hill and Kettle Hill. Maxfield's balloon, which had been severely damaged, played no further role in the short-lived war.

The Twentieth Century

During the First World War balloons were again used by the Army for reconnaissance and artillery control, and by the U.S. Navy for detection of submerged submarines, but the craft were largely replaced by aircraft as reconnaissance platforms. No further intelligence use was made of the craft until the 1950s when high-altitude unmanned balloons were sent on photoreconnaissance missions over the Soviet Union. This program, known as the Moby Dick Program, produced useful results but was abandoned in 1956 in favor of the U-2 reconnaissance aircraft (see OVERHEAD RECONNAISSANCE).

(Bidwell, "History of the Military Intelligence Division, Department of the Army General Staff"; Glines, *Compact History of the United States Air Force*; Mac-Closkey, *From Gasbags to Spaceships*; Davis, *Our Incredible Civil War*; O'Toole, *The Spanish War*; DAH.)

REDDICK, WILLIAM H.: soldier, Union secret agent

Corporal Reddick of the Third Division, Army of the Ohio, volunteered to take part in a paramilitary operation behind Confederate lines aimed at severing the rail line between Atlanta and Chattanooga in April 1862 (see ANDREWS'S RAID). Dressed in civilian clothing he and a party of twenty other Union troops led by JAMES J. ANDREWS hijacked a locomotive and attempted to destroy railroad tracks and bridges between the two cities. He was captured by Confederate troops and imprisoned. Though An-

drews and six of the others were hanged, he and five others escaped, were recaptured, and exchanged for Confederate prisoners of war in March 1863. Reddick and the other five were awarded the newly created Medal of Honor by Secretary of War Edwin Stanton. They were the first to receive that decoration.

(Bryan, *The Spy in America*; Boatner, *Civil War Dictionary*; O'Neill, *Wild Train*.)

REVERE, PAUL (January 1, 1735–May 10, 1818): craftsman, Army officer, secret agent, and courier

A native of Boston, Revere attended local schools before following his father's trade of silversmithing. He served as a lieutenant of artillery in the British army during the French and Indian War.

Revere was active in underground politics prior to the American Revolution and was prominent among the Boston Whigs. His famous engraving of the Boston massacre in 1770 was an inaccurate version of the event, but proved to be an effective piece of anti-British propaganda. He was a member of the SONS OF LIBERTY and served as a courier for the Boston committees of Correspondence and Safety (see COMMITTEES OF CORRESPONDENCE). As a member of the former group, he was a leader of the Boston Tea Party in December 1773.

In the fall of 1774 Revere was one of approximately thirty Boston Whigs, chiefly "mechanics" (i.e., skilled workers, in the usage of the eighteenth century), who formed a SECRET INTELLIGENCE network to observe the activities of the British military forces and Tories in and around Boston. The principal function of this organization was to warn the militant patriots in the area of any British moves against them, such as the September 1, 1774 raid on their secret military supply depot at Charlestown. The organization also conducted sabotage and guerrilla operations against British military installations, e.g., the destruction and theft of cannon at Boston's North Battery on September 15, 1774.

The most important operation of the Revere organization took place in mid-April 1775, when it detected British preparations to raid the Patriot military depot at Concord, Massachusetts. On April 16th Revere was sent by Dr. Joseph Warren, who may have been the leader of the Revere organization, to Lexington to warn John Hancock and Samuel Adams of the imminent British operation. As a result, the military stores were moved from their Concord locations.

Two days later, on April 18th, Warren dispatched

Revere on his famous "midnight ride" to warn the patriots beyond Boston that several hundred British troops were about to march out of the city, apparently to raid Concord. Revere and another courier alerted the countryside between Boston and Lexington, but Revere was captured by a British patrol between the latter town and Concord. However, a Lexington patriot who had been alerted by Revere made his way to Concord and spread the alarm.

Revere was released, without his horse, later that night. He could not return to Boston while the British occupied the city, but he was active as a courier for the committees of Correspondence and Safety. He printed the first issue of Continental currency and supervised a gunpowder mill at Canton, Massachusetts. During 1778–79 he commanded Castle William, a fortification in Boston harbor. As a lieutenant colonel of artillery he took part in military expeditions to Rhode Island and Penobscot Bay.

After the war Revere returned to his silversmithing and other crafts.

(Bakeless, *Turncoats, Traitors and Heroes*; Boatner, *Encyclopedia of the American Revolution*; Forbes, *Paul Revere and the World He Lived In*; WAMB.)

RHODES, ROY A. (March 11, 1917–): soldier, Soviet espionage agent

A native of Oilton, Oklahoma, Rhodes enlisted in the U.S. Army in 1943 and served in the Signal Corps. In 1951 he was assigned to the U.S. embassy in Moscow as "motor sergeant," i.e., he was in charge of the embassy's fleet of automobiles.

During the Christmas season of 1951 he attended an impromptu party with several Soviet citizens and subsequently awoke in bed with a Russian woman. The incident had been staged by Soviet intelligence in order to blackmail Rhodes into cooperating. Rhodes succumbed to the overture and furnished the Soviets with cryptographic and other information. He was paid a total of between $2,500 and $3,000, for which he signed receipts.

After Rhodes returned to the United States he refused to continue to work for the Soviets. RUDOLF ABEL, a Soviet intelligence officer operating covertly in New York City during the 1950s, made an unsuccessful attempt to contact him. Rhodes's work for the Soviets was disclosed to the U.S. authorities by REINO HEYHANAN, a Soviet intelligence officer and Abel's courier, who defected to the United States in 1957.

Rhodes was court-martialed and sentenced to a dishonorable discharge and five years in prison.

(Donovan, *Strangers on a Bridge*; Bernikow, *Abel*.)

RHYOLITE RECONNAISSANCE SATELLITE

Rhyolite is a signals intelligence (SIGINT) satellite designed to intercept foreign telemetry and communications signals. It travels in a geosynchronous orbit that permits it to remain over a fixed position on the surface of the earth. The satellite was developed for the Central Intelligence Agency by TRW Inc., under contract to the NATIONAL RECONNAISSANCE OFFICE. The first Rhyolite was launched on March 6, 1973 and positioned over the horn of Africa, from which vantage point it could monitor Soviet microwave communications in western Russia and telemetry from Soviet missile tests. A second Rhyolite was launched on May 23, 1977 and reportedly positioned over Borneo, where it could monitor signals from both the Soviet Union and China. Two more Rhyolite satellites were launched on December 11, 1977 and April 7, 1978.

The Rhyolite satellite plays an important role in verifying Soviet compliance with the SALT I strategic arms limitation agreement with regard to the numbers and types of Soviet strategic missiles.

(Bamford, *The Puzzle Palace*; *New York Times*, January 13, 1985, Section 6, p. 54).

RICHARDS, ATHERTON (September 29, 1894–): businessman, intelligence officer

A native of Honolulu, Hawaii, Richards graduated from Wesleyan University in 1915. He worked in the New York City Bureau of Municipal Research in 1915–16, and in the San Francisco Bureau of Governmental Research in 1916–17. In 1917–18 he served as a first lieutenant in the U.S. Army. Afterward he pursued a variety of business interests in New York and Honolulu, and was president of the Hawaiian Pineapple Company from 1932 to 1941.

In 1941 he was recruited into the Office of the Coordinator of Information, the predecessor to the Office of Strategic Services, and was placed in charge of the Visual Presentation Branch, a briefing unit. In 1942 he was commissioned as a lieutenant colonel in the U.S. Army and served as a deputy director of the OSS until 1945. He was discharged with the rank of colonel. Richards returned to Hawaii and resumed his business activities.

(Roosevelt, *War Report of the OSS*; Cline, *CIA: Reality vs. Myth*; *Who's Who in America*, v. 28.)

RICHARDSON, JOHN: intelligence officer

Richardson attended Whittier College in California during the early 1930s (he was a classmate of Richard

M. Nixon). He joined the Central Intelligence Agency during its earliest days in the late 1940s and was assigned to the Office of Policy Coordination, as the Agency's COVERT ACTION department was then known. Richardson served in Vienna, Austria, circa 1949, as chief of station. During the early 1950s he was chief of the Southeast Europe Division of CIA/OPC, and later chief of station in Athens, Greece.

In 1959 Richardson left Athens to become chief of station in Manila. He succeeded WILLIAM E. COLBY as chief of the Saigon station in 1962. There he became closely associated with Ngo Dinh Nhu, the brother of President Ngo Dinh Diem and his closest advisor. In 1963 Henry Cabot Lodge, the American ambassador to Saigon, demanded the removal of Richardson on the grounds that the Ngo brothers were using him as a private channel to Washington and thus frustrating Lodge's work. Richardson was succeeded in Saigon by PEER DE SILVA.

Richardson served as chief of the CIA's Office of Training in the late 1960s.

(Smith, *Portrait of a Cold Warrior*; Hunt, *Undercover*; Colby and Forbath, *Honorable Men*; De Silva, *Sub Rosa*.)

RINTELEN, FRANZ VON (ca. 1877–1949): naval officer, banker, intelligence officer

The son of an aristocratic German family, von Rintelen served as a German naval officer before embarking on a career in international banking. After several years with the Deutsche Bank he came to America in 1906 as a representative of the Disconto Gesellschaft, Germany's second largest bank. He lived in New York City for three years, then spent a year in Latin America, after which he returned to Germany.

Von Rintelen was a captain-lieutenant in the German Naval Reserve. At the outbreak of the FIRST WORLD WAR he returned to active duty with the Navy as financial advisor to the Admiralty General Staff. In March 1915 he was sent to the United States to carry out COVERT ACTION aimed at ending American arms and munitions sales to the Allies. Von Rintelen told the German intelligence chiefs who dispatched him on this mission, "I'll buy up what I can, and blow up what I can't."

Using the pseudonym "Emile V. Gache" and a Swiss passport, he arrived in the United States on April 3, 1915 posing as a businessman. He soon discovered that sabotage was far more effective than preemptive purchasing in interdicting the flow of munitions from the United States to the Allies. With the help of Carl von Kleist, a retired German sea

Capt. Franz von Rintelen. Source: Author's collection.

captain, von Rintelen made contact with the captains and crews of all the German vessels that had been interned in New York harbor under the neutrality laws since the outbreak of hostilities in Europe. Von Rintelen enlisted one ship, the S.S. *Friedrich der Grosse*, and her officers and crew to serve as a factory for the production of incendiary devices. Dr. Walter T. Scheele, a chemist and German secret agent who had been living in the United States since before the war, designed the bombs and supervised their manufacture. Officials of the Hamburg-American and the North German Lloyd steamship lines recruited dockworkers willing to plant the bombs in the cargoes of ships carrying munitions to Europe.

The incendiary bombs were planted in nonexplosive cargo, since von Rintelen's sabotage was not aimed at blowing up the ships but at forcing the captains to flood the munitions holds, thus rendering the cargoes useless, or causing them to abandon and scuttle the ships. The technique proved highly effective. Von Rintelen later stated that none of the sabotaged ships reached its destination, and in every case its cargo of munitions was denied to the Allies.

Von Rintelen organized similar firebombing rings in the ports of Baltimore and New Orleans. With his sabotage operation well under way, he turned to other types of covert action against the American munitions trade. One of these was the creation of "Labor's National Peace Council," a political action group that worked for an embargo on the shipment of munitions abroad and fostered strikes in munitions factories. Samuel Gompers, the American labor leader, discovered the Council's German sponsorship, however, and succeeded in thwarting von Rintelen's plan.

Von Rintelen attempted similar political operations involving agitation among dockworkers and Irish-

Americans, but was equally unsuccessful in them. His most ambitious undertaking (Tuchman says it was his principal mission in the United States) was a plan to foment a revolution in Mexico, restore former President Victoriano Huerta to power, and thereby incite war between Mexico and the United States. (Huerta had seized power in 1913, murdered his predecessor, and became the bête noire of President Woodrow Wilson who worked diligently to help bring about his downfall in 1914.) This operation was penetrated by agents of EMANUEL V. VOSKA, who was cooperating with both British Intelligence and the U.S. State Department. Huerta, who had been living in exile in the United States, was arrested and the plan failed.

During his mission in the United States, von Rintelen quarreled with FRANZ VON PAPEN and Karl Boy-Ed, the German military and naval attachés in the United States, respectively, who had been running a similar covert action operation under their official cover. Von Papen's complaints to Berlin about his rival led to von Rintelen's recall on July 6, 1916, two days after Huerta's arrest. Berlin stated that von Rintelen's activities were becoming known and he was in danger of arrest, and he was indeed arrested by the British authorities when the Dutch ship on which he was returning to Europe arrived at Falmouth, England.

Von Rintelen was interned in England as a prisoner of war. After American entry into the war in 1917 he was extradited to the United States, tried and convicted of conspiracy to foment labor agitation, passport fraud, and conspiracy to firebomb ships (the ESPIONAGE ACTS had not yet been passed at the time of his activities in the United States). He was imprisoned in the federal penitentiary at Atlanta, Georgia, until November 1920, when his sentence was commuted.

Von Rintelen took up residence in England and became a naturalized British citizen.

(Landau, *The Enemy Within*; Tuchman, *The Zimmerman Telegram*; Rintelen, *Dark Invader*.)

RIVINGTON, JAMES (1724–July 4, 1802): bookseller, businessman, printer, journalist, publisher, British propagandist, American secret intelligence agent

A native of London, England, Rivington entered the printing trade, made a fortune publishing Tobias Smollett's *History of England*, and lost it all betting on horse races. He was advised by London author and lexicographer Dr. Samuel Johnson that there were no booksellers of note in the American colonies, and he

moved to America in 1760 and opened bookstores in Philadelphia and New York City. Two years later he opened a third shop in Boston.

Rivington's business ventures flourished, partly through the publication of pirated editions of such popular works of the time as *Robinson Crusoe*, and partly through his expansion into such nonliterary lines as medicinal nostrums, violins, pickled sturgeon, live poultry, and even sealing wax. In 1766, having consolidated his book business in New York City, he moved to Maryland to pursue a land lottery scheme that soon returned him to bankruptcy. He quickly recovered, however, partly by means of marrying a wealthy widow, Elizabeth Van Horne, the daughter of an influential New York family.

In 1773 Rivington started a newspaper, *Rivington's New-York Gazetteer*. During the years immediately preceding the American Revolution, when New York was politically divided along Whig and Tory lines, the *Gazetteer* was decidedly Tory in its editorial policy. After his shop was wrecked by a mob of angry patriots in 1775, Rivington sailed for England, returning two years later with a royal commission as the King's Printer in New York (New York City was occupied by the British throughout most of the war). He resumed publication of his newspaper under the new name, *Rivington's New York Loyal Gazette*, which he changed a few months later to the simpler, *The Royal Gazette*. He established a mutual arrangement with other New York newspaper publishers which, in effect, resulted in the first daily newspaper in America.

Rivington's paper reported American defeats in great detail, ignored American victories, and published anti-American satires, sketches, and doggerel. One of the authors of the last was British intelligence officer, Major JOHN ANDRÉ. Another contributor to *The Royal Gazette* was ROBERT TOWNSEND, a principal agent of the CULPER SPY RING, who found the Tory newspaper to be excellent cover for his secret intelligence work for Gen. GEORGE WASHINGTON.

Just when Rivington himself began working for the Culper Ring is unknown, but it may have been as early as 1779 when he and Townsend opened a coffee shop a few doors away from Rivington's bookshop-newspaper office at the corner of Wall and Queen Streets. British military personnel, anxious to see their names in the *Gazette*, understood that patronage of the publisher's coffee shop was the route to such celebrity. The proprietor's unquestioned devotion to the King removed any inhibition the soldiers may have felt about freely discussing British plans and operations, and what was discussed in the Wall Street shop may have been promptly recorded and dispatched through the Culper network to General Washington.

The only specific piece of intelligence for which Rivington is known to have been the source was one of enormous value. In September 1781 he turned over to Maj. Allan McLane, one of Washington's intelligence officers, the Royal Navy's signal code. McLane promptly delivered this item to Count de Grasse, the admiral commanding the French fleet. When the British fleet under Adm. Thomas Graves encountered de Grasse's ships in the battle of the Chesapeake Capes a few days later, the French inflicted severe damage on the British fleet and drove it back to New York. The departure of the British ships permitted a French convoy under Admiral Barras to land reinforcements for the Continental Army, a move that led to the defeat of Cornwallis at Yorktown a few weeks later.

After the war Rivington became the target of American patriots unaware of his true wartime role, despite General Washington's efforts to protect him. He was assaulted, threatened with death, and eventually driven out of business. In 1797 he was confined to debtors' prison. His reason for not disclosing his wartime secret service to Washington is unknown. Espionologist COREY FORD has noted that Rivington had arranged with Sir Guy Carleton, the British commander, for his (Rivington's) sons to receive commissions in the British army and receive half pay for life, despite the fact they had never seen active service. Ford offers the plausible theory that this was the reason for Rivington's silence.

Despite Rivington's unpopularity in post-Revolutionary New York City, a street in lower Manhattan was named after him and still bears his name.

Rivington's secret service became known in 1959 through the research of Dr. Catherine Snell Crary of Finch College.

(*Who Was Who in America*, historical volume; Boatner, *Encyclopedia of the American Revolution*; Corey Ford, *A Peculiar Service*; Crary, "The Tory and the Spy.")

ROBERTSON, SAMUEL (ca. 1843–June 18, 1862): soldier, Union secret service agent

A native of Bourneville, Ohio, Robertson enlisted in the Ohio Volunteer Infantry, a part of the Army of the Ohio, in 1861. In April 1862 he volunteered to take part in a paramilitary operation behind Confederate lines aimed at severing the rail line between Atlanta and Chattanooga (see ANDREWS'S RAID). He and a party of twenty other Union troops in civilian clothes and led by JAMES J. ANDREWS

hijacked a locomotive and attempted to destroy railroad tracks and bridges between the two cities. He was captured by Confederate troops and imprisoned. Robertson, Andrews, and six others of the party were hanged.

(Bryan, *The Spy in America*; Boatner, *Civil War Dictionary*; O'Neill, *Wild Train*.)

ROBINSON, BEVERLY (January 11, 1722–April 9, 1792): planter, army officer, British secret agent and intelligence officer

A native of Middlesex County, Virginia, and the son of a prominent Virginia family, Robinson married into the wealthy New York Philipse family in 1748. Having increased his wife's fortune through good management, he had retired as one of New York's wealthiest landowners before the American Revolution.

Of Tory sympathies, Robinson refused to take the American oath of allegiance and was therefore forced to relinquish his home, just across the Hudson River from West Point, to the Continental Army and take refuge in British-occupied New York City. There he raised the Loyal American Regiment, of which he became colonel, and later another loyalist unit, the Guides and Pioneers. He distinguished himself in combat on several occasions, including the storming of Fort Montgomery, an American stronghold a few miles down the Hudson River from West Point, in October 1777.

Robinson's greater contribution to the British cause, however, lay in his work as intelligence officer. Intimately familiar with the countryside along the Hudson River in the vicinity of West Point, where his former home was located, he was able to provide Sir Henry Clinton with essential BASIC INTELLIGENCE in support of British military moves in that region. Further, he had many friends, acquaintances, and tenants in the area, some of whom agreed to observe the activities of the continental Army there and report back to him in New York City. He was also involved in arranging the defection of American officers and men to the British side. In this role he unsuccessfully attempted to persuade the legendary Gen. Israel Putnam to defect.

Robinson was involved in BENEDICT ARNOLD's plan to surrender West Point to the British. Arnold had established his headquarters, not at West Point, but in Robinson's house across the river, which had been confiscated by the Continental Army. On the pretext of wishing to discuss the disposition of his household property, Robinson requested a meeting with Arnold. This provided a cover for Robinson's

Capt. Joseph J. Rochefort. Source: Naval Historical Center.

trip to Haverstraw with Maj. JOHN ANDRÉ, and André's fateful meeting with Arnold.

After the war Robinson moved to England, where he was compensated for the loss of his estate. He settled near Bath.

(*Who Was Who in America,* historical volume; Boatner, *Encyclopedia of the American Revolution.*)

ROCHEFORT, JOSEPH JOHN ca. 1898–1976), Navy officer, intelligence officer

After attending the University of California, Rochefort began his career as an enlisted man in the U.S. Navy and advanced to officer's rank. He had a talent for cryptology and headed the Code and Signal Section of the Office of Naval Communications (see NAVAL INTELLIGENCE) during 1925–27. Because he was also an able linguist he was sent to Japan to study Japanese during 1929–32. In June 1941 Lt. Comdr. Rochefort was given command of the Combat Intelligence Unit (later the Fleet Radio Unit, Pacific, or FRUPAC) of the Fourteenth Naval district in Hawaii. The function of the Unit was to collect communications intelligence disclosing the disposition of operations of the Japanese navy.

Rochefort and his Unit succeeded in breaking some of the Japanese naval cryptosystems and in tracking some Japanese warships through radio direction-finding and traffic analysis, but they failed to discover the movements of the Japanese carrier task force that launched the PEARL HARBOR ATTACK. However, Rochefort's work during the following year provided much crucial intelligence to Adm. Chester W. Nimitz, commander of the U.S. Pacific Fleet. In March 1942 he and his unit identified Port Moresby as the objective of an upcoming Japanese carrier operation, thus forewarning Nimitz shortly before the battle of the Coral Sea. Very soon thereafter Rochefort's unit pieced together almost the whole of the Japanese operation plan for the BATTLE OF MIDWAY, an accomplishment that made possible the American victory at Midway. Historians regard this feat as the greatest single intelligence success in the naval war with Japan.

Rochefort was recommended for the Distinguished Service Medal by Adm. Chester Nimitz for his work in the battle of Midway, but he was denied the award by the Navy Department, reportedly for reasons of internal Navy politics. Rochefort's unit became the object of a bureaucratic power struggle within the Navy shortly thereafter, and Rochefort was relieved of its command and assigned to sea duty in October 1942. He was subsequently returned to intelligence work in Washington and was awarded the Legion of Merit in 1946. He later retired with the rank of captain.

In 1958 Admiral Nimitz again tried and failed to obtain the Distinguished Service Medal for Rochefort. However, Rochefort's wartime associates continued to intercede in his behalf, and he was given the award posthumously in 1985.

(Kahn, *The Codebreakers;* Spector, *Eagle Against the Sun;* Holmes, *Double-Edged Secrets;* Rochefort, "As I Recall . . . Learning Cryptanalysis"; Potter, "The Crypt of the Cryptanalysts"; Layton, *"And I Was There."*)

ROOSEVELT, ARCHIBALD BULLOCH, JR. (February 18, 1918–): newspaperman, banker, intelligence officer

A native of Boston and a grandson of Theodore Roosevelt, Archibald Roosevelt graduated from the Groton School in 1936 and from Harvard University in 1939. He worked as a newspaperman until 1942, when he was commissioned as a second lieutenant in the U.S. Army. He was discharged with the rank of captain in 1947.

Roosevelt served with the Central Intelligence Agency, where, like his cousin KERMIT ROOSEVELT, he was a specialist in the Middle East. He was an attaché at the American embassy in Beirut, Lebanon, in 1947–49, and consul at Istanbul, Turkey, in 1951–53. He served at the American embassy in Madrid and in 1962 became chief the CIA station in London. In 1966 he was replaced in that post by Bronson Tweedy.

Roosevelt left government service in 1974. Since 1975 he has been vice-president and director of international relations for the Chase Manhattan Bank.

(Wise and Ross, *The Espionage Establishment*; Alsop, *The Center*; *Who's Who in America*, 42nd ed.)

ROOSEVELT, KERMIT (February 16, 1916–): historian, businessman, intelligence officer, covert operations officer

Roosevelt, a grandson of President Theodore Roosevelt, was born in Buenos Aires, Argentina. He attended the Groton School, and graduated from Harvard University in 1938. He taught history at Harvard from 1937 to 1939, and at the California Institute of Technology from 1939 to 1941. In 1941 he joined the Office of the Coordinator of Information, which soon became the Office of Strategic Services, and he stayed with the organization until 1946. He was assigned to the OSS SECRET INTELLIGENCE BRANCH and served as assistant to Dr. STEPHEN PENROSE, chief of SI in the Near East.

While recuperating from a Jeep accident he suffered in Italy just after V-E Day, Roosevelt wrote the official history of the OSS. In 1947 he visited Iran in the course of writing a book entitled, *Arabs, Oil, and History*.

Roosevelt joined the newly formed Central Intelligence Agency and became a special assistant in political operations to the chief of the CIA CLANDESTINE SERVICE. His experience and knowledge of the Near East was soon put to good use. By one account he engineered the operation that put Gamal Abdel Nasser in power following the 1952 coup in Egypt that forced out King Farouk.

In 1953 Roosevelt organized and directed the Agency's IRAN COUP, which resulted in the overthrow of the leftist premier of Iran, Mohammed Mossadegh, and secured the throne of Shah Mohammed Reza Pahlevi. He was awarded the National Security Medal in recognition of his role in this operation.

Roosevelt remained with the CIA as a specialist in the Near East until 1957 when he left to join Gulf Oil

as vice-president for governmental relations. In 1964 he became a partner in a Washington public relations firm representing, among other international clients, the government of Iran.

(Roosevelt, *Countercoup*; Smith, *OSS*; Smith, *Portrait of a Cold Warrior*; Powers, *The Man Who Kept the Secrets*; *Who's Who in America*, 37th ed.)

ROPER, ELMO BURNS, JR. (July 31, 1900– April 30, 1971): market research and public opinion specialist, intelligence officer

A native of Hebron, Nebraska, Roper attended the University of Minnesota in 1919–20, and the University of Edinburgh (Scotland) in 1920–21. He operated a retail jewelry store in Creston, Iowa, from 1921 to 1928, then worked as a salesman for the Seth Thomas Clock Company and other clock manufacturers. While in sales he developed techniques for market research, and in 1933 he formed a market research consulting firm. His correct prediction of the outcome of the presidential election of 1936 gained him national recognition as an expert in the field of public opinion measurement.

In 1942 Roper was appointed deputy director of the Office of the Coordinator of Information, the predecessor to the Office of Strategic Services. COI Director WILLIAM J. DONOVAN recruited Roper because he wished to use his management skills in organizing the agency. He thus became a charter member of Donovan's "brain trust," and remained with the OSS as deputy director until the agency was dissolved in 1945.

Roper returned to private consulting after the war, continued his *Fortune* surveys and election polls, taught journalism at Columbia University, and was a radio commentator and newspaper columnist.

(*Current Biography*, 1945, 1971; *Who's Who in America*, v. 34; Roosevelt, *War Report of the OSS*.)

ROSENBERG CASE

Summary: In 1951 Julius Rosenberg and his wife, Ethel, American members of the Communist party, were convicted of espionage, viz., transmittal of classified information regarding the U.S. nuclear weapons program to Soviet Intelligence during the Second World War. Despite lengthy appeals and international protests they were executed in 1953, thus becoming the only Americans to receive the death penalty in peacetime for espionage.

Background and Discussion: During 1944–45 the Federal Bureau of Investigation intercepted enciphered messages exchanged between the Soviet consulate in New York City and Soviet intelligence headquarters in Moscow. Unable to break the Soviet cryptosystem at that time, the FBI kept the intercepted cables in its files. In 1947 the Bureau enlisted the help of a cryptanalyst of the Army Security Agency (see ARMY INTELLIGENCE, NATIONAL SECURITY AGENCY) in trying to read them, and met with some success.

The cryptanalyzed material disclosed, among other things, that Soviet Intelligence had penetrated the British Mission to the Manhattan Project (the wartime nuclear weapons development program) in 1944. Subsequent investigation by the FBI revealed that the PENETRATION AGENT was Klaus Fuchs, a German-born Communist who had fled Nazi Germany before the war and settled in Britain where he worked for the government as a physicist. The FBI conveyed this information to British intelligence, and in 1949 Fuchs was arrested, tried, convicted of espionage, and imprisoned.

The intercepts also disclosed to the FBI that, while in the United States, Fuchs had reported to Soviet intelligence through a courier whom the FBI suspected to be Harry Gold, a Swiss-born chemical technician who had been raised in Philadelphia and had been recruited by the Soviets in 1935. In 1950 Fuchs confirmed to the FBI that Gold had been his Soviet contact. Gold was arrested. He confessed, pleaded guilty to espionage, and was imprisoned. He agreed to cooperate with the FBI, and his information led the Bureau to David Greenglass, a former Army enlisted man who had worked as a machinist on the Manhattan Project at Los Alamos, New Mexico. Greenglass had turned over to the Soviets details of the secret triggering mechanism used to detonate the first fission weapons.

Greenglass was arrested and charged with espionage. In an effort to obtain leniency he disclosed that he had been recruited into the espionage network by his sister, Ethel, and her husband, Julius Rosenberg, a New York-born electrical engineer and a longtime member of the Communist Party of the United States. Julius Rosenberg had served as a civilian employee of the U.S. Army Signal Corps during 1940–45, and apparently had been recruited by Soviet intelligence prior to that period. He is believed to have reported to Anatoly Yakovlev, an employee of the Soviet consulate in New York.

The FBI had collateral information confirming Rosenberg's involvement with Soviet intelligence and indicating that he was, in fact, the head of a Soviet espionage network operating in the United States. The Rosenbergs were arrested and charged with espionage, along with codefendants David Greenglass and Morton Sobell, the latter an engineer who had worked as part of Rosenberg's network but had not been directly involved in stealing nuclear weapons information.

The four defendants were tried in March–April 1951 and convicted. Greenglass was sentenced to fifteen years imprisonment, Sobell to thirty years. The Rosenbergs were sentenced to death, although the government made it clear that their sentences would be reduced if they cooperated and revealed details of their work for Soviet intelligence. However, they continued to insist on their innocence and, after a series of appeals, were executed in Sing Sing Prison at Ossining, New York, on June 19, 1953.

The Rosenbergs' supporters, and especially their two children, Robert and Michael Meeropol, continue to insist that they were innocent of the charges on which they were convicted.

(Lamphere, *The FBI-KGB War*; Radosh and Milton, *The Rosenberg File*; Meeropol and Meeropol, *We Are Your Sons*.)

ROSITZKE, HARRY AUGUST (February 25, 1911–): intelligence officer

A native of Brooklyn, New York, Rositzke graduated from Union College in 1931 and Harvard University in 1935. From 1936 to 1942 he taught English at Harvard, the University of Omaha, and the University of Rochester. He served in the U.S. Army from 1942–46, and during the last two years was assigned to the Office of Strategic Services in London, Paris, and Germany. After the dissolution of the OSS he was transferred to the Special Services Unit and then to the Central Intelligence Group, the interim intelligence agencies that bridged the gap between the OSS and the CENTRAL INTELLIGENCE AGENCY. In 1947 he moved to the newly formed CIA as a member of its Office of Special Operations, the original name of the agency's SECRET INTELLIGENCE BRANCH.

Appointed chief of Soviet operations at the CIA base in Munich, West Germany in May 1952, Rositzke became responsible for agent operations in the Soviet Union, counterespionage, and agent recruitment. From 1957 to 1962 he was chief of the CIA station at New Delhi, India, where he was involved in working against the Soviet and Chinese intelligence services. In 1962 he returned to Washington to work on domestic intelligence operations against Soviet and East European officials in the United States, and coordinate operations against Communist parties abroad.

Rositzke retired from the CIA in 1970 and has since written several books.

(Rositzke, *CIA's Secret Operations; Contemporary Authors*, vol. 45.)

ROSS, MARION A.(October 9, 1832–June 18, 1862): schoolteacher, soldier, Union secret service agent

Ross attended Antioch College and was a schoolteacher in Champaign County, Ohio, before the Civil War. In 1861 he enlisted in the Ohio Volunteer Infantry, which was part of the Army of the Ohio. He had attained the rank of sergeant major by April 1862, when he volunteered to take part in a paramilitary operation behind Confederate lines aimed at severing the rail line between Atlanta and Chattanooga in April 1862 (see ANDREWS'S RAID). He and a party of twenty other Union troops in civilian clothes and led by JAMES J. ANDREWS hijacked a locomotive and attempted to destroy railroad tracks and bridges between the two cities. He was captured by Confederate troops and imprisoned. Ross, Andrews, and six others of the party were hanged.

(Bryan, *The Spy in America*; Boatner, *Civil War Dictionary*; O'Neill, *Wild Train*.)

ROSTOW, WALT WHITMAN (October 7, 1916–): economist, intelligence analyst

A native of New York City, Rostow received a B.A. and a Ph.D. from Yale University in 1936 and 1940, respectively. He attended Balliol College, Oxford as a Rhodes scholar from 1936 to 1938. In 1940 and 1941 he was an instructor in economics at Columbia University. In 1942 he was given a commission in the U.S. Army and assigned to the Office of Strategic Services, where he served in the OSS RESEARCH AND ANALYSIS BRANCH. He was discharged with the rank of major in 1945.

After the war Rostow held several academic and government posts. Between 1961 and 1966 he was chairman of the State Department Policy Planning Council. Between 1966 and 1969 he acted as special assistant to the President for national security affairs. He was one of the principal architects of the Vietnam policy of the Johnson administration. More recently he has been teaching political economics at the University of Texas.

(*Who's Who in America*, 42nd ed.; Smith, *OSS*.)

ROWAN, ANDREW SUMMERS (April 23, 1857–January 10, 1943): Army officer, intelligence officer

A native of Gap Mills, Virginia (now West Virginia), Rowan graduated from the U.S. Military Academy in 1881 and served for eight years as an infantry officer in Texas and the Dakotas. On orders from the War Department in 1890, he made a covert reconnaissance of the full length of the Canadian Pacific Railroad, collecting information of military interest about the line and the region it traversed. During 1891–92 he was a member of the International Railway Commission and did survey work in Central America.

In 1893 Rowan was assigned to the Military Information Division of the Adjutant General's Office (see ARMY INTELLIGENCE) and became chief of the Map Section. In April 1898 he was appointed military attaché to Chile, but before departing for this post he was sent on a special mission to Cuba by MID chief, Maj. ARTHUR L. WAGNER.

Rowan had specialized knowledge of Cuba and was the author of *The Island of Cuba*, a book about the country. The purpose of his secret mission to Cuba was to collect military information regarding the island on the eve of the SPANISH-AMERICAN WAR. He joined a party of Cuban insurgents in Jamaica and traveled to Cuba with them by open boat, landing in Oriente Province on the southeast coast on April 24, two days after the war began. He met Cuban Gen. Calixto Garcia in the town of Bayamo and was furnished with maps and other intelligence by the insurgent leader. Garcia sent along a delegation of Cuban officers with Rowan on his return trip to Washington to coordinate Cuban insurgent operations with those of the U.S. Army and Navy. The information Rowan collected while in Cuba contributed important basic intelligence to "Military Notes on Cuba," a compendium of such information compiled by the MID and distributed to the officers of the American expedition that landed in Cuba in June.

Rowan, who had been promoted to the rank of captain during his Cuban mission, was appointed lieutenant colonel of volunteers shortly after his return. He served on the staff of Gen. Nelson A. Miles and took part in the Puerto Rican campaign in July. After a tour with the American occupation forces in Cuba after the war, he served in the Philippines until 1902. During 1902–03 he taught military science at Kansas State Agricultural College (now Kansas State University). After several other assignments he returned to the Philippines in 1905 and was promoted to the rank of major. He returned to the United States in 1907 and was stationed at Fort Douglas, Utah, until his retirement in 1909.

Rowan was awarded the Distinguished Service Cross for his mission to Cuba and was also decorated for gallantry in combat in the Philippine Insurrection.

In 1899 Rowan's modest Cuban exploit caught the

fancy of businessman-dilettante Elbert Hubbard, who celebrated it as an example of pluck in his essay "A Message to Garcia," which he published in his magazine, the *Philistine*. The essay, which scrambles most of the facts, became a best-seller when half a million reprints were ordered by the New York Central Railroad for distribution to its own employees and other workers who might benefit by Rowan's example. Rowan thereby inadvertently became the central figure in a myth that obscured his real accomplishments and valorous acts.

(*WAMB; Who Was Who in America*, v. 2; Bidwell, "History of the Military Intelligence Division, Department of the Army General Staff" O'Toole, *The Spanish War*.)

ROWLETT, FRANK BYRON (May 2, 1908–): cryptologist

A native of Rose Hill, Virginia, Rowlett graduated from Emory and Henry College in 1929. In 1930 he was the first junior cryptanalyst to be hired by WILLIAM F. FRIEDMAN, director of the newly established Signal Intelligence Service of the U.S. Army Signal Corps. During the Second World War he received a commission in the U.S. Army and advanced to the rank of colonel while continuing to serve with the SIS and its successors, the Signal Security Agency and the Army Security Agency. During 1953–58 he served with the Central Intelligence Agency. In 1958 he became the special assistant to the director of the NATIONAL SECURITY AGENCY, in which post he worked for the establishment of a National Cryptologic School. He served briefly as commandant of the school until his retirement in December 1965.

Rowlett was awarded the Distinguished Intelligence Medal, the National Security Medal, and other awards and decorations, and he holds patents on cryptographic devices and equipment.

(Bamford, *Puzzle Palace*; Kahn, *Codebreakers*; *Who's Who in America*, 37th ed.)

RUBENSTEIN, SIDNEY SIMON (April 5, 1905–): counterespionage officer

A native of Baltimore, Maryland, Rubenstein earned an LL.B. from the University of Maryland in 1931. He practiced law and accountancy in Baltimore until 1934 when he joined the Federal Bureau of Investigation as a special agent.

In 1941 Rubenstein took military leave from the FBI and was commissioned in the U.S. Army Air Corps. He served with the Counterintelligence Division of the Air Force (see AIR FORCE INTELLI-GENCE) and taught security at the Air Intelligence School at Harrisburg, Pennsylvania, and at Austin, Texas. In 1944 he was assigned to the Office of Strategic Services, where he served with the OSS COUNTER-ESPIONAGE BRANCH in the China-Burma-India theater. In 1945–46 he served with the war crimes branch of the judge advocate general of U.S. Army.

After the war Rubenstein left the FBI and accepted a commission in the U.S. Air Force. He served first as chief of the Counterintelligence Division of the Office of Special Investigations, and later as commandant of the OSI training school in Washington. He later served in several security positions in the Department of Defense, and in 1958–61 was security advisor to the U.S. mission to NATO. He retired from the Air Force in 1962 with the rank of colonel. He later acted as a security consultant to the Department of Defense and to the Mosler Safe Company.

Rubenstein was awarded the Legion of Merit three times for his service in the Second World War.

(Smith, *OSS: Who's Who in America*, v. 34)

RUTH, SAMUEL (1818–August 14, 1872): railroad official, Union secret agent

A native of Pennsylvania, Ruth received some training as a mechanic before moving to Virginia in 1839. He went to work for the Richmond, Fredericksburg and Potomac Railroad and achieved the rank of superintendent by 1858.

Ruth remained in Virginia and his railroad position after the outbreak of the Civil War, although he was secretly loyal to the Union. Through dilatory tactics and deliberate inefficiency, he effected slowdowns on the R.F.& P. railroad, a vital transportation service of the Confederate Army.

Although he apparently undertook his sabotage activities on his own initiative, Ruth eventually became a member of the Union intelligence network in Richmond run by ELIZABETH VAN LEW. Among the items of vital military intelligence that he supplied to Union intelligence officer Gen. GEORGE H. SHARPE was advance notice of Gen. Robert E. Lee's attack on Fort Steadman in March 1865, a disclosure that enabled Grant to inflict heavy casualties on the Confederate force. About the same time, Ruth informed Sharpe that a trainload of tobacco was to be hauled to Fredericksburg to be illegally exchanged with Northern blockade-runners for bacon. Union forces raided the site of the planned trade and seized the tobacco, thus denying the Confederates some much needed food.

Ruth also ran an underground escape route by

which refugees from the Confederacy could safely make their way to Union territory. It was this activity that led to his arrest and imprisonment in Castle Thunder, a Richmond prison for Union captives and sympathizers, in January 1865. However, the evidence against him on the charges of treason and espionage was judged insufficient and he was released within ten days.

After the war Sharpe officially informed Secretary of War Edwin Stanton that he estimated Ruth's services as having been worth no less than $40,000 to the Union. However, Ruth's petition to Congress for compensation for his underground work was denied on the grounds that other citizens had rendered similar services without expectation of reward.

Ruth continued in his position with the R.F.& P. after the war, despite the fact that his wartime service to the North had become known in Virginia. In 1869 the administration of President Grant appointed him collector of internal revenue for the Second District of Virginia, a position he held until shortly before his death.

(Johnston, "Disloyalty on Confederate Railroads in Virginia"; Stuart, "Samuel Ruth and General R.E. Lee: Disloyalty and the Line of Supply to Fredericksburg, 1862–1863.")

S

S-2

An intelligence officer attached to the staff of a command level below division in the U.S. Army. See also G-2, ARMY INTELLIGENCE.

ST. ALBANS RAID

On October 19, 1864 a party of about thirty Confederate raiders led by Lt. BENNETT H. YOUNG struck the town of St. Albans, Vermont, near the Canadian border. The raid was part of a larger Confederate operation known as the NORTHWEST CONSPIRACY, and had been ordered by Confederate intelligence officer George N. Sanders, partly in retaliation for General Sheridan's depredations in Virginia. The objective of the raid was to loot the banks and burn the town.

The raiders, traveling incognito, arrived in St. Albans in small groups between October 15th and 18th. Early in the afternoon of the 19th Lt. Young stood on the steps of the American House, the hotel at which he had been staying, and proclaimed the town a Confederate possession. The raiders later claimed they had donned Confederate uniforms for the occasion; the St. Albans townspeople said they had been wearing civilian garb.

The raiders rounded up some of the 5,000 residents and herded them into a park in the town square. They robbed the First National Bank, the St. Albans Bank, and the Franklin County Bank of a total of about $200,000. When the townspeople began to resist, some gunfire was exchanged with the raiders and one St. Albans man was killed. The raiders set fire to several buildings, but did not succeed in start-

ing a general conflagration. As the resistance of the townspeople increased, the raiders stole horses from the local livery stable, fled across the border into Canada, and dispersed in several small groups.

Twelve of the raiders were arrested by the Canadian authorities near Philipsburg, Quebec. Lt. Young was captured near Philipsburg on Canadian soil by a posse from St. Albans, but was turned over to the Canadian authorities on the informal promise that he and the other captives would be escorted back to St. Albans the next day. Instead the raiders were held in Montreal until December, when extradition to the United States was denied by the Canadian government and the men were released. Seventy-five thousand dollars of the stolen money was recovered and returned to the banks.

The minor action had a major military effect, forcing the North to divert troops for the protection of the Canadian border. It also caused a further chilling of relations between the U.S. and Great Britain.

(Horan, *Confederate Agent*; Stern, *Secret Missions of the Civil War*; Bemis, *A Diplomatic History of the United States*.)

SALOMON, HAYM (ca. 1740–January 6, 1785): merchant, banker, financier, secret agent

A native of Lissa, Poland, Salomon was a Jew who fled persecution in his homeland and settled in New York circa 1773. He opened a brokerage and a mercantile business. After Gen. GEORGE WASHINGTON evacuated Manhattan in mid-September 1776,

Salomon remained as a STAY-BEHIND agent for Washington.

On September 22, 1776—coincidentally, the day NATHAN HALE was hanged—Salomon was arrested by the British authorities and charged with espionage. After a short period of imprisonment he was released to the custody of Gen. Leopold Philip von Heister, commander-in-chief of the Hessian mercenary troops serving the British in America, in order to serve as a German-English interpreter in the Hessian commissary department.

Salomon continued to work as an American secret intelligence agent in New York. He also persuaded several Hessian troops to desert and join the Patriots, and he gave financial assistance to his fellow patriots held prisoner in New York. In August 1778 he was again arrested, this time charged with conspiracy to burn the British fleet and destroy British storehouses in New York. He was sentenced to death.

Salomon escaped and fled to Philadelphia. There he resumed his business activities. He became an important financier of the Revolution, reportedly lending more than $650,000. He was also paymaster to the French expeditionary force under Gen. Rochambeau in 1781.

The U.S. government had not yet repaid Salomon's loans at the time of his death, and he is reported to have died in bankruptcy.

(Central Intelligence Agency, *Intelligence in the War of Independence*; *Who Was Who in America*, historical volume; Lancaster and Plumb, *American Heritage Book of the Revolution*; Russell, *Haym Salomon and the Revolution*.)

SAMOS RECONNAISSANCE SATELLITE

SAMOS (Satellite and Missile Observation System) was a reconnaissance satellite program inaugurated by the U.S. Air Force in the mid-1950s concurrent with the DISCOVERER RECONNAISSANCE SATELLITE program (see OVERHEAD RECONNAISSANCE). While the aim of the Discoverer program was to recover films from orbit by means of a capsule ejected from the satellite, photographs made by the SAMOS's cameras were transmitted back to a ground station by a radio signal.

On January 31, 1961, SAMOS-2, the first successful SAMOS satellite, was placed into a polar orbit varying in altitude between 295 and 343 miles, with an orbital period of ninety-five minutes. The satellite carried between 300 and 400 pounds of instruments, including a camera/film-processor built by Eastman Kodak, and a video scanner built by CBS Laboratories. It was launched by an Atlas/Agena rocket from Vandenberg Air Force Base in California.

Reconnaissance photographs sent by the SAMOS series satellite augmented the photographs recovered from the Discoverer satellites. The SAMOS program reportedly continued into the early 1970s (see KH-11 RECONNAISSANCE SATELLITE)

(Klass, *Secret Sentries in Space*; Taylor and Mondey, *Spies in the Sky*; Greenwood, "Reconnaissance and Arms Control.")

SAMPSON, RICHARD S. (October 15, 1919–): clandestine service officer

A native of Iowa, Sampson graduated from Cornell University in 1941 and later served with the CIA CLANDESTINE SERVICE.

Sampson was posted to São Paulo, Brazil, in 1959–62, and was attached to the American embassy in Bogotá, Colombia, in 1965–68, and Montevideo, Uruguay, in 1968–70. He served as chief of the CIA station in Mexico City in the mid-1970s.

(Smith, *Portrait of a Cold Warrior*; *Who's Who in Government*, 1st ed.)

SANFORD, HENRY SHELTON (June 15, 1823–May 21, 1891): American diplomat and intelligence officer

A native of Woodbury, Connecticut, Sanford began his diplomatic career in 1847 as an attaché with the American legation at St. Petersburg, and in 1853 was appointed chargé d'affaires in Paris. In 1861 he was appointed minister resident to Belgium by President Lincoln. Secretary of State Seward characterized him as the minister of the United States in Europe during the first year of the Civil War. One of Sanford's principal assignments during the war was to prevent Confederate agents in Europe from obtaining warships, arms, munitions, and other supplies. With the help of a London private detective agency run by former English police officer Ignatius Pollaky, he organized an extensive intelligence network with agents in European textile mills, factories, shipyards and ports, and postal and telegraph offices. The major target of Sanford's operations was JAMES D. BULLOCH, chief of the Confederate secret service in Europe, who was procuring warships in Europe for the Confederate Navy. Sanford's principal method of countering the Confederates was to gather information on activities of theirs that violated the neutrality of the countries involved, and turn it over to

Henry S. Sanford. Source: Library of Congress.

the respective governments. His activities seriously damaged Confederate supply lines.

In 1870 Sanford bought a large tract of land on the St. John's River in Florida where he built a sawmill and a store, the beginnings of the town of Sanford, Florida. He also established a colony of Swedish immigrants at New Upsala, Florida.

Sanford also took an interest in the exploration and development of central Africa. He participated as a representative of the U.S. government in international efforts to end the slave trade and control the sale of firearms and liquor in central Africa.

(Owsley, "Henry Shelton Sanford and Federal Surveillance Abroad"; *DAB; Who Was Who in America,* historical volume.)

SANITIZE

To delete information from a message or document for reasons of security. A document might bear a top

secret classification, for example (see SECURITY CLASSIFICATION SYSTEM), even though only one sentence or paragraph contains information of that security level; if that information were deleted the document would be *sanitized* and given some lower classification, or be declassified.

Documents are often sanitized to protect or disguise the source of the intelligence they contain. For example, one government might release to an allied government *order of battle* intelligence collected by means of satellite photoreconnaissance, but it might withhold the actual photographs in order to conceal the photographic capabilities (e.g., resolution) of the reconnaissance system. And certain specifics might be deleted from a counterintelligence report to local security forces in order to conceal the fact that the intelligence had been collected through communications interception.

SATELLITE CONTROL FACILITY

The Satellite Control Facility is a command post that controls the operation of U.S. reconnaissance satellites, performing such functions and turning satellite cameras on and off as the satellite passes over an area of intelligence interest, and sending the signal that causes the satellite to eject and de-orbit a film capsule. The SCF communicates with the orbiting satellite through a network of eight tracking stations located around the world. Known informally as "the Blue Cube," the SCF is located in Sunnyvale, California, and is operated by the Air Force for the NATIONAL RECONNAISSANCE OFFICE.

See OVERHEAD RECONNAISSANCE.

(Klass, *Secret Sentries in Space; New York Times,* January 13, 1985, Section 6, p. 50)

SAWYER, JOHN EDWARD (May 5, 1917–): educator, foundation official, intelligence analyst

A native of Worcester, Massachusetts, Sawyer graduated from Williams College in 1939, and earned an LL.D. from Harvard University in 1941. In 1942 he was commissioned as an ensign in the U.S. Naval Reserve. Assigned to the OSS RESEARCH AND ANALYSIS BRANCH, he served in Washington and North Africa as a specialist in French affairs. He was awarded the Bronze Star.

He was one of the intelligence analysts transferred to the State Department after the OSS was dissolved in 1945 (see STATE DEPARTMENT INTELLIGENCE). In 1946 he was discharged with the rank of lieutenant and left the State Department.

Sawyer was a member of the faculty of Harvard University until 1953. From 1953 to 1961 he was associate professor of economic history at Yale University, and he served as president of Williams College during 1961–73. In 1974 he joined the Andrew Mellon Foundation as vice-president, and since 1975 has been president of the Foundation.

(Smith, *OSS*; *Who's Who in America*, 42nd ed.)

SCHLESINGER, ARTHUR MEIER, JR. (October 15, 1917–): author, historian presidential advisor, intelligence officer.

A native of Columbus, Ohio, Schlesinger graduated summa cum laude from Harvard University in 1938. In 1942 he joined the Office of War Information, the "overt" propaganda group headed by Robert E. Sherwood that had been split off when the Office of the Coordinator of Information was transformed into the Office of Strategic Services. In 1942 he transferred to the OSS and worked as a political intelligence analyst in the OSS RESEARCH AND ANALYSIS BRANCH.

After the war Schlesinger became a professor of history at Harvard University. His *Age of Jackson* won the Pulitzer prize for History in 1946, and he wrote a three-volume history of the administration of President Franklin D. Roosevelt. In 1961 President Kennedy appointed him as his special assistant. In 1965 he published a history of the Kennedy administration, *A Thousand Days*.

(Smith, *OSS*; *Who's Who in America*, 42nd ed.)

SCHLESINGER, JAMES RODNEY (February 15, 1929–): economist, government official, intelligence officer

A native of New York City, Schlesinger attended the Horace Mann School and graduated from Harvard University in 1950. He earned an M.A. and Ph.D. in economics from Harvard in 1952 and 1956, respectively. From 1955 to 1963 he was a member of the faculty of the University of Virginia, and during that time he lectured at the Naval War College and served as a consultant to the board of governors of the Federal Reserve System.

Schlesinger's lectures at the Naval War College were published as a book, *The Political Economy of National Security; A Study of the Economic Aspects of the Contemporary Power Struggle*. The book led to an invitation from the Rand Corporation. Schlesinger joined Rand as a senior staff member in 1963 and eventually became the company's director of strategic studies. While at Rand he also served as a consultant to the Bureau of the Budget.

James R. Schlesinger—oil portrait by Lloyd Embry. Source: Central Intelligence Agency.

In 1969 Schlesinger left Rand to take up an appointment as assistant director of the Bureau of the Budget, and he continued in that position in the Bureau's successor agency, the Office of Management and Budget. One of the projects he supervised while in that position was a survey and management study of the INTELLIGENCE COMMUNITY. In 1971 he was appointed chairman of the Atomic Energy Commission.

In January 1973, reportedly at the suggestion of Henry Kissinger, President Nixon appointed Schlesinger to succeed RICHARD HELMS as director of the CENTRAL INTELLIGENCE AGENCY. The new position gave Schlesinger the opportunity to implement the reforms recommended in his OMB study of intelligence. His appointee as chief of the CIA CLANDESTINE SERVICE, WILLIAM E. COLBY, helped him shift the Agency's focus from traditional covert operations to sophisticated technical intelligence collection such as reconnaissance satellites (see OVERHEAD RECONNAISSANCE).

In May 1973, just four months after his appointment as director of central intelligence, Schlesinger left the post to become secretary of defense in a reshuffling of the Nixon administration precipitated by the resignation of Attorney General Richard Kleindienst because of his involvement in the Watergate affair. Schlesinger was succeeded as DCI by William Colby, who continued to implement many of the reforms begun by Schlesinger, including the termination or early retirement of some 2,000 CIA employees. Among those forced out were most of the surviving ''charter members'' of the Agency, the veterans of the Office of Strategic Services and others who joined the CIA during the first few years of its existence.

While DCI, Schlesinger directed the compilation of the ''Family Jewels,'' a list of nearly seven hundred illegal or otherwise questionable operations that the CIA carried out over the years. The disclosure of some items from this list during 1974 and 1975 led to the investigation of the CIA by a presidential commission and two congressional committees, caused a ''siege atmosphere'' to prevail within the intelligence community for several years, and brought about some reforms.

Schlesinger left the post of secretary of defense in 1975 to become a visiting scholar at the Johns Hopkins School of International Studies. In 1977–79 he was director of the Department of Energy. Since 1979 he has acted as senior advisor at the Center for Strategic and International Studies of Georgetown University, and a senior advisor to Shearson Lehman Brothers, Inc.

(*Who's Who in America*, 43rd ed.; *Current Biography*, 1973; Colby and Forbath *Honorable Men*; Cline, *The CIA: Reality vs. Myth*.)

SCHOW, ROBERT ALWIN (October 19, 1898–): Army officer, intelligence officer

A native of Hoboken, New Jersey, Schow graduated from the U.S. Military Academy in 1918. During 1939–44 he was assistant military attaché and military attaché in France and in 1945–46 he was assistant chief of staff for intelligence to the Fifteenth U.S. Army (see ARMY INTELLIGENCE). During 1949–51 he served with the Central Intelligence Agency as assistant director for special operations, i.e., chief of the Office of Special Operations, as the SECRET INTELLIGENCE department of the CIA was then called.

During 1951–54 Schow was assistant chief of staff for intelligence in SHAPE (Supreme Headquarters Allied Powers in Europe). He became deputy assistant chief of staff for intelligence in the Department

of the Army (i.e., the number two officer in Army Intelligence) in 1954, and in 1956 he moved into the post of assistant chief of staff for intelligence (i.e, the chief of Army intelligence).

In 1958 Schow retired from the Army with the rank of major general, which he had held since 1954. Among his many decorations are the Legion of Merit and the French Legion of Honor, croix de guerre, and Medal of the Resistance.

After his retirement from the Army Schow worked for the Radio Corporation of America.

(Smith, *OSS: Who's Who in America*, v. 32.)

SCHWARZKOPF, H. NORMAN (1895– November 25, 1958): Army officer, businessman, law enforcement official

Schwarzkopf graduated from the U.S. Military Academy in 1917. After serving with the American forces in Europe and reaching the rank of captain, he left the Army and took a job with a New Jersey department store. Shortly thereafter, New Jersey Governor Edward I. Edwards gave him the job of organizing and heading the New Jersey State Police.

Schwarzkopf played a prominent role in the investigation of the 1932 kidnapping of the son of Charles Lindbergh and at the trial of Bruno Hauptmann, the man convicted of the crime. Schwarzkopf came under criticism for his performance in the case by New Jersey Governor Harold G. Hoffman, who refused to reappoint him to the State Police post when his term expired in June 1936.

Schwarzkopf worked as a trucking company executive until shortly before the Second World War, when he joined the New Jersey National Guard and was promoted to the rank of lieutenant colonel. During the war he was assigned to Iran, where he reorganized and trained the national police force, the Imperial Iranian Gendarmerie, and served as its head from 1942 to 1948. In 1948 he was promoted to brigadier general and subsequently served in West Germany and Italy.

In 1951 Schwarzkopf returned to New Jersey, where he was appointed administrative director of the state's Department of Law and Public Safety. In 1953 he became commanding general of the Seventy-eighth Division of the Army Reserve Corps, an all-New Jersey unit.

In August 1953, ostensibly on a round-the-world tour, Schwarzkopf visited Iran and played a key role in the Central Intelligence Agency's IRAN COUP.

Schwarzkopf retired in 1956.

(obituary, *New York Times*, November 27, 1958, p. 29; Roosevelt, *Countercoup*.)

SCOTT, JOHN M. (ca. 1840–June 18, 1862): soldier, Union secret service agent

Scott lived in Findlay, Ohio, before the Civil War. In 1861 he enlisted in the Ohio Volunteer Infantry, which was part of the Army of the Ohio. He had attained the rank of sergeant by April 1862 when he volunteered to take part in a paramilitary operation behind Confederate lines aimed at severing the rail line between Atlanta and Chattanooga (see ANDREWS'S RAID). He and a party of twenty other Union troops in civilian clothes and led by JAMES J. ANDREWS hijacked a locomotive and attempted to destroy railroad tracks and bridges between the two cities. He was captured by Confederate troops and imprisoned. Scott, Andrews, and six others of the party were hanged.

(Bryan, *The Spy in America*; Boatner, *Civil War Dictionary*; O'Neill, *Wild Train*.)

SCOVILLE, HERBERT ("PETE"), JR. (March 16, 1915–July 30, 1985): physical chemist, arms control specialist, government official, intelligence officer

A native of New York City, Scoville graduated from Yale University in 1937, did postgraduate work at Cambridge University in 1937–39, and earned a Ph.D. in physical chemistry from the University of Rochester in 1942. He worked for the Atomic Energy Commission at Los Alamos during 1946–48. As technical director of the Armed Forces Special Weapons Project of the Department of Defense from 1948 to 1955 he helped develop nuclear weapons.

In 1955 Scoville joined the CENTRAL INTELLIGENCE AGENCY and served as director of the Office of Scientific Intelligence, a CIA unit that kept track of developments in nuclear energy and missile technology. He was an outspoken critic of HUMINT (human intelligence agents) as a means of collecting scientific intelligence, advocating instead such technical collection methods as OVERHEAD RECONNAISSANCE. In 1962 he was appointed deputy director for research, i.e., chief of the Research Directorate that CIA Director JOHN A. MCCONE had just created in an attempt to consolidate and integrate the Agency's scientific and technical functions. This consolidation effort was temporarily stalled owing to bureaucratic resistance, however, and Scoville left the Agency before the problem was solved with the creation of the CIA SCIENCE AND TECHNOLOGY DIRECTORATE in 1963.

From 1963 to 1969 Scoville served as assistant director for science and technology with the U.S. Arms Control and Disarmament Agency. He was responsible for developing positions on such matters as the 1963 treaty on a limited nuclear test ban, the 1969 treaty aimed at curbing the spread of nuclear weapons, and the strategic arms limitation talks with the Soviet Union.

Scoville left government service in 1969, and until 1971 was director of the Arms Control Program of the Carnegie Endowment for International Peace. He was a well-known advocate of nuclear arms control, which he promoted until his death in 1985.

(*Who's Who in America*, 43rd ed.; Powers, *The Man Who Kept the Secrets*; obituary, *New York Times*, July 31, 1985, p. A14.)

SCULLY, JOHN: detective and Union secret agent

A native of England, Scully was in the United States circa 1853 when he was hired by ALLAN PINKERTON to work as a detective for PINKERTON'S NATIONAL DETECTIVE AGENCY. He was one of the detectives who accompanied Pinkerton to Cincinnati in May 1861 to establish the secret service of the Army of the Ohio under Gen. George B. McClellan, and shortly thereafter he was sent into Confederate territory to collect military intelligence.

In September 1861 Scully worked with Pinkerton agent TIMOTHY WEBSTER to infiltrate secessionist circles in Baltimore. About the same time he took part in the investigation of Confederate secret service agent ROSE O'NEAL GREENHOW.

In February 1862 Pinkerton sent Scully and PRYCE LEWIS to Richmond to make contact with Webster, who was operating in the Confederate capital as a penetration agent and had not been heard from for some time. Scully and Lewis were recognized as Pinkerton agents and arrested by the Confederate authorities. To save his own life Scully betrayed Webster, who was hanged. Scully and Lewis were incarcerated in Castle Thunder, the Confederate prison in Richmond for Union prisoners and sympathizers until September 1863, when they were released in an exchange of prisoners of war.

After the war Scully lived in Chicago where he worked as a guard in City Hall.

(Horan and Swiggett, *The Pinkerton Story*; Horan, *The Pinkertons*; Bryan, *The Spy in America*.)

SEA SUPPLY COMPANY

A PROPRIETARY COMPANY of the Central Intelligence Agency, based in Thailand, which provided *commercial cover* (see COVER) for the CIA's Office of Policy Coordination in the Far East during the 1950s.

(Smith, *Portrait of a Cold Warrior*.)

SEBOLD, WILLIAM G. (1899–): American double agent

A native of Muehlheim, Germany, Sebold was born Wilhelm Georg Debowski. He served in the German army during the FIRST WORLD WAR, and later worked as a merchant seaman. In 1922 he jumped ship in Galveston, Texas, and remained in the United States. He changed his name to William Sebold, married, and became an American citizen. He settled in San Diego, California, and got a job as a mechanic with the Consolidated Aircraft Corporation.

In 1939 Sebold visited his family in Germany. Because he listed his occupation as aircraft mechanic on his travel documents he attracted the attention of German Intelligence. He rejected the first overtures of the German intelligence officers, who considered him potential secret intelligence agent material, but he was eventually blackmailed by the Gestapo (the Nazi secret police), which had turned up a twenty-year-old criminal record (he had done time in Germany for smuggling and other felonies) and threatened to disclose this information to the U.S. immigration authorities, thus jeopardizing his American citizenship.

Sebold agreed to work for the Abwehr (German military intelligence) and was given three months of training in Hamburg, including courses in operating a clandestine radio transmitter. However, he also managed to visit the American consulate in Cologne where he disclosed his predicament to the vice-consul. The official advised Sebold to pretend to go along with the Abwehr, and to serve as a DOUBLE AGENT for the Federal Bureau of Investigation after his return to the United States.

Sebold was met by FBI agents when he arrived in New York City in February 1940. He turned over to them rolls of microfilm he had carried from Germany—messages from Abwehr headquarters to agents and officers in New York. The FBI copied the films and returned them to Sebold for delivery, having learned not only the names and addresses of the Abwehr operators but the intelligence collection requirements they had been given.

Following Abwehr instructions, Sebold set up a clandestine radio transmitter in a house in a secluded section of Centerport, Long Island. He also opened offices at 152 West 42nd Street in the name of the fictitious Diesel Research Company in order to have a convenient and secure place to meet with other Abwehr agents in New York. His performance as a radio operator was so satisfactory to the Abwehr that other German networks in the United States often "borrowed" him to transmit their reports to headquarters. All his transmissions were first screened by the FBI, however, to insure that no vital intelligence was sent. The Bureau also used Sebold's Diesel Research offices for clandestine audio and photographic surveillance of the German agents who met there.

In June 1940 the FBI harvested the results of Sebold's double role, rounding up thirty-three Abwehr agents operating in the United States. In addition to Sebold's testimony, the government presented the evidence of the documents he had intercepted and the audio and video records of the incriminating meetings in the Diesel Research offices. The operation virtually neutralized the German secret intelligence apparatus in the United States.

After the trial of the agents Sebold returned to private life.

(Farago, *The Game of the Foxes*; Hynd, *Passport to Treason*; Kahn, *Hitler's Spies*.)

SECOND WORLD WAR

The War: In September 1939 Germany invaded Poland in violation of an agreement with Britain and France, thereby precipitating a war with those two countries. At the same time, under a secret agreement signed with the Hitler regime, the Soviet Union occupied part of Poland and seized parts of Finland. The following spring German forces overran Belgium, Holland, Luxembourg, and most of France. In September 1940 the German Luftwaffe mounted a massive aerial bombardment of London that failed to achieve its objective of bringing about a British surrender. In June 1941 Hitler turned on his Soviet ally, reneged on the nonaggression pact he had signed with Soviet dictator Stalin, and invaded Russia. In East Asia the Japanese exploited the fall of France by occupying French Indochina, while simultaneously pursuing the war they had launched against China in 1937. (Japan had signed an alliance with Germany and its fascist ally, Italy, in 1940, thereby creating the "Berlin-Tokyo-Rome Axis.")

Pearl Harbor

American public opinion was divided regarding these events between a segment sympathetic toward Britain, China, and the other victims of Axis aggression, and a segment firmly opposed to the United States being drawn into another overseas conflict as it had been in the First World War. The administration of President Franklin Roosevelt shared the views of the former segment, but was forestalled from military intervention by the strength of the latter. It did achieve the repeal of some provisions of the recently enacted Neutrality Laws, however, and thereby was able to sell arms to Britain and France. It also embargoed the export of scrap iron and other strategic materials to Japan, and in July 1941 froze Japan's financial assets and credit in the United States. In eventual response to this step Japan carried out the surprise PEARL HARBOR ATTACK on December 7, 1941, precipitating a war with the United States and abruptly ending all significant isolationist sentiment in America. Three days later Germany and Italy declared war on the United States.

Japanese forces overran Thailand, Burma, Hong Kong, Malaya, and the Dutch East Indies. The Japanese onslaught in the Pacific soon included the capture of such American possessions as Wake Island and Guam, and by May 1942 the Philippine Islands. A month later, however, the U.S. Navy halted the Japanese eastward thrust at the battle of MIDWAY.

The Mediterranean

In November 1942 an Anglo-American force liberated French North Africa. By the following May, the British and American Allies had retaken all of North Africa from the Axis. Meanwhile, the German invasion of Russia faltered at Stalingrad. The Allies captured Sicily in August 1943, and in early September a British force landed on the extreme southern tip of Italy. These victories precipitated a government crisis in Italy, and on September 8th a new Italian government surrendered to the Allies. Anticipating this development, the Germans sent a force to occupy Italy from the Alps to Naples, and when an Allied force landed at Salerno on September 9th it met bitter German resistance that was to continue and slow the Allies' advance up the Italian peninsula during the next eighteen months.

The Pacific War

In the southwest Pacific American forces began a general offensive in June 1943, and by the end of the year had taken parts of the Bismarck and Solomon island groups. In the northern Pacific, Japanese-held islands in the Aleutians were reclaimed by American forces. By December 1943 the American forces in the Pacific had undertaken a policy of leapfrogging islands strongly defended by the Japanese to hit at softer targets within bomber range of Japan. The Gilbert Islands fell to the American advance in mid-November, the Marshall Islands the following February, and the Marianas in June 1944.

Early in the war the China-Burma-India theater had seemed to promise the Allies a springboard for attacking Japan, but several years of bitter fighting in the zone failed to open the land route from India to China needed to support such a strategy. By 1944 Allied aims in the theater were limited to keeping Chinese resistance alive in order to distract the Japanese from the Pacific, by then clearly the route for the main thrust against the Japanese mainland.

By mid-June 1944 the U.S. air forces were able to carry out aerial bombardment of the Japanese home islands from bases in the Pacific. The U.S. Navy engaged the Japanese fleet in several encounters and dealt it an overwhelming defeat at the battle of the Philippine Sea. By the end of August the United States had taken the important Pacific bases of Saipan, Tinian, and Guam.

In the southwest Pacific much of the Japanese navy was destroyed in October 1944 at the battle of the Leyte Gulf, and the way was cleared for reclaiming the Philippine Islands. By the end of December 1944 American forces had taken the islands of Leyte and Mindoro, setting the stage for the invasion of the major Philippine island of Luzon.

Victory in Europe

In the European theater the Allies carried out aerial bombardment of strategic targets during 1943–44, while the Anglo-American invasion force continued to struggle up the Italian peninsula. At the same time some 1.2 million American troops crossed the Atlantic to staging areas in Britain in preparation for the major Allied cross-channel attack that was launched on June 6, 1944. Early in 1944 the Red Army, with American strategic air support, opened a drive that carried it across the Ukraine, pushing the Germans back into Poland and behind the Carpathian Mountains to the south. By the end of the year all German forces had been driven from France and the USSR.

By April 1945 British forces had crossed the Rhine, the American advance had reached the Elbe—about sixty miles from Berlin—and the Red Army had advanced to a line formed by the Oder and Neisse rivers some hundred miles to the east of the German capital. German resistance in northern Italy began to crumble, and the Allied advance now swept northward. On May 2 the German forces in Italy surrendered and Berlin fell to the Red Army; six days later all other German forces followed suit, bringing the war in Europe to an end.

The Fall of Japan

In the Pacific U.S. forces met determined Japanese resistance during the spring and summer of 1945. By early March Manila was retaken and the Japanese forces in the Philippines were driven into the mountains of the islands of Luzon and Mindanao. In the central western Pacific, the strategic islands of Iwo Jima and Okinawa were captured in March and July, respectively, at an enormous cost in casualties to American forces in some of the bloodiest fighting of the Pacific war. In March the U.S. air forces based in the Marianas began striking at cities on the Japanese mainland—Tokyo, Osaka, Kobe, and Nagoya. Japanese resistance in southeast Asia crumbled; British and Australian forces had taken most of Burma, New Guinea, the Bismarcks, the Solomons, and the Dutch East Indies by mid-year.

Although defeat was now obviously inevitable, the Japanese government refused Allied demands for unconditional surrender and prepared to resist the coming Allied invasion of the Japanese mainland with the same sort of desperate and suicidal campaign that Japanese forces had waged at Iwo Jima and Okinawa, but on a vastly larger scale. However, in early August the U.S. air forces dropped a nuclear bomb on the Japanese military center at Hiroshima, completely destroying it and the surrounding city, and three days later did the same to the seaport of Nagasaki. Within a few days of the nuclear attacks Japanese Emperor Hirohito overrode his military advisors and accepted the Allied surrender terms, bringing the war to an end.

U.S. Intelligence in the War: More personnel and more separate organizations were involved in American intelligence and related operations during the war than at any earlier time in history. Much of the official record of these operations remains classified more than forty years after the end of the war. For example, in June 1984 the Central Intelligence Agency released 195 cubic feet of OSS files to the public through the National Archives. This was the first installment of some 2,500 cubic feet of OSS files to be released over a period of several years, a small portion of the hundreds of thousands of cubic feet of OSS files that will remain classified. Similar security considerations have slowed the release of intelligence records of other government agencies. Because so much relevant material remains unavailable, no comprehensive history of American intelligence during the war has been undertaken for general publication, and were such an account available it would be difficult to make an adequate summary of it for the purpose of this encyclopedia. It is therefore possible only to present the briefest compilation and summary of the relevant information discussed in greater depth elsewhere in this work.

Counterintelligence and Countersubversion

As the war approached, counterintelligence and countersubversion received first priority by the American intelligence services. The countersubversion role of the FEDERAL BUREAU OF INVESTIGATION, dormant since 1924, was restored by order of President Roosevelt in 1937; the FBI was authorized to investigate subversive activities carried on by Communists, Fascists, and the agents of foreign governments within the United States. The number of espionage cases handled by the Bureau increased dramatically from an average of thirty-five cases per year during 1933–37 to 634 cases in 1938. In 1939 Roosevelt established a committee comprised of the heads of the FBI, the Army's Military Intelligence Division (see ARMY INTELLIGENCE), and the Office of NAVAL INTELLIGENCE to coordinate all espionage and counterespionage matters.

FBI counterespionage was greatly aided by WILLIAM G. SEBOLD, a German-born American recruited by German intelligence to serve as an espionage agent in the United States who volunteered to work as a DOUBLE AGENT for the FBI. As a result of Sebold's work, the Bureau rounded up thirty-three German agents in June 1940, virtually neutralizing the entire German espionage apparatus in the United States for the duration of the war.

German intelligence made some effort to reestablish an apparatus in the United States, especially for the purpose of sabotage (see PASTORIUS). However the problem of Axis sabotage and subversion in the United States during the war never approached the magnitude that the Central Powers had achieved during the FIRST WORLD WAR.

Latin America

Axis subversion in Latin America was another matter that received early intelligence attention by the U.S. government. In 1938 the Office of Naval Intelligence (see NAVAL INTELLIGENCE) recognized the threat, expanded its activities in the region, and established naval attaché offices in every major Latin American capital. In June 1940 President Roosevelt established the OFFICE OF THE COORDINATOR OF INTER-AMERICAN AFFAIRS under Nelson A. Rockefeller to counter Axis economic penetration and propaganda in the region. Also in 1940 Roosevelt made the FBI responsible for positive, nonmilitary foreign intelligence (see INTELLIGENCE TAXON-OMY) throughout the western hemisphere; the Bureau established the FBI Special Intelligence Service for this purpose, sending its agents into Latin America under both official and commercial cover. FBI/SIS carried out extensive and effective counterespionage and countersubversion operations in Mexico, Brazil, Chile, Argentina, Central America, and the Caribbean during the war.

The FBI's operations against the Axis in the western hemisphere were aided by British intelligence through Sir WILLIAM STEPHENSON, the British service's liaison officer in the United States. Under cover of the British Passport Control office in New York City, Stephenson operated British Security Coordination, a covert intelligence and counterintelligence unit that also conducted liaison, propaganda operations, and secret diplomacy aimed at bringing the United States into the war.

Stephenson worked closely with WILLIAM J. DONOVAN, a prominent Wall Street lawyer who served as an unofficial presidential advisor during 1939–40 regarding the strategic situation in Europe and Britain's prospects for survival. Stephenson persuaded Donovan—who in turn persuaded Roosevelt—that the United States needed a SECRET INTELLIGENCE and COVERT ACTION agency modeled on the British Secret Intelligence Service, and as a result the Office of the Coordinator of Information (COI) was established in July 1941 with Donovan as its director. A quasi-agency of the Executive Office of the President, COI became the OFFICE OF STRATEGIC SERVICES under the Joint Chiefs of Staff in June 1942.

The Japanese Threat

Although the American armed forces had been neglected by the government after the First World War, the intelligence services of the Army and Navy managed to maintain a moderate level of activity focused on Japan during the 1920s and 1930s. Japan had been seen as a potential strategic threat to the U.S. since the 1890s. In 1912 the Office of Naval Intelligence produced War Plan Orange, a detailed plan for an all-out war with Japan, and the plan had been updated regularly by ONI and the Navy's War Plans Division through the 1930s. Communications intelligence was the major source of information on Japan's strategic capabilities and intentions during the 1930s; beginning in 1922 the Navy had conducted a long-term program to develop a cadre of specialists in Japanese language, military and naval affairs, and cryptosystems. This program yielded a rich harvest with the approach of war, as Op-20-G, the Office of

Naval Communications' Code and Signal Section, intercepted and deciphered a large volume of highly important Japanese diplomatic, naval, and military communications. The Army's Signal Intelligence Service also devoted much time and attention to Japanese communications, and in 1940 SIS director WILLIAM FRIEDMAN and his cryptanalysis staff broke "Purple," the high-level Japanese diplomatic cipher. However, despite the wealth of communication intelligence collected by the Army and Navy cryptologic units, and a considerable amount of collateral information, U.S. intelligence failed to anticipate the PEARL HARBOR ATTACK.

Communications Intelligence

In the wake of the Pearl Harbor disaster, the War Department established the SPECIAL BRANCH within the Military Intelligence Service (see ARMY INTELLIGENCE) to improve the processing and dissemination of U.S. communications intelligence. The Special Branch worked closely with the British communications intelligence service and received most of its strategic communications intelligence regarding Germany through this liaison.

In the Pacific, the Navy's FRUPAC (Fleet Radio Unit, Pacific) under Lt. Comdr. JOSEPH ROCHEFORT produced communications intelligence that was crucial to the American naval victory at MIDWAY, the turning point in the Pacific war. FRUPAC and other Navy communications intelligence units were also instrumental in the YAMAMOTO INTERCEPTION, supplied the Navy's submarine fleet with the intelligence needed to destroy the Japanese merchant marine in the Pacific, and guided the American amphibious advance across the western Pacific through the Japanese-held islands.

In the southwest Pacific the CENTRAL BUREAU, a joint Australian-American unit under Brig. Gen. Spencer B. Akin, collected and processed communications intelligence for Gen. Douglas MacArthur's command. The Central Bureau had a direct radio link to the Arlington, Virginia, headquarters of the Army's Signal Intelligence Service (SIS).

The SIS also provided tactical communications intelligence in other theaters of the war. SIS detachments in Europe operated close to the front, and their interception of enemy tactical communications repeatedly frustrated German counterattacks.

The OSS

Reflecting the character of its founder and director, Gen. William Donovan, the OSS was an energetic and innovative agency, staffed by talented amateurs, guided to some extent by some seasoned covert operators of British intelligence, and unfettered by established military doctrine or tradition. An extensive OSS program of espionage, sabotage, and subversion in North Africa insured the success of the Allied landings in November 1942. The agency provided similar support for the invasions of Sicily and Italy the following year. Teams of the OSS SPECIAL OPERATIONS BRANCH infiltrated European countries to organize and assist local resistance groups in guerrilla warfare against the German occupation. SO Branch agents worked with the French Resistance in support of the Allied cross-channel invasion in June 1944 (see JEDBURGH OPERATION). OSS OPERATIONAL GROUPS fought behind the lines in every theater of the war, and were especially useful in disrupting the transport and logistics of the retreating German forces in Italy and France during the final year of the war.

The OSS SECRET INTELLIGENCE BRANCH operated networks of espionage agents worldwide. SI agents in Europe furnished reports that enabled Allied air forces to pinpoint their targets, provided early warning of the German missile development program, conducted extensive counterintelligence operations against German intelligence, and brought about the early surrender of all German and Italian Fascist forces in northern Italy (see ALLEN DULLES). SI agents provided valuable tactical intelligence from behind German lines during the Allied advance across Europe.

The OSS RESEARCH AND ANALYSIS BRANCH produced important strategic intelligence. For example, early in the war Allied strategists had assumed that Germany's limited food production capability and not her manpower supply would prove the critical factor in sustaining a prolonged war effort. However, by studying openly available agricultural statistics OSS intelligence analysts were able to determine that the German food supply would never fall so low as to affect Germany's ability to fight. The analysts were also able to make highly accurate estimates of the German army's manpower strength from such available information as published obituaries of officers, and thereby correctly determined that a shortage of manpower would be the critical factor.

In China and Southeast Asia OSS detachments worked with local guerrillas against the Japanese and supplied target intelligence to the Allied air forces.

Army Intelligence

Though OSS agents contributed tactical intelligence to Allied ground forces, especially in Europe, the OSS did not take over the field intelligence role of ARMY INTELLIGENCE, which continued to participate in the Army's command structure through G-2 and S-2 staffs, and through Counter Intelligence Corps (CIC) and Signal Intelligence Service (SIS) detachments. The activities of field intelligence personnel were not at all limited to the sort of work generally associated with headquarters staffs. For example, CIC agents landed with the first waves of the Thirty-sixth Infantry Division at Salerno and were among the first Allied troops to enter Rome.

Army intelligence played a proportionately larger role in the Southwest Pacific theater—generally, Australia, the Solomon Islands, New Guinea, the Netherlands East Indies, and the Philippines—from which the OSS had been excluded by Gen. Douglas MacArthur, the theater commander. Paramilitary operations, irregular warfare, secret intelligence, and other functions performed elsewhere by the OSS were the responsibility of the ALLIED INTELLIGENCE BUREAU, a joint U.S.-Australian coordinating agency headed by MacArthur's G-2, Maj. Gen. CHARLES A. WILLOUGHBY. Willoughby established the ALLIED GEOGRAPHICAL SECTION to provide basic geographic intelligence on the uncharted or poorly mapped areas of the theater; the ALLIED TRANSLATOR AND INTERPRETER SECTION, which translated captured Japanese documents and interrogated Japanese prisoners of war; the Central Bureau (previously noted); and the ALAMO SCOUTS, an elite unit that carried out reconnaissance and commando operations.

Although the Army's field intelligence activities were decentralized and integrated within the theater commands, the Army retained some centralized intelligence functions within the Military Intelligence Division of the General Staff and the related Military Intelligence Service (the MIS was a separate unit created in February 1942 to carry out operational tasks for the MID; MID was supposed to become a purely planning and policy staff, but it gradually lost its distinct identity as the war progressed). The MID/MIS established and operated schools to train field intelligence officers for overseas assignments, supervised the Counter Intelligence Corps within the United States, conducted background investigations of government personnel, carried out counterintelligence investigations and was responsible for the security of the Manhattan Project (see BORIS T. PASH, PEER DE SILVA). A special CIC unit that accompanied the American advance into Germany was responsible for collecting intelligence regarding the state of the German nuclear program and for keeping German technology and technical personnel in this field out of Soviet hands.

The MID/MIS also conducted strategic secret intelligence operations in Europe, independent of those of the OSS (see GROMBACH ORGANIZATION).

Naval Intelligence

The role of the Office of Naval Intelligence was downgraded as the result of bureaucratic squabbling with the Office of Naval Communications and the Navy's War Plans Division before American entry into the war. ONI was consequently relegated almost completely to a domestic counterintelligence and security agency during the war. Positive strategic intelligence was the sole responsibility of the War Plans Division until 1942, when Adm. Ernest J. King—named to the newly created post of commander-in-chief of the Navy (which combined the roles of chief of naval operations and commander-in-chief of the fleet)—established an intelligence division within his staff.

Notwithstanding this setback, ONI managed to break new ground in the field of psychological warfare. Op-16-W, the Special Warfare Branch of ONI, was established to perform this function. Its most notable success was a psychological campaign directed against the crews of German U-boats in the North Atlantic. The campaign consisted of a series of radio propaganda broadcasts by "Commander Norden," who was in fact German-speaking Commander RALPH G. ALBRECHT of Op-16-W.

Op-16-W apparently came close to a much greater psychological warfare success early in 1945 in a campaign devised by Capt. ELLIS ZACHARIAS that was calculated to persuade the Japanese leaders—who by then foresaw their country's eventual defeat—that "Unconditional surrender does not mean the extermination or enslavement of the Japanese people," and, specifically, that it did not mean the removal of their emperor. Although the campaign did not bring about the Japanese surrender before the costly battles of Okinawa and Iwo Jima had been fought and the cities of Hiroshima and Nagasaki destroyed by atom bombs, there is some evidence that it was an important factor in the Japanese decision to surrender after those defeats.

Naval Group China

A separate Navy intelligence organization was established to train, equip, and lead guerrillas in China. Naval Group China, under the command of Comdr. MILTON E. MILES, worked with Chinese Nationalist leader Chiang Kai-shek to establish the SINO-AMERICAN COOPERATIVE ORGANIZATION (SACO), a joint U.S.-Chinese intelligence and covert action agency. SACO was briefly a subordinate unit of the OSS during 1943, when Miles was also serving as OSS coordinator for China. However differences between OSS Director Donovan and Miles led to OSS withdrawal from the project, after which American participation in SACO was purely a Navy matter. By war's end SACO reached a strength of more than 50,000 Chinese guerrillas, with 2,500 American trainers and advisors. The organization harassed Japanese forces throughout China, thereby helping to divert them from the main Allied thrust in the Pacific.

The Navy's largest and most important intelligence undertaking was in the field of communications intelligence, however. As noted above, the Navy's communications intelligence activities were carried out by the Office of Naval Communications and detachments such as FRUPAC.

Air Intelligence

A-2, the Intelligence Division of the Army's Air Staff (see AIR FORCE INTELLIGENCE), had been given the task of identifying profitable potential targets within prospective enemy countries before the war, and after hostilities commenced this activity became the Strategic Target Objective Folder program. Because strategic bombing was the principal role of the Army Air Forces during the war, target intelligence became the major activity of A-2 and the air intelligence staffs of subordinate commands.

Aerial photoreconnaissance became a major method of intelligence collection during the war. In 1942 the Army Air Forces replaced the slow, obsolete aircraft that had previously been used for this function with high-speed interceptors and high-altitude bombers, modified for photoreconnaissance use. The long-range bomber-type aircraft were used to identify prospective strategic targets and to assess post-strike bomb damage. The interceptors flew tactical reconnaissance missions and became a major source of field intelligence for the ground forces commanders.

The great value of tactical photoreconnaissance was proven early in the war, during the North African campaign, and it was regarded as indispensable thereafter. By 1944 the growth of this technique in field intelligence made it necessary to create a separate section within the G-2 staffs at Army and Corps levels, the G-2 Air.

Consequences: The Pearl Harbor attack demonstrated that war could come to America with stupefying suddenness and without the nicety of diplomatic preliminaries; the development of nuclear weapons showed that war could now devastate a nation in a matter of days or even hours; and Soviet postwar expansionism in Europe and the consequent cold war provided a tangible, not an abstract, future threat. These developments profoundly influenced U.S. national security and foreign intelligence doctrine after the war.

1. *Central Intelligence:* In 1955 the Hoover Commission noted, "The CIA may well attribute its existence to the surprise attack on Pearl Harbor and to the postwar investigation into the part Intelligence or lack of Intelligence played in the failure of our military forces to receive adequate and prompt warning of the impending Japanese attack." The concept of a single, centralized agency for the coordination of national intelligence had actually been proposed before Pearl Harbor by Col. William Donovan, and the COI and OSS were the result. Those agencies did not survive postwar demobilization, but the National Security Act of 1947, which established the CIA and the NATIONAL SECURITY COUNCIL, was passed while the painful lessons of Pearl Harbor and its postmortems were still fresh in the minds of American leaders.

2. *Covert Action:* During the war covert political, psychological, paramilitary, and economic warfare was waged at a level unprecedented in American history. The establishment of the OSS SPECIAL OPERATIONS BRANCH gave the U.S. its first formal covert action unit, and many OSS SO veterans brought their experience to the CIA CLANDESTINE SERVICE after the war. U.S. policymakers recalled the demonstrated effectiveness of covert action in the war during the late 1940s and early 1950s when they were faced with the dilemma of either fighting a possible nuclear war with the USSR or tolerating further Soviet expansionism; covert action then seemed to offer an ideal "third option" to formal warfare or ineffectual diplomacy, a way to meet Communist subversion through Western countersubversion. Although the limitations of covert action were demonstrated by the BAY OF PIGS INVASION and similar failures, it remains a major weapon in the arsenal of American intelligence.

3. *Technical collection:* Technical methods of intelligence collection underwent enormous advancement during the war. The vital role communications intelligence played in the Allied victory led directly to the establishment of the NATIONAL SECURITY AGENCY in 1952. The techniques and equipment of aerial reconnaissance were greatly refined and developed during the war, and it became a major method of collecting both strategic and tactical intelligence. Development continued after the war and it was eventually wed to the artificial satellite, which evolved from yet another innovation of the war, the ballistic missile (see OVERHEAD RECONNAISSANCE).

Radar, yet another product of the war, has also become an instrument of intelligence collection. The electronic digital computer, another innovation developed under the pressures of the war, eventually became a major tool for processing intelligence. At the same time that much advanced technology was being introduced into the methods of intelligence collection, technology was becoming central to the strategic capabilities of potential adversaries. This has meant that the very substance of much of the information collected has taken on a scientific and technical character. The war may be seen, therefore, as the beginning of the marriage of technology and intelligence that has flourished in the subsequent decades.

4. *Intelligence Professionalism:* Before the war intelligence was the exclusive domain of diplomats and military officers, very few of whom could qualify as professional intelligence officers. The experience of the war, especially as formulated by such OSS veterans as SHERMAN KENT (in his *Strategic Intelligence for American World Policy*), established the role of the intelligence officer as a distinct professional specialty. The emergence of such subspecialties within the intelligence field as economic intelligence, estimative intelligence, and imagery analysis has been one result. Another has been the establishment of intelligence as a career specialty by the armed services, thereby concentrating and conserving the military and naval intelligence experiences of officers and enlisted personnel. Perhaps the most important consequence of the advent of professionalism in intelligence work has been the development of a body of theory, doctrine, and literature in the field of intelligence and the establishment of such institutions as the DEFENSE INTELLIGENCE COLLEGE, which foster intelligence as an academic discipline.

(Persico, *Piercing the Reich*; Kahn, *The Codebreakers*; Lewin, *The American Magic*; Spector, *Eagle Against the Sun*; Troy, *Donovan and the CIA*; Dorwart, *Conflict of Duty*; Ford, *Donovan of OSS*; Overy, *The Air War*; Infield, *Unarmed and Unafraid*; Corson, *Armies of Ignorance*; Powe and Wilson, *The Evolution of American Military Intelligence*; Holmes, *Double-Edged Secrets*; Layton, *"And I Was There"*; Cave Brown, *The Last Hero, Secret War Report of the OSS*; Hymoff, *The OSS in World War Two*; Smith, *OSS*; Ind, *Allied Intelligence Bureau*; Zacharias, *Secret Missions*; Finnegan, *Military Intelligence*; Rout and Bratzel, *The Shadow War*; Bidwell, "History of the Military Intelligence Division, Department of the Army General Staff"; Roetter, *The Art of Psychological Warfare, 1914–1945*.)

SECRET COMMITTEE

On September 18, 1775 the Continental Congress created the Secret Committee for the procurement of war supplies for the Patriots in the AMERICAN REVOLUTION. It was originally chaired by Thomas Willing of Philadelphia, a banker and merchant, and included BENJAMIN FRANKLIN and SILAS DEANE. In December Willing was succeeded by his business partner, Robert Morris. The Committee was authorized to spend large sums of money in secret for the purchase of weapons, munitions, medical supplies, blankets, and other supplies and equipment, and it shortly took control of all foreign trade. It was also authorized to arm and man vessels in foreign countries for privateering.

The biggest contracts let by the Committee went to the firm of Willing & Morris (the Committee's first and second chairmen), while other business was given to friends and relatives of Deane and firms connected with other members of the Committee. This favoritism and profiteering drew angry criticism from other members of Congress.

In December 1775 the Committee (and the COMMITTEE OF SECRET CORRESPONDENCE, with which it is sometimes confused) met with French secret service agent JULIEN ACHARD DE BONVOULOIR in Philadelphia to discuss the possibility of French military aid to the United States. As a result the committees jointly dispatched SILAS DEANE to France, where he worked with PIERRE CARON DE BEAUMARCHAIS to establish secret arrangements for the trading of American agricultural commodities for French weapons and supplies through a cover corporation, Hortalez & Cie.

In 1777, after the Committee's covert duties had been taken over by the American ministers in France —Franklin, Deane, and Arthur Lee—the Committee became the Committee of Commerce, which later evolved into the U.S. Department of Commerce.

(Augur, *The Secret War of Independence*; Boatner, *The Encyclopedia of the American Revolution*.)

SECRET INTELLIGENCE

Intelligence collected by covert means, usually by human agents. When used adjectivally, e.g., *secret intelligence agent* or *secret intelligence operation*, the term is generally synonymous with *espionage*.

> The object of secret intelligence activity is to obtain by secret means information which cannot otherwise be secured and which is not elsewhere available.
> —Kermit Roosevelt, *War Report of the OSS*

However, the term is not commonly used to refer to information collected by technical means, e.g., communications intelligence, even though those means might be secret. Lately *espionage* and HUMINT are used more often than *secret intelligence*.

See also OSS SECRET INTELLIGENCE BRANCH.

SECRET LINE

A *network* of couriers and secret intelligence agents run by the CONFEDERATE SECRET SERVICE during the Civil War. It was an "underground railway" linking the Confederate government in Richmond with safe houses, agents, Southern sympathizers, and other Confederate assets in the North and in foreign countries.

(Gaddy, "William Norris and the Confederate Signal and Secret Service.")

SECRET SERVICE (U.S.)

Not to be confused with the CIVIL WAR counterintelligence unit organized by LAFAYETTE C. BAKER and sometimes unofficially referred to by the same name (see NATIONAL DETECTIVE BUREAU), the U.S. Secret Service was established in 1865 as a unit of the Department of the Treasury to enforce the federal laws against counterfeiting currency (the U.S. government had begun printing paper money three years earlier).

The Secret Service was the only federal law enforcement agency in existence until the creation of the Justice Department's Bureau of Investigation in 1908 (see FEDERAL BUREAU OF INVESTIGATION). For that reason the federal government occasionally called upon it to provide investigative or other police services needed in cases other than counterfeiting. During the SPANISH-AMERICAN WAR the Secret Service was in charge of domestic counterintelligence, both within the military services and the civilian population (see MONTREAL SPY RING). In May 1915 President Woodrow Wilson called on the Secret Service to investigate the massive sabotage and subversion campaign of German Intelligence in the United States during the FIRST WORLD WAR.

The Secret Service took on the duty of protecting the person of the President of the United States in 1894 after detecting a conspiracy to assassinate President Grover Cleveland; such protection, at first furnished on an ad hoc basis in response to specific threats and hazards, became a permanent full-time duty in 1902. The presidential protection assignment was formalized by Congress in 1906. Similar protection was extended to the President-elect in 1913, to members of the President's immediate family in 1917, to the vice-president in 1951, and to major presidential candidates in 1968.

The Secret Service continues to be responsible for the suppression of counterfeiting and the security of all Treasury Department installations. It has no foreign intelligence responsibilities, although it receives intelligence from other members of the INTELLIGENCE COMMUNITY in support of its executive protection and other duties.

(Bowen and Neal, *The United States Secret Service*.)

SECRET WAR IN LAOS

General: Between 1962 and 1972 the Central Intelligence Agency supported and directed a major military campaign fought in Laos by mountain tribesmen against the Communist Pathet Lao and armed forces of North Vietnam, thereby forestalling the Communist takeover of that country.

Background: The renewed program of North Vietnamese subversion in Indochina in 1957 (see VIETNAM WAR) was not limited to South Vietnam but extended into Laos, a small former French colony at the western border of northern and central Vietnam. A narrow diagonal strip of territory lying between Vietnam and Thailand, and following the Mekong Valley southward to Cambodia, Laos was regarded by strategic experts as the "gateway to Southeast Asia." Its immediate value to North Vietnam was as an infiltration and supply route that bypassed the heavily defended Demilitarized Zone between North and South Vietnam and led into South Vietnam, the route that came to be known as the Ho Chi Minh Trail.

Formerly an independent state within the French Union, Laos was made neutral by the same Geneva Agreements that ended the French war in Indochina in 1954. Since then the Pathet Lao, as the Laotian Communists were called, had violated the terms of the Agreements by taking over—with North Vietnamese help—the Laotian provinces of Phong Saly and Sam Neua, bordering North Vietnam and China. There they established a base from which they hoped eventually to conquer the rest of the country by force. The Pathet Lao were aided by a Vietminh (i.e. Vietnamese Communist) force that remained in the country after 1954, also in violation of the Agreements. The generally toothless and ineffective International Control Commission (ICC) set up to insure adherence to the Geneva Agreements failed to stop the Communist violations. Under the Agreements, all decisions of the ICC had to be unanimous; thus Poland, the Communist member of the Commission, could and did veto any move against the North Vietnamese government.

At the same time that they were pursuing this military policy in Laos, the Pathet Lao made great political gains in the country, despite American diplomatic and economic efforts to make Laos a pro-Western ally. The political and social situation in the country, too intricate and convoluted to be recounted adequately here, presented formidable obstacles to American policy (which was further confounded by bickering and non-coordination between the State Department, the CIA, the Agency for International Development, and the Defense Department, all of which took a hand in it), while providing the Communists—i.e., North Vietnam, China, and the Soviet Union—with favorable conditions to advance their interests.

In 1957 the neutralist government of Prince Souvanna Phouma entered into a coalition with the Pathet Lao (which was led by Souvanna's half-brother, Prince Souphanouvong), a development that alarmed the Eisenhower administration. Unable to challenge effectively the North Vietnamese violations of the Geneva Agreements in Laos through the ICC or other international organizations, unable to counter Communist political gains in the country through purely diplomatic means, and unwilling to meet the Communist incursion with overt military intervention, the Eisenhower administration sought to counter the Communists through covert action by the CIA. In 1958 a CIA mission was established in Laos as the Program Evaluation Office (PEO), ostensibly a unit of the State Department, and actually a DEVISED FACILITY of the CIA to provide cover for the mission. CIA officers operating under cover of the PEO recruited among the Meo, the largest single tribal group in Laos, to establish a force to fight against the Pathet Lao and NVA (North Vietnamese army). By 1959 the CIA had developed a small pilot program in which the Meo conducted intelligence-gathering operations in mountain villages near the strategic Plain of Jars in northern Laos.

The CIA also established the Committee for the Defense of the National Interests, an ostensibly Laotian political organization, and through it engineered a parliamentary crisis in July 1958, bringing about the replacement of Souvanna's neutralist-Communist coalition government with a pro-Western regime. Unfortunately this did not amount to a permanent or long-term solution, and there followed a period during which Laotian governments succeeded one another through coups d'état or rigged elections while American policymakers squabbled over the merits of seeking a pro-Western Laos (the CIA and the Defense Department) or a neutral one (State and the Agency for International Development). (Noting that CIA backing of the pro-Western faction is sometimes cited as an example of the Agency making its own foreign policy, Powers states that the contretemps between State and CIA was "first, a dispute between Washington and the field, and, second, an instance, one of many, in which the President elected to use the CIA without fully informing the State Department what he was up to.") Meanwhile, in 1959, the North Vietnamese strengthened Communist control of the northern Laotian provinces of Phong Saly and Sam Neua by sending NVA troops to back up the Pathet Lao.

In response to the North Vietnamese incursion, the Laotian government—at that moment still the pro-Western regime installed through CIA covert action—called on the United States for more military aid and for military advisors and technicians. U.S. Army Special Forces teams were sent into Laos under PEO cover as civilians to train both the Royal Lao army and the CIA's Meo guerrillas.

However, the Royal Lao army's efforts to retake the two provinces from the Pathet Lao and drive out the North Vietnamese were hamstrung by the political instability of the Laotian government and the disarray of American policy. North Vietnam and the USSR stepped up their aid to the Pathet Lao. A major military defeat of the royal Laotian Army by the Pathet Lao in the Plain of Jars in 1961 brought the Kennedy administration to the brink of open military intervention. After a second Geneva conference in 1961–62—in which Laos, the United States, Britain, Thailand, Burma, the USSR, China, North Vietnam, and six other nations participated—the situation eventually stabilized into an uneasy stalemate: in theory Laos was neutralized by the new Geneva Agreements, the country was not to enter into any foreign military alliance, and all foreign troops were to be withdrawn; in practice the North Vietnamese had tacitly agreed to postpone their plans to take over Laos completely (after yet another military onslaught in 1963, in which they alienated the Laotian nationalists from the Communists) and for the time being were prepared to observe a de facto partition of the country giving them control of the two northern provinces and the Ho Chi Minh Trail, which they would continue to use to supply their forces in South Vietnam. For its part, the United States would not undertake a major military intervention in Laos, but would continue to resist the Pathet Lao and the NVA through clandestine paramilitary warfare.

The Secret War: In 1962 the Kennedy administration placed the CIA in overall charge of the clandestine war in Laos. The nucleus of the anti-Communist force was the Meo guerrillas, whom the CIA and the U.S. Army Special Forces had begun to organize, train, and equip in 1958. Within a year or two after training had begun the Meo force consisted of some 9,000 guerrillas led by Lt. Col. (later Gen.) Vang Pao, a Laotian officer who had served with the French against the Vietminh. Supplementing the CIA and Special Forces advisors attached to the Meo force were thirteen teams—totaling ninety-nine men—from the Police Aerial Resupply Unit (PARU), a Thai commando force organized and trained by the CIA for the government of Thailand. Air support—both combat and logistical—for the anti-Communist forces was provided by Air America, a civil airline and the major CIA AIR PROPRIETARY in East Asia.

After the CIA assumed main responsibility for resisting a Pathet Lao/NVA takeover in Laos in 1962, the Agency greatly enlarged the Meo force, eventually expanding it to 30,000 Meo and other Laotian troops who operated in battalion-size units, augmented by some 17,000 Thai mercenaries. L'Armée Clandestine (the Secret Army), as it came to be called, was under the overall direction in the field of a few score officers of the Far East Division of the CIA CLANDESTINE SERVICE.

According to Branfman (a severe critic of the CIA and U.S. policy in Laos who lived in the country and interviewed many of the American military and civilian personnel there during 1967–71), "The CIA's regional office in Bangkok, Thailand, was in overall charge of CIA activities in Laos, which must, of course, be conceived of on a *regional* basis [italics in original]." He states that the CIA paramilitary operation in Laos was "an integral part of the much larger Secret Army, including KMT [i.e., Nationalist Chinese, or Kuomintang, troops, thousands of whom remained in Burma, Laos, and Thailand after the Communist victory in China in 1949] and irregular Thai forces in Thailand, Shan tribes in Burma, irregular units in Cambodia, and what was once a force of Montagnards, ethnic Cambodians, Vietnamese, and Nung [Chinese hill people], totaling at least forty-five thousand in South Vietnam."

The CIA's command post for its operations in Laos was located in the Agency's Laos station in the Laotian capital of Vientiane. Covert air operations in Laos (conducted by Air America and Continental Air Service, the latter not a CIA air proprietary but a private firm chartered by the Agency) were headquartered in an Agency compound at the Udorn Air Force Base in Thailand (Branfman says it was under cover of a devised facility known as the 4802nd Joint Liaison Detachment). According to Branfman, CIA activities in Laos went beyond field command of L'Armée Clandestine, and included participation—targeting and, in some cases, direction—in U.S. Air Force bombing operations against the Ho Chi Minh Trail and other targets in Laos; operation of Tacan (tactical air navigation, an electronic system using

UHF signals) sites in Laos in support of the air operations; and direction of small-unit commando raids into China and North Vietnam.

But the principal role of the CIA in Laos was the support and direction of L'Armée Clandestine in its operations against the Pathet Lao and NVA. (WILLIAM E. COLBY, chief of the Far East Division of the CIA CLANDESTINE SERVICE during 1962–67, writes that Meo operations against the Ho Chi Minh Trail were quite limited because the tribesmen were unfamiliar with the territory through which the trail was routed, and the use of Meo as spotters for U.S. Air Force attacks on the Trail "proved of only minor value.") Initially, at least, the objective of the secret war was to hold the Communists in check in Laos. Powers states that later "the CIA's program grew into a much larger effort to use [L'Armée Clandestine] as an asset in the war against the North Vietnamese." Ranelagh writes:

Ultimately a secret war was effectively fought in Laos, with CIA support for hill tribesmen being geared to bringing them into the fight against the Vietcong rather than simply helping the tribes resist the Pathet Lao, the Laotian communists. The calculation was that this would force the North Vietnamese and the Vietcong to divert men and resources from the war in South Vietnam. . . . By 1970 the secret war had effectively been won by the Pathet Lao and North Vietnamese, but—as the CIA had calculated—at significant cost to the communist effort in South Vietnam."

However, Breckinridge, a twenty-six-year veteran of the CIA, takes a somewhat different view: "Laotian forces supported by the U.S. Government achieved their main mission of holding the Laotian communists, supported by North Vietnam, away from the main population centers in the country." Colby takes a similar view:

And the result [of the Secret War]: the battle lines at the end of ten years of fighting against an enemy whose strength increased from 7,000 to 70,000 in that time, were approximately where they were at the outset, and the Communists were forced to accept a second agreement to recognize a neutral and independent Laos and the coalition government that America had pledged to support in 1962. To be sure, the end was not victory, but neither was it the defeat that the Communists had sought. (But when the Communist forces resumed military and subversive pressure *after* the 1973 agreement, CIA was *not* directed to respond, and Laos is under Communist rule today, with CIA's tribal friends in exile, dead, or living under oppression.)

The "second agreement" and "1973 agreement" to which Colby refers is the agreement between the Laotian government and the Pathet Lao of February 1973 that ended the war in Laos, formed a new coalition government including the Pathet Lao, and called for the withdrawal of all foreign troops; and the Paris Peace Agreement of January 1973 that ended American participation in the Vietnam war, and by which the participants agreed to withdraw all "troops, military advisers and military personnel, armaments, munitions and war material" from Laos and Cambodia. With the 1973 Agreements the CIA was ordered to terminate its operations in Laos. Breckinridge observes that "the Laotians were left to their own devices." Gen. Vang Pao, commander of L'Armée Clandestine, left Laos soon after the agreements were signed and later settled in the United States.

A provisional coalition government, headed by King Savang Vatthana and including the Pathet Lao, was formed in 1974. However, the Pathet Lao took complete control in 1975, at which time Savang signed a letter of abdication and the Communists proclaimed a People's Democratic Republic of Laos.

The CIA's secret war in Laos has been a favorite issue of critics of the Agency, who follow Sen. Stuart Symington's denunciation of it. Symington, a member of the Senate Foreign Relations Committee, expressed surprise, shock, and anger when he purportedly first learned of the secret war in the early 1970s. In fact, Symington had been fully briefed on the operation as early as September 1966; had subsequently visited Laos, where he was the houseguest of CIA station chief THEODORE SHACKLEY; and had arranged for Shackley to brief the Armed Services Committee in closed session in October 1967, after which briefing Symington had praised the CIA's conduct of the secret war. In any case, the war ceased to be secret in the mid-1960s when, due to its sheer size, the undertaking could no longer practically be hidden from the media and other observers in Laos (see, for example, ANTHONY POE).

Also incidental to the secret war was the charge that the CIA cooperated in the distribution of Laotian opium, the production of which is a major industry among the Meo. However, the Senate committee that investigated alleged wrongdoing by the CIA and other intelligence agencies in 1975 found no evidence to support the charge.

(Hilsman, *To Move a Nation*; Schlesinger, *A Thousand Days*; New York Times, *The Pentagon Papers*; Branfman, "The President's Secret Army: A Case Study—the CIA in Laos, 1962–72," in Borosage and Marks, *The CIA File*; Powers, *The Man Who Kept the Secrets*; Colby, *Honorable Men*; Marchetti and Marks,

The CIA and the Cult of Intelligence; Breckinridge, *The CIA and the U.S. Intelligence System;* Ranelagh, *The Agency;* Generous, *Vietnam: The Secret War;* McGehee, *Deadly Deceits.*)

SECURITY CLASSIFICATION SYSTEM

General: The United States government—including U.S. intelligence agencies—restricts the disclosure of information affecting national security according to a system of security classifications established by presidential directive. The three major classifications, in ascending order of the importance of the information involved, are: Confidential, Secret, and Top Secret. Additional classifications, sometimes called compartmentation codes, may be appended to these hierarchical categories to reflect some particularly sensitive kind of information. For example, Restricted Data is the classification used for information pertaining to nuclear weapons technology or procedures; thus a document containing such information might be classified Secret–Restricted Data or Top Secret–Restricted Data.

Employees and contractors of the U.S. government who need access to classified information are subjected to a background investigation, and if the authorities uncover nothing objectionable, security clearances are granted. The thoroughness of such background investigations varies, ranging from a relatively cursory check for access to Confidential data to a detailed and thorough vetting of anyone who is to have access to Top Secret information. Clearance for compartmentation classifications and other special categories of information is granted when an individual already holding an appropriate security clearance establishes his or her need to know the information.

Generally, U.S. intelligence documents are classified with the primary concern of protecting the sources of the information or the methods used to obtain it. For example, the information obtained by Army and Navy cryptanalysts prior to and during the SECOND WORLD WAR through breaking the Japanese diplomatic and naval codes and ciphers was assigned the code word MAGIC. In order to keep this intelligence secure and thus prevent the Japanese from changing their codes and ciphers, American military and civilian personnel who had not been granted the MAGIC compartmentation clearance were not permitted to know of the information, regardless of the level of the hierarchical security clearance they held. (The restriction of MAGIC information is blamed in part for the U.S. military's failure to foresee the PEARL HARBOR ATTACK.)

Dissemination control is yet another type of security classification. It keeps a document from being automatically distributed to certain persons who might otherwise be authorized to see it. The most common dissemination control, NOFORN (i.e., No Foreign Dissemination), withholds the document from routine dissemination to foreign nationals, e.g., military or intelligence officers in the service of an allied government. NODIS (i.e., No Dissemination) indicates that the document is not to be disseminated at all.

History: Article II, Section 2 of the Constitution has been interpreted as giving the President of the United States authority to restrict the dissemination of information relating to defense and foreign policy. This power was first exercised in 1790 when President Washington presented, for Senate approval, a secret article to be inserted into a treaty with the Creek Indians.

The first security classification system was established during the War of 1812 when the categories Secret, Confidential, and Private were used. The restriction of defense information in peacetime began in 1869 when a War Department order prohibited the unauthorized photographing or drawing of Army forts. In 1897, during the period of tension preceding the Spanish-American War, the War Department restricted public access to lake and coastal defense installations.

In 1912 the War Department classified as Confidential information pertaining to submarine mine projects; land defenses; tables, maps, and charts showing defense location, number of guns, and types of armament. In 1917 the Department adopted a security classification based on the British and French systems, which categorized information as Secret (not to be disclosed), Confidential (might be circulated to certain authorized persons), and For Official Circulation Only (might be distributed to government officials, but not to the press or public). Also in 1917, Congress passed the Espionage Act, which made it unlawful in time of peace to disclose certain "classified information" to a foreign government, faction, or citizen with the knowledge or intent that the information would injure the United States; or, in time of war, to disclose such information to an enemy. Among the classified information included in the Act was that relating to CRYPTOLOGY and communication systems.

In 1940 President Franklin Roosevelt issued an executive order giving the secretary of war and the secretary of the Navy the authority to classify certain military or naval information. Three categories of classification were then in use: Restricted (the lowest level, and not to be confused with Restricted Data, i.e., the special category established later for information related to nuclear weapons), Confidential, and Secret. In 1950 President Truman issued another executive order that added the classification Top Secret, a classification that had come into use during the Second World War. The following year Truman extended the security classification system to non-military agencies, permitting any executive department or agency to classify any "official information the safeguarding of which is necessary in the interest of national security, and which is classified for such purposes by appropriate classifying authority."

In 1953 President Eisenhower narrowed the scope of Truman's executive order by replacing the term "national security" with "national defense," and limiting the number of agencies authorized to classify information. Eisenhower's order eliminated the Restricted category and refined the definitions of the remaining three security classifications:

Top Secret: Information the unauthorized disclosure of which could result in exceptionally grave damage to the nation such as leading to a definite break in diplomatic relations affecting the defense of the United States, an armed attack against the United States or its allies, a war, or the compromise of military or defense plans, or intelligence operations, or scientific or technological developments vital to the national defense.

Secret: Information the unauthorized disclosure of which could result in serious damage to the Nation, such as by jeopardizing the international relations of the U.S., endangering the effectiveness of a program or policy of vital importance to the national defense, or compromising important military or defense plans, scientific or technological developments important to national defense, or information revealing important intelligence operations.

Confidential: Information the unauthorized disclosure of which could be prejudicial to the defense interests of the Nation.

The following year Congress passed the Atomic Energy Act of 1954, which provided, among other things, for a special security classification, Restricted Data, which was defined as "all data concerning (1) design, manufacture, or utilization of atomic weapons; (2) the production of special nuclear material; or (3) the use of special nuclear material in the production of energy. . . ." This is the only instance in which a security classification was established by statute, rather than by presidential order.

President Kennedy modified Eisenhower's executive order to provide for the automatic downgrading and declassification of classified documents. His order established four categories for this purpose, des-ignated as Groups. Groups 1 and 2 were for information too sensitive to be downgraded and declassified automatically. Group 3 documents were to be downgraded (e.g., from Top Secret to Secret, or from Secret to Confidential) at twelve-year intervals. Group 4 documents were to be downgraded at three-year intervals and declassified after twelve years. In practice, however, most intelligence information was not placed in Groups 3 or 4, and intelligence documents retained their original classification unless and until the agency involved decided to declassify them.

In 1972 President Nixon further modified the automatic declassification process, establishing a schedule by which a Top Secret document moves down to Secret in two to three years, to Confidential in four to five years, and is declassified in ten to twelve years. However, the order retained the provision that some documents remain exempt from any automatic downgrading or declassification.

During the 1960s, as such technical intelligence-collection methods as satellite reconnaissance photography and sophisticated ELINT techniques came into increasing use, there was a proliferation of compartmentation codes to protect these sources. Code words like DINAR, UMBRA, and TRINE were appended to the Top Secret or Secret designations to indicate that the information contained in a document disclosed, implicitly or explicitly, the source or method used to collect it. This comparmentation was intended to conceal further such specifics as the resolution of American satellite cameras or the ability to intercept some particular foreign communication channel.

Code words were also used to limit the individuals who had access to information on a given subject. For example, State Department cables and documents concerning a particular series of negotiations aimed at resolving the Vietnam War were designated by the code word MARIGOLD.

(Cox, *The Myths of National Security;* Wise, *The Politics of Lying;* Frank and Weisband, *Secrecy and Foreign Policy.*)

SEITZ, ALBERT BLAZIER (August 16, 1898–July 16, 1962): engineer, writer, intelligence officer

A native of Springfield, Ohio, Seitz attended Wittenberg College in 1916–17 and the U.S. Military Academy in 1918–19. In 1919–20 he served with the Royal Canadian Northwest Mounted Police. He attended the University of Wisconsin in 1924–25. Seitz worked as an engineer in Ohio from then until 1940, during which period he studied at Franklin University (1933–34) and Ohio State University (1934–35).

Seitz was commissioned as a captain in the U.S. Army in 1940 and subsequently served in the Office of Strategic Services, rising to the rank of colonel. In 1943 he parachuted into German-occupied Yugoslavia to work as the OSS representative to the partisans led by Gen. Draza Mihajlovíc. The following year he served with the French Resistance. He was awarded the Legion of Merit and the Serbian Order of the White Eagle in recognition of his wartime service.

After the war Seitz remained in Europe with the Strategic Services Unit, the War Department organization that preserved the remnants of the OSS, and he was with the SSU when it became part of the Central Intelligence Group and, later, the Central Intelligence Agency. He served with the Allied Control Commission in Romania, was chief of civil censorship in Berlin, and assistant military attaché in Greece.

Seitz left the CIA in 1952 and published a book based on his wartime experiences, *Mihailovic—Hoax or Hero?* He later wrote *Children of the Mist*, a book about U.S. Civil War guerrillas. In 1957 he joined the U.S. International Cooperation Administration, the State Department's foreign aid agency. He served as chief of the Laos Training Assistance Group of the U.S. Operations Mission (See SECRET WAR IN LAOS).

(*Who Was Who in America*, v. 4; Smith, *OSS*.)

SHACKLEY, THEODORE GEORGE, JR. (July 16, 1927–): Clandestine Service officer

A native of Massachusetts, Shackley served in the U.S. Army in 1945–47 and graduated from the University of Maryland in 1951. He again served in the Army in 1951–53 and was discharged with the rank of first lieutenant.

Shackley served in the CIA CLANDESTINE SERVICE. He was chief of JM/WAVE, the large CIA base established in Miami after the BAY OF PIGS INVASION for the purpose of mounting covert operations against the Cuban regime of Fidel Castro.

Shackley was attached to the American embassy in West Berlin in 1965–66. In 1966–68 he was in Vientiane, Laos, as chief of the CIA station. He was assigned to Saigon in 1968 and served as chief of the CIA station there. He later served in Chile.

In 1972 Shackley returned to Washington to become chief of the Western Hemisphere Division of the Clandestine Service. His most pressing task in that position was repairing the damage done to the Division by the disclosures of PHILIP AGEE. He was succeeded as division chief by DAVID A. PHILLIPS in mid-1973.

Shackley later was chief of the East Asia Division of the Clandestine Service then deputy to the chief of the Clandestine Service and finally a member of the CIA's Policy and Coordination Staff. He retired from the CIA in 1979 and later worked in the import-export business.

In 1981 Shackley published a book, *The Third Option*, an analysis of counterinsurgency and covert action as instruments of American foreign policy.

Shackley was thrice awarded the Distinguished Intelligence Medal.

(*Who's Who in Government*, 1st ed.; Smith, *Portrait of a Cold Warrior*; Snepp, *Decent Interval*; Martin, *Wilderness of Mirrors*; Goulden, *The Death Merchant*; Shackley, *The Third Option*.)

SHAHEEN, JOHN MICHAEL (October 25, 1915–November 1, 1985): businessman, diplomat, covert operations officer

A native of Lee County, Illinois, Shaheen attended the University of Illinois in 1934–36, and the University of Chicago in 1937–38. In 1941 he was commissioned in the U.S. Naval Reserve and assigned to the OSS SPECIAL OPERATIONS BRANCH.

Together with MARCELLO GIROSI, Shaheen planned the operation code-named MacGregor and led the team that carried it out (also see MICHAEL BURKE). The operation involved the infiltration of an advance undercover team into German-held Italy with the mission of persuading the anti-Nazi commander of the Italian Navy, who happened to be Marcello Girosi's brother, Massimo, to surrender his fleet when the Allies landed in Salerno. The project failed to achieve this objective because, unknown to the OSS, negotiations between Admiral Girosi and the Allies were already under way. However, Shaheen and his team succeeded in a secondary objective: they smuggled a group of Italian weapons specialists out of Italy and back to Washington.

In August and September 1945, Shaheen was in charge of the short-lived Reports Declassification Section, which was charged by WILLIAM J. DONOVAN with the task of "sanitizing" some of the files of the Special Operations Branch and the Operational Groups. The sanitized files would then be used as the basis or inspiration for stories of the OSS exploits intended for public consumption. Donovan's hope was that this publicity would further his plan for a peacetime centralized intelligence agency. However, the Section and its efforts came to halt on October 1, 1945 when the OSS was dissolved.

Shaheen was discharged in 1945 with the rank of commander, having been awarded the Silver Star and the Legion of Merit. After the war he founded Tele-Trip Insurance, a company that sold life insurance from airport vending machines. Later he was active in the oil business—the Shaheen Natural Resources Company, the Macmillan Ring-Free Oil Company, and the Golden Eagle Refining Company. In 1974 he was the special U.S. ambassador to Colombia.

(*Who's Who in America,* 42nd ed.; Hymoff, *The OSS in World War II;* Smith, *OSS;* obituary, *New York Times,* Nov 4, 1985, p. D14.)

SHARPE, GEORGE HENRY (February 26, 1828–January 12, 1900): lawyer, diplomat, government official, Army officer, intelligence officer

A native of Kingston, New York, Sharpe attended schools in that city and in Albany, New York, before entering Rutgers, from which he graduated in 1847. He studied law at Yale University, then practiced law in New York City with the firm of Bidwell and Strong.

Sharpe went to Europe and served as secretary of the U.S. legation in Vienna, Austria, in 1851–52. In 1854 he returned to the United States and entered into the practice of law at Kingston, New York. In May 1861 he raised a company of volunteers, which he led with the rank of captain as part of the Ulster Guard, the Twentieth New York Regiment. He saw action at the first battle of Bull Run in July 1861. He was mustered out in August 1861 (the end of his term of enlistment) and returned to Kingston. In August 1862 he raised the 120th New York Regiment, of which he was named colonel. The regiment became part of the Army of the Potomac under General George B. McClellan.

In February 1863 Gen. Joseph Hooker, who had just been put in command of the Army of the Potomac, appointed Sharpe deputy provost marshal general and put him in charge of intelligence (the secret service organization Allan Pinkerton had organized for McClellan a year and a half earlier had been disbanded with the departure of McClellan and Pinkerton). Sharpe assembled a staff of seventy intelligence officers, scouts, and agents, which became known as the BUREAU OF MILITARY INFORMATION.

Under Sharpe, the Bureau became a true military intelligence service in the modern sense, collecting information from all possible sources: prisoners of war, Confederate deserters and refugees, Southern newspapers (see NEWSPAPERS IN THE CIVIL WAR), the Army of the Potomac's balloon corps (see RECONNAISSANCE BALLOONS), Signal Corps observation posts, communication intercepts (see WIRETAPPING AND COMMUNICATIONS INTELLIGENCE IN THE CIVIL WAR), liaison with other commands, as well as from the spies and informers who worked for the Bureau behind Confederate lines.

The Bureau issued highly useful (and well used) estimates of Confederate orders of battle and movements. In the planning of the Chancellorsville campaign (April-May, 1863) and the pursuit of the Confederate invasion of Pennsylvania (June-July 1863), the Bureau provided the Union commanders with crucial intelligence.

After Gettysburg, Sharpe's Bureau became so highly regarded that, when Gen. Ulysses S. Grant took overall command of the Union Army in March 1864, he arranged for Sharpe to join his staff as his intelligence officer (the Bureau continued to function as a unit, however, serving both George Meade and U.S. Grant, the latter having taken the field with the Army of the Potomac and other Union forces in the eastern theater).

In December 1864 Sharpe was breveted a brigadier general of volunteers. After Appomattox he was in charge of paroling Lee's army, i.e., releasing Confederate prisoners of war upon receiving their individual pledges to cease bearing arms against the United States. He was mustered out of the service in June 1865.

In 1867 U.S. Secretary of State William Seward sent Sharpe to Europe on a confidential mission to identify any American citizens there who might have taken part in the assassination of President Lincoln, and to secure information regarding the whereabouts of John H. Surratt, a fugitive who had been charged in the matter (see LINCOLN CONSPIRACY). The following year Seward sent him to Vermont to investigate rumors of a planned raid on Canada by Irish nationalists.

In 1870 President Grant appointed Sharpe U.S. marshal for the Southern District of New York State. In that post he fought the Tweed ring of New York City, combatting election fraud and putting two of the most notorious members of the ring in prison.

Sharpe later held several other government posts: surveyor of the Port of New York, chairman of a federal commission to promote trade between the United States and Central and South America (a post that carried the rank of envoy extraordinary and minister plenipotentiary). From 1879 to 1883 he was a member of the New York State Assembly, and he was assembly speaker during 1880–81. During 1890–

99 he was a member of the board of United States General Appraisers.

(Fishel, "The Mythology of Civil War Intelligence"; Schmidt, "G-2, Army of the Potomac"; Wriston, *Executive Agents in American Foreign Relations*; Bidwell, "History of the Military Intelligence Division, Department of the Army General Staff"; Boatner, *Civil War Dictionary*; obituary, *New York Times*, January 15, 1900, p. 7.)

SHAW, HENRY B. (ca. 1822–?): business man, Confederate secret service agent and intelligence officer

Shaw was the owner of a Mississippi steamboat and lived in Nashville, Tennessee, before the Civil War. During the war he worked as a secret agent for Gen. Earl Van Dorn in Mississippi, and for Gens. Nathan B. Forrest and Joseph Wheeler in Tennessee. In April 1863, Gen. BENJAMIN F. CHEATHAM appointed Shaw to organize a company of scouts (i.e., secret service agents) for the Confederate Army of Tennessee. Shaw assembled a group of at least forty-five (and perhaps more) soldiers from the ranks of various Confederate commands. All were familiar with the Tennessee-Kentucky area and acquainted with its people, and all stood ready to volunteer for the very hazardous duty of operating out of uniform behind Union lines. Shaw adopted the pseudonym of "E. C. Coleman" (sometimes "Colman"), and the unit therefore became known as COLEMAN'S SCOUTS.

In November 1863 Shaw was captured by counterespionage officers of Union Gen. GRENVILLE M. DODGE near Nashville. Although the Federals were suspicious of Shaw, they did not know he was E. C. Coleman, a name they had learned from captured Confederate dispatches. SAMUEL DAVIS, one of the Coleman's Scouts who was also in Dodge's custody, refused to disclose Coleman's true identity (and was consequently hanged for espionage). Alexander Greig (sometimes Gregg) succeeded Shaw as chief of Coleman's Scouts.

Shaw was sent to the Union prisoner-of-war camp at Johnson's Island, near Chicago. He was released in a prisoner exchange in February 1865. After the war he returned to the steamboat business and was killed in a boiler explosion on one of his boats.

(Bakeless, *Spies of the Confederacy*; Bryan, *The Spy in America*.)

SHEEPDIPPING

The term applies to the process of establishing a specialized form of cover. When a covert operation requires the employment of individuals who, because of their special skills or other unique qualifications, happen to be members of the uniformed armed services, and when the possible disclosure of the involvement of U.S. military personnel in the operation could embarrass the U.S. government, the individuals are "sheepdipped." The individual goes through the motions of resigning from the service. His records are removed from the regular service files and transferred to a special file, while dummy records are processed to reflect the individual's resignation or discharge. This, in turn, triggers the process by which all other public and private records relating to the individual—credit, bank, social security, income tax, etc.—are eventually updated to reflect his purported new civilian status, and it thus becomes impossible to prove that he is still a member of the armed forces. In the meantime, his real military records continue to be processed clandestinely, reflecting such promotions, increases in pay or benefits, and other changes that his increasing time in service warrant. The situation becomes much more complicated if he is killed or captured while in the "sheepdipped" status, because such items as insurance and other benefits to dependents or survivors must be handled without disclosing his true status.

Sheepdipping was used in transferring Air Force pilots to the CIA's U-2 program in 1956 (see OVERHEAD RECONNAISSANCE, FRANCIS GARY POWERS), and in U.S. ground operations in Laos in the 1960s and 1970s.

(Prouty, *The Secret Team*.)

SHEINWOLD, ALFRED: bridge columnist, cryptographer, intelligence officer

Sheinwold, later well-known as the author of the syndicated columns, "Scheinwold on Bridge," and "Scheinwold on Backgammon," served in the Office of Strategic Services and its predecessor, the Office of the Coordinator of Information. A talented cryptographer, he was in charge of the Cryptographic Security Section of the OSS Message Center (see OSS COMMUNICATIONS BRANCH). The functions of the Section were to untangle badly garbled messages from OSS stations, to insure that the ciphers used by the OSS were secure, and to train OSS cryptographers.

Sheinwold subsequently became bridge editor of the *Los Angeles Times*. In addition to the syndicated columns previously noted, he is the author of two books on playing bridge.

(*Who's Who in America*, 42nd ed.; Kahn, *The Codebreakers*; Cave Brown, *The Last Hero*; Roosevelt, *War Report of the OSS*.)

SHEPARDSON, WHITNEY HART (October 30, 1890–May 29, 1966): lawyer, businessman, diplomat, intelligence officer

A native of Worcester, Massachusetts, Shepardson graduated from Colgate University in 1910 and attended Oxford University as a Rhodes scholar. He graduated from Oxford in 1913. During 1913–14 he taught at St. Mark's School, Southborough, Massachusetts. After graduating from Harvard Law School in 1917, Shepardson was an attorney with the U.S. Shipping Board, and was commissioned as a second lieutenant in the U.S. Army in 1918. He attended the Paris Peace Conference in 1919 as special assistant to Col. Edward M. House, President Wilson's advisor. He worked for the New York City firm of P.N. Gray and Company during 1920–23, with the International Education Board during 1923–27, and with the General Education Board during 1925–27. From 1928 to 1930 he was president of Bates International Bag Company and then held the position of vice-president of the International Railways of Central America during 1931–42.

In 1942 Shepardson joined the Office of Strategic Services. He was chief of the OSS SECRET INTELLIGENCE BRANCH in London in 1942, and in Washington, D.C., during 1943–46.

From 1946 to 1953 he was director of the Carnegie Corporation's British Dominions and Colonies Fund. In 1953 he became president of the Committee for a Free Europe, the Central Intelligence Agency's cover organization that ran RADIO FREE EUROPE and carried out "gray propaganda" (see COVERT ACTION) operations in Eastern Europe. He held that post until 1956.

Shepardson was a trustee of the Council on Foreign Relations. In 1960 he published *The Early History of the Council on Foreign Relations*. He is also the author of several books on foreign affairs.

Shepardson held the Medal for Merit, the French Legion d'Honneur, the croix de guerre, and the Dutch Order of the Orange.

(Smith, *OSS*; Cave Brown, *The Last Hero*; *Who Was Who in America*, v. 4.)

SIBERT, EDWIN LUTHER (March 2, 1897–): Army officer, intelligence officer

A native of Little Rock, Arkansas, Sibert attended Cornell University during 1914–15 and graduated from the U.S. Military Academy in 1918. He served with the Allied Expeditionary Force in Germany in 1919, and was an ROTC instructor at Cornell University in 1922–26. During 1931–33 he was aide-de-camp to the commanding general in Panama, and

during 1933–35 he attended the Army's Command and General Staff School. He served at West Point during 1936–38 and attended the Army War College during 1938–39. Sibert served on the General Staff during 1939–40 and was military attaché in Brazil during 1940–41. He was chief of staff of the Seventh Division in 1942 and advanced to the rank of brigadier general that year. In 1943 he commanded the Ninety-ninth Artillery Division.

Sibert was chief of staff for intelligence (see ARMY INTELLIGENCE) in the European Theater during 1943–44, and held the same post with the Twelfth Army in Europe during 1944–45. During 1945–46 he was again chief of staff for intelligence in the European Theater. In that capacity he was instrumental in establishing the Gehlen Organization, the West German intelligence service that worked for U.S. intelligence in the late 1940s and 1950s.

In 1946 Sibert became assistant director of the Central Intelligence Group and continued in that post when the CIG became the CIA in 1947. In 1948 he left the CIA to become commanding general of the Pacific Sector of Panama in 1948, after which he became commanding general of U.S. Army forces in the Antilles. During 1950–52 he was staff director of the Inter-American Defense Board. He became the commanding general of Camp Edwards in 1952.

Siebert was twice awarded the Distinguished Service Medal and held the Legion of Merit, the Bronze Star, and several foreign decorations.

(*Who's Who in America*, v. 28; Smith, *OSS*; Höhne and Zolling, *The General Was a Spy*.)

SIDE-LOOKING AIRCRAFT RADAR (SLAR)

Conceived in the early 1950s, SLAR systems project a radar signal to either side of the aircraft on which they are carried. Such side-directed radar signals transmitted from a moving vehicle were discovered to provide much higher resolution "pictures" than conventional radar systems. Photos of terrain made with SLAR have such high resolution that to the untrained eye they seem to have been made by an optical camera.

SLAR systems are widely used in OVERHEAD RECONNAISSANCE by aircraft, and are reportedly also used in some reconnaissance satellites.

(Klass, *Secret Sentries in Space*; Gunston, *Spy Planes*.)

SIGINT

Signals intelligence (see -INT). This general category includes any intelligence collected from intercepted communications (e.g., microwave, landlines, secret writing) or electromagnetic emanations (e.g., foreign radar signals or telemetry) from an object of intelligence interest. There are two major categories within SIGINT—COMINT and ELINT.

COMINT, or communications intelligence, is officially defined by NATIONAL SECURITY COUNCIL INTELLIGENCE DIRECTIVE No. 6 as "the interception and processing of foreign communications passed by radio, wire, or other electromagnetic means, and by the processing of foreign encrypted communications, however transmitted. . . ." Unencrypted written communications, press reports, and propaganda broadcasts are excluded from this category.

Thus, COMINT would include, for example, intelligence gained from listening to the routine unencrypted voice communications between a foreign military aircraft and a ground station, as well as the interception and cryptanalysis of foreign diplomatic telegrams. It would also include the inspection of an intercepted letter for concealed communications in invisible ink or microdots.

ELINT, or electronics intelligence, is officially defined by NSCID No. 6, as "the collection (observation and recording) and the processing for subsequent intelligence purposes of information derived from foreign, noncommunications, electromagnetic radiations emanating from other than atomic detonation or radioactive sources." ELINT includes information collected regarding the frequency and other characteristics of foreign radar systems and navigational radio beacons. Within the ELINT subcategory there falls a sub-subcategory, TELINT, or telemetry intelligence. TELINT would include, for example, information on foreign missile tests obtained by intercepting telemetry sent by the test missiles while in flight.

See NATIONAL SECURITY AGENCY.

(Bamford, *The Puzzle Palace*.)

SIGSBEE, CHARLES DWIGHT (January 16, 1845–July 19, 1923): naval officer

A native of Albany, New York, Sigsbee graduated from the U.S. Naval Academy in 1863 and saw action during the Civil War. He was commander of the *Maine* when the battleship was blown up at Havana on February 15, 1898, and he commanded the auxiliary cruiser *St. Paul* during the Spanish-American War. During 1900–03 he was chief of the Office of NAVAL INTELLIGENCE, where he formalized the intelligence lessons learned during the recent war, improved security and organization, and oriented ONI toward the potential naval threat of Germany.

(*WAMB*; Dorwart, *Office of Naval Intelligence*.)

Rear Adm. William Sowden Sims—an oil portrait by Irving R. Wiles, circa 1920. Source: Sims, *The Victory at Sea*.

SIMS, WILLIAM SOWDEN, (October 15, 1858–September 28, 1936): naval officer

The son of an American father, Sims was born in Port Hope, Ontario. He graduated from the U.S. Naval Academy in 1880 and in 1897 was made ONI's naval attaché in Paris. During the SPANISH-AMERICAN WAR Lt. Sims ran an agent network in Europe that reported mainly on Spanish preparations to send a task force to relieve Manila, which was blockaded by the American Asiatic Squadron under Adm. George Dewey. Sims's intelligence accomplishments were eclipsed by his later fame as American naval commander in Europe during the FIRST WORLD WAR.

(Dorwart, *Office of Naval Intelligence*; *WAMB*.)

SINGLAUB, JOHN KIRK (July 10, 1921–): Army officer, association official, intelligence officer

A native of Independence, California, Singlaub graduated from the University of California at Los Angeles in 1942. In 1943 he was commissioned as a second lieutenant in the U.S. Army. He served in the OSS SPECIAL OPERATIONS BRANCH of the Office of Strategic Services and, in 1944, led Resistance guerrillas behind German lines in France. In 1945 he led Chinese guerrillas against the Japanese forces in China. During 1946–48 he was an American observer of the Chinese civil war.

Singlaub commanded an infantry battalion in the Korean War during 1952–53. He graduated from the Army's Command and General Staff College in 1954, and served on the faculty of the College during 1954–57. He was a U.S. military advisor in Vietnam during 1966–68. During 1966–67 he commanded the STUDIES AND OBSERVATION GROUP (see VIETNAM WAR).

Singlaub was chief of staff of U.S. Forces in Korea during 1976–77. He was removed from that post after airing his differences with President Jimmy Carter over the proposed reduction of American forces in Korea, a move he believed might tempt North Korea to attack the South.

Singlaub retired from the Army in 1978 with the rank of major general. He subsequently became chairman of the United States Council for World Freedom, a private anti-Communist organization that provides material support to the anti-Sandinista guerrillas in Nicaragua. He is also chairman of the World Anti-Communist League, an international organization.

Singlaub holds many decorations, American and foreign, including the Distinguished Service Medal, the Silver Star, the Soldiers Medal, the Bronze Star, the Air Medal, the Army Commendation Medal, and the Purple Heart.

(*Who's Who in America*, 42nd ed.)

SINKOV, ABRAHAM (August 21, 1907–): mathematician, educator, cryptanalyst, intelligence officer

A native of Philadelphia, Sinkov graduated from the City College of New York in 1927. He worked as a schoolteacher in New York City while doing postgraduate work at Columbia University, where he earned a master's degree in mathematics in 1929. In 1930 he was one of the first four junior cryptanalysts hired by WILLIAM F. FRIEDMAN to serve in the newly established Signal Intelligence Service (see ARMY INTELLIGENCE).

In the late 1930s Sinkov was in charge of the SIS's signal intercept station in Panama. During the SECOND WORLD WAR he was commissioned as a major in the U.S. Army, was promoted to colonel, and

served as an assistant director of the CENTRAL BUREAU, which he later headed. By war's end he was cryptanalytic officer, U.S. Army Forces in the Far East.

Sinkov served with SIS's successor organizations, the Army Security Agency, the Armed Forces Security Agency, and the NATIONAL SECURITY AGENCY, and was at one time deputy director of NSA's Office of Production. He retired from government service in 1962, but continued to serve as a consultant to NSA.

Concurrent with his service with NSA, Sinkov was a member of the staff of the National War College during 1954–55, and a lecturer at the University of Maryland during 1957–63. After his retirement he joined the faculty of Arizona State University as a professor of mathematics. Since 1977 he has been emeritus professor of mathematics at Arizona State.

Sinov was awarded the Legion of Merit and the Order of the British Empire for his service in the war.

(*American Men and Women of Science*, 15th ed.; Kahn, *The Codebreakers*; Lewin, *American Magic*; Bamford, *The Puzzle Palace*.)

SINO-AMERICAN COOPERATIVE ORGANIZATION (SACO)

A U.S.- Nationalist Chinese intelligence and special operations organization in China during the SECOND WORLD WAR.

Background and Discussion: In April 1942 (then) Comdr. MILTON E. MILES was sent to Chunking, China, as a naval observer with secret orders to establish weather stations and a system of coastwatchers to support the Pacific Fleet and prepare for amphibious landings three or four years thereafter. Miles received the cooperation of Gen. Tai Li, Chiang Kai-shek's intelligence chief, in carrying out this task, and Miles agreed to Tai Li's proposal that the U.S. Navy train, equip, and share in the command of a guerrilla force of some fifty thousand Chinese.

In September 1942 Miles was appointed coordinator for the OFFICE OF STRATEGIC SERVICES in China. The following April the agreement he had reached with Tai Li was formalized as the Sino-American Special Technical Cooperation Agreement, by which China and the United States agreed to work together against the Japanese in the fields of intelligence and clandestine warfare. The United States was to supply arms, equipment, and training; the Chinese were to furnish manpower and facilities. The organization created to carry out this agreement was called the Sino-American Cooperative Organization, and it was under the joint command of Tai Li, who became its director, and Miles, the deputy director.

The OSS played a subordinate role in this arrangement. Under the initial arrangement between OSS Director WILLIAM J. DONOVAN and Miles, Miles was in charge of all OSS activities in China, as well as commanding a naval unit—eventually elevated to Naval Group China—and reporting directly to Adm. Ernest J. King, the commander-in-chief of the Navy. The OSS and Navy personnel under Miles's command comprised the American component of SACO. Also, at least in theory, Miles was subordinate to Gen. Tai Li, and thus the OSS (and Navy) personnel were under his ultimate authority.

This arrangement soon proved extremely unsatisfactory to all concerned. Miles had serious differences in both substance and style with Donovan and many senior officers of the OSS, and the feeling was mutual. Donovan and his associates generally regarded Tai Li—whom Miles admired—as a ruthless cutthroat. Tai Li was extremely suspicious of Donovan and the OSS, whom he suspected of being under the influence of his personal bête noire, the British. After a year of noncooperation with Miles and Tai Li, Donovan dismissed Miles from the post of OSS/China coordinator, withdrew the OSS from SACO, and integrated OSS/China with Gen. Claire Chennault's Fourteenth U.S. Air Force.

Miles continued as commander of Navy Group China and as deputy director of SACO. SACO flourished, by war's end reaching a strength of 2,500 American trainers and advisors, and more than fifty thousand Chinese guerrillas. SACO operated ten guerrilla training camps, organized into "columns" of about one thousand men with a handful of American advisors. They conducted guerrilla operations from the China coast to the Mongolian borders, ambushing and harassing Japanese convoys and raiding Japanese supply dumps, as well as fighting Chiang Kai-shek's domestic enemies, the Chinese Communists. SACO also operated a network of coastwatchers and weather stations to supply needed information to U.S. Navy units in the Pacific.

Although there seems to be no question that SACO was a highly effective special operations organization, some of Miles' claims regarding the organization's human intelligence collection have been questioned.

(Miles, *A Different Kind of War;* Spector, *Eagle Against the Sun;* Smith, *OSS;* Dunlop, *Donovan;* Constantinides, *Intelligence and Espionage: An Analytical Bibliography.*)

SKINNER, CORTLANDT (1728–1799): lawyer, government official, British army and intelligence officer

Prior to the American Revolution, Skinner was a prominent citizen and large landowner in New Jersey. He served as attorney general of the colony in 1775.

Skinner was a Loyalist, and he worked secretly with William Franklin, BENJAMIN FRANKLIN's Tory son and the formal royal governor of New Jersey, to pass intelligence to London, including secret records of the Continental Congress. In June 1776, the Patriots captured some of these documents and Skinner's complicity was revealed. He was forced to flee to the British stronghold on Staten Island where he was welcomed by General William Howe, who commissioned him a major and put him in charge of Loyalist troops. The Continentals soon captured him, but they released him in a prisoner exchange in September 1776.

The British then promoted Skinner to brigadier general of provincials and authorized him to raise and lead a brigade of Loyalist troops that became known as Skinner's Brigade, or the West Jersey Volunteers. The Brigade, which included the redoubtable JAMES MOODY, conducted reconnaissance, guerrilla, and secret intelligence operations throughout New Jersey and the surrounding area. Throughout the war, Skinner ran highly effective intelligence networks throughout New Jersey and Pennsylvania from his Staten Island headquarters.

After the war Skinner moved to England. He was compensated for his lost landholdings and put on half pay as a brigadier for life. His son, Philip Kearny Skinner, served in the British army and rose to the rank of lieutenant general.

(Boatner, *Encyclopedia of the American Revolution;* Bakeless, *Turncoats, Traitors and Heroes.*)

SLAVENS, SAMUEL (ca. 1836–June 18, 1862): soldier, Union secret service agent

Slavens lived in Wakefield, Ohio, before the CIVIL WAR. In 1861 he enlisted as a private in the Ohio Volunteer Infantry, a part of the Army of the Ohio. In April 1862 he volunteered to take part in a paramilitary operation behind Confederate lines aimed at severing the rail line between Atlanta and Chattanooga (see ANDREWS'S RAID). He and a party of twenty other Union troops in civilian clothes led by JAMES J. ANDREWS hijacked a locomotive and attempted to destroy railroad tracks and bridges between the two cities. He was captured by Confederate troops and imprisoned. Slavens, Andrews, and six others of the party were hanged.

(Bryan, *The Spy in America*; Boatner, *Civil War Dictionary*; O'Neill, *Wild Train*.)

SMITH, ABBOTT EMERSON (June 20, 1906–): historian, intelligence officer

A native of Portland, Maine, Smith graduated from Colby College in 1926, and studied at the Eastman School of Music in 1926–27 and at Harvard University in 1927–28. He attended Oxford University as a Rhodes scholar, earning a B.A. in 1930 and a D. Phil. in 1932. He taught history at Bard College from 1932 to 1943, when he was commissioned in the U.S. Naval Reserve. He was discharged with the rank of lieutenant commander in 1948.

In 1948 Smith joined the newly formed Central Intelligence Agency. He served on the staff of the Office of National Estimates until 1958, when he became vice chairman of the Board of National Estimates under SHERMAN KENT (see NATIONAL INTELLIGENCE ESTIMATE). In 1968 he succeeded Kent as chairman of the Board of National Estimates.

(Cline, *The CIA: Reality vs. Myth*; *Who's Who in America*, 37th ed.)

SMITH, JAMES (ca. 1843–?): soldier, Union secret agent of the Civil War

Private Smith of the Third Division, Army of the Ohio, volunteered to take part in a paramilitary operation behind Confederate lines aimed at severing the rail line between Atlanta and Chattanooga in April 1862 (see ANDREWS'S RAID). Dressed in civilian clothing, he and a party of twenty other Union troops led by JAMES J. ANDREWS hijacked a locomotive and attempted to destroy railroad tracks and bridges between the two cities. He was captured by Confederate troops and imprisoned (Andrews and six of the party were hanged).

(Bryan, *The Spy in America*; Boatner, *Civil War Dictionary*; O'Neill, *Wild Train*.)

SMITH, JOSEPH BURKHOLDER (June 16, 1921–): propaganda and political action specialist, Clandestine Service officer

A native of Harrisburg, Pennsylvania, Smith graduated from Harvard University in 1943 and served in the U.S. Army as a Japanese-language specialist. After his discharge in 1946 he taught history at Dick-

inson College until 1951, when he joined the Central Intelligence Agency.

Smith was assigned to the Office of Policy Coordination, as the agency's COVERT ACTION department was then called. He served on the Plans Staff of the Far East Division and was trained in psychological warfare, propaganda, and other covert techniques. In 1954 he was assigned to the Singapore station, where he was in charge of propaganda operations until 1956. In October 1956 he became chief of the Malaya desk at CIA headquarters in Washington. Soon thereafter Smith was made deputy chief of the Indonesia/Malaya Branch of the FE Division, and he served in that capacity during the preparations for the abortive CIA-sponsored INDONESIA REBELLION.

In 1958 Smith was assigned to the Manila station to replace GABRIEL KAPLAN as chief of CIA political action in the Philippines. In 1960 he returned to CIA headquarters and took over as chief of the Propaganda Guidance Section, a unit of the Covert Action Staff of the CIA CLANDESTINE SERVICE. The function of the Section was to establish the themes for the CIA's worldwide "black" and "gray" propaganda assets see (COVERT ACTION).

In 1961 Smith took charge of the Venezuelan desk of the Clandestine Service's Western Hemisphere Division. The following year he was assigned to the Agency's Buenos Aires station to manage a propaganda project run jointly by the CIA and the Secretaria de Informacion del Estado (SIDE), an Argentine security agency. He remained in Buenos Aires for four years, running propaganda and other political action operations.

In 1967 Smith returned to CIA headquarters to serve in the Office of Training, where he conducted seminars in propaganda and political action. In 1969 he was assigned to the Agency's Mexico City station. He retired from the CIA in 1973.

In 1976 Smith published a book of memoirs of his CIA career, *Portrait of a Cold Warrior*.

(Smith, *Portrait of a Cold Warrior*.)

SMITH, JOSHUA HETT (1736–1818): lawyer, intelligence officer

Smith was the son of prominent New York lawyer William Smith and the brother of New York Supreme Court Chief Justice William Smith, both of whom were Tories. Joshua Smith, however, was a Patriot of the American Revolution and ran a secret service for Gen. Robert Howe when Howe commanded West Point. Smith continued this operation after Howe was succeeded by BENEDICT ARNOLD as commander of the fortress and consequently played an (apparently) unwitting role in Arnold's treason.

Smith escorted Maj. JOHN ANDRÉ to his fateful meeting with Arnold at Haverstraw, New York, on the night of September 21–22, 1780. Apparently ignorant of the purpose of the meeting, Smith was under the misapprehension that it was somehow part of an American intelligence operation. When André was unable to rejoin the British sloop that had brought him to Haverstraw, Arnold sent Smith to escort the British officer through the American lines, and Smith was with André when the latter was captured by American militiamen.

Smith was tried by the military court and acquitted of complicity in the Arnold affair, but was arrested and jailed by the New York authorities on suspicion of being a Tory. He escaped after a few months and made his way to British-occupied New York City. In 1783 he went to England.

He returned to America in 1801 and spent his final years in obscurity.

(Boatner, *Encyclopedia of the American Revolution;* Van Doren, *Secret History of the American Revolution.*)

SMITH, R(USSELL) JACK (July 4, 1913–): intelligence officer

A native of Jackson, Michigan, Smith graduated from Miami University (Oxford, Ohio) in 1937 and received a Ph.D. from Cornell University in 1941. He taught English at Williams College from 1941 until 1945 when he joined the OSS RESEARCH AND ANALYSIS BRANCH. He worked with RAY S. CLINE, preparing current intelligence reports.

In 1946–47 Smith returned to academia as assistant professor of English at Wells College. In 1947 he joined the newly formed Central Intelligence Agency, where he was put in charge of CURRENT INTELLIGENCE in the Office of Reports and Estimates. He was instrumental in recruiting his friend and former OSS colleague Ray S. Cline into the CIA. Smith later served in the Office of National Estimates and in 1954–56 was the U.S. representative to the British Joint Intelligence Committee on the Far East in Singapore. From 1957 to 1962 he was a member of the Board of National Estimates. During the CUBAN MISSILE CRISIS in 1962 he was sent to West Germany to brief Chancellor Konrad Adenauer on the situation in Cuba and American intentions in the crisis.

Smith served as director of the Office of Current Intelligence from 1962 until 1966, and then succeeded Cline as the deputy director for intelligence. He re-

Gen. Walter Bedell Smith. Source: Library of Congress.

mained in the latter post until the early 1970s, when Edward W. Proctor succeeded him.

(*Who's Who in America*, 37th ed.; Cline, *The CIA: Reality vs. Myth.*)

SMITH, WALTER BEDELL (October 5, 1898– August 9, 1961): Army officer, intelligence officer

A native of Indianapolis, Indiana, Smith enlisted in the Indiana National Guard in 1910 and rose from the rank of private to first sergeant. In 1917 he enrolled in the Army ROTC and was commissioned as a second lieutenant in the infantry. He served in France in 1918 and was wounded. He was promoted to first lieutenant and assigned to the Military Intelligence Division of the General Staff (see ARMY INTELLIGENCE) in Washington, D.C.

Smith served in a variety of Army staff positions until 1929, when he was promoted to captain and sent to the Philippines. He returned in 1931 and attended the Infantry School at Fort Benning, Georgia, staying on for a year as an instructor. He graduated from the Command and General Staff School at Fort Leavenworth, Kansas, in 1935, and from the

Army War College in 1937. In 1939 he was promoted to major and assigned to the Army General Staff.

In August 1941, having reached the rank of lieutenant colonel, Smith was named secretary of the General Staff. The following year, promoted to the temporary rank of brigadier general, he was made secretary of the U.S.-British Combined Chiefs of Staff. In September 1942 he became chief of staff under General Eisenhower. He served as chief of staff of the Allied North African campaign and as chief of staff of the Supreme Headquarters, Allied Expeditionary Force (SHAEF). In the latter capacity he was chief planner and executive officer of the entire Allied command in Europe. In December 1945 he was promoted to the permanent rank of major general.

In 1946 President Truman appointed him ambassador to the Soviet Union, and he remained in that post until 1949. In September 1950 he was appointed director of the CENTRAL INTELLIGENCE AGENCY. The CIA, only two years old at the time, had several serious organizational defects. Smith set to work to correct these flaws. One of his first acts was to bring the Office of Policy Coordination—the Agency's COVERT ACTION department—under the complete and direct control of the CIA; up to that point it had answered to a joint State and Defense Department management team. Smith brought veteran OSS intelligence officer WILLIAM LANGER to Washington on a one-year leave of absence from Harvard to establish the Office of National Estimates and the Board of National Estimates (see NATIONAL INTELLIGENCE ESTIMATES). Perhaps the most far-reaching step Smith took was to recruit OSS veteran ALLEN DULLES as a deputy director of CIA, and eventually to accept Dulles's recommendation that the Office of Policy Coordination and the Agency's SECRET INTELLIGENCE unit, known as the Office of Special Operations, be merged into a single department, the CIA CLANDESTINE SERVICE.

Smith presided over the CIA during the KOREAN WAR, a period of rapid growth of the Agency. He left in 1953, but the Agency would retain for the next ten years the basic structure he had given it through his reforms.

In 1953 President Eisenhower appointed Smith under-secretary of state under John Foster Dulles. The following year he headed the U.S. delegation to the Geneva conference on the war in Indochina. He retired in October 1954.

(*Who Was Who in America*, v. 4; *WAMB*; Cline, *The CIA: Reality vs. Myth*.)

SONS OF LIBERTY

A complex of patriotic secret societies in pre-revolutionary America.

The first group calling itself the Sons of Liberty was organized in Boston in 1765 to protest the Stamp Act. It took its name from a line in Isaac Barré's speech in opposition to the Act in the House of Commons (Barré, a British army officer and politician strongly sympathetic to the American cause, and his similarly disposed colleague, John Wilkes, inspired the citizens of Wilkes-Barre, Pennsylvania, to name their city after them). Affiliated groups using the same name were established soon thereafter in Connecticut, New York, Rhode Island, New Jersey, South Carolina, and elsewhere in the colonies. In most cases these groups had existed as political or public service organizations under different names long before 1765; e.g., in Boston as the Caucus Club; in Charleston, South Carolina, as the Fireman's Association; in Philadelphia as the Heart-and-Hand Fire Company; in Baltimore as the Ancient and Honorable Mechanical Company. Britain's passage of the Stamp Act gave them a common name and purpose.

The Sons of Liberty resisted enforcement of the Stamp Act through various means, almost all of them violent and illegal, e.g., rioting, seizing and destroying the stamps, and attacking public officials charged with enforcing the Act. When rumors began to circulate that the British government intended to enforce the Act with troops, the New York chapter of the Sons of Liberty entered into a mutual military defense pact with their Connecticut and New Jersey counterparts. In North and South Carolina, the Sons actually stormed British forts and garrisons, but met no armed resistance. All of the British stamp agents in the colonies soon resigned. In the face of such violent opposition, the British Parliament had no choice but to repeal the Act in March 1766.

The Sons of Liberty did not go out of existence with the attainment of their original goal, but continued to operate as a patriot underground in the colonies, conducting COVERT ACTION and eventually espionage against the British government's apparatus in America. Such early American secret intelligence networks as PAUL REVERE's Boston spy ring were formed from the ranks of the Sons of Liberty, and many individual agents, e.g., HERCULES MULLIGAN, began in the Sons. The organization may therefore be regarded as the ultimate precursor of all subsequent American intelligence services.

The Sons of Liberty adopted a more formal organization as the COMMITTEES OF CORRESPONDENCE in 1772, and the Committees of Safety in 1775. (See AMERICAN REVOLUTION.)

(Miller, *Sam Adams: Pioneer in Propaganda*; Boatner, *Encyclopedia of the American Revolution*; DAH.)

SONS OF LIBERTY (CIVIL WAR)

See KNIGHTS OF THE GOLDEN CIRCLE.

SOUERS, SIDNEY WILLIAM (March 30, 1892–January 14, 1973): journalist, businessman, Navy officer, intelligence officer

A native of Dayton, Ohio, Souers studied at Purdue University in 1911–12, but graduated from Miami (of Ohio) University in 1914. After a year as a reporter for the *New Orleans Item*, he began a career in business. He joined the Mortgage Security Company in New Orleans and after five years became its president. He subsequently served in senior executive positions and on the boards of several large national corporations. In 1928 he became commissioner of the Port of New Orleans, a position he held in addition to his business pursuits. In 1929, while working in this capacity, he was commissioned as a lieutenant commander in the U.S. Naval Reserve.

Souers remained in the Naval Reserve after moving to St. Louis, Missouri, and in 1932 he was named senior intelligence officer for that general area. This assignment included investigative work, the development of an intelligence organization, and public relations.

Called to active duty in 1940, Souers was appointed intelligence officer for the Ninth Naval District, Great Lakes, Illinois. In 1942 he was made intelligence officer for the Sixth Naval District in Charleston, South Carolina. Later that year he became intelligence officer for the Caribbean Sea Frontier, headquartered in San Juan, Puerto Rico. His achievements in developing submarine countermeasures led first to his promotion to the rank of rear admiral in 1943, and then to the position of assistant director of the Office of Naval Intelligence in Washington, D.C. In 1944 he was made deputy chief of Naval Intelligence.

In January 1946 President Truman appointed Souers director of the newly established Central Intelligence Group, the organization that was shortly to become the CENTRAL INTELLIGENCE AGENCY. Thus, Souers became the first director of central intelligence. Souers, who was eager to return to civilian life, accepted the position with the understanding that he had committed himself to stay no more than six months, a period judged sufficient to organize the new agency and get it started.

Souers's efforts were hampered by the exceedingly awkward organizational arrangement of the CIG within the government. The CIG, which had no

Rear Adm. Sidney W. Souers—oil portrait by C.L. MacNelly. Source: Central Intelligence Agency.

budget, reported to the National Intelligence Authority, a governing body composed of the secretaries of state, war, and the Navy, and the President's personal representative, Adm. William D. Leahy. The CIG's task was vaguely defined as the correlation, evaluation, and planning for the coordination of intelligence within the government. After the agreed-upon six months, Souers left the CIG, having accomplished little beyond demonstrating that a central intelligence function could not be run by committee. He was succeeded by Gen. HOYT VANDENBERG, whose personal prestige and connections enabled him to obtain a degree of autonomy for the CIG.

Souers returned to civilian life and his business undertakings, but in May 1947 President Truman recalled him to government service to set up an intelligence service for the Atomic Energy Commission. That same year he was appointed executive secretary of the NATIONAL SECURITY COUNCIL, a post he held until 1950, when he again resumed his private pursuits.

Among the decorations awarded Souers were the Distinguished Service Medal and the Legion of Merit.

(*Current Biography*, 1949; *Who Was Who in America*, v. 5; Troy, *Donovan and the CIA*, Braden, "The Birth of the CIA.")

SPANISH-AMERICAN WAR

Background: The revolution of Cuban insurgents against Spanish rule in 1895–98 found sympathy and material aid in the United States, brought domestic pressure to bear on the U.S. government to intervene, and pushed Spanish-American relations near to the breaking point. On February 15, 1898 the battleship U.S.S. *Maine*, which had been sent to Havana as a show of force and to protect American lives and property, was destroyed by an explosion that took the lives of 266 crewmen and two officers. A U.S. Navy court of inquiry found that the explosion was the result of a submerged mine, a finding that seemed to implicate the Spanish authorities. After an unsuccessful two-month effort to persuade Spain through diplomatic channels to grant independence to Cuba and so defuse the popular demand for war in the United States, President McKinley yielded to political pressure and declared war on April 22nd.

The War: Executing war plans devised jointly during 1894–97 by the Naval War College and the Office of NAVAL INTELLIGENCE, the U.S. North Atlantic Squadron blockaded the major Cuban ports on April 22nd, and on May 1st the U.S. Asiatic Squadron under Comm. George Dewey completely destroyed the Spanish Asiatic Fleet in Manila Bay and then proceeded to blockade the port of Manila.

Throughout May and June the Army assembled a large expeditionary force at Tampa under Maj. Gen. Rufus Shafter for an invasion of Cuba, and a second force at San Francisco under Maj. Gen. Wesley Merritt to land in the Philippines and capture the city of Manila. During the same period the Spanish prepared a land-sea task force at Cadiz, Spain, under Adm. Manuel de la Camara to attack the American squadron at Manila Bay and relieve the city, while a squadron of four cruisers and three torpedo boat destroyers under Adm. Pascual Cervera y Topete left the Cape Verde Islands en route to the Caribbean in the hope of harassing the American blockade or bombarding ports along the Eastern Seaboard.

U.S. Intelligence Objectives: There were three major U.S. intelligence missions. The first was to track the progress of Admiral Camara's task force at Cadiz. Camara was of special concern to Washington because the armor and guns of his squadron were superior to those of Dewey's force at Manila. Mc-

Kinley intended to use the Philippines as a bargaining chip to bring the war to an early end, and the successful Spanish relief of Manila would set back those plans.

The second major intelligence target was Adm. Cervera's squadron, which seemed, first of all, to offer a significant threat to the Eastern Seaboard and so caused general panic in many coastal cities, and, secondly, threatened Army plans to send a large fleet of transports carrying the expeditionary force to Cuba. Though Cervera's fleet was known to be inferior in numbers and destructive power to the North Atlantic Squadron, so long as its whereabouts remained unknown, American operations in the Caribbean were threatened with disruption.

The third intelligence mission was to maintain liaison with the Cuban insurgents for the purposes of supplying them and obtaining detailed information on Spanish strength and disposition in Cuba, as well as BASIC INTELLIGENCE of the Cuban countryside.

U.S. Intelligence Operations: The task of tracking Camara's fleet fell to the Office of NAVAL INTELLIGENCE (ONI), in the persons of the U.S. naval attachés in London and Paris, Lts. John C. Colwell and WILLIAM S. SIMS, respectively. Although ONI had in the past gathered naval information only from open soruces in an overt and systematic way, Colwell and Sims met the new need for the covert collection of intelligence with inspired amateurism. Through the lavish expenditure of secret service funds, Sims soon established a network of agents stretching from the Canary Islands, where "an Italian citizen" reported Spanish naval movements for $300 per month, to Port Said, where "a reliable gentleman," a former Swedish army officer, watched and waited for Camara's squadron to pass through the Suez Canal en route to Manila. A French aristocrat and retired naval officer reported to Sims from Madrid. Colwell ran a second network and sent at least three agents into Spain, recruited a PENETRATION AGENT in the Spanish embassy in London, and had an assortment of high and low level informers throughout England and the Continent. Sims and Colwell produced reasonably accurate intelligence of Camara's progress (the task force sailed on June 17th, but progress was slow through the Mediterranean), made some useful reports of Spanish strategic plans, and disseminated disinformation in Spain at Washington's request.

In the matter of Adm. Cervera's squadron, ONI failed to learn the most significant fact, viz., that it had sailed for the Caribbean in a state of serious disrepair and unreadiness, and constituted a negligible naval threat. The Army and Navy chiefs in Washington continued to make and alter their plans based on the assumption that it was well-armed, well-equipped, fully coaled, and bringing supplies for the relief of Havana. None of this was true. Meanwhile a large naval force was split from the North Atlantic Squadron to blockade the southern Cuban port of Cienfuegos, where it was erroneously believed Cervera was headed, and the Army's invasion flotilla was delayed at Tampa for fear of encountering the Spanish fleet en route to Cuba.

Cervera's ships arrived in the southeast Cuban port of Santiago on May 19th almost out of coal and in need of considerable repairs and refitting. In the one real intelligence coup of the war, President McKinley received word of Cervera's arrival that same day through the diligence of Capt. MARTIN L. HELLINGS of the Signal Corps. Hellings, formerly the manager of the Western Union telegraph office at Key West, had organized a network of agents before the war among the Western Union telegraphers in Cuba; Cervera's telegram announcing his arrival to the Spanish commander at Havana had been received there by one of his agents and relayed to the Signal Corps in Key West, and from there on to the White House. The discovery enabled the U.S. Navy to blockade Cervera in Santiago harbor, effectively neutralizing whatever naval potential he may have possessed. The Army landed an invasion force of some 16,000 men near Santiago on June 22, and there followed the battles of Las Guasimas on June 24th, El Caney and San Juan on July 1st, and the siege of Santiago, commencing on July 1st. On July 3rd Cervera's squadron tried to escape from the harbor and run the American blockade, and was completely destroyed. This development forced Madrid to recall Camara's task force, now en route to Manila, to defend the Spanish coasts from possible attack by the North Atlantic Squadron. With Manila and the eastern end of Cuba in American hands and beyond hope of Spanish reclamation, Madrid was forced to capitulate.

The relatively easy task of reconnaissance and liaison with the Cuban insurgents was handled primarily by the Army's Military Information Division (see ARMY INTELLIGENCE), which early in the war sent Lt. ANDREW S. ROWAN into Cuba to contact Gen. Calixto Garcia. Rowan's exploit was celebrated inaccurately and disproportionately by Elbert Hubbard in his famous and popular essay "A Message to Garcia." Liaison with Gen. Maximo Gomez in the central provinces of the island was accomplished separately by *New York Herald* correspondent Fred O. Somerford and Navy Lt. VICTOR BLUE. Blue undertook another behind-the-lines reconnaissance near Santiago in mid-June to investigate the report that some of Cervera's ships were not in Santiago Bay; he learned the report was erroneous, but it had

already caused the Army invasion force to delay a week in sailing from Tampa.

Lt. HENRY F. WHITNEY of the Military Information Division carried out a covert reconnaissance of Puerto Rico early in the war disguised as a British merchant marine officer. Whitney was nearly caught by the Spanish authorities when the story of his mission leaked from the War Department and was published in the newspapers, but he nonetheless managed to carry out a two-week survey of Spanish military strength and defenses. His information proved of some value to Gen. Nelson Miles in his invasion of Puerto Rico.

Spanish Intelligence Operations: Lt. Ramon Carranza, former naval attaché at the Spanish embassy in Washington, ran an operation of short duration and limited value out of a hastily established intelligence station in Montreal. See the MONTREAL SPY RING.

(O'Toole, *The Spanish War*, "Our Man in Havana.")

SPECIAL ACTIVITIES

A term often synonymous with COVERT ACTION; also *special operations* (the latter term is used more often to refer to paramilitary operations than to other forms of covert action, and may have come from the British during the Second World War—British subversion and sabotage operations were conducted by the Special Operations Executive (SOE), an organization distinct from the British Secret Intelligence Service).

The term *special activities* has come into increasing use in recent years, perhaps because many American paramilitary operations, e.g., support of the anti-Sandinista guerrillas in Nicaragua, have been too well-publicized to be properly called "covert."

See OSS SPECIAL OPERATIONS BRANCH.

(Jordan and Taylor, *American National Security;* Richelson, *The U.S. Intelligence Community.*)

SPECIAL BRANCH

A unit of the Military Intelligence Service (see ARMY INTELLIGENCE), which exploited highly sensitive communications intelligence during the SECOND WORLD WAR.

Background and Discussion: After the failure of American intelligence to anticipate the PEARL HARBOR ATTACK despite the fact that Army and Navy cryptanalysts were reading enciphered Japanese diplomatic and naval traffic long before the event, Secretary of War Henry L. Stimson commissioned a review of the War Department's communications intelligence processing system by New York attorney ALFRED MCCORMACK.

In March 1942, after a two-month study, McCormack recommended the expansion and improvement of the communications intelligence operations of the Signal Corps. He recommended, furthermore, that the entire process of collecting, evaluating, and analyzing communications intelligence; integrating it with intelligence from collateral sources; and producing and disseminating the resulting finished intelligence, should be considered as a single process and placed under the control of a single agency, viz., the Military Intelligence Service of the War Department (see ARMY INTELLIGENCE). Finally, McCormack urged the recruitment and training of highly qualified individuals to perform the analysis and dissemination of this intelligence.

In response to McCormack's recommendations, Stimson established the Special Branch of the Military Intelligence Service under Col. Carter W. Clarke, a Signal Corps officer who had assisted McCormack in the study. McCormack was given a direct commission as a colonel in the U.S. Army and assigned as Clarke's deputy.

McCormack went beyond the military establishment to staff the Branch, recruiting fellow lawyers and academic scholars, and others with the special qualifications or talents required. By March 1943 the Branch consisted of twenty-eight officers and fifty-five civilians. Initially Clarke organized the Branch along broad geographical lines, but later streamlined it into three sections: A, which had the responsibility for diplomatic and clandestine traffic, and which produced the Magic Summary, a daily publication that contained all the important spot intelligence gleaned from each day's batch of intercepted messages; B, which processed intercepted Japanese army traffic and issued the Japanese Army Supplement to the Magic Summary; and C, which processed German military traffic collected by the British.

McCormack, TELFORD TAYLOR, and WILLIAM FRIEDMAN, director of the Army's Signal Intelligence Service, visited England in April 1943 and spent two months studying British communications intelligence methods. As a result the Special Branch thereafter worked very closely with the British at their Bletchley Park COMINT center and received much of the Ultra material, as the British intercepts of German communications were called.

Also as a result of McCormack's British visit, the Special Branch adopted the British practice of assigning intelligence officers on detached duty to the staffs of field commanders in order to insure both that the Branch's intelligence product was safeguarded and that it was properly disseminated to those who needed

it. These liaison officers received their rations and quarters from the local command, but remained under the operational control of the MIS in Washington, with which they communicated through the Special Branch's own secure channel.

In June 1944 the Special Branch was reorganized to make it a more homogenous component of the MIS.

(Lewin, *American Magic, Ultra Goes to War*; Bamford, *The Puzzle Palace*).

SR-71 RECONNAISSANCE AIRCRAFT ("the Blackbird")

The development of the SR-71 was begun in 1959 in response to improvements in the altitude and guidance systems of Soviet SAMs (surface-to-air missiles), and in anticipation of the time when even the high altitude of the U-2 RECONNAISSANCE AIRCRAFT would no longer protect it from interception. The SR-71 was intended to evade interception through a combination of high-altitude and very high speed.

The aircraft was developed by U-2 designer C. L. ("KELLY") JOHNSON at the Lockheed Aircraft Company's "Skunk Works" in Burbank, California. A prototype model, designated the A-11, first flew on April 26, 1962. Early versions of the plane were also known as the YF-12 research interceptor. The reconnaissance version, the SR-71A, made its maiden flight on December 22, 1964.

The SR-71 has a delta-shaped wing, 55 feet, 7 inches in span; is 107 feet, 5 inches long; has an empty weight of about 65,000 pounds and weighs 170,000 pounds when loaded. It is powered by two Pratt & Whitney J58 afterburning turbojets, each delivering 32,500 pounds of thrust. It holds the world aircraft records for speed (2,193 miles per hour, or Mach 3.31) and sustained height (85,069 feet). Its range, without midair refueling, is 2,982 miles, while flying at 1,983 miles per hour. The body of the SR-71 is made almost entirely of titanium to withstand the heat generated by air friction at its high speed, and the aircraft incorporates many technological innovations developed specifically for its supersonic mission.

The SR-71 carries a crew of two: a pilot and a reconnaissance systems officer. It is regarded as a difficult and demanding aircraft to fly, and a trainer version, the SR-71B, was developed to prepare pilots for it. The types of reconnaissance systems with which the plane is equipped have not been disclosed, but they presumably include advanced photographic and electronic systems. Likewise, the missions on which the plane has flown have not been disclosed,

SR-71 Blackbird reconnaissance aircraft. Source: Lockheed Aircraft.

but some SR-71s have been observed bearing the Air Force snake emblem, denoting service in Southeast Asia during the Vietnam War.

The SR-71s are assigned to the Air Force's Ninth Reconnaissance Wing at Beale Air Force Base in California.

(Gunston, *Spy Planes;* Taylor and Mondey, *Spies in the Sky.*)

STAGER, ANSON (April 20, 1825–March 26, 1885): telegrapher, businessman, Army officer, cryptographer

A native of Ontario County, New York, Stager went to work in 1841 as a clerk, and later a bookkeeper, for a Rochester, New York, newspaper publisher who established telegraph service in Pennsylvania between Philadelphia and Harrisburg. Stager taught himself telegraphy and worked as a telegrapher in Lancaster, Pennsylvania, and later managed the telegraph company's offices in Pittsburgh. By 1852 he had become general superintendent of the New York and Mississippi Valley Printing Telegraph Company, and he became general superintendent of the Western Union Telegraph Company when that company absorbed the other in 1856.

At the outbreak of the Civil War Stager was commissioned captain of volunteers in the U.S. Army, and placed in charge of the southern Ohio and western Virginia telegraph service, which had been mobilized for use by the military. At the request of Gen. George B. McClellan he devised a telegraph cipher for military use. The cipher, believed to be "the first army cipher ever used telegraphicaly in war" (Plumb), was a simple, yet effective, word transposition system (see CRYPTOLOGY). It was somewhat elaborated by War Department telegraphers DAVID

HOMER BATES, ALBERT B. CHANDLER, CHARLES A. TINKER, and others, and used throughout the war.

In October 1861 Stager was made head of the War Department's military telegraph service, an agency established then to handle strategic and administrative telegraph communications, and which took over responsibility for field telegraph service from the U.S. Army Signal Corps in March 1864 (see WIRETAPPING AND COMMUNICATIONS INTELLIGENCE IN THE CIVIL WAR).

In 1865 Stager was brevetted a brigadier general of volunteers. After the war he returned to civilian life and moved to Chicago, where he founded the Western Electric Company, and later was president of the Western Edison Electric Light Company and the Chicago Telephone Company.

(*Who Was Who in America*, historical volume; *National Cyclopedia of American Biography*, v. 4; Harlow, *Old Wires and New Waves*; Plumb, *The Military Telegraph During the Civil War in the United States*; Kahn, *The Codebreakers*.)

STANSBURY, JOSEPH (January 9, 1750–November 1809): poet, songwriter, businessman, British secret agent and courier

A native of London, England, Stansbury moved to America and settled in Philadelphia in 1767. He opened a shop, dealing in glassware, china, and crockery, and soon became well-known and popular for the humorous and satirical songs he wrote and sang.

Stansbury's sympathies remained with the British during the American Revolution, and he was jailed briefly in 1776 when an informer reported he had led in singing "God Save the King" at a gathering in his home. During the British occupation of Philadelphia he was rewarded for his loyalty with a number of minor official positions. When the British evacuated the city, however, he took the oath of allegiance to Pennsylvania in order to avoid further trouble with the American authorities.

Stansbury was acquainted with Philadelphia Tory Elizabeth (Peggy) Shippen, who became the wife of BENEDICT ARNOLD, and it may have been for this reason that Arnold selected him to carry his treasonous overtures to Sir Henry Clinton in New York City. Throughout much of 1779 and 1780 he carried Arnold's intelligence reports to Maj. JOHN ANDRÉ, Clinton's aide-de-camp in New York, and Clinton's messages back to Arnold in Philadelphia. In mid-1780 he was jailed in Philadelphia "for treasonable practices," although the authorities were certainly unaware at the time of both Arnold's treason and Stansbury's role in it. He was released the following December and banished from Philadelphia.

Stansbury moved to New York City where the British gave him rations, lodgings, and a stipend of $2 a day as a reward for his services. He continued to write political songs and prose. After the war he was again imprisoned upon returning to Philadelphia. Upon his release he returned to New York City, spent some time in Nova Scotia, and journeyed to England to apply for compensation as a Loyalist. His request was denied by the British government on the grounds that his loyalty to the King seemed to have lacked ardor. In disallowing his claim, the Commission on Loyalist Claims remarked, "He seems at no time to have been true to his allegiance, and however you may like the treason it is impossible to approve the traitor."

Stansbury returned to Philadelphia in 1785 and resumed his business there. In 1793 he moved once again to New York City where he served as secretary of the United Insurance Company until his death.

(*Who Was Who in America*, historical volume; Boatner, *Encyclopedia of the American Revolution*; Flexner, *The Traitor and the Spy*; Van Doren, *Secret History of the American Revolution*.)

STATE DEPARTMENT INTELLIGENCE

By the very nature of its function, the State Department has always been intimately concerned with foreign intelligence, although intelligence was not recognized as a distinct professional specialty or organizational entity within the Department until the twentieth century.

Before the adoption of the U.S. Constitution in 1788, American foreign affairs were handled by committees of the Continental Congress. The earliest of these was the COMMITTEE OF SECRET CORRESPONDENCE, which was established on November 29, 1775 and later renamed the Committee on Foreign Affairs. In addition to its diplomatic functions, the Committee carried out foreign intelligence collection and propaganda operations in France and elsewhere in Europe during the AMERICAN REVOLUTION.

The Department of Foreign Affairs was established as an executive department of the U.S. government by an act of Congress on July 27, 1789. On September 15th of that year the Department was assigned additional responsibilities in the domestic area—e.g., the Patent Office and the Census Bureau—and was renamed the Department of State (with the creation of the Department of Interior in 1849, State was relieved of most of its domestic duties and since has been almost exclusively concerned with foreign affairs).

The Department remained quite small during the first half of the nineteenth century—its staff consisted of fifteen persons in 1820, for example, and until 1853 the ranking officer in the Department under the secretary of state was the chief clerk. Consequently the tasks of intelligence collection and intelligence research and analysis were not specialized and differentiated functions but generally remained among the miscellaneous duties of diplomats abroad and Department staff members in Washington. When intelligence collection needs arose that could not be handled on this basis, the Department resorted to the ad hoc means of special executive agents.

Executive Agents

Executive agents—private persons sent abroad on public business—were employed by the State Department from its earliest days. They did not have the powers of an ambassador, a minister, or other diplomatic representatives, but the fact that they could be appointed by the secretary of state without the consent (or knowledge) of the Senate protected the confidentiality of their business. They were often paid out of the President's contingent, or "secret service," fund, thereby avoiding the public disclosure of their identities or missions. Executive agents were used by State for a variety of tasks, most of which were of some special sensitivity: opening relations with a foreign power, dealing with nations with whom the United States had broken off relations, dealing with the colonies of a foreign power, etc. And they were sent abroad, often undercover, to gather intelligence regarding matters of particular interest to the Department.

For example, in 1823 the Department sent GEORGE B. ENGLISH, a former U.S. Marine Corps officer who had embraced the Islamic religion and served as an officer in the Turkish army, back to Turkey with secret orders to report on the Ottoman Empire's attitude toward a possible commercial treaty with the United States covering American trade in the Black

Office of the chief clerk, Department of State, in the 1880s. Intelligence coordination and analysis fell among his miscellaneous duties during the nineteenth century. Source: National Archives.

Sea. He managed to obtain a copy of the trade agreement Turkey had signed with France, an important piece of intelligence. Another agent was sent to Europe that same year to discover the plans of the European powers regarding the former Spanish colonies in the western hemisphere that had recently achieved independence. In 1826 a secret agent was sent to the West Indies to collect economic intelligence regarding potential trade with the United States. And the following year the Department sent an agent to Cuba to investigate the likelihood that Mexico and Colombia might invade the island.

In at least one instance the Department sent abroad a sort of "intelligence agent at large" to investigate a variety of matters. Austrian-born journalist Francis J. Grund was sent to Europe by Secretary of State Lewis Cass in 1858 to make inquiries, in the guise of a private citizen, regarding British naval operations in the West Indies, the termination of a commercial treaty with the German kingdom of Hanover, European plans for a canal across the Central American isthmus, and sundry other affairs about which the Department required more information than could be obtained by its legations in Europe.

The State Department also employed executive agents for intelligence missions that had more to do with domestic law enforcement than foreign affairs. For example, Secretary of State William H. Seward sent veteran Civil War intelligence officer GEORGE H. SHARPE to Europe in 1867 in search of John Surratt and other American citizens who might have been involved in the LINCOLN CONSPIRACY. Seward also sent Sharpe to Vermont shortly thereafter to investigate reports that the Fenians—Irish nationalists in America—were planning to launch an invasion of Canada from the United States.

Covert Action

The nineteenth-century missions of some State Department agents were more concerned with what is today called COVERT ACTION than with SECRET INTELLIGENCE. William Eaton's 1805 mission to North Africa was not quite covert, but it was a paramilitary operation aimed at a political objective. Eaton, who had served as a counterespionage agent for the State Department in the United States, and later as American consul in Tunis, led a small army of Arabs, Greeks, European adventurers, and eight U.S. Marines across the Libyan desert and captured the port of Derna. The object of his operation—which was sanctioned by the Department and President Jefferson—was to overthrow the pasha of Tripoli who had been carrying out a campaign of piracy, kidnapping, and extortion against American shipping in the

Mediterranean, and replace him with the pasha's more reasonable brother. Although Eaton did not achieve his objective, his operation convinced the pasha to reform his policy regarding the United States.

Propaganda, rather than paramilitary operations, was the more common form of State Department covert action abroad during the nineteenth century. In 1845 the Polk administration secretly sent former Postmaster General Charles A. Wickliffe to Texas to promote the cause of U.S. annexation of the then independent republic. The following year American businessman Thomas O. Larkin performed the same covert mission in California.

The Civil War

The CIVIL WAR occasioned extensive covert action and secret intelligence operations abroad by the State Department. In fact, Secretary of State Simon Cameron assumed some domestic counterespionage functions for a time, early in the war, hiring LAFAYETTE C. BAKER to organize a secret service for that purpose within the State Department (Baker and his unit were transferred to the War Department shortly thereafter). Cameron's successor, William H. Seward, secretly sent several executive agents to Europe during the war for a variety of purposes ranging from propaganda to secret diplomacy.

HENRY S. SANFORD, the American minister to Belgium, ran an extensive secret service in England and France aimed at thwarting Confederate efforts to obtain warships and other war material in Europe. JOHN BIGELOW, an American journalist, worked under cover as the American consul general in Paris while conducting pro-Union "gray" propaganda operations in France and elsewhere on the continent. Seward sent New York journalist and Republican leader Thurlow Weed to England as a covert propaganda agent.

The Twentieth Century

With the FIRST WORLD WAR State Department intelligence was placed on a permanent formal footing. In 1915 Secretary of State Robert Lansing assigned the intelligence function to Frank K. Polk, who as counselor was the second-ranking officer in the Department. Polk's primary task was to coordinate the work of the SECRET SERVICE, ARMY INTELLIGENCE, the Justice Department's Bureau of Investigation (see FEDERAL BUREAU OF INVESTIGATION), and other federal agencies that were collecting foreign intelligence. Together with presidential advisor Col. Edward M. House, Polk was also responsible for liaison with British intelligence through

Sir WILLIAM WISEMAN, the British Secret Intelligence Service's representative in Washington. Anglo-American intelligence liaison was also one of the tasks of Polk's assistant, Gordon Auchincloss, who was sent to London for that purpose. But other State Department intelligence activity continued to be carried out on an ad hoc basis; coordination with EMANUEL V. VOSKA's private counterespionage service was done through Charles R. Crane, a confidant of President Wilson who happened to know Voska and was the father of Secretary Lansing's private secretary.

While Lansing was attending the 1919 Paris Peace Conference, Polk, as acting secretary of state, played an important role in preserving M.I.8, the wartime cryptanalysis unit of the Army's Military Intelligence Division, and establishing it as the Cipher Bureau, a joint State/War Department agency (see AMERICAN BLACK CHAMBER, HERBERT O. YARDLEY).

In 1919 Congress created the position of under secretary of state, a post with more responsibility and authority than that of counselor. Polk was made the first incumbent in the job, and he brought with him the intelligence functions that had been attached to the counselor's office since 1915. State Department intelligence was thereby put on a permanent peacetime footing for the first time. A unit within the under secretary's office—designated U-1—was established to carry on the coordination and liaison function, a prototypical "central intelligence agency." Polk created the Office of the Chief Special Agent to carry out counter-espionage and countersubversion investigations both within the United States and abroad (the Office was later designated U-3).

In 1927 State Department intelligence was reorganized by Secretary of State Frank B. Kellogg. U-1 was abolished. In place of the central coordinating unit, the Department's geographic desks were to take over the analysis of intelligence bearing on their respective areas. High priority intelligence reports from other U.S. government agencies were to be handled by the secretary himself. U-3, the counterespionage unit, was retained under the title Bureau of the Chief Special Agent, but matters relating to Communist subversion became the special responsibility of ROBERT F. KELLEY, chief of the Department's Division of East European Affairs.

The decentralized intelligence organization established by Kellogg remained generally in effect until after the SECOND WORLD WAR (though Kelley's East European Affairs Division was abolished in 1937). In September 1945, with the termination of the Office of Strategic Services, the OSS RESEARCH AND ANALYSIS BRANCH was transferred to the State Department. State was also the recipient of the OSS Presentation Branch (an audiovisual briefing unit), as well as remnants of the OFFICE OF THE COORDINATOR OF INTER-AMERICAN AFFAIRS, the Office of War Information, and the Foreign Economic Administration, all of which had some foreign intelligence functions. This abrupt accretion of intelligence files and personnel was the result of President Truman's decision to concentrate foreign intelligence within the Department. In all, some 1,600 persons were transferred into the Department and became the Interim Research and Intelligence Service, which shortly thereafter was called the Office of Research and Intelligence. Veteran Army intelligence officer Col. ALFRED MCCORMACK was put in charge of the unit as special assistant to the secretary of state for research and intelligence.

The Centralization Question

The arrangement proved unworkable, in part because veteran diplomats and foreign service officers distrusted the newcomers and regarded them as academic and impractical in their concept of foreign affairs, and in part because a centralized intelligence service within the Department was perceived by some senior State officials as a threat to their bureaucratic prerogatives. In April 1946 the Office of Research and Intelligence was broken up and most of its staff was assigned to the various geographical divisions of the Department, essentially a return to the decentralized arrangement that had existed since 1927. The remainder became the Office of Intelligence Coordination and Liaison. Colonel McCormack resigned in protest of the move.

When Gen. George C. Marshall became secretary of state the following year State's intelligence was yet again reorganized, this time as a single staff unit. The unit, eventually known as the Office of the Special Assistant, Intelligence, was much smaller than the defunct Office of Research and Intelligence, and a much less formidable competitor with the Department's geographical divisions for power, prestige, and funds. The Office had no intelligence collection responsibilities, but was involved entirely in intelligence research and analysis.

Much of State's intelligence activity during the immediate postwar years involved interagency undertakings. In January 1946 the Department, along with the War and Navy departments, became a participant in the National Intelligence Authority, which was created to direct the Central Intelligence Group (see CENTRAL INTELLIGENCE AGENCY). The CIG derived its personnel from the participating departments, and thereby received many of the people who had been transferred to State when the OSS was dissolved. Of course, State Department's role ended when the CIA succeeded the CIG, although the secretary of state continued to participate in CIA matters as a member of the NATIONAL SECURITY COUNCIL.

When the Office of Policy Coordination was created in 1949, the State and the Defense departments shared the responsibility for directing the covert action operations of the new agency, with State playing the major role in peacetime (see CENTRAL INTELLIGENCE AGENCY). But this direct involvement ended when CIA Director WALTER BEDELL SMITH assumed full control of OPC late in 1950.

State may have been one of the departments that participated in the support and direction of the GROMBACH ORGANIZATION during this period, although any such involvement must have ended when that Organization became a contract service to the CIA.

Bureau of Intelligence and Research

In 1957 intelligence was again given a more prominent role within the State Department's organization with the creation of the BUREAU OF INTELLIGENCE AND RESEARCH. The director of the new Bureau was Hugh S. Cumming, Jr., a veteran diplomat and foreign service officer. Under Cumming, the Bureau made some progress in overcoming the stigma that had attached to State Department intelligence in the recent past, viz., that the end product was excessively academic and of little use to foreign policy-makers. Nonetheless, the Bureau remained something of a bureaucratic stepchild in terms of personnel and budget.

In 1961 Cumming was succeeded as director by OSS veteran and foreign affairs specialist ROGER HILSMAN, JR. Hilsman reorganized the Bureau, ridding it of many tasks in biographic intelligence and BASIC INTELLIGENCE that duplicated work done by the CIA and focusing its resources on research and intelligence production directly related to the formulation of foreign policy (the Bureau has no intelligence collection responsibilities). Under Hilsman the Bureau achieved an importance equivalent to that of the geographical divisions and other major units within the State Department. In recognition of this, the post of director of the Bureau was elevated to the level of assistant secretary of state in 1963.

Hilsman was succeeded as director in 1963 by his deputy, Thomas L. Hughes. In 1969 the job was taken over by veteran CIA intelligence officer, RAY S. CLINE, who held it until 1973.

(Wriston, *Executive Agents in American Foreign Relations*; Jeffreys-Jones, *American Espionage*; Troy, *Donovan and the CIA*; Ransom, *Central Intelligence and National Security*, *The Intelligence Establishment*; Hilsman, *To Move a Nation*.)

STATION

The field headquarters of an intelligence service within a foreign country. In the CIA CLANDESTINE SERVICE, every station is managed by a chief of station, who is nominally subordinate to the American ambassador to the host country, and who reports to the chief of a geographical area division within the Clandestine Service at CIA headquarters. Often the chief of station conducts liaison with senior officials of the host country, while the deputy chief of station handles relations with the host's police forces and intelligence services. The station is organized along functional lines into Operations, Support, and Administration.

Operations consists of CASE OFFICERS, who are concerned with positive intelligence collection, counterintelligence, and COVERT ACTION. Reports officers, who extract useful intelligence from case officer reports and process it into reports to CIA headquarters, are considered Support, as are the communications officers, who handle secure communications between the station and CIA headquarters, and technicians, who provide expertise in various specialized kinds of TRADECRAFT, e.g., electronic surveillance and surreptitious entry. The Administration officers are responsible for the station's "housekeeping," e.g., personnel management, disbursements, and office administration.

Any unit of the same intelligence service located elsewhere in the host country is subordinate to the station and is known as a BASE.

(Beck, *Secret Contenders*; De Silva, *Sub Rosa*.)

STAY-BEHIND NET

A network of espionage and/or sabotage agents and their equipment established in an area expected to be occupied by an adversary. The network can be activated any time after the adversary's forces have entered the area. Stay-behind nets obviate the risks associated with infiltrating AGENTS into a DENIED AREA.

According to former CIA Director WILLIAM E. COLBY, the CIA CLANDESTINE SERVICE in the early 1950s

had undertaken a major program of building, throughout those Western European countries that seemed likely targets for Soviet attack, what in the parlance of the intelligence trade were known as "stay-behind nets," clandestine infrastructures of leaders and equipment trained and ready to be called into action as sabotage and espionage forces when the time came.

The term may be of recent (i.e., Second World War) origin, but the idea of the stay-behind net is not new. During the American Revolution Gen. Thomas Mifflin established a *stay-behind net* in Philadelphia on the orders of Gen. GEORGE WASHINGTON, shortly before that city was occupied by the British.

(Colby and Forbath, *Honorable Men.*)

STEINBERG, SAUL (June 15, 1914–): artist, architect, intelligence officer

A native of Romanic-Sarat, Romania, Steinberg studied philosophy at the University of Bucharest and received a doctorate in architecture from the Reggio Politecnico, Facoltà di Architettura in Milan, Italy, in 1940. He practiced architecture in Milan until 1941, when he fled Fascist Italy. He settled in New York City in 1942.

Steinberg had been contributing drawings to *Harper's Bazaar* and *Life* for several years, and in 1943 he held a one-man show in New York. That same year he became a naturalized American citizen and was commissioned as an ensign in the U.S. Naval Reserve.

Steinberg was assigned to the United States Navy Group China and served with the SINO-AMERICAN COOPERATIVE ORGANIZATION in China from mid-1943 through late 1944. He taught Chinese guerrillas the techniques of explosive demolition of bridges and other structures. Afterward he was assigned to the Office of Strategic Services and served in North Africa and Italy, where he drew propaganda cartoons for the OSS MORALE OPERATIONS BRANCH. In 1945 he was discharged with the rank of lieutenant.

After the war Steinberg's drawings and cartoons became well-known, appearing frequently in the *New Yorker* and other publications.

(*Current Biography*, 1957; *Who's Who in America*, 37th ed.; Miles, *A Different Kind of War.*)

STEPHENS, SIR PHILIP (1725–November 20, 1809): British naval official and intelligence officer

Born in Alphamstone, Essex, where his father was a clergyman, Stephens at an early age was appointed clerk in the navy victualing office. He became a protege of Rear Adm. George Anson and later Anson's secretary. In 1763 he became secretary of the Admiralty. During a period encompassing the AMERICAN REVOLUTION he supervised the Admiralty's secret service through *Frouw* Marguerite Wolters, a Dutch widow who ran an intelligence station in Rotterdam under cover of a bookshop. The Rotterdam station (which was moved to Ostend and run by Wolters's clerk L.C. Hake in 1780, when the British declared war on the Dutch) operated a far-flung agent network throughout Europe. One of the major targets of Sir Philip's operation were the shipments of arms and supplies leaving French ports for America.

(*DNB*; Morris, *The Peacemakers.*)

STEPHENSON, SIR WILLIAM SAMUEL (January 11, 1896–): inventor, industrialist, British intelligence officer

A native of Point Douglas (near Winnipeg), Canada, Stephenson left high school at the outbreak of the First World War in 1914 to enlist in the Royal Canadian Engineers. He was commissioned as a second lieutenant, saw action in France, and was promoted to captain. After recovering from a gassing he transferred to the Royal Flying Corps, learned to fly, and was assigned to a fighter squadron in France in 1916. He shot down numerous German planes and, in July 1918, was himself shot down and captured by German troops. He escaped from a prisoner-of-war camp and made his way back to his squadron.

After the war Stephenson returned to Canada and pursued a boyhood interest in radio and electronics. In 1921 he settled in England, where he invented and patented a device for the radio transmission of still photographs. Royalties from his patents made him a millionaire by the time he was thirty. He was involved in several other successful commercial ventures, including aircraft manufacture, film production, and steel mills.

Early in the Second World War Stephenson put his knowledge of the European steel industry, which was then supplying the German rearmament program, at the disposal of the British Secret Intelligence Service. After his involvement in an abortive SIS attempt to sabotage Swedish iron ore shipments to Germany in 1939, the Service asked him to undertake a mission to Washington to establish high-level liaison between British intelligence and the FEDERAL BUREAU OF INVESTIGATION. The proposed relationship was for the purpose of Anglo-American cooperation in uncovering Axis espionage and sabotage activities in the United States. With the approval of President Franklin Roosevelt, but with the misgivings of the secretary of State and the State Department, FBI Director J. EDGAR HOOVER agreed to the liaison arrangement.

In 1940 British Prime Minister Winston Churchill persuaded Stephenson to take charge of the British intelligence apparatus in the United States in a role closely similar to that played by SIR WILLIAM WISEMAN in America during the FIRST WORLD WAR. Under the cover of the British Passport Control officer in New York City, Stephenson established the British Security Coordination office at 630 Fifth Avenue in New York.

BSC was the New York station of SIS, and it also included liaison officers from the British Security Service and the Special Operation Executive (the British wartime paramilitary agency), as well. It carried out the Anglo-American liaison function Stephenson had arranged for with the FBI. Furthermore, Stephenson's job, like that of his First World War predecessor, Wiseman, included propaganda operations and secret diplomacy aimed at bringing the United States into the war. But Stephenson and the BSC had an even larger responsibility, viz., direct SECRET INTELLIGENCE, COUNTERINTELLIGENCE, AND COUNTERESPIONAGE operations against the Axis in the United States, Canada, and Latin America.

One of Stephenson's earliest and most important accomplishments was to serve in the role of midwife in the birth of the Office of the Coordinator of Information, the U.S. agency that became the OFFICE OF STRATEGIC SERVICES. In December 1940 he accompanied WILLIAM J. DONOVAN on a trip to London. Donovan, a Wall Street lawyer with considerable knowledge of European military and political affairs, was serving as an unofficial White House advisor, and was en route to England and the Mediterranean to assess the strategic situation at the request of President Roosevelt. Stephenson had ample time to meet with him when their plane was delayed in Bermuda for eight days by the weather and it was apparently during these meetings that he persuaded Donovan of the need for an American intelligence and COVERT ACTION agency on the model of the British Secret Intelligence Service and Special Operations Executive. After Donovan returned with a proposal to Roosevelt for the plan that eventually became the OSS, Stephenson lent his good offices to the proposal and brought to bear the considerable influence of the British government in gaining approval for it. After the creation of the Office of the Coordinator of Information, he saw to it that BSC provided all necessary assistance to the new organization in the way of intelligence expertise, training, and counterintelligence files. He became so close a collaborator with Donovan that associates dubbed him "Little Bill" and Donovan "Big Bill" in order to distinguish between them.

BSC was disbanded in 1946 and Stephenson returned to his business ventures, which he pursued in the West Indies, Canada, and elsewhere. He was knighted in 1945 and also awarded the U.S. Medal of Merit and the French Legion of Honor. He had earlier been awarded the Military Cross and the Distinguished Flying Cross for his service in the First World War. In 1980 he was made a Companion of the Order of Canada.

(Hyde, *Room 3603*; Stevenson, *A Man Called Intrepid*; Troy, *Donovan and the CIA*; Who's Who 1982–1983.)

STIDGER, FELIX A. (ca. 1837–?): businessman, Union secret agent

A native of Taylorsville, Kentucky, Stidger owned a dry goods store in Mattoon, Illinois, at the outbreak of the Civil War. An ardent supporter of the Union, he enlisted in the U.S. Army and served as a clerk in the Office of the Adjutant General in Washington, and a provost marshal's office in Tennessee.

In April 1863 Brig. Gen. HENRY B. CARRINGTON, the Union military commander at Indianapolis who had served with Stidger in the Adjutant General's Office, requested that Stidger be assigned to assist him in an investigation of the subversive activities of the Copperheads, as the anti-war wing of the Democratic Party was called. Carrington assigned Stidger to work undercover, posing as a rabid Copperhead, and penetrate the KNIGHTS OF THE GOLDEN CIRCLE, a secret society involved in sabotage, terrorism, and other illegal acts aimed at crippling the Union war effort in the Northwest (i.e., the Midwest, in today's usage).

Stidger succeeded in his imposture and was accepted into the Knights in Indiana. Within a month he was reporting back to Carrington on the plans and operations of the society. By June he had been elevated to the post of grand secretary of the organization, which by then had changed its name to the Order of American Knights. Through Stidger, Carrington and the War Department learned that the society was far better organized and more dangerous than they had previously suspected. (However, a recent study by historian Frank L. Klement finds that the organization was far smaller and less dangerous than has been supposed.)

During the late spring and summer of 1864 the society, by then calling itself the Sons of Liberty, was working with Confederate secret service agents based in Canada on a plan to foment revolution in Indiana, Illinois, and Ohio, overthrow the governments of those states, and split them off from the Union (see NORTHWEST CONSPIRACY). Stidger's penetration of the society enabled the Union authorities to keep abreast of the progress of the conspiracy, and to arrest, try, and convict the Copperhead leaders involved in it. Stidger, abandoning his cover, was the chief witness for the government at the trial.

Stidger then returned to civilian life. After the war he was frequently the target of Copperhead and Confederate vengeance, and was once nearly murdered on a Louisville street. He settled in Chicago and established the Stidger Progressive American Twentieth Century Shorthand School. In 1903 he published an account of his wartime service, *Treason History of the Order of Sons of Liberty*.

(Horan, *Confederate Agent*; Corson, *Armies of Ignorance*; Klement, *Dark Lanterns*.)

STILWELL, RICHARD GILES (February 24, 1917–): Army officer, intelligence officer

A native of Buffalo, New York, Stilwell attended Brown University in 1933–34 and graduated from the U.S. Military Academy in 1938. He saw combat in the Second World War and advanced in rank rapidly. After the war he was assigned to the Central Intelligence Agency, and in the early 1950s was chief of the Far East Division of the Office of Policy Coordination, as the agency's COVERT ACTION department was then called. His deputy in the FE Division was DESMOND FITZGERALD.

In 1952–53 Stilwell returned to regular Army duty and commanded the Fifteenth Infantry Regiment in Korea. He later served on the faculty of the Army War College. In 1961–65 he served with the U.S. Military Assistance Command in Vietnam, and in 1965–67 he commanded the U.S. Military Assistance Command in Thailand. He was later U.S. Army deputy chief of staff for military operations. After retiring from the Army he served as a deputy under secretary of defense during the Reagan administration. Stilwell attained the rank of lieutenant general and received numerous decorations, including the Distinguished Service Medal, Silver Star, Bronze Star, Legion of Merit, Distinguished Flying Cross, Air Medal, the Purple Heart, and nineteen foreign decorations.

(Smith, *Portrait of a Cold Warrior*; Powers, *The Man Who Kept the Secrets*; *Who's Who in America*, 37th ed.)

STORMONT, LORD (David Murray, second Earl of Mansfield, seventh viscount Stormont (October 9, 1727–September 1, 1796) British diplomat, intelligence officer

Stormont graduated from Christ Church, Oxford in 1748 and entered the British diplomatic service. In 1772 he was made ambassador to the French court. During 1775–78 he ran an agent network targeted on American efforts to establish an alliance with France against England. His most valuable agent, EDWARD BANCROFT, penetrated the American ministry at Passy and became secretary to BENJAMIN FRANKLIN and the other American commissioners in France.

With the French entry into the war in 1778, Stormont returned to London, but continued to function as a senior officer of the British Secret Service until the fall of Lord North's ministry in 1782.

(*DNB*; Morris, *The Peacemakers*.)

STRATEGIC INTELLIGENCE

According to the Joint Chiefs of Staff's *Dictionary of Military and Associated Terms*, "intelligence which is required for the formulation of policy and military plans at national and international levels." SHERMAN KENT defined it as "high-level foreign positive intelligence."

See TACTICAL INTELLIGENCE; INTELLIGENCE TAXONOMY.

(Kent, *Strategic Intelligence for American World Policy*; Hopple and Watson, *The Military Intelligence Community*.)

STRINGFELLOW, (BENJAMIN) FRANKLIN (June 18, 1840–June 8, 1918): schoolteacher, clergyman, Confederate intelligence officer and secret agent

A native of Culpeper County, Virginia, Stringfellow attended school in Albemarle County and the Episcopal High School of Alexandria. After graduation he taught Latin and Greek in the Stanton School in Shuqualak, Mississippi.

At the outbreak of the Civil War Stringfellow returned to Virginia to enlist in the Confederate Army, but was rejected several times because of his delicate appearance (he was short, and, at ninety-four pounds, very lean). He was eventually accepted as a private in the Virginia Cavalry in May 1861 and saw action as a courier in the battle of Bull Run in July. Afterward he was assigned to the staff of Gen. J.E.B.

Stuart who, by some accounts, commissioned him a captain.

Stringfellow served as a secret agent for Stuart. Historian and espionologist Edwin C. Fishel characterizes Stringfellow as "an outstanding example of a special group—agents of undoubted success, undoubted value, on whom there is a very little contemporary documentation, and about whom a great body of myth has grown up, most of it untrue." The task of separating the facts from the abundant fiction in Stringfellow's story remains to be done. The traditional account is summarized here:

Sometime in the latter part of 1861 Stringfellow was detailed to the CONFEDERATE SECRET SERVICE and sent to Alexandria, Virginia, where he assumed the identity of "Edward Delcher," the assistant to a local dentist who was a Confederate sympathizer. Stringfellow's job was to search the large numbers of Northern newspapers gathered in Alexandria by the Secret Service for information of military or political intelligence value (see NEWSPAPERS IN THE CIVIL WAR), extract it, and forward it by secret courier to Richmond.

Stringfellow remained in this capacity through the early part of 1862, but was eventually betrayed to the Union authorities by the dentist, who apparently believed his wife had become too fond of his new assistant. Stringfellow left Alexandria one jump ahead of a Union patrol, made his way back to Confederate lines, rejoined General Stuart in mid-April, and, for a time, served as a uniformed scout. He took part in Stuart's reconnaissance sortie around the Army of the Potomac as Gen. George B. McClellan advanced on Richmond during June 1862.

In July 1862 Stringfellow was again sent on an undercover mission deep into Union territory. By August he was able to send Gen. Thomas J. ("Stonewall") Jackson a detailed report on the capabilities and intentions of Union Gen. John Pope, who was then advancing southward through the counties just east of the Blue Ridge Mountains in Virginia. Stringfellow's reports were instrumental in the Confederate victory there. He continued to operate behind Union lines throughout August 1862, providing both Jackson and Gen. Robert E. Lee with intelligence of great value in the campaign that culminated in the Confederate victory at the second battle of Bull Run (August 29–30, 1862).

In February 1863 Stringfellow was sent to Washington to establish a secret communication network between Stuart and his agents in the capital. While carrying out this mission he spent considerable time in Alexandria, Virginia, and was nearly captured there when recognized by a Union officer he had taken prisoner earlier in the war.

Stringfellow carried out several other undercover missions for Stuart during 1863. On some of these occasions he crossed into Union territory dressed in female attire, a disguise that his small frame and stature permitted. He was captured during the Gettysburg campaign, a few days before the battle, but released soon after the battle in a prisoner exchange. His undercover reconnaissance during the Wilderness campaign of May 1864 is regarded as having nearly caused the defeat of Gen. Ulysses S. Grant in that engagement. When Stuart was killed in May 1864 Stringfellow was attached to the staff of General Lee as a principal scout.

In March 1865 Confederate President Jefferson Davis sent Stringfellow on a secret mission to Washington to deliver a message to a foreign legation (apparently part of a last-ditch attempt to bring about the intervention of England, France, or some other European power on behalf of the Confederacy). He was also to make contact with a Union officer working for the Confederacy. Stringfellow completed both tasks but was captured by Union detectives (possibly of the NATIONAL DETECTIVE BUREAU) while attempting to make his way back to Confederate territory in April. He escaped and was a fugitive in Union-held Maryland and Virginia for several weeks, during which time President Lincoln was assassinated. Federal suspicion was directed at him as a possible member of the Lincoln conspiracy, and was heightened by the fact that he had spent a brief time while in Washington at the house of Mary Surratt, who cooperated with the Confederate Secret Service.

Stringfellow prudently fled to Canada and remained there until the postwar and post-assassination hysteria was over. He returned home, settled in Fairfax County, Virginia, and entered the Episcopal Seminary in Virginia, from which he graduated in 1876. He served in many parishes throughout Virginia and was pastor in Mechanicsville when he died.

In his later years he was also a popular speaker throughout the South, where he gave public lectures on his wartime experiences.

(*DAB*; *WAMB*: Bakeless, *Spies of the Confederacy*.)

STRONG, GEORGE VEAZEY (March 14, 1880–January 10, 1946): Army officer, intelligence officer

A native of Chicago, Strong attended the Michigan Military Academy in 1898–1900 and graduated from the U.S. Military Academy in 1904. He was assigned to the Sixth Cavalry at Fort Meade, South Dakota, and saw service, participating in the capture of some 300 Ute Indians who had left the Uintah reservation in Wyoming. In 1907 he was transferred to the Philippines, where he fought against the Moros.

In April 1908 Strong was ordered to Tokyo, and he served there as military attaché at the American embassy until 1911. He studied the Japanese language and, in 1911, published two works: *Japanese-English Military Dictionary*, and *Common Chinese-Japanese Characters*. He attended Army service schools at Fort Leavenworth, Kansas, served in Iowa and Texas, and was assigned to the Office of the Judge Advocate General in Chicago in 1916.

In July 1918 Strong, who had risen to the rank of major, went to France, served with the Fourth Army Corps, and was awarded the Distinguished Service Medal. In April 1919 he was assigned to the U.S. Military Academy as a professor of law. He left West Point in 1923 to join the Military Affairs Section of the Judge Advocate General's Office in Washington, D.C. After a few months he enrolled in the Army War College and, upon graduation, was assigned to the War Plans Division of the General Staff.

In 1925–27 Strong acted as technical advisor to the American delegation to several international conferences on disarmament and related matters at Geneva, Switzerland. In 1928 he was promoted to lieutenant colonel and assigned to the Twenty-fourth Infantry at Fort Benning, Georgia. Later he enrolled in the Command and General Staff School, from which he graduated in June 1931. The following year he was again sent to Geneva to serve as technical advisor at a disarmament conference, and he remained there until 1935. In 1937 he returned to Washington, D.C., to serve as chief of the intelligence group of the Military Intelligence Division (see ARMY INTELLIGENCE). He was promoted to brigadier general and became chief of the War Plans Division in 1938.

After command assignments in Nebraska and Texas in 1940–41, Strong was promoted to major general. In June 1942 he was made assistant chief of staff, G-2, i.e., chief of Army intelligence, and he served in that capacity until 1944. Strong was one of the most dedicated opponents of the Office of the Coordinator of Information, the predecessor organization of the OFFICE OF STRATEGIC SERVICES, which he saw as a dangerous rival to Army intelligence. His proposal to split the COI into three parts to be divided among other government agencies was rejected.

Strong retired in February 1944. In addition to the Distinguished Service Medal, he was awarded the Purple Heart, the Legion of Merit, and the French Legion of Honor.

(*Who Was Who in America*, v. 2; Troy, *Donovan and the CIA*; obituary, *New York Times*, January 12, 1946, p. 15.)

STUDIES AND OBSERVATION GROUP

Ostensibly created to study the activities of the U.S. Military Assistance Command, Vietnam (USMACV) during the VIETNAM WAR, the SOG was in fact a joint-service organization with a large Army component that conducted cross-border COVERT ACTION missions into Laos, Cambodia, and North Vietnam, and perhaps elsewhere in Southeast Asia. Established in January 1964 during a period in which many of the large paramilitary operations of the CIA CLANDESTINE SERVICE were being transferred to the Department of Defense, the SOG performed four primary missions: cross-border missions to disrupt enemy activities, e.g., North Vietnamese supply lines on the Ho Chi Minh Trail; locating American POWs and downed airmen in preparation for escape and evasion missions; training and dispatching agents into North Vietnam to establish resistance groups; and "black" and "gray" psychological warfare operations (see COVERT ACTION).

Although nominally a part of USMACV, the SOG was directly controlled by the commander-in-chief, Pacific, and was ultimately under the special assistant (to the secretary of defense) for counterinsurgency and special activities. As a joint-service unit, it included personnel from the Army Special Forces, Air Force Special Warfare Units, Navy SEALS (Sea/Air/Land Teams), the South Vietnamese Special Forces, and other South Vietnamese. At its peak strength the SOG consisted of 2,000 American personnel and 8,000 Vietnamese.

The SOG was composed of sub-units called "studies groups," each specializing in a particular form of covert action. The Air Studies Group flew clandestine missions into DENIED AREAS to dispatch and recover agents, and to carry out other covert activities. The Psychological Studies Group ran the "black" and "gray" psychological operations. The Maritime Studies Group used high-speed boats to infiltrate and exfiltrate agents and commando teams into and out of North Vietnam and other Communist controlled areas. The Ground Studies Group carried out OVER-THE-FENCE missions, many of which were directed at interdiction of the Ho Chi Minh Trail in Laos.

The SOG, as such, was dissolved before the United States withdrawal from Southeast Asia in 1973.

(Generous, *Vietnam: The Secret War*; Bowman, *The World Almanac of the Vietnam War*; Finnegan, *Military Intelligence*.)

STUDIES IN INTELLIGENCE

This quarterly professional journal for U.S. intelligence officers, inaugurated circa 1956, was first called

Intelligence Articles. Studies contains articles written by U.S. intelligence officers and other professionals on intelligence history, procedures, TRADECRAFT, and even reviews of spy fiction. It is published by the Central Intelligence Agency and classified Secret, and hence not available to the general public.

(Marchetti and Marks, *The CIA and the Cult of Intelligence;* Wise and Ross, *The Invisible Government.*)

SUBVERSION IN THE CONFEDERACY

Support for secession was far from unanimous in the Confederate states during the CIVIL WAR. Even the vice-president of the Confederacy, Alexander H. Stephens, was anti-secession and pro-peace, although he never put these philosophical positions into action. However, many dissident Southerners engaged in the same sort of "fifth column" activities in the South as the Southern sympathizers of the KNIGHTS OF THE GOLDEN CIRCLE carried out in the North, but on a smaller scale.

Soon after the outbreak of the war an organization of Unionists called the Peace and Constitutional Society was formed in Arkansas. Its aims were the encouragement of desertion from the Confederate Army, recruitment for the Union Army, and promotion of the overthrow of the Confederate government. By the end of 1861 the Society had 1,700 members in Alabama, Georgia, North Carolina, and Tennessee. A similar organization, the Heroes of America, operated in Virginia.

Yet another subversive secret organization, the Peace Society, operated in Alabama, Georgia, and Tennessee (it is not clear how or whether this group was related to the Peace and Constitutional Society). The Society seems to have been, by far, the most sophisticated of the dissident groups, with elaborate systems of recruitment, communication with the Union Army, and membership that included men serving in the Confederate Army and civilian officials of the Confederate government.

The details of the cooperation of these organizations with Union secret service units have thus far eluded historical investigation. ELIZABETH VAN LEW, who operated a secret intelligence network in Richmond, Virginia, for the Army of the Potomac throughout the war, seems to have been the leader of one such group in that city. It is likely that Gen. GRENVILLE M. DODGE's secret service of the Army of the Tennessee and the Department of Missouri had contacts with the Peace Society, but whether the agents and informers who worked for Dodge's chief of scouts, L.A. NARON, were part of an infrastructure organized by that Society is not known.

Though it remains unclear whether these organizations cooperated institutionally with Union intelligence, it is certain that they had a considerable negative effect on the Confederate war effort through the encouragement of draft-dodging and desertion. Nonetheless, the success of Southern subversives in reducing Confederate manpower seems to have been far smaller, even proportionally, than that of the Northern dissidents on the strength of the Union Army.

(*DAH;* Tatum, *Disloyalty in the Confederacy.*)

T

TACTICAL INTELLIGENCE

According to the Joint Chiefs of Staff's *Dictionary of Military and Associated Terms*, "intelligence which is required for the planning and conduct of tactical operations."

See STRATEGIC INTELLIGENCE.

(Hopple and Watson, *The Military Intelligence Community*.)

TALLMADGE, BENJAMIN (February 25, 1754–March 7, 1835): Army officer, congressman, intelligence officer

A native of Brookhaven, New York, Tallmadge graduated from Yale in 1773 and became superintendent of a high school in Wethersfield, Connecticut. He was commissioned a lieutenant in a Connecticut regiment in June 1776 and saw action during the AMERICAN REVOLUTION at the battles of Long Island, White Plains, Brandywine, Germantown, and Monmouth. In December 1776 he was commissioned as a captain in Col. Elisha Sheldon's Second Regiment of Light Dragoons in the Continental Army. He was commended by Gen. GEORGE WASHINGTON and Congress for his raid on Fort St. George, Long Island, in November 1780.

In 1778 Tallmadge recruited ABRAHAM WOODHILL of Setauket, Long Island, to serve as his principal secret intelligence agent and thereby began the establishment of what became known as the CULPER SPY RING. He continued to run the Culper ring through the end of the war, at which time he had been advanced to the rank of colonel.

Boatner, Ford, and many other writers characterize

Tallmadge as chief of Washington's secret service, but Constantinides joins a host of careful espionologists who point out that Washington himself was the chief of his own secret service, and Tallmadge was

Col. Benjamin Tallmadge. Source: Library of Congress.

but one of several case officers who ran the Culper ring and other networks.

Tallmadge played a crucial role in apprehending Maj. JOHN ANDRÉ and thereby discovering the treason of BENEDICT ARNOLD. He was in charge of André while the latter was a prisoner of the Continental Army, and developed a deep friendship for the condemned Englishman.

After the war Tallmadge was a businessman in Litchfield, Connecticut, where he became president of a bank and the town's first postmaster. He served as a congressman from Connecticut during 1801–1817.

(Who Was Who in America, historical volume; Boatner, Encyclopedia of the American Revolution; Tallmadge, Memoir of Colonel Benjamin Tallmadge; Constantinides, Intelligence and Espionage; Bakeless, Turncoats, Traitors and Heroes; Ford, A Peculiar Service; Pennypacker, General Washington's Spies On Long Island and in New York.)

TAYLOR, TELFORD (February 24, 1908–): lawyer, government official, writer, Army officer, intelligence officer

A native of Schenectady, New York, Taylor graduated from Williams College in 1928, and received an LL.B. from Harvard Law School in 1932. After serving as a law clerk for Judge Augustus Hand of the Second (New York) Court of Appeals, he entered government service and held a series of posts with the U.S. Department of the Interior, the Agricultural Adjustment Administration, the Senate Interstate Commerce Committee, the Department of Justice, and the Federal Communications Commission.

In October 1942 Taylor was commissioned as a major in the U.S. Army and assigned to the Military Intelligence Service of the War Department's General Staff (see ARMY INTELLIGENCE). He served in the SPECIAL BRANCH of MIS, which exploited highly sensitive communications intelligence. He was promoted to the rank of lieutenant colonel in March 1943, and the following May was made chief of the London office of the Special Branch and became responsible for the exchange of COMINT with British intelligence.

In June 1945 Taylor, who had been promoted to colonel, was assigned to the Office of the Chief Counsel of the international war crimes trials in Nuremburg, Germany. He worked with former U.S. Attorney General Robert H. Jackson and, in October 1946, succeeded him as chief prosecutor.

Taylor, who had been promoted to the rank of brigadier general in April 1946, returned to civilian life and the private practice of law in 1949. He became a professor at Columbia Law School in 1963. He has held several other public and educational posts, and has written extensively on the Nuremburg trials, the Second World War, and other subjects.

(Current Biography, 1948; Who's Who in America, 42nd ed.; Lewin, American Magic, Ultra Goes to War.)

THAYER, ROBERT HELYER (September 22, 1901–): lawyer, government official, diplomat, intelligence officer

A native of Southboro, Massachusetts, Thayer graduated from St. Mark's School in 1919, and attended Amherst College in 1918–19. He graduated from Harvard University in 1922 and from Harvard Law School in 1926, joining the New York law firm of Cadwalader, Wickersham and Taft the same year. In 1929 he joined Donovan, Leisure, Newton and Lumbard, the Wall Street law firm of WILLIAM J. DONOVAN, and he became a member of the firm in 1932. In 1937 he became an assistant district attorney for New York County, and the following year the chief of the indictment bureau.

In 1941 he was commissioned as a lieutenant commander in the U.S. Naval Reserve and discharged in 1945 with the rank of commander. In 1946 he was assistant New York State commissioner of housing and an unsuccessful candidate for Congress from Brooklyn, New York. Thayer returned to Cadwalader, Wickersham and Taft in 1947. In 1949 he became commissioner against discrimination in New York State, a post he held until 1951.

Thayer then served with the Central Intelligence Agency. He was chief of station in Paris, France, during 1951–54, and during 1954–55 he was the officer in charge of Western European affairs of the Operations Coordination Board, an interagency panel for the review of covert operations.

In 1955 Thayer was appointed U.S. minister to Romania, a post he held until 1958. He was assistant secretary of state during 1958–61, and later served as a consultant to the secretary of state. From 1961 to 1971 he served with the American Field Service International.

Thayer is a member of the Council on Foreign Relations.

(Smith, OSS; Who's Who in America, 43nd ed.)

THOMPSON, BENJAMIN (COUNT RUMFORD) (March 26, 1753–August 21, 1814): physicist, Army officer, government official, British secret agent

A native of Woburn, Massachusetts, Thompson served as an apprentice to a shopkeeper in Salem and taught school before marrying, at age nineteen, a wealthy widow several years his senior and settling on a farm at Rumford (now Concord), New Hampshire. In 1773 he was commissioned as a major in a New Hampshire provincial regiment.

As the American Revolution approached local self-appointed patriots accused Thompson of being unfriendly to the American cause. As a consequence he was persecuted and imprisoned for a time, and his application to Gen. GEORGE WASHINGTON for a commission in the Continental Army was denied. Whatever the original validity of the charges against him, he fulfilled them by becoming a British secret agent. Operating from his home in Woburn, Massachusetts (where the hostility of his New Hampshire neighbors had forced him to flee), he reported to Gen. Thomas Gage in Boston on the strength, condition, movements, and plans of the Continental Army.

Thompson served as a secret agent for only a few months. In October 1775 he fled to Boston. When the British evacuated the city the following March he sailed to England. In London he became the protégé and friend of British Secretary of State Lord George Germaine. He was appointed to the secretaryship of the province of Georgia in 1779, and was made under-secretary of state for the Northern Department in 1780. In 1781 Thompson was commissioned a lieutenant colonel in the British army. Returning to America, he saw action near Charleston, South Carolina, in 1782, and later commanded the Queen's Rangers, a Tory unit, on Long Island, and then a regiment, the King's American Dragoons, in New York City.

After the war Thompson returned to London where he was rewarded with a knighthood and a full colonelcy. Resolved to pursue the profession of arms despite British postwar demobilization, he traveled to the Continent and served in the Bavarian army, where he rose to the ranks of major general, privy councillor, court chamberlain, and minister of police and of war. He was created a count of the Holy Roman Empire and assumed the name Rumford, after his erstwhile home in New Hampshire. Thompson, however, is best known to history for his scientific work, which included disproving the caloric theory of heat and establishing that heat was a form of energy. He spent his last years in Paris, where he was married to the widow of the French scientist Antoine Lavoisier.

(*Who Was Who, in America*, historical volume; Bakeless, *Turncoats, Traitors and Heroes*; Einstein, *Divided Loyalties*.)

THOMPSON, EDMUND RANDALL (May 29, 1930–): Army officer, intelligence officer

A native of New Rochelle, New York, Thompson graduated from the U.S. Military Academy in 1952. He was commissioned as a second lieutenant in the Artillery and served with the U.S. Army in Korea during 1954–55. He earned an M.A. and Ph.D. in Geography from Syracuse University in 1959 and 1962, respectively, and was an instructor at West Point. He served in Vietnam and Cambodia in 1964.

Thompson later transferred to Military Intelligence (see ARMY INTELLIGENCE). During 1968–69 he was the G-2 of the Twenty-fifth Infantry Division in Vietnam. Later he was commander of the 116th Military Intelligence Group. He was promoted to the rank of brigadier general in 1975 and was commander of the U.S. Army Intelligence Agency during 1975–77. He became assistant chief of staff for intelligence, U.S. Army, in 1977 and held that post until 1981, a longer tenure than any previous incumbent. In November 1981 he was assigned to a senior post in the Defense Intelligence Agency, remaining there until his retirement from the Army with the rank of major general in April 1984.

Since his retirement Thompson has been active in the National Military Intelligence Association and the Association of Former Intelligence Officers. He is a student of the intelligence and espionage of the American Revolution.

Thompson was decorated with the Distinguished Service Medal, Legion of Merit, Bronze Star, Meritorious Service Medal, Air Medal, and Commendation medal.

(*Who's Who in America*, 42nd ed.)

THOMPSON, JACOB (May 15, 1810–March 24, 1885): lawyer, congressman, government official, Confederate army officer and secret service agent

A native of Leasburg, North Carolina, Thompson graduated from the University of North Carolina in 1831. He practiced law in Pantotoc, Mississippi, and served as a congressman from Mississippi during 1839–51. Active in the Democratic Party, he played an important part in the Democratic National Conventions of 1854 and 1856. He was secretary of the Interior under President James Buchanan during 1857–61.

Thompson served in the Confederate Army as chief inspector under Lt. Gen. John Pemberton until 1863. In that year he was elected to the Mississippi legislature, and the following year Confederate Pres-

Jacob Thompson. Source: Author's collection.

ident Jefferson Davis sent him to Canada to serve as chief of a three-man quasi-diplomatic commission (the other members were Clement C. Clay and James P. Holcombe). He was, in fact, the chief Confederate secret service agent in Canada, and his main assignment was to foment revolution in Indiana, Illinois, and Ohio, in order to split those states off from the Union and the Northern war effort (see NORTHWEST CONSPIRACY).

Thompson also undertook other COVERT ACTION operations against the Union. In one, an economic operation, he sent an agent to New York with instructions to purchase gold. The gold was shipped to England where it was sold for sterling bills of exchange that were converted into dollars and sent back to the agent in New York to buy more gold. In this way Thompson arranged for the export of $5 million worth of gold at an overhead cost (i.e., shipment and handling) of $25,000. This artificially created demand drove gold prices up, prompted people to convert their paper money into gold, and created a mild panic in Northern gold markets. Thompson

did not achieve his ultimate objective of destabilizing the Northern economy, however, because federal authorities intervened and put an end to the gold export operation.

Thompson mounted a "gray propaganda" operation (see COVERT ACTION) by bribing the editor of the *New York Daily News* to publish anti-war editorials. He also provided financial support to anti-war candidates in the national elections of 1864.

Thompson lived in Canada and Europe after the war, returning to his home in Oxford, Mississippi, in 1868. In 1865 the military court that tried the eight defendants charged with the conspiracy in the assassination of President Lincoln indicted Thompson for complicity in the case (see LINCOLN CONSPIRACY). Most of the evidence presented against him was fraudulent; the rest was circumstantial. The government made no further effort to prosecute him after his return to the United States in 1868.

(*Who Was Who in America*, historical volume; Horan, *Confederate Agent*; Roscoe, *The Web of Conspiracy*; Stern, *Secret Missions of the Civil War*.)

THUERMER, ANGUS MACLEAN (July 17, 1917–): journalist, diplomat, intelligence officer

A native of Quincy, Illinois, Thuermer graduated from the University of Illinois in 1938 and did postgraduate study at the Kaiser Friederich Wilhelm University in Berlin in 1939. He worked for the Associated Press as a foreign correspondent during 1939–42, and as an editor in Chicago during 1946–50, and in Washington, D.C. during 1951–52. Thuermer studied at Harvard University in 1951, joined the U.S. Foreign Service in 1952, and was vice-consul in Bombay, India, during 1953–58. He served with the State Department in Washington during 1958–61, and was political officer at the American embassy in Accra, Ghana, during 1961–64. He served as political officer at the embassies in Munich, West Germany, and New Delhi, India, during 1964–67 and 1967–71, respectively.

In 1971 Thuermer became assistant to the director of central intelligence, who was then RICHARD M. HELMS. He served as the spokesman to the press for the Central Intelligence Agency, continuing in that post through JAMES SCHLESINGER's and WILLIAM E. COLBY's terms as directors of Central Intelligence.

(*Who's Who in Government*, 2nd ed.)

THYRAUD DE VOSJOLI, PHILIPPE L. (ca. 1921–): French intelligence officer

A native of France, Thyraud de Vosjoli was living with his parents in 1940 in the small town of Romorantin within the German-occupied zone when he joined the French underground and began smuggling Jewish refugees to the relative safety of the Vichy-controlled zone. His activities eventually became known to the Gestapo and he was forced to flee the country. In December 1943, after a period of imprisonment in Spain and service in the French army in Morocco, he joined the Bureau Central de Renseignement et d'Action (Central Bureau of Intelligence and Action), the intelligence service of the Free French under Gen. Charles de Gaulle.

Thyraud de Vosjoli served throughout the war in the BCRA and its successor agency, the Direction Générale des Études et Recherches (Central Agency for Studies and Research). In Algiers and later in London he was chief of its Far East and Western Hemisphere section. After the war he remained with the French intelligence service, which began operating under yet another name, the Service de Documentation Extérieure et de Contre-Espionage.

In 1951 Thyraud de Vosjoli was sent to Washington to serve as the SDECE's liaison officer with the Central Intelligence Agency and the Federal Bureau of Investigation. During 1951–54 he established intelligence networks in several Caribbean and Central American countries, including Cuba, aimed at monitoring Soviet intelligence activities in those areas.

In July 1962 Thyraud de Vosjoli's networks in Cuba apprised him of the Soviet military buildup that led to the CUBAN MISSILE CRISIS. After a trip to Cuba he was able to advise CIA Director JOHN A. MCCONE of the likelihood that the Soviet Union had introduced offensive nuclear weapons to the island. This information may have been the basis for McCone's early disagreement with CIA National Estimates discounting the possibility of such a Soviet move.

Soon after the missile crisis Thyraud de Vosjoli was ordered to terminate his Cuban networks, and in September of 1963 he was ordered to end his liaison functions in Washington and return to France. He attributed both of these developments to Soviet penetration of the SDECE in particular and the De Gaulle government in general, a situation of which he had already seen evidence. Further, he was convinced that his life would be in jeopardy if he returned to France. He therefore resigned from the SDECE and remained in the United States.

Thyraud de Vosjoli's role in the Cuban missile crisis was dramatized by Leon Uris in his novel *Topaz*.

(Thyraud de Vosjoli, *Lamia;* Powers, *The Man Who Kept the Secrets.*)

TIBET OPERATION

Background: In 1951 Tibet, over which China had held suzerainty since 1907, was invaded and occupied by Red Chinese troops. The fierce opposition of the Tibetans was crushed, and the Dalai Lama, Tibet's traditional ruler, was forced to sign an agreement in Peking incorporating Tibet into China as an autonomous region. According to this arrangement, China was to be responsible for Tibet's foreign affairs, but there was to be a (theoretically) independent internal Tibetan government. Many of the Khamba tribesmen of Tibet, who had resisted the Chinese most fiercely, fled into India, Nepal, and Thailand.

The Operation: Circa 1953 the Central Intelligence Agency recruited some of the Khamba refugees, trained them as intelligence agents, and sent them back into Tibet to assess the political situation and the possibility of reversing the Chinese Communist takeover. Some agents, equipped with clandestine radio transmitters, provided a communication channel between the Dalai Lama and the CIA. The Agency also supported Tibetan guerrillas within the country who were harassing the Chinese occupation force. Civil Air Transport, an Agency AIR PROPRIETARY, was used to airdrop guerrillas and supplies into the country. Many of the guerrillas were brought to the United States and given training in mountain fighting at a secret CIA base at Camp Hale, a disused U.S. Army installation high in the Rocky Mountains near Leadville, Colorado.

In 1959 the Chinese moved to replace the Dalai Lama with the twenty-one-year-old Panchen Lama, a Tibetan leader more docile and sympathetic to the Communist occupation. An uprising ensued, which Chinese troops crushed. The Dalai Lama, accompanied by some of the CIA-trained agents and guerrillas, fled to India. He was joined there by several thousand of his followers, including a force of Khamba troops. With his departure, the Chinese dissolved the Dalai Lama's government and installed the Panchen Lama in his place. The move provoked a general uprising against the Chinese throughout Tibet.

The CIA stepped up its support for the Tibetan forces. This included the training at Camp Hale and logistical supply (through Civil Air Transport and another CIA Air Proprietary, Air Ventures) of the guerrillas, and the occasional participation of CIA contract paramilitary specialists who entered Tibet to lead the operations (see ANTHONY A. POE).

The Tibetan guerrillas focused their effort on communications and the two major roads linking China and Tibet, using land mines and ambushes to impede the flow of support to the Chinese occupation. The Chinese responded with a massive counterattack, and the fighting spilled across the Tibetan borders into India, Bhutan, and Sikkim. The CIA-supported guerrillas did not succeed in driving the Chinese from their country, but their efforts brought unfavorable world attention to the Chinese government (e.g., the UN voted to express its grave concern over the Chinese suppression of human rights in Tibet). The Chinese tightened their grip on Tibet, replacing the Panchen Lama with a secular government in 1964. During the Cultural Revolution in China in 1966, the Chinese Red Guards overran the country, destroying temples and trying to eradicate all vestiges of the traditional religion and culture of Tibet.

CIA-supported guerrilla operations continued sporadically throughout the 1960s and were eventually terminated. By some accounts the operation fell victim to the deemphasis of COVERT ACTION within the U.S. government following the failure of the BAY OF PIGS INVASION.

According to Victor Marchetti, a former senior CIA official who was serving with the Agency at the time, the operation was undertaken for the purpose of harassing the Chinese, and without any realistic expectation of achieving larger goals. But HARRY ROSITZKE, who was chief of the CIA station in New Delhi during 1957–62 (i.e., the senior CIA officer in India during much of the Tibet Operation), implied in his memoirs that destabilizing the Chinese occupation of Tibet had been the aim, albeit an unrealistic one, of the operation.

(Marchetti and Marks, *The CIA and the Cult of Intelligence*; Rositzke, *The CIA's Secret Operations*; Robbins, *Air America*; Wise, *The Politics of Lying*.)

TINKER, CHARLES ALMERIN (January 8, 1838–March 12, 1916): telegrapher, businessman, cryptanalyst

A native of Chelsea, Vermont, Tinker was raised in Michigan where he attended local schools. He learned telegraphy and worked as a telegrapher for several railroads and telegraph companies. At the outbreak of the CIVIL WAR he entered the War Department's Military Telegraph Service, and served in the field as a telegrapher for the Army of the Potomac. He was later assigned to the War Department's telegraph office in Washington.

ALBERT B. CHANDLER, DAVID HOMER BATES, and Tinker were the self-styled "Sacred Three," the principal telegraphers in the War Department's tele-

graph office during the CIVIL WAR. In addition to sending and receiving telegrams, and enciphering and deciphering some of them, they were occasionally called upon to solve intercepted Confederate cryptograms, and they achieved some success in doing so (see WIRETAPPING AND COMMUNICATIONS INTELLIGENCE IN THE CIVIL WAR).

At the end of the war Tinker was placed in charge of the demobilization of the Military Telegraph Service and the return of its facilities to private telegraph companies. Thereafter he became manager of the Washington office of the Western Union Telegraph Company, a post he held until 1872. He subsequently held supervisory positions in several telegraph companies and railroads. He was one of the founders, along with millionaire Jay Gould, of the American Union Telegraph Company.

(*National Cyclopedia of American Biography*, v. 2; Kahn, *The Codebreakers*; Harlow, *Old Wires and New Waves*.)

TIROS RECONNAISSANCE SATELLITE

TIROS (Television and Infra-Red Observation Satellite) was one of the earliest U.S. reconnaissance satellite programs. Sponsored by the U.S. Army beginning in the late 1950s, the TIROS program was aimed at developing an orbiting surveillance platform equipped with television cameras to photograph the earth's surface, and a transmitter to send the pictures back to a ground station.

Before it became operational the TIROS program was reoriented from intelligence-gathering to meteorological work (e.g., the photography of cloud formations) and was transferred to NASA. The first TIROS was orbited in April 1960.

The program was subsequently turned over to the Weather Bureau (later known as National Weather Service), where it developed into the now-familiar weather satellite program.

(Klass, *Secret Sentries in Space*; Taylor and Mondey, *Spies in the Sky*.)

TOFTE, HANS V. (ca. 1912–August 24, 1987): intelligence officer

A native of Copenhagen, Denmark, Tofte joined the East Asiatic Company, a Danish shipping firm, at age nineteen. He was sent to Peking circa 1930 to learn Chinese as the first step in a planned lifetime career with the firm. After two years in Peking he was transferred to Kirin, Manchuria, where he spent most of the next eight years, and from where he made frequent trips through China and northern Korea.

Tofte returned to Denmark at the outbreak of the Second World War and served briefly in the anti-German Danish underground. He made his way to the United States and was recruited in New York City by WILLIAM STEPHENSON, then chief of the British Secret Intelligence Service in America. Tofte went to Singapore for the SIS with the rank of major in the Indian army (India was then still a British possession). He established operations to supply Chinese forces fighting the Japanese and organized guerrilla forces to assist them. After the fall of Singapore he returned to the United States.

Tofte enlisted in the U.S. Army and, because of his background and fluency in several languages, including Chinese and Russian, he was assigned to the Office of Strategic Services. Tofte served in the OSS SPECIAL OPERATIONS BRANCH in Cairo, Egypt, and received parachute training in Palestine. In October 1943 he organized a small flotilla of schooners and trawlers that transported arms and supplies across the Adriatic and through the German blockade to the partisans in Yugoslavia. The operation also supported anti-Nazi partisans in Albania.

The following summer Tofte was in the OSS SECRET INTELLIGENCE BRANCH in London, England. He was deputy chief of the Division of Intelligence Procurement, a unit created by London OSS SI chief WILLIAM CASEY for the purpose of carrying out espionage operations in Germany. From an American air base in Dijon, France, Tofte dispatched agents by air into Nazi-occupied Germany. He was discharged from the Army with the rank of major.

After the war Tofte returned to Denmark where he worked as traffic manager for American Overseas Airlines. A few years later he married an American woman and moved to Mason City, Iowa, to run his in-laws' printing business. He joined the U.S. Army Reserve and, with the outbreak of the Korean War in June 1950, accepted an assignment to the Central Intelligence Agency.

Tofte served in the Office of Policy Coordination, as the Agency's COVERT ACTION department was called. He was assigned to the Far East Division and was chief of covert action operations in Japan, Korea, and China. His initial task was to establish an escape-and-evasion network to assist American airmen brought down in enemy territory, and to begin organizing guerrilla warfare operations in North Korea. He established six CIA bases in Japan, the major one housed on the U.S. Naval Air Station at Atsugi, fifty miles south of Tokyo.

Tofte recruited guerrillas from among the thousands of North Koreans who had been evacuated to refugee camps around Pusan, South Korea. He selected hundreds of young men from among them for guerrilla training at a CIA base on Yong-do Island, off the South Korean coast. By December 1951 he had sent forty-four guerrilla teams (a total of 1,200 men) into North Korea. They operated south of the Yalu River from Antung in the west to Rashin and Yuki in the northeast (an area with which Tofte happened to be familiar from his days in China with the East Asiatic Company), sabotaging trains, ambushing truck convoys, and disrupting the flow of supplies from Manchuria and eastern Siberia to the Communist forces fighting in Korea. Tofte also ran Operation Tropic, the support of "third force" guerrillas (i.e., anti-Communists not affiliated with the Nationalist Chinese regime on Taiwan) on the Chinese mainland.

Tofte remained with the CIA CLANDESTINE SERVICE, moving on to the Western Hemisphere Division. He served in Argentina in the 1950s, and later in Colombia where he supervised a CIA project to train government forces in the use of helicopters in counterinsurgency operations. In the mid-1960s he served in the newly formed Domestic Operations Division.

In 1966 Tofte, living in Washington, offered to rent a basement apartment in his house to a recently recruited CIA employee. The recruit noticed classified CIA documents in the house—a violation of Agency security regulations—and reported it to the CIA's director of security. A CIA security officer visited the house the next day and obtained entry through a pretext offered to Tofte's elderly mother-in-law. He removed the classified documents and returned them to CIA headquarters.

Tofte charged that some $30,000 worth of jewelry had also been removed during the officer's visit and took legal action against the Agency. The affair was soon a public embarrassment to the Agency and Tofte was discharged in September 1966.

(Persico, *Piercing the Reich;* Smith, *OSS;* Cave Brown, *The Last Hero;* Goulden, *Korea;* Leary, *Perilous Missions;* Smith, *Portrait of a Cold Warrior;* Powers, *The Man Who Kept the Secrets;* obituary, *New York Times,* August 28, 1987, p. A17.)

TOMPKINS, PETER (April 29, 1919–): writer, journalist, intelligence officer

Tompkins was born in the United States but raised in Italy, where his parents lived as expatriates. He attended Stowe School in Buckinghamshire, England, and Harvard University. In 1939 he left Harvard to work as a war correspondent in Rome for the *New York Herald Tribune,* and later for the Mutual

Broadcasting System in Italy and the National Broadcasting System in Greece.

In 1941 Tompkins joined the Office of the Coordinator of Information, the predecessor of the Office of Strategic Services, and he continued with that agency when it became the OSS in 1942. At first Tompkins was attached to the Anglo-American Psychological Warfare Branch at Allied headquarters in Algiers in 1943, but his fluency in Italian and familiarity with Italy prompted the OSS SECRET INTELLIGENCE BRANCH to tap him for a parachute mission into Italy.

Though the mission was cancelled, Tompkins remained involved in OSS Italian operations. He took part in Operation MacGregor (see JOHN SHAHEEN) and served as an assistant to DONALD DOWNES in Naples, recruiting anti-Fascist Italians for espionage missions into northern Italy. In mid-January 1944 he was selected by Gen. WILLIAM J. DONOVAN to undertake a secret mission to Rome—then still occupied by the Germans—to coordinate the intelligence and sabotage operations of the partisans with the planned Allied landings at Anzio and the advance on Rome.

Tompkins landed on the Italian coast some forty miles from Rome on the night of January 21–22, and was met by the partisans. Arriving in the city he made contact with the several underground groups active there, but soon discovered his task was complicated by the failure of the OSS Italian headquarters to clarify his authority to other OSS elements operating in German-occupied Italy. This situation worsened when the Allied advance was stalled immediately after the Anzio landings on January 22nd.

On March 17th German counterespionage officers discovered the clandestine radio station Tompkins was using to communicate with OSS Headquarters, and several of the partisans working with Tompkins were arrested. Tompkins was forced to flee, moving from place to place in Rome, one step ahead of the Germans. He survived through the audacious decision to enlist in the Fascist Italian African Police under an alias. He later deserted from that organization, but remained in Rome until the city was liberated by the Allies on June 4. On June 3rd, as the Allies approached, Tompkins prevailed upon the Italian army authorities to prevent sabotage by the retreating Germans. He later discovered that none of the intelligence reports he had sent back to OSS Headquarters over the clandestine radio had been circulated or used, and that, consequently, his mission had largely been a waste. He later served in Germany with the OSS.

Tompkins became a writer after the war, and he has published books on such various subjects as George Bernard Shaw, Mexican archeology, and his wartime experiences.

(*Contemporary Authors*, New Revision Series, v. 12; Tompkins, *A Spy in Rome*; Smith, *OSS*; Cave Brown, *The Last Hero*.)

TORDELLA, LOUIS WILLIAM (May 1, 1911–): Navy officer, mathematician, cryptologist, intelligence officer

A native of Garrett, Indiana, Tordella graduated from Loyola University in Chicago, from which he also earned a master's degree, and he earned a doctorate in mathematics from the University of Illinois. He became a member of the Loyola mathematics faculty. In 1935 he joined the University of Illinois faculty, where he taught mathematics until 1942.

In 1942 Tordella was commissioned as an officer in the U.S. Navy, assigned to cryptologic duties with the Navy Security Group and rose to the rank of lieutenant commander. After the war he worked as a civilian employee of the Navy Department and was involved in the formation of the Armed Forces Security Agency and its successor, the National Security Agency.

Tordella was the first NSA employee selected to attend the National War College, where he studied during 1953–54. In 1958 he became deputy director of NSA, the senior civilian post in that agency. He held the job until his retirement in 1974, the longest tenure of any deputy director.

(Bamford, *The Puzzle Palace*; Kahn, *The Codebreakers*.)

TOWNSEND, ROBERT (ca. 1754–March 7, 1838): businessman, journalist, American espionage agent

The son of a merchant of Oyster Bay, Long Island, Townsend became a partner in Oakman and Townsend, a dry goods business in New York City, in 1779. He also worked as a writer for JAMES RIVINGTON's New York Tory newspaper, *The Royal Gazette*.

Townsend's true allegiance was to the Patriots, however, and he worked as an espionage agent for Gen. GEORGE WASHINGTON, and was a charter member and principal agent of the CULPER SPY RING. Washington, who never met him, knew him only by his pseudonym, "Samuel Culper, Jr."

As a New York merchant, Townsend was well-situated to collect military intelligence regarding the British forces occupying the city. His affiliation with the Tory *Gazette* provided him additional espionage opportunities, as well as a cover. (He was also a silent partner in Rivington's Wall Street coffee shop, where the printer apparently gathered intelligence by listening to the conversations of its military clientele.) And the fact that his father lived in Oyster Bay gave him an excuse for frequent trips to Long Island, where he reported to "Samuel Culper, Sr.," i.e., ABRAHAM WOODHULL, at Setauket (although Townsend's reports were usually carried to Woodhull by Culper Ring courier Austin Roe).

Townsend's common-law wife, known to history only by her communication code number, 355, was also a member of the Culper Ring. Townsend was also aided in his espionage by his younger sister, Sarah, who attracted the amorous attentions of British intelligence officer Maj. JOHN ANDRÉ, and so may have had the benefit of information André occasionally let slip.

For some as yet undiscovered reason, Townsend resigned from the Culper Ring sometime in the winter of 1779–80, but he resumed his work after a few months upon the urging of Woodhull.

After the war Townsend sold his dry goods business and retired to live in Oyster Bay. His wish that his espionage role remain secret was honored by Woodhull and Maj. BENJAMIN TALLMADGE, the only persons who knew of it. It remained unknown until discovered in the 1930s by historian and espionologist Morton Pennypacker through handwriting identification.

Townsend's son by his common-law marriage, Robert Jr., became a member of the New York State legislature.

(Ford, *A Peculiar Service;* Bakeless, *Turncoats, Traitors and Heroes;* Pennypacker, *General Washington's Spies.*)

TRADECRAFT

The methods of the covert operator. The term includes the techniques of surveillance and countersurveillance, and communications between CASE OFFICERS and AGENTS. It is also used to include certain technical specialties, e.g., wiretapping, lockpicking, and alarm neutralization. In general, tradecraft is the sum total of the skills the case officer or agent must master in order to operate in the field.

TRUDEAU, ARTHUR GILBERT (July 5, 1902–): Army officer, engineer, businessman, intelligence officer

A native of Middlebury, Vermont, Trudeau graduated from the U.S. Military Academy in 1924. He served in the Army Corps of Engineers and earned an M.S. in civil engineering from the University of California in 1928. During the 1930s he served in the Works Projects Administration in New York City and supervised river and harbor construction in the Pacific Northwest and Alaska. He held a variety of engineering and staff positions during the Second World War and saw duty in Australia, North Africa, Europe, and the Philippines.

After the war Trudeau served on a war crimes commission in Japan. During 1948–50 he commanded the 1st Constabulary Brigade in West Germany. During the Korean War he commanded the Seventh Infantry Division and was decorated for his heroism in the battle of Pork Chop Hill.

From 1953 to 1955 Trudeau was assistant chief of staff for intelligence, i.e., chief of ARMY INTELLIGENCE. While serving in this post he directed a study of repatriated American prisoners of war who had been subjected to Communist brainwashing while in North Korean or Chinese captivity during the Korean War. This study led to the issuance of the Code of Conduct for members of the armed forces in combat and captivity.

According to Blackstock, Trudeau was embroiled in a dispute with CIA Director ALLEN DULLES growing out of his private conversations with West German Chancellor Konrad Adenauer during the latter's visit to the United States in 1954. Blackstock reports that Trudeau expressed his concern to Adenauer that the Gehlen Organization (the West German intelligence organization that worked for the CIA during the late 1940s and 1950s) had been penetrated by Soviet agents, and that Dulles's objections to Trudeau's intervention in the matter led to his removal from his Army Intelligence post by President Eisenhower. However, CIA intelligence officers familiar with the affair claim that Blackstock has exaggerated it, that it was a minor issue, and it was not the reason that Trudeau's term as chief of Army Intelligence came to an end.

In 1958 Trudeau was made chief of the Army Research and Development Command. He held that post until his retirement in 1962. After his retirement from the Army he served as president of the Gulf Research and Development Company.

Trudeau was awarded numerous decorations during his military career, including the Legion of Merit, the Distinguished Service Medal, the Air Medal, the Silver Star, and the Bronze Star.

(*Current Biography,* 1958; *Who's Who in America,* v. 34; De Gramont, *The Secret War;* Blackstock, *The Strategy of Subversion;* Constantinides, *Intelligence and Espionage.*)

TRUESDAIL, WILLIAM (?–1886): law enforcement officer, banker, businessman, intelligence officer

Before the Civil War Truesdail was a banker and real estate speculator in Erie, Pennsylvania, where he had also served as a deputy sheriff and police justice and earned a reputation as an effective investigator of fraud and embezzlement.

During the war Truesdail served under Union Gen. William S. Rosecrans as chief of police of the Army of the Mississippi in 1862 and of the Army of the Cumberland in 1862–63. Although he was addressed as "colonel," Truesdail held a civilian post that included the functions of intelligence collection and counterespionage.

Truesdail ran a small but effective network of scouts, secret service agents, and informers, which included PHILIP HENSON and PAULINE CUSHMAN.

(Bakeless, *Spies of the Confederacy*; Kane, *Spies for the Blue and Gray*; Bryan, *The Spy in America*.)

TRUSCOTT, LUCIAN KING 2nd (January 9, 1895–September 12, 1965): Army officer, paramilitary specialist, intelligence officer

A native of Chatfield, Texas, Truscott grew up there and in Oklahoma. After several years teaching school in Oklahoma, he enlisted in the Army in 1917. He attended officers' training camp, was commissioned as a second lieutenant of cavalry, and advanced through grades to lieutenant colonel by 1936.

During the Second World War, Truscott served with the British commandos under Lord Louis Mountbatten. Then, using the techniques learned from the British, he recruited and trained a brigade of U.S. Army Rangers. In August 1942 he led his Rangers in a joint Anglo-American raid across the English Channel on the French port of Dieppe. In November of that year he led a special task force in the capture of Port Lyautey, French Morocco, during the Allied landings in North Africa.

Truscott, in the rank of temporary major general, later commanded the Third Infantry Division in the landings in Sicily and at Anzio. He commanded the Sixth Corps during the landings on the French coast, and the Fifth Army during the attack across the Po Valley in Italy in the spring of 1945. In October of that year he succeeded General Patton in command of the Third Army in occupation duty in Bavaria. He was awarded many decorations in recognition of his heroism during the war, including the Distinguished Service Medal, the Legion of Merit, the Purple Heart, and the French croix de guerre. He retired from the Army in 1947.

Truscott then served with the Central Intelligence Agency. In 1951 Director WALTER BEDELL SMITH appointed him the CIA CLANDESTINE SERVICE chief of station in West Germany. The station, at that time the focus of the Clandestine Service's major area of operations, consisted of some 1,200 persons. Truscott served as umpire during the merger, then in progress, of the West German components of the Office of Policy Coordination and Office of Special Operations (see CENTRAL INTELLIGENCE AGENCY), and worked to resolve jurisdictional conflicts with Army Intelligence, which was also active in the area.

In 1954 President Eisenhower appointed Truscott to the job of resolving jurisdictional disputes between the CIA and the military intelligence services. Truscott reportedly also served in the capacity of Eisenhower's unofficial watchdog of the CIA, reporting directly to the President on planned COVERT ACTION. According to Corson, Truscott was effective in thwarting ill-considered plans to assassinate Communist Chinese leader Chou En-lai and to foment Eastern European uprisings in the late 1950s, which the United States was not in a position to support militarily.

(WAMB; *Who Was Who in America*, v. 4; Corson, *Armies of Ignorance*; Powers, *The Man Who Kept the Secrets*; Cline, *The CIA: Reality vs. Myth*.)

TRUTH DRUGS

The search for a potion that can compel a person to speak the truth is as old as history. For centuries the only substance to come close to filling this requirement was alcohol, the tongue-loosening properties of which were well-known in antiquity. In the first century, A.D., Pliny the Elder observed: "It has become quite a common proverb that in wine there is truth."

In vino veritas seems to have remained the only prescription for a truth drug (in the West, at least) until the nineteenth century. At the close of the Civil War Charles E. Cady, a surgeon who had served with the 138th Pennsylvania Volunteers reported:

> During an experience of 3 years in the Army, I have upon numerous occasions procured from Rebel officers and soldiers much important information while they were partly under the influence of chloroform. . . . Pure unadulterated chloroform should be used—such as in use in the Army—it should be carefully but rapidly administered; & while the patient is semi-

anaesthetized he should be questioned bluntly and pointedly.

Cady discovered a principle fundamental to most subsequent use of drugs in interrogation: in a condition of "twilight sleep," a subject's ability to withhold information from an interrogator is greatly weakened.

In 1922, Dr. Robert House, a Dallas, Texas, physician, experimented with the use of scopolamine, a narcotic alkaloid obtained from plants of the nightshade family, in the interrogation of criminal suspects. However, scopolamine was found to have several undesirable side effects, especially the production of hallucinations.

Late in 1941, researchers at the office of the Coordinator of Information, the predecessor of the Office of Strategic Services, experimented with scopolamine and a combination of scopolamine and morphine as truth drugs in intelligence investigations. However, the research was temporarily suspended when the drugs were judged to be too dangerous.

In September 1942 the research was resumed by OSS Director of Research and Development STANLEY LOVELL. Lovell and his associates undertook to find a substance meeting these requirements:

1) It must be administered without the subject's knowledge; 2) It must induce a talkative mood and if possible a full exposé of the truth, as the subject knew the truth; 3) It must not be habit-forming or physiologically harmful; 4) It must leave no remembrance or suspicion of any kind.

Scores of drugs were tested, singly and in combination, including mescaline, various barbiturates, scopolamine, benzadrine, and marijuana. The only substance that showed any promise of meeting the OSS requirements was tetrahydrocannabinol acetate, a derivative of marijuana, which could be covertly administered to a subject in his food or cigarettes. Lovell described the effects of the drug:

A few minutes after administration, the subject gradually becomes relaxed, and experiences a sensation of well-being. In a few minutes this state passes into one in which thoughts flow with considerable freedom, and in which conversation becomes animated and accelerated. Inhibitions fall away, and the subjects talk with abandon and indiscretion. During this talkative and irresponsible period, which lasts from one to two hours, skillful interrogation usually elicits information which would not be revealed under other circumstances.

The experiments were done on Army enlisted men who believed they had volunteered to participate in a search for a shell-shock remedy. OSS officer George H. White also tried out the drug on an unwitting New York gangster, August "Little Augie" Del Gaizo, a notorious drug smuggler and dealer who prided himself on the fact that he would never inform on his partners in crime. But White reported that, under the influence of the drug, Little Augie reeled off a long, detailed account of the operations of the mob, complete with names, dates, places, and other particulars. White reported:

All of [Little Augie's revelations] could be damaging to the subject, and is a class of information that subject would never give under ordinary circumstances. There is no question but that the administration of the drug was responsible for loosening the subject's tongue.

Summarizing the OSS experiments with tetrahydrocannabinol acetate, Lovell reported:

The treatment is by no means a magic key to the secrets of the mind, but it does constitute an assistance to interrogation of inestimable value to the government of the United States. Certain disclosures of the greatest value are in the possession of our military intelligence as a result of this treatment, which it is felt would otherwise not be known. It is believed that use of this method under proper secrecy and only on problems involving the vital interests of our country will further confirm this preliminary conclusion. Properly employed . . . it may be a national asset of incalculable importance.

Apparently the drug was put into operational use by the OSS, possibly in the interrogation of captured German submarine crews, but the program was terminated by OSS chief Gen. WILLIAM J. DONOVAN, who may have feared that any leak of the operation would be used by Germany to justify the use of drugs on American POWs.

In 1950 the Central Intelligence Agency resumed truth-drug experiments as part of its behavior control program. The CIA researchers experimented with sodium pentothal and tetrahydrocannabinol, LSD, and possibly other drugs. Between 1955 and 1958, as part of the research program LSD and marijuana were tested on child molesters and other criminal sexual psychopaths incarcerated at the Ionia State Hospital in Michigan. The theory underlying this experimental program was that the reluctance of such individuals to confess their crimes was closely analogous to the resolve of a captured agent to resist interrogation.

Whatever success the Agency may have achieved in such programs, it apparently fell short of the

Adm. Stansfield Turner—oil portrait by William F. Draper. Source: Central Intelligence Agency.

discovery of a completely reliable and effective truth drug. One case that has been cited as evidence of the limitations of such drugs is that of Uri Nosenko, a Soviet defector who was subjected to three years of continuous interrogation by the CIA. His disclosures nonetheless remain a matter of contention within the Agency.

(Freedman, "'Truth' Drugs"; Cave Brown, *The Last Hero;* Marks, *The Search for the "Manchurian Candidate".*)

TURNER, STANSFIELD (December 1, 1923–): Navy officer, intelligence officer

A native of Highland Park, Illinois, Turner attended Amherst College during 1941–43 and graduated from the U.S. Naval Academy in 1946. A Rhodes scholar, he attended Oxford University, from which he received a master's degree in 1950.

During his career as a naval officer he commanded a mine sweeper, a destroyer, a guided-missile cruiser, and a carrier task group. He served as president of the Naval War College during 1972–74, commanded the U.S. Second Fleet during 1974–75, and was commander and chief of NATO forces in southern Europe when he was appointed director of central intelligence by President Carter in 1977.

Turner succeeded GEORGE BUSH as DCI at a time when the CENTRAL INTELLIGENCE AGENCY and the rest of the INTELLIGENCE COMMUNITY were recovering from the ordeal of the congressional investigations of 1975–76, and trying to repair the damage resulting therefrom. Turner's lack of experience as a professional intelligence officer, and the perception within the intelligence community that President Carter was hostile toward the CIA, did not help the process of recovery. Turner understood and managed technical intelligence operations effectively, but some intelligence "insiders" felt he did not deal equally well with the activities of the CIA CLANDESTINE SERVICE. Observers also point out that vital liaison with friendly foreign intelligence services, which had been badly jeopardized by the leaks and disclosures of the congressional investigating committees, might have been repaired more effectively by a DCI with a background in clandestine operations.

Turner's differences with his deputy director of central intelligence, veteran CIA officer E. HENRY KNOCHE, led him to replace Knoche with FRANK C. CARLUCCI, another "outsider." Turner further isolated himself from the CIA "insiders" by appointing Robert "Rusty" Williams, a civilian without intelligence experience who had worked with him at the Naval War College, as his special assistant, and by bringing in other naval officers without intelligence backgrounds to serve in senior staff positions.

In October 1977 Turner reduced the size of the Clandestine Service by abolishing 820 positions, an action that involved the early retirement of 147 officers and the discharge of an additional seventeen. This reduction in force, which became known as the "Halloween massacre" because it was done at the end of October, removed virtually all of the OSS veterans and other "charter members" who had served in the Agency since its earliest years. It was seen in the Agency and throughout the government as a purge of the senior clandestine operators, and it adversely affected CIA morale and Turner's relations with veteran CIA officials.

Turner's tenure as DCI was not regarded as unremittingly negative by intelligence "insiders," however. For example, he is praised for having established the National Intelligence Council. This unit is similar in concept to the Board of National Estimates, which Director WILLIAM E. COLBY abolished, a move that many experienced intelligence analysts regard as a mistake.

President Reagan appointed WILLIAM CASEY to succeed Turner in January 1981. Turner has since worked as a private consultant, lecturer, writer, and television commentator on national security matters, and serves on the boards of directors of several corporations. He holds the Distinguished Intelligence Medal, the Distinguished Service Medal, the Legion of Merit, and the Bronze Star.

(*Who's Who in America*, 42nd edition; Cline, *CIA: Reality vs. Myth*; Ranelagh, *The Agency*; Turner, *Secrecy and Democracy*.)

U

U-2, reconnaissance aircraft

The U-2 was developed to meet the continuing requirements of the Central Intelligence Agency for strategic intelligence on the Soviet Union after the agent air-dispatch program was terminated in the early 1950s (see CENTRAL INTELLIGENCE AGENCY). Advances in photographic technology had made possible the collection of useful intelligence by aerial reconnaissance flights at altitudes beyond the effective ceilings of Soviet intercepter aircraft. What the CIA now required was a reconnaissance aircraft that could attain such altitudes and maintain them over routes several thousand miles long.

The U-2 program, jointly funded by the CIA and the U.S. Air Force, was managed by CIA officer RICHARD M. BISSELL. The aircraft was designed and developed by C.L. ("KELLY") JOHNSON at the Lockheed Aircraft Company's "Skunk Works" in Burbank, California.

Johnson began work on the plane in the spring of 1954. Essentially, his design consisted of a very light, single-seat sailplane powered by a jet engine. The earliest model, the U-2A, had a wingspan of 80 feet; a length of 49 feet, 7 inches; and an empty weight of 9,920 pounds. It was powered by Pratt & Whitney J57 turbojet with a thrust of 11,200 pounds. It had a maximum speed of 494 miles per hour, a maximum range of 2,200 miles, and an operational ceiling of 70,000 feet. The landing gear was a tandem bicycle type—a tail wheel and a single main gear beneath the fuselage just ahead of the wing (a pair of outrigger wheels near the wingtips kept the plane level during the first part of its takeoff run, but were jettisoned thereafter to conserve weight; landing

therefore involved the difficult and hazardous maneuver of tipping the craft onto a downturned wingtip just before it came to a full stop).

The project was carried out in complete secrecy (the letter U in the plane's designation stood for "utility," a measure to disguise the plane's real function). The first U-2A was test-flown at the remote Watertown Strip in Nevada on August 1, 1955. Soon thereafter Lockheed began turning out the production model, the U-2B, which was faster (528 miles per hour), heavier (11,700 pounds), and had a higher operational ceiling (85,000 feet) and a longer range (3,000 miles). The initial government order was for forty-eight of the planes, plus five two-seater versions, the U-2D (the second seat carrying an observer or systems operator). Twenty-two of the aircraft were delivered to the CIA during the first half of 1956; the initial flight over Soviet territory, made on July 1, 1956, covered Moscow, Leningrad, and the Soviet Baltic seacoast.

In 1959 a more powerful (17,000 pound thrust) jet engine was installed in the U-2C. Because the U-2 is one of the most difficult aircraft to fly, a two-seater, dual-control training version, the U-2CT, was built.

ARTHUR C. LUNDAHL, a CIA photographic specialist, supervised the development of the special camera, films, and lenses carried by the U-2. The camera, scanning continuously through seven apertures, was able to record a 125-mile-long strip of land on a single piece of film, resolving detail so accurately that golf balls could be identified on a green from an altitude of 55,000 feet. The U-2 also carried a "black box," i.e., a system for the collection of SIGINT data—radar and radio signals emanating from the ground.

The U-2s were operated under the cover of the National Advisory Committee for Aeronautics (NACA), a civilian agency that was the predecessor of the National Aeronatics and Space Administration (NASA). The ostensible purpose for the flights was meteorological observation. The CIA conducted many flights along the periphery of Soviet territory, from which vantage useful long-range photography could be done. Additionally, a reported twenty to thirty flights over Soviet territory were carried out between July 1, 1956 and May 1, 1960, when a U-2 flown by FRANCIS GARY POWERS was shot down over Sverdlovsk, USSR. No further U-2 flights were made in Soviet airspace. Although the Powers incident was politically damaging to the United States, the U-2 reconnaissance program during 1956–60 succeeded in collecting intelligence regarding the Soviet nuclear and missile programs that was vital to U.S. national security.

Soviet ability to intercept an aircraft flying at the U-2's operational ceiling remained in doubt after the Powers incident; some intelligence officials theorized that an engine malfunction had forced Powers to descend to a lower altitude, within the range of Soviet interception. However, when a SAM (surface-to-air missile) downed a U-2 flown by a Chinese Nationalist pilot over the Chinese mainland on September 9, 1962, and a Soviet SAM downed a U.S. Air Force U-2 over Cuba on October 27, 1962 (see CUBAN MISSILE CRISIS, RUDOLPH ANDERSON), the U.S. government became convinced that the U-2 was no longer invulnerable by reason of its high altitude.

Beginning in the early 1960s, the U-2 was supplanted in its original mission—collecting intelligence on Soviet strategic developments—by reconnaissance satellites (see OVERHEAD RECONNAISSANCE). However, U-2 aircraft continued to be used—mainly by the U.S. Air Force—in reconnaissance missions over areas in which the threat of interception remained small or nonexistent. A special version of aircraft, the WU-2, was actually used for weather research and observation.

Because of high attrition (due largely to accidents),

The U-2R, a larger and more advanced version of the U-2 reconnaissance aircraft. Source: Lockheed Aircraft.

the government ordered twelve more U-2s in 1968. This model, the U-2R, was considerably larger (103 foot wingspan; 63 feet in length; 14,990 pounds in weight) and capable of greater performance (operational ceiling 90,000 feet; range 3,500 miles) than the earlier versions. The U-2R also was equipped with a pair of wing pods that could be used to carry reconnaissance systems or an additional 105 gallons of fuel.

The latest evolution of the U-2 is the TR-1, which was first flown in September 1981. The TR-1 is very similar to the U-2R, but has a greater range (4,000 miles) and is equipped with sophisticated new electronics systems. Among the latter are the ASARS (Advanced Synthetic-Aperture Radar System), a SIDE-LOOKING AIRCRAFT RADAR that yields high-resolution images of the ground, and ECM (electronic countermeasures) systems to counter enemy radar. The TR-1 is used by the U.S. Air Force. The ER-2, a civilian version of the plane, is used by NASA for earth-resource research.

(Gunston, *Spy Planes*; Prados, *The Soviet Estimate*; Taylor and Mondey, *Spies in the Sky*.)

ULMER, ALFRED CONRAD (August 26, 1916–): businessman, covert operations officer

A native of Jacksonville, Florida, Ulmer graduated from the Hill School in 1935 and worked as a reporter for the *Jacksonville Journal* until 1937. He graduated from Princeton University in 1939 and worked on the public relations staff of the Benton & Bowles advertising agency until 1941, when he was commissioned as an ensign in the U.S. Naval Reserve. Ulmer was assigned to the Office of Strategic Services. He served in Cairo in a joint American-British unit composed of personnel from the OSS and the British paramilitary unit, the Special Operations Executive. Later, when stationed in Italy, he ran the special Germany-Austria Section of the OSS SECRET INTELLIGENCE BRANCH. He was promoted to the rank of lieutenant commander and awarded the Bronze Star.

After the war Ulmer remained in Austria and maintained the skeletel remnants of the Secret Intelligence Branch there while the OSS was dissolved, turned into the Strategic Services Unit, and later revived as the Office of Special Operations of the Central Intelligence Group (see CENTRAL INTELLIGENCE AGENCY). Thus he became one of a small handful of OSS officers who served in the CIA without a postwar return to civilian life.

Ulmer was the CIA's first chief of station in Vienna. From 1948 to 1950 he served as chief of station in Madrid, and in 1953 he was assigned to Athens, where he was chief of station until 1955. In 1956 he became chief of the Far East Division of the CIA CLANDESTINE SERVICE, replacing GEORGE AURELL in that position.

Ulmer was regarded within the CIA as one of the most active and dedicated covert operations officers. His colleagues judged him a likely candidate to succeed FRANK WISNER as chief of the Clandestine Service. However Ulmer planned and managed the CIA's involvement in the INDONESIA REBELLION in 1958, and his association with this notable failure is believed to have damaged his prospects for further advancement. In 1958 DESMOND FITZGERALD succeeded him as chief of the Far East Division. From 1958 to 1962 Ulmer was chief of station in Paris.

Ulmer resigned from the CIA in 1962 to serve as director of Niarchos Ltd., a company owned by Greek shipping magnate Stavros Niarchos, whose close friend he had become while chief of station in Athens. Ulmer also pursued other business interests and, since 1975, he has been with the Swiss banking firm of Lombard, Odier et Cie.

(Smith, *OSS*; Smith, *Portrait of a Cold Warrior*; Powers, *The Man Who Kept the Secrets*; *Who's Who in America*, 43rd ed.)

V

VALERIANO, NAPOLEON DIESTRO (1917?–January 20, 1975): Army officer, paramilitary specialist

A native of the Philippines, Valeriano served in the U.S. Army during the Second World War, and with the Philippine army after the country gained its independence in 1946. He later became an American citizen and served with the Central Intelligence Agency. In the early 1950s he worked with the CIA Manila station chief, EDWARD G. LANSDALE, to establish Filipino counterinsurgency combat teams to fight the Huks, the Communist guerrillas who were attempting to take over the Philippines. He was personal aide and military advisor to the Philippine President Ramon Magsaysay and held the rank of full colonel in both the U.S. and Philippine armies.

Valeriano subsequently worked with Lansdale in Vietnam during the early days of the Diem regime. In 1960 he was in charge of training Cuban exiles in guerrilla warfare, but when the plans for a Cuban operation were enlarged into the BAY OF PIGS INVASION, Valeriano was replaced in the training post. He worked with Lansdale in the post-Bay of Pigs Cuban operation code-named MONGOOSE.

Valeriano is the author of *Counterinsurgency, the Philippine Experience.*

(Smith, *Portrait of a Cold Warrior;* obituary, *New York Times,* January 22, 1975, p. 42.)

VAN DEMAN, RALPH HENRY (September 3, 1865–January 22, 1952): physician, Army officer, intelligence officer

A native of Delaware, Ohio, Van Deman studied at Ohio Wesleyan University during 1883–86, graduated from Harvard in 1888, read law for a year, then entered the Miami Medical School in Cincinnati, Ohio. He received his M.D. in 1893 and went on duty as a surgeon in the U.S. Army (in 1891, while still in medical school, he had been commissioned as a second lieutenant for that purpose.)

After service as an Army surgeon Van Deman attended the Army's Infantry and Cavalry School at Fort Leavenworth, Kansas, in 1895. In June 1897 he was assigned to the Military Information Division of the Adjutant General's Office, which then comprised ARMY INTELLIGENCE. He served in MID's Mapping Section for about a year, then was sent to Cuba during the final phase of the brief Spanish-American War.

Van Deman served in the Philippines during the Filipino insurrection against the U.S. Army forces occupying the islands after the Spanish-American War. In February 1901 he was promoted to captain and assigned to the Bureau of Insurgent Records, the intelligence unit of the Army's Philippines Department, which was shortly thereafter designated the Military Information Division of the Philippines. While serving in that unit he became aware of Japanese intelligence activity in the Philippines, and Japanese strategic interest in the islands. Van Deman took a major part in transforming the MID of the Philippines into a true tactical intelligence and counterintelligence unit.

Van Deman served in the MID of the Philippines until 1903. In 1905 he attended the Army War College in Washington, D.C. The following year he was sent on a covert mission to China for the War Department MID to collect basic intelligence regarding topography, roads, and railroads, vital information that the Army had lacked six years earlier when it joined in

Col. Ralph Van Deman. Source: National Archives.

the international expedition to rescue foreign nationals in Peking during the Boxer Rebellion. He continued to serve in the War Department MID for several years. During the Japanese war scare in 1907 he was responsible for providing President Theodore Roosevelt with weekly memoranda on Japanese activities. The intelligence contained in these reports convinced Roosevelt to send the U.S. "Great White Fleet" around the world to demonstrate American naval strength.

In May 1915, after several years of troop duty, Van Deman (then having achieved the rank of major) was assigned to the War College Division of the War Department's General Staff. He recognized the neglected state of military intelligence—the MID had been swallowed up by the War College Division in a 1908 reorganization of the General Staff, and intelligence work had since stopped almost completely. He undertook a one-man campaign to restore the MID as a separate division of the General Staff and reactivate intelligence work in the Army. Van Deman achieved a measure of success in May 1917—less than a month after American entry into the FIRST WORLD WAR—when a Military Intelligence Section was established within the War College Division and he was placed in charge of it.

Van Deman managed the Section—later called the Military Intelligence Branch—during most of the war and was responsible for its growth, organization, and its extensive counterespionage and countersubversive operations within the United States. In June 1918 he was succeeded by Col. MARLBOROUGH CHURCHILL as chief of the Branch. Van Deman was sent to France for a tour with the G-2 division of General Pershing's staff (see ARMY INTELLIGENCE).

During the PARIS PEACE CONFERENCE OF 1919 Van Deman was responsible for security and counterespionage in the staff of the American Peace Commission. He also participated in the extensive positive intelligence collection activities of the Commission staff.

Van Deman returned to Washington in August 1919 and served briefly under Brigadier General Churchill as deputy chief of the unit that had become the War Department's Military Intelligence Division in August 1918. In March 1920 he went to the Philippines to command the Thirty-first Infantry. He held a variety of infantry commands until his retirement with the rank of major general in 1929.

Van Deman settled in San Diego, California, where he established a private counterespionage and countersubversion organization. With the assistance of former members of the AMERICAN PROTECTIVE LEAGUE—the private counterespionage organization that had worked with Van Deman during the First World War—and other private investigators, informants, and researchers, as well as some local police departments, he compiled voluminous files (reportedly containing more than 100,000 entries) on suspected subversives and foreign agents. He put his private counterespionage service at the disposal of Army Intelligence, Naval Intelligence, and the Federal Bureau of Investigation.

In December 1941 Van Deman became an advisor on intelligence matters to the War Department, and he continued in this capacity until May 1946. No details of his wartime service are openly available, but he received the Legion of Merit for these activities, which were officially described as of "the highest importance" for having "materially assisted the war effort."

Van Deman also held a number of other awards and decorations for his service in uniform, including the Distinguished Service Medal and the French Legion of Honor. He is regarded as "the father of American military intelligence."

(Van Deman, *Memoirs*; *Who Was Who in America*, v. 5; Corson, *Armies of Ignorance*; Bidwell, "History of the Military Intelligence Division, War Department General Staff"; Powe, "Emergence of the War Department Intelligence Agency: 1885–1918"; Powe and Wilson, *The Evolution of American Military Intelligence*.)

VAN LEW, ELIZABETH L. (October 17, 1818–September 25, 1900): government official, Union secret agent

Although a native of Richmond, Virginia, Van Lew was the daughter of two transplanted Northerners: her father was a New Yorker who had settled in Richmond as a young man, opened a hardware business, and become one of the city's most prosperous residents; and her mother was the daughter of a former mayor of Philadelphia.

Van Lew was schooled in Philadelphia, and, in the great national debate that preceded the Civil War, she held firmly abolitionist opinions. After the death of her father she freed all of the family's slaves, and also purchased and freed those relatives of her family's slaves who were offered for sale.

During the Civil War Van Lew became the central figure in what has since become known as the Richmond underground, a group of Union sympathizers that worked actively against the Confederacy through various means including sabotage and espionage (see SAMUEL RUTH). She obtained the permission of the Confederate authorities to visit and nurse the Union prisoners of war held in Richmond in Castle Thunder, Libby Prison, and Belle Isle, and to provide the prisoners with food, books, and other comforts. However, she also aided in the escape of some of the men and reportedly had a secret room built in her house where fugitives could stay until they were spirited back to the Union lines by other federal secret service agents.

There is no question that Van Lew engaged extensively in espionage for the Union during the war, but the details of this service have been lost, a consequence of her own wish that the matter continue to be concealed from her Richmond neighbors after the war; in 1866 she requested and was given all the War Department documents relating to her secret service. She presumably destroyed these, and may have obtained and destroyed papers held privately by some of the Union officers with whom she cooperated. It is known, however, that she reported to Gen. Benjamin Butler at Fort Monroe, Virginia, during 1863 or 1864, and this may have marked the beginning of her espionage work.

She established a network of agents in Richmond,

Elizabeth Van Lew in later life. Source: The Valentine Museum.

including, by some accounts, clerks in the Confederate War and Navy departments. However, she protected the identities of her agents so well most of their names are lost to history. She is said to have placed an agent, Mary Elizabeth Bowser, one of her former slaves, as a servant in the home of Confederate President Jefferson Davis.

Information furnished by Van Lew may have led the Union to attempt the ill-fated Kilpatrick-Dahlgren raid on Richmond during February 28–March 4, 1864, in which an attempt was made to release the Union prisoners of war and (according to Confederate charges based on some disputed captured documents) burn the city and assassinate Jefferson Davis and his Cabinet. She and her associates in the Richmond underground retrieved the body of Col. Ulric Dahlgren, one of the leaders of the mission, and secreted it for later delivery to Adm. John A. Dahlgren, the officer's father.

As Grant advanced on Richmond a few months later, Van Lew sent frequent reports to the general in response to his repeated requests for specific information regarding the Confederate defenses. Grant's intelligence officer, Gen. George H. Sharpe, later

Lt. Gen. Hoyt S. Vandenberg—oil portrait by C.L. MacNelly. Source: Central Intelligence Agency.

asserted that "the greater portion [of the intelligence received by Grant in this campaign] in its collection and in good measure in its transmission, we owed to the intelligence and devotion of Miss Van Lew." Sharpe added, "For a long, long time she represented all that was left of the power of the United States government in the city of Richmond."

Van Lew financed her wartime operations from her own pocket. After the war Grant tried unsuccessfully to get Congress to reimburse her with a payment of $15,000. After he became President, he appointed her postmaster of Richmond to help alleviate the financial straits in which her patriotism had placed her. She was replaced in this position, over Grant's protests, by his successor, President Rutherford Hayes.

Van Lew held a civil service post in Washington for some years, then returned to Richmond, where she lived out her life in diminished circumstances, ostracized by the community because of her service to her country.

(*WAMB*; obituary, *New York Times*, September 26, 1900; Stuart, "Colonel Ulric Dahlgren and Rich-mond's Union Underground"; Beymer, *On Hazardous Service*; Corson, *Armies of Ignorance*.)

VANDENBERG, HOYT SANFORD (January 24, 1899–April 2, 1954): Army and Air Force officer, intelligence officer

A native of Milwaukee, Wisconsin, Vandenberg graduated from the U.S. Military Academy in 1923 and immediately underwent flight training. After graduating from the Advanced Flying School at Kelly Field, Texas, he began serving in a series of military aviation assignments including command of a pursuit squadron at Schofield Barracks, Hawaii, and as flight instructor at Randolph Field, Texas. Vandenberg entered the Air Tactical School at Maxwell Field, Alabama, and graduated in 1935. He graduated from the Command and General Staff School at Fort Leavenworth, Kansas, in 1936 and from the Army War College in 1939.

During the Second World War Vandenberg served on the staff of Gen. Henry H. Arnold and as chief of staff of Gen. James H. Doolittle's Twelfth Air Force. He served in England and North Africa and flew combat missions over Tunisia, Sardinia, Sicily, and Italy.

In August 1943, Vandenberg, then with the temporary rank of brigadier general, was made a deputy chief of the Air Staff in Washington, D.C., and in that capacity accompanied Ambassador W. Averell Harriman on a diplomatic mission to the Soviet Union. In March 1944 he was promoted to temporary major general and sent to England as deputy commander of the Allied Expeditionary Air Forces. In August 1944 he took command of the Ninth Air Force, then flying close air support and bomber escort missions in Europe. In July 1945 he was named assistant chief of staff for operations of the Army Air Forces.

In January 1946 Vandenberg became Army assistant chief of staff for intelligence (i.e. chief of ARMY INTELLIGENCE), and in June of that year he was appointed director of the Central Intelligence Group (CIG), the predecessor to the CENTRAL INTELLIGENCE AGENCY.

By his own preference, Vandenberg's term as director of CIG was brief, but his personal prestige, coupled with the fact that he was the nephew of the influential Sen. Arthur H. Vandenberg, enabled him to increase considerably the power of the agency. He succeeded in getting a specific allocation of funds for the CIG and the right of the agency to conduct intelligence research and analysis independent of the military services. Most important of all, he won for the CIG the role of intelligence collection in Latin America, a function that had previously been the jealously guarded province of the FEDERAL BUREAU OF INVESTIGATION.

In May 1947 Vandenberg got the job he wanted, Air Force chief of staff. He was succeeded as director of CIG by Rear Adm. ROSCOE H. HILLENKOETTER. Vandenberg retired from the Air Force in 1953, having been awarded the Distinguished Service Medal, the Silver Star, the Distinguished Flying Cross, the Air Medal, the Legion of Merit, and the Bronze Star.

(WAMB; Who Was Who in America, v. 3; Braden, ''The Birth of the CIA.'')

VARDILL, JOHN (1749–January 16, 1811): clergyman and British intelligence officer

A native of New York City, Vardill graduated from King's College (today Columbia University) in 1766. He went to England and received a master of arts at Oxford in June 1774, having been ordained a priest of the Church of England the previous April. He was unanimously elected assistant minister of Trinity Church (New York City) in December 1774, but he remained in England to promote university status for his alma mater, King's College. He was a Tory ideologue and propagandist, and possibly for that reason he was recruited by the British secret service to spy on Americans in London suspected of Whig or revolutionary tendencies. As a reward for his services he was made Regius Professor of Divinity at King's College, a position he expected to assume after the British had succeeded in suppressing the American Revolution.

Vardill proved adept at his espionage role. He spied on BENJAMIN FRANKLIN'S agent, Johnathan Austin, when the latter was in London; recruited fellow New Yorker Jacobus Van Zandt to the British secret service, and spied on the American community in London during the Revolution. His major contribution, however, was in masterminding the Hynson Affair, in which Capt. Joseph Hynson, a Maryland sea captain, stole dispatches that the American commissioners in France had sent to the Continental Congress, and turned them over to the British.

Because of the outcome of the American Revolution Vardill was forced to remain in England and forfeit the professorship at King's College.

(DAB; Einstein, Divided Loyalties.)

VELA RECONNAISSANCE SATELLITE

The Vela satellite program was inaugurated in 1961 for the purpose of detecting nuclear explosions in space, in order to verify Soviet compliance with nu-clear test-ban treaties. The satellite was developed by TRW Inc. and equipped with nuclear detection instrumentation developed by the Atomic Energy Commission and Western Electric's Sandia Laboratories.

The first pair of Vela satellites were launched on October 16, 1963 and placed in a near circular orbit 60,000 miles above the earth. The two satellites, each weighing 300 pounds, were spaced 180 degrees apart in order to provide simultaneous coverage of space on both sides of the earth. A second and third pair of Vela satellites were placed in orbit on July 17, 1964 and July 20, 1965.

On April 28, 1967 a pair of advanced model Vela satellites were placed in 70,000-mile-high orbits. The new Vela was heavier (500 pounds) and able to detect nuclear explosions in the earth's atmosphere, as well as in space. Additional pairs of the advanced Vela satellites were orbited on May 23, 1969 and April 8, 1970.

The Vela series was subsequently discontinued and the nuclear-detection function was combined with the missile-launch detection function of the early warning satellites in use since the early 1970s (see MIDAS EARLY WARNING SATELLITE).

(Klass, Secret Sentries in Space; Bamford, The Puzzle Palace.)

VELASQUEZ, LORETA JANETA (1840–?): Confederate Army officer and secret agent(?)

Velasquez's story of having served in the Confederate Army disguised as a man, and later having operated as a Confederate secret agent is supported by little but her own ghostwritten book, The Woman in War, which is suspiciously similar to the commercially successful and equally improbable memoirs of S. EMMA EDMONDS.

According to her memoirs, Velasquez was apprehended in Washington by War Department provost marshal LAFAYETTE C. BAKER. However, there is no record of this arrest. She further claims to have worked as a supposed double agent for Baker (while in fact continuing to work for the Confederacy), but there is no record of her having been on his payroll. Her claim that she played a part in the Northwest Conspiracy is also unsupported.

Velasquez published her memoirs in 1876, eight years after Baker's death.

See CIVIL WAR MYTHOLOGY.

(Corson, Armies of Ignorance; Boatner, Civil War Dictionary.)

Loreta Velasquez. Source: Author's collection.

Loreta Velasquez as she purportedly appeared disguised as a Confederate soldier. Source: Library of Congress.

VICTORIA, MARIA DE (ca. 1882–August 12, 1920): German secret service agent

Victoria was the youngest daughter of Baron Hans von Kretschmann, a general in the German army. She was well educated, widely traveled, and spoke several languages fluently. In 1910 she was recruited by the intelligence department of the German War Office. Her first assignment was in Chile, where she married Manuel de Victoria, an Argentine citizen whom she recruited into the German secret service.

After her return to Germany with her husband in 1914, Victoria successfully carried out a mission in Russia. On January 21, 1917 she arrived in the United States on a mission to conduct secret intelligence and sabotage operations. Information supplied by British intelligence led the War Department's Military Intelligence Division (see ARMY INTELLIGENCE) to intercept letters intended for her from German secret service headquarters in Berlin. The Secret Ink Section of MID's Codes and Ciphers unit found invisible writing (see CRYPTOLOGY) in the letters, disclosing her role in the German secret service. She was traced to a hotel in Long Beach, Long Island (where she may have been observing the movements of troop and supply ships leaving New York harbor) and arrested on April 27, 1918.

Victoria was indicted for conspiracy to commit espionage but was never brought to trial. She was released in 1920. Her death in that year reportedly resulted from drug addiction.

Victoria's husband was captured in France en route to Argentina, tried by a military court, and sentenced to life imprisonment on April 25, 1918.

(Landau, *The Enemy Within;* Bryan, *The Spy in America;* Yardley, *The American Black Chamber.*)

VIETNAM WAR

Background: In 1940 the Vichy French regime consented to Japan's occupation of the part of French Indochina now called Vietnam. During the Second World War there was considerable underground resistance to the Japanese occupation by several nationalist, revolutionary, and Communist organizations. In 1941 a coalition of these groups, the Vietminh League, was established by the Communists. Shortly before the end of the war the Japanese permitted the Vietminh to seize power from the Vichy French authorities and establish the Democratic Republic of Vietnam, consisting of the French Indochinese states of Tonkin, Annam, and Cochin China. After the war France agreed to recognize Vietnam as a free state within the French Indochinese federation, but failed to sign a definitive agreement implementing that recognition. A protracted guerilla war between the Vietminh and the French followed.

The French War: In 1949 France established an ostensibly independent Republic of Vietnam as part of the French Union, and appointed Bao Dai, the former emperor of Annam, as head of the Vietnamese state. This move failed to satisfy the Vietminh who continued to fight the French, soon with the support of the newly victorious Communist government of neighboring China.

The Vietminh employed the guerrilla strategy that Mao Tse-tung had devised and used with success in China. In this mode of warfare the object is not to take and hold a piece of territory but to undermine the enemy's authority and control therein and to win the allegiance and support of the local people; the enemy's army is not destroyed through a series of major battles in a few crucial places, but through a campaign of ambush and harassment throughout a large area; and the guerrilla forces do not seek a quick victory, but instead entangle the enemy in a long conflict that will become for him costly, frustrating, and politically insupportable.

By the end of 1953 the war had gone on for nearly eight years, during which time it had lost popular support in France and had become a major issue of French domestic politics. The French National Assembly had adopted regulations prohibiting draftees from being sent to Indochina, thereby limiting the Army fighting the war to regular troops and the French foreign legion.

With the end of the Korean War in July 1953 the Chinese Communists were free to increase their aid to the Vietminh in the form of manpower and equipment, especially artillery. The Vietminh hoped to complete their victory over the French before a promised increase in American aid materialized (the United States had begun to furnish economic and military aid to the French in Indochina with the outbreak of the Korean War; American strategists saw the Indochina and Korean wars as two interlocking aspects of Chinese Communist expansion in East Asia). The Vietminh therefore chose this moment to transform their war of harassment into a conventional main force war, a step that Mao's strategy prescribed as the final stage of his "people's war."

Dien Bien Phu

During December 1953–January 1954 the Vietminh attacked with four infantry divisions and an artillery-engineering division, invading Laos—a French Indochinese state that borders northern Vietnam on the west. In response the French reinforced a string of bases throughout the Indochinese countryside, thereby dispersing their forces. The Vietminh then suspended their general invasion of Laos and concentrated their forces on one of the French bases,

Dien Bien Phu, located on the Vietnamese-Laotian border and athwart the main route between China and Laos. Surrounded and outnumbered by the Vietminh, isolated from the main French stronghold of Hanoi 200 miles to the east, and supportable only by airdrops (after the airstrip came under artillery attack) that became increasingly vulnerable to Vietminh anti-aircraft fire, the French garrison at Dien Bien Phu fell after a fifty-six day siege, on May 7, 1954.

The fall of Dien Bien Phu marked the end of the French war for Indochina. In July representatives of France and the Vietminh attending an international conference at Geneva signed a cease-fire agreement that established an International Control Commission (India, Poland, and Canada) to oversee the truce, and provided for the temporary partitioning of Vietnam by means of a Demilitarized Zone along the seventeenth parallel. Pending nationwide elections to be held no later than July 1956, Vietnam north of the partition was to be under the control of the Vietminh, while the southern portion of the country remained under the French-sponsored government of Bao Dai.

Shortly before the Geneva Agreements were signed, Bao Dai appointed as his prime minister Ngo Dinh Diem, a French-educated Roman Catholic and former colonial government official who was also a Vietnamese nationalist and had previously refused to align himself with either the French or the Vietminh. By the end of 1955 Diem had deposed Bao Dai by means of a rigged referendum and had emerged as president of the Republic of Vietnam. Meanwhile the Vietminh consolidated their control in the north through a campaign of political oppression (Fall writes that some 50,000 North Vietnamese were executed by the Communist regime, while twice that number were sent to forced labor camps). The lack of freedom in the north, and the fact that South Vietnam had not been a signatory to the Geneva Agreements were cited by Diem as justification for refusing to participate in the nationwide elections that had been scheduled for July 1956.

As the French presence in Vietnam ended, the United States moved in to fill the vacuum. As early as February 1950 the NATIONAL SECURITY COUNCIL had formulated the "domino theory," the premise that the fall of Indochina to the Communists would precipitate the fall of Thailand and Burma like a row of dominoes and endanger all other Southeast Asian countries. Soon after Diem took control the U.S. government declared its support for him and began channeling aid directly to the South Vietnamese government, bypassing the French. In January 1955 a U.S. Military Assistance Advisory Group (US-MAAG) arrived in South Vietnam and took over the training of the armed forces. By April 1956 the last French troops had been withdrawn from Vietnam, and the American military advisors had completely taken over their role.

The American War: In 1957, having consolidated its control in the north, the Communist government of North Vietnam began a renewed campaign of terrorism and subversion in the south through the Vietcong, a Communist force consisting of guerrillas newly infiltrated into South Vietnam and Communist STAY-BEHIND NETS established in the south soon after the Geneva Agreements. Local government officials in outlying districts were murdered by the Vietcong to illustrate the powerlessness of the Saigon government to secure the countryside, and the Communists began mounting guerrilla attacks against ARVN (Army of the Republic of Vietnam) outposts. The U.S. suffered the first American casualties on October 22, 1957 when a bomb exploded in the quarters of the USMAAG personnel and wounded a number of Americans. Two USMAAG advisors were killed on July 8, 1959, the first American fatalities of the war. In January 1960 the Vietcong overran several ARVN outposts. Soon thereafter President Diem requested more American military advisors, and the strength of the USMAAG contingent was increased from 327 to 685, and then to 900 by the end of the year.

Vietcong terrorism continued to escalate. An increasing number of guerrillas infiltrated from the north, most by way of the "Ho Chi Minh Trail" (named after the North Vietnamese head of state), which ran through the mountains and jungles of eastern Laos in order to bypass the heavily defended Demilitarized Zone between North and South Vietnam. The strength of the Vietcong tripled during 1959–61 to an estimated 15,000 and most of the countryside came under the covert influence of the National Liberation Front (NLF), as the Vietcong's political arm was called. During the same period the annual toll of South Vietnamese murdered by the Vietcong increased tenfold to about five hundred.

When President John F. Kennedy took office in 1961 he sent Gen. Maxwell Taylor and WALTER W. ROSTOW to Vietnam on a fact-finding mission. On the basis of their recommendation Kennedy decided to send additional military advisors to Vietnam, and to emphasize the techniques of counterinsurgency over conventional warfare. By the end of 1961 there were 3,200 American advisors in the country; a month later 4,000. The USMAAG was reorganized as the U.S. Military Assistance Command, Vietnam (USMACV) in February 1962.

The Vietcong's campaign of revolutionary war, following the principles of Mao Tse-tung, was at this time still at the stage where the insurgents were trying to gain the support and allegiance of the South Vietnamese people. Their effort in this regard was greatly abetted (unintentionally) by President Diem and his government officials, who were frenchified, and therefore reminiscent of colonialism; Roman Catholic, and therefore alien to most South Vietnamese; and corrupt. Even before the North Vietnamese guerrilla offensive of 1957, some non-Communist South Vietnamese insurgents rose against the Diem government. And even within Diem's regime there was discord: the South Vietnamese armed forces mounted unsuccessful coups against him in November 1960 and February 1962.

During 1962 Diem inaugurated a "strategic hamlet" program in which South Vietnamese peasants living in Vietcong-controlled areas were relocated from their home villages to fortified villages in more secure areas, a technique of counterinsurgency that had succeeded elsewhere. However, the strategic hamlets proved to be no more secure from Vietcong attack than other villages, and the resentment peasants felt on being sometimes forcibly removed from their ancestral homes may actually have worked to the advantage of the insurgents (the failure of the strategic hamlet program was due in part to the fact that Col. Pham Ngoc Thao, Diem's chief lieutenant for the program, was one of many North Vietnamese PENETRATIONS of the ARVN). By the end of 1962 the American advisors in USMACV had been increased to 11,300, but no progress against the Vietcong was discernible. The Communists increased their own strength in South Vietnam and stepped up their attacks, while the South Vietnamese armed forces remained unable to deal with them.

The Fall of Diem

During 1963 Diem compounded his difficulties in the war by a campaign of religious oppression against the Buddhists, the religious majority in South Vietnam. On May 8th the national police (the force was headed by one of Diem's brothers; another brother was chief of the secret police) fired into a crowd at Hue protesting the government's anti-Buddhist actions; the police killed nine persons and wounded twenty others. A month later a Buddhist monk publicly burned himself to death to protest the government's actions, and several other monks followed suit during the next few weeks. In response Diem stepped up his campaign against the Buddhists. On August 21st Diem's private army attacked Buddhist temples and sanctuaries throughout the country, beating, jailing or murdering hundreds of monks, nuns, students, and others. Several South Vietnamese officials, including the foreign minister and ambassador to the United States, resigned to protest the raids. Diem rejected official American protests against his actions and refused to discuss government reforms proposed by the United States. In November a group of ARVN generals, having been assured that the United States would not interfere, overthrew the Diem government and installed a military junta. Diem and one of his brothers—the secret police chief—were assassinated.

A rapid series of coups followed as the military leaders jockeyed for position. Meanwhile the USMACV took an increasing role in both the direction and the prosecution of the war. By July 1964 the number of American military advisors had been increased to 21,000. The Vietcong also stepped up their activity and began directing it more often against Americans in South Vietnam. Early in August, in response to reported attacks on U.S. Navy vessels in the Gulf of Tonkin by North Vietnamese torpedo boats, the U.S. bombed bases in North Vietnam. As a result of the incident the U.S. Congress passed the Southeast Asia Resolution (better known as "the Gulf of Tonkin Resolution"), authorizing President Lyndon Johnson "to take all necessary measures to repel any armed attack against the forces of the U.S. and to prevent future aggression . . . and to take all necessary steps" to assist in the defense of South Vietnam or other Southeast Asian nations. The Resolution amounted to an open-ended American commitment to the war.

The American Role Changes

In February 1965 Vietcong attacks against US-MACV installations resulted in more than thirty American deaths and 130 wounded. In retaliation the U.S. and South Vietnamese air forces bombed military targets in North Vietnam, and on March 2nd President Johnson launched Operation Rolling Thunder, an ongoing series of air strikes against North Vietnam. A bomb exploded outside the U.S. embassy in Saigon on March 30, killing two Americans. Shortly thereafter the Johnson administration took the major decision to change the role of U.S. ground forces in South Vietnam from advising and defense to direct military engagement of the enemy. At about the same time North Vietnam introduced regular army units into the south, preparing to take the final step of conventional warfare. However, the North Vietnamese regular forces suffered major defeats at the hands of the U.S. Army and Marines at Plei Me and the Ia Drang Valley during October–November. The Communists then reverted to the more successful guerrilla warfare stage of Mao's revolutionary war formula.

A pattern was then established that was to persist throughout most of the duration of the American military involvement in the war: American ground forces, using helicopters, artillery, and ground vehicles, took the major role in the war, conducting "search and destroy" operations aimed at liquidating the Vietcong in South Vietnam, while the ARVN took charge of security functions in areas under nominal government control; the Vietcong survived and flourished, nonetheless, and continued to engage in terrorism, carry out guerrilla operations, and to control large areas of the countryside whenever and wherever the Americans or ARVN were not present in strength; U.S. air strikes against the Ho Chi Minh Trail attempted to interdict the flow of replacements and supplies from the north, which, however, continued generally unabated; an "on-again-off-again" campaign of strategic bombing of North Vietnam was aimed at forcing the North Vietnamese to negotiate a settlement of the war but did not have that effect; increasing numbers of American troops were sent into Vietnam, reaching a peak of about half a million in 1968–69; the number of American casualties rose rapidly—14,000 were killed in 1968 alone, and the total American combat fatalities in the war reached more than 47,000; the war increasingly became an issue of American domestic politics as support for American involvement dwindled, active opposition to it grew, and millions of eligible American men avoided the draft through means both legal and illegal.

The Tet Offensive

The long series of coups and military juntas ended and the political situation in South Vietnam stabilized somewhat in 1967 when Nguyen Van Thieu was elected president and the country returned to constitutional government, but the steady increase of Vietcong terrorism—e.g., 3,820 murders in 1967—continued to deny the government the popular support it needed. On January 30, the first day of a mutually agreed upon truce for Tet, the Vietnamese Lunar New Year, Vietcong and North Vietnamese regular forces launched a major campaign of coordinated attacks on urban areas—the seven largest cities, including Saigon and Hue, and thirty provincial capitals throughout the length and breadth of the country. In Saigon Vietcong commandoes occupied the American embassy buildings for six hours before being killed by U.S. forces, but other Vietcong elsewhere in the city held out for a week. In Hue Communist forces held out and fought a bitter block-by-block battle until February 24th. The Tet offensive was considered a military defeat for the Communists, since the Vietcong failed to hold any of the areas they attacked. The operation may also have reflected a political failure, since it did not trigger a popular uprising against the Thieu government in support of the Vietcong. But Tet was a psychological and propaganda victory for the Communist insurgents in that it demonstrated that even the urban strongholds of South Vietnam were not safe from terrorism and guerrilla attack.

Concurrent with the Tet offensive, the Communists again attempted to move into the main-force phase of Maoist warfare with an attack by North Vietnamese regulars on the U.S. Marine outpost at Khesanh, located in the remote northwest corner of South Vietnam. The Communists may have seen Khesanh as an opportunity to repeat their 1954 victory at Dien Bien Phu; but the siege of Khesanh, which lasted from January 20th until April 6th, was unsuccessful, and demonstrated once again that the North Vietnamese could not succeed in the final, main-force stage of revolutionary warfare in the face of overwhelming American military strength and firepower. However, time and American war-weariness were on the side of the Communists.

The Tet offensive set off a new wave of anti-war sentiment in the United States. At the end of March President Johnson announced his withdrawal from the presidential election campaign of 1968 and another halt in the strategic bombing of North Vietnam. Shortly thereafter North Vietnam agreed to preliminary peace negotiations with the United States; the talks began in Paris in May but soon became deadlocked.

Vietnamization of the War

American military policy shifted from the large search-and-destroy operations to an emphasis on defending the urban centers while striking at Vietcong concentrations whenever they were located, with mobile helicopter-borne ground forces. The Americans launched a long-term program to achieve the "Vietnamization" of the war, i.e., returning the major burden of the fighting to the ARVN. In June 1969, President Richard Nixon, having promised to bring about an honorable end to U.S. involvement in Vietnam, announced the withdrawal of 25,000 American troops, the first of a series of such withdrawals. He announced further withdrawals of 35,000 and 50,000 troops in September and December, respectively.

In April 1970, however, Nixon ordered an invasion of Cambodia, a former French Indochinese state immediately to the west of Vietnam used as a sanctuary and staging area by the Vietcong and North Vietnamese army. Nixon acted in response to a request from anti-Communist Gen. Lon Nol, who had recently seized power in Cambodia. Some 32,000 American troops and 40,000 ARVN troops crossed into Cambodia and attacked North Vietnamese sanctuaries and supply bases. Large amounts of weapons and ammunition were seized, but the Communist troops generally retreated to avoid a main-force confrontation with the invaders. The American-South Vietnamese expedition withdrew in June, but the U.S. continued to support Cambodian forces against the North Vietnamese through air strikes and military and economic aid.

The invasion of Cambodia triggered new anti-war protests and demonstrations in the United States, including one on the campus of Kent State University on May 2nd in which the ROTC building was burned to the ground. Two days later, as rioting continued on the campus, Ohio National Guardsmen called out to maintain order fired on student protesters, killing four and wounding eleven. The incident further rallied anti-war protest. On June 24th the Senate repealed the Southeast Asia (i.e., Gulf of Tonkin) Resolution and a week later passed the Cooper-Church amendment barring future U.S. military operations in or aid to Cambodia without congressional approval.

Anti-war sentiment was further heightened by the disclosure of a massacre of Vietnamese civilians at My Lai by an American infantry platoon in March 1968 and by the subsequent unfolding of details of the atrocity during the court-martials of the officers responsible during 1970–71, and by the leak and publication in 1971 of the "Pentagon Papers," a collection of official U.S. government documents disclosing official public deception in regard to American involvement in Vietnam. Nixon's program of Vietnamization and American withdrawal continued, and by the end of 1971 fewer than 160,000 U.S. troops remained in Vietnam.

During April–March 1971 the ARVN undertook a major operation to interdict the Ho Chi Minh Trail in Laos, meeting fierce resistance and sustaining heavy losses (by some accounts, fifty percent casualties). The operation succeeded in dealing a major blow to the Communist forces, but soon after the forty-five-day ARVN operation was concluded the flow of traffic on the Ho Chi Minh Trail returned to normal.

The American program to Vietnamize the war did not fully compensate for the withdrawal of U.S. troops, and the military capabilities of South Vietnam were weakened. By early 1972 the North Vietnamese believed the south had been sufficiently weakened for them to attempt once again to escalate to a main-force conflict. On March 30th North Vietnam launched a major coordinated offensive across the Demilitarized Zone, attacking in the Central Highlands, along the Cambodian border, and elsewhere in South Vietnam. The North Vietnamese offensive involved long-range, heavy artillery; 500 tanks and twelve divisions of North Vietnamese regulars—150,000 troops; as well as thousands of Vietcong. The spearheads drove deeply into South Vietnam during April, meeting little resistance from the ARVN. The U.S. responded to the onslaught by increasing the bombing of North Vietnamese supply lines and strategic targets in the north, and mining Haiphong and other North Vietnamese harbors. By midsummer the South Vietnamese were able to recover and turn back the Communist offensive, and by autumn the military situation had stabilized. On August 11th the last American ground combat unit was withdrawn from South Vietnam. Fewer than 44,600 American armed forces personnel remained.

Meanwhile, the peace talks that had been going on intermittently in Paris for several years had begun to bear fruit. After the United States and North Vietnam tentatively agreed to a draft peace treaty in October 1972, President Nixon ordered a temporary halt to all bombing north of the twentieth parallel. When the North Vietnamese objected to some subsequent amendments to the draft and proposed some modifications of their own in December, Nixon ordered a resumption of full-scale bombing of the north. The talks resumed on January 8, 1973, and on January 27th the peace treaty was signed by the United States, South Vietnam, North Vietnam, and the Provisional Revolutionary Government of South Vietnam, i.e., the new name of the political arm of the Vietcong. It called for a cease-fire, an international control commission (Canada, Hungary, Poland, and Indonesia), the withdrawal of all U.S. troops and advisors from Vietnam and all foreign troops from Laos and Cambodia, the release of American prisoners, and the eventual reunification of Vietnam.

The U.S. Withdraws

For the United States the treaty meant the end of direct involvement in the war, although material support to South Vietnam was to continue. The last American troops departed South Vietnam in March. On August 15th the United States terminated all American military operations elsewhere in Indochina, i.e., in Cambodia and Laos. The North Vietnamese built up their forces in the south in violation of the cease-fire, however, and in December 1974 launched a series of main-force attacks that continued through the spring of 1975. The South Vietnamese armed forces, whose material support by the United States had been severely cut by Congress earlier in 1974, was unable to resist the North Vietnamese

offensive, and on April 30, 1975 South Vietnam surrendered unconditionally. In Cambodia, the government of Lon Nol had surrendered to the Communist insurgents two weeks earlier. On December 3rd Communist insurgents in Laos took over the government of that country and established the People's Democratic Republic of Laos.

The fall of Indochina to Communism did not end warfare in the region, however. Traditional national antagonisms between Vietnam and Cambodia were exacerbated by the ideological and political differences between the USSR and China. In 1977 fighting broke out between Vietnam, a Soviet client state, and Cambodia, an ally of China. In 1979 Vietnamese forces captured the Cambodian capital of Phnom Penh. Thereafter the Khmer Rouge—the formerly Communist Cambodian faction—entered into a coalition with other Cambodian groups and waged a guerrilla war against the Vietnamese occupation forces.

Intelligence in the War: The involvement of U.S. intelligence services in Vietnamese events began as early as the Second World War with the Office of Strategic Services. The Vietminh underground supplied the OSS with military intelligence on Japanese troop movements and aided downed American airmen during the war. In June 1945 Capt. LUCIEN CONEIN of the OSS led five OSS sabotage experts and one hundred French and Vietnamese commandos on a successful raid of a Japanese headquarters in northern Vietnam. As the end of the war approached in July and early August 1945 the OSS sent a liaison team into northern Vietnam to contact Ho Chi Minh, the Vietminh leader. Finding Ho seriously ill and near death, the OSS medics nursed him back to health. The OSS liaison team trained two hundred Vietminh guerrillas in American commando tactics and supplied them with small arms. Shortly after the Japanese surrender several OSS "mercy teams" were sent to Vietnam to collect intelligence and protect the 10,000 Allied prisoners of war held in Japanese prison camps.

OSS relations with Ho and the Vietminh were complicated by postwar international politics. France intended to reimpose colonial dominion over Vietnam and the rest of Indochina, while the Vietminh were committed to achieving independence. The United States government, opposed in principle to colonialism but a wartime ally of France, was caught in the middle. Further confounding the situation was American wariness of Ho's known Communist affiliation. In October 1945, amid escalating violence between the French, the Vietminh, and other factions, the OSS evacuated its teams from the country.

American ambivalence toward the Vietnam situation ended with the advent of the cold war in the late 1940s, and even before the beginning of the Korean War in June 1950 U.S. policymakers saw the continued French dominance in Indochina as important to the containment of Communist expansion in East Asia. American aid to the French in Vietnam did not include intelligence support, however, although the CIA-owned airline, Civil Air Transport (see AIR PROPRIETARIES), provided logistical air support to the besieged French force at Dien Bien Phu and elsewhere in Indochina during 1953–54 (these contract air operations were overt and not run by the CIA).

American intelligence returned to Vietnam on June 1, 1954, soon after the fall of Dien Bien Phu, in the person of (then), Col. EDWARD G. LANSDALE, a U.S. Air Force officer detailed to the Central Intelligence Agency, who had succeeded in countering Communist insurgency in the Philippines during 1950–53. Under the official cover of air attaché, Lansdale was sent to Vietnam to try to repeat what he had accomplished in the Philippines, i.e., the selection and promotion of a strong national leader to rally the democratic forces in the country against the Communists and the defeat of the insurgents through the use of the psychological warfare, civic action, community development, and counterinsurgency programs that had worked against the Filipino Huks.

The Saigon Military Mission

Lansdale was head of the Saigon Military Mission (SMM), a unit attached to the U.S. embassy, created to provide official cover for the CIA team in Vietnam. His deputy was Maj. Lucien Conein, the former OSS officer who had led guerrilla raids against the Japanese in Vietnam during the Second World War. The SMM, consisting of Lansdale, Conein, and ten other American military personnel, organized, trained, and led two Vietnamese paramilitary teams in sabotage, psychological warfare, and guerrilla operations. During the 300-day regroupment period provided by the terms of the Geneva Agreements of 1954 all Vietnamese were free to choose to live in either the south or the Communist north; the SMM conducted an extensive black propaganda (see COVERT ACTION) operation that caused many northerners to flee to the south (transportation for much of this migration was provided by the CIA air proprietary, Civil Air Transport). SMM agents sabotaged the North Vietnamese transportation network—railroads and bus lines—and organized STAY-BEHIND NETS in the north. The SMM also established the ARVN's First Armed Propaganda Company, a unit whose men infiltrated North Vietnam in the guise of Vietnamese civilians

to carry out "black" psychological warfare operations (i.e., to disseminate black propaganda.)

In the newly appointed South Vietnamese prime minister, Ngo Dinh Diem, Lansdale thought he had found another Magsaysay (the Filipino leader Lansdale had supported in the campaign against the Huks, who, with Lansdale's help, became the highly effective president of the Philippines). He threw his full support and that of the CIA behind Diem, determined to build a fully functioning democracy around the Vietnamese leader.

Lansdale established the FREEDOM COMPANY OF THE PHILIPPINES, a DEVISED FACILITY that enabled him to introduce a large staff of experienced Filipino advisors into South Vietnam, personnel who would have been excluded from the country by the terms of the Geneva Agreements were their sponsorship by the U.S. government known. The Freedom Company, ostensibly a private Filipino people-to-people civic action and community development project, was composed of Filipinos who had fought as guerrillas against the Japanese during the Second World War, and experienced counterinsurgency troops who had taken part in the suppression of the Huk rebellion in the Philippines. They helped draft a constitution for the Republic of South Vietnam, trained Diem's palace guard and other ARVN personnel, and organized the Vietnamese Veterans Legion, a political veterans group that supported Diem. The Freedom Company also ran "Operation Brotherhood," which resettled the Vietnamese who had fled the north. Freedom Company teams improved roads, furnished medical care, and distributed food and other government assistance throughout war-torn South Vietnam, while at the same time carrying out propaganda and psychological warfare operations and assisting ARVN counterintelligence and security forces in identifying Vietminh stay-behind agents. The Company, which operated in Laos and Thailand as well as Vietnam, also scouted for potential intelligence agents to be recruited by SMM. In 1957 the Freedom Company was transformed into a commercial firm, the Eastern Construction Company, a profit-making firm no longer receiving direct support from the CIA, but retaining close ties with the Agency.

Closely coordinated with the Freedom Company was the Security Training Center, a countersubversion, counterinsurgency, and psychological warfare school run by the CIA under the cover of a project of the Philippine government. The Center, which had a staff of twelve instructors, was located at Fort McKinley on the outskirts of Manila.

Lansdale guided Diem through the treacherous first two years of his tenure. He steered him clear of a planned coup by a French-sponsored rival, Gen.

Nguyen Van Hinh, and worked closely with him in suppressing a criminal organization of river pirates and in crushing or coopting the private armies of several quasi-religious sects.

Lansdale and the SMM organized and trained the Vietnamese First Observation Group, a 300-man elite unit separate from the ARVN, reporting directly to Diem through the Vietnamese Presidential Survey Office. It was originally created to operate undercover in fifteen-man teams in the event of a North Vietnamese main-force invasion across the Demilitarized Zone; the teams would serve as stay-behind nets in Communist-controlled territory. In 1957 a team from the newly formed U.S. Special Forces (the "Green Berets") trained fifty-eight members of the First Observation Group, thereby creating the nucleus of the Vietnamese Special Forces, or Lac Luong Dac Biet (LLDB). The LLDB was given combat missions against the Vietcong in South Vietnam, as well as clandestine border-crossing missions into North Vietnam and Laos. It was also, in effect, Diem's palace guard.

Against the threat of renewed Communist insurgency in South Vietnam, the SMM helped Diem to develop security and counterinsurgency forces. Through a program run under covert CIA contract by Michigan State University the SMM set up a 50,000-man Civil Guard to maintain law and order, collect intelligence, and conduct countersubversion operations at the province level in areas under ARVN control. The Village Self-Defense Corps—later renamed the Popular Forces—was established under SMM auspices, arming villagers loyal to the Saigon government and training them to take a hand in their own defense against Communist insurgency. Unfortunately, Diem also employed these security forces and the First Observation Group to suppress legitimate political opposition to his administration. In 1956, having realized he had made a serious mistake in supporting Diem, and unable to persuade or force the Vietnamese president to make the needed democratic reforms to his repressive regime, Lansdale left Vietnam for another assignment.

Following Lansdale's departure, liaison with the Diem regime continued to be a major function of the CIA's Saigon station, which was headed by NICHOLAS A. NATSIOS during 1956–60. WILLIAM E. COLBY, who was assigned to the Saigon station in 1959 and served as its chief during 1960–62, recalls that collecting intelligence on the Vietcong and North Vietnamese Army (NVA) through liaison with the intelligence services of the government of South Vietnam (GVN), and on the domestic political situation in South Vietnam through unilateral operations (see LIAISON AND UNILATERAL OPERATIONS) were the principal functions of the Saigon station during that period. However, in May 1961 President Kennedy approved a plan that included a general expansion of U.S. and GVN intelligence, counterintelligence, and covert action operations in Vietnam.

Civilian Irregular Defense Group

The new program called for the CIA and U.S. Special Forces to train the South Vietnamese in counterinsurgency techniques, and particularly to prepare those living in the countryside to resist the Vietcong. One result was the development of the Civilian Irregular Defense Group (CIDG). The initial CIDG was organized in February 1962 among the Rhadé, one of the largest groups of Montagnards—as the Vietnamese hill tribesmen were called—of the village of Buon Enao in the southern highlands. The CIDG program encompassed both military training and civil action. The tribesmen were taught how to defend their villages against the Vietcong, how to carry out limited offensive operations in their local areas against the Vietcong, and also a large assortment of "civic action" skills, e.g., paramedical techniques, to improve the quality of life in the villages. Within six months of its initiation, the CIDG program had expanded to 129 Rhadé hamlets centered on Buon Enao, which was protected by nearly 10,000 trained and armed tribesmen. A roving strike force of 1,800 Rhadé took a more active combat role against the Vietcong, patrolling between villages, setting ambushes, gathering intelligence, and standing ready to come to the aid of any village under Vietcong attack. Two hundred and eighty Rhadé had been trained as paramedics.

The initial success of the Buon Enao project led to an enlargement of the CIDG program by the CIA and Special Forces to include other Montagnards and other ethnic minorities throughout South Vietnam. By 1964 there were 75,000 trained and armed irregulars in the CIDG. In the Montagnard areas located along the remote and mountainous western border areas through which the Vietcong infiltrated South Vietnam, the CIDG was virtually the only GVN presence, and in many CIDG areas the Vietcong threat was virtually eliminated.

The success of the CIDG program led to the creation of several other CIA-Special Forces projects involving Montagnards. One, known as the Mountain Scouts, was an irregular force that undertook long-range intelligence gathering missions in remote areas of South Vietnam. The Trailwatchers, later known as the Border Surveillance force, was composed of Montagnards trained to observe and report Vietcong movements in their localities, and when possible to capture or destroy Vietcong units. The Combat Intelligence Teams and the Civilian Airborne Rangers were Montagnard irregulars who performed covert intelligence and sabotage missions in Laos and Cambodia.

Covert infiltration of Laos to attack Communist bases and supply lines was one of the tasks specified by the Kennedy plan of May 1961 for expanded covert operations in Southeast Asia. The plan also called for clandestine missions into North Vietnam to "form networks of resistance, covert bases and teams for sabotage and light harassment." These border-crossing operations were carried out by the elite Vietnamese First Observation Group under the direction of CIA and U.S. Special Forces personnel. The CIA's Operation Haylift involved the airdrop of South Vietnamese agents into North Vietnam; but the operation seems to have been generally ineffective, and many of the Haylift agents were captured soon after arriving in the north.

The Kennedy plan also called for an expansion of communications intelligence activities in Vietnam, including the training of ARVN units in such COMINT skills as radio interception and direction finding, and the sharing of COMINT with the GVN. In 1961 the Third Radio Research Unit of the U.S. Army Security Agency (see ARMY INTELLIGENCE, NATIONAL SECURITY AGENCY) was sent to Vietnam to serve with the USMAAG and advise the Vietnamese Military Security Service, the ARVN military COMINT agency.

In August 1963, Diem had the CIA-trained First Observation Group commandoes disguise themselves as regular ARVN troops and raid Buddhist temples. This misuse of the commandoes exacerbated discord between the Diem regime and the Kennedy administration. Through the CIA's Saigon station, Kennedy learned of a planned coup d'état by a group of ARVN generals and informed them that the U.S. would not oppose the move. The fall of Diem on November 2, 1963 was followed three weeks later by the assassination of President Kennedy and the succession of Lyndon Johnson to the presidency. Thereafter the role of intelligence in the war—and the war itself—underwent major changes.

Under a program begun by the Kennedy administration, many of the CIA's large paramilitary operations were turned over to the Department of Defense during 1963–64. This included the CIDG and LLDB (Vietnam Special Forces) programs, which became exclusively projects of the USMACV, as well as smaller programs such as the People's Action Teams (the PAT program was similar in concept to the CIDG, but involved Vietnamese, as opposed to Montagnard, participation).

Studies and Observation Group

The enlarged role of USMACV in paramilitary operations coincided with President Johnson's National Security Action Memorandum #273 of November 26, 1963, which called for, inter alia, support for GVN clandestine operations in North Vietnam and up to fifty kilometers into Laos, the latter actions intended to interdict the Ho Chi Minh Trail. In January 1964 an organization called the STUDIES AND OBSERVATION GROUP (SOG) was established within USMACV. Ostensibly created to study the U.S. military advisory experience in Vietnam, SOG was in fact a covert action (or SPECIAL ACTIVITIES, a term apparently preferred by the Defense Department) unit that conducted cross-border missions into Laos, Cambodia, and North Vietnam, as well as other covert action operations. SOG also conducted "black" psychological operations, e.g., Project Eldest Son, which involved the insertion of rigged ammunition rounds, set to explode on use, into enemy supply dumps: the rigged rounds made the Vietcong and NVA troops fearful when using any of their ammunition; at the same time SOG fed the Communist troops rumors that the defective ammunition was the result of production flaws in China caused by Mao's Cultural Revolution.

One of the principal activities of SOG was long-range reconnaissance OVER-THE-FENCE MISSIONS into Laos aimed at interdicting the flow of Communist supplies along the Ho Chi Minh Trail. These operations, code-named Leaping Lena (1964) and Shining Brass (1965), involved the insertion of SOG teams into Laos to reconnoiter the Trail and coordinate U.S. air strikes against truck parks and convoys. The operations were effective in identifying the targets, although aerial bombardment of the Trial was never able to reduce the flow of supplies below the minimum the Vietcong required to continue the war in the south.

Under a project known as OPLAN 34A, the SOG's Maritime Studies Group conducted commando raids against the North Vietnamese coastline using Swift boats, high-speed vessels built in Norway. One such mission carried out on the night of July 31-August 1, 1964 on a North Vietnamese radar station and other facilities on the islands of Hon Me and Hon Ngu in the Gulf of Tonkin provoked a response by North Vietnamese torpedo boats, which, while pursuing the fleeing SOG craft, encountered the U.S.S. *Maddox*, a destroyer on an unrelated SIGINT mission in the same waters. The engagement between the North Vietnamese craft and the *Maddox*, and a subsequent engagement involving a second American destroyer, the U.S.S. *C. Turner Joy*, were the incidents that led

Congress to pass the Southeast Asia Resolution (better known as "the Gulf of Tonkin Resolution"), which authorized an open-ended American commitment to the war.

The American Buildup

The escalation of American involvement in the war from the role of advisor to principal combatant in 1965 brought an increased emphasis on military intelligence (as opposed to counterinsurgency and covert action, the foci of American intelligence activity in Vietnam up to that point). The Army established the Continental Army Command Tactical Intelligence Center at Fort Bragg, North Carolina, to prepare and deploy tactical intelligence units to Vietnam; the center eventually deployed more than thirty such units.

Armed forces intelligence in Vietnam was organized on a theater level by Maj. Gen. Joseph A. McChristian, the assistant chief of staff, intelligence (i.e., the J-2) of USMACV. McChristian established theater-level intelligence centers in Saigon for the coordination of all military intelligence, e.g., prisoner interrogation, captured documents, aerial reconnaissance. The Saigon-based 525th Military Intelligence Group, which was under McChristian's command, controlled four other major units: the 135th MI Group, which performed counterintelligence functions; the 149th MI Group, which collected positive intelligence; the First MI Battalion, an aerial reconnaissance unit; and the 519th MI Battalion, which furnished personnel to joint U.S./South Vietnamese intelligence centers. The 509th Radio Research Group of the Army Security Agency was established in Vietnam to provide direct COMINT support to Army elements down to the brigade level.

Aerial Reconnaissance

The U.S. Army was equipped with its own aerial reconnaissance—the Army's term is "aerial surveillance"—units in Vietnam. The Seventy-third Aerial Surveillance Company and four other companies operated the OV-1 Mohawk, a STOL (short-takeoff-and-landing) aircraft designed for tactical reconnaissance missions and equipped with a variety of sensor systems, including cameras, infrared scanners, and SIDE-LOOKING AIRCRAFT RADAR. The Army employed several other aircraft types in reconnaissance, including the UH-1 "Huey" and the OH-6 "Loach" helicopters, sometimes equipped with a so-called "people-sniffer" system, a device developed by the U.S. Army Limited War Laboratory at the Aberdeen (Maryland) Proving Ground, which could identify hidden troop concentrations by detecting the pres-

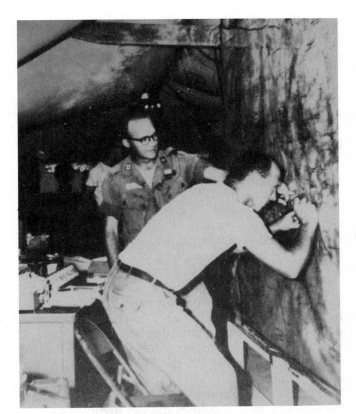

Members of the Twenty-fifth Military Intelligence Detachment plot suspected enemy positions on a map at the Chu Chi Base Camp, Vietnam, in 1966. Source: Department of Defense.

ence of certain chemical components of human perspiration and urine in the air above the jungle (by some accounts the device could not distinguish between human and animal emanations, and therefore was of limited reliability).

Aerial reconnaissance for target identification and post-strike damage assessment, as well as in support of ground operations, was carried out by both the U.S. Air Force and Navy. The RF-101 Voodoo aircraft was widely used for photoreconnaissance during the early 1960s, but it was restricted to missions in South Vietnam and Laos after the buildup of air defenses in North Vietnam in 1967 made sorties in that area too hazardous for the aircraft. The faster and therefore less vulnerable RF-4C Phantom aircraft was used for such missions thereafter. The Phantom was also equipped with the newly developed Terrain Following Radar, which enabled it to fly at high speed at treetop level, beneath the effective altitude of enemy radar and therefore safe from interception by surface-to-air missiles.

The Phantom was not invulnerable, however, and for reconnaissance missions over heavily defended targets, or deep into Communist territory, the Air Force used Remotely Piloted Vehicles (RPVs), unmanned drone aircraft controlled by microwave signal from a distant aircraft. As part of a program code-named Lightning Bug and later Buffalo Hunter, a family of RPVs were developed for photoreconnaissance and SIGINT missions. Typically a DC-130 Hercules transport aircraft carrying one or more RPVs beneath its wings would fly from a base in South Vietnam and enter North Vietnamese airspace, remaining beyond the range of enemy radar detection or interception. The RPV was launched and proceeded under control of personnel in the Hercules to the target area, where it would photograph objects and installations of interest, and in some cases collect SIGINT. Its mission complete, the drone would return to South Vietnamese airspace where an HH-3E "Jolly Green Giant" helicopter would take over its control. On a microwave command signal from the helicopter the RPV would shut down its engine and deploy a parachute, permitting midair recovery of the drone by the helicopter. After the film and other recordings were removed, the RPV was prepared for another flight.

The small RPVs proved to be less vulnerable to interception and, of course, did not involve any risk of crew loss. They eventually became the principal means of photoreconnaissance of North Vietnam and were also used for a variety of nonreconnaissance missions, e.g., distributing propaganda leaflets.

Aerial reconnaissance in support of the Navy's air operations against North Vietnam was carried out by carrier-based aircraft launched from Yankee Station, an area in the South China Sea adjacent to the Gulf of Tonkin. Most such flights were made by the RA5C Vigilante, a modification of the Navy's A5A fighter, or by the RF-8, the reconnaissance version of the F-8 Crusader fighter, but the navy also used unmanned RPVs, launched from carriers, for this mission. The venerable P2V, a Second World War-vintage patrol bomber, was used to monitor shipping in the waters off North Vietnam.

The task of more general intelligence gathering was accomplished through high-altitude photoreconnaissance flights over North Vietnam by U-2 RECONNAISSANCE AIRCRAFT beginning in 1965, and later by SR-71 RECONNAISSANCE AIRCRAFT.

The special requirements for surveillance of the Ho Chi Minh Trial in Laos led to the development of the YO-3 "Q-Star" aircraft, a modified sailplane powered by a small, well-muffled engine, and driven by a large-diameter, slowly rotating propeller designed to produce the least possible noise when operating. The function of the YO-3 was to fly under power to the vicinity of the Trail at night, then, proceeding in unpowered flight, glide silently and undetected at low altitude over the trail while searching for the presence of enemy personnel and vehicles with an assortment of sensors, including infrared heat emission detectors. Several YO-3 aircraft were deployed to Vietnam during 1969-70 but did not receive extensive use.

The Electronic Battlefield

More extensive surveillance of the Ho Chi Minh Trail was undertaken through a project code-named Muscle Shoals, and later known as Igloo White. It involved the development and placement along the Trail of devices called Unattended Ground Sensors (UGS), which could detect the passage of personnel or vehicles and report the event to a distant command post from which an air strike could then be directed.

Muscle Shoals grew out of plans for the McNamara Line, a proposed physical barrier across the Demilitarized Zone and extending westward across Laos to prevent Vietcong infiltration. Although the Line was never built, related studies done by the Institute for Defense Analysis, a Department of Defense think tank, demonstrated the feasibility of an electronic anti-infiltration barrier on the Ho Chi Minh Trail. The system was designed by the Pentagon's Defense Communications Planning Group and put in place late in 1967 by Task Force Alpha, a special unit of the Seventh Air Force, along a segment of the Trail some thirty miles inside Laos and extending northward from slightly above the sixteenth parallel to a point midway between the seventeenth and eighteenth parallels.

The UGS were placed by air from Navy SP2Vs and other aircraft. Four types were used: the Spikebuoy, a five-and-a-half-foot long listening device that buried itself in the ground on impact, leaving a camouflaged transmitting antenna above ground; the three-foot long Acoubuoy, also an acoustic sensor, which was dropped by parachute into the jungle treetops; the Adsid (Air Delivered Seismic Detection Sensor), a smaller device that buried itself in the ground and registered the vibrations of passing troops and vehicles; and the Acousid, which combined both acoustic and seismic detection. To enhance the effectiveness of the acoustic sensors, small antipersonnel mines were scattered along the Trail by air; these bomblets were not primarily intended to kill or injure the infiltrators, but to insure that the passing troops made enough noise to be detected by the sensors.

Signals from the UGS were monitored by an EC-121R electronic surveillance aircraft kept on station continuously over Laos (later the smaller and less-expensive-to-operate Beechcraft QU-22—a modified

Lockheed EC-121 SIGINT reconnaissance aircraft similar to the ones used in the Muscle Shoals and Igloo White programs in Vietnam. Source: Lockheed Aircraft.

Beechcraft Bonanza—performed this task). The signals were relayed to Task Force Alpha's Infiltration Surveillance Center at Nakhon Phanom, Thailand, where they were processed by a pair of IBM 360/65 computers. The computers analyzed the raw seismic and acoustical data, and immediately identified the nature of the activity on the Trail and pinpointed its location. The information sometimes triggered an immediate air strike; otherwise the information was compiled to identify truck parks, troop concentrations, or bottlenecks on the Trail, which were then targeted for subsequent air strikes.

The Muscle Shoals/Igloo White system proved highly effective in focusing American air power against Communist traffic on the Ho Chi Minh Trail, and although it did not completely interdict the Vietcong's supply line, it enormously increased the cost

of the war to the North Vietnamese. A second system was deployed around the Marine stronghold of Khesanh during the North Vietnamese siege of that installation in 1968, and was extremely effective in directing air and artillery strikes against the Communist force.

Order of Battle

The electronic surveillance of the Ho Chi Minh Trail also provided one of the few direct counts of the number of Vietcong and NVA regulars infiltrating into South Vietnam, and, from that, the most accurate indication of the Communist ORDER OF BATTLE, i.e., strength, composition, organization, location, and disposition of Communist forces in South Vietnam.

SR-71 reconnaissance aircraft that reportedly flew high-altitude photointelligence missions over North Vietnam. Source: Lockheed Aircraft.

OB intelligence estimates proved to be particularly elusive in Vietnam, owing to the nature of the Maoist "people's war," in which the guerrilla strives to be indistinguishable from the local populace and the locals often hide their allegiance. The Communist force actually consisted of a spectrum of personnel types, ranging from the North Vietnamese regulars and Vietcong elite forces through NLF political cadres, supply officers, medics, recruiters, and even tax collectors, to the local Communist "militia" and peasant sympathizers, representing a broad range of actual military threat.

In Vietnam, OB estimates took on a political importance they do not usually possess; in a war of counterinsurgency, the number of insurgents remaining at large is the best, and one of the few, quantitative measures of progress, and therefore intelligence analysts were under conscious and unconscious pressures to minimize Communist strength. For similar political reasons, the Communists announced greatly exaggerated reports of their strength in South Vietnam.

Raw OB intelligence was collected primarily through prisoner and defector interrogations, and from captured documents. Collecting these data was the job of intelligence components of USMACV and ARVN. OB estimates were produced by USMACV J-2, and also by the Office of Current Intelligence of the CIA INTELLIGENCE DIRECTORATE. Until 1967 these estimates were in general agreement, but apparently they fell seriously short of stating the true degree of Communist strength.

During 1966–67 CIA intelligence analyst Samuel A. Adams visited Vietnam several times and concluded that USMACV and the CIA had underestimated Vietcong and North Vietnamese strength in the south by as much as half. His analysis precipitated a dispute between the USMACV and the CIA over the enemy strength figures to be used in a 1967 NATIONAL INTELLIGENCE ESTIMATE entitled "Capabilities of the Vietnamese Communists for Fighting in South Vietnam." The Defense Intelligence Agency representative to the Board of National Estimate favored the use of USMACV's previous strength estimate of 270,000, while the CIA member proposed the new figure, based on Adams's research, of more than 500,000.

Coming at a moment when domestic opposition to

the war was increasing rapidly, the USMACV-CIA dispute took on powerful political overtones. Doubling the previous estimates of Communist strength would create the appearance that the United States and the GVN had not only failed to make progress in the war but that they were rapidly losing it. Furthermore, the new and larger figure would imply the need to draft perhaps a million or more additional American men over and above projected draft calls to fight in the war, because established counterinsurgency doctrine held that such wars could be won only when regular forces outnumbered the insurgents by ratios estimated variously between three to one and ten to one.

The CIA eventually capitulated and agreed to use the USMACV figure in the estimate, which was signed by RICHARD M. HELMS in his capacity as director of central intelligence and chairman of the United States Intelligence Board (see NATIONAL FOREIGN INTELLIGENCE BOARD). This was done over the most emphatic personal protests of Adams, who later filed formal charges with the CIA's inspector general against Helms (no action resulted). Adams's charges that Gen. William Westmoreland, commander of US-MACV, had deliberately falsified the OB figures, were made in a CBS television documentary aired in 1982 and resulted in an unsuccessful libel suit by Westmoreland against CBS, Adams, and others.

Adams's estimate of Communist strength was apparently vindicated by the Communist's Tet offensive of January–February 1968, after which the military revised official estimates of Vietcong and North Vietnamese regular strength upward to the level Adams had estimated. These new OB figures benefitted from COMINT, which the NATIONAL SECURITY AGENCY had begun furnishing in November 1967. The NSA COMINT reports initially pertained only to enemy units, but following Tet the reports included figures on the number of personnel North Vietnam dispatched to South Vietnam. These reports began to become available at about the same time as the Muscle Shoals/Igloo White system became operational, which may have added independent collateral confirmation of the data.

(Regarding CIA intelligence analysis in the Vietnam War, Karalekas notes

> While the DDP [CIA Clandestine Service] effort was increasing in proportion to the American military buildup, DDI [CIA Intelligence Directorate] estimates painted a pessimistic view of the likelihood of U.S. success with repeated escalations in the ground and air wars. At no time was the institutional dichotomy between the operational and analytical components more stark.)

CORDS and the Phoenix Program

Although emphasis shifted from counterinsurgency to conventional warfare after the American military buildup of 1965, the United States continued to develop programs aimed at pacification of the countryside, i.e., securing villages against Vietcong terrorism. In May 1967 the Civil Operations and Revolutionary Development Support program (CORDS), a joint undertaking of the State Department's Agency for International Development and USMACV, was initiated. CORDS was the brainchild of ROBERT W. KOMER, the program's first director, who had been a CIA analyst before joining the National Security Council staff and becoming a presidential advisor. The following March he was joined by William E. Colby, who had been chief of the CIA Saigon station before becoming head of the Clandestine Service's Far East Division; Colby was temporarily transferred from the CIA to AID at Komer's request.

Like the Civilian Irregular Defense Groups and the People's Action Teams, CORDS combined the themes of civic action and local militia, thereby aiming at improving both the quality of life and the security of the villagers. However, CORDS assumed the additional function of targeting the so-called Vietcong infrastructure, the Communist political and military cadres that lived and operated covertly in South Vietnam. To accomplish this, CORDS initiated the Intelligence Coordination and Exploitation Program (ICEX) in cooperation with the CIA, Army Intelligence, and the GVN's security services. ICEX was renamed Phoenix by Komer, and was alternately known as *Phung Hoang*, the name of a bird of Vietnamese mythology roughly similar to the phoenix.

Before Phoenix, several South Vietnamese agencies working in complete independence of each other collected counterintelligence and arrested suspected Vietcong cadres. Phoenix brought these scattered efforts together under one centralized and coordinated program. The first step in the Phoenix program was the centralization of counterintelligence records. District intelligence operations coordination centers were established to coordinate intelligence record-keeping in each of South Vietnam's four military regions; reporting to them were province intelligence operations coordination centers in each of the country's forty-four provinces. These centers were staffed by Vietnamese security personnel and U.S. military intelligence advisors (in 1970 a Military Assistance Security Advisor Course was inaugurated at Fort Bragg to provide trained personnel to work in the coordination centers).

Phoenix made use of an already existing program,

Chaumont, France, to serve in the G-2 section of the American Expeditionary Force under (then) Col. DENNIS NOLAN. He ran a secret intelligence organization behind enemy lines, consisting of several hundred agents in several European countries. He remained in Army Intelligence during 1919 and was sent to Prague to investigate German involvement in the events that had brought on the war.

Voska left the Army in 1919 and settled in Prague, where he founded the Czechoslovakia Commercial Corporation, a marketing firm that represented such American companies as Underwood Typewriters and Monroe Calculating Machines. He was arrested by the Nazis when they invaded Czechoslovakia in 1939, but managed to obtain his release and fled to the United States. During the Second World War he served in Turkey with the Office of War Information (see OFFICE OF STRATEGIC SERVICES).

After the war Voska returned to Prague and resumed his business activities. An ardent anti-Communist, he was arrested and imprisoned by the Czechoslovakian government in 1950. Seriously ill after ten years in prison, he was released in December 1959 and died shortly thereafter.

(Voska and Irwin, *Spy and Counterspy;* Jeffreys-Jones, *American Espionage;* obituary, *New York Times,* April 5, 1960, p. 37.)

W

WAGNER, ARTHUR LOCKWOOD (March 16, 1853–June 17, 1905): Army officer, intelligence officer

A native of Ottawa, Illinois, Wagner graduated from the U.S. Military Academy in 1875. He served with the infantry in the campaigns against the Sioux and the Ute Indians during 1876–77 and 1880–81. He was assigned to the post of professor of military science and tactics at the East Florida Seminary (now the University of Florida) during 1882–85, and taught at the Army's Infantry and Cavalry school at Fort Leavenworth, Kansas, from 1886 to 1897. During that period he published several books on military matters (including *The Service of Security and Information,* an intelligence-related text) that became standard texts, and he is credited with raising the standards of the school. Wagner came to be regarded in the Army as the final authority on military tactics and strategy.

In 1896 Wagner achieved the rank of major and the post of assistant adjutant general of the Army. The following year he was put in charge of the Military Information Division of the Adjutant General's Office (see ARMY INTELLIGENCE). As the SPANISH-AMERICAN WAR approached, he took several steps to improve the Army's intelligence of the situation in Cuba and Puerto Rico. Shortly before the outbreak of hostilities he dispatched Lt. ANDREW S. ROWAN on the celebrated mission to contact the Cuban insurgent leader, Gen. Calixto Garcia, obtain needed military intelligence from him, and establish the basis for the subsequent liaison between Garcia and the American expeditionary forces in the Santiago campaign. In April Wagner dispatched Lt. HENRY H. WHITNEY on a covert reconnaissance mission to Puerto Rico. Shortly thereafter Wagner,

who had been promoted to lieutenant colonel in February 1898, left the Military Information Division to serve as an intelligence officer on the staffs of Gens. Henry Lawton and Nelson Miles during the Santiago and Puerto Rico campaigns, respectively.

After the war Wagner served briefly as adjutant

Gen. Arthur L. Wagner. Source: National Archives.

Lt. Comdr. Richard Wainwright. Source: Author's collection.

general of the Department of the Dakotas and was assigned to the Philippines in December 1899. He served there in a number of intelligence posts during the Philippine Insurrection. In 1902, having achieved the rank of colonel, he returned to the United States and was adjutant general of the Lakes at Chicago until 1904 when he was assigned to the faculty of the newly established Army War College in Washington, D.C. He was promoted to the rank of brigadier general on the day that he died.

There is an often-repeated story that Wagner's career fell victim to the vindictiveness of Secretary of War Russell A. Alger, with whom he is supposed to have had a difference of military opinion regarding intelligence about Cuba during the early weeks of the Spanish-American War. Alger is supposed to have vowed to block Wagner from any future promotions. Whether or not Alger did in fact make such a promise, he was gone from the War Department by August 1899, long before Wagner could have expected further promotion, and Wagner's subsequent career advancement seems to have proceeded without adverse incident.

(*WAMB*; *Who Was Who in America*, v. 1; Bidwell, "History of the Military Intelligence Division, Department of the Army General Staff"; Ganoe, *History of the United States Army*; Ind, *A Short History of Espionage*.)

WAINWRIGHT, RICHARD (December 17, 1849–March 6, 1926): Navy officer

A native of Washington, D.C., Wainwright was the son of a distinguished naval officer of the same name. Appointed to the U.S. Naval Academy by President Lincoln on the recommendation of Admiral David Farragut, Wainwright graduated in 1868. After a long and distinguished career both at sea and ashore he was made chief of the Office of NAVAL INTELLIGENCE in April 1896. He did much to shift the focus of ONI from the mere collection of data on foreign fleets to a broader engagement in analyzing naval power and international politics, and systematically developing strategic war plans. He was a personal friend of Assistant Secretary of the Navy Theodore Roosevelt, and this association was instrumental in the development of ONI's planning for the SPANISH-AMERICAN WAR, plans which influenced basic policy decisions of the McKinley administration.

Wainwright left ONI in November 1897 to become executive officer of the *Maine*, and survived the destruction of that ship in Havana harbor on February 15, 1898. During the Spanish-American War he commanded the *Gloucester*, formerly the *Corsair*, the yacht of J.P. Morgan, which had been converted to a warship at the outbreak of hostilities. Under Wainwright's command the *Gloucester* took part in the sea battle of Santiago (July 3, 1898) and sank two Spanish destroyers.

Wainwright was later superintendent of the Naval Academy. He was promoted to rear admiral in July 1908, and retired in December 1911.

Wainwright's mother, Sally Franklin (Bache) Wainwright, was a great-granddaughter of BENJAMIN FRANKLIN.

(Dorwart, *The Office of Naval Intelligence*; *DAB*.)

WALK-IN

An individual, usually a foreigner, who contacts an intelligence service (sometimes by "walking into" the embassy, but usually by a more circumspect route) and volunteers to work as an AGENT. The walk-in is greeted with deep suspicion initially because of the likelihood that he or she is actually a PROVOCATION. Nonetheless, many of the most valuable DEFECTORS-IN-PLACE and PENETRATION

AGENTS of both the West and the USSR have been walk-ins (see OLEG PENKOVSKY).

WALLER, JOHN H.: intelligence officer

Waller joined the Office of Strategic Services in 1944 and was assigned to the OSS COUNTER-ESPIONAGE BRANCH. He served as deputy theater commander in the Middle East.

Waller later served with the CIA CLANDESTINE SERVICE in Iran, the Sudan, and India. He was chief of the Africa Division during 1964–68, and of the Near East Division during 1971–75. He was inspector general of the CIA during 1976–80, after which he retired from the Agency.

Waller was awarded the Distinguished Intelligence Medal and the National Civil Service Award.

WALLIS, SAMUEL (?–1798): businessman, frontiersman, British secret agent

Wallis's origins are obscure, apart from the facts that he was a native of Maryland and a Quaker. He was a shipper and speculator in Philadelphia, and owned a farm or plantation in Muncy, a frontier community on the bank of the Susquehanna River in central Pennsylvania.

During the American Revolution Wallis was a captain in the Northumberland militia and otherwise openly espoused the American cause, but he remained secretly loyal to Britain. During the British occupation of Philadelphia he provided some valuable and, apparently, secret service to Gen. William Howe, the British commander in chief. In 1779, when Maj. Gen. John Sullivan was planning an American expedition against the Iroquois, who had allied themselves with the British and were harassing American settlers on the frontier, Wallis was called upon to furnish Sullivan with a map of the Iroquois country. Wallis drew a false map calculated to mislead the American expedition, while sending a correct map to Sir Henry Clinton in New York through British secret courier JOSEPH STANSBURY. However, the false map failed to mislead Sullivan and had no effect upon the expedition.

In the course of his treasonous correspondence with Sir Henry Clinton, BENEDICT ARNOLD grew suspicious of Stansbury, who had been carrying the messages back and forth between the two, and he occasionally enlisted Wallis to act as his courier instead.

Wallis's role was not disclosed when Arnold's treasonous conspiracy failed. He continued to work as a British secret agent and covertly supplied food to the British army while maintaining strong personal con-

nections with the Continental Congress and an unsullied reputation as a staunch patriot.

After the war he moved to his plantation at Muncy, which he enlarged while engaging in profitable land speculation in the west. His treason did not become publicly known until the release of documents from British archives in the twentieth century.

(Boatner, *Encyclopedia of the American Revolution;* Van Doren, *Secret History of the American Revolution.*)

WAR OF 1812

Background: The war between the United States and Great Britain during 1812–15 was ancillary to Britain's wars with France in 1793–1801 and 1803–15; the causes of the War of 1812 sprang from the British struggle with Napoleon, and the course of the war in North America was strongly influenced by British preoccupation with the conflict in Europe.

Both Britain and France tried to prevent the United States from trading with their opponent, but only Britain was in a practical position to enforce her wishes. Britain exacerbated tense Anglo-American relations by boarding American ships in international waters to impress (i.e., kidnap) crewmen arbitrarily deemed to be British subjects, and by encouraging Indian depredations against American frontier settlers in the Northwest (i.e., Ohio and the territories of Indiana, Illinois, and Michigan).

Through these transgressions the British played into the hands of American expansionist interests in the Northwest who sought to acquire Canada, and to those in the South and West who coveted parts of Florida owned by Spain (a British ally in the war with France). These interests were represented by the "war hawks," a group of young Southerners and Westerners sent to Congress in 1811.

Relations with Britain worsened late in 1811. President James Madison's efforts to reverse British policy by diplomatic means failed, and on June 1, 1812 he asked Congress to declare war on Britain. Support for the move was far from unanimous; the New England Federalists were strongly opposed to the expansionist aims of the war hawks and to Madison's war proposal. The declaration eventually was passed by a close vote (19 to 13 in the Senate, 79 to 49 in the House) on June 18th.

The War: Although the war had been long anticipated, the U.S. government had not taken any steps to prepare the Army and Navy to fight it. The Army was undermanned, ill-equipped, poorly trained, and poorly led, and no plan (worthy of the name) for the conduct of the war existed at the outbreak of hostilities. Gen. William Hull's invasion of Canada in July

1812 accomplished nothing but the loss of Detroit and the Michigan Territory to the British in August. Attempted invasions of Canada in October across the Niagara River and at Lake Champlain also failed when the New York militia refused to support the federal regulars. The psychological impact of these defeats was somewhat mitigated by individual victories of the U.S. Navy in engagements with vessels of the British naval blockade of the East Coast. But the Navy, far outmatched in numbers of fighting ships, failed to lift the blockade that continued to inflict heavy damage on the American economy and left the coast open to the threat of invasion.

The American military situation improved in 1813, chiefly as the result of Capt. Oliver Hazzard Perry's naval victories on the Great Lakes, and Gen. William Henry Harrison's recovery of Detroit and defeat of a British force in Ontario. However, the British struck back the following year, advancing into Maine as far south as the Penobscot River, establishing a naval base on Cape Cod, and even raiding and burning Washington.

Only Britain's war-weariness and preoccupation with Napoleon prevented her from exacting a high price for America's lack of military preparedness. In the event the Treaty of Ghent, which officially ended the war in December 1814 (the battle of New Orleans was fought in January 1815), was in the nature of an armistice that neither side could claim as evidence of its victory over the other. The end of British interference with American trade resulted not from the Treaty but from the end of Britain's war with France. The port of Mobile and western Florida (the latter had been annexed by the United States before the war) became American territory, but Spain retained her possessions in eastern Florida until 1821, when she ceded them to the United States. And, of course, Canada remained British.

Intelligence: American unpreparedness at the outbreak of the war extended to military intelligence, especially that required by the Army for the planned invasion of Canada. Not only was there a nearly total absence of intelligence on British strength and disposition north of the border, the War Department lacked basic intelligence—maps and terrain studies of southern Canada, and realistic estimates of the sympathies of settlers and Indians in the border areas. Therefore there was nothing that could be called a war plan in existence when war was declared.

With the barest minimum of foresight the War Department sent a small column of ill-trained and ill-equipped Ohio militia under Gen. William Hull to Detroit a few weeks before the declaration of war.

The "plan" called for Hull to launch an invasion of Canada from that point after Congress passed the declaration. It is symptomatic of the entire comedy of errors that Hull did not receive word that the declaration was in force until two days after the British commander in Canada was officially notified of it by Washington. Worse, the American commander, en route to Detroit, managed to lose a trunk containing his orders and his muster roll, and the documents were in the hands of the British before the American column even arrived at its destination.

British intelligence had not ceased its collection activities in the United States since the close of the Revolutionary War, and was therefore well-equipped with both the basic and the military intelligence it needed. To this advantage was added another: Gen. Isaac Brock, the British commander in Canada, had a keen sense of Hull's intelligence failures, and he proved to be a master of the art of military deception. By various means he fed Hull persuasive disinformation, causing the American commander to overestimate greatly the strength of the British force he was facing. Consequently Hull failed to pursue the initiative after he crossed into Canada unopposed in mid-July. Although only a tiny British force held the area he had entered, he was convinced he was seriously outnumbered and fell back to Detroit. Brock followed him and laid siege to the city with a force no larger than that which Hull commanded inside its walls. The British commander then concocted a phony dispatch to his headquarters stating that he had 5,000 Indians prepared to fight alongside him, and therefore would not need reinforcements. Brock contrived to permit this document to fall into Hull's hands, with the result that the American commander immediately surrendered Detroit to the British without offering any resistance.

The other American expeditions into Canada in 1812 had little better intelligence than Hull had. Although better BASIC INTELLIGENCE of Canadian areas bordering New York State *was* available, it was simply because this region had been longer settled than that adjacent to Michigan, and not through any preparation by the War Department. But as to the question of determining British strength and intentions, the American commanders seem to have ignored even the need for such intelligence during the war.

The role of intelligence failure in the poor American military performance should be placed in perspective, however. It was merely another sign of the poor state of readiness of the Army at the beginning of the war. Even had much better intelligence been available, it is unlikely that it would have offset the handicaps of poor leadership, insufficient manpower and training, and inadequate material from which the United States suffered.

New England Subversion

Had the war developed into a protracted land conflict fought in the Northeast, the British might have had the advantage of an American fifth column among the Federalists of the New England states who continued to oppose the war in ways bordering on treason. British intelligence was well aware of the pro-British sentiment that had existed in New England since long before the declaration of war. For example, in 1809 the governor-general of Canada sent an agent—a former American artillery officer named JOHN (or James) HENRY—into the United States to assess public opinion in New England in the event of an Anglo-American war. Henry lived and traveled in Massachusetts and Vermont during 1809–11 and reported to his Canadian principal that there was considerable pro-British sentiment among the Federalists of the region, perhaps sufficient to a scheme to split New England from the Union and form a Northern Confederacy that would align itself with Great Britain. (Henry subsequently had a falling out with the British and sold copies of his reports to President Madison early in 1812; Madison paid $50,000 of public funds for the documents in the mistaken belief that they constituted evidence of treason on the part of his political enemies, the Federalists.)

Federalist opposition to the war continued for its duration and took such forms as the refusal of the State of Massachusetts to permit its militia to be called up for federal service, and the refusal of large Boston banks—Federalist controlled—to lend money to the U.S. government during the war. Commodore Stephen Decatur claimed that the New Englanders went even further in their subversion: according to him, they warned the British blockade by means of blue lights along the Connecticut shore when he attempted to put to sea. The so-called "blue-light Federalists," if they in fact existed, would have presented a serious counter-espionage and countersubversion problem had the war been fought on land in New England.

Through its intelligence operations in America, the British government was aware of its potential allies in New England. However, it could not exploit this advantage without risking the continuing of a war it did not want.

(Bidwell, "History of the Military Intelligence Division, Department of the Army General Staff"; Bryan, *The Spy in America*; Ind, *A Short History of Espionage*; Beirne, *The War of 1812*.)

WARNE, KATE (ca. 1833–1868): detective, Union secret agent

Warne's origins are mysterious, and even her maiden name is unavailable. One day in 1856 she called upon ALLAN PINKERTON, described herself as a widow, and applied for a job with PINKERTON'S NATIONAL DETECTIVE AGENCY. She pointed out that in many circumstances a woman could be more effective than a man in the role of undercover investigator. Pinkerton hired her, making her probably the first American female detective, and possibly the first in the world. He later recalled that "she succeeded far beyond my utmost expectations." Her effectiveness prompted Pinkerton to hire other women, and by 1860 he had assembled a small staff of female detectives headed by Warne.

In February 1861 Warne played an important part in thwarting the BALTIMORE PLOT to assassinate President-elect Abraham Lincoln en route to his inauguration. Posing as the sister of Lincoln, who was himself traveling incognito, she accompanied the President-elect on the train trip from Philadelphia to Washington and kept curious railroad conductors and others away from "her brother" on the pretext that he was an invalid.

In May 1861 Warne was one of the detectives who accompanied Pinkerton to Cincinnati to organize the Secret Service of the Army of the Ohio under Gen. George B. McClellan. Apparently she was also one of the agents he sent into Confederate territory to collect military intelligence shortly thereafter.

Warne is buried in the Pinkerton family plot in Graceland Cemetery in Chicago, evidence of the bond of affection that existed between her and the Pinkertons.

(Horan and Swiggett, *The Pinkerton Story*; Horan, *The Pinkertons*.)

WASHINGTON, GEORGE (February 22, 1732–December 14, 1799): first President of the United States, farmer, government official, Army officer, intelligence officer

A native of Virginia, Washington received little formal schooling and was largely self-educated. He worked as a surveyor, and in 1749 he was appointed official surveyor of Culpeper County, Virginia. During the French and Indian (Seven Years) War he served with distinction as an officer in the Virginia militia, achieving the rank of brigadier.

Gen. George Washington. Source: U.S. Army.

The death of his elder brother in 1752 made Washington heir to the family estate, Mount Vernon, and after his marriage to a wealthy widow in 1759 he was one of America's richest men. He served in the House of Burgesses and became identified with the Patriot element in Virginia politics before the American Revolution. He served as a Virginia delegate to the Continental Congresses in 1774–75, and was an advocate of military preparedness for the coming war with Britain.

In June 1775 Washington was unanimously selected by the Continental Congress to be commander in chief of the Continental Army. His ability as a commander became apparent at the battle of Trenton in December 1776 and was demonstrated often thereafter.

Washington was keenly aware that in facing a larger, better trained and equipped, and more mobile foe, good military intelligence would be vital to success and even to survival. This was especially evident to him during the New Jersey campaign of late 1776, and he then took personal charge of recruiting, instructing, and running secret intelligence agents and establishing agent networks. As his biographer, James Thomas Flexner, notes, "Washington had a passion

for intelligence that would enable him to foresee, and, as far as his possibilities went, he was an excellent spymaster." Washington personally recruited JOHN HONEYMAN, for example, who played so important a role in the crucial victory at Trenton, and Joshua Mersereau, who organized the MERSEREAU SPY RING in Staten Island and Manhattan. Washington was concerned with the most minute details of intelligence TRADECRAFT, and he instructed his agents in such particulars as the use of invisible inks (see CRYPTOLOGY) and the establishment of COVER.

However, Washington's secret intelligence requirements expanded so rapidly that he soon delegated the role of CASE OFFICER to selected subordinates who established and ran secret intelligence networks for him, e.g., ELIAS DAYTON, who took over the Mersereau ring and established other networks in New York; Nathaniel Sackett and Gen. Charles Scott, who ran still other networks in Manhattan and Long Island; Maj. BENJAMIN TALLMADGE, who established one of the most effective networks of the war, the CULPER SPY RING; and Gen. Thomas Mifflin, who established a STAY-BEHIND NET in Philadelphia that operated during the brief (September 1777–June 1778) British occupation of that city.

Although he delegated these secret intelligence functions to subordinates, Washington continued to act as his own chief intelligence officer, i.e., he did his own intelligence analysis, piecing together the fragments of information supplied by his subordinates into a comprehensive picture of British strength, position, and intentions. He has been criticized for this by some military historians who cite, for example, the intelligence failure that led to Washington's defeat at the battle of Brandywine (September 1777). They argue that one officer cannot divide his attention between the line function of command and the staff function of intelligence without neglecting one or the other. The counterargument is that no professional staff officers competent to the task were to be found among the citizen soldiers of the Continental Army, and therefore Washington had no alternative.

Washington was a master of military deception and counterintelligence, and he often misled the British by furnishing false information to their intelligence agents. When his greatly depleted army was wintering at Morristown, New Jersey, early in 1777, he discouraged General Howe from attacking by planting grossly inflated reports of his troop strength on two separate unsuspecting British agents, and arranged to have it confirmed to Howe by a double agent. The following winter Washington executed an even more elaborate deception operation to convince the British commanders that he was preparing attacks on both Philadelphia and New York, when in fact his army, badly beaten at Brandywine and Germantown, was licking its wounds at Valley Forge. And during August 1781 he skillfully convinced British Gen. Henry Clinton that he planned an assault on New York City at the very moment he was moving his army to Virginia for the climactic battle of Yorktown.

After the war Washington resigned his commission and returned to the private life of a Virginia planter. In 1787 he was unanimously chosen to preside over the Federal Constitutional Convention in Philadelphia. In 1789 he was made the first President of the United States by the unanimous vote of the Electoral College. He was reelected in 1792 and served a second term, but declined invitations to serve a third time. He returned to Mount Vernon, serving again only briefly as Army commander in chief during a French war scare in 1798.

Washington's role as the Revolution's most important intelligence officer is little known, having been obscured by generations of biographers and myth-makers who preferred to depict him as a man so essentially veracious as to be incapable of guile, even in the service of his country. However, the revision of public attitudes in the mid-twentieth century toward spying and secret warfare has apparently encouraged biographers and historians to examine this previously neglected side of the Father of His Country.

(Flexner, *George Washington in the American Revolution*; Thompson, "George Washington, Master Intelligence Officer"; Bakeless, *Turncoats, Traitors and Heroes*; Ford, *A Peculiar Service*; Bryan, *The Spy in America*; Boatner, *Encyclopedia of the American Revolution*; *WAMB*.)

WEBSTER, TIMOTHY (1821–April 28, 1862): private detective, Union double agent

A native of Newhaven, Sussex, England, Webster was brought to the United States by his parents in 1833 and raised in Princeton, New Jersey. He was working as a sergeant of police at the Crystal Palace, an exposition hall in New York City, in 1856 when he met ALLAN PINKERTON who hired him as a detective with the PINKERTON'S NATIONAL DETECTIVE AGENCY.

Webster played an important part in uncovering the BALTIMORE PLOT to assassinate President-elect Abraham Lincoln en route to his inauguration in February 1861. In May 1861, after the beginning of the CIVIL WAR, he accompanied Pinkerton to Cincinnati to help organize the Secret Service of the

Timothy Webster. Source: Author's collection.

Department of the Ohio under Gen. George B. McClellan. Shortly thereafter Pinkerton sent him through Confederate lines into Kentucky and Tennessee to gather military intelligence. A little later he was sent to Baltimore, where he was already established as a secessionist sympathizer as a result of his cover in the Baltimore Plot investigation. He penetrated the secessionist underground there, and his intelligence reports led to the arrest of the leaders, who were plotting with the Confederate secret service.

Webster, whose true role was still unsuspected by the Baltimore secessionists, was invited to join the Knights of Liberty, a secret society of Confederate sympathizers similar to the KNIGHTS OF THE GOLDEN CIRCLE. Armed with the credentials of this society and letters of introduction from some of the Baltimore secessionists, he traveled to Richmond, the capital of the Confederacy, in October. There he met Confederate leaders, including the Secretary of State, Judah Benjamin, and offered the latter his services as a secret courier between Richmond and Baltimore. Benjamin accepted the offer, and Webster was at once given the opportunity both to report regularly to Pinkerton in Washington on the intelligence he had collected in Virginia, and to read the secret Confederate communications before passing them along to the addressees.

Webster made four round trips between Richmond and Baltimore during the winter of 1861–62, collecting information that, according to historian and espionologist Edwin C. Fishel, justifies Pinkerton's rating of him as the top agent of that period. In February 1862 he was stricken with inflammatory rheumatism while in Richmond and confined to bed. Alarmed by Webster's long silence, Pinkerton dispatched two other agents, PRYCE LEWIS and JOHN SCULLY, to Richmond to investigate. Lewis and Scully located Webster, but were recognized as Pinkerton agents and arrested. To save his life, Scully betrayed Webster, and Lewis, seeing that the damage had already been done, did the same. The two were imprisoned for a time in Richmond and then released in an exchange of prisoners of war. Webster was tried and convicted of espionage, and hanged.

(Horan and Swiggett, *The Pinkerton Story*; Horan, *The Pinkertons*; Bryan, *The Spy in America*.)

WEBSTER, WILLIAM HEDGCOCK (March 6, 1924–): lawyer, jurist, intelligence officer

A native of St. Louis, Missouri, Webster was commissioned as an officer in the U.S. Naval Reserve, serving during 1943–46 and 1951–52. He graduated from Amherst College in 1947 and from Washington University law school in 1949. He practiced law in St. Louis until 1971, except for 1960–61 when he served as U.S. attorney, Eastern District, Missouri. In 1971 he was appointed judge in the U.S. District Court, Eastern District, Missouri. In 1973 he was appointed to the U.S. Court of Appeals, Eighth Circuit, a post he held until 1978, when President Jimmy Carter appointed him director of the FEDERAL BUREAU OF INVESTIGATION.

Webster took charge of an FBI suffering from the loss of prestige that followed disclosure in the mid-1970s of the Bureau's illegal or improper domestic intelligence activities under J. EDGAR HOOVER, activities that included illegal entries, warrantless wiretaps, and the infiltration and surveillance of noncriminal political dissident groups. Webster instituted many reforms in the Bureau and continued others that had been instituted by his predecessor, Clarence M. Kelly. He focused the Bureau's activities on white-collar crime and political corruption, recruited members of minority groups, and steered clear of the excesses of the past. During the mid-1980s the Bureau, under Webster, was notably successful in its work against organized crime and Soviet espionage, and had reclaimed most or all of its lost prestige.

In March 1987 President Ronald Reagan appointed Webster to succeed WILLIAM J. CASEY as director of central intelligence (see ROBERT M. GATES).

(*Who's Who in America*, 43rd ed.; *New York Times*, March 4, 1987, p. A1.)

WELCH, RICHARD SKEFFINGTON (December 14, 1929–December 23, 1975): intelligence officer

A native of Hartford, Connecticut, Welch attended the Classical High School in Providence, Rhode Island, before enrolling in Harvard, from which he graduated in 1951. He joined the CENTRAL INTELLIGENCE AGENCY soon after graduation and served in the CIA CLANDESTINE SERVICE.

Welch served at CIA headquarters in Washington, and later at the CIA station in Athens, and on Cyprus. In 1966 he was assigned to Guatemala and in 1967 to Guyana. After three years back at headquarters in Washington, he was sent to Peru as chief of station in 1972. In June 1975 he was made chief of station in Athens, Greece (a classical scholar, he was fluent in both ancient and modern Greek).

Six months after his arrival in Greece, Welch was assassinated by terrorists in front of his home while he and his wife were returning from a Christmas party at the American ambassador's residence. A leftist group calling itself "the Revolutionary Organization of November 17" (in reference to the date of a student uprising in 1973) later claimed responsibility for the assassination. The same group carried out a series of other political assassinations in Greece, including the 1983 murder of U.S. Navy Capt. George Tsantes.

Welch's name, address, telephone number, and CIA affiliation had been published along with those of other CIA officers in the English-language *Athens News* a month before the murder. About a year before the incident he had been identified as a CIA officer in Peru by *CounterSpy*, the publication of the Fifth Estate, a Washington-based group opposed to all U.S. intelligence activities. The same issue contained an editorial by PHILIP AGEE urging the "identification, exposure, and neutralization" of CIA people working overseas, so that "the people themselves will . . . decide what they must do to rid themselves of CIA."

There has been considerable speculation that these publications were directly or indirectly responsible for Welch's murder. Those who dispute this theory point out that the official Foreign Service cover assigned to Welch and most other CIA station chiefs could easily be penetrated through an analysis of their curricula vitae in official State Department bio-graphic directories, which, in fact, is the means the Fifth Estate said it used to identify Welch. The November 17th group claimed to have had Welch under surveillance since shortly after his arrival in Greece in June 1975.

Welch lived in the same house that several previous Athens station chiefs had occupied, and this has been suggested as yet another possible explanation of how his murderers identified him.

(*Newsweek,* January 5, 1976, p. 26; *New York Times,* December 24, 1975, p. 1; February 22, 1985, p. 6; Phillips, *The Night Watch.*)

WENTWORTH, PAUL (?–1793): British intelligence officer

Wentworth's origins are obscure, but he is believed to have been a cousin or brother of John Wentworth, royal governor of New Hampshire. Wentworth was a Harvard classmate of John Adams. He owned considerable land in New Hampshire and a plantation in Surinam, but he preferred living in Europe, especially Paris. He spoke perfect French. He also lived for some time before the American Revolution in London, where he was colonial agent for New Hampshire. In that capacity he came to know and befriend fellow agent BENJAMIN FRANKLIN. Shortly before the Revolution he joined the British secret service. He was paid a salary of 500 pounds per year, but his real motivation seems to have been the prospect of becoming a baronet and getting a seat in Parliament. At the outbreak of the Revolution he was sent to Paris, where as a cover for his operations he played the role of a wealthy businessman (which, in fact, he was), man-about-town and bon vivant. He took a mistress—one Mlle. Desmaillis—and used her house in Rue Traversière to entertain a wide circle of French and American notables whom he found useful in one way or another. BEAUMARCHAIS and the French foreign minister, the Count de Vergennes, were among his circle of friends and acquaintances.

Wentworth's chief intelligence targets were Franklin and the American ministry at Passy. He recruited numerous agents within the ministry, but the most successful of them by far was his Connecticut protégé, EDWARD BANCROFT, secretary to Franklin and the American legation. The intelligence gathered by Wentworth's operation was of superior quality, providing complete and timely reporting of all significant dispatches between Passy and Philadelphia, and developments in French-American relations. However, much of this intelligence was disregarded by George III because he distrusted the motives of

both Wentworth and Bancroft, suspecting them of trying to manipulate events in order to profit from the resulting rise or fall of the London stock market. Consequently, British policy never took full advantage of this valuable intelligence asset.

When France joined the United States in the war against Britain, Wentworth came under close surveillance by French counterespionage agents and he soon returned to London, where he continued to run his agent networks in Europe. He prospered well enough to buy Hammersmith, a riverside estate outside London, but he never received the title and station in British society he longed for. In 1790 he went to live on his plantation in Surinam, by some account with a nephew, Nathaniel Wentworth. He died in 1793, reportedly of natural causes.

(Einstein, *Divided Loyalties;* Currey, *Code Number 72;* Young, *Revolutionary Ladies.*)

WESTERN ENTERPRISES

A Central Intelligence Agency, PROPRIETARY COMPANY based in Taiwan, which provided commercial cover for the CIA CLANDESTINE SERVICE in the Far East during the 1950s.

(Smith, *Portrait of a Cold Warrior.*)

WHEELON, ALBERT DEWELL (January 18, 1929–): aerospace executive, intelligence officer

A native of Moline, Illinois, Wheelon received a bachelor's degree from Stanford University in 1949 and a Ph.D. from the Massachusetts Institute of Technology in 1952. He taught at MIT from 1949 to 1952 when he joined the Douglas Aircraft Company. Between 1953 and 1962 he worked for the Ramo-Wooldridge Corporation, a major aerospace company. In 1962 he was recruited by Director JOHN MCCONE of the CENTRAL INTELLIGENCE AGENCY to serve as the Agency's first deputy director for Science and Technology. Wheelon's term with the CIA marked the increasing shift in emphasis away from covert operations and toward technical collection of intelligence that followed the departure of ALLEN DULLES in the wake of the BAY OF PIGS.

Wheelon served with the CIA until 1966, when he returned to private industry and joined Hughes Aircraft. He was awarded the Distinguished Intelligence Medal at the time of his departure from CIA.

See also CIA SCIENCE AND TECHNOLOGY DIRECTORATE, HERBERT SCOVILLE.

(*Who's Who in America,* 43rd ed.)

John E. Wilkie. Source: Author's collection.

WHITNEY, HENRY HOWARD (December 25, 1866–April 2, 1949): Army officer

A native of Hopewell, Pennsylvania, Whitney graduated from West Point in 1892. On April 1, 1896 he was assigned to special duty with the Army's Military Information Division (see ARMY INTELLIGENCE). In May 1898, shortly after the beginning of the SPANISH-AMERICAN WAR, he was sent on a covert reconnaissance of Puerto Rico. When he arrived on the island aboard a British merchant ship the Spanish authorities were waiting for him, having learned of his mission through a leak in the War Department that was picked up by the American press. However, he disguised himself as one of the ship's coal stokers and so avoided capture. Later he managed to get ashore in the guise of "H.W. Elias," a British merchant marine officer. During his sojourn in Puerto Rico he learned that there were relatively few Spanish troops on the island, almost no artillery, and only a handful of small, antiquated naval vessels. This information was of value to Gen. Nelson Miles who commanded the invasion force that landed in Puerto Rico late in July.

Whitney rose to the rank of brigadier general before his retirement. He died in Madison, New Jersey.

(O'Toole, *The Spanish War; Who's Who in America, 1899–1900.*)

WILEY, JOHN COOPER (September 26, 1893–February 3, 1967): diplomat, intelligence officer

Wiley was born in Bordeaux, France, the son of American parents. He was educated by private tutors and attended Union College in 1916. In 1915 he was appointed clerk at the American embassy in Paris, and secretary at the embassy the following year. He served at a variety of foreign posts, including Madrid, Warsaw, Berlin, Moscow, and Vienna, until 1940 when he returned to Washington.

Wiley was assigned on temporary duty from the State Department to the Office of the Coordinator of Information—the predecessor to the Office of Strategic Services—and continued with the OSS during the SECOND WORLD WAR. He served on the OSS Board of Analysts and, together with DEWITT CLINTON POOLE, established the OSS FOREIGN NATIONALITIES BRANCH, which Poole headed.

Wiley was U.S. ambassador to Colombia in 1944–47, to Portugal in 1947–48, to Iran in 1948–51, and to Panama from 1951 until his retirement in 1954.

(Roosevelt, *War Report of the OSS; Who Was Who in America*, v. 4.)

WILKIE, JOHN ELBERT (April 27, 1860–December 13, 1934): businessman, journalist, Secret Service chief

A native of Elgin, Illinois, Wilkie began his newspaper career on the *Chicago Times* in September 1877 and traveled abroad as a foreign correspondent. In 1881 he joined the *Chicago Tribune* as a reporter, and was later city editor and commercial editor of the paper. In 1893 he went to London and engaged in banking and steamship businesses. He returned to Chicago in 1896 and again worked as a reporter, making a specialty of criminal investigations.

In February 1898 Wilkie was made chief of the SECRET SERVICE at the request of Assistant Secretary of the Treasury Frank A. Vanderlip, who had once worked as a reporter for the *Chicago Tribune* under Wilkie. Vanderlip and Secretary of the Treasury Lyman J. Gage selected an outsider for the job becaused they wanted a major reorganization of the Service, and Wilkie offered a combination of administrative skill and a background in criminal investigation.

In April 1898, two months after Wilkie took office, the SPANISH-AMERICAN WAR broke out and the Secret Service was faced with a major counterespionage task. The Service met the challenge successfully and broke the MONTREAL SPY RING, the only espionage operation mounted by Spain during the brief war.

Shortly after its Spanish-American War success, however, the Service under Wilkie experienced a notable failure: on September 6, 1901 President William McKinley was fatally shot by an anarchist at the Pan American Exposition ion Buffalo, New York, despite the nearby presence of three Secret Service agents. (It should be noted that at this date the Secret Service was not officially responsible for the full-time protection of the President; it received that duty only after the McKinley assassination).

Wilkie served as Secret Service chief until 1912, during which period the agency was primarily involved in its traditional role of catching counterfeiters, smugglers, and bootleggers. Later he returned to Chicago and became the vice-president of a local streetcar company.

(Wilkie, *American Secret Service Agent; Who Was Who in America*, v. 1; O'Toole, *The Spanish War*.)

WILLAUER, WHITING (November 30, 1906– August 6, 1962): businessman, diplomat, intelligence officer

A native of New York City, Willauer graduated from Princeton University in 1928 and from the Harvard Law School in 1931. He joined the Boston law firm of Bingham, Dana and Gould, where he specialized in the investigation and trial of transportation cases. He left the firm in 1939 and went to Washington, where he worked as an attorney for several government agencies. In 1941 he joined China Defense Supplies, Inc., a lobbying organization for Chiang Kai-shek's Nationalist Chinese regime. He helped Gen. Claire Chennault establish the American Volunteer Group, popularly known as the Flying Tigers, and spent most of the Second World War in China helping Chennault deal with logistical problems.

In 1944 Willauer became director of the Far East and Special Territories Branch of the U.S. Foreign Economic Administration, which collected economic intelligence, procured strategic materials, and did postwar planning. In 1945 he joined with several of his former associates in the Chinese lobby to pursue business ventures in China. The following year he and General Chennault founded an airline to do business in China and the Far East. The line was eventually called Civil Air Transport.

In 1950 CAT, near bankruptcy after four years of struggling to do business in a China wracked by civil war, was purchased by the Office of Policy Coordination, as the Central Intelligence Agency's COVERT ACTION department was then known. The airline was to provide air support and cover for CIA/ OPC's operations in the Far East (see AIR PROPRIETARIES). Willauer and Chennault stayed on with the company in the capacity of president and chairman of the board, respectively. Willauer became, in effect, a contract employee of the CIA.

Willauer remained in the CAT post until 1953, when personal and medical problems forced him to leave. He presided over this CIA PROPRIETARY COMPANY during the KOREAN WAR, a period in which it was especially active in the Agency's covert operations in the Far East.

Willauer became U.S. ambassador to Honduras in 1954 and took part in the GUATEMALA COUP. During 1958–60 he was ambassador to Costa Rica. Late in 1961 he returned to Washington to serve as a special assistant to the secretary of state. Willauer reviewed the CIA's plans for the BAY OF PIGS INVASION and expressed some misgivings about the project.

(Leary, *Perilous Missions*.)

WILLIAMS, JAMES ARTHUR (March 29, 1932–): Army officer, intelligence officer

A native of Paterson, New Jersey, Williams graduated from the U.S. Military Academy in 1954 and later earned an M.A. in Latin American studies at the University of New Mexico. He served as an assistant Army attaché at the U.S. embassy in Caracas, Venezuela, and was an exchange officer in an exchange program established by the departments of State and Defense.

Williams served as deputy director of estimates in the Defense Intelligence Agency, deputy assistant chief of staff for intelligence of the Department of the Army (see ARMY INTELLIGENCE), and deputy chief of staff for intelligence of U.S. Army, Europe, and the Seventh Army in West Germany before becoming director of the Defense Intelligence Agency.

Williams retired with the rank of lieutenant general in 1986. He holds the Legion of Merit, the Bronze Star, Air Medal, and the Army Commendation Medal.

(*Who's Who in America*, 42nd ed.)

Gen. Charles A. Willoughby, left, conferring with Eighth Army commander Gen. Matthew Ridgway (wearing sunglasses), and Director of Central Intelligence Walter Bedell Smith (right) during the Korean War. Source: Department of Defense.

WILLOUGHBY, CHARLES A. (March 8, 1892–1972): Army officer, intelligence officer

A native of Heidelberg, Germany, Willoughby was born Karl Weidenbach, but subsequently adopted his mother's maiden surname. He became a naturalized American citizen in 1910. He graduated from the Gettysburg (Pennsylvania) College in 1914 and was commissioned as a second lieutenant in the U.S. Army in 1915. He served on the Mexican border in 1916–17, and in France during the First World War.

Willoughby attended the Army's Command and General Staff School in 1931, and the Army War College in 1936. He advanced through grades to the rank of colonel by 1939 when he became Gen. Douglas MacArthur's chief of staff for intelligence. He served as MacArthur's chief of intelligence through the Philippine and Southwest Pacific campaigns. He presided over a substantial intelligence establishment, largely of his own creation, which included

the ALLIED INTELLIGENCE BUREAU, the ALLIED TRANSLATOR AND INTERPRETER SECTION, and the ALLIED GEOGRAPHICAL SECTION. His proprietary interest in this establishment may have prompted him to urge MacArthur to refuse the Office of Strategic Services permission to operate in the Southwest Pacific theater, and his appeal succeeded.

Willoughby reached the temporary rank of major general, and reverted to the permanent rank of brigadier general after the war. He continued to serve as chief intelligence officer of MacArthur's Far East Command and served in that post during the KOREAN WAR. His earlier antipathy toward the OSS apparently carried over to the Central Intelligence Agency when that Agency began operations in the Far East in 1950. Relations were strained between Willoughby and GEORGE E. AURELL, the chief of the CIA's Office of Policy Coordination (as the COVERT ACTION unit was then designated) in Japan. When HANS V. TOFTE arrived in Japan in mid-1950 to organize CIA/OPC escape-and-evasion networks and guerrilla operations in North Korea, Willoughby reportedly threatened to throw the CIA out of the Far East. However, Tofte ignored the threat and Willoughby apparently was unable to make good on it.

Among Willoughby's many decorations were the Distinguished Service Cross, the Distinguished Service Medal, the Silver Star, the Legion of Merit, and a variety of foreign decorations.

(*Who Was Who in America*, v. 5; Spector, *Eagle Against the Sun*; Ind, *Allied Intelligence Bureau*; Manchester, *American Caesar*; Leary, *Perilous Missions*; Goulden, *Korea*.)

WILSON, FRANK JOHN (May 19, 1887–June 22, 1970): law enforcement officer, security specialist, Secret Service director

A native of Buffalo, New York, Wilson attended local schools and worked in the real estate business in Buffalo until 1917. After brief service in the U.S. Army, he attended the University of Buffalo.

In 1920 Wilson joined the U.S. Treasury Department and was assigned to the Intelligence Unit. He served as a special agent in Chicago, San Francisco, Baltimore, and New Orleans. In 1933–35 he was in charge of the Department's Intelligence Unit in Cleveland, Ohio. In 1937 Wilson became director of the SECRET SERVICE and he remained in that capacity until his retirement in 1946. During 1947–48 he was a security consultant to the Atomic Energy Commission.

(Bowen and Neal, *The United States Secret Service*; *Current Biography*, 1946; *Who Was Who in America*, v. 5.)

WILSON, GEORGE D. (ca. 1830–June 18, 1862): shoemaker, soldier, Union secret service agent

Prior to the Civil War, Wilson spent many years traveling as a journeyman shoemaker. In 1861 he enlisted as a private in the Ohio Volunteer Infantry, which was part of the Army of the Ohio. In April 1862 he volunteered to take part in a paramilitary operation behind Confederate lines aimed at severing the rail line between Atlanta and Chattanooga (see ANDREWS'S RAID). He and a party of twenty other Union troops in civilian clothes and led by JAMES J. ANDREWS hijacked a locomotive and attempted to destroy railroad tracks and bridges between the two cities. He was captured by Confederate troops and

imprisoned. Wilson, Andrews, and six others of the party were hanged.

(Bryan, *The Spy in America*; Boatner, *Civil War Dictionary*; O'Neill, *Wild Train*.)

WILSON, JOHN A. (July 25, 1832–?): businessman, Union secret service agent

A native of Franklin County, Ohio, Wilson lived in Wood County before the Civil War. In 1861 he enlisted in the Ohio Volunteer Infantry, which was a part of the Army of the Ohio. In April 1862 he volunteered to take part in a paramilitary operation behind Confederate lines aimed at severing the rail line between Atlanta and Chattanooga (see ANDREWS'S RAID). He and a party of twenty other Union troops in civilian clothes and led by JAMES J. ANDREWS hijacked a locomotive and attempted to destroy railroad tracks and bridges between the two cities. He was captured by Confederate troops and imprisoned (Andrews and seven of the party were hanged).

After the war Wilson ran a grocery store in Haskins, Ohio.

(Bryan, *The Spy in America*; Boatner, *Civil War Dictionary*; O'Neill, *Wild Train*.)

WINDER, JOHN HENRY (February 21, 1800–February 8, 1865): Army officer, Confederate intelligence officer

A native of Somerset County, Maryland, Winder graduated from the U.S. Military Academy in 1820. He served in the U.S. Army in the Mexican War. In 1860 he attained the rank of major of artillery. He resigned from the Army at the outbreak of the Civil War and went to Richmond, Virginia, where he applied for a commission in the Confederate Army. He was commissioned a brigadier general and made provost marshal and commander of the Confederate prisons in Richmond.

Winder, who reported directly to the Confederate secretary of war, was also responsible for a large secret service department headquartered in Richmond, which conducted both espionage and counterespionage. No detailed account of this department is available because the Confederate leaders destroyed the records before they evacuated Richmond in 1865; however, the little information extant suggests that it functioned on a large scale and included a wide assortment of agents and detectives.

In 1864 Winder was put in charge of all Confederate prisons and prisoner-of-war camps east of the Mississippi, including the notorious Andersonville

Prison Camp near Americus, Georgia. The question of the degree of his responsibility for the suffering and death in these institutions is the subject of debate among historians. Winder was never called to account by the U.S. government in the matter; he died of natural causes before the Confederacy was defeated.

(*DAB*; *Who Was Who in America*, historical volume; Boatner, *Civil War Dictionary*; Bidwell, "History of the Military Intelligence Division, Department of the Army General Staff.")

WIRETAPPING AND COMMUNICATIONS INTELLIGENCE IN THE CIVIL WAR

Background: Samuel Morse's magnetic telegraph was nearly thirty years old at the outbreak of the Civil War, but it had received only limited military use (by the British) in the Crimean War (1853–56) and the Indian Mutiny (1857–58). The Civil War saw the first extensive military application of telegraphy.

An extensive civilian telegraph network, growing throughout the United States since 1844, was in place in the North and South by 1861. The American Telegraph Company lines linked points on the Eastern Seaboard, while Western Union's system ran westward through the Allegheny Mountains. Smaller telegraph companies served areas not covered by the two big companies. Most towns and cities served by the railroad were also linked by telegraph.

On May 20, 1861, U.S. government agents entered telegraph company offices throughout the North and seized copies of all telegrams that had been sent or received in the past twelve months, in order to investigate secessionist subversion. The following day the American Telegraph Company cut off communications between Washington and Richmond as a security measure. Telegraphic communication between the Union and the Confederacy was terminated for the duration of the war. The War Department took control of all telegraph lines on February 25, 1862.

At the outbreak of the war the U.S. Army Signal Corps had been in existence for less than a year. Commanded by Maj. A.J. Myer, the Corps was responsible for the Army's communications in the field, including both portable field telegraphs and visual flag signalling. In October 1861 a Military Telegraph Service was established in the War Department as a civilian unit under the Quartermaster Corps. Headed by ANSON STAGER, former general superintendent of the Western Union Telegraph Company, the Service was originally intended to provide only strategic communications between headquarters, while the Signal Corps would continue to be responsible for tactical communications in the field. However, bureaucratic rivalry between Myer and Stager led in March 1864 to the Signal Corps' loss of all telegraphic responsibilities, which were thereafter assigned to the Military Telegraph Service.

In September 1862 the Military Telegraph Service established a telegraph office in the War Department building next door to the White House. It was supervised by Stager's deputy, then Maj. Thomas T. Eckert. The office became the hub of Union military communications, and hence a place that President Lincoln visited daily and where he passed much of his time during the war. It was thus the prototype of the modern national command and control center. The office also had a cryptanalytical function (see Cryptanalysis and Communication Security below).

The civilian telegraph companies in the Confederacy continued to operate throughout the war. However, some of their facilities and personnel were pressed into military service for field communications early on by Confederate commanders. In April 1862 the Confederate Signal Bureau was established as part of the Adjutant General's Department and was placed under the command of Maj. WILLIAM NORRIS. The Bureau, which also had SECRET INTELLIGENCE and cryptological functions, was responsible for both telegraph and semaphore communications (see CONFEDERATE SECRET SERVICE). However, most Confederate Army commands did not have field telegraph units but relied instead upon the private commercial companies to handle their telegraphic communications throughout the war.

Wiretapping: Some telegraph wiretapping was practiced by both sides. Most tapping was done only for the purpose of communications intelligence, but taps were also occasionally used to originate false messages to deceive the other side.

One well-documented interception operation was carried out by two civilian employees of the Union's Military Telegraph Service, F.S. Van Valkenberg and Patrick Mullarkey, in 1863. The pair were dispatched by Gen. William S. Rosecrans to learn whether Gen. Braxton Bragg was detaching troops to reinforce the Confederate garrison at Vicksburg, Mississippi. Van Valkenbergh and Mullarkey passed through Confederate lines and tapped the telegraph lines between Chattanooga and Knoxville, Tennessee. They listened to the Confederate communications for a week, at the end of which time they intercepted an order to search the area for Union spies. The two escaped but were several weeks evading capture behind Confederate lines before they could make good their return to Union territory.

In mid-July 1864 Confederate telegrapher Charles

A. Gaston was sent to tap the Union telegraph lines between the War Department in Washington and General Grant's headquarters outside the besieged Confederate capital of Richmond, Virginia. Guarded by a small detachment of Confederate troops in civilian disguise, Gaston remained at his intercept post through August, September, and part of October, copying the Union messages and sending the intercepts to Lee by courier. However, most of the Union telegrams were in cipher, and the Confederate cryptanalysts were unable to read them. Nonetheless, administrative telegrams sent in the clear provided some useful military intelligence to the Confederates.

The most ambitious wiretapping operation of the war apparently never got past the planning stage. Confederate telegrapher D.F.S. Ways proposed tapping "all wires leading out of Baltimore to the various cities" and connecting them to a secret line leading to Confederate headquarters. But there is no record that this plan was ever carried out.

Telegraph Deception: The transmission of false orders and messages from telegraph wiretaps was a more difficult undertaking than the simple interception of enemy telegrams, because individual telegraphers acquire a distinctive "fist," which can be recognized by other telegraphers who are in regular communication with them. Nonetheless, each side occasionally managed to send false orders that the other side accepted and carried out. Gen. Ormsby M. Mitchel captured two large Confederate railroad trains by sending false messages from Huntsville, Alabama, and Gen. Truman Seymour captured a Confederate train near Jacksonville, Florida, in the same way.

On the other hand, an enemy wiretap, once detected, could be used to feed disinformation to the other side. Bakeless recounts an incident in March 1864 when Gen. William T. Sherman learned that Confederate agents of Gen. Nathan B. Forrest had tapped the telegraph lines near Memphis, Tennessee. Sherman reportedly sent orders by telegraph dispatching one of his divisions to Savannah, Tennessee. Knowing that Forrest would learn of the move through his tap, and anticipating that he would lead his cavalry to Savannah to cut off the isolated Union force, Sherman secretly ordered a strong cavalry force into the Shavannah area. When Forrest arrived he encountered an overwhelming and unexpected Union force, and barely managed to escape the trap.

Semaphore Interception: Alphabetic signalling by flag, torch, or light was an important means of communication by both sides. Signalling was done from the tops of tall buildings, hills, mountains, and specially constructed wooden towers that often rose more than one hundred feet above the ground (the high vantage points used by Civil War signalmen often provided direct visual intelligence to commanders; Confederate signalmen prevented General Beauregard from being surprised at the first battle of Bull Run). The use of telescopes permitted the reception of semaphore signals over great distances.

Obviously the semaphore offered no inherent security whatsoever because messages could be intercepted by anyone who could see the signalmen. Both sides encrypted semaphore messages, but confidence in the security of the cryptosystems used was so low that commanders rarely entrusted important information to them. Historian Edwin C. Fishel says that although visual interception of semaphore signals was the main medium of interceptions in the war, little intelligence was acquired this way during the first year or so.

As with the telegraph, disinformation was sometimes sent by semaphore to deceive the enemy. Fishel reports that this was done often, although sometimes the false messages failed to convince the opposition, whose skepticism was raised by the unusual prospect of an important message being sent by the relatively insecure signal-flag method. On the other hand, as in the case of telegraph intercepts, the enemy's genuine semaphore messages were sometimes thought to be disinformation and were therefore ignored. Lee's departure from Fredericksburg, for example, was betrayed by a Confederate semaphore message read by Union signalmen, but Gen. Joseph Hooker discounted the intelligence as a hoax, and only realized his error after Capt. John McEntee confirmed the information through prisoner interrogation a week later.

Cryptanalysis and Communication Security: Compared to the advanced state of the cryptological art in Europe at the time of the Civil War, both the Union and Confederacy were relatively unsophisticated. Compared only to the Confederacy, however, the Union probably possessed superior codes, ciphers, and code-breaking skills.

At the outbreak of the war Anson Stager devised a cipher for Gen. George B. McClellan, and with some modifications and elaboration, it remained the principal Union cipher throughout the war. It was a simple yet effective word transposition system (see CRYPTOLOGY) that the Confederacy's cryptanalysts apparently never broke. (Fishel believes that if the Confederates indeed failed to break this cryptosystem, it was for some reason other than its difficulty— e.g., failure to intercept a sufficient number of encrypted messages—because his research establishes that the Stager word transposition system is actually quite easily broken.)

The Confederates employed several different communications code and cipher systems, and it is a mark of their naiveté that one of these, established by Gen. Albert S. Johnston and Gen. P.G.T. Beauregard, was a Caesar substitution (see CRYPTOLOGY), which may have protected the communications of the Roman general for which it was named but would offer no real obstacle to any alert schoolboy who had read Edgar Allan Poe's "The Gold Bug."

The Confederates made wider use of the Vigenere substitution system, which, although it had been devised in the sixteenth century, still offered some measure of security at the time of the Civil War. But three of the telegraphers in the War Department's telegraph office—DAVID H. BATES, CHARLES A. TINKER, and ALBERT B. CHANDLER (the self-styled "Sacred Three")—usually had no trouble in breaking the system whenever a Confederate message fell into their hands. The Union Army in the field also had a degree of cryptanalytic know-how; writing of the intercepted Confederate telegrams and other communications in his memoirs, General Grant recalled, "It would sometimes take too long to make translations of [them]. But sometimes they gave useful information."

Summary: Telegraph wiretapping was common, and an important intelligence source for both sides in the Civil War. The Confederates seemed to have done more tapping than the Federals, probably because the Union Army had more telegraph lines than did their opponents. However, the Confederates were rarely able to read encrypted Union messages, while Union code-breakers were almost always able to crack the simple cipher systems used by the Confederates.

Even more semaphore traffic was intercepted by both sides, but due to the obvious ease with which this medium could be intercepted and widespread distrust of the simple cryptosystems used in flag signalling, relatively little information of value was transmitted or intercepted in this way.

Both sides, however, practiced deception by transmitting both false orders and disinformation, both by telegraph and semaphore. Consequently communications intelligence was often suspected unless and until it was confirmed by a collateral source, e.g., agent's reports or prisoner interrogations.

(Harlow, *Old Wires and New Waves;* Miller (ed.), *Soldier Life and the Secret Service;* Bakeless, *Spies of the Confederacy;* Kahn, *The Codebreakers;* Fishel, "The Mythology of Civil War Intelligence"; Boatner, *Civil War Dictionary.*)

WISE, JOHN (February 24, 1808–September 29, 1879?): balloonist

A native of Lancaster, Pennsylvania, Wise worked as a cabinetmaker before pursuing his boyhood in-

terest in ballooning. He made his first ascent at Philadelphia in 1835 and, accompanied by fellow balloonist JOHN LA MOUNTAIN, set a distance record in 1859 with an 804-mile flight from St. Louis, Missouri, to Henderson, New York.

Wise was a proponent of the military use of balloons. In 1848, during the Mexican War, he proposed the aerial bombardment of Vera Cruz, but the city was taken by American forces before the idea could be considered. In June 1861, shortly after the outbreak of the Civil War, he was called to Washington by Maj. Hartman Bache, acting chief of the Bureau of Topographic Engineers of the Army of the Potomac, and asked to submit a proposal for a large balloon. Wise's proposal was accepted, he delivered the balloon within two weeks, and the Bureau hired him as a civilian employee to pilot it (see RECONNAISSANCE BALLOONS). He made his first successful reconnaissance flight on July 24th above Arlington, Virginia, where he was able to observe Confederate Army movements and spot enemy artillery emplacements.

Two days later the balloon was inadvertently released while being towed to an advanced position and had to be shot down to prevent it from falling into Confederate hands. Wise was severely upbraided by Maj. Amiel W. Whipple, chief of the Topographical Engineers, and he resigned soon afterward. He returned home, raised a cavalry troop, and served on the ground for several months before retiring because of ill health.

After the war Wise resumed ballooning and supported himself by staging public aerial exhibitions. His dream was to cross the Atlantic Ocean by balloon, but he failed in one attempt in 1873 and landed in Canaan, Connecticut. In 1879, at the age of 71, he disappeared while attempting to fly across Lake Michigan.

Wise was the author of two books on ballooning and is credited with inventing the rip panel, a safety device for balloons.

(*Who Was Who in America,* historical volume; MacCloskey, *From Gasbags to Spaceships;* Glines, *The Compact History of the United States Air Force.*)

WISEMAN, SIR WILLIAM (February 1, 1885–June 1962): banker, diplomat, British intelligence officer

A native of Hatfield, Essex, England, Wiseman was the son of a prominent Royal Navy family and the tenth holder of a baronetage dating from 1628. He studied at Winchester College and attended Cambridge University during 1904–05. During 1906–08 he worked as a reporter for the *London Daily Express.*

In 1909 he switched to investment banking in Canada and Mexico.

At the outbreak of the FIRST WORLD WAR Wiseman was commissioned as an artillery lieutenant in the British army. He was gassed in Flanders in 1915 and, while recuperating in England, was recruited by the British Secret Intelligence Service. He was sent to the United States and put in charge of SIS operations here early in 1916. Operating in New York City under the pseudonym of "Walter Wisdom," director of W. Wisdom Films, and in Washington under his true name and the cover of the Purchasing Commission of the British Ministry of Munitions, Wiseman performed much the same functions as did SIR WILLIAM STEPHENSON a generation later during the SECOND WORLD WAR, i.e., counterespionage and counterintelligence operations against German Intelligence in America, propaganda operations aimed at getting the United States into the war, and liaison with U.S. intelligence. However, Wiseman's role expanded into the area of diplomacy when the close and long-standing friendships of the British ambassador in Washington, Sir Cecil Spring Rice, with prominent Republicans proved an impediment to his dealings with the Democrat administration of President Woodrow Wilson (Spring Rice had served in Washington during the Harrison and second Cleveland administration, was a close friend of John Hay and Henry Cabot Lodge, and had been best man at the 1886 wedding of Theodore Roosevelt).

Wiseman developed a personal friendship with Col. Edward M. House, Wilson's closest and most influential advisor. The Englishman filled a need perceived by House for a channel between the White House and 10 Downing Street that would bypass both Spring Rice and Walter Hines Page, the American ambassador in London in whom House and Wilson had little confidence. The British Foreign Office seized the opportunity thus presented and made Wiseman a special emissary to the White House.

The arrangement provided something more than an efficient Anglo-American channel for urgent and sensitive communications; Wiseman was a keen observer of the American scene and a wise advisor to the British government regarding its American policies. His good offices facilitated the collaboration between the two governments as the United States entered the war in 1917, and for the duration of the wartime alliance.

Wiseman's diplomatic activity did not supplant his intelligence duties, which he continued to carry out throughout the war and afterward. Notable among them was his arrangement to send the writer and British secret intelligence agent, W. SOMERSET MAUGHAM, to Russia on behalf of the U.S. State Department to assess the prospects of a Russian alliance against Germany after the fall of the Czar's government. Maugham also served as a courier for funds provided by the British government in an attempt to bolster the provisional Russian government of Alexander Kerensky.

After the war Wiseman remained in the United States. In 1929 he became a partner in the Wall Street investment banking firm of Kuhn, Loeb and Company. In 1940 he was briefly called upon by his successor, Sir William Stephenson, to take part in a covert operation aimed at the defection of the German consul general in San Francisco. Although the operation did not succeed, Wiseman was able to obtain valuable political intelligence from the official regarding German plans in the Mediterranean.

(*Who Was Who in America*, v. 4; Fowler, *British-American Relations, 1917–1918*; Jeffreys-Jones, *American Espionage*; Landau, *The Enemy Within*; Hyde, *Room 3603*; West,. *MI6*.)

WISNER, FRANK GARDINER (1909–October 29, 1965): intelligence officer

A native of Laurel, Mississippi, Wisner graduated from the University of Virginia in 1931, and from the University's law school in 1934. He practiced law in New York City with the Wall Street firm of Carter, Ledyard and Milburn until 1941, when he joined the U.S. Naval Reserve.

In 1943 Commander Wisner obtained a transfer to the Office of Strategic Services. He was assigned to the OSS SECRET INTELLIGENCE BRANCH and was sent to istanbul to establish a new OSS network there in the wake of German penetration of the Cereus network, which had been run from that city. He successfully rebuilt the network, extending it throughout the German-occupied countries of southeastern Europe. In September 1944 he was sent to Bucharest to take over the OSS team there, and to run an OSS operation that evacuated Allied airmen downed behind enemy lines.

Until March 1945 Wisner remained in Bucharest, while the Soviet Army sacked the city and the Communists took over Romania. His agents penetrated the Romanian Communist Party and Soviet army headquarters in Bucharest, providing Washington with high-grade intelligence reports on Soviet plans and operations in the region.

Immediately after the German surrender Wisner was sent to Wiesbaden, West Germany, to take charge of OSS liaison with the Gehlen Organization, the remnants of the branch of German military intelligence with agents in Eastern Europe and the USSR. After the termination of the OSS in September 1945 he remained in Germany with the Strategic Services

Unit, the caretaker unit that took over the OSS secret intelligence assets. However, in 1946 he returned to civilian life and the Carter, Ledyard law firm.

Wisner had acquired a deep interest in foreign affairs, and in pursuit of this interest he joined the Council on Foreign Relations. Many other OSS veterans belonged to the Council, and its president at this time was former OSS/Switzerland chief ALLEN DULLES. In 1947 Wisner joined the State Department as the deputy assistant secretary of state for occupied countries, a post that involved him with the problems of refugees from the USSR and Soviet-dominated countries in Eastern Europe.

In September 1948 Wisner transferred to the recently formed CENTRAL INTELLIGENCE AGENCY and was made chief of the Office of Policy Coordination, the CIA department then responsible for foreign COVERT ACTION operations. Under him the OPC grew rapidly: at the end of one year it had three hundred employees, seven overseas stations, and a budget of $4.7 million; at the end of three years it had grown to 2,812 employees, forty-seven overseas stations, and a budget of $82 million.

Many of the OPC staff members were OSS veterans, and the organization under Wisner was largely responsible for the emphasis on covert action (as contrasted with SECRET INTELLIGENCE) that characterized much of the CIA's activity during the 1950s. In 1952 OPC and the Office of Special Operations, the CIA's intelligence and counterespionage department, were merged into the Plans Directorate, i.e., the CIA CLANDESTINE SERVICE. Wisner was made deputy director for plans (DDP), chief of the new organization.

Under Wisner the Clandestine Service achieved two of its earliest and most famous successes: the IRAN COUP and the GUATEMALA COUP. The successful U-2 RECONNAISSANCE AIRCRAFT program was also launched during Wisner's stewardship (see OVERHEAD RECONNAISSANCE).

Late in 1956, apparently depressed by the Soviet suppression of the Hungarian uprising in October of that year, Wisner began to show signs of a mental and physical breakdown. He was hospitalized, but returned to work early in 1957. His symptoms were again apparent in 1958 (perhaps aggravated by the failure of the INDONESIA REBELLION), and he entered the Shepherd Pratt hospital for six months of therapy, including electroshock.

After his second hospitalization, CIA Director Allen Dulles reassigned Wisner to the job of chief of the CIA's London station, a job Dulles believed would be less detrimental to his mental and physical health. However, his problems continued, and in 1961 he resigned from the Agency. Four years later he died

from a self-inflicted shotgun wound at his Galena, Maryland, farm.

(Smith, *OSS*; Cave Brown, *The Last Hero*; Powers, *The Man Who Kept the Secrets*; obituary, *New York Times*, October 30, 1965, p. 35.)

WITTING

Aware. In CIA and other American intelligence usage the word describes a person who is aware of the intelligence role of an organization or individual serving an intelligence agency undercover. Thus, an airline employee who knows that the company he is working for is a CIA AIR PROPRIETARY is said to be "witting."

WITZKE, LOTHAR (1895–): German secret agent and saboteur

A native of Posen, East Prussia, Witzke attended the Posen Academy. At the age of seventeen he entered the German naval academy as a cadet. Witzke, was serving aboard the German cruiser *Dresden* at the beginning of the First World War. He survived the sinking of the ship and was interned in Valparaiso, Chile. He escaped in 1916 and made his way to the United States, where he contacted the German consular service and was introduced to KURT JAHNKE, a German secret agent.

Witzke worked for the German Secret Service throughout the war in Mexico and the United States. His principal area of activity apparently was COVERT ACTION, especially arson and sabotage. He started fires in Oregon logging camps late in 1916, was involved in a plot to incite a widespread uprising by the International Workers of the World throughout the United States, and blew up a black powder magazine at the Mare Island Naval Station near San Francisco. Witzke's most spectacular achievement, however, was the BLACK TOM EXPLOSION, in which two million pounds of munitions, stored on Black Tom Island in New York harbor while awaiting shipment to Russia for use against Germany, exploded, causing some $14 million worth of damage and killing three men and a child.

Witzke was arrested by Army intelligence agents in 1918 in Arizona, after crossing the Mexican border with a false passport. He was tried by a military commission on charges of espionage. Part of the evidence offered against him was a coded letter found in his possession. Decrypted by Captain John M. Manley of the Military Intelligence Division's Cable and Telegraph Section, the letter identified him as a German secret agent. Witzke, who had refused a deal with the U.S. government in which he would exchange information on German intelligence operations for his life, was sentenced to death by hanging. He thus became the only German spy sentenced to death in the United States during the First World War. However, President Wilson commuted his sentence to life imprisonment in 1920. In 1923 Witzke was released, partly in recognition of an act of heroism he performed during a boiler explosion in Leavenworth prison.

Witzke was subsequently employed by an oil company in Venezuela and the Hamburg-America steamship line in China.

(Landau, *The Enemy Within.*)

WOLLAM, JOHN (ca. 1841–?): soldier, Union secret service agent

Wollam lived in Jackson County, Ohio, before the Civil War. In 1861 he enlisted as a private in the Ohio Volunteer Infantry, which was part of the Army of the Ohio. In April 1862 Wollam volunteered to take part in a paramilitary operation behind Confederate lines aimed at severing the rail line between Atlanta and Chattanooga (see ANDREWS'S RAID). He and a party of twenty other Union troops in civilian clothes and led by JAMES J. ANDREWS hijacked a locomotive and attempted to destroy railroad tracks and bridges between the two cities. He was captured by Confederate troops and imprisoned (Andrews and seven of the others were hanged). Wollam and several others escaped.

After the war Wollam lived in Topeka, Kansas.

(Bryan, *The Spy in America;* Boatner, *Civil War Dictionary;* O'Neill, *Wild Train.*)

WOOD, MARK (ca. 1840–ca. 1867): soldier, Union secret agent

Wood was born in England and came to the United States before the Civil War. He lived in Ohio and Kentucky and, in 1861, he enlisted in the Ohio Volunteer Infantry, which was a part of the Army of the Ohio. In April 1862 he volunteered to take part in a paramilitary operation behind Confederate lines aimed at severing the rail line between Atlanta and Chattanooga in (see ANDREWS'S RAID). He and a party of twenty other Union troops in civilian clothes and led by JAMES J. ANDREWS hijacked a locomotive and attempted to destroy railroad tracks and bridges between the two cities. He was captured by Confederate troops and imprisoned (Andrews and seven of the party were hanged).

Wood lived in Toldedo, Ohio, after the war, and

died there of tuberculosis, which he had contracted while in prison.

(Bryan, *The Spy in America;* Boatner, *Civil War Dictionary;* O'Neill, *Wild Train.*)

WOODHULL, ABRAHAM (ca. 1750–1826): farmer, jurist, intelligence officer

A native of Setauket, Long Island, Woodhull served briefly in the New York militia early in the American Revolution, but resigned to work the family farm in British-occupied Setauket. In August 1778 he was recruited by Maj. BENJAMIN TALLMADGE to serve as the leader of what came to be known as the CULPER SPY RING.

A naturally cautious and timorous man, Woodhull overcame his fears and ran one of the most successful American secret intelligence networks of the Revolution. Initially he carried out covert reconnaissance of British garrisons and installations in New York City, using the rooming house of his brother-in-law, Amos Underhill, as both a safe house and a listening post. However, there was not sufficient pretext for a Long Island farmer to visit the city very often, so Woodhull recruited New York dry goods merchant ROBERT TOWNSEND to serve as his principal agent in the city. Woodhull and Townsend used the respective pseudonyms, "Samuel Culper, Senior," and "Samuel Culper, Junior," in their communication with Tallmadge.

Townsend sent his reports to Woodhill via Austin Roe, a Setauket tavernkeeper who frequently visited New York to purchase supplies for his establishment. Woodhull would retrieve the reports from a "dead drop" on his property and turn them over to Caleb Brewster, a Setauket blacksmith, who carried them across Long Island Sound in his whaleboat, and delivered them to Tallmadge or his couriers.

Woodhull ran this apparatus successfully and without detection for the duration of the war. Tallmadge respected Woodhull's wishes not to disclose his wartime services during his lifetime. Woodhull continued to work his farm in Setauket. In 1799 he was appointed first judge of Suffolk County, New York, and served until 1810.

(Pennypacker, *General Washington's Spies;* Ford, *A Peculiar Service;* Bakeless, *Turncoats, Traitors and Heroes;* Bryan, *The Spy in America.*)

WRIGHT, PATIENCE LOVELL (1725–March 23, 1786): sculptor, American secret agent(?)

Born Patience Mehitabel Lovell, she was a native of Bordentown, New Jersey (or, by some accounts, Oyster Bay, New York). She married John Wright, a New Jersey tradesman, in 1748, and lived in Bordentown until his death in 1769. She then set up portrait studios in Philadelphia and New York, and earned her living sculpting in wax, a talent she had discovered in childhood.

In 1772 Wright moved to London and set herself up there to sculpt wax likenesses of the rich and famous. She befriended BENJAMIN FRANKLIN, then serving as colonial agent for Pennsylvania, Georgia, and Massachusetts, and became well acquainted with many powerful Englishmen, including William Pitt and Lord North. Her eccentric outspokenness (when the King and Queen visited her studio she addressed them as "George" and "Charlotte") was indulged by the doting London demimonde who found her amusing, and her pro-American declarations were tolerated (although the King is said to have avoided her studio after she sternly scolded him for making war on the Americans).

Wright was well-situated to hear much of the gossip of the English ruling classes during the American Revolution. That she collected intelligence of value to the United States and passed it on to Franklin as she claimed and her biographer and other writers later asserted is doubtful. Einstein estimates that "she was probably only a useful informant in her own estimation." Long speculates that she may have been used by the British to feed the Americans deceptive material, and concludes that the information she did pass along to Franklin had no effect on American policy decisions.

In 1781 Wright went to Paris where, sponsored by Franklin, she tried to establish herself as she had done in London. After a year she returned to London, however. She died while preparing to return to America.

(*Who Was Who in America*, historical volume; Sellers, *Patience Wright*; Einstein, *Divided Loyalties*; Long, "Patience Wright of Bordentown.")

WYMAN, WILLARD GORDON (March 21, 1898–March 29, 1969): Army officer, intelligence officer

A native of Augusta, Maine, Wyman attended Bowdoin College in 1917 and graduated from the U.S. Military Academy in 1919. He studied Chinese while attached to the Office of the U.S. military attaché in Peking, China, in 1928–32.

During the Second World War Wyman served as assistant commanding general of the First U.S. Infantry Division in 1943–44, and commanded the Seventy-first Infantry Division in 1944–45. In 1945–46 he served as chief of intelligence for the Army Ground Forces.

Wyman was subsequently assigned to the Central Intelligence Agency, where he served as assistant director of Special Operations. He was in charge of the Office of Special Operations, as the SECRET INTELLIGENCE department of the CIA was then designated, during the first years of the Agency's existence. In 1951 he left the CIA to command the Army's Ninth Corps in Korea. He was succeeded in his CIA post by LYMAN B. KIRKPATRICK. Wyman later held several other senior command assignments in the Army and retired with the rank of general in 1958.

Among many other decorations, Wyman was awarded the Distinguished Service Cross, the Silver Star, the Bronze Star, and the Legion of Merit.

(Powers, *The Man Who Kept the Secrets*; *Who Was Who in America*, v. 5.)

Y

YAMAMOTO INTERCEPTION

On April 18, 1943 Adm. Isoroku Yamamoto, commander in chief of the Japanese Combined Fleet, died when the plane in which he was traveling to Bougainville in the Solomon Islands was shot down by American fighter aircraft. This interception was made possible by U.S. Navy cryptanalysts who had deciphered a Japanese radio message containing Yamamoto's detailed itinerary.

The message was intercepted on April 13th by the Fleet Radio Unit, Pacific Fleet (FRUPAC), as the Pearl Harbor Combat Information Unit of the Navy's Communication Security Section was then called (see NAVAL INTELLIGENCE). The message, which had been sent by the commander of the Japanese Eighth Fleet, announced that Yamamoto would conduct a one-day inspection tour of bases in the upper Solomon Islands five days hence, and it included the exact route and arrival times he would follow. It was enciphered in JN25, a high-security Japanese naval code that the American cryptanalysts at Pearl Harbor had broken. Because Yamamoto was known to be compulsively punctual, the message amounted to a guarantee that the Japanese commander would follow the specified route at the stated times. Part of the route passed within range of American interceptors based on Guadalcanal.

There was some question among American naval intelligence officers whether to exploit this opportunity to kill Yamamoto. The admiral had planned the PEARL HARBOR ATTACK—a brilliant operation—but he had also planned the battle of MIDWAY, which had been a Japanese defeat. However, the intelligence officers concluded that any successor would be a less capable commander.

The possibility that the interception of Yamamoto might disclose to the Japanese that their naval cipher

Japanese Adm. Isoroku Yamamoto. Source: U.S. Navy.

Herbert O. Yardley in Army uniform during the First World War. Source: National Archives.

had been broken raised a more difficult question. If the Japanese changed systems as a consequence of the Yamamoto interception, the Americans might be denied more valuable intelligence in the future. However, Adm. Chester W. Nimitz, commander in chief of the U.S. Pacific Fleet, decided that the potential benefits of removing Yamamoto—depriving the Japanese of a very capable commander and, at the same time, striking a severe blow to their morale—were worth this risk.

Early on the morning of April 18th, eighteen Army Air Force P-38 fighters took off from Henderson Field on Guadalcanal. Flying over the ocean at wave-top height to evade Japanese radar, the planes flew a semicircular route to the west and north, avoiding the Japanese-held islands of Munda, Rendova, and Shortland. The route and speed of the P-38s had been worked out to bring them to a point on the Bougainville coast at the precise moment the two bombers carrying Yamamoto and his party were due to arrive.

The precision paid off: the American fliers sighted the bombers and their fighter escort just as the Bougainville coast came into view. While fourteen of the P-38s engaged the escort, the remaining four attacked

the two bombers. Yamamoto's plane was shot down and Yamamoto was killed. His death had the expected impact on the the Japanese war effort.

The American command sought to conceal the circumstances of the operation from the Japanese by, first of all, appearing to be unaware that Yamamoto had been aboard the downed bomber, and secondly, by putting out the cover story that the interception had been based on information radioed by Australian coastwatchers stationed along the plane's route. However, the true story was leaked in Washington, where it became familiar cocktail party fare, although Japanese intelligence apparently failed to pick it up.

(Kahn, *The Codebreakers;* Holmes, *Double-Edged Secrets.*)

YARDLEY, HERBERT OSBORN (April 13, 1889–August 7, 1958): writer, cryptologist

A native of Worthington, Indiana, Yardley attended a local high school before becoming a railroad telegrapher. In 1912 he moved to Washington, D.C., and was employed as a telegrapher and code clerk in the State Department.

Yardley had no formal training in higher mathematics or cryptology, but he attempted the cryptanalysis (see CRYPTOLOGY) of State Department codes simply to amuse himself, and quickly succeeded in breaking the most trusted of the Department's codes. He then composed a long treatise, "Solution of American Diplomatic Codes," which he presented to his astonished State Department supervisor in the form of a 100-page memorandum. When the Department instituted an improved code in response to Yardley's discoveries, he demonstrated that this, too, could be broken.

After American entry into the First World War, Yardley persuaded Maj. RALPH H. VAN DEMAN to arrange his transfer to the U.S. Army, get him commissioned as a captain, and put him in charge of MI-8, the newly created cryptological section of the Military Intelligence Division (see ARMY INTELLIGENCE). Under Yardley MI-8 quickly grew in both staff and functions. It compiled new code systems for use by the Army, established secure communications with some forty military attachés and intelligence officers overseas, was capable of reading more than thirty shorthand systems, developed chemicals for reading invisible writing, and, of course, broke foreign codes and ciphers, and read intercepted communications, including a large volume of Latin American diplomatic traffic.

After the Armistice, Yardley took charge of a code bureau attached to the American Commission to the

Peace Conference in Paris. The bureau encrypted and deciphered American dispatches to and from Washington, and solved and read those of other Allied nations.

After the war and its aftermath, Yardley and Gen. MARLBOROUCH CHURCHILL argued for the retention of MI-8 as a permanent peacetime cryptological department. They were successful, and the unit became the Cipher Bureau, a branch of the Military Intelligence Division jointly funded by the War and State departments. The Bureau was informally known as "the American Black Chamber," a name coined by Yardley in reference to the code-breaking Black Chambers of Europe. Because of a technicality the State Department could not legally spend its component of the funds within the District of Columbia, so the Bureau was established in New York City. The location was within convenient reach of the transatlantic cable offices of the Western Union and Postal Telegraph companies, both of which surreptitiously cooperated in supplying the Bureau with copies of enciphered foreign diplomatic traffic carried on their lines. The very existence of the Bureau was a secret, and it operated under the cover of a private business, the Code Compilation Company, which actually managed to make a profit by producing a commercial code.

In December 1919, Yardley succeeded in breaking Japan's diplomatic codes, an achievement that permitted American negotiators to read Tokyo's instructions to the Japanese representatives at the Washington Conference on the Limitation of Armaments (1921–22). One objective of the conference, in which Japan, the United States, Great Britain, France, Italy, and several other nations took part, was to fix a limit to the tonnage of capital warships (i.e., battleships, aircraft carriers, and heavy cruisers) of the participants. The Five-Power Naval Treaty that resulted established a 5:5:3 tonnage ratio among the United States, Britain, and Japan, respectively. The fact that this ratio represented the final Japanese bargaining position was known to the American negotiators as a result of Yardley's intercepts, and they were therefore able to press successfully for this figure.

During the decade of the 1920s the Bureau intercepted and read more than 45,000 telegrams in the codes of more than twenty foreign governments. However, with the advent of the administration of President Herbert Hoover in 1929, Secretary of State Henry L. Stimson withdrew State Department funding from the Bureau because, as he explained many years later, "Gentlemen do not read each other's mail." Consequently, the Bureau went out of existence shortly thereafter.

Abruptly unemployed and in financial straits, Yar-dley sought relief through writing a revealing memoir, *The American Black Chamber*, which soon became a best-seller. (According to some accounts, he sold information about the Bureau's code-breaking to the Japanese before publication of the book.) The embarrassed U.S. government, although rejecting Yardley's position that because the Bureau had been dissolved there was no longer any reason to protect its secrets, did not prosecute Yardley or his publisher, but instead denied that the Bureau had ever existed.

Yardley continued to pursue his literary career, writing two novels, *The Red Sun of Nippon* and *The Blonde Countess*. The latter was made into a 1935 film called *Rendezvous*, starring William Powell, Rosalind Russell, and Cesar Romero. MGM retained Yardley as technical advisor on the film.

In 1938 he went to China to work as a cryptanalyst for Chiang Kai-shek. Two years later he returned to the United States, then went to Canada to establish a cryptological unit for the Canadian Department of External Affairs. From 1941 to 1945 he worked in Washington, D.C., for the wartime Office of Price Administration. He collaborated on another novel, *Crows Are Black Everywhere*, and held a variety of jobs in the Washington area. A talented poker player since his boyhood, he published the very successful *The Education of a Poker Player* in 1956.

(Kahn, *The Codebreakers*; Yardley, *The American Black Chamber*; Bamford, *The Puzzle Palace*; Layton, *"And I Was There"*; Lewin, *American Magic*; *Who Was Who in America*, v. 3.)

YOUNG, BENNETT HENDERSON (May 25, 1843–February 23, 1919): lawyer, businessman, historian, Confederate secret service agent

A native of Nicholasville, Kentucky, Young attended the Centre College of Kentucky in Danville, Kentucky. At the outbreak of the CIVIL WAR he was commissioned as a lieutenant in the Kentucky cavalry of Gen. John Hunt Morgan (the unit known as Morgan's raiders). Young led the ST. ALBANS RAID, in which a party of Confederate guerrillas based in Canada crossed into Vermont and raided the border town of St. Albans, robbing three banks of a total of $200,000, and burning several buildings.

Young was captured on Canadian soil by a posse from St. Albans. He was turned over to the Canadian authorities, who refused to extradite him back to the United States. After being held for several weeks in Montreal, he and other Confederate raiders who had participated in the raid were released. The raid had a major military effect, in that it forced the Union to divert troops to guard the Canadian border. It also

Bennett H. Young. Source: Author's collection.

precipitated a minor diplomatic crisis between the United States and Great Britain.

After the war Young studied at Queens College in Toronto, Canada, and graduated from the Law Department of Queens College, Belfast, Ireland. He returned to Kentucky and became president of the Monon Route, a railroad line between Louisville and Chicago. He was later president of the Louisville Southern Railroad, and of the Kentucky and Indiana Bridge Company. He received an LL.D. from King's College in Tennessee in 1891 and practiced law in Louisville. Young was active in Confederate veterans' affairs and became president of the Confederate Veterans Association. In 1914 he dedicated the Confederate Monument in Arlington Cemetery.

Young wrote several works of history. One, *Confederate Wizards of the Saddle,* is a collection of cavalry stories. However, he never wrote an account of the St. Albans Raid.

(*Who Was Who in America,* v. 1; Horan, *Confederate Agent.*)

YOUNGER, EVELLE JANSEN (June 19, 1918–): lawyer, law enforcement officer, counterespionage officer

A native of Nebraska, Younger attended the University of Nebraska, receiving an A.B. and an LL.B. in 1940. He joined the Federal Bureau of Investigation as a special agent in 1940 and supervised the National Defense Section. In 1942 he was commissioned in the U.S. Army and assigned to the Office of Strategic Services. He served in the OSS COUNTER-ESPIONAGE BRANCH in the Far East until 1946.

Younger held the position of Los Angeles deputy city attorney and city prosecutor in 1946–50. He began the private practice of law in 1950 but returned to active duty with the U.S. Air Force in 1951. He was discharged with the rank of major in 1952. Younger served as a judge in Los Angeles until 1964, as Los Angeles County district attorney until 1970, and as attorney general of California until 1978. He then returned to private law practice in Los Angeles.

(*Who's Who in America,* 42nd ed.; Smith, *OSS.*)

Z

ZACHARIAS, ELLIS MARK (January 1, 1890–June 27, 1961): Navy officer, intelligence officer

A native of Jacksonville, Florida, Zacharias graduated from the U.S. Naval Academy in 1912. He served in various capacities aboard battleships and cruisers until 1919, when he was assigned to the marine engineering faculty of the Naval Academy.

In 1920 Zacharias was assigned to the Office of NAVAL INTELLIGENCE and appointed assistant naval attaché to the American embassy in Tokyo for the purpose of learning the Japanese language and studying Japanese affairs. During his tour in Tokyo he gathered information on Japanese attitudes toward arms limitations. Shortly before leaving this post he took part in the rescue work that followed the great Japanese earthquake of 1923.

In 1926, after two years of sea duty, Zacharias served a brief tour in Washington with ONI's cryptanalysis and communications intelligence unit. That same year he returned to duty with the Navy's Asiatic station. Aboard the U.S.S. *Marblehead*, he headed the first comprehensive radio communication interception unit, monitoring Japanese carrier and fleet training radio communications.

Zacharias again served in Tokyo for a brief term as acting naval attaché in 1928, after which he returned to ONI in Washington, where he served as chief of the Far Eastern Division during 1928–31 and 1934–36. In the intervening period he commanded the destroyer *Dorsey* and attended the Naval War College. During 1938–40 he was district intelligence officer of the Eleventh Naval District in San Diego, California. In the latter capacity he established net-

works of informers to counter the espionage activities of Japanese, Communist, and Nazi agents aimed at the Pacific Fleet and the California defense industry.

Zacharias commanded the heavy cruiser *Salt Lake City* from November 1940 to May 1942, during which

Ellis M. Zacharias. Source: U.S. Navy.

The Zimmermann telegram inspired this political cartoon in the *New York Evening World*. **Source: Author's collection.**

time he saw action against the Japanese in the Gilbert and Marshall islands in the Second World War. In June 1942 he returned to Washington to serve as deputy director of ONI, a post he held until August 1943. In that position he was instrumental in bringing about a reorganization of ONI and involving the Agency in such activities as psychological warfare.

In September 1943 Zacharias left ONI to command the battleship U.S.S. *New Mexico* and saw action in the Gilberts and Marianas. During October 1944–April 1945 he was chief of staff of the Eleventh Naval District.

In April 1945 Zacharias returned to ONI and headed a psychological warfare campaign against the Japanese until V-J Day. After his retirement in 1946 he lectured and wrote articles and books on naval and national security affairs, including *Secret Missions*, a memoir of his service as an intelligence officer.

(Zacharias, *Secret Missions*; Dorwart, *Conflict of Duty*; *Who Was Who in America*, v. 4; Schuon, *U.S. Navy Biographical Dictionary*.)

ZIMMERMANN TELEGRAM

On January 16, 1917 German Foreign Minister Arthur Zimmermann sent an enciphered dispatch to Heinrich J.F. von Eckardt, the German minister in Mexico, instructing him to deliver a secret proposal to the Mexican government. Anticipating that the United States would soon be drawn into the FIRST WORLD WAR on the Allied side, Zimmermann proposed a German-Mexican military alliance against America aimed at Mexico's recovery of Texas, New Mexico, and Arizona, the territories it lost in the Mexican War.

The Zimmermann telegram was intercepted and deciphered by British intelligence, and the British government turned it over to the U.S. government on February 24th. The subsequent publication of the message inspired American indignation toward Germany and contributed to the popular support for the Wilson administration's decision, several weeks later, to enter the war.

The proposed German-Mexican alliance never materialized, and the German government replaced Zimmermann as foreign minister.

(Tuchman, *The Zimmermann Telegram*; Kahn, *The Codebreakers*.)

ABBREVIATIONS

A-2   See entry A-2.
ACOUSTINT   acoustic intelligence
ADSID   Air Delivered Seismic Detection Sensor
AEC   Atomic Energy Commission
AEF   American Expeditionary Force
AFIS   Air Force Intelligence Service
AFSA   Armed Forces Security Agency
AIB   Allied Intelligence Bureau
AID   Agency for International Development
ARVN   Army of the Republic of South Vietnam
ASA   Army Security Agency
ATIS   Allied Translator and Interpreter Section
AVC   American Veterans Committee

BND   Bundesnachrichtendienst (West German Federal Intelligence Service)
BNE   Board of National Estimate
BSC   British Security Coordination

CAT   Civil Air Transport
CB   Central Bureau
CD   Censorship and Documents Branch
CEWI   Combat Electronic Warfare and Intelligence
CFI   Committee on Foreign Intelligence
CIA   Central Intelligence Agency
CIC   Counter Intelligence Corps
CID   Central Information Division
CIDG   Civilian Irregular Defense Group
CIG   Central Intelligence Group
CNO   Chief of Naval Operations
COI   Office of the Coordinator of Information
COINTELPRO   Counterintelligence Program
COMINT   communications intelligence
COMIREX   Committee on Imagery Requirements and Exploitation
COMOR   Committee on Overhead Reconnaissance
COMPADRE   Committee for Philippine Action in Development, Reconstruction and Education
COMSEC   communications security
CORDS   Civil Operations and Revolutionary Development Support

D/DIRNSA   Deputy Director of the National Security Agency
DAB   Dictionary of American Biography
DAH   Dictionary of American History
DCI   Director of Central Intelligence

DCID   Director of Central Intelligence Directive
DDCI   Deputy Director of Central Intelligence
DDI   Deputy Director for Intelligence
DDO   Deputy Director for Operations
DDP   Deputy Director for Plans
DDS&T   Deputy Director for Science and Technology
DEA   Drug Enforcement Agency
DEFCON   defense condition
DEFSMAC   Defense Special Missile and Astronautics Center
DIA   Defense Intelligence Agency
DIRNSA   Director of the National Security Agency
DNB   Dictionary of National Biography

ELINT   electronic intelligence
ERA   Economic Research Area
EXCOMAIR   Executive Committee for Air Proprietary Operations
EXCOMM   National Reconnaissance Executive Committee

FBI   Federal Bureau of Investigation
FBIS   Foreign Broadcast Information Service
FE   Far East
FN   Foreign Nationalities Branch
FOSIC   Fleet Ocean Surveillance Information Center
FRD   Frente Revolucionario Democrático (Cuban Democratic Revolutionary Front)
FRUPAC   Fleet Radio Unit, Pacific
FTD   Foreign Technology Division

G-2   See entry G-2.
GID   General Intelligence Division
GRU   Soviet military intelligence
GVN   Government of South Vietnam

HUAC   House Un-American Activities Committee
HUMINT   human intelligence

IC   Intelligence Community
ICC   International Control Commission
ICEX   Intelligence Coordination and Exploitation
IG   Inspector General
INR   Bureau of Intelligence and Research

INSCOM Army Intelligence and Security Command
IOB Intelligence Oversight Board
IRBM Intermediate Range Ballistic Missile
IRIS Interim Research and Intelligence Service

J-2 See J-2 entry.
JCS Joint Chiefs of Staff
JIC Joint Intelligence Committee
JTAG Joint Technical Advisory Group

KGB Komitet Gosudarstvennoi Bezopastnosti (Soviet Committee for State Security).

LLDB Lac Luong Dac Biet (South Vietnamese Special Forces)

MI Military Intelligence
MI5 Military Intelligence, Department Five (British Security Service)
MI6 Military Intelligence, Department Six (British Secret Intelligence Service)
MID Military Intelligence Division
MIDAS Missile Detection and Surveillance
MIO Military Intelligence Organization
MIS Military Intelligence Service
MO Morale Operations Branch
MRBM Medium Range Ballistic Missile
MVD Ministerstvo Vnutrennikh Del (Soviet Ministry of Internal Affairs)

NACA National Advisory Committee for Aeronautics
NAMFREL National Movement for Free Elections
NASA National Aeronautics and Space Administration
NIA National Intelligence Authority
NIC National Intelligence Council
NIE National Intelligence Estimate
NIO National Intelligence Officer
NIPE National Intelligence Programs Evaluation
NKVD Narodnyi Kommissariat Vnutrennikh Del (Soviet People's Commissariat for Internal Affairs)
NLF National Liberation Front
NODIS no dissemination
NOFORN no foreign dissemination
NPIC National Photographic Interpretation Center
NRO National Reconnaissance Office
NSA National Security Agency
NSC National Security Council
NSCID National Security Council Intelligence Directive
NVA North Vietnamese Army

OACSI Office of the Assistant Chief of Staff, Intelligence
OB order of battle
OCI Office of Current Intelligence
OCIAA Office of the Coordinator of Inter-American Affairs
OELR Office of European Labor Research
OG Operational Group
OGPU Obiedinennoye Gosudarstvennoye Politicheskoye Upravlenie (Soviet State Political Administration)
ONC Office of Naval Communications
ONE Office of National Estimates
ONI Office of Naval Intelligence
OP-12 War Plans Division, Office of the Chief of Naval Operations
OP-16 Office of Naval Intelligence
OP-20 Office of Naval Communications
OPC Office of Policy Coordination
ORE Office of Reports and Estimates
ORR Office of Research and Reports
OSO Office of Special Operations
OSR Office of Strategic Research
OSS Office of Strategic Services
OWI Office of War Information

PARU Police Aerial Resupply Unit
PB/7 Program Branch Seven
PEO Program Evaluation Office
PFIAB President's Foreign Intelligence Advisory Board
PHOTINT photographic intelligence
PNG persona non grata
PSE Psychological Stress Evaluator

R&A Research and Analysis Branch
RAAF Royal Australian Air Force
RADINT radar intelligence
RFE Radio Free Europe
RL Radio Liberty
RPV Remotely Piloted Vehicle

S&T Science and Technology Directorate
S-2 See S-2 entry.
SAC Strategic Air Command
SACO Sino-American Cooperative Organization
SAM surface-to-air missile
SAMOS Satellite and Missile Observation System
SCA Service Cryptologic Agency
SCF Satellite Control Facility
SD Sicherheitdienst (Nazi security service)
SEALS Sea/Air/Land Teams
SHAEF Supreme Headquarters, Allied Expeditionary Forces

SHAPE Supreme Headquarters, Allied Powers, Europe
SI Secret Intelligence Branch
SIG Senior Interagency Group
SIGINT signals intelligence
SIS British Secret Intelligence Service
SIS Army Signal Intelligence Service
SIS FBI Special Intelligence Service
SO Special Operations Branch
SOE Special Operations, Executive
SOG Studies and Observation Group
SOSUS Sound Surveillance System
SSU Strategic Services Unit
STOL Short Takeoff and Landing
SWG Special Wireless Group

TELINT telemetry intelligence

UGS Unattended Ground Sensor
USAFE U.S. Air Force in Europe
USAINTC U.S. Army Intelligence Command
USIB United States Intelligence Board
USMAAG U.S. Military Assistance Advisory Group
USMACV U.S. Military Advisory Command, Vietnam

WAMB Webster's American Military Biographies
WH Western Hemisphere Division
WIN Wolność i Niepodleność (Polish Freedom and Independence movement)

X-2 Counter Espionage Branch

BIBLIOGRAPHY

Abel, Elie. *The Missile Crisis.* Philadelphia: Lippincott, 1966.

Agee, Philip. *Inside the Company: CIA Diary.* Harmondsworth, Eng.: Penguin Books, 1975.

Agee, Philip, and Louis Wolf, eds. *Dirty Work: The CIA in Western Europe.* Secaucus, N.J.: Lyle Stuart, 1978.

Agular, Luis, ed. *Operation Zapata.* Frederick, Md.: University Publications of America, 1981.

" 'Ah, Sweet Intrigue!' Or Who Axed State's Prewar Soviet Division?" *Foreign Intelligence Literary Scene,* v.3, n.5 (October 1984), 1–2.

Allison, Graham T. *Essence of Decision: Explaining the Cuban Missile Crisis.* Boston: Little, Brown, 1971.

Alsop, Stewart. *The Center: People and Power in Political Washington.* New York: Harper & Row, 1968.

Alsop, Stewart, and Thomas Braden. *Sub Rosa: The OSS and American Espionage.* New York: Reynal & Hitchcock, 1946.

Ambrose, Stephen E. *Ike's Spies: Eisenhower and the Espionage Establishment.* Garden City, N.Y.: Doubleday, 1981.

American Men and Women of Science, 15th ed. New York: R.R. Bowker, 1982.

Andrews, J. Cutler. *The North Reports the Civil War.* Pittsburgh: U. Pittsburgh Press, 1955.

―――. *The South Reports the Civil War.* Princeton, N.J.: Princeton U. Press, 1970.

Armbrister, Trevor. *A Matter of Accountability: The True Story of the Pueblo Affair.* New York: Coward-McCann, 1970.

Augur, Helen. *The Secret War of Independence.* Boston: Little, Brown, 1955.

Bakeless, John. *Spies of the Confederacy.* Philadelphia: Lippincott, 1970.

―――. *Turncoats, Traitors and Heroes.* Philadelphia: Lippincott, 1959.

Baker, Lafayette C. *History of the United States Secret Service.* Philadelphia, privately published, 1867. Revised edition, *The United States Secret Service in the Late War.* Philadelphia: John E. Potter, 1889. Also several other editions, titles, publishers, and dates.

Bamford, James. *The Puzzle Palace.* Boston: Houghton Mifflin, 1982. Revised edition. Harmondsworth, Eng.: Penguin, 1983.

Barnum, H.L. *The Spy Unmasked; or, Memoirs of Enoch Crosby, Alias Harvey Birch.* New York: J.&J. Harper, 1828. Reprinted with additional material. Harrison, N.Y.: Harbor Hill Books, 1975.

Bauer, K. Jack. *The Mexican War, 1846–1848.* New York: Macmillan, 1974.

Beck, Melvin. *Secret Contenders: The Myth of Cold War Counterintelligence.* New York: Sheridan Square Pubs., 1984.

Becket, Henry S.A. (pseud.). *The Dictionary of Espionage.* Briarcliff Manor, N.Y.: Stein and Day, 1986.

Beirne, Francis F. *The War of 1812.* New York: Dutton, 1949.

Bemis, Samuel F. "The British Secret Service and the French-American Alliance." *American Historical Review,* v.29 (1923–24), pp. 474–495.

―――. *A Diplomatic History of the United States.* Revised edition. New York: Holt, 1942.

Bendiner, Elmer. *The Virgin Diplomats.* New York: Knopf, 1976.

Bernikow, Louise. *Abel.* New York: Trident Press, 1970.

Bernstorff, Count Johann. *My Three Years in America.* New York: Scribner's, 1920.

Beschloss, Michael R. *Mayday: Eisenhower, Khrushchev and the U-2 Affair.* New York: Harper & Row, 1986.

Beymer, William Gilmore. *On Hazardous Service: Scouts and Spies of the North and South.* New York: Harper & Bro., 1912.

Bidwell, Bruce W. "History of the Military Intelligence Division, Department of the Army General Staff." Unpublished manuscript prepared for the Military Intelligence Division and the Office of Military History, U.S. Army, 1959–61. Library of Congress Photoduplication Service.

―――. *History of the Military Intelligence Division, Department of the Army General Staff: 1775–1941.* Frederick, Md.: University Publications of America, 1986 (Parts 1 through 4 of Bidwell's previously listed 8-part manuscript).

Bittman, Ladislav. *The Deception Game: Czechoslovak Intelligence in Soviet Political Warfare.* Syracuse, New York: Syracuse Research Corp., 1972.

Blackstock, Paul W. *Agents of Deceit: Frauds, Forgeries and Political Intrigue Among Nations.* Chicago: Quadrangle, 1966.

―――. *The Strategy of Subversion: Manipulating the Politics of Other Nations.* Chicago: Quadrangle, 1964.

Boatner, Mark M., III. *Civil War Dictionary*. New York: McKay, 1959.

———. *Encyclopedia of the American Revolution*. New York: McKay, 1974.

Bowen, Walter S., and Harry Edward Neal. *The United States Secret Service*. Philadelphia: Chilton, 1960.

Bowman, John S., ed. *The World Almanac of the Vietnam War*. New York: World Almanac, 1985.

Boyd, Julian P. *Number 7: Alexander Hamilton's Secret Attempts to Control American Foriegn Policy*. Princeton, N.J.: Princeton U. Press, 1964.

———. "Silas Deane: Death by a Kindly Teacher of Treason?" *William and Mary Quarterly*, 3rd Ser., v.16 (1959), pp. 165–187, 319–342, and 515–550.

Braden, Tom. "The Birth of the CIA," *American Heritage*, v28. n.2 (February 1977), pp. 4–13.

Brandt, Ed. *The Last Voyage of the USS Pueblo*. New York: Norton, 1969.

Branfman, Fred. "The President's Secret Army: A Case Study—The CIA in Laos, 1962–72," in Robert Borosage and John Marks. *The CIA File*. New York: Grossman-Viking, 1976.

Breckinridge, Scott D. *The CIA and the U.S. Intelligence System*. Boulder, Colorado: Westview, 1986.

Brewin, Bob, and Sydney Shaw. *Vietnam on Trial: Westmoreland vs. CBS*. New York: Atheneum, 1987.

Brogan, Patrick, and Albert Zarca. *Deadly Business: Sam Cummings, Interarms, and the Arms Trade*. New York: W.W. Norton, 1983.

Brook-Shepherd, Gordon. *The Storm Petrels: The Flight of the First Soviet Defectors*. New York: Harcourt Brace Jovanovich, 1977.

Bryan, George S. *The Great American Myth*. New York: Carrick & Evans, 1940.

———. *The Spy in America*. Philadelphia: Lippincott, 1943.

Bucher, Lloyd M. *Bucher: My Story*. Garden City, N.Y.: Doubleday, 1970.

Bulloch, James D. *The Secret Service of the Confederate States in Europe*. New York: Putnam's, 1884. Reprinted. New York: Thomas Yoseloff, 1959.

Buranelli, Vincent, and Nan Buranelli. *Spy/Counterspy: An Encyclopedia of Espionage*. New York: McGraw-Hill, 1982.

Burke, Michael. *Outrageous Good Fortune: A Memoir*. Boston: Little, Brown, 1984.

Campbell, Kenneth. "Ethan Allen Hitchcock: Intelligence Leader—Mystic," *Intelligence Quarterly*, v.2, n.3 (October 1986), pp. 13–14.

Campbell, Rodney. *The Luciano Project: The Secret Wartime Collaboration of the Mafia and the U.S. Navy*. New York: McGraw-Hill, 1977.

Canan, Howard V. "Confederate Military Intelligence," *Maryland Historical Magazine*, v.59, n.1, March 1964, pp. 34–51.

Canan, James. *War in Space*. New York: Harper & Row, 1982.

Carter, Samuel III. *The Riddle of Dr. Mudd*. New York: Putnam's, 1974.

Case, Lynn M., and Warren F. Spencer. *The United States and France: Civil War Diplomacy*. Philadelphia: U. Penn. Press, 1970.

Casey, William J. *Where and How the War Was Fought: An Armchair Tour of the American Revolution*. New York: Morrow, 1976.

Cave Brown, Anthony. *The Last Hero: Wild Bill Donovan*. New York: Times Books, 1982.

———, ed. *The Secret War Report of the OSS*. New York: Berkley, 1976.

Central Intelligence Agency. *Directors and Deputy Directors of Central Intelligence: Dates and Data, 1946–1983*. Washington: CIA History Staff, November 1983.

———. *Fact Book on Intelligence*. Washington: CIA Office of Public Affairs, May 1986.

———. *Intelligence in the War of Independence*. Washington: CIA Office of Public Affairs, n.d.

———. *Intelligence: The Acme of Skill*. Washington: CIA Office of Public Affairs, n.d.

Childs, Harwood L., and John B. Whitton, eds. *Propaganda by Short Wave*. Princeton, N.J.: Princeton U. Press, 1942.

Clapp, Margaret. *Forgotten First Citizen: John Bigelow*. Boston: Little, Brown, 1947. Reprinted. New York: Greenwood Press, 1968.

Clark, Ronald William. *The Man Who Broke Purple: The Life of the World's Greatest Cryptologist, Col. William F. Friedman*. Boston: Little, Brown, 1977.

Cline, Ray S. *The CIA: Reality vs. Myth*. Washington: Acropolis, 1982 (revision of the author's *Secrets, Spies and Scholars*).

Coffin, William Sloane. *Once to Every Man*. New York: Atheneum, 1978.

Colby, William, and Peter Forbath. *Honorable Men: My Life in the CIA*. New York: Simon and Schuster, 1978.

Commission on CIA Activities Within the United States. *Report to the President*. Washington: U.S. Government Printing Office, June 1975.

Constantinides, George C. *Intelligence and Espionage: An Analytical Bibliography*. Boulder, Colorado: Westview, 1983.

Contemporary Authors. Detroit, Michigan: Gale Research Co., 1962 to date.

Cook, Blanche Wiesen. *The Declassified Eisenhower*. Garden City, N.Y.: Doubleday, 1981.

Cook, Fred. *The FBI Nobody Knows*. New York: Macmillan, 1964.

Cooke, Alistair. *A Generation on Trial: USA vs. Alger Hiss.* New York: Knopf, 1952.

Cookridge, E.H. (pseud.). *Spy Trade.* New York: Walker, 1971.

———. *The Third Man.* New York: Putnam's, 1968.

Coon, Carleton S. *A North Africa Story.* Ipswich, Mass.: Gambit, 1980.

Cooper, Chester L. *The Lost Crusade: America in Vietnam.* New York: Dodd, Mead, 1970. Revised. Greenwich, Conn.: Fawcett Publications, 1972.

Copeland, Miles. *The Game of Nations: The Amorality of Power Politics.* New York: Simon and Schuster, 1969.

———. *Without Cloak or Dagger.* New York: Simon and Schuster, 1974. Revised. New York: Pinnacle, 1975.

Corson, William R. *The Armies of Ignorance: The Rise of the American Intelligence Empire.* New York: Dial Press, 1977.

Costello, John E. "Remember Pearl Harbor," *Proceedings of the U.S. Naval Institute,* v.109/9/967, pp. 52–62.

Cox, Arthur Macy. *The Myths of National Security.* Boston: Beacon, 1975.

Cox, Cynthia. *The Real Figaro: The Extraordinary Career of Caron de Beaumarchais.* New York: Coward-McCann, 1963.

Crary, Catherine Snell. "The Tory and the Spy: The Double Life of James Rivington," *William and Mary Quarterly,* v.16, n.1 (January 1959), pp. 61–72.

Cullum, George W. *Biographical Register of the Officers and Graduates of the U.S. Military Academy at West Point, New York, Since Its Establishment in 1802.* Various publishers. 1891–1950.

Cummins, Light. "Spanish Espionage in the South During the American Revolution," *Southern Studies,* v.19, n.1, 1980. pp. 39–49.

Current Biography. New York: H.W. Wilson Co., 1940 to date.

Currey, Cecil B. *Code Number 72: Ben Franklin: Patriot or Spy?* Englewood Cliffs, N.J.: Prentice-Hall, 1972.

Daniel, James, and John G. Hubbell. *Strike in the West: The Complete Story of the Cuban Crisis.* New York: Holt, Rinehart and Winston, 1963.

Dannett, Sylvia G.L. *Profiles of Negro Womanhood.* Yonkers, N.Y.: Educational Heritage, 1964.

———. *She Rode with the Generals: The True and Incredible Story of Sarah Emma Seelye, alias Franklin Thompson.* Nashville, Tenn.: Thomas Nelson, 1960.

Davidson, James West, and Mark Hamilton Lytle. *After the Fact: The Art of Historical Detection.* New York: Knopf, 1982.

Davidson, Philip. *Propaganda and the American Revolution, 1763–1783.* Chapel Hill, N.C.: U. North Carolina Press, 1941.

Davis, Burke. *Our Incredible Civil War.* New York: Holt, Rinehart and Winston, 1960.

Davis, Curtis Caroll, "The Civil War's Most Over-Rated Spy," *West Virginia History,* v.28, n.1 (October 1965), pp. 1–9.

———. "Companions of Crisis: The Spy Memoir As a Social Document," *Civil War History,* v.10, n.4, (December 1964) pp. 385–400.

———. "The Pet of the Confederacy Still? Fresh Findings about Belle Boyd," *Maryland Historical Magazine,* v.78, n.1, (Spring 1983), pp. 35–53.

De Gramont, Sanche. *The Secret War: The Story of International Espionage Since World War II.* New York: Putnam's, 1962.

De Silva, Peer, *Sub Rosa: The CIA and the Uses of Intelligence.* New York: Times Books, 1978.

De Toledano, Ralph. *J. Edgar Hoover: The Man in His Time.* New Rochelle, N.Y.: Arlington House, 1973.

Deriabin, Peter, and Frank Gibney. *The Secret World.* Garden City, N.Y.: Doubleday, 1959.

Dictionary of American Biography. New York: Scribner's, 1928–1958.

Dictionary of American History, second rev. ed. New York: Scribner's 1942–1961.

Dictionary of National Biography. London: Oxford U. Press, 1922.

Divine, Robert A., ed. *The Cuban Missile Crisis.* Chicago: Quadrangle, 1971.

Donner, Frank J. *The Age of Surveillance: The Aims and Methods of America's Political Intelligence System.* New York: Knopf, 1980.

Donovan, James B. *Strangers on a Bridge: The Case of Colonel Abel.* New York: Atheneum, 1964.

Dorwart, Jeffery M. *Conflict of Duty: The U.S. Navy's Intelligence Dilemma, 1919–1945.* Annapolis: Naval Institute Press, 1983.

———. *The Office of Naval Intelligence: The Birth of America's First Intelligence Agency, 1865–1918.* Annapolis: Naval Institute Press, 1979.

Downes, Donald. *The Scarlet Thread: Adventures in Wartime Espionage.* New York: British Book Centre, 1953.

Dulles, Allen. *The Craft of Intelligence.* New York: Harper & Row, 1963.

———. *The Secret Surrender.* New York: Harper & Row, 1966.

Dunlop, Richard. *Behind Japanese Lines: With the OSS in Burma.* Chicago: Rand McNally, 1979.

———. *Donovan: America's Master Spy.* Rand McNally, 1982.

Edmonds, S. Emma E. *Nurse and Spy in the Union*

Army: The Adventures and Experiences of a Woman in Hospitals, Camps, and Battle-Fields. Hartford, Conn.: W.S. Williams, 1865.

Einstein, Lewis. Divided Loyalties: Americans in England During the War of Independence. Boston: Houghton Mifflin, 1933.

Eisenschiml, Otto. In the Shadow of Lincoln's Death. New York: Wilfred Funk, 1940.

———. Why Was Lincoln Murdered? Boston: Little, Brown, 1937.

Eliot, Ellsworth, Jr. West Point in the Confederacy. New York: G.A. Baker, 1941.

Encyclopedia of American Biography. New York: Harper & Row, 1974.

Ennes, James M., Jr. Assault on the "Liberty": The True Story of the Israeli Attack on an American Intelligence Ship. New York: Random House, 1979.

Falkner, Leonard. "A Spy for Washington," American Heritage, v.8, n.8 (August 1957), pp. 58–64.

Fall, Bernard B. The Two Viet-Nams: A Political and Military Analysis. Revised edition. New York: Praeger, 1964.

Farago, Ladislas. Burn After Reading: The Espionage History of World War II. New York: Walker, 1961.

———. The Game of the Foxes: The Untold Story of German Espionage in the United States and Great Britain During World War II. New York: McKay, 1971.

———. War of Wits: The Anatomy of Espionage and Intelligence. New York: Funk & Wagnalls, 1954.

Felix, Christopher (pseud.). A Short Course in the Secret War. New York: Dutton, 1963.

Finnegan, John Patrick. Military Intelligence: A Picture History. Arlington, Va.: U.S. Army Intelligence and Security Command, 1985.

Fishel, Edwin C. "The Mythology of Civil War Intelligence," Civil War History, v.10, n.4 (December 1964), pp. 344–367.

Flexner, James Thomas. George Washington in the American Revolution (1775–1783). Boston: Little, Brown, 1968.

———. The Traitor and the Spy: Benedict Arnold and John André. New York: Harcourt, Brace, 1953.

"For Your Information," Foreign Intelligence Literary Scene. v.3, n.6 (October 1984), p. 12.

Forbes, Esther. Paul Revere and the World He Lived In. Boston: Houghton Mifflin, 1942.

Ford, Corey. Donovan of OSS. Boston: Little, Brown, 1970.

———. A Peculiar Service. Boston: Little, Brown, 1965.

Fowler, W.B. British-American Relations, 1917–1918: The Role of Sir William Wiseman. Princeton: Princeton U. Press, 1969.

Frank, Thomas M., and Edward Weisband, eds. Secrecy and Foreign Policy. New York: Oxford U. Press, 1974.

Frazier, Howard, ed. Uncloaking the CIA. New York: Free Press, 1978.

Freedman, Lawrence Zelic. " 'Truth' Drugs," Scientific American, v.202, n.3, (March 1960), pp. 145–154.

Freeman, Douglas Southall. Lee's Lieutenants: A Study in Command. New York: Scribners, 1942–44.

Friedman, William F., and Elizabeth S. Friedman. The Shakespearean Ciphers Examined. Cambridge, Eng.: Cambridge U. Press, 1957.

Gaddy, David G. "William Norris and the Confederate Signal and Secret Service," Maryland Historical Magazine, v.70, n.2. (Summer 1975) pp. 167–188.

Ganoe, William Addleman. The History of the United States Army. New York: Appleton-Century, 1942.

Generous, Kevin M. Vietnam: The Secret War. New York: Gallery Books, 1985.

Glines, Carroll V. The Compact History of the United States Air Force. New York: Hawthorn, 1973.

Goulden, Joseph C. The Death Merchant: The Rise and Fall of Edwin P. Wilson. New York: Simon and Schuster, 1984.

———. Korea: The Untold Story of the War. New York: Times Books, 1982.

Green, James Robert. "The First Sixty Years of the Office of Naval Intelligence." Master's thesis. Washington: American University, 1963.

Greenwood, Ted. "Reconnaissance and Arms Control," Scientific American, v.228, n.2, (February 1973), pp. 14–25.

Grendel, Frederic. Beaumarchais: The Man Who Was Figaro. London: Macdonald and Jane's, 1973.

Gunston, Bill. An Illustrated Guide to Spy Planes and Electronic Warfare Aircraft. New York: Arco, 1983.

Halberstam, David. The Best and the Brightest. New York: Random House, 1972.

Hall, James O. "The Spy Harrison," Civil War Times, v. 24, n.10 (February 1986), pp. 18–25.

Hall, Roger. You're Stepping on My Cloak and Dagger. New York: Norton, 1957.

Harlow, Alvin F. Old Wires and New Waves. New York: Appleton-Century, 1936.

Hatch, Robert McConnell. Major John André: A Gallant in Spy's Clothing. Boston: Houghton Mifflin, 1986.

Headley, John William. Confederate Operations in Canada and New York. New York: Neale, 1906. Reprinted (with accompanying unbound biographic material on Headley prepared by the reprint editors). Alexandria, Va.: Time-Life Books, 1984.

Hilsman, Roger. To Move A Nation: The Politics of

Foreign Policy in the Administration of John F. Kennedy. Garden City, N.Y.: Doubleday, 1967.

Hinckle, Warren, and William Turner. *The Fish is Red: The Story of the Secret War Against Castro.* New York: Harper & Row, 1981.

Höhne, Heinz, and Hermann Zolling. *The General Was a Spy: The Truth About General Gehlen and His Spy Ring.* New York: Coward-McCann, 1972.

Holmes, W.J. *Double-Edged Secrets: U.S. Naval Intelligence Operations in the Pacific during World War II.* Annapolis: Naval Institute Press, 1979.

Hood, William. *Mole.* New York: Norton, 1982.

Hopple, Gerald W., and Bruce W. Watson. *The Military Intelligence Community.* Boulder, Colo.: Westview, 1986.

Horan, James D. *Confederate Agent: A Discovery in History.* New York: Crown, 1954.

————. *The Pinkertons: The Detective Dynasty That Made History.* New York: Crown, 1967.

Horan, James D., and Howard Swiggett. *The Pinkerton Story.* New York: Putnam's, 1951.

House of Representatives. *Hearing Before the Committee on Expenditures in the Executive Departments, Eightieth Congress, First Session, on H.R. 2319 (National Security Act of 1947), June 27, 1947.* Washington: U.S. Government Printing Office. 1982.

————. *Inquiry Into the Alleged Involvement of the Central Intelligence Agency in the Watergate and Ellsberg Matters: Report of the Special Subcommittee on Intelligence of the Committee on Armed Services, Ninety-third Congress, First Session, October 23, 1973.* Washington: U.S. Government Printing Office, 1973.

Hunt, E. Howard. *Give Us This Day.* New Rochelle, N.Y.: Arlington House, 1973.

————. *Undercover: Memoirs of an American Secret Agent.* New York: Berkley/Putnam, 1974.

Hyde, H. Montgomery. *Room 3603: The Story of the British Intelligence Center in New York During World War II.* New York: Farrar, Straus: 1963.

Hymoff, Edward. *The OSS in World War II.* New York: Ballantine Books, 1972.

Hynd, Alan. *Passport to Treason: The Inside Story of Spies in America.* New York: Robert M. McBride, 1943.

Ind, Allison. *Allied Intelligence Bureau: Our Secret Weapon in the War Against Japan.* New York: McKay, 1958.

————. *A Short History of Espionage.* New York: McKay, 1963.

Infield, Glenn B. *Unarmed and Unafraid.* New York: Macmillan, 1970.

Jeffreys-Jones, Rhodri. *American Espionage: From Secret Service to CIA.* New York: Free Press, 1977.

————. "The Montreal Spy Ring of 1898 and the Origins of 'Domestic' Surveillance in the United States," *Canadian Review of American Studies,* v.5 (Fall 1974).

Jensen, Joan M. *The Price of Vigilance.* Chicago: Rand McNally, 1968.

Johnson, Haynes, with Manuel Artime, José Perez San Roman, Erneido Oliva, and Enrique Ruiz-Williams. *The Bay of Pigs: The Leaders' Story of Brigade 2506.* New York: W.W. Norton, 1964.

Johnson, Lyndon Baines. *The Vantage Point: Perspectives of the Presidency, 1963–1969.* New York: Holt, Rinehart and Winston, 1971.

Johnston, Angus J., II. "Disloyalty on Confederate Railroads in Virginia," *Virginia Magazine of History and Biography,* v.63, n.4 (October 1955), pp. 410–426.

Jones, John Price, and Paul Merrick Hollister. *The German Secret Service in America, 1914–1918.* Boston: Small, Maynard & Co., 1918.

Jordan, Amos A., and William J. Taylor, Jr. *American National Security: Policy and Process.* Baltimore: Johns Hopkins U. Press, 1981.

Kahn, David. *The Codebreakers: The Story of Secret Writing.* New York: Macmillan, 1967.

————. *Hitler's Spies: German Military Intelligence in World War II.* New York: Macmillan, 1978.

Kane, Harnet T. *Spies for the Blue and Gray.* Garden City, N.Y.: Doubleday, 1954.

Karalekas, Anne. *History of the Central Intelligence Agency.* Laguna Hills, Calif: Aegean Park Press, 1977. Reprinted in Leary, William M., ed., *The Central Intelligence Agency: History and Documents.* University, Ala.: U. Alabama Press, 1984.

Karnow, Stanley. *Vietnam: A History.* New York: Viking Press, 1983.

Katz, Friedrich. *The Secret War in Mexico: Europe, the United States, and the Mexican Revolution.* Chicago: U. Chicago Press, 1981.

Kaufman, Louis, Barbara Fitzgerald, and Tom Sewell. *Moe Berg: Athlete, Scholar, Spy.* Boston: Little, Brown, 1974.

Keesing, Hugo A. "The Defense Intelligence College: Winning the Silent War," *Military Intelligence,* v.12, n.1 (January–March 1986), pp. 27–28.

Kennan, George F. *Memoirs, 1925–1950.* Boston: Little, Brown, 1967.

Kennedy, Robert F. *Thirteen Days: A Memoir of the Cuban Missile Crisis.* New York: Norton, 1969.

Kennedy, William V., David Baker, Richard S. Friedman, and David Miller. *Intelligence Warfare: Today's Advanced Technology Conflict.* New York: Crescent Books, 1983.

Kent, Sherman. *Strategic Intelligence for American World Policy.* Princeton: Princeton U. Press, 1949, 1966.

Kirkpatrick, Lyman B., Jr. *The Real CIA.* New York: Macmillan, 1968.

———. *The U.S. Intelligence Community: Foreign Policy and Domestic Activities.* New York: Hill and Wang, 1973.

Kissinger, Henry. *White House Years, 1969–1973.* Boston: Little, Brown, 1979.

Klass, Philip J. *Secret Sentries in Space.* New York: Random House, 1971.

Klein, Alexander. *The Counterfeit Traitor.* New York: Holt, 1958.

Klement, Frank L. *Dark Lanterns: Secret Political Societies, Conspiracies, and Treason Trials in the Civil War.* Baton Rouge, La.: Louisiana State U. Press, 1984.

Kwitny, Jonathan. *Endless Enemies: The Making of an Unfriendly World.* New York: Congdon and Weed, 1984.

Lamphere, Robert J., and Tom Shachtman. *The FBI-KGB War: A Special Agent's Story.* New York: Random House, 1986.

Lancaster, Bruce, and J.H. Plumb. *The American Heritage Book of the Revolution.* New York: American Heritage, 1958.

Landau, Henry. *The Enemy Within: The Inside Story of German Sabotage in America.* New York: Putnam's, 1937.

Lansdale, Edward Geary. *In the Midst of Wars: An American's Mission to Southeast Asia.* New York: Harper & Row, 1972.

Layton, Edwin T. *"And I Was There": Pearl Harbor and Midway—Breaking the Secrets.* New York: Morrow, 1985.

Leacacos, John P. *Fires in the In-Basket: The ABC's of the State Department.* Cleveland: World, 1968.

Leary, William M. *Perilous Missions: Civil Air Transport and CIA Covert Operations in Asia.* University, Ala.: U. of Alabama Press, 1984.

Lemaitre, Georges. *Beaumarchais.* New York: Knopf, 1949.

Lerner, Daniel. *Sykewar: Psychological Warfare Against Germany, D-Day to VE-Day.* New York: G.W. Stewart, 1949.

Lewin, Ronald. *The American Magic: Codes, Ciphers and the Defeat of Japan.* New York: Farrar, Straus & Giroux, 1982.

———. *Ultra Goes to War: The First Account of World War II's Greatest Secret Based on Official Documents.* New York: McGraw-Hill, 1978.

Long, John Cuthbert. "Patience Wright of Bordentown," New Jersey Historical Society, *Proceedings,* Vol. 79 (1961), pp. 118–119.

Lord, Walter. *Day of Infamy.* New York: Holt, 1957.

Lovell, Stanley. *Of Spies and Strategems.* Englewood Cliffs, N.J.: Prentice-Hall, 1963.

Lukas, J. Anthony. *Nightmare: The Underside of the Nixon Years.* New York: Viking, 1976.

MacCloskey, Monro. *The American Intelligence Community.* New York: Richards Rosen Press, 1967.

———. *From Gasbags to Spaceships: The Story of the U.S. Air Force.* New York: Richards Rosen Press, 1968.

Manchester, William. *American Caesar: Douglas MacArthur, 1880–1964.* Boston: Little, Brown, 1978.

Marchetti, Victor, and John D. Marks. *The CIA and the Cult of Intelligence.* New York: Knopf, 1974.

Marks, John D. *The CIA's Corporate Shell Game.* Washington: The Center for National Security Studies, 1976. Reprinted from the *Washington Post,* July 11, 1976.

———. *The Search for the "Manchurian Candidate": The CIA and Mind Control.* New York: Times Books, 1979.

Martin, David C. *A Wilderness of Mirrors.* New York: Harper & Row, 1980.

Mashbir, Sidney Forrester. *I Was an American Spy.* New York: Vantage, 1953.

McGehee, Ralph W. *Deadly Deceits: My 25 Years in the CIA.* New York: Sheridan Square Pubs., 1983.

McMaster, John Bach. *History of the People of the United States During Lincoln's Administration.* New York: Appleton-Century, 1927. Reprinted as *Our House Divided.* New York: Premier Books, 1961.

Meeropol, Robert, and Michael Meeropol. *We Are Your Sons.* Boston: Houghton Mifflin, 1975.

Meyer, Cord. *Facing Reality: From World Federalism to the CIA.* New York: Harper & Row, 1980.

Miles, Milton. *A Different Kind of War: The Little-Known Story of the Combined Guerrilla Forces Created in China by the U.S. Navy and the Chinese During World War II.* Garden City, N.Y.: Doubleday, 1967.

Miller, Francis Trevelyan, ed. *Soldier Life and the Secret Service* (vol.8 of *The Photographic History of the Civil War.* A.S. Barnes, 1911). Reprinted. New York: Castle Books, 1957.

Miller, John G. *Origins of the American Revolution.* Boston: Little, Brown, 1943.

———. *Sam Adams: Pioneer in Propaganda.* Boston: Little, Brown, 1936.

———. *Triumph of Freedom, 1775–1783.* Boston: Little, Brown, 1948.

Millis, Walter. *Road to War: America, 1914–1917.* Boston: Houghton Mifflin, 1935.

Mogelever, Jacob. *Death to Traitors: The Story of General Lafayette C. Baker, Lincoln's Forgotten Secret Service Chief.* Garden City, N.Y.: Doubleday, 1960.

Monaghan, Jay. *Diplomat in Carpet Slippers: Abra-*

ham Lincoln Deals with Foreign Affairs. Indianapolis: Bobbs-Merrill, 1945.

Morgan, William J. The OSS and I. New York: Norton, 1957.

Morn, Frank. "The Eye That Never Sleeps": A History of the Pinkerton National Detective Agency. Bloomington, Ind.: Indiana U. Press, 1982.

Morris, Richard B. The Peacemakers: The Great Powers and American Independence. New York: Harper & Row, 1965.

Mosley, Leonard. Dulles: A Biography of Eleanor, Allen and John Foster Dulles and Their Family Network. New York: Dial Press, 1978.

————. Power Play: Oil in the Middle East. New York: Random House, 1973.

Murphy, Robert. Dipolmat Among Warriors. Garden City, N.Y.: Doubleday, 1964.

National Cyclopedia of American Biography. Clifton, N.J.: James T. White, from 1898.

New York Times. The Pentagon Papers. New York: Quadrangle, 1971.

————. The Watergate Hearings: Break-in and Cover-up. New York: Viking, 1973.

Nicolosi, Anthony A. "The Spirit of McCarty Little," Proceedings of the U.S. Naval Institute, v.110/9/979 (September 1984), pp. 72–80.

Nixon, Richard M. The Memoirs of Richard Nixon. New York: Grosset & Dunlap, 1978.

O'Brien, Michael J. Hercules Mulligan: Confidential Correspondent of General Washington. New York: P.J. Kennedy & Sons, 1937.

————. In Old New York: The Irish Dead in Trinity and St. Paul's Churchyards. New York: American Irish Historical Society, 1928.

Office of Strategic Services. "Prominent Persons in the OSS," Record Group 226, Modern Military Records, U.S. National Archives and Records Agency, Washington, D.C.

O'Neill, Charles Kendall. Wild Train: The Story of Andrews' Raiders. New York: Random House, 1956.

O'Toole, G.J.A. "Our Man in Havana: The Paper Trail of Some Spanish War Spies," Intelligence Quarterly, v.2, n.2 (July 1986), pp. 1–3.

————. The Spanish War: An American Epic, 1898. New York: Norton, 1984.

Overstreet, Harry, and Bonaro Overstreet. The FBI in Our Open Society. New York: Norton, 1969.

Overy, R.J. The Air War, 1939–1945. Briarcliff Manor, N.Y.: Stein and Day, 1981.

Owsley, Harriet Chappell. "Henry Shelton Sanford and Federal Surveillance Abroad, 1861–1865," Mississippi Valley Historical Review, v.48, n.2 (September 1961), pp. 211–228.

Padover, Saul Kussiel. Experiment in Germany:

The Story of an American Intelligence Officer. New York: Duell, Sloan and Pearce, 1946.

Page, Bruce, David Leitch and Phillip Knightley. The Philby Conspiracy. Garden City, N.Y.: Doubleday, 1968.

Paige, Glenn D. The Korean Decision (June 24–30, 1950). New York: Free Press, 1968.

Papen, Franz von. Memoirs. New York: Dutton, 1953.

Patrick, Louis S., "The Secret Service of the American Revolution." Journal of American History, v.1 (1907), pp. 497–508.

Peake, Hayden B. "The Putative Spy," Foreign Intelligence Literary Scene, v.5, n.2 (March/April 1986), 1, pp. 7–8; v.5, n.3 (May/June 1986), pp. 3–4.

Peers, William R., and Dean Brelis. Behind the Burma Road: The Story of America's Most Successful Guerrilla Force. Boston: Little, Brown, 1963.

Penkovskiy, Oleg. The Penkovskiy Papers. Garden City, N.Y.: Doubleday, 1965.

Pennypacker, Morton. General Washington's Spies on Long Island in New York. Brooklyn, N.Y.: Long Island Historical Society, 1939.

————. General Washington's Spies on Long Island and in New York, Volume II. Privately printed, 1948.

Persico, Joseph E. Piercing the Reich: The Penetration of Nazi Germany by American Secret Agents During World War II. New York: Viking Press, 1979.

Philby, Kim. My Silent War. New York: Grove-Dell, 1968.

Phillips, David Atlee. Careers in Secret Operations: How to Be a Federal Intelligence Officer. Frederick, Md.: University Publications, 1984.

————. The Night Watch: 25 Years of Peculiar Service. New York: Atheneum, 1977.

Pinkerton, Allan. The Spy of the Rebellion: History of the Spy System of the United States Army During the Late Rebellion. New York: G.W. Carlton, 1883.

Plumb, William R. The Military Telegraph During the Civil War in the United States. Chicago, 1882.

Political Profiles: The Truman Years, The Eisenhower Years, The Kennedy Years, The Johnson Years, The Nixon-Ford Years. New York: Facts on File, 1978, 1978, 1976, 1976, 1979.

Potter, E.B. "The Crypt of the Cryptanalysts," Proceedings of the U.S. Naval Institute, v.109/8/966 (August 1983), pp. 52–56.

Powe, Marc B. "The Emergence of the War Department Intelligence Agency: 1885–1918." Master's thesis; Department of History; Kansas State University, Manhattan, Kansas, 1974.

Powe, Marc B., and Edward E. Wilson. The Evolution of American Military Intelligence. Fort Huachuca, Ariz.: The U.S. Intelligence Center and School, 1973.

Powers, Francis Gary, with Curt Gentry. *Operation Overflight: The U-2 Spy Pilot Tells His Story for the First Time.* New York: Holt Rinehart & Winston, 1970.

Powers, Thomas. *The Man Who Kept the Secrets: Richard Helms and the CIA.* New York: Knopf, 1979.

Prados, John. *The Soviet Estimate: U.S. Intelligence Analysis and Russian Military Strength.* New York: Dial Press, 1982.

Prange, Gordon W. *At Dawn We Slept: The Untold Story of Pearl Harbor.* New York: McGraw Hill, 1981.

———. *Pearl Harbor: The Verdict of History.* New York: McGraw-Hill, 1986.

Pratt, Fletcher. *Secret and Urgent: The Story of Codes and Ciphers.* Garden City, N.Y.: Blue Ribbon Books, 1942.

Prouty, L. Fletcher. *The Secret Team: The CIA and Its Allies in Control of the United States and the World.* Englewood Cliffs, N.J.: Prentice-Hall, 1973.

Radosh, Ronald, and Joyce Milton. *The Rosenberg File: A Search for the Truth.* New York: Holt, Rinehart, 1983.

Ranelagh, John. *The Agency: The Rise and Decline of the CIA.* New York: Simon and Schuster, 1986.

Ransom, Harry Howe. *Central Intelligence and National Security.* Cambridge, Mass.: Harvard U. Press, 1965.

———. *The Intelligence Establishment* (revised edition of previous work). Cambridge, Mass.: Harvard U. Press, 1970.

Ray, Ellen, William Schaap, Karl van Meter, and Louis Wolf, eds. *Dirty Work 2: The CIA in Africa.* Secaucus, N.J.: Lyle Stuart, 1979.

Reader's Digest. *Secrets & Spies: Behind-the-Scenes Stories of World War II.* Pleasantville, N.Y.: Reader's Digest Assn., 1964.

Richelson, Jeffrey T. *The U.S. Intelligence Community.* Cambridge, Mass.: Ballinger, 1985.

Ridgway, Matthew B. *The Korean War.* Garden City, N.Y.: Doubleday, 1967.

Rintelen, Franz. *The Dark Invader: Wartime Reminiscences of a German Naval Intelligence Officer.* London: Lovat Dickson, 1933.

Robbins, Christoper. *Air America.* New York: Putnam's, 1979.

Rochefort, Joseph. "As I Recall . . . Learning Cryptanalysis," *Proceedings of the U.S. Naval Institute,* v. 109/8/966 (August 1983), pp. 54–55.

Roetter, Charles. *The Art of Psychological Warfare, 1914–1945.* Briarcliff Manor, N.Y.: Stein and Day, 1974.

Roosevelt, Kermit. *Countercoup: The Struggle for the Control of Iran.* New York: McGraw-Hill, 1979.

———. *War Report of the OSS (Office of Strategic Services).* New York: Walker, 1976.

Roscoe, Theodore. *The Web of Conspiracy: The Complete Story of the Men Who Murdered Abraham Lincoln.* Englewood Cliffs, N.J.: Prentice-Hall, 1959.

Rositzke, Harry. *The CIA's Secret Operations: Espionage, Counterespionage, and Covert Action.* New York: Reader's Digest Press, 1977.

———. *The KGB: The Eyes of Russia.* Garden City, N.Y.: Doubleday, 1981.

Ross, Ishbel. *Rebel Rose: Life of Rose O'Neal Greenhow, Confederate Spy.* Harper & Bros., 1954.

Rostow, W.W. *Open Skies: Eisenhower's Proposal of July 21, 1955.* Austin, Tex.: U. Texas Press, 1982.

Rout, Leslie B., Jr., and John F. Bratzel. *The Shadow War: German Espionage and United States Counterespionage in Latin America during World War II.* Frederick, Md.: University Publications, 1986.

Russell, Charles Edward. *Haym Salomon and the Revolution.* New York: Cosmopolitan Book Corp., 1930.

Safire, William. *On Language.* New York: Times Books, 1980.

Sampson, Anthony. *The Sovereign State of ITT.* Briarcliff Manor, N.Y.: Stein and Day, 1973. Revised. Greenwich, Conn.: Fawcett, 1974.

Sandberg, Carl. *Abraham Lincoln: The War Years.* New York: Harcourt, Brace, 1939.

Schellenberg, Walter. *The Labyrinth: Memoirs of Walter Schellenberg.* New York: Harper and Bros., 1956.

Schlesinger, Arthur M., Jr. *A Thousand Days: John F. Kennedy in the White House.* Boston: Houghton Mifflin, 1965.

Schlesinger, Stephen, and Stephen Kinzer. *Bitter Fruit: The Untold Story of the American Coup in Guatemala.* Garden City, N.Y.: Doubleday, 1982.

Schmidt, C.T., "G-2, Army of the Potomac," *Military Review,* v.28 (July 1948), pp. 45–56.

Schoenbrun, David. *Triumph in Paris: The Exploits of Benjamin Franklin.* New York: Harper & Row, 1976.

Schuon, Karl. *U.S. Navy Biographical Dictionary.* New York: Franklin Watts, 1964.

Sears, Stephen W. *Landscape Turned Red: The Battle of Antietam.* New Haven: Ticknor & Fields, 1983.

Sellers, Charles Coleman. *Patience Wright: American Artist and Spy in George III's London.* Middletown, Conn.: Wesleyan U. Press, 1976.

Senate, U.S. *Alleged Assassination Plots Involving Foreign Leaders: An Interim Report of the Select Committee to Study Governmental Operations With Respect to Intelligence Activities.* Ninety-fourth Congress, First Session. Report No. 94-465. Washington: U.S. Government Printing Office, November 20, 1975.

Seth, Ronald. *Unmasked! The Story of Soviet Espionage.* New York: Hawthorn, 1965.

Shackley, Theodore. *The Third Option: An American View of Counterinsurgency Operations*. New York: Reader's Digest Press, 1981.

Sims, William Sowden. *The Victory at Sea*. Garden City, N.Y.: Doubleday, Page, 1920.

Smith, Burke M. "The Polygraph," *Scientific American*, v.216, n.1 (January 1967), pp. 25–31.

Smith, George Gardner, ed., *Spencer Kellogg Brown*. New York: Appleton, 1903.

Smith, Joseph Burkholder. *Portrait of a Cold Warrior*. New York: Putnam's, 1976.

Smith, R. Harris. *OSS: The Secret History of America's First Central Intelligence Agency*. Berkeley, Calif.: U. California Press, 1972.

Snepp, Frank. *Decent Interval: An Insider's Account of Saigon's Indecent End Told by the CIA's Chief Strategy Analyst in Vietnam*. New York: Random House, 1977.

Special Operations Research Office. *U.S. Army Area Handbook for Indonesia*. Washington: U.S. Government Printing Office, 1964.

Spector, Ronald H. *Eagle Against the Sun: The American War with Japan*. New York: Free Press, 1985.

Starr, Stephen Z. *Colonel Grenfell's Wars*. Baton Rouge, La.: Louisiana State U. Press, 1971.

State Department. *Papers Relating to the Foreign Relations of the United States: The Paris Peace Conference, 1919*. v.11. Washington: U.S. Government Printing Office, 1945.

Stern, Philip M., with Harold P. Green. *The Oppenheimer Case: Security on Trial*. New York: Harper & Row, 1969.

Stern, Philip Van Doren. *The Confederate Navy: A Pictorial History*. Garden City, N.J.: Doubleday, 1962.

———. *Secret Missions of the Civil War: First-hand Accounts by Men and Women Who risked their Lives in Underground Activities for the North and the South*. Chicago: Rand McNally, 1959.

Stevenson, William. *A Man Called Intrepid: The Secret War*. New York: Harcourt Brace Jovanovich, 1976.

Stockwell, John. *In Search of Enemies: A CIA Story*. New York: W.W. Norton, 1978.

Stuart, Meriwether. "Colonel Ulric Dahlgren and Richmond's Union Underground, April 1864," *Virginia Magazine of History and Biography*, v.72, n.2 (April 1964). pp. 152–204.

———. "Of Spies and Borrowed Names: The Identity of Union Operatives in Richmond Known as 'The Phillipses' Discovered," *Virginia Magazine of History and Biography*, v.89, n.3 (July 1981), pp. 308–327.

———. "Samuel Ruth and General R.E. Lee: Disloyalty and the Line of Supply to Fredericksburg, 1862–1863," *Virginia Magazine of History and Biography*, v.71, n.1, (January 1963), pp. 35–109.

Sweeney, Walter C. *Military Intelligence: A New Weapon in War*. New York: Frederick A. Stokes, 1924.

Symonds, Craig L. *A Battlefield Atlas of the Civil War*. Annapolis: Nautical and Aviation Publishing Co., 1983.

Szulc, Tad. *Compulsive Spy: The Strange Case of E. Howard Hunt*. New York: Viking, 1974.

Szulc, Tad, and Karl E. Meyer. *The Cuban Invasion: The Chronicle of a Disaster*. New York: Praeger, 1962.

Tallmadge, Benjamin. *Memoir of Colonel Benjamin Tallmadge*. New York, 1858. Reprinted. New York: New York Times & Arno Press, 1968.

Tatum, Georgia Lee. *Disloyalty in the Confederacy*. Chapel Hill, N.C.: U. North Carolina Press, 1934. Reprint. New York: AMS Press, 1970.

Taylor, Charles E. "The Signal and Secret Service of the Confederate States," *North Carolina Booket*, v.2, n.11. Hamlet, N.C., 1903.

Taylor, John W.R., and David Mondey. *Spies in the Sky*. New York: Scribner's, 1972.

Thomas, Hugh. *Cuba: The Pursuit of Freedom*. New York: Harper & Row, 1971.

Thompson, Edmund R., "George Washington, Master Intelligence Officer," *American Intelligence Journal*, v.6, n.2., pp. 3–8.

———. "Intelligence at Yorktown," *Defense 81*, October 1981, pp. 25–28.

———. "Sleuthing the Trail of Nathan Hale," *Intelligence Quarterly*, v.2, n.3 (October 1986), pp. 1–4.

Thyraud de Vosjoli, P.L. *Lamia*. Boston: Little, Brown, 1970.

Time-Life Books (The Editors). *The Civil War: Spies, Scouts and Raiders*. Alexandria, Va.: Time-Life Books, 1985.

Tompkins, Peter. *A Spy in Rome*. New York: Simon and Schuster, 1962.

Troy, Thomas F. *Donovan and the CIA: A History of the Establishment of the Central Intelligence Agency*. Frederick, Md.: University Publications, 1981.

Truman, Harry S. *Memoirs: Vol. II, Years of Trial and Hope*. Garden City, N.Y.: Doubleday, 1956.

Tuchman, Barbara W. *Stilwell and the American Experience in China, 1911–1945*. New York: Macmillan, 1971.

———. *The Zimmermann Telegram*. New York: Viking, 1958.

Tully, Andrew. *The FBI's Most Famous Cases*. New York: Morrow, 1965.

———. *The Super Spies*. New York: Morrow, 1969.

Turner, Stansfield. *Secrecy and Democracy: The CIA in Transition*. Boston: Houghton Mifflin, 1985.

Ungar, Sanford J. *FBI*. Boston: Little, Brown, 1976.

Van Deman, Ralph. "Memoirs of Major General R.H. Van Deman." Unpublished manuscript. U.S. Army CIC Center, Ft. Holabird, Md., 1950–1956.

Van Doren, Carl. *Benjamin Franklin*. New York: Viking, 1938.

―――. *Secret History of the American Revolution: An Account of the Conspiracies of Benedict Arnold and Numerous Others drawn from the Secret Service Papers of the British Headquarters in North America now for the first time examined and made public*. New York: Viking, 1941.

Voska, Emanuel Victor, and Will Irwin. *Spy and Counterspy*. New York: Doubleday, Doran, 1940.

Wagner, William. *Lightning Bugs and other Reconnaissance Drones*. Fallbrook, Calif.: Armed Forces Journal International in cooperation with Aero Publishers, 1982.

Wallace, Willard M. *Appeal to Arms: A Military History of the American Revolution*. New York: Harper & Bros., 1951.

Weber, Ralph E. *United States Diplomatic Codes and Ciphers, 1775–1938*. Chicago: Precident Publishing, 1979.

Webster's American Military Biographies. Springfield, Mass.: G & C Merriam, 1978.

Weigley, Russell F. "American Strategy from Its Beginnings through the First World War," in Peter Paret, ed. *Makers of Modern Strategy from Machiavelli to the Nuclear Age*. Princeton: Princeton U. Press, 1986.

Weinstein, Allen. *Perjury: This Hiss-Chambers Case*. New York: Knopf, 1978.

West, Nigel (pseud.). *MI6: British Secret Intelligence Service Operations, 1909–1945*. New York: Random House, 1983.

Wheelon, Albert D. "PFIAB: A History," *Periscope* (Association of Former Intelligence Officers), v.10, n.3 (Summer 1985), p. 4.

Whitehead, Don. *The FBI Story: A Report to the People*. New York: Random House, 1956.

Who's Who: An Annual Biographical Dictionary, with Which is Incorporated Men and Women of the Time. London: A.&C. Black, 1849 to date.

Who's Who in America. Chicago: Marquis, 1899 to date.

Who's Who in Consulting. second edition. Detroit: Gale Research, 1973.

Who's Who in Government, first and second editions. Chicago: Marquis, 1972 and 1973.

Who's Who in the East (and Eastern Canada). Chicago: Marquis, 1948 to date.

Who's Who in New York (City and State). Eighth edition. New York: Who's Who Publications, 1924.

Who Was Who in America. Chicago: Marquis. Historical Volume (1607–1896), v.1 (1897–1942), v.2 (1943–1950), v.3 (1951–1960), v.4 (1961–1968), v.5 (1969–1973), v.6 (1974–1976), v.7 (1977–1981).

Wilkie, Don. *American Secret Service Agent*. New York: Frederick A. Stokes, 1934.

Wise, David. *The American Police State: The Government Against the People*. New York: Random House, 1976.

―――. *The Politics of Lying: Government Deception, Secrecy, and Power*. New York: Random House, 1973.

Wise, David, and Thomas B. Ross. *The Espionage Establishment*. New York: Random House, 1967.

―――. *The Invisible Government*. New York: Random House, 1964.

―――. *The U-2 Affair*. New York: Random House, 1962.

Wohlstetter, Roberta. "Cuba and Pearl Harbor: Hindsight and Foresight," *Foreign Affairs*, v.43 (July 1965), pp. 691–707.

―――. *Pearl Harbor: Warning and Decision*. Stanford, Calif.: Stanford U. Press, 1962.

Wriston, Henry Merritt. *Executive Agents in American Foreign Relations*. Baltimore: Johns Hopkins, 1929. Reprinted. Gloucester, Mass: Peter Smith, 1967.

Wyden, Peter. *Bay of Pigs: The Untold Story*. New York: Simon and Schuster, 1979.

―――. *Day One: Before Hiroshima and After*. New York: Simon and Schuster, 1984.

Wynne, Greville. *Contact on Gorky Street*. New York: Atheneum, 1968.

Yardley, Herbert O. *The American Black Chamber*. Indianapolis: Bobbs-Merrill, 1931. Reprint. New York: Ballantine, 1981.

Young, Philip. *Revolutionary Ladies*. New York: Knopf, 1977.

Youngblood, Rufus W. *20 Years in the Secret Service: My Life With Five Presidents*. New York: Simon and Schuster, 1973.

Zacharias, Ellis M. *Secret Missions: The Story of an Intelligence Officer*. New York: Putnam's, 1946.

INDEX